MARKETING COMMUNICATIONS

A EUROPEAN PERSPECTIVE

Patrick **De Pelsmacker** Maggie **Geuens** Joeri **Van den Bergh**

PEARSON

Harlow, England • London • New York • Boston • San Francisco • Toronto • Sydney • Auckland • Singapore • Hong Kong
Tokyo • Seoul • Taipei • New Delhi • Cape Town • São Paulo • Mexico City • Madrid • Amsterdam • Munich • Paris • Milan

PEARSON EDUCATION LIMITED
Edinburgh Gate
Harlow CM20 2JE
United Kingdom
Tel: +44 (0)1279 623623
Fax: +44 (0)1279 431059
Web: www.pearson.com/uk

First published 2001 (print)
Second edition published 2004 (print)
Third edition published 2007 (print)
Fourth edition published 2010 (print)
Fifth edition published 2013 (print and electronic)

ISBN: 978-0-273-77322-1 (print)
  978-0-273-77324-5 (PDF)
  978-0-273-79484-4 (eText)

British Library Cataloguing-in-Publication Data
A catalogue record for the print edition is available from the British Library

Library of Congress Cataloging-in-Publication Data
A catalog record for the print edition is available from the Library of Congress

10 9 8 7 6 5 4 3
17 16 15 14

Print edition typeset in 10/12 pt Minion Pro by 35
Printed and bound by DZS Grafik, Slovenia

NOTE THAT ANY PAGE CROSS REFERENCES REFER TO THE PRINT EDITION

MARKETING COMMUNICATIONS

We dedicate this book to Isabel, Vita, Jina, Jan, Jolien and Jelle

CONTENTS

11 Sponsorship   344

12 Brand activation   373

13 Direct marketing   422

14 Exhibitions and trade fairs   458

15 E-communication   484

16 Ethical issues in marketing communications   555

Companion Website

For open-access **student resources** specifically written
to complement this textbook and support your learning,
please visit **www.pearsoned.co.uk/depelsmacker**

Lecturer Resources

For password-protected online resources tailored to support
the use of this textbook in teaching, please visit
www.pearsoned.co.uk/depelsmacker

ABOUT THE AUTHORS

Patrick De Pelsmacker (b. 1957) holds a PhD in economics (University of Ghent, Belgium). He is Professor of Marketing at the University of Antwerp, Belgium and part-time Professor of Marketing at the University of Ghent. He is a regular guest lecturer at various institutes, such as the Solvay Business School (University of Brussels, Belgium), the Rotterdam School of Management (The Netherlands), the Swedish Institute of Management (Brussels, Stockholm), the Centre for Management Training (University of Warsaw, Poland), the Institute of Business Studies (Moscow, Russia), the University of Lugano (Lugano, Switzerland), the Copenhagen Business School (Copenhagen, Denmark), The University of Geneva (Switzerland) and Ca'Foscari University (Venice, Italy). He also has teaching experience in management and marketing programmes in France, Thailand, Indonesia, the Philippines, Vietnam, Italy, the Czech Republic, Hungary and Romania. He has undertaken numerous in-company training and consultancy assignments.

His field of interest is in marketing research techniques, consumer behaviour and marketing communications. He has co-authored textbooks on marketing communications and marketing research techniques, and has written over one hundred articles in various journals, including *Applied Economics, International Journal of Research in Marketing, Journal of Advertising, Psychology and Marketing, International Journal of Advertising, Journal of Marketing Communications, Advances in Consumer Research, Journal of Business Ethics, Journal of Consumer Affairs, Journal of International Consumer Marketing, International Marketing Review, Marketing Letters, Journal of Business Research, Journal of Advertising Research, Cyberpsychology and Behavior, Accident Analysis and Prevention, Health Communication, Journal of Business and Psychology, Journal of International Advertising, Journal of International Marketing, Educational and Psychological Measurements* and *Psychological Reports*. He has contributed to more than twenty books and over sixty research reports and working papers on various marketing-related topics.

Maggie Geuens (b. 1969) holds a PhD in Applied Economics at the University of Antwerp, Belgium, where she also worked as an assistant professor. Currently she is Professor of Marketing at the University of Ghent. She is the academic director of the Brand Management Centre at the Vlerick Leuven Gent Management School. She also has teaching experience in The Netherlands, Italy, Kazakhstan, Russia and Vietnam. She is involved in consultancy on a regular basis.

Her main field of research interest is in advertising, branding and consumer behaviour. She has co-authored a book on *Marketing Management*, has contributed to over sixty papers and research reports in her interest field, and has published in journals such as *Journal of Consumer Research, International Journal of Research in Marketing, Journal of the Academy of Marketing Science, Journal of Health Communication, Psychology and Marketing, Journal of Advertising, International Journal of Advertising, Journal of Business Research, Journal of Marketing Communications, International Marketing Review, PsychologicaBelgica, Tourism Management, Advances in Consumer Research, Journal of Business and Psychology, Psychological Review, Educational and Psychological Measurement, Applied Psychological Measurement, International Journal of Advertising and Marketing to Children* and *Journal of Consumer and Market Research*.

Joeri Van den Bergh (b. 1971) holds a master's degree in marketing (University of Ghent and the Vlerick Leuven Gent Management School). He started his career as a researcher at the Marketing Communication Research Centre, and later became senior researcher, involved in the activities of this Centre, as well as the Kids and Teens Marketing Centre, and the Senior Consumer Marketing Centre. He is co-founder and managing partner of InSites Consulting, the European online market research pioneer. He is now director of InSites Consulting ON SNEAKERS, the children and youth division where he manages European accounts such as MTV Networks and Nokia. He is a regular teacher on various marketing programmes, has been involved in in-company training and consultancy, and is Secretary of the Board of AncienneBelgique (AB), one of Europe's leading music venues.

His main field of interest is marketing communications, especially Internet communications, research techniques and children and youth marketing. He has contributed to various books and to over thirty research reports in these fields. He has published in journals including *International Journal of Advertising* and the *Journal of International Consumer Marketing*.

PREFACE

Marketing communications are not only one of the most visible and widely discussed instruments of the marketing mix, with an overwhelming impact on both society and business, they are also one of the most fascinating. Every private consumer and business executive is exposed to advertising. They make use of sales promotions, are approached by sales persons, visit trade fairs and exhibitions, buy famous or not so famous brands, are a target of public relations activity, are exposed to sponsorship efforts, receive direct mail, telemarketing or research calls and visit stores in which no stone is left unturned to influence their buying behaviour. Furthermore, almost every consumer is a regular user of the Internet.

Marketing executives constantly face the challenge of integrating their promotional effort into strategic management and marketing plans. They must integrate the various instruments of the marketing communications mix, build successful brands, try to find out how marketing communications can be instrumental in achieving company objectives, and how they can be applied in specific marketing situations.

Following the success of the first four editions, this fifth edition of *Marketing Communications: A European Perspective* continues to offer a comprehensive overview of the cornerstones, techniques and applications of marketing in a European context.

The market

This text is geared to undergraduate and postgraduate students who have attended introductory courses in marketing, and who want to extend their knowledge to various aspects of marketing communications. The text can also be used by marketing communications professionals who want an overview of the whole field and may find inspiration and new angles to their marketing communications practice in the many examples, cases and research results that are covered in this text.

Organisation

The text is organised as follows. Chapter 1 provides a global overview of marketing communications and discusses the crucial topic of the integration of marketing communications activity. One of the major objectives of marketing communications is to build and maintain strong brands. Branding is covered in Chapter 2. Chapter 3 discusses the groundwork of all marketing communications activity. It is devoted to the intriguing question of how communications influence consumers.

In subsequent chapters the different steps in the marketing communications plan and the various instruments and techniques of marketing communications are covered. Separate chapters are devoted to the definition of target groups (4) and objectives (5) and to budgeting issues (6).

Chapters 7–15 cover each of the marketing communications instruments. Chapters 7–9 address advertising-related issues, including media planning and advertising research. Subsequent chapters each cover one tool of the marketing communications mix: public relations (10), sponsorship (11), brand activation (12), direct marketing (13), exhibitions and trade fairs (14) and e-communications (15). In Chapter 16 the increasingly important ethical side of marketing communications is discussed.

Pedagogy

To help reinforce key learning points, each chapter includes the following:

- Chapter Outline, which presents the contents of the chapter graphically.
- Chapter Objectives, Summaries and Review Questions and references to interview videos assist the reader in understanding the important elements and help test one's knowledge.
- Main text organised in sections and sub-sections to help students digest and retain the information.
- Tables, figures, outlines and other illustrative material help the reader grasp the essential facts.
- Separate highlights throughout the text cover extended examples, mini-cases, interesting research results or more technical issues.
- Suggested further readings offer the opportunity to refer to other, more specialised or specific sources of information on many subjects.
- An extensive European or global case study.

Distinctive characteristics

- This is not just a text about advertising, supplemented by a brief discussion of the other instruments of the marketing mix. Although advertising-related topics are thoroughly discussed, this text is comprehensive in that it covers *all* instruments of the marketing communications mix.
- The text has a consistent European focus. Although research results and examples from other parts of the world are covered, the main focus is the application of marketing communications concepts in a European environment.
- Every chapter contains an extensive European or global case study in a wide variety of industries, markets and countries. Most of these cases contain original and in-depth material, often provided by the marketing executives of the brands and companies discussed. Challenging case questions are designed to encourage the reader to apply the concepts from the chapter to the solution of the case at hand. Furthermore, many of these cases can be used with more than one chapter.
- A number of chapters focus extensively on particularly important and/or relatively new fields of interest related to marketing communications. This is the case for the chapters on branding, how communications work, brand activation, e-communications and ethics.
- Throughout the text, numerous examples, case studies and research results from various countries, industries and markets are given, to illustrate and make the concepts as practice-oriented as possible.

New to the fifth edition

While the structure of the fifth edition of this text and its chapters has largely remained the same as the fourth edition, case studies, vignettes, examples and references have been updated and new material has been added to every chapter. Some of the new material draws upon the following companies and organisations: Hyundai, Angry Birds, Samsung, HTC, PWC, Caja Madrid, Belgian Post, Coop, Speedo, Lotus Bakeries, Nivea, Mamas & Papas, Dunkin' Donuts, Britney Spears, Quechua, Coca-Cola, Sainsbury's, KLM, Pinterest, Tipp-Ex, AS Adventure, Heinz, O'Neill, Kaiser Chiefs, Gulf Stream, Magnum, Sonera, Kleenex, Argos, Cornetto, Red Cross, British Airways, Burger King, Yeo Valley, Taco Bell, Axe, Cheerios, Cadbury, Bavaria, Shisheido, Abercrombie & Fitch, Philips, Rugbeer, Adidas and Lay's.

Furthermore, most end-of-chapter cases have been updated and several new cases and vignettes have been added: Walkers crisps, Club Med, Yellow Pages New Zealand, and the Global Fund to fight Aids, malaria and tuberculosis. New theories, frameworks and research results have been added in many chapters, and these include gender role stereotyping, branding and celebrity endorsement in India, how children react to new advertising formats, probability markers, integrating emotions and habits into the theory of planned behaviour, two-sided messages, experience positioning of electric cars, response to online reviews, health communications, the RFM-model, measuring online campaigns and user-generated content. The chapter on e-communications has been thoroughly updated and extended and includes a large section on social media communications, to reflect the most recent evolutions and best-practice applications in this fast-growing area. A thoroughly revised chapter on brand activation has been added.

Finally, we are proud to offer instructor and student support materials on our website: http://www.pearsoned.co.uk/depelsmacker. Visit this site to find valuable teaching and learning materials on *Marketing Communications*.

AUTHORS'
ACKNOWLEDGEMENTS

While we assume full responsibility for the content of the whole text, important parts of it could not have been written without the help and support of numerous people. We would particularly like to thank the following people, and hope we have not forgotten anyone.

Guy Geerts (Darwin BBDO)
Koen Helsen, Lieven Bertier (Barco)
Isabel Raes
Yves Van Landeghem (Saatchi & Saatchi)
Bert Denis (TBWA)
Claudia Gonzalez (The Global Fund to Fight Aids, Malaria and Tuberculosis)
DespinaSpanou (European Commission)
Derek Gosselin, Rick Grant, Julie Vitek, Katja Damman (Suez)
Nigel Lawrence (Dunnhumby)
Luc Suykens, Nicolas Frèrejean, Nada Dugas (Procter & Gamble)
Marc Frederix, (National Lottery Belgium)
Lars Vervoort, Tine Nelissen (Carrefour Belgium)
Christine Edier (Unicef)
Alain Heureux (IAB Europe)
Marc Michils (Quattro Saatchi and Saatchi)
Jorgen NygaardAndreassen (Fedma)
Joëlle Van Ryckevorsel, Teresa di Campello (L'Oréal)
A number of reviewers: Paul Copley, University of Northumbria; Claude Pecheux, Les Facultés Universitaires Catholiques de Mons; Jane Underhill, University of Northumbria; Tania Van den Bergh, Arteveldehogeschool, Flanders, Belgium

Finally, we would like to thank Pearson Education for supporting and publishing the fifth edition of this text. In particular we thank the following: Rufus Curnow, Acquisitions Editor; Tim Parker, Project Editor; Kelly Miller, Designer for cover and text; Kerrie Morton, Project Controller and Christopher Kingston, Editorial Assistant.

PUBLISHER'S ACKNOWLEDGEMENTS

We are grateful to the following for permission to reproduce copyright material:

Figures

Figure on page 9 from A method for the selection of appropriate business-to-business integrated marketing communications mixes, *Journal of Marketing Communications*, Vol. 8 (1), pp. 1–18 (Garber, L.L. and Dotson, M.J. 2002), Copyright © 2002 Routledge, reprinted by permission of the publisher (Taylor & Francis Ltd., http://www.tandf.co.uk/journals); Figure 1.1 from Integrated marketing communications and the evolution of marketing thought, *Journal of Business Research*, Vol. 37 (3), pp. 155–62 (Hutton, J.G. 1996), Copyright © 1996, Elsevier, with permission from Elsevier; Figure 1.3 from Determinants of the corporate identity construct: A review of the literature, *Journal of Marketing Communications*, Vol. 9 (4), pp. 195–220 (Melewar, T.C. 2003), Copyright © 2003 Routledge, reprinted by permission of the publisher (Taylor & Francis Ltd., http://www.tandf.co.uk/journals); Figure 2.1 from *PLMA Yearbook 2012*; Figure 3.1 after How advertising works: A planning model, *Journal of Advertising Research*, Vol. 20 (5), pp. 27–33 (Vaughn, R. 1980), www.warc.com/jar; Figure 3.3 after The Elaboration Likelihood Model of Persuasion, *Advances in Experimental Social Psychology*, Vol. 19, pp. 123–205 (Petty, R.E. and Cacioppo, J.T. 1986), Copyright © 1986, with permission from Elsevier; Figure 3.6 after The role of attitude toward the ad as a mediator of advertising effectiveness: a test of competing explanations, *Journal of Marketing Research*, Vol. 23, p. 131 (MacKenzie, S.B., Lutz, R.J. and Belch, G.E. 1986), American Marketing Association; Figure 4.1 from Recycling the family life cycle: A proposal for redefinition, *Advances in Consumer Research*, Vol. 9, pp. 271–6, Figure 1 (Gilly, M. and Enis, B. 1982), Association for Consumer Research, reproduced with permission of Association for Consumer Research, permission conveyed through Copyright Clearance Center, Inc.; Figure 4.4 from GFK significant, November 2011; Figure 5.2 from *Defining Advertising Goals for Measured Advertising Results*, New York: Association of National Advertisers (Colley, R.H. 1961); Figures 6.4, 6.5 after Ad spending: growing market share, *Harvard Business Review*, Vol. 68 (1), pp. 44–8 (Schroer, J. 1990), Copyright © 1990 Harvard Business School Publishing Corporation, all rights reserved, reprinted by permission of Harvard Business Review Figure 8.5 from JFC Informatique & Media, Paris, France (2003); Figure 12.2 from Shopping and saving strategies around the world, The Nielsen Company (2011), http://www.nielsen.com/content/corporate/us/en/insights/reports-downloads/2011/global-shopping-survey-oct-2011.html; Figure 13.2 after *The Loyalty Effect: The hidden force behind growth, profits and lasting value* (Reichheld, F.F. 2001) Copyright © 2001 by the Harvard Business School Publishing Corporation, all rights reserved, reprinted by permission of Harvard Business School Press; Figure 13.4 from Development of addressed mail items in the five largest European markets, The Boston Consulting Group, as found at http://www.post.at/gb2009/en/Postmarkt_Europa.php; Figure 13.7 from The mismanagement of customer loyalty, *Harvard Business Review*, July, pp. 86–94 (Reinartz, W. and Kumar, V. 2002), Copyright © 2002 by the Harvard Business School Publishing Corporation, all rights reserved, reprinted by permission of Harvard Business Review; Figures 13.8, 13.9 from *Annual Report 2011*, Lotus Bakeries p. 33; Figure 13.10 from *Annual Report 2011*, Lotus Bakeries p. 11; Figures 14.3, 14.4 from Geert Maes, CEO, FISA; Figure on page 494 from *Measuring the effectiveness of online advertising: Study conducted by PwC for IAB France and the SRI* (2010) p. 13; Figure on page 494 from *Measuring the effectiveness of online advertising:*

Study conducted by PwC for IAB France and the SRI (2010) p. 22; Figure 15.2 from InSites Consulting, www.insites-consulting.com; Figure 16.2 from *Statistics Report 2010: European trends in advertising complaints, copy advice and pre-clearance*, European Advertising Standards Alliance (EASA) (2010) p. 11, Figure 1, http://www.easa-alliance.org/, European Advertising Standards Alliance – The single voice for advertising self-regulation; Figure 16.3 from *Statistics Report 2010: European trends in advertising complaints, copy advice and pre-clearance*, European Advertising Standards Alliance (EASA) (2010) p. 28, Figure 13, http://www.easa-alliance.org/, European Advertising Standards Alliance – The single voice for advertising self-regulation; Figure 16.4 from *Statistics Report 2010: European trends in advertising complaints, copy advice and pre-clearance*, European Advertising Standards Alliance (EASA) (2010) p. 25, Figure 9, http://www.easa-alliance.org/, European Advertising Standards Alliance – The single voice for advertising self-regulation

Screenshots

Screenshot on page 498 from GAIA chicken squeeze screenshot, http://www.gaia.be/nl/nieuws/gaia-lanceert-chicken-squeeze-, the image can only be used to address the welfare problems of chickens in cages for the production of eggs

Tables

Table 1.3 adapted from W.F. van Raaij, Integratie van Communicatie: vanuit de Zender of vanuit de Ontvanger' (Integration of Communication: Starting from the Sender or the Receiver?), in *Effectiviteit in Communicatie management (Effectiveness in Communication Management)*, pp. 169–84 (Damoiseaux, V.M.G., van Ruler, A.A. and Weisink, A. (eds) 1998), Deventer: Samson, ISBN: 9014058411, 9789014058412; Table 6.2 after Ad spending: maintaining market share, *Harvard Business Review*, 68 (1), pp. 38–43 (Jones, J.P. 1990), Copyright © 1990 Harvard Business School Publishing Corporation, all rights reserved, reprinted by permission of Harvard Business Review; Table 6.3 after *Advertising Media Planning*, Lincolnwood, IL: NTC Business Books (Sissors, J.Z. and Surmanek, J. 1986) © The McGraw-Hill Companies, Inc.; Table 6.4 from Statistics Belgium, http://statbel.fgov.be/nl/modules/publications/statistiques/verkeer_vervoer/inschrijvingen_nieuwe_en_tweedehandse_voertuigen_2008-2011.jsp; Table 6.5 from with thanks to Wendy Van Dyck, Communication Channel Expert, Space Brussels, for providing advertising budgets of the car industry; Table 11.1 after Sports sponsorship development in leading Canadian companies: issues and trends, *International Journal of Advertising*, 17 (1), pp. 29–50 (Thwaites, D., Anguilar-Manjarrez, R. and Kidd, C. 1998), reproduced with permission of WARC; Table 14.2 after Selecting and evaluating trade shows, *Industrial Marketing Management*, vol. 21 (4), pp. 335–41 (Shoham, A. 1992), Copyright © 1992, Elsevier, with permission from Elsevier; Table 15.2 from Users of the world, unite! The challenges and opportunities of social media, *Business Horizons*, Vol. 53 (1), pp. 59–68 (Kaplan, A.M. and Haenlein, M. 2010), p. 62, Copyright © 2010, with permission from Elsevier; Table on page 579 after I. Doukakis, M. Krambia-Kapardis and M. Katsioloudes, Corporate Social Responsibility: A pilot study into the realities of the business sector in Cyprus, in, *New Challenges for Corporate and Marketing Communications. Proceedings of the Eighth International Conference on Corporate and Marketing Communications*, pp. 64–80 (Bennett, R. 2003), London Metropolitan University

Text

Box on page 132 from *InSites Consulting 2008 lifestyle segmentation of Dutch youngsters for MTV Networks*, Rotterdam, InSites Consulting (Van den Bergh, J. and Verhaeghe A. 2008); Box on page 528 adapted from 'Sainsbury's changes Tiger Bread to "Giraffe Bread" following advice from 3-year-old', *The Telegraph*, 01/02/2012 (O'Hare, S.), http://www.telegraph.co.uk/news/newstopics/howaboutthat/9053800/Sainsburys-changes-Tiger-Bread-to-Giraffe-Bread-following-advice-from-3-year-old.html, Copyright © Telegraph Media Group Limited 2012

Photos

The publisher would like to thank the following for their kind permission to reproduce their photographs:

(Key: b-bottom; c-centre; l-left; r-right; t-top)

12 Getty Images: Chinafoto Press. 14 The Absolut Company: Vincent Dixon. 19 InSites Consulting. 32 BBDO: (t). 49 Getty Images: AFP. 51 Patrick De Pelsmacker. 67 Reproduced with permission of Barco. 90 Gesamtverband Werbeagenturen GWA & McCann Erickson Europe. 94 Getty Images: Max Nash / AFP. 129 Getty Images. 131 Alamy Images: Michael Dwyer. 144 Rex Features: Crollalanza. 158 Gesemtverband Werbeagenturen GWA & J Walter Thompson. 161 Corbis: Richard Klune. 162 Corbis: Henry Diltz. 204 Corbis: Tony Savino. 208 Reproduced with permission of Nissan. 210 Reproduced by permission of V.F. Corporation: AMVBBDO. 211 Reproduced with permission of De Lijn, Belgium. 220 AMVBBDO. 222 Image courtesy of The Advertising Archives. 229 Grey Communications Group Ltd. 232 Reticel NV. 244 L'Oreal UK. 268 James Davies. 270 Corbis: John Hicks. 314 Nationale Loterij, Belgium. 327 Getty Images. 328 Getty Images. 354 Getty Images: Guinness (t). 375 Alamy Images: Anthony Hatley. 380 Getty Images. 384 Alamy Images: Alex Segre. 385 Corbis: Richard Cummins. 414 NV Mars Belgium SA. 434 Lotus Bakeries. 477 Reproduced with permission by FISA, Belgium. 540 The Global Fund. 557 Getty Images. 565 Getty Images. 584 Pampers. 585 Pampers

Cover images: *Front:* iStockphoto

All other images © Pearson Education

In some instances we have been unable to trace the owners of copyright material, and we would appreciate any information that would enable us to do so.

LIST OF ACRONYMS

ABC	Audit Bureau of Circulations
ACC	Association of Communication Companies
AIM	Affect Infusion Model
AIO	activities, interests and opinions
ANOVA	analysis of variance
ATR	awareness trial reinforcement
B2B	business-to-business
B2C	business-to-consumer
BOGOF	buy one get one free
BPS	Brand Personality Scale
CARU	Children's Advertising Review Unit
CEEMEA	Central and Eastern Europe, Middle East and Africa
CEIR	Centre for Exhibition Industry Research
CEO	chief executive officer
CPM	cost per thousand
CPM-TM	CPM in target market
CPT	cost per thousand
CRM	customer relationship marketing
CSR	corporate social responsibility
CTLC	Community-based Technology and Learning Centres
CTR	click-through rate
DAGMAR	Defining Advertising Goals for Measured Advertising Results
DAR	Day After Recall
DEA	data envelopment analysis
DM	direct mail
DOSS	degree of overall similarity of strategy
DRTV	direct response television
EASA	European Advertising Standards Alliance
EDLP	every day low prices
ELM	Elaboration Likelihood Model
EMEA	Europe, the Middle East and Africa
ERP	effective rating points
ESP	emotional selling proposition
FCB	Foot–Cone–Belding
FMCG	fast-moving consumer goods
GRP	gross rating points
HILO	high–low
HSM	Heuristic–Systematic Model
HTML	Hypertext Mark-up Language
IAB	Interactive Advertising Bureaux
IAT	Implicit Association Test
ICC	International Chamber of Commerce
IMC	integrated marketing communications
IP	Internet Protocol

JEP	Jury of Ethical Practices
LNG	liquefied natural gas
MAO	motivation, ability and opportunity
MC	marketing communications
MMA	Mobile Marketing Association
MMORPG	massively multiplayer online role-playing game
MNT	mother and newborn tetanus
MPU	Mid-Page Unit
MUSH	Municipal, University, Social, Hospital
NGO	non-governmental organisation
OOH	out-of-home
OTS	opportunity to see
PBC	perceived behavioural control
PEOU	personalised ease of use
PI	product involvement
PKM	Persuasion Knowledge Model
PLC	product life cycle
PMT	Protection Motivation Theory
POP	point-of-purchase
POPAI	Point-of-Purchase Advertising Institute
POS	point-of-sales
PPC	pay per click
PR	public relations
PU	perceived usefulness
PURL	personalised website (URL)
RE	Reading Ease
RFID	radio frequency identification
RFM	recency–frequency–monetary value
RNR	Radio News Release
ROI	return on investment
RQ	Relationship Quality
RSS	Really Simple Syndication
SEA	search engine advertising
SEM	search engine marketing
SEO	search engine optimisation
SMS	Sports Marketing Surveys; Short Message Service
SOM	share of market
SOV	share of voice
SRO	self-regulatory organisation
SRC	self-reference criterion
STAS	Short-Term Advertising Strength
STP	segmenting–targeting–positioning
SWOT	Strengths, Weaknesses, Opportunities and Threats
TAM	Technology Acceptance Model
TOMA	Top-of-Mind Awareness
TORA	Theory of Reasoned Action
TPB	Theory of Planned Behaviour
UGC	user-generated content
USP	unique selling proposition
VNR	Video News Release
WAP	Wireless Application Protocol
WFA	World Federation of Advertisers
WFL	Win for Life
WOM	word of mouth
VOD	video-on-demand

CHAPTER 1
Integrated communications

CHAPTER OUTLINE

The marketing mix

The communications mix

Communications across cultures

Integration of marketing communications

Integration of corporate communications

Factors leading to integrated marketing and corporate communications

Levels of integrated communications

Barriers to integrated communications

The integrated communications plan

CHAPTER OBJECTIVES

This chapter will help you to:

- Situate marketing communications in the marketing mix
- Get an overview of the instruments of the marketing communications mix
- Understand what integrated (cross-cultural) marketing and corporate communications mean, and their organisational implications
- Learn the factors leading to integrated communications
- Get an overview of the different levels of integration
- Understand why fully integrated communications are not easily implemented
- Get an overview of the essential steps in the marketing communications plan

Introduction

The integration of the various instruments of the marketing mix is one of the major principles of sound marketing strategy. Obviously, this integration principle also applies to the various instruments of the communications mix. In fact, integrated communications have been practised by good marketing communicators for decades. Why, then, has the concept of 'integrated marketing communications' (IMC) in recent years developed into one of the basic new trends in marketing communications? Is IMC really fundamentally new? Or is it an old idea which has rarely, if ever, been realised? In other words, is it something everybody agrees on which should have been activated years ago, but for all kinds of practical reasons was not? Or is it nothing more than traditional marketing and advertising dressed up in fancy words and a new language?[1] Whatever the case, the integration of the various instruments of the communications mix is favourably influenced and necessitated by a number of important trends in marketing today. At the same time, barriers to change, and to the successful implementation of IMC, remain strong. The latter may explain why such an obvious concept as IMC, leading to a more homogeneous and therefore more effective communications effort, has not been put into practice much earlier. As a result, integrated communications have a number of practical and organisational consequences that influence the way in which communicators organise their communications function, the way in which they deal with communications consultants such as PR and advertising agencies and, indeed, the way in which communications consultants organise themselves.

Marketing and the instruments of the marketing mix

Marketing is the process of planning and executing the conception, pricing, promotion and distribution of ideas, goods and services to create and exchange value, and satisfy individual and organisational objectives.[2]

Given the marketing objectives and goals, the target segments and the market position that has to be defended, the tools of the marketing plan have to be decided upon. The marketer has a number of tools to hand: the instruments of the marketing mix. Traditionally, these instruments are divided into four categories, called the 4Ps of the marketing mix. Some of the tools of the marketing mix are shown in Table 1.1.

Table 1.1 Instruments of the marketing mix

Product	Price	Place	Promotion
Benefits	List price	Channels	Advertising
Features	Discounts	Logistics	Public relations
Options	Credit terms	Inventory	Sponsorship
Quality	Payment periods	Transport	Brand activation
Design	Incentives	Assortments	Direct marketing
Branding		Locations	Point-of-purchase
Packaging			Exhibitions and trade fairs
Services			Personal selling
Warranties			Electronic communication

The product tool consists of three layers. The **core product** is the unique benefit that is being marketed. In fact it is the position, the unique place in the mind of the consumer, that will be focused upon. Often the brand is a summary, a visualisation of this core benefit and all the associations it leads to. The core product has to be translated into a **tangible product**. Product features, a certain level of quality, the available options, design and packaging are important instruments by which a core benefit can be made tangible. Finally, the **augmented product** gives the tangible product more value and more customer appeal. The augmented product can be defined as the 'service layer' on top of the tangible product. It includes elements such as prompt delivery, installation service, after-sales service and management of complaints.

Price is the only marketing instrument that does not cost anything, but provides the resources to spend on production and marketing activities. The **list price** is the 'official' price of a product. However, discounts and incentives of all kinds can be used to make the product more attractive. Systems of down payments and payment periods, combined with attractive interest rates, can also be used to make the offering more attractive and ensure that the immediate budget constraint is less of a problem for the consumer. The price instrument is an ambiguous tool. On the one hand, price cuts are an effective way to attract consumers. On the other, price cuts mean losing margin and profit. Furthermore, the customer gets used to discounts and may gradually be educated to buy on price and be a brand-switcher. The regular use of the price instrument is incompatible with building a strong position and a strong brand on the basis of product characteristics or benefits. Therefore good marketing can be defined as avoiding the price tool as much as possible.

By means of place or distribution, the company manages the process of bringing the product from the production site to the customer. This involves transporting the product, keeping an inventory, selecting wholesalers and retailers, deciding on which types of outlet the product will be distributed in, and the assortment of products to be offered in the various outlets. Distribution strategy also implies maintaining co-operation between the company and the distribution channel, and finding new ways to distribute products, such as infomercials (programme-length advertising and selling) and e-commerce.

Promotion or marketing communications (MC) are the fourth and most visible instruments of the marketing mix. They involve all instruments by means of which the company communicates with its target groups and stakeholders to promote its products or the company as a whole. The instruments of the communications mix are introduced in the next section.

Good marketing is integrated marketing. Two principles are important when designing and implementing a marketing mix, namely **consistency** and **synergy**. Marketing instruments have to be combined in such a way that the company's offering is consistently marketed. In other words, all marketing instruments have to work in the same direction, and not conflict with each other. The ice cream brand Häagen-Dazs is positioned as a high-quality treat for sophisticated young adults. This core product or basic positioning is reflected in the whole marketing mix. The product itself is of excellent quality and made from the best ingredients. The **brand name** sounds – at least to an American public – exotic, maybe Scandinavian. The price is high, emphasising the exclusive character and the top quality of the brand. Distribution is relatively exclusive. The product is available in special shops or in separate freezers in supermarkets. Marketing communications reflect the sophistication and special, erotic atmosphere of the brand positioning. Similarly, a watch, the basic benefit of which is low cost, will be a very simple product with no special features or design. No strong brand name will be developed, and the basic marketing instrument will be price. The watch will have to be widely available, especially in discount stores and hypermarkets. Promotion will be limited to in-store communications or a simple presentation of the product in the retailer's advertising campaign.

The second important principle is synergy. Marketing mix instruments have to be designed in such a way that the effects of the tools are mutually reinforcing. A brand will become stronger if it is advertised and available in the appropriate distribution outlets. Sales staff will be more successful if their activities are supported by public relations activity, price incentives or advertising campaigns. The effect of sponsorship will be multiplied if combined with sales promotion activity and public relations campaigns generating media exposure of the sponsored event. Intensive distribution will be more effective when combined with in-store communications and advertising, etc. Successful marketing depends on a well-integrated, synergetic and interactive marketing mix.

The same principles apply to marketing communications. In each of the chapters on communication instruments attention will be devoted to consistency and synergy in integrating communications instruments.

The communications mix

Often advertising is considered a synonym for marketing communications because it is the most visible tool of the communications mix. But, of course, a large variety of communications instruments exist, each with its own typical characteristics, strengths and weaknesses. The tools of the communications mix were presented in the last column of Table 1.1.

Advertising is non-personal mass communications using mass media (such as TV, radio, newspapers, magazines, billboards, etc.), the content of which is determined and paid for by a clearly identified sender (the company).

Brand activation is the seamless integration of all available communications means in a creative platform in order to activate consumers by stimulating interest, initiating trial and eventually securing consumer loyalty. It is a tool used to build brands through interaction with target audiences as it helps increase frequency, consumption and penetration of the brand. It is a marketing process of bringing a brand to life through creating brand experience. **Sales promotions**, as a part of brand activation, are sales-stimulating campaigns, such as price cuts, coupons, loyalty programmes, competitions, free samples, etc.

Sponsorship implies that the sponsor provides funds, goods, services and/or know-how. The sponsored organisation will help the sponsor with communications objectives such as building brand awareness or reinforcing brand or corporate image. Sports, arts, media, education, science and social projects and institutions, and TV programmes, can be sponsored. Events are often linked to sponsorship. A company can sponsor an event or organise its own events, for instance for its sales team, its clients and prospects, its personnel, its distribution network, etc.

Public relations consist of all the communications a company instigates with its audiences or stakeholders. Stakeholders are groups of individuals or organisations with whom the company wants to create goodwill. Press releases and conferences, some of the major public relations tools, should generate publicity. Publicity is impersonal mass communications in mass media, but it is not paid for by a company and the content is written by journalists (which means that negative publicity is also possible).

Point-of-purchase communications are communications at the point of purchase or point of sales (i.e. the shop). It includes several communications tools such as displays, advertising within the shop, merchandising, article presentations, store layout, etc.

Exhibitions and **trade fairs** are, particularly in business-to-business and industrial markets, of great importance for contacting prospects, users and purchasers.

Direct marketing communications are a personal and direct way to communicate with customers and potential clients or prospects. Personalised brochures and leaflets (with feedback potential), direct mailings, telemarketing actions, direct response advertising, etc., are possible ways of using direct marketing communications.

E-communications offer new ways to communicate interactively with different stakeholders. The Internet, together with e-commerce, combine communicating with selling. Mobile

Table 1.2 Personal versus mass marketing communications

	Personal communications	Mass communications
Reach of big audience		
Speed	Slow	Fast
Costs/reached person	High	Low
Influence on individual		
Attention value	High	Low
Selective perception	Relatively lower	High
Comprehension	High	Moderate–low
Feedback		
Direction	Two-way	One-way
Speed of feedback	High	Low
Measuring effectiveness	Accurate	Difficult

marketing uses the possibilities of text, video and sound transfer to mobile phones. Interactive digital television has the potential to transform traditional advertising into interactive communications on TV.

Marketing communications try to influence or persuade the (potential) consumer by conveying a message. This message transfer may be directed to certain known and individually addressed persons, in which case it is called **personal communications**. The message transfer may also be directed to a number of receivers who cannot be identified, using mass media to reach a broad audience. This is called **mass communications**. Personal communications are mainly direct and interactive marketing actions and personal selling. All other promotional tools are mass communications. Table 1.2 compares personal and mass marketing communications using different criteria. This comparison does of course generalise. The practical implications of the selection mix depend on the situation and the creative implementation and execution of the communications instruments. For instance, a bad mail shot could also lead to higher selective perception and lower attributed attention.

Another way of categorising marketing communications instruments is to differentiate between theme or image communications and action communications.

In **image or theme communications** the advertiser tries to tell the target group something about the brand or products and services offered. The goal of image communications could be to improve relations with target groups, increase customer satisfaction or reinforce brand awareness and brand preference. This might eventually lead to a positive influence on the (buying) behaviour of the target group. Theme communications are also known as above-the-line communications, as opposed to below-the-line or action communications. This difference (the line) refers to the fee an advertising agency used to earn. All above-the-line promotional tools used to lead to a 15% commission fee on media space purchased. Consequently, above-the-line communications are synonymous with mass media advertising (TV, radio, magazines, newspapers, cinema, billboards, etc.). Below-the-line or **action communications** tools were communications instruments for which the 15% rule was not applicable. This terminology has since lost its importance because most agencies now charge a fixed fee or hourly fee rather than using the commission system.

Action communications seek to influence the buying behaviour of target groups and to persuade the consumer to purchase the product. The primary goal is to stimulate purchases. In practice, theme and action campaigns are not always that easy to distinguish. Sometimes the primary goal of advertising is to sell, as in advertisements announcing promotions or direct response ads. Visits from sales teams may also have the purpose of creating goodwill rather than selling. Theme promotions such as sampling gadgets to increase brand awareness are also used.

BUSINESS INSIGHT
Eurocard/MasterCard: imbuing a well-known brand with richer emotional qualities

Europay International and its local partners market the Eurocard/MasterCard all across Europe. All countries differ in terms of the relative strength of the Eurocard/MasterCard, its target audiences and its major marketing objectives. For example, in Central Europe, the main objective is to introduce the concept of credit cards; in Germany to motivate and capture first-time card applicants; in France to maintain market share. This has meant that locally generated campaign and media strategies and tactics have been applied throughout the years. In 2000, a global campaign was launched to build brand awareness and to create a stronger emotional bond with the target audiences. This image-building campaign was intended to differentiate an essentially generic brand with well-known functional qualities from its competitors. The European-wide target group for the campaign was defined as people who use their credit cards intelligently and responsibly, essentially to achieve good things in their lives for their families, their friends, their colleagues and themselves. Eurocard/MasterCard users are supposed to be more family-oriented, more in line with values of personal balance and harmony, rather than hedonistic and materialistic. The basic selling idea is 'Eurocard/MasterCard: the best way to pay for everything that matters'. The creative expression is: 'There are some things that money can't buy – for everything else there's Eurocard/MasterCard.'

TV advertising has been used to launch, consolidate and leverage the concept of higher-level emotional values throughout Europe. The concept has been leveraged across all media and has also been used in below-the-line campaigns. Eurocard/MasterCard was a sponsor of the UEFA Euro 2000 and the UEFA Champions League soccer competitions. In all countries, the campaign was extended into various other media. For instance, in France, print and outdoor advertising have become a key part of the media schedule; in the UK, cinema and national press were added; in Italy, radio and press were used. Both in Italy and Germany, an Internet site was set up, linked to the sponsorship of the Champions League. Research indicates that consumers value the campaign as sensitive and intelligent. It is considered to be advertising that clearly understands people as individuals and addresses them in an adult and positive manner. After the advertising campaign, unprompted brand awareness in nine European markets had increased by 3% to 37%. Unprompted advertising awareness had moved up from 5% to 11%.[3]

Integration of marketing communications

Integrated marketing communications have been defined in a number of ways, stressing various aspects, benefits and organisational consequences of IMC. Putting it very generally,

> it is a new way of looking at the whole, where once we saw only parts such as advertising, public relations, sales promotion, purchasing, employee communication, and so forth, to look at it the way the consumer sees it – as a flow of information from indistinguishable sources.[4]

It is the integration of specialised communications functions that previously operated with varying degrees of autonomy. It is seamless, through-the-line communications.[5] The American Association of Advertising Agencies uses the following definition of IMC:

> a concept of marketing communication planning that recognizes the added value of a comprehensive plan that evaluates the strategic roles of a variety of communication disciplines, e.g., general advertising, direct response, sales promotion and public relations – and combines these disciplines to provide clarity, consistency and maximum communication impact.[6]

The various definitions incorporate the same core idea: communications instruments that traditionally have been used independently of each other are combined in such a way that a synergetic effect is reached, and the resulting communications effort becomes 'seamless' or homogeneous. The major benefit of IMC is that a consistent set of messages is conveyed to all target audiences by means of all available forms of contact and message channels. Communications should become more effective and efficient as a result of the consistency and the synergetic effect between tools and messages. In other words, IMC have an added value when compared with traditional marketing communications.[7]

BUSINESS INSIGHT
Brighter mornings for brighter days

To reinforce its claim 'We bring brighter mornings', Tropicana developed a full-round integrated marketing communications campaign. On its website it explains the healthiness of its orange juice. As a juicy, delicious, nourishing orange only needs water and bright sunshine, Tropicana claims its juice is actually a bit of sunshine which brings mornings to life with a nutritious boost. Why? Because *brighter mornings develop into brighter days*. This message is also stressed in its TV commercials. To further bring the message alive, Tropicana organised several events in which it literally brought sunshine to people in the farthest reaches of Canada, but also in a more iconic place, Trafalgar Square in London. The event in London was on the same day that the TV campaign kicked off. A giant helium sun was installed which was 30 000 times bigger than a football, had a surface area of 200 m² and weighed over 2500 kg. The internal light source of the Trafalgar sun produced the equivalent of 60 000 light bulbs: 4 million lumens of light. The sun rose an hour earlier than normal sunrise and set three hours later than normal sunset, giving people in London four additional hours of sunlight. Next to delivering this unique brand experience to people, informing them on the website and bringing the message in advertisements, the claim that a glass of Tropicana tastes delicious and energises your day was reinforced by digital and point-of-purchase communications, free samples, a PR campaign, a movie on YouTube, and a Facebook action.

Who would not believe that if Tropicana can bring sunshine to the darkest places of Canada and enlighten London like this, it would not be able to bring a little bit of sunshine to your breakfast table?[8]

The rationale behind this new way of looking at marketing communications – and certainly the most relevant issue in the whole IMC discussion – is the consumer's point of view. The consumer does not recognise the subtle differences between advertising, sponsorship, direct mailing, sales promotions, events or trade fairs. To him or her, these are all very similar and indistinguishable ways that a company employs to persuade people to buy its products. Therefore, it is very confusing and less persuasive to be confronted with inconsistent messages. Consumers may be more sensitive to commonalities and discrepancies among messages than to the specific communications vehicles used to transmit them.[9] IMC may therefore also be defined from the customer's point of view. It is in the field of communications where the receiver is offered sources, messages, instruments and media in such a way that an added value is created in terms of a faster or better comprehension of the communication. Integration occurs at the consumer or perceiver level. It is the task of the communicator to facilitate this integration at the consumer level by presenting the messages in an integrated way.[10] In fact, there is a need to manage each point of contact between the consumer and the product or organisation.[11] In Figure 1.1, an overview is given of various elements of the communications mix, and the potentially integrating role of marketing communications.[12]

IMC do not happen automatically. All the elements of the communications mix have to be carefully planned in such a way that they form a consistent and coherent integrated communications plan. As a consequence, IMC can only be implemented successfully if there is also a strategic integration of the various departments that are responsible for parts of the communications function. Indeed, advertising, public relations, sales promotions and personal

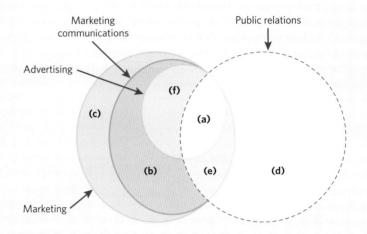

(a) Corporate advertising

(b) Sales force and channel communications, trade shows, packaging, direct marketing, sales promotions, etc.

(c) Distribution, logistics, pricing, new-product development, etc.

(d) Investor relations; community relations; employee communications; public affairs/government relations; most media relations; crisis communications and corporate identity; executive communications; charitable contributions, etc.

(e) Product publicity; brochures and other collateral materials; parts of media relations, crisis communications and corporate identity, sponsorships, etc.

(f) Traditional mass-media advertising

Figure 1.1 The marketing mix and integrated marketing communications

Source: Hutton, J.H. (1996), 'Integrated Marketing Communication and the Evolution of Marketing Thought', *Journal of Business Research*, 37, 155–62.

selling in most companies are traditionally managed by separate divisions that seldom communicate with each other, let alone take account of each other's priorities or integrate their efforts. Successful IMC rest on the existence of one communications manager who has the authority to supervise and integrate all the specialised communications functions of the organisation. Often this will imply a radical change in the structure of the organisation, and that may be the most important reason why IMC have not been implemented in most companies.

RESEARCH INSIGHT
Perception of IMC in the US motor carrier industry

In a study of the perception of US motor carrier marketing managers, 192 respondents were asked to report for which communications functions they used each of the marketing communications tools they employed. The subjects framed five communications functions as the steps of the individual-level new product adoption model. Sixteen marketing communications tools were mentioned. The map below was generated by means of correspondence analysis on the basis of the number of times a communications tool was assigned to a specific communications function. It is a graphical representation of how appropriate the marketing managers perceive the role of each tool in each stage of the new product adoption process. The horizontal axis of the map primarily represents the various stages in the adoption process. All mass communications tools are clustered on the left-hand side of the map, close to the first stages of the adoption process (awareness and interest). Internet and e-mail are positioned close to the interest and evaluation stages. Telemarketing is more closely associated with generating trials while personal selling is more closely associated with gaining adoption. Although IMC advocate consistency in all the communications tools used, each tool still has a specific role to play in the communications strategy accompanying the launch of a new product.[13]

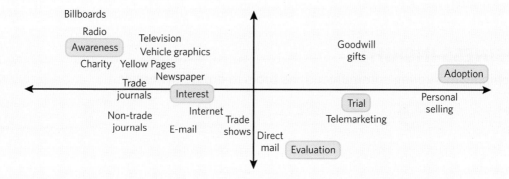

Source: Garber, L.L. and Dotson, M.J. (2002), 'A Method for the Selection of Appropriate Business-to-Business Integrated Marketing Communications Mixes', *Journal of Marketing Communications*, 8(1), 1–18.

In Table 1.3, some major differences between 'classic' communications and integrated communications are summarised.[14] In this overview, the focus is on the changing nature of communications and the changing attitude of the consumer. Both necessitate a seamless integration of communications instruments. Traditional communications strategies are based on mass media delivering generalised transaction-oriented messages. Integrated communications

Table 1.3 Classic and integrated communications

Classic communications	Integrated communications
Aimed at acquisition	Aimed at retention, relationship management
Mass communications	Selective communications
Monologue	Dialogue
Information is sent	Information is requested
Information provision	Information – self-service
Sender takes initiative	Receiver takes initiative
Persuasive 'hold up'	Provide information
Effect through repetition	Effect through relevance
Offensive	Defensive
Hard sell	Soft sell
Salience of brand	Confidence in brand
Transaction-oriented	Relationship-oriented
Attitude change	Satisfaction
Modern: linear, massive	Postmodern: cyclical, fragmented

Source: Based on van Raaij, W.F. (1998), 'Integratie van Communicatie: vanuit de Zender of vanuit de Ontvanger?' (Integration of Communication: Starting from the Sender or the Receiver?), in Damoiseaux, V.M.G., van Ruler, A.A. and Weisink, A. (eds) *Effectiviteit in Communicatie Management* (*Effectiveness in Communication Management*). Deventer: Samson, 169–84.

are much more personalised, customer-oriented, relationship-based and interactive. They are aimed not only at changing awareness and attitudes, but also at directly influencing behaviour. Integration is not synonymous with relationship marketing, satisfaction management or interactive communications. These principles may well be put in practice by means of a 'classic' communications strategy. However, by means of integrated communications the key objectives of modern marketing can be reached much more effectively.

BUSINESS INSIGHT
Combining marketing communications tools to create synergies

Integrating the various tools can lead to synergies in a number of ways. Here are some examples:

- The sales team have an easier job if their product or company is well known as a result of sponsorship or advertising.
- In-store or point-of-purchase communications that are consistent with advertising are much more effective.
- A promotional campaign that is supported by advertising is generally more successful.
- Direct mailing is more effective when prepared by an awareness-increasing advertising campaign and supported by a sales promotion campaign.
- Public relations, corporate advertising and sponsorship can have synergetic effects on company image building.
- Websites will be more frequently visited when announced in mass media advertising.
- Advertising for a trade show will be more effective if an incentive to visit the stand is offered.

Integrating marketing communications across cultures

More and more companies are operating internationally. Following this trend, international communications have also grown enormously. International marketing communications management differs from domestic communications management in that one has to operate in a different environment with different demographic, economic, geographic, technological, political and legal conditions. Cultural and legal differences between a company and its foreign marketplace can cause many problems and difficulties. The translation from the message strategy 'what to say' into a creative strategy 'how to say it' is even more problematic in international marketing communications than it is in domestic communications. Different cultural components can have a major impact on international communications campaigns. Different regulations regarding communications instruments are also important. Furthermore, marketing communications have to consider differences in media availability and the popularity of different media. Due to differences in the international marketing environment, a company has to consider the major question: to what extent should it localise (adapt) or globalise (standardise or integrate) its marketing communications across different cultures?

Cultural difference are among the most important factors that impact international marketing communications. Hofstede[15] describes **culture** as the 'collective programming of the mind which distinguishes the members of one group or category of people from those of another'. In order to succeed in international communications, marketing communications managers have to understand these cultural differences. The reason for this is that, since consumers grow up in a certain culture and are used to that culture's values and beliefs, they will respond differently to marketing communications.[16] Often, marketers and marketing communications executives fall victim to the self-reference criterion (SRC). The **self-reference criterion** refers to our unconscious tendency to refer everything to our own cultural values.[17] People often expect that foreigners have the same values, same interests, etc., as they do themselves, and if this is not the case, they consider their own habits, values, etc., to be superior. In order to be able to understand other cultures, the marketer has to try to avoid the self-reference mistake, and not take for granted everything he or she is used to. The impact of culture on advertising will be more extensively discussed later (see Chapter 7).

BUSINESS INSIGHT
Marketing and the Chinese

China is becoming an increasingly important market for many companies. However, marketers have to take into account Chinese habits and sensitivities. To increase the number of visitors in Hong Kong Disneyland, the dresses of Mickey and Minnie Mouse were adapted. An American–Chinese designer developed a frivolous cherry-red dress that reminds many of the traditional Moa outfit. In that way, the management hopes to appeal more to local culture and to attract more visitors from mainland China.[18]

The French car maker Citroën placed an advertisement in the Spanish newspaper *El Pais* featuring the Chinese leader Mao Zedong. The text said: 'it is true, we are the leaders. But revolution never stops at Citroën.' The Chinese protested because they found the ad insulting, and Citroën had to withdraw it.[19]

Standardisation or adaptation

Once a company decides to go international, one of the most important strategic decisions to be made is to what extent a global or cross-culturally integrated marketing strategy in the foreign market(s) must be followed. A **standardised campaign** can be defined as a campaign that is run in different countries, using the same concept, setting, theme, appeal and message, with the possible exception of translations (Photo 1.1). A local approach implies that elements of the communications strategy are adapted to local circumstances. A major advantage of **globalisation** is the cost savings that can be realised. Standardisation across the world induces economies of scale and might lead to huge savings in manufacturing costs, personnel costs and communications costs. Not only can the price of the communications programme be reduced, but also the quality can be enhanced. Really good creative ideas are scarce. Global campaigns offer the advantage of globally exploiting a great creative idea. Other advantages are that global campaigns make things simpler for the company in the sense that co-ordination and control of the communications programme in the different countries become easier. Moreover, a global image can be created across different parts of the world. Brands that have communicated globally include: Nivea, Martini, L'Oréal, Xerox, Parker pens, etc.

Often the international marketer will have to adapt or localise his or her marketing mix to a different foreign environment. People living in different cultures differ in their beliefs, previous experiences, attitudes, values, etc. Different values might lead to different needs and

Photo 1.1 H&M: A global brand.
Source: Getty Images: Chinafoto Press.

different consumption behaviour. Even in cases where consumers' needs are homogeneous, this does not automatically mean that people want to satisfy these needs in a similar way. Nescafé, for example, offers more than 100 varieties since consumers in different countries prefer different blends and flavours. Furthermore, different cultures have different attitudes towards instant coffee. One analysis of instant coffee's share of the total coffee market found it to be more than 90% in the UK, 85% in Japan, 50% in Canada, 35% in France, 32% in the USA and 10% in Germany,[20] making global advertising less obvious. Philishave modifies its ads because of the different shaving habits in different countries.[21] Nokia adapted its 6100 series mobile phones and, for example, raised the ring volume for noisy crowds in Asia.[22] Komatsu enlarged the door handles of its mechanical shovels for the Finnish market because Finnish workers often wear gloves against the cold.[23]

BUSINESS INSIGHT
The Chinese image of global brands

Since the majority of Chinese consumers are not familiar with the Roman alphabet, the first requirement when international companies enter the Chinese market is to choose a proper Chinese name. This is not an easy task and a company has several possibilities. First of all, the brand name can be directly translated. In this case, the Chinese name sounds like the original name, but has no specific meaning in Chinese. This strategy is followed by Nike, for example. Secondly, the company can opt for free translation. In this case, the name is translated according to its meaning, but has no phonetic link with the original brand name. Schindler, for example, sounds like 'Xunda' in Chinese and means 'quick arrive'. Finally, the company can go for a mixed translation. This is the most popular alternative and results in a name that both sounds like the original brand name and has a meaning in Chinese. For example, Gucci's Chinese name sounds like 'Guzi' and means 'Classic looks', while Nivea sounds like 'Niweiya' and means 'Girl keep elegance'.

Besides deciding on the translation method, a company also has to decide on the sound of the new name. Every Chinese syllable can be pronounced with four different intonations. So, a two-syllable name can have 16 different tone combinations, having an impact not only on the ease of pronunciation but also on the connotations. Next, different combinations of characters have to be selected. Although different combinations can have the same pronunciation, they have completely different meanings. For example, Ford sounds like 'Fute' in Chinese and can have two different meanings: 'happiness' and 'bending over'. Since neither really fits Ford, it opted for a direct translation without a meaning. Ford's competitors fared better and have strong meanings. BMW is renamed as a 'horse', which in Chinese legend is connected with speed. Citroën is a 'dragon', referring to power, and Rover is a 'tiger', which is linked with prestige. So, it is important to realise that by giving the brand a Chinese name, not only is a local name given, but also a local image and a local identity, which can be very different from the original one. Only 7% of Chinese names have an almost identical meaning to the original one. A good example here is Volkswagen, for which the Chinese name means 'the masses' or 'the people'. More than 50% of Chinese names have a positive connotation that is absent in the original name. For example, Polaroid does not have a real meaning in the Roman language but its Chinese name 'Shoot get instant photos' accurately describes Polaroid's benefits. About 12% have a different connotation. Examples here are Yahoo!, which in Chinese means 'elegant tiger', and Lux soap, which is called 'strong man'. It is interesting to note that Lux is pronounced with exactly the same sound and tone in Taiwan but has a different meaning. In Taiwan, Lux refers to 'beauty', a meaning that fits the brand better. However, when Lux entered the Chinese market in the 1980s, 'beauty' was not an acceptable name since it referred to 'decadent bourgeois aesthetics' under the orthodox communist doctrine. Another example of different meanings in Chinese and Taiwanese is Johnson & Johnson. It is called 'strong life' in China and 'tender/delicate life' in Taiwan. The company opted for 'strong life' in China because, in view of the 'one-child' policy, parents would rather have strong than delicate babies.

The foregoing illustrates that obtaining a global image is not always easy. For 2 million Chinese consumers, BMW is not 'the ultimate driving machine' but 'a treasure horse'. If the same image is not possible, try to go for a meaningful name since it enhances image and association formation. Moreover, if possible, emphasise a Western image rather than a local image in the new name, since the Chinese regard Western products very favourably.[24]

Probably the best way to approach international markets is not to adhere to one of the extreme strategies of globalisation or localisation, but to opt for a 'global commitment to a local vision',[25] or in other words to 'think global, but act local' (**glocalisation**). If the brand positioning is a good one, the brand should be rolled out in most countries. Also, an excellent creative idea can work nearly everywhere. However, advertisers should always look at the creative idea through the eyes of the locals. Even the best ideas might need some adaptation in execution to get into the mind set of local people or to respect their cultural values.[26] An example would be to work out a global creative idea, but to adapt the advertising so that local

Photo 1.2 Absolut Vodka: think global, act local.

Source: The Absolut Company: Vincent Dixon.

presenters, experts or celebrities are employed, or that reference is made to local history or national symbols; Big Ben in London, the Eiffel Tower in Paris, the Atomium in Brussels, the gondolas in Venice (Photo 1.2). Coca-Cola records radio spots in about 40 languages and uses 140 different music backgrounds.[27] Goodyear and Kraft develop a pool of ads from which each country selects the most appropriate one.[28] Miele runs campaigns with a different pay-off line. In Germany, Spain and Switzerland Miele is 'a decision for life', in Austria Miele is 'reliability for many years', and in the Netherlands, Belgium, the USA and Canada 'there is no better one'.[29]

BUSINESS INSIGHT
Globalising and standardising at Unilever and Procter & Gamble

For decades, Unilever adapted both its 'brand hardware' and 'software' to local markets. Due to cost considerations, local Unilever companies are no longer allowed to adapt the brand hardware, consisting of product formula, packaging and product range. However, a brand's software, such as the brand name, advertising, PR and event marketing, is still localised. For example, although standardised products are used, Unilever decided to retain different brand names for its fabric softener in each country (Lenor in the UK, Kuschelweich in Germany, Coccolino in Italy, Mimosin in Spain, Snuggle in the USA and Robijn in Belgium). Also, the Coccolino teddy used in the Italian market and the puppets Darren and Lisa used for the UK market were retained because the cloth puppets and teddy have been used for years and connect well with local people. Dumping them would be throwing away valuable brand equity. Moreover, cost savings that can be achieved by standardising brand hardware are much higher than can be achieved by globalising an advertisement campaign.

Similar reasoning is followed by Unilever's competitor, Procter & Gamble. It learned the hard way that globalisation is not always the way to go. Changing the name of the Mexican soap brand Escuda into Safeguard led to a serious sales decrease. After the name was changed back to Escuda again, sales went back up. Since then, P&G has been thinking of the hard points it wants to keep consistent across regions. For example, the machine used to make Bounty has to be standardised, but the brand name, the colours, etc., can be adapted to meet local needs, as can the advertising. For Pampers, for example, widely varied copy is used for the Middle Eastern, Latin American and South African campaigns.[30]

Some product categories seem to lend themselves better to a global approach than others (Figure 1.2).[31] Some products can be sold to similar target groups across countries. This boils down to global segmentation or finding groups of consumers that share similar opinions, values, interests, etc., across borders instead of looking for different target groups in different countries. Young people or people with a higher education, for example, are very similar, whether they are French, Italian, German, Belgian or American. The reason for this is that these groups, in general, are more open-minded, less culturally bound, more receptive to international media, make more use of international media, have more international contacts and/or go abroad more often. This factor explains the success of MTV, Calvin Klein and Dell computers. Products that can be sold on the basis of image appeals are also more suited for global communications.

Images, visual messages and international music lend themselves more to standardisation than a spoken or written message. Examples of successful campaigns in this category are Marlboro, Levi's, Coca-Cola, Martini, Smirnoff vodka, perfume ads and airline campaigns. Luxury products are targeted at upper-class people who buy the product for the status it brings. Because only the status and no product information needs to be communicated, these appeals are easier to standardise. Although innovative, high-tech products, such as the latest computers, the latest software, etc., need an informational appeal, these products seem to be used everywhere in the same way, which can justify a global appeal. Products with a country-of-origin appeal can be more easily globalised. Belgium is famous for its chocolate, France for its wine, Japan for its technology, Germany for its durability, Switzerland for its watches. Products that use a country-of-origin positioning may well be advertised by means of a global approach.

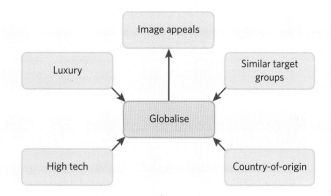

Figure 1.2 Product suitability for global approach

Based on: Fannin, R. (1984), 'What Agencies Really Think of Global Theory', *Marketing and Media Decision* (December), 74–82.

RESEARCH INSIGHT
Glocalisation is the best branding strategy in India

The expansion of multinational companies into international markets has resulted in a large literature on positioning strategies in different cultures or markets.[32] An important question is to what degree branding and marketing communications in these markets should be standardised (globalisation), locally adapted (localisation) or glocalised. The latter refers to 'global localisation',[33] a global brand identity strategy that allows for country-specific flexibility in communications mix decisions. India, with a population of more than 1 billion people, which is growing at 1.41% per year, is one of the booming markets of the twenty-first century. Moreover, the increasing purchasing power of Indian consumers at the rate of 7.2% in 2010–11 indicates the ability of these consumers to purchase high-quality products in the near future. The liberalisation of the Indian market from 1991 onwards, and the growth of domestic demand, have provided the prerequisites for the entrance of multinational companies into this market.[34] Success in such a lucrative market needs proper understanding of effective communications and branding strategies. For international companies, India is therefore a very relevant context to study these strategies.

In a sample of 327 Indian consumers, the effectiveness of communications and branding strategies (globalisation, glocalisation and localisation) was studied by assessing the effect of different types of endorsers and types of brand communications and their interaction on consumer responses.[35]

Three types of endorsers were studied: an unknown Indian model, a local (Indian) celebrity and a global celebrity. In an advertisement they were each combined with a global and a local brand communication for a home cinema system. Brand globalness was manipulated by globalising or localising all the written elements (websites, names of cities, language used, etc.) of the ads except the brand name. The experimental conditions represent globalisation or complete standardisation (combination of a global endorser and a global brand), localisation or complete adaptation (combination of a local model or celebrity and a global brand) and glocalisation (combination of a local model or celebrity and a global brand; combination of a global celebrity and a local brand).

Previous studies of standardisation and adaptation of communications strategies reveal that both standardisation and localisation are able to positively affect a consumer's attitudes and purchase intention towards advertised products. On the one hand, it has been reported that adapted or localised messages are more persuasive and result more often in positive attitudes than global ones.[36] On the other hand, other studies show that brands that are perceived as global can create associations of wide availability and recognition which strongly affect a consumer's decision to purchase such brands through brand prestige and brand quality.[37] India is an ethnocentric country.[38] It can therefore be expected that these ethnocentric tendencies lead to preference of local elements in brand advertising. On the other hand, Indians are status conscious.[39] If global elements in the ad create a perception of brand globalness, they may lead to more positive attitudes and a higher purchase intention than localised brands.

Testing the six ads (three types of endorsers with two types of brands) reveals that a glocalisation strategy (a combination of a global brand with a local endorser) engenders the most positive consumer responses over complete globalisation (a combination of a global brand and a global endorser). Moreover, highly ethnocentric Indians prefer both glocalisation and localisation (a combination of a local brand and a local endorser) over globalisation, while the attitudes and purchasing intentions of Indians who scored low on ethnocentrism do not differ for any of the strategies.

Integration of corporate communications

Corporate communications can be defined as the total integrated approach to the communications activity generated by all functional departments of a company, targeted at all company stakeholders, and aimed at establishing and maintaining the link between strategic objectives, the corporate identity and the corporate image in line.[40] Corporate communications have three main objectives:

1. To establish joint strategic starting points of the organisation that will have to be translated into consistent communications; in other words, to define a corporate identity that is in line with corporate strategy.

2. To reduce the gap between the desired identity and the image of the company (corporate image) that exists with its target groups.

3. To organise and control the implementation of all the communications efforts of a company, in line with the two above-mentioned principles.

In an organisation, corporate communications have to be integrated with marketing communications. All communications efforts, whether for the benefit of the whole company and all types of stakeholders, or to support the marketing of the company's products towards customers and potential customers, should be consistent and synergetic, and aim at communicating the same company values and propositions to all.

Corporate vision and mission, culture, personality and identity

Corporate communications can be defined as the visualisation of corporate identity. To understand what the core concept of corporate identity means, its link with a number of related concepts has to be discussed. This is presented in Figure 1.3.[41]

Just as individuals have personalities, so do organisations. Corporate identity is derived from strategic priorities, corporate culture, corporate structure and industry identity. **Corporate culture** can be defined as 'the deeper level of basic assumptions and beliefs that are shared by members of an organisation, that operate unconsciously and define in a basic "taken-for-granted" fashion an organisation's view of itself and its environment'.[42] Put more simply, corporate culture can be defined as 'the way we do things around here'. It is determined by factors such as the corporate philosophy, values, mission, principles, guidelines, history, the founder of the company and the country of origin.[43] Corporate culture consists of a number of levels. The first level includes the physical aspects of the company, such as the atmospherics of the building (look and style) and the way visitors are treated. The second level consists of the values held by employees, such as the importance of honesty in doing business, the service-mindedness of the sales staff and the responsiveness to customer complaints. The third level is achieved when everyone in the company develops a firm belief in the corporate culture characteristics, and behaves accordingly without questioning them. This third level is sometimes considered to be synonymous with **corporate personality**. This concept refers to the values held by personnel within the organisation. It is defined as the collective, commonly shared understanding of the organisation's distinctive values and characteristics. It encompasses corporate philosophy, mission, strategy and

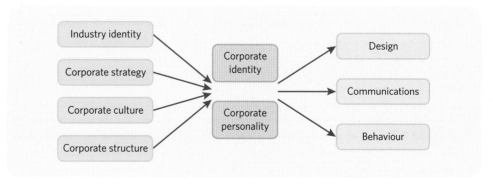

Figure 1.3 Corporate strategy, culture, personality, and corporate identity and its components

Source: Melewar, T.C. (2003), 'Determinants of the Corporate Identity Construct: A Review of the Literature', *Journal of Marketing Communications*, 9(4), 195–220.

principles, and as such is a major component of the corporate identity or even its main determining factor.[44]

Corporate identity is also embedded in **corporate strategy**. Long-term strategic objectives will determine and shape the desired corporate personality: the company's mission will reflect the desired personality and corporate culture; positioning decisions will reflect the priorities that companies hold as to their chosen personality. On the other hand, the corporate personality will also determine the strategic options. Corporate culture and corporate personality are a very persistent part of the internal company environment, and as such cannot be changed overnight. Corporate strategy will always to a certain extent have to be based on the most persistent elements of the corporate personality, or at least take them into account.

Corporate identity is also influenced by industry identity and corporate structure. **Industry identity** involves underlying economic and technical characteristics of an industry, such as industry size, growth, competitiveness, culture and technology levels. A strong generic or industry-wide identity (e.g. the banking industry) often forces companies to have similar strategies and missions. **Corporate structure** consists of organisational structure and brand structure. Organisational structure is concerned with the lines of communication and reporting responsibilities within the organisation. It relates to the degree of centralisation and decentralisation, and often has a major influence on brand structure (see also the next chapter).

Obviously, the choice of a specific type of corporate identity will depend on the strategic priorities defined, and will have a great impact on brand strategy and marketing and corporate communications.

Corporate identity is the set of meanings by which a company allows itself to be known and through which it allows people to describe, remember and relate to it. It is the way the company chooses to present itself to its relevant target audiences by means of symbolism, communications and behaviour. It is the tangible manifestation, the visual statement, of the personality (shared values) or corporate culture of an organisation. Corporate identity is what the company is, what it does and how it does it. It relates to the products and brands a company offers, how they are distributed, how the company communicates with the public or stakeholders, and how the company behaves.[45]

Corporate communications, but also marketing communications, have to be based on, and be consistent with, the important elements of the corporate identity of the company. For

BUSINESS INSIGHT
CEOs and their families don't buy their competitors' products

One of the obvious ways to show commitment to your own company and its products and services is not to buy, use or wear competitive brands. Word has it that Bill Gates from Microsoft forbids his wife to buy big competitor Apple's iPhone. CEOs from Belgian companies seem to agree. Jef Colruyt, the CEO of one of the largest retailers in Belgium that carries his name, says he buys 99% of what he needs in his own supermarkets. The products he cannot find in his own shops, like fresh lobster, he buys at the local fish store, and not in a competitive supermarket, and he expects the same from his family. The CEO of the outdoor supermarket chain AS Adventure occasionally enters a store of his biggest competitor, Decathlon, but says it feels like cheating. Barbara Torfs, CEO of the shoe store chain Torfs, only wears shoes from her own brand and expects other family members to do the same. Wearing other shoes at family parties is barely tolerated and regarded as blasphemy, she says. Anthony Vanherpe, CEO of Panos (a chain of take-out sandwich shops), says he eats at competitors Délifrance once or twice a year to monitor the competition in terms of product assortment, marketing and look and feel, but wouldn't appreciate it if his family did the same.[46] CEOs buying and using their own products is a strong and obvious sign of commitment that can enhance corporate identity and reputation.

instance, companies that are committed challengers in the markets in which they operate will be more aggressive communicators, maybe using more direct guerrilla types of marketing and thus communications strategies involving head-on sales promotion and comparative advertising techniques. Also the principles of value marketers, like The Body Shop, will be reflected in all their communications efforts. Sponsorship will be used to link the company's image to environmental causes such as wildlife concerns, and in-store communications techniques will be used to convey the message of avoiding waste by recycling and simple, low-cost packaging.

Building and maintaining a corporate identity is more than just consistently using the traditional tools to communicate a company's core elements. Everything it does, and all the material it uses, should be an integral part of the effort to convey a homogeneous and consistent identity. **Corporate symbolism** or **corporate design**, more specifically a consistent house style on business cards, letterheads, vehicles, gifts, clothes, equipment, packaging, etc., is an integral part of the corporate identity, or at least of the way in which it is made visible.

BUSINESS INSIGHT
The visualisation of the corporate identity: logos and slogans

The company name, logo and slogan are vital elements of the house style of a company and important elements of corporate design. They are the visualisation of the corporate identity.

Logos and slogans should have a number of characteristics:

- A logo should be the long-term visualisation of the company's strategy. One logo and one slogan should be used for the whole company. The slogan should be a perfect summary of the company's identity.

- Logos and slogans have to be distinctive. They are tools of differentiation between the company and its competitors. As a result, slogans that are relevant but too general should be avoided, as well as logos that are too similar to the ones used by the competition. The same goes for company names, for that matter. Often, images and colours are much more important factors in recognising a logo or a brand and attributing it to the correct product than the verbal elements of a brand (the brand name).

- Additionally, slogans should be relevant for the consumer, otherwise they will not be able to contribute to the development of a distinctive corporate image.

- The logo and slogan should be timeless, but modifiable. All too often, logos refer to a short-term objective, or to an issue that seemed important at the time the logo was designed, but loses all its relevance after some time. Since logos and slogans should visualise the long-term image of a company, they should have a timeless capacity that allows them to be used for a long period of time. Having said that, the perception of what is beautiful changes over time. Logos should be modifiable in that the corporate design should be adaptable to changing aesthetic preferences over time, without radically altering the whole house style.

- Slogans, but especially logos, should be usable in all circumstances and in all communications instruments and tools. This includes advertisements, mailings and annual reports, but also business cards, letterheads, envelopes, brochures, trucks, walls, films, ties, pens, press releases, etc. They should be equally distinctive on a business card and on a large truck. The company should be able to combine them with other logos, to include them in communications tools with different colours, with all kinds of letter formats and shapes.

Source: InSites Consulting.

Corporate design is not just a matter of logos and slogans. Here are a number of examples in which intelligent design has contributed to the corporate or brand identity:

- the shape of the container (Toilet Duck, Absolut Vodka);
- a distinctive opening device (Grolsch beer);
- the packaging material (Ferrero Rocher; Absolut Vodka);
- the colour of the packaging (Marlboro);
- the use of a personality (KFC and Colonel Sanders, the Marlboro cowboy).

Besides communications and corporate design, **corporate behaviour** is also an important factor in making the corporate identity visible. The saying 'actions speak louder than words' is very applicable to corporate identity issues. The way in which the employees of a McDonald's restaurant behave is an integral part of the corporate identity of the company. The self-proclaimed customer-friendliness of a bank (e.g. by means of an advertising campaign) may be completely destroyed by behaviour that is inconsistent with this principle. A mineral water, using 'purity' as its main selling proposition, cannot afford actions that may be perceived as a threat to this purity, e.g. manufacturing processes involving potentially toxic chemicals or a lack of hygiene during the bottling process. Internal marketing, and internal communications as a part of it, will be extremely important in convincing and training staff to develop behaviour that is consistent with the desired corporate identity.

Paying attention to the corporate identity is of growing importance for a number of reasons:

- The business environment is undergoing rapid changes, altering the structure and the strategic direction of companies. Mergers, acquisitions, changing competitive environments, etc., change the nature of markets in radical ways. Corporate identity should therefore be constantly monitored and reviewed, along with the rapidly changing strategies.
- It is increasingly difficult for companies to differentiate themselves and their products from each other. Developing a distinctive corporate identity can be of crucial importance in developing a unique market position.
- Companies tend to become more global, and hence the danger of inconsistent communications by the various business units becomes greater. Developing a common corporate identity can be the basis of a more consistent communications strategy.
- Important economies of scale can be achieved by ensuring that all forms of communication by a company are consistent with one another. A good starting point is the development of a common base, i.e. a common corporate identity that is based on well-defined strategic options.
- A well-established corporate identity can lead to increased motivation of the company's own employees. Feeling 'part of a family' may stimulate them to do a better job.
- A corporate identity that is communicated convincingly creates confidence and goodwill with external target groups of stakeholders. Shareholders and investors may have more confidence, relations with the government may be better, higher-quality employees may be attracted, and the general public may have a more favourable attitude.

Corporate image and corporate reputation

The **corporate image** is the stakeholder's perception of the way an organisation presents itself. It is the result of the interaction of all experiences, beliefs, feelings, knowledge and impressions of each stakeholder about an organisation. It is a subjective and multidimensional impression of the organisation. The corporate identity resides in the organisation, but the

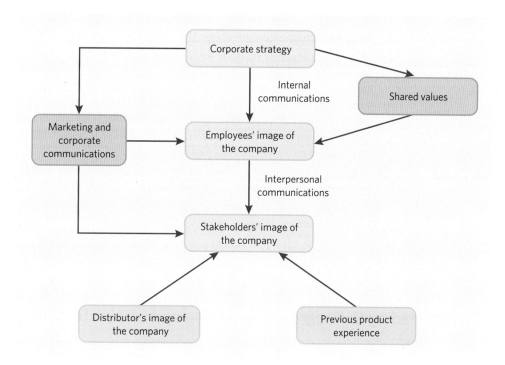

Figure 1.4 Factors influencing the corporate image

Source: Based on Dowling, G.R. (1986), 'Managing Your Corporate Images', *Industrial Marketing Management*, 15, 109–15.

corporate image resides in the heads of the stakeholders.[47] The corporate image is not always consistent with the desired corporate identity; in other words, an image gap may exist.

Corporate reputation is the evaluation or esteem in which an organisation's image is held. It is based on experience with the company and/or exposure to communications, behaviour and symbolism. While corporate image can be quite transient and short term in nature, corporate reputation is more firmly embedded in the mind of an individual. Images may change, but the corporate reputation is not easily altered in the short run. It implies credibility, trustworthiness, reliability and responsibility.[48] It refers to how stakeholders view and believe in the core identity and image components of the company.

The corporate image is influenced by a number of factors, the corporate identity and its communication being only two of them. These factors are presented in Figure 1.4.[49]

Corporate identity or corporate culture and corporate strategy are important determining factors or cornerstones of the corporate image, as well as marketing and external corporate communications. But the company's employees also play an important role. Their communications with external target groups and their behaviour in their contacts with these groups will to a large extent determine how the company is perceived. Therefore, internal communications are very important to corporate identity building and corporate communications. Misfits between the perception of the employees and the desired corporate identity may therefore lead to an undesirable image gap.

Besides a company's own staff, other intermediate audiences, such as the distribution channel or advertising agencies, may have an influence on the corporate image. Finally, reality is an important factor: product experience is, to put it in operant conditioning terms, a powerful reinforcer or punisher in the development of a corporate image.

What is the value of a positive corporate image?

- It gives the company authority and is the basis for success and continuity.
- Consumers buy products, often not just because of their intrinsic quality, but also because of the reputation and the value the consumers attach to the company marketing the products.

A positive corporate image creates an emotional surplus, which can be a more persistent long-term competitive advantage than any specific product characteristic.

- A positive corporate image is particularly important for companies whose customers are not deeply involved in the product category. Such customers will base their buying decisions on limited information, such as the impression they have of the company's value. But even when the customer is highly involved, but does not have the capability of judging the value of the company's offerings (because the available information is too complex, or product quality is difficult to assess, as in the case of services), the corporate image can be the decisive factor in the customer's decision.

- It creates a surplus of goodwill which avoids or diminishes problems with government, pressure groups, consumer organisations, etc., in times of crisis.

- It supports the company in attracting more easily the people who are crucial for its success, such as investors, analysts, employees and partners.

Integrated corporate communications should take all these considerations into account.

Factors leading to integrated marketing and corporate communications

A number of important changes and trends have created the need and urge to integrate marketing and corporate communications and to facilitate them. Table 1.4 lists key IMC drivers.

There is a widespread belief that mass media communications are becoming increasingly less effective. Communications clutter, resulting from increasing advertising pressure, leads to increased irritation and advertising avoidance behaviour and to a situation in which advertising in traditional, undifferentiated and impersonalised media is less and less capable of attracting attention, let alone of convincing consumers. As a result of more and more advertisers claiming media time and space, mass media are increasingly expensive. Furthermore, traditional mass media communications are primarily capable of stimulating awareness and attitudes, but much less of stimulating or directly influencing demand. The need for marketing strategies influencing behaviour directly has further eroded the attractiveness of traditional mass media. Using more media and more channels and tools to reach the consumer effectively increases the need for integration of these tools.

Table 1.4 Key drivers of integrated communications

Loss of faith in mass media advertising
Media cost inflation
Need for more impact
Need for more cost-effectiveness and efficiency
Media fragmentation
Audience fragmentation
Increased reliance on highly targeted communications methods
Low levels of brand differentiation
Increased need for greater levels of accountability
Technological evolutions: online and social media communications, mobile communications
Greater levels of audience communications literacy
Overlapping audiences
More complex decision-making units
Need to build more customer loyalty
Move towards relationship marketing
Globalisation of marketing strategies

There is an increased cost awareness and a need for more cost-effective and efficient marketing. The time horizon of companies has become more short-term-oriented. As a result, there is a greater need for directly effective marketing strategies and for instruments the effectiveness of which can be assessed and can be assessed instantaneously. There is, in other words, a growing need for increased levels of accountability. Consequently, mass media are supplemented with, or replaced by, other communications tools with allegedly more impact, that focus much more on influencing the behaviour of individual consumers directly, and the effectiveness of which can be measured precisely, such as direct marketing and interactive marketing communications. Adding more and more diversified tools to the communications mix leads to more media being used and more fragmented media, and increases the need for integration of marketing communications. As a spin-off from this integration of fragmented communications tools, it becomes less and less relevant to measure the effect of one single element in the communications mix, such as advertising. The measurement of communications effectiveness will have to focus on techniques such as monitoring and tracking, which assess the effectiveness of a total campaign at the brand level.

BUSINESS INSIGHT
Non-traditional forms of marketing communications

Branded content

Consumers react increasingly cynically to traditional advertising, and pay less and less attention to it. Therefore, advertisers try to 'hide' commercial messages in media content. This is called 'advertainment' or 'branded content'. Product placement in movies and shows on TV is one example. And this is even practised in books: Fay Weldon got a lot of criticism because she was paid to mention the luxury brand Bulgari in one of her books. Brands are also integrated in computer games. Some computer games are even specifically developed to promote a brand. They are called 'advergames'. 'Plugs' are media formats in which celebrities are paid to talk about a brand.[50]

Entire TV programmes can be produced to promote a brand or a company. In the TV format 'Project Runway', candidates have to design their own fashion clothing products and are judged by a professional jury. At the end of a series of ten programmes, there is a winner, who gets the resources to develop his or her own clothing line. The local Belgian version of this format (called 'De Designers') was largely financed by JBC, a fashion retailer. In return, JBC could appoint one of the members of the jury and received a lot of visibility and brand mention. The winner could design his or her fashion clothing line which would then be sold in JBC stores. Also the Belgian electricity producer Electrabel financed a programme, 'Under high voltage XL' in which families participated in experiments to reduce their electricity consumption.[51]

Walt Disney Studios sponsor an entertaining movie news show. At the end of the show it is revealed that it was paid for by Buena Vista (Disney's film distribution company). Of course, most consumers are not aware of the close link between Disney and Buena Vista.[52] The Belgian cinema group Kinepolis experiments with scent marketing. During the Axe Instinct commercial the deodorant is blown into the theatre through the ventilation system. Similar campaigns for Dove and Magnum ice cream are planned.[53]

Some companies experiment with personalised branded content. The German game producer Software Entertainment develops games in which the brands placed are adapted to the individual's preference. For instance, in a car game, Ford can be replaced by BMW if the player appears to be a BMW fan. Also, interactive brand placement is possible. If the viewer watches a programme on a digital platform, and an actor drinks a bottle of beer, for instance by clicking on the bottle, the viewer can enter an advertising message, a promotion offer, or a Wikipedia-like environment in which comments of other users can be read and own comments can be added.[54]

Buzz marketing

Word of mouth has always been important in steering the behaviour of people, but it has become increasingly important also in people's buying behaviour. More than two-thirds of all consumer buying behaviour is influenced by word-of-mouth advertising.[55] People look for others they can relate and aspire to. Traditionally, media figures, celebrities, sports heroes, etc., play an important role in commercial communications. But recently, consumers seem to relate more to 'ordinary' people than to celebrities. This is the origin of buzz marketing. The essence of buzz marketing is the fact that the spontaneous networks that make up our society constitute the most effective way to meaningfully reach people and influence consumers. Buzz marketing is aimed at spreading the message through the personal network of consumers. It is 'organised word of mouth'. Buzz marketing works on the basis of the principle 'give them something to talk about'. It works on the basis of individuals who like to receive messages and like to spread the word. What do people want to talk about? Here are the six magic buttons of buzz marketing: Play with taboos: intimacies, sex . . . ; talk about the extraordinary; look for the unusual, but keep the link with the brand; give people something to laugh about that makes them enjoy and talk about it to others; bring a story with a special angle; keep it 'secret', people like to talk about secrets. Buzz is not something that just happens to companies, it can be organised. A typical example of buzz marketing is blogging (weblogging): individuals who give their opinion in real time on Internet diaries.

Stealth advertising

Stealth advertising is a marketing activity in which the commercial content is hidden. For instance, people are paid to go to trendy bars and to promote a new drink by offering it to other visitors, without saying that they work for the company that launched it. For instance, Sony Ericsson, Wal-Mart and Procter & Gamble have used this technique in the past to support the launch of a new product, to improve their image, or to build a stronger connection with their customers (see Chapter 16 on ethical issues for more details).

Audiences and markets tend to become more and more fragmented, making mass media less effective and increasing the need for more specialised and fragmented media. Communications tend to become customised for narrower and narrower markets, and customer contact is established by means of multimedia methods. There is an increasing reliance on highly targeted communications methods, such as database techniques and boutique channel (highly targeted TV channel) advertising.[56] IMC are about co-ordinating multiple and diverse tools targeted at multiple and diverse audiences.[57]

Most markets in well-developed countries are mature. This means that a lot of products and brands are of similar quality. Low levels of brand differentiation increase the need to make the difference by means of communications. Therefore, some argue 'that the basic reason for [the increased attention for] integrated marketing communications is that marketing communications will be the only sustainable competitive advantage of marketing organisations in the 1990s and into the twenty-first century'.[58]

Mainly as a result of technological evolutions and innovations, new marketing and marketing communications tools are becoming available. Scanning and database technology allow more in-depth knowledge of the consumer and, especially, a more personalised and direct approach to the consumer. Interactive media, such as the Internet, have contributed to a situation in which the relationship between the sender and the receiver of messages is less unidirectional. Social media and mobile applications have profoundly changed the way companies communicate with their stakeholders. Direct marketing and direct response communications also lead to a situation in which communications become more and more receiver-directed.[59] Together with increased communications literacy on the part of the consumer, this leads to a market situation in which much of the power is at the receiving end, i.e. the receiving consumer decides what he or she will be exposed to and how he or she will react to it. Indeed, the marketing situation has gradually shifted from a situation in which all the power of knowledge and control was in the hands of the manufacturer to a market in which the retailers are the strongest party. Today the balance is shifting towards a market in which the consumer is the most powerful agent.[60] In fact, one could argue that integration is mainly technology-driven. New technologies and applications, such as the Internet, make the consumer less accessible, and force companies into a more integrated approach towards a fragmented and increasingly interactive communications situation which will make marketing communications more credible and more convincing.

Organisations are increasingly communicating with multiple audiences and stakeholders. Many of these stakeholders overlap. An employee may be a shareholder, a community leader may be a supplier, members of stakeholder groups are target customers, and all of them are exposed to different media. Furthermore, decision-making units in many of these stakeholder groups are increasingly complex, implying that they have to be reached by means of different communications tools and channels. It is not necessary to give exactly the same message to all these audiences; on the contrary, messages will have to be adapted to the stakeholders' needs. Nevertheless, it is very important not to convey contradictory messages. Consistent communications have to reflect the mission, corporate identity and core propositions of the organisation to all target groups. Integrated communications provide a mechanism for identifying and avoiding message conflicts when communicating with these overlapping and complex target groups.

One of the trends in marketing today is the increasing importance of building customer loyalty instead of attracting and seducing new customers. This trend towards relationship marketing implies a much more 'soft sell' approach. IMC focus upon building a long-term relationship with target groups by means of consistent interactive communications, rather than aggressively persuading the consumer to buy a company's products.

Finally, markets are becoming increasingly global. Phenomena such as the Internet, but also the globalisation of mass media and the increasing exposure of consumers and stakeholders to international communication stimuli, increase the need for consistency in everything the company communicates in all countries in which it markets its products.[61]

Levels of integration

Companies cannot be expected to integrate their communications efforts fully overnight. Several stages or levels of integration can be distinguished. In Table 1.5 seven categories or levels of integration are distinguished.

The first five levels imply the integration of the communications effort mainly at the consumer or marketing communications level. The first two levels focus on conveying the same image and brand awareness through all the marketing communications tools. The next step is the functional integration of all the tools (advertising, sales promotions, sponsorship) into one marketing communications department. In the fourth stage, the marketing tools and the marketing PR function are co-ordinated. Finally, in the fifth stage marketing communications and marketing PR are functionally integrated into one system through which harmonised and consistent messages are conveyed to all actual and potential consumers. In the last two stages, corporate communications and marketing communications efforts are integrated into one system. Indeed, companies communicate not only with (potential) customers, but with all stakeholders. In fully integrated communications messages, tools, instruments and media, targeted to all stakeholders, are co-ordinated and eventually integrated into a comprehensive system of consistent relationship marketing.[62]

Another way of looking at integration levels implies four stages.[63] First of all, the company can define an integrated *mission*, i.e. the basic values and objectives of the company, which are based on the corporate identity. From this basic mission a number of *propositions* are derived, i.e. concrete propositions to the target groups. A 'one-voice' approach implies the

Table 1.5 Levels of integration

- Awareness
- Image integration
- Functional integration
- Co-ordinated integration
- Consumer-based integration
- Stakeholder-based integration
- Relationship management integration

Source: Duncan, T. and Caywood, C. (1996), 'The Concept, Process and Evolution of Integrated Marketing Communication', in Thorson, E. and Moore, J. (eds), *Integrated Communication: Synergy of Pervasive Voices.* Mahwah, NJ: Lawrence Erlbaum Associates, 13–34.

consistent integration of mission and propositions. Propositions can be creatively translated into *concepts* or messages with a certain content and format. A concept can be a theme, a core message, a specific style or a slogan. The fourth level is the integration of *execution*. This implies uniformity in layout, design, typography, logo, colours, visual triggers and other elements of the house style. Successful IMC imply that a 'one-voice' approach is developed, which serves as a starting point for integrated concepts and execution.

Evidently, a company's communications are more than communicating with marketing target groups. A variety of other audiences and stakeholders need to be considered too. In the next integration stage, all communications to all target groups are harmonised. In a truly integrated communications environment, corporate identity definition, corporate reputation and image-building, stakeholder communications and marketing communications are fully integrated. The integration of marketing communications in an international company is not complete until it is achieved across national and international boundaries.

Barriers to integrated communications

IMC are far from a reality in most companies. A number of strong barriers prevent IMC being implemented quickly and efficiently. They are listed in Figure 1.5.

Over many years, companies have grown used to extreme specialisation in marketing communications. The various instruments of the communications mix are managed by separate individuals or departments. Traditionally, strategic power is the exclusive domain of advertising, PR is largely reactive and sales promotion and personal selling are mainly tactical. Specialisation is rewarded and highly regarded, and the need for, or benefits of, integration are overlooked.

The various instruments of the communications mix have traditionally been managed by different organisational entities as discrete activities. Financial structures and frameworks have been in place for many years.[64] Often the idea of IMC is incompatible with traditional hierarchical and brand management structures. These structures may or may not be changed easily. Ideally, IMC can best be effected when all communications activities are physically integrated into one department. But people are generally conservative and reluctant to change. Turf wars and ego problems are important barriers to IMC. The parochialism of managers and their fear of budget cutbacks in their areas of control, and of reductions in authority and power, lead to defending the status quo. PR departments especially are reluctant to integrate because they often consider IMC as the encroachment of ad people on PR professionals and a form of marketing imperialism.[65]

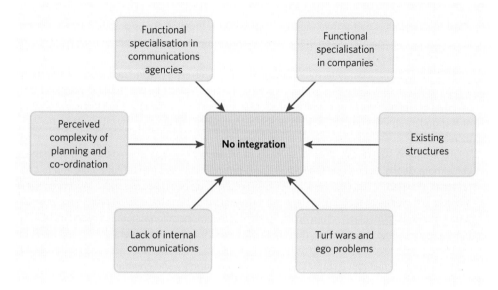

Figure 1.5 Barriers to integrated communications

BUSINESS INSIGHT
IMC and the role of communication agencies

In April 2012, consultant Deepblue presented its Communication Agency Tracking study in which the role of Belgian agencies in IMC is highlighted by advertisers.[66] The study was based on 56 depth interviews and 170 online interviews. It contained four main parts: personal perceptions regarding the evolution of the latest communications business trends in the market; how the communications practices have evolved and how they are likely to keep evolving; the advertisers' opinion on the roles of communications agencies; and the advertisers' evaluation of agency performance.

The advertisers find that agencies adapted themselves well to the evolution of advertisers' needs and that creativity has become more relevant and is more deeply linked with the business objectives of the advertisers. The structure of agencies facilitates a better use of specialised and diversified skills and agencies are capable of initiating new trends and making advertisers activate new marketing solutions. However, they also note a number of weaknesses. Industry fragmentation among mainstream and specialised agencies makes it increasingly difficult to judge the agencies' added value. Agencies tend to overestimate their capability of establishing or managing integrated communications strategies and plans. The agency–advertiser relationship is weakened by a lack of (human) resources, managers' availability and account stability. Impact models to justify the return on investment of campaign activities are usually poor.

The vast majority of the interviewees consider the '360°' claim of agencies as merely a marketing label. A 360° or 'full service' agency is an 'ideal concept' that can, however, not be realised in the market. They consider it a waste of time for one single agency to ensure the capabilities to deliver a true 360° communications plan. These attempts only lead to excessive increases of fees on the basis of the 360° promise. There is a manifest lack of consistency in the co-ordination of 360° plans. Agencies usually give priorities to the service they feel most comfortable with. On top of that, there is a marked difference in how to operationalise the 360° concept itself. Agencies think that 360° means that every communications touchpoint should be used to reach the consumer, while advertisers prefer to embrace all opportunities and touchpoints, but then select the best options. According to the latter, integration of a few touchpoints is better than merely using as many touchpoints as possible. Agencies should better and more honestly position themselves on the basis of their unique skills and not pretend they are experts in all communications tools and tactics.

In 2012, 33% of communications budgets were still invested in traditional above-the-line advertising, and another 21% in below-the-line with point-of-sales and 10% in below-the-line without POS. Another 19% were invested in digital/online communications. These especially are expected to increase moderately as strongly (66% of respondents), while less than 30% of the respondents predict that investments in the other tools are going to increase.

According to advertisers, the top priorities of an agency manager should be to position the agency and its added value more clearly, to engage in the advertiser's environment and marketing vision, and to create a structure based on areas of expertise, i.e. clearly establish a structure of units of specialisation. Moreover, agencies should invest in a better knowledge of their customers (advertisers), in better strategic planning and internal organisation, and in better methods to measure return on investment and remuneration schedules based on ROI. The ideal communications agency should focus on ROI, think out of the box (surprise consumers, go beyond traditional codes, go beyond traditional channels), have a long-term vision, focus on a realistic 360° approach, listen to advertisers and understand them, and maintain a correct balance between strategy and creation.

If not all communications activities of a company are integrated into one department, at least the sharing of information, the communications across divisions and the co-ordination of all communications activities have to be organised. Often, the combination of lack of internal communication and the perceived complexity of planning and co-ordination are important barriers to the organisation of IMC.

Finally, the functional specialisation of external communications agencies and their fragmentation in overspecialised disciplines make the full integration of communications even more cumbersome. The role of communications consultants is discussed in the following section.

The integrated communications plan

The different communications tools will be used in an IMC mix, according to a communications plan that will have to be integrated into the strategic marketing plan. The essential steps in the communications plan are listed in Table 1.6.

Since marketing communications have to be embedded in the strategic marketing plan, the first step is to analyse the marketing communications environment and the marketing strategy, and assess where the marketing communications activity should fit in. From this analysis, target groups and objectives and goals of the marketing communications effort can be derived. Next, which instruments, techniques and media to use and to what extent will be agreed. On the basis of this plan, a budget can be established, and the communications plan and timing can be implemented. Finally, the effectiveness of the campaign has to be assessed.

In the following chapters, branding (see Chapter 2) and how communications can influence consumers (see Chapter 3) are discussed. Branding is an important core issue, since brands are often the link between marketing strategy and its communication. In subsequent chapters, the various stages in the marketing communications plan are discussed, and per instrument a detailed overview of the planning stages is provided. The components of the marketing communications plan are discussed in more depth in the following chapters: target groups (see Chapter 4), objectives (see Chapter 5), budgets (see Chapter 6) and tools (see Chapters 7–15). In each of these chapters the various stages in planning and executing the campaign are detailed and highlighted. The last chapter focuses upon ethical issues in marketing communications.

Table 1.6 The communications plan

- Situation analysis and marketing objectives: *Why?*
- Target groups: *Who?*
- Communications objectives: *What?*
- Tools, techniques, channels and media: *How and where?*
- Budgets: *How much?*
- Timing: *When?*
- Measurement of results: *How effective?*

Summary

Integrated communications are the integration of formerly specialised communications functions into one organisational system that conveys a consistent set of messages to all target audiences. Integrated marketing and corporate communications manage each point of contact between the consumer or other target groups and the product or the organisation. Several key drivers of IMC can be identified, such as loss of faith in mass media advertising, the need for enhanced cost-effectiveness, media and target audience fragmentation and over-lap, more complex decision-making units, the need to build customer loyalty, relationship marketing and, last but not least, the evolution of technology. Integrating the marketing effort is not an easy process. Companies evolve only gradually to a truly integrated communications system. This slow evolution is caused by a number of important barriers to integration, such as the functional specialisation in companies, existing structures, the lack of internal communications and the perceived complexity of planning and co-ordination. In integrated communications many instruments are used. They are embedded in a communications plan that has to be integrated in the strategic marketing plan.

REVIEW QUESTIONS

1. Give a brief overview of the instruments of the communications mix.
2. What are the main concerns in a cross-cultural communications context?
3. What are integrated communications and in what way do they differ from 'classic' communications?
4. How do corporate strategy, culture and personality influence corporate identity?
5. How does corporate identity influence corporate communication?
6. What factors have to be taken into account in corporate image management, and what is the role of communications?
7. What are the factors that reinforce the need for integrated communications, and how can the latter provide an answer to contemporary marketing communications problems?
8. What are the levels of integration a company can go through?
9. What are the barriers to integrated marketing communications?

Further reading

Argenti, P. and Forman, J. (2002), *The Power of Corporate Communication: Crafting the Voice and Image of your Business*. Maidenhead: McGraw-Hill Trade.

De Mooij, M. (2005), *Global Marketing and Advertising: Understanding Cultural Paradoxes*, 2nd edition. Thousand Oaks, CA: Sage.

Hofstede, G. (2003), *Culture's Consequences: Comparing Values, Behaviors, Institutions and Organizations Across Nations*. Thousand Oaks, CA: Sage.

Hofstede, G.J., Pedersen, P.B. and Hofstede, G. (2002), *Exploring Culture. Exercises, Stories and Synthetic Cultures*. Yarmouth, ME: Intercultural Press.

Kitchen, P.J. and De Pelsmacker, P. (2005), *Integrated Marketing Communication: A Primer*. London: Routledge.

Kitchen, P.J., De Pelsmacker, P., Schultz, D.E. and Eagle, L. (eds) (2006), *A Reader in Marketing Communications*. London: Routledge.

Mueller, B. (2004), *Dynamics of International Advertising*. New York: Peter Lang.

Schultz, D.E. and Kitchen, P.J. (2000), *Communicating Globally: An Integrated Marketing Approach*. Lincolnwood, IL: NTC Business Books.

Usunier, J.C. and Lee, J.A. (2005), *Marketing Across Cultures*. Harlow: Pearson Education.

Wright, R. (2004), *Business-to-Business Marketing*. Harlow: Addison-Wesley.

Corporate Reputation Review, http://www.palgrave-journals.com/crr/index.html.

Industrial Marketing Management, http://www.elsevier.com/wps/find/journaldescription. cws_home/505720/description#description.

CASE 1:
Walking the walk: how Walkers proved it can make *any* sandwich more exciting

A new approach for a snack that has only been communicating new flavours and prize promotions for years

Walkers is the top snack brand in the UK, enjoyed by over 10 million people every day. In recent times, the brand's marketing approach has focused on the development of limited edition flavours and price promotions. These have been very successful at delivering short-term sales spikes, but often have not delivered a sustained uplift. The brand had lost its momentum in recent years. In 2002, new

flavours sales were £20 million; in 2007 they were down to £6.7 million.

In 2009, Walkers identified a new opportunity for growth in the profitable 'singles' segment of the business. Research showed that many consumers already had a latent appreciation of a benefit: 60% of them agreed a packet of Walkers would improve their lunchtime sandwich. Yet only 12% of sandwiches were eaten with an accompanying bag of crisps at lunch. There was a huge opportunity to increase this figure – getting more people to make a habit out of the dual purchase of sandwich + Walkers at lunch. Not an easy task when the average lunch break is only 27 minutes, and people's decision process seems to be limited to their choice of sandwich, making it very easy to forget about crisps. It was clear that two things stood in the way: mental availability (saliency – they were not thinking of the two together at the crucial moment); and physical availability (crisps were not sitting near enough to sandwiches in-store).

AMVBBDO's communications objective was to help Walkers meet its 'singles' segment revenue growth target of 15%. A campaign was developed with two main objectives:

1. Take the favourable but latent association between crisps and sandwiches and make it top of mind, prompting consumers to think about the two at lunchtime.

2. Encourage retailers to site Walkers next to their sandwiches in store.

Success would mean capturing the imagination of four key audiences:

- The Great British public, including sub-groups who required differing depths of engagement.
- Journalists, who needed to be attracted by a story they could not resist writing about, in order to get a greater return from the campaign budget.
- The Walkers sales force, who needed emboldening in their crucial task of securing incremental merchandising near to sandwich chillers.
- The people responsible for buying at the UK's biggest supermarkets.

The key business challenge is summarised in Figure 1.6.

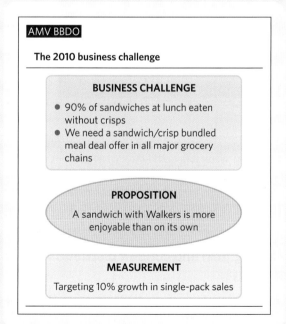

Figure 1.6 The 2010 key business challenge

The creative idea

To ensure the message was registered, Walkers and AMVBBDO felt it required a different style of approach. Their ambition was to surprise: to get consumers saying '*Walkers did what?!?!*' The basic idea behind the campaign was to prove Walkers can make *any* sandwich more exciting, even the town of Sandwich, Kent. Through a series of surprise events over three days, Walkers and AMVBBDO turned the sleepy town of Sandwich into the most exciting town in the UK. Each event featured a celebrity fulfilling a typical community role: JLS (a British band who won second place in the fifth season of the British talent show *The X Factor*) took the sixth-form college assembly; Frank Lampard, a famous football player, coached the college football team; Jenson Button, the Formula one driver, got behind the wheel of a black cab; Marco Pierre White, a British celebrity chef and TV personality, sold gourmet sandwiches from a market stall; Pamela Anderson, the movie star, pulled pints at the local pub; while the British comedian Al Murray hosted the quiz. There was something for everyone.

The idea was to capture the genuine surprise and excitement of the locals on film, and to produce TV commercials and online video content. To ensure reactions were genuine, a great deal of effort went into keeping the plans under wraps, and the events were filmed unscripted and unrehearsed. Regional media were engaged before and during the campaign to ensure they were taken on the journey with Walkers and felt part of the proceedings. To build on the natural spread of news that would occur once the events started happening, Walkers and AMVBBDO set up to prepare and distribute content in near real time. This was made possible by having journalists embedded, and video editing and social media activation teams on site, along with all key decision-makers. Walkers also invited along the buyers from the UK's biggest supermarkets to enjoy the event. Capturing their imaginations would be key to persuading them to site Walkers next to sandwiches in-store.

At its basic level, the communications model was this: the events would generate content, which would then be released through a focused set of channels, according to a phasing plan designed to maximise the campaign's buzz creation and longevity.

Teamwork in action

The nature of this campaign, the need for rapid distribution of event coverage and total synchronicity between TV, online and PR channels, meant that tight collaboration was a fundamental requirement for success. The various parties involved – PepsiCo, AMVBBDO (core idea and creative direction), Freud (PR), OMD (Media planning and buying), Jigsaw (website production) and TRA (video seeding and social media activation) worked as a true team, characterised by a fluid exchange of information, ideas and decisions. The boundaries between disciplines were often blurred. To →

Source: BBDO.

Source: BBDO.

build on the natural spread of news that was expected to occur once the events started happening, the team put in place a range of dedicated resources to ensure speed and flexibility in how they managed the campaign unfolding:

- Round the clock, a social media team fuelled and responded to conversations, some of which were initiated by local residents as soon as the afternoon of the first day of shooting.

- A PR team, located on site, were able to facilitate live event reporting opportunities for the embedded journalists, including interviews with the celebrities. The instant news flows that resulted helped maximise the 'live' impact of the campaign.

- A video/TV editing team, located on site and in London, were able quickly to deliver content ready for distribution while other filming activity was still taking place. All approvers were on call to allow rapid turnround and sign-off, with TV stations lined up for last minute play-out.

Phasing plan and content distribution strategy

The phasing plan involved three discrete stages, *tease→reveal→extend*, and was guided by two principles: (1) surprise – reflecting the nature of the core idea; (2) the tactics used by major motion pictures (preview with trailers →

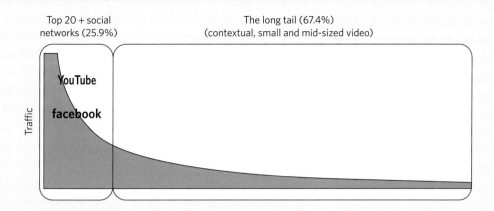

Figure 1.7 Division of total video views across websites

reveal the feature-length version → offer 'DVD' extras for those who want to engage more deeply).

In phase 1, teaser stories from the embedded journalists in Sandwich were in the papers the very next day. And just 24 hours later, ten-second teaser adverts were broadcast on TV and released online, creating the opportunity for viewers exposed to both the news stories and the adverts to connect the dots. After just a further five days, the reveal phase began, with full feature stories in the press and the release of a 60-second advert, again on TV and online. The extend phase then comprised the steady release of 26 pieces of video content across the Web, and housed on the campaign's YouTube channel, which functioned as the content hub. Catering for audience members who seek a deeper level of engagement, the content was also made available on an immersive website at walkers.co.uk. The site featured a 3-D town of Sandwich, within which the content could be discovered. All the TV ads pointed to the website; all the online videos linked to the YouTube channel content hub.

The campaign was conceived with PR-'ability' at its heart. There was a high degree of both integration and synchronisation between it and the other channels used. Throughout the phases, PR collateral ran across print, online and broadcast news media, and comprised event features, profile pieces and bespoke daily webisodes from behind the scenes. Involving a cross-section of talent allowed the team to tap into a vast range of publications catering to different passions, e.g. sport and music.

'Online' encompasses a bundle of channels all by itself, and required a sub-set of principles. The team leaned towards a decentralised approach to content release, seeding the videos widely and encouraging their free circulation around the Web. Particular videos were, however, focused towards the relevant communities, for instance those passionate about football got more of the videos featuring Frank Lampard. The resulting appreciation and advocacy from JLS's fan base was especially strong. The majority of

the total video views actually came from the long tail of small video-hosting sites that were seeded to, not from YouTube (Figure 1.7).

Supplementing the above seeding approach, the team used paid rich media display to boost the reach of the videos, and got the celebrities to point their Twitter fans in the direction of the campaign's YouTube content hub, to see them surprising the Sandwich locals. The team also benefited from indirect reach (earned media) both instantly and as the campaign progressed, the latter because of the general sharing of the videos amongst friends, the former because some of the Sandwich locals shared user-generated photos and videos on Facebook directly from their mobile phones, and because of the work of the on-site social media team, who were posting photos and starting conversations from the word 'go'.

Figure 1.8 summarises the activities under each phase. Figure 1.9 shows the 360° integrated marketing communications logic behind the campaign.

A short video summary of the campaign can be viewed at http://digital.151awards.com/awards/WalkersSandwich/ Assets/AH107542_Walkers_Sandwich_CYBER_B01.mov.

Results

The campaign turned out to be very successful in many respects and engaged all the target groups of the campaign.

The Great British public:

- ranked third in Adwatch, with a modest TV spend of £960 000;
- 80% '*enjoyed watching it a lot*' (Millward Brown post-test, vs UK norm of 65%);
- the campaign channel was the most popular sponsored channel on YouTube throughout March (YouTube);
- the campaign resulted in 1.7 million complete video views, equivalent to 3.3 million minutes in viewing time.

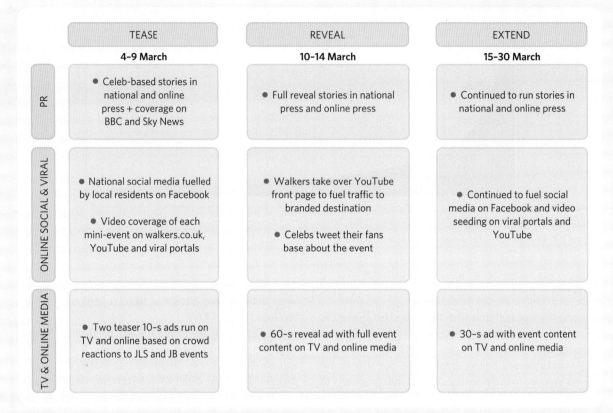

Figure 1.8 Communications activities under each phase

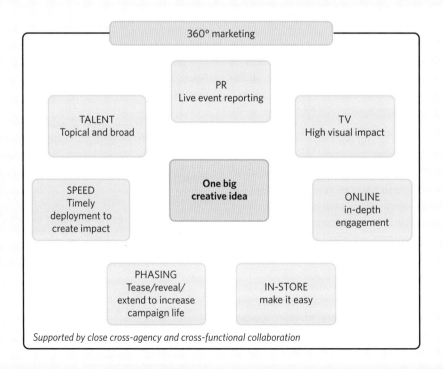

Figure 1.9 The 360° integrated marketing communications logic behind the campaign

The impact of the campaign is illustrated by the following quotes from the Sandwich locals:

- 'It's something they will remember for the rest of their lives' (Veronica Gomez, Headmistress, Sandwich Sixth Form Technical College);

- 'Thanks for making my little town of Sandwich more exciting!! I had a fab week meeting all the celebs especially bumping into JLS on my lunch break :) come back again soon x' (carolinerose99, Walkers Sandwich YouTube channel);

- 'We couldn't believe it when Frank [Lampard] came over and pulled his hood down . . . There was quite a lot of pressure for the goalie in that game!' (Daniel Langiano, Sandwich Tech Football Team);

- 'I didn't know what to do up there, so I just hugged them and started singing with them . . . They all kissed me on the cheek. Afterwards I texted everyone to tell them!' (Stephanie, Sandwich Tech student).

Also journalists were impressed:

- Jason Richards, VP of Sales, PepsiCo UK said: 'The unique and exciting nature of the campaign really captured the imagination of our sales teams and our customers, leading to fantastic execution of Walkers meal deals across multiple channels';

- 'Sandwich was such a brilliant idea. At one point I feared for my life as a small group of girls suddenly grew into a mob as word got out that the hottest boys in pop were actually in the sleepy town!' (*Now Magazine*);

The results of the campaign were impressive:

- 350 pieces of coverage across press, TV and online;

- £3.3 million advertising equivalent value generated.

- 10 000 new meal deals activated (PepsiCo) as illustrated by the following table:

Tesco	Addition of permanent stackers at front of store
JS	Meal deals back on at front of store
Co-op	Walkers replaces McCoys in meal deal
ASDA	Box at front of store
Morrisons	Walkers launches meal deals
Impulse	Meal deals secured with strong POS support

The campaign helped build the sense that Walkers is a modern, innovative brand:

- Walkers' highest ever result for 'would talk about with friends' (Millward Brown post-test, 50% vs the UK norm of 29%);

- won a Gold 'Direct Lion' and Silver 'Promo & Activation Lion' at Cannes.

It landed its message and built the saliency of the favourable link between sandwiches and Walkers:

- 'Makes my sandwich more enjoyable' +18pts (Millward Brown tracking).

It helped Walkers to grow its revenue from the 'singles' segment by 26%, beating the target of 15%. But even more telling was the increase in singles-segment value share, which went up by 6%, against a background of overall segment decline in 2009.

QUESTIONS

1. Describe and assess the problem identification of Walkers and AMVBBDO, and the solution they propose in terms of objectives, target groups and creative ideas.

2. Describe the main components of the campaign. Was the campaign well integrated, consistent and synergetic? Could other instruments have been used, or the same instruments in a different way? Which ones and how?

3. Explore the various campaign results. Do you think the campaign was successful?

4. Suppose you were responsible for a follow-up campaign. What changes would you make compared with the previous campaign and why?

Sources: Marketing Society Awards for Excellence 2011, category M: 360° Marketing, Client: PepsiCo, Agency: Abbott Mead Vickers BBDO, Authors: George Roberts and Tom White (AMV), Adam Warner (PepsiCo), Guy Geerts, Darwin BBDO Belgium.

References

1. Schultz, D.E. (1996), 'The Inevitability of Integrated Communication', *Journal of Business Research*, 37, 139–46.

2. American Marketing Association (1985).

3. Euro Effie (2001), Berlin: Gesamptverbrand Werbeagenturen GWA eV, http://www.euro-effie.com.

4. Schultz, D.E., Tannenbaum, S.I. and Lauterborn, R.F. (1992), *Integrated Marketing Communication: Putting it Together and Making it Work*. Lincolnwood, IL: NTC Business Books.

5. Duncan, T.R. and Everett, S.E. (1993), 'Client Perceptions of Integrated Marketing Communication', *Journal of Advertising Research* (May/June), 30–9.

6. Duncan, T.R. and Everett, S.E. (1993), 'Client Perceptions of Integrated Marketing Communication', *Journal of Advertising Research* (May/June), 30–9.

7. Payne, A. and Holt, S. (2001), 'Diagnosing Customer Value: Integrating the Value Process and Relationship Marketing', *British Journal of Management*, 12, 159–82.

8. Brady, S. (2012), 'Here Comes the Sun: Tropicana Wakes Up London', http://www.brandchannel.com/search_result.asp?cx=000980657010496705841%3Avvjr5rsv4ws&cof=FORID%3A10&ie=UTF-8&q=tropicana+sun; http://www.tropicana.ca/EN/brighter.php (accessed July 2012).

9. Englis, B.G. and Solomon, M.R. (1996), 'Using Consumption Constellations to Develop Integrated Communication Strategies', *Journal of Business Research*, 37, 183–91.

10. Schultz, D.E. (1996), 'The Inevitability of Integrated Communication', *Journal of Business Research*, 37, 139–46.

11. Englis, B.G. and Solomon, M.R. (1996), 'Using Consumption Constellations to Develop Integrated Communication Strategies', *Journal of Business Research*, 37, 183–91.

12. Hutton, J.H. (1996), 'Integrated Marketing Communication and Evolution of Marketing Thought', *Journal of Business Research*, 37, 155–62.

13. Garber, L.G. and Dotson, M.J. (2002), 'A Method for the Selection of Appropriate Business-to-Business Integrated Marketing Communications Mixes', *Journal of Marketing Communications*, 8(1), 1–18.

14. Based on: van Raaij, W.F. (1998), 'Integratie van Communicatie: vanuit de zender of vanuit de Ontvanger?' ('Integration of Communication: Starting from the sender or the receiver?'), in Damoiseaux, V.M.G., van Ruler, A.A. and Weisink, A. (eds), *Effectiviteit in Communicatiemanagement* (*Effectiveness in Communication Management*). Deventer: Samson, 169–84.

15. Hofstede, G. (1991), *Cultures and Organizations: Software of the Mind*. London: McGraw-Hill.

16. Zhang, Y. and Gelb, B.D. (1996), 'Matching Advertising Appeals to Culture: The Influence of Products' Use Conditions', *Journal of Advertising*, 25(3), 29–46.

17. Lee, J.A. (1966), 'Cultural Analysis in Overseas Operations', *Harvard Business Review* (March–April), 106–14.

18. *De Morgen*, 23 January 2008.

19. *De Morgen*, 17 January 2008.

20. Rijkens, R. (1992), *European Advertising Strategies: The Profiles and Policies of Multinational Companies Operating in Europe*. London: Cassell.

21. Rijkens, R. (1992), *European Advertising Strategies: The Profiles and Policies of Multinational Companies Operating in Europe*. London: Cassell.

22. Kotler, P. (2003), *Marketing Management*, 11th edition. Upper Saddle River, NJ: Prentice Hall.

23. Kotler, P., Armstrong, G., Saunders, J. and Wong, V. (2001), *Principes van Marketing*, Schoonhoven: Academic Service.

24. Fan, Y. (2002), 'The National Image of Global Brands', *Brand Management*, 9(3), 180–92.

25. Keegan, W.J. (2002), *Global Marketing Management*, 7th edition. Upper Saddle River, NJ: Prentice Hall.

26. White, R. (2000), 'International Advertising: How Far Can it Fly?', in Jones, J.P. (ed.), *International Advertising. Realities and Myths*. Thousand Oaks, CA: Sage, 29–40.

27. Keegan, W.J. (2002), *Global Marketing Management*, 7th edition. Upper Saddle River, NJ: Prentice Hall.

28. Kotler, P. (2003), *Marketing Management*, 11th edition. Upper Saddle River, NJ: Prentice Hall.

29. Rijkens, R. (1992), *European Advertising Strategies: The Profiles and Policies of Multinational Companies Operating in Europe*. London: Cassell.

30. Taylor, D. (2003), 'An Italian Teddy Weakens Global Brand Logic', *Marketing*, 27 February, 18; Neff, J. (2002), 'P&G Flexes Muscle for Global Branding', *Advertising Age*, 73(22), 53.

31. Fannin, R. (1984), 'What Agencies Really Think of Global Theory', *Marketing and Media Decisions* (December), 74–82.

32. Akaka, M.A. and Alden, D.L. (2010), 'Global Brand Positioning and Perceptions: International Advertising and Global Consumer Culture', *International Journal of Advertising*, 29(1), 37–56; Griffith, D.A. and Yalcinkaya, G. (2010), 'Resource-Advantage Theory: A Foundation for New Insights into Global Advertising Research', *International Journal of Advertising*, 29(1), 15–36; Zou, S. and Volz, Y.Z. (2010), 'An Integrated Theory of Global Advertising: An Application of the GMS Theory', *International Journal of Advertising*, 29(1), 57–84.

33. Sinclair, J. and Wilken, R. (2009), 'Strategic Regionalization in Marketing Campaigns: Beyond the Standardization/Glocalization Debate', *Continuum: Journal of Media & Cultural Studies*, 23(2), 147–57.

34. Nag, B. (2011), 'Trade Liberalization and International Production Networks: Experience of the Indian Automotive Sector', *Fighting Irrelevance: The Role of Regional Trade Agreements in International Production Networks in Asia – A Study of Asia-Pacific Research and Training Network on Trade*. ESCAP. United Nations Economic and Social Commission for Asia and the Pacific.

35. Rajabi, M., Dens, N. and De Pelsmacker, P. (2012), 'Endorser Type and Brand Globalness Effects in India: Think Global or Act Local?', *Proceedings of the 2012 EMAC Conference, Lisbon*.

36 Butt, M.M. and de Run, E.C. (2010), 'Ethnic Advertising: Adolescents' Attitudes Towards Target and Non-target Advertisements', *Young Consumers: Insight and Ideas for Responsible Marketers*, 11(3), 189–203; Noriega, J. and Blair, E. (2008), 'Advertising to Bilinguals: Does the Language of Advertising Influence the Nature of Thoughts?', *Journal of Marketing*, 72(5), 69–83.

37 Demir, K.D. and Tansuhaj, P. (2011), 'Global vs. Local Brand Perceptions among Thais and Turks', *Asia Pacific Journal of Marketing and Logistics*, 23(5), 667–683; Özsomer, A. and Altaras, S. (2008), 'Global Brand Purchase Likelihood: A Critical Synthesis and an Integrated Conceptual Framework', *Journal of International Marketing*, 16(4), 1–28; Johansson, J.K. and Ronkainen, I.A. (2005), 'The Esteem of Global Brands', *Journal of Brand Management*, 12(5), 339–54; Steenkamp, J.-B.E., Batra, R. and Alden, D.L. (2003), 'How Perceived Brand Globalness Creates Brand Value', *Journal of International Business Studies*, 33(1), 35–47.

38 Upadhyay, Y. and Singh, S.K. (2006), 'Preference for Domestic Goods: A Study of Consumer Ethnocentrism', *Vision: The Journal of Business Perspective*, 10(3), 59–68.

39 Ramaswamy, V., Alden, D.L., Steenkamp, J.-B.E.M. and Ramachander, S. (2000), 'Effects of Brand Local and Nonlocal Origin on Consumer Attitudes in Developing Countries', *Journal of Consumer Psychology*, 9(2), 83–95.

40 Jackson, P. (1987), *Corporate Communications for Managers*. London: Pitman.

41 Melewar, T.C. (2003), 'Determinants of the Corporate Identity Construct: A Review of the Literature', *Journal of Marketing Communications*, 9(4), 195–220.

42 Schein, E.H. (1984), 'Coming to a New Awareness of Corporate Culture', *Sloan Management Review*, 25 (winter), 3–16.

43 Melewar, T.C. (2003), 'Determinants of the Corporate Identity Construct: A Review of the Literature', *Journal of Marketing Communications*, 9(4), 195–220.

44 Cornelissen, J. and Harris, P. (1999), *Two Perspectives on Corporate Identity: As the Expression of the Corporate Personality and as the Essential Self*, ICCIS Working Paper Series. Glasgow: University of Strathclyde.

45 Olins, W. (1990), *Corporate Identity: Making Business Strategy Visible through Design*. London: Thames & Hudson.

46 *Het Nieuwsblad*, 5 March 2009.

47 Cornelissen, J. and Harris, P. (1999), *Two Perspectives on Corporate Identity: As the Expression of the Corporate Personality and as the Essential Self*, ICCIS Working Paper Series. Glasgow: University of Strathclyde.

48 Fombrun, C. (1996), *Reputation: Realising Value from the Corporate Image*, Harvard, MA: Harvard Business School Press.

49 Dowling, G.R. (1986), 'Managing Your Corporate Images', *Industrial Marketing Management*, 15, 109–15.

50 Roehm, L., Roehm, H. Jr and Boone, D. (2004), 'Plugs vs. Placements: A Comparison of Alternatives for Within-Program Brand Exposure', *Psychology and Marketing*, 21(1), 17–28.

51 *De Morgen*, 20 February 2008.

52 Zinkhan, G.M. and Watson, R.T. (1996), 'Advertising Trends: Innovation and the Process of Creative Destruction', *Journal of Business Research*, 37, 163–71.

53 *De Morgen*, 18 March 2009.

54 *De Morgen*, 12 October 2007.

55 Mees, M. (2006), 'Buzz Marketing or Bullshit Marketing', in Van Tilborgh, C. and Duyk, R. (eds), *Management Jaarboek*. Brussels: Vlaamse Management Associatie, 123–9.

56 De Pelsmacker, P. and Roozen, I. (1993), 'Trends in Marketing Technieken van Vandaag' ('Trends in Marketing Techniques Today'), *No Ideas No Marketing, congresverslagen 12e congres van Stiching Marketing*, 75–88.

57 Stewart, D.W. (1996), 'Market-Back Approach to the Design of Integrated Communications Programs: A Change in Paradigm and a Focus on Determinants of Success', *Journal of Business Research*, 37, 147–53.

58 Schultz, D.E., Tannenbaum, S.I. and Lauterborn, R.F. (1992), *Integrated Marketing Communications: Putting it Together and Making it Work*. Lincolnwood IL: NTC Business Books.

59 Low, G.S. (2000), 'Correlates of Integrated Marketing Communications', *Journal of Advertising*, 40, 27–39; Liechty, J., Ramaswamy, V. and Cohen, S.H. (2001), 'Choice Menus for Mass Customisation: An Experimental Approach for Analysing Customer Demand with an Application to a Web-based Information Service', *Journal of Marketing Research*, 38, 183–96.

60 Schultz, D.E. (1996), 'The Inevitability of Integrated Communication', *Journal of Business Research*, 37, 139–46.

61 Schultz, D.E. and Kitchen, P.J. (2000), *Communicating Globally: An Integrated Marketing Approach*. Lincolnwood IL: NTC Business Books.

62 Duncan, T. and Caywood, C. (1996), 'The Concept, Process and Evolution of Integrated Marketing Communication', in Thorson, E. and Moore, J. (eds), *Integrated Communication; Synergy of Pervasive Voices*. Mahwah, NJ: Lawrence Erlbaum Associates, 13–34.

63 van Raaij, W.F. (1997), 'Globalisation of Marketing Communication?', *Journal of Economic Psychology*, 18, 259–70.

64 For a discussion of the structural relationship between PR and advertising departments in organisations, see Grunig, J.A. and Grunig, L.A. (1998), 'The Relationship Between Public Relations and Marketing in Excellent Organisations: Evidence from the IABC Study', *Journal of Marketing Communications*, 4(3), 141–62.

65 Hutton, J.H. (1996), 'Integrated Marketing Communication and the Evolution of Marketing Thought', *Journal of Business Research*, 37, 155–62.

66 Deepblue (2012), Communication Agency Tracking.

CHAPTER 2
Branding

CHAPTER OUTLINE

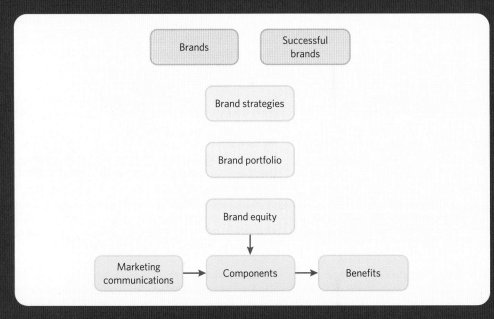

CHAPTER OBJECTIVES

This chapter will help you to:

- Understand the various aspects of branding
- Learn about the characteristics of successful brands
- Make the distinction between major types of brand strategies and their advantages and disadvantages
- Form an idea of the composition of a brand portfolio
- Understand the concept of brand value or brand equity and its major components
- Assess the benefits of branding for the consumer and the manufacturer
- Get an overview of how marketing communications contribute to brand strength

Introduction

Since the early days of marketing, brands have always been important. Consistent and long-term investment in brand awareness and brand image resulted in famous brands that survived the storms of changing marketing environments and were powerful instruments of marketing strategy. Later, the pressure for short-term results and the changing power balance between manufacturers and retailers has led to a situation in which patient and long-term investment in brand value no longer seems to be a priority. Short-term profit goals seem to be at least as important as long-term investments in goodwill. However, the value of brands in modern marketing strategy, and the important role of marketing communications in building and maintaining brand value, are still recognised. Brands are powerful instruments of strategic marketing and important vehicles on the road to long-term profitability.

What is a good brand? What are suitable branding strategies? Why are brands so important, and for whom? What is the value of a brand (often referred to as brand equity)? What is a brand portfolio and what different functions can brands fulfil in a portfolio? And, last but not least, what is the role of marketing communications in building and supporting brands?

Brands

The American Marketing Association defines a **brand** as 'a name, term, sign, symbol or design, or a combination of these, intended to identify the goods or services of one seller or group of sellers, and to differentiate them from those of a competitor'. Defined like this, a brand is a set of verbal and/or visual cues, and as such it is a part of a product's tangible features. A brand name is that part of a brand that can be spoken, including letters, words and numbers, like BMW, Danone or HP. A **brand mark** is the element of a brand that cannot be spoken, often a symbol, design or specific packaging, like the Mercedes logo or the Absolut Vodka bottle. A trademark is the legal designation indicating that the owner has exclusive use of the brand.

However, Keller goes beyond the pure constituting brand elements and defines a brand as an identifier that adds either rational and tangible dimensions (related to product performance) or symbolic, emotional and intangible dimensions (related to what the brand represents) that differentiate it from other products designed to fulfil the same need.[1]

RESEARCH INSIGHT
A brand is a bundle of meanings

A brand can be defined as 'a cluster of meanings', or a cluster of associations concerning attributes, benefits and values. These associations are created or enhanced by every contact or experience the consumer has with the brand. Batey describes the difference between a brand and a product as follows:[2]

Product	Brand
You buy a product for what it does	You choose a brand for what it means
A product sits on retailers' shelves	A brand exists in consumers' minds
A product can quickly be outdated	A brand is timeless
A product can be copied by a competitor	A brand is unique

Brand names, as well as other brand elements such as logos, URLs, symbols, characters, spokespeople, jingles, packages and signages, should be memorable, meaningful, likable, adaptable, transferable and protectable.[3] A good brand name is easy for customers to say, spell and recall. Excellent examples are Dell, Bic, Nokia and Ford. To enhance brand recognition and avoid brand confusion, a brand name should also be distinctive and be able to differentiate the product from the competition. Besides being memorable, it is an advantage that brand elements are meaningful; for example, Mr Clean cleaning product, Vanish stain remover, Head & Shoulders shampoo and *Newsweek* magazine reinforce an attribute or benefit association related to the brand positioning. Brand elements should also be tested on their visual and/or verbal likability or, in other words, on their aesthetic appeal. Over time, brand elements may lose their appeal, calling for an update. As a consequence, logos, symbols, characters and even brand names often have to be adapted. Texaco, Nike and Michelin are just a few examples of brands that updated their logo/character over time. Preferably a brand is transferable both across product categories and geographic boundaries. The more specific the brand name, the more difficult it may be to extend the brand to other product categories. Nivea could easily extend its brand to the shampoo, skin care and other markets, but it will be difficult for Head & Shoulders to extend its shampoo brand into skin care. To build a successful global brand, the brand name should be easy to pronounce in different languages. This is not the case for the soft drink brand Mountain Dew in many non-English-speaking countries nor the Polish vodka brand Wyborowa in non-Polish-speaking countries. Global brand names also have to be culture- or language-neutral in the sense that they do not evoke strange or undesirable connotations in foreign languages. Kodak, Mars and IBM are good examples of this linguistic neutrality. On the other hand, the Rolls-Royce Silver Mist model name sounds strange in Germany (where *Mist* means manure), as does the Finnish defroster Super-Piss in certain European countries, and the toilet paper brand Kräpp in English-speaking parts of the world. Other examples are the Spanish bread brand Bimbo that is associated with an attractive, unintelligent lady in English; the Dutch bread brand Bums reminds English-speaking people of a person's backside and German-speaking people of sex; the Egyptian airline company Misair is not appealing to French-speaking consumers because *misère* means misery to them.[4] Finally, a brand should be available and easy to protect through registration. Therefore, no generic words should be used. Really successful brand names often become household names, i.e. the brand name is used to indicate the product category in which it was a pioneer. Examples are Xerox, Aspirin and Hoover.

BUSINESS INSIGHT
Bacardi's good fortune Bat

In 1862, Don Facundo Bacardi bought a small tin-roofed distillery in Santiago de Cuba. When his wife first stepped in the distillery, she saw a colony of fruit bats living in the roofing. For the local people, bats represented good fortune, health and family unity. She suggested that her husband take the bat as the trademark for his rum. Because of high levels of illiteracy at the time, a strong, distinctive, memorable and likeable trademark was very important to identify and sell the product. The bat fulfilled all these criteria. Positive word-of-mouth reports of the excellent rum spread soon and the bat made it easy for consumers to find the right product. More importantly, in line with local beliefs and traditions, local storytellers reinforced positive brand associations by claiming that the bat brought good fortune to the drink and gave it magical powers. Magic or not, the company had good fortune and, more than 140 years later, Bacardi's bat is one of the best-known trademarks world wide.[5]

Three categories of brands can be distinguished:

1. **Manufacturer brands** are developed and marketed by manufacturers of the product. They are supported by integrated marketing, including pricing, distribution and communications. Levi's, Danone and BMW are examples of manufacturer brands.

2. **Own-label brands** (also called **private label brands**, store or dealer brands) are developed and marketed by wholesalers or retailers. There is no link between the manufacturer and the brand. Retailers develop own-label brands to gain more power. It enables them to enhance their store image, generate higher margins and be more independent of the manufacturers of premium brands. Originally, they only competed on the basis of a price benefit compared with manufacturer brands. St Michael (Marks & Spencer, UK), Clever (Billa, Austria) and Derby (Delhaize, Belgium) are examples of such store brands. Now, however, most European retailers have adopted sub-branding strategies.[6] For example, a three-tier strategy concerning quality is popular, consisting of the regular private label, a price-aggressive budget or value label (e.g. No. 1 from Carrefour) and a quality-focused premium label (e.g. Tesco's Finest, Albert Heijn's Excellent, Safeway's Select). Further, several retailers have thematic private labels, such as a health and wellness sub-brand (e.g. Tesco Organic, Loblaw's President's Choice Green, Carrefour Bio), an ethical sub-brand (e.g. Axfood's Aware fair trade label, Wal-Mart's Sam's Choice fair trade and Rainforest Alliance label), and a culinary sub-brand (e.g., Fior Fiore from Coop Italia, De Nuestra Terra from Carrefour Spain). In many product categories, own-label brands pose a serious threat to well-established manufacturer brands. Some retailers are using their own-label brands as the key element in their marketing strategy, and support their own brand with a limited number of well-established manufacturer brands to optimise their store image and consumer traffic. In Europe, private label brands hold high market shares as Figure 2.1 shows.

Research indicates that a country's private label share goes up during economic downturns and shrinks when the economy is flourishing. However, consumers switch more

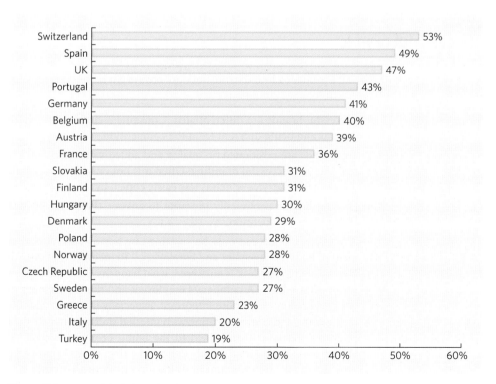

Figure 2.1 Private label shares in Europe
Source: PLMA Yearbook 2012.

extensively to store brands during recession times than they switch back to national brands in a subsequent recovery.[7] Indeed, recent Nielsen results indicate that 60% of European shoppers say to buy more private label products during the current economic downturn and 92% agree to continue buying them as the economy recovers.[8]

As a consequence, brand manufacturers have to take the competition of private labels seriously at all times. Six strategic options can be chosen: (1) increase distance from private labels through innovation; (2) increase distance from private labels by investing in brand equity (offer 'more value for money' by stressing brand image, changing packaging, etc.); (3) reduce the price gap; (4) introduce a value-flanker as a me-too strategy; (5) wait and do nothing; and (6) produce (premium) private labels. A study in the Netherlands shows that the best strategy for national brands might be to react by investing in innovations and brand image. This is preferred to 'wait and do nothing', although the latter may sometimes be effective (e.g. wait until the company is ready to come up with the next innovation). Producing private labels may also be a viable option, especially in product categories with high private label market shares or many possibilities for technological differentiation. Producing private labels for retailers has the advantage that it strengthens the ties with the retailer. Furthermore, it can also be very profitable for the company if it has excess capacity. Finally, companies seem to react to the competition with private labels in a subtler way than to other brands. Decreasing the distance from private labels by price reductions and value-flankers is less used. Obviously the latter would sour the relationship with the retailer. Furthermore, it often also seems to have a detrimental impact on the company's and market profitability.[9]

3. **Generic brands** indicate the product category. In fact, the concept is a contradiction in terms. Generics are in fact brandless products. They are usually sold at the lowest prices. In pharmaceutical products, generics are quite successful. The end of the legal protection of a patent allows the introduction of generics at lower prices. Depending upon the country, generics account for a substantial share of pharmaceutical product sales.

Successful brands

Giving a product a brand name does not always guarantee success. Successful brands have to meet a number of conditions:[10]

- Successful brands are differentiated. Consumers clearly perceive them as having unique benefits and being different from the competition.
- Top brands are positioned on quality and added value. Superior product quality is a prerequisite for successful branding. Often it is not only the product that is superior but also the additional service which is less easily copied by competitors.
- Leading brands continually innovate to answer changing consumer tastes and to keep ahead of the competition.
- A leading position can only be sustained by having full support and complete commitment of both management and employees.[11] Remember that every brand contact matters: how a call to a helpdesk is answered, what happens when advice is sought or when a complaint is raised, etc. A company's employees and the engagement they show to the brand has never before been more important. Especially in service branding, internal marketing (i.e. training and communicating with internal staff to convince them of the basic strategic priorities and keep them tuned to the brand promise) is vital. The success of a bank, an airline or a restaurant largely depends upon the motivation and quality of the service provider (bank clerk, steward or waiter) to satisfy the customer.
- Brands cannot become success stories without long-term, consistent communications support, making customers aware of their uniqueness and keeping the brand's value

trustworthy. Both long-term support and the significant contribution of communications are important. Successful brands are not built overnight. Long-term communications, and more particularly advertising support, are a key factor in the development of successful brands. As already mentioned, brand managers are often tempted to cut investments in brands to increase short-term profitability, thereby affecting the long-term profit potential.

BUSINESS INSIGHT
Building a strong brand

A brand that clearly understood the fact that successful brands need to be differentiated and have high quality is Hyundai. In its early days, Hyundai was perceived as a lower-quality brand. Taking Japanese automakers as an example, Hyundai seriously invested in quality and kept making its cars better and better. In the late 1990s, Hyundai surprised the industry by offering the best automobile warranty in the industry, a safety net that created consumer confidence. As an extension of this value-building strategy, Hyundai introduced Hyundai Assurance Plus early in 2009. While other brands were competing on price discounts, Hyundai offered its customers peace of mind. Hyundai's Assurance Plus assured the customers that if they lose their income, Hyundai would make instalment payments for three months while they got back on their feet. If this was not enough time, Hyundai would take back the car. The company broadly defined income loss as involuntary unemployment, physical disability, self-employed personal bankruptcy, accidental death, etc. Hyundai was not the automaker that enjoyed highest market share or highest awareness, but its value-adding programme did set the brand apart and had a positive impact on sales. After the introduction of Assurance Plus, Hyundai's sales were up 14% as compared with the same period one year before. In fact, it realised the highest sales increase in the industry, and was one of only three automakers to make an increase at all.[12] Also, in the following years Hyundai made sure to keep on investing in quality and innovative designs, leading to a consistent increase in brand value. In 2011, its brand value increased no less than 19% as compared with 2010.[13]

Table 2.1 gives an overview of Interbrand's 2011 ranking of 25 of the world's most valuable brands. Interbrand calculates brand values on the basis of cash flows. Absolute winners in the top 100 ranking are Apple (8), Amazon.com (26) and Google (4), which respectively gained 58%, 32% and 27% in brand value as compared with 2010. The biggest losers in 2011 were Nokia (14), Nintendo (48) and Sony (35) which saw their brand value decline by respectively 15%, 14% and 13%. Nokia hopes to counter this negative evolution by its strategic partnership with Microsoft, while Nintendo is looking at a further take-off of the Nintendo 3DS and Sony is betting on PlayStation Vita to turn the tide.[14]

BUSINESS INSIGHT
Most impactful and fast-growing brands

In 2008, Brandchannel organised a brand poll in which 4310 consumers from several countries participated. The consumers were asked to vote for the brands that had most impact on them. Apple came out as an absolute winner. Apple was judged top in (1) offering the best retail environment, (2) having produced the most innovative

Table 2.1 Top 25 brands worldwide

2011 rank	2010 rank	Brand	Country of origin	2011 brand value ($M)	Change in brand value (%)
1	1	Coca-Cola	USA	71 861	2
2	2	IBM	USA	69 905	8
3	3	Microsoft	USA	59 087	−3
4	4	Google	USA	55 317	27
5	5	General Electric	USA	42 808	0
6	6	McDonald's	USA	35 593	6
7	7	Intel	USA	35 217	10
8	17	Apple	USA	33 492	58
9	9	Disney	USA	29 018	1
10	10	HP	USA	28 789	6
11	11	Toyota	Japan	27 764	6
12	12	Mercedes	Germany	27 445	9
13	14	Cisco	USA	25 309	9
14	8	Nokia	Finland	25 071	−15
15	15	BMW	USA	24 554	10
16	13	Gillette	USA	23 997	3
17	19	Samsung	South Korea	23 430	20
18	16	Yves Saint Laurent	France	23 172	6
19	20	Honda	Japan	19 431	5
20	22	Oracle	USA	17 262	16
21	21	H&M	Sweden	16 459	2
22	23	PepsiCo	USA	14 590	4
23	24	American Express	USA	14 572	5
24	26	SAP	Germany	14 542	14
25	25	Nike	USA	14 528	6

Source: Adapted from Interbrand, Best Global Brands 2011, http://www.interbrand.com/nl/best-global-brands/best-global-brands-2008/best-global-brands-2011.aspx (accessed July 2012).

and enticing packaging, (3) being able to rebound from a crisis and (4) being the most inspiring brand. This may not be too surprising: Apple's iPods, iPhone and MacBook bridged the gap between being cool and being a mass product. Moreover, Apple Genius bars exceeded customers' expectations of what after-sales service can be. With its iPad, Apple moved on in the same direction, further creating innovative products that seamlessly fit in with people's lifestyles. In 2012 Apple came out as the most valuable brand in Millward Brown Optimor's BrandZ™ survey. The second most valuable brand was Google, whereas the fastest-growing brands were Facebook and Baidu (i.e. China's Google); 30% of the BrandZ top 100 brands were to be technology brands.[15]

Brand strategies

A brand strategy starts with the decision whether or not to put a brand name on a product. It can be argued that, for some product categories, branding is not essential and may even be useless. This is especially true for undifferentiated and homogeneous products. Since branding is an essential element in pull marketing strategies, the products for which a push strategy is indicated have less need of formal branding. The latter may be the case for industrial products such as steel and raw materials, or complex machinery like transmission equipment or capacitors. However, except for generics, hardly any brandless consumer product can be imagined, although in some consumer product categories such as fresh fruit, vegetables, meat and bread, branded goods are the exception rather than the rule, although also in these product categories branding is on the rise. Marketers cannot live with undifferentiated products and will always look for extra marketable value. A brand is an excellent vehicle by means of which a product can be differentiated from the competition.

Once the decision to go for branded products has been taken, a company must decide on its overall brand strategy. This strategy will also guide the branding of new product introductions. Figure 2.2 shows the basic brand strategies. First of all, a product can be given one brand name, or several (mostly two) brands can be used to position it. In the case of one brand name, four different strategies can be followed. Sticking to existing product categories and using the same brand name for all new product introductions in a product category is called **line extension**. This strategy is used very frequently. Examples are Magnum's flavours Temptation Chocolate and Strawberry White, or Kellogg's K Chocolate delight and Kellogg's K Fruit & Yoghurt cereals. Marketers may want to expand the variety of their offerings, try to accommodate the needs of new consumer segments, react to successful competitive products, crowd the product space and deter competitive entry, enhance the image of the parent brand or try to command more shelf space from retailers. Overall, it improves the competitive position of the brand by offering consumers more variety, as a result of which they are not inclined to look to competitive brands to satisfy their needs. Moreover, there seem to be strong spillover effects from advertising the line extension on choice of the parent brand. Advertising of Yoplait non-fat yoghurt, for example, increased sales of Yoplait yoghurt even more than advertising of Yoplait yoghurt itself.[16] Line extension strategies have a number of obvious advantages. The favourable image of the brand is carried over to the new products that are marketed with the same brand name, and the past communications investments in the brand are more efficiently used to market more products. However, a line extension also has a number of disadvantages, the

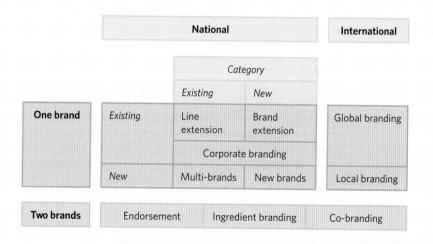

Figure 2.2 Basic brand strategies

most important being that the original brand loses its meaning and clear positioning.[17] Another disadvantage is the risk of cannibalisation. A new product may cannibalise the company's other products instead of taking market share away from the competition, the net result of which could be that the line extension is not very profitable. An unsuccessful extension can also harm sales of the parent brand.[18] Finally, too many line extensions can lead to over-choice, confusing consumers about which option would be ideal for them, the end result of which could be that consumers put off their choice or become less satisfied with their final choice (with too many options around, choosing means losing . . .).[19]

BUSINESS INSIGHT
Angry Birds conquer the skies

Take some angry birds, green pigs and a castle, program a game, and cash in. That seems to be the story behind the immensely popular 'Angry Birds'. 'Angry Birds' was developed by Rovio, a small Finnish developer of computer games, and started its career in 2009 as an iPhone game. The concept is simple, but also bizarre. With a catapult you shoot angry birds to a castle in which pigs that stole the birds' eggs are hiding. In mid-2011 the game had been downloaded 700 million times and played by 30 million people worldwide. The new 'Angry Birds Space' in which the birds circle around planets was downloaded 20 million times within a week after its launch.

In 2010 Zynga, the company that developed and marketed, among others, 'Farmville', offered $2 billion for Rovio, but the owners refused. Their plan is to become 'much bigger than Disney'. They made a series of animated 'Angry Birds' cartoons of 2½–3 minutes each and are planning a full movie by 2014. Moreover, they opened the first Angry Birds Amusement Park in Tampere, Finland, and plan to open more of them across the globe. The game is also available on Facebook where different kinds of players are reached. Rovio and Samsung agreed to install the game on Samsung TV sets. In 2010 about 25 million plush birds were sold. The brand is the most counterfeited one in China.

What is the successful recipe behind the game? First of all, the game is based on a well-known and popular idea: conquer a castle. The weird birds are the heroes of the game and therefore lend themselves to all kinds of extensions, such as movies, cartoons, amusement parks and merchandising. Once a critical mass of players picked up the game, it featured in the top lists of downloaded apps, and therefore got a lot of visibility and momentum. With the increasing penetration of smart phones, so-called 'casual games' have become a huge market. Casual games are simple games that people play on mobile devices as an easy and short pastime.

Will the success of 'Angry Birds' continue? Analysts predict that, like any other fad, it will continue to be successful for some years, and also because of its extensions into other activities and products, but will then fade away and be replaced by the then latest thing. Others believe that, since 'Angry Birds' is now part of the lives of so many people, it will continue to appeal to the nostalgic feelings of these players for a long time.[20]

Brand extension, or **brand stretching**, occurs when an existing brand is used to market products in a different product category. Examples are Harley-Davidson footwear, Armani underwear, Godiva ice cream and Nesquick cereals. The basic rationale behind brand extensions is the same as the one behind line extensions, i.e. limiting the risk of failure of new product introductions by capitalising upon the image and reputation of a successful existing brand, and at the same time trying to save the huge advertising expenses of launching a totally new brand. Research indicates that brand extensions tend to be more effective than new brand introductions in the sense that they capture more market share and require less advertising.[21] However, the risks of brand extensions are great. First of all, if the brand image does not fit well the new product category or the new market segments the new introduction may not be successful.[22] Bic tried to launch a low-price perfume and failed. The same thing happened when the company launched Bic underwear. Research, however, shows that an incongruent brand extension can overcome initial negative responses if the extension is backed by sufficient advertising support. Respondents who were exposed to an ad five times responded significantly more positively (or less negatively) than respondents who saw the ad only once.[23] Furthermore, other studies show that some individuals are more sensitive to incongruent extensions than others. Consumers from East Asian countries and females, for example, are more likely to seek a connection and consequently respond more positively to moderate incongruent extensions than Western consumers and males.[24] Secondly, there is the risk of **brand dilution**. This occurs when the brand name is used for so many different product categories that the brand personality becomes fuzzy and the brand's value deteriorates.[25] If Virgin had not continuously articulated the abstract characteristics of its origin (i.e. fun, hip and subversive) in all its products, it could have been detrimental to use the brand name Virgin for products so fundamentally different as airlines, compact discs and soft drinks. By stressing its abstract characteristics, Virgin seems to become virtually product independent, embodying a mere brand concept or image.[26]

BUSINESS INSIGHT
Brand extension losers and winners

A survey on brand extensions in which branding and marketing professionals could vote for the best and worst brand extensions showed that key factors for successful extensions are a strong brand and a loyal consumer. Moreover, the most successful extensions came from 'companies that really know their customers, and know the limitations of their brands even more so'. Winners were, among others, Coppertone, extending its suncare brand to sunglasses, and Mr Clean Performance Car Washes. Burger King men's apparel and Kellogg's hip-hop streetwear won the votes for worst brand extensions.[27]

A special case of extension strategies is **corporate branding**. In this case, the name of the company is used for all the company's products. This strategy is often used by service companies like banks and insurance companies for which the reputation and the endorsement of a reliable company is very important. For the same reason, it is also very valuable for high-technology products. Potential customers have more faith in a long-established and experienced company with a good reputation, which will be able to offer consistent high-quality support in the future. Corporate branding is very similar to the other extension strategies and therefore has the same advantages and disadvantages. One additional disadvantage is that a corporate branding strategy is relatively inflexible. Specific niches that are not associated with the corporate reputation cannot be efficiently targeted on the basis of a corporate branding strategy.[28]

BUSINESS INSIGHT
Samsung, the new electronics giant

In the mid-1990s, Samsung Electronics Co. was still a lower-end consumer electronics producer bringing its product onto the market under a handful of brand names including Wiseview, Tantus and Yepp. To move up the value chain, the company had to build a stronger identity. Therefore, the company got rid of its other brands and invested in building a strong corporate brand. Next, it focused on better quality, a nicer design and innovation. To be visible to users 24 hours a day, seven days a week, the company chose first to focus on a new line of mobile phones and digital TVs. These are also products with which consumers are more likely to form a strong bond. Building a strong image in these categories opens doors to other categories. Samsung's strategy is clearly paying off. Currently Samsung holds 17th place in the Best Global Brands ranking, leaving Sony behind in overall brand value in 35th place. Samsung has become the clear leader in flat-panel TVs and continues its focus on mobile devices. Through a strong flagship brand strategy around Galaxy smart phones and tablet devices under the Android platform, Samsung hopes to gain a strong foothold in the market. Also in other markets, such as digital appliances, digital imaging, IT solutions, B2B, and especially semiconductors, Samsung continuously offers innovative and relevant solutions.[29]

A brand strategy in which different brands are used for products or product ranges in the same product category is called **multi-branding**. This is frequently used by companies like Procter & Gamble and Mars. Procter & Gamble, for instance, has a number of different detergent brands. However, the traditional multi-branding companies also use brand stretching. For instance, Fairy and Dreft are brands used in both dishwashing liquids and laundry detergents. The advocates of multi-branding argue that this strategy permits finer segmentation and positioning. Each brand is fully capable of building its own personality and perceived benefit and of appealing to the specific segment it is targeted at. The obvious disadvantage of this strategy is that individual brands cannot benefit from the leveraging effect of existing brands.

Companies using the multi-branding strategy will also be inclined to use new brands when they introduce a product in a new product category. But introducing new brands may also be called for when none of the company's brands is suitable for use in the new product category. For instance, Toyota established a new name for its luxury car range, the Lexus.

Western brand thinking has mainly been shaped by Procter & Gamble, Unilever, Henkel and Mars. The key feature here was differentiation: every possible segment should be serviced with a new brand. Japanese brand thinking, on the other hand, used to focus on harmony and loyalty: trust, authenticity, credibility and expertise is based on the company and the values it stands for. Therefore, all products refer to the company and are not stand-alone items.[30] In the 1990s, some claimed that the corporate brand would be the only successful option for brand building in the future.[31] However, this does not appear to be true, at least not as far as fast-moving consumer goods are concerned. Comparing brand strategies of the 20 top suppliers of UK grocery retailers (involving about 400 products) between 1994 and 2004 showed a significant drop in the use of corporate brands to the advantage of mixed brands. More than 60% of the products used some form of mixed branding in 2004. The researchers assume that the reason for the recent shift away from corporate brands can be sought in risk avoidance (inspired by recent scandals that broke brands like Enron), the need for precise targeting and the benefits of mixed branding.[32]

When a company introduces a product abroad, it can also choose between an extension or a 'new brand' strategy. If the existing brand has the required global characteristics, is already known in the new country, or if the company is committed to building global brands (Photo 2.1), a global strategy will be used. Globalisation increases the value of the brand (see below) and enables the company to benefit from transnational efficiencies in advertising, since TV channels targeted at consumer segments in different countries, such as Eurosport and MTV, increase the 'footprint' of ads broadcast through these channels. Examples of global brands are Coca-Cola, Nike and Gillette. Global brands can range from being globally consistent to locally adapted. Gillette is consistent around the world because men's shaving needs are, world wide, more or less the same. YouTube can be situated in the middle of the continuum: it has global reach, but pursues a localisation strategy because it realises that people sharing the same culture will be more likely to share content. McDonald's is locally adapted: it does use the same logo and colours, but adapts its service and products to fit local needs. For example, it is an upscale delivery service in Brazil, offers teriyaki chicken strips in Japan, and its German coffee shops are better than Starbucks.[33]

Photo 2.1 HSBC: A global brand with a local touch
Source: Getty Images: AFP.

Local brands often have a long tradition in specific countries and are often market leaders in their home country. Thumbs Up is the leading soft drink in India leaving Coca-Cola behind; Efes Pilsen and Cola Turka are leading in Turkey; Valentine is a more powerful paint brand in France than Dulux; Dreft is a powerful detergent brand and Côte d'Or a very attractive chocolate brand in Belgium and the Netherlands; Larios was leader in the Spanish gin market when it was bought by Pernod-Ricard. DBS has a 30% market share in the Norwegian bicycle sector while Crescent accounts for 20% of the Swedish bicycle sector and Kildamoës has 15% of the Danish market. Local brands benefit, among other things, from (1) the deep-rooted and powerful bond that has been established with local consumers (i.e. consumers often buy the brand their parents bought), (2) being perfectly adapted to unique local tastes or needs, (3) local operational and logistical advantages and (4) strong community ties. These local brands are very attractive for global companies, and more and more global companies extend their brand portfolio with local brands.[34]

A recent study indicates that whether consumers prefer a local brand such as Mecca Cola (France) or Fei-Chang (China) above a global brand such as Pepsi or Coca-Cola depends on whether they are global- or local-minded. The tendency towards a global or local mindset is related to people's desire to be different (local) versus similar to others (global). Consequently, companies benefit from positioning their products in a way compatible with the mindset of their target group.[35]

Companies can also opt for **dual branding strategies**. Three categories of dual strategies can be distinguished. In **endorsement branding** two brand names of the same company are used, one of them serving as a quality label or endorsement.[36] In fact, this strategy can be situated somewhere between an extension and a multi-brand strategy, and combines the advantages of both, although the disadvantages of the two combined strategies should be taken into account. An example is Kellogg's (Cornflakes, Rice Krispies, Coco Pops, etc.).

With **ingredient branding**, a brand of a basic ingredient of the product is mentioned next to the actual product's brand name. Examples are Intel, Nutrasweet, Woolmark, Goretex and Tetrapak. The advantages are that both brands can benefit from the synergy effects of combining the two strong brands. Furthermore, communications costs can be shared. A prerequisite for ingredient branding is that the ingredient has to be essential, differentiating and of consistently high quality.[37]

Finally, in **co-branding**, two or more brands are simultaneously presented on one product. Co-branding can range from advertising multiple brands in one ad (e.g. featuring Shell and Ferrari together) to co-developing a product (e.g. Philips and Inbev who came up with the Perfect Draft, or Braun and Oral B launching an electric toothbrush). Forming an alliance may be driven, for example, by the desire to leverage positive brand equity of the partner brand (e.g. LG working together with Prada to launch an exquisitely designed phone), to share or decrease advertising or development costs (e.g. Coca-Cola and Heinz Plant Bottle™ partnership in which Coca-Cola is partly reimbursed for its development costs of the Plant Bottle whereas Heinz can use the bottle without having any development costs) or to gain access to new markets or distribution channels (e.g. the Belgian women's magazine *Libelle* which asked the apparel retailer E5 to launch jointly a women's collection, giving Libelle access to the fashion market and to the outlets of E5). Obviously, the combination should result in a perfect perceptual fit, from a product or image point of view.[38]

BUSINESS INSIGHT
HTC with a Beats experience

To differentiate itself from the competition, HTC decided to put the spotlight on the audio features of its smart phones. To this end, HTC invested $300 million in Beats™ Electronics LLC, the company that redefined the audio market with its iconic Beats by Dr.Dre™ audio experience. This resulted in the superb Beats earbuds being packed with HTC's Android smart phones. Unfortunately, this branding alliance did not give HTC the expected advantages. Consumers simply do not buy a smart phone for its premium earphones. Further, including the premium accessory forced HTC to raise prices while competitors offered similar smart phones at lower prices. Therefore, despite the major investment in Beats, HTC decided that the iconic Beats Audio earbuds for several of its models will no longer be included in the box. However, the partnership may take a step forward with the acquisition of Mog, a music subscription service that has a catalogue of over 14 million tracks that subscribers can listen to on a computer and Android devices. This would allow HTC and Beats to challenge the likes of iTunes and Spotify and to stick to a premium audio differentiation in comparison with competitive smart phones.[39]

Photo: San Pellegrino and
Bulgari join forces in Switzerland
Source: Patrick De Pelsmacker.

Brand portfolio

Building a strong brand is one thing, sustaining brand equity in the long run is something else. Besides a well-balanced marketing programme and continuous and consistent integrated marketing communications support, it may be necessary to adapt the brand portfolio over time. A **brand portfolio** can be defined as the set of all brands and brand lines that a company possesses. The rationale behind every brand portfolio should be threefold. First of all, a company should try to maximise market coverage in the sense that different market segments can be serviced. Secondly, brand overlap has to be minimised in such a way that brands are not competing among themselves. Furthermore, some overlap may be necessary, or as the CEO of Liz Claiborne put it: 'Cannibalization is inevitable, but it's much better to steal market share from yourself than to sit back and let somebody else do it.'[40] Thirdly, every brand in the brand portfolio should have an added value for the company. For example, in 2000 Unilever decided to trim its brand portfolio from about 1600 to 400 leading brands. Two criteria were used to select the leading brands: (1) *brand appeal*, meaning the appeal of the brand to the consumer and how well the brand meets the expected consumer needs over five to ten years; and (2) *prospects for sustained growth*, indicating the brand potential to justify significant investments in technology, innovation and brand communications. Focusing on the 400 brands with a positive growth rate (such as Dove, Lipton, Magnum, Calvin Klein) allowed Unilever to reduce overheads and to focus resources where they were most effective.[41]

Brands in a portfolio usually serve different functions and can be classified as bastion, flanker, fighter and prestige brands (see Figure 2.3). **Bastion brands** provide most profit for the company, often follow a premium price strategy, are characterised by a high level of psycho-social meaning and are generally considered as high-performance brands. In order to

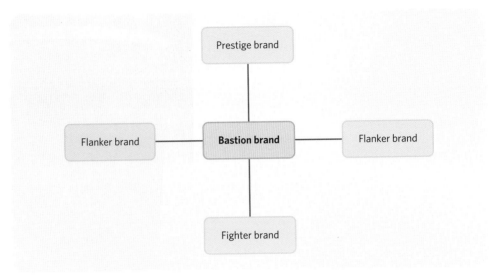

Figure 2.3 A brand portfolio model
Source: Riezebos 1995, cited in Riezebos 2003.

protect bastion brands, flanker, fighter or prestige brands can be introduced. A **flanker brand** follows a similar price–profit ratio as the bastion brand, is also characterised by a high psycho-social meaning and perceived performance level, but usually appeals to a different, smaller market segment (niche). **Fighter brands** are sold at a lower price, situated between the price of the bastion and discount brands. Their quality perception is usually lower than that of the bastion and flanker brands. **Prestige brands** are high-quality, luxury brands targeted at a smaller segment, looking for status and high psycho-social meaning.[42]

Procter & Gamble's shampoo bastion brand is Pantène, while Head & Shoulders can be considered as a flanker brand. Philip Morris introduced Basic as a fighter brand to protect Marlboro, just as Procter & Gamble launched Bonux to protect Dash, and the Volkswagen Group acquired Seat and Skoda to safeguard Volkswagen. Finally, Toyota and Nissan have Lexus and Infinity as prestige brands.[43]

Brand equity

In the previous sections it has been argued that brands are valuable assets for marketing. Brand equity is a concept that is used to indicate the value of a brand. It is the value added to a product by virtue of its brand name.[44] In fact, a distinction should be made between **consumer brand equity** and **financial brand equity**.[45] The latter refers to the financial value of the brand for the company, the former to the underlying customer- and marketing-related components of brand equity. In practice, the concept of brand equity is used to describe both. Economically speaking, the value of a brand is the sum of all discounted future income streams attributable to the brand.

Financial brand equity

When looking at the balance sheet of companies marketing branded products, one generally finds only buildings, machines and inventories there. Seldom is the goodwill built up in well-known brands shown. However, whenever a company is involved in mergers or acquisitions, the financial value of the brand portfolio becomes of great importance. Some say that the brand portfolio is the most valuable asset of a company. John Stuart, former president of

Quaker Oats, illustrated this by stating: 'If we were to split up the company, you can have all the buildings, I will take the brands. I am sure I will be more successful than you.' As a result, huge amounts of money are paid for brand portfolios. Nestlé took over Rowntree (KitKat, After Eight, Rolo) for $4.5 billion, while analysts estimated the value at $3 billion. Similarly, the physical assets of Jaguar represented only 16% of the price Ford paid for it.[46] This brand value can also easily change. For example, in 2008 HP was valued at $23.509 billion, Apple at $13.723 billion and Dell at $11.695 billion, whereas in 2011 these brands were valued at $28.479 billion, $33.492 billion and $8.347 billion respectively, noting a spectacular increase in the value of the Apple brand.[47]

BUSINESS INSIGHT
Building a strategic brand portfolio

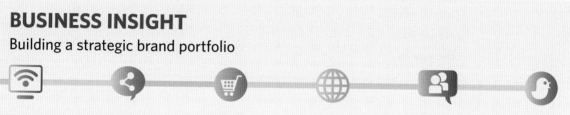

The German company Adidas-Salomon bought Reebok in 2005 for €3.1 billion, 34% on top of Reebok's shares. It was clear why Adidas-Salomon was willing to pay such a surplus. Nike was number 1, Adidas number 2 and Reebok number 3; consequently it would be easier to compete with Nike if Adidas and Reebok joined forces. With Reebok, Adidas hoped to close the gap with Nike in the USA. Nike held a market share of 36%, Adidas 8.9% and Reebok 12.2% of the US market. Furthermore, Reebok had already made great strides in emerging markets such as China, Korea and Malaysia. Reebok was not only complementary to Adidas concerning geographic markets and foreign distribution channels, but also complementary in terms of market segments. Reebok was, for example, much stronger than Adidas in basketball, football, hockey and fashion/athletic segments. As a result, the acquisition looked like a perfect fit and certainly justified the money that has been paid for it.[48]

How can the financial brand value be calculated? Different calculation methods exist. Interbrand, one of the leading brand valuation companies, uses four criteria:[49]

- A *financial analysis* to identify business earnings.
- A *market analysis* to determine what proportion of those earnings is attributable to the brand ('branding index').
- A *brand analysis*, to find out how strong the brand is in the perception of consumers ('brand strength score').
- A *legal analysis*, to establish how well a brand is legally protected.

Using these four categories, experts determine financial brand equity. In Table 2.2 an example is given of the importance of the brand (branding index), relative to other assets, in a number of industries.[50] Especially in consumer product companies, the brand accounts for a large part of the business earnings. In IT and pharmaceutical companies, other intangibles, such as patents and the quality of personnel, are relatively more important. In industrial sectors, tangible assets play a major role. Obviously these percentages are only averages, and the situation may be significantly different from one company to the next. The higher the branding index or the importance of a brand for a company, the more branding strategy and brand support in terms of marketing communications will be important for the company's economic success.

Another important aspect of the brand valuation system is the brand strength score. This is based on seven criteria with different weights. They are summarised in Table 2.3. The most important criteria are leadership and internationality (each accounting for 25% of the score). Obviously, a leading brand is generally a more stable and valuable property. Additionally,

Table 2.2 The relative importance of brands (%)

Industry	Tangibles	Brand	Other intangibles
Utilities	70	0	30
Industrial	70	5	25
Pharmaceutical	40	10	50
Retail	70	15	15
Info tech	30	20	50
Automotive	50	30	20
Financial services	20	30	50
Food and drink	40	55	5
Luxury goods	25	70	5

Source: Perrier, R. (1997), *Brand Valuation*. London: Premier Books and Interbrand Group.

Table 2.3 The brand strength index

Factor	Relative importance (%)
Leadership	25
Internationality	25
Stability	15
Market	10
Trend	10
Support	10
Protection	5

Source: Perrier, R. (1997), *Brand Valuation*. London: Premier Books and Interbrand Group.

brands that have proved to be successful in different countries are assumed to be a more stable and robust asset. Customer loyalty accounts for 15%. Strong brands are brands with a loyal customer base. Brands that have been supported consistently by marketing investments, that show an increasing long-term trend and that are in markets in which branding is relatively important are also assumed to be more valuable. Finally, the value of well-protected brands is, of course, more secure.

Consumer brand equity

For a marketer, consumer brand equity is more important than financial brand value. The former type of brand equity, representing the 'marketing value' of a brand, can be measured in different ways, all of them trying to capture the extent to which the brand gives the product extra marketing strength. Figure 2.4 presents the components of consumer brand equity.[51] Each of the brand equity factors is determined and influenced by marketing communications strategy, and leads to a number of benefits. These are discussed in the following sections. In this section, the components of brand equity are looked at more closely.

A well-known brand is more valuable than an unknown brand. Consumers have more faith in a well-known brand. A distinction can be made between deep and broad brand awareness. **Deep brand awareness** means that the brand comes to mind easily and enjoys high top-of-mind awareness. **Broad brand awareness** refers to the fact that the brand comes to mind

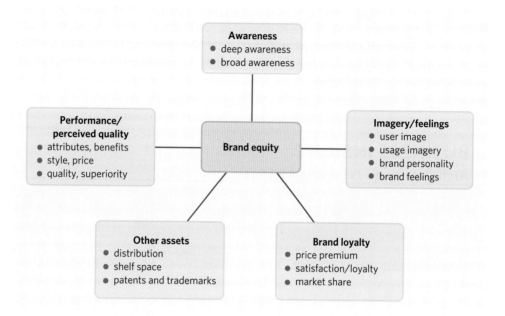

Figure 2.4 Components of consumer brand equity
Source: Based on Aaker, D.A. (1996), *Building Strong Brands.* New York: Free Press.

often, in different usage situations.[52] Deep and broad awareness are necessary to penetrate the consideration set of consumers. The more a brand is in the consideration set of consumers, the greater the chance that it will be purchased and that consumers will become loyal to it.[53] Furthermore, brand awareness leads to more interest and processing of advertising for the brand, thereby enhancing the effectiveness of marketing communications.[54] **Brand awareness** is more than just being aware of the fact that the brand exists. It also includes knowing what the product stands for, and its attributes and characteristics, such as the brand logo, the manufacturing company, functional, situational and symbolic characteristics, price, quality, performance and advertising characteristics.

Performance refers to the extent to which the product meets the customer's utilitarian, aesthetic and economic needs and wants.[55] The utilitarian needs are largely grasped by the attributes and the benefits that the product provides (number of calories, customer friendliness, number of flights a day, a smooth shave, etc.). Besides attributes and benefits, there are also other dimensions that differentiate the brand and determine a brand's performance. A nice style and design can be important to fulfil the consumer's aesthetic needs (think of how Apple changed the computer landscape by introducing colours and frivolous designs). Price is important because consumers may infer from the price whether the product is cheap or expensive, and whether they can trust it or not. Perceived quality is the consumer's subjective judgement about a product's overall quality, its excellence and superiority relative to alternatives.[56] Quality and superiority are extremely important because they largely determine brand purchase.[57]

Brand imagery[58] is related to how well the brand fulfils consumers' psychological and social needs. It refers to how consumers think about a brand in an abstract way rather than to what consumers believe the brand really does. Brand imagery pertains to intangible brand aspects that can become linked to the brand by customer experience, marketing communications, word of mouth, etc. A first intangible association that consumers can make with a brand is user image. For example, the stereotypical user of Oil of Olay is seen as 'a pretty, down-to-earth, solid, female citizen'.[59] It goes without saying that a brand's user image should correspond to the target group's actual or ideal self to be effective.[60] A second type of intangible association pertains to usage imagery. Usage imagery indicates which usage situations consumers associate with a brand or product. For example, most consumers would think that it is more appropriate to drink a soft drink in the afternoon or evening than at breakfast. Likewise, a smoking jacket would be highly unsuitable to visit an amusement park, but has a perfect fit with a gala party. Private label products may also be perfect for private use, but not for gift giving.

BUSINESS INSIGHT
Arch Deluxe: an expensive McFlop

McDonald's has focused on kids and families for many years. In response to the greying of the population and an expanding older market, McDonald's tried to capture the more adult audience. To this end, the company launched the Deluxe line, 'hamburgers for adults', with a sophisticated, grown-up taste. The line included the Fish Filet Deluxe, Grilled Chicken Deluxe, Crispy Chicken Deluxe and as flagship the Arch Deluxe. The new line was launched by a $100 million ad campaign. Both the products and the campaign were very different from what people expected and were used to from McDonald's. The ads showed kids looking puzzled at the complex hamburger and making 'yucky faces'. Ronald was even shown in 'adult' activities like golf and pool. McDonald's key values and key consumer associations are friendliness, cleanliness, consistency, simplicity and convenience. That is what people expect to get from McDonald's and that is the reason why they go to McDonald's – not to get a sophisticated burger at a high price. McDonald's gradually discontinued the line and currently only a few sandwiches (such as Chicken McGrill) are still available. It is estimated that McDonald's lost about $300 million in research, production and marketing for the Deluxe line. The Deluxe line is considered as one of the biggest marketing flops in history, on the same level as New Coke.[61]

As a third type of intangible associations, brands can also have a symbolic meaning or a personality. **Brand personality** can be defined as the set of 'human personality traits that are both applicable to and relevant for brands'.[62] A brand's personality is stronger if its elements are deliberately co-ordinated and if the personality is kept consistent over time. In 1997, Jennifer Aaker developed the Brand Personality Scale (BPS) to measure a brand's personality.[63] The BPS distinguishes five personality dimensions: (1) sincerity (down-to-earth, honest, wholesome and cheerful), (2) excitement (daring, spirited, imaginative and up-to-date), (3) competence (reliable, intelligent and successful), (4) sophistication (upper class and charming) and (5) ruggedness (outdoorsy and tough). In her US study, MTV scored highly on excitement, CNN on competence, Levi's on ruggedness, Revlon on sophistication and Campbell on sincerity. However, in a later cross-cultural study in Japan and Spain, only three of the five factors emerged. Furthermore, Aaker did include not only personality items in her scale, but also user characteristics such as male, female, upper class, Western, etc. To solve the foregoing shortcomings, a new scale was developed and it proved to be robust in the USA and the ten different European countries in which it was tested. The new measure also consists of five dimensions, but shows more affinity with the Big Five of human personality than Aaker's dimensions do: (1) responsibility (down-to-earth, stable, responsible), (2) activity (active, dynamic, innovative), (3) aggressiveness (aggressive, bold), (4) simplicity (ordinary, simple) and (5) emotionality (romantic, sentimental).[64] In the current competitive environment, engineering brand symbolism and a brand personality are becoming more important. The success of Lego, for example, is linked not only to its physical attributes, being the simple and distinctive Lego bricks, but also to the psychological meaning of a company committed to fostering creative imagination.[65]

Table 2.4 Means–end chains and brand association structures

	Concrete attributes	Abstract attributes	Functional benefits	Psycho-social benefits	Instrumental values	End-values
Bacardi Breezer	Less alcohol	Filling	I drink less alcohol	I avoid the negatives of alcohol	I am more able to socialise and can really enjoy my friends	I get the feeling I belong to the group
50 cl cola can	Too much to drink	Cola gets warm	I cannot drink it all	I throw it away	I am wasting money	I feel irresponsible
Spicy Doritos	Flavour	Strong taste	I eat less	I don't get fat	I maintain a good figure	I feel good about myself

Source: Based on Reynolds, T.J. and Gutman, J. (2001), 'Laddering Theory, Method, Analysis, and Interpretation', in Reynolds, T.J. and Olson, J.C. (eds), *Understanding Consumer Decision Making: The Means-End Approach to Marketing and Advertising Strategy*, Mahwah, NJ: Lawrence Erlbaum Associates, 25–62.

Finally, **brand feelings** or consumers' emotional responses to the brand are an important element of brand equity. For example, warmth, fun, excitement, self-respect, social approval and security are considered as important types of brand-building feelings.[66] These feelings may have become associated to the brand by means of its marketing communications programme or the experiences the consumer had with the brand. They may also stem from the attributes or benefits consumers associate with the brand. The relation between attributes and consumers' end-values/feelings can be revealed by the 'means–end chain'. The structure of the 'ladder' of meanings that a brand can deliver is often presented as a 'means–end chain', with six levels (associations) (Table 2.4).[67] First of all, a brand suggests a number of both concrete and abstract attributes. Concrete attributes can be the Absolut Vodka bottle or the lubricating strip on a Gillette razor. Abstract attributes can be the level of technology in a Saab car or the good taste of Danone yoghurt. These attributes lead to functional and psycho-social benefits. A functional benefit of Elsève hairspray is that you avoid sticky hair. The psycho-social benefit of Nespresso coffee may be that guests feel happy and have more fun drinking it. Finally, brands are also associated with instrumental and end-values. Using Dolce and Gabbana perfume may enable you to impress others (instrumental values), leading to a higher level of self-esteem (end-value). The concept of means–end chains is derived from the fact that the attributes (means) lead to benefits, which eventually lead to values (ends). For instance, Dorito crisps are made of corn and have a special flavour; as a result, they are tasty and guests have more fun and enjoy visiting you, which makes you a good host, leading to the desired end-value of higher self-esteem. The final goal of consumption and brand choice is to satisfy end-value needs.

In assessing brand association structures, not only should the evoked associations be measured, but also their desirability, strength and uniqueness,[68] i.e. the extent to which customers value the associations they make, and the extent to which the brand is perceived to be the only one that evokes that particular set of associations.

Other assets also determine brand equity, such as the number of stores carrying the brand, the percentage of people that have easy access to the brand, shelf space, patents and trademarks, quality of staff, labels, etc.

The first four factors of brand equity do not imply any real behaviour on the part of the consumer. Evidently, real brand strength will be translated into consumers buying the brand and being loyal to it. Behind every powerful brand stands a group of loyal consumers. In fact, the real company asset is **brand loyalty**, not the brand itself.[69] Different levels of loyalty can be distinguished (Figure 2.5). Evidently, a strong brand implies that as many customers as

Figure 2.5 The loyalty pyramid

possible are satisfied, committed buyers. Not only will committed buyers repurchase the brand, but also they will actively promote your brand to others and function as real ambassadors. Striving for customer loyalty is also a cost-saving strategy. Research indicates that the cost of attracting new customers can be as much as six times greater than the cost of retaining existing customers.[70] One way to retain loyal customers and committed buyers is to address marketing programmes in such a way that consumers are offered an experience instead of a product. For example, marketers and consumers can jointly build brand communities where brand experiences can be built and/or shared. A **brand community** is 'a specialised, non-geographically bound community, based on a structured set of social relationships among users of a brand'.[71] Jeep, for example, organises brand fests such as Jeep Jamborees (regional rallies focusing on off-road trail driving), Camp Jeep (national rally offering lifestyle and product-related activities) and Jeep 101 (off-road driving course), all attracting a wide range of Jeep owners and their friends. Even Jeep owners who come to the event with a feeling of being different from the others seem to leave the event believing they belong to a broader community. Brand communities also exist for Harley-Davidson (Harley Owner Groups, HOGs) and Apple. By managing their communities in the right way, companies can build fierce loyalty, enhance marketing efficiency and increase their brand's equity.[72] Certainly, customers who feel they belong to a brand community will remain brand loyal. Moreover, the experiences gathered by means of the brand community increase word of mouth, leading to many friends also buying the brand.

Benefits of branding

Strong brands have a number of benefits for the company, the retailer and the consumer.[73] Strong brands help the consumer to locate and identify products and evaluate their quality. This makes it easier for the consumer to develop attitudes and expectations. A brand name serves as a shorthand label for a large bundle of associations and the whole brand personality.

Table 2.5 Brand equity components and branding benefits

Brand equity components	Benefits
Brand awareness	• Brand in evoked set • Influence on attitude and perceptions • Anchor for associations • Signal of substance/commitment
Product performance/perceived quality	• Price premium • Differentiation/positioning • Reason to buy • Channel member interest • Brand extension potential
Imagery associations (user type, brand personality, history, feelings)	• Differentiation/positioning • High price premium • Memory retrieval potential • Reason to buy • Brand extension potential
High brand loyalty	• Reduced marketing costs • Trade leverage • Attracting new customers • Time to respond to competitive threats

Branding makes shopping more efficient in that it reduces the amount of decision-making time required and the perceived risk of purchase, as a result of the fact that a brand promises a constant level of quality. It gives consumers the ability to assess quickly the value and quality of new products by association with a well-known brand name. Furthermore, the consumer derives a psychological reward, since some brands, like Rolex or Lexus, are regarded as status symbols. Finally, branding increases the innovation potential of manufacturers, thus leading to more variety and consumer choice.

Retailers also benefit from strong brands because they improve the image of the store, and as a result attract customers. Strong brands often result in lower selling costs and a higher inventory turn. Furthermore, retailers benefit from the marketing support the brand gets, by means of advertising, sales promotion and in-store communications.

Last but not least, manufacturers benefit greatly from high-equity brands.[74] In Table 2.5, the benefits for the manufacturer are summarised per brand equity component. High brand awareness puts the brand in the evoked set of many consumers, and may even give it a prominent place in this evoked set. The more a brand is in the evoked set of consumers, the more probable it becomes that the consumer is going to buy it. Promotional support is facilitated.

Well-known brands are also capable of developing favourable attitudes and perceptions more easily, again leading to more sales. Additionally, well-known brands can lead to more interest and trust by retailers, resulting in easier access to the distribution channel. Well-known brands also increase the power of the manufacturer over the retailer. As already mentioned, a brand name serves as a shorthand signal for favourable brand associations. Brand awareness also gives the company and the brand a sense of trustworthiness and the image of commitment.

Good product performance and higher perceived quality give the consumer a good reason to buy the product, but also the right user image or brand personality induces people to buy the product. Higher perceived quality as well as a positive brand personality and higher customer loyalty give the company the opportunity of charging a premium price. Furthermore, it protects the company against future price competition. Positive brand imagery, strong brand-evoked feelings, good performance and high-quality perceptions enable the manufacturer to create a differential advantage, to build up a defence against the competition and to target and position products in a more sophisticated way. The same brand equity components also give the manufacturer an efficient base for line or brand extensions. The image and personality of the brand are easily carried over to the new product, giving it a head start. An extensive set of brand associations helps the consumer retrieve information from memory, thus facilitating the purchasing process and biasing it towards the brand.

A strong brand is capable of fostering brand loyalty. It is a vehicle in forging stable relationships between the consumer and the manufacturer. It reduces the marketing cost, because it is cheaper to retain an existing loyal customer than to win over a new one. Brand loyalty leads to more support from the distribution channel and makes the company less vulnerable to competitive action. Overall, the most important consequence of possessing strong brands is that it can generate higher and more stable sales and profits.

Marketing communications and brand equity

Marketing communications are the voice of a brand. In general, the role of marketing communications is to inform, persuade and remind consumers of the brand essence, to engage consumers in a dialogue and to build relationships, or even a brand community.

A number of communications tools can be used to build and reinforce brand equity. Others, however, should be avoided or used carefully. Taking a long-term perspective of brand management, managerial efforts can be classified in two types of activities: brand-building and brand-harming activities.[75] High advertising spending and investing in corporate social responsibility initiatives are examples of brand-building activities. Frequent use of price promotions, on the other hand, dilutes the brand in the long run and can therefore be classified as a brand-harming activity. Indeed, price cuts and other types of immediate material incentives may reduce the quality perception of brands and the potential of the brand to command a premium price. On the other hand, loyalty promotions may serve both as a reward for loyal customers and as a means of enhancing the loyalty-creating effect of brand strength with new customers.

Direct mailings used in a 'junk mail' way could also harm the brand. A beautiful and convincing image campaign may be completely overturned and destroyed by frequent, straightforward, hard sell direct mailing campaigns. On the other hand, public relations, if well handled, and corporate image-building can be valuable brand-building activities for corporate brands. McDonald's did not open a restaurant in Moscow because of its immediate profit potential. The worldwide coverage of the event in the media gave it massive free publicity and positioned the company as very international and forward-looking. On the other hand, Perrier reacted so clumsily to the problem of benzene in its mineral water that the image of the brand was seriously damaged. Consistent corporate identity and corporate image-building through packaging and design add to building and maintaining the long-term network of associations, one of the factors of brand equity.[76]

BUSINESS INSIGHT
Colours and symbols as brand-building tools

Corporate identity-building can lead to powerful associations between colours or symbols and brand names. Consider the following examples:

- Golden arches symbolise McDonald's.
- The circle with the triangular star is Mercedes.
- Three stripes on a shoe is Adidas.
- A stylised lion is the ING Bank.

- IBM owns dark blue in business machines.
- Red is Coca-Cola and blue is Pepsi in the soft drink market.
- In batteries, bronze and black is Duracell.

Marketing communications are crucial contributors to brand equity in several ways. A first step in brand-building is creating deep and broad brand awareness.[77] Deep awareness means that the brand is strongly linked with its product category and enjoys high top-of-mind awareness. Frequent advertising using slogans, baselines or jingles that make reference to the product category help to build top-of-mind awareness. British Airways, for example, used as a baseline 'the world's favourite airline'. Broad awareness refers to the fact that consumers easily think of the brand in different situations. When Febreze was launched, P&G used ads showing that the product could be used to prevent bad odours in laundry, in shoes, in curtains, in carpets, in cars, etc., which stimulated broad awareness. Once a brand node is well established in memory, it is easier to create additional links. Therefore, focusing on brand meaning or brand image comes in only after brand awareness has been established. Also for building brand image, advertising is an excellent tool (Figure 2.6). Brand image communications can focus on product performance (stressing ingredients, attributes, benefits such as product reliability, product durability, service, style, price, etc.) or on imagery (who is the typical user, when and where can the product be used, brand personality and brand values, brand history, feelings, etc.). Miele, for example, works more on performance than on imagery, stressing the durability of its products. Coke Zero ads show that the product is meant for men, whereas Coke Light ads have always made clear that females are the target users. In general, print, factual ads are better for performance-building, and TV and cinema advertising are more suited to build imagery. For more on specific advertising types (e.g. emotional ads, demonstrations, etc.), see Chapter 7.

BUSINESS INSIGHT
Alternating performance and imagery communications

To form a rich network of associations around a brand, it is advisable to alternate performance and imagery communications. For example, when the Belgian airline SN Brussels Airlines was founded, it used print ads to create performance. The performance ads stressed how convenient it is to book an SN Brussels Airline's ticket, its cheap price, etc. Further, TV ads and viral marketing were used to create imagery. For example, the passionate personality of the airline was shown in an emotional TV ad where the ground crew hurried up to form the sentence 'Mr Jones, it's a boy' when the passenger could not be reached by phone because the flight had just taken off. This same ad was used in viral marketing allowing consumers to adapt the 'it's a boy' message and send it to their partner, friends, etc.

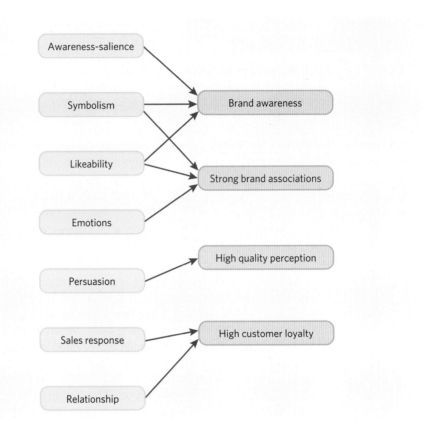

Figure 2.6 Brand equity components and advertising models

Source: Based on Franzen, G. (1998), *Merken en Reclame* (*Brands and Advertising*). Kluwer Bedrijfsinformatie.

Also, when a brand has been on the market for a long time, investing in communications that strengthen deep and broad awareness, and that reinforce brand performance and imagery, remains necessary.[78] For example, for many brands, enhancing the breadth of awareness is an important basis for future growth. If consumers choose Special K cereals not only for breakfast, but also as a snack in the afternoon, this can seriously drive up sales volume. Also, when a brand node is not regularly accessed it will become less likely that it is activated in purchase situations.

Although advertising is the key tool of marketing communications when it comes to building and sustaining strong brands, it is not the only tool that can or should be used. In the spirit of integrated marketing communications (see Chapter 1), different communication tools should be mixed and matched to reach an optimal effect. Red Bull, for example, invested more in below- than above-the-line communications to support its brand.[79] It used buzz or rumour marketing (e.g. one of the product's ingredients, taurine, was not allowed at first in the EU; this created a forbidden fruit effect: What would the product be like? Would it really give an energy boost? Would it be harmful?, etc.), outdoor marketing (e.g. Minis driving in the city with a big can of Red Bull installed on the vehicle, hiring youngsters to put empty cans in discotheques and trendy places), point-of-purchase materials (e.g. Red Bull insisted on having its own fridge in discotheques and fancy clubs), and sampling in colleges and universities to create awareness. Its TV ads also served to build awareness, but added a humorous touch at the same time which helped to convey the brand personality. Sponsoring of extreme sports events and sports athletes helped to build credibility that the brand indeed revitalises the body. Fuel nozzles in petrol stations broadened brand awareness and reminded people that Red Bull is not only about energizing the body, but also the mind. No doubt, the combined effect of all these communications tools on Red Bull's brand equity was higher than any single communications tool could have generated. In current times, social media should also not be forgotten. Involving customers and potential customers, providing them with both interesting and fun information, and having them generate unexpected or cool experiences are crucial to build a bond, make them revisit the web page and have them not only press the 'I like' button but talk about the brand to other people.

In the next chapter and the chapters on specific communications tools, these issues will be explored in more depth.

Summary

A brand is a bundle of meanings; it adds either rational and tangible aspects or symbolic, emotional and intangible dimensions to a product that differentiate it from competitive products. Brand names should be memorable, meaningful, likeable, adaptable, transferable and protectable. There are different categories of brands. To compete with manufacturer brands, distributors introduce own-label brands and generic products. Successful brands have a number of common characteristics. The products are original, of good quality and differentiated from the competition, and the brand is supported by the management, employees and characterised by additional service and integrated communications support in a long-term perspective. Companies can choose different strategies for their brands. Besides co-branding with other brands, an extension or multi-brand strategy can be adopted. Also corporate branding, i.e. using the same company name for all company products, is a possibility. Not only does brand equity have to be built, but also it has to be sustained over time. In this respect, the brand portfolio may have to be adapted once in a while. It is important that the portfolio maximises market coverage, minimises brand overlap and is efficiently composed. To protect the main brand (bastion brand), flanker, fighter and prestige brands may be useful. Brand strength is measured on the basis of a number of factors, such as leadership, internationality and stability. The marketing value of a brand, or brand equity, is composed of five factors: brand awareness; product performance and perceived quality; imagery associations and brand feelings; high brand loyalty; and other assets such as legal protection and a good distribution network. Strong brands lead to a number of benefits for the company, the consumer and the retailer. Brand equity is developed and supported by means of consistent, long-term, integrated marketing communications. It is important to build deep and broad awareness first before creating a positive image.

REVIEW QUESTIONS

1. What is a brand? What are the characteristics of a good brand? What types of brand can be distinguished?

2. What are the characteristics of successful brands?

3. What are the benefits and disadvantages of line and brand stretching versus multi-branding? What are the implications of the two types of strategy for marketing communications?

4. What is a brand portfolio and what different functions can the composing brands serve?

5. What is brand equity and what are its main components?

6. How can marketing communications influence brand equity?

7. What are the benefits of strong brands for the consumer and for the manufacturer?

Further reading

Aaker, D. (2011), *Brand Relevance: Making Competitors Irrelevant*. New York: Wiley.

Davis, J.A. (2010), *Competitive Success: How Branding Adds Value*. Chichester: Wiley.

Keller, K.L., Aperia, T. and Georgson, M. (2012), *Strategic Brand Management: A European Perspective*, 2nd edition. Harlow: Financial Times Press.

Kumar, N. and Steenkamp, J.B. (2007), *Private Label Strategy*. Harvard, MA: Harvard Business School Press.

Laforet, S. (2010), *Managing Brands: A Contemporary Perspective*. Maidenhead: McGraw-Hill.

Journal of Brand Management, http://www.palgrave-journals.com/bm/index.html.

Journal of Product and Brand Management, http://www.emeraldinsight.com.

CASE 2:
Barco, projecting the magic

Barco was founded in Belgium in 1934 by Lucien De Puydt, who specialised in the assembly of radios with American components. He called the company 'The Belgian-American Radio Corporation', or Barco. In the 1940s, Barco picked up with an innovation in communication technology, namely television. From the 1960s onwards, Barco started to diversify into different industries. Today, Barco is a world leader concerning visualisation solutions for a variety of selected professional markets, such as control rooms, defence and aerospace, digital cinema, health care, media and entertainment, and simulation and virtual reality. These markets are served by Barco's four main divisions: Entertainment, Healthcare, Control Rooms & Simulation, and Defence & Aerospace. Worldwide, Barco has about 3500 employees and its sales amounted to about €1.041 billion in 2011. The latter denotes a sharp increase of €400 million in just two years.

Barco is present in more than 90 countries and is visible almost everywhere: screens at pop concerts and sports events, screens in aircraft, projectors in movie theatres, screens in hospitals, screens for company presentations, screens to monitor industry processes, etc. For example, U2, Madonna and Bon Jovi all use Barco screens for their concert tours, Barco's screens are used for the Eurovision Song Contest; six times in a row Barco has been the exclusive partner of the Berlin International Film Festival; Barco was omnipresent at the Shanghai World Expo; China uses Barco to help monitor the country's electricity network;

Barco ensures the safety of a million travellers on the Sao Paulo metro; Delhi's police surveillance centre relies on Barco; major hospitals all around the world use Barco equipment. However, since Barco is active in business-to-business markets, hardly any consumer knows the company. Consequently, Barco is one of the world's best-kept secrets.

To become more visible and to build a stronger brand, Barco adopted a corporate branding strategy in 2010, which has clearly paid off as its recent success in digital cinema shows. In the following paragraphs, we describe Barco's strategic and branding orientation of the past and at present and how this brand focus helped it to gain leadership in digital cinema.

The Barco brand: past and present

Barco used to adhere to a product orientation, firmly believing that high-quality products and technologies would automatically result in market success. Concerning brand identity, the following elements were considered as core building blocks: quality, reliability, technological advantage, performance and being the category reference. As many of Barco's employees are engineers, such a product orientation was largely supported by managers and personnel alike. Moreover, since Barco's products had easily 'sold themselves' in the past, Barco was convinced that customers' perceptions matched its own beliefs. Although high-quality products and technologies are obviously important, unfortunately they cannot make Barco unique since they can be easily copied. Further, even in a high-tech B2B environment, high quality is not the only thing that matters. An image study in 2002 made this painfully clear to Barco. The study showed that Barco was perceived as company-centred, technical, technology-driven, purely factual without an emotional link, not containing a 'feelgood' factor or possessing much likeability. In short, a rather distant and boring brand. Some customers even said they just bought Barco because there was not yet a competitor for some of the products, adding 'as soon as an alternative comes onto the market, we will buy from them'. No need to stress that this was an unpleasant message for Barco.

As well as these image problems, each division appeared to have its own 'look and feel' and communicated in different ways to the customers: different colours were used; the corporate slogan 'Innovators in Image Processing' was used by some but not all divisions; company presentations were made in completely different templates, etc. The divisions not only looked different, but also felt as if they belonged to different companies. For example, when a customer asked for information about projectors at a show where LCD screens were on display, an employee simply answered, 'Oh, that's not us, you need to talk to the Barco projector guys', without trying to help the customer.

Barco responded with a corporate branding programme to give the company 'one face' and to move from a product-oriented company towards a customer-oriented company. To this end, first a unified vision and mission were spelled out that explicitly incorporated the customer-orientation aspect. Barco's vision is that, as imaging is revolutionising the world, accurate processing and display of visual information have become critical in the business world. This inherent complexity demands user-friendly solutions. In line with this vision, Barco's mission is 'to create value through the design and delivery of user-friendly imaging solutions to selected professional markets on a global basis'.

Building further on the vision and mission, four general principles were articulated underlying the new branding strategy.

Principle 1: One brand

Barco is the one powerbrand across all segments and categories in all divisions. Sub-brands can be installed, but only in a secondary role to support the Barco brand. One logo, one baseline, one website, one overall look and feel are installed.

Principle 2: One company

The corporate brand defines the end promise of all products, in all markets, segments and product categories. The branding strategy needs to be applied in all divisions and all markets, so that it is clear, for example, that it is Barco and not the division Control Rooms & Simulation that is launching a new product.

Principle 3: Customer centred

The new branding strategy is driven and inspired by Barco's customers. It is based on customer insights, customer language, customer decision processes and customer buying behaviour.

Principle 4: Focus on Barco strategy

The branding strategy is an important contributor to Barco's mid-term and long-term corporate objectives. An important objective of Barco is to be number one or a strong number two in all the markets it serves.

Rucci, Kirn and Quinn (1998) demonstrated that the engagement and commitment of employees towards the brand and the company have a significant impact on how they treat customers and, consequently, on customers' perceptions and business performance. They showed that companies that were rated by their employees as a great place to work witnessed a 25% growth in share and dividend returns compared with 6.3% for other companies. Keeping this in mind, Barco continuously delivered important efforts to involve employees in each of the brand process steps. Further, to reinforce the brand story and to increase employee commitment, an internal 'to be one' branding programme was installed consisting of the following internal brand identity guidelines:

'to be one': internal brand identity guidelines	
One team	Barco has a team of 3500 dedicated professionals
One vision	Barco leads the way in digital visualisation for professionals
One image	Barco stands for innovation, quality and customer intimacy
One culture	Barco shares a common set of strong values: accountability, customer focus, innovation, integrity, team spirit, trust
One goal	Barco aims for global leadership in all its target markets
One future	Barco continuously invests in new technologies
One billion	Barco is a €1 billion revenue company

According to a recent employee survey, Barco managed to keep high employee engagement after the brand redirections. For example, 72% of the employees agree or strongly agree that they feel proud to work for Barco, 65% feel motivated to go beyond their formal job responsibilities, 71% feel their job provides them with the opportunity to do challenging and interesting work, 73% agree they are treated with respect as individuals, and 89% agree that the people in their team are committed to delivering high-quality products and services. These findings are also reflected in the fact that CRF Institute (an independent company specialising in international working conditions research) named Barco as one of Belgium's 'Top Employers' in 2011.

Next, it was time for Barco to practise what it preached. The marketing communications campaigns for digital cinema projectors launched in 2010 was the first test case of the new strategy.

Digital cinema: from challenger to market leader

Barco launched the first digital projector in 1999. Shortly afterwards, the first generation of digital cinema projectors followed. However, the market was not very interested at that time. The main reason was that, for conventional projection, movie studios pay the costs of the film reels whereas, for digital projection, the movie theatres themselves had to bear the huge costs of the expensive digital projectors, with studios saving on distribution costs (a film reel costs up to $1000 a theatre). With the launch of the 3-D movie *Avatar*, demand took off. At that time, there were four digital projector manufacturers in the market: Christie (the historic market leader in the cinema market), Sony (strong consumer brand holding a dominant market position from cameras to movie production), NEC (strong consumer brand) and, as an underdog, Barco. Initially, all offerings were technology-focused, with none of the companies having a clear technological advantage as most players – except Sony – used the same chipset from Texas Instruments. Sony had an advantage as it had access to 4K resolution technology (i.e. an image size of 4096 × 2160 pixels as compared with 2K or 2048 × 1080 resolution for the other companies). However, digital cinema was not driven by resolution but by 3-D. For 3-D there is 80% light loss, therefore brightness is more important than resolution. As Barco was strong in brightness, it held a competitive advantage here. In contrast to the other three players, it did not focus on the technical advantage though, but built a brand-centred campaign. To strengthen the link between Barco and digital cinema, the central element of the campaign was a stinger movie which was shown at tradeshows, at customer demonstrations, in Barco offices and, most important of all, in cinema theatres before the main movie. In line with the new branding strategy, Barco looked at what its technology could do for the end-user. Therefore, the stinger movie showed the magic of cinema as experienced by a young boy and fireflies were used as a metaphor for the light Barco was bringing. The headline was 'Projecting the magic'. Instead of overwhelming potential customers with the exact technological details, the movie stressed the result of the extra brightness and focused on emotion.

The stinger movie was not the only tool Barco used. To maximise the impact of the campaign and to ensure all target groups were reached, the stinger movie was accompanied by an integrated marketing communications campaign. To this end, Barco also made use of the following marketing communications tools:

- Direct mailing to *Film Echo* magazine subscribers
- Ads in various trade press worldwide
- Dedicated website: www.projectingthemagic.com
- Online advertising (Manice, Cinema Today)
- Barco quarterly digital cinema e-newsletter
- Video on YouTube
- Social media: Twitter, Facebook (screensaver and wallpaper)
- Presence and screenings at tradeshows (e.g. Showest, USA; Cinema Expo, the Netherlands)
- Press release announcing the new projector range

The tradeshows were very important for Barco, resulting in more than 1000 visitors a day. Importantly, it was able to reach the whole industry at only four key tradeshows and to generate 1200 leads, of which 250 were qualified. The online campaign resulted in 6500 web visitors with more than 34 000 page views. The stinger on YouTube resulted in more than 2400 views with more than 800 downloads of source files from barco.com. E-blasts had a read rate of 47% and a click-through rate of 23% (as compared with an industry average of 1%). But, most importantly, Barco created massive credibility in the industry.

How did the competitors try to counter Barco's attack? Sony played even more on 4K and Christie copied Sony by announcing 4K projectors as well, even though Texas Instruments would not have the chip for 4K ready. However, according to industry specialists, 4K is nothing more than a marketing hype and brightness is more important as far as 3-D projection is concerned. Barco would soon have 4K projectors ready, but did not want to comprise the sales of its 2K projectors. To this end, Barco responded to Christie and Sony in a three-phased approach: (1) a viral campaign; (2) the launch of the 4K projector at the opening night of Cinemark; and (3) a Guinness world record. For the viral campaign, Barco hired Peter Knight, a free lance projectionist and valued guest writer in industry magazines. He travelled from Europe to Orlando (where Barco will later launch its 4K projector) and interviewed key

Source: Reproduced with permission of Barco.

stakeholders in the industry on the value of 4K. Every day he reported his findings on www.the4Kdiaries.com and Twitter. The 4K diaries website received 2250 visitors. Examples of posts are:

Indeed, there is more to image quality than resolution. There are other things to consider as Michael Karagosian explained, such as colour and contrast, which are probably more important than pure resolution as they are perceived by the human eye first.

I started this quest not knowing much about 4K, and what I have discovered is that where 4K is concerned, you need to look at much more than just resolution and even the image on the screen. You need to consider the whole cinema going experience as a concept which could provide additional revenue for cinema owners.

For the launch of Barco's 4K projector, the company managed to get established parties in the industry as sponsors. This enhanced Barco's credibility even more as →

it was not just Barco who was announcing a new digital cinema projector, but the whole industry. Third and most importantly, Barco managed to get a new category inserted in the *Guinness Book of World Records*: the brightest projector. Barco set a new record in this category with 43 000 lumens of light (as compared with 20 000 lumens for competitive brands), which is comparable with the combined light output of about 1700 regular flashlights. From then on, Barco started advertising with the slogan 'brightest projector on the planet'. Christie and Sony did not respond.

What about the results? Firstly, in terms of sales, the campaign supported Barco's rapid market expansion and boosted the company's image in the cinema market. Barco became industry leader with a 40% market share and 25 000 projectors installed by the end of 2011. Importantly, Barco obtained these spectacular results with a modest budget of about €400 000. Approximately half of the budget was spent on tradeshow participation, 35% on advertising and a modest 15% on campaign creation and collateral. Further recognition of the campaign was the LACP Spotlight Award Barco received (LACP is a global communications competition) and inclusion by MLC (Marketing Leadership Council) in its top 50 of B2B campaigns.

Secondly, Barco displayed one consistent and recognisable brand image in the digital cinema sector (and not different images for the different types of projectors the company has for this industry). According to a customer loyalty study conducted by an independent research firm in 2011, Barco's secured loyalists in the digital cinema industry grew from 33% in 2009 to 55% in 2011, a customer loyalty mark that is 12 points above the industry benchmark. Barco's image proved to be the most impactful loyalty driver in the digital cinema market with products

achieving third place (in other industries served by Barco, products consistently form the top loyalty driver) (see also Figure 2.7). Nevertheless, Barco needs to keep on improving its projectors and that is exactly what it does. Right now, it already has a projector that produces 55 000 lumens of light. Barco also incorporated laser technology into the light engines and integrated media servers and theatre management systems software to offer its customers the capability of integrated systems. By consistently putting customers' needs first, Barco has become a more customer-oriented (and less a mere product-oriented) company.

Thirdly, in terms of in-house confidence the campaign was also a big success. 'Projecting the magic' was the first campaign for a specific product that Barco launched after the new branding strategy was installed. The smooth co-operation between the different divisional, regional and corporate Barco teams was seen as one of the success factors of the campaign. The spectacular results reinforced the company's belief that 'to be one' was the right way to go and recognised the new Corporate Marketing organisation as an important sparring partner for other divisions. In this sense, the campaign also resulted in a significant motivational boost for all Barco's employees.

To conclude, in a couple of years Barco managed to move from a merely technology-focused to a more customer-focused organisation. Technology remains important, but, unlike in the past, one face for the whole organisation and one brand image in terms of providing the right customer solution in all its markets have become important as well. By following the 'one brand', 'one company', 'customer centred' and 'focus on Barco's mid-term and long-term strategy', the 'Projecting the magic' campaign for digital cinema became a big success.

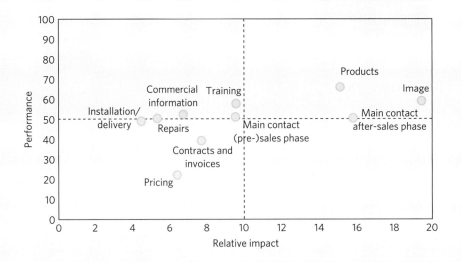

Figure 2.7 Drivers of performance and impact

QUESTIONS

1. What branding strategy did Barco use in the past? Which one is it currently using?

2. What are the advantages and disadvantages of the current branding strategy?

3. Currently Barco is active in several markets. Would you advise Barco to do more brand extensions in the future? Would you advise it to focus on fewer markets?

4. What are the major strengths of the Barco brand?

5. Do you think Barco has a high Brand Strength Index? What about its customer brand equity?

6. What communications tools does Barco use in its 'Projecting the magic' campaign? Do you think this was a good choice? Why (not)? What else would you suggest, if any?

7. To what extent is the campaign in line with the principles of the new branding strategy?

Sources: Based on Information provided by Koen Helsen, VP Corporate Marketing, and Lieven Bertier, Brand & e-Marketing Manager, Annual Report 2009, 2010 and 2011, www.barco.com; Rucci, A.J., Kirn, S.P. and Quinn, R.T. (1998), 'The Employee–Customer Profit Chain at Sears', *Harvard Business Review*, 76(1), 82; the 2010 Employee Survey (HayGroup), and the Customer Loyalty 2011 Study, Focus on Digital Cinema (Synovate).

References

[1] Keller, K.L., Aperia, T. and Georgson, M. (2012), *Strategic Brand Management: A European Perspective*, 2nd edition. Harlow: Financial Times Press.

[2] Batey, M. (2008), *Brand Meaning*. New York: Routledge.

[3] Keller, K.L., Aperia, T. and Georgson, M. (2012), *Strategic Brand Management: A European Perspective*, 2nd edition. Harlow: Financial Times Press.

[4] Riezebos, R. (2003), *Brand Management*. Harlow: Financial Times/Pearson Education.

[5] Batey, M. (2008), *Brand Meaning*. New York: Routledge.

[6] de Jong, K. (2007), *Private Labels in Europe*. Vught: International Private Label Consult; Kumar, N. and Steenkamp, J.B. (2007), *Private Label Strategy*. Harvard, MA: Harvard Business School Press.

[7] Lamey, L., De Leersnyder, B., De Kimpe, M. and Steenkamp, J.-B.E.M. (2007), 'How Business Cycles Contribute to Private-Label Success: Evidence from the United States and Europe', *Journal of Marketing*, 71 (January), 1–15.

[8] Private label today, http://www.plmainternational.com/en/private_label_en.htm (accessed July 2012).

[9] Verhoef, P.C., Nijssen, E.J. and Sloot, L.M. (2002), 'Strategic Reactions of National Brand Manufacturers towards Private Labels: An Empirical Study in the Netherlands', *European Journal of Marketing*, 36(11), 1309–26.

[10] Doyle, P. (2008), *Value-based Marketing*, 2nd edition. Chichester: Wiley; Keller, K.L., Aperia, T. and Georgson, M. (2012), *Strategic Brand Management: A European Perspective*, 2nd edition. Harlow: Financial Times Press.

[11] Interbrand, *Best Global Brands 2008*, http://www.interbrand.com/images/BGB_reports/BGB_2008_EURO_Format.pdf (accessed June 2009); de Chernatony, L. (2006), *From Brand Vision to Brand Evaluation*. Oxford: Butterworth–Heinemann; Tellis, G.J. and Golder, P.N. (1996), 'First to Market, First to Fail? Real Causes of Enduring Market Leadership', *MIT Sloan Management Review*, 37(2), 65–75.

[12] Thompson, J. (2009), *Brandchannel's 2009 brandjunkie awards results*, http://www.brandchannel.com/features_ effect.asp?pf_id=470 (accessed June 2009); Interbrand, *Best Global Brands 2008*, http://www.interbrand.com/images/BGB_reports/BGB_2008_EURO_Format.pdf (accessed 9 April 2009); Silverstein, B. (2009), *Marketing strategies that build value*, April, http://www.brandchannel.com/features_effect.asp?pf_id=472 (accessed June 2009).

[13] Interbrand, *Best Global Brands 2011*, http://www.interbrand.com/nl/best-global-brands/best-global-brands-2008/best-global-brands-2011.aspx (accessed July 2012).

[14] Interbrand, *Best Global Brands 2011*, http://www.interbrand.com/nl/best-global-brands/best-global-brands-2008/best-global-brands-2011.aspx (accessed July 2012).

[15] Millward Brown (2012), BrandZ™ Top 100 Most Valuable Global Brands, http://www.millwardbrown.com/BrandZ/Top_100_Global_Brands.aspx (accessed July 2012).

[16] Balachander, S. and Ghose, S. (2003), 'Reciprocal Spillover Effects: A Strategic Benefit of Brand Extensions', *Journal of Marketing*, 67(1), 4–13.

[17] Ries, A. and Trout, J. (2002), *The 22 Immutable Laws of Marketing*. New York: HarperCollins.

[18] Swaminathan, V., Fox, R.J. and Reddy, S.K. (2001), 'The Impact of Brand Extension Introduction on Choice', *Journal of Marketing*, 65(4), 1–15.

[19] Goedertier, F., Geskens, K., Weijters, B. and Geuens, M. (2012), 'Increasing Choice Satisfaction through Goal-Based Labeling', *Marketing Letters*, 23(1), 119-36; Iyengar, S.S. and Lepper, M.R. (2000), 'When Choice is Demotivating: Can One Desire Too Much of a Good Thing?', *Journal of Personality and Social Psychology*, 79(6), 995–1006; Reutskaja, E. and Hogarth, R.M. (2009), 'Satisfaction in Choice as a Function of the Number of Alternatives: When "Goods Satiate"', *Psychology and Marketing*, 26(3), 197–203; Schwartz, B. (2004), *The Paradox of Choice: Why More Is Less*. New York: HarperCollins.

[20] *De Standaard*, 3 April 2012.

[21] Keller, K.L., Aperia, T. and Georgson, M. (2012), *Strategic Brand Management: A European Perspective*, 2nd edition. Harlow: Financial Times Press.; Smith, D.C. and Park, C.W. (1992), 'The Effects of Brand Extensions on Market

Share and Advertising Efficiency', *Journal of Marketing Research*, 29 (August), 296–313.

22 Ahluwalia, R. (2008), 'How Far Can a Brand Stretch? Understanding the Role of Self-construal', *Journal of Marketing Research*, 45 (June), 337–50; Grime, I., Diamantopoulos, A. and Smith, G. (2002), 'Consumer Evaluations of Extensions and their Effects on the Core Brand: Key Issues and Research Propositions', *European Journal of Marketing*, 36(11), 1415–38.

23 Lane, V.R. (2000), 'The Impact of Ad Repetition and Ad Content on Consumer Perceptions of Incongruent Extensions', *Journal of Marketing*, 64 (April), 80–91.

24 Ahluwalia, R. (2008), 'How Far Can a Brand Stretch? Understanding the Role of Self-construal', *Journal of Marketing Research*, 45 (June), 337–50.

25 Keller, K.L., Aperia, T. and Georgson, M. (2012), *Strategic Brand Management: A European Perspective*, 2nd edition. Harlow: Financial Times Press.

26 Berthon, P., Holbrook, M.B. and Hulbert, J.M. (2003), 'Understanding and Managing the Brand Space', *MIT Sloan Management Review*, 44(2), 49–54.

27 Tischler, L. (2009), *Best and Worst Brand Extensions of 2008*, 30 January, http://www.fastcompany.com/blog/linda-tischler/design-times/best-and-worst-brand-extensions-2008 (accessed June 2009).

28 Keller, K.L., Aperia, T. and Georgson, M. (2012), *Strategic Brand Management: A European Perspective*, 2nd edition. Harlow: Financial Times Press.

29 Berner, R. and Kiley, D. (2005), 'Global Brands: Interbrand Rank the Companies that Best Built Their Images – and Made Them Stick', *Business Week*, 1 August, 86–9; Interbrand, *Best Global Brands 2008*, http://www.interbrand.com/images/BGB_reports/BGB_2008_EURO_Format.pdf (accessed June 2009); Interbrand, *Best Global Brands 2011*, http://www.interbrand.com/nl/best-global-brands/best-global-brands-2008/best-global-brands-2011.aspx (accessed July 2012).

30 Kapferer, J.N. (2000), *(Re)Inventing the Brand: Can Top Brands Survive the New Market Realities?* London: Kogan Page; Tanaka, H. (1993), 'Branding in Japan', in Aaker, D.A. and Biel, A.L. (eds), *Brand Equity and Advertising: Advertising's Role in Building Strong Brands*. Hillsdale, NJ: Lawrence Erlbaum Associates, 51–66.

31 King, S. (1991), 'Brand-building in the 1990s', *Journal of Marketing Management*, 7(3), 3–13.

32 Laforet, S. and Saunders, J. (2005), 'Managing Brand Portfolios: How Strategies Have Changed', *Journal of Advertising Research* (September), 314–27.

33 Hollis, N. (2008), *The Global Brand*. New York: Palgrave Macmillan.

34 Hollis, N. (2008), *The Global Brand*. New York: Palgrave Macmillan; Kapferer, J.N. (2001), *(Re)Inventing the Brand: Can Top Brands Survive the New Market Realities?* London: Kogan Page.

35 Zhang, Y. and Khare, A. (2009), 'The Impact of Accessible Identities on the Evaluation of Global Versus Local Products', *Journal of Consumer Research*, 36 (October), 524–37.

36 Riezebos, R. (2003), *Brand Management: A Theoretical and Practical Approach*. Harlow: Financial Times/Prentice Hall.

37 Keller, K.L., Aperia, T. and Georgson, M. (2012), *Strategic Brand Management: A European Perspective*, 2nd edition. Harlow: Financial Times Press.

38 Geylani, T., Inman, J.J. and TerHofstede, F. (2008), 'Image Reinforcement or Impairment: The Effects of Co-branding on Attribute Uncertainty', *Marketing Science*, 27(4), 730–44; Geuens, M., Pêcheux, C., Vermeir, I. and Faseur, T. (2008), 'Co-branding in Advertising: the Issue of Category and Image Fit', *Latin-American Advances in Consumer Research*, 133–34; Simonin, B.L. and Ruth, J.A. (1998), 'Is a Company Known by the Company It Keeps? Assessing the Spillover Effects of Brand Alliances on Consumer Brand Attitudes', *Journal of Marketing Research*, 35(2), 30–42.

39 Alan, F. (2012), *HTC executive says it plans to drop Beats Audio headphones from some smartphone boxes*, http://www.phonearena.com/news/HTC-executive-says-it-plans-to-drop-Beats-Audio-headphones-from-some-smartphone-boxes_id28864 (accessed July 2012); Olivarez-Giles, N. (2012), 'HTC and Beats to Take on Spotify, iTunes to Boost Phone Sales?', *LA Times*, http://articles.latimes.com/2012/feb/15/business/la-fi-tn-htc-beats-music-streaming-service-rumor-20120215 (accessed July 2012); Sadewo, B. (2012), *HTC and Beats Audio set to acquire music subscription service Mog?*, http://www.androidauthority.com/htc-and-beats-audio-set-to-acquire-music-subscription-service-mog-65757/ (accessed July 2012); Sullivan, M. (2012), 'Beats Audio (HTC) Acquisition of MOG All But Done, Sources Say', *PCWorld*, http://www.pcworld.com/article/252298/beats_audio_htc_acquisition_of_mog_all_but_done_sources_say.html (accessed July 2012).

40 Keller, K.L., Aperia, T. and Georgson, M. (2012), *Strategic Brand Management: A European Perspective*, 2nd edition. Harlow: Financial Times Press.

41 www.unilever.com/pressreleases/2000/EnglishNews_988.asp (accessed July 2009). See also 'Unilever Slashes its Brand Portfolio from 1600 to 400', *Eurofood*, 7 October 1999, http://findarticles.com/p/articles/mi_m0DQA/is_1999_Oct_7/ai_56904871/ (accessed July 2009).

42 Riezebos, R. (2003), *Brand Management: A Theoretical and Practical Approach*. Harlow: Financial Times/Prentice Hall.

43 Riezebos, R. (2003), *Brand Management: A Theoretical and Practical Approach*. Harlow: Financial Times/Prentice Hall.

44 Yoo, B., Donthu, N. and Lee, S. (2000), 'An Examination of Selected Marketing Mix Elements and Brand Equity', *Journal of the Academy of Marketing Science*, 28, 195–212.

45 Keller, K.L., Aperia, T. and Georgson, M. (2012), *Strategic Brand Management: A European Perspective*, 2nd edition. Harlow: Financial Times Press.

46 Batey, M. (2008), *Brand Meaning*. New York: Routledge.

47 Interbrand, *Best Global Brands 2008*, http://www.interbrand.com/images/BGB_reports/BGB_2008_EURO_Format.pdf (accessed June 2009); Interbrand, *Best Global Brands 2011*, http://www.interbrand.com/nl/best-global-brands/best-global-brands-2008/best-global-brands-2011.aspx (accessed July 2012).

48 Kiley, D. (2005), 'Reebok and Adidas: A Good Fit', *BusinessWeek*, 4 August, http://www.businessweek.com/

bwdaily/dnflash/aug2005/nf2005084_8340.htm (accessed June 2009).

49 Interbrand, *Best Global Brands 2011*, http://www.interbrand.com/nl/best-global-brands/best-global-brands-2008/best-global-brands-2011.aspx (accessed July 2012); Perrier, R. (1997), *Brand Valuation*. London: Premier Books and Interbrand Group.

50 Perrier, R. (1997), *Brand Valuation*. London: Premier Books and Interbrand Group.

51 Based on: Keller, K.L., Aperia, T. and Georgson, M. (2012), *Strategic Brand Management: A European Perspective*, 2nd edition. Harlow: Financial Times Press; Aaker, D.A. (1996), *Building Strong Brands*. New York: Free Press.

52 Keller, K.L., Aperia, T. and Georgson, M. (2012), *Strategic Brand Management: A European Perspective*, 2nd edition. Harlow: Financial Times Press.

53 Keller, L.K. (1993), 'Conceptualizing, Measuring and Managing Customer Based Brand Equity', *Journal of Marketing*, 57(1), 1–22.

54 De Pelsmacker, P. and Geuens, M. (1999), 'The Advertising Effectiveness of Different Levels of Intensity of Humour and Warmth and the Moderating Role of Top of Mind Awareness and Degree of Product Use', *Journal of Marketing Communication*, 5, 113–29.

55 Keller, K.L., Aperia, T. and Georgson, M. (2012), *Strategic Brand Management: A European Perspective*, 2nd edition. Harlow: Financial Times Press.

56 Aaker, D.A. (1996), *Building Strong Brands*. New York: Free Press.

57 Kotler, P. and Armstrong, G. (2010). *Principles of Marketing*, 13th edition. Upper Saddle River, NJ: Prentice Hall.

58 Keller, K.L., Aperia, T. and Georgson, M. (2012), *Strategic Brand Management: A European Perspective*, 2nd edition. Harlow: Financial Times Press.

59 Plummer, J.T. (2000), 'How Personality Makes a Difference', *Journal of Advertising Research*, 40 (November/December), 79–83.

60 Solomon, M.R., Bamossy, G., Askegaard, S. and Hogg, M.K. (2007), *Consumer Behaviour: A European Perspective*, 3rd edition. Harlow: Pearson Education.

61 Haig, M. (2005), *Brand Failures: The truth about the 100 biggest branding mistakes of all time*. London: Kogan Page; Horowitz, A., Athitakis, M. and Lasswell, M. (2004), *The Dumbest Moments in Business History*. New York: Portfolio; http://en.wikipedia.org/wiki/Arch_Deluxe (accessed June 2009).

62 Azoulay, A. and Kapferer, N.N. (2003), 'Do Brand Personality Scales Really Measure Brand Personality?', *Brand Management*, 11 (November), 143–55.

63 Aaker, J.L. (1997), 'Dimensions of Brand Personality', *Journal of Marketing Research*, 63 (August), 347–56.

64 Geuens, M., Weijters, B. and De Wulf, K. (2009), 'A New Measure of Brand Personality', *International Journal of Research in Marketing*, 26(2), 97–107.

65 Anonymous (2002), 'Branding @ Lego, McDonald's and JCB', *Strategic Direction*, 18(10), 7–9.

66 Keller, K.L., Aperia, T. and Georgson, M. (2012), *Strategic Brand Management: A European Perspective*, 2nd edition. Harlow: Financial Times Press.

67 Reynolds, T.J. and Olson, J.C. (2001), *Understanding Consumer Decision Making: The Means–End Approach to Marketing and Advertising Strategy*, Mahwah, NJ: Lawrence Erlbaum Associates.

68 Keller, K.L. (2008a), *Building, Measuring, and Managing Brand Equity*, 3rd edition. Upper Saddle River, NJ: Prentice Hall.

69 Perrier, R. (1997), *Brand Valuation*. London: Premier Books and Interbrand Group.

70 Dekimpe, M.G., Steenkamp, J.-B.E.M., Mellens, M. and VandenAbeele, P. (1997), 'Decline and Variability in Brand Loyalty', *International Journal of Research in Marketing*, 11(3), 261–74.

71 Muniz, A. and O'Guinn, T. (2001), 'Brand Community', *Journal of Consumer Research*, 27 (March), 412–32.

72 Fournier, S. and Lee, L. (2009), 'Getting Brand Communities Right', *Harvard Busines Review*, 87(4), 105–111.

73 Webster, F.E. (2000), 'Understanding the Relationships Among Brands, Consumers and Resellers', *Journal of the Academy of Marketing Science*, 28(1), 17–23.

74 Brassington, F. and Pettitt, S. (2003), *Principles of Marketing*. London: Pitman; Keller, K.L. (2008a), *Building, Measuring, and Managing Brand Equity*, 3rd edition. Upper Saddle River, NJ: Prentice Hall.

75 Yoo, B., Donthu, N. and Lee, S. (2000), 'An Examination of Selected Marketing Mix Elements and Brand Equity', *Journal of the Academy of Marketing Science*, 28, 195–212.

76 Biel, A.L. (1993), 'Converting Image into Equity', in Aaker, D.A. and Biel, A.L. (eds), *Brand Equity and Advertising: Advertising's Role in Building Strong Brands*. Hillsdale, NJ: Lawrence Erlbaum Associates, 67–82.

77 Keller, K.L., Aperia, T. and Georgson, M. (2012), *Strategic Brand Management: A European Perspective*, 2nd edition. Harlow: Financial Times Press.

78 Keller, K.L., Aperia, T. and Georgson, M. (2012), *Strategic Brand Management: A European Perspective*, 2nd edition. Harlow: Financial Times Press.

79 Keller, K.L., Aperia, T. and Georgson, M. (2012), *Strategic Brand Management: A European Perspective*, 2nd edition. Harlow: Financial Times Press.

CHAPTER 3
How marketing communications work

CHAPTER OUTLINE

> Hierarchy of effects
>
> Attitude formation and change
>
> | High elaboration likelihood Cognitive attitude formation | Low elaboration likelihood Cognitive attitude formation |
> | High elaboration likelihood Affective attitude formation | Low elaboration likelihood Affective attitude formation |
> | High elaboration likelihood Behavioural attitude formation | Low elaboration likelihood Behavioural attitude formation |
>
> Irritation
>
> Brand confusion

CHAPTER OBJECTIVES

This chapter will help you to:

- Get an idea of how hierarchy-of-effects models describe how communications work
- Understand the importance of attitude formation in the consumer persuasion process
- Distinguish the basic types of attitude formation and change processes and marketing communications models
- Learn about the importance of elaboration likelihood and cognitive, affective and behavioural processes for marketing communications
- Understand the causes and consequences of ad-evoked irritation
- Learn what causes brand confusion in advertising

Introduction

Often it is hard to predict how a consumer will respond to advertising or how someone will process a communications message. Several factors have an impact on this: consumer goals, characteristics of the product type, the situation the consumer is in (hurried or distracted by others, for example), involvement in the product category and social, psychological or cultural factors. In this chapter an overview of the different ways in which a consumer might process marketing communications is given. One type of explanatory framework that has dominated the marketing communications literature for decades is the hierarchy-of-effects models. Later, modifications of these models were presented, and the focus has shifted towards attitude formation models of response to marketing communications. Consumer involvement and cognitive, affective and behavioural aspects of message processing have been studied intensively. One thing we have learnt so far is that no single theory can explain it all. Some models are applicable in some situations for some kinds of people and for some categories of products. Because of this complexity, it is not surprising that marketing communications do not always work as they should. At the end of the chapter, two phenomena an advertiser would like to avoid – irritation and brand confusion – are discussed.

Hierarchy-of-effects models

Hierarchy-of-effects models[1] are some of the oldest marketing communications models. The first was published in 1898, and their influence on marketing thought remained important until the 1980s. In general, a hierarchy-of-effects model assumes that things have to happen in a certain order, implying that the earlier effects form necessary conditions in order for the later effects to occur.[2] According to these models, consumers go through three different stages in responding to marketing communications, namely a cognitive, an affective and a conative stage, or a think–feel–do sequence. During the cognitive stage consumers engage in mental (thinking) processes which lead to awareness and knowledge of the brand communicated. In the affective stage emotional or feeling responses occur which are associated with the advertised brand and attitudes towards the brand are formed. A difference with the previous stage is that consumers may become aware and gather information continuously and effortlessly, while affective reactions may only be formed when the need for an evaluation arises. The conative or behavioural stage refers to undertaking actions with respect to the advertised brand, such as buying it.

Consumers are assumed to go through the three stages in a well-defined sequence. The majority of the hierarchy models claim a cognitive–affective–conative sequence. In other words, consumers should first learn or become aware of a brand such as Fitnesse breakfast cereal, for instance. Afterwards they develop affective responses or form an attitude towards Fitnesse, which might be that Fitnesse is tasty and healthy. Finally, this feeling or attitude makes the consumers want to buy Fitnesse. The task of marketing communications is then to lead the consumers through these successive stages. Table 3.1 gives some examples of hierarchy models that follow this traditional sequence. The Lavidge and Steiner model is the one most frequently referred to in the literature.

However, a lot of disagreement exists regarding the sequence of the different stages, and several researchers have developed alternative models. An example is the **low-involvement hierarchy-of-effects model** according to which consumers, after frequent exposure to marketing messages, might buy the product, and decide afterwards how they feel about it (cognitive–conative–affective hierarchy). Another possibility is the **experiential hierarchy-of-effects model** in which consumers' affective responses towards a product lead them to buy it and, if necessary, they reflect on it later. This would suggest an affective–conative–cognitive sequence.

Table 3.1 Hierarchy-of-effects models

Year	Model	Cognitive	Affective	Conative
1900	AIDA, St Elmo Lewis	Attention	Interest, desire	Action
1911	AIDAS, Sheldon	Attention	Interest, desire	Action, satisfaction
1921	AIDCA, Kitson	Attention	Interest, desire, conviction	Action
1961	ACCA (or DAGMAR), Colley	Awareness, comprehension	Conviction	Action
1961	Lavidge and Steiner	Awareness, knowledge	Liking, preference, conviction	Purchase
1962	AIETA, Rogers	Awareness	Interest, evaluation	Trial, adaption
1971	ACALTA, Robertson	Awareness, comprehension	Attitude, legitimation	Trial, adoption

Source: Based on Barry, T.E. and Howard, D.J. (1990), 'A Review and Critique of the Hierarchy of Effects in Advertising', *International Journal of Advertising*, 9, 121–35.

Vaughn[3] proposed an integration of the different sequence models and presented a model, known as the **Foot-Cone-Belding (FCB) grid**. Four different situations are distinguished, based on two dimensions, i.e. the high–low involvement and the think–feel dimension. **Involvement** can be defined as the importance people attach to a product or a buying decision, the extent to which one has to think it over and the level of perceived risk associated with an inadequate brand choice. The **think-feel dimension** represents a continuum reflecting the extent to which a decision is made on a cognitive or an affective basis. Here Vaughn takes into account that for certain products, such as sugar, mineral water, paper towels, soap and banks, cognitive elements are important, while for products such as cakes, ice cream and perfume, affective elements seem to have more impact on the buying decision process. For example, consumers may wonder whether they are running out of water, or whether they will need paper towels during the next week. This is in contrast to considerations such as what to buy the children for a treat: Kinder Delight or chocolate mousse? Figure 3.1 shown the different sequences in each of the four situations.

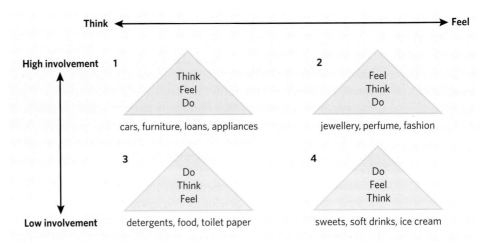

Figure 3.1 The FCB grid

Source: Based on Vaughn, R. (1980), 'How Advertising Works: A Planning Model', *Journal of Advertising Research*, 20(5), 27–33, www.warc.com/jar.

Purchase decisions in the first quadrant are characterised by high involvement and rational decision criteria. Here, the consumer first wants to learn about the product. This could be the case for deciding on an insurance policy or a loan or for buying a new computer or major household appliances. In this quadrant, the classical hierarchy of effects would hold. The second quadrant concerns product decisions of high involvement, but for which less information is needed. In this case, the consumer first wants to be emotionally attracted by the brand image, then he or she collects information, and finally undertakes some action. Jewellery, perfume, fashion and holidays may be examples that fit in this category. In the third quadrant, product decisions are located that require a minimum of cognitive effort and tend to become routinised because of habit formation. The assumed sequence is first buying the product, then learning what its major advantages and disadvantages are, and finally developing an attitude after product or brand usage. Toilet paper, sugar, paper tissues and detergents are expected to be bought without much reflection and only after product experience will an attitude be formed. The fourth quadrant reflects decision-making regarding products which can be termed 'life's little pleasures'. The assumed sequence here is: buy the product, experience an affective response and gather product knowledge afterwards. Examples that fit this category might be soft drinks, ice cream and chocolate bars. For example, consumers buy cake or pizza, eat it and realise that they are really fond of it, but learn afterwards that it makes them fat.

The **Rossiter–Percy grid** is an alternative to, or a modification of, the FCB grid which again classifies products and buying decisions in four categories, based on the dimensions of high–low involvement and fulfilling a transformational or informational buying motive.[4] **Transformational buying motives** consist of positive motivations, such as sensory gratification, social approval or intellectual stimulation, while **informational buying motives** refer to reducing or reversing negative motivations such as solving or avoiding a problem, or normal depletion. Examples of products for which transformational motives prevail are products that give consumers pleasure, such as ice cream, cosmetics and perfume. Examples of informational products are detergents, babies' nappies and insurance products.

The advantage of hierarchy-of-effects models and related frameworks is that they incorporate what is their most important contribution, i.e. recognition of the importance of brand awareness. Hierarchy-of-effects models consider brand awareness as a prerequisite for brand attitude formation. They correctly assume that affective responses cannot be formed or that a purchase cannot take place without having an awareness of the brand.[5] In this respect, it should be mentioned that most companies strive to reach **Top-of-mind awareness (TOMA)** in consumers. TOMA indicates which brand is most salient within a product category. It reflects the first brand that comes to mind when thinking of a particular product category. It is generally acknowledged that brands that are top of mind are more likely to be purchased.

BUSINESS INSIGHT
The reintroduction of God in Singapore

You could assume that God does not need to be introduced and that awareness of God is high. This is not what the Love Singapore Movement (a group of 150 churches) thought. It decided to reintroduce God to Singaporean teenagers and young professionals by advertising. The objective of the campaign was first to increase top-of-mind awareness of God, and secondly to change God's image of 'schoolteacher' into 'someone you wouldn't mind putting on the guest list of your dinner party'. Budgeting for 17 TV commercials and 24 ads in newspapers, Ogilvy & Mather came up with witty, playful, approachable God spreading messages like: 'I hate rules. That's why I only made ten of them', 'Bring your umbrella, I might water the plants today', and 'Of course I have a sense of humour. I gave you baboons with bright red asses, didn't I?' Before the ads were on air for a week, the Singapore authorities pulled them out. Therefore, Ogilvy & Mather started using non-traditional media. Buses were painted with the message 'Please don't drink and drive. You're not quite ready to meet me yet'. Subway waiting places were plastered with the message 'I'm here. God', and SMS was used to spread text messages such as: 'Thank me. It's Friday. God'; 'Even I rested on the 7th day. Enjoy. God'; and 'Are you coming over to my place later?' (on Sundays). The campaign received incredible attention both in the traditional media and on the Internet. The campaign was awarded two gold lions at the Cannes Advertising Festival and achieved a cult status in no time.[6]

Notwithstanding the important contribution of the classical hierarchy models, several shortcomings have been formulated. A major critique is that empirical support for the fact that consumers go through each stage is still lacking. Significant relations have been observed between ad characteristics and recall, and between ad characteristics and attitudes and purchase intentions, but not between recall and attitudes. This leads to the conclusion that, empirically, no hierarchy of cognitive, affective and conative effects can be observed.[7] Furthermore, hierarchy models do not allow interactions between the different stages, which is very unlikely. Purchase will lead to experience, which will have an important impact on beliefs and attitudes, for example. Therefore, to base marketing communications on hierarchy-of-effects models may not be the most effective or relevant strategy.

Attitude formation and change

Since the 1980s, attitudes have received more and more attention. An **attitude** is as a person's overall evaluation of an object, a product, a person, an organisation, an ad, etc. In this view, an attitude towards a particular brand (Ab) can be considered as a measure of how much a person likes or dislikes the brand, or of the extent to which he or she holds a favourable or unfavourable view of it. The reason for this interest in, for example, brand attitudes is the belief that the more favourable brand attitudes are, the more likely a purchase of the brand becomes. Although brand attitudes are relatively stable, they can be changed over time. So, the ultimate challenge for marketing communications is to change attitudes in favour of the company's brand.

Attitudes play an important role in hierarchy-of-effects models too, but in these models they are primarily defined as affective reactions in a hierarchical setting. In fact, an attitude can be assumed to consist of three components (Figure 3.2).[8] The cognitive component reflects knowledge, beliefs and evaluations of the object; the affective component represents

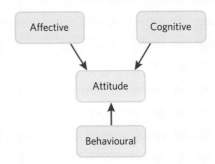

Figure 3.2 Attitude components

the feelings associated with the object; and the behavioural component refers to action readiness (behavioural intentions) with respect to the object.

An example may clarify the distinct components. You may love Timberland shoes (affective component) because you know they are durable and convenient to wear (cognitive component) and that is why you intend to buy Timberland the next time you go shopping (behavioural component). To change attitudes, marketers might concentrate on changing one of the three components. Gap might stress the fact that its clothes are neat, cool and stylish, thereby trying to influence the feelings associated with it by image-building. Communications campaigns trying to influence the consumer on an affective basis often use emotional ads containing no or very few product arguments. Miele might address the quality and durability of its appliances to change consumers' beliefs and evaluations. Marketing communications will probably use many and strong arguments to illustrate the numerous benefits of Miele. Coca-Cola might run a promotion campaign in which consumers can receive a fabulous Coke mobile phone or a Coke sofa in return for a certain amount of cola caps, to induce consumers to buy (a lot of) the brand.

As mentioned before, consumers follow different processes. Not surprisingly, a lot of communications models have been developed, most of them giving an adequate explanation for particular situations only. These different communications models regarding attitude formation and attitude change can be classified along two dimensions.[9] The first refers to the way attitudes are formed – primarily cognitive, affective or behavioural; the second is about the level of elaboration of a message, or central-route versus peripheral-route processing.

RESEARCH INSIGHT

How to get the message through? Promoting dental hygiene to kids

In a study of 190 children between 7 and 9 years old, the effect of dental hygiene messages was measured. The study investigated the impact of a low versus high threat appeal and the medium through which subsequent health information is conveyed (game, information brochure, narrative story), on the adaptive behaviour of 7–9 year old children concerning dental hygiene.[10]

Threat appeals are 'persuasive messages designed to scare people by describing the terrible things that can happen to them if they do not do what the message recommends.'[11] Empirical research shows that, in general, stronger threat appeals are more persuasive than weaker ones.

Computer games have become an important part of children's lives. Gaming is not just one of their favourite pastime activities, but games are also increasingly used by marketers in an attempt to influence children's purchase behaviour. Today, almost every food and beverage brand targeting children has an advergame on its website. **Advergames** are 'computer games specifically created to function as advertisements to promote brands', containing brand identifiers such as logos and characters.[12] Games can also be powerful learning tools. Several authors[13] argue that computer games can be more enjoyable, more interesting and thus more effective than traditional learning modes to increase children's knowledge. Previous research shows that playing advergames can affect children's food preferences and eating patterns. The question in the study was whether computer games can be used to promote dental hygiene. Therefore, the impact of interactive games as a medium to provide health information was compared with the impact of other media types, such as a traditional information brochure and a narrative story (for instance, told in a classroom).

The children were randomly exposed to one of six conditions (low and high threat appeal combined with three communication formats). After receiving some basic information about the study, the children were exposed to either a weak or a strong threat message. In the high threat condition, children were informed about the consequences of untended teeth, stressing the related dangers and risks. In this high threat condition, children saw a picture of affected teeth with caries. In the low threat condition, the consequences were described as less severe. In this condition, children saw a picture of healthy teeth. All children were told that they could avoid these negative consequences by brushing their teeth regularly and eating healthy food in the same way in all experimental conditions, thereby controlling for perceived efficacy. Following the threat message, the respondents were randomly assigned to one of three media, i.e. they played a computer game, read a brochure or listened to a narrative story in class. Afterwards, each participant was asked to fill in a standardised questionnaire and to choose a snack as a reward for participating. By making them choose between candy or a piece of fruit, (non-)adaptive behaviour was measured. For the interactive game condition, an existing computer game was used that was developed to teach children the importance of brushing teeth, going to the dentist and eating healthy food through interactive game play. The information brochure and narrative story were developed in such a way that both contained the same information as the computer game, only presented in a different way. In all three media, a beaver named Ben was introduced, who explained the importance of dental hygiene, eating healthy food and going to the dentist on a regular basis. In the computer games, the children were challenged, for example, to brush teeth using the mouse and distinguish healthy from unhealthy food, receiving bonus points when succeeding. The same information was incorporated in the story, but this time it was told in a more narrative, descriptive way ('once there was a beaver named Ben', etc.). For the brochure, the same format was followed as in a traditional classroom textbook.

The results of the experiment show that children pay significantly more attention to the game than to the narrative story and the brochure. The children who played the computer game and read the brochure showed no significant difference in snack choice after being exposed to either the low or the high threat condition. However, after being exposed to the narrative story, 19% of the children in the low threat condition chose a healthy snack, while in the high threat condition 67% preferred the healthy snack over the candy. The results show that, although children pay more attention to games and brochures than to a story, a strong perceived threat about the risks of bad dental hygiene has a more positive effect on children's adaptive behaviour (choosing fruit instead of sweets) than a weaker threat appeal, especially when they are exposed to a subsequent narrative health-related story.

Under high levels of efficacy, a high threat appeal leads to more adaptive behaviour than a low threat appeal. However, when children are provided with additional health-related information after the threat message, the effectiveness of this threat message appears to depend on the medium used to communicate this extra health information. The results only show a positive effect of a stronger threat appeal on adaptive behaviour when the children listened to a story. For children who played the game or read the brochure, the level of perceived threat had no effect on their snack choice. This can be explained by the attention-demanding task of playing a game and reading a brochure. Games are immersive and interactive, and children devote a lot of attention to them. Reading a brochure also requires the reader to focus attention on the reading material, certainly for children within the age category of 7-9 years. Indeed, the results show that active reading or game-playing leads to high focused attention. This interference with the preceding threat message weakens its effect. Listening to a story, however, is a rather passive activity which requires less attention, therefore allowing the threat appeal to 'stay in' better. This study implies that for children who are afraid of dental caries, the combination of a strong threat appeal and a supplementary narrative story is the best communication strategy among the ones tested. Games, pleasant and attention-getting as they may be, are not the most effective medium to reinforce a strong threat appeal.

Broadly stated, these dimensions are comparable with the ones used in the FCB grid, but no hierarchical conclusions are derived from them. The think–feel dimension of the FCB grid is transformed into a distinction between cognitive, affective and behavioural attitude formation. The involvement dimension of the FCB grid is extended to motivation, ability and opportunity (MAO). By **motivation**, a willingness to engage in behaviour, make decisions, pay attention, process information, etc., is meant. Motivation is to a large extent influenced by consumer needs and goals. Consumer needs can be categorised as functional, symbolic or hedonic.[14] Functional needs can be compared with the informational motivation dimension of the Rossiter–Percy grid and pertain to solving consumer problems. Consumers buy detergents to clean dirty clothes and hire a baby-sitter because they cannot leave their baby unattended. Symbolic needs relate to how we see ourselves and how we would like to be perceived by others. Youngsters may wear Calvin Klein jeans to show they are trendy. Hedonic needs reflect consumers' desires for sensory pleasure. Many tourists buy Belgian chocolates when visiting Belgium because of the delicious taste. Needs/goals can also be classified as approach or promotion goals, and avoidance or prevention goals.[15] The former pertain to positive outcomes while the latter relate to avoiding negative outcomes. For example, consumers can decide to shop at Carrefour because it offers them a nice shopping experience (= approach, promotion) or because they do not have to drive far (= avoidance, prevention). A consumer who plans to buy a new car is probably motivated to process marketing communications on cars. However, the needs or higher-order goals that this particular consumer is pursuing have an important impact on information processing and the benefits he or she is receptive to.[16] If the consumer is mainly driven by functional needs, he or she may want clear information on price, safety, fuel consumption, etc., while a status appeal or an ad showing driving sensations may be more effective when symbolic or hedonic needs prevail. The same goes for approach/promotion goals and avoidance/prevention goals: when the former are prevalent then marketing communications should bring a message focused on positive outcomes (you feel the excitement when driving this car), while for the latter goals a message should emphasise negative outcomes (the excellent air bags will protect you during a crash).[17] So, in order to be persuasive, marketing communications should tap into consumers' motivational concepts and marketers need to understand what goals consumers are trying to accomplish by buying the product.[18]

BUSINESS INSIGHT

Being a teenage mum is not that much fun

Teenagers getting pregnant is not a problem in developing countries alone; in many developed countries it also happens more than society would like. Many young girls see babies as cute and lovely (approach motivation), but do not realise the responsibilities and problems that having a baby at such a young age can bring. To convert the approach to a prevention motivation, encourage contraceptive use and raise awareness about teenage pregnancy, Duval Guillaume created for the Belgian public health department a TV spot that promotes a fictitious game. The game is inspired by the Simms, a game that is very popular among teenage girls. The ad starts out like a normal video game commercial: 'Get ready for teenage mum, your ultimate gaming experience . . .'. The player is invited to change diapers around the clock, try to study while the baby cries all night, and manage relationships with friends while looking after the child. The player sees the girl in the game having to choose between picking up the phone or letting her baby have a little accident. Choosing the baby results in 'friend lost'. The next challenge is to feed the baby, who spits food in his mum's face. At the end, the mum is on her knees, totally exhausted. The voiceover ends with 'your ultimate challenge: not having a nervous breakdown'. Next the text 'Being a teenage mum is not that much fun. Use contraceptives. http://www.laura.be' appears. The ad clearly shows the difficulties of balancing teenagers' needs and wants with the responsibility of a baby. The campaign provoked a lot of discussion, was mentioned on many weblogs and received an award for its creativity and effectiveness.[19]

Although someone is motivated to do something, he or she may be unable to do it. **Ability** refers to the resources needed to achieve a particular goal. One may be motivated to process a computer ad, but when it is full of technical details one may not be able to process and understand it because of a lack of technical knowledge. A person may be motivated to buy a particular house, but after learning what it is going to cost after renovation, stamp duty, land registration fees, etc., might be unable to buy it because of insufficient money.

Finally, **opportunity** deals with the extent to which the situation enables a person to obtain the goal set. A consumer may be motivated to buy Danette of Danone, but if the supermarket runs out of Danette, the consumer does not have the opportunity to buy it. A consumer may be motivated to process the information of a particular ad, but if the phone rings, he or she does not have the opportunity to pay attention to it. Also, when the ad contains little or no information, it does not provide the opportunity to elaborate on it.

The effects of the MAO factors on attitude formation and marketing communications processing are presented in the **Elaboration Likelihood model** (ELM) (Figure 3.3).[20] If motivation, ability and opportunity are all high, the elaboration likelihood is said to be high and consumers are expected to engage in **central-route processing**. This means that they are willing to elaborate on the information, to evaluate the arguments and find out what the information really has to offer. Depending on the quality and credibility of the arguments, consumers will react by producing counter-, support or neutral arguments, which induce a negative, positive or no attitude change, respectively. For example, when thinking of McDonald's consumers might think of how good McDonald's burgers and fries taste: a support argument. On the other hand, consumers might also think of how unhealthy fast food is: a counter-argument. Furthermore, consumers might just think of the red and yellow colours of a McDonald's restaurant: in effect, a neutral argument. Attitudes formed via the central route prove to be good predictors of later behaviour and are fairly resistant to other persuasive messages.

On the other hand, if one or more of the MAO factors is/are low, consumers are more likely to process the information peripherally. The result of the latter is no real information

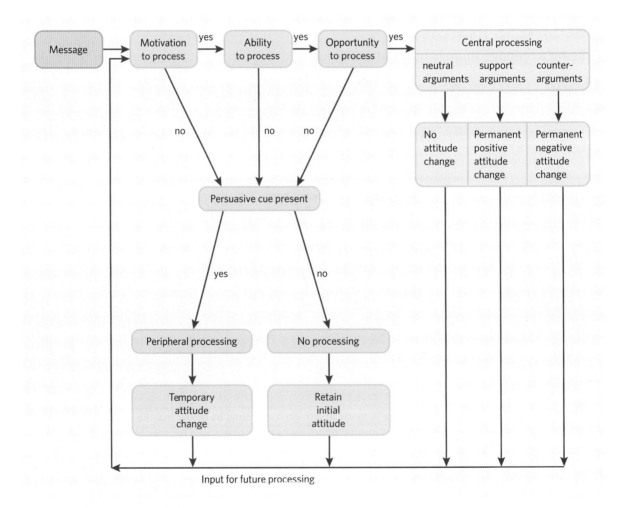

Figure 3.3 The Elaboration Likelihood model

Source: Based on Petty, R.E. and Cacioppo, J.T. (1986), 'The Elaboration Likelihood Model of Persuasion', *Advances in Experimental Social Psychology*, 19, 123–205.

processing, but an evaluation based on simple, peripheral cues, such as background music, humour, an attractive source or endorser, the number of arguments used, etc.[21] In other words, a favourable brand attitude might be formed because the consumer liked the music in a Levi's commercial or the erotic setting in a Häagen-Dazs ad or because the consumer is fond of the polar bears in the Coca-Cola commercial, or because he or she assumed that the high price of the Miele washing machine is a sign of superior quality, or that French wine is invariably good. However, such attitudes do not necessarily last long. If Pepsi launches a campaign with a cute animal, a celebrity or a nice song, consumers may forget about Coca-Cola's nice polar bears and switch their attitude in favour of Pepsi. The reason why consumers start paying more attention to peripheral cues is that in many ads peripheral cues form the only processable information under circumstances of low motivation, limited ability or limited opportunity. Ads without attractive peripheral cues, but with an easy-to-process, product-related message, might also work under low MAO, simply because the cognitive resources to form counter-arguments are lacking.

RESEARCH INSIGHT

Probability markers have a different effect depending on the type of service and the tolerance for ambiguity of individual consumers

Probability markers are specific words or phrases in advertising used to signal to what degree it is likely that a given claim or argument is true. Those markers that indicate the probable, rather than absolute, truth of a claim are known as *hedges*, whereas the markers that indicate complete commitment to the truthfulness of the claim are known as *pledges*. Hedges, which can be adverbs ('possibly', 'probably'), verbs ('can', 'may', 'help'), particles ('about', 'sort of'), or other expressions ('9 out of 10', '85% of', etc.), weaken the impact of a claim by allowing for exceptions or avoiding total commitment. Pledges, on the other hand, examples of which also include some adverbs ('definitely', 'undoubtedly'), verbs ('will', 'guarantee'), and other expressions ('have been proven to', 'you can be sure'), are absolute in nature and signal total confidence in the truthfulness of the claim.[22] Probability markers are frequently used in advertising.[23] Some well-known examples include the Carlsberg campaign ('Probably the best beer in the world'), a similar slogan used by a Belgian brand of beer, Delirium Tremens ('Voted as best beer in the world'), numerous drug advertisements (such as a Nutra-Life ad stating 'Nutra-Life Cold and Flu fighter may reduce the severity and duration of colds'), as well as cosmetics ads (such as an Oil of Olay ad stating 'Proven to help you look revitalised').

A study was conducted with 331 Belgian and 374 Croatian students;[24] 55.7% of the participants were female. The majority of them (45.9%) were between the ages of 22 and 26. The remainder fell into the following age groups: 33.1% between the ages of 18 and 21; 6.7% between the ages of 27 and 30; 12.4% under 18; and 1.9% over 30. The purpose of the study was to assess to what extent the type of service (hedonic vs utilitarian), the involvement with the service (high vs low), the type of probability marker (hedge, pledge and none), and tolerance for ambiguity affected consumer responses.

Language power, just like emotions, has been empirically proven to act as a peripheral cue.[25] It is, therefore, likely that involvement would act as a moderator to the effectiveness of the usage of probability markers in advertising, namely that the impact of probability markers on advertising effectiveness would be greater in low-involvement situations than in those where involvement is high. This assumption finds support in a previous study.[26]

Hedonic services, often also referred to as experiential services, are characterised by high levels of people orientation, employee contact and customisation. The quality of and satisfaction with a hedonic service rely on the sensations derived from the consumption of the service,[27] and are highly person-specific. As such, they are hard to assess objectively, being dependent on personal, subjective tastes and experiences. Using pledges, markers of absolute certainty, and thus implying universal applicability of the advertising claims, in ads of hedonic services might attract the consumers' attention to the inappropriateness of such claims and cause them to question the absolute and categorical conclusion of the truth of the claim. On the other hand, placing a claim with a hedge into a hedonic service ad might reduce the tendency of the consumers to counter-argue the claim and increase the perceived honesty/credibility of the advertiser.[28] Utilitarian services are, however, much more pragmatic and practical than hedonic ones. They are characterised by low levels of employee–customer contact, moderate customisation and higher product orientation than hedonic services. All this makes them much less individualised and person-specific, enabling easier objective assessment of service quality and customer satisfaction, which depend mainly on the functionality of their consumption,[29] based on an almost universal set of characteristics that ensure optimal functionality. Using pledges in ads of utilitarian services, therefore, signals the advertisers' full confidence in the truthfulness of the claim, thus enhancing its persuasive power. A hedge in advertising copy for a utilitarian service, on the other hand, might create the impression that the advertiser is not willing to stand totally behind the claim, weakening the claim itself, and undermining the advertiser's authority, credibility and status.[30] This would result in decreased efficiency of the ad.

The third dimension studied is uncertainty avoidance, defined by Hofstede as 'the extent to which people feel threatened by uncertainty and ambiguity and try to avoid these situations'.[31] Since probability markers are linguistic expressions of various degrees of certainty vs probability or ambiguity (i.e. uncertainty), the question arises whether the cultural dimension of uncertainty avoidance or tolerance for ambiguity could cause higher or lower acceptance of pledges and hedges in different cultures, and, therefore, influence the effectiveness of ads containing hedges or pledges on consumers from different country markets.

Two 2 (service type: hedonic/utilitarian) × 2 (involvement: high/low) × 3 (probability marker: hedge, pledge, no marker) between-subjects experiments were set up, one in Croatia, and one in Belgium (Flanders). The two experiments used the same stimuli, although the verbal part was translated into the local languages. A graduate school ad was used as a utilitarian high-involvement service, a copy/printing shop as a utilitarian low-involvement service, a bar as a hedonic high-involvement service, and a sandwich shop as a hedonic low-involvement service. Twelve different groups were each exposed to one of the ads, and responses were measured.

As expected, hedges and pledges do not have an effect in case of high-involvement services. This is not surprising, as probability markers are considered peripheral cues that are expected mainly to have an effect in low-involvement situations. However, probability markers do have an effect in case of low-involvement services, and this effect is moderated by the tolerance for ambiguity. More tolerance for ambiguity improves the attitude towards the brand and purchase intention for low-involvement services ads in which hedges are used. More tolerance for ambiguity leads to a lower attitude towards the brand and purchase intention for low-involvement services ads in which pledges are used. For hedonic low-involvement services, which are experiential, subjective and very person-specific in nature, advertising claims that include hedges have been found to be the most effective, resulting in the highest levels of brand attitude and purchase intentions. It seems that such claims may be inciting heightened perceptions of honesty/credibility of the advertiser in the eyes of the consumer, whereas a claim containing an absolutistic pledge would not only be easy to counter-argue and dismiss, but also have the opposite effect on the perceived credibility of the advertiser. On the contrary, ads for utilitarian low-involvement services seem to work better when they include a claim containing a pledge. Pledges in this case, where the service is much less customised and person-specific, and considerably easier to evaluate objectively (making it also easier to compare its universal functional characteristics with other similar services with certainty), signal the strength of the advertisers' convictions in the absolute truthfulness of the claims contained in the advertising copy.

The above-mentioned results have some interesting practical implications for advertising professionals and executives in both countries. As Croatian consumers, being in general rather tolerant of ambiguity, seem to react positively to ads containing probability markers, advertising campaigns in Croatia would benefit from inclusion of probability markers in advertising copy. This ought to be especially the case for ads for hedonic products or services, for which arguments with hedges have been proven to be the best choice. On the other hand, a comparatively low tolerance for ambiguity among Belgian consumers should cause advertisers in Belgium to be cautious in the use of probability markers in advertising campaigns designed for the Belgian market. An exception to this might be the use of pledges, which leave little room for uncertainty and ambiguity, and which, according to the results of this study, would be especially well suited to arguments used in ads of utilitarian products/services.

At first sight, the above might suggest that the central route pertains to cognitive attitude formation (people think carefully about the substance of the message), while **peripheral-route processing** is more likely to give rise to affective attitude formation (people rely on how the ad makes them feel instead of what the ad really tells). However, reality reveals a more complicated picture. The ELM, as well as other models such as Chaiken's Heuristic–Systematic model (HSM), and Forgas's Affect Infusion model (AIM), assume that, under different MAO conditions, both arguments and affect may give rise to peripheral and central (and even biased) processing.[32] It is not so much the MAO factors, but consumers' goals that might determine whether consumers rely on the substance of the message (i.e. the strength of the claims, the compellingness of the product attributes, etc.) to form a judgement or on their affective responses (i.e. ad-evoked feelings, aesthetic of the product design, charisma of the endorser, etc.). Recent research shows that when individuals focus on ideals (promotion goals, relating to one's hopes, wishes and aspirations, such as dreaming of a nice house, an exotic holiday, etc.), they consider affective information as more relevant than the substance of the message and, as a consequence, are more likely to base their evaluation on affect. On the other hand, when consumers' 'oughts' (prevention goals, relating to one's duties, obligations and responsibilities, such as providing for a child's education, looking professional at work) are their driving goal, the opposite result is found.[33]

RESEARCH INSIGHT
The impact of self-regulatory focus in health campaigns

In health campaigns, a fear–relief appeal is often used. This message starts by focusing on negative consequences of a risk behaviour and ends with offering a solution via behavioural recommendations. However, due to mixed results, there is a lot of discussion about its overall effectiveness. It is often suggested that a valuable contribution could result from adopting a segmentation approach in which an individual differences perspective is taken.

A recent study examined whether taking into account individuals' chronic self-regulatory focus could contribute to the effectiveness of health messages. Although previous research indicates that promotion people tend to rely more on affect than prevention people, it was argued that, by using ads with an emotional tone that is compatible with a prevention focus in the stimuli, affect could work for prevention people as well. Therefore, in line with the regulatory relevancy principle, the emotional tone of the test ads was matched to the chronic self-regulatory focus of the audience. More specifically, it was expected that fear–relief ads would work better for prevention people because these emotions are more compatible with their regulatory focus, whereas sadness-joy ads were expected to have more impact in promotion people because dejection and cheerfulness emotions match better with a promotion focus.

A first study focused on anti-smoking campaigns. The results of an experiment with 256 student smokers indeed indicated a congruency effect: smokers with a promotion focus felt more involved with the sadness-joy than with the fear–relief campaign leading to a more positive attitude towards the sadness-joy campaign than towards the fear–relief campaign, and vice versa for smokers with a prevention focus. A second study focused on sun protection campaigns, and 1386 women aged between 24 and 38 participated in the experiment. Also here, an emotion–congruency trend appeared, but only for high users of sun beds. The conclusion of both studies is that emotional health campaigns can work for promotion *and* prevention people on the condition that the ad-evoked emotions match consumers' regulatory focus and consumers feel highly and affectively involved in the subject matter.[34]

Table 3.2 Six types of attitude formation and change

		Elaboration likelihood based on motivation/involvement, ability and opportunity	
		High elaboration central-route processing	Low elaboration peripheral-route processing
Attitudes based on:	*Cognitions*	• Multi-attribute models • Self-generated persuasion	• Heuristic evaluation
	Affect	• Feelings-as-information model	• Ad transfer • Feelings transfer • Classical conditioning • Mere exposure effect
	Behaviour	• Post-experience model • Perception–Experience–Memory model	• Reinforcement model • Routinised response behaviour

How exactly the message substance or affective responses are processed is likely to depend on consumers' elaboration likelihood. Therefore, we distinguish six types of marketing communications models based on two dimensions (see Table 3.2). The first dimension pertains to elaboration likelihood which can be either high or low. The second dimension is related to the attitude component on which attitude formation is mainly built, i.e. cognition, affect or behaviour.

High elaboration likelihood, cognitive attitude formation

The models that will be discussed here are relevant if the consumer's motivation, ability and opportunity are high and especially when cognitive elements are important for attitude formation. An example is someone who is going to buy a home video installation and tries to compare objectively the different brands available on several attributes (price, sound quality, etc.) before making a decision.

Multiple attribute models

The most famous multiple attribute model is no doubt the Expectancy–Value model, or **Fishbein model**.[35] In this model, brand attitudes are made up of three elements: relevant product attributes, the extent to which one believes the brand possesses these attributes, and the evaluation of these attributes or how good/bad one thinks it is for a brand to possess these attributes. More specifically, brand attitude is represented by the weighted sum of the products of brand beliefs and attribute evaluations:

$$A_o = \sum_{i=1}^{n} b_{oi} e_i$$

where: A_o = attitude towards object o
  b_{oi} = belief of object o possessing attribute i
  e_i = evaluation of attribute i
  n = number of relevant attributes

In other words, since not all product attributes are equally important for a consumer, product beliefs are weighted by the importance that the consumer attaches to the different product attributes. Table 3.3 shows an example of an attitude towards going to university and going to a polytechnic. In this case, beliefs and evaluations are measured by means of a seven-point Likert scale. A Likert scale is an ordinal scale but, if the scale contains enough categories, it is usually considered an interval scale, as a result of which calculating mean scores across respondents is allowed.[36] An example of a seven-point (going from 1 to 7 or from −3 to +3) Likert scale, is:

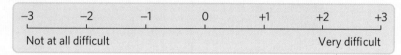

To what extent do you think it is difficult to succeed at university?

| −3 | −2 | −1 | 0 | +1 | +2 | +3 |

Not at all difficult   Very difficult

In this example, the quality of the teachers is most valued ($e = 7$) and the perception that it is difficult to get a degree seems to be the least important attribute ($e = 2$). Multiplying these evaluations by the beliefs regarding universities and polytechnics as possessing these characteristics gives the results in the fourth and sixth columns. Summing these products results in a more positive attitude towards going to a university. So, if all relevant attributes are measured and correctly evaluated, a university would eventually be chosen.

The **Theory of Reasoned Action (TORA)** is an extension of the Expectancy–Value model.[37] The model was developed to provide a link between attitude and behavioural intention. The latter is determined not only by attitudes, but also by the subjective norm. A **subjective norm** comprises the belief one holds regarding what different reference groups consider as socially desirable behaviour, weighted by the consumer's need or willingness to behave according to the norms of the particular reference group. The latter is referred to as social sensitivity. Certain personalities are more sensitive to social pressure and, as a consequence, are more willing to comply with the rules, norms and beliefs of reference groups than others. An example of socially influenced behaviour is that, even though a child might not be particularly fond of piano lessons, the child might take these lessons to please the parents. And although a teenager might not hold a favourable attitude towards smoking, he or she might do so

Table 3.3 An illustration of the Fishbein model

		Attitude towards going to a university/polytechnic			
		University		Polytechnic	
Attribute	e_i	b_i	$e_i \times b_i$	b_i	$e_i \times b_i$
Difficulty	2	+2	+4	+1	+2
Prestige	6	+2	+12	0	0
High cost	3	+1	+3	0	0
Quality of teachers	7	+1	+7	−1	−7
Number of friends	5	−1	−5	+2	+10
High study time	3	+2	+6	0	0
Business-oriented	5	−1	−5	+1	+5
Attitude			22		10

e_i is measured on a seven-point bipolar scale (1 = bad, 7 = good)
b_i is measured on a seven-point unipolar scale (−3 = unlikely, +3 = likely)

Table 3.4 An illustration of subjective norm effects

	Subjective norm = social sensitivity (ss) × others' opinions (oo)				
		University		Polytechnic	
Reference group	ss_i	oo_i	$ss_i \times oo_i$	oo_i	$ss_i \times oo_i$
Friends at school	6	+2	+12	−1	−6
Friends in youth club	5	0	0	+1	+5
Friends in sports club	5	−1	−5	+1	+5
Parents	4	+2	+8	−2	−8
Family	4	+1	+4	0	0
Current teachers	3	+2	+6	0	0
Business	5	+2	+10	+1	+5
Subjective norm			+35		+1

ss_i is measured on a seven-point bipolar scale (1 = low, 7 = high)
oo_i is measured on a seven-point bipolar scale (−3 = negative, +3 = positive)

because his or her friends regard it as 'cool' to smoke. Again, some teenagers will be more likely to let themselves be led by the opinions of others.

Table 3.4 illustrates how a subjective norm can influence the choice between going to university and going to a polytechnic. The reference group valued most highly is the friends at school ($ss = 6$), while the sensitivity or motivation to comply with the opinion of current teachers is the lowest ($ss = 3$). Multiplying social sensitivity by the opinions of significant others for the different reference groups, and summing all these products, results in a subjective norm of +35 for going to university and +1 for going to a polytechnic. In view of these results as well as the results of Table 3.3, the attitude towards a university is more favourable than the attitude towards a polytechnic.

RESEARCH INSIGHT
Integrating emotions into the Theory of Planned Behaviour and predicting electric car usage intention

In the context of the adoption (intention) of innovations and (new) behaviour, two conceptual frameworks have been extensively studied. In the Technology Acceptance Model (TAM), the attitude towards and the adoption or continuous use (intention) of an innovation are determined by three antecedents: perceived ease of use (PEOU), perceived usefulness (PU) and compatibility.[38] PEOU is the degree to which a person believes that using the system will be effortless. PU is the degree to which a person believes that using a particular technology will enhance his or her job performance. Compatibility is the degree to which the innovation fits with the potential adopter's existing values, previous experiences and current needs.[39] The Theory of Planned Behaviour (TPB) is a second conceptual framework that has often been used for analysing and predicting a variety of intentions and behaviours. The TPB predicts behavioural intention which, in turn, is assumed to be a predictor of actual behaviour.[40] Behavioural intention is explained by three general dimensions: the *attitude* towards the behaviour, the *social influence (subjective norm)* on the behaviour and the *perceived behavioural control* in conducting the behaviour. Attitudes are evaluative responses to the behaviour. The subjective norm stands for perceived social pressure by significant others or differ-ent reference groups to perform or not to perform a certain behaviour. A reference group is a group that serves as a comparison point and the opinion of which is perceived as important for the individual. Perceived behavioural control over performing the behaviour is a person's perception about whether different aspects of the behaviour are in his or her control or are easy or difficult. It is related to the perceived ability and the external source constraints and facilitators of the behaviour.[41]

Notwithstanding the overwhelming evidence of the role of affective reactions in consumer decision-making, conceptual models and empirical research on the adoption (intention) of innovations or (new) behaviour have largely ignored the role of emotions.[42] Perugini and Bagozzi argue that 'although there is little question that the TPB offers a parsimonious account of purposive behaviour, its sufficiency can be questioned'.[43] Bagozzi states that the TPB has seemingly seduced researchers into overlooking the fallacy of simplicity.[44] Therefore, various authors suggest extending the TPB with other factors. One of the most often suggested improvements is extending the TPB with measures of emotional responses to the product or the issue for which the intention to use is predicted. According to Wood and Moreau, the affective influence is often stronger and more far-reaching than previously considered and the addition of emotional responses benefits traditional models of diffusion.[45]

In a sample of 1202 Belgians the determining factors of the usage intention of an electric car and the differences between early and late usage intention segments are investigated.[46] The TPB framework is extended with emotional reactions towards the electric car and car-driving in general. Emotions and the attitude towards the electric car appear to be the strongest determinants of usage intention, followed by the subjective norm. Reflective emotions towards car-driving and perceived behavioural control factors also play a significant role. Differences in the relative importance of the determinants of usage intention between sub-groups based on environmental concern and behaviour and social values were also studied. In general, people in segments that are more inclined to use the electric car are less driven by emotions towards the electric car and more by reflective emotions towards car-driving, and take more perceived behavioural concerns into account.

The TORA has been further extended to the TPB.[47] Fishbein and Ajzen felt this extension was necessary to be able to deal with behaviours over which people have incomplete volitional control. Indeed, behavioural intention can result in actual behaviour only if the consumers themselves can decide to perform or not perform the behaviour. For many consumer behaviours this prerequisite does not pose a problem (e.g. choosing between Coke Vanilla or Coke Lemon), but often behaviour also depends on non-motivational factors, such as resources (time, money, skills, infrastructure, etc.). For example, a consumer may be willing to go to work by means of public transport, but when he or she lives in a remote village in which hardly any public transport facilities are available, this may be difficult to do. Or, a consumer and his or her significant others may hold very favourable attitudes towards buying a Lamborghini, but when this consumer lacks the money, a cheaper car will be bought in the end (so, in fact, the extension resembles the 'ability' and 'opportunity' factors of MAO). That behavioural control as perceived by the consumer is more predictive of behaviour than actual behavioural control is very important. **Perceived behavioural control (PBC)** can be defined as 'the perceived ease or difficulty of performing the behaviour and it is assumed to reflect past experience as well as anticipated impediments and obstacles'.[48] Two individuals enrolling for a foreign-language course may have equally strong intentions to learn the foreign language, but if one feels more confident than the other that he or she can master it, he or she is more likely to persevere than the one who feels less confident. Therefore, not actual control but perceived behavioural control is added to TORA to build the TPB. Perceived behavioural control is computed by multiplying control beliefs by perceived power of the particular control belief to pose the behaviour, and the resulting products are summed across the salient control beliefs. For example, for jogging, salient control beliefs appeared to be 'being in poor physical shape' and 'living in an area with good jogging weather'. Figure 3.4 presents the TPB model graphically.

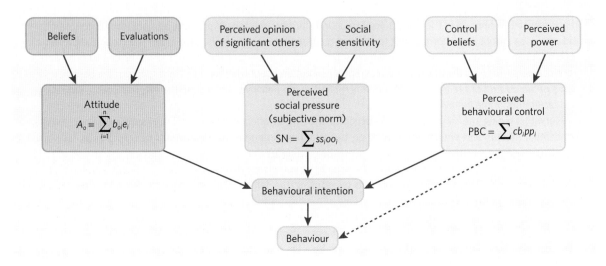

Figure 3.4 The Theory of Reasoned Action (TORA)

BUSINESS INSIGHT
Handicap International

Handicap International was founded in 1982 in France. Afterwards, a network was created with sections in Belgium, Germany, Luxembourg, Switzerland, the UK and the USA. Currently, Handicap International is active in about 60 countries with aid programmes for people with disabilities. To collect money for clearing up cluster bombs, a mine awareness programme and a physical rehabilitation centre in Afghanistan, Handicap International used direct mail (DM) as a communication tool. It sent citizens a paper bomb, not bloody pictures or crying people. A strong accompanying letter and a reference to the expertise of Handicap International were also included. Since Handicap International is well aware that many people believe their individual efforts do not matter, it clearly indicated what could be done with small sums of money and gave people the option to choose one of them. For example, €30 meant crutches for one of the victims; with €40 about 10 square metres could be cleared of mines; and for €55 a prosthesis could actually be given to a cluster bomb victim. This increased donors' perceived behavioural control. The DM action clearly paid off: the response rate amounted to more than 10%, and 37% more money than expected was collected. Handicap International received a Cuckoo Award for the effectiveness of the campaign.[49]

The TPB has received considerable attention in the literature. Ajzen constructed a website with more than 400 articles in which TPB was used.[50] These studies deal with a variety of activities, from predicting eating behaviour to condom use, from job-seeking behaviour to speeding, from helping to health behaviour, etc.[51] From a database of 185 of these independent studies, it has been shown that the TPB accounted for 27% and 39% of the variance in behaviour and intention, respectively. Moreover, the PBC construct and attitudes in particular seem to have predictive value, while the subjective norm in general accounts for only a small part of the variance in behaviour and intention.[52]

RESEARCH INSIGHT
The explanatory power of the TPB versus the Relationship Quality model in an apparel context

The effectiveness of the TPB model has been shown in a variety of contexts. However, comparisons with more specific models that are often used in certain research areas are very scarce. Using a combination of real-life purchase behaviour data and survey information of 634 customers, a recent study compared the TPB with the more specific Relationship Quality (RQ) model to predict apparel purchases. The RQ or the Satisfaction–Profit Chain model is one of the most often used models to explain purchase intention and/or behaviour in a non-contractual customer–firm relationship. It indicates that high levels of relationship quality result in correspondingly high levels of purchase intention and behaviour.

The results point out that despite the more specific character of the RQ model and the more general character of the TPB model, the TPB constructs (attitude towards the behaviour, subjective norm and perceived behavioural control) proved to predict behavioural intentions better than the RQ constructs (trust, commitment and satisfaction). Secondly, the RQ and TPB constructs are fully mediated by behavioural intentions. Thirdly, taking 'buy–not buy' as the dependent variable, intentions had a significant impact on apparel purchase behaviour, above and beyond the effects of past behaviour. This proves the importance of measuring the TPB constructs, even in situations when data on past behaviour are available.[53]

Based on the TPB model, marketing communicators can try to change consumers' attitudes and influence their behaviour in several different ways (Figure 3.5). Firstly, they can try to change brand beliefs. For example, suppose a university has a reputation for granting degrees too easily and not taking the education task seriously enough. If an independent quality control committee finds that this university is offering students a good-quality education, the university might use this conclusion in an advertising campaign in order to influence existing beliefs. A second possibility is changing attribute evaluations. For

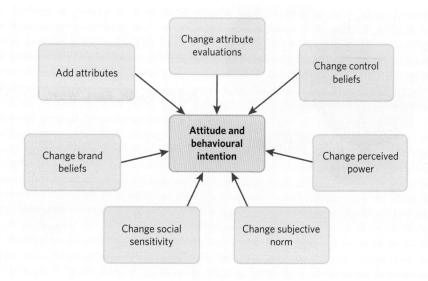

Figure 3.5 Marketing communications and the TORA model

example, when people have the impression that a large university has to be good since it is able to attract so many students, a small university can try to change this evaluation by emphasising the benefits of small classes (more personal contact, more time per student, greater supervision, etc.). Finally, attitudes can be changed by adding attributes. For example, if a university has an exchange contract with foreign universities so that foreign students can take part of the courses while its own students can follow courses abroad, the university can emphasise the multicultural environment. By doing so, it might create an additional attribute that students take into account when choosing between universities. When Levi's, for example, saw its market share decline, it emphasised its pioneering role in the jeans market and tried to add the fact that Levi's was the first jeans brand as a product attribute that consumers might consider when buying jeans. An example in the beer market is Labatt Ice which underscores the freshness of the beer, rather like Cola Light claims 'you have never been refreshed like this before'.

Besides trying to change attitudes, marketers can focus on changing the opinion of others. To counter the increase in smoking of young girls, for example, the UK government tried to change the opinions of youngsters by means of a communications campaign of which the main message was that smoking makes you less attractive to the opposite sex. One ad pictured two pairs of kissing lips with the message 'Ever kissed a non-smoker? Taste the difference.' A more recent campaign tries to counter alcohol abuse in teenage girls (to avoid getting pregnant while being drunk) with the message 'if you drink like a man, you might end up looking like one'. Raising or lowering social sensitivity for specific significant others is another possibility. For example, while buying a new car used to be a decision made by the parents, Opel stresses how comfortable, exciting and cool the Opel Safira is perceived by children, hoping that parents will take the opinion of their children into account when choosing a particular type and brand of car. Finally, perceived behavioural control can be influenced. Marketers could change control beliefs by showing how easy or convenient to use certain products are. For example, MasterCard uses the slogan 'North. South. East. West. No card is more accepted' to indicate you can pay everywhere with MasterCard (Photo 3.1). Another possibility is to focus on increasing perceived power or the confidence of consumers that they can master the activity. Nike stresses 'Just do it', meaning that everyone can be an athlete.

North. South. East. West. No card is more accepted.

MasterCard
www.mastercard.com

Photo 3.1 MasterCard: influencing perceived behavioural control
Source: Reproduced with permission of Gesamtverband Werbeagenturen GWA and McCann-Erickson Europe.

RESEARCH INSIGHT
Two-sided messages work better, but is refutation necessary?

Two-sided messages give both sides of an issue or a product. Empirical studies show that this type of message is generally more effective in terms of credibility than when only one side is provided.[54] Two sub-types of two-sided messages can be distinguished: refutational and non-refutational ones. In non-refutational messages, advertisers simply present positive and negative information. In refutational messages, the advertiser subsequently refutes or discounts the negative information that was added to the message. Empirical results regarding the credibility of refutation in two-sided messages are mixed. Some previous studies found no different effects on credibility for both a refutational and a non-refutational two-sided message. Other studies emphasise that a refutational statement makes receivers take the message and the source more seriously, implying that a two-sided refutational message is more credible.[55] These heterogeneous results show that two-sided messages' effects on credibility are complex.

In a study conducted with 853 teenagers (15–19 year olds, 63.4% females), two-sided refutational and non-refutational rational and emotional messages were tested by means of ads that warn against the dangers of binge drinking (a non-controversial issue) and marijuana use (a controversial issue). This study tested if issue ambivalence has an effect on the responses to refutational and non-refutational two-sided messages.[56] Pre-tests showed that binge drinking is not at all ambivalent, since most people condemn it. Marijuana use, on the other hand, is clearly an ambivalent issue for people. One could argue that, for an ambivalent issue, a two-sided message is 'normal' or 'expected', as this type of issue is known to have obvious pro and contra arguments. Hence, an advertiser who uses a two-sided message for an ambivalent issue is not regarded as giving both sides of the issue voluntarily, but just as acknowledging the inherent ambivalence of the issue. On the other hand, univalent issues are less obviously dual: they are characterised by either strong pro arguments (univalent positive issue) or strong contra arguments (univalent negative issue). When counter-information about a univalent issue is disclosed, this might be perceived as more 'voluntary', as the source is not expected to disclose information on both sides of the issue.[57] Therefore, two-sided messages about univalent issues might be considered as more voluntary, and thus more credible, than two-sided messages about ambivalent issues.

Besides the sidedness and refutational factors, also the tone of the argumentation was manipulated. Pham found that the relevance of the arguments (emotional vs rational) depends on the type of consumption motive underlying the behaviour or the issue. He distinguishes between consummatory motives (i.e. underlying behaviour that is pleasant as such), which are more affectively driven, and instrumental motives (i.e. underlying behaviour that is undertaken to achieve well-considered further goals), which are more cognitively driven. Consequently, when an issue is primarily associated with consummatory motives, affective considerations will be more relevant than cognitive considerations.[58] In other words, for consummatory behaviour, emotional arguments are more credible than rational arguments. Like most unrestrained behaviour, binge drinking and marijuana use are inherently consummatory, because the act of binge drinking or smoking marijuana holds little if any instrumental value.[59] Studies show that individuals mostly indulge in drugs for emotional, impulsive, social reasons instead of rational reasons.[60] So, for the issues of binge drinking and marijuana use, emotional arguments would appear to be more relevant, and thus more credible than rational arguments.

A 2 × 2 × 2 between-subjects factorial experimental design was set up, manipulating refutation within a two-sided message (two-sided non-refutational vs two-sided refutational), message tone (rational vs emotional), and ambivalence of the issue (ambivalent vs univalent issue), leading to eight different messages. Each of the messages contained a main argument against the issue (the directional argument, which is against binge drinking or against marijuana use) and a secondary argument in favour of the issue (the counter-argument). In the refutational two-sided messages, this secondary positive argument was refuted. Argument tone (rational vs emotional) was manipulated through the types of arguments used: general, rational, factual arguments versus personal, emotional, subjective arguments. Ambivalence of the issue was manipulated through the use of two distinct issues.

The results of the experiment show the following. When the issue is univalent and the arguments are emotional, a refutational and a non-refutational two-sided message lead to no difference in source credibility and message credibility. When rational arguments are used, a refutational two-sided message leads to a significantly higher source credibility and message credibility than a non-refutational two-sided message. When the issue is ambivalent, and the arguments are emotional, a refutational two-sided message leads to a higher source credibility and message credibility than a non-refutational two-sided message. When rational arguments are used, a refutational and a two-sided message lead to no difference in source credibility and message credibility.

The results of the study show that the need for refutation depends on the ambivalence of the issue and the consistency of the argument tone in the message with the motivation to conduct the behaviour at hand. When the health risk issue is univalent, a two-sided message is regarded as more voluntary (because the source is not 'supposed' to give both sides of the issue), leading to more credibility. When such a univalent issue is combined with highly relevant, emotional arguments, the overall credibility is high, regardless of whether the message is refutational or not. Hence, in this case, refutation is not needed, as the credibility is already high. When, however, such a univalent issue is communicated with less relevant, rational arguments, refutation is needed in order to enhance the overall credibility. Conversely, for an ambivalent issue, characterised by a lower perceived voluntariness, credibility might be lower: an ambivalent issue is obviously dual, making a two-sided message more the 'expected' way of acknowledging this duality, rather than a sign of honesty or voluntariness. When, for an ambivalent issue, the more relevant, emotional arguments are used, refutation is a helpful tool to increase the credibility. When, however, less relevant rational arguments are used, refutation vs non-refutation does not have a different impact on source and message credibility.

Self-generated persuasion[61]

Another form of central-route, cognitively based processing is **self-generated persuasion**. In this case, the consumer is not persuaded by strong brand arguments, but by his or her own thoughts, arguments or imagined consequences. These thoughts go beyond the information offered in the ad. The consumer combines the information in the message with previous experience and knowledge, and tries to imagine him- or herself consuming the product and the consequences thereof. Sometimes consumers even come up with new product uses. For example, when seeing an ad for canned lobster soup, a consumer might think of using the soup not as a soup, but as an ingredient for a sauce to use in a fish pasta. In other words, the persuasive process is imagery-based. These self-generated thoughts and the cognitive and affective responses evoked by the imagined brand experience give rise to fairly strong brand beliefs. These beliefs are believed to have a considerable impact on brand attitude.

Low elaboration likelihood, cognitive attitude formation

In this case, one of the MAO factors is low, leading or forcing the consumer to concentrate on peripheral cues. The consumer will try to make inferences on the basis of the cue in order to form a cognitively based attitude. For example, when consumers do not have the time to compare all available brands on relevant attributes, they may infer from a high price that the brand is a high-quality brand and therefore form a positive attitude towards it. This process is called **heuristic evaluation**.[62] When MAO is low, central information processing is very unlikely to occur and consumers will probably process the communication peripherally. This means that they do not elaborate on the message, but try to make inferences on the basis of ad characteristics. In other words, peripheral cues in the ad are used as a heuristic cue to evaluate the quality of the message and to form a general evaluation of the brand advertised. These inferential beliefs have a significant influence on the attitude people form towards the brand. Heuristic evaluation has also been referred to as the satisficing choice process.[63] Since consumers' MAO factors are not optimal, they lack the motivation, ability or opportunity to

Table 3.5 Potential heuristic cues

Characteristics	Peripheral cue	Heuristic
Source	Attractiveness Expertise Status Number of sources	The more attractive, the better The more expertise, the better The higher the status, the better The more, the better
Message	Number of arguments Repetition Layout	The more, the better The more, the better The more attractive, the better
Product	Price Design Country of origin	The higher, the better The more attractive, the better German is good (cars) The Netherlands is good (cheese) Italian is good (fashion, leather)

Source: Based on Pieters, R. and van Raaij, F. (1992), *Reclamewerking* (*How Advertising Works*). Leiden/Antwerp: StenfertKroeseUitgevers.

gather and process information to find the best choice. They are not looking for direct evidence of performance superiority in this case, but settle for a satisfactory or acceptable brand choice. Therefore, they seek for reassurance or credibility in heuristic cues such as brand name reputation, experts endorsing the brand, price level, etc. Table 3.5 summarises a few ad characteristics that can be used as a heuristic cue (Photo 3.2).

Another example is the use of celebrities. The heuristic in this case might be 'if George Clooney loves Nespresso, it has to be good' or 'if Anna Kournikova wears a Shock sportsbra because "only the ball should bounce", it has to be a comfortable and good bra'.

RESEARCH INSIGHT
Automatic and unintentional country-of-origin effects

It is generally accepted that consumers think products are better when they are made in countries holding a positive image. These effects have been found in a huge variety of countries. One explanation for these effects is that consumers use country stereotypes as a heuristic to simplify the decision process. An additional and more recent explanation is that a reference to the country in which the product is made spontaneously activates country stereotypes, and that these stereotypes influence the evaluation of the product even when consumers do not intend to use this information in their judgement. In a recent experimental study, consumers had to classify eight fictitious brands of notebooks as either good or bad. In a first stage, consumers were exposed to brand characteristics (processor speed, hard drive capacity and RAM size). On the basis of these characteristics they were taught how they could easily make a distinction between a good and a bad brand. After an unrelated task, consumers were in a second stage re-exposed to the eight brands, but now information was added concerning where the brand was manufactured (either a positive- or a negative-image country). Next, consumers had to classify the brands again. Half of the respondents were distracted during this task, while the other half could pay full attention to the classification task. The results showed that the negative or positive effect associated with the country of origin involuntarily influenced brand judgements. This effect was larger in the distracted group who could not pay full attention to the brand categorisation. This suggests that in cases where respondents' MAO factors are high (high motivation or involvement, high ability and opportunity) and consumers follow central-route processing, automatically activated country stereotypes are more likely to be inhibited, while their impact is largest when one of the MAO factors is low.[64]

Photo 3.2 The Mini, built in Oxford and sold in 75 countries
Source: Getty Images: Max Nash/AFP.

High elaboration likelihood, affective attitude formation

In this category, central processing of affective elements is predominant.

Affect-as-Information

Affect has long been considered as a peripheral cue, having an impact only when people have low involvement. However, it is increasingly recognised that affect may play a fundamental role in decision-making. People may judge objects by monitoring their subjective feelings to the target. The **Affect-as-Information model** posits that consumers may use feelings as a source of information to form an overall evaluation of a product or brand, not by means of a simple association, but through a controlled inferential process or, in other words, in an informed, deliberate manner.[65] A feeling-based inference often referred to is the 'how-do-I-feel-about-it' model. According to this model, consumers evaluate brands/objects by imagining the brand in their minds and asking themselves 'How do I feel about this brand/object?' Next they infer like/dislike or satisfaction/dissatisfaction from the valence of their feelings.[66] Consumers may even infer the strength of their preference from the strength of the feelings that the brand or object evokes.[67] Note that we are talking about real feelings (i.e. 'subjective experiences of affective states and responses with a somato-visceral component'), not about affective or hedonic beliefs (such as 'It would be great to spend a weekend in Stockholm').[68] These feelings can be evoked either integrally by looking at the product or imagining the product, or by a pre-existing or contextually induced mood.[69] However, a prerequisite of the Affect-as-Information model is that when people inspect their feelings to judge a brand or object, they do not inspect their mood states at that moment, but their feelings in response to the brand or object. So, if consumers decide not to go to the movies, it is because the thought of going to the movies makes them feel unpleasant, not because they happen to be in a bad mood. As a consequence, for feelings to influence the product evaluation, they must be perceived as representative of the product, i.e. consumers must be convinced that these feelings are genuine affective responses to this product. Moreover, feelings not only need to be representative, but also have to be relevant for the evaluation at hand and match consumers' goals.[70] For example, when a consumer has made an appointment to go to the dentist, the fact that he or she does not feel happy about going may not be considered to be relevant by this person, and he or she might still go. In fact, when consumers' purchase motivations are hedonic rather than functional, the likelihood that they will perceive their feelings as relevant and follow the 'how-do-I-feel-about-it' model is much more likely.[71]

It should be obvious that feelings should not be assigned a heuristic or peripheral role here. Under high elaboration likelihood, people use their feelings because they believe they contain valuable information. When consumers closely scrutinise the arguments in a message, mood and ad-evoked emotions can be considered as an argument or a central cue.[72] One way to elicit strong ad-evoked feelings is to make consumers think of pleasant things in the past, such as the birth of a baby, a wedding, a first romance, etc. Another way is to use nostalgic ads. Nostalgic ads make use of music, movie stars, fashion products, symbols or styles that were popular during a consumer's youth. Research has indicated that early experience performs a determining role in shaping subsequent preferences and actually can influence consumers' lifelong preferences.[73] For example, it has been shown that consumers retain a lifelong attachment to the styles of popular music they experienced in their late teens and early twenties.

Low elaboration likelihood, affective attitude formation

While central-route processing and cognitively based attitude formation predominated in the 1960s and 1970s, models characterised by peripheral processing of mainly affective elements received a lot of attention in the 1990s. The attitude towards the ad (Aad) and feelings transfer, classical conditioning and the mere exposure effect are some models that have been frequently referred to in the literature.

Aad transfer

From the 1980s onwards, research on low-involvement, affective processing has boomed. Among the first to indicate that how one evaluates an ad may be transferred to how one evaluates the brand were Mitchell and Olson.[74] They used an ad picturing a kitten and a

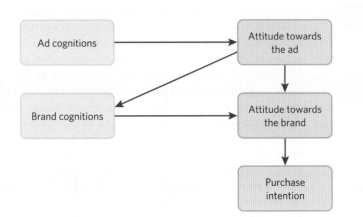

Figure 3.6 Dual mediation hypothesis

Source: Based on and reprinted with permission from 'The role of attitude toward the ad as a mediator of advertising effectiveness: a test of competing explanations', *Journal of Marketing Research*, published by the American Marketing Association, MacKenzie, S.B., Lutz, R.J. and Belch, G.E., 1986, vol. 23, p. 131.

purely informative ad. Their conclusion was that both brand attitude (Ab) and purchase intention were influenced not only by brand beliefs, but also to a great extent by the attitude towards the ad (Aad). Another study found that the difference in brand preference before and after exposure to advertising was twice as positive for consumers who liked the ad a lot as compared with consumers who had a neutral Aad.[75] When consumers feel indifferent towards the available brands as a consequence of low brand differentiation or insignificant consequences of a non-optimal choice, their choice goal is likely to be to buy the first brand that they like.[76]

Ad likeability might be an important factor because of its ability to attract attention and facilitate information processing. Peripheral cues such as humour, music, animals and children may attract attention, induce curiosity which leads consumers to watch the whole ad, and induce a favourable Aad[77] which can lead to a favourable Ab.

The Aad transfer model receiving most empirical support is the **dual mediation model** (Figure 3.6).[78] According to this model, the evaluation of the ad has not only an immediate impact on the evaluation of the brand, but also an indirect effect on brand attitude via brand cognitions. The reasoning behind this model is that consumers who hold a positive attitude towards the communication are more likely to be receptive to arguments in favour of the brand advertised. For example, if you like the Frisk commercial in which a cook accidentally drops a Frisk (a mint) in an aquarium, a fish eats it and gets so much energy out of it that the fish jumps into the next aquarium, then the next, and at the end out of the window, you might be less inclined to think of counter-arguments, or you might find yourself thinking of more support arguments (e.g. Frisk gives energy, Frisk is refreshing) because you think the commercial is clever, original and humorous.

Feelings transfer

In line with the foregoing, some researchers suggest that the feelings an ad evokes may be transferred to the attitude towards the ad, the brand attitude and the purchase intention without much deliberation.[79]

Why consider ad-evoked feelings? Several studies show that people in a positive mood make decisions more quickly, use less information, avoid systematic processing, evaluate everything more positively, accept a persuasive message more easily and pay less attention to details.[80] According to some researchers, ad-evoked feelings might even have a greater impact on communications effectiveness than mood.[81] Mood affects brand evaluation only if this evaluation takes place when watching the ad. Since ad-evoked feelings and the brand are associated in a consumer's memory, emotional advertising might influence brand evaluation no matter when the brand evaluation takes place. In this way, thinking of the brand in another situation might activate the feelings associated with it.

Empirical studies investigating the influence of ad-evoked feelings usually find that feelings exert a significant influence on the different stages in the communications process. A study investigating 23 000 responses to 240 ads shows that ad-evoked feelings (pleasure, arousal, dominance) explain 3% to 30% of the variance in brand interest and purchase intention while brand knowledge and beliefs explained 2% to 13%.[82] The magnitude of the influence of ad-evoked feelings depends on the product category advertised, the specific feelings that are evoked and the type of ad that is tested. Also, whether ad-evoked emotions are measured by means of self-report or autonomic measures makes a difference.[83] Neverthe-less, we can conclude that affective responses might be predictive of brand choice and, as a consequence, are a valuable tool for message testing and brand tracking.[84]

Emotional conditioning

Emotional conditioning can be considered an extreme case of feelings transfer, and is based on Pavlov's classic conditioning theory.[85] When dogs see food they begin to salivate. This is called an unconditioned response since it happens automatically. By frequently pairing a conditioned stimulus (a bell) with an unconditioned stimulus (meat powder), Pavlov was able to get dogs salivating just by hearing the bell (conditioned response). In a marketing context, communications practitioners sometimes try to pair a brand with an emotional response. Figure 3.7 explains the strategy DaimlerChrysler followed. Being aware of the fact that Celine Dion was a very popular singer, DaimlerChrysler paid Celine Dion between $10 million and $20 million to use songs such as 'I Drove All Night' in a three-year 'Drive and Love' campaign. Chrysler hoped that by frequently pairing Celine Dion's songs with the brand, the love feeling that her songs evoked would be transferred to Chrysler and would make the brand classy again.[86] On the premise of a high exposure frequency and strong emotional content, attitudes towards saturated brands are said to be predominantly formed on the basis of emotional conditioning.[87] The findings of a recent study indicate that emotional conditioning can indeed alter brand choice, but only when initially no strong preferences for competitive brands were formed and when brand choice is made under cognitive load (i.e. when consumers lack the cognitive resources to carefully think over their choice).[88] Examples of brands that try to benefit from emotional conditioning are Martini, Bacardi Breezer and Häagen-Dazs, which try to associate sexual arousal with their brands.

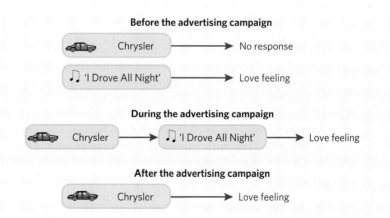

Figure 3.7 Emotional conditioning at work

BUSINESS INSIGHT
Emotional conditioning worked out well for Häagen-Dazs

Häagen-Dazs has used erotic advertising for several years. One of its campaigns features a couple indulging in sexual foreplay. The ice cream is their main attribute, which is put on each other's body and licked off by the other. By frequently combining the ice cream with foreplay, the ice cream itself has sexual connotations for some people. This is illustrated by the statements of some university students who completely identify Häagen-Dazs with sex. In an interview one of those students said:[89]

> It was very nice ice cream, we really enjoyed the ice cream and the advertising had a lot of sexual connotations in it and I think we basically liked the connotations of the ads and we liked the idea of that and we believed the idea that Häagen-Dazs was sexy because the ads told us it was sexy, so when we had the ice cream in front of us we felt that the pot was very sexy, a sexy pot.

Furthermore, when the students had a date, they always made sure to buy Häagen-Dazs in advance. Successful strategies are quickly copied. Besides Häagen-Dazs, Magnum also opted for eroticising its ice cream.[90]

Mere exposure

Hundreds of studies have demonstrated that prior exposure to stimuli (nonsense syllables, words, slogans, pictures, faces, sounds, smells, etc.) increases positive affect towards these stimuli.[91] In the same vein, ad and brand exposures can increase liking of the ad and the brand, and can make it more likely that the advertised brand enters consumers' consideration set.[92] In other words, the mere exposure of consumers to a particular ad, without the consumer actively elaborating on the ad, can influence consumer preferences and behaviour. Indeed, studies show that respondents who were exposed to an ad more than once, as compared with respondents who saw the ad for the first time, appeared to evaluate the ad as more favourable and less dull.[93] For a while, it has been assumed that prior exposure to stimuli acquaints consumers with the stimuli and that this familiarity causes the more positive attitude towards the stimuli. However, several studies indicate that the **mere exposure effect** on brand attitude does not occur through a subjective feeling of familiarity. When a respondent has been exposed to a particular stimulus before, this exposure can result in a more positive stimulus evaluation even if the respondent cannot remember having seen the stimulus before.[94] A more recent explanation of the mere exposure effect is that prior exposure increases processing fluency at the time consumers have to make a judgement.[95] The fact that consumers have been frequently exposed to a certain ad or brand results in a representation of this stimulus in consumers' memory. When consumers later on want to evaluate the stimulus, e.g. during a shopping trip, the representation of the stimulus in their memory will facilitate the encoding and processing of the stimulus. As a consequence, processing of the stimulus will be easier and more fluent. Since consumers often do not realise that prior exposure increases processing fluency, they misattribute the source of the processing fluency (i.e. the previous exposure) to liking, truth or acceptability of the ad or brand, especially when they have been incidentally exposed to the ad or brand and are not aware of this exposure.[96] Of course, the mere exposure effect is limited and should be seen as a function of learning and satiation.[97] The more novel a stimulus, the more consumers can learn and the more positive the affective response will be.[98] When consumers are confronted too often with a particular message or ad, there is no longer any learning opportunity and they get bored. This can have a boomerang effect on ad and brand attitude. The latter effect is called **wear-out** and indicates that there is a certain threshold of exposure after which additional exposure results in negative instead of positive communications effects (see Chapter 8).

RESEARCH INSIGHT
The impact of brand attitudes versus brand accessibility on brand choice

Marketing actions are often designed to change people's attitudes towards certain brands or products. Marketers do this on the assumption that inducing a positive attitude towards a brand will result in attitude-consistent buying behaviour. Hence, by changing attitudes, they actually want to sway choices in the direction of their products. This is a reasonable approach since attitudes are often easier to change than actual behaviour. However, a lot of social, psychological and consumer research has already shown that the link between attitudes and behaviour is not that straightforward, and that behaviour is often not in line with reported attitudes.

A study investigated to what extent consumers' choice depends on their attitudes or on the accessibility of a certain brand in the decision environment. The research was set up around two data collections, separated from each other by one week. In the first phase, 346 respondents' attitudes towards different charities were measured. In the second phase the researchers manipulated the accessibility of the charities by getting respondents to answer questions about either their most preferred choice or their fourth most preferred choice (254 students fully completed both questionnaires).

Subsequently, participants were asked to decide on a charitable organisation to receive a donation of €250. Next, they were asked about the perceived importance of the decision they had to make. Participants were split into two groups to create a high- and a low-involvement group, based on the median of the perceived importance of the decision.

The results show that simply making a choice option relatively more accessible or salient in the decision context compared with its competitors increases the likelihood that the alternative becomes part of the consideration set for both low- and high-involvement respondents. For low-involvement individuals, also the choice for the alternative that was made more accessible increased. High-involvement respondents were more likely to choose their most preferred charity, irrespective of whether another charity was made more accessible.

This study once again underscores the importance of creating positive attitudes in high-involvement respondents or for high-involvement products. On the other hand, for low-involvement individuals and low-involvement situations, high brand accessibility by means of repeated ad exposure or being salient in the purchase environment (e.g. by means of floorboards, shelf presence, etc.) may be sufficient.[99]

High elaboration likelihood, behavioural attitude formation

The theories discussed above have often been tested for hypothetical products and/or hypothetical brands, which makes them more relevant for new than for established brands. Although using hypothetical stimuli is ideal for eliminating research biasing effects such as brand knowledge, the extent to which the brand has been advertised in the past and the influence of previous campaigns, it disregards a source of information that might have important consequences for the way a consumer processes and evaluates a new marketing message, more specifically personal brand experience through previous brand usage. Post-experience models assume central-route processing of prior brand experiences. So, in this case the consumers are motivated, willing and able to think of previous brand experience and will take this into account in forming an attitude towards the brand, as well as in deciding what brand to buy in the future.

Although incorporating the influence of brand experience is a much more realistic approach to consumer information processing, brand experience has been neglected by most researchers. As a consequence, only a few communications models exist that try to explain its effect on the communications process. However, it is straightforward that brand satisfaction or dissatisfaction will have an impact on the next purchase. For example, if you have been driving a Ford for six years and you are really satisfied with its design, petrol consumption and after-sales dealer service, the probability that you will buy a Ford next time is much higher than if you find out that your Ford consumes much more petrol than your friend's Mazda, spare parts are more expensive than Opel's and your Ford broke down five times in six months. Another example is that when you buy Lay's crisps you expect them to be fresh, otherwise you are very likely to switch brands.

An example of a model that incorporates brand experience is the **post-experience model**.[100] This model assumes relations between the current purchase, on the one hand, and previous purchase, previous advertising, previous promotion, current advertising and current promotion, on the other. The post-experience model was tested using scanner panel data for an 84-week period on ketchup and detergent brands. The data included household purchase records, store environment information on price and promotion, and advertising exposure records. The results revealed that the current purchase is significantly influenced by previous purchase behaviour, current advertising and current promotion, but not by previous advertising, and negatively by previous promotion. The fact that a brand was previously bought in a promotion diminished the probability that the consumer would purchase the brand again in the next period. The latter can be explained by the fact that people who take advantage of promotions are more likely to be brand-switchers who are less inclined to buy the same brand in subsequent purchases. Current advertising also enhanced brand-switching. The results of this study seem to suggest that previous purchase behaviour is indeed the most important explanatory factor of current behaviour and that advertising mainly serves to remind people who have not recently purchased the brand of the fact that it exists.

However, what is the role marketing communications can play for first buys, on the one hand, and for other than first-time purchases, on the other? The **Perception-Experience-Memory model** (see Figure 3.8) tries to formulate an answer to this.[101] When consumers do not yet have brand experience, the main function of advertising consists of framing perception. Framing can affect consumers' expectation, anticipation and interpretation. Expectation is concerned with notifying consumers that a particular brand in a certain product category is available and putting the brand in a frame of reference so that consumers expect to see it. Next, marketing communications should try to create anticipation or generate hypotheses. Research indicates that exposing consumers to an attribute-based ad before brand trial makes consumers more curious about the brand ('Would Red Bull really energise my body and mind, and give me wings?'), it helps consumers to formulate hypotheses about the brand

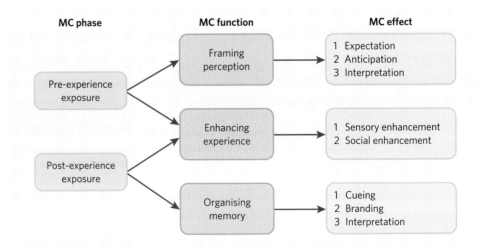

Figure 3.8 The Perception–Experience–Memory model

Source: Based on Hall, B.F. (2002), 'A New Model for Measuring Advertising Effectiveness', *Journal of Advertising Research*, 42 (March/April), 23–31.

('Red Bull will give me a kick'), and it induces the consumers to test their hypotheses during a subsequent trial experience.[102] Besides expectation and anticipation, pre-experience communications may offer an interpretation or a rationale for the anticipation the brand generates. For example, an unfamiliar computer brand could use the Intel Inside logo to assure consumers that it is a trustworthy and high-quality brand.

A next critical function of both pre-experience and post-experience communications is enhancing sensory and social experience. Products may taste better, function better or look nicer and the service may be perceived as friendlier or more knowledgeable just because consumers expect to experience this and anticipate the experience.[103] Moreover, consumers may focus their brand trial evaluation on attributes that they would not have used without the pre- or post-experience ad (instead of evaluating Red Bull on taste, carbonation, sugar level, etc., it may be evaluated on the uplifting experience it gives because of the advertising campaign), or marketing communications may change the weight that the advertised attributes receive at evaluation (valuing the uplifting experience as more important than taste, refreshment, etc.). On the basis of experiments in which respondents were exposed to an ad alone, to an ad and a product trial, or to a product trial alone, it appeared that a pre-experience ad combined with brand trial resulted in significantly more favourable brand responses than either a brand trial alone or an ad alone. More specifically, when an ad and brand trial were combined, the pre-trial ad led consumers to process the brand trial information in a more focused and meaningful way, resulting in more confidently held brand beliefs, a higher expectancy value from the brand (as measured by the Fishbein model) and higher purchase intentions. Moreover, ads appeared to be better in fostering confidently held beliefs about non-experiential attributes (such as the number of calories), while trial was more powerful in creating confidently held experiential attribute beliefs (such as taste).[104] Also, post-experience ads have been shown to enhance the experience of a previous brand trial. This happens when a consumer evaluates his or her brand experience as more favourable when he or she has been exposed to advertising after brand usage as compared with the situation when no advertising followed the brand experience. For example, if you have had Fitnesse cereal for breakfast and afterwards you see an ad for Fitnesse which shows all the ingredients and stresses the fact that no sugar is added, it might improve your evaluation of Fitnesse as a healthy breakfast choice.

A second role of post-experience communications is to organise memory. It offers verbal and visual cues such as jingles, slogans, user imagery, etc., enriching the brand schema and making it more likely that afterwards the brand will be recalled. Increasing brand recall and top-of-mind awareness can increase the possibility that consumers stop buying the competitor's brand and change to the company's brand; in other words, it can stimulate brand-switching.[105] Pepsi, for example, tried to change taste beliefs by stressing 'nothing else is a Pepsi'. On the other hand, post-experience communications may also prevent consumers switching to the competitor's brand.[106] Finally, post-experience communications also help consumers to interpret their experiences: 'The advertisement not only influences the consumer to feel that the sensory or social experience was a good one, but it also provides reasons to believe that it was.'[107] It is important to remember that marketing communications really are able to improve and reshape objective sensory experience. In an era in which consumers have the feeling that in the majority of product categories brands are converging instead of becoming more distinct,[108] post-experience advertising may offer the extra element for a brand to be perceived as better or more unique than the rest.

Low elaboration likelihood, behavioural attitude formation

In this case, at least one of the MAO factors is low, making well-thought-through processing less likely. Consumers will rather concentrate on elements of previous brand experience to form an attitude and purchase intention. A typical model for this low-involvement–behavioural-oriented processing is Ehrenberg's **reinforcement model**. According to this model, awareness leads to trial and trial leads to reinforcement. Product experience is the dominant variable in the model, and advertising is supposed to reinforce habits, frame experience (see previous section) and defend consumers' attitudes.[109] A similar model is called the **routinised response behaviour model** and assumes that a large number of product experiences can lead to routinised response behaviour, especially for low-involvement, frequently purchased products such as toilet paper, toothpaste, paper tissues, mineral water or chewing gum.[110] In this case, consumers do not spend much time on deciding which brand to buy, but buy a particular brand out of habit. In other words, previous behaviour guides future behaviour. Although the initial brand choice may have been thoroughly elaborated, routinised response behaviour is characterised by no or very low cognitive effort in which very few possibilities are considered. The fact that routinised response behaviour is a frequently used purchase strategy is illustrated by a study observing consumers who were buying detergents in a supermarket:[111] 83% of the 120 consumers observed took only one brand while no more than 4% picked up more than one brand to investigate them a bit closer. It took the consumers on average 13 seconds to walk down the aisle and choose a detergent. Obviously, no extended problem-solving was used here. Building brand awareness and trying to become top of mind is very important here in order to be included in the limited set of brands that a consumer is willing to consider, to retain brand loyalty and to enhance brand-switching to the own brand.

As becomes obvious from previous sections, a lot of communications models have been presented and all of them found empirical support in some circumstances. However, the key seems to be to define which variables influence the way a consumer deals with marketing communications. Motivation, ability and opportunity certainly are very important variables, although an even more important factor – previous brand experience – has been neglected most of the time. Future research will no doubt try to integrate this variable further and will propose new models. One thing is certain: communications processing is a complex subject and predicting how someone is going to respond to a certain stimulus will always be a cumbersome task. As is the case with consumer behaviour, theories and models can only help us to understand consumers and their responses a bit better. Attention will be devoted now to two phenomena that are major concerns to advertisers, namely irritation and brand confusion.

Causes and consequences of irritation evoked by advertising

When ad-evoked feelings were discussed above, in general only positive feelings were considered. In this section, frequently experienced negative feelings are addressed. Irritation can be defined as 'provoking, annoying, causing displeasure, and momentary impatience'.[112] As mentioned before, many researchers use different feeling scales and, as a consequence, come up with different feeling dimensions. However, a striking result is that in many studies investigating consumers' responses to advertising, an irritation dimension appears.[113] In other words, irritation seems to be a basic reaction to marketing communications. Two questions arise: What causes irritation? And what are the consequences of ad-evoked irritation for advertising effectiveness?

Causes of irritation

A number of factors can cause irritation. They are shown in Figure 3.9. As for media, consumers mention television as one of the most irritating communications media, the reason being that commercials interrupt programmes.[114] For the same reason, interruption of an ongoing task, as well as for the intrusive character, pop-up ads are also considered to be rather irritating.[115] Concerning irritating ad content, several elements can be identified.[116]

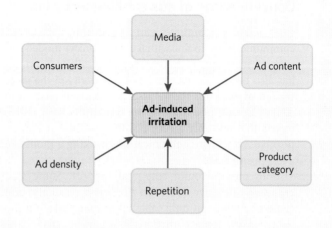

Figure 3.9 Causes of ad-evoked irritation

Firstly, unbelievable, exaggerated, overdramatised situations such as expert endorsements, testimonials and slice-of-life commercials increase irritation. A good example is a housewife confirming how white Daz makes her laundry. Secondly, unsympathetic characters in the ad, or picturing an uncomfortable situation such as a quarrel, enhance irritation, as well as hectic, nervous spots. Thirdly, brand comparisons in which the advertised brand always claims to be the best, or showing the brand name too often, leads to more irritation. Fourthly, information-oriented appeals seem to irritate more than transformational or image-dominant appeals. Furthermore, if information cues are used, it is advisable to follow a 'soft sell' (e.g. availability, quality, taste, etc.) rather than a 'hard sell' (performance, price, etc.) approach and stick to no more than five arguments (four arguments seem to be ideal). Fifthly, satire, provocation and eroticism increase irritation, while music, sentimental humour and warmth created by the use of animals or children seem to have an irritation-reducing effect.

With respect to the product category, research results are not really surprising. Products that seem to elicit on average more irritation are female hygiene products, female underwear, laxatives, toothpaste, mouthwash, personal care products, detergents and cleansers.[117] Concerning repetition, consumers seem to react negatively to an ad at low exposure frequency because of the newness of the stimulus. After repeated exposures the ad responses become more and more positive, a phenomenon called **wear-in**. However, after a certain number of exposures, 'wear-out effects' occur in the sense that negative responses show up again[118] (see also Chapter 8). However, wear-out effects (leading to a higher level of irritation) seem to be more prominent for some types of commercials than others. Complex messages, minor changes in ad execution, short or slow commercials, very warm spots and non-food ads do not seem to experience negative effects of higher exposure levels,[119] while humorous, long, fast-paced, image-dominant and transformational commercials suffer more from high repetition levels.[120] Ad density or the fact that consumers are exposed to many ads in a short period can also evoke irritation. An experiment in which respondents were exposed to a 30-minute documentary on capital punishment with either 3 or 30 embedded ads indicated significant differences in evoked irritation.[121]

Consumers react differently to advertising. For instance, a study trying to define consumer segments on the basis of the general attitude towards advertising found a segment of advertising haters as well as a segment of advertising lovers.[122] On the basis of the foregoing, it is obvious that some consumers are more likely to be irritated by advertising than others. Some research results suggest that men and consumers in the 34–41 age group are more irritated by commercials, while irritation seems to increase with increasing levels of education and income.

Consequences of ads evoking irritation

Contradictory hypotheses can be found in the literature regarding the effects of irritating communications. In line with feelings transfer models, one can expect negative evoked feelings, such as irritation, to have a negative influence on ad- and brand-related responses. This has also been referred to as **'the superiority of the pleasant' hypothesis**. On the other hand, **the law of extremes theory** assumes that the relationship between the attitude towards the ad and the attitude towards the brand follows a J-shaped curve (Figure 3.10).[123] The latter means that not only a very positive, but also a very negative Aad can eventually lead to a positive Ab, while communications evoking a moderate instead of an extreme Aad result in a less positive Ab.

Both models found empirical support. Some studies show negative feelings lead to exclusively negative effects on Ab, brand recall and brand confusion.[124] Moreover, irritation caused by either an unlikeable ad or many ads in a short time period has also been shown to negatively impact unrelated subsequent ads.[125] These results can be explained by the law of extremes theory or the feelings transfer that is likely under low elaboration likelihood, affective attitude formation. Another study[126] found that the effect of irritating communications depends on the type of buying motive the ad appeals to. As mentioned before, transformational buying motives consist of positive motivations such as sensory gratification, social approval or intellectual stimulation, while informational buying motives refer to reducing or turning of negative motivations such as solving or avoiding a problem, or normal depletion.[127] It turns out that ad-related responses are negatively affected by irritation in any case, but correct brand recall, the attitude towards the brand and purchase intention are only affected negatively by irritating commercials when transformational buying motives are appealed to. In other words, for informational motives, the law of extremes theory seems to be confirmed. People did not like the ad, but the negative feelings were not transferred to the brand. This corresponds with the Affect-as-Information model that can be expected to apply under high elaboration likelihood, affective attitude formation. Consumers experienced negative feelings but, depending on their motive, they considered these feelings relevant or irrelevant. Only when the feelings were deemed relevant were they taken into account, resulting in a negative impact for transformational purchase motivations. For informational purchase motivations, feelings apparently were not perceived to be relevant and therefore they did not serve as information input. Again, the important role of consumer motivations is shown.

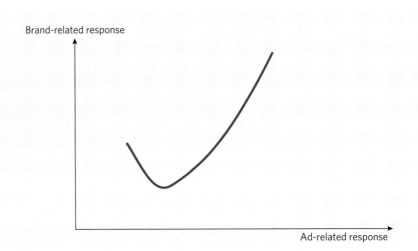

Figure 3.10 The J-shaped relationship between Aad and Ab

Advertising and brand confusion

The goal of advertising is to stimulate demand for the brand advertised. However, similar products and similar advertising appeals may generate brand confusion, which in turn can lead to an increase in sales of a competitor's instead of the advertiser's brand. Therefore, attention should be devoted to how brand confusion can be avoided by finding out which factors are most likely to cause it.

Brand confusion refers to the fact that a communication for brand X is regarded by the consumer as being a communication for a different brand, Y.[128] In other words, the consumer attributes a wrong brand name to a particular communications stimulus. Besides brand confusion, product confusion can also occur. **Product confusion** is the phenomenon of attributing a stimulus to the wrong product category. A consumer might, for instance, think that a particular ad is for a bank, while it is in fact for an insurance company. Furthermore, a distinction has to be made between positive and negative brand confusion.[129] Negative brand confusion refers to the extent to which a consumer wrongly thinks that your advertising message is an ad for a competitor's brand, while positive confusion is about wrongly assuming that a competitor's communications campaign is actually a campaign for your brand. It has to be added, though, that positive confusion is not necessarily positive, since the confusion with another brand can harm the current or desired positioning or image of your brand.

A study[130] regarding facial care products and perfumes shows that brand confusion is a serious problem. Up to 35% of the people who thought they knew which brand was advertised in an ad in which the brand name was covered, actually confused brands. Another study[131] investigated correct attribution for print ads. For several of the print ads tested, correct brand attribution came to less than 10%. Especially for insurance companies, banks and facial care products, correct brand attribution is low, while for clothing and beer some of the brands are able to get a correct recognition score of 50%. It has to be added, though, that the low numbers in the latter study do not completely relate to brand confusion, since the people who did not have the faintest idea are also included in the analyses. However, the latter group was excluded in the former study.

A number of factors can cause brand confusion (Figure 3.11). Examples are brand and product category-related, consumer-related, message and campaign-related factors. As for brand and product category-related factors, brand name similarity, reduced inter-brand

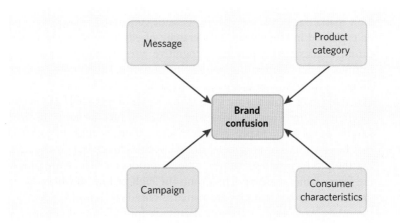

Figure 3.11 Factors affecting brand confusion

differences with respect to functionality and product presentation,[132] wilful brand imitation by imitating package shape and size, label print style and layout, and package colour,[133] and a high degree of competition in the product category[134] (which is often accompanied by a high advertising clutter) seem to increase the risk of brand confusion. Furthermore, brand confusion often occurs to the disadvantage of low-market-share brands to the advantage of market leaders or other large-market-share brands. Message-related factors refer to differences between ads in emotional and informational content, but also in format. With respect to emotional content, for example, it is generally agreed that emotional appeals attract more attention, but when the emotional content distracts the consumers, less brand recall and more brand confusion may result, leading to the phenomenon where everybody knows the ad, but nobody knows the brand advertised. As mentioned before, too much information causes irritation, which in turn can lead to more brand confusion.[135] Format factors that have been shown to lower the level of brand confusion are a clear headline, the use of pictures and showing the product in use. Furthermore, 'the degree of overall similarity of strategy' (DOSS) in information content seems to have increased over time, although ads seem to differ more and more in emotional content.[136] Therefore, the more unique an ad is in terms of content and execution, the less likely brand confusion is to occur.[137]

As for campaign-related factors, the campaign budget is negatively related to brand confusion, and the same can be expected for total **gross rating points (GRP)** or share of voice (see also Chapters 6 and 8).[138] Furthermore, using multiple communications media and a consistent communications strategy, over time as well as over the different media, may be important factors in reducing or avoiding brand confusion. Concerning consumer characteristics, individuals with a negative attitude towards advertising in general are more likely to confuse brands, since they are more likely to avoid or block out most of the advertising targeted at them. Not only the attitude towards advertising in general, but also the attitude towards a particular ad are of major importance, since a more positive Aad seems to lead to less brand confusion.[139] Furthermore, people who feel more involved or who are more familiar with the product category are less likely to confuse brands since they have more brand and product knowledge.[140] Brand-loyal consumers, on the other hand, are more focused on their favourite brand and, as a consequence, confuse brands more easily.[141] Rather surprisingly, the fact that a consumer had been exposed to an ad a few or several times did not impact the level of brand confusion.

Summary

How marketing communications persuade consumers is largely a black box process that can be explained in many ways. In hierarchy-of-effects models, the consumer is assumed to go through a hierarchical process of cognitive, affective and behavioural responses to communications stimuli. Depending on the type of product and buying situation, this hierarchy may differ. A crucial role in this persuasion process is the formation and change of attitudes. The extent to which attitudes are formed in a stable or less stable way depends on the elaboration likelihood of information processing, which in turn depends on the motivation, the ability and the opportunity to process information. If one of these factors is not present, consumers may be convinced by peripheral stimuli, such as the colours in the ad or the celebrity endorsing the product, rather than by rational product information. The way in which attitudes are formed and changed depends on the high or low likelihood of elaboration, on the one hand, and whether attitudes are primarily based on cognitive, affective or conative factors, on the other. As a result, six types of attitude formation and communications models can be distinguished. Among the most important of these models are the cognitively based high elaboration likelihood model of Fishbein–Ajzen and the Theory of Planned Behaviour, the affectively oriented feelings-as-information and feeling transfer models. The post-experience, the perception–experience–memory and the routinised response behaviour models focus on the behavioural aspects of attitude formation. Communications do not always have positive effects. A number of media, product and ad characteristics can cause irritation and brand confusion, which affect advertising effectiveness.

REVIEW QUESTIONS

1. What are the contributions and shortcomings of hierarchy-of-effects models, such as the Lavidge and Steiner model and the FCB grid?
2. How are attitudes formed and changed? How can the ELM explain how communications work?
3. How can the elements in the Theory of Planned Behaviour be used in marketing communications?
4. What is heuristic evaluation and how can it be used in marketing communications?
5. How can the feelings-as-information theory be used in marketing communications?
6. What is the importance of ad-evoked feelings and emotional conditioning in marketing communications?
7. What is the mere exposure effect?
8. How can pre- and post-experience advertising influence brand choice?
9. What causes irritation and what are its consequences for advertising effectiveness?
10. What is brand confusion and what are the factors affecting it?

Further reading

Ajzen, I., 'Theory of Planned Behavior: A Bibliography', http://people.umass.edu/aizen/tpbrefs.html (accessed June 2009).

Chaudhuri, A. (2006), *Emotion and Reason in Consumer Behavior*. Burlington, MA and Oxford: Elsevier Butterworth Heinemann.

Crano, W.D. and Prislin, R. (2008), *Attitudes and Attitude Change*. New York: Psychology Press.

Petty, R.E., Fazio, R.H. and Brinol, P. (2008), *Attitudes; Insights from the New Implicit Measures*. New York: Psychology Press.

Ratneshwar, S. and Mick, D.G. (2005), *Inside Consumption: Consumer Motives, Goals and Desires*. New York: Routledge.

Wänke, M. (2008), *Social Psychology of Consumer Behavior*. New York: Psychology Press.

Journal of Advertising, http://ja.memphis.edu/.

Journal of Consumer Psychology, http://www.elsevier.com/wps/find/journaldescription.cws_home/713950/description#description.

Journal of Consumer Research, http://www.journals.uchicago.edu/toc/jcr/current.

CASE 3:
Club Med: a 'true creator of happiness' fights non-consideration

Club Méditerranée: a strong brand with a rich history

In 1950, Gérard Blitz, the son of an Antwerp diamond merchant, introduced a new style of holiday for 'developing a taste for living outdoors and doing physical training and sport', and, together with his partner Gilbert Trigano, founded 'Club Méditerranée' (Club Med). This idea gave birth to the spirit: 'Our purpose in life is to be happy. The place to be happy is here. And the time to be happy is now.' This phrase coined by Gérard Blitz received considerable endorsement in the post-war context. By freeing people from their restrictions, allowing them to get together, recharge their batteries and return to original pleasures, happiness by Club Med was born. Club Med invented a new way to bring people together and an unprecedented vacation style: all-inclusive holidays in resorts in the world's most beautiful venues, where every guest or Great Member (GM) could unwind through contact with nature, sports and others, surrounded by the friendliness of the staff, or Gentils Organisateurs (GO).

In 2005, Club Med refocused its activity on high-end global tourism to become the world specialist in upscale, friendly, multicultural, all-inclusive holidays. This new position placed Club Med in a new international competition range comprising luxury hotels, holiday clubs, resorts and tour operators. Club Med targets the clients of upscale hotels who are seeking a friendlier atmosphere and the guests of holiday clubs who require higher-quality service within an upscale, all-inclusive formula.

To accompany its new upscale position, Club Med adopted in late December 2007 a new signature and launched a global communications campaign, bold and poetic: 'Where happiness means the world' represented this strong promise of happiness 'by Club Med'. Deployed in the 40 countries where the group was present, the new Club Med campaign expressed powerfully, in the style typical of the Club Med 'label', all the feelings, the happiness, that can be experienced through the vast collection of offers, activities and discoveries available in the resorts.

In 2011, the company operated 72 holiday villages in 26 countries around the world, where 1.2 million customers were served by 15 000 staff members of 100 different nationalities. The turnover of the company was €1423 million, 45% of which was in France. Club Med occupied a strong position in the universe of luxury brands.

Consumers do not understand the brand and do not consider it

For a number of years, Club Med has been in decline in the Dutch-speaking part of Belgium. Compared with other tour operators, the brand has not been very visible in that part of the market. In 2010, its share was 6% in Flanders, while Jetair had 35%, Thomas Cook 15%, Neckermann 11% and Sunjets 10%.

In 2010 qualitative and quantitative consumer research was undertaken. A qualitative study with potential customers of higher social classes led to the following insights:

- The marketing challenge of Club Med in Flanders was not brand awareness or the perception of high prices, but the fact that potential customers did not consider Club Med when they thought of booking a holiday (mental zapping).

- People perceived Club Med as a 'UCPA upscale' (UCPA is a low-end travel organisation) which turned part of the target group off. People did not know the Club Med concept very well, and associated it with noisiness and forced intimacy.

- At the same time, the expectations of the target group were consistent with the strong points of the Club Med concept, such as openness to the world, and a level of intimacy that customers could freely choose themselves.

In other words, the study revealed that the problem was not so much brand awareness or price perception, but a lack of understanding of the concept and the Club Med brand. To corroborate these qualitative findings, a quantitative study was conducted in a sample of 485 respondents: well-off Flemish couples or families with children less than 12 years old, the core target group of Club Med. This study largely confirmed the insights from the qualitative phase. First of all, the study showed that Club Med's brand awareness was as high as that of its main competitors (Figure 3.12). Also the price perception was in line with the competition (Figure 3.13). However, the main problem was that the brand was not considered by the target group as much as the competition (Figure 3.14).

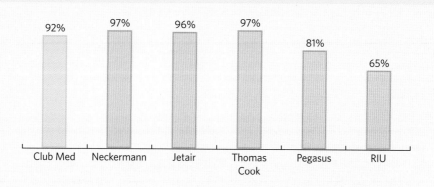

Figure 3.12 Brand awareness of Club Med and its main competitors

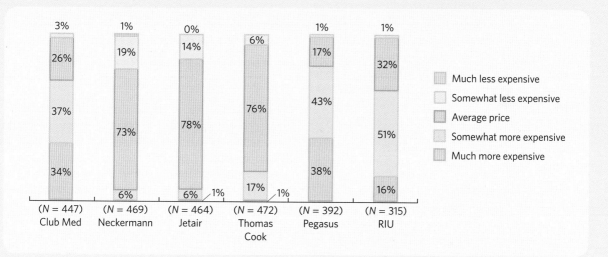

Figure 3.13 Price perception of Club Med and its competitors: How do you think the price of their offer compares with other travel agencies/resort hotels?

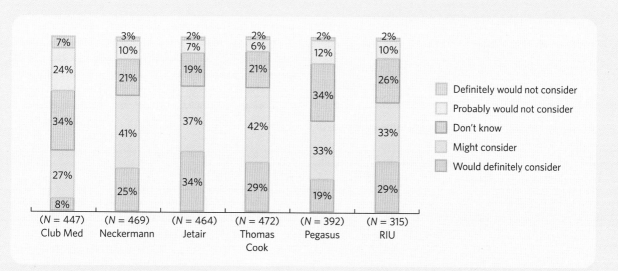

Figure 3.14 Brand consideration of Club Med and its competitors: To what extent would you consider booking a holiday with each of these travel agents/resort hotels?

Table 3.6 Image of Club Med in target group (those who know Club Med)

	Also acknowledged by target group	Average	Less acknowledged by target group
Personality	Active Full of life Dynamic Adventurous	Friendly	
Satisfaction	Enables getting to know new people Creates a festive, happy atmosphere Stimulates new experiences	Creates an atmosphere where I can forget my worries	Handles everything and makes sure I don't have to worry
Offer	Has a lot of sport activities Has an all-inclusive formula Separate activities for the whole family		A well-known and respected chain

Moreover, as was also found in the qualitative study, Club Med was perceived as an upmarket version of UCPA, an image that Club Med definitely does not want (Table 3.6). Not knowing Club Med and the characteristics of its offer appeared to be the main reason not to consider the brand (Figure 3.15).

A campaign to put Club Med on the map again

In 2011 the company decided to redress the lack of consideration and misperceptions about Club Med by means of a marketing communications campaign. The campaign was targeted at the affluent Flemish families with children younger than 12. The objectives were set out to be reached in three stages, as follows:

1. Take away the barriers to consideration of Club Med as a travel organisation.

2. Reinforce the uniqueness of the brand.

3. Reinforce word of mouth.

A further ambition was to become an iconic brand by 2013.
   Derived from these three pillars, the following specific objectives were formulated:

- Maintain brand awareness at least at the same level of the competitors.

- The image of the brand should improve, more specifically on the following key attributes:
  - Happy atmosphere
  - Experience new things
  - Safe and secure
  - Closer to my family
  - Discovery
  - Feel unique

- Improvement of the price perception – Club Med should be perceived as relatively expensive.

- Improvement of the value-for-money perception.

- Improvement of product quality perception.

The campaign used a combination of traditional mass media and online tools. A billboard teaser campaign was supplemented by inserts and ads in a number of major newspapers and banners on selected Internet sites. A PR campaign targeting travel journalists was rolled out and a direct mailing was sent to key prospects. All these efforts were geared at attracting prospects to the Internet site www.ontdekclubmed.be ('discover club med') and to invite people to share their thoughts on social media.

A campaign well received by the target group

Various measures indicate that the campaign was well processed by the target group. Since its launch, the website has received 33 000 unique visitors who visit the site on average for one minute (Figure 3.16). Visitor peaks are seen as a result of campaign efforts (mailings, newspaper inserts, etc.). By the end of March 2011, the Facebook page had more than 130 000 visitors and 6800 fans. Word of mouth on Facebook, blogs, etc., evolved positively during the campaign period. The evolution of word-of-mouth quality during the campaign is shown in Figure 3.17.
   The campaign in the newspaper *De Morgen* scored the best ever of the 300 campaigns tested for this newspaper. Three out of four respondents saw the ad and 94% could attribute it to the campaign, leading to a useful score of 72% (Figure 3.18). Another newspaper ad scored a recognition of 54%, a correct attribution of 72%, and hence a useful score of 39%, well above the average of 27% for all the ads in this newspaper.

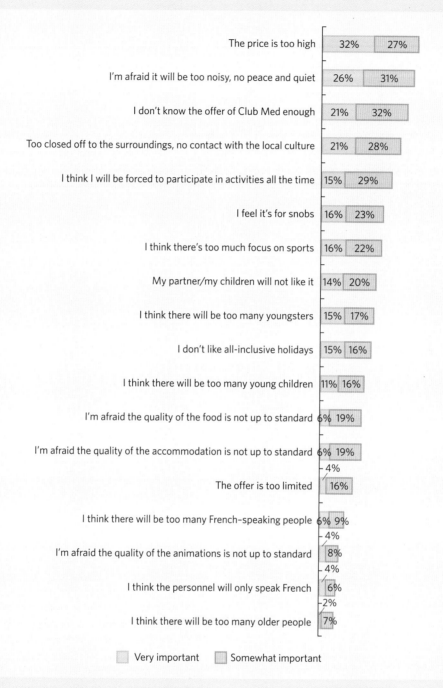

Figure 3.15 Reasons not to consider Club Med for holidays

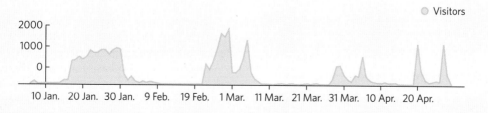

Figure 3.16 Evolution of number of unique visitors to the website (www.ontdekclubmed.be)

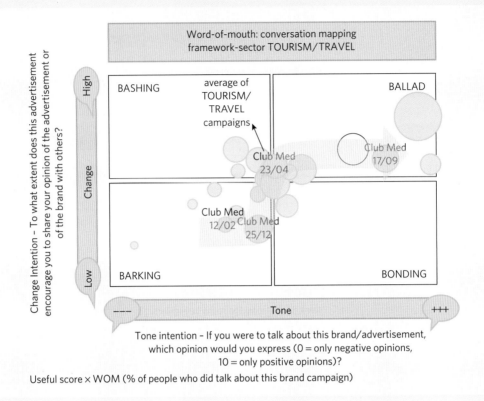

Figure 3.17 Evolution of Club Med word-of-mouth quality during the campaign

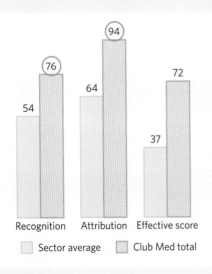

Figure 3.18 Recognition, correct attribution and useful score of the *De Morgen* newspaper campaign

Moving in the right direction

After the campaign, in June 2011, key indicators of effectiveness were measured. Brand awareness did not change after the campaign. Club Med maintained its high awareness score of more than 90%, and is still equally as well known as its competitors. General brand attitude improved: among families with kids, the brand opinion of Club Med is significantly less neutral and more favourable than in the previous measurement (March 2010) (Figure 3.19). In 2010, 27% of the respondents found Club Med 'somewhat less expensive'. In June 2011, this decreased to 18%. Although not impressive, the price perception evolved in the desired direction. Similarly the 'value for money' perception had improved. In 2010, 28% felt that Club Med was good value for money. In 2011, this had increased to 33%. The brand associations in terms of the attributes put forward as important did not significantly change between March 2010 and June 2011. The image thus largely stayed the same, and the campaign did not succeed in altering the perception of the core target group (Figure 3.20).

The commercial results of Club Med also evolved positively. After two years of severe decline in Flanders, the number of customers slightly increased in 2011 (Figure 3.21). Similarly, turnover substantially increased after two years of substantial decline (Figure 3.22). Combining the recruitment and sales figures leads to the conclusion that sales primarily increased as a result of a higher unit price per holiday sold.

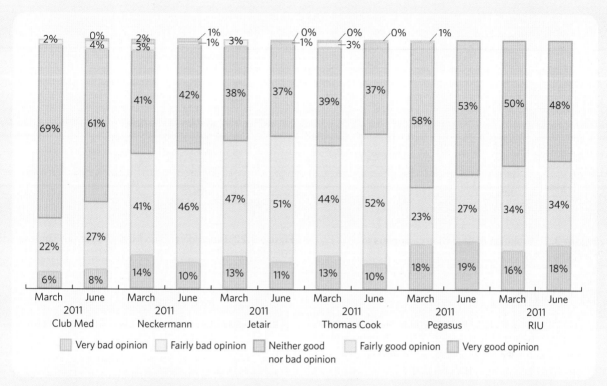

Figure 3.19 Image of Club Med and its competitors, March 2010 versus June 2011

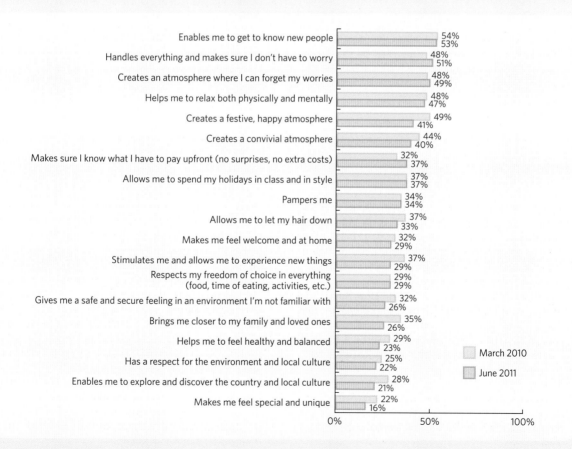

Figure 3.20 Evolution of Club Med image attributes, 2010–11

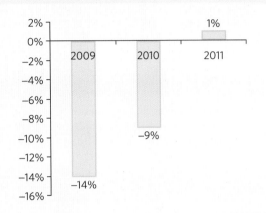

Figure 3.21 Evolution of Club Med customers in Flanders, 2009–2011

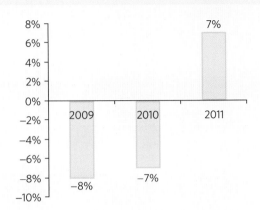

Figure 3.22 Evolution of Club Med turnover in Flanders, 2009–2011

QUESTIONS

1. Describe and assess Club Med's problem identification and the research it is based on. Given its desired positioning and business problem, did Club Med draw the right conclusions from the research?

2. In Club Med's campaign, did it follow a hierarchy-of-effects approach? If yes, which one? Is such an approach needed?

3. In which cell of the FCB grid would you classify travel solutions? In which cell can Club Med be situated or does it aim to be situated? Has it been successful?

4. Using the classification of attitude formation models in this chapter, which models seem most relevant to explain the processing and impact of the Club Med campaign?

5. In terms of the Theory of Planned Behaviour, how is Club Med trying to form the intentions towards its brand? What is the role of attitudes, subjective norms and perceived behavioural control?

6. Does Club Me aim at central or peripheral processing? Why?

7. Would you say Club Med has been effective in reaching its targets, and is this effectiveness attributable to its communication campaign?

Sources: www.clubmed-corporate.com (accessed 22 June 2012); Bert Denis, TBWA.

References

[1] Barry, T.E. and Howard, D.J. (1990), 'A Review and Critique of the Hierarchy of Effects in Advertising', *International Journal of Advertising*, 9, 121–35; Barry, T.E. (2002), 'In Defense of the Hierarchy of Effects: A Rejoinder to Weilbacher', *Journal of Advertising Research*, 42(3), 44–7.

[2] Vakratsas, D. and Ambler, T. (1999), 'How Advertising Works: What Do We Really Know?', *Journal of Marketing*, 63(1), 25–43.

[3] Vaughn, R. (1986), 'How Advertising Works: A Planning Model Revisited', *Journal of Advertising Research*, 26(1), 57–66.

[4] Rossiter, J.R. and Percy, L. (1997), *Advertising and Promotion Management*. New York: McGraw-Hill.

[5] Keller, K.L. (2008), *Building, Measuring, and Managing Brand Equity*, 3rd edition. Upper Saddle River, NJ: Prentice Hall.

[6] Yoon, S.K. (2001), 'Prophet Warning: Is Nothing Sacred?', *Far Eastern Economic Review*, 10 May, http://www.singapore-window.org/sw01/010510re.htm (accessed June 2009).

[7] Barry, T.E. and Howard, D.J. (1990), 'A Review and Critique of the Hierarchy of Effects in Advertising', *International Journal of Advertising*, 9, 121–35; Barry, T.E. (2002), 'In Defense of the Hierarchy of Effects: A Rejoinder to Weilbacher', *Journal of Advertising Research*, 42(3), 44–7.

[8] Bamossy, S. and Hogg, A. (2007), *Consumer Behaviour: A European Perspective*, 3rd edition. Harlow: Pearson Education.

[9] Hoyer, W.C. and MacInnis, D.J. (2007), *Consumer Behavior*, 4th edition. Boston, MA: Houghton Mifflin.

[10] Panic, K., Cauberghe, V. and De Pelsmacker, P. (2011), 'Promoting Dental Hygiene to Children: Investigating the Impact of Threat Appeals in Combination with Traditional vs. Interactive Media', *Proceedings of the 2011 Icoria Conference, Berlin*, CD-ROM.

[11] Witte, K. (1992), 'Putting the Fear Back into Fear Appeals: The Extended Parallel Process Model (EPPM)', *Communication Monographs*, 59(4), 329–49.

[12] Kretchmer, S.B. (2005), 'Changing Views of Commercialization in Digital Games: In-Game Advertising and Advergames as Worlds in Plays', Paper presented at *DIGTAR Conference 'Changing Views: Worlds in Play'*, Vancouver.

[13] Gee, J.P. (2003), *What Video Games Have to Teach Us about Learning and Literacy*. New York: Palgrave Macmillan; Prensky, M. (2005), 'Computer Games and Learning: Digital Game-based Learning', in Raessens, J. and Goldstein, J. (eds), *Handbook of Computer Games Studies*, Cambridge, MA: MIT Press, 59–79.

[14] Hoyer, W.D. and MacInnis, D.J. (2007), *Consumer Behavior*, 4th edition, Boston, MA: Houghton Mifflin; Park, C.W., Jaworski, B.J. and MacInnis, D.J. (1986), 'Strategic Brand Concept–Image Management', *Journal of Marketing*, 50 (October), 135–45.

[15] Pham, M.T. and Higgins, E.T. (2005), 'Promotion and Prevention in Consumer Decision Making: State of the Art and Theoretical Propositions', in Ratneshwar, S. and Mick, D.G. (eds), *Inside Consumption: Perspectives on Consumer Motives, Goals and Desires*, London: Routledge, 8–43; Aaker, J.L. and Lee, A.Y. (2001), '"I" Seek Pleasures and "We" Avoid Pains: The Role of Self-Regulatory Goals in Information Processing and Persuasion', *Journal of Consumer Research*, 28 (June), 33–49; Higgins, E.T. (1997), 'Beyond Pleasure and Pain', *American Psychologist*, 52 (December), 1280–300.

[16] Huffman, C., Ratneshwar, S. and Mick, D.G. (2000), 'Consumer Goal Structures and Goal Determination Processes', in Ratneshwar, S., Mick, D.G. and Huffman, C. (eds), *The Why of Consumption: Contemporary Perspectives on Consumer Motives, Goals and Desires*, New York: Routledge, 1–35.

[17] Pham, M.T. and Higgins, E.T. (2005), 'Promotion and Prevention in Consumer Decision Making: State of the Art and Theoretical Propositions', in Ratneshwar, S. and Mick, D.G. (eds), *Inside Consumption: Perspectives on Consumer Motives, Goals and Desires*, London: Routledge, 8–43.

[18] Baumgartner, H. (2002), 'Toward a Personology of the Consumer', *Journal of Consumer Research*, 29 (September), 286–92.

[19] Cuckoo Awards (2005).

[20] Petty, R.E. and Cacioppo, J.T. (1986), 'The Elaboration Likelihood Model of Persuasion', *Advances in Experimental Social Psychology*, 19, 123–205.

[21] Petty, R.E. and Cacioppo, J.T. (1986), 'The Elaboration Likelihood Model of Persuasion', *Advances in Experimental Social Psychology*, 19, 123–205.

[22] Berney-Reddish, I.A. and Areni, C.S. (2006), 'Sex Differences in Responses to Probability Markers in Advertising Claims', *Journal of Advertising*, 35(2), 7–16.

[23] Areni, C.S. (2002), 'The Proposition-Probability Model of Argument Structure and Message Acceptance', *Journal of Consumer Research*, 29(2), 168–87.

[24] Bušljeta Banks, I. and De Pelsmacker, P. (2011), 'Tolerance for Ambiguity and the Effects of Probability Markers in Services Advertisements: A Study of Belgian and Croatian Consumers', *Proceedings of the 2011 International Conference on Research in Advertising, Berlin*, CD-ROM.

[25] Areni, C.S. (2003), 'The Effects of Structural and Grammatical Variables on Persuasion: An Elaboration Likelihood Model Perspective', *Psychology & Marketing*, 20 (April), 349–75; Areni, C.S. and Sparks, J.R. (2005), 'Language Power and Persuasion', *Psychology & Marketing*, 22(6), 507–25; Sparks, J.R. and Areni, C.S. (2008), 'Style Versus Substance: Multiple Roles of Language Power in Persuasion', *Journal of Applied Social Psychology*, 38(1), 37–60.

[26] Bušljeta Banks, I., De Pelsmacker, P. and Purnawirawan, N.A. (2011), 'Probability Markers in Advertising Have a Different Effect on the Purchase Intention for Hedonic and Utilitarian Low and High Involvement Services', *Proceedings of the 40th European Marketing Academy Conference Ljubljana*, CD-ROM.

[27] Voss, K.E., Spangenberg, E.R. and Grohmann, B. (2003), 'Measuring the Hedonic and Utilitarian Dimensions of Consumer Attitude', *Journal of Marketing Research*, 11(3), 310–20.

[28] Areni, C.S. (2002), 'The Proposition-Probability Model of Argument Structure and Message Acceptance', *Journal of Consumer Research*, 29(2), 168–87.

[29] Voss, K.E., Spangenberg, E.R. and Grohmann, B. (2003), 'Measuring the Hedonic and Utilitarian Dimensions of Consumer Attitude', *Journal of Marketing Research*, 11(3), 310–20.

[30] Berney-Reddish, I.A. and Areni, C.S. (2006), 'Sex Differences in Responses to Probability Markers in Advertising Claims', *Journal of Advertising*, 35(2), 7–16.

[31] De Mooij, M. and Hofstede, G. (2010), 'The Hofstede Model: Applications to Global Branding and Advertising Strategy and Research', *International Journal of Advertising*, 29(1), 85–110.

[32] Bosmans, A. (2002), 'Affective Persuasive Communication: Multiple Roles of Affect in Persuading the Consumer', Unpublished Doctoral Dissertation, Ghent University; Forgas, J.P. (1995), 'Mood and Judgment: The Affect Infusion Model (AIM)', *Psychological Bulletin*, 117(1), 39–66; Chaiken, S. (1980), 'Heuristic versus Systematic Information Processing in the Use of Source versus Message Cues in Persuasion', *Journal of Personality and Social Psychology*, 39, 752–66; Petty, R.E. and Cacioppo, J.T. (1986), 'The Elaboration Likelihood Model of Persuasion', *Advances in Experimental Psychology*, 19, 123–205.

[33] Pham, M.T. and Avnet, T. (2004), 'Ideals and Oughts and the Reliance on Affect versus Substance in Persuasion', *Journal of Consumer Research*, 30 (March), 503–18.

[34] Adams, L., Faseur, T. and Geuens, M. (2008), 'The Influence of Self-regulatory Focus in the Effectiveness of Emotional Health Campaigns: It's a Matter of Context too', *Proceedings of the Association for Consumer Research Conference, San Francisco*.

35   Ajzen, I. (2002), 'Attitudes', in Fernandez Ballesteros, R. (ed.), *Encyclopedia of Psychological Assessment*, vol. 1. London: Sage, 110–15; Ajzen, I. (1991), 'The Theory of Planned Behavior', *Organizational Behavior and Human Decision Processes*, 50, 179–211; Fishbein, M. and Ajzen, I. (1975), *Belief, Attitude, Intention, and Behavior: An Introduction to Theory and Research*. Reading, MA: Addison-Wesley.

36   De Pelsmacker, P. and Van Kenhove, P. (2006), *Marktonderzoek: Technieken en Toepassingen* (*Marketing Research: Techniques and Applications*). Amsterdam: Pearson Education Benelux.

37   Ajzen, I. (2002), 'Attitudes', in Fernandez Ballesteros, R. (ed.), *Encyclopedia of Psychological Assessment*, vol. 1. London: Sage, 110–15; Ajzen, I. (1991), 'The Theory of Planned Behavior', *Organizational Behavior and Human Decision Processes*, 50, 179–211.

38   Taylor, S. and Todd, P. (1995), 'Understanding Information Technology Usage: A Test of Competing Models', *Information Systems Research*, 6, 144–76.

39   Rogers, E.M. (1995), *Diffusion of Innovations*. New York: Free Press.

40   Ajzen, I. (1991), 'The Theory of Planned Behavior', *Organizational Behavior and Human Decision Processes*, 50, 179–221.

41   Bandura, A. (1986), *Social Foundations of Thought and Action*. Englewood Cliff, NJ: Prentice Hall.

42   Perlusz, S. (2011), 'Emotions and Technology Acceptance: Development and Validation of a Technology Affect Scale', jgxy.usx.edu.cn/DAOM/046_StefanoPerlusz.pdf (accessed 1 July 2011); Bagozzi, R.P., Gopinath, M. and Nyer, P.U. (1999), 'The Role of Emotions in Marketing', *Journal of the Academy of Marketing Science*, 27(2), 184–206; Kim, H.W., Chan, H.C. and Chan, Y.P. (2007), 'A Balanced Thinking-Feelings Model of Information Systems Continuance', *International Journal of Human Computer Studies*, 65, 511–25.

43   Perugini, M. and Bagozzi, R.P. (2001), 'The Role of Desires and Anticipated Emotions in Goal-directed Behaviours: Broadening and Deepening the Theory of Planned Behaviour', *British Journal of Social Psychology*, 40, 79–98.

44   Bagozzi, R.P. (2007), 'The Legacy of the Technology Acceptance Model and a Proposal for a Paradigm Shift', *Journal of the Association for Information Systems*, 8(4), 244–54.

45   Wood, S.L. and Moreau, C.P. (2006), 'From Fear to Loathing? How Emotion Influences the Evaluation and Early Use of Innovations', *Journal of Marketing*, 70 (July), 44–57.

46   Moons, I. and De Pelsmacker, P. (2012), 'Emotions as Determinants of Electric Car Usage Intention', *Journal of Marketing Management*, 28(3–4), 195–237.

47   Ajzen, I. (1991), 'The Theory of Planned Behavior', *Organizational Behavior and Human Decision Processes*, 50, 179–211.

48   Ajzen, I. (2002), 'Perceived Behavioral Control, Self-Efficacy, Locus of Control, and the Theory of Planned Behavior', *Journal of Applied Social Psychology*, 32, 665–83.

49   http://www.handicapinternational.be (accessed 28 April 2006); Cuckoo Awards 2005.

50   http://people.umass.edu/aizen/tpbrefs.html (accessed 19 September 2012).

51   Yao, M.Z. and Linz, D.G. (2008), 'Predicting Self-protections of Online Privacy', *CyberPsychology & Behavior*, 11, 615–17; White, K.M., Robinson, N.G., Young, R.M., Anderson, P.J., Hyde, M.K., Greenbank, S. *et al.* (2008), 'Testing an Extended Theory of Planned Behaviour to Predict Young People's Sun Safety in a High Risk Area', *British Journal of Health Psychology*, 13, 435–48; Warner, H.W.N. and Åberg, L. (2008), 'Drivers' Beliefs About Exceeding the Speed Limits', *Transportation Research Part F: Traffic Psychology and Behaviour*, 11, 376–89; Van Hooft, E.A.J., Born, M.P., Taris, T.W. and Van der Flier, H. (2006), 'The Cross-cultural Generalizability of the Theory of Planned Behavior: A Study on Job Seeking in the Netherlands', *Journal of Cross-Cultural Psychology*, 37, 127–35; Tuu, H.H., Olsen, S.O., Thao, D.T. and Anh, N.T.K. (2008), 'The Role of Norms in Explaining Attitudes, Intention and Consumption of a Common Food (Fish) in Vietnam', *Appetite*, 51, 546–51; Townsend, L. and Dawes, A. (2007), 'Intentions to Care for Children Orphaned by HIV/AIDS: A Test of the Theory of Planned Behavior', *Journal of Applied Social Psychology*, 37, 822–43; Knussen, C. and Yule, F. (2008), '"I'm Not in the Habit of Recycling": The Role of Habitual Behavior in the Disposal of Household Waste', *Environment and Behavior*, 40, 683–702.

52   Ajzen, I. (1991), 'The Theory of Planned Behavior', *Organizational Behavior and Human Decision Processes*, 50, 179–211.

53   De Cannière, M.H., De Pelsmacker, P. and Geuens, M. (2009), 'Relationship Quality and the Theory of Planned Behavior Models of Behavioral Intentions and Purchase Behavior', *Journal of Business Research*, 62, 82–92.

54   Crowley, A.E. and Hoyer, W.D. (1994), 'An Integrative Framework for Understanding Two-sided Persuasion', *Journal of Consumer Research*, 20, 561–74; Eisend, M. (2006), 'Two-sided Advertising: A Meta-analysis', *International Journal of Research in Marketing*, 23, 187–98.

55   Eisend, M. (2006), 'Two-sided Advertising: A Meta-analysis', *International Journal of Research in Marketing*, 23, 187–98.

56   Cornelis, E., Cauberghe, V. and De Pelsmacker, P. (2012), 'The Impact of Refutation on Credibility: The Moderating Role of Issue Ambivalence', *Proceedings of the 41st EMAC Conference, Lisbon*, CD-ROM.

57   Allen, M. (1991), 'Meta-analysis Comparing Effectiveness of One and Two-sided Messages', *Western Journal of Speech Communication*, 55, 390–404.

58   Holbrook, M.B. and Hirschman, E.C. (1982), 'The Experiential Aspects of Consumption: Consumer Fantasies, Feelings, and Fun', *Journal of Consumer Research*, 9, 132–40; Pham, M.T. (1998), 'Representativeness, Relevance, and the Use of Feelings in Decision Making', *Journal of Consumer Research*, 25, 144–59.

59   Ricciardelli, L.A., Williams, R.J. and Finemore, J. (2001), 'Restraint as Misregulation in Drinking and Eating', *Addictive Behaviors*, 26, 665–75.

60 Williams, A. and Clark, D. (1998), 'Alcohol Consumption in University Students: The Role of Reasons for Drinking, Coping Strategies, Expectancies, and Personality Traits', *Addictive Behaviors*, 23, 371–78.

61 MacInnis, D.J. and Jaworski, B.J. (1989), 'Information Processing from Advertisements: Toward an Integrative Framework', *Journal of Marketing*, 53, 1–23.

62 MacInnis, D.J. and Jaworski, B.J. (1989), 'Information Processing from Advertisements: Toward an Integrative Framework', *Journal of Marketing*, 53, 1–23.

63 Baker, W.E. and Lutz, R.J. (2000), 'An Empirical Test of an Updated Relevance-Accessibility Model of Advertising Effectiveness', *Journal of Advertising*, 29(1), 1–14.

64 Liu, S.C. and Johnson, K.F. (2005), 'The Automatic Country-of-origin Effects on Brand Judgements', *Journal of Advertising*, 34(1), 87–97.

65 Schwarz, N. and Clore, G.L. (1996), 'Feelings and Phenomenal Experiences', in Higgins, E.T. and Kruglanski, A.W. (eds), *Social Psychology: Handbook of Basic Principles*, New York: Guilford, 433–65.

66 Pham, M.T. (1998), 'Representativeness, Relevance, and the Use of Feelings in Decision Making', *Journal of Consumer Research*, 25(2), 144–60.

67 Gorn, G.J., Pham, M.T. and Sin, L.Y. (2001), 'When Arousal Influences Ad Evaluation and Valence Does Not (and Vice Versa)', *Journal of Consumer Psychology*, 2(3), 237–56.

68 Pham, M.T., Cohen, J.B., Prajecus, J.W. and Hughes, D.G. (2001), 'Affect Monitoring and the Primacy of Feelings in Judgment', *Journal of Consumer Research*, 28(2), 167–88.

69 Pham, M.T., Cohen, J.B., Prajecus, J.W. and Hughes, D.G. (2001), 'Affect Monitoring and the Primacy of Feelings in Judgment', *Journal of Consumer Research*, 28(2), 167–88.

70 Pham, M.T. (1998), 'Representativeness, Relevance, and the Use of Feelings in Decision Making', *Journal of Consumer Research*, 25(2), 144–60; Bosmans, A. and Baumgartner, H. (2005), 'Goal-relevant Emotional Information: When Extraneous Affect Leads to Persuasion and When it Does Not', *Journal of Consumer Research*, 32 (December), 424–34.

71 Pham, M.T. (1998), 'Representativeness, Relevance, and the Use of Feelings in Decision Making', *Journal of Consumer Research*, 25(2), 144–60.

72 Bagozzi, R.P., Gopinath, M. and Nyer, P.U. (1999), 'The Role of Emotions in Marketing', *Journal of the Academy of Marketing Science*, 27(2), 184–206; Forgas, J.P. (1995), 'Mood and Judgment: The Affect Infusion Model (AIM)', *Psychological Bulletin*, 117(1), 39–66.

73 Schindler, M.R. and Holbrook, M.B. (2003), 'Nostalgia for Early Experience as a Determinant of Consumer Preferences', *Psychology and Marketing*, 20(4), 275–302.

74 Mitchell, A.A. and Olson, J.C. (1981), 'Are Product Attribute Beliefs the Only Mediator of Advertising Effects on Brand Attitude?', *Journal of Marketing Research*, 18, 318–32.

75 Biel, A.L. (1990), 'Love the Ad: Buy the Product?', *Admap*, 21–5.

76 Baker, W.E. and Lutz, R.J. (2000), 'An Empirical Test of an Updated Relevance-Accessibility Model of Advertising Effectiveness', *Journal of Advertising*, 29(1), 1–14.

77 Lancendorfer, K.M., Atkin, J.A.L. and Reece, B.B. (2008), 'Animals in Advertising: Love Dogs? Love The ad!', *Journal of Business Research*, 61(5), 384–91.

78 Brown, S.P. and Stayman, D.M. (1992), 'Antecedents and Consequences of Attitude towards the Ad: A Meta-Analysis', *Journal of Consumer Research*, 19, 34–51.

79 Bagozzi, R.P., Gopinath, M. and Nyer, P.U. (1999), 'The Role of Emotions in Marketing', *Journal of the Academy of Marketing Science*, 27(2), 184–206.

80 Frijda, N.H. (1987), *The Emotions*. Cambridge: Cambridge University Press; Bower, G.H. (1991), 'Mood Congruity of Social Judgment', in Forgas, J. (ed.), *Emotion and Social Judgment*. Oxford: Pergamon, 31–53.

81 Mitchell, A.A. (1988), 'Current Perspectives and Issues Concerning the Explanation of "Feelings" Advertising Effects', in Hecker, S. and Stewart, D.S. (eds), *Nonverbal Communication in Advertising*. Lexington, MA: Lexington Books, 122–44.

82 Morris, J.D., Woo, C., Geason, J.A. and Kim, J. (2002), 'The Power of Affect: Predicting Intention', *Journal of Advertising Research*, 42(3), 7–17.

83 Poels, K. and Dewitte, S. (2006), 'How to Capture the Heart? Reviewing 20 Years of Emotion Measurement in Advertising', *Journal of Advertising Research*, 46(1), 18–37.

84 Morris, J.D., Woo, C., Geason, J.A. and Kim, J. (2002), 'The Power of Affect: Predicting Intention', *Journal of Advertising Research*, 42(3), 7–17.

85 Pavlov, I. (1927), *Conditioned Reflexes*. London: Oxford University Press.

86 Freeman, S. (2003), 'Celine Dion Sings "I Drove All Night" for Chrysler', *Wall Street Journal*, 16 January.

87 Kroeber-Riel, W. (1984), 'Effects of Pictorial Elements in Ads Analyzed by Means of Eye Movement Monitoring', *Advances in Consumer Research*, 11, 591–6.

88 Gibson, B. (2008), 'Can Evaluative Conditioning Change Attitudes Toward Mature Brands? New Evidence from the Implicit Association Test', *Journal of Consumer Research*, 35(1), 178–88.

89 Elliott, R. and Ritson, M. (1995), 'Practicing Existential Consumption: The Lived Meaning of Sexuality in Advertising', *Advances in Consumer Research*, 22, 740–5.

90 Furnival, J. (2009), 'Lick "n" Tell', *Daily Telegraph*, 26 September, http://www.telegraph.co.uk/foodanddrink/4809908/Lick-n-tell.html (accessed June 2009).

91 Janiszewski, C. and Meyvis, T. (2001), 'Effects of Brand Logo Complexity, Repetition, and Spacing on Processing Fluency and Judgment', *Journal of Consumer Research*, 28 (June), 18–32.

92 Shapiro, S. (1999), 'When an Ad's Influence Is Beyond Our Conscious Control: Perceptual and Conceptual Fluency Effects Caused by Incidental Ad Exposure', *Journal of Consumer Research*, 26 (June), 16–36.

93 Mano, H. (1996), 'Assessing Emotional Reactions to TV Ads: A Replication and Extension with a Brief Adjective Checklist', *Advances in Consumer Research*, 23, 63–9.

94 Zajonc, R.B. and Markus, H. (1988), 'Affect and Cognition: The Hard Interface', in Izard, C.E., Kagan, J. and Zajonc, R.B. (eds), *Emotions, Cognition and Behaviour*. Cambridge: Cambridge University Press, 73–102.

95 Janiszewski, C. and Meyvis, T. (2001), 'Effects of Brand Logo Complexity, Repetition, and Spacing on Processing Fluency and Judgment', *Journal of Consumer Research*, 28 (June), 18–32.

96 Ferraro, R., Bettman, J.R. and Chartrand, T.L. (2009), 'The Power of Strangers: The Effect of Incidental Consumer Brand Encounters on Brand Choice', *Journal of Consumer Research*, 35(5), 729–41.

97 Hoyer, W.C. and MacInnis, D.J. (2001), *Consumer Behaviour*. Boston, MA: Houghton Mifflin.

98 Berlyne, D.E. (1970), 'Novelty, Complexity, and Hedonic Value', *Perception and Psychophysics*, 8 (November), 279–86.

99 Van Kerckhove, A., Vermeir, I. and Geuens, M. (2008), 'Combined Influence of Selective Focus and Decision Involvement on Attitude-behaviour Consistency in a Context of Memory-based Decision Making', in Perks, K.J. and Shukla, P. (eds), *Marketing Landscapes: A Pause for Thought, Proceedings of the 37th Annual Conference of the European Marketing Academy (EMAC), Brighton.*

100 Deighton, J., Henderson, C.M. and Neslin, S.A. (1994), 'The Effects of Advertising on Brand Switching and Repeat Purchasing', *Journal of Marketing Research*, 31, 28–43.

101 Hall, B.F. (2002), 'A New Model for Measuring Advertising Effectiveness', *Journal of Advertising Research*, 42 (March/April), 23–31.

102 Kempf, D.S. and Laczniak, R.N. (2001), 'Advertising's Influence on Subsequent Product Trial Processing', *Journal of Advertising*, 30(3), 27–38.

103 Hall, B.F. (2002), 'A New Model for Measuring Advertising Effectiveness', *Journal of Advertising Research*, 42 (March/April), 23–31.

104 Kempf, D.S. and Laczniak, R.N. (2001), 'Advertising's Influence on Subsequent Product Trial Processing', *Journal of Advertising*, 30(3), 27–38.

105 Keller, K.L. (2008), *Building, Measuring, and Managing Brand Equity*, 3rd edition. Upper Saddle River, NJ: Prentice Hall.

106 Deighton, J., Henderson, J.M. and Neslin, S.A. (1994), 'The Effects of Advertising on Brand Switching and Repeat Purchasing', *Journal of Marketing Research*, 31(2), 28–43.

107 Kempf, D.S. and Laczniak, R.N. (2001), 'Advertising's Influence on Subsequent Product Trial Processing', *Journal of Advertising*, 30(3), 27–38.

108 Clancy, K.J. and Trout, J. (2002), 'Brand Confusion', *Harvard Business Review*, 80(3), 22.

109 Ehrenberg, A.S.C. (1974), 'Repetititve Advertising and the Consumer', *Journal of Advertising Research*, 14 (April), 25–34; Vakratsas, D. and Ambler, T. (1999), 'What Do We Really Know?', *Journal of Marketing*, 63 (January), 26–43.

110 Bamossy, S. and Hogg, A. (2007), *Consumer Behaviour: A European Perspective*, 3rd edition. Harlow: Pearson Education.

111 Hoyer, W.D. (1984), 'An Examination of Consumer Decision Making for a Common Repeat Purchase Product', *Journal of Consumer Research*, 11, 822–9.

112 Aaker, D.A. and Bruzzone, D.E. (1985), 'Causes of Irritation in Advertising', *Journal of Marketing*, 49 (Spring), 47–57.

113 De Pelsmacker, P. and Van den Bergh, J. (1998), 'Ad Content, Product Category, Campaign Weight and Irritation: A Study of 226 TV Commercials', *Journal of International Consumer Marketing*, 10(4), 5–27.

114 Pasadeos, Y. (1990), 'Perceived Informativeness of and Irritation with Local Advertising', *Journalism Quarterly*, 67, 35–9.

115 Edwards, S.M., Li, H. and Lee, J.H. (2002), 'Forced Exposure and Psychological Reactance: Antecedents and Consequences of the Perceived Intrusiveness of Pop-Up Ads', *Journal of Advertising*, 31(3), 83–95.

116 Aaker, D.A. and Bruzzone, D.E. (1985), 'Causes of Irritation in Advertising', *Journal of Marketing*, 49 (Spring), 47–57; De Pelsmacker, P. and Van den Bergh, J. (1998), 'Ad Content, Product Category, Campaign Weight and Irritation: A Study of 226 TV Commercials', *Journal of International Consumer Marketing*, 10(4), 5–27.

117 De Pelsmacker, P. and Van den Bergh, J. (1998), 'Ad Content, Product Category, Campaign Weight and Irritation: A Study of 226 TV Commercials', *Journal of International Consumer Marketing*, 10(4), 5–27.

118 Pechmann, C. and Stewart, D.W. (1990), *Advertising Repetition: A Critical Review of Wear-In and Wear-Out*, Working paper. Cambridge, MA: Marketing Science Institute.

119 Cox, D.S. and Cox, A.D. (1988), 'What Does Familiarity Breed? Complexity as a Moderator of Repetition Effects in Advertisement Evaluation', *Journal of Consumer Research*, 15, 111–16; Anand, P. and Sternthal, B. (1990), 'Ease of Message Processing as a Moderator of Repetition Effects in Advertising', *Journal of Marketing Research*, 27, 345–53; Schumann, D.W., Petty, R.E. and Clemons, D.S. (1990), 'Predicting the Effectiveness of Different Strategies of Advertising Variation: A Test of the Repetition-Variation Hypothesis', *Journal of Consumer Research*, 17, 192–202.

120 De Pelsmacker, P. and Van den Bergh, J. (1998), 'Ad Content, Product Category, Campaign Weight and Irritation: A Study of 226 TV Commercials', *Journal of International Consumer Marketing*, 10(4), 5–27.

121 Fennis, B.M. and Bakker, A.B. (2001), 'Stay Tuned – We Will Be Back after These Messages: Need to Evaluate Moderates the Transfer of Irritation in Advertising', *Journal of Advertising*, 15(3), 15–25.

122 De Pelsmacker, P. and Geuens, M. (1997), 'Affect Intensity and the General Attitude Towards Advertising', in De Pelsmacker, P. and Geuens, M. (eds), *The Changing World of Marketing and Corporate Communication, Proceedings of the Second International Conference on Marketing and Corporate Communication*. Antwerp: RUCA, 60–2.

123 Moore, D.L. and Hutchinson, J.W. (1983), 'The Effect of Ad Affection Advertising Effectiveness', *Advances in Consumer Research*, 10, 526–31.

124 Burke, M.C. and Edell, J.A. (1989), 'The Impact of Feelings on Ad-Based Affect and Cognition', *Journal of Marketing Research*, 26, 69–83; Stayman, D.M. and Aaker, D.A. (1988), 'Are All the Effects of Ad-Induced Feelings Mediated by Aad?', *Journal of Consumer Research*, 15, 368–73; Aaker, D.A. and Bruzzone, D.E. (1985), 'Causes of Irritation in Advertising', *Journal of Marketing*, 49

(Spring), 47–57; De Pelsmacker, P. and Van den Bergh, J. (1997), *Advertising Content and Brand Confusion*, Research report, Marketing Communication Research Centre. Ghent: De Vlerick School voor Management.

125 Fennis, B.M. and Bakker, A.B. (2001), 'Stay Tuned – We Will Be Back after These Messages: Need to Evaluate Moderates the Transfer of Irritation in Advertising', *Journal of Advertising*, 15(3), 15–25.

126 De Pelsmacker, P., Van den Bergh, J. and Anckaert, P. (1998), *Irritation, Product Type, Consumer Characteristics and Advertising Effectiveness*, Working paper, Marketing Communication Research Centre. Ghent: De Vlerick School voor Management.

127 Rossiter, J.R. and Percy, L. (2000), *Advertising and Promotion Management*, New York: McGraw-Hill.

128 Poiesz, T.B.C. and Verhallen, T.M.M. (1989), 'Brand Confusion in Advertising', *International Journal of Advertising*, 8, 231–44.

129 Poiesz, T.B.C. and Verhallen, T.M.M. (1989), 'Brand Confusion in Advertising', *International Journal of Advertising*, 8, 231–44.

130 Brengman, M., Geuens, M. and De Pelsmacker, P. (2001), 'The Impact of Consumer Characteristics and Campaign Related Factors on Brand Confusion in Print Advertising', *Journal of Marketing Communications*, 7, 231–43.

131 De Pelsmacker, P. and Van den Bergh, J. (1997), *Advertising Content and Brand Confusion*, Research report, Marketing Communication Research Centre. Ghent: De Vlerick School voor Management.

132 Poiesz, T.B.C. and Verhallen, T.M.M. (1989), 'Brand Confusion in Advertising', *International Journal of Advertising*, 8, 231–44.

133 Diamond, S.A. (1981), *Trademark Problems and How to Avoid Them*. Chicago: Crain Communication, Inc.

134 De Pelsmacker, P. and Van den Bergh, J. (1997), *Advertising Content and Brand Confusion*, Research report, Marketing Communication Research Centre. Ghent: De Vlerick School voor Management.

135 De Pelsmacker, P., Van den Bergh, J. and Anckaert, P. (1998), *Irritation, Product Type, Consumer Characteristics and Advertising Effectiveness*, Working paper, Marketing Communication Research Centre. Ghent: De Vlerick School voor Management.

136 De Pelsmacker, P. and Geuens, M. (1997), 'Emotional Appeals and Information Cues in Belgian Magazine Advertisements', *International Journal of Advertising*, 16(2), 123–47.

137 Poiesz, T.B.C. and Verhallen, T.M.M. (1989), 'Brand Confusion in Advertising', *International Journal of Advertising*, 8, 231–44.

138 Poiesz, T.B.C. and Verhallen, T.M.M. (1989), 'Brand Confusion in Advertising', *International Journal of Advertising*, 8, 231–44.

139 Brengman, M., Geuens, M. and De Pelsmacker, P. (2001), 'The Impact of Consumer Characteristics and Campaign Related Factors on Brand Confusion in Print Advertising', *Journal of Marketing Communications*, 7, 231–43.

140 Foxman, E.R. and Muehling, D.D. (1990), 'An Investigation of Factors Contributing to Consumer Brand Confusion', *Journal of Consumer Affairs*, 24(1), 170–89.

141 Brengman, M., Geuens, M. and De Pelsmacker, P. (2001), 'The Impact of Consumer Characteristics and Campaign Related Factors on Brand Confusion in Print Advertising', *Journal of Marketing Communications*, 7, 231–43.

CHAPTER 4
Target groups

CHAPTER OUTLINE

The segmenting-targeting-positioning framework

Market segmentation

Effective segmentation

Targeting strategies

Selecting target groups

Positioning strategies

CHAPTER OBJECTIVES

This chapter will help you to:

- Understand the process of segmenting, targeting and positioning
- Get an overview of the criteria for segmenting markets
- Understand the requirements for good segmentation
- Distinguish the strategies for targeting market segments
- Choose a positioning strategy

Introduction

The first step in the strategic marketing planning process is the study of market needs, a situation analysis of current and future market conditions. This can be done by using **SWOT analysis**, which consists of an internal analysis – strengths and weaknesses of the company or brand – and an external analysis – opportunities and threats in the marketplace. This analysis leads to opportunities for existing product lines in new or existing markets, or new product ideas for new or current markets. In most circumstances a market has different groups of customers or prospects with different needs and subject to different trends. Identifying these different groups and deciding at which group(s) to target the marketing and communications efforts is a major task of communications planning. Companies can define target markets in a number of ways, based on multiple criteria. Segmenting a market, deciding on target groups or segments to focus on and establishing a position to defend vis-à-vis these target groups are at the same time vital components of the strategic marketing plan and basic cornerstones of a communications strategy. Understanding buying motives and behaviour of target groups is an essential element of this groundwork and requires thorough preliminary analysis. The choice of well-defined target groups and positioning decisions should, later in the communications planning, be reflected in the selection of communications objectives, communications instruments, campaign execution and media planning.

The segmenting–targeting–positioning framework

Table 4.1 lists the various steps in the segmenting–targeting–positioning (STP) process. The STP exercise starts with a definition of potentially relevant factors on the basis of which a market can be segmented. **Market segmentation** should ideally lead to more homogeneous sub-groups in that the members of one group should react in the same way to marketing stimuli and differ in their reactions to these stimuli from the members of other segments. In other words, it is not sufficient for men and women to be physiologically different. If there is no systematic difference between the two groups in the way they react to marketing stimuli, there is no sound reason to distinguish between them. For example, the furniture market includes different segments such as home and business markets. These segments can be further divided: home markets include student home furniture, design furniture, classic furniture, etc.; business markets include, for instance, office furniture (for small/large companies), hotel furniture, etc.

In stage 2 of the STP process, segmentation variables can be combined to form segmentation profiles. In fact, by combining segmentation variables, multivariate segmentation takes place. Various analytical techniques, such as cluster analysis, conjoint analysis, multidimensional scaling and automatic interaction detection, are being used to identify segments on the basis of multiple variables.[1] Once segment profiles have been identified, their attractiveness can be assessed. Segment attractiveness will depend on the size and predicted evolution of sales, buying power and the amount of competition targeted at the same segment.

Table 4.1 Segmenting, targeting and positioning

1. Definition of segmentation criteria
2. Definition of segment profiles
3. Assessment of the attractiveness of segments
4. Selection of target groups
5. Definition of the desired unique position in the mind of targeted consumers

On the basis of this analysis of attractiveness, the marketer will select a number of target groups to focus on, based on their attractiveness and for which the company has relevant strengths. This is called **targeting**. All further communications objectives, strategies and tactics will be aimed at these specific groups. Hence, the promotional mix may differ depending on the different target markets a company is focusing on in its communications programme. For example, IKEA, the Swedish international 'takeaway' furniture distributor, could target the segment of young home users with a limited budget interested in designer furniture by offering a special designer furniture line. Or it could capitalise on the trend that teleworking and self-employment are increasing and develop a home office furniture line for this targeted segment.

Finally, the company has to define a unique and relevant position for its products in the mind of the target group. **Positioning** can be defined as the way a product is perceived by the target group on important attributes, the 'place in the mind' a product occupies relative to its competitors. Positioning is a core element of marketing strategy and hence of marketing communications. Indeed, marketing management can be defined as finding and sustaining a unique and defendable image or position for a product. Unlike imitating successful competitors, positioning attempts to claim exclusive 'ownership' of a benefit in the mind of the customer which differentiates it from the competition.[2] This position is the brand or product personality, which should always be claimed and supported in the communications strategy.[3] Several examples of successful positioning can be given. Mercedes stands for luxury, Volvo for safety, Miele (dishwashers, washing machines, etc.) for quality, Levi's for the original American jeans and Duracell batteries for power.

Market segmentation

Market segmentation is the process of dividing consumers into homogeneous groups, i.e. groups that share needs or react in a comparable way to marketing and communications efforts. Different variables or criteria can be used to segment a market. Table 4.2 presents a framework and some examples of variables used to segment consumer markets.[4] Objective segmentation variables are variables that can be measured objectively and straightforwardly. Inferred constructs have to be defined before people can be classified into groups. For instance, the construct 'lifestyle' has to be operationalised before any one consumer can be attributed to a lifestyle group.

General factors are segmentation variables that hold in all behavioural circumstances. A person is always male or female, no matter what buying situation he or she is in. On the basis of specific or behaviour-related variables, consumers can belong to different segments depending on the product class or buying situation concerned. For instance, a person can be a loyal buyer or a heavy user of chocolate or a chocolate brand, but an infrequent and brand-switching consumer of margarine.

Table 4.2 Consumer market segmentation variables

	Objective	Inferred (psychographic)
General	Geographic Demographic (income, gender, age, education, profession, life cycle)	Social class Personality Lifestyle
Specific (behavioural)	Occasion Loyalty status User status Usage rate	Benefit Buyer readiness

Markets can be divided into different **geographic segments** such as continents, climate, nations, regions or neighbourhoods. Consumer behaviour and buying patterns often denote cultural differences and therefore the place where consumers live may require other marketing mix approaches. For instance, Starbucks Corporation has faced some challenges when opening international franchises in several European countries that have strong traditions of coffee bars, such as Italy and Spain. Locals were not accustomed to Starbucks' core concept of take-away coffees. This segmentation method is often combined with other criteria. A marketing area is first defined geographically and subsequently other segments within this broad geographic area are identified.

Demographic segmentation divides the market on the basis of sex, age, family size, religion, birthplace, race, education or income. These segmentation variables are frequently used, not only because they correlate with other variables such as consumer needs, but also because they are less difficult to measure than others.

BUSINESS INSIGHT
Children have a strong impact on buying behaviour

A Belgian study found that families with children account for 46% of fast-moving consumer purchases, although they are only 37% of the population. Moreover, the more children in a family, the higher the ticket price per store visit. Young children under 12 influence not only the type of products bought, but also the brands chosen. They identify needs, they also provide information and advice, and they put pressure on parents ('pester power'). For instance, the penetration of new technologies such as flat-screen TVs is higher than average in families with young children. Due to the decreasing number of children, co-shopping occurs more frequently than before, leading to on average a more than 17% increase in shopping value. This is due to not only more different products bought, but also larger quantities per product type. Moreover, the impact of each child increases when there are fewer children in the family ('little-prince effect'). Families also tend to become more 'democratic': children are increasingly allowed to have a say in family decisions. Single or divorced parents tend to feel guilty and compensate for this by giving in to their children's requests. Families with young children also have a lower-than-average perceived strong loyalty, less than 20%, as opposed to up to 40% for families without children and retired persons. They also shop more in discount stores than other groups. Children predominantly form their preferences and attitudes about products and brands through TV advertising. In general, they are more sensitive to emotional messages than to rational ones. In families with children, in-store decision rates are 25% lower than in families without children. In other words, purchases are more often planned in advance at home, probably due to the impact of children on shopping intentions.[5]

BUSINESS INSIGHT
Axe introduces a fragrance for women

Since its introduction in 2002, Unilever's body spray brand Axe (Lynx in the UK) has been pitched squarely at young men, with commercials depicting women getting a whiff of Axe users and then aggressively pursuing them. In 2012, Axe introduced a fragrance for women. The new scent, Anarchy, is being marketed in different versions for women and men. The launch campaign included print and online ads and commercials on YouTube. A teaser commercial was scheduled for movie theatres. To start the campaign, Axe introduced a branded serialised graphic novel on YouTube and Facebook in partnership with the publisher Aspen Comics. New sequences were uploaded every few days. The plots were based partly on consumers' suggestions and votes, and some fans were even depicted in the comic. Previously, an Axe commercial was always about a guy spraying himself and a girl being attracted, and Axe facilitating the contact between both. Now, however, women also have something to spray on themselves, and consequently there is more of an equilibrium between the sexes. Of the 2.3 million 'likes' Axe has on Facebook, about a quarter are by women. Apparently Unilever has been hearing for some time that women have been asking for and looking for their very own scent of Axe. Axe has a 74% market share in the men's body spray category. While only about 17% of American men use body spray (65% use aftershave and 62% use cologne), it is most popular among men 18 to 24 years old, with 28% using it. As for women, 47% use body spray, second to body lotion with fragrance, which is used by 59%.

Unilever launched Axe Anarchy, the women's body spray, in a 'limited edition', with the possibility of being offered permanently based on sales. Anarchy will also be available as a deodorant, antiperspirant, shower gel and shampoo, but only for men.[6]

For instance, Diamond targets women in the UK by offering a cheaper car insurance because women are better drivers and female accidents imply less severe damage. Colgate produces strawberry-flavoured toothpaste for children. BMW launched the BMW 1 series for 'smaller' budgets.

Besides differences between younger and older consumers, one can also distinguish between generations or age groups born in a particular period. This makes their buying responses, needs and interests different from those of people of the same age, living in a different time period. Table 4.3 shows the characteristics of three generations, i.e. baby boomers, generation X and generation Y.

RESEARCH INSIGHT

Men might be from Mars, but women are definitely from Venus – influence of gender on effectiveness of probability markers in advertising

Two studies were conducted in which ads using different types of probability markers (hedge, pledge, no probability marker) were tested with a sample of men and women. In the first study a convenience sample of 638 Belgians was collected via an online survey: 53.1% of the respondents were female, and the average age was 27. In the second study the participants were 331 Belgian undergraduate students (51.4% were female).[7]

According to the selectivity model,[8] women tend to process information and form judgements comprehensively, taking into account all the available cues, assigning equal importance to information relevant to themselves and to others, and exhibiting great sensitivity to detail and all relevant information. Women encode a greater number of claims than men do and process each of the claims more extensively.[9] In other words, women could be considered as more systematic (central) processors. Men most often do not use comprehensive processing of all available information when forming judgements. They instead tend to make use of heuristic (peripheral) processing, relying on a highly available, salient single cue or sub-set of cues. Hence, the expectation is that the presence of probability markers (both hedges and pledges) in advertising copy will have a greater impact on brand attitude and purchase intention towards advertised products for men than for women.

Studies have shown that both genders are more easily persuaded when the message content is relevant to the opposite gender's social role than to their own. More specifically, Carli found that women who use powerless language in an attempt to persuade men are considered more likeable and can influence men better than women who use more powerful language.[10] Moreover, men are less likely than women to rely on the opinions of others in making a judgement,[11] and have been described as more risk-seeking and competitive than women.[12] Therefore it can be expected that men will show a higher preference for hedges and will dislike pledges the most.

Utilitarian consumption is less person-specific, enabling easier objective assessment of product/service quality and customer satisfaction. Using pledges in ads of utilitarian products/services, therefore, shows the advertisers' full confidence in the truthfulness of the claim.[13] A hedge in an ad for a utilitarian product/service, on the other hand, might signal that the advertiser does not stand behind the claim, weakening the claim itself and undermining the advertiser's credibility.[14] Women, especially, might favour pledges for utilitarian products, as they are generally risk-averse,[15] and pledges can serve as strong arguments, which are likely to influence judgements under central processing. Men, on the other hand, are usually described as competitive risk-takers who prefer to rely on their own judgements.[16] Hedges may be more effective targeted at men even for a utilitarian product/service ad, as hedges represent an opportunity to take a risk and men form their own evaluation. A pledge, on the other hand, can be considered as a challenge to their status/authority and an attempt, on the part of the advertiser, to control their opinions, which might result in a form of rebellion. It can therefore be expected that, for women, ads for hedonic products/services with hedges will result in the most positive brand attitude and purchase intention (compared with ads with pledges or probability markers), while for utilitarian products/services pledges will be most effective. For men, ads using hedges will result in the most positive brand attitude and purchase intention, compared with ads with pledges or no probability markers, while ads with pledges will be the least effective.

The results of the first study show that, as expected, the impact of probability markers in advertising copy is very significant for men, but not for women. Men have a pronounced preference for hedges over pledges and a significant preference for hedges over the no probability marker condition. Men are more strongly affected by the use of probability markers in advertising than women, and they show a significant preference for hedges. For women, the differences between the levels of brand attitude and purchase intention for the three manipulation conditions (no probability marker, hedge, pledge) are not significant. Women, in other words, are virtually unaffected by the presence or absence of a probability marker in advertising copy. In the second study for services, the results show that women are not particularly sensitive to probability markers in the case of hedonic buying motivation. Men, however, display a clear dislike of pledges, in both the cases of hedonic and utilitarian services. Men again display a strong preference for hedges and especially dislike pledges, while there is no difference for women.

In order to be able to deliver products and services that match the differing needs and wants of men and women, as well as to create promotional materials that will appeal to the targeted gender, marketers need to understand how gender differences influence information processing and the effectiveness of promotional claims. When targeting men, hedges are the best strategy and pledges especially must be avoided. As women do not seem to be influenced very much by these language tactics, hedges may be an effective strategy for marketers targeting a mixed gender audience. When catering to women specifically, the focus should be on other aspects than probability markers in the claims, as no benefit in terms of brand attitude or purchase intention can be gained by any strategy here.

Table 4.3 Baby boomers, generation X and generation Y

Present age	Generation name	Characteristics
40–60	Baby boomers	Luxury, high-quality products, not bargain hunters, less critical of marketing techniques and advertising
30–40	Generation X	High spending, materialistic, ambitious, need for individualism, critical of marketing techniques and advertising
15–30	Generation Y	High buying power, high expectations of services and relationships, marketing and technologically savvy, less brand loyal, viral marketing key

Source: Based on Herbig, P., Koehler, W. and Day, K. (1993), 'Marketing to the Baby Bust Generation', *Journal of Consumer Marketing*, 10(1), 4–9; www.petersheahan.com; and Krotz, J.L., 'Tough customers: how to reach Gen Y,' http://www.microsoft.com/smallbusiness/resources/marketing/market-research/tough-customers-how-to-reach-gen-y.aspx#ToughcustomershowtoreachGenY (accessed June 2009).

Baby boomers were born in the years immediately after the Second World War. North America and Europe in particular saw a huge boom in the number of births in these years. Today baby boomers are aged between 45 and 65 years and form a large and wealthy group of consumers. As a group they prefer quality products and tend not to look for bargains (unlike their parents), on average they have few children and more women go out to work.[17] This makes baby boomers an ideal market for luxury and high-quality products, as well as for products for working households: a smaller car meant as the second family car, easy-to-prepare meals, child minders, etc.

From 1965 to 1980 birth rates in the USA and Europe declined, due inter alia to effective contraception and an increased number of divorces; people born during this period are referred to as baby busters, generation X or X'ers.[18] Although this segment is smaller than the baby boomers', it is an interesting target market since almost 85% of busters over the age of 15 have a job, but do not seem to be particularly inclined to save much. Furthermore, they often get allowances from their parents, resulting in quite high spending per capita. Baby busters seem to have different characteristics from baby boomers at the same age. Firstly, they hold different values. Baby busters are more materialistic, ambitious and show a greater need for individualism, for keeping their own identity within the society. Secondly, baby busters have more marketing knowledge; they acknowledge the meaning of marketing and advertising. Thirdly, baby busters as compared with baby boomers are said to be more cynical and more critical of advertising. They reject any attempt to lump them together in a target segment.

BUSINESS INSIGHT
Long live time bandits!

In this day and age of new gadgets, clean and simple modern design, some people, including young ones, want to escape to the reliability of decent old products. 'Old' is in. The brochure of AS Adventure, a chain of outdoor stores, is full of high-tech gear, but has the look and feel of an old photo album, with sepia colours and ruffled photos with brown edges. J.K. Rowling's book *The Tales of Beedle the Bard* has a dowdy cover, as if the book has been lying around in a flea market for years. Also, the book that was published following the 40-year writing career of John Irving looks like it was found in a basement where it had lain for decades: old-fashioned typography, wrinkled paper and a dusty cover. Of course, these are digital technology products, but they illustrate that 'retro' and 'vintage' are in. Cookbooks and restaurants increasingly focus on grandmothers' menus and old vegetables like earth pear and horseradish. The Belgian supermarket Delhaize sells 'unprofessionally baked' cakes that look as if they were made at home. Good old Marseille soap is immensely popular. Estée Lauder's new Tuberose Gardenia perfume is based on the favourite flowers of grandma Lauder. Many children have never seen a conventional telephone, but that did not stop Fisher Price from launching its classical toy phone again, as well as its traditional school clock, with indicators and without batteries. 'Time' is the new currency, and there is a new generation of 'time bandits'.[19]

In many rich countries, the 1980s and 1990s were a period of rapidly falling birth rates. In Southern Europe and Japan, and less markedly in Northern and Eastern Europe, generation Y (also known as millennials or echo boomers) is dramatically smaller than any of its predecessors. In the Soviet Union during the 1980s, there was a 'baby boom echo' similar to that in the USA, and generation Y there is relatively large. In the USA more than 70 million of them comprise about a quarter of all Americans and the largest demographic cohort since the baby boomers.[20] In their book on *Connecting to the Net.Generation*, Junco and Mastrodicasa included research-based information about the personality profiles of generation Y. In their survey, they found that 97% of students owned a computer, 94% owned a mobile phone and 56% owned an MP3 player (iPod, Zune, Sansa, etc.).[21] This generation has never known a world without computers, e-mail or the Internet. Their priorities are simple: they want whatever the next new product or gadget is and they want it first. Millennials do not pay much attention to marketing although this generation is the most marketed to in history. The following companies have targeted them and interacted with them effectively: Apple, Converse, Facebook and Nintendo. They all personalised their products so that each millennial youngster could fit the product to their ideas, looks and independence. This generation is fully aware of all kinds of marketing. The trick is to approach millennials openly and creatively.[22] Lots of gen Y choices come from peer-to-peer recommendations, which explains why viral marketing is quite successful in this age group. Living in an age where information is everywhere and where everyone can reach them, millennials are very selective about who they listen to. Via their Facebook and Google+ accounts, they get their information from one another – and not from the media. The endorsement by their friends is what they care about. They do not get this peer-to-peer information through e-mails, they instantly text one another, using SMS, Facebook chat or instant messaging. E-mail is too slow and old fashioned for them. They watch each other on YouTube. And sometimes they do all three at the same time! Millennials multitask and they are good at it.[23]

RESEARCH INSIGHT
Children's reaction towards traditional and hybrid advertising

Children spend an increasing amount of time on media usage. A study conducted in Germany demonstrates that children between the age of 3 and 13 years spend on average over one hour a day watching television.[24] A European study showed that children between 6 and 14 years old spend on average 88 minutes per day surfing the Internet.[25] The impact of advertising on children and young teenagers has raised considerable concern among governmental institutions and professional organisations such as the American Psychological Association.[26] Recent studies have shown that advertising directed at children impacts on their brand preferences[27] and food choices.[28] Moreover, exposure to advertising messages might also encourage children to pester their parents to purchase the advertised product.[29] Children are now exposed to commercial messages through new online techniques and hybrid forms of advertising. One of the most frequently employed and most interactive techniques is the advergame, a custom-built online mini-game designed to promote a brand.[30]

An experiment with 125 children (11–14 years old) compared the effects of traditional TV advertising, a trailer promoting an advergame, and the advergame itself.[31] A large amount of research has investigated the role of 'advertising literacy' in determining children's responses to persuasive messages.[32] Researchers generally take a developmental psychological point of view, stating that children lack both cognitive and information processing skills to fully comprehend commercial messages, making them more susceptible to persuasive attempts.[33] Younger children are thought to be more influenced by advertising than older children, because children acquire advertising literacy over years. Moreover, past research has revealed that with increasing knowledge of advertising's intent comes an enhanced ability to resist or elaborate upon commercial messages.[34] The study also explored the role of 'persuasion knowledge' in processing these formats.

The experiment consisted of five different experimental treatments. The experimental manipulation consisted of exposure to different types of advertising techniques for Unilever's popsicle and ice cream brand Ola. The employed stimuli were all existing commercial materials for the Ola brand. Group 1 was exposed to a 30-second trailer in which a fictitious cartoon character encouraged the children to visit the website (www.olakids.be) and play an advergame. Group 2 was put in front of a computer to play the actual Ola advergame. The goal of the advergame was to slide down an icy slope and collect as many Ola popsicles as possible. It took children about two minutes to complete the game. Children in the third treatment were asked to play the advergame, and afterwards they were shown the trailer. In the fourth treatment, children were asked to watch the trailer and to play the advergame afterwards. Group 5 was shown a traditional TV ad for Ola. All 125 children were randomly assigned to one of the five treatments. The experiment was conducted using groups of four children. They were taken to a room where they were given the experimental treatment, depending on the group to which they were assigned. After the experimental treatment, every child was taken separately to a freezer, where they were allowed to pick one popsicle. They were taken there individually to avoid their choice being influenced by that of others. The freezer contained three brands of popsicles: a generic store brand (Carrefour), an 'IJsboerke' or an 'Ola'. All popsicles were rocket shaped. The child's preference was registered. Subsequently, the children were administered a survey.

A one-way analysis of variance (ANOVA) was conducted to test whether the different experimental treatments had an effect on children's ability to recall the advertised brand. The number of prompts needed before correct identification of the brand was used as a dependent measure for recall. The average number of prompts needed by children in the advergame condition was significantly higher than that of children in the traditional ad condition. Children who were exposed to the advergame needed significantly more help to recall the brand behind the persuasive message than children who got to see a traditional TV ad. Advergames engage children and induce feelings of telepresence, a sensation of being present in the gaming environment.[35] Since advergame playing is an enjoyable experience, a feeling of being present in the advergame can produce more positive evaluations of the brand and the game. The focus in the advergame is on actively engaging with the brand or the product, rather than on passive exposure to brand identifiers. This implies that gamers receive less explicit cues that could give away persuasive intentions or information about the brand, which might explain why explicit recall memory for Ola is significantly lower in the advergame condition.

It was also investigated whether persuasion knowledge moderated the effect of the experimental treatments on brand attitude. A 5 (experimental treatments) × 2 (persuasion knowledge, yes/no) full-factorial, one-way ANOVA was performed using the attitude towards Ola as the dependent variable. Children without persuasion knowledge develop a significantly more positive attitude towards the brand than children with persuasion knowledge. Within the group of children without persuasion knowledge, children that were exposed to the trailer and played the advergame afterwards developed a significantly more positive attitude towards Ola than children that were exposed to only the trailer and the traditional TV commercial. Children without persuasion knowledge developed a significantly more positive attitude towards the brand than their counterparts when they were shown a trailer followed by playing the advergame. These results are consistent with the literature on integrated marketing communications. Carefully designed interplay between different forms of marketing communications may lead to a seamless communication process which minimises consumer irritation and has beneficial effects on consumers' reactions towards the brand. People with persuasion knowledge are thought to be more resilient to such persuasive efforts; those who are less knowledgeable about advertisers' tactics are more susceptible to these techniques.

BUSINESS INSIGHT
Obama's campaign spoke to millennials . . . and they listened

In 2008, Obama approached American voters by consistently delivering a message of 'Change'. He did not *talk* to his audience but *interacted* with them. He spoke to the younger generations directly through his website my.barackobama.com (MYBO). By using the keyword 'my' at the beginning of his domain name, he brought it to a personal level. The site allows users to take control of their relationship with the Obama brand by customising and personalising the site when they log on. The site offers the use of tagging, discussion boards, photo uploads and other interactive Web 2.0 elements. Obama also hit the millennials' hearts by talking about ending the war in Iraq, about the environment, improving education and his philosophy that every person can make a difference. This allowed youngsters to feel independent in thinking and knowing that they affect the world and are not just another number. It became trendy to vote for Obama, because youngsters saw their favourite celebrities, music groups and peers supporting him. Barack Obama also did a great service in establishing the importance of voting among youngsters who felt that their vote would not count in the big picture. He was right! Youngsters played a huge role in clinching the presidency.

Learning from Obama's campaign

The millennial generation is attracted to something smart, fresh and different and has found these qualities in President Obama. His success is a result of both product and uniform branding. Obama showed he was consistent with his message. He was able to reach not only the millennials, but also the baby boomers who had a chance to reminisce about memories of the 1960s and what they wanted to change then. There are parallel issues to hand with the war, corruption and health care, and Obama addressed the baby boomers as much as the millennials. Even though they are opposed to marketing and advertising efforts, there are ways to get into contact with them. Cut the mass branding and start niche marketing, so they feel they are 'learning' about the next cool music device or clothing trend. Catch them on Facebook, not by advertising, but by starting a 'group' about your business or product and invite those who would be potential customers to join. Try appealing to college students by tailoring a line to the top colleges, as Victoria's Secret did with Pink: OnCampus (see www.vspink.com). If Barack Obama can inspire action and earn votes from historically inactive young voters together with the support of older generations, his brand strategy may turn out to be absolute and a great model for marketers to follow to reach millennials.[36]

In his new election campaign, Barack Obama is enlarging his presence on social media networks, to get fully into contact with 'young' Americans. He, or rather the Obama campaign staff, joined Instagram in January 2012 (Photo 4.1). By doing so, the 2012 campaign tried to prove it had not lost touch with the hip digital tools that kids are using today. In less than a day, and with just two uploads, Obama already had more than 15 000 followers.[37] By the end of June, after posting 72 photos, his fan club increased to 930 000 followers.[38]

In April 2012, Barack Obama also joined Pinterest, the wildly popular social network where users pin links to items they love or find inspirational on an online board. Some of his boards include Pet Lovers for Obama, Obama-inspired recipes, The First Family, ObamArt and Faces of Changed. More than 24 000 people follow his account.[39]

Photo 4.1 Obama wins the presidency
Source: Getty Images.

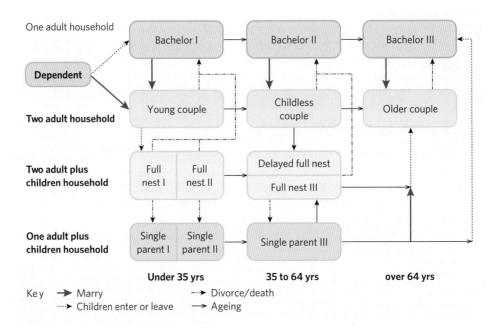

Figure 4.1 A model household life cycles

Source: Gilly, M. and Enis, B. (1982), 'Recycling the Family Life Cycle: A Proposal for Redefinition', in Mitchell, A. (ed.), *Advances in Consumer Research*, 9, Association for Consumer Research, Ann Arbor, MI, 271–6.

Consumer markets can also be segmented on the basis of household life-cycle criteria. This concept has its origin in sociology in the decade of the 1930s and has been applied in market research since the 1950s. It is founded on the fact that family changes (for instance, marriage, birth and emancipation of children, break-up of the marriage, etc.) affect both income and expenditure of households.[40] Consequently, each stage will imply different needs and therefore consumers can be segmented in this manner. Life-cycle segmentation and marketing is extremely popular in the financial sector where CRM software tools (customer relationship marketing; see Chapter 13) allow marketers to track changes in the life cycles of clients as input for a targeted marketing campaign.[41] Studies revealed that the importance attributed to financial choice criteria and financial services varies as consumers pass through the life-cycle stages.[42]

The conceptual framework of household life-cycle stages has been modernised a few times, the most recent consensus being found on the model of Gilly and Enis since it excluded only 0.5% of households.[43] Figure 4.1 illustrates this model.

BUSINESS INSIGHT
Cheerios targeting young mums

In 1941, General Mills was the first to introduce an oat-based ready-to-eat breakfast cereal, Cheerios. Since then, several fruit and chocolate varieties have supplemented the original. General Mills is also known for its long history of philanthropy, with its foundation having given more than $420 million to non-profit organisations since its founding. In November 2009, Cheerios ran a campaign on Facebook designed to strengthen its relationship with its key demographic of mothers with young kids, the generation Y mums. Facebook was seen as the best platform to start a conversation with this target group. The campaign wanted to encourage more people to connect to the Cheerios Facebook page. Completely in line with the General Mills' philanthropic tradition, Cheerios promised to donate a free book to First Book (books for children in need), for every new person who connected to the Cheerios Facebook page. Cheerios ran the campaign via Facebook's 'reach block', which guaranteed that Cheerios would reach its target audience over a 24-hour period. The company took advantage of Facebook's anonymised targeting to target women over 25 years old.

Several ads were developed: ads to communicate with the Facebook page to 'help donate a free book'; and ads to stress the healthful qualities (no artificial flavours or colours) of the cereal.

This campaign resulted in:

- an increase in Facebook connections from 8854 people on the day before the campaign, up to 133 129 after the first day of the campaign on the 'reach block';
- an engagement rate of 0.19% – the highest recorded by General Mills at that time;
- 84.5 million delivered impressions;
- more than 124 000 books donated to First Book.

Facebook has given the brand another way of staying in touch with its target group. Cheerios is convinced that it can deliver content and messages to its core target of generation Y mums, which they would not be able to deliver via traditional media. By partnering with its fans, the company is able to tap into the collective intelligence of thousands of mums to gather and share parenting ideas with the entire Cheerios community. The company believes that real people saying real things can trump traditional brand messages, especially within social platforms. Its ability to be a catalyst for creating this valuable and authentic content is important for Cheerios.[44] By June 2012, Cheerios had more than 780 000 fans on its Facebook page.

Source: Alamy Images: Michael Dwyer.

Segmenting markets using lifestyle or personality criteria is called **psychographic segmentation**. Psychographic research was developed when traditional demographic segmentation was shown to have strong limitations in predicting consumer behaviour. **Lifestyle segmentation** describes how people organise their lives and spend their time and money. These external characteristics (playing sports, going to the theatre or restaurant) are linked to a person's personality (e.g. a risk-averse person will not take up dangerous sports). Lifestyle measurement is based on the activities, interests and opinions (AIO) of consumers. AIO combine internal and external characteristics to map the lifestyle of a consumer. Activities include how people spend their money and time, e.g. work, leisure, product use, shopping behaviour, etc. Interests can be in fashion, housing, food, cars, culture, etc. Opinions are attitudes, preferences and ideas on general subjects such as politics or economics, on more specific subjects or on oneself and one's family.

RESEARCH INSIGHT
Value segmentation of young people in the Netherlands

In July 2008 InSites Consulting studied the lifestyle of the Dutch youth population (aged 14–24) for MTV Networks. The basis for this psychographic segmentation was Schwartz's theory of human values, and InSites measured the ten values (universalism, benevolence, conformity, tradition, security, power, achievement, hedonism, stimulation and self-direction) using a *K*-means clustering based on utilities scores for the different Schwartz value statements. Six psychographic clusters within this young population in the Netherlands were found:

- popu kids: 20% of the Dutch 14–24 year olds
- hedonists: 25%
- social explorers: 14%
- idealists: 6%
- conservatives: 17%
- wizz kids: 20%

Popu kids (20%)

Popu kids score high on achievement and stimulation. They feel it is important to be the best and attach great value to the brands of clothes they are wearing. They are quite self-confident and popular; 62% are male. Popu kids are interested in gaming, computers, mechanics and new technologies, fitness and football. They tend to drink a lot when going out. Important brand characteristics to them are: representing a high status; and an image of luxury and glamour.

Hedonists (25%)

Hedonists have high scores on the Schwartz values hedonism, stimulation and self-direction. They feel they have to live now and prefer to be out of the house as much as possible. They like nightlife and partying, hanging around and going to pubs. Online they look for new music, recommended by peer youngsters. Luxury, glamour and safety are brand attributes that hedonists do not like at all.

Social explorers (14%)

Social explorers have higher scores on values such as stimulation, self-direction and universalism. They also feel it is important to be the best but would like to make the world a better place and are open and tolerant to youngsters that are different. They love to meet lots of new people, like to play musical instruments or perform on stage; 62% are female. Social explorers are interested in cooking, music festivals (such as the Dutch festival Pinkpop), concerts, playing music, dancing, art and culture, adventurous travel and psychology. They love visiting friends or acquaintances. In brands they want to identify with, they tend to appreciate social awareness and corporate responsibility.

Idealists (6%)

Idealist youngsters have higher scores on universalism, benevolence and tradition. They like spirituality and playing musical instruments. They are interested in reading books, going to concerts, playing music, adventurous travel, history, philosophy, politics and graffiti. They identify with brands that give them a safe and secure feeling.

Conservatives (17%)

Conservative youngsters score higher on Schwartz's values of universalism, tradition, conformity and security. They like making music and identify with brands that are honest and give them a safe feeling.

Wizz kids (20%)

Wizz kids score high on power and achievement; 68% are male. They think it is important to be the best and the brands of their clothes are important to them. They love gaming and watching video clips online. They look for brands that deliver high standards and status to identify themselves with.[45]

Source: InSites Consulting 2008 lifestyle segmentation of Dutch youngsters for MTV Networks, Rotterdam, InSites Consulting (Van den Bergh, J. and Verhaeghe A. 2008).

When a company divides its market into segments referring to product or brand preferences, or involvement with categories, it adopts a **behavioural segmentation**. Consumers can be segmented on the basis of the occasion when they use a product or a brand. For instance, a brand of orange juice can be targeted at a segment of consumers drinking juice at breakfast, but there will also be a segment using orange juice in cocktails in the evening etc. Minute Maid found out that there was an opportunity for fruit juice at home during the evening.

The Coca-Cola Company launched Minute Maid Hot & Cold as a world premiere in Belgium. It is an apple juice with cinnamon that is positioned as a refreshing cold drink during the breakfast moment and as a relaxing hot drink in the evening (tea moment), a product that can be used in different ways for different occasions.

Markets can also be divided into segments on the basis of customer loyalty. Customers can be loyal to one brand, loyal to a set of brands or brand-switchers. Obviously, marketing communications efforts can be different when targeting these different groups. Brand-switchers are mainly influenced by material incentives. Sales promotions will therefore be an important tool to get them to buy a product. Brand-loyals, on the other hand, do not have to be convinced. Advertising to keep the brand top of mind and loyalty promotions will be the main communications instruments to be used with this group. Consumers that are loyal to a set of brands will have to be approached with a combination of communications tools. Advertising will keep the company's brand in their choice set, while in-store communications and sales promotions will make them choose the company's brand rather than competing brands.

Markets can also be segmented on the basis of the user status of customers. An individual can be a non-user, a potential user, a first-time user, a regular user or an ex-user. Non-users are consumers who will never buy a product. They should therefore be avoided in a marketing communications plan. Men, for example, will never buy sanitary towels for themselves. As a result, a communications plan should avoid talking to them as much as possible. Ex-users are more a target group for customer satisfaction research than for a marketing communications campaign. It will be very hard to regain a customer who has deliberately decided not to use the product anymore. Potential users need to be persuaded to try the product for the first time. Advertising, building awareness and attitude, trial promotions and in-store communications may convince them to have a go. First-time users should be converted into regular users. Advertising, building a favourable attitude and a preference for the brand, together with loyalty promotions, might do the job. Regular users should be confirmed in their favourable attitude and buying behaviour. They may be approached by means of advertising and loyalty promotions.

Markets can also be segmented on the basis of usage rate. Heavy users are of particular interest to a company because they make up the largest part of sales. Light users may be persuaded to buy and consume more of the product by means of special offers or 'basket-filling' promotions, increasing the number of items they buy.

Segmenting on the basis of benefits looked for by consumers can be done by researching all benefits applicable to a certain product category, e.g. a salty snack should be crunchy, taste good and not be expensive. For each of these benefits consumers preferring that benefit are identified and for each benefit products or brands offering that benefit are defined. This segmentation links psychographic, demographic and behavioural variables. A specific benefit for which a brand has a unique strength can be defined, and the communications effort can be targeted at the customer group preferring that particular benefit. As such, benefit segmentation is conceptually very close to positioning.

Finally, consumers can be divided into more homogeneous sub-groups on the basis of their buyer readiness. When a potential customer is unaware of a brand, awareness-building advertising and sponsorship will have to be used. For a group of customers already aware of the product, attitude-building campaigns are called for. People who are interested in and like the product should be persuaded to try it by means of sales promotions and in-store communications.

Requirements for effective segmentation

In stage 2 of the STP process, segmentation variables can be combined to form segmentation profiles. Segment profiles have to meet a number of requirements to be effective (Figure 4.2). Segments have to be measurable. It should be possible to gather information about segmentation criteria and about the size, composition and purchasing power of each segment. Segments have to be substantial enough to warrant separate and profitable marketing campaigns to be developed particularly for that segment. Segment profiles have to be attainable, i.e. accessible and actionable. The marketing manager must be able to identify the segment members and target the marketing action programme at them separately. Unless most members of the segment visit similar places, shop in similar supermarkets or read similar media, it will be difficult to reach them separately and develop specific stimuli for them. In other words, the chosen segments must be within reach of communications media and distribution channels. Finally, market segmentation should ideally lead to more homogeneous sub-groups in that the members of one group should react similarly to marketing stimuli and differ in their reactions to these stimuli from the members of other segments.

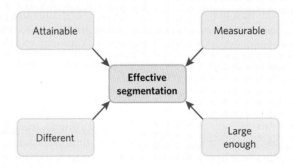

Figure 4.2 Requirements for effective segmentation

BUSINESS INSIGHT
Coca-Cola Zero aiming at men

In 2006, the Northern European market for carbonated soft drinks was in worrying decline, but the sub-sector of light soft drinks was still growing, especially within the cola category. Perceived as a feminine brand, Coca-Cola Light was experiencing fierce competition as men increasingly turned to competing brands with more masculine overtones. Coca-Cola needed to create a macho brand in order to maintain and grow its share of light colas and to avoid losing the young male sector. Coca-Cola Zero was the answer. The key concept was 'Life as it should be' – unlimited enjoyment with zero compromise and no negative consequences, aimed at 18–29 year old men concerned for their health, image, masculinity and waistlines. They dream of a better life – being richer, having hotter girlfriends and succeeding in fulfilling their childhood dreams.

Initially, the drink was marketed with a tagline of 'everybody chill' – a nice but vague emotional message. It did not work. Consumers were confused about what the brand stood for, what was meant by 'Zero'. The company came back to Coke Zero's intrinsic value with the message 'real Coke taste, zero calories'. Five years on, the marketing story remains the same. Coke Zero's packaging was initially white. But there was a problem as the colour connoted diet drinks, and among the coveted young male demographic, diet connoted 'female'. The company quickly borrowed the idea from its Australian division to have the packaging in black. Its packaging needed to evoke a subconscious masculinity: Black – good; white – bad. Within six months, the new marketing and packaging were in place, and the brand took off.[46]

Thanks to a communications strategy based on three key principles (to quickly generate attention, build awareness and encourage frequency of use), Coca-Cola Zero grew to double the target set for it in Germany and exceeded the target by 38% in Denmark, while unit sales in Germany and Denmark, and Coca-Cola share overall, grew significantly.[47] One year after the launch (July 2006) of 'Coca-Cola Zero' in the UK the sales of Coca-Cola's sugar-free cola were on the cusp of overtaking those of regular Coke for the first time ever, which, if achieved, would make the UK the first Coca-Cola market worldwide to achieve this landmark. Total sales for the first full 12 months of 'Coke Zero' reached 68 million litres, helping the company's sugar-free sales grow 4.4% year on year. Over 49% of Coke Zero's sales were new or additional purchases of the Coke brands, a testimony to the growing role of diet sparkling drinks in people's diets. Coca-Cola Zero was launched in the UK with a major, men-oriented marketing plan: 'Buy-A-Player' football promotion, the Wayne Rooney TV spot and iTunes promotion. A year later the campaign was extended with the 'Win a Real Saturday' promotion, providing a million tickets to watch English Football League and Scottish Premier League matches. The success of the Coke Zero launch has been widely recognised throughout the industry. Coca-Cola's biggest launch in over 20 years became the most successful food and beverage launch in recent history, and picked up the coveted 'Star Product of the Year Award' at the annual Gold Awards by leading industry magazine *The Grocer*.[48] In 2008, two years after its launch in the UK, Coca-Cola Zero was hailed as the biggest new product development launch in three years by AC Nielsen. Having grown by 49% since launch, the brand was at that time worth £60 million.[49] And the success continues. Coke Zero's sales increased in 2010 with 17 straight quarters of double-digit growth. It is sold in 130 countries, including big markets like Brazil and Mexico. It is surely the most successful new soft drink of the last decade, a billion-dollar brand mentioned in the same breath as Coca-Cola, Diet Coke, Sprite and Fanta. In the USA, its sales are about six times larger than Pepsi Max, introduced in 1993 in international markets and in the USA in 2007. In 2009, when the overall soda market shrank by about 2%, Coke Zero sales jumped 20% in the USA. Coke Zero was listed in 12th place in the carbonated soft drinks market in the USA.

Marketing can take a brand far, but the product itself has to deliver on the promise. Taste is often tricky with diet soft drinks, but in this case the taste was right. Fans say Coke Zero tastes much like Coca-Cola Classic, albeit perhaps a little sweeter. The future looks bright. Based on the expanding popularity of diet and 'light' drinks, Coke Zero is expecting further growth. In 1982, the year of the launch of Diet Coke, diet drinks made up only 1% of sales at the Coca-Cola Company. Today, that share has increased to 42% and the company expects it to hit 50% by 2020. On top of this, the brand's sales are especially strong among Hispanics and African-Americans, two growing demographics.[50]

After segmenting the market, opportunities for each segment should be singled out. The next stage in the process is targeting segments.[51] There are two decisions here: how many segments will the company target, and which segments are most attractive to that company?

Targeting strategies

Market concentration is used when the company chooses one segment and tries to be a market leader within that segment. Market differentiation involves directing the marketing effort to different segments with different marketing and communications strategies. Undifferentiated marketing is using the same strategies in all segments. There are five basic types of targeting strategies.

- **Concentration on one segment**. A company chooses one segment (one product for one market) and develops a marketing mix for that segment. This strategy has some positive aspects. The company will be able to build up expertise and enjoy learning effects. On the other hand, it will be dependent on a single segment (which could suddenly stop growing) and vulnerable to competitors. For instance, Jaguar was a company concentrating on one segment until it was acquired by Ford.

- **Selective specialisation**. A company chooses a number of segments that look attractive. There is no synergy between the segments, but every segment looks profitable. Activities in one segment can compensate for other, slower-growing segments. For instance, Richard Branson started with a music label (Virgin) which he sold while launching new services in different segments: travel (holidays, trains, flights and travel guides), entertainment (a new music label V2, Virgin Megastores, books, radio and Internet service provision), telecoms (mobile and fixed lines), lifestyle (soft drinks, wines, cosmetics and fitness clubs), energy (water, gas and electricity), finance (credit cards, loans, insurance, etc.) and motoring (retailing of cars and bikes).

- **Product specialisation**. A company concentrates on one product and sells it to different market segments. For instance, a company can sell microscopes to companies, hospitals, universities, schools, labs, etc.

- **Market specialisation**. A company concentrates on one market segment and sells different products to that group of customers, e.g. a company selling microscopes, oscilloscopes, etc. to hospitals.

- **Full market coverage**. A company tries to target all customer groups with all the products they need. For instance, General Motors makes cars (in different classes), four-wheel-drive cars, vans, agricultural machines, etc.

BUSINESS INSIGHT
'Wii Fit' looking for the non-typical purchasers of video games

'Wii Fit' is one of a series of games launched by Nintendo focusing on socialisation and activities designed to appeal to consumers who do not typically purchase video games. Looking to expand beyond family-oriented sports video games such as 'Wii Tennis' and 'Wii Golf', Nintendo launched in April–May 2008 (December 2007 in Japan) 'Wii Fit'. This game consists of a balance board and software containing 48 fitness training-related games and activities for workouts at home. 'Wii Fit' stresses four main categories of physical activity – balance, aerobics, yoga and strength training – and, while Nintendo executives are not billing the game as a replacement for exercise, they are positioning it as a pastime that promotes a healthy lifestyle. Users can track their weight and training progress and receive points for performing tasks using good form and increased intensity. The game allows users to measure their weight and body-mass index, and guides them through activities such as yoga poses and muscle-toning exercises.

According to the NPD Group, GfK Chart-Track and Enterbrain, the game has sold 1.433 million copies in the USA, 624 000 in the UK and 1.547 million in Japan, respectively, for a total of 3.604 million copies sold from January to July 2008. As of December 2008, 'Wii Fit' is the Wii's third best-selling game, with 14 million copies sold world-wide.[52] Research International looked at the introduction of 'Wii Fit' in the Netherlands, one year after the launch in April 2008. It found that awareness was very good: 8 out of 10 adults indicated that they knew, had seen or even read something about this game. The survey found that 1 out of 14 people used 'Wii Fit', a figure which it was felt could be higher. There are some interesting socio-demographical differences: Research International found the biggest usergroup among women, youngsters (under 35) and owners of game PCs. Men and people older than 35 years contained the biggest group of non-users.[53]

Selecting the right target groups

The second decision is to select the most attractive target groups. To evaluate segments, companies have to look at four elements: size and growth of segments; structural attractiveness of a segment; objectives and budgets of a company; and stability of market segments. Current turnover, potential growth and profitability of segments are the first important conditions a marketer should evaluate for each segment. For small companies, it could be wiser to target smaller or less attractive niche segments when competition is strong in the larger segments. Structural attractiveness can be analysed by using Porter's model. Current competitors, potential entrants, substitution products and the power of customers and suppliers influence the attractiveness of segments. Some attractive segments may not fit with the strategic objectives or long-term goals of a company.

BUSINESS INSIGHT
The repositioning of MySpace

In 2005, MySpace ruled the social media world and was bought by News Corp. for nearly $600 million. But MySpace tried to be everything to too many people, which is difficult with one single product, unless the product is a true commodity (e.g. milk) that nearly everyone wants. In the social media world, customers were not looking for the same product. They wanted a product that was customisable to their own styles. Facebook took advantage of this situation and surpassed MySpace in web traffic in 2007. MySpace was forced to reposition itself. It changed its marketing strategy – new website design, new content and more emphasis on entertainment (games, music, movies) – and adopted a more targeted approach. The company hoped to appeal to the under 35 market, and in particular the under 25s.

According to ComScore, more than 50% of the MySpace users are 25 and younger.[54] In June 2011, MySpace was sold for $35 million to the digital media company Specific Media and investors including Justin Timberlake. Their 'new' focus for MySpace was music.[55] In February 2012, MySpace added more than 1 million new users in one month, taking it to 25 million registered users. The website claimed that about 40 000 people a day had signed since it introduced apps with the social networks Twitter and Facebook. This represented a dramatic turnaround for MySpace.[56] Music had always been MySpace's biggest attraction, especially as a hub for independent artists looking to make their music available to the masses. CEO Tim Vanderhook put it as follows: 'the one million-plus new user accounts we've seen in the last 30 days validates our approach. MySpace is building meaningful social entertainment experience around content, where consumers can share and discover the music they love. Consumers are getting excited about MySpace again – a testament to a great music product.'[57] MySpace is claiming to offer the biggest free music collection online, ahead of popular streaming services such as Spotify and Deezer. MySpace has a music catalogue of more than 42 million songs; Spotify has about 15 million songs in the USA. As MySpace's Music Player (with Facebook connection) becomes more popular, users might not need to visit the site. This would enable MySpace to continue to grow even without having direct traffic statistics to show for it.[58] To help build growth and momentum, MySpace started a new partnership with Panasonic to create MySpace TV (movies, news, sports and reality programming). This app will offer music video and audio streaming alongside social features such as online chat and virtual viewing parties.[59]

While a million new members is an impressive milestone, MySpace is still on a downward trend overall. Once the biggest social medium, MySpace sunk to fourth place behind Facebook, LinkedIn and Twitter with more than 24 million visitors in December 2011. If MySpace can keep adding users, there might be life left yet in what was once the world's most popular social network.[60]

Positioning

Positioning a brand or product is differentiating it from competitors in the minds of consumers, e.g. Volvo is a safe car, Duracell batteries last longer, etc. Positioning means taking into account a complicated set of perceptions, feelings and impressions that a consumer has about a brand or product. Consumers will position brands in certain associative schemes even if a company is not actively promoting the competitive advantage of its products.

Positioning strategies

Six basic questions should be asked when creating a market position:[61]

1. What position, if any, do we already have in our customer's or prospect's mind?
2. What position do we want?
3. What companies must be outgunned if we are to establish that position?
4. Do we have enough marketing budget to occupy and hold that position?
5. Do we have the guts to stick with one consistent positioning strategy?
6. Does our creative approach match our positioning strategy?

A frequently used visual tool that helps companies position products and brands is 'mapping', based on axes representing the dimensions important to consumers. Every product or brand is given a score on both dimensions and the map shows which products or brands have the same characteristics. Figure 4.3 is a map of the salty snacks market. In the eyes of a consumer, there seems to be a big difference between peanuts and cocktail snack nuts. The latter are competing with fantasy snacks (snacks in different shapes). There is no product considered as natural and different. This is a hole in the market, but to be attractive it should be a profitable hole. There are a number of positioning strategies that a company can use.[62] They are summarised in Table 4.4.

Positioning by product attributes and benefits is based on a unique selling proposition which makes a company's brand or product special for the target market. For example, Vidal Sassoon Wash&Go was the first shampoo (introduced by Procter & Gamble) offering a unique combination of shampoo and conditioner. Positioning by price/quality means offering the same or better quality at a lower price than competitors. For instance, Virgin Coke offers a 'good' coke with a brand image comparable with Coca-Cola and Pepsi but at a lower price.

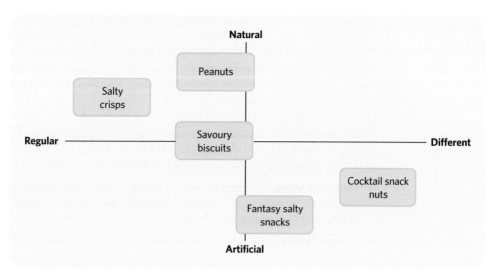

Figure 4.3 Mapping the salty snack market

Table 4.4 Positioning strategies

● Product attributes or benefits	● Product user
● Price/quality	● Competitor
● Use or application	● Cultural symbols
● Product class	

Positioning by use or application implies emphasising a specific use or application of the product. For instance, Kellogg's introduced cereals as a snack at hours other than breakfast by offering little variety packages that kids can take to school. Positioning by product class is an alternative to positioning against another brand, e.g. Eurostar offers a fast train connection as an alternative to airline connections. Positioning by product user is associating a product with a specific group of users, e.g. Aquarius, a thirst-quenching isotone drink for sporting men and women, is positioning a brand by a group of product users. In positioning by competitor, comparative advertising is often used. A well-known example is Avis, which uses the slogan 'we try harder' to position itself against the market leader in car and truck rental, Hertz. The drink 7 UP was positioned as 'the un-cola' and became number 3 in the soft drinks market. Cultural symbols refer to brand personalities or branding devices such as Tony the Tiger (Kellogg's Frosties), Mr Clean, Captain Iglo, Bibendum (Michelin). These symbols are a visual way of successfully differentiating from competitors. The brand personality or cultural symbol often visualises the key benefit of a product. For instance, Mr Clean is a powerful, clean symbol. Tony the Tiger gives power and strength.

A company may possibly detect different competitive edges, in which case it will have to choose one or more competitive advantages for its positioning strategy. A company can focus on one single advantage for a target group. This exclusive **unique selling proposition (USP)** will be easier to remember by the target group, especially in low-involvement buying situations. Other companies will stress more than one competitive advantage. This is necessary when two or more competitors claim to be the best in the same attributes. Volvo, for example, claims to be both safe and durable.

Not all differences with competitors are meaningful for an effective differentiation. Every difference could mean an increase in costs to a company, therefore the way a company differentiates its products and brands should be well considered. The chosen USP(s) should be important to the target group, clearly different from what a competitor is offering, superior, easy to communicate, difficult to imitate or copy, affordable for the target group of consumers and profitable for the company.

The more claims a company makes about its brands, the greater the risk of disbelief. Moreover, the different product benefits should be compatible in a consumer's mind: a superstrong detergent that also claims to be mild for the hands will not have any credibility.

There are indeed three possible positioning mistakes a company or brand can make:

- **Underpositioning**. A company fails to make a clear differentiation with competitors, e.g. Korean car brands such as Kia or Hyundai: how do they position themselves against Japanese or European cars?

- **Overpositioning**. Extreme positioning on one benefit will reduce the number of interested consumers, e.g. if IKEA only claimed low prices and not quality (Möbelfakta guarantee, for example), it would deter people looking for a durable dining room suite.

- **Confusing positioning**. Inconsistent communications or an inconsistent choice of distribution channels would give a customer a confused image of a company or brand. For example, bath towels claiming exclusive quality but also sold in hypermarkets will have difficulty keeping their positioning.

Developing a positioning strategy

There are seven consecutive steps in the development of a positioning strategy (Table 4.5). Firstly, the company has to identify its major competitors. This competition analysis should go further than the brands in exactly the same product category, but should also include generic competition, i.e. products in different product categories that nevertheless satisfy the same need. For instance, a gift box of chocolates (e.g. Ferrero) is competing not only with other chocolate gift boxes, but also with wine, champagne and flowers, which people take when visiting friends or relations. All possible competitors and their effects and evolutions on consumer target group behaviour should be taken into account. Secondly, the consumers' perception of the products and brands of competitors should be assessed. Questions such as which attributes or benefits are important in this market segment and how a competitor's product or brand is evaluated on these criteria are important.

Table 4.5 Stages in the development of a positioning strategy

- Identification of competitors
- Assessment of the consumers' perception of competitors
- Determination of positions of competitors
- Analysis of consumers' preferences
- The positioning decision
- Implementation of the positioning
- Monitoring the position

RESEARCH INSIGHT
Developing different types of anticipated experience positioning for electric cars

One of the options to counter the trend of deploying natural resources and polluting the air is the partial or complete shift to electric vehicles. Car manufacturers have started to develop and launch electric cars. They face the challenge of developing and positioning a new product type that is responsive to consumer needs. In this context, product design and advertising are boundary spanning functions between companies and consumers. Product categories and brands are often categorised as either functional (e.g. lawnmowers) or symbolic (e.g. cars).[63] A functional product possesses mainly product-related or concrete functional associations[64] and is bought primarily to satisfy utilitarian needs since they emphasise physical product features, performance and benefits.[65] Products or brands with a symbolic positioning internally generate needs for self-enhancement, role position, group membership, or ego-identification and usually entail non-product-related or abstract, image-based associations.[66] Symbolic motivations are more important determinants of car use than instrumental motivations. This enables car manufacturers to differentiate their products beyond differences in concrete functional needs. Brand experience is one of the important cornerstones of symbolic brand identity. Brakus *et al.* conceptualise brand experience as subjective consumer responses that are evoked by specific brand-related experiential attributes (sensory, behavioural and intellectual).[67]

A conjoint measurement study explored how to evoke different types of anticipated experiences for designing and advertising electric cars.[68] Firstly, brainstorming sessions were organised in six groups of between 6 and 10 participants (all masters students) to identify electric car features that would be capable of evoking three different types of anticipated experiences, i.e. sensory, behavioural and intellectual. Only those ideas that were deemed to be both original and workable in the near future were considered. A number of the most often elicited characteristics were chosen that could be used to design and position an electric car as sensory, behavioural or intellectual. These characteristics served as input for the conjoint analyses.

The purpose of these conjoint analyses was to identify a relatively limited number of combinations of electric car characteristics that would evoke a relatively exclusive sensory, behavioural or intellectual anticipated experience. Three conjoint designs were set up, one for each experience type. In each of these designs, four two-level attributes were defined. For each analysis, an orthogonal conjoint design was generated in which eight car types were defined as combinations of the two levels of each of the four attributes. For each of the conjoint measurements, a sample of 100 individuals, representative of the Flemish (Belgium) population in terms of gender, age and level of education, was selected by a professional marketing research agency. They received an online questionnaire. Firstly they were asked to read a general description of a person who was going to buy an electric car. They were then exposed to the eight car-type descriptions. These eight descriptions were randomised across respondents to avoid order effects. Respondents were asked to indicate their anticipated experiences. One item was selected to represent each of the three experience types. Consequently, in each of the three conjoint analyses, the respondents were asked to score each car type on a five-point Likert scale (completely disagree to completely agree) on the following items: 'This car makes a strong impression on my senses' (sensory); 'This car incites me to action' (behavioural); 'This car makes me think and incites me to solve problems' (intellectual). Finally, respondents were asked to indicate their gender, age and level of education.

Two car descriptions were identified that were capable of evoking relatively exclusively a sensory and an intellectual anticipated experience. No car could be identified that evokes an exclusively behavioural anticipated experience. These characteristics could thus be used to develop experientially different electric car propositions in advertising. However, this can only be effectuated for the sensory and intellectual car type, but not for the behavioural positioning. The two cars have the following characteristics.

Sensory

- The electric engine of this car makes no sound. Silence, or the music from the high-quality sound system, can be experienced optimally.

- The electric car is designed with elements that are specifically developed for the car, such as hard carbon materials outside, soft tanned leather for the seats, and hardened plant fibre inside.
- The electric car makes a technically advanced and dynamic impression because of the fluent lines, the large glass surfaces, the LED headlights, and the remarkable radiator grill that does not serve to cool the engine but behind which a blue light is installed.
- The electric car is equipped with the latest communications technology. For instance, with your smart phone you can ask it to turn on the heating or defrost the windows in the morning. When you drive home in the evening, you can program your oven or TV.

Intellectual

- The electric car allows you to drive into the city centre and park for free. This will no longer be possible with a car with a combustion engine.
- The electric car has an accounting system. Via your smart phone you can look up the total cost of your car during the last month.
- The electric car drives silently. Therefore you do not cause any noise pollution.
- The electric car has a clearly visible eco-label with information about its environmental friendliness, so that other people can easily see that you have chosen an environmentally-friendly way of driving.

Determining the positions of competitors' brands and products with respect to each of the relevant attributes is the third step in a positioning development. Consumer research through in-depth interviews, focus groups or full quantitative assessment should be used in this stage. Often, this analysis leads to a 'map' of consumers' perceptions about the relative position of each brand, as illustrated in Figure 4.3. It is not just the relative position of each brand that is important. Each of the targeted segments may have different buying motives or needs and will find other attributes important. Therefore, relative preferences of target groups towards the competing brands have to be studied.

After the first four stages of what is essentially market and consumer research, the company has to decide which position it is going to defend. Ideally, the company will select a position on the basis of one or more attributes that are important in the mind of a consumer and for which the brand is at least as strong as its major competitors. As a positioning decision should be a brand's direction for a number of years, a marketer should consider whether the positioning is appropriate and attainable. Positioning should be based on important attributes, not on fads, and on attributes for which the company can hope to defend and maintain its relative strength and reputation. Once a position is chosen, a company has to implement it by supportive marketing and communications activities. All communications instruments, in synergy with all other marketing tools, will have to reflect the selected positioning strategy. The last step in the positioning process is the monitoring stage. The image of the brand and its competitors on important attributes will have to be tracked on a continuous basis to reveal changes in consumer perceptions and in the competitors' positions.

As a result of this tracking analysis, a company may have to alter the position of its brands to keep up with the changing consumer or competitive landscape. There are a number of ways to change a positioning strategy or to reposition a brand:[69]

- *A company can introduce a new brand.* For instance, after major price cuts in its PC branch IBM introduced a new brand 'Ambra' to be competitive in a new context of consumers expecting cheap computers for daily use. Procter & Gamble reintroduced its old Bonux brand as a cheaper laundry powder to counter the competition of own-label brands.
- *A company can change an existing brand.* Compaq used a different strategy to cope with the changing computer trends. Compaq lowered the prices of its existing brand and made basic versions of its computers.

- *Changing beliefs with regard to own-brand benefits.* Japanese car brands such as Honda and Toyota changed their image of cheap, small and poor-quality cars to an excellent price/quality appreciation.

- *Companies may also attempt to change beliefs with regard to the benefits of competing brands.* The Body Shop created a less environmentally-friendly and animal-friendly image about the cosmetic products of competitors.

- *The importance of attributes may be changed.* Volvo succeeded in increasing the importance of safety as a car attribute.

- *New attributes can be added to the 'perceptual map' of consumers.* Procter & Gamble introduced the Vizirette to measure out the amount of detergents used in washing machines by explaining to the public that it would improve washing results.

BUSINESS INSIGHT
The Cadbury Snack brand repositioned

Since the 1950s, Cadbury Snack was positioned as one of the leading confectionery brands. However, over the years Cadbury saw a decline in its consumer loyalty. Research revealed that consumers perceived the Snack brand as being for an 'older/established customer segment'. Cadbury wanted the Snack appeal to a younger target market (ages 25–35). Therefore, Cadbury refreshed Snack by updating the look of its packaging, displays and marketing communications to give it a more cheerful and lively appearance, and by incorporating a communications campaign that depicted the product being enjoyed in a work environment. The repositioning proved to be successful, as the company increased its customer loyalty rating by 5%. It is important to set out realistic goals and steps for what a company is trying to achieve with its new positioning strategy. If Cadbury Snack had launched an athletic food bar instead of repositioning its original product's brand, its existing and potential customers might have become confused about the link to the other Cadbury products, which are seen as a sweet treat. This could have had a serious impact not only on Cadbury Snack but also on other Cadbury products.[70]

The latter four repositioning strategies are based on the components of the Fishbein model, discussed earlier. Defending a brand position or image will often be one of the major objectives of a communications campaign. Marketing communications objectives are further explored in the next chapter.

BUSINESS INSIGHT
Lingerie brand Playtex rebrand targets over 50s

In 2011, Playtex ran a £1 million campaign in the UK to reposition Playtex as the underwear brand for women over 50. The 'Feeling better than ever' campaign was run both on the Web and in print advertising and it included British celebrities. The campaign was targeted at women using messages about being 'young at heart' and 'coping with a changing body shape'. Playtex was founded in 1932 and its roots are in latex. Playtex became a dominant brand of girdles. For decades, it was one of the most popular brands of bras. Playtex was 'Cross your heart' and 'It lifts and separates'. It extended its brand into areas such as baby goods and tampons. In today's world of Victoria's Secret and Agent Provocateur, it is hard to remember that Playtex pushed the limits. But it was Playtex that, as the first major brand, used actual women (and not models) in bra advertising, and was the first brand to advertise a tampon on TV. The aim of the new UK campaign was to reposition Playtex as the lingerie label for British women in their 50s, which is an admirably tight target, considering that so many brands go for too wide demographic targets and, consequently, fall short. In line with the new positioning, Playtex has moved away from using a 20-something model, and is now using a 42 year old mother of three, who embodies the values of the brand to appeal to women who are young at heart but coping with their changing body shape. While Playtex is still the brand of the Playtex18 Hour® Bra and Playtex Cross Your Heart® Bra, it is also the brand of the Playtex Diaper Genie and Playtex® Sport® Tampons. So the biggest challenge facing Playtex is the fragmentation of the brand itself.[71,72]

Source: Rex Features: Crollalanza.

Summary

The segmenting–targeting–positioning process is one of the core elements of the strategic marketing plan. Market segmentation is the process of dividing consumers into homogeneous segment profiles. This can be done on the basis of one characteristic of potential consumers, or multiple characteristics can be combined. Segmentation criteria can be behavioural (such as buying occasion, loyalty status, usage rate, buyer readiness or benefit sought) or general (such as demographics and psychographics – lifestyle, personality, etc.). Market segments have to be measurable, substantial, attainable, different and large enough. The next stage in the process is to target one or more of these customer groups. Marketing communications can concentrate on one segment, specialise selectively, specialise in specific markets or products, or fully cover the market. Marketers have to define a unique position for their products in the mind of the consumer, based on product attributes or benefits, price/quality, use or application, product class, product users, competitors or cultural symbols. Developing, monitoring and adapting an appropriate position for a brand, a product or a company is a crucial prerequisite for effective marketing communications.

REVIEW QUESTIONS

1. What are the stages in the segmenting–targeting–positioning process, and what is the relevance of this process for marketing communications?
2. On the basis of what criteria can markets be segmented? How can market segmentation influence the communications mix?
3. What are segment profiles, and what are the requirements for effective segmentation?
4. Discuss the most important targeting strategies and the selection of target groups.
5. What positioning strategies can a company develop, and what are the consequences for communications strategies?
6. What are the stages in the development of a positioning strategy?
7. How can a product be repositioned?

Further reading

Brennan, B. (2009), *Why She Buys: The New Strategy for Reaching the World's Most Powerful Consumers*. New York: Crown Business.

Dibb, S. and Simkin, L. (2007), *The Market Segmentation Workbook: Making it happen*. London: Routledge.

Trout, J. (2008), *Differentiate or Die: Survival in Our Era of Killer Competition*, 2nd edition. New York: Wiley.

Tungate, M. (2008), *Branded Male: Marketing to Men*. London: Kogan Page.

Van den Bergh, J. and Behrer, M. (2013), *How Cool Brands Stay Hot: Branding to Generation Y*, 2nd edition. London: Kogan Page.

Weinstein, A. (2004), *Handbook of Market Segmentation*. London: Haworth Press.

CASE 4:
The 'Ex-smokers are Unstoppable' campaign across 27 European Union countries

Background

Every year, 695 000 Europeans die because of smoking. Smoking continues to be the largest single cause of preventable death and disease in the European Union (EU). Research shows that, on average, 21% of European smokers have tried to quit at least once in the past year. However, research also indicates that they are not always successful.

Anti-tobacco campaigns are not new but until recently they focused only on how bad smoking is and how it can negatively impact on health and lifestyles. The European Commission has been funding campaigns against tobacco since 2002. The first campaign, 'Feel free to say no', ran from 2002 to 2004. The second, 'Help: for a life without tobacco', ran from 2005 to 2010 and focused on smoking prevention, smoking cessation and passive smoking, targeting, in particular, young Europeans between 15 and 25 years old.

The latest is the 'Ex-smokers are Unstoppable' campaign. It was launched on 16 June 2011 and will run until the end of 2013 in all EU countries. It shifts the focus from the dangers of smoking to the benefits of giving up.

For the first time, the message is a positive one in that it aims to support a long-term motivation to stay away from tobacco. The focus is on the positive aspects of the new life which opens up to ex-smokers. The campaign celebrates ex-smokers and portrays them as inspiring role models to encourage other smokers to quit. The large number of smokers who want to quit no longer need convincing about the need to stop. The challenge is to find the right motivation to get them to act on their desire to give up smoking.

In addition to the motivational message, free practical help and guidelines on how to stop are provided through iCoach. Created with input from leading scientists, psychologists and communications experts, the iCoach online tool guides smokers through a five-stage process that offers motivation, advice and tips and sends daily help by e-mail so that they stay on course.

Objectives

The overall objective of the campaign is to help smokers get rid of their addiction and lead happier and healthier lives. The campaign is built around four elements:

1. **Appeal**. It must be appealing and perceived by the audience to be different to other campaigns.

2. **Recommendation**. As word of mouth and advice from a friend can be very persuasive, it is essential that the audience pick up the message and talk about it (conversations and recommendations).

3. **Reflection**. The campaign needs to make people think about their own behaviour (consider quitting); it must have a direct effect on their attitudes.

4. **Quitting**. The ultimate goal is that people quit smoking with the help of iCoach. The European Commission set a target of helping 111 851 smokers to quit smoking (i.e. iCoach registrations).

Communications strategy

The campaign is aimed at smokers, and the target group is 25–34 year olds. Research shows that younger people are more likely to smoke and tend to be less susceptible to scare tactics; many of the negative effects of smoking, like chronic diseases or cancer, do not present themselves in the young, who often believe these problems do not concern them.

The new and positive campaign message has been communicated in print, audio-visual media (TV and seeding) and online (display ads, banners, search engine, social media), as well as at national and international events. A variety of motivational messages have enabled the use of different triggers in different contexts. All channels aim to generate traffic to the official website of the campaign, where visitors are immediately directed to the iCoach programme to turn intention into behaviour.

As the campaign has progressed, interesting and inspiring material has come to light: stories from real ex-smokers, with their dreams and ambitions and what they have achieved since giving up. Facebook pages provide a virtual place to share these stories and comment on them.

In the first phase (June 2011), the campaign was launched with print and bannering as these channels proved the most manageable budget-wise and provided full European coverage.

Metro (or newspapers with a similar profile) became the print partner, as this free newspaper is handed out on a daily basis in urban areas. Cover wraps and multiple executions highlighted the advantages of quitting and, crucially, encouraged the press to dedicate influential column inches to the campaign.

Facebook was a central platform for all campaign activity with 29 national pages. In August 2011, Facebook fans were recruited for a photo shoot organised by the world renowned photographer Rankin to identify national ambassadors willing to share their ex-smokers' stories with the rest of the world. The call for stories was shared virally and seeded via anti-smoking, health and sports bloggers. The personal stories were used in the autumn phase of the campaign and

the winners became the ambassadors of the campaign. From mid-September until mid-October, print and online/digital media were the key media used – cover wraps, print ads, Facebook ads, online performance bannering, homepage takeovers and searches.

In addition, two TV ads demonstrated ex-smokers' achievements and were featured on pan-regional TV channels, Eurosport and Euronews. They were also seeded online with Go Viral and EBuzzing to extend the reach and enlarge the potential for discussion. Once again, all media were directed to the website where visitors could immediately register on iCoach.

EX-SMOKERS LOOK BETTER

Out with the grey skin and yellow stains on your fingers and in with the whiter teeth and shinier hair! Quitting smoking is simply the most effective beauty treatment on earth.

EX-SMOKERS TRAVEL MORE

When you stop smoking you start saving lots of money. If you smoke a pack a day, and each pack costs €8, you could save around €2,920 a year. That could buy you a lovely holiday, including palm trees, tropical fruit cocktails and plenty of unforgettable experiences. And the following year you will save the same amount again, and the year after that, and so on until the day you die. That means lots of holidays – especially since non-smokers live longer, too.

EX-SMOKERS HAVE MORE MONEY

A pack of 20 cigarettes costs about €8. That's not cheap, but the average European can afford it. Now let's say you smoke a pack a day. That's €56 a week, which still doesn't hurt your wallet too badly. Now let's calculate what that comes to per year: 365 x 8 = €2,920. Wow – that's more than the average net monthly wage in the European Union. So if you quit smoking you gain an extra month's salary, every year, starting now.

EX-SMOKERS ARE LESS NERVOUS

Oddly enough, smokers often light up when they are feeling nervous, which doesn't make much sense because nicotine works as a stimulant. It helps release adrenaline into your blood which makes you even more nervous. Besides that, living with an addiction is hardly ever relaxing. So wind down and put out that cigarette!

EX-SMOKERS ARE MORE CONFIDENT

Quitting is anything but easy. So ex-smokers are usually proud of themselves – and rightly so. It's a big achievement so why not feel good about yourself? By quitting you have shown that you are everything but a quitter. Your friends and family will be proud, too. And, by the way, you'll smell better and look better, which is another boost for your confidence.

EX-SMOKERS SMELL BETTER

When you stop smoking you stop smelling like a cigarette or an ashtray. And that's a great improvement. For a smoker, smelling like a cigarette or an ashtray isn't a big problem. Their houses smell like that and so do their clothes, so for them it is a comfortably familiar smell. Even your kids smell like cigarettes when you smoke indoors. But to the 71% of Europeans who don't smoke, smelling like a cigarette simply means you stink!

EX-SMOKERS ARE HEALTHIER

Old news, agreed. But it's no secret either that each year 650,000 Europeans die of smoking-related diseases. And only a small number of them actually grows old first. The health benefits of those who quit smoking include increased lung capacity, greater stamina, and fewer respiratory infections. Those who quit smoking also decrease the risk of cancer, strokes, and cardio-vascular diseases.

EX-SMOKERS HAVE MORE FREEDOM

It's a free world – nobody is forcing you to quit. But think about it: what else makes you bother complete strangers, frantically search for a light, slip out of restaurants between every course, become nervous on long flights, or ties you to a hospital bed for a very long time? So why not make your escape while you can?

EX-SMOKERS SLEEP BETTER

When you are young, smoking doesn't keep you awake at night. But things change when you get older – your impaired breathing makes you feel more tired in the morning, while your evening cigarettes create too much adrenaline which means it takes you longer to fall asleep.

BECOME AN EX-SMOKER BECOME UNSTOPPABLE

If you can beat your cigarette habit, you can do almost anything. Ex-smokers are healthier, feel younger and have more confidence. They look better, smell better, have more money and a more positive outlook. Basically, ex-smokers are unstoppable!

With help from our free health-coaching platform iCoach, you can become an ex-smoker, too. More than 30% who start the programme quit smoking.

Go to www.exsmokers.eu and become unstoppable.

EX. SMOKERS ARE UNSTOPPABLE

BECOME UNSTOPPABLE ON EXSMOKERS.EU

An initiative of the European Commission

Source: http://www.exsmokers.eu/uk-en/downloads.

Source: http://www.runwithjess.com/2011/09/ex-smokers-are-unstoppable.html.

The total budget was split into three categories: print (49%), TV (17%) and digital (34%); 19.4 million 25–34 year old smokers and 347.3 million adults were reached across the EU's 27 countries.

Results

To assess the effectiveness of the campaign, two sources of information have been taken into consideration. Firstly, statistics on website visits and subscriptions to iCoach were collected. Secondly, the campaign was post-tested in all 27 EU Member States.

Objective 1: appreciation of the new approach

Post-test results (Figure 4.4) show that smokers who have seen the campaign on TV, on banners or in print have indicated that they are really interested in the initiative, want to find out more and have got some new and positive motivation from it. TV advertising has performed exceptionally well. The majority of the public see a breath of fresh air in this campaign, and smokers in particular identify new elements. More than 50% of the smokers who have seen the campaign acknowledge that it is telling them new things about giving up smoking. The large majority (67%) of the sample are convinced that this new approach will persuade more people to stop, while an even larger group (80%) think that this campaign is doing a better job than previous efforts.

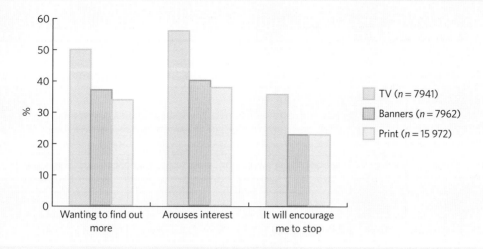

Figure 4.4 Percentage of smokers agreeing and totally agreeing with the statements after seeing a TV ad, a banner or a print ad
Source: GFK significant, November 2011 – Base: smokers.

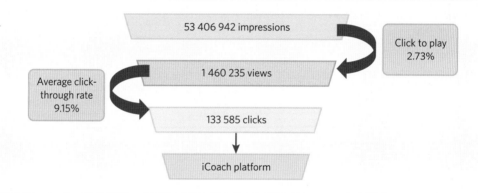

Figure 4.5 Viral reach and click-through rate
Source: GoViral, November 2011.

Objective 2: conversation and sharing potential

The post-test indicates positive results with both smokers and non-smokers, as 44% and 36% respectively say that they talked about the campaign. Moreover, 97% of all conversations about the campaign have been positive. On average, 18% of the smokers who have seen the campaign have recommended it to someone else.

Objective 3: effect on attitude and intention to stop

Having seen this campaign, an average of 28% of smokers are considering quitting smoking. TV and print have proved to be the most effective media in this respect. An average of 20% of the smokers claimed that they visited the website after seeing the campaign, which indicates that they actively searched for information.

The two TV ads led to an average click-through rate online of 9.15% compared with a GoViral benchmark of 2% to 3% (Figure 4.5). The TV commercials encouraged people to find out more on the website.

Objective 4: iCoach registrations

In the period from 15 June to 31 October 2011, more than 1 million unique visitors visited the website (www.stop smokingcoach.eu). There were 359 545 visits to the registration page, resulting in a total of 145 491 registrations on iCoach, which means that 40% of the visitors actually registered on iCoach. This is 30% above the target that was set by the European Commission. In June 2012, there were already 212 000 registered users on iCoach, with the campaign proving most effective in the target 25–34 age group (Figure 4.6).

Every time a new campaign wave has been launched it has boosted the registrations on iCoach (Figure 4.7). →

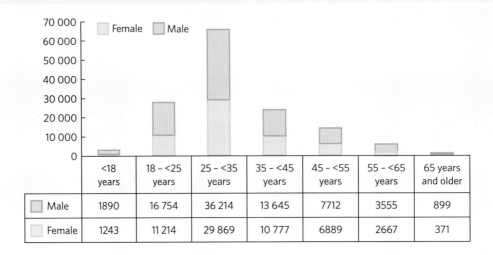

	<18 years	18 – <25 years	25 – <35 years	35 – <45 years	45 – <55 years	55 – <65 years	65 years and older
Male	1890	16 754	36 214	13 645	7712	3555	899
Female	1243	11 214	29 869	10 777	6889	2667	371

Figure 4.6 iCoach registrations, by gender and age
Source: Brand New Day, November 2011.

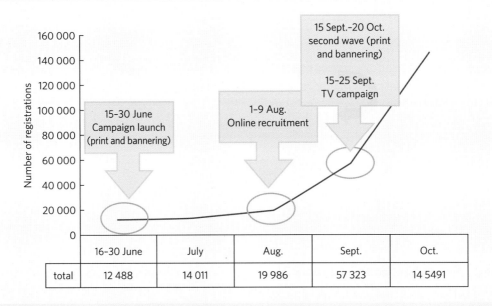

	16–30 June	July	Aug.	Sept.	Oct.
total	12 488	14 011	19 986	57 323	14 5491

Figure 4.7 Cumulated number of registrations on iCoach during first campaign year
Source: Brand New Day, November 2011.

Conclusion

Post-tests and registration results demonstrate that the positive campaign on quitting smoking is being well received and is proving successful.

The results indicate that people recognise it as a break from the traditional 'quit smoking' communications.

The core target group is showing an increased interest in giving up smoking. This has been turned into reality through registrations on iCoach.

QUESTIONS

1. To attain (reach) goals of marketing communications, a good target group definition is essential. Describe the core target group for the 'Ex-smokers are Unstoppable' campaign and why it was chosen. Was it a good decision to select that particular age group?

2. Suppose you are responsible for this campaign in your country. What will your off and online communications plan look like? Which channels will you use and why?

3. The total budget for this campaign was split as follows: print (49%), TV (17%) and digital (34%). Based on the results, was this a good decision? Would you do it differently? Why/why not?

4. The approach of the 'Ex-Smokers are Unstoppable' campaign has proven successful. Explain.

5. What could be a good follow-up to this campaign in the future?

Sources: Isabel Raes prepared this case study based on the following sources: Information received from Despina Spanou, Principal Advisor for Communication and Stakeholders, Health & Consumers at the European Commission; Yves Van Landeghem, Strategy Director, Saatchi & Saatchi Brussels, 27 June 2012, Euro-Effie case 2012; http://europa.eu/rapid/pressReleasesAction.do?reference=MEMO/11/405&formal=HTML&aged=0&language=en.

References

1 Malhotra, N. (2008), *Marketing Research: An Applied Orientation*. Upper Saddle River, NJ: Pearson Education.

2 Ries, A. and Trout, J. (2001), *Positioning: The Battle for Your Mind*, 2nd edition. New York: McGraw-Hill.

3 Bovée, C.L., Thill, J.V., Dovel, G.P. and Wood, M.B. (1995), *Advertising Excellence*. Englewood Cliffs, NJ: McGraw-Hill.

4 Dibb, S. and Simkin, L. (2007), *The Market Segmentation Workbook: Making it happen*. London: Routledge; Cathelat, B. (1993), *Socio-Styles: The New Lifestyles Classification System for Identifying and Targeting Consumers and Markets*. London: Kogan Page.

5 *IP Backstage*, 26 October 2008, 4–9.

6 http://www.nytimes.com/2012/01/09/business/media/axe-adds-fragrance-for-women-to-its-lineup.html (accessed 20 September 2012).

7 Banks, I.B., De Pelsmacker, P. and Dens, N. (2012), 'Men Might Be from Mars, but Women Are Definitely from Venus – Influence of Gender on Effectiveness of Probability Markers in Advertising', *Proceedings of the 2012 AMA Conference, Tampa, FL*.

8 Meyers-Levy, J. and Sternthal, B. (1991), 'Gender Differences in the Use of Message Cues and Judgments', *Journal of Marketing*, 28 (February), 84–96.

9 Darley, W.K. and Smith, R.E. (1995), 'Gender Differences in Information Processing Strategies: An Empirical Test of the Selectivity Model in Advertising Response', *Journal of Advertising*, 24(1), 41–56.

10 Carli, L. (1990), 'Gender, Language, and Influence', *Journal of Personality and Social Psychology*, 59(5), 941–51.

11 Meyers-Levy, J. (1989), 'Gender Differences in Information Processing: A Selectivity Interpretation', in Cafferate, P. and Tybout, A.M. (eds), *Cognitive and Affective Responses to Advertising*. Lexington, MA: Lexington.

12 Areni, C.S. and Kiecker, P. (1993), 'Gender Differences in Competitiveness and Risk Aversion: Theoretical Foundations and Some Preliminary Findings', in *Gender and Consumer Behavior Volume 2*. Duluth, MN: Association for Consumer Research, 30–43; Tannen, D. (1991), *You Just Don't Understand: Women and Men in Conversation*. New York: Ballantine.

13 Areni, C.S. (2002), 'The Proposition-Probability Model of Argument Structure and Message Acceptance', *Journal of Consumer Research*, 29(2), 168–87.

14 Berney-Reddish, I.A. and Areni, C.S. (2005), 'Effects of Probability Markers on Advertising Claim Acceptance', *Journal of Marketing Communications*, 11(1), 41–54.

15 Areni, C.S. and Kiecker, P. (1993), 'Gender Differences in Competitiveness and Risk Aversion: Theoretical Foundations and Some Preliminary Findings', in *Gender and Consumer Behavior Volume 2*. Duluth, MN: Association for Consumer Research, 30–43.

16 Meyers-Levy, J. (1989), 'Gender Differences in Information Processing: A Selectivity Interpretation', in Cafferate, P. and Tybout, A.M. (eds), *Cognitive and Affective Responses to Advertising*. Lexington, MA: Lexington.

17 Peter, J.P. and Olson, J.C. (1993), *Consumer Behavior and Marketing Strategy*. Burr Ridge, IL: Irwin.

18 Herbig, P., Koehler, W. and Day, K. (1993), 'Marketing to the Baby Bust Generation', *Journal of Consumer Marketing*, 10(1), 4–9.

19 *De Morgen*, 27 December 2008.

20 www.wikipedia.com, Generation Y.

21 Junco, R. and Mastrodicasa, J.M. (2007), *Connecting to the Net.Generation: What Higher Education Professionals Need to Know About Today's Students*. Washington, DC: NASPA.

22 Novak, R. (2009), 'Marketing to Millennials: A Lesson Learned from the Obama Campaign', *The Daily Anchor*, 19 January, http://www.thedailyanchor.com/2009/01/19/marketing-to-millennials-a-lesson-learned-from-barack-obama/ (accessed June 2009).

23 Fields, B. 'Marketing to Gen Y: What You Can't Afford Not to Know', http://www.startupnation.com/articles/9011/1/marketing-GenY.htm (accessed June 2009).

24 Feierabend, S. and Chan-Olmsted, S. (2008), 'Was Kinder sehen', *Media Perspektiven, 2008*(4), 190–204.

25 Livingstone, S., Haddon, L., Görzig, A. and Olafsson, K. (2011), *EU Kids Online II*. London: EU Kids Online.

26 Kunkel, D., Wilcox, B.L., Joanne, C., Edward, P., Linn, S. and Dowrick, P. (2004), *Report of The American Psychological Association Task Force on Advertising and Children*. Washington, DC: American Psychological Association.

27 Buijzen, M. and Valkenburg, P. (2000), 'The Impact of Television Advertising on Children's Christmas Wishes', *Journal of Broadcasting & Electronic Media*, 44(3), 456–70.

28 Ferguson, C.J., Muñoz, M.E. and Medrano, M.R. (2011), 'Advertising Influences on Young Children's Food Choices and Parental Influence', *Journal of Pediatrics*, 160(3), 452–5.

29 McDermott, L., O'Sullivan, T., Stead, M. and Hastings, G. (2006), 'International Food Advertising, Pester Power and its Effects', *International Journal of Advertising*, 25(4), 513–40.

30 Mallinckrodt, V. and Mazerski, D. (2007), 'The Effects of Playing an Advergame on Young Children's Perceptions, Preferences and Requests', *Journal of Advertising*, 36(2), 87–100; Moore, E.S. and Rideout, V.J. (2007), 'The Online Marketing of Food to Children: Is it Just Fun and Games?', *Journal of Public Policy & Marketing*, 26(2), 202–20.

31 Verhellen, Y., Oates, C., De Pelsmacker, P. and Dens, N. (2012), 'Does Persuasion Knowledge Moderate Children's Reactions towards Traditional versus Hybrid Advertising?', *Proceedings of the 2012 Icoria Conference, Stockholm*, CD-ROM.

32 Eagle, L. (2007), 'Commercial Media Literacy: What Does it Do, to Whom – and Does it Matter?', *Journal of Advertising*, 36(2), 101–10; Livingstone, S. and Helsper, E.J. (2006), 'Does Advertising Literacy Mediate the Effects of Advertising on Children? A Critical Examination of Two Linked Research Literatures in Relation to Obesity and Food Choice', *Journal of Communication*, 56, 560–84; Oates, C., Blades, M. and Gunter, B. (2001), 'Children and Television Advertising: When Do They Understand Persuasive Intent?', *Journal of Consumer Behaviour*, 1(3), 238–45; Roozendaal, E., Buijzen, M. and Valkenburg, P. (2008), 'Reclamewijsheid in Ontwikkeling: Een vergelijking van de cognitieve reclamevaardigheden van kinderen en volwassenen', *Tijdschrift voor Communicatiewetenschap*, 36(4), 270–83.

33 Eagle, L. (2007), 'Commercial Media Literacy: What Does it Do, to Whom – and Does it Matter?', *Journal of Advertising*, 36(2), 101–10; Kunkel, D., Wilcox, B.L., Joanne, C., Edward, P., Linn, S. and Dowrick, P. (2004), *Report of The American Psychological Association Task Force on Advertising and Children*. Washington, DC: American Psychological Association.

34 Friestad, M. and Wright, P. (1994), 'The Persuasion Know-ledge Model: How People Cope With Persuasion Attempts', *Journal of Consumer Research*, 21(1), 1–31.

35 Grigorovici, D.M. and Constantin, C.D. (2004), 'Experiencing Interactive Advertising beyond Rich Media: Impacts of Ad Type and Presence on Brand Effectiveness in 3D Gaming Immersive Virtual Environments', *Journal of Interactive Advertising*, 5(1), 22–36; Nelson, M.R., Yaros, R.A. and Keum, H. (2006), 'Examining the Influence of Telepresence on Spectator and Player Processing of Real and Fictitious Brands in a Computer Game', *Journal of Advertising*, 35(4), 87–99.

36 Novack, R. (2009), 'Marketing to Millenials: A lesson learned from the Obama Campaign', 19 January via www.thedailyanchor.com.

37 http://mashable.com/2012/01/04/barack-obama-joins-instagram/ (accessed 20 September 2012).

38 http://web.stagram.com/n/barackobama/ (accessed 20 September 2012).

39 http://www.nydailynews.com/news/politics/president-obama-joins-pinterest-article-1.1051750 (accessed 20 September 2012).

40 Redondo-Bellon, I., Royo-vela, M. and Aldas-Manzano, J. (2001), 'A Family Life Cycle Model Adapted to the Spanish Environment', *European Journal of Marketing*, 35(5/6) 612–38.

41 Dumont, E. (2001), 'Is Life Cycle Marketing Outdated?', *Bank Marketing* (April), 12–13.

42 Javalgi, R.J. and Dion, P. (1999), 'A Life Cycle Segmentation Approach to Marketing Financial Products and Services', *The Services Industries Journal*, 19 (July), 74–96.

43 Gilly, M. and Enis, B. (1982), 'Recycling the Family Life Cycle: A Proposal for Redefinition', in Mitchell, A. (ed.), *Advances in Consumer Research*, 9. Ann Arbor, MI: Association for Consumer Research 271–6.

44 http://www.scribd.com/doc/97390183/Cheerios-Facebook-Ad-Case-Study#download (accessed 20 September 2012).

45 Van den Bergh, J. and Verhaeghe, A. (2008), *InSites Consulting 2008 lifestyle segmentation of Dutch youngsters for MTV networks*. Rotterdam: InSites Consulting.

46 http://www.thestar.com/business/article/862906--coke-zero-becomes-a-hero-for-coca-cola-co (accessed 20 September 2012).

47 www.adforum.com, Euro Effies 2008.

48 '"Coke Zero" Anniversary Sees Sugar-Free Sales on Brink of Overtaking Original Coke', http://presscentre.coca-cola.co.uk/viewnews/coke_zero_anniversary, 27 July 2007 (accessed June 2009).

49 '"Coca-Cola Zero" "Launch" A taste of life as it should be! Campaign', http://www.cokecce.co.uk/media-centre/news-and-press-releases/2008/coke-zero-campaign.aspx (accessed June 2009).

50 http://www.thestar.com/business/article/862906--coke-zero-becomes-a-hero-for-coca-cola-co (accessed 20 September 2012).

51 Kotler, P. and Keller, K.L. (2006), *Marketing Management*. Englewood Cliffs, NJ: Prentice Hall.

52 'Financial Results Briefing for the Six-Month Period Ended December 2008', http://www.nintendo.co.jp/ir/pdf/2009/090130e.pdf#page=6 (accessed June 2009).

53 www.marketingonline.nl.

54 http://www.knowthis.com/blog/postings/to-regain-importance-myspace-tries-a-repositioning-strategy/ (accessed 20 September 2012).

55 http://www.guardian.co.uk/technology/2012/feb/14/myspace-one-million-users (accessed 20 September 2012).

56 http://www.guardian.co.uk/technology/2012/feb/14/myspace-one-million-users (accessed 20 September 2012).

57 http://www.seo-micrositez.com/blog/post-name/tim-vanderhook/ (accessed 20 September 2012).

58 http://www.guardian.co.uk/technology/2012/feb/14/myspace-one-million-users (accessed 20 September 2012).

59 http://www.seo-micrositez.com/blog/post-name/tim-vanderhook/ (accessed 20 September 2012).

60 http://www.pcworld.com/article/249849/myspace_the_next_hot_social_network.html (accessed 20 September 2012).

61 Ries, A. and Trout, J. (2001), *Positioning: The Battle for Your Mind*, 2nd edition. New York: McGraw-Hill.

62 Aaker, D.A., Batra, R. and Myers, J.G. (1992), *Advertising Management.* Englewood Cliffs, NJ: Prentice Hall.

63 de Ruyter, K. and Wetzels, M. (2000), 'The Role of Corporate Image and Extension Similarity in Service Brand Extensions', *Journal of Economic Psychology*, 21(6), 639–59; Park, C.W. and Young, S. (1986), 'Consumer Response to Television Commercials: The Impact of Involvement and Background Music on Brand Attitude Formation, *Journal of Marketing Research*, 23(1), 11–24.

64 de Ruyter, K. and Wetzels, M. (2000). 'The Role of Corporate Image and Extension Similarity in Service Brand Extensions', *Journal of Economic Psychology*, 21(6), 639–59; Park, C.W., Jaworski, B.J. and MacInnis, D.J. (1986), 'Strategic Brand Concept-image Management', *Journal of Marketing*, 50(4), 135–45.

65 Bhat, S. and Reddy, S.K. (2001), 'The Impact of Parent Brand Attribute Associations and Affect on Brand Extension Evaluation', *Journal of Business Research*, 53(3), 111–22.

66 de Ruyter, K. and Wetzels, M. (2000), 'The Role of Corporate Image and Extension Similarity in Service Brand Extensions', *Journal of Economic Psychology*, 21(6), 639–59; Bhat, S. and Reddy, S.K. (2001), 'The Impact of Parent Brand Attribute Associations and Affect on Brand Extension Evaluation, *Journal of Business Research*, 53(3), 111–22; Dijk, M. and Yarime, M. (2010), 'The Emergence of Hybrid-electric Cars: Innovation Path Creation through Coevolution of Supply and Demand', *Technological Forecasting & Social Change*, 77, 1371–90.

67 Brakus J.J., Schmitt, B.H. and Zarantonello; L. (2009), 'Brand Experience: What Is it? How Is it Measured? Does it Affect Loyalty?', *Journal of Marketing*, 73(3), 52–68.

68 Moons, I. and De Pelsmacker, P. (2012), 'Developing Different Types of Anticipated Experience Positioning for Electric Cars', *Proceedings of the 2012 Icoria Conference, Stockholm*, CD-ROM.

69 Leeflang, P.S.H. (1990), *Probleemgebied marketing* (*Problem Field Marketing*). Houten: StenfertKroese.

70 http://www.bandagroup.com/ideas/advisor-2007-spring.html (accessed 20 September 2012).

71 http://www.brandchannel.com/home/post/2011/03/25/Playtex-Looks-to-Lift-and-Separate-Branding.aspx (accessed 20 September 2012).

72 http://www.lingerieinsight.com/article-525-playtex-woos-ignored-50-something-british-women/ (accessed 20 September 2012).

CHAPTER 5
Objectives

CHAPTER OUTLINE

A hierarchy of marketing communications objectives

Stages in the product life cycle and marketing communications objectives

Consumer choice situation and communications objectives

CHAPTER OBJECTIVES

This chapter will help you to:

- Get an overview of the various goals and objectives of marketing communications campaigns
- Understand the relation between stages in the product life cycle (PLC) and communications objectives
- Understand how the consumer choice situation affects communications objectives

Introduction

Once the target group of the marketing communications plan is well defined, it is crucial to the planning process to set the main communications objectives. These goals will determine the choice of the right communications and media mix and will consequently influence message and strategy development, budgeting and effectiveness research issues. Communications goals will always have to fit in with the marketing objectives such as market share, estimated return figures or market penetration (the number of people or percentage of the target group buying the product) goals. These marketing objectives, in turn, are formulated to contribute to the overall company goals, such as making profits, providing earnings for shareholders, etc. Formulating marketing communications objectives is also important in judging the effectiveness of a campaign. The question of whether an advertising campaign, promotional action or whatever other communications plan has been 'good' or 'effective' depends on the goals that were defined for that specific campaign. It is therefore impossible to judge campaigns or individual communications executions without a thorough knowledge of the objectives. Different categories and types of objectives can be distinguished. Furthermore, the product life cycle stage and the consumer's choice situation will also influence the marketing communications objectives.

Marketing communications objectives

Marketing communications objectives can be broadly divided into three categories: **reach goals**, **process goals** and **effectiveness goals** (Figure 5.1). The reach goal of communicating is to reach the target groups in an effective and efficient way. For this purpose a good segmentation and audience definition are needed, as well as insights into the media behaviour of the desired segments. Part of this problem was discussed earlier on target groups; the detailed considerations of media planning will be the subject of a later chapter (Chapter 8). Process goals are conditions which should be established before any communications can be effective. All communications should capture the attention of the target group, then appeal or be appreciated, and last but not least be processed (and remembered). The third type of communications goals are the effectiveness goals. They arc, of course, the most important ones, since reach goals only assure sufficient exposure, and process goals only ensure enough processing of the message to make the effectiveness goals possible.

Evidently, long-term sales and market share growth are the ultimate objectives of most marketing communications campaigns. However, sales are influenced by other marketing mix instruments, such as product quality, design, benefits, packaging, distribution and pricing strategies, as well as the market evolution, technology and innovations, and of course competitive

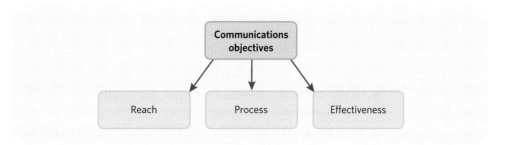

Figure 5.1 Categories of communications objectives

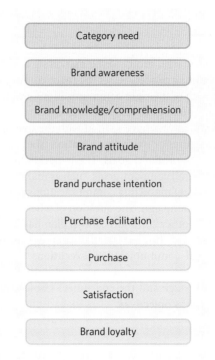

Figure 5.2 Communications objectives: the DAGMAR model

Source: Colley, R.H. (1961), *Defining Advertising Goals for Measured Advertising Results.* New York: Association of National Advertisers.

action. Since the DAGMAR[1] (Defining Advertising Goals for Measured Advertising Results) model was published in 1961 by Russell Colley, communications goals have emphasised the current stage of the buyer or potential buyer in the purchase process rather than just immediate sales effects. This insight also helped marketers to use measurable goals since communications effects on sales were all but impossible to isolate due to interaction effects with other marketing mix variables.[2] The communications effects or goals that are distinguished in the DAGMAR model are shown in Figure 5.2.

The **DAGMAR model** is essentially a hierarchy-of-effects model, similar to those discussed earlier. It is frequently used as a framework to define communications goals. To get a person or organisation to buy a product that was not bought before, or to increase the frequency or quantity of repeat buying, a consumer will normally go through the phases shown in Figure 5.2.

According to the DAGMAR model, during the communications process nine effects can be established. When a marketer is defining his or her communications strategies, he or she will have to select the most appropriate communications effect or goals from the list above. Every promotional campaign should be organised with one of these communications objectives in mind. The choice of the right goals depends on the problems that have arisen in the preliminary situation analysis of the market, brand positions, competition, opportunities and threats. In that sense, communications objectives are only an intermediary way to reach marketing goals of a higher order, such as sales volumes, market share, distribution penetration, etc.

A good set of communications goals should have a number of characteristics. It should:[3]

- fit in with the overall company and marketing goals;
- be relevant to the identified problems and specific to cope with threats or to build on opportunities in the market;
- be targeted at different target audiences, which implies that different target groups (such as countries, socio-demographic groups, heavy and light users) could need different communications objectives;

- be quantified in order to be measurable, which allows a precise evaluation of the campaign results to be made;
- be comprehensive and motivating to all involved persons but at the same time be realistic and achievable;
- be timed to enable specific scheduling of the campaign as well as planning the evaluation of results;
- be translated into sub-goals when necessary.

The communications objectives are guidelines for everyone who is involved in campaign development and realisation: marketers, advertising agencies, PR officials and sales promotion agencies, media planners and buyers, and researchers. They are also fundamental to campaign strategy: all phases of the marketing communications plan, such as creative, media and budgeting decisions, should be built on the goals.

As communications objectives are also the criteria against which a campaign's success (or failure) is evaluated, it is important that they are well defined and quantified. Only when goals are measurable are they a management tool enabling returns to be gauged against investments.

Developing category wants

The first basic condition to be fulfilled by a brand is that it should fit within category needs and wants. If buyers cannot perceive the communicated product or brand as an appropriate answer to their needs and demands, they will not be motivated to buy it. Category wants or needs can be defined as the existence of one or more of these buying motives and the perception of the product category as a good means of meeting these motives (Photo 5.1). Of course, although category need is always necessary before other brand-related objectives work, it is clear that in most cases, i.e. when promotional actions and communications are targeted at category users, it can be considered as already present and thus can be ignored. Indeed, it can be assumed that category wants are already well developed in product categories such as food, detergents, insurance and cars. However, in product categories that are infrequently purchased or infrequently used, such as painkillers, communicating category needs to remind buyers of their present but forgotten need may be useful.

Using category need as a primary communications objective is a must for innovations. Consumers should first understand which need is satisfied by an innovation and the difference between the 'new category' and known categories should be stressed. When Sony invented the CD player, the first thing to communicate, before building awareness for the Sony brand, was the difference in sound quality compared with the cassette player. Creating category awareness is also an appropriate goal when non-category users are addressed. For instance, when telecom operators of cellular phone networks communicate to a group of non-owners of a cellular phone they will stress the need for mobile telephones. When they address owners they will stress other benefits such as special rates and special services. Sometimes a manufacturer repositions a product or service to meet other usage occasions or methods of use. Kellogg's introduced Variety cereals in small packages to broaden its cereal market from the breakfast moment to other snack and school moments and consequently takes part in the between-meals market. Category wants can be omitted, refreshed or actively used in market communications in the different situations described above. The following communications goals are not on a category level but focus on the brand.[4]

Brand awareness: recognition and recall

Brand awareness is the association of some physical characteristics such as a brand name, logo, package, style, etc., with a category need. There are two ways brand awareness can be defined. For example, if people think of a soft drink, they may spontaneously think of Coca-Cola,

Photo 5.1 Coral Black Velvet: innovations call for communicating category needs

Source: Reproduced with permission of Gesamtverband Werbeagenturen GWA and J. Walter Thompson.

Fanta or Lipton Ice Tea. This is their top-of-mind brand awareness. In an unaided context, people may recall several brands spontaneously. This is brand recall or unaided spontaneous awareness. But it is also possible that people recognise a brand by its package, colour, logo, etc. This is brand recognition or aided awareness. Aided brand awareness is of course less difficult to achieve. Less repetition and thus smaller investments are needed to establish it than brand name recall. Research has shown that the correlation between recall and recognition is on average 50%. Buyers will be better able to recognise brands than to recall brand names spontaneously.[5] On the other hand, brand recall is not a guarantee that the buyer will recognise the brand in a shop.

The question of which awareness goal should be aspired to by a marketer depends on the situational circumstances in which the product or brand is bought. If the purchase decision is made at another time and location than the point of sales (at the office, at home), or when a buyer has to ask explicitly for a certain product or service (e.g. at a drugstore or a pharmacist), brand name recall is needed. This is also true when a shopping list with preferred brand names for every category is made prior to going to a shop, or when somebody is making purchases by phone (airline tickets, courier services, etc.). When the purchase decision is made in the store (and according to a POPAI study this is the case for 60% to 80% of all fast-moving consumer goods bought in the supermarket, and the buyer can use visual cues such as packages, displays, colours, and logos, brand recognition is more important than brand recall.

BUSINESS INSIGHT
The Smart Fortwo

The Smart Fortwo city car was revolutionary at the time it was introduced and still remains one of a kind, but was reaching the end of its product life cycle, necessitating a reinvention in 2007. The integrated launch campaign's main objective was to introduce the new Smart Fortwo in Europe with a pre-launch phase to create awareness and interest and a launch phase to convert this interest into sales. In order to achieve a significant sales growth, Smart wanted to convert people who like Smart as a brand into those who have the Smart Fortwo in their relevance set when thinking about purchasing a new small car. The campaign needed to work deeply in the decision process, starting with brand awareness and ending with the purchase of the product. A mix of classic media and customer relationship marketing (CRM) activities combined TV and cinema, radio, print (mainly consumer magazines) with PR, online and further CRM activities such as direct mailings.

The Smart Fortwo was designed as an urban mobility solution, tailor-made for life in the city, so the core campaign thought was 'Discover a new city' – the new Smart car enables the driver to see his or her city with new eyes. Where others may see limitations, Smart drivers see opportunities. The campaign increased sales figures in Germany, France and Italy by more than 20% (in Germany it was 70% higher) with a lower 'media spend per unit sold' than main competitors Mini and Toyota Aygo. Smart even managed to outgrow Toyota Aygo in all three markets, as well as Mini in Italy and Germany. The CRM activities were also outstandingly successful, generating almost three times more leads than expected and selling almost 20 times more cars than one could normally expect.[6]

To stimulate brand recognition, showing the product package or logo in advertising and other communications in exactly the same colours and formats is crucial. The latter implies that media such as radio advertising are less appropriate for brand recognition goals. To build brand recall, repetition of the association between the category and the brand is necessary. Sign-off slogans should therefore always integrate category and brand name. In some cases a marketer should try to attain both brand recall and recognition. A consumer then recalls a brand at home and will search for it at the supermarket or store. For this search process to be successful, brand recognition is needed. Sometimes this dual brand awareness objective is required, since for many product categories consumers limit their search activity based on loyalty to a limited set of brands.

Every communications activity should take brand awareness into account. Even if brand attitude or other objectives are more dominant, it will still be important to support brand awareness. A brand can never have too much brand awareness. Brand awareness should also be established prior to brand attitude and the other communications objectives. If a brand is not known, it will be impossible to build an image, preference or attitude towards that brand. The effect of brand awareness on brand choice and brand purchases is substantial. If two brands are equally valued, the brand with the highest awareness will be purchased more often.[7]

Brand knowledge

Brand knowledge and comprehension mean that target consumers are aware of the most essential brand characteristics, features and benefits. They know the strengths of the brands as compared with competitive brands; they know why they should buy brand X instead of brand Y or Z. Essentially, consumers should be able to recall the brand's positioning. This knowledge may be based on very objective information, but also on brand image and lifestyle positioning. It is clear that what people know about a brand is very subjective and based on past experiences or on beliefs and perceptions.

BUSINESS INSIGHT
Sony Ericsson's objectives in the handheld market

Nokia, Sony Ericsson, Samsung and Motorola are all competing aggressively for leadership in the mobile handset markets in Europe. In 2006, Nokia had a 30.6% volume share in Russia and 38.9% in Poland. Sony Ericsson was number 2 in Poland with 20% and number 3 in Russia with 11.7%. Consumers perceived Nokia as leader in all relevant brand image criteria. Mobile handset advertising is seen as functional, with no brand having yet fully explored the emotional territory, so the opportunity for Sony Ericsson was to exploit this lack of differentiation in communications. Business objectives for Sony Ericsson were to grow faster than Nokia in the total CEEMEA region, especially in Russia and Poland in 2007, with at least a double-digit market share growth. The campaign also aimed to overtake Nokia in the 'leadership in music' brand criterion and increase brand purchase consideration scores in Russia and Poland, by at least 20% in both markets.

In a category driven by technological innovation, it was decided to pursue a strategy focused around the music category. At the end of 2006, a new brand identity was introduced, Sony Ericsson 'Walkman' phones, a new and innovative portfolio to challenge market leader Nokia, aimed at two key target audiences: opinion-forming 'Pioneer Youth' and 'Mainstream Youth'. The media strategy, 'Brighten Your Day', focused on delivering mood enhancement to their daily routine by bringing fun, colour and music enjoyment. There were three key phases in Sony Ericsson's campaign: 'Announce' focused on awareness and on ensuring high visibility; 'Showcase' transformed key urban commuter travel hubs; and 'Engage' was a fully integrated strategy including music concerts, on out-of-home channels and online, in the lead-up to MTV European Music Awards Sponsorship. The key message of 'You can't get closer to your music!' was designed to increase the awareness of Sony Ericsson Walkman phones and take consumers on an exciting 'musical mind trip'. In both markets, the goal of a 10% market share increase was exceeded. The communications strategy achieved significant gains in the 'leadership in music' criterion, overtaking Nokia in both markets. This significantly drove brand purchase consideration, which led to a bigger market share growth rate as compared with Nokia, all with a significantly lower budget.[8]

Brand attitude

If consumers are equally aware of a number of brands in a certain product category they will base their brand choice on an evaluation of the different brands. The result of this evaluation is called **brand attitude**. Brand attitude is the perceived value of a brand to a consumer. Because a brand is stronger (and thus has more loyal customers) when the differentiation with another brand is bigger, brand attitude is an important communication objective (see also Chapter 2).

A marketer should study the current brand attitudes and perceptions and then decide what to do. If there is no brand attitude, and people are unaware of brand benefits, a brand attitude should be created (Photo 5.2). If there is a moderately favourable brand attitude, the attitude should be reinforced through adapted communications. Improving attitudes among these benefit-aware target groups will lead to more frequent buying and hopefully make customers loyal. A very favourable brand attitude should be maintained to keep all loyal customers satisfied (Photo 5.3). In marketing practice there is no such thing as a permanently very favourable brand attitude because attitudes are liable to change as a consequence of dynamic markets and competition power. When a certain brand attitude cannot be improved, it could be a strategic decision to switch to another attitude by repositioning the brand and perhaps find a better brand proposition for the targeted market.

Photo 5.2 Guinness: developing brand attitude
Source: Corbis: Richard Klune.

Photo 5.3 Cool-Aid: national brand benefit
Source: Corbis: Henry Diltz.

Existing brand attitudes can also be adapted to appeal to other and new target groups. For instance, Wolverine World Wide, the American company behind Wolverine shoes for workers and Hush Puppies, a brand of casual footwear, began building the Caterpillar footwear brand in 1994 under licence from Caterpillar Inc., the heavy equipment and engine manufacturer. Caterpillar boots and shoes are now sold in 100 countries on six continents, reflecting the original brand attitude of Caterpillar in a totally different product category. In 1998, the company also acquired the licence from Harley-Davidson to transfer the legendary motorcycles' brand image to shoes and boots; in 2000, Wolverine started to manufacture Stanley footwear, positioned as footwear helping workers to 'make something great', bringing the slogan of the well-known manufacturer of construction tools to life in a new category.

If there is a negative prior brand attitude, changing the attitude is necessary. This is a very difficult objective to realise. It might be better – especially when the negative attitude is based on negative experiences – to modify the brand attitude and reposition the brand by appealing to different buying motivations.[9] In January 2003, Christian Dior had to change major elements of its advertising campaign for Dior Addict perfume and cosmetics. The TV spot for the fragrance originally showed a bikini model dipping her finger into a substance on a mirror and holding it up to her nose, then grabbing a bottle of Addict perfume while a voice whispers 'addict' and 'Will you admit it?' The ad initiated the 'Addiction is Not Fashionable' protest campaign and boycott co-ordinated by Faces and Voices of Recovery and MOMStell, a group of parents concerned with addiction and recovery issues. In response to this protest, Dior stopped using the tagline 'admit it' in its marketing communications and altered the ads to emphasise the full name of the product 'Dior Addict' instead of 'addict' as a single word.[10]

Purchase intention

The intention of the buyer to purchase the brand or the product or take other buying-related actions (going to the store, asking for more information) can also be enhanced. For low-involvement buying situations (see Chapter 3), **purchase intention** should not be stressed in communications. In this case, when a brand is known and a favourable brand attitude exists, this will in many cases lead to buying behaviour whenever the need for a certain category is aroused. In high-involvement situations, however, when perceived buying risks are high, the intention to buy is typically a necessary mediating step between a favourable attitude and the actual purchase. In this case, generating purchase intention and trial is necessary.[11] Advertising and sales promotion can stimulate the consumer in that direction.

BUSINESS INSIGHT
Intel stimulates purchase intention of Centrino Duo PCs

Consumers in Europe, the Middle East and Africa who purchase computers at retail often spend less than planned as salespeople persuade them to trade down. Consumers had the cash to upgrade to the best Intel-powered computer so Intel had to make them demand it. Intel's core targets are consumers who are passionate about using technology to pursue creative interests. The campaign targeted tech-savvy digital musicians – individuals, aged around 25–35 years, who rely on their computers. The goal for the four-month campaign was to get consumers to engage with Intel and to express a stronger preference for Centrino Duo processors at retail. Research revealed that MySpace was the preferred destination for Intel's target audience, who spend 10% of their total online time there. Intel aimed to win consumer support by giving MySpace users tools to make better music while educating them about Centrino Duo. The campaign ran with MySpace in a six-market programme designed to create an Intel SuperGroup, with voting determining the band members, the song, the name and the artwork. It rolled out in three stages to engage influencers and content creators, drive wider awareness and broaden reach. There were more than 66 000 content engagement episodes, well ahead of the initial target of 25 000. Post-campaign research showed awareness at 33% among all MySpace users in the six markets where it was promoted. Consumers in 46 markets were reached. Intel signed up more than 60 000 friends and had more than 25 000 unique users on its blog. Total submissions and votes to the online competition hit 171 000, 180% ahead of target. Intel SuperGroup was pioneering – it was the first multi-market campaign on MySpace. It was bold – it took Intel into a brand-averse environment. It was efficient – cost per profile view was $0.12. And it was very successful – 29% of the target audience will definitely upgrade.[12]

Purchase facilitation

Purchase facilitation is about assuring buyers that there are no barriers hindering product or brand purchase. These barriers could be other elements of the marketing mix, such as price, product and place (distribution).

Sometimes availability or price is a problem, preventing consumers from buying a product. Communications in this case should minimise the perceived problems. For example, if a certain brand is not widely available in all stores, a list of approved dealers might help the consumers.[13] Point-of-purchase communications may also help to facilitate purchases.

BUSINESS INSIGHT
Purchase facilitation in lingerie shops

A lot of men consider lingerie a sexy present for their loved ones. However, buying bras usually turns out to be a painful and embarrassing experience. Contrary to popular belief (among women) most men do not have the faintest idea about the size of the 'natural wealth' of their girlfriends or wives. When asked about size, they give vague indications such as 'more or less like that woman over there' or 'about a handful'. The consequence is that 90% of women who receive a lingerie set as a present (mostly in December or on Valentine's Day) take it back to the shop because it does not fit. A female student of the 'Piet Zwart Institute for Retail and Interior Design' in Rotterdam developed a new retail concept that aims at facilitating the buying process for men. In the middle of the shop a 'breast wall' is installed. On this wall, breasts of different sizes and shapes are modelled in gel, and men can 'experience' which size is closest to the one they need. Furthermore, most men do not feel comfortable in lingerie shops and find it difficult to make their way around. Therefore, the shop is more or less conceived as a do-it-yourself store. There are separate aisles per cup size, and the size is clearly illustrated by means of pictures in each aisle. 'Men know everything about HP's of cars, but have a selective memory about the anatomy of their wives and girlfriends', the designer says. 'We should assist them as much as we can.' In the meantime, the new concept has raised the interest of lingerie retailers and manufacturers all over the world.[14]

Purchase

Sales are, of course, the main marketing objective. However, in most circumstances it is difficult to use sales goals as a primary communications objective. Nevertheless, there are situations in which, due to the action-oriented context of communications tools, sales could be a good objective. For instance, the main objective of most sales promotions like couponing, price cuts and premiums is the short-term effect on sales. Some direct marketing tools such as direct response advertising may be evaluated by generated sales. Indeed, in these situations direct sales are the main goal.

BUSINESS INSIGHT
Reviving the sales of Vicks

In early 2007, Vicks had little presence in the big, growing respiratory category (cough, cold and flu) and a dwindling presence in decongestants. The brand was suffering from terminally declining relevance and sales while employing different communications ideas for each product initiative. Resurrecting this brand would require the simultaneous launch of new products to fill gaps in the Vicks portfolio where it would face strong market leaders. And this in a challenging health-care environment where people exhibit high loyalty (three times the fast-moving consumer goods average) and have a low buying frequency of the category of 1.2 times a year. The new products had to achieve immediate payback on the investment but also be united under a single idea to create a brand that stretched across the range. By early 2008, Vicks was a coherent brand with products in both respiratory and decongestant sectors and sales growth in the UK/Ireland of 31% (versus an objective of 25%), value share improvement by 7% in Austria and 19% in the Netherlands. Vicks' use of media was highly efficient. In each of the countries, gross rating points fell – by 3% in the UK/Ireland, 20% in Austria and 13% in the Netherlands – while value share growth was still achieved. This efficient and effective scenario was achieved with a new communications model that was targeted towards 21% of the population who have a high desire to soldier on when they have a cold. Most are women aged 25–45 with young children and an active lifestyle. The following media were deemed the most crucial for success of the campaign: TV to promote the new brand point of view and to introduce hero products; the Web to add visibility, information and reassurance; and in-store to encourage cross-range sales. The single brand idea, 'At Vicks we focus on solutions not problems; we are for people not symptoms', was employed for all advertised products. This idea drove sales of advertised products and also drove sales of the entire Vicks range.[15]

Satisfaction

When a consumer buys a product or service he or she has certain expectations about the purchase. When the product or service lives up to the required and desired benefits or surpasses expectations, the consumer will be satisfied and thus inclined to choose the same brand whenever he or she buys the product again. Dissatisfied consumers will probably buy a different brand on the next occasion and will complain to relatives and friends. Most marketers are satisfied when consumers finally buy and stop communicating at that point. But it is clear that communications should also be directed to existing customers. The most important reason is that clients are advocates of the brand and products they buy. Word-of-mouth communications can be stimulated and approved by communicating with current customers. Moreover, it is important to reassure consumers about their choice. Cognitive dissonance, i.e. the fact that – due to a choice situation – buyers start to have doubts about that choice, should be avoided to enhance brand loyalty.

Brand loyalty

Brand loyalty is defined as the mental commitment or relation between a consumer and a brand. But there are different types of brand loyalty. Repeat purchase is not the same as brand loyalty. The former is often the result of habit or routine buying rather than of brand preference or brand loyalty. Instead of evaluating alternatives and choosing a new brand for every new purchase, in low-involvement, fast-moving packaged goods consumers tend to buy the same brands again without having a commitment to the brand. This is how brand habits develop. By always using and buying the same brands, a positive attitude towards those brands is initiated. Longitudinal tracking in the USA, UK and Germany has shown that brand loyalty is not a characteristic of a brand but of a product category. Brands with a higher market share in that category have a higher 'loyalty' because of their higher penetration rate and not necessarily because the emotional bond with the customer is better. Brand 'loyalty' can indeed be the result of habit formation.[16]

RESEARCH INSIGHT
Organisational responses to negative online reviews

Research on complaint management has emphasised the importance of service recovery, i.e. restoring customer trust after a service failure. A well-executed recovery effort not only is capable of influencing customer satisfaction positively, but can also convert dissatisfied customers into satisfied and loyal ones.[17] Customer satisfaction after a service recovery depends on customers' fairness perception (i.e. the extent to which they perceive themselves as being treated fairly compared with other customers; the extent to which they perceive that the output is in balance with the input) and attribution of accountability (i.e. the perceived causes of success or failure, who is to blame).[18] Research on recovery management has usually measured satisfaction after service failure of the duped customer in a one-to-one relationship. With the growing use of the Internet, everybody can post a negative comment online, for everyone with an Internet connection to read. Negative online WOM by a dissatisfied customer due to a service failure can have serious consequences, as this can harm brand image, companies' reputations and consumers' attitudes and purchase intentions.[19] Thus, it is one of the major challenges for companies to develop appropriate response strategies to negative e-WOM.[20] When online reviews are read by so many potential customers, it is critical not only to satisfy the initial client, but also to remove barriers with the readers of these online reviews. People who intend to buy a service are likely to reconsider their decision after reading negative reviews, especially when these potential customers realise that the organisation does not respond properly to these negative comments.

In a Belgian study, prospective customers' perceived trust, attitudes and intentions were measured following organisational responses to consumer review sets varying in their degree of negativity.[21] Using a 3 (positive, neutral, negative online review set) × 6 (online managerial response to reviews: no reaction, refutation, apology, apology and promise that it will not happen again, apology and compensation, apology and promise of compensation) full factorial, between-subjects design, the study investigates how a company (in this case, a restaurant) should react to counter different degrees of negative online WOM, and what kind of response is advisable to regain the trust and business of prospective customers.

When the number of positive reviews outweighs the number of negative reviews, the results showed that there are no significant differences in terms of perceived trust, attitude and purchase intention between the different response strategies. Due to the fact that the negative WOM is outnumbered by positive comments, the readers believe that the service failure would not reoccur, thus offering an apology or even compensation to the dissatisfied customer would not enhance the purchase intention of the reader. Based on the social validation theory,[22] the reader may attribute the accountability to the complaining customers, instead of the service provider: 'some people are just naggers'. When the numbers of positive and negative reviews are equal, it is more difficult to assign accountability and thus to evaluate whether justice is served. The results revealed that both the apology and promise strategy and the apology, promise and compensation response result in a significantly higher perception of trust than refutation. The combination of an apology and a promise also results in the most positive attitude and purchase intention score. These results indicate that the apology–promise response significantly enhances trust, attitude and purchase intention. However, offering compensation on top of an apology and a promise does not significantly improve attitude and purchase intention. According to the justice theory, perceived distributional justice will be optimal when there is a balance between the input and the output. When the outcome of the recovery is more substantial than the damage experienced, people may feel guilty and less comfortable about accepting compensation. As the opinion of the customers is divided, it is possible that the reader is not sure who is accountable and perceives the failure as less severe. Assurance of a fair service in the future is enough to enhance the perceived trust, attitude and purchase intention of the prospective customer. When the number of dissatisfied customers is higher than the number of satisfied ones, it is easy to blame the service provider for the failure. The findings showed that, compared with the refutation strategy, the apology and compensation strategy and the apology, promise and compensation strategy significantly enhance the perceived trust in the manager. The apology, promise and compensation strategy results in significantly more positive attitude and intention scores than no reaction, refutation and even the apology responses.

Overall, the findings suggest that different response strategies are needed depending on the ratio of the positive and negative reviews, to increase the perceived trust, attitude and purchase intention of readers of online reviews. When the reviews are mostly positive, no reaction is needed to counter the few negative comments. When the balance is neutral, an apology combined with a promise that the failure will not happen again appears to be the appropriate thing to do. Offering compensation in this situation is found to be unnecessary (from the bystander's perspective). Finally, when the majority of reviews are negative, not only an apology, but also a promise and compensation are desirable to convince the readers that the service is actually worth considering.

Instead of focusing solely on higher market penetration rates, many high-penetration brands are now using advertising campaigns to encourage their loyal consumers to use the brand more frequently, as well as suggesting new ways to use the brand or new situations in which it can be consumed. The more frequent use of a brand may be a much more cost-effective way to build sales. Recent publications have therefore argued that when dealing with brands with a high degree of market penetration, consumption intentions are more likely to capture consumption-related responses (and success of a campaign) than attitudes towards the brand or purchase intentions. Volume estimates would then best approximate the actual consumption of heavy users and likelihood estimates are best used with light users or with infrequently consumed brands.[23]

Of course, not all communications objectives should be present in a communications plan or campaign. A marketer should choose which of the above goals is most appropriate in the market and communications situation. Marketers will therefore need a clear view based on

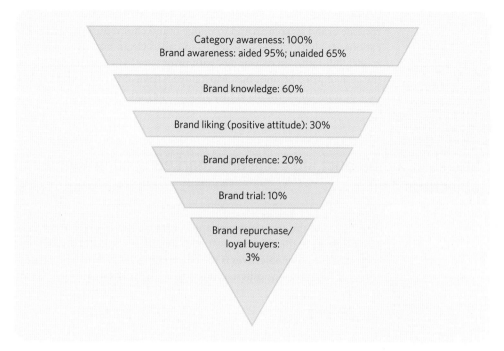

Figure 5.3 Percentage of the target group in each stage of the DAGMAR model

situation analysis and prior research among the target audience to decide which goals a campaign should focus upon. If awareness levels are low, they should focus on that goal; if preference is a problem, the campaign should stress liking. Brand awareness and brand attitude will always be part of the goals, as both effects should be maintained in every promotional campaign. As these objectives should be quantified to make them measurable, marketing communications objectives could be: to increase the percentage of unaided recall or aided recognition among the target group; to increase the number of target consumers preferring the brand above the competitive brands; to stimulate current buyers to stay loyal and purchase the products again or buy them more frequently; and to encourage non-buyers to try the brand for the first time. The number of people in each step of the hierarchy of objectives can be expected to decrease, as is illustrated in Figure 5.3.[24]

The DAGMAR model has the merit that, instead of sales goals which are hard to correlate with communications expenditures, other quantifiable measures for effectiveness, such as awareness and image ratings, are introduced. These other measures are assumed to be inter-mediate effects, and thus indicators of future sales. An increase in awareness and brand ratings would be ahead of sales increases. However, in practice it can be seen that awareness and image ratings are highly associated with usage, but that sales fluctuate sooner than awareness and image ratings. Attitude changes were even found to follow behaviour changes and can be considered to be caused by them.[25] This change in the communications effects hierarchy was extensively described earlier (see Chapter 3) (e.g. the Foot–Cone–Belding or FCB grid).

Further criticism of the so-called traditional 'strong theory of communications', as pre-sented in the DAGMAR model, was formulated by Ehrenberg.[26] He states that there is no evidence that consumers experience a strong desire or conviction before they purchase a product or a service. The traditional model is a conversion model, i.e. turning non-users into users, whereas advertising is directed at experienced consumers. Jones[27] and Ehrenberg present an alternative 'weak theory of marketing communications': the **ATR model** (Awareness→Trial →Reinforcement). Marketing communications first arouse awareness, then induce consumers towards a first trial purchase and then reassure and reinforce those users after their first pur-chase. According to Ehrenberg, involvement is basically product involvement and very rarely brand involvement. Consequently, the goal of marketing communications is to create or recreate brand awareness and to nudge brand choice during purchases. Marketing communications are almost never directed to so-called virgin non-users as is implied in the DAGMAR model, but rather to consumers with prior experience of different brands. This is also true in the case of price promotions. Most buyers have already bought the brand before. Even when new or unfamiliar brands are promoted, they are rarely chosen.[28]

Stages in the product life cycle and marketing communications objectives[29]

The choice of the most appropriate communications goals depends on a number of factors that originate in the marketing strategy and the situation analysis. One of the more important factors in choosing objectives is the phase of the life cycle of a brand or product. In this section, different strategies for different life stages are explored. They are summarised in Figure 5.4.

Introduction

A company that is marketing a completely new product will have to develop the market. Consumers will have to learn what the new product is about: which needs will be fulfilled by the product and what the differences are compared with the products that the consumers were used to before the innovation or launch of the new product or brand. The major communications objectives in this market situation will be creating category need (explaining which needs are better fulfilled with the innovation), brand awareness and brand knowledge. With daily consumed goods, consumers will have to be persuaded to try the new product. The communications strategy has to stress the basic selling points, i.e. the central functional advantages of the products.

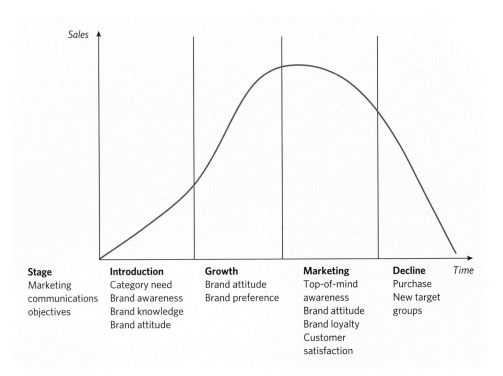

Stage	Introduction	Growth	Marketing	Decline
Marketing communications objectives	Category need Brand awareness Brand knowledge Brand attitude	Brand attitude Brand preference	Top-of-mind awareness Brand attitude Brand loyalty Customer satisfaction	Purchase New target groups

Figure 5.4 Stages in the product life cycle and communications objectives

For instance, the R8 was Audi's first entry into the high-end sports car market. In a market dominated by the Porsche 911, the R8 was to establish Audi as *the* German sports car, achieve the number 2 spot and bolster the Audi brand. The R8 contains Audi innovations that have changed motor sports and car manufacturing in key ways. The communications centred on the idea of the R8 as innovative and an embodiment of the brand's technological competence. They promoted consumer interest that reflected on the brand as a whole, providing convincing evidence that this same technological competence and innovative energy goes into every single car. In the year of its launch, the R8 topped the rankings for the most popular sports car. It has closed the gap on the Porsche 911, and has energised the Audi brand.[30]

Most introductions are new brand launches rather than real product innovations. Evidently, in this case it is not necessary to communicate the central functional product features as consumers are aware of them from their experience with other brands. The goals are to create brand awareness and support psycho-social brand image connotations. This is done by associating a brand with a certain projected lifestyle. When Nivea first launched the colour cosmetic sub-brand Nivea Beauté onto the European market in 1997, the objective was to utilise the Nivea core competencies of skin care expertise and emotional values to build a care-based decorative cosmetic brand focusing on products offering gentle formulae and classic colours in the eye, nail, lip and face segments. By 2000 stronger focus had to be placed on category-specific drivers such as modernity, new colours, fashion trends and innovative products to cope with the continued pressure from local competitors, global heavyweight L'Oréal Perfection and the US top brand Maybelline, using heavy advertising investments to support a global rollout after merging with Jade (Germany, Austria and Switzerland) and Gemey (France and Belgium). Apart from TV ads spreading the 'the most beautiful me' message, the print communications were especially important in demonstrating colour and fashion competence. In Germany and France, Nivea Beauté was the only brand in 2000 notably to improve brand image values on all levels. Not only the core Nivea values but also category drivers such as 'colours are modern and up to date' saw improvements. Brand likeability, brand usage and brand awareness also improved after the campaign.[31] A study[32] on what kinds of communications stimulate sales of new products came up with four factors. It should be clearly communicated that it is a new product and is thus different from other products. This difference should be specifically linked to the category such as 'the refreshing soft drink' or 'the strongest mint'. Thirdly, differences in characteristics are not enough; they should be translated into real benefits for the consumer and communicated in that way. The last important factor is the support given to that beneficial point of difference. Some objective endorsements should give consumers the reason why a certain claim should be believed. Typical endorsements are demonstrations, scientific evidence, celebrity endorsements, testimonials of experts or 'normal' users in a slice-of-life setting.

Growth

In the growth stage, a different situation leads to other strategies. Consumers are aware of the brand, the product and the most important characteristics and features. Other brands have entered the market with a comparable offer. Communications strategies in this stage of the product life cycle will be aimed at defending the brand's position against possible competitive attacks. Marketers will have to create brand preference by emphasising the right product features and benefits to differentiate the brand from competitors and position it as unique.

Maturity

A brand in the mature stage of its life cycle has to cope with strong competition in a market that is scarcely growing. This implies that an increase in the return of one manufacturer will be reflected in a decrease in a competitor's revenues. Communications strategies will focus on increasing the brand loyalty of consumers. Customers should be induced to be less open to the advantages of competing brands. There are six possible communications objectives in this particular product life-cycle stage:

- High spontaneous brand awareness, top-of-mind awareness.
- Claim a clear and unique brand benefit, a characteristic on which the brand is better than competing brands.
- If there are no or only small product differences, stressing a lower price might be a good strategy.
- Get attention by offering small product innovations.
- Reinforce the psycho-social meaning for product categories such as cigarettes, beer and coffee. These brands differ very little in functional characteristics but the experience of the brands by consumer groups might be very different. The strategy of these brands is positioning by supporting the transformational meaning of a brand.
- Communications strategies could also be more defensive in this stage of the product life cycle. Current customers should be reassured of their choice and their positive experience of and satisfaction with the brand.

BUSINESS INSIGHT
Repositioning a mature brand

Until 1954, Marlboro was a cigarette for women: it had no national distribution and a small share of the market. Philip Morris then developed a new filter. Most filter cigarettes were thought to be directed to women, but the Marlboro filter cigarette seemed to be appreciated by male smokers too. The advertising professional Leo Burnett therefore advised Marlboro to position the brand as a cigarette for real men. After trying out some less successful symbols, Burnett and Philip Morris chose the symbol that was mostly associated with virility: a cowboy. Consumer response was extraordinary with exploding market shares in the USA and all over the world as a result.

Decline

When manufacturers are confronted with declining products or brands and decide to milk or harvest the brand, they will probably turn to sales promotions such as prizes and lotteries. If they decide to renew the life of the declining product or brand (and believe in life-cycle stretching), they can use the following strategies:

- communicate an important product adaptation or change;
- draw attention to new applications or moments of use (e.g. beer as a recipe ingredient instead of as a drink);
- increase the frequency of use;
- attract new target groups (e.g. Bacardi Breezer for youngsters).

Coral (Robijn in the Netherlands) is a light-duty detergent brand, long established in Germany, the Netherlands, Austria, Belgium, France, Switzerland and more recently in Sweden, Finland and Norway. Germany and the Netherlands represent two-thirds of global sales. Coral had a stable market share over time and nothing had been done to create a dynamic over the last decade, resulting in a drastically ageing consumer profile, with a core group of people aged 50 and over. To ensure a future for the brand, Coral had to recruit, and create a strong bond with, young European women between 25 and 35 years old. This target group has absolutely no interest in washing, as they are certainly not housewives. Coral had to find another value that would speak emotionally to this young target group. Research showed Lever Fabergé, the company behind Coral, that clothes reflect personality, self-expression and self-confidence to young women. Hence, taking care of clothes is taking care of themselves. As black and dark clothes represent one-third of a modern woman's wardrobe, Coral decided to launch the first washing specialist for black clothes: Coral Black Velvet. In this way Coral was no longer a detergent, but an essential fashion accessory helping young women to take care of their precious clothes. In order to demonstrate that Coral Black Velvet could be part of the strong emotional relationship between clothes and women, Lever used a media strategy that created contacts in locations where young women care about clothes, appearance and fashion: women's magazines, parties, fashion shows and bars. In Germany Coral's share of market moved from 3.8% to 6.2% in six months; in the Netherlands Robijn moved from a share of 9.6% to 14.2% in the same period. Because of the huge success of Coral Black Velvet, soon several 'me-toos' were introduced on the German fabrics market.[33]

Consumer choice situations and marketing communications objectives[34]

The effectiveness of communications goals may be determined not only by the product or brand life cycle, but also by the consumer choice situation. Figure 5.5 shows six important variables affecting the consumer choice situation. Firstly, this is determined by the choice process a consumer follows. This situational characteristic is, for instance, different for high- versus low-involvement products. In the former case, an extended choice process with a longer orientation and information processing phase is typical. Influencing consumers in this process and consequently communicating with them will also differ in these different situations.

Consumer characteristics are, for instance, experiences, knowledge and socio-economic characteristics. Consumer–product relationships have to do with involvement from low to extremely high, and routine purchases versus intensively considered purchases. The speed, frequency and modalities of choice, from often and superficial to once in a while and attentive, are elements of the choice process. Characteristics of the outlet or point of purchase (shop, home, office) are important, as well as advice involved with the purchase: is there any kind of personal advice (from a salesperson, friends, family, neighbours) involved with the purchase process? Finally, product characteristics, such as articles bought daily, known brands or speciality goods, can have an impact. Based on these six groups of variables, a number of frequently occurring choice situations as well as their impact on the communications goal-setting can be described:

- *Standard mass products.* Fast-moving consumer goods, such as detergents and food products, are typically low-involvement situations in which mass communications focus on building brand awareness and brand knowledge. Generating trial and routine repeat purchases is also important.

- *Standard services.* Services targeted at a broad mass market, like restaurants, shoe repairers, hairdressers, etc. Building brand awareness and stimulating trial through price cuts and other actions are often used.

- *Mail order products.* Mass products like clothing and non-food interior articles for mass markets but ordered through mail and catalogue sales. The awareness of the company is important, but stimulating catalogue enquiries is the first goal. Once the catalogue is mailed, it will be the main communications tool. Sales depend on the quality of this catalogue. The same idea applies for e-commerce shops, where next to the usability of the site, the brand awareness and the product quality are key.

- *Impulse products.* Products that seduce buyers into an impulse purchase. Consumers need not be convinced. The confrontation of consumers with the product is crucial: out-of-stock situations should be avoided. After creating brand awareness, creating confrontations is the most essential communications goal. Early in 2009, Delhaize, a major retailer in Belgium, decided to take 300 Unilever products off the shelves because of stuck price negotiations. Unilever reacted via a media campaign and informed its consumers that its products were still available in other retailers. The communications agency Brandhome did some research on the impact of the out-of-stocks and found that 31% of the Delhaize customers went to other supermarkets to buy the Unilever products; 19% were not happy with the situation but were considering what to do; and 47% bought alternative products in Delhaize from Unilever competitors like Danone and P&G.[35]

- *Quality products.* Valuable quality products and brands for relatively small markets of categories such as garments, design products, cosmetics, shoes, accessories, etc., bought for their quality, for aesthetic reasons and because they symbolise a certain lifestyle. As customers are more involved with this kind of product, the marketer should focus on creating and supporting brand awareness.

- *Quality services.* Complex or special services for relatively small markets including travel agencies, tax advisers, etc. In the introductory phase of a quality service, network relations are crucial. Many people buy a service after being advised by friends or relations. For retention, after-sales communications, such as direct marketing, are important.

- *International luxury products.* World-famous brands such as Chanel, Dior, Yves Saint Laurent, Gucci, Vuitton, etc., that appeal to customers. Initially, word-of-mouth communications are important, and generating traffic in the special stores is crucial. Later, direct marketing becomes important.

- *Special niche products.* Brands and products for specific segments of people (children, the elderly, hobbyists, etc.) cannot be mass communicated because this strategy would lead to too much 'waste'. Special interest magazines and trade magazines offer an efficient way of creating brand awareness. Direct, personal contact is also very important.

- *Showroom products.* The main objective of the marketer is to attract people to the showroom. Building brand awareness and reputation is the first step; subsequently, invitations to the showroom are made. The sales team will then have the major part in the communications process, persuading visitors to buy the products.

- *Products with new techniques.* Products such as audio and video equipment with technical innovations bought by early adopters. All the marketer has to do is introduce the new product lines and their propositions to interested people and attract them to the retail outlets.

- *Investment products.* For products that are bought once or twice in a lifetime, such as houses, boats, university education, etc., word-of-mouth communications and personal contacts and selling are far more important than mass communications.

- *Unsought products.* Complex products and services such as insurance and maintenance services which are bought because they are imposed or because they are needed, not because people actually want them. The first objective is to explain the use of the products, to change the negative perceptions of consumers and to create confidence.

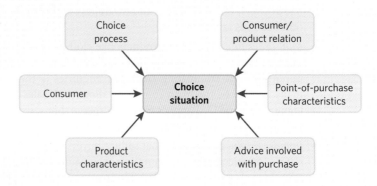

Figure 5.5 Factors affecting the consumer choice situation

BUSINESS INSIGHT

Accenture's 'We know what it takes to be a tiger' campaign

To win business in the management consulting, technology services and outsourcing market, topping the consideration list is crucial. Accenture's communications had to help it own the category in a distinctive, relevant and compelling way, and capture the attention and consideration of a busy, frequently travelling, international audience.

The campaign 'We know what it takes to be a Tiger' was aimed at the demanding and results-driven 'change drivers' who occupy the 'C-Suite' (i.e. CEO, COO, CFO, etc.) in the world's largest companies. Business-wise, the campaign needed to increase Accenture's brand valuation year on year. It needed to help Accenture to increase revenue, achieve higher margins and deepen existing client relationships. Next to these objectives, the following communications goals were set: increase advertising awareness and beat competition on cost per awareness; double the consideration for Accenture among the advertising-aware in core markets; increase association with key brand personality traits; and own the concept of 'high performance delivered'. To own this benefit, the idea of 'high performance delivered' was created to brand the unique type of success that Accenture can help deliver for its clients. To bring this to life creatively, Tiger Woods was employed to be the personification of high performance. Tiger Woods (for golfers and non-golfers alike) gave Accenture's campaign great power. The campaign ran in out-of-home (e.g. airports), print, TV, radio and online media in France, Germany, Spain, Italy and the UK. The campaign was Accenture's most successful to date, doubling consideration in each of the core markets. Retention was excellent – all of Accenture's top 100 clients have now been working with the company for at least five years. The advertising awareness goal was met and Accenture widened the gap over a key competitor in the UK, France and Italy.[36]

Summary

A marketing communications campaign can have several objectives that are consistent with the stages in the consumer decision-making process: stimulating product category need, increasing brand awareness and brand knowledge, improving brand attitude or image, increasing purchase intention and facilitating purchases, and maximising customer satisfaction and brand loyalty. Different objectives will require a different communications mix. The objectives of a communications campaign differ according to the stage in the product life cycle. While awareness-building is more important in the introductory and growth stages, brand image and brand preference building will be crucial in the growth and the maturity stages, and purchase-directed objectives will prevail in the decline stage. On the basis of the consumer choice situation, 12 types of products can be distinguished for which marketing communications objectives are essentially different.

REVIEW QUESTIONS

1. Describe the various stages in the DAGMAR model. What is the consequence of this model for marketing communications objectives?

2. What are the characteristics of a good set of marketing communications objectives?

3. How does the definition of marketing objectives fit into the marketing communications plan?

4. In what circumstances is it useful to stress category needs and wants in marketing communications?

5. In what circumstances is brand recall rather than brand recognition the more important communications goal?

6. In what circumstances is the stimulation of purchase intention a good marketing communications objective?

7. What are the shortcomings of the DAGMAR model as a framework for marketing communications objectives?

8. To what extent should marketing communications objectives be adapted in the introductory, growth, maturity and decline stages of a product life cycle?

9. How can consumer choice situations influence communications objectives?

10. What corporate objectives can be distinguished?

Further reading

Ehrenberg, A.S.C., Hammond, K.A. and Goodhardt, G.J. (1992), 'The After-Effects of Large Consumer Promotions', *Journal of Advertising Research*, 34(4), 11–21.

Jones, D.B. (1994), 'Setting Promotional Goals: A Communication Relationship Model', *Journal of Consumer Marketing*, 11(1), 38–49.

Jones, J., Slater, J. and Clarck, H. (2003), *What's in a Name: Advertising and the Concept of Brands.* Armonk, NY: M.E. Sharpe.

Joyce, T. (1991), 'Models of the Advertising Process', *Marketing and Research Today*, 19(4), 205–13.

Percy, L., Rossiter, J. and Elliott, R. (2002), *Strategic Advertising Management.* Oxford: Oxford University Press.

CASE 5:
Yellow Pages: an old-fashioned brand that is revived through a ground-breaking campaign

New Zealand Yellow Pages in trouble

It was the perfect product for the twentieth century: a giant yellow book in which whatever you needed . . . some asbestos for the ceiling . . . a man to repair your telex machine . . . your nearest waterbed stockist . . . could be found. It was updated every single year and efficiently delivered by hand to every home in the country. A big yellow helper, without which our parents' lives would have been even more arduous and toilsome. As we entered 2008, Yellow Pages was realistic about the public's view of the brand.

Yellow Pages was something your mum kept in the cupboard underneath the telephone, and pulled out when something went wrong with the plumbing. It was an icon of the pre-Internet age, and both consumers and businesses were questioning their need for it in a world where they could find anything they wanted on Google. Businesses were being dissuaded from Yellow Pages by all manner of new Internet directory services, and consumers saw Google as a much more modern, relevant way to search for anything. Across the world, Yellow Pages businesses were in sharp decline.

Throughout the world, Yellow Pages businesses faced a tumultuous 2009. As online search became increasingly mobile and ubiquitous, the relevance of the printed Yellow Pages product declined further, resulting in inevitable declines in usage as people migrated to the Internet to look up a business. With the recent arrival of multiple new online and digital advertising channels available to businesses both small and large, the need to be in Yellow Pages decreased, resulting in inevitable declines in advertiser numbers and revenue. This challenge was made even more difficult in 2009 as businesses across the board faced a recession and chose to spend significantly less on advertising. Total New Zealand advertising spend declined by 12% overall, and 17% in the case of other print-based media, the most comparable with Yellow Pages' core offering. Online advertising did grow, but only at 11%, and off a very small base. New Zealand's Yellow Pages Group faced serious and widely touted problems with its yellow.co.nz search experience, which frequently provided inaccurate or incomplete results, turning online Kiwis back to Google for their searches.

Clearly, communications could not address any of these fundamental business and marketplace issues. So Yellow Pages got going on print innovations to improve the relevance of the print product, broader advertiser packages to address advertiser declines and technology investment to fix the online search problems. These innovations and improvements would drive greater usage and revenue in the future, but they would take at least a year to develop and launch. So, in the meantime, the decision was taken to continue to use communications to improve perceptions of the Yellow Pages brand. Communications and brand perception alone would not be enough to turn the business around, but a stronger brand would facilitate a much more successful launch of those improvements in 2010 and beyond.

The global challenge is to give Yellow Pages a genuine place in the twenty-first century, or haemorrhage business at the current rate and see the death of the brand within a decade. For Yellow Pages to have a place in the twenty-first century it was necessary to challenge the deeply entrenched attitudes and behaviours that surrounded the brand:

From	To
A thing of the past	Modern and relevant
A book	Online and mobile
Lagging way behind Google	A leader in search
Used when there is a problem	Used when there is an opportunity
Used when not found on Google	Used for first search

There had been a major push earlier in 2008, spending NZ$2.3 million on a TV advertising campaign, and it had had no discernible effect on brand health or usage. With a fraction of that budget and such firmly held consumer perceptions, Yellow Pages needed to do something completely different.

Yellow Pages had seen great success with its 'Treehouse Restaurant' campaign in 2008. To prove that Yellow Pages is still the best way to get any job done, the ad agency challenged Aucklander Tracey Collins to build a restaurant halfway up a redwood pine tree, using nothing but contacts from Yellow Pages website, mobile app and book. The agency publically followed her progress and, in January 2009, opened the Treehouse Restaurant to a sellout two-month season. The campaign drew unprecedented attention, being featured on over 20 000 websites internationally and in the pages of over 100 different magazines. It was reviewed on every major NZ TV property and was the lead story on the front page of the *NZ Herald*. From a media spend of only NZ$436 000 the campaign achieved 61% awareness of the campaign, showing the idea to be almost twice as efficient as Yellow Pages' historic traditional TV advertising. The perceptions of that 61% towards the brand have been enhanced significantly, proving that Yellow Pages was persuading New Zealanders to re-evaluate their view of an old and deeply entrenched brand. As a result of the largely online campaign, monthly unique visitors to the whebsite (yellow.co.n2) were driven above 1 million for the first time ever, and have grown the website's share of first search at the cost of their goliath competitor Google. It had improved relevance and modernity perceptions significantly, leaving brand health in a far stronger position. And so the agency was tasked with producing a follow-up campaign, and challenged to improve on the performance of the Treehouse, but with a budget 17% smaller. While $2.4 million was spent on the Treehouse, only $2 million could be spent in 2009.

This case history describes a follow-up campaign launching a chocolate brand through Yellow Pages to put the brand on the map as a relevant and modern way to build a business.

Campaign objectives

The overall objective of the 2009 campaign was to continue to challenge New Zealanders' deeply entrenched perceptions of Yellow Pages and earn the brand a place in the twenty-first century. Specifically, the objectives were to:

- Get New Zealanders to think of Yellow Pages as more of a leader in search, rather than a laggard to Google, and improve its brand tracking score for 'Leading the way in search'.

- Get New Zealanders to see Yellow Pages as a modern, contemporary, innovative brand and improve brand tracking scores across the board, but specifically the measure 'is modern/of today'.

- Increase awareness of Yellow Pages' online and mobile products and improve brand tracking scores: 'There is →

much more to Yellow Pages than the printed directory' and 'Is up with the latest technology'.

The campaign also aimed to spread this message further than with the previous year's Treehouse campaign by engaging more New Zealanders, and by using the campaign to actively engage staff and advertiser customers. If successful, this would help the wider business in remaining New Zealanders' first choice when searching for a business, continuing to be perceived as the most effective advertising medium in the minds of small and medium-size businesses and performing better financially than the rest of the advertising media category.

Target audience

Yellow Pages has two targets: businesses wanting to advertise and people wanting to find a business. Yellow Pages makes its money from business advertisers, but only if those businesses believe that their customers use Yellow Pages. To make sure they do, it produces specific advertiser campaigns to communicate the effectiveness of advertising in Yellow Pages. But to maintain that effectiveness it is critical that the consumer audience sees it as a modern, relevant option in today's digital world. And so the challenge was to improve brand health among the consumer audience. Given that there are few people who never have the need to look for a business listing, the target is wide – all people aged 25–54.

What the Yellow Pages staff know about those people is that they have all grown up with Yellow Pages, they have all just been through the Internet revolution, and many of them still think of the brand as 'the way you found stuff before the Internet'.

The strategic thinking that inspired the idea

In a nutshell, the communications strategy for earning the Yellow Pages brand a place in the twenty-first century was to prove that it is the best way to get any job done today. It is about actions, not words, about truly demonstrating the power of Yellow Pages, and about playing up those more modern online and mobile Yellow Pages products. The Treehouse was proof of concept. It had been enormously effective in terms of its media efficiency, its ability to get into the conversations of New Zealanders, and ultimately its effect on brand health. But Yellow Pages could not just do the same thing again. It needed to build on the success of that campaign with an updated strategy that would improve perceptions among many more New Zealanders this time. The Treehouse had touched 46% of New Zealanders in total, a pretty good number considering that Yellow Pages used very little traditional media. But it could not just speak to those people again. It needed to grow that total awareness. Also, only 2000 people – predominantly Aucklanders –

actually got to eat at the restaurant and really live the whole campaign experience end to end. The company needed many more people to have the full, end-to-end experience.

The brief to the ColensoBBDO creatives in 2009 was to create a 'job done' that could be experienced by thousands more people, all over New Zealand, and to make it even more participatory by using online, events and social networking tools to a greater extent.

The winning idea

On 14 September 2009, Yellow Pages and ColensoBBDO challenged ordinary Kiwi Josh Winger to create the world's first chocolate bar that tasted of the colour yellow, using only contacts from Yellow Pages' online, mobile and print products. Between October and March, Josh worked out of his Mt Eden office with 45 businesses listed in Yellow Pages, the media and thousands of New Zealanders, to create Yellow Chocolate. With flavour technologists Sensient, and taste tests throughout the country, he determined what the colour yellow tasted like. With Donovan's Chocolate he had that taste made into a chocolate bar. With Seven Design he created the packaging and retail displays. With Progressive Enterprises he cut a distribution deal which saw the bar stocked in Foodtown, Countdown and Woolworths supermarkets and Gull service stations throughout the country. With Special Problems he created and launched an advertising campaign for the bar.

The winning media strategy and marketing mix/execution

The media objective was to reach and involve as many New Zealanders as possible, utilising as many media touchpoints as possible. The heart of the media strategy was a completely new channel – a chocolate bar. The bar was of course the culmination of the entire campaign, but also a highly impactful piece of communication. As tens of thousands of New Zealanders paid their $2 at Foodtown and then sat down to bite into a bar of Yellow Chocolate, they had read about Josh's mission and learnt about Yellow Pages' products and how they are still the best way to get any job done.

Along the way, Yellow Pages put particular emphasis on progressive media such as online, social networking, TV content partnerships and of course the chocolate bar itself. Yellow Pages was the first New Zealand brand to create a live Twitter billboard, and it designed Facebook integration that is now being used by Facebook itself as a case study example. The primary reason for that emphasis on new media was to achieve the brand objective of being perceived as modern and relevant to this century. Of course, these touchpoints would also be more involving and in many cases more credible than traditional media. The full media mix was as follows:

Television	$517 340
Online	$225 517
Press	$120 279
Outdoor	$119 170
Radio	$104 000
Ambient	$32 358
Total media spend	*$1 118 664*

Results and ROI

Perceptions of the Yellow Pages brand were lifted among the majority of New Zealanders as tens of thousands of them paid $2 for a piece of direct communications that demonstrated that Yellow Pages is still the best way to get any job done:

- Over 100 000 bars of Yellow Chocolate were sold in four days, creating New Zealand's fastest ever chocolate bar launch.
- Over 100 000 New Zealanders actively followed the campaign by visiting the website, following Josh on Facebook or Twitter, or signing up for a chocolate trial.
- Over 10% of New Zealanders claim to have talked about the campaign in conversations with their friends, family and colleagues.
- Ultimately 61% of New Zealanders were exposed to the campaign.
- Those 61% feel significantly better about the Yellow Pages brand than those who were not exposed to the campaign.
- Brand health improvements centred around the key metrics of 'Modern and of today', 'There's more to Yellow Pages than the printed directory' and 'Up with the latest technology and innovations'.
- As a result, that 61% of New Zealand consumers and business people see Yellow Pages as being much more of 'a leader in search'.
- Today, Yellow Pages remains the number one place where New Zealanders search for a business and the top, most effective advertising medium in the minds of New Zealand businesses.
- Across the financial year, Yellow Pages outperformed the tough advertising media market, with a smaller decline in traditional revenues compared with the average across other traditional media channels, and a greater growth in online revenues than the market in general, demonstrating that although the business suffered a recessionary impact, that impact was smaller than the rest of the category.

These results are reviewed in more detail below.

Campaign participation, awareness, talkability and brand perception

Participation in the campaign was huge, with 81 000 unique visitors to the website (www.yellowchocolate.co.nz), 17 000 followers on Facebook and Twitter, and 11 000 people signing up to be the first to get a taste of Yellow Chocolate. Once launched, the 100 000 bars sold out in just four days, each one a powerful piece of direct marketing that told the full story of Josh using only Yellow Pages to get his job done. The bar was New Zealand's fastest-selling chocolate bar launch ever, outselling favourites like Cadbury Crunchie and Dairy Milk by two to one. Yellow Chocolate went on to sell on Trade Me for up to $40 for a single bar, and $320 for a pack of 20 bars. The campaign was ultimately seen by 61% of the country. Well over 1 in 10 New Zealanders claim to have talked about the campaign in their conversations with friends, family and colleagues.

Brand health among that 61% of New Zealanders is significantly better than among those that were not exposed to the campaign, particularly among those critical measures of 'Modern and of today' and 'more to Yellow Pages than the printed directory' (Figure 5.6).

Compared with the Treehouse campaign, the improvement in brand health between those that saw the campaign and those that did not is much greater for the Chocolate campaign:

	Treehouse	Chocolate
Is modern and of today	4% better	32% better
More than the print directory	13% better	18% better
Up with the latest technology	11% better	29% better

With the Chocolate campaign, Yellow Pages made more New Zealanders feel better about the Yellow Pages brand than they had in the previous year, demonstrating that the Chocolate campaign built on the success of the Treehouse and grew brand health further again.

Perceptions of Yellow Pages being a 'leader in search' are significantly stronger among those exposed to the campaign (Figure 5.7).

Product usage

Despite consumers being given many more on- and offline ways to search for businesses, Yellow Pages remains the number one choice for New Zealanders (Figure 5.8).

Again, despite continued efforts from other advertising media, small and medium-size businesses in New Zealand still perceive Yellow Pages to be by far the most effective advertising medium for them (Figure 5.9).

Across the campaign recallers are more likely to associate Yellow Pages with being trusted, modern, more than just print and up with the latest technology

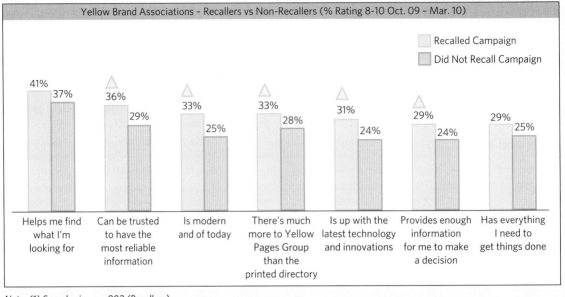

Note: (1) Sample size n = 802 (Recallers)

△ Significantly higher than non-recallers
▽ Significantly lower than non-recallers

Figure 5.6 Yellow Pages brand associations: recallers vs non-recallers of the campaign
Source: TNS Conversa.

Perceptions of Yellow Pages leadership are significantly stronger amongst recallers of the campaign

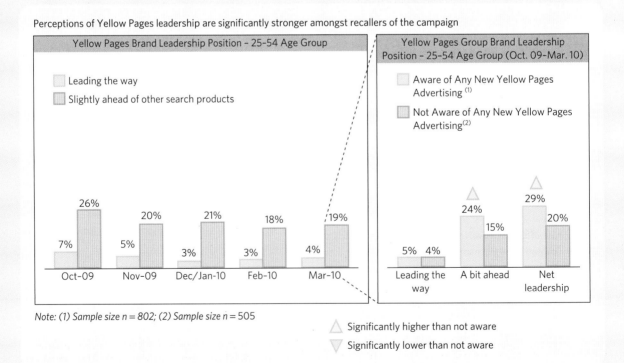

Note: (1) Sample size n = 802; (2) Sample size n = 505

△ Significantly higher than not aware
▽ Significantly lower than not aware

Figure 5.7 Perceptions of Yellow Pages leadership
Source: TNS Conversa.

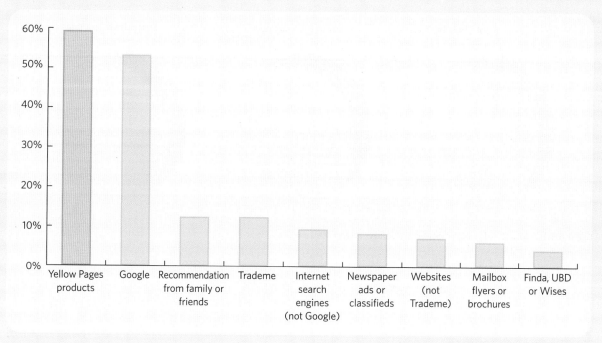

Figure 5.8 Information sources used when searching for a business – June 2009 to May 2010
Source: TNS Conversa.

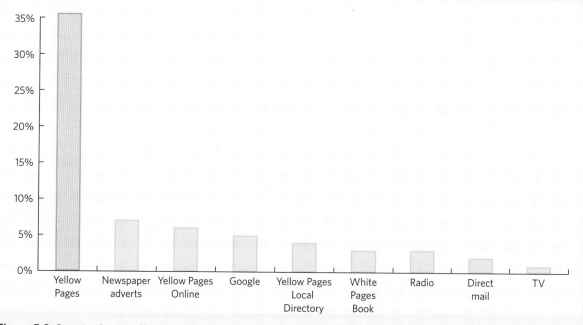

Figure 5.9 Perceived most effective advertising media for small and medium-size businesses – June 2010
Source: TNS Conversa.

Staff and customer engagement

As part of the campaign, activities were used to create staff involvement and interest. This started with clues for staff to guess what product the new campaign was going to be for, trialling the potential product and ending with a treasure hunt for Yellow Pages Chocolate. A survey was carried out

with 415 Yellow Pages staff to assess the impact of the campaign: 81% of staff followed the campaign; 87% talked about it with family and friends; 35% bought a bar; and overall 79% thought the campaign successfully promoted Yellow Pages (Figure 5.10).

Of Yellow Pages' high-value advertiser customers, 120 had a sales rep deliver them a bar before they were made →

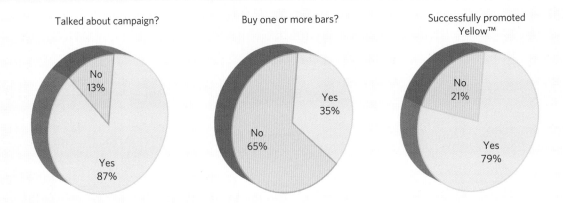

Figure 5.10 Impact of the campaign on Yellow Pages staff
Source: Yellow internal staff survey.

available to the public. The response from advertiser customers was unanimously positive.

Business performance

Given significant industry commentary and speculation surrounding Yellow Pages' business performance, it is important to note that across the 2009 calendar year, Yellow Pages far outperformed the rest of the advertising media industry. Bruce Cotterill, CEO, Yellow Pages Group, stated in August 2010:

> *During the later half of the Yellow® chocolate campaign there was a considerable amount of negative PR about the financial stability of the Yellow business. To be clear, these issues relate to YPG Finance Limited, and are a result of the high purchase price paid for the business ($2.24B) and an overall softening in the economy. The core Yellow operating business continues to perform strongly and is very profitable, with profit in excess of $150M in the financial year ending June 2010.*

As a consequence of the recession, the traditional media market declined by 14%, with print media hardest hit, falling 17%. Across the same period, Yellow Pages' print revenues declined by just 8%. Online, the market grew by 11%, but Yellow Pages' online growth was over 38%. These successes led to Yellow Pages increasing its share of the New Zealand media market from 11% in 2008 to 12.2% in 2009. During the period January–June 2010, it was 1.6% ahead of forecast sales.

Wrapping up

The Yellow Chocolate campaign engaged over 60% of New Zealanders in the Yellow Pages brand, and perceptions of

that large majority are measurably and significantly better as a result of being exposed to the campaign. Importantly, the campaign improved on the successes of the earlier Yellow Treehouse campaign, engaging many more New Zealanders, and making those people feel even better about the Yellow Pages brand. This was achieved with a budget 17% lower than the Treehouse. Yellow Pages remains the number one place where New Zealanders look for a business, and the top, most effective advertising medium in the minds of small and medium-size businesses. As a result, Yellow Pages continues to significantly outperform the advertising media category.

QUESTIONS

1. Describe and assess Yellow Pages' problem identification. Did it make the right analysis, come to the right conclusion and identify the right target groups?

2. At which stage in the product life cycle was the Yellow Pages brand in 2009? Which communications objectives are relevant at that stage? Which objective did Yellow Pages choose with its chocolate campaign? Was that consistent with the product life-cycle stage of Yellow Pages?

3. Imagine you were responsible for relaunching Yellow Pages in your country. Which of the nine communication goals would you include in your marketing communications plan?

4. Which consumer choice situation is applicable to Yellow Pages? What is the influence of this situation on the communication objectives for Yellow Pages?

5. Was the Yellow Pages campaign successful? Why or why not?

6. What could be creative ideas for a new campaign? Think of ideas that can bring in a local touch (in your home country).

Sources: Guy Geerts, Darwin BBDO, ColensoBBDO, Yellow Effie award case New Zealand, 2010.

References

1   Colley, R.H. (1961), *Defining Advertising Goals for Measured Advertising Results*. New York: Association of National Advertisers.

2   Jones, D.B. (1994), 'Setting Promotional Goals: A Communication Relationship Model', *Journal of Consumer Marketing*, 11(1), 38–49.

3   Pickton, D. and Broderick, A. (2009), *Integrated Marketing Communications*, 3rd edition. Harlow: Financial Times/Prentice Hall.

4   Rossiter, J.R. and Percy, L. (1997), *Advertising Communication and Promotion Management*. Sydney: McGraw-Hill.

5   Hefflin, D.T.A. and Haygood, R.C. (1985), 'Effects of Scheduling on Retention of Advertising Messages', *Journal of Advertising*, 14(2), 41–7.

6   Euro Effie (2008), Brussels: European Association of Communications Agencies, http://www.euro-effie.com.

7   Rossiter, J.R. and Percy, L. (1997), *Advertising Communication and Promotion Management*. Sydney: McGraw-Hill.

8   Euro Effie (2008), Brussels: European Association of Communications Agencies, http://www.euro-effie.com.

9   Rossiter, J.R. and Percy, L. (1997), *Advertising Communication and Promotion Management*. Sydney: McGraw-Hill.

10   Curley, B. (2002), ' "Addict" Perfume Targeted by Anti-stigma Campaign', *Join Together*, 21 October, http://www.jointogether.org/news/features/2002/addict-perfume-targeted-by.html (accessed June 2009).

11   Rossiter, J.R. and Percy, L. (1997), *Advertising Communication and Promotion Management*. Sydney: McGraw-Hill.

12   Euro Effie (2008), Brussels: European Association of Communications Agencies, http://www.euro-effie.com.

13   Rossiter, J.R. and Percy, L. (1997), *Advertising Communication and Promotion Management*. Sydney: McGraw-Hill.

14   *De Morgen*, 13 January 2006.

15   Euro Effie (2008), Brussels: European Association of Communications Agencies, http://www.euro-effie.com.

16   Franzen, G. and Moriarty, S.E. (2008), *The Science and Art of Branding*. New York: M.E. Sharpe.

17   Sparks, B.A. and McColl-Kennedy, J.R. (2001), 'Justice Strategy Options for Increased Customer Satisfaction in a Services Recovery Setting', *Journal of Business Research*, 54(3), 209–18.

18   Swanson, S.R. and Kelley, S.W. (2001), 'Service Recovery Attributions and Word-of-mouth Intentions', *European Journal of Marketing*, 35(1/2), 194–211.

19   Lee, M. and Youn, S. (2009), 'Electronic Word of Mouth (eWOM)', *International Journal of Advertising*, 28(3), 473–99;

Sen, S. and Lerman, D. (2007), 'Why Are You Telling Me This? An Examination into Negative Consumer Reviews on the Web', *Journal of Interactive Marketing*, 21(4), 76–94.

20   Hennig-Thurau, T., Malthouse, E.C., Friege, C., Gensler, S., Lobschat, L., Rangaswamy, A. and Skiera, B. (2010), 'The Impact of New Media on Customer Relationships', *Journal of Service Research*, 13(3), 311–30.

21   Purnawirawan, N., De Pelsmacker, P. and Dens, N. (2012), 'To Respond or Not to Respond: The Effectiveness of Organizational Responses to Negative Online Reviews', *Proceedings of the 2012 AMA Conference, Tampa, FL.*

22   Cialdini, R. (1993), *Influence: Science and Practice*. New York: HarperCollins.

23   Wansink, B. and Ray, M. (2000), 'Estimating an Advertisement's Impact on One's Consumption of a Brand', *Journal of Advertising Research*, (November/December), 106–13.

24   Belch, G.E. and Belch, M.E. (2008), *Advertising and Promotion: An Integrated Marketing Communication Perspective*, 8th edition. New York: McGraw-Hill.

25   Joyce, T. (1991), 'Models of the Advertising Process', *Marketing and Research Today*, 19(4), 205–13.

26   Ehrenberg, A.S.C. (1992), 'Comments on How Advertising Works', *Marketing and Research Today*, 20(3), 167–9.

27   Jones, J.P. (1991), 'Over-promise and Under-delivery', *Marketing and Research Today*, 19(40), 195–203.

28   Ehrenberg, A.S.C., Hammond, K.A. and Goodhardt, G.J. (1992), 'The After Effects of Large Consumer Promotions', *Journal of Advertising Research*, 34(4), 11–21.

29   Floor, K. and Van Raaij, F. (1993), *Marketing communicatie-strategie* (*Marketing Communications Strategy*). Houten: StenfertKroese.

30   Euro Effie (2008), Brussels: European Association of Communications Agencies, http://www.euro-effie.com.

31   Euro Effie (2001), Berlin: Gesamptverbrand Werbeagenturen GWA eV, http://www.euro-effie.com.

32   Andrews, K. (1986), 'Communication Imperatives for New Products', *Journal of Advertising Research*, 26(5), 29–32.

33   Euro Effie (2001), Berlin: Gesamptverbrand Werbeagenturen GWA e.V, http://www.euro-effie.com.

34   Koopmans, A.J., Stoevelaar, A.I. and Holzhauer, F.F.O. (1994), 'Voorwaarden voor Effectieve Marketing-communicatie' ('Conditions for Effective Marketing Communication'), *Tijdschrift voor Marketing* (October), 32–5.

35   www.tijd.be, 16 February 2009.

36   Euro Effie (2008), Brussels: European Association of Communications Agencies, http://www.euro-effie.com.

CHAPTER 6
Budgets

CHAPTER OUTLINE

> How communications budgets affect sales
>
> Communications budgeting methods
>
> Factors influencing budgets
>
> Budgeting for new brands or products

CHAPTER OBJECTIVES

This chapter will help you to:

- Understand how communications budgets may influence communications effectiveness
- Get an overview of theoretical and practical marketing communications budgeting methods
- Optimise share-of-voice decisions
- Identify factors that influence budgeting decisions
- Decide upon a communications budget for a new product or brand

Introduction

In this era of globalising, scaling-up and increasing competition, companies are continuously looking for new ways to economise. Restructuring and rationalisation have dominated companies' policies during the recession years of the new millennium. Costs were cut dramatically in areas such as employment and production. Companies tend to save most in those expenses that may be influenced in the short term. Hence, communications budgets are often first in line to be reviewed. The importance of the communications budget and the consequences of changes in this budget on a company's results are regularly marginalised or neglected. However, the communications budget level is one of the determinants of the communications mix effectiveness and thus of company sales and profits. Many researchers, academics and practitioners have been confronted with the difficulty of assessing the appropriate budgets for communications campaigns. Since returns are hard to identify, allocation of funds for promotion is one of the primary problems and strategic issues facing a marketer. This chapter discusses the elements that a marketer should consider when making budget allocations, and offers some insights into the relation between communications intensity and communications effectiveness.

Deciding on the communications budget is not a one-off activity and certainly does not come at the end of the marketing communications planning cycle. The financial resources of a company or brand influence the communications programme, and plans should be continuously assessed against financial feasibility at all stages in the planning process.

There is no ideal formula for making the best budgeting decision. Deciding on the budget requires experience and judgement. Therefore, the budgeting process should be well considered and based on concrete marketing and communications objectives defined in the communications plan. These goals, together with knowledge of past budgets and their effectiveness and competitive actions, will be an important input for the rest of the budgeting process. The second step is to apply one of the budgeting methods discussed in the next section. Using more than one method could help a marketer set minimum and maximum budgets which will be a guide to the rest of the process, such as planning concrete actions. The last step is to evaluate and possibly revise the budget and objectives, and adapt them to specific circumstances.[1] It is better to scale down the objectives (for instance, to reach a smaller target in a more effective way than was planned) than to try to reach the same objectives with a smaller budget. Finally, budgeting decisions should always take into account the long- and short-term effects of communications efforts on sales and profits.

How the communications budget affects sales

To be able to assess the size of the budget, it is important to understand how communications efforts influence sales. **Sales response models** depict the relationship between these two factors. Figure 6.1 shows a concave sales response model. In this model it is hypothesised that sales behave in a microeconomic way, following the law of diminishing returns: the incremental value of added communications expenditures decreases. An explanation for this relation is that, once every potential buyer is reached with the communications mix, they either will or will not buy, and beyond that optimal point prolonged communications will not change the non-buyers' minds. This model suggests that smaller budgets may be as effective as much bigger ones.[2]

Another way to model sales responses to communications efforts is the S-shaped relation (Figure 6.2). This model assumes that, initially, when the level of effort is low, there is no

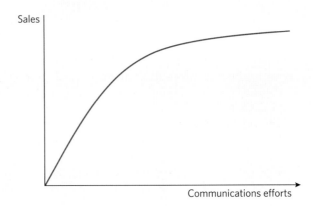

Figure 6.1 Concave sales response model

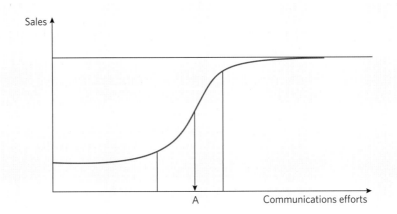

Figure 6.2 The S-shaped sales response model

communications effect at all. Even if communications effort is zero, there will be a certain level of sales, and a minimum investment is needed to enjoy any results of the communications programme and to increase sales. When that level is reached, sales will start to increase with incremental communications expenditures. The higher the investments, the greater the additional sales will be. At point A, increased investments start to lead to smaller changes in sales. It is impossible, even with very high communications investments, to exceed a certain saturation level of sales. This is due to the market and the cultural and competitive environment. Exorbitant communications investments may even lead to negative effects, such as irritation and consumer resistance.[3]

Estimating the relationship between the communications budget or effort and sales or market share is not easy. First of all, marketing communications are not the only marketing mix instrument influencing sales. Prices, product line decisions and changes in the distribution strategy will also influence sales. Furthermore, an effective marketing mix implies that synergy and interaction exist between the various marketing tools. In a well-designed marketing plan each tool reinforces another. A communications plan may lead to better results if the distribution strategy is optimised or the price is lowered. A rearrangement of the product line may result in more effective communications, etc. As a result of this interaction, it is very difficult to isolate the effect of the communications budget on commercial results. Furthermore, sales response models do not take the effect of competitive actions and environmental factors into account.

Finally, and at least as importantly, communications efforts may have both an immediate short-term and a long-term effect on sales and market share. Traditional theories consider communications as a long-term investment in goodwill.[4] Cumulative investments are needed to lead to sales returns, and the long-term effects of communications efforts are much higher than the short-term effects.[5]

This traditional view is challenged by John Philip Jones,[6] who proposes a controversial theory on the short-term effects of advertising, claiming that paradigms stating that sales are mainly influenced by accumulated advertising campaigns of the past are mistaken. He tried to prove that immediate communications effects on sales exist. According to Jones, the whole idea of long-term effects was due to a lack of scanner data. All other advertising testing methods were too irregular and too slow to discover short-term effects. Fluctuations in two-monthly data were explained as seasonal effects. Promotion effects, on the other hand, were traceable and thus researchers deduced that promotions had short-term effects and advertising long-term effects. This belief had serious repercussions on the ratio of advertising to promotions, because marketers confronted with recession and mature markets chose short-term immediate effects on sales instead of long-term image-building advertising. Jones used single-source data[7] relating advertising exposure (a test group with ad confrontation and a control group without ad exposure based on TV viewing behaviour tracking) with scanner data of the same test subjects. Differences in purchases between the two groups were considered to be a measurement of ad effectiveness.

In the survey, there were 142 brands, of which 78 were advertised. Calculations were made on 110 000 observations. Jones introduced a new measurement tool called STAS (Short-Term Advertising Strength). The baseline STAS for brand X is the share of brand X in the budget of families who have not seen an ad for brand X in a seven-day period before purchase. Jones then calculated the share of brand X in the budget of families who were exposed to an ad at least once during the same period. This is called 'stimulated STAS'. The difference between baseline STAS and stimulated STAS is the 'STAS differential', expressing the immediate sales-generating effect of an ad campaign. STAS is calculated as an index by multiplying the ratio stimulated STAS/baseline STAS by 100. A brand with a market share of 6% without advertising and a share of 9% after one week of advertising had a STAS (differential) of $9/6 \times 100 = 150$.[8] Based on these calculations, Jones discovered that 70% of all ad campaigns were able to generate immediate advertising effects. Mostly these effects were small and temporary. When looking at the distribution in deciles of differential scores, 20% had good differential scores, 30% on average a positive score, 30% no definite positive or negative score, and 20% had a negative score and were not effective in beating competing ad campaigns. Only 46% of brands created a long-term effect, defined as an increase in market share compared with that of the previous year. Jones concluded that when a brand is not able to hold its STAS differential constant, this is often caused by lack of continuity in its advertising campaigns.

He also came to the rather surprising conclusion that the first exposure of an ad causes the largest part of sales returns, and that additional exposures will only lead to small effects on sales. The sales response curve would then be a concave degressive function (Figure 6.1).[9] The most effective frequency of an ad campaign according to Jones is one single exposure.

Jones believes that long-term effects will only come about when an ad campaign is also effective in the short term and does not believe in the sleeper effects of marketing communications. This statement is radically opposed to the widespread belief that a higher ad frequency is needed to gain any effects on sales. Therefore, Jones's statements on short-term communications effects are very controversial, and may be an over-reaction to the widespread belief that there are mainly carry-over effects of communications efforts. In reality, both short-term and long-term effects are important.[10]

RESEARCH INSIGHT
Calculating the short-term and long-term effects of advertising

A frequently used and simple sales response model, taking long-term and short-term effects into account, is the following (numbers are exemplary):

$S_t = 250 + 1.4A_t + 0.6S_{t-1}$

where: S_t = sales in period t
            S_{t-1} = sales in period $t - 1$
            A_t = advertising in period t
            250 = constant term expressing that even if there were no advertising at all in period t or in the past, sales would still be €250

The short-term effect of advertising is the coefficient of A_t. Every €1000 invested in advertising results in €1400 extra sales. The coefficient of S_{t-1} summarises the effect of all advertising efforts in the past. The long-term effect of advertising on sales is calculated as $1.4/(1 - 0.6) = 3.5$. This means that, in the long run, every €1000 invested in advertising results in 3500 extra sales.

Communications budgeting methods

Table 6.1 lists the various communications budgeting methods.

Marginal analysis

The basic principle of **marginal budgeting analysis** is quite obvious: to invest resources as long as extra expenses are compensated by higher extra returns. Marketers should invest in promotional or communications efforts as long as their marginal revenue exceeds the marginal communications cost (optimum point indicated in Figure 6.3). Profit is calculated as the difference between gross margin and communications expenditures. It is clear that sales and gross margin will increase with higher communications efforts, but will level off, which leads to lower profits and eventually loss. This analysis has the advantage of estimating the effect of advertising on profits, and derives a normative rule of optimal advertising efforts. However, the analysis remains largely theoretical because of the problems involved in estimating the sales response relation. As a result, marginal analysis is seldom used as a practical budgeting method.[11]

Table 6.1 Communications budgeting methods

- Marginal analysis
- Inertia
- Arbitrary allocation
- Affordability
- Percentage of sales
- Competitive parity
- Objective and task

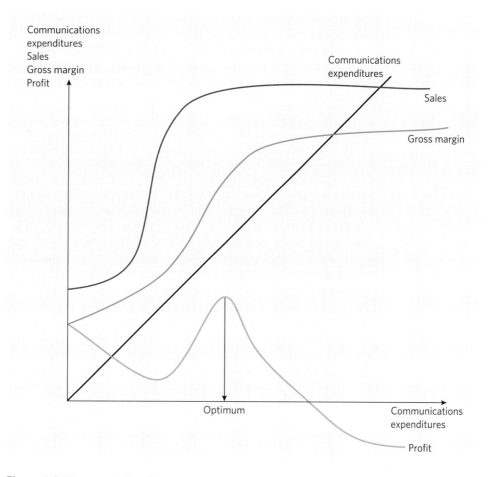

Figure 6.3 The marginal analysis

In addition to the theoretical marginal approach, there are a number of techniques that are relatively easy to use without requiring difficult calculations. Some of the techniques that practitioners commonly use when developing communications budgets are the following.

Inertia

The **inertia budgeting method** is to keep budgets constant year on year, while ignoring the market, competitive actions or consumer opportunities. Needless to say, this is not a very strategic method.

Arbitrary allocation

Again, this is one of the simplest of all budgeting methods, but also one of the least appropriate. Whatever the general manager or managing director decides will be implemented. This very subjective way of deciding how to spend promotional funds does, of course, lack critical analysis and overall strategy. The technique is mostly used by small companies where the managing director's personal preferences (e.g. sponsoring a golf event) and contacts over-rule more strategic processes that take the marketing and competitive environment and customer wants into account.

Affordability method

In this method 'leftover' resources, after all input costs (i.e. human resources, operational and financial costs), are invested in communications. This method is often used in small and medium-size enterprises. Marketing communications are considered to be a pure cost rather than an investment and are mostly not part of the strategic plan, neither are any concrete communications goals defined. As a result, it is a technique without any focus on strategic market or brand issues. This approach will never lead to optimal budgeting, since some opportunities will be lost because of lack of investment-proneness.

Percentage of sales

In this technique, budgets are defined as a percentage of the projected sales of the next year. An alternative to this technique is to take the communications outlays of the past year as a basis and then add a certain percentage, based on the projected sales growth of the following year. These techniques are very popular in many companies due to their ease of use. The percentages used by companies differ. Some sources indicate that they fluctuate around an average of 5%.[12] Other authors speak of percentages between 0.5% and 10%.[13] Although they are commonly used and, like the **affordability method**, ensure that costs do not threaten profits, these budgeting methods have some notable disadvantages. The **percentage of sales budgeting method** could lead to overspending in markets in which these kinds of investments are not needed and at the same time communications budgets might be too small where they might have had a major impact. Decreasing returns on sales will lead to smaller communications budgets, which will certainly not help to change the negative sales evolution. Communications budgets should not be the result of sales but rather should create demand and thus push up sales. This technique also defends the theoretical insight that sales are dominated by communications investments and that other marketing mix elements do not have an impact on sales. This technique does not consider any potential sales growth areas and will limit sales performance.

Another common way of using the percentage of sales method is to take the sales of the past year instead of projected sales, but that is even worse. This method uses past performance as a *ceteris paribus* situation. Therefore, it is unlikely that the company will make progress (unless a lucky wind changes the competitive environment or consumer demands in the right direction).

A last variant of this method is to take a percentage of profits instead of sales. This has the same disadvantages, as an existing brand might need less advertising than a recently launched brand which is not making any profit at all during the first year. Losses will lead to cancelling communications budgets and thus to abandoning all hope instead of investing in brand communications to make them profitable again.

Competitive parity

Competitive parity budgeting means that companies look at the amount of money competitors spend on communications and then copy their budgets. The logic of this method lies in the fact that the collective behaviour of a market will not skew much of the budget optimum. The advantage of this method is that the market will not be destabilised by over-investments or extremely low promotional budgets. This method is often used in fast-moving consumer goods where sales are believed to be highly influenced by advertising and communications spending.

Nevertheless, the theoretical basis of this method has some disadvantages. The underlying assumption is again that promotional spendings are the only variable that influences sales. Furthermore, a company assumes that the competitor's communications budget was set in an effective and efficient way. Lastly, this method implies that resources, operational methods, opportunities and objectives of competitors used as a benchmark are exactly the same as those of the company itself. These are three quite dangerous assumptions. Companies may have other market definitions or other targets, leading to other activities and products in other stages of their life cycle, which make comparisons a difficult and unreliable technique for financial decisions. The parity method is also based on historical data and not on competitors' plans for the future. Believing that competitors will adhere every year to the same communications efforts is probably not the best analytical way to make marketing plans.

Some researchers have developed paradigms that are of practical use to marketers wanting to assess the effects of their share of voice (SOV) on their share of market (SOM). Share of voice is calculated as the ratio of own communications investments divided by the communications investments of all market players. A study on the impact of advertising of competitors with comparable products on market share, not taking into account the advertising quality or any formal or content characteristics of advertising, came to the following conclusions.[14] Ad spendings will only influence market share (SOM) when there is a different advertising intensity over a long period. Marginal budget changes do not affect SOM. If competitors aggressively augment their communications budgets, this can be countered by following with increasing communications expenditure. If, however, there is no reaction to this attack, the increase in SOV will lead to a higher SOM. This means that market leaders will have to track the expenditures of competitors and react to changes to prevent them from gaining market share.

As shown in Figure 6.4, the largest and the smallest player in the market are located above the 45° line. This means that their SOV is smaller than their SOM. The follower in a market is located in a position where it has a higher SOV than market share. Leaders enjoy economies of scale and have a smaller advertising cost per unit. The smallest players should focus on niches because they do not have the resources to compete with the leader and are only profitable if they concentrate on specific niches and forget growth ambitions. If followers want to increase their market share, they will have to increase their SOV above their SOM. This will put pressure on their profitability, which could be dangerous for their competitive positions. This is why stuck-in-the-middle positions are very difficult to hold and market consolidation will lead to two or three large leaders, like Coca-Cola and Pepsi in the cola market. These leaders will have to compete with local or national strong brands (niche players). A market will stay in equilibrium as long as the market leaders keep their SOV within a certain range. Market shares and positions will only change with a minimum of 20 or 30 percentage-point differences in SOV.

In Figure 6.5 a matrix is proposed with strategic recommendations for communications budgets in different market situations.

The relation between SOV and SOM in different market situations was also studied by Jones.[15] Brands with a higher SOM than SOV are called profit-taking brands. Brands with the opposite relation are investment brands. In his study of 23 countries, data on 1096 brands in repeat-purchase packaged goods markets were collected (Table 6.2).

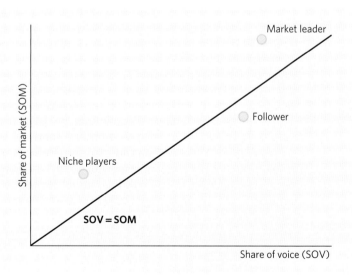

Figure 6.4 Relation between SOM and SOV in market dynamics

Source: Reprinted by permission of *Harvard Business Review*. Based on 'Ad Spending: Growing Market Share' by Schroer, J.C. 68(1), 1990. Copyright © 1990 by the Harvard Business School Publishing Corporation. All rights reserved.

Figure 6.5 SOV effect and strategies for different market positions

Table 6.2 The relation between SOV and SOM

	All brands	Profit-taking brands % in total	Investment brands % in total
Total	1096	44	56
SOM 3% and less	224	27	73
SOM 4%–6%	218	37	63
SOM 7%–9%	153	41	59
SOM 10%–12%	112	45	55
SOM 13%–15%	77	56	44
SOM 16% and more	312	59	41

In Table 6.2, it can be seen that the percentage of profit-takers among brands with a small market share is low. The higher the market share, the more profit-taking brands will appear: 59% of brands with a market share of 16% or more have an SOV that is lower than their SOM. Some explanations can be offered to explain this phenomenon. Small brands have to invest in communications to create brand awareness. Larger and usually older brands are often being 'harvested'. Communications budgets are cut in order to make the brand more profitable. Among brands with market shares larger than 13%, harvesting could be a valid explanation for their profit-taking status. Twenty-eight per cent of profit-taking brands are able to charge a price premium and two-thirds of profit-takers are able to gain market share. Economies of scale in advertising are explained by Jones as a tendency for popular brands to benefit from above-average purchase and repurchase frequency. He calls this phenomenon 'penetration supercharge' and illustrates his theory with Unilever's Lux brand. Lux is sold in 30 countries and has an average market share of 17% and an average SOV of 14%. Unilever is able to keep the market share stable and occasionally enjoys sales increases. In some markets, Lux tried to economise by lowering SOV. In markets where SOV was below 12%, SOM began to fragment. The conclusion is that the under-investment barrier is 5% (17 − 12%).

The relation between SOM and SOV provides an objective tool for companies to compare their communications spend with the budgets of other players in the market. This allows marketers to make a better analysis. The average SOV helps to estimate the maximum under-investment that big brands can afford without losing too much of their market position.

BUSINESS INSIGHT
Relating budgets to top-of-mind brand awareness

Besides sales effects, the result of the marketing communications effort can also be measured in other terms, such as brand awareness. In the following graph the efficiency of the advertising campaigns of different banks is analysed. On the horizontal axis budgets are measured. The vertical axis shows top-of-mind awareness of bank names. For two consecutive years, the relationship between the two factors is shown. The more a bank moves to the upper left corner of the graph, the more efficiently it is spending its resources. The analysis also permits a comparison of the own company with competitors.

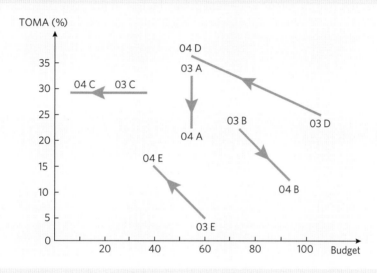

Top-of-mind awareness and advertising budgets

Objective and task method

This method is one of the least arbitrary methods, which makes it a difficult technique to use. It differs from the other methods in that it starts from communications objectives and the resources that are needed to reach these planned goals. All needed investments are then added and this will lead to the overall communications budget. It requires more strategic planning and investment analysis and is therefore clearly superior to all the other methods. Moreover, budgets can be evaluated each year, and this feedback will lead to improved decision-making and more efficient budgeting in the future. The difficulty in this method lies in the estimation of profit impacts of different communications actions and tactics. Therefore it is of the utmost importance that historical data on, for instance, sales promotion responses in each market are stored. But estimating all costs of every action needs some effort and often the final costs of an action are difficult to foresee.[16]

Table 6.3 shows the three most frequently used budgeting methods in the USA.[17] Percentage of sales is the most commonly used communications budgeting technique. It is likely that variants such as percentage on last year's returns and percentage on profits are also commonly

Table 6.3 Budgeting methods most often used in the USA

Budgeting method	Consumer goods	Business-to-business
1. Percentage of expected sales	50%	28%
2. Affordability method	30%	26%
3. Arbitrary method	12%	34%

Source: after *Advertising Media Planning*, Lincolnwood, IL: NTC Business Books (Sissors, J.Z. and Surmanek, J. 1986)
© The McGraw-Hill Companies, Inc.

used. Spending what is left after all other costs are covered is also popular, and the **arbitrary budgeting method** is frequently used in smaller companies and business-to-business contexts. A survey by Belgian Business & Industry revealed that 40% of all business-to-business companies had no preset communications budget: funds were allocated according to needs. Eighteen per cent said they had a budget, but admitted that the funds were not allocated to specific tasks and objectives.

BUSINESS INSIGHT
Experimental budgeting

Experimental budgeting implies using different budgets on different locations or in separate markets. Comparing results of split-run test groups will allow a company to gain insights that will enable it to identify optimal communications budgets. Of course, as in every split-run experiment, test groups should be fully comparable and other possible influential variables should be kept constant. A well-known example of experimental budgeting is the case of Budweiser beer.[18] Anheuser-Busch, manufacturers of Budweiser, split the USA into 200 geographic areas. In the experiment test areas were randomly assigned to experimental groups. One of the areas, the control group, received a communications budget level which was believed to be the optimal level. All other groups received budgets ranging from −100% to +300% of that of the control group. Tests lasted from 12 to 24 months and were evaluated by sales responses compared with the five-year, seasonally adjusted sales trend line. The results of these experiments indicated that the advertising expenditures of Anheuser-Busch were too high. Reducing the communications budgets would have only a minor effect on sales. By lowering the advertising costs, the total cost per draft Budweiser beer also decreased. This allowed Anheuser-Busch to drop the price, which led to increased sales and market share. The Budweiser case demonstrates that experimental budgeting can be very effective and, when overspends are found, budget cuts might lead to increased market share.

However, there are some fundamental disadvantages with this method. Firstly, experiments tend to be expensive. To test different budget levels it would be necessary to assign an amount of non-optimal budgets. High budgets will lead to a spill of resources and low budgets could affect market positions. Moreover, experiments and the data-gathering process require additional investments. When cutting costs through reducing the number of test groups and/or the test period, less accurate and thus less reliable results will be achieved. A second disadvantage is that experiments are hard to control and that uncontrollable factors such as competitive actions, distribution influences, etc., are likely to skew the experimental settings. It is also very difficult to reach each of the test groups with different isolated communications channels and, when regional media are used, communications impacts might not be comparable with the traditional national media coverage.

Factors influencing budgets

A number of factors may influence the budgeting decision or may call for budget adjustments.[19] They are summarised in Figure 6.6.

The smaller the targeted markets, the easier it is to reach the targets in a cost-efficient way. Spending too much in small markets leads to saturation, and overspends are likely to be ineffective. Larger markets imply more dispersed target groups which are more difficult to reach and thus more expensive. When particular markets have higher potential, it may be a good idea to allocate more money to these specific markets. Brands with smaller market shares and new brands require a high communications budget; larger well-established brands and 'harvested' brands in the mature stage of their life cycle could do with a lower allocation of communications funds.

Some studies[20] show that companies and brands with larger market shares have an advantage in communications costs (such as better media space buying, synergy between different communications mix elements on different company brands, better media rental rates and lower production costs) and can thus spend less money on promotional activities while having the same or even better sales. However, other research[21] claims that there is no evidence that larger companies are able to support their brands with lower advertising costs than smaller ones. A number of organisational factors that have a potential influence on the budgeting decision can be identified:[22] the organisational structure (centralised vs decentralised, formalisation and complexity), the use of experts such as consultants, the organisational hierarchy, preferences and experiences of decision-makers and decision-influencers, and pressure on management to reach certain budgets.

Sometimes it is necessary to make adjustments to the planned budgets during the year or during the communications campaign. If sales and profits lag behind projected and budgeted figures (planning gap), cutting communications efforts is often the easiest and fastest way to increase profits. Of course, this will only have an immediate effect in the short term. In the

Figure 6.6 Factors influencing communications budgets

Source: Based on Belch, G.E. and Belch, M.A. (1998), *Advertising and Promotion. An Integrated Marketing Communication Perspective.* New York: Irwin/McGraw-Hill.

long run this might lead to eroding competitive edges and market and brand positions. Crisis situations such as troubles with production or distribution might need exceptional investments in public relations and crisis communications. Other internal occurrences such as financial scandals, strikes, ecological catastrophes, etc., might also demand budget adjustments.

Unexpected opportunities or threats in the market might change strategic plans and communications budgets, as well as unexpected moves by competitors, new legislation, new media and changes in media costs.

Economic recessions will often have serious consequences for communications budgets. Consumers spend less money, and shrinking markets mean stronger competitive battles in which price is a commonly used weapon. Companies may react in one of two ways with regard to their promotional spending. Some try to economise in every way possible. A substantial amount of all costs are fixed and cannot be lowered in the short term. Most companies are attracted by a budget that is quite easy to bring down: the communications budget. Other companies react by increasing their budget, believing that extra investment will drive sales up. A crisis is regarded as the ideal moment to establish their position. This is called anti-cycle budgeting. Market share is gained during recessions and then defended in periods of a booming economy. Some multinationals such as PepsiCo, Coca-Cola, General Mills, Kellogg's and Procter & Gamble have a strong belief in long-term investments in marketing communications.

Some companies prepare contingency budgets. These are reserve budgets provided for financing quick management actions as necessary. These crisis actions are planned in so-called contingency plans. They stipulate which actions must be taken when, for instance, significant drops in sales occur or an important competitor switches to aggressive promotional actions or launches a new product. Reaction time will be substantially lower in such cases when all appropriate actions and budgeting have been foreseen.

Budgeting for new brands or products

Although budgeting for existing brands in established product categories is the most common task for marketers, often they are confronted with the problem of budgeting for a brand or product launch. This is even more difficult than the former. Historical data on the budget settings that have been successful are not available and consequently easy-to-use schemes as discussed above are not appropriate for estimating required budgets.[23]

The primary budgeting method for launching new brands or products should be the objective-and-task method. But given the uncertainty and lack of historical data, this is not only a difficult budgeting method but also one that is not risk-free. Therefore, other methods are good back-ups to compare estimations made earlier. A marketer may, for instance, examine the industry advertising-to-sales (A/S) ratio (advertising intensity) for the market in which a brand is to be launched. The marketer may decide to set a budget that is higher than the industry average in order to make an impact. Doubling the A/S ratio is considered a safe guideline for the first year of introduction. In the second year, overspending the ratio by 50% should do. Of course, it could be even more informative to make comparisons with particular competing brands or products.

Peckham, a consultant with AC Nielsen, developed a rule of thumb for new, fast-moving, consumer good brands.[24] Peckham's 1.5 rule recommends setting the SOV of the brand to be launched at 1.5 times the desired SOM at the end of the brand's first two years. A limitation of Peckham's rule is that it is only applicable in markets or product categories for which there is a strong correlation between SOV and SOM. A study of 638 firms across 20 industries[25] found a strong relationship between SOV and SOM across a broad range of industries for consumer as well as industrial products.

It is quite easy to calculate SOV once the industry communications budgets are known, but to estimate target market shares, the brand's order of entry on a market should be studied.[26] In almost all markets, a brand's competitive advantage is determined by the order of entry on a market. Pioneer brands often enjoy market share leadership, the second brand gets the second-largest market share, etc.[27] The market share of a brand entering a category is on average 0.71 times the share of the previous entrant, although for frequently purchased (fast-moving) consumer products it is 0.92.[28] Overcoming this order-of-entry effect by later entrants is difficult and can only be achieved when introducing a product of superior quality, by spending a lot more on advertising or by making advertising of better quality. Quality of advertising – that is, advertising that gets better results in getting the message across and creating better awareness, being more persuasive or getting higher purchase intentions or sales results – depends on the creative work of advertising agencies and the media planning job of media agencies. These factors have not been considered here but are, of course, of huge importance and influence the effectiveness of and consequently the required budget. However, according to some studies,[29] in about 76% of all product categories order-of-entry advantages in market share are never overcome.

Summary

Sales response models have been developed to describe the relationship between communications budgets and communications effects. However, the extent to which sales respond to advertising depends on a number of other factors, such as the product range, price and distribution strategies, the marketing environment and the competition. As a result, it is very difficult to decide on communications budgets on the basis of these models because the effects of communications efforts on sales cannot be isolated. Furthermore, traditionally, advertising is assumed to affect sales only in the long run (although this point of view is radically contradicted by the works of Jones), which makes it even harder to decide on budgets in terms of effectiveness. Therefore, companies often resort to more practical and easier, but not very relevant, budgeting methods such as inertia, arbitrary allocation, affordability and percentage of sales. In the objectives and task method, the communications needs are assessed, after which a task-related budget is defined. In the competitive parity method, companies analyse their market position and decide on their share of voice accordingly. Communications budgets are influenced by multiple factors, such as a crisis situation, contingencies, unexpected opportunities, economic recessions and other market and company factors, and companies should always be alert and prepared to adapt budgets to changing situations.

REVIEW QUESTIONS

1. What is a sales response model and why is it not easy to estimate?
2. Discuss Jones's theory on the short-term and long-term relationship between advertising budgets and sales.
3. Discuss the various communications budgeting methods that are frequently used by practitioners.
4. What is the relationship between share of voice and share of market, and how does it affect budgeting?
5. What are the factors that influence the budgeting decision?
6. How should the communications budget for a new product launch be determined?

Further reading

Butherfield, L. (2003), *AdValue*. New York: Butterworth–Heinemann.

Jones, J.P. (2006), *When Ads Work: New Proof that Advertising Triggers Sales*, 2nd edition. Armonk, NY: M.E. Sharpe.

Krieger, A.M. and Green, P.E. (2006), 'A Tactical Model for Resource Allocation and its Application to Advertising Budgeting', *European Journal of Operation Research*, 175(3), 1782–97.

Pringle, H. and Marshall, J. (2011), *Spending Advertising Money in the Digital Age: How to Navigate the Media Flow*. London: Kogan Page.

CASE 6:
Budgeting in the automobile industry

ACEA's report of 2008 reveals a heavy impact of the current financial and economic crisis on Europe's passenger car and commercial vehicle manufacturers. Production as well as demand for vehicles, which had grown in 2007, began to dip in the first quarter of 2008, affected mainly by the rise in oil prices. By the beginning of the third quarter, the European economy slipped into reverse, which resulted in a steeper decline. This accelerated in a turbulent final three months. By March 2009, government scrappage incentive schemes had been introduced in ten countries to boost flagging markets and help sustain the transition to 'greener' cars. However, the effect is mainly seen in the segment of small–medium-sized cars, and measures are still needed to encourage fleet renewal in all segments, boosting demand for the cleanest, safest models. The world economy had a strong recovery in the first half of 2010 but slowed down again in the second half of the year. The deceleration that was noted in Q3 was expected due to the withdrawal of stimulus measures and the fading away of positive impulses from the inventory cycle. The positive evolution of economic growth remained gradual and uneven across EU Member States. Germany is leading this recovery, while other countries are still facing the economic crisis.

European (EU27, no figures for Malta and Cyprus) new passenger car registrations dropped by 5.5% to 13 360 599 units in 2010 compared with the previous year. These results varied across the major markets. Spain and the UK saw an increase of new car registrations by respectively 3.1% and 1.8%, whereas Germany recorded a serious drop by 23.4%. The Italian (−9.2%) and the French (−2.2%) markets also experienced a decline. The biggest increase

was tracked in Ireland where new car registrations grew by 54.7%, after a major drop of 62.1% in 2009. In 2011, most of the significant markets experienced a decrease in new car registrations, from −2.1% in France to −4.4% in the UK, −10.9% in Italy and −17.7% in Spain. The exception to this decline was Germany with an increased demand for new cars of 8.8%. It is still the largest market with a total of 3 173 634 new registrations. Germany is followed by France with 2 251 669 units and by the UK with 1 941 253 registrations.

Consumer choices reflected concerns about the economy. Market penetration of small cars was the highest ever in 2009 at 45% but decreased slightly in 2010 to a level of 43.4%; 4 × 4 penetration, which had peaked in 2007 at 9.9%, fell back to 8.8% in 2010, with a dramatic fall in France from 7.2 to 4.2%. In the EFTA countries (Iceland, Norway and Switzerland), the average 4 × 4 penetration is 26.6%. Iceland has the highest penetration level of 4 × 4 vehicles at 39.3%. Average engine size fell to 1639 cc, from 1706 cc a year earlier, while average power output, which had risen steadily since 1990, fell to 85 kW and is at the same level as in 2006. More than half of all new cars sold in Western Europe were diesel models (51.8%), compared with 40.9% in 2002; the diesel boom continues. New cars with diesel models have the highest penetration in Belgium (75.9%) and Norway (74.9%).

During 2010 a total of 15.1 million vehicles were produced in the EU, representing 26% of the total world production. With an increase of 8%, the automobile industry has not yet attained the pre-crisis levels. The total produced units in 2010 were still down by 6% compared with

2008, and reached the lowest level recorded since 1997, with the exception of 2009. After a dramatic drop in Austria (125 836 in 2008 to 56 620 in 2009), output recovered by 52% to 86 000 units in 2010. Europe's biggest passenger car producer is Germany with 5.6 million cars in 2010, up by 11.8%.

Evolution of number of new passenger cars in Belgium

In 2011 a total of 577 382 new passenger cars were registered in Belgium. The average age of the Belgian passenger car is increasing: in 2011 it was 7 years, 11 months and 24 days, while in 1991 the average age was 6 years and 21 days. Table 6.4 summarises the number of registrations of new private cars in Belgium for the period 2008-11.

Evolution of advertising budgets of car brands in Belgium

The car industry is one of the largest advertising spenders in Belgium, together with government, financial services (banking and insurance), telecoms, retail distribution and fast-moving consumer goods. Table 6.5 gives an overview of total advertising budgets spent by the major car makes in Belgium. These budgets are an aggregation of all traditional above-the-line media: TV, radio, magazines, newspapers, billboards, cinema and Internet advertising.

Table 6.4 Registration of new private cars in Belgium, 2008-11

Brands	2008		2009		2010		2011	
Volkswagen	53 465	9.9%	42 713	8.9%	53 842	9.8%	62 330	10.8%
Renault	49 019	9.1%	46 839	9.7%	58 400	10.6%	61 541	10.7%
Peugeot	52 993	9.8%	44 751	9.3%	52 702	9.6%	48 805	8.5%
Citroën	49 171	9.1%	43 541	9.1%	48 595	8.8%	45 656	7.9%
Opel	45 265	8.4%	40 896	8.5%	40 733	7.4%	42 922	7.4%
Ford	39 563	7.3%	37 808	7.9%	38 531	7.0%	39 065	6.8%
Audi	27 482	5.1%	26 975	5.6%	29 548	5.4%	31 800	5.5%
BMW	31 274	5.8%	25 957	5.4%	29 123	5.3%	29 721	5.1%
Toyota	23 904	4.4%	20 443	4.3%	20 373	3.7%	21 966	3.8%
Mercedes	23 574	4.4%	18 921	3.9%	21 802	4.0%	21 270	3.7%
Volvo	12 423	2.3%	13 214	2.8%	17 227	3.1%	19 786	3.4%
Skoda	13 281	2.5%	12 302	2.6%	15 797	2.9%	19 758	3.4%
Nissan	11 213	2.1%	12 550	2.6%	15 589	2.8%	18 490	3.2%
Hyundai	10 407	1.9%	8 815	1.8%	9 981	1.8%	14 540	2.5%
Dacia	3 483	0.6%	4 050	0.8%	10 215	1.9%	13 980	2.4%
Fiat	15 174	2.8%	12 767	2.7%	15 857	2.9%	13 230	2.3%
Kia	9 825	1.8%	9 593	2.0%	9 684	1.8%	12 407	2.1%
Seat	11 082	2.0%	9 472	2.0%	10 122	1.8%	10 405	1.8%
Suzuki	6 248	1.2%	7 783	1.6%	9 295	1.7%	7 174	1.2%
Mini	7 187	1.3%	5 475	1.1%	6 329	1.1%	6 825	1.2%
Alfa Romeo	4 654	0.9%	3 886	0.8%	6 032	1.1%	6 234	1.1%
Mitsubishi	3 495	0.6%	2 879	0.6%	3 927	0.7%	4 766	0.8%
Chevrolet	4 859	0.9%	4 276	0.9%	5 323	1.0%	4 336	0.8%
Honda	4 808	0.9%	4 466	0.9%	3 676	0.7%	3 358	0.6%
Mazda	5 109	0.9%	3 460	0.7%	3 784	0.7%	2 480	0.4%
Land Rover	2 670	0.5%	1 910	0.4%	2 208	0.4%	2 246	0.4%
Lancia	2 404	0.4%	2 303	0.5%	1 750	0.3%	1 726	0.3%

Table 6.4 (*cont'd*)

Brands	2008		2009		2010		2011	
Porsche	997	0.2%	974	0.2%	1 324	0.2%	1 567	0.3%
Smart	1 868	0.3%	1 393	0.3%	1 196	0.2%	1 304	0.2%
Lexus	823	0.2%	510	0.1%	659	0.1%	1 130	0.2%
Saab	2 607	0.5%	1 264	0.3%	1 091	0.2%	847	0.1%
Jaguar	1 638	0.3%	1 091	0.2%	1 092	0.2%	612	0.1%
Subaru	481	0.1%	584	0.1%	605	0.1%	479	0.1%
Jeep	828	0.2%	491	0.1%	460	0.1%	495	0.1%
MC Louis	341	0.1%	274	0.1%	311	0.1%	343	0.1%
Ssangyong	309	0.1%	268	0.1%	61	0.0%	329	0.1%
Burstner	235	0.0%	193	0.0%	230	0.0%	234	0.0%
Chrysler	1 059	0.2%	541	0.1%	597	0.1%	199	0.0%
Chausson	146	0.0%	120	0.0%	128	0.0%	162	0.0%
Trigano	305	0.1%	176	0.0%	198	0.0%	194	0.0%
Hymer	149	0.0%	152	0.0%	112	0.0%	159	0.0%
Rimor	256	0.0%	183	0.0%	176	0.0%	154	0.0%
Daihatsu	974	0.2%	483	0.1%	300	0.1%	147	0.0%
Ferrari	75	0.0%	89	0.0%	98	0.0%	126	0.0%
Infiniti	12	0.0%	40	0.0%	91	0.0%	123	0.0%
Benimar	27	0.0%	29	0.0%	36	0.0%	118	0.0%
Aston Martin	134	0.0%	86	0.0%	105	0.0%	92	0.0%
Elnagh	44	0.0%	48	0.0%	80	0.0%	88	0.0%
Giottoline	26	0.0%	35	0.0%	74	0.0%	87	0.0%
Adria	120	0.0%	60	0.0%	97	0.0%	85	0.0%
Quattro	128	0.0%	59	0.0%	73	0.0%	85	0.0%
Capron	60	0.0%	72	0.0%	70	0.0%	84	0.0%
Maserati	111	0.0%	93	0.0%	69	0.0%	81	0.0%
Dethleffs	86	0.0%	92	0.0%	87	0.0%	81	0.0%
Dodge	878	0.2%	776	0.2%	607	0.1%	74	0.0%
Euramobil	73	0.0%	72	0.0%	47	0.0%	70	0.0%
Carthago	27	0.0%	18	0.0%	50	0.0%	60	0.0%
Possl	1	0.0%	3	0.0%	23	0.0%	59	0.0%
Challenger	60	0.0%	58	0.0%	90	0.0%	51	0.0%
Rapido	77	0.0%	51	0.0%	59	0.0%	50	0.0%
LMC	31	0.0%	46	0.0%	22	0.0%	48	0.0%
Mobilvetta	18	0.0%	39	0.0%	25	0.0%	41	0.0%
TEC	29	0.0%	39	0.0%	31	0.0%	40	0.0%
Bentley	75	0.0%	45	0.0%	31	0.0%	37	0.0%
Lotus	59	0.0%	43	0.0%	68	0.0%	35	0.0%

Table 6.4 (cont'd)

Brands	2008		2009		2010		2011	
LADA	37	0.0%	13	0.0%	64	0.0%	34	0.0%
Itineo	23	0.0%	43	0.0%	42	0.0%	34	0.0%
Knaus	53	0.0%	39	0.0%	26	0.0%	32	0.0%
Laika	34	0.0%	34	0.0%	35	0.0%	27	0.0%
Morgan	21	0.0%	35	0.0%	29	0.0%	20	0.0%
Cadillac	164	0.0%	73	0.0%	44	0.0%	19	0.0%
VAZ Lada	24	0.0%	13	0.0%	0	0.0%	0	0.0%
MB	953	0.2%	1 029	0.2%	0	0.0%	0	0.0%
Others	634	0.1%	549	0.1%	503	0.1%	429	0.1%
Total	**541 142**	**100%**	**480 463**	**100%**	**551 661**	**100%**	**577 382**	**100%**

Source: From Statistics Belgium, htttp://statbel.fgov.be/nl/modules/publications/statistiques/verkeer_vervoer/inschrijvingen_nieuwe_en_tweedehandse_voertuigen_2008-2011.jsp (accessed May 2012).

Table 6.5 Advertising budgets per year (all media) in Belgium, 2008–11 (€)

Brand	2008	2009	2010	2011
Gillet	30 016	0	0	0
Saab	1 819 302	934 612	2 247 108	783 907
BMW	19 597 054	17 177 907	12 772 607	16 723 090
Mini	4 049 959	3 962 242	2 846 650	4 246 611
Chevrolet	5 972 175	3 772 578	3 443 444	3 902 545
Chrysler	1 258 505	519 912	88 044	0
Chrysler Jeep Dodge	184 231	450 578	134 207	0
Dodge	2 418 768	548 799	101 107	0
Jeep	1 480 329	67 099	2 690	1 569 645
Citroën	16 561 728	20 182 166	21 715 952	25 786 952
Audi	7 900 808	6 224 083	5 844 075	8 230 708
Bentley	3 900	4 100	4 500	0
D'Ieteren Car Centers	51 520	66 866	345 083	300 214
Lamborghini	0	0	4 500	0
Porsche	478 231	640 755	561 438	346 544
Seat	4 075 779	6 498 581	7 233 629	8 582 230
Skoda	5 364 052	3 541 912	6 600 748	7 742 586
VW	17 708 904	18 376 325	21 994 243	25 334 709
VW Commercial Vehicles	0	0	226 754	986 354
Daihatsu	201 264	25 952	3 440	40 779
Mercedes – Benz	12 385 687	7 496 604	8 238 167	12 358 541
Smart	859 943	620 226	1 043 960	1 271 238
Abarth	0	136 532	149 805	59 458

Table 6.5 (*cont'd*)

Brand	2008	2009	2010	2011
Alfa Romeo	3 199 565	3 997 884	5 369 904	6 125 286
Alfa Romeo Fiat Lancia Jeep	0	8 175	41 496	175 699
Ferrari	0	0	3 790	0
Fiat	5 428 752	7 775 307	6 966 174	6 351 272
Lancia	4 346 145	2 730 317	3 014 773	4 114 320
Maserati	79 612	85 543	81 590	79 640
Ford	11 918 615	11 920 675	14 816 280	16 543 587
Cadillac	555 642	0	0	13 082
General Motors	80 135	0	0	0
Honda	3 781 115	2 880 175	1 959 139	1 376 197
Isuzu	36 600	23 713	48 477	34 649
Jaguar	1 892 233	1 358 553	2 423 222	1 914 318
Kia	9 777 815	13 876 799	10 780 670	8 115 447
Hyundai	7 116 927	7 035 385	8 229 257	10 718 717
Hyundai Suzuki Mitsubishi	0	68 506	0	0
Land Rover	4 187 128	2 801 369	1 532 203	2 229 002
Ligier	17 805	26 445	40 871	65 135
Lotus	0	7 244	10 490	0
Mazda	4 717 960	2 932 539	2 165 642	1 163 821
Rover	0	4 830	0	0
Mitsubishi	2 558 938	1 098 444	851 637	1 917 185
Hyundai	0	0	485 197	0
Moorkens Car Division	4 878	1 826	4 195	19 359
Suzuki	3 541 985	1 860 403	2 802 359	1 997 283
Infiniti	192 000	518 794	554 100	2 327 861
Nissan	12 197 401	7 282 914	10 024 540	15 958 628
Opel	12 700 364	11 991 472	12 742 610	14 898 967
Peugeot	14 115 623	14 791 673	26 026 696	26 770 722
Dacia	1 698 216	1 393 528	2 399 295	1 959 414
Renault	23 989 341	22 831 626	18 038 786	20 784 802
Ssangyong	198 646	0	0	85 785
Subaru	1 589 039	364 968	641 550	151 577
Lexus	1 776 878	1 121 752	776 659	3 106 774
Toyota	12 895 701	12 490 697	8 305 282	8 184 642
Volvo	6 634 359	7 796 554	12 902 531	13 155 177
Total	**253 631 572**	**232 325 942**	**249 641 563**	**288 604 458**

QUESTIONS

1. Using Tables 6.4 and 6.5, carry out a share of voice/ share of market analysis of the automobile industry for 2008, 2009, 2010 and 2011. Indicate the profit-taking car makes and the investment makes for each year. Do they match the leaders and followers in this market?

2. Study the figures of German car manufacturers BMW and Audi. What budgeting method would you assume

they are using: a percentage of sales method or a competitive parity method? Why do you think this?

3. Suppose you want to launch the Smart brand on the Belgian market. Your goal is to capture a market share of 1.5% by the year 2011. What budget would you suggest to reach this goal? Consider two methods: the A/S ratio method on the one hand and Peckham's law on the other.

4. What factors might influence advertising budgets in the car industry?

Sources: ACEA economic report for year 2011, www.acea.be; Febiac, www.febiac.be. Thanks to Wendy Van Dyck, Communication Channel Expert, Space Brussels, for providing advertising budgets of the car industry.

References

[1] Bovée, C.L., Thill, J.V., Dovel, G.P. and Wood, M.B. (1995), *Advertising Excellence*. New York: McGraw-Hill.

[2] Arndt, J. and Simon, J. (1983), 'Advertising and Economies of Scale: Critical Comments on the Evidence', *Journal of Industrial Economics*, 32(2), 229–41.

[3] Longman, K.A. (1971), *Advertising*. New York: Harcourt Brace Jovanovich.

[4] Jegers, M. and De Pelsmacker, P. (1990), 'The Optimal Level of Advertising, Considering Advertising as an Investment in Goodwill', *Ekonomicko Matematicky Obzor (Review of Econometrics)*, 26(2), 153–63.

[5] Aaker, D.A., Batra, R. and Myers, J.G. (1987), *Advertising Management*. Englewood Cliffs, NJ: Prentice Hall.

[6] Jones, J.P. (1995), *When Ads Work: New Proof that Advertising Triggers Sales*. New York: Free Press/Lexicon Books.

[7] Jones, J.P. (1995), Editorial, *Harvard Business Review* (January–February), 53–66.

[8] François, J. (1996), 'Forecasting Effect of Advertising on Sales: Reporting on a Large-scale US Research', *Media Line News*.

[9] McDonald, C. (1995), 'Advertising Response Functions: What are They, What do They Mean, and How Should we Use Them?', *Admap* (April), 10.

[10] Dekimpe, M.G. and Hanssens, D.M. (1995), 'The Persistence of Marketing Effects on Sales', *Marketing Science*, 14(1), 1–21.

[11] Belch, G.E. and Belch, M.A. (1998), *Advertising and Promotion: An Integrated Marketing Communication Perspective*. New York: Irwin/McGraw-Hill.

[12] Aaker, D.A., Batra, R. and Myers, J.G. (1987), *Advertising Management*. Englewood Cliffs, NJ: Prentice Hall.

[13] Kaynak, E. (1989), *The Management of International Advertising: A Handbook and Guide for Professionals*. New York: Quorum Books.

[14] Schroer, J.C. (1990), 'Ad Spending: Growing Market Share', *Harvard Business Review*, 68(1), 44–8.

[15] Based on Jones, J.P. (1990), 'Ad Spending: Maintaining Market Share', *Harvard Business Review*, 68(1), 38–43.

[16] Fill, C. (1995), *Marketing Communication: Frameworks, Theories and Applications*. London: Prentice Hall.

[17] Sissors, J.Z. and Surmanek, J. (1986), *Advertising Media Planning*. Lincolnwood, IL: NTC Business Books.

[18] Aaker, D.A., Batra, R. and Myers, J.G. (1987), *Advertising Management*. Englewood Cliffs, NJ: Prentice Hall.

[19] Belch, G.E. and Belch, M.A. (1998), *Advertising and Promotion: An Integrated Marketing Communication Perspective*. New York: Irwin/McGraw-Hill.

[20] Brown, R.S. (1978), 'Estimating Advantages to Large Scale Advertising', *Review of Economics and Statistics*, 60, 428–37.

[21] Boyer, K.D. and Lancaster, K.M. (1986), 'Are There Scale Economies in Advertising?', *Journal of Business*, 59(3), 509–26.

[22] Low, G.S. and Mohr, J.J. (1991), 'The Budget Allocation between Advertising and Sales Promotion: Understanding the Decision Process', *AMA Educators' Proceedings*. Chicago, 448–57.

[23] Rossiter, J.R. and Percy, L. (1998), *Advertising Communication and Promotion Management*. Sydney: McGraw-Hill.

[24] Peckham, J.O. (1981), *The Wheel of Marketing*. Scarsdale, NY: self-published.

[25] Simon, C.J. and Sullivan, M.M. (1993), 'The Measurement and Determinants of Equity: A Financial Approach', *Marketing Science*, 12(1), 28–52.

[26] Rossiter, J.R. and Percy, L. (1998), *Advertising Communication and Promotion Management*. Sydney: McGraw-Hill.

[27] Parry, M. and Bass, F.M. (1990), 'When to Lead or Follow? It Depends', *Marketing Letters*, 1(3), 187–98.

[28] Urban, G., Carter, T., Gaskin, S. and Mucha, Z. (1986), 'Market Share Rewards to Pioneering Brands: An Empirical Analysis and Stratgeic Implications', *Management Science*, 32(6), 645–59.

[29] Buzell, R.D. (1981), 'Are There Natural Market Structures?', *Journal of Marketing*, 45(1), 42–51.

CHAPTER 7
Advertising

CHAPTER OUTLINE

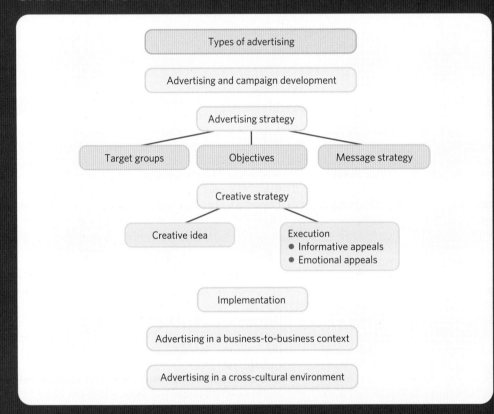

Types of advertising

Advertising and campaign development

Advertising strategy

Target groups   Objectives   Message strategy

Creative strategy

Creative idea

Execution
- Informative appeals
- Emotional appeals

Implementation

Advertising in a business-to-business context

Advertising in a cross-cultural environment

CHAPTER OBJECTIVES

This chapter will help you to:

- Distinguish the various stages in advertising campaign development
- Learn about the information that is needed about the target groups of an advertising campaign
- Understand the various objectives of an advertising campaign and the characteristics of a good set of objectives
- Understand the importance of creativity in advertising
- Evaluate the effectiveness of various execution strategies for rational appeals
- Understand the effectiveness of emotional execution strategies such as humour, eroticism and warmth

Introduction

Advertising is one of the oldest, most visible and most important instruments of the marketing communications mix. Large sums of money are spent on advertising, and no other marketing phenomenon is subject to so much public debate and controversy. Huge amounts of research are devoted to the question of what makes advertising effective and to the role of advertising characteristics on its effectiveness.

As is the case with other communications instruments, special attention has to be devoted to the different steps in advertising campaign development and to the fit between the strategic marketing plan and the advertising campaign. The most crucial step in this process is translating the creative idea in an advertising execution. To this end, it is important to devote a lot of attention to different formal and content techniques and their effectiveness in advertising. But first of all, an overview is given of the different types of advertising.

Types of advertising

Advertising can be defined as any paid, non-personal communications through various media by an identified company, non-profit organisation or individual.[1] Advertising is a good marketing communications tool to inform and persuade people, irrespective of whether a product (Nestlé's Fitnesse keeps you slim), a service (Avis: We try harder) or an idea (Come up against cancer) is promoted. Not surprisingly, advertising is a commonly used tool. Compared with early 2011, in 2012 global advertising spending is on the rise in most parts of the world except Europe (Figure 7.1). Compared with 2010, in which global ad spend was $475.7 billion, ad spends in 2012 were predicted to increase to $529.5 billion, and even to $603.1 billion in 2015.[2]

Different types of advertising can be distinguished on the basis of four criteria, as shown in Table 7.1. First of all, advertising can be defined on the basis of the sender of the message. **Manufacturer advertising** or product advertising is initiated by a manufacturing company that

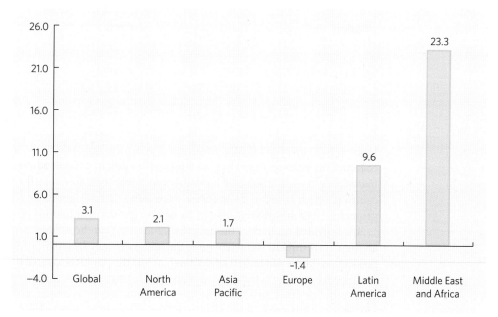

Figure 7.1 Growth in global advertising spend across the world, first quarter 2012 vs first quarter 2011
Source: www.statista.com (accessed 9 July 2012).

Photo 7.1 Outdoor advertising to communicate an idea for a generic 'product category'
Source: Corbis: Tony Savino.

Table 7.1 Types of advertising

Sender	Message
● Manufacturer	● Informational
● Collective	● Transformational
● Retailer	● Institutional
● Co-operative	● Selective vs generic
● Idea	● Theme vs action
Receiver	**Media**
● Consumer	● Audio-visual
● Business-to-business	● Print
– industrial	● Point-of-purchase
– trade	● Direct

promotes its own brands. If a government takes the initiative for a campaign, this is called **collective advertising**. Retail organisations also advertise (**retail advertising**). Sometimes two manufacturing companies, or a retailer and a manufacturer, jointly develop an advertising campaign. This is called **co-operative advertising**. Besides goods and services, ideas can be promoted (**idea advertising**), mostly by not-for-profit organisations (Photo 7.1).

The intended receiver of the advertising message can be either a private end-consumer or another company. In the latter case, the company may buy the products to use in its own production process (**industrial advertising**), or buy the products to resell them (**trade advertising**).

Different types of advertising can also be distinguished according to the type of message conveyed. The difference between advertising focused on informational and transformational consumer motives was explained earlier (see Chapter 3). **Institutional advertising** is the term used to describe government campaigns. **Selective advertising** campaigns try to promote a specific brand, while **generic advertising** campaign promotes a whole product category, such as Dutch cheese, British beef or French wine. **Theme advertising** attempts to build a reservoir of goodwill for a brand or a product. **Action advertising** tries to stimulate consumers to buy a product immediately. Often, the latter is used in support of a sales promotion campaign.

Finally, different types of campaigns can be distinguished on the basis of the medium in which the ad is placed. Two main categories of traditional or above-the-line advertising can be distinguished: audio-visual and print. Other forms of advertising, such as in-store communications (see Chapter 12) and direct advertising (see Chapter 13), are called below-the-line advertising.

Campaign development

Developing an advertising campaign, like any other communications plan, consists of a sequence of steps (Figure 7.2).[3] The starting point is the marketing strategy, on the basis of which a specific advertising strategy needs to be developed. The three main points in the advertising strategy are: the target group (to or with whom are we going to communicate?), the advertising objectives (why are we going to communicate or what are we trying to reach?) and the message strategy (what are we going to communicate?). The most difficult step is translating the advertising strategy into a creative strategy or, in other words, going from 'what to say' to 'how to say it'.

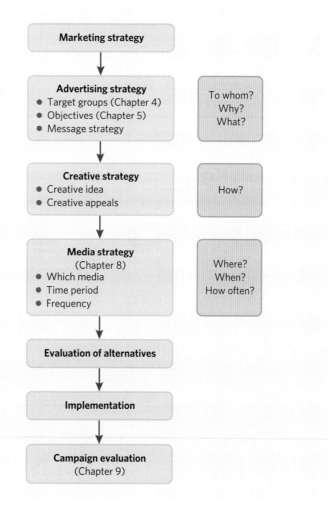

Figure 7.2 Stages in campaign development

Afterwards the media strategy is developed. The different ideas will be evaluated on the basis of the creative brief and objectives stated, and the winning idea will be produced and implemented. In the process, the ads in the campaign may be tested, and often the effectiveness will be assessed after the campaign. Target groups, objectives, media planning and campaign testing are discussed separately (see Chapters 4, 5, 8 and 9, respectively).

Message strategy

What are we going to say to the consumers? The message strategy or advertising platform is a very important element of advertising strategy since it has to convince consumers. They have to know why they should buy the product, to learn in what way it is special, how it is beneficial or advantageous for them, how it can help them, what characteristics it has or what benefits and value it offers, etc. In order to answer the question 'what to communicate?' the advertiser has to know and understand the target group very well: he or she has to know what the product can do for the target group, what the product can mean to them and how the product can help the consumers to reach their goals. Indeed, advertising can only be effective if it benefits the consumer. Therefore, the message cannot be focused on seller objectives, but has to start from the target consumers' motives.[4] Some customers see a car just as a functional vehicle, a means of getting them from A to B. This target group can perhaps be convinced by communicating the brand's attributes (airbag, engine, etc.) or benefits (reliability, safety, etc.). Other customers do not want to buy a car; they want to buy an image, a status. Obviously, communications to the latter group should be different from those to the former group. Communicating a lifestyle, an image or a product's identity might be more suitable than telling customers about attributes or benefits.

Knowing the problems, preferences and aspirations of the target group may be essential for deciding on the right message.

RESEARCH INSIGHT
Advertising to specific target groups: kids and teens and senior citizens

Both kids and teens and senior citizens require a specific advertising approach. The table below outlines some dos and don'ts.

ADVERTISING DO'S AND DON'TS

Kids and teens		Senior citizens	
Dos	**Don'ts**	**Dos**	**Don'ts**
1. Tell a basic story	1. Long dialogues	1. Positive message	1. Remind of getting older
2. Entertain kids	2. Complex messages	2. Intergenerational approach	2. Use senior positioning
3. Surprise kids	3. Imitate kids' talk	3. Focus on cognitive age	3. Age labels
4. Use older models	4. Patronise	4. Promote benefits to overcome guilt	4. Make long story short
5. Remember mum and dad	5. Execution mistakes	5. Use symbols of their youth	5. Take physical consequences of getting older into account

Kids and teens want to hear a basic story (a product is a solution to a problem or a reward for good behaviour), but not a long dialogue or complex message. Children want to be entertained and surprised. They continually look for new experiences and details, and like the use of music, humour, animation, colours, jingles, games, puzzles, etc. Although they do like catchy slogans and are fond of slang and kids' talk, it is better for an advertiser to avoid using it since by the time he or she discovers their sayings they are already out of date. The aspirational age of children is about four years older than they actually are; therefore it is better to cast older children to avoid reactions like 'This is not for me, this is for babies.' Kids hate being patronised, so do not pretend to be one of them or to know better than them. Although you want children to be fond of your brand, it is usually the parents who have to buy it. Therefore, make sure that your appeal is also attractive to parents by mentioning arguments pertaining to health, durability, lifetime value, values, etc. Finally, try to avoid 'wrong executions' such as showing children who are too young or the wrong gender (remember that boys have difficulty identifying with girl characters while girls can identify with both boys and girls) and not using enough visuals (children listen with their eyes!).[5]

Senior citizens represent a group that accounts for 80% of personal wealth and about 40% of consumer spending. Since 80% of consumers over the age of 50 perceive contemporary advertising as irrelevant to them, it is about time to take their needs and motivations into account.[6] Senior citizens know they are getting older and that this will bring inconveniences; they do not want advertising to remind them of this or to confront them with these negative life aspects. Rather, focus on what the product can do for them, what the main benefits are. Another possibility is to stress positive aspects of getting older, such as friendships, children and grandchildren, wisdom and experience.[7] An intergenerational approach may tap into these perfectly, such as featuring grandparents enjoying a certain product or service with the rest of the family,[8] certainly much better than using a senior positioning. Seniors are not looking for a product 'ideal for seniors' because they still want to belong to society and do not want to form an isolated group or, as Ahmad put it: 'Older consumers like to be respected as people and not because they are old in terms of chronological age.'[9] Moreover, many seniors do not feel old (actually, at an age of 55 they feel about eight years younger than they are) and do not want to be addressed as old or senior citizens, certainly not if they have not yet reached the age of 65. Unfortunately, in practice the age of 50 or 55 is often chosen as the boundary.[10] European seniors have lived through war situations and recessions and know what poverty and scarcity mean. As a consequence, many of them still feel guilty about spending money. Therefore, advertising should try to take away the feeling of being thrifty by providing them with good reasons to buy. Many senior citizens are rather critical and want objective, extended information and compelling reasons why they should buy the brand.[11] Nostalgic appeals showing symbols, heroes, music groups, etc., from the seniors' youth can be very powerful. Finally, although seniors do not like to admit it, they do encounter problems when ageing, e.g. sight and hearing problems. Therefore, it is better to use high contrast levels between text and background, a serif font not smaller than 10 points, and slower-paced TV and radio commercials, in which background noise is avoided.[12]

Furthermore, it is important not to confuse consumers. Therefore, most companies stick to promoting one unique benefit of their brand, which can be functional or non-functional. A functional benefit, also called a unique selling proposition (USP), usually refers to functional superiority in the sense that the brand offers the best quality, the best service, the lowest price, the most advanced technology. For example, Gillette is 'the best a man can get'; there is 'no better washing machine' than Miele; Durex Avanti 'gives the most natural feeling'; no card is more accepted than MasterCard, etc. A non-functional benefit usually reflects a unique psychological association to consumers and is referred to as an **emotional selling proposition (ESP)**.[13] CenterParcs is a state of happiness, you buy L'Oréal because 'you are worth it' and you buy a PlayStation 3 because 'this is living'. Other examples of brands that are promoted on the basis of non-functional benefits include Porsche, Rodania, Rolls-Royce, Louis Vuitton, and Van Cleef & Arpels.

In order to know which USP or ESP to go for, the advertiser needs to have a clear consumer insight. These are often revealed by qualitative research. For example, for Dove a consumer insight was that tiny, perfect models in advertising lower women's self-esteem. Therefore, Dove came up with its real beauty campaign showing normal women of all ages, shapes and sizes in an attempt to inspire consumers to feel comfortable with themselves. The

Luxembourg fixed-line operator, TELE2 AB, was well aware of the fact that heavy phone users are sensitive about the cost that the phone represents in their monthly household budget. These heavy users would love to call more if they did not have to worry about the cost. Therefore, TELE2 positions itself on the promise of providing the 'best price offer' and the 'most simple and clear offer'. A pan-European campaign with the slogan 'TELE2, simply phone for less' proved to be very successful in France, Germany, Italy, Austria, Switzerland and the Netherlands.[14]

BUSINESS INSIGHT

Nissan Qashqai: 'urbanproof' for city conquerors

In 2006, Nissan's sales were sliding. It decided to withdraw its Almera and launch a new car for the city segment that had to replace the vacuum left by the Almera. Moreover, the new car formed a nice opportunity for Nissan to take in younger customers. Almera's customer base consisted more of older consumers and, because Nissan did not want to grow old with its consumers, it had to make sure to regularly take in young consumers. To this end, Nissan developed a car that stood out: a combination of a passenger car with the styling of an SUV, a tough car that at the same time was urbanproof.

To help generate sales of 93 000 units across European markets, drive awareness and interest in the Qashqai, attract new, younger consumers with whom Nissan had never connected before, and to avoid cannibalisation of the Nissan's 4 × 4 X-trail, Nissan created a two-phase communications programme. The target group consisted of 25–35 year old, urbanite males in 21 European markets. A consumer insight was that these males enjoy the city and all the challenges it brings; they like to rule the city. Moreover, they want to stand out, and attitude and style are more important to them than functionality. In the pre-launch phase the objective mainly consisted of building awareness. In view of the target group, an online campaign was deemed to be most effective. Therefore, Nissan used viral films with a focus on branding and product details, an official website and blogs on which debates were stimulated. In the second phase, a clear positioning or brand meaning was built to further increase awareness and trigger interest. At this stage, a real integrated campaign was deemed to be most suitable. The communications budget, which was 50% smaller than its strongest competitors (such as the VW Golf), was divided as follows: 48% TV advertising, 13% online, 18% outdoor, 15% print and 6% other. Nissan took over metro stations, wrapped cinemas, used digital floor media at train stations, launched an event and invested in PR. The idea behind the campaign was 'urbanproof'. Keeping the consumer insights in mind, Nissan wanted to link the toughness of the car with the target group's attitude of wanting to conquer the city. The TV ad, for example, featured the car being used as a skateboard and showed its agility at getting around, parking, etc., in a busy city centre. By positioning the Qashqai as urban, Nissan also differentiated the car from the X-trail.

The campaign was very effective in the sense that within two months it became Nissan's top-selling model, without cannibalising the X-trail, and taking in many new, young customers. Between March 2007 and March 2008, 24% of Nissan's cars sold were a Qashqai. The second and third best-selling models were Note with 16% and Micra with 14%. The campaign was awarded a Gold Euro Effie.[15]

Source: Reproduced with permission of Nissan.

Creative idea

Before an advertising agency can start thinking of a creative strategy, the advertiser must give the agency a creative brief. The necessary elements of a creative brief are summarised in Figure 7.3. The **creative brief** or the document that forms the starting point for the advertising agency should contain not only information on the target group, advertising objectives and message strategy, but also sufficient information concerning the background of the company, the product, the market and the competitors. This implies information concerning the past, present and future in order to give the agency as accurate a view of the brand and its environment as possible. Some examples of necessary elements are the long-term company and brand strategy, past, current and desired positioning, former advertising campaigns, message strategies and execution styles, desired media, available budget and timing of the different steps (creative idea, execution strategies, campaign running, etc.).

The first step of the creative strategy is to develop a creative idea. But what is a creative idea? It is hard to give an accurate definition, but let us consider some attempts. A **creative idea** can be defined as an 'original and imaginative thought designed to produce goal-directed and problem-solving advertisements and commercials'.[16] According to others, a creative advertising idea has to be attention-grabbing and should work as a catalyst in the sense that it should create a 'chemical reaction' of immediately understanding the brand's position.[17] According to the jazz musician Charlie Mingus, 'Creativity is more than just being different. Everybody can play weird, that's easy. What's hard is to be as simple as Bach. Making the simple complicated is commonplace, making the complicated simple, awesomely simple, that's creativity'.[18] In essence, a creative idea seems to boil down to a proposition which makes it possible to communicate a brand's position in an original, attention-getting, but easy-to-catch way (Photo 7.2). Several researchers argue that creativity probably is the most important aspect of advertising.[19] An expert panel even held the opinion that 'the selling power of a creative idea can exceed that of an ordinary idea by a multiple of 10'.[20]

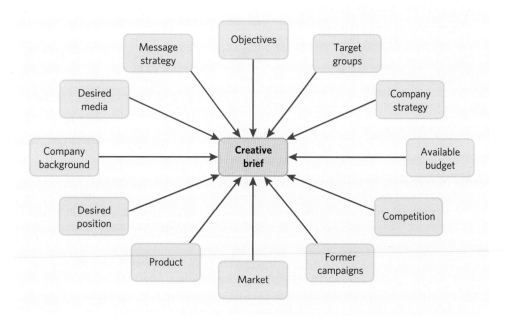

Figure 7.3 The creative brief

Photo 7.2 Eastpak: the selling power of a creative idea

Source: Reproduced with permission of VF Corporation: AMVBBDO.

BUSINESS INSIGHT
Creativity in advertising

A few examples may clarify what is meant by creative advertising ideas:

- Miller beer has a screw cap instead of a crown cap. Miller promoted its beer in TV commercials with the slogan 'twist to open', showing a fat man in his underwear twisting in front of his bottle of Miller beer, pausing a moment to see whether his bottle had opened, and then starting to twist again.

- Volkswagen promoted its Beetle with the slogan 'think small', turning the small size into a competitive advantage, just as Smart tried to do with 'reduce to the max'. Nissan did the opposite, promoting its new pick up using print ads and billboards. To stress the size of the pick up, a countryside picture features a man and, no, not his dog, but his hippopotamus playing with a stick. The baseline reads 'Think Bigger'. Nissan won a Gold Clio Award for this campaign.

- To make clear to the Spanish audience that children should watch less TV and play more, an ad was run in which a little boy is shown watching TV while his dog is watching him. After having waited a while to get a bit of attention, the dog turns away and starts packing its bags. With the bag in its mouth, the dog waits a few minutes in front of the boy, but when the boy does not even look up, the dog sadly leaves.

- Oslo Sporveier wanted to encourage existing users to use public transport more often, as well as encourage new users to take up the habit of using public transport. To reach these objectives, public transport had to be made easier since at that time tickets could be purchased at only one place. Therefore, Oslo Sporveier started to sell season tickets through newsagents. The communications campaign promoting this season ticket featured a ticket collector on a bus. A smug-looking, self-satisfied woman holds her ticket ready for the collector. Just before the collector arrives, a punk seated next to the woman grabs the ticket, eats it, and then shows his season ticket to the collector. The pay-off slogan reads 'Smart people buy season tickets - not single tickets.'[21] A Belgian animated advertising campaign to promote the public bus featured penguins on a flake of ice. Suddenly, a killer whale shows up and prepares for a nice penguin dinner, already slightly opening its mouth. All the penguins smartly move backwards, as a consequence of which the flake of ice tilts up and the killer whale bumps into it as if it were a wall. The ad ends with the baseline 'It's smarter to travel in groups. Take the bus.'

- Nicorette, a product to help smokers give up the smoking habit, received a Silver Euro Effie for its Beat Cigarettes campaign. Instead of showing quitters suffering cravings, they were shown beating a giant cigarette. In some ads the giant cigarette represented a boxing-ball; in others it was used as a battering ram. All ads showed happy quitters in a humorous setting, while the baseline 'Beat cigarettes one at a time. You're twice as likely to succeed with Nicorette' summed it all up.[22]

- Frisk Mints received a Gold Clio Award for its campaign in which an imbecilic-looking guy is brought into a laboratory to test his response latency. In the laboratory, a real horse and a fictitious horse played by humans are shown. The imbecile first has to eat a Frisk and is then asked to distinguish between the real horse and the fictitious horse by pushing a button. Amazingly he succeeds in pressing the right button, after which the slogan 'Frisk sharpens you up' appears.[23]

Source: Reproduced with permission of De Lijn, Belgium.

Besides the need for a creative idea to develop effective advertising, one can question how creative the ad itself has to be. Indirect evidence of the belief in the success of creative ads might be the fact that advertising seems to be more creative than a few decades ago.[24] However, attention-grabbing, originality and imagination do not suffice. In the end, advertising must help to accomplish marketing objectives. The existing studies do not convey consistent results. Some studies[25] claim creativity has a positive impact on ad likeability, brand awareness, brand liking and purchase intentions, but other studies could not find a relation between ad creativity on the one hand and attitude towards the ad, brand attitude, purchase intention or firm profitability on the other.[26] Although it is clear that a creative idea is needed to express a brand's positioning statement attractively, the question remains as to how creative the ad itself should be. Also, research indicates that practitioner views on advertising creativity differ from those of consumers.[27] It often happens that consumers rank commercials differently to creative directors. The latter are often quite surprised that the public do not select the ads perceived as most creative by themselves. The foregoing illustrates that more research is called for to find out how important creativity is in the eyes of consumers and what creativity means to them.

RESEARCH INSIGHT
The relationship between winning a Clio Award and firm profitability

Measuring the return on investment of advertising campaigns is a long-standing issue with marketing professionals. A clear link between advertising expenditures and financial performance is often difficult to establish. Taking it one step further, although there is a common belief that advertising creativity is an essential element of advertising success, the link between creativity in advertising and advertising effectiveness is not an obvious one. The evidence of an impact of creative advertising on the bottom line of companies is anecdotal at best. In the USA, the Clio Awards recognise advertising excellence worldwide in mass media, integrated media, design and on the Internet. The campaigns are judged by a jury of industry experts. Many thousands of campaigns are submitted each year. The winners are made public during an awards ceremony lasting three days. It can be assumed that winning a Clio signals a firm's quality, effectiveness and innovativeness in advertising, and that this information reaches all the stakeholders quickly. In a study of 126 Clio Award-winning companies that were also traded on the New York Stock Exchange, the relationship between winning Clio Awards and the evolution of stock price was examined. The general conclusion of the study was that, in terms of adding value to the winning firms, Clio Awards did not seem to generate any substantial attention from the investment community. The only exception was the group of 16 food advertisers for which a cumulative excess return of 2% was measured. Surprisingly, some of the results seem to indicate that winning an award affects stock prices negatively, for instance for retailers and manufacturers. This may reflect the financial market's bias against perceived overspending on advertising, or even the prejudice that spending too much on advertising is wasteful. The study illustrates that establishing a relationship between advertising efforts, let alone creative ones, and financial results is not obvious.[28]

Creative appeals

BUSINESS INSIGHT
Too powerful to stay in its own commercial

P&G had a hit in 2010 with its award-winning Old Spice ad 'The Man Your Man Could Smell Like', generating almost 42 million views (so far). Who does not remember the atypical ad language 'Hello ladies. Look at your man. Now back to me. Now back at your man. Now back to me. Sadly, he isn't me. But if he stopped using lady scented body wash and switched to Old Spice, he could smell like he is me' going on, showing that anything is possible when a man smells like Old Spice and not a lady.

The success of the first commercial was followed by a successful second ad, and another successful ad, etc. The ads quickly went viral and the brand surprised everybody by posting dozens of improvised scenes of the main actor giving personal responses to everyone who had commented on the Old Spice ads via social networks. All this led to a sales increase in Old Spice products of 170%.

Building on what the public came to expect from Old Spice, P&G's 2012 ad again excels in creativity and originality while keeping on stressing the power of Old Spice. This time, the Old Spice man takes over ads for other P&G products such as Bounce and Charmin. The Charmin ad, for example, features the Old Spice man's head bursting through a box of Freshmates and his hand smashing through the wall showing a can of Old Spice while shouting 'Old Spice is too powerful to stay in its own commercial!' Soon consumers started tweeting messages like 'the Old Spice Man in other commercials = pure brilliance', 'amazing haha', 'disruption earns attention', etc. It looks like creativity is really appreciated by the general public.[29]

Table 7.2 Creative advertising appeals, advertising formats and endorsers

Rational appeals	Emotional appeals
• Talking head	• Humour
• Demonstration	• Fear
• Problem solution	• Warmth
• Testimonial	• Eroticism
• Slice of life	• Music
• Dramatisation	• Etc.
• Comparative ads	
• Etc.	
Endorsers	
• Expert endorsement	
• Celebrity endorsement	

In trying to generate the established advertising objectives, agencies or creatives can use a multitude of appeals, formats and execution strategies to express or translate their creative idea.[30] Broadly speaking, two different types of creative appeals can be distinguished: rational appeals and emotional appeals. **Emotional advertising appeals** are advertisements whose main purpose is to elicit affective responses and to convey an image. **Rational advertising appeals**, on the other hand, contain features, practical details and verifiable, factually relevant cues that can serve as evaluative criteria. Referring to the difference between action and image communications as discussed earlier (see Chapter 1), many image communications make use of emotional appeals, while most action communications use rational appeals. Also, with respect to the difference between product performance and imagery communications, most product performance ads use rational elements, whereas imagery communications most often consist of emotional ads. However, mixed appeals also exist, employing both rational and emotional elements. Both for emotional and rational appeals, different formats or execution strategies and different types of endorsers can be used (see Table 7.2). Also, it has to be added here that several of the formats that can be used for rational appeals could just as well be used for emotional appeals, although they are discussed only once. For example, a comparative ad can be purely factual, describing own and competitive prices, but could also be humorous, such as Virgin Atlantic's campaign featuring large billboards in airports with the message 'Enjoy your overpriced flight'.

Rational appeals

Rational ads may contain one or several information cues. The most widely used classification system of information cues is the one presented in Table 7.3, which has been applied in more than 60 studies.[31] The classification consists of 15 different types of information.

Table 7.3 Resnik and Stern's information classification

• Price	• Special	• offers
• Quality	• Taste	• Independent research
• Performance	• Nutrition	• Company research
• Components	• Packaging	• New ideas
• Availability	• Warranties	• Safety

Source: Based on Abernethy, A.M. and Franke, G.R. (1996), 'The Information Content of Advertising: A Meta-Analysis', *Journal of Advertising*, 25(2), 1–17.

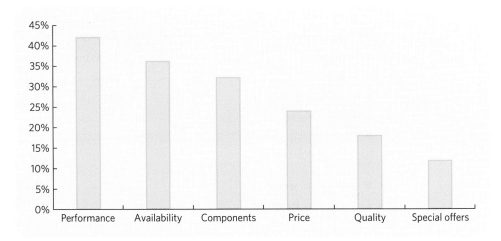

Figure 7.4 Most frequently used information cues in advertising

Source: Based on Abernethy, A.M. and Franke, G.R. (1996), 'The Information Content of Advertising: A Meta-Analysis', *Journal of Advertising*, 25(2), 1–17.

Abernethy and Franke performed a meta-analysis on 59 studies in 24 different countries, including the USA, most Western countries and the Pacific Rim, in which this classification had been used, and revealed the following.[32] The mean number of information cues (over the different countries and over different media) is 2.04, and the cues most frequently used are performance (in 43% of the cases), availability (37%), components (33%), price (25%), quality (19%) and special offers (13%) (Figure 7.4).

As might be expected, ads for durable goods contain significantly more information cues than ads for non-durable goods (2.7 versus 2.0). Ads in developed countries (the USA, Canada, Southern and Western Europe, Japan, Australia, New Zealand) are more informative than ads in less developed countries (China, Taiwan, South Korea, India, Saudi Arabia, parts of Latin America). Another study showed that rational appeals are more effective than emotional appeals when a product is new to the market, while the opposite holds true in markets in which consumers are already very familiar with the product.[33] Moreover, ads for intangible products (e.g. services) contain more information cues than for tangible products. The same conclusion holds for low as compared with high competitive markets.[34] One study shows that a diagnostic product element (= information that helps consumers to assess product quality) stimulates message involvement and enhances ad and brand evaluations for high, but not for low Need for Cognition individuals (i.e. consumers that do not like to engage in cognitive activities). Two diagnostic information elements, however, did not further improve involvement or evaluations as compared with one information element, leading to the conclusion that one diagnostic information element seems sufficient.[35] Finally, the level of information varies between different advertising media (see also Chapter 8).

RESEARCH INSIGHT
Advertising for brand extensions

The optimal advertising appeal for brand extensions depends, among others, on the fit between the parent brand and the extension. In an experimental study with 208 participants, the effectiveness of different advertising appeals was studied for extensions varying in fit with the parent brand. A 2 (parent brand concept: functional, symbolic) × 2 (extension product category: functional, symbolic) × 2 (advertising strategy: parent brand focus, extension focus) experiment was set up. Eight different ads were created, two for each new brand extension (sunscreen – functional and champagne – symbolic), introduced by a highly symbolic brand (Louis Vuitton, a French luxury label in handbags and fashion accessories), or a more functional brand (H&M, a Swedish fashion and accessories brand which is relatively low budget). For each possible brand extension combination, the ads differed in their focus on either the parent brand or the new extension. The test brands were chosen based on a pre-test, which showed both brands were highly familiar. The test brands as well as the product categories used differed significantly in terms of functionality and symbolism.

The results show that perceived fit positively affects extension evaluation in terms of credibility, attitude and purchase intention in that these effects are found in case of a match between the parent brand concept and the extension product category in terms of symbolism and functionality. An incongruent extension also significantly damages the parent brand, measured as the difference between pre- and post-extension brand attitude. However, advertising focus moderated the results of matching versus mismatching extension categories. A focus on the extension mitigated the negative effects of a mismatch on credibility, attitude towards the extension and purchase intention. When the ad focused prominently on the brand name, mismatching extensions were significantly more negatively evaluated than a matching counterpart. In other words, a highly fitting extension is most effectively communicated with a brand focus. Lowly fitting extensions are best communicated with an extension focus. Advertising messages that focus on the brand are indeed unlikely to compensate for products that are obviously not congruent. In line with categorisation theory, a mismatch between the parent brand and the extension in terms of brand concept should result in more difficult categorisation and more piecemeal processing. Consumers will, in this case, base their evaluation of the extension more on the core attributes and benefits of the extension itself. Providing this information in an ad should positively influence evaluation of the extension. Moreover, a mismatching extension significantly dilutes the parent brand, especially when the ad focuses on attributes of the extension. This will increase the salience of these attributes, which may be especially incongruent with the parent brand.

In sum, these results suggest that the best advertising strategy is a function of the specific extension situation (brand extension match or not), and of the main objective the ad wishes to achieve. If the goal is – as with most extension ads – to induce positive communications effects for the extension, then a matching extension benefits most from a positioning close to the parent brand, whereas a mismatching extension is better advertised with its own attributes and features. However, one should keep in mind that the latter situation may strongly dilute the parent brand attitude in general, as it will link incongruent extension associations with the brand schema. Only a matching extension, advertised with an extension focus, enhances the parent brand. This is a potential way to build brand equity. It should be noted that extensions in any case are a risky strategy for the parent brand, and conditions under which enhancement effects occur should be carefully considered. Whether focusing on the brand or on the extension, brand managers need to focus on creating extension ads that are well liked, as the attitude towards the extension ad positively influences evaluation of the extension, and consequently general parent brand attitude.[36]

Turning to the advertising formats noted in Table 7.2, a **talking head** refers to an ad in which the characters tell a story in their own words: monologue, dialogue or interview techniques could be used.

In a **demonstration**, consumers are shown how a product works. It is an easy way to focus on product attributes, and talk about the benefits and product uses while demonstrating the product. For example, when Febreze was launched in Europe, ads showed consumers that the product could be used for preventing disturbing odours in clothes, sofas, curtains, cars, etc.

A **problem solution** shows how a problem can be solved or avoided. Problem solution is sometimes combined with a fear appeal showing consumers what happens if the brand is not used.[37] For example, the ads for Head & Shoulders feature an elegant-looking business professional wearing a nice dark suit. Unfortunately he has a dandruff problem which clearly shows on the suit. Head & Shoulders can solve this problem.

A **testimonial** features ordinary people saying how good a product is. Typical products which are advertised in this way are detergents: 'I really was amazed, my clothes have never been so white.' SlimFast ('You really can') also used ads featuring local testimonials of how much weight people lost to introduce or relaunch the brand in the UK, Germany, France and the Netherlands.[38] Testimonials are often effective because they rely on the positive membership reference group effect. The latter is especially the case for consumers who are highly susceptible to normative influence. For these consumers a testimonial is more impactful than attribute information, whereas the reverse holds true for people scoring low on susceptibility to normative influence.[39] In general, it is advisable to carefully pre-test testimonials on believability and the emotions they evoke because research shows that testimonials often lead to irritation in consumers.[40]

BUSINESS INSIGHT
Reaching the consumer with new advertising media

Advertising professionals seek to break through the advertising clutter by trying to find evermore creative channels to reach their target audience.

In the UK a campaign was launched for a new video game which used 'bleeding' bus stop posters. For a full week, a red blood-like fluid dripped out of the posters, generated by an ink cartridge that was built into the ad. The campaign generated a lot of 'rumour around the brand'. The agency did clean the pavements afterwards.

A US advertising agency pays people $19.50 to walk around with an advertising message on their forehead five days in a row and for three hours per day. The message is tattooed on the forehead with vegetable ink, and disappears by itself after one week. The concept is called Fan Branding or Headvertising, and has already been used by, among others, Dunkin Donuts and the British TV channel CNX. A 37 year old Australian sold the right part of his face to a Mexican restaurant for €6000. He allowed the restaurant to tattoo its name on his face.[41]

The Belgian agency Rapid-Affichage writes advertising messages on pavements in fluorescent paint. For instance, at the entrance to a music store, visitors can read: 'Soulwax. Nite Versions. Out now.' Some public authorities do not like the idea, because they consider it as 'damaging the public domain', but the company meticulously removes all traces after the campaign period.

The American company Convex Group patented LidRock, a system to attach CD-ROMs or DVDs to the lid of cardboard cups in fast food restaurants, cinemas, sport stadiums and amusement parks. The lid is adjusted to allow the CD to be clicked on it. The market potential is enormous. In 2005 in North America, 634 drinks were sold every second.

Destroying or damaging bank notes is not allowed in the USA, but attaching removable stickers to them is allowed. That is all it takes to create a new advertising medium. Research showed that 95% of consumers noticed the message on their bank notes and 56% did not remove it, thus generating extra exposure with other consumers.

The Belgian company Activemedia invented a wheel cover that does not turn along with the wheel when the car is moving. For €150, a message is attached to the four wheels of one of the hundreds of co-operating Antwerp taxis.[42]

Slice-of-life ads feature the product being used in a real-life setting, which usually involves solving a problem. The effectiveness of this type of ad is attributed to the fact that the product is shown in a real-life context that the target group can relate to. An example would be a family putting picnic hampers, blankets, toys, etc., in their new Mercedes space van to go out for a picnic on a Sunday afternoon. Another example shows a boy playing soccer with his friends, then he comes home with his clothes so dirty one would think they will never be clean again. Fortunately, the boy's mother has Dreft, which cleans the clothes without a problem. Although slice-of-life advertising is used quite often, research shows that such ads are more likely to cause irritation.[43]

Dramatisation advertising is rather similar to a slice of life. Both first present a problem and afterwards the solution, but a dramatisation builds suspense and leads consumers to a climax. The difference between a slice of life and/or a drama (which just tells a story) and a dramatisation lies in the intensity. The AlldaysTanga campaign is an example of a dramatisation. A young woman is dancing on a stage amid a large crowd, wearing extremely close-fitting clothes. Suddenly, in front of everyone, her panty liner gets dislodged, causing her a lot of embarrassment while other girls make fun of her. The spot ends showing several other girls dancing without any worries. The solution becomes obvious in the base line 'Should've worn ALLDAYS TANGA'.[44]

BUSINESS INSIGHT
Wash&Go is the best of traditions

Wash&Go, the mid-tier shampoo leader in the Balkans market, became crushed between a stronger than ever premium tier and an impressively large low tier. In response to this situation, other mid-tier competitors launched premium ingredients-based variants. Wash&Go decided to do the opposite: it launched Wash&GoReviva, a nettle-based variant. The nettle ingredient had already existed for more than 30 years in the market and was especially popular among low-tier users. Importantly, all existing nettle-based shampoos were priced at least four times cheaper than Wash&GoReviva.

Wash&Go was the only shampoo brand that positioned itself on an ESP. Capitalising on this heritage and on Balkan women's desire to have enduring appeal to their partners, Wash&Go launched an emotional campaign that dramatised how women can hold on to their men. The 'Best of Traditions' campaign made a humorous comment on old, absurd rituals and superstitions to keep a partner, presenting the nettle extract as the only solution to keep your beloved one. The campaign objective was to increase sales volume by 25%. The appeal resonated very well in the target group, surpassing the sales objective by 210.6% in Bulgaria and 88.3% in Romania. The company received a Bronze Euro Effie for its 'Best of Traditions' campaign.[45]

Comparative advertising can be used as a means to differentiate a brand from a competitor. A direct comparative ad explicitly names the comparison brand (often a well-known competitive brand) and claims that the comparison brand is inferior to the advertised brand with respect to a specific attribute. An indirect comparative ad does not explicitly mention a comparison brand, but argues to be superior on a certain attribute compared with other brands ('Gillette, the best a man can get'). For a long time, directly comparative advertising was an American phenomenon. However, the European Commission has decided to allow comparative advertising in certain circumstances. A study points out that consumers in countries in which comparative advertising is not allowed, or is used infrequently, have a much more negative attitude towards comparative ads than American consumers.[46] Taylor Nelson Sofres found in 2001 that two-thirds of UK consumers find comparable ads unacceptable; women were most opposed and youngsters aged between 16 and 24 minded least that brands criticise competitors.[47] Research in France showed that direct comparative ads led to more positive brand attitudes than indirect or non-comparative ads.[48] However, French advertisers remain unconvinced of the effectiveness of comparative advertising on French consumers and do not intend to use it more often in the future.[49] Also in Spain, comparative advertising does not seem to be well received. A study revealed that the more intense the comparative claim, the less consumers believed the propositions, the more counter-arguments were formed, and the more negative attitudes and brand intentions became.[50] This seems to suggest that advertisers should be careful about using this technique in Europe.

RESEARCH INSIGHT
The advantages and disadvantages of comparative advertising

Are comparative ads more effective than non-comparative ads? A short review of research results reveals the following:

The advantages and disadvantages of comparative advertising

Advantages	Disadvantages
More attention	Less credible
Better brand and message awareness	Comparison of similar brands confuses people
More elaborate processing	Less favourable attitude towards the ad
Association with comparison brand	Possibility of increasing brand confusion
Differentiation	Possibility of aggressive media wars
More favourable attitude towards the brand	Costs due to law suits
Purchase behaviour more likely	

Consumers seem to devote more attention to a comparative than to a non-comparative ad. The reason is that since at least two brands are being compared, the ad is relevant to more consumers (users of both the sponsored and comparison brand).[51] Because of more attention, comparative ads lead to a better message and brand awareness, evoke more cognitive responses and, as a consequence, enhance a more central communications processing.[52] However, it should be noted that consumers perceive comparative advertising as less credible.[53] A recent study shows that elaborate processing and credibility of comparative advertising may be different for men and women. For men, comparative advertising seems to increase brand evaluations and purchase intentions because it increases their brand involvement and enhances processing. For women, on the other hand, comparative advertising leads to heightened persuasive intent perceptions and these perceptions decrease brand evaluation and purchase intentions.[54]

Concerning product positioning, positive effects can be observed. With new brand introductions, advertisers often stress the superiority of the new brand over a more familiar competitor on a typical attribute. By doing so, two desirable goals seem to be reached: (1) the new product is associated with the comparison brand and, as a consequence, more easily included in the consideration set of the target consumers; (2) the brand advertised is different from, and is more likely to be preferred to, the comparison brand.[55]

The attitude towards the brand usually is positively influenced by comparative ads, while the contrary holds for the attitude towards the ad.[56] The latter is perceived to be less personal, less friendly and amusing, less honest and more aggressive.[57] Although conative or behavioural effects have not been extensively studied, it seems that comparative ads have a positive influence on purchase intention.[58] Furthermore, comparative as opposed to non-comparative ads seem to enhance purchase behaviour, as indicated by coupon redemption.[59]

Although the balance of advantages and disadvantages turns out to be in favour of comparative advertising, one should also take into account the following threats. The use of comparative advertising may lead to aggressive, competitive media wars when the comparison brand feels attacked (the so-called boomerang effect). Furthermore, comparative advertising may be misleading and confusing for consumers.[60] One should try to avoid promoting a competitive brand. This occurs when, as a result of the ad, the consumer wrongly thinks the ad sponsor is the comparison brand. Costs may also rise because of lawsuits etc. Finally, remember that comparative ads are not appreciated to the same extent in different cultures and countries. The findings reported in US studies may not hold at all for Europe, Asia, etc.

Emotional appeals

Emotional advertising refers to advertising that tries to evoke emotions in consumers rather than to make consumers think. Emotional ads mainly consist of non-verbal elements such as images and emotional stimuli. It should be clear that there is a difference between the intended emotional content of a stimulus, or the emotional technique used, and the emotions experienced by a consumer as a result of being exposed to an ad. Emotional appeals do not necessarily evoke emotions in all people, although they are designed to do so.

Humour

Humorous advertising can be defined as an appeal created with the intent to make people laugh, irrespective of the fact that the humour is successful (people indeed perceive the ad as humorous) or unsuccessful (people do not think the ad is funny). Humour seems to be one of the most frequently used emotional techniques throughout the world. A survey in 1992 in 33 countries revealed that approximately 35% of all magazine and outdoor advertising contained humour. No significant differences could be detected between the different countries, nor between the two media.[61] More current estimates also indicate that humorous advertising takes a share of about 10% to 30% (Photo 7.3).[62]

Are humorous appeals effective? No doubt most people appreciate a good joke, but can humorous ads convey a brand message? Or do they leave people remembering the joke, but neither the brand nor the brand message? Can humour be used for 'serious' products, or does a humorous approach make a clown of the advertising company? Humour seems to raise a

Photo 7.3 Nicorette: giving up smoking with a smile
Source: AMVBBDO.

lot of questions, and unfortunately not a lot of straight answers can be given. Humour has been studied by many researchers, and overall there is only one aspect on which agreement between the researchers can be found: humour attracts attention.[63] However, the question remains as to what extent humour also attracts attention to the brand. As far as recall and recognition, creating positive ad and brand attitudes and increasing purchase intention are concerned, no conclusive results can be drawn.[64] This can partly be explained by several moderating variables (Figure 7.5).

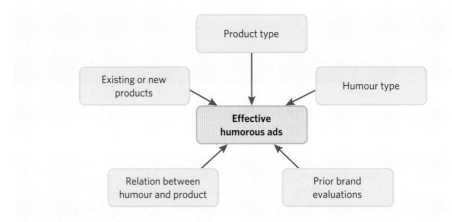

Figure 7.5 Moderating variables affecting the effectiveness of humour in advertising

Different types of humour exist, e.g. cognitive humour. In this case, there is an incongruity, an unexpected element as a result of which the consumer has to follow different lines of reasoning to solve the incongruity;[65] for example, an advert for Amstel Light beer showed products that normally belong in the refrigerator in an unexpected spot because Amstel Light has taken their place in the refrigerator. One example features a woman who is sleeping in bed. When she wakes up and turns on the light, she screams when she finds a plate of meatloaf next to her in bed. The next scene shows the refrigerator where a 12-pack of Amstel Light is jammed into the meatloaf's position.[66] There is also sentimental humour: for example, a little kitten that tries to catch the ball in a football game on TV; a satire, meant to be funny and insulting at the same time; sexual humour, making fun of the other sex, etc. The different types of humour are appreciated by the target consumers to a different extent leading to different communications effects. While sentimental humour is quite innocent, satire or sexual humour is more aggressive and, not surprisingly, not everyone finds the latter types of humour funny.

The effectiveness of humour also depends on the product type. The prevailing opinion seems to be that humour is more appropriate for low- than for high-involvement products, and for transformational rather than for informational products, and that humour, in any case, should be avoided for high-involvement/informational products, such as banking and insurance.[67]

In general, humour seems to be more effective for existing and familiar brands than for new and unfamiliar brands.[68] In other words, building brand awareness using humour is more difficult, since the humour might gain too much attention, leading to inferior brand attention. Humour that is in one way or another related to the product is more effective than unrelated humour.[69] Finally, humour may have a detrimental effect when prior brand evaluations are negative.[70] In other words, if you are convinced that a Lion bar tastes awful and sticks to your teeth, you are more likely to think that the company wants to be funny, but is not funny at all, while a positive brand attitude leads to more tolerance and acceptance.

Eroticism

Defined very broadly, an ad can be classified as erotic if one or more of the following elements are present: partial or complete nudity, physical contact between two adults, sexy or provocatively dressed person(s), provocative or seductive facial expression, and suggestive words or sexually laden music, etc. (Photo 7.4). Although some people seem convinced that eroticism is being used more and more in European advertising, content analyses show that this is only in the eyes of the beholder.[71]

How effective is an ad showing a seductive Claudia Schiffer in front of the Citroën Xsara, the erotic style of the Martini campaigns, the nude Sophie Dahl for Opium or the full-frontal nude model for Yves Saint Laurent's scent H7? As was the case with humour, no clear guidelines can be provided for the use of eroticism. However, an indisputable conclusion is that **erotic advertising** attracts attention, even to the extent that more car accidents occur near erotic billboards.[72] One may wonder, though, whether any attention is directed at the brand or the brand message. Indeed, most researchers agree that eroticism reduces brand and message recall.[73] Another negative aspect on which most researchers agree is that eroticism has a negative impact on the image of the advertiser.[74] For other communications objectives such as the attitude towards the ad or the brand, and purchase intention, mixed research results have been reported.[75]

An explanation can be found in a number of moderating factors. For instance, the more intense the eroticism or, in other words, the more overt the sex appeal in the form of nudity or suggestion of sexual intercourse, the more negative the responses to the ad become.[76] However, a study for suntan lotion found exactly the opposite, suggesting that advertisers would do better opting for 'the full monty' rather than for partial nudity.[77] Perhaps this result can be explained by the product promoted, namely suntan lotion. Previous research results reveal that the more the erotic appeal is related to the product, the more positive the responses to

Photo 7.4 Using erotic appeal for underwear
Source: The Advertising Archives.

it become.[78] In other words, functional products such as underwear, bath foam, shower cream, etc., and romantic products such as perfume, aftershave, alcohol, cosmetics, etc., are expected to benefit more from an erotic appeal than other product categories such as coffee, a lawnmower, a lathe, etc. Notwithstanding the foregoing, a study in which the effectiveness of eroticism for social marketing topics (as diverse as eating healthily, public library and museum attendance, HIV/AIDS prevention, etc.) was tested showed that sexual appeals were more persuasive than matched non-sexual appeals.[79] So for this variable research results are also inconclusive.

Which target group can most effectively be addressed with an erotic appeal? One study shows that erotic appeals lead to better memory and superior attitudes and purchase intent among low-involvement consumers, whereas high-involvement consumers show superior attitudes and purchase intent towards non-sexual appeals.[80] Further, in general, men respond significantly more positively to eroticism than women.[81] However, in most of the studies, ads with seductive or naked women were used. Handsome men as product endorsers might have completely altered the picture. In fact, lately more and more advertisers are using men as sex objects to please women. Examples are the Cola Light 11.30 break commercial, the Australian ad for Underdaks men's underwear in which two female airport officers have a man stripped to his underwear by sounding a false alarm each time he passes through the control gate, the Gini ad in which a female passionately grabs a guy, starts opening the buttons of his shirt, unhooks his belt, pulls the belt out of his trousers and . . . uses the belt to open her bottle of Gini. However, the differences between men and women cannot be fully explained by the sex of the model. Women seem to respond favourably to erotic ads only when there is a strong fit between the ad and the brand. Men, on the other hand, respond favourably to eroticism irrespective of the level of fit.[82]

To conclude, among marketing practitioners there seems to be agreement that sex sells, but some are wondering for how much longer. According to them, sex is becoming a commodity that is no longer able to shock or convey indulgent sensuality.[83]

Warmth

Warm advertising can be described as advertising that consists of elements evoking mild, positive feelings such as love, friendship, cosiness, affection and empathy. Although warmth now seems to be used less than it was a few decades ago, it is still a frequently used emotional technique.[84] Is this frequent use of warmth justified? The answer is, clearly, yes. Although mixed results have been reported as to the effect of warmth on message and brand recall and recognition, warmth leads to more positive affective responses, less negative feelings such as irritation, a more positive attitude towards the ad and towards the brand, and sometimes an enhanced purchase intention.[85] Target groups most responsive to warm appeals are females, emotional individuals and individuals with a lot of cognitive empathy (meaning that they can understand the situation of others).[86]

RESEARCH INSIGHT
The role of affect in Alzheimer's disease message processing

Alzheimer's disease is a devastating, incurable disease. The disease pathway is typically characterised by a long pre-clinical phase in which patients experience mild cognitive impairments. Medical research states that through early diagnosis of symptoms the disease process can be slowed down.[87] The main concern is then to make the population at risk aware of the importance of early diagnosis and stimulate them to take responsible actions at the earliest stage of the onset of the disease. Very little is known about the role of affective communication stimuli in the domain of a fatal disease, where one can merely intervene in order to lengthen the time period in which the patient can still enjoy a reasonable quality of life.

Forgas's Affect Infusion Model (AIM) distinguishes four judgemental strategies, two low-affect infusion strategies (direct access and motivated processing) and two high-affect infusion strategies (heuristic and substantive processing). Affect should have an effect when heuristic or substantive processing is used.[88] Two underlying mechanisms of affect infusion are affect-as-information and affect priming. The affect-as-information theory suggests that rather than computing a judgement on the basis of recalled features of a target, individuals may ask themselves 'How do I feel about it?' and, in doing so, may be guided by their feelings to judge a message. In the affect priming theory, affect can indirectly inform judgements by facilitating access to related cognitive categories.[89] Hence, affect can prime the encoding, retrieval and selective use of information in the constructive processing of judgements. Within the AIM, it is implied that it is in the course of substantive, constructive processing that affect is most likely to play a significant informational role in what is perceived, learned and recalled, and how stimulus information is interpreted. Thus stimuli that are perceived as positively affective should lead to paying closer attention to positive information, better learning such details, and making more positive interpretations of ambiguous information. The AIM also implies that judgements about more complex stimuli (substantive processing context), requiring more elaborate processing and made without the benefit of objective evidence, should show greater affective effects. According to this principle, substantive processing is more likely when the message is personally relevant.

A study with Belgian and Spanish participants aimed at exploring the role of message affect and message thoughts in the processing of Alzheimer awareness messages varying in argument strength and affective tone of visuals.[90] The study compares two target groups. The first one is older people (hereafter referred to as the 'General Public'), an age cohort that is a prime target group for Alzheimer awareness messages. The second group are Caregivers of Alzheimer patients. The study investigates differences in message processing depending on the level of experience with Alzheimer's disease. The first sample consisted of 495 Belgian and Spanish seniors. The second sample, the Alzheimer Caregivers sample, consisted of 243 Belgian and Spanish Caregivers for patients with Alzheimer's disease.

Six Alzheimer awareness messages were developed in which two levels of argument strength (weak and strong) were combined with three pictures of different affective valence (negative, neutral and positive). These messages were aimed at convincing people to seek early treatment. A 2 (message strength: weak–strong) × 3 (affective valence of image: negative–neutral–positive) between-subjects design was used to collect the data. Participants received an e-mail with a link to a Web survey. After answering a number of demographic questions, they viewed one of the six Alzheimer's disease messages, to which they were randomly assigned. Subsequently, they answered questions on scales evaluating their responses to the message.

One of the main conclusions of the study is that the affective reaction to an Alzheimer message is very important for its effectiveness. Affect plays an important role in the development of message thoughts and message outcomes such as Alzheimer thoughts, perceived message substance and the attitude towards the ad. However, what causes this affective reaction, the process by means of which the affective reactions lead to message outcomes, and the role of message thoughts in this process differ according to groups with varying levels of Alzheimer's disease experience. For the non-experienced General Public participants, processssing Alzheimer messages is to a certain extent affect-driven, but message thoughts play an important mediating role in processing the message. The afffective reaction to the message and argument strength substantially determine message thoughts. Partly through the development of message thoughts, affective reactions positively transfer to perceived message substance, Alzheimer thoughts and the attitude towards the message, suggesting affect priming and infusion as well as central biased processing. In the case of experienced Caregiver participants, processing Alzheimer messages is more exclusively affect-driven in that affect plays a much more prominent role in the development of Alzheimer thoughts, perceived message substance and the attitude towards the message, and the development of message thoughts is not influenced by affective reactions, neither do they mediate their effect.

The results of the study have implications for health communication professionals. Processing health messages and forming health issue judgements following these messages is largely an affect-driven process for both experienced and non-experienced subjects. In the General Public, positive affective reactions are an important prerequisite for the development of positive attitudes and thoughts. Nevertheless, argument strength remains an important driver of positive message processing too, and special care should be taken that positive message thoughts are also developed. Secondly, various message components may evoke positive affective reactions. Argument strength is one of them, but also the type of visual is an important driver of affective responses. On the basis of the study, neutrally valenced images seem to be the optimal choice in this type of message. For the subjects with Alzheimer's disease experience, affect is the main driver in forming judgements about Alzheimer's disease messages. The development of messages for groups with Alzheimer experience should pay close attention to evoking a positive affective reaction to the message, and not so much to developing positive message thoughts.

Fear

Fear appeal advertising (or threat-based advertising) refers the consumer to a certain type of risk (threat) that he or she might be exposed to and which he or she usually can reduce by buying (e.g. insurance) or not buying (e.g. not drinking when driving) the product advertised (coping efficacy). Typical risks that might be used in a fear appeal are:[91]

- *Physical.* The risk of bodily harm, often used for burglar alarms, toothpaste, analgesics, etc. An example would be 'When are you going to install an alarm? After they break in?'
- *Social.* The risk of being socially ostracised, often used for deodorants, dandruff shampoo, mouthwash, etc.
- *Time.* The risk of spending a lot of time on an unpleasant activity while the activity can be performed in less time. During the introduction period of dishwashers, messages frequently read 'Do you realise that most people spend X years of their life washing the dishes?'
- *Product performance.* The risk that competitive brands do not perform adequately. Dyson vacuum cleaners are promoted as having no bag, which makes them the only cleaner to maintain 100% suction, 100% of the time.
- *Financial.* The risk of losing a lot of money, typically used by insurance companies.
- *Opportunity loss.* Pointing out to consumers that they run the risk of missing a special opportunity if they do not act right away. For example, the Belgian mobile phone provider Proximus ran a campaign with the following message: 'Subscribe now to Proximus, and pay nothing until April.'

Are threat appeals effective? Most studies point in an affirmative direction. Several studies confirm that threat appeals are capable of sensitising people to threats and of changing their behaviour.[92] For example, a fairly recent study shows that these appeals succeed in lowering alcohol consumption in students.[93]

RESEARCH INSIGHT
How threat appeals work

Threat appeals are 'persuasive messages designed to scare people by describing the terrible things that will happen to them if they do not do what the message recommends'.[94] Fear appeals and threat appeals are often incorrectly used as synonyms. However, threats illustrate undesirable consequences from certain behaviours (threat appeal); fear is a potential emotional response of an individual to a threat.[95] Threat appeals are often used as persuasive messages in public service announcements or social profit campaigns, for instance anti-smoking, HIV, speeding, drunk driving, etc., but also commercial companies such as banks and insurance companies occasionally use threat appeals. The objective is always to increase the involvement of people with an issue or a problem by presenting it as threatening, and to offer a credible solution, such as the adaptation of certain behaviour, or purchasing a certain brand.

In earlier models of how threat appeals work, fear is considered as the only factor that influences adaptive behaviour. These 'Drive models'[96] attribute the effectiveness of threat appeals to evoked fear. Drive models claim that there is an inverted U-shaped relationship between the fear level of a message and attitudes and behaviour. In other words, moderate fear appeals work best: some fear is needed to motivate people to reach a negative drive state. However, the fear has to be able to be reduced (drive reduction). If fear is too high, maladaptive behaviour will follow as a result of 'reactance', the motivation to resist any perceived threat to one's freedom to make up one's own mind about an issue.[97] The 'Terror Management Theory'[98] also offers a potential explanation of why high fear messages are counter-productive. According to this theory, people deny their fear of death and attempt to enhance their positive self-esteem, for instance by means of speeding, as a way of managing this fear.

The Protection Motivation Theory (PMT),[99] on the other hand, prescribes that four independent cognitive responses mediate the impact of a threat appeal on coping attitudes, intentions and behaviour: *perceived severity*, an individual's beliefs about the seriousness of the threat; *perceived susceptibility or probability of occurrence*, an individual's beliefs about his or her chances of experiencing the threat; *perceived response efficacy*, an individual's beliefs as to whether a response effectively prevents the threat; and *perceived self-efficacy*, an individual's belief in his or her ability to perform the recommended response. Perceived severity and susceptibility represent the perceived level of threat, perceived response efficacy and self-efficacy represent the perceived level of efficacy. Threat messages consequently lead to protection motivation which, in turn, has an impact on attitudes and coping intention and behaviour. Evoked fear may affect attitudes and behaviour through its impact on perceived severity and probability of occurrence, but fear is not a necessary prerequisite for compliance with the message recommendation.

The PMT does an excellent job in explaining the factors leading to message acceptance, but fails to explain the specific factors leading to message rejection. The 'Extended Parallel Processing Model'[100] defines two reactions to threat appeals: a mainly cognitive one (danger control), where people think about the threat and ways to avert it; and a mainly emotional one (fear control) in which people react to their fear and engage in strategies (reactance, defensive avoidance) to control their fear. Threat appeals may evoke fear that leads to fear control, or they may lead to higher perceived threat that leads to fear and, in turn, again to increased perceived threat (feedback loop) and danger control. Too high levels of evoked fear may immediately lead to fear control and thus to ineffective messages. High levels of threat (caused by or inducing fear), combined with high levels of coping efficacy perception ('I can do something about it'), lead to danger control and message acceptance: people feel threatened, but have the impression they can do something about it. On the other hand, high levels of threat combined with low levels of perceived coping efficacy lead to fear control and message rejection. People feel threatened and get the impression they cannot do anything about it, hence ignore or reject the message.

Recent empirical work on threat appeals[101] leads to the conclusion that perceived threat and coping efficacy, and evoked fear, each have a separate and independent effect on message processing (involvement, credibility), and hence on adaptive attitudes and behaviour. Scaring people seems to be particularly effective in grabbing their attention, involving them in the message and having them perceive the message as credible. The defensive avoidance or reactance phenomenon, as claimed by some of the above-mentioned models, has seldom been found in empirical research. But also an increased perception of threat (even without evoking fear) can do the same thing, as well as an improved impression of coping efficacy. Fear can be evoked by different types or stimuli: a higher social or physical threat in the message, a negatively framed message, a fear-evoking or negative emotional or threatening context.[102]

Music

Who has not caught themselves singing an ad jingle: 'whenever there is fun, there is always Coca-Cola', 'I feel Cointreau tonight', etc., or thinking about one of the songs used in a commercial? For example, Celine Dion's 'I Drove All Night' for DaimlerChrysler, Steppenwolf's 'Born to Be Wild' in the Ford Cougar ad, 'L'air du Temps' for the champagne brand Bernard Massard, Marvin Gaye's 'I Heard it through the Grapevine' in the California Raisin ad, etc. Music is extensively used in TV and radio commercials. For example, a study found that 84.5% of US commercials and 94.3% of the ads in the Dominican Republic contained music.[103]

The major reasons why advertisers make use of music is because they believe that it can gain attention, create a mood, a sense of relaxation, or it can set an emotional tone that enhances product evaluations and facilitates message acceptance, send a brand message and convey a unique selling point, signal a certain lifestyle and build a brand personality, and communicate cultural values.[104]

Although there seems to be general agreement that the right music may have a significant impact on an ad's effectiveness, not much empirical evidence exists to support this claim. The only point of agreement seems to be that music induces more positive feelings.[105] As far as brand recall is concerned, for example, one could expect that jingles may have a positive influence because by singing the jingle yourself afterwards, you actually rehearse the brand name and brand message over and over again. However, empirical studies show mixed results: sometimes music seems to have a positive effect, sometimes a negative effect and sometimes no effect at all on ad recall.[106] Regarding behavioural consequences, Gorn[107] demonstrated experimentally that consumers were more likely to choose a specific colour of pen if they had been exposed to an ad in which that pen had been paired with pleasant rather than unpleasant music. Other researchers were not able to replicate his findings, however.[108]

Two moderating variables may partly account for these contradictory results.[109] The effectiveness of music may depend on the attention-gaining value referring to the arousal or activation potential of the musical sound. Fast, loud music, for example, can be expected to have a higher attention-gaining value. However, although this type of music might initially attract attention to the ad, it also distracts the listener, which leads to an impairment of cognitive processing and brand information recall.[110] A second factor is music/message congruence, referring to the extent that the music and the ad copy convey the same message. Incongruence may lead to distraction from, instead of attention to, the brand message.

Endorsers

Experts can be used to demonstrate the quality or high technology of a product. For example, toothpaste brands are often promoted by means of someone in a white lab coat to imply a dentist's opinion. The effectiveness of this type of ad is assumed to be based on the perceived credibility of the experts' judgement.[111] In contrast with testimonials, **expert endorsements** do not seem to be perceived as irritating. On the contrary, one study even suggests experts evoke more positive affective responses.[112]

Celebrities can also be used to endorse a product. Their effectiveness is based on the 'aspiration group' effect. Examples of **celebrity endorsement** are George Clooney for Nescafé and Martini, Tiger Woods for Nike and Accenture, David Beckham for Vodafone, etc.

RESEARCH INSIGHT
Endorser type and brand globalness effects in India: think global or act local?

Emerging markets such as India are important drivers of future sales growth. One important question is to what degree branding and marketing communications in these markets should be standardised (globalisation), locally adapted (localisation) or glocalised ('globally localised'),[113] a global brand identity strategy that allows for country-specific flexibility in communications mix decisions. Brand globalness is often associated with prestige and quality.[114] The use of celebrity endorsement is considered a powerful tool in creating or managing brand equity. At the same time, the effectiveness of celebrity endorsement may differ across cultures.[115]

In two experiments with representative samples of the Indian urban population, it was examined how these two factors, brand globalness (global or local) and type of endorser (international celebrity, local celebrity and local non-celebrity), interact to influence consumer responses to brand communications.[116] In the first study, an experiment was conducted on the basis of a 3 (local non-celebrity, local celebrity, global celebrity) × 2 (local brand, global brand) full factorial, between-subjects design. Firstly, a pre-test was conducted to select one local and one global celebrity who were equally familiar and one non-celebrity endorser who was not familiar. To avoid confounds, the potential endorsers were also pre-tested to be equally attractive, equally credible and equally fitting with the advertised product. The actors Leonardo DiCaprio (global celebrity), Akshay Kumar (local celebrity) and a local non-celebrity model were selected. Using each of these three endorsers, two identical ads were created for a new brand of home cinema systems (TFX) that was positioned as either 'global' or 'local'. A new brand was used to avoid potential confounds of prior brand associations. The global brand ad was drafted in English, mentioning the cities of New York, London and Delhi, and referring to a website tfx.com. The local brand condition was completely in Hindi, referred to three Indian cities (Delhi, Mumbai and Kolkata) and directed people to the website tfx.in. The advertising copy was translated and back-translated by four native Hindi speakers to ensure that the ads transferred the same meaning in Hindi and English. In this study, a glocalisation strategy (a combination of a global brand with a local endorser) engenders the most positive consumer responses over complete globalisation or localisation.

In the first study, brand globalness was merely manipulated through the language in the ad, geographic locations and website, but the brand name was kept constant. In the second study, this time for fashion, brand globalness was more extremely manipulated by also manipulating the brand name. Two fictitious proper names that represented either a local (Ram Lal) or international, global (Jack Dixon) fashion designer were selected. The other brand manipulations were identical to study 1, and also the same three endorsers were used. The design was again a 3 × 2 full factorial, between-subjects design.

When brand globalness is moderate (all verbal elements in the ad except the brand name), global brands do not score significantly better than local brands in India. Local brands in India are generally not as positively received as global brands, and the type of endorser does not really seem to make any difference. Global brands, however, should glocalise their ads by engaging a local celebrity, as ad and brand responses are significantly more positive when a local celebrity endorses a global brand than with a global celebrity or a local non-celebrity endorser. This glocalisation strategy may have triggered both the higher prestige of a global brand and a sense of uniqueness among the Indian participants. When also the brand name is globalised, a global brand is more favourably perceived than a local brand and there are no endorser differences whatsoever. It seems that the effect of outspoken brand globalness on brand attitudes is so strong that it suppresses endorser-type effects.

It is clear that celebrities are used extensively. For example, one in four ads in US and one in five UK campaigns feature celebrities.[117] But how effective are celebrity endorsements? They certainly attract a lot of attention, not only from the target group, but also from the media. The latter is very interesting since it can give rise to free publicity. For example, when the 'Won't Kiss Off Test' campaign for Revlon's Colorstay Lipsticks was launched, Cindy Crawford kissed reporters, leading to massive free publicity.[118] Moreover, several studies have shown that celebrities can have a direct positive impact on ad likeability and also an indirect effect on brand attitude and purchase intentions.[119] For instance, the management of Pepsi attributes its 8% increase in sales in 1984 to the Michael Jackson endorsement, while the Spice Girls were good for a 2% global market share increase in 1997.[120] However, not all celebrities are effective for all products or all situations. Several factors play a role.[121] According to the Source Credibility Model, the celebrity should be credible in the sense that he or she has expertise and is trustworthy. The trustworthiness of an endorser is defined as the degree to which the endorser is perceived to be honest and believable. Tiger Woods has proved that he has mastered how to play golf, which makes him highly credible for promoting golf equipment and sportswear. In a study in which both an actor and an athlete promote a candy bar and an energy bar, it was found that the ad featuring the athlete was more effective when an energy bar was promoted, while the type of endorser did not matter for the candy bar.[122]

Besides credibility, attractiveness may also be important. According to the Source Attractiveness Model, attractiveness refers in this context to the degree that the celebrity is known (awareness and familiarity), is physically perceived to be attractive and is liked by the target group. Although all adults agree that Sean Connery is a great movie star, Will Smith will no doubt have more impact on teenagers. Several studies found support for this model, although a recent study warns that one should be cautious about using highly attractive models. Using very thin models, for example, may reduce the self-image of the target group and evoke negative feelings towards both the celebrity and the product.[123]

Finally, as is summarised in the Product Match-Up Hypothesis, there should be an appropriate fit between the endorser's image, personality, lifestyle, etc., and the product advertised. In this respect, it should be added that the behaviour of the celebrity may turn against a brand that he or she is associated with. Eric Cantona, for example, was prosecuted for kicking a soccer fan. Although this could have been a disaster for Nike, the company cleverly managed the problem and even succeeded in turning it to an advantage by starting to sell sportswear showing the word 'punished'. Youngsters who like rebels, and who still admire Cantona for his soccer skills, were extremely fond of these shirts. Tiger Woods got himself into trouble with his love life. As a result, the long-standing relationship between Woods and Accenture was ended. The potential risk of negative celebrity information is expected to be especially great for new or unfamiliar brands for which the celebrity is the primary cue on which consumers base their brand evaluations.[124]

BUSINESS INSIGHT
Corega, leading the way in the fixatives and denture care market

Denture fixatives are creams that fix dentures to the gums. They hold the teeth in place, securing a good 'bite'. The product is functional, but at the same time it offers peace of mind and social confidence to wearers who are afraid of 'losing' their false teeth. About 10% of Central and Eastern European citizens have false teeth. However, only 13% of them wore fixatives, as compared with 29% in Germany and 21% in the USA. Therefore, the overall objective of Corega was to develop the denture fixative market (+15%) and become market leader.

In contrast to competing brands that made use of patronising ads, Corega decided to use real people talking in an authentic way about their teeth issues. Corega chose celebrities famous in the 1960s and the 1970s. The target group grew up with these celebrities, which would make it easier to connect with them. The campaign ran in Poland, Russia, Ukraine, Romania, Bulgaria, Estonia and the Czech Republic. In each country, a different celebrity was used to take into account local, cultural nuances. The campaign had a tremendous success. Category sales increased by 22% (as compared with an objective of 15%), and Corega took overall brand leadership in the total denture care market with a sales increase of 75% (vs an objective of 30%). The campaign was awarded a Bronze Euro Effie.[125]

Source: Grey Communications Group Ltd.

Campaign implementation

After advertising agencies have come up with creative and executional ideas, the advertiser has to evaluate the different alternatives on the basis of the creative brief. This means that the idea ultimately chosen needs to be suitable for and appealing to the target group, be capable of reaching the advertising objectives, and be a kind of catalyst, making the brand's position immediately clear in a simple, eye-catching manner. The idea must also fit with the company's and the brand's long-term strategy and with previous campaigns. It has to be adaptable to the different media to be used, and financially implementable within the given advertising budget and within the given time limits.

When agreement is reached on the creative idea to be used for the different media, the ads need to be produced. Since ad production needs special skills, this job is typically carried out by technical experts. Photography, typography and sound recording need to be well thought through, so that headline, baseline, copy, background music, packshots, presenters, characters, the set, etc., form an integrated and consistent ad. As soon as the advertiser approves of the ad proposal, the ads are produced and handed over to the media.

After the campaign has run, it has to be evaluated for its effectiveness. In order to do this, it is very important to have clear, measurable objectives at the beginning of the campaign development process, as well as accurate data of the situation prior to the campaign launch. The important aspect of media planning is discussed later (see Chapter 8), as is advertising research (see Chapter 9).

BUSINESS INSIGHT
Saving XL commercials

Advertising agencies often make long commercials that are then cut back to the traditional 30-second format shown on TV. However, many advertising professionals feel that they would be able to bring a more convincing message if they were allowed to expose their target groups to these longer commercials. A movie theatre is the ideal medium to show long commercials. Screenvision, the company that sells advertising space in Belgian movie theatres, worked together with the advertising agency Markee to build a website on which advertising agencies could place the long versions of their commercials. The public could vote for the best commercial. The ten highest-scoring commercials end up in a short list, and a professional jury picks a winner. The winning commercial is then shown in Belgian cinemas for free during one month. During the contest, every advertiser can show two-minute commercials for the price of a 30-second one in all Belgian cinemas.[126]

Advertising in a business-to-business context

Traditionally, business-to-business advertising has been described as 'heavy, ponderous, deadly serious and boring'.[127] This qualification can be attributed to the specific characteristics of the business environment, i.e. the importance of technical aspects of products and services, the importance of the products for the economic performance of the buyer and the complex decision-making units. Business ads, for that reason, tend to be more factual and rational, and tend to emphasise the company name rather than its products, because customers are also buying reliability, after-sales service and technical support; in other words, a relationship with a trustworthy partner.

On the other hand, there are a number of reasons why business advertising should not be so different from consumer advertising. After all, the human element is present in both situations, and some of the functions of advertising are common to both markets. As to the second factor, in business-to-business communications, advertising is used to create awareness and interest, and to build preference or reinforce the attitude after the customer has purchased the product. As far as the first factor is concerned, people are not all that different on and off the job, and are always subject to emotions, values and even biases. Some studies even suggest that once basic performance criteria are met, business decisions are largely based on psychological factors, such as earlier experience with a vendor, vendor credibility, experience, flexibility and reliability to serve customers in the future, and vendor commitment to a particular technology.

BUSINESS INSIGHT
Advertising business-to-business consultancy services: PWC

In recent years, the consultancy industry has witnessed important mergers and acquisitions, accompanied by renaming and rebranding of the companies involved. Rebranding and repositioning tasks are always accompanied by major communication campaigns in which a variety of tools can be used. This is illustrated by the story of PWC.

In 1999, a number of companies merged into PricewaterhouseCoopers (PWC). The merger was accompanied by a creative advertising campaign intended to build brand awareness and brand image among its high-profile business customers worldwide. The 2001 'PWC Corporate Finance and Recovery' campaign in the European business press was shortlisted as Best Business Press Campaign for the prestigious European Media and Marketing Awards. The company supplements its advertising efforts by sponsoring various initiatives, such as the Fast Track 100 and Profit Track league tables, which identify the fastest-growing and most profitable UK companies. PWC also produces reports and survey results that are of interest to the boardrooms of its clients, and is strongly involved in the World Economic Forum at Davos and the European Business Forum. PWC's website is used to promote stakeholder dialogue and supports the company's extensive community programme, such as sponsorship of the Web-based Maths Enhancement Programme with the University of Exeter. PWC also places a lot of importance on internal marketing to inform and motivate its 20 000 employees.[128]

All in all, studies show that the content and format of business ads are significantly different from consumer ads in a number of ways. The most striking differences seem to be that fewer people are depicted in business ads, the proportion of advertising space devoted to copy tends to be greater in business advertising, product characteristics are more frequently mentioned and psychological – as opposed to functional – appeals are seldom used in business advertising.[129]

What are the dimensions of an effective business-to-business ad? Research shows that a successful business ad should score on four dimensions: characteristics of the ad, the reader's feelings about his or her relationship with the ad, the selling proposition and the company's orientation or visibility. To score positively on each of the dimensions, business ads should clearly use a rational approach. The ad should explain the product and the benefits of the product, its quality and performance. The information should be presented in a logical order. On the one hand, the size of the text should be closely monitored. Too much text and too much information decrease ad effectiveness. On the other hand, the use of illustrations and pictures, as long as they are relevant to the target group, enhances ad effectiveness. Including too many people in the ad reduces its impact and, when people are shown, the target group should be able to identify with them. All in all, business ads differ and should differ from consumer ads, but there is no reason to assume that business ads should be dull, and packed with text and information overload.[130]

Comfort Bultex: sits like it fits. Business-to-business advertising.

Advertising in a cross-cultural environment

Figure 7.6 shows some important components of culture. Each of these culture components may have an impact on how advertising messages are perceived and should be framed to be correctly understood by consumers in different cultures.

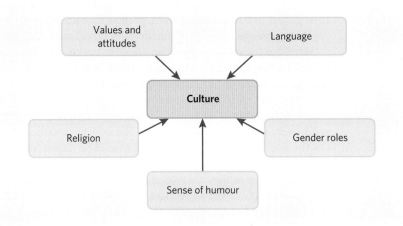

Figure 7.6 The major components of culture

BUSINESS INSIGHT
Maybe today's youth are not so global after all

Coca-Cola tested more than 30 commercials using a panel of Singaporean teens. Assuming that contemporary youth are global and Asian youngsters can be mirrored to American ones, ads showing things that are typical of American youth, such as body-pierced, grungy kids in a car listening to rock music and head-banging, shirtless youngsters crowd-surfing at a concert and youngsters going down a store aisle on a grocery cart, were shown to Singaporean youngsters. However, the ads were not really appreciated by the Singaporean teens. They considered the ads far too rebellious and unruly. The head-banging car scene was particularly disliked. One 18 year old made the comment 'They look like they're on drugs constantly. And if they're on drugs, then how can they be performing at school?' Coke concluded that ads have to be 'within bounds of societal approval' in order to be liked by young Singaporeans. According to the managing director of Viacom's MTV India, Asian teens are far more conservative than American or European youngsters. Rebellion, anger or the need to question authority, which are all elements of global youth culture, do not appeal in Asia. Asian youngsters may wear earrings, belly-button rings and ponytails, but they are still very conformist, a value deeply seated in Asian culture.[131]

Bajaj Auto, India's largest scooter and motorcycle producer, fared better. Its commercial pictured an Indian boy and his Caucasian girlfriend cruising around on a Bajaj motorbike. Since in India most marriages are still arranged and strict caste codes still operate, this scene is pretty provocative. However, this provocation is set off by the next scene: the youngsters arrive at a temple and the boy covers his girlfriend's head with a shawl. The commercial shows rebellion, but it does not push it too far. According to the creator of the ad, the message of the commercial is 'we are changing, testing boundaries, but we have pride in our core values'. Indian youth loved the ad and Bajaj motorcycles achieved a sales increase of 25% during the seven months following the launch.

Verbal language

Subtle differences or different pronunciations may convey totally different meanings. In Asian countries such as Japan and Thailand, language differs according to who is speaking. The suffixes Thai women use are different from those Thai men use. In Japan the level of formality of the language depends on the gender and the status of the speaker.[132] For marketing communications, this means that the seller always has to place him- or herself in an inferior position. Furthermore, translation of words may lead to more space requirements, which can alter the overall layout of the ad. For instance, 25% more space is needed when translating from English into a Romanesque language and 30% from English into German. Furthermore, the meaning of words may alter as a result of translation. For example, Germans associate *ruhig* with a forest, sleep, church, a cemetery and a bed, while *tranquille* makes the French think of the countryside, a forest, a house, a library.[133] Also, non-verbal language is important.[134] Non-verbal language includes timing, special orientation, gestures, touch, colours and eye contact.

Timing

Is time money or do people consider it to be indefinitely available? A time-is-money person (such as in Europe and the USA) may find an ad that appeals to 'saving time' convincing, in contrast to people who do not adhere to this time concept. Also, a distinction can be made between a time orientation towards the past, present or future. Many European countries have an orientation towards the past, using the past to explain where they are now. Americans are more future-oriented, while Muslim countries are rather fatalistic and adhere to a present-time orientation. History-related advertising appeals may not work so well in the USA.

Space

Asian and Arab people tend to stand very close to one another, Western and American people leave more space and find it rather threatening when people stand close to them. According to Hall's 'proxemics', Western countries are characterised by three primary zones of space: the intimate zone (0–45 cm), the personal zone (45 cm–1 m) and the social zone (1–2 m). However, within Europe differences concerning optimal space also appear: the further south you go, the smaller the distance gets. Northern Europeans, the English and Americans are said to have a low-touch culture, demonstrating low contact in public, while Southern Europeans, Arabs and Eastern Europeans are said to have a high-touch culture. However, although a country may belong to a high-touch culture, one should keep in mind subtleties in touching rules in advertising. Touching a woman is usually a more sensitive area and, especially in Arab countries, this may cause problems.[135] Moreover, who touches who also depends on the culture. In Europe it is usual to see people of the opposite sex (a couple) walking hand in hand on the street. This is not the case for many Asian and Arab countries. Here you would rather see people of the same sex (not a couple, but just acquaintances) holding hands.

Colours

Colours have different meanings in different cultures. For instance, in the USA and Europe, green is often associated with freshness and good health, but in countries with dense green jungles it is associated with disease instead. Red suggests good fortune in China but means death in Turkey. White stands for purity and cleanliness in many European countries, but suggests death in many Asian countries. Black has negative connotations in Japan, India and Europe, but is perceived positively in the Middle East.[136]

Gestures

Cultures differ in the way they greet each other: shaking hands, bowing, kissing, etc. Furthermore, moving the head back and forth is an affirmative sign in most Western countries, but means 'no' in Greece and Bulgaria. Patting a child on the head is a sign of affection in Western cultures, but an insult in Islamic countries. Raising three fingers when ordering a drink means you want three drinks in Western countries, but in Japan you would be ordering two drinks since Japanese count the number of fingers that are down instead of up.

Eye contact

Looking someone straight in the eye is regarded positively by Europeans and Americans because it is perceived as a sign of honesty. However, in Japan you show respect by lowering your eyes.

BUSINESS INSIGHT
Slogan translation mistakes

Despite the fact that translators usually know the foreign language quite well, translation errors frequently occur. One way to avoid such errors is to translate and back-translate, which should result in the same words or sentence(s) as the original one(s). Some examples of translation errors are:[137]

- The Pepsi slogan 'Come alive, you're in the Pepsi generation' was translated into German in 1960. The result became 'Come alive out of the grave'.
- GM's brand Chevy Nova translates in Spanish as 'doesn't go', while Nescafé was understood as 'no es café'.
- A Copenhagen airline office promises to 'take your bags and send them in all directions'.
- A Hong Kong dentist claims to extract teeth 'by the latest Methodists'.
- A Japanese hotel left the following notice to hotel guests: 'You are invited to take advantage of the chambermaid'.
- 'Let Hertz put you in the driving seat' became 'Let Hertz make you a chauffeur'.
- The truck brand Fiera from Ford became 'ugly old woman' when translated into Spanish.
- Mitsubishi renamed its Pajero model in Spanish-speaking countries because Pajero is related to masturbation.

Values and attitudes

Values and attitudes are our guide in determining what is right and what is wrong, what is important and desirable, and how we behave. Therefore, it is important to understand different cultural values and beliefs. Some researchers claim that cultural values form the core of advertising messages and that advertising reinforces cultural values.[138] Since different cultures cherish different values, they often emphasise different communications appeals. Even in the USA and the UK, two countries in which the marketing environment is very similar (economic development, language, legal restrictions, marketing institutions, technology, etc.), differences in culture lead to different types of advertising appeals. A study investigating beer ads in the two countries found that American ads predominantly depict American values such as achievement, individualism/independence and modernity/newness, while British ads show British values such as tradition/history and eccentricity (acting strangely or whimsically, often to humorous ends). Furthermore, in British ads the beer is more often shown being drunk on regular occasions, while in American ads product use is depicted during special occasions or the usage is not shown at all.[139] Empirical studies show that consumers seem to respond more positively to culture-congruent appeals.[140]

Religion[141]

Religion influences what is allowed to be said or shown in a marketing message. For example, Seiko got into trouble when it ran its worldwide advertising campaign in Malaysia saying 'Man invented time, Seiko perfected it'. According to Islam, God and not man invented time, so the message had to be changed to 'Man invented timekeeping, Seiko perfected it'. In France, Volkswagen had to withdraw its billboards for the new Golf since it was said to mock the Last Supper. A modern version of the Last Supper is shown, the last meal Jesus had with his disciples. Instead of 'Drink, this is my blood', Jesus says 'Let's rejoice since the new Golf is born'. Secondly, religion influences the value people attach to material goods. According to Islam and Buddhism, material wealth is immoral, while in the Western world wealth is a symbol of achievement. Therefore, status appeals can be expected to be more successful in Western countries than in Islamic or Buddhist countries. Thirdly, religion has an influence on what products can and cannot be consumed. An ad for a refrigerator should not show beef or pork inside the refrigerator if the ad is meant to run in countries with a Hindu or Islamic culture.

Sense of humour

Some countries make more use of humour than others. Ads in the UK, for instance, are more likely to contain humour than in the USA or France, while a higher percentage of ads in the latter countries are more humorous than in Germany. Furthermore, different cultures seem to appreciate different types of humour. Incongruent humour is more often used in Germany (92%) and Thailand (82%) than in the USA (69%) and Korea (57%). The English like black humour, the Germans slapstick and demeaning humour, while the Japanese seem to prefer black humour and dramatisations.[142]

Gender roles

A review of content analyses in different countries leads to the conclusion that gender roles in advertising differ to a great extent from one country to another. In Malaysia, women are usually depicted in the home taking care of the children. In Singapore, women are concerned with looking beautiful and are often shown in white-collar and service occupations. German and Japanese advertising sticks much more to traditional gender roles than ads in Denmark, France, New Zealand and the USA. Australian and Swedish ads have a more balanced and non-traditional way of presenting men and women in advertising.[143] Using traditional gender roles, such as talking about the 'lady's kitchen', the 'lady's vacuum cleaner', etc., when trying to sell a house to a young European couple, will not be appreciated by these women since more and more men and women share household chores, while in Muslim countries, such as Malaysia, it would be unwise to imply that men could have a role in the housekeeping.

High- and low-context cultures

A high-context communication or message is one in which most of the information is either in the physical context or internalised in the person, while very little is in the coded, explicit, transmitted part of the message. A low-context communication is just the opposite; that is, the mass of the information is vested in the explicit code.[144] In other words, in **low-context cultures**, a lot of emphasis is placed on words. One is as accurate, explicit and unambiguous as possible so that the receiver can easily decode the message and understand what is meant. In **high-context cultures** words are one part of the message, the other part is formed by body language and the context, i.e. the social setting, the importance and knowledge of the person. In the latter case, the message is more ambiguous and implicit. The Japanese, for example, have 16 ways to avoid saying 'no'.[145] Advertising appeals differ to a great extent in different context cultures. For example, Japanese ads have been shown to contain fewer information cues, less emphasis on the product's benefits, fewer comparisons and to consist of more emotional appeals than American ads.[146] In other words, in Japan a soft sell approach is preferred, while in the USA a hard sell approach is more frequently encountered.

Cultural dimensions[147]

According to Hofstede, five cultural dimensions can be distinguished which can explain the differences in cultural components across countries (Figure 7.7).

The characteristic of an **individualist culture** is that there are loose ties between people and that they look after themselves and their immediate family only. In a **collectivistic culture** people belong to strong, cohesive in-groups (often extended families) who look after and protect each other in exchange for unquestioning loyalty. Central to individualism is giving priority to personal goals over the goals of the group, as well as an emphasis on differentiation and achievement, while collectivism stands for the reverse: harmony, conformism, group goals, participation and teamwork above all. This leads to differences in advertising appreciation. An empirical study shows that Americans respond more favourably to an individualistic appeal, while Chinese people react more positively to a collectivistic appeal. It should be added, though, that a culturally incongruent appeal is less harmful when the appeal matches the product use condition. For example, a Chinese individualistic appeal for a toothbrush is less harmful than a Chinese individualistic appeal for a camera.[148]

The degree of **power distance** refers to the extent to which authority plays an important role, and to what extent less powerful members of the society accept and expect that power

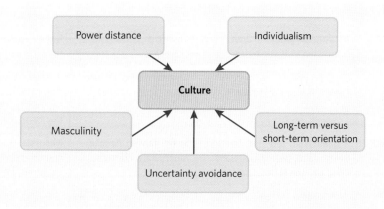

Figure 7.7 Hofstede's five cultural dimensions

is distributed unequally. In high-power-distance cultures (e.g. Malaysia), a few people have all the power and make all the decisions. The other people carry out orders. In low-power-distance cultures (e.g. Denmark, Austria) power is not concentrated in the hands of a few and interactions between people occur on a more equal basis. In the latter case, people are used to evaluating information and making decisions themselves. For advertising, this might mean that expert endorsers are more appropriate in high-power-distance cultures in which people are used to being and expect to be told what to do, while information-dense ads might be more appropriate in low-power-distance cultures in which people appreciate making decisions on the basis of information offered.[149]

In **masculine cultures**, assertiveness, competitiveness and status are valued highly, while in **feminine cultures**, caring for others and quality of life are central values. In feminine cultures men's and women's values and roles coincide, while there is a larger gap in their roles in masculine cultures. **Uncertainty avoidance** refers to the extent to which people feel uncomfortable with uncertainty and ambiguity and have a need for structure and formal rules in their lives. Communications for uncertainty avoidance cultures can focus on expert appeals and providing information and guarantees to reassure consumers. **Long-term versus short-term orientation** deals with values such as pragmatic future-oriented thinking, virtue, thrift, perseverance and a sense of shame versus conventional, historical or short-term thinking, fulfilling social obligations, respect for tradition and a sense of security and stability. Table 7.4 shows how different countries are positioned on Hofstede's dimensions and on the communications context dimension.[150]

IMC INSIGHT
Integrating advertising in IMC

Advertising as the classic instrument to reach a large audience, and as one of the most flexible communications tools, is the obvious channel to support and supplement other communications efforts. Advertising can be used to reinforce sponsorship campaigns, by using events and celebrities in advertising, by capitalising on product placement in movies and TV programmes, or by pointing out the corporate social responsibility efforts of the company. Advertising can also be used to monopolise the broadcast of the sponsored event. Shareholder meetings, points of view on societal issues and press releases can be referred to in advertising campaigns. Sales promotions can be announced in ads, and ads can build traffic for in-store and promotion campaigns. The latter can be reinforced by referring to the ads on the shop floor ('as seen on television'). Offline advertising can be used to build traffic to websites and as an introduction to interactive advertising formats. In general, advertising can be used to build the necessary awareness and brand image to provide the fertile soil for other communication efforts.

Table 7.4 Positioning of countries on cultural dimensions

	Countries scoring high on left-dimension attributes	Countries scoring average	Countries scoring high on right-dimension attributes	
Collectivism	East and West African countries Latin American countries Portugal	Arab countries, Greece, Japan, Spain, Turkey	Australia, Switzerland, Scandinavian countries, France, UK, USA, Germany, the Netherlands, Belgium	**Individualism**
Low power	Scandinavian countries, Austria, Switzerland, Germany, Ireland, USA, UK, the Netherlands	Spain, Taiwan, Greece, Japan, Italy, Portugal	Malaysia, Guatemala, Arab countries, West African countries, Philippines	**High power**
Feminine	Scandinavia, Portugal, the Netherlands, Turkey	Belgium, France, Greece, Spain, Arab countries	Austria, Canada, UK, Ireland, Italy, Japan, Switzerland, USA	**Masculine**
Uncertainty tolerant	Scandinavian countries, UK, USA, Ireland, Canada, India	Arab countries, Austria, Switzerland, Germany	Belgium, France, Greece, Japan, Portugal, Spain	**Uncertainty avoidance**
Short-term orientation	Pakistan, Nigeria, Canada, UK, USA, Australia, Germany, Poland, Sweden	India, Thailand, Hungary, Singapore, the Netherlands	China, Hong Kong, Taiwan, Japan, South Korea	**Long-term orientation**
High context	Japan, China, Arab countries, Latin American countries	Italy, Spain, France, UK	North American countries, Scandinavian countries, Germany, Switzerland	**Low context**

Summary

Advertising is any paid, non-personal communications through various media by an identified brand or company. It is one of the most visible tools of the communications mix. Advertising campaign development consists of a number of stages. Firstly, advertising strategy has to be decided on: who are the target groups of the campaign; what are the objectives; and what messages are going to be conveyed? At the very core of the advertising process is the development of a creative idea. Companies have to write a creative brief before the advertising agency can start to do its job. Creativity is hard to describe, but bringing the message in an original, novel and appealing way comes close. In general, two broad types of creative appeals, rational and emotional, can be used to develop a campaign, although mixed forms also exist. Emotional appeals are ads whose main purpose is to elicit affective responses and to convey an image. Rational appeals, on the other hand, contain information cues such as price, value, quality, performance, components, availability, taste, warranties, new ideas, etc. For both rational and emotional appeals, different formats or execution strategies can be used. Rational appeals may, for instance, make use of a talking head, a demonstration, a problem solution, a testimonial, a slice of life, a drama or a (direct or indirect) comparison with competitors. Emotional appeals may be based on humour, fear, warmth, eroticism, music or the like. Rational and emotional appeals may further feature different types of endorsers: ordinary people, experts or celebrities. None of the execution strategies works in all situations and for all target groups; for example, although everyone agrees that emotional techniques are capable of attracting attention, it is by no means certain that they get the message across in the manner intended. Therefore caution should be taken to select the right technique. In cross-cultural advertising campaigns, substantial differences in cultural characteristics have to be taken into account.

REVIEW QUESTIONS

1. What are the various stages in advertising campaign development?
2. Is creativity in advertising important?
3. What are the necessary elements in a creative brief?
4. What are the most frequently used execution strategies for rational appeals and why are they supposed to be effective?
5. What are the advantages and disadvantages of comparative advertising?
6. Are humorous advertising appeals effective? What about erotic ones?
7. To what extent are fear appeals effective advertising techniques?
8. On the basis of what criteria would you select a celebrity?
9. What are the components of culture and how can they influence international advertising?
10. According to Hofstede, on the basis of which dimensions can culture be distinguished, and what is their impact on cross-cultural advertising?

Further reading

Belch, M. and Belch, G. (2008), *Introduction to Advertising and Promotion: An Integrated Marketing Communications Perspective*, 6th edition. New York: McGraw-Hill.

De Mooij, M. (2005), *Global Marketing and Advertising: Understanding Cultural Paradoxes*, 2nd edition. Thousands Oaks, CA: Sage.

Hofstede, G. and Hofstede, G.J. (2004), *Cultures and Organizations: Software for the Mind*, 2nd edition. New York: McGraw-Hill Professional.

Mueller, B. (2004), *Dynamics of International Advertising*. New York: Peter Lang.

O'Guinn, T., Allen, C.T. and Semenik, R.J. (2008), *Advertising and Integrated Brand Promotion*, 4th edition. Mason, OH: Thomson/South-Western.

International Journal of Advertising, http://www.internationaljournalofadvertising.com/.

International Marketing Review, http://info.emeraldinsight.com/products/journals/journals. htm?id=IMR.

Journal of Advertising, http://ja.memphis.edu/.

Journal of Advertising Research, http://www.marketingpower.com/Community/ARC/Pages/ Research/Journals/Other/JournalofAdvertisingResearch.aspx.

Journal of International Marketing, http://www.journalofinternationalmarketing.com/.

Journal of Marketing Communications, http://www.tandf.co.uk/journals/titles/13527266.asp.

CASE 7:
L'Oréal's Biotherm and Biotherm Homme: a global brand of skin care products

The L'Oréal Group

The L'Oréal Group, with headquarters in Clichy, France, was founded in 1907, and is the world's foremost company in cosmetics. In 2011, the group had 68 900 employees in 58 countries and 42 production facilities around the world. It is present in 130 countries with almost 300 subsidiaries. In 2011, group turnover was €20.3 billion, €3.3 billion of which was profit. The competition is heavy and global, with companies such as Procter & Gamble, Unilever, Beiersdorf, Wella, Estée Lauder and LVMH.

L'Oréal's vision is that cosmetics are part of the universal quest for beauty and well-being. As a form of self-expression, they are personal, part of social life, and they serve a daily need for self-confidence and contact with others. L'Oréal claims to put all its expertise and research resources to work for the well-being of men and women, in all their diversity, around the world. Consequently, the company's focus centres around three important principles:

- Unfailing attention to consumers and understanding and anticipating their individual needs and aspirations.

- Respect for personal diversity; the company strives to match personal diversity with the diversity of its products and brands (age, type of skin, over time, culture, etc.).

- The effectiveness of the products is built upon in-depth research and a dedication to investing in innovation, product safety and the highest standards of reliability and product quality.

With respect to R&D, in 2008 about 3300 employees of 60 nationalities worldwide were working in 30 different research disciplines; €580 million was invested in R&D, one-third of which is devoted to advanced research. In 18 research centres and 13 evaluation centres around the world, each year 5000 formulae are developed and in 2011, as in preceding years, more than 600 new patents were registered. L'Oréal has 100 active co-operations with leading academic and research institutions.

Attention to consumer needs and personal diversity is reflected in the branding and product range strategy of the group. The company markets 27 global brands, i.e. brands with annual sales of over €50 million. They can be divided into four categories (Table 7.5). Each brand has its own well-designed brand proposition, and brand equity is continuously built and supported by means of advertising and other forms of marketing communications. L'Oréal also recognises that there is no single model of beauty. Each culture has unique personal care segments, unique styles

Table 7.5 Four categories of cosmetics

Type of product	Consumer products	Professional products	Luxury products	Active cosmetics
Definition	Are priced competitively and distributed through mass market retailing channels	Meet the requirements of hair salons and provide customers with a wide range of innovative products	Offer customers products and premium service in department stores and specialty stores	Dermo-cosmetic products sold in pharmacies and specialist retailers
Brands	L'Oréal Paris Garnier Maybelline NY Softsheen Carson CCB Paris	L'Oréal professional Kérastase Redken Matrix Mizani	Lancôme Biotherm Helena Rubinstein Kiehl's ShuUemura Giorgio Armani Ralph Lauren Cacharel Viktor & Rolf	Vichy La Roche – Posay Innéov SkinCeuticals

of dress and self-expression, unique traditions in cosmetics and, above all, its own unique vision. The company tries to serve these diverse needs by designing a diverse product range with products attuned to each culture and its needs. For example:

- SoftSheen.Carson: The world leader in hair care products for people of African descent.
- Lancôme and L'Oréal Paris: European taste and traditions.
- ShuUemura: Standard bearer for Japanese style.
- Maybelline NY & Redken: Trendsetters in the USA.
- Armani: Italian style.

L'Oréal products are available in supermarkets, hair salons, pharmacies, cosmetic boutiques and other specialist outlets, and also online and through mail order distribution. Brands are available in different outlets, depending on the category they belong to (see Table 7.5).

Biotherm

Biotherm is one of L'Oréal's luxury brands. It was founded in 1950 and covers a comprehensive range of face care (53% of sales), body care (20%), sun care (4%), make-up (6%) and skin care for men (16%). The brand originated with the discovery of an active ingredient found in thermal springs in the French Pyrenees, which was called 'Pure extract of thermal plankton'. This basic component contains essential trace elements, minerals salts, proteins and vitamins, and is mixed with natural ingredients. Due to its biological affinity with the skin, Biotherm has a soothing, regenerating and stimulating effect. Its three basic functions are: cleansing, toning and treating. It is claimed to lead to a clearer, healthier,

softer, silky, vital and energised skin and a flawless complexion. Biotherm is positioned on the basis of the following verbatims: young, well-being, positive attitude (de-dramatised, wink), simple, fresh, pure, minimalistic, direct, assertive and complicity. The product range is organised by skin type (dry, normal, etc.) and also on the basis of special needs and lifestyle elements. For instance, the following specialised products belong to the Biotherm programme: Age Fitness (anti-ageing), Densit Lift (anti-wrinkle) and Acnopur (to treat skin imperfections). Lifestyle products are Hydra-Detox (to eliminate toxins generated by urban pollution), D-stress (against stress-induced skin fatigue) and Aqua Sport (to keep the body toned and fit). Biotherm is distributed in almost 14 000 stores worldwide, 12 000 of which are in Europe. Sales in 2003 totalled about €350 million, and were predicted to show double-figure growth in the years thereafter. Figure 7.8 shows a positioning map, based on two dimensions: 'serious–sensation' and 'new luxury–classic luxury'. Biotherm is positioned in the 'serious–new luxury' corner of the map. Its largest most direct competition is Clinique (16.4% market share). Table 7.6 gives the market position of Biotherm and its main competitors in a number of European countries and for a number of product categories.

The Biotherm brand image in different countries

In February 2003, focus group studies were conducted with 80 women in various countries. The objective of this qualitative research project was to explore the brand image of Biotherm, and to assess the strengths and weaknesses of the brand and brand communications. The focus groups were composed of users of both Biotherm and competitive

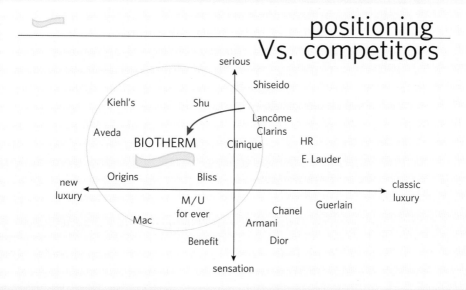

Figure 7.8 Biotherm's positioning versus the competition

Table 7.6 Biotherm and the top three other brands in selected European countries and markets (2002) (percentages are market shares)

Product category	France	%	Germany	%	Italy	%	Spain	%
Care	Clarins	20.5	Shiseido	12.8	Shiseido	11.9	Lancôme	13.7
	Lancôme	12.0	Biotherm	12.1	Lancôme	9.9	Clarins	10.3
	Sisley	9.5	Lancôme	11.4	Lauder	9.9	Clinique	9.9
	Biotherm	7.6	Clarins	8.3	Biotherm	5.9	Biotherm	9.4
Face care	Clarins	16.4	Shiseido	15.0	Shiseido	12.6	Lancôme	14.6
	Lancôme	12.7	Lancôme	10.7	Lauder	11.5	Lauder	11.3
	Sisley	10.2	Lauder	8.9	Lancôme	10.4	Clinique	11.0
	Biotherm	6.1	Biotherm	8.7	Biotherm	4.8	Biotherm	8.4
Body care	Clarins	45.3	Biotherm	35.5	Clarins	29.2	Clarins	30.3
	Biotherm	14.5	Clarins	14.8	Biotherm	13.1	Biotherm	20.4
	Dior	8.6	Lancôme	14.1	Dior	7.9	Lancôme	9.6
	Lancôme	6.0	Dior	5.8	Lancôme	7.4	Dior	6.0

Table 7.7 Composition of focus groups on the Biotherm brand image in Germany, Spain and France

France Paris 3 groups	Spain Madrid 3 groups	Germany Düsseldorf 4 groups
• 7 Biotherm users 25–35 years old	• 7 Biotherm users 25–35 years old	• 7 Biotherm users 20–30 years old
• 6 Clinique users 25–35 years old	• 7 Biotherm users 30–40 years old	• 7 Biotherm users 35–45 years old
• 6 Origins Aveda users 25–35 years old	• 6 Clinique users 25–35 years old	• 6 Clinique users 25–35 years old
		• 6 Shiseido users 25–35 years old

Table 7.8 Brand image of Biotherm in Germany

	☺ Strengths	Weaknesses
• Image/value	• Rich and stable mental picture	• Risk of being too insipid, featureless
	• French endorsement	
	• Real consistency between fundamental values (naturalness, purification, softness, sobriety) and their expression through products (colours, smells, feel: lightness, etc.)	
• Product offer	• Clear, readable instructive offering, complete, accessible	• Lack of distinct benefits
	• Legitimacy for face and body	• Problem of product descriptions not in German
	• Powerful hydration benefits, 'intelligent' freshness, skin care, respect, softness, safety, calming	
• Ads		• Lack of life, of movement, of dynamism, of emotion
• Target	• Woman aged 30–40, sweet, natural, young-minded, rather sporty, healthy, easy-going	• Club biotherm not personalised enough

products. Tables 7.7–7.10 give the composition of the focus groups in Germany, France and Spain along with the results of the survey. Although the composition of the groups was similar in the three countries, the results differ in some respects. For instance, while in Germany the brand is accused of being featureless, in Spain consumers complain about the origin of the brand and the water, and in France the perception is that there is a lack of seduction, femininity and sensuality. In terms of product offering, German consumers believe that there is a lack of distinct benefits, and they complain that the product description is not in German. French women feel that there is a lack of status

Table 7.9 Brand image of Biotherm in Spain

	Strengths	Weaknesses
• Image/value	• Eau Naturelle Bienfaisante (more sea-water) at the heart of life → Freshness, Cleanliness, Health, Physical and psychological effects Research: confidence, scientific	• What about origins – of the water – of the brand?
• Product offer	• Simple and serious offering • Enhancement of Make-up offer • 'Mission' for hydration + refreshing, regenerating and relaxing actions • Good value for money	• Lack of substance (Well-being, health)
• Ads	• Attractive colour (Celluli-choc, Hair Resource) • Central role of regenerating water	• Agua! Too much water, pale, lack of consistency
• Target	• Woman aged 30–40, natural, spontaneous, sporty Bohemian (20–30) and non-conformist (ut.Clinique)	• Women are too smooth, disincarnate, not convivial enough, lack seduction • Lack of assertion

Table 7.10 Brand image of Biotherm in France

	Strengths	Weaknesses
• Image/value	• Natural, simplicity, freshness, dynamism, healthy	• Lack of seduction, feminity, sensuality
• Product offer	• Strong water, tonifying, hydrating, freshness, relaxing • Natural ingredients	• Lack of status for younger • Too pharmaceutical
• Ads	• More selective; more modern	• Lack of dream • Lack of sensoriality
• Target	• More young people: 25–35	• Not fashion

for younger consumers, and the product has too 'phar-maceutical' a feel. Consumers in all three countries agree that the advertisements for Biotherm lack life, emotion, dynamism, dream and sensoriality.

Men and body care

In a 2003 study, Publicis investigated which taboos had disappeared from the masculine mind the years before, and what significant new behavioural patterns appeared to have emerged; in other words, what were the new ways in which men could be addressed? Four key points of communication were identified. They are summarised in Figure 7.9. Almost half of the men today like the idea of having a masculine and feminine side, especially young men. The result is a 'blurring' of behaviour: muscles and health, but also youth, perfection and facial beauty are important. There is a growing trend among men to care for their appearance and to care about themselves. Skin care is considered to be at the crossroads of physical hygiene and the desire to seduce. Being authentic, good-looking and seductive is increasingly

important. A large proportion of men want to have more free time to take care of themselves. And sport, along with gay culture, is one of the main points of attention of the New Man. But the 'eternal man' remains eternal. Values such as being in control, strong, ambitious, forceful, and full of authority are still positively valued, and preferred to a man who is passive, hesitating and lost in dreams.

Biotherm Homme

The skin and skin treatment of men and women are funda-mentally different in a number of ways. Men have between 6000 and 25 000 facial hairs, much more than women. Typically, men spend 3000 hours of their lives shaving (i.e. 140 days). A man's skin is more oily and more susceptible to acne, and is 16% to 20% thicker than a woman's skin, and therefore less fragile. On the other hand, a man's skin tends to age more rapidly, and wrinkles appear more quickly. Therefore, there is a need for a skin care product especially designed for men. Additionally, the aforementioned evolu-tion in men's attitude towards body care signals a market

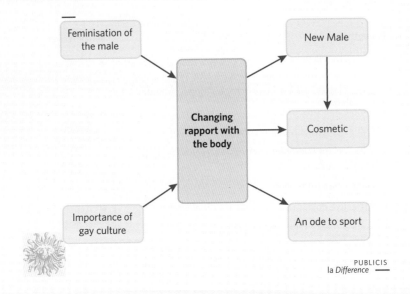

Figure 7.9 New ways to address men and the link with cosmetics

Photo 7.5 Biotherm Homme Force Suprème, Anti-Ageing Eye Care and Daily Anti-Wrinkle Moisturizer

Source: L'Oreal UK.

potential for a specific male body care product. Biotherm Homme (Photo 7.5), a skin care programme for men launched in 1985, has experienced strong growth in recent years. This complete line of skin care products for the face and the body was the world's market leader in men's care (2004, value shares). The men's skin care market has been growing steadily since the mid-1990s (twice as fast when one includes the men who borrow products from their girlfriends or wives).

The positioning of Biotherm Homme can be summarised as follows: 'There is more to skin care than aftershave. You have no qualms about your individuality. You are comfortable looking after your body, skin and general wellbeing. You want to keep things simple, quick and effective. You want immediate results that make you feel good about yourself.' The brand

statement is: 'Biotherm Homme, men's skin care coach', because only a coach can provide men with a custom-made programme that respects and soothes their skin. This coach is 'the creator of men's skin care treatment'. It has created personalised programmes specifically for men: high-precision shaving formulae, face care treatments with extremely targeted ingredients, technical body care products. Each individual should be able to find the product that is best suited to his personal skin care needs.

In March 2003, a qualitative brand study in four focus groups of men aged 20–45 was carried out in Germany. In this study, the brand statement was tested as well as a number of advertising campaigns for both Biotherm and some of its competitors, merchandising programmes and product offers. The conclusion was that the idea of a 'coach' was too business-like and authoritative, did not fit into the need for autonomy of men, and lacked pleasure, character, sensuality and emotionality. However, the notion of personalisation, and the description of ingredients and scientific research, were noted as strong points. In terms of advertising effects, the conclusions were that they were identifiable, attractive, aesthetic, masculine, informative and simple. However, the non-German name of the product, the 'coach' idea and the non-selective packaging were negative points, leading to low spontaneous recognition. The conclusion was that the brand statement needed to be redefined, using elements such as: skin care specialist, scientific knowledge, innovation, highlighting skin care benefits and sensations. The communications elements to stress were the specific characteristics of the product, the sensuality of the product and the models, and the key colour codes on each product. It was further concluded that, in order to build brand loyalty, the identification of men with the product needed to be enhanced by means of clear claims, visible skin results, identification of skin types, needs and benefits, and identification of products offer.

QUESTIONS

1. Is the vision and branding strategy of Biotherm and Biotherm Homme mainly global (standardised) or local (adapted to local cultures)? Explain and give examples.

2. Looking at the different types of needs that people can experience (for instance, consider Maslow's hierarchy with physiological as the most basic followed by safety, love/belonging, esteem and finally self-actualisation – see http://www.businessballs.com/maslow.htm). To which needs do L'Oréal in general, and Biotherm and Biotherm Homme in particular, appeal? Do you believe these needs are universal?

3. Clinique is mentioned as one of the closest competitors of Biotherm. Why? In what ways is the positioning of Biotherm and Clinique similar or different (use communications materials, websites, etc., to illustrate)?

4. Summarise the main similarities and differences of the results of the focus group discussions in the three countries studied. Can you find a relationship between the cultural characteristics of the countries and the attitudes and perceptions of the group members from these countries?

5. Is Biotherm Homme positioned differently in different countries (consult communications materials, websites, etc.)? Why or why not?

6. Are the conclusions and the marketing communications implications of the German Biotherm Homme study correct? Would you adapt the communications strategy in a different way?

Sources: Materials provided by Teresa di Campello and Joëlle Van Rijckevorsel, L'Oréal. www.loreal.com; www.biotherm.com; http://www.loreal.com/_en/_ww/pdf/Rapport_Annuel_2008_FR.pdf; www.loreal.com (accessed 9 July 2012).

References

[1] Kotler, P. and Armstrong, G. (2010), *Principles of Marketing*, 13th edition. Upper Saddle River, NJ: Prentice Hall.

[2] www.statista.com (accessed 9 July 2012).

[3] Many organisations offer software to help companies to plan their advertising campaigns. See, for instance, www.paloalto.com.

[4] Solomon, B. and Askegaard, H. (2007), *Consumer Behaviour: A European Perspective*, 3rd edition. Harlow: Pearson Education.

[5] Geuens, M., De Pelsmacker, P. and Mast, G. (2003), 'Family Structure as a Moderator of Parent–Child Communication about Consumption', *International Journal of Advertising and Marketing to Children*, 4(1), 1–6; Roedder John, D. (1999), 'Consumer Socialization of Children: A Retrospective Look at Twenty-five Years of Research', *Journal of Consumer Research*, 26(3), 183–213; McNeal, J.U. (1999), *Kids Market: Myths and Realities*, Ithaca, NY: Paramount Market; Gunter, B. and Furnham, A. (1998), *Children as Consumers: A Psychological Analysis of the Young People's Market*, London: Routledge; Acuff, D.S. (1997), *What Kids Buy and Why: The Psychology of Marketing to Kids*. New York: Free Press.

[6] Clegg, A. (2006), *Mining the Golden Years*, 24 April, http://www.brandchannel.com/features_effect.asp?pf_id=311 (accessed June 2009).

[7] Weijters, B. and Geuens, M. (2003), 'Evaluation of Age-Related Labels by Senior Citizens', Working paper, Vlerick Leuven Gent Management School; Young, G. (2002), 'Ageing and the UK Economy', *Bank of England Quarterly Bulletin*, 42(3), 285–92.

[8] Walker, M.M. and Macklin, M.C. (1992), 'The Use of Role Modeling in Targeting Advertising to Grandparents', *Journal of Advertising Research*, 32(4), 37–45.

[9] Ahmad, R. (2002), 'The Older Ageing Consumers in the UK: Are They Really that Different?', *International Journal of Market Research*, 44(3), 337–60; Moschis, G.P. and Mathur, A. (1997), 'Targeting the Mature Market: Opportunities and Challenges', *Journal of Consumer Marketing*, 14(4), 282–93.

[10] Weyters, B. and Geuens, M. (2003), 'Evaluation of Age-Related Labels by Senior Citizens', Working Paper, Vlerick Leuven Gent Management School; Szmigin, I. and Carrigan, M. (2001), 'Time, Consumption and the Older Consumer: An Interpretive Study of the Cognitively Young', *Psychology & Marketing*, 18(10), 1091–1116; Barak, B., Mathur, A., Lee, K. and Zhang, Y. (2001), 'Perceptions of Age-Identity: A Cross-Cultural Inner-Age Exploration', *Psychology & Marketing*, 18(10), 1003–30.

[11] Lewis, H.G. (1996), *Silver Linings: Selling to the Expanding Motive Market*. New York: Bonus Books.

[12] Yoon, C. and Cole C.A. (2008), 'Aging and Consumer Behavior', in Haughtvedt, C.P., Herr, P.M. and Kardes, F.R. (eds), *Handbook of Consumer Psychology*. New York: Lawrence Erlbaum Associates; Lumpkin, J.R. (1989), *Direct Marketing, Direct Selling, and the Mature Consumer: A Research Study*. Westpoint, CT: Quorum Books.

[13] Kotler, P. and Armstrong, G. (2010). *Principles of Marketing*, 13th edition. Upper Saddle River, NJ: Prentice Hall.

[14] Euro Effie (2001), Berlin: Gesamtverband Werbeagenturen GWA eV, http://www.euro-effie.com.

[15] Euro Effie (2008), Brussels: European Association of Communications Agencies, http://www.euro-effie.com.

[16] Reid, L.N., King, K. and DeLorme, D.E. (1998), 'Top-Level Agency Creatives Look at Advertising Creativity Then and Now', *Journal of Advertising*, 27(2), 1–15.

[17] Rossiter, J.R. and Percy, L. (2000), *Advertising Communication and Promotion Management*. New York: McGraw-Hill.

[18] Centlivre, L. (1988), 'A Peek at the Creatives of the '90s', *Advertising Age*, 18 January, 62.

[19] Otnes, C., Oviatt, A.A. and Treise, D.M. (1995), 'Views on Advertising Curricula from Experienced Creatives', *Journalism Educator*, 49 (Winter), 21–30.

[20] *Management and Advertising Problems in the Advertiser–Agency Relationship* (1985). New York: Association of National Advertisers.

[21] Ind, N. (1993), *Great Advertising Campaigns: How They Achieve Both Creative and Business Objectives*. London: Kogan Page.

[22] Euro Effie (2001), Berlin: Gesamtverband Werbeagenturen GWA eV, http://www.euro-effie.com.

[23] Anonymous (2003), 'Belgisch Regisseursduo Gooit Hoge Ogen op Amerikaans Reclamefestival' ('Belgian Producers Amaze at American Advertising Awards'), *De Morgen*, 22 May 2003.

[24] Reid, L.N., King, K. and DeLorme, D.E. (1998), 'Top-Level Agency Creatives Look at Advertising Creativity Then and Now', *Journal of Advertising*, 27(2), 1–15.

[25] Smith, R.E., Chen, J. and Yang, X. (2008), 'The Impact of Advertising Creativity on the Hierarchy of Effects', *Journal of Advertising*, 37(4), 47–61; Heiser, R.S., Sierra, J.J. and Torres, I.M. (2008), 'Creativity via Cartoon Spokespeople in Print Ads: Capitalizing on the Distinctiveness Effect', *Journal of Advertising*, 37(4), 75–84; Leather, P., MacKechnie, S. and Amirkhanian, M. (1994), 'The Importance of Likeability as a Measure of Television Advertising Effectiveness', *International Journal of Advertising*, 13(3), 265–80.

[26] Biel, A.L. and Bridgwater, C.A. (1990), 'Attributes of Likeable Television Commercials', *Advances in Consumer Research*, 11, 4–10; De Pelsmacker, P. and Van den Bergh, J. (1998), 'Ad Content, Product Category, Campaign Weight and Irritation: A Study of 226 TV Commercials', *Journal of International Consumer Marketing*, 10(4), 5–27; Till, B.D. and Baack, D.W. (2005), 'Recall and Persuasion: Does Creative Advertising Matter?', *Journal of Advertising*, 34(3), 47–57; Tippens, M.J. and Kunkel, R.A. (2006), 'Winning a Clio Award and its Relationship to Profitability', *Journal of Marketing Communications*, 12(1), 1–14.

[27] West, D.C., Kover, A.J. and Caruana, A. (2008), 'Practitioner and Customer Views of Advertising Creativity; Same Concept, Different Meaning?', *Journal of Advertising*, 37(4), 35–45.

[28] Tippins, N.J. and Kunkel, R.A. (2006), 'Winning a Clio Award and its Relationship to Firm Profitability', *Journal of Marketing Communications*, 12(1), 1–14.

[29] Sauer, A. (2012), *Brand Bites: Old Spice Man Video-Bombs Other Commercials*, http://www.brandchannel.com/home/post/2012/02/03/Brand-Bites-020312.aspx; Hutchings, E. (2012), *Old Spice Man Crashes Other Product's Commercials*, http://topsy.com/www.psfk.com/2012/02/old-spice-man-commercials.html (accessed July 2012).

[30] De Pelsmacker, P., Decock, B. and Geuens, M. (1998), 'Advertising Characteristics and the Attitude Towards the Ad – A Study of 100 Likeable TV Commercials', *Marketing and Research Today*, 27(4), 166–79.

[31] Abernethy, A.M. and Franke, G.R. (1996), 'The Information Content of Advertising: A Meta-Analysis', *Journal of Advertising*, 25(2), 1–17.

[32] Abernethy, A.M. and Franke, G.R. (1996), 'The Information Content of Advertising: A Meta-Analysis', *Journal of Advertising*, 25(2), 1–17.

[33] Chandy, R.K., Tellis, G.J., MacInnis, D.J. and Thaivanich, P. (2001), 'What to Say When: Advertising Appeals in Evolving Markets', *Journal of Marketing Research*, 38(4), 399–414.

[34] Pickett, G.M., Grove, S.J. and Laband, D.N. (2001), 'The Impact of Product Type and Parity on the Informational Content of Advertising', *Journal of Market Theory and Practice*, 9(3), 32–43.

[35] Chang, C. (2007), 'Diagnostic Advertising Content and Individual Differences', *Journal of Advertising*, 36(3), 75–84.

[36] Dens, N. and De Pelsmacker, P. (2008), '*Advertising for Extensions: The Moderating Role of Extension Type, Product Type, and Type of Advertising Appeal on Extension Evaluation*', *Proceedings of the 37th European Marketing Academy Conference, Brighton*; Dens, N. and De Pelsmacker, P. (2008b), 'How Attitude toward the Extension Mediates Parent Brand Feedback Effects for Line and Brand Extensions in Response to Extension Advertising, in Acevedo, C.R., Hernandez, J.M.C. and Lowrey, T.M. (eds), *Latin America Advances in Consumer Research*, Sao Paulo: Association for Consumer Research, Vol. 21, 142–3. Dens, N. and De Pelsmacker, P. (2009), 'Extension Attitude and Feedback Effects in Response to Extension Advertising: The Moderating Role of Product and Brand Symbolism',

Proceedings of the 14th International Corporate and Marketing Communications Conference, Nicosia.

[37] Brassington, B. and Pettitt, S. (2003), *Principles of Marketing*, 3rd edition. Harlow: Pearson Education.

[38] Ball, D. (2003), 'Unilever Sees Hefty Profit in SlimFast', *Wall Street Journal*, 23 April.

[39] Martin, B.A.S., Wentzel, D. and Tomczak, T. (2008), 'Effects of Susceptibility to Normative Influence and Type of Testimonial on Attitudes Toward Print Advertising', *Journal of Advertising*, 37(1), 29–43.

[40] De Pelsmacker, P. and Van den Bergh, J. (1998), 'Ad Content, Product Category, Campaign Weight and Irritation: A Study of 226 TV Commercials', *Journal of International Consumer Marketing*, 10(4), 5–27; Aaker, D.A. and Bruzzone, D.E. (1985), 'Causes of Irritation in Advertising', *Journal of Marketing*, 49 (Spring), 47–57.

[41] *De Morgen*, 15 April 2008.

[42] *Bizz*, March 2004, 34–5; *De Morgen*, 8 December 2005.

[43] De Pelsmacker, P. and Van den Bergh, J. (1998), 'Ad Content, Product Category, Campaign Weight and Irritation: A Study of 226 TV Commercials', *Journal of International Consumer Marketing*, 10(4), 5–27; Aaker, D.A. and Bruzzone, D.E. (1985), 'Causes of Irritation in Advertising', *Journal of Marketing*, 49 (Spring), 47–57.

[44] Euro Effie (2001), Berlin: Gesamtverband Werbeagenturen GWA eV, http://www.euro-effie.com.

[45] Euro Effie (2008), Brussels: European Association of Communications Agencies, http://www.euro-effie.com.

[46] Donthu, N. (1998), 'A Cross-Country Investigation of Recall and Attitude Toward Comparative Advertising', *Journal of Advertising*, 27(2), 111–22.

[47] Brabbs, C. (2001), 'Two-thirds Find Comparative Ads "Unacceptable"', *Marketing*, 20 September, 4.

[48] Dianoux, C. and Herrmann, J.L. (2001), 'The Influence of Comparative Advertising on Memorization and Attitudes: Experimentation in the French Context', *Recherche et Applications en Marketing*, 16(2), 33–50.

[49] Dianoux, C. (2002), 'What Is the Future for Comparative Advertising in France?', *Décisions Marketing*, 25 (Janvier–Mars), 93.

[50] del Barrio-Garcia, S. and Luque-Martinez, T. (2003), 'Modelling Consumer Response to Differing Levels of Comparative Advertising', *European Journal of Marketing*, 37(1), 256–74.

[51] Grewal, D., Kavanoor, S., Fern, E., Costley, C. and Barnes, J. (1997), 'Comparative Versus Non-Comparative Advertising: A Meta-Analysis', *Journal of Marketing*, 61(4), 1–15; Barry, T. (1993), 'Comparative Advertising: What Have We Learned in Two Decades?', *Journal of Advertising Research*, 33(2), 19–27.

[52] Putrevu, S. and Lord, K. (1994), 'Comparative and Non-Comparative Advertising: Attitudinal Effects Under Cognitive and Affective Involvement Conditions', *Journal of Advertising*, 23(2), 77–90.

[53] Grewal, D., Kavanoor, S., Fern, E., Costley, C. and Barnes, J. (1997), 'Comparative Versus Non-Comparative Advertising: A Meta-Analysis', *Journal of Marketing*, 61(4), 1–15.

[54] Chang, C. (2007), 'The Relative Effectiveness of Comparative and Non-Comparative Advertising. Evidence for Gender Effects in Information-Processing Strategies', *Journal of Advertising*, 36(1), 21–35.

[55] Pechmann, C. and Ratneshwar, S. (1991), 'The Use of Comparative Advertising for Brand Positioning: Association Versus Differentiation', *Journal of Consumer Research*, 18(2), 145–60.

[56] De Pelsmacker, P., Van den Bergh, J. and Anckaert, P. (1998), *Vergelijkende Reclame: Een Literatuurstudie* (*Comparative Advertising: Review of the Literature*), Research report, Marketing Communication Research Centre. Ghent: De Vlerick School voor Management.

[57] Droge, C. (1989), 'Shaping the Route to Attitude Change: Central versus Peripheral Processing Through Comparative versus Non-Comparative Advertising', *Journal of Marketing Research*, 26 (May), 193–204.

[58] Droge, C. (1989), 'Shaping the Route to Attitude Change: Central versus Peripheral Processing Through Comparative versus Non-Comparative Advertising', *Journal of Marketing Research*, 26 (May), 193–204.

[59] Swinyard, W. (1981), 'The Interaction Between Comparative Advertising and Copy Claim Variation', *Journal of Marketing Research*, 18 (May), 175–86.

[60] Pechmann, C. and Stewart, D. (1990), 'The Effects of Comparative Advertisements on Attention, Memory, and Purchase Intentions', *Journal of Consumer Research*, 17(2), 180–91.

[61] McCullough, L.S. (1992), 'The Use of Humor in International Print Advertising: A Content Analysis', Working paper, Miami University.

[62] Krishnan, H.S. and Chakravarti, D. (2003), 'A Process Analysis of the Effects of Humorous Advertising Executions on Brand Claims Memory', *Journal of Consumer Psychology*, 13(3), 230–45.

[63] Cline, T.W. and Kellaris, J.J. (2007), 'The Influence of Humor Strength and Humor-Message Relatedness on Ad Memorability: A Dual Process Model', *Journal of Advertising*, 36(1), 55–67; Weinberger, M.G. and Gulas, C.S. (1992), 'The Impact of Humor in Advertising – A Review', *Journal of Advertising*, 21(4), 35–59.

[64] Geuens, M. and De Pelsmacker, P. (2002), 'The Moderating Role of Need for Cognition on Responses to Humorous Appeals', in Broniarczyk, S. and Nakamoto, K. (eds), *Advances in Consumer Research*. Provo, UT: Association for Consumer Research, 29, 50–56.

[65] For a typology of humour types, see Speck, P.S. (1991), 'The Humorous Message Taxonomy: A Framework for the Study of Humorous Ads', *Current Issues and Research in Advertising*, 14(1), 1–44.

[66] Beirne, M. (2003), 'Heineken's Headlines are Humorous, but Amstel Light Spots are a Scream', *Brandweek*, 44(19), 8.

[67] Spotts, H.E., Weinberger, M.G. and Parsons, A.M. (1997), 'Assessing the Use and Impact of Humor on Advertising Effectiveness', *Journal of Advertising*, 26(3), 17–32.

[68] Weinberger, M.G. and Gulas, C.S. (1992), 'The Impact of Humor in Advertising – A Review', *Journal of Advertising*, 21(4), 35–59.

[69] Cline, T.W. and Kellaris, J.J. (2007), 'The Influence of Humor Strength and Humor-Message Relatedness on

Ad Memorability: A Dual Process Model', *Journal of Advertising*, 36(1), 55–67.

[70] Chattopadhyay, A. and Basu, K. (1990), 'Humor in Advertising: The Moderating Role of Prior Brand Evaluation', *Journal of Marketing Research*, 27, 466–76.

[71] De Pelsmacker, P. and Geuens, M. (1997), 'Emotional Appeals and Information Cues in Belgian Magazine Advertisements', *International Journal of Advertising*, 16(2), 123–47.

[72] Anonymous (2001), 'Sexy Vrouwelijk Strijkerskwartet Zorgt voor Mannelijke Blikschade' ('Sexy Female Musicians Cause Male Car Accidents'), *De Morgen*, 6 April 2001.

[73] De Pelsmacker, P. and Geuens, M. (1996), 'The Communication Effects of Warmth, Eroticism and Humour in Alcohol Advertisements', *Journal of Marketing Communication*, 2(4), 247–62.

[74] Ford, J.B., LaTour, M.S. and Lundstrom, W.J. (1993), 'Contemporary Women's Evaluations of Female Sex Roles in Advertising', *Journal of Consumer Marketing*, 8(1), 15–28.

[75] De Pelsmacker, P. and Geuens, M. (1996), 'The Communication Effects of Warmth, Eroticism and Humour in Alcohol Advertisements', *Journal of Marketing Communication*, 2(4), 247–62.

[76] Smith, S.M., Haughtvedt, C.P. and Jadrich, J.M. (1995), 'Understanding Responses to Sex Appeals in Advertising: An Individual Difference Approach', *Advances in Consumer Research*, 22, 735–9.

[77] Dudley, S.C. (1999), 'Consumer Attitudes toward Nudity in Advertising', *Journal of Marketing Theory and Practice*, 7(4), 89–96.

[78] Geuens, M. (1997), 'Erotische Reclame: Een Effectieve Strategie?' ('Erotic Advertising: An Effective Strategy?'), *Tijdschrift voor Economie en Management*, 42(1), 57–79.

[79] Reichert, T., Heckler, S.E. and Jackson, S. (2001), 'The Effects of Sexual Social Marketing Appeals on Cognitive Processing and Persuasion', *Journal of Advertising*, 30(1), 13–27.

[80] Putrevu, S. (2008), 'Consumer Responses Toward Sexual and Nonsexual Appeals: The Influence of Involvement, Need for Cognition (NFC), and Gender', *Journal of Advertising*, 37(2), 57–69.

[81] De Pelsmacker, P. and Geuens, M. (1996), 'The Communication Effects of Warmth, Eroticism and Humour in Alcohol Advertisements', *Journal of Marketing Communication*, 2(4), 247–62.

[82] Putrevu, S. (2008), 'Consumer Responses Toward Sexual and Nonsexual Appeals: The Influence of Involvement, Need for Cognition (NFC), and Gender', *Journal of Advertising*, 37(2), 57–69.

[83] Benady, D. (2002), 'Playing the Game', *Marketing Week*, July 25, 24–27.

[84] De Pelsmacker, P. and Geuens, M. (1997), 'Emotional Appeals and Information Cues in Belgian Magazine Advertisements', *International Journal of Advertising*, 16(2), 123–47.

[85] De Pelsmacker, P. and Geuens, M. (1998), 'Different Markets, Different Communication Strategies? A Comparative Study of the Communication Effects of Different Types of Alcohol Ads in Belgium and Poland', *International Marketing Review*, 15(4), 277–90; De Pelsmacker, P. and Geuens, M. (1996), 'The Communication Effects of Warmth, Eroticism and Humour in Alcohol Advertisements', *Journal of Marketing Communication*, 2(4), 247–62; Geuens, M. and De Pelsmacker, P. (1998), 'Feelings Evoked by Warmth, Eroticism and Humour in Alcohol Advertisements', *AMS Review*, www.ams.review.org/articles/geuensol-1998.pdf; De Pelsmacker, P. and Van den Bergh, J. (1998), 'Ad Content, Product Category, Campaign Weight and Irritation: A Study of 226 TV Commercials', *Journal of International Consumer Marketing*, 10(4), 5–27.

[86] Geuens, M. and De Pelsmacker, P. (1999), 'Individual Differences and the Communication Effects of Different Types of Emotional Stimuli: Exploring the Role of Affect Intensity', *Psychology and Marketing*, 16(3), 195–209.

[87] Bain, L.J., Barker, W., Loewenstein, D.A. and Douara, R. (2008), 'Towards an Earlier Diagnosis of Alzheimer Disease', *Proceedings of the 5th MCI Symposium 2007, Alzheimer Disease & Associated Disorders*, 22(2), 99–110.

[88] Schwarz, N. and Clore G.L. (2003), 'Mood as Information: 20 Years Later', *Psychological Inquiry*, 14 (3&4), 296–303; Forgas, J.P. (1995), 'Mood and Judgment: The Affect Infusion Model (AIM)', *Psychological Bulletin*, 117(1), 39–66.

[89] Isen, A. (1987), 'Positive Affect, Cognitive Processes and Social Behaviour', in L. Berkowitz (ed.), *Advances in Experimental Social Psychology*, San Diego, CA: Academic Press, Vol. 20, 203–253.

[90] Lewi, T. and De Pelsmacker, P. (2010), 'Affect Is an Important Factor in Processing Alzheimer Disease Awareness Messages', *Proceedings of the 2010 Icoria Conference, Madrid*, CD-ROM.

[91] Mowen, J.C. (1993), *Consumer Behavior*. New York: Macmillan.

[92] Stephenson, M.T. and Witte, K. (2001), 'Creating Fear in a Risky World', in Rice, R. and Atkin, C.K. (eds), *Public Communication Campaigns*. Thousand Oaks, CA: Sage, 88–102.

[93] Moscato, S., Black, D.R., Blue, C.L., Mattson, M., Galer-Unti, R.A. and Coster, D.C. (2001), 'Evaluating a Fear Appeal Message to Reduce Alcohol Use among "Greeks"', *American Journal of Health Behavior*, 25(5), 481–91.

[94] Witte, K. (1992), 'Putting the Fear Back into Fear Appeals: The Extended Parallel Processing Model', *Communication Monographs*, 59(4), 329–49.

[95] Lewis, I., Watson, B. and Tay, R. (2007), 'Examining the Effectiveness of Physical Threats in Road Safety Advertising: The Role of Third-Person Effect, Gender, and Age', *Transportation Research Part F*, 10(1), 48–60.

[96] Janis, I. (1967), 'Effects of Fear Arousal on Attitude Change: Recent Developments in Theory and Experimental Research', in Berkowitz, L. (ed.), *Advances in Experimental Social Psychology 3*. New York: Academic Press, 166–255.

[97] Dillard, J.P. and Shen, L. (2005), 'On the Nature of Reactance and its Role in Persuasive Communication', *Communication Monographs*, 72(2), 144–68.

[98] Taubman Ben-Ari, O., Florian, V. and Mikulincer, M. (1999), 'Does a Threat Appeal Moderate Reckless Driving? A Terror Management Theory Perspective', *Accident Analysis and Prevention*, 32(1), 1–10.

99 Rogers, R. (1983), 'Cognitive and Physiological Processes in Fear Appeals and Attitude Change: A Revised Theory of Protection Motivation', in Cacioppo, J. and Petty, R. (eds), *Social Psychophysiology*. New York: Guilford, 153–76.

100 Witte, K. (1992), 'Putting the Fear Back into Fear Appeals: The Extended Parallel Processing Model', *Communication Monographs*, 59(4), 329–49; Witte, K. (1994), 'Fear Control and Danger Control: A Test of the Extended Parallel Process Model (EPPM)', *Communication Monographs*, 61, 113–34; Witte, K. (1998), 'Fear as Motivator, Fear, as Inhibitor: Using the Extended Parallel Processing Model to Explain Fear Appeal Successes and Failures', in Anderson, P.A. and Guerrero, L.K. (eds), *Handbook of Communication and Emotion: Research, Theory, Application, and Contexts*. San Diego, CA and London: Academic Press, 423–50.

101 Cauberghe, V., De Pelsmacker, P., Janssens, W. and Dens, N. (2009), 'Fear, Threat and Efficacy in Threat Appeals: Message Involvement as a Key Mediator to Message Acceptance', *Accident Analysis and Prevention*, 41(2), 276–85.

102 Janssens, W., De Pelsmacker, P. and Cauberghe, V. (2009), 'The Effect of Prime, Frame and Death-relatedness in Threat Appeals on Ad-evoked Fear and Message Credibility', *Proceedings of the 2009 Icoria Conference, Klagenfurt*, CD-ROM.

103 Murray, N.M. and Murray, S.B. (1996), 'Music and Lyrics in Commercials: A Cross-Cultural Comparison Between Commercials Run in the Dominican Republic and in the United States', *Journal of Advertising*, 25(2), 51–63.

104 Braithwaite, A. and Ware, R. (1997), 'The Role of Music in Advertising', *Admap* (July/August), 44–7; Alpert, J.I. and Alpert, M.I. (1990), 'Music Influences on Mood and Purchase Intentions', *Psychology and Marketing*, 7(2), 109–33; Bruner, G.C. (1990), 'Music, Mood and Marketing', *Journal of Marketing*, 54(4), 94–104.

105 De Pelsmacker, P. and Van den Bergh, J. (1998), 'Ad Content, Product Category, Campaign Weight and Irritation: A Study of 226 TV Commercials', *Journal of International Consumer Marketing*, 10(4), 5–27.

106 Walker, D. and von Gonten, M.F. (1989), 'Explaining Related Recall: New Answers from a Better Model', *Journal of Advertising Research*, 29(30), 11–21.

107 Gorn, G.J. (1982), 'The Effects of Music in Advertising on Choice Behavior: A Classical Conditioning Approach', *Journal of Marketing*, 46(4), 94–101.

108 Kellaris, J.J. and Cox, A.D. (1989), 'The Effects of Background Music in Advertising: A Reassessment', *Journal of Consumer Research*, 16(1), 113–18.

109 Kellaris, J.J., Cox, A.D. and Cox, D. (1993), 'The Effect of Background Music on Ad Processing: A Contingency Explanation', *Journal of Marketing*, 57(4), 114–25; MacInnis, D.J. and Park, C.W. (1991), 'The Differential Role of the Characteristics of Music on High and Low Involvement Consumers' Processing of Ads', *Journal of Consumer Research*, 18 (September), 161–73; Anand, P. and Sternthal, B. (1990), 'Ease of Message Processing as a Moderator of Repetition Effects in Advertising', *Journal of Marketing Research*, 27 (August), 345–53.

110 Oakes, S. and North, A.C. (2006), 'The Impact of Background Musical Tempo and Timbre Congruity upon Ad Content Recall and Affective Response', *Applied Cognitive Psychology*, 20, 505–20.

111 Wang, A. (2005), 'The Effects of Expert and Consumer Endorsements on Audience Response', *Journal of Advertising Research*, 45 (December), 402–12.

112 Aaker, D.A. and Bruzzone, D.E. (1985), 'Causes of Irritation in Advertising', *Journal of Marketing*, 49 (Spring), 47–57.

113 Sinclair, J. and Wilken, R. (2009), 'Strategic Regionalization in Marketing Campaigns: Beyond the Standardization/Glocalization Debate', *Continuum: Journal of Media & Cultural Studies*, 23(2), 147–57.

114 Steenkamp, J.-B. E. M., Batra, R. and Alden, D. L. (2003), 'How Perceived Brand Globalness Creates Brand Value', *Journal of International Business Studies*, 33(1), 35–47.

115 Biswas, S., Hussain, M. and O Donnell, K. (2009), 'Celebrity Endorsements in Advertisements and Consumer Perceptions: A Cross-cultural Study', *Journal of Global Marketing*, 22(2), 121–37.

116 Rajabi, M., Dens, N. and De Pelsmacker, P. (2012), 'Endorser Type and Brand Globalness Effects in India: Think Global or Act Local?', *Proceedings of the 2012 EMAC Conference, Lisbon*, CD-ROM.

117 Erdogan, Z., Baker, M.J. and Tagg, S. (2001), 'Selecting Celebrity Endorsers: The Practitioner's Perspective', *Journal of Advertising Research*, 41(3), 39–48.

118 Erdogan, Z., Baker, M.J. and Tagg, S. (2001), 'Selecting Celebrity Endorsers: The Practitioner's Perspective', *Journal of Advertising Research*, 41(3), 39–48.

119 Lafferty, B.A., Goldsmith, R.E. and Newell, S.J. (2002), 'The Dual Credibility Model: The Influence of Corporate and Endorser Credibility on Attitudes and Purchase Intentions', *Journal of Marketing Theory and Practice*, 10(3), 1–12.

120 Erdogan, B.Z. (1999), 'Celebrity Endorsements: A Literature Review', *Journal of Marketing Management*, 15(4), 291–314.

121 Erdogan, Z., Baker, M.J. and Tagg, S. (2001), 'Selecting Celebrity Endorsers: The Practitioner's Perspective', *Journal of Advertising Research*, 41(3), 39–48.

122 Till, B.D. and Busler, M. (2000), 'The Match-Up Hypothesis: Physical Attractiveness, Expertise, and the Role of Fit on Brand Attitude, Purchase Intent and Brand Beliefs', *Journal of Advertising*, 29(3), 1–13.

123 Bower, A.B. (2001), 'Highly Attractive Models in Advertising and the Women Who Loathe Them: The Implications of Negative Affect for Spokesperson Effectiveness', *Journal of Advertising*, 30(3), 51–63.

124 Till, B.D. and Shimp, T.A. (1998), 'Endorsers in Advertising: The Case of Negative Celebrity Information', *Journal of Advertising*, 27(1), 67–82.

125 Euro Effie (2008), Brussels: European Association of Communications Agencies, http://www.euro-effie.com.

126 *De Morgen*, 26 March 2009.

127 Lambert, D.R., Morris, M.H. and Pitt, L.F. (1995), 'Has Industrial Advertising Become Consumerized? A Longitudinal Perspective from the USA', *International Journal of Advertising*, 14, 349–64.

128 www.pwcglobal.com and www.superbrands.org (accessed 9 June 2003).

129 Lambert, D.R., Morris, M.H. and Pitt, L.F. (1995), 'Has Industrial Advertising Become Consumerized? A Longitudinal Perspective from the USA', *International Journal of Advertising*, 14, 349–64.

130 Lohtia, R., Johnston, W.J. and Aab, L. (1995), 'Business-to-Business Advertising: What Are the Dimensions of an Effective Print Ad?', *Industrial Marketing Management*, 24, 369–78.

131 Prystay, C. (2002), 'Selling to Singapore's Teens is Tricky – What Works in the US (Grunge, Anger, Rebellion) Doesn't Necessarily Click', *Wall Street Journal*, 4 October.

132 Mueller, B. (1996), *International Advertising: Communicating Across Cultures*. Belmont, CA: Wadsworth.

133 Walliser, B. and Usunier, J.C. (1998), 'The Standardization of Advertising Execution: A Review of the Empirical Literature', in Andersson, P. (ed.), *Proceedings of the 27th EMAC Conference, Marketing Research and Practice, Track 2: International Marketing, Stockholm*, 517–36.

134 Usunier, J.C. and Lee, J.A. (2005), *Marketing Across Cultures*. Harlow: Pearson Education.

135 Mueller, B. (1996), *International Advertising: Communicating Across Cultures*. Belmont, CA: Wadsworth.

136 Brengman, M. (2002), 'The Impact of Colour in the Store Environment: An Environmental Psychology Approach', Doctoral Dissertation, Ghent University.

137 Hollensen, S. (2004), *Global Marketing: A Market-Responsive Approach*. Harlow: Pearson Education; Keller, K.L. (2008), *Strategic Brand Management: Building, Measuring and Managing Brand Equity*. Upper Saddle River, NJ: Prentice Hall.

138 Pollay, R.W. and Gallagher, K. (1990), 'Advertising and Cultural Values: Reflections in the Distorted Mirror', *International Journal of Advertising*, 9, 359–72.

139 Caillat, Z. and Mueller, B. (1996), 'Observations: The Influence of Culture on American and British Advertising: An Exploratory Comparison of Beer Advertising', *Journal of Advertising Research*, 36(3), 79–88.

140 Zhang, Y. and Gelb, B.D. (1996), 'Matching Advertising Appeals to Culture: The Influence of Products' Use Conditions', *Journal of Advertising*, 25(3), 29–46.

141 Mueller, B. (1996), *International Advertising: Communicating Across Cultures*. Belmont, CA: Wadsworth.

142 Walliser, B. and Usunier, J.C. (1998), 'The Standardization of Advertising Execution: A Review of the Empirical Literature', in Andersson, P. (ed.), *Proceedings of the 27th EMAC Conference, Marketing Research and Practice, Track 2: International Marketing, Stockholm*, 517–36.

143 Walliser, B. and Usunier, J.C. (1998), 'The Standardization of Advertising Execution: A Review of the Empirical Literature', in Andersson, P. (ed.), *Proceedings of the 27th EMAC Conference, Marketing Research and Practice, Track 2: International Marketing, Stockholm*, 517–36.

144 Hall, E.T. (1976), 'How Cultures Collide', *Psychology Today* (July), 66–97.

145 Usunier, J.C. and Lee, J.A. (2005), *Marketing Across Cultures*. Harlow: Pearson Education.

146 Hong, J.W., Muderrisoglu, A. and Zinkhan, G.M. (1987), 'Cultural Differences and Advertising Expression: A Comparative Content Analysis of Japanese and US Magazine Advertising', *Journal of Advertising*, 16(1), 55–62, 68; Ramaprasad, P. and Hazegawa, K. (1990), 'An Analysis of Japanese Television Commercials', *Journalism Quarterly*, 67 (Winter), 1025–33; Mueller, B. (1992), 'Standardization versus Specialization: An Examination of Westernization in Japanese Advertising', *Journal of Advertising Research*, 32(1), 15–24.

147 Hofstede, G. (2001), *Culture's Consequences*, 2nd edition. Thousand Oaks, CA: Sage; Hofstede, G. (1991), *Cultures and Organizations: Software of the Mind*. London: McGraw-Hill.

148 Zhang, Y. and Gelb, B.D. (1996), 'Matching Advertising Appeals to Culture: The Influence of Products' Use Conditions', *Journal of Advertising*, 25(3), 29–46.

149 Zandpour, F. and Harich, K. (1996), 'Think and Feel Country Clusters: A New Approach to International Advertising Standardization', *International Journal of Advertising*, 15, 325–44.

150 See, for details about countries, www.geert-hofstede.com, and Hofstede, G. and Hofstede, G.J. (2005), *Cultures and Organizations: Software for the Mind*, 2nd edition. New York: McGraw-Hill Professional.

CHAPTER 8
Media planning

CHAPTER OUTLINE

The media planning process

Media objectives

Frequency | Reach | Weight | Continuity | Cost

Selecting media | Media context

CHAPTER OBJECTIVES

This chapter will help you to:

- Distinguish the various steps in the media planning process
- Understand the technical details of media objectives, such as frequency, reach, weight, continuity and cost
- Learn about the criteria on the basis of which the media mix can be composed
- Understand the advantages and disadvantages of the different advertising media
- Get an overview of the criteria to be used in media planning
- Understand the importance of media context for advertising effectiveness

Introduction

Media planning is receiving more and more attention. This is not surprising since the cost of buying advertising time and space makes up 80% to 90% of the advertising budget.[1] The latter also explains the recent attention paid to integrated marketing communications, the purpose of which is to use all advertising media, as well as other communications tools, as effectively and efficiently as possible. Attention is paid to each of the different steps in a media plan. Media planning is not just a matter of selecting the appropriate media, given the target group of the advertising campaign and the characteristics of the different advertising media. It is also a technical issue in which the components of media objectives (such as frequency, reach, weight, continuity and cost) are calculated and compared. Both technical media objectives and criteria for selecting the media mix and characteristics of the different media are discussed. Furthermore, the importance of creativity in the use of media and possible influences of the media context are highlighted.

The media planning process

The purpose of media planning is to draw up an adequate media plan. A **media plan** can be defined as a document specifying which media and vehicles will be purchased when, at what price and with what expected results. It includes such things as flow charts, the names of specific magazines, reach and frequency estimates and budgets.[2] Creating a media plan is a process which consists of different steps (Figure 8.1).

Just as an environmental analysis is necessary to formulate the marketing strategy and to create a marketing plan, the communications environment needs to be screened to formulate a media plan. First of all, media planners should be acquainted with all regulations and legal aspects, as well as with local habits. Is TV advertising allowed; do people watch predominantly TV, read magazines or listen to the radio, etc.?

Secondly, media planners should be able to judge the communications efforts of the competition. In this respect, the following elements are important:[3]

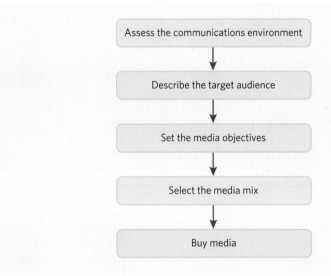

Figure 8.1 Steps in media planning

- **Category spending**. What is the advertising spending in the product category, and how has it evolved over the last five years? Did category spending increase, decrease or remain stable?

- **Share of voice**. What is the relative advertising spending of the different competitive brands in the product category? Share of voice (SOV) is calculated by dividing a particular brand's advertising spending by the total category spending. Besides the share of voice, one should also investigate the share of market (SOM) and how share of voice relates to share of market. Some researchers assume that share of market follows share of voice, while others argue that the share of market should always be smaller than the share of voice in order to be able to maintain growth (see also Chapter 6 on budgets).

- **Media mix**. Identify how each competitor divides its advertising spending across the different media and analyse the trend in media mix composition.

Target groups were extensively discussed earlier (see Chapter 4). Although all segmentation variables mentioned there remain valid, a variable that needs special attention at this stage is the media behaviour of the target audience. Do the target consumers listen to the radio or watch TV and, if so, which programmes do they listen to or watch, at what time and on which days? Do the target consumers read newspapers or magazines and, if so, which ones do they read? Do the target consumers use electronic media, do they often go the cinema, etc.? This information is indispensable.

Media objectives

Media objectives are derived from the communications objectives, and ought to be concrete, measurable and realistic. Media objectives are usually formulated in terms of the characteristics shown in Figure 8.2.

Frequency

Frequency indicates how many times a consumer of the target group, on average, is expected to be exposed to the advertiser's message within a specified time period. It is important to know that frequency is estimated on the basis of the number of times one could be exposed to the media vehicle, and not to the message itself. For example, if a consumer has a newspaper subscription and a certain campaign has one ad a week for six weeks in that newspaper, we could expect that the particular consumer will be exposed to the ad six times during the

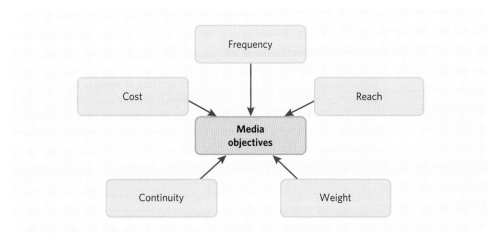

Figure 8.2 Media objectives

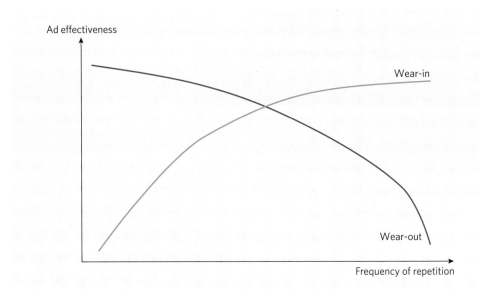

Figure 8.3 Ad frequency and ad effectiveness

six-week period. However, if the consumer does not always read the full newspaper and occasionally omits the pages in which the ad appears, the actual number of times he or she will be exposed to the message will be lower than six.

When deciding on the objective of how many times the target group has to be reached, a first question that arises is: How often should a consumer be exposed to a message for it to be effective? And how does a consumer respond to frequent exposures to the same message? Research shows that advertising repetition initially increases learning, but may lead to boredom and irritation later.[4] According to the **two-factor model**, an inverted-U relationship exists between the level of exposure on the one hand, and advertising effectiveness (cognitive responses, attitudes, purchase) on the other (Figure 8.3). Wear-in and wear-out effects explain the nature of this relationship.[5] At low levels of exposure, consumers develop rather negative responses (e.g. counter-arguments) due to the novelty of the stimulus. After a few exposures, the reaction becomes more positive. This is referred to as **wear-in**. More frequent exposures again lead to more negative responses, a phenomenon called **wear-out**. Negative responses, such as irritation, can be expected to be the highest both at low and high exposure levels, while positive responses are optimal at intermediate exposure levels. One way to counter or delay the wear-out effect is to make minor changes to the ad so that the consumer is not exposed to the same ad over and over again or to use executional cues that evoke positive emotional responses.[6] One study shows that in cases where consumers process messages in a superficial or shallow way (e.g. when they are hardly aware of the fact that there is an ad), wear-out may not occur at all.[7]

Another way of thinking about advertising repetition lies in the economic **signalling theory**, which assumes that consumers take advertising repetition as a signal of the quality of a brand. In this view, higher advertising costs signal greater manufacturer effort and higher manufacturer confidence and trust in quality.[8] In other words, consumers think that if a manufacturer is willing to spend a lot of money on advertising, it must be convinced that it will get the money back in the long run. The latter is only possible if consumers not only try, but also repurchase the product, which can only occur with a high-quality product. However, at extremely high levels of repetition, consumers find the advertising expenses excessive. At that point, people think something must be wrong, and perceptions about the advertising company as well as about the quality level of the brand deteriorate. It is interesting to note that the attitude towards the ad seems to wear out more quickly than the perception of brand quality.[9] In this sense, repetition beyond ad wear-out can make sense.

RESEARCH INSIGHT
Wear-in and wear-out effects in advergames

Besides brand placements in magazines, movies and TV game shows, digital games have been discovered for brand placements too. Advergames are computer games specifically created to function as ads to promote brands, where the entertainment content mimics traditional game forms.[10] Since advergames are rather simple in their design (no complex rules, short playing time, etc.), they can be easily distributed on different platforms, such as on web-sites, via e-mail (tell a friend, viral marketing), on cell phones and on interactive digital TV, e.g. during a commercial break. Integrating brands in games is a growing business. PricewaterhouseCoopers estimated that in-game brand placements was a $3 billion business in 2009, which is not surprising given that 69% of the American heads of household claim to play games.[11] According to Yankee Group, the advergame industry, as part of the in-game industry, generated $312.2 million in 2009. Strong brands such as Coca-Cola, Honda, Burger King and Gillette have already invested in advergames.[12] For instance, in the Coca-Cola advergame, the player has to catch soda bottles that drop off a conveyer belt.

The effects of repeatedly playing an advergame on brand recall and brand attitude were tested in two experiments. In experiment 1 (480 participants), game repetition was manipulated by requesting that the respondents play the game either two or four times. In experiment 2 (88 participants), the respondents could freely decide how often they wanted to play the game. In both experiments the game 'Snag' was used. This game has a simple design, and there are no complex rules. The main goal of the game is that the 'snag' (which is under control of the gamer) has to catch as many objects as possible that appear at sudden intervals on the screen. However, the tail of the snag becomes longer and longer and may not touch the boundaries of the game or itself. The game can be played in a few minutes, with different rehearsals, called 'lives', making the repeated playing a natural looking action. The game was played in two versions, one with a car and one with a coffee brand logo. In both experiments, e-mails were sent to a convenience sample of Belgian university students containing the URL link to the game and the questionnaire. After the gaming experience, the participants completed a self-administrated questionnaire.

Berlyne's two-factor model states that in the 'wear-in' or learning phase, the consumer becomes familiar with the advertising message, leading to an increase in recall rates. After a first level of message repetition, the initial hostility and uncertainty towards the message declines and positive habituation increases, and also more positive brand responses develop. Contrary to this observation in traditional advertising, playing the advergame more frequently did not have a significant impact on brand recall in either experiment. The wear-in or learning process was apparently very fast in an advergame, which can be explained by the focused attention of the individual on the interactive content. Also, the lack of complexity in the advergame might have accelerated the wear-in and wear-out phases. Consequently, recall did not increase between two and four plays and reached its maximum after two exposures.

In the 'wear-out' or tedium phase, advertising effectiveness declines with continuing repetition due to boredom, irritation and/or consumer reactance towards the message. The interactive nature of the gaming environment increases the focused attention and the likeability of the experience, leading to a high motivation and ability to process the interactive content and to fast wear-in. In addition, advergames are rather simple in their design. Therefore, it can be expected that the wear-out phase is achieved relatively quickly, leading to the development of negative brand attitudes even after low levels of exposure. This expectation was confirmed. Compared with the low game repetition level, higher levels of repetition had a negative effect on brand attitudes. These brand attitude results were again found under both forced game repetition and voluntary game repetition.

Although the premise may exist that repeatedly playing an advergame increases advertising effectiveness, this study found support for the opposite. Playing the game several times had no positive influence on brand recall, but impacted the development of brand attitudes negatively. Consequently, advertisers should avoid a situation where the consumer can repeatedly play the same simple game. Therefore, advertisers could work with more complex advergames or build in variations in the advergame, for instance by displaying different 'play worlds'. The technological possibilities nowadays even allow the advertising messages to be customised to the consumers, which might counter the negative effects on the brand attitude of repetitive playing of an advergame.[13]

In conclusion, several reasons have been reported in the literature as to why a high (but not excessive) repetition level of advertising might be beneficial:

- It makes the message more memorable and raises brand recall.[14]
- It makes attitudes more accessible and raises consumers' confidence in their attitudes,[15] making them more resistant to attitude change and brand switching.
- It increases the believability of the ad claims.[16]
- It leads to a greater top-of-mind brand awareness.[17]
- It functions as a signal or cue for brand quality.[18]

However, the difficulty remains to determine the optimal frequency level, which is inevitably linked to the advertising objective, the type of message used, media clutter, the product category, the competition level, the target group and the media used. Controversy also exists concerning the frequency level that is sufficient to evoke the intended response in the consumer. This frequency level is also referred to as the motivational frequency or the **effective frequency**, defined as 'the minimum number of exposures, within a purchase cycle, considered necessary to motivate the average prospect in the target audience to accomplish an advertising objective'.[19] Some researchers think one exposure is sufficient, while others assume an effective frequency of at least three.[20] One exposure may be sufficient if the consumer is reached at the right moment, with the right message. For example, a consumer is driving home from work and a small stone shatters the car window. One ad for Car Glass mentioning that it repairs car windows 24 hours a day may be very effective at that moment. On the other hand, a consumer may need to see a yoghurt ad 15 times before it becomes effective. Moreover, two exposures may be sufficient for market leadership or an established brand image, while at least four might be necessary for new campaigns targeted at infrequent users, if the objective is to increase the usage of a product or when medium clutter is high.[21] In other words, situational variables play an important role.

RESEARCH INSIGHT

Is advertising money used efficiently?

Given the large amount of money that is annually spent on advertising, the question of possible inefficiency in the use of advertising money is a very relevant one. However, it is not easy to measure such efficiency or inefficiency and the resulting loss of sales as a consequence of inefficient use of advertising money. Measuring, minimising inputs, maximising outputs and benchmarking are vital to detect and correct problems. Defining efficiency as the ratio between outputs (sales attributed to advertising) and inputs (advertising media expenditures), a recent study used data envelopment analysis (DEA) to evaluate and benchmark the efficiency of the top 47 US advertisers' ad expenditures in print (magazines and newspapers), broadcast (TV and radio) and the Internet. The advantage of DEA is that it can handle multiple inputs and multiple outputs, and that it is capable of calculating the efficiency of the 47 advertisers relative to each other. The results showed several clear inefficiencies. More specifically, 34 of the 47 advertisers appeared to be inefficient in their ad expenditures and they were least efficient with Internet advertising. As compared with the other advertisers, Federated Department Stores, for example, would have to reduce print media investments by $2.3 billion, broadcast media expenditures by $68 million and Internet ad spending by $7 million to become an efficient advertiser. John Wanamaker's famous saying, 'Half of every dollar spent on advertising is wasted; the problem is I just don't know which half', could well be true. The good news is that with recent techniques such as DEA, advertisers can get an idea of which part they need to cut down.[22]

One technique to judge the effectiveness of the media is **β-coefficient analysis**, developed by Morgensztern, in which the relationship between the number of exposures and the degree of memorisation (i.e. the percentage of the target group that remembers the ad) is analysed. The mathematical form of the β-coefficient model is as follows:

$$M_n = 1 - (1 - \beta)^n$$

where: M_n = memorisation after n exposures
β = medium-specific memorisation rate

Figure 8.4 illustrates the evolution of memorisation, given a β-coefficient of 12%. As the figure illustrates, total recall increases decreasingly as a function of exposure.

The β-analysis takes into account that memorisation of a message depends on the medium used. It is assumed that each exposure is able to make a constant percentage (β) of the consumers who previously could not remember the message of a campaign actually remember the message. Table 8.1 gives a few examples of media and their β-coefficients while Figure 8.5 shows the relation between the number of exposures and the memorisation rate for different

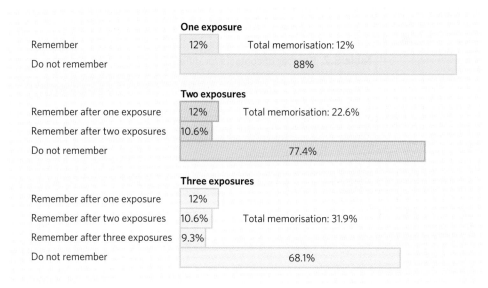

Figure 8.4 The β-coefficient: exposure and memorisation

Table 8.1 β-coefficients for different media

Medium	β-coefficient
Cinema	70%
Magazines	10%
Daily papers	10%
TV	15%
Radio	5%
Outdoor	2%

Source: Quattro Saatchi, Brussels (2003).

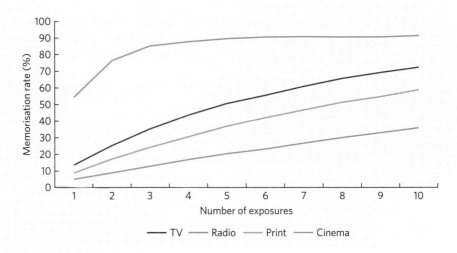

Figure 8.5 The relation between exposures and memorisation for different media
Source: JFC Informatique & média, Paris, France (2003).

Table 8.2 Number of contacts for different media

Medium	Not enough contacts	Too many contacts	Suggested contacts
Radio	4	15	5–14
Press	3	10	4–9
TV	2	7	3–6
Cinema	1	3	2

Source: Quattro Saatchi, Brussels (2003).

media. Cinema advertising is by far the most effective medium to make people memorise an advertising message, while outdoor seems to be the least effective. Applying the formula shown above suggests that the number of people who have memorised a message after three exposures is 97.3% for cinema advertising, but only 27.1% for daily papers.

Morgensztern not only developed different β-coefficients for different media, but also used these coefficients to suggest the minimum and maximum number of exposures for the different media in order for a message to be effective. Table 8.2 shows the suggested number of contacts.

Reach and weight

Total reach of a medium vehicle can be defined as the number or percentage of people who are expected to be exposed to the advertiser's message during a specified period.

BUSINESS INSIGHT
Audience shares of the leading European channels

Total reach refers to the audience one can expect to reach with a certain medium. The following table shows those TV channels with the highest share of the adult population for different European countries.[23]

Audience shares of the leading European channels

Country	Channel	Reach	Country	Channel	Reach
Austria	ORF 2	29.8	Luxembourg	RTL Télé Letzebuerg	52.9
Belarus	ONT	52.8	Macedonia	A 1	28.9
Belgium N	TV1	29.2	Netherlands	RTL4	16.8
Belgium S	RTL TVI	23.2	Norway	NRK1	40.2
Bulgaria	BTV	37.9	Poland	TVP 1	25.8
Croatia	HTV 1	43.8	Portugal	SIC	29.3
Czech Rep	Nova	43.4	Romania	Romania 1	28.4
Denmark	TV2	36.2	Russia	PERVY	26.8
Estonia	TV3	22.1	Serbia and Montenegro	PINK	21.2
Finland	MTV3	38.1	Slovakia	Markiza	45.9
France	TF1	30.6	Slovenia	POP TV	29.0
Germany	RTL	15.0	Spain	TVE 1	24.0
Greece	Antenna	22.5	Sweden	TV4	25.6
Hungary	RTL KLUB	29.5	Switzerland F	TSR 1	25.8
Iceland	RUV	42.7	Switzerland G	SF 1	24.8
Ireland	RTE 1	27.4	Switzerland I	TSI 1	26.7
Italy	RAI 1	24.2	Turkey	KANAL D	15.0
Latvia	LNT	22.2	Ukraine	INTER	29.3
Lithuania	LNK	27.0	UK	BBC 1	26.3

Whether these channels are the best to include in the media plan depends on the target group. If the target group consists of children and teens, an ad on a youth channel may be more efficient than the leading channels shown in the table. Moreover, some of these channels are public channels which do not take advertising. In this case, companies have to look for other options.

The difference between total and **useful reach of a medium vehicle** is important. Useful reach is not about how many consumers will probably see the message (total reach), but how many consumers from the target group (useful reach) are likely to see the message. As was the case for frequency, only exposure to the media vehicle can be estimated, not exposure to the message itself. Furthermore, one should realise that, although total reach may be higher for a TV campaign, useful reach may be higher for a campaign in specialised magazines. Even within the same medium type, total and useful reach can differ enormously for different media vehicles. For instance, for a target group of youngsters aged between 3 and 14 years, the reach shown in Table 8.3 can be obtained with an ad on the Swedish TV channels SVT1 and SVT2.

Table 8.3 Example of reach by medium

	Total reach (thousands)	(Useful) reach (thousands)	(Useful) reach (%)
SVT1	2193	409	30.9%
SVT2	1234	69	5.2%

Source: Based on IP Peaktime (2004), *Television 2004. European Key Factors*. Neuilly-sur-Seine, Cedex, Brussels: IP.

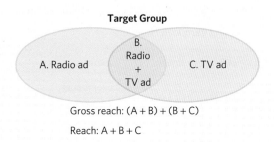

Gross reach: (A + B) + (B + C)

Reach: A + B + C

Figure 8.6 Gross reach and net reach

When the same message comes in different media or multiple times in the same vehicle, a distinction can be made between gross reach and (net) reach. As illustrated in Figure 8.6, **gross reach** is the sum of the number of people in the target group that each individual medium reaches, regardless of how many times an individual is reached. In other words, a person who is reached by medium *x* and medium *y* counts as two. **Net reach**, often simply referred to as 'reach', is the sum of all people reached at least once (a person reached by *x* and *y* counts as one). In other words, reach equals gross reach minus the duplicated audience. Gross reach, expressed as a percentage of the target group, is referred to as gross rating points (GRP). The weight of a campaign is typically expressed by GRP. For example, an objective of Gatorade could be to realise a total of 400 GRP in a month for a target group of sports people. These GRP can be realised by means of different media and different media vehicles.

A measure often used by media planners is **opportunity to see** (OTS). OTS is defined as the average probability of exposure that an average reached target consumer has. It is calculated by dividing gross reach by net reach. For instance, suppose that Bacardi Breezer wants to reach the adult Polish population. Reach of an ad during the break of the daily soap *Clan* on the Polish TV channel TVP1 is 57.2%, of an ad during the break of the daily soap '*L*' *like love* on TVP2 is 51.5%, of an ad on Polskie Radio is 17.3% and of an ad on Radio RMF FM is 22.6%.[24] A four-week campaign consisting of four ads during the *Clan* and *For Better or for Worse* programmes, six ads on Polskie Radio and eight ads on radio RMF FM results in 719.4 GRP. To compute reach, we cannot just add the reach of the four vehicles since we can expect that some people will watch several channels or watch TV and listen to the radio. Assume therefore that reach is not 100% but 65%. In this case, OTS would be 11.1 (GRP divided by reach in percentage, or 719.4 divided by 65). To come back to GRP, the latter means that GRP can actually be calculated in two different ways:

- By multiplying reach (in percentage) and frequency for the different media vehicles used:

$$GRP = \sum_{i=1}^{n}(f_i \times r_i)$$

  where: n = number of media vehicles
  f_i = frequency of media vehicle i
  r_i = percentage reach of media vehicle i

- By multiplying reach (in percentage) and opportunity to see:

  $GRP = Reach \times OTS$

  where: Reach = audience across different media vehicles minus duplicated audience

Table 8.4 Reach and frequency distribution

Exposures	Reach
1	20.0%
2	16.0%
3	11.5%
4	6.0%
5	3.5%
6	1.8%
7	1.2%

Effective reach is the number of target consumers who are expected to be exposed to the advertiser's message at an effective frequency level. Suppose an advertising campaign reached 60% of its target consumers with the frequencies reported in Table 8.4. If the consumer needs to be exposed at least three times to be effective, then the effective reach is 24.0% (11.5% + 6.0% + 3.5% + 1.8% + 1.2%).

BUSINESS INSIGHT
Calculating gross reach, OTS and effective gross reach

A company defines its target group as all males aged between 30 and 40. The total size of the target group is 10 million consumers. The company plans a newspaper campaign. The newspaper has a total readership of 18 million and a useful readership of 5 million. Ten ads are placed in the newspaper. The table below gives the distribution of percentage reach as a function of the exposure frequency.

The reach of the campaign is 5 million or 50% of the target group. The weight of the campaign is 238 GRP (5 × 1 + 6 × 2 + 3 × 3 + 9 × 4 + 8 × 5 + 7 × 6 + 6 × 7 + 3 × 8 + 2 × 9 + 1 × 10). As a result, the gross reach is 23.8 million exposures (238% × 10 million). OTS is 4.76 (238/50 or 23.8/5). Effective rating points (ERP), or effective gross reach, defined as at least three exposures, are 221 GRP.

Frequency	Newspaper reach (% of target group)
1	5
2	6
3	3
4	9
5	8
6	7
7	6
8	3
9	2
10	1

Continuity

Concerning campaign continuity, advertisers have three possibilities: a continuous, a pulsing or a flighting schedule:

- A **continuous schedule** means that the advertiser spends a continuous amount of money throughout the whole campaign period (Figure 8.7). However, since most companies have budget constraints, a continuous schedule might result in too low expenditures per period to be effective.
- A **pulsing schedule** indicates that a certain level of advertising takes place during the whole campaign period, but during particular periods higher advertising levels are used (Figure 8.8).
- A **flighting schedule** is used when advertising is concentrated in only a few periods and not during the whole campaign period (Figure 8.9). This might be preferred due to budget constraints, for example. In other words, during some months no advertising takes place in order to be able to spend higher levels during peak demand months.

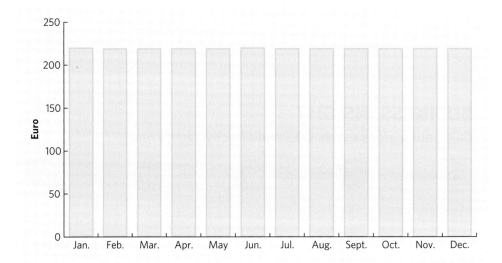

Figure 8.7 Continuous advertising

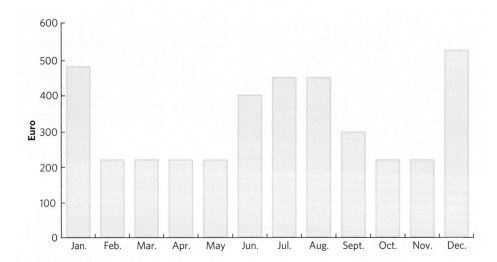

Figure 8.8 Pulsing advertising

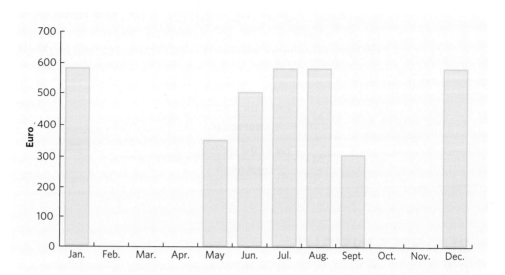

Figure 8.9 Flighting advertising

As mentioned before, some researchers argue that the most important thing is to reach consumers near the point of purchase. Jones[25] suggests that one exposure is sufficient and may have a much greater influence than frequent exposures. According to him, trying to reach as many people in the target group within the period near their purchasing is more effective than trying to reach a particular segment more frequently during the same time period. Ephron[26] shares this view and compares being off-air, as is the case with a flighting schedule, with being out of stock at the sales point. According to him, advertisers reach this week's buyers with this week's advertising, and next week's buyers only with next week's advertising, and not with this week's advertising. Also, a recent study investigating the impact of 1482 radio commercials reveals that media consistency and spending the advertising budget in complementary media and radio channels, i.e. focusing on reach rather than frequency of exposure (and, as a consequence, using a continuous rather than a flighting or pulsing schedule), are important explanatory factors for both ad and brand recognition.[27] Others argue that both reach and frequency remain important.[28] When the purpose of advertising is to give information, frequent exposure can be important; when the objective of advertising is to remind people (e.g. in the case of mature products), one exposure may be enough.[29] But, even in the latter case, a positive effect of frequent exposure can be measured.[30] Moreover, it cannot be stressed enough that a drop in ad spending during recessions is not a wise decision. More and more studies find strong support for the argument that recessions provide special opportunities for maximising the benefit of advertising euros.[31]

Another aspect worth considering when deciding on whether to use a continuous, pulsing or flighting schedule is how long people remember the message. Too much focus on a certain period of time without any repetitions during the rest of the year can be detrimental, since people easily forget the communications they have been exposed to.

Two scheduling tactics worth mentioning are **double-spotting** and **roadblocking**.[32] With double-spotting, two spots are placed within the same programme to increase the likelihood of obtaining the effective frequency. Roadblocking refers to placing the same ad across many channels at the same time. In this case, reach can be seriously increased since everyone watching TV at, for example, 9 p.m., will be confronted with the ad. Moreover, it is also a partial solution to the zapping phenomenon since even zapping will not help consumers to avoid the ad.

Cost

The cost of a medium is usually expressed as the cost per thousand (CPT), meaning the cost of reaching 1000 people. **Cost per thousand** (CPT) is usually referred to as CPM, the 'M' referring to the Roman symbol for thousand. CPM is calculated by dividing the cost of the medium (the air cost of a 15- or 30-second commercial, the cost of a one-page magazine ad, etc.) by the medium's audience. More interesting to know is the **cost per thousand in the target market**, represented by CPM-TM. In this case, the cost of the medium has to be divided by the useful reach:

$$\text{CPM-TM} = \frac{\text{Cost of the medium}}{\text{Useful reach}} \times 1000$$

$$\text{CPM} = \frac{\text{Cost of the medium}}{\text{Total reach}} \times 1000$$

BUSINESS INSIGHT
Calculating cost per thousand useful contacts

Suppose a fashion chain wants to reach young females (between 16 and 30 years of age). An ad is inserted in three women's magazines, in a TV guide and in a special interest magazine. The following CPMs can be calculated. Although the CPM for the TV guide is the lowest, calculation of the CPM-TM shows that, for reaching the young female audience, *Woman I* may be more cost efficient.

Type of magazine	Magazine	Cost (€)	Total reach (000s)	CPM	(Useful) reach	CPM-TM
Women's magazines	*Woman I*	3250	230	14.13	115	28.26
	Woman II	1995	116	17.19	58	34.39
	Woman III	1800	106	16.98	53	33.96
TV guide	*TV One*	3900	585	6.67	117	33.33
Special interest	*Modern Lifestyle*	2260	44	51.36	7	322.8

As was the case with the other concepts, only taking CPM and CPM-TM into account can lead to major errors. CPM and/or CPM-TM may be low because the medium vehicle is very cheap and does not reach the target medium in an effective way. Using billboards near minor roads does not cost a lot, but only a very small percentage of the target audience may be reached.

Selecting media

There is a difference between media and vehicles. Advertising media refer to types of communications channels that can distribute a message. Examples are newspapers, magazines, TV, etc. On the other hand, vehicles are particular programmes, magazines, etc., such as *The Simpsons, The Osbournes, Pop Idol, Cosmopolitan, Star*, etc. This section is mainly devoted to media, and not so much to specific vehicles. The percentages presented in Figure 8.10 reveal that worldwide TV is the medium to which most of advertising spending is devoted,

Medium	2009	2010	2011	2012	2013
Newspapers	96 973	95 416	92 802	91 911	91 334
Magazines	43 633	43 741	43 224	43 060	42 909
Television	160 199	178 826	184 929	196 182	207 056
Radio	31 778	32 169	32 899	33 906	35 117
Cinema	2 107	2 315	2 423	2 564	2 718
Outdoor	27 774	29 917	31 503	33 357	35 155
Internet	54 683	84 026	72 531	83 457	96 392
Total	**417 147**	**444 410**	**460 311**	**484 436**	**510 648**

Source: http://www.marketingcharts.com/direct/global-web-ad-spend-to-rise-33-by-13-19491/zenithoptimedia-advertising-expenditure-by-medium-2009-2013-oct11gif/.

Figure 8.10a Global advertising spend per medium type ($ million, 2010 average conversion rate), 2009–13

Medium	2009	2010	2011	2012	2013
Newspapers	23.24	21.47	20.16	18.97	17.89
Magazines	10.46	9.84	9.39	8.89	8.40
Television	38.40	40.24	40.17	40.50	40.55
Radio	7.62	7.24	7.15	7.00	6.88
Cinema	0.51	0.52	0.53	0.53	0.53
Outdoor	6.66	6.73	6.84	6.89	6.88
Internet	13.11	18.91	15.76	17.23	18.88
Total	**$417 147**	**$444 410**	**$460 311**	**$484 436**	**$510 648**

Source: http://www.marketingcharts.com/direct/global-web-ad-spend-to-rise-33-by-13-19491/zenithoptimedia-advertising-expenditure-by-medium-2009-2013-oct11gif/.

Figure 8.10b Percentage spend on advertising media worldwide, 2009–13

followed by online, newspapers and magazines. The share of online advertising is on the rise, mainly at the expense of newspaper advertising and, to a lesser extent, magazine and radio advertising.

Media mix criteria

Before deciding which media will and will not be included in the media mix, the different media should be evaluated on several criteria. These criteria can be categorised as quantitative, qualitative and technical criteria. Table 8.5 gives an overview of several potential criteria.

Quantitative criteria deal with factors such as how many people can be reached, how often and how quickly the target group can be reached, whether the advertising message

Table 8.5 Mixed media criteria

Quantitative criteria	Reach Frequency Selectivity Geographic flexibility Speed of reach (delayed or not) Message life Seasonal influence
Qualitative criteria	Image-building capability Emotional impact Medium involvement Active or passive medium Attention devoted to the medium Quality of reproduction Adding value to the message (by means of the context) Amount of information that can be conveyed Demonstration capability Extent of memorisation of the message (β-coefficient) Clutter
Technical criteria	Production cost Media buying characteristics (lead time, cancellation, etc.) Media availability

can be adapted for different geographic regions, whether the medium is more effective during certain periods of the year than during others, and how selective the advertising medium is.

Medium selectivity refers to the extent that a medium is directed towards the target group. Medium selectivity can be represented by a selectivity index showing how well the target group is represented in the medium reach, relative to the universe:[33]

$$\text{Selectivity index} = \frac{\% \text{ of the target group in total reach}}{\% \text{ of the target group in the universe}} \times 100$$

Selectivity index < 100:   The target group is under-represented;
                            The vehicle is not selective on the target group

Selectivity index = 100:   The target group is proportionally represented

Selectivity index > 100:   The target group is over-represented;
                            The vehicle is selective on the target group

Qualitative criteria to evaluate different media are the extent to which the medium is capable of building a brand image and a brand personality, the impact the medium has on the audience, how involved the audience are with the medium and, as a consequence, whether the audience are active or passive and whether the audience pay a lot of or only minor attention to the messages conveyed by the medium. Qualitative criteria are also about whether or not the vehicle can add value to the brand or product due to the context in which the brand or product is shown (see also further in this chapter), whether or not the quality of reproduction is sufficiently high, how much and what type of information can be conveyed to the consumer (e.g. can the use and customer friendliness of the product be demonstrated?), how many exposures are needed to make consumers remember the message (β-coefficient) and whether or not the medium is characterised by a lot of advertising clutter resulting in a need for more exposures in order to become reasonably effective.

BUSINESS INSIGHT
Calculating medium selectivity

Media vehicle	Population size young adults (12–30) (000s)	% young adults (12–30) of total TV population	Reach for young adults (12–30) (%)	% of young adults in total reach	Selectivity index (fifth column/ third column)
TV2	1240	23.0	32.2	22.6	98.3
Zulu	1240	23.0	3.8	45.2	196.5

Source: Based on IP Peaktime (2004), *Television 2004. European Key Factors.* Neuilly-sur-Seine, Cedex, Brussels: IP.

Consider the Danish TV channels TV2 and Zulu. How selective are they for a target group consisting of young adults aged between 12 and 30?

TV2 reaches 32.2% of the youngsters and Zulu only 3.8%. However, Zulu appears to be very selective for the target group of youngsters while TV2 is not. The latter can be explained as follows: TV2 has a large audience and, although almost one in three youngsters watch this channel, other age groups are better represented. Zulu, on the other hand, has a very limited audience and, although it reaches only 3.8% of the youngsters, they are the age group that is most represented in Zulu's audience.

Technical criteria refer to the production costs of the message, often expressed as CPM or CPM-TM, the convenience or problems related to media buying (is it difficult to book media time or space; how long in advance do you have to book media time in order to be sure that you can distribute your message; can this media time or space be cancelled and, if so, how long in advance, etc.?). Another criterion is media availability or what the penetration rate of the medium is among the population. If people do not own a TV or a radio, or never buy a newspaper, it is no use spending a lot of money advertising in these media.

Every vehicle has its own audience which form a market. The seller tries to sell the vehicle by claiming that the vehicle audience (e.g. people who read the *Financial Times*) consist of a relatively high number of people with buying power, although the seller also has the responsibility of giving the buyer an accurate overview of what the audience look like. The buyer's task is to find out whether or not the vehicle audience match the target group or whether or not the target group is sufficiently represented in the vehicle audience. Every vehicle is also related to its medium and inherits the characteristics associated with that medium. Therefore, the starting point for discussing the medium can be the advantages and disadvantages of each medium (see below). However, buyer and seller must go further than that and try to form a clear picture of the medium's social role and expression capacity.

Knowing that the target group reads magazines every week is not sufficient; it is necessary to know what magazines they read. If the target audience like to watch TV, which channels do they watch, at what time of the day do they watch, which programmes do they select, etc.? The different vehicles should be compared with each other within the same medium, between the different media and in relation to the target audience. The price must be understood in terms of value and not in terms of cost. Therefore comparisons are made to direct (other vehicles within the same medium) and indirect (vehicles within other media) competitors.

Care must be taken that media planning is more than just selecting the vehicles with the most promising results. The different media and vehicles must be considered in conjunction with each other. Is it wise, for instance, to plan the TV campaign after the radio campaign, or vice versa? Is it better first to explain the message in more detail in magazines before the out-of-home campaign starts? How important is it to have several TV commercials during prime time in the first week of the launch of a new product? Research on β-coefficient issues is very important to get some insight into the consequences of planning one medium before the other, or to decrease the GRP of radio to the advantage of TV. Furthermore, for a media planner, media consumption should be far more important than GRP cost. The most important questions are: Which radio channel does a target consumer listen to in the morning? Which billboards does he or she come across on the way to work? Which magazines or newspapers are read in the evening? Which TV programmes are watched in the evening? What events that can be sponsored does the target consumer go to etc? In Table 8.6 an example is given of a preparatory analysis for a media plan. The different advertising media are listed. The use, advantages and disadvantages of these media will now be discussed in more detail.

Outdoor

Outdoor advertising consists of media such as billboards, but also transit media in the form of messages on buses, trams, in stations, etc. (Photos 8.1 and 8.2). Outdoor advertising has the advantage of reaching a lot of people. As a consequence, effective reach can be very high. Not only reach, but also frequency can be quite high. The lifetime of a message is very long, and the same message can be seen over and over again. For instance, on the way to school or office you might encounter the Nokia message of 'connecting people' every day. Or you might see a bus or tram with the announcement of the film *The Matrix Reloaded* over and over again. The time period to reach the audience is very short and the costs are moderate. For certain types of billboards there is the obligation to work nationally, but for others a regional approach is obtainable.

Photo 8.1 L'Oréal: a tower in Berlin is a spectacular advertising medium
Source: James Davies.

Table 8.6 Advertising media and media planning criteria

Criteria	Importance	Daily papers	Magazines – General interest	Magazines – Specialised	Magazines – Women	Magazines – Men	Billboards – City	Billboards – Other	Cinema	Radio – Local	Radio – National	TV – Local	TV – National	Transit
Quantitative														
Reach*	++	+	+	O	+	+	+	O	O	O	+	+	+	+
Frequency	+	−	O	O	O	O	+	+	−	−	−	−	−	+
Selectivity**	++	O	+	+	+	+	+	O	+	+	O	−	−	−
Geographic flexibility	+	+	−	−	−	−	+	O	+	+	−	+	−	+
Speed of reach	+	+	O	O	O	O	+	+	+	+	+	+	+	+
Message life	+	O	+	+	+	+	+	+	−	−	−	−	−	+
Seasonal influence	+	+	+	+	+	+	+	+	O	−	+	−	−	+
Qualitative														
Stage building	++	+	+	+	+	+	+	+	+	O	+	O	+	O
Impact (emotional or formational)	++	+	O	+	O	O	−	−	++	O	O	+	++	O
Involvement	+	+	O	+	O	O	−	−	+	O	O	+	+	−
Attention	++	+	O	+	O	O	−	−	+	O	O	+	+	O
Active medium	+	+	O	+	+	+	O	O	+	−	−	−	−	−
Adding value	++	O	O	O	O	O	O	O	+	O	O	+	+	O
Quality of reproduction	+	O	+	+	+	+	+	+	+	O	+	+	+	+
Amount of information	+	+	+	+	+	+	−	−	O	O	O	O	O	−
β-coefficient	++	+	+	+	+	+	−	−	++	O	O	+	+	−
Clutter		−	−	−	−	−	−	−	−	O	−	+	+	−
Technical														
CPM	+	+	+	+	+	+	+	+	−	+	O	−	−	+
Flexibility in buying***	+	+	+	+	+	+	+	+	+	+	+	+	+	+

* x < 30%: −   30% ≤ x < 60%: O   x ≥ 60%: +
** x < 100: −   100 ≤ x < 110: O   x ≥ 110: +
*** Differs for different countries

Photo 8.2 TioPepe advertises outdoors
Source: Corbis: John Hicks.

BUSINESS INSIGHT

Indoor Media: advertising in toilets and fitting cubicles

One of the challenges of effective advertising is to find media that are selective and result in a guaranteed, undisturbed high-quality exposure of the message to the target group. Since the late 1990s, Indoor Media, a Belgian advertising agency that specialises in 'indoor media' applications, has successfully run the Vespasius network: thousands of posters in the toilets of movie theatres, cafés and discotheques. You cannot ignore the posters. They are at eye level, and everyone spends enough time at the toilet to enable them to read the ad. At first, mainly products for young people were thought suitable for advertising through this channel. But recently more 'serious' companies have also discovered the potential of this medium. For instance, Axa-bank uses Vespasius advertising. For €50 000, Axa is on 2200 Vespasius posters for two weeks, making it a very cost-effective medium. But companies like Dior are not convinced. They fear the 'the medium is the message' effect: a toilet is hardly a supportive context for selling a luxury product. Indoor Media does not agree, saying: 'Where do you think women use perfume when they go out? In the toilet, of course!' Recently, the company has also run a network of posters in fitting cubicles. A credit card company was the first to advertise. These cubicles have the same advantage as toilets. They are separate for men and women, just like toilets, and, depending on the shop or the café, they allow exposure to different lifestyle and age groups. People are more inclined to give their undivided attention to the message in toilets than in fitting cubicles but, to guarantee maximum exposure, the ads are placed as close as possible to the row of pegs. Further, since people walk in and out of the cubicles frequently during one shopping visit, there is repetitive exposure to the message in a short period of time.[34]

However, people do not feel highly involved in billboards or transit advertising and usually do not pay a lot of attention to them. Furthermore, only a limited amount of information can be conveyed. Targeting or selective reach is not possible, since all kinds of people will see the messages. Usually, there is no context that can add value to the message.

BUSINESS INSIGHT
Grolsch: using outdoor to shine a light on sales promotions

In November 2001, the beer brand Grolsch ran an integrated marketing communications campaign in the Netherlands. The objective of the campaign was to increase home consumption of Grolsch in men aged between 20 and 34. To reach this objective a sales promotion ran for three weeks (weeks 47, 48 and 49) consisting of a free lamp for every case of Grolsch beer purchased. The sales promotion was supported by point-of-purchase material, information on the website, TV advertising, an ad in a regional newspaper and an outdoor Abribus campaign. The Abribus campaign ran for one week in the middle of the sales promotion campaign (week 48). During this week, media investments in the product category amounted to €1.3 million, with the following shares of voice: Heineken 30%, Grolsch 25%, Amstel 13%, Brand 10%, Bavaria 3% and another six competitors 19%. Heineken, Grolsch and Amstel are also the largest players in the Dutch beer market, each enjoying a brand awareness of over 97%. Did the outdoor campaign reach its objectives? It sure did. Comparing top-of-mind awareness for Grolsch at the beginning and at the end of week 48 showed an increase from 25% to 31%. The spontaneous awareness of the sales promotion doubled from 15% to 30%. Total awareness of the promotion amounted to 37%, while awareness in the target group reached 46%. As the source of the sales promotion awareness, 41.3% of the respondents mentioned outdoor advertising, 46.0% in-store communications and 23.8% TV advertising. Intention to buy Grolsch during the promotion action did not increase, though.[35]

Magazines

Magazines have the advantage that a large audience can be reached. Furthermore, special interest magazines or magazines directed at a specific target group, such as females or youngsters, create the possibility of a selective approach for different target groups. Depending on the type of magazine, a high-quality context can be offered, making it a good medium for image building (e.g. *Vogue*). Special interest magazines, such as computer magazines, also have the advantage of inducing a high involvement level and being perceived as highly credible, adding a certain value to the inserted ads. For magazines in general, the quality of reproduction is high and a lot of information can be distributed. The message life is relatively long, people can process the messages at their own pace, and the same message or ad may be seen several times, since it is very likely that a reader does not read the magazine only once, but rather takes it up several times before he or she disposes of it.

Major disadvantages are that it is a rather slow medium, which leads to a delay in reach. People can buy a monthly magazine this week, but not read it for the next two weeks. Furthermore, the medium is not so flexible in the sense that last-minute changes are not tolerated and regional versions are impossible. Some magazines also suffer from high clutter, rendering an advertising message less effective.

BUSINESS INSIGHT
Customer media magazines add experiences to a brand

Customer media, previously called 'sponsored magazines', are magazines that are produced to communicate a company's brands by featuring articles that endorse the brands and targeting the audiences that are target groups for the brands. Also in-house magazines that are mainly targeted at internal stakeholders can be considered as customer media. According to the British Association of Publishing Agencies, the market for customer media was €910 million in 2004, and €1.3 billion in 2011. Customer media are financed by the issuing company or, in the case of retailers, by means of ads that are placed by the brands sold in the retailer's shops and promoted in the magazine.

In the Netherlands and the UK especially, customer media have a long tradition. The Dutch retailer Albert Heijn has distributed the magazine *Allerhande* (*All kinds of things*) since 1983. Around Christmas, about 2.5 million copies are distributed, and it reaches one in three Dutch households. The magazine is fully paid for by ads of brands sold in Albert Heijn. *A.S. Magazine*, issued by A.S. Adventure, a Belgian chain of outdoor stores, focuses on adventurous travellers, and has featured articles about, for instance, rafting in Sweden and the diary of a pharmacist who climbed Mount Everest to raise money for Médecins sans Frontières. After each article, a list of products that relates to the article is given. Of course, only gear that can be found in A.S. Adventure shops is featured. Ads of, among others, Gore-Tex, North Face and Suzuki provide the budget for the magazine.

Customer media are ideal media to support the image of a company and its products and to place the products and brands in an experiential context, adding emotional depth to the brand perception and experience. Research indicates that a professionally made and well-targeted magazine is read on average for half an hour, a substantial and high-quality level of exposure.[36]

Newspapers

The major advantage of newspapers is the number of people that can be reached in a very short period of time. Furthermore, newspapers are a flexible medium in the sense that last-minute changes are possible in case the company's needs change or when the company wants to take advantage of, or make use of, recent events. Ads referring to recent events are called **top topicals** and can usually count on more attention. The readers are usually highly involved in their newspaper, and the objective, informational context makes newspapers a credible medium with a high impact, not only for ads but also for PR messages. Newspapers also provide the possibility of working regionally. In contrast with several other media, newspapers can convey large amounts of information.

Disadvantages of newspapers are the limited selectivity of the medium and the low quality of reproduction. Furthermore, they are a transient medium in the sense that the message has a very short life since a newspaper lasts only one day.

BUSINESS INSIGHT
Compaq wins award for best use of newspapers

In 2002, Compaq won an award for the best use of newspapers. Full-page newspaper ads were created that resembled actual news reports. The ads contained testimonials from leading businesses and governments indicating that Compaq had never been more dependable. For example, one of the headlines read 'Hong Kong SAR: Government Teams with Compaq to Deliver Online Public Services to Hong Kong Citizens'. Moreover, in some newspapers Compaq had fixed positionings on a certain day of the week, always featuring the same headline, e.g. 'BT: Business Tuesday from Compaq'. In the first instance, Compaq wanted to go for business magazines and information technology trade magazines. In the end it chose newspapers because of their 'credibility and immediacy'.[37]

Door-to-door

Door-to-door advertising periodic publications (once a week, once a month, etc.) are distributed locally and free of charge. Advertisers in this medium are usually local merchandisers or local service organisations. Door-to-door publications have the advantage of being geographically flexible and of obtaining a fairly high reach. Furthermore, the medium provides the opportunity to deliver a lot of information at a fairly low cost. The promotional context in which the message appears may be useful for reaching consumers interested in promotional offers.

Limitations are that the medium is not at all selective and people may only be marginally involved in door-to-door publications and may not pay much attention unless they are interested in certain promotions. Furthermore, the quality of reproductions is often doubtful. Because of the overload of such publications, people often react negatively to this form of irresponsible use of paper and 'environmental pollution', and more and more people are putting a note on their mailbox stating 'no advertising please'.

Television

A clear advantage of TV is the communication power of an audio-visual message which, in general, leads to a fairly high (especially emotional) impact. TV is a passive medium, making it ideal for transferring a brand image or brand personality. The context surrounding the message can also add value to the message by inducing in the audience a certain mood (e.g. by the programme or movie during which the message is shown). Furthermore, a lot of people can be reached in a fairly short period of time. Local TV makes it possible to exert a regional approach. Research on viewing habits reveals that different personalities and people with different lifestyles watch different programmes, creating the possibility of using TV as a selective medium.

Major drawbacks are the high production costs that are involved and the fact that it is not always possible to direct a message at a selective target group. Often, a lot of occasional viewers are reached, which results in a low effective reach. Furthermore, the lifetime of a message is extremely short: 15 or 30 seconds pass very quickly and often nothing is left of the message afterwards. Increasing advertising clutter further impedes the effectiveness of messages, making more exposures a necessity, which adds to total costs. TV also has a seasonal influence. During the summer people spend more time outdoors instead of spending their evenings in front of the TV screen. In other words, during winter a TV commercial will reach a greater audience than in the summer.

RESEARCH INSIGHT
Can advertising reach the whole target group?

Advertising clutter is becoming a real problem.[38] Before you can convince consumers to buy, you have to build a brand. To build a brand, you need to create awareness. To create awareness, you need to attract attention. To attract attention, you have to find a way to break through the massive amount of other messages known as advertising clutter. One way to do this is to create original ads. Although this has been a long-held conviction by copywriters and art directors, only recently has the power of original ads to attract attention been empirically demonstrated.[39] Several advertisers do not opt for originality but react to the increasing clutter by outspending their competitors and launching even more ads. The result of all this is that in the UK, on TV alone, 17 278 730 ads were broadcast in

2004, in Spain 2 601 972 were broadcast, in Germany 1 255 084, in France 2 002 739 and in Italy 1 415 507.[40] Not surprisingly, consumers are not too keen on this and some of them start rejecting ads. A segmentation that seems to enjoy some consistency across studies classifies TV viewers into 'acceptors', 'rejectors', 'players' and 'uninvolved' on the basis of their answers to statements such as:[41]

1. I find TV advertising interesting and quite often it gives me something to talk about.

2. Nearly all TV advertising annoys me.

3. I find some TV advertising is OK but I think quite a lot of it is devious.

4. Quite often I find TV advertising more entertaining than the programmes.

Studies in 1996 and 2001 describe these segments as follows: *Players* form the largest group (between 35% and 50%) and want to be entertained and challenged. They do not have a negative attitude towards advertising as long as it is good advertising. *Acceptors* (between 19% and 22%) think TV advertising is interesting, moderately entertaining and rarely annoying. *Uninvolved* (between 11% and 23%) do not think TV advertising can be considered as interesting, entertaining or involving. *Rejecters* (20%) feel TV advertising is annoying, is not interesting or enter-taining at all and is often devious.[42] Unfortunately, the latter group is an interesting target group for marketers since they seem to have considerable spending power. Are TV rejectors a lost group for advertising? For TV advertising: yes. For advertising in other media: no. Indeed, 56% of the TV rejectors and 60% of the TV uninvolved appear to be acceptors or players for press advertising, while 38% of TV rejectors and 46% of TV uninvolved are acceptors or players for radio advertising.[43] Therefore, an easy solution seems to be to combine TV advertising with other media such as press and/or radio.

Cinema

As is the case with TV, cinema benefits from the audio-visuality of the message, having a greater impact on the audience. The impact of cinema advertising is even increased by the fact that the audience pay much more attention to the message than in any other circum-stances, while distraction is less likely to occur. The surroundings and context further add to the value of the message, because of the mood and expectations of the audience. As will be discussed later in this chapter, a positive mood can lead a viewer to process all incoming information more positively than when the viewer is in a neutral or a negative mood. Going to the cinema is fun; people have a lot of expectations and are, in a sense, quite excited. This can lead to more positive processing of the advertising messages. Another important advantage of cinema advertising is the fact that this medium is fairly selective to a young and upmarket audience. Furthermore, this audience seem to like cinema advertising, and consider it as a part of their cinema visit that cannot be missed.[44]

The disadvantages are that the potential reach is limited, and that the speed and frequency of reaching the audience are very slow. The lifetime of a message is very short. Furthermore, relatively high production costs are encountered.

Radio

The major benefit of radio advertising is that potentially a lot of people can be reached. Furthermore, the production costs are low and radio is a very dynamic medium. Different people (not only in terms of demographic characteristics, but also in terms of lifestyle etc.) seem to listen to different radio stations, making it a selective medium for targeting a specific consumer group.

Limitations are that the lifetime of a message is very short and that people use the radio as background noise. The latter means that the potential attention that will be paid to a message is fairly low.

RESEARCH INSIGHT
The importance of qualitative criteria in media planning

For many years, quantitative criteria such as reach, frequency, CPT, etc., have dominated media planning. Recently, more and more media planners have become convinced of the importance of qualitative criteria such as the context, capacity of image-building, creativity, etc. Creativity is very important because several media have become increasingly cluttered. Some advertisers succeed in running a very effective and efficient advertising campaign with relatively low costs due to creative use of the different media. Some examples are the following:

- Several years ago the newly launched Fiat Regata was promoted by attaching a life-size car to a billboard. In the press, consumers were encouraged to walk near these billboards while filling out questions for a contest. The campaign received media exposure in the press worth five times more than the actual media investment.[45]

- In 1992, every time someone passed a tram shelter with a promotion for 3 Suisses, the billboard began to sing a Jacques Dutronc song '*J'aime les filles dans les abribus, j'aime les filles qu'on croise dans les trams . . .*' (I love the girls in bus shelters, I love the girls I encounter on the tram . . .). The campaign ran for seven days and was a huge success. It is said that some people were so surprised that they even forgot to get on the tram.[46]

- In Denmark, Carlsberg used an Abribus campaign in 2003 where the ad looked different during daytime than at night-time. During the day, a pint of Carlsberg was shown on a black background. The pint itself was 80% filled with white foam. At night-time, the same ad on the same black background was shown, but the pint was now 80% filled with the gold Carlsberg beer.[47]

- In 2002, Virgin Express used a similar approach with newspaper ads. To promote the airline company, a full-page ad was created with different fictitious news reports. All reports mentioned the low attendance on occasions where normally many people are present. Headlines ran as follows: 'Problem of the traffic jams finally solved. Highways empty, except in the neighbourhood of the airport'; 'Major peace manifestation attracts only 7 participants'; 'Nobody attends erotica fair'; 'Sudden idling swept our cities'; and 'Members of Parliament play truant as never before'. In the middle of the page readers found the explanation for the situation: Virgin Express's extremely low fares to attractive cities such as Madrid, Milan, Nice, Rome, Athens, Barcelona, Lisbon, etc.[48]

- In 2002, Procter & Gamble's anti-dandruff shampoo, Head & Shoulders, was promoted by means of fragrance-emitting ads on bus shelters. The posters showed a happy young lady with the wind in her hair inviting consumers to press a button to dispense the scent of new citrus fresh.[49] By 2003, scent advertising was being used more and more. In the Netherlands, the advertising agency Senta ran a magazine campaign for the fabric softener Robijn (also known as Snuggle and Cocolino). When consumers rubbed the ink, the scent was released. About 80% of readers noticed the ad and also seemed to remember it.[50]

- Marketers also invent new media. In 2003, a London ad agency recruited university students to wear brand logos on their foreheads, turning their heads into living billboards. In exchange for wearing these ads in public places for three or four hours, students received about £6.50 an hour.[51]

Media context

Advertising always forms part of a surrounding context. An advertising context consists of the **receiver context** and the **medium context**.[52] The receiver context refers to the situational circumstances in which a person is exposed to an advertisement (e.g. at home, in the company of friends, on one's way to work, when one is in a bad mood, etc.). The importance of the receiver's context (especially the psychological state) was dealt with earlier (see Chapter 3). The medium context is the topic of this section and refers to characteristics of the content of

Table 8.7 Impact of media context variables

Media context variable	Impact on ad effectiveness
Objective context variables	
● Medium itself	Context effects more pronounced for TV
● Vehicle content	Violence, humour and sex have a negative impact
● Media clutter in vehicle	The more the clutter, the less positive the ad results
● Type of ad block	Context effects more pronounced for interrupting than shoulder blocks
● Sequence within ad block	Primacy and recency effects
● Congruence between context and ad	Product involvement (PI) moderates impact: for low PI, congruency is best; for high PI, contrast is best
Subjective context variables	
● Intensity of response	Mixed results, balance in direction of higher intensity, better ad results
● Valence of response	Positive valenced context improves ad effectiveness

Source: Based on Moorman, M. (2003), 'Context Considered: The Relationship Between Media Environments and Advertising Effects', Doctoral Dissertation. University of Amsterdam.

the medium in which an ad is inserted, as they are perceived by the individuals who are exposed to the ad.[53] TV commercials appear before, after or between TV programmes or other commercials, magazine or newspaper ads are inserted between articles, billboards are placed on the wall of a building or in a bus shelter, transit advertising forms part of the bus, tram, etc. Several studies indicate that the media context has an influence on how people perceive, interpret and process an advertising message. Since the effectiveness of the same ad may depend on the context surrounding the ad, it is useful for the advertiser to get a clearer view of what these context effects might look like. The conclusions outlined in Table 8.7 are made on the basis of an extensive literature review.[54]

Context effects seem to be more prevalent in one medium than another. Although most studies so far focus on TV, there seems to be some evidence that context variables matter more in a TV than in a print environment.[55]

Besides the medium, the content of the medium vehicle also plays a role. Concerning how interesting and involving a programme is, a recent study found that violent and sexual programmes, as compared with neutral programmes, impair TV viewers' memory for TV ads.[56] This was found to be the case for males and females, for all age groups and for people who like and dislike programmes containing violence and sex. One possible explanation for this finding is that sex and violence attract so much attention that there is not enough processing capacity left to process the embedded ads. Another explanation is that sexual and violent programmes evoke sexual and violent thoughts. By being occupied with thinking about sex and violence, consumers' memory for commercials could be seriously reduced. A similar conclusion also seems to hold for humorous programmes, although in the past comedies have been shown to lead to a higher ad recall than news or dramas.

As discussed earlier, **advertising clutter** has increased significantly in most media. A problem is that, due to this enormous clutter, ads become less effective. The more the clutter, the lower the motivation and opportunity to pay attention to an ad. Too many marketing messages compete for the attention of the consumer. As a consequence, less attention will be devoted to individual ads.[57]

Concerning ad blocks, a distinction can be made between interrupting blocks (a commercial block in the middle of the programme) or shoulder blocks (a commercial block between two different programmes). Although some researchers hypothesise that commercials in interrupting blocks are less effective because viewers do not want to be disturbed at that moment, this does not seem to be true. Intense and positive responses towards the context carry over more easily to ads in an interrupting break than in a shoulder break. An explanation for the latter is that during the programme viewers experience more arousal and interest than between programmes.[58]

As for the sequence within a block, the earlier an ad appears in the block, the higher the motivation to pay attention to the ad and process the information. Furthermore, the placement of an ad also determines the opportunity to pay attention to it. The primacy effect, suggesting that ads that come early in a magazine or early in a sequence of TV commercials are more effective, has been confirmed on several occasions.[59] However, for TV advertising the last position can also be beneficial since the consumer has more time to process the ad due to the fact that it is not followed by another ad, but by a short silence.[60] Because of inherent characteristics of the medium, certain places can raise the opportunity to pay attention; for example, the upper-left corner of a magazine (people normally start reading from the left to the right), the right-hand page (this is the flat page when a magazine is open) or the cover page.[61]

RESEARCH INSIGHT
Context effects in split-screen TV formats

It is common for people to be exposed simultaneously to both audio-visual stimuli and interactive information in many media-rich websites that contain a video sequence and clickable commercial information. Furthermore, people are increasingly watching movies, programmes, and other content via web links. Interactive digital TV, the merging of TV and Internet technology, has led to an integration of interactivity within the audio-visual content. These evolutions have led to many new entertainment and advertising formats. One of these new advertising formats is the telescopic ad. By means of a click on the call-to-action button in a traditional ad, content appears on screen that provides additional information.[62] This interactivity embedded in the persuasive information has the capacity to evoke a cognitively involving experience.[63] To avoid viewers missing part of their programming, this new advertising format allows people to follow the broadcasting content using the picture-in-picture technology.

When people are simultaneously exposed to interactive persuasive information and a programme context, they will divide their attention between both tasks. This can lead to an interference effect. Interference can be defined as the process by which our ability to recollect information is hindered by our exposure to some other information.[64] Advertising researchers distinguish between different types of interference. *Perceptual interference* is related to the simultaneous processing of information of different modalities (e.g. reading, listening) and/or different representation formats (verbal or non-verbal). *Semantic interference* takes place when an ad is placed within a programme of similar content; elements of the programme and ad merge together in a phenomenon known as meltdown, resulting in impaired recall. Besides the negative interference effects of simultaneous exposure to ad and context, positive reinforcement effects have also been observed. For example, prior research has shown that integrated multisensory cues can enhance learning and experience.[65] Congruent context information may also cognitively prime the embedded ad, leading to more attention and information processing.[66]

In two experiments, the effect of simultaneous exposure to a TV programme and an interactive ad on self-reported attention and clicking behaviour was studied. Experiment 1 examined perceptual interference/reinforcement, and Experiment 2 investigated semantic interference/reinforcement. In the first experiment (208 participants) a sequence (six minutes) from the movie *Taxi* was shown. After participants responded to the call to action, in the audio-visual programme context condition, the programme appeared in the upper-right-hand corner of the screen, by means of the picture-in-picture technology. In the auditory programme context condition, the programme was not visible, and the interactive information was available on the whole screen. The users could only hear the programme in the background. The advertising stimuli were combinations of a traditional 30-second ad, with an integrated call to action ('Click here for more information'), followed by an interactive part with clickable additional information related to the advertising message. The message was about the selective use of antibiotics given the threat of immunity to antibiotics over time. In the interactive part of the ad, participants could select five information buttons related to the advertising message. The interactive part of the ad was manipulated by adding pictures (non-verbal) to the textual information (verbal). The textual information was the same in both conditions. The participants received an e-mail with a web link to the stimuli, followed by a questionnaire. The results showed that, in the case of an interactive ad containing text and pictures, a simultaneous audio-visual programme context leads to less attention and clicking than an auditory context. In other words, the audio-visual programme context interferes more with the verbal/pictorial interactive ad than the auditory programme context, implying a lower self-reported level of attention to the information and fewer clicks than in the auditory programme context.

In the second experiment (133 participants), the same 30-second ad from Experiment 1, with an integrated call to action followed by an interactive information part with clickable information, was used. The layout of the interactive part was a combination of text and pictures and was the same in all experimental conditions. A thematically incongruent programme context appeared in the same sequence as in Experiment 1 (a sequence from the movie *Taxi* in which there was a conversation between a man and a woman sitting in a taxi). The message of the ad ('the correct use of antibiotics') was thematically incongruent with the taxi sequence. The thematically congruent programme context was a sequence featuring patients in a hospital who received medication. The use of medicines to counter a virus and the medical context of the programme sequence were thematically congruent with the ad message about the use of antibiotics. The audio-visual programme context appeared simultaneously with the interactive information on screen, by means of picture-in-picture technology. Also the participants' search goals were manipulated by using different calls to action. To evoke a goal-directed motivation to search in the information, a promotional incentive was embedded in the call to action ('Click here and have a chance to win a bicycle'). Consequently, participants had a definite end goal: that is, correctly answering the questions in the interactive part for a chance to win a bicycle. Experiential motivation was induced by inviting participants to view more information ('Click here for more information'). The study was administered in the same way as in Experiment 1. The results showed that, in the case of goal-directed browsing, a congruent programme context leads to more attention and clicking than an incongruent context, while there were no differences in attention and clicking when people were experientially motivated. Goal-directed people are less likely to be distracted from their primary task when the programme context is congruent than when it is incongruent. When the context is incongruent with the interactive ad, more attention and elaboration are necessary to encode and dissolve the incongruent context. When the user has an experiential goal to browse through information in the interactive ad, he or she is not focused on any specific information or stimulus. Thus, the user's attention will be drawn to the audio-visual programme regardless of the (in)congruency between the interactive information and the audio-visual programme.[67]

Studies on the impact of media-style–ad-style congruency are scarce and reveal contradictory conclusions. Some researchers claim that the better the fit between the ad and the media context, the more motivated consumers will be to process the ad and the easier this job will be for them. A computer ad inserted in a computer magazine, for instance, increases the likelihood that the reader wants to pay attention and is willing to process the ad, since the computer magazine makes the need for a computer or information on computers more salient and this evoked need stimulates the motivation to pay attention to stimuli that are relevant to the need. Similarly, people reading a magazine that evokes transformational needs, such as a beauty magazine, are more likely to look for transformational cues in ads, such as the attractiveness of the hair after using a certain shampoo, while reading a health magazine is more likely to make people pay attention to cues such as the revitalisation of damaged hair.[68] Also, contexts evoking the same feeling as the ad appear to enhance ad responses as compared with contexts evoking a different feeling.[69] According to the priming principle, an ad can be interpreted on the basis of schemas (knowledge structures) activated or primed by the context.[70] Congruency between the ad and the context means that the ad can be more easily interpreted since the relevant knowledge structures are already activated. However, some studies found no effects or even a positive impact associated with placing an ad in a style that is incongruent with the media context. This relation between ad–context congruency and ad effectiveness can be explained as follows: the novelty of the ad or the unexpectedness of the information given its context increases the attention to the ad because consumers see the ad as innovative and interesting. How can the contradictory results be explained and what should an advertiser go for: a context-congruent or a context-incongruent ad? The solution can be found in moderator variables. Apparently, people react differently depending on how involved they are with the product category.[71] When product involvement is low, consumers go for the peripheral route of processing and it helps them if context and ad style are congruent. On the other hand, when product involvement is high, they are more likely to follow the central route. In this case, they are willing to expend more cognitive resources and seem to appreciate a context-incongruent ad more.

Concerning the **intensity of context responses**, two opposing views are held. Some claim that the more intense context responses are, the less capacity will be left for consumers to process the ad. As a consequence, less attention will be paid to the ad and the ad will be less effective. An exciting context inducing high arousal in respondents has been shown to lead to less positive ad responses than a romantic or cosy context which induced a significantly lower arousal level.[72] However, other researchers claim that the more intense consumer responses to the context are, the more attentive and aroused they are and, as a result, the better the ads will be processed. Research results are mixed, but the majority of the findings point in the direction of a positive impact of intensity of context responses on attitudes and purchase intention.[73] Besides the intensity, the valence of context-induced responses (whether they are positive or negative) may also matter.[74] Some researchers suggest that a context that evokes a positive mood induces less elaborate processing of embedded ads and a less positive attitude towards the ad. Two theories try to explain this.[75] According to the cognitive capacity theory, a positive mood activates a whole bunch of information in memory that limits the consumer's processing of incoming information. A second theory proposes that when people are in a positive mood, they try to keep this mood and, as a consequence, avoid all stimuli (such as ads) that could alter this situation. The opposite can be expected when they are in a neutral or a bad mood. On the other hand, there is also evidence that people who are in a good mood evaluate ads more positively and are more capable of, and willing to, process ad-related information. This can be explained by affect transfer (see Chapter 3) by means of which the positive evaluation of the context is transferred (or misattributed) to the ad. However, the majority of the studies investigating the impact of context-induced mood on embedded ads find that emotional responses to the context indeed carry over to the ad, but not to the brand.[76]

RESEARCH INSIGHT
'The medium is the message'

Instead of facilitating or inhibiting consumers' processing of advertising messages, the medium itself can also be the message. A recent study investigated the impact of creative media choice. In this study, creative media choice refers to the fact that the brand logo and slogan are shown, but that brand associations are primed by the medium and, as a consequence, implicitly instead of explicitly communicated. Advantages of creative medium choice could be that:

1. The ad context is intentionally rather than incidentally processed.

2. The distinctiveness of the medium increases the transfer from associations from the medium to the brand.

3. The indirect approach creates less negative cognitive responses and enhances ad credibility and attitudes.

In the study, two products were investigated: an insurance company and an energy drink. The insurance company was promoted either on an egg or in a traditional newspaper. An egg was chosen because of its protective shell and the fact that it is a fragile and easily breakable product. The energy drink was promoted either on an elevator or in a traditional newspaper. An elevator was chosen because it is powerful, moves quickly and reminds people of the energy that is needed to walk up or down the stairs. About 600 students participated in the experiment. Results confirmed the hypotheses: the creative media enhanced the brand associations more than did the traditional medium (newspaper). Moreover, the creative media increased ad credibility significantly and induced significantly more positive ad and brand attitudes as compared with the traditional medium.[77]

Summary

In media planning, the decision is taken about what media and vehicles will be purchased, at what time and at what price. Media planning consists of a number of steps. After assessing the communications environment and describing the target audience, media objectives have to be set, and media vehicles have to be selected and bought. Media objectives refer to criteria, such as the frequency with which the target group has to be exposed to the message, and the reach or weight of a campaign, i.e. the number of desired contacts with the target group. Furthermore, the continuity or schedule of the campaign has to be decided on, and media costs have to be taken into account. Media selection is based on quantitative criteria, such as frequency, reach and seasonal influences, but also on qualitative criteria, such as image-building capacity, emotional impact, demonstration capacity and quality of reproduction. Technical criteria, such as production costs and media buying characteristics, also have to be taken into account. Each type of advertising medium (newspapers, magazines, TV, radio, etc.) has its advantages and disadvantages. Furthermore, the media context can have a considerable impact on advertising effectiveness. The role of arousal, mood and compatibility of media and ads appears to be important.

REVIEW QUESTIONS

1. What are the various steps in the media planning process?
2. How does ad message repetition affect advertising effectiveness?
3. How can β-coefficient analysis be used to optimise message repetition?
4. What is the relationship between reach, net, gross and effective reach, opportunity to see, and gross and effective rating points?
5. How can media scheduling or continuity affect advertising effectiveness?
6. On the basis of which criteria should a media plan be composed?
7. What are the main advantages and disadvantages of print and audio-visual media?
8. Why is cinema advertising effective?

Further reading

Calder, B.J. and Kotler, P. (2008), *Kellogg on Advertising and Media*. Hoboken, NJ: Wiley.

Katz, H.A. (2006), *The Media Handbook: A Complete Guide to Advertising Media Selection, Planning, Research and Buying*. Mahwah, NJ: Lawrence Erlbaum Associates.

Kelley, L.D. and Jugenheimer, D.W. (2008), *Advertising Media Planning: A Brand Management Approach*. New York: M.E. Sharpe.

Sissors, J. and Baron, R. (2002), *Advertising Media Planning*, 6th edition. Chicago and New York: McGraw-Hill.

CASE 8:
Maes: a challenger brand with more character

Maes: a Belgian lager beer with character in decline

Jupiler (AB Inbev) is the market leader in the Belgian lager market. MaesPils is the number 2 brand and is brewed and marketed by the Alken-Maes Brewery. For many years, this brewery was owned by the British group Scottish & Newcastle, but in early 2008 was taken over by the Heineken Group.

Since 2002 the Belgian lager market has been in decline, with an average decrease in volume sold of 2% per year.

This decline is mainly due to the on-trade channel (pubs and restaurants), while the off-trade channel (supermarkets) partly compensates for this trend (Figure 8.11).

At the same time Maes has lost 30% of volume sold in six years, a much larger decline than the average market. This is partly due to the fact that Maes has a greater share in on-trade than in off-trade. On the other hand, Maes also loses sales substantially in the off-trade channel. In the remainder of this case study, only the off-trade channel is considered. The decreasing volume sales in supermarkets

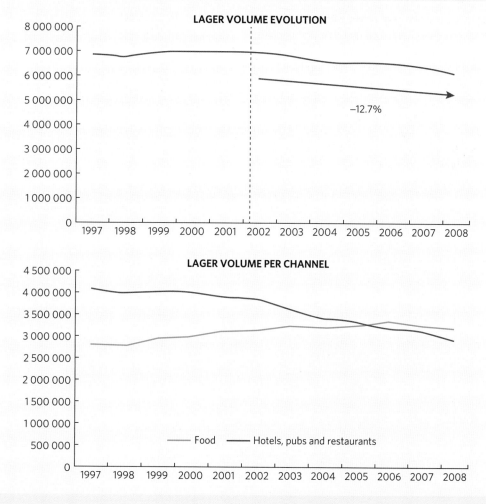

Figure 8.11 Evolution of lager volume per channel

have a severe negative impact on Maes's market share: from 9.7% in 2005 to 7.8% in 2008. Competition in the beer market is strong and has substantially changed over the last 20 years. In 1985 Maes had a volume market share of 17.8%, Jupiler (the market leader) 39.8% and the private labels 12.2%. In 2008, there was one undisputable market leader that kept growing every year (Jupiler), and the private labels had a market share of about 33% (Figure 8.12). Maes is stuck in the middle and experiences pressure from both sides. The reason for the success of Jupiler is manifold. With its central brand promise 'Men know why', Jupiler has succeeded in appealing to a broad male audience. Its communications are consistent and synergetic and for many years the brand maintained a high share of voice in Belgian beer advertising (50% in 2008 as opposed to 21% for Maes). Moreover, for many years Jupiler has sponsored the major football league in Belgium, therefore called the 'Jupiler League'.

Ambitious objectives for a facelifted Maes

In April 2009 MaesPils was relaunched with the ambition to position Maes again as a strong brand. The product and packaging went through a thorough facelift and a new and modern house style was developed. The product now contains more malt and has a fuller, more bitter taste. The price was increased by 8%. The case describes the relaunch of Maes in two campaign waves: May–June and October–November 2009.

The commercial objective of the campaign was to half the 25-year continuous decline in off-trade market share within the campaign period. At the end of 2008, the projected market share for 2009 without any campaign was 7.2%. During the first few months of 2009, the situation got worse. Without any additional efforts, in March the projected market share was 6.3%. The aim was to reach a market share of 7.8% (the same as in 2008) in 2009. Therefore, during the last eight months of 2008, substantial growth had to be realised to attain this objective.

The year-long decline of Maes resulted in a loss of social consensus around the brand. Consumers doubted Maes's taste and even Maes drinkers no longer wanted to admit their preference in public. Maes had become a loser brand, and consumers chose the leader. The communications strategy of the new campaign therefore aimed at restoring the social consensus. Beer drinkers should again trust and love Maes. The communications strategy was built on three pillars:

1. **Brand credentials**. Restore trust in the beer and the brand. The product is at the focus of the campaign. Maes has changed and we are confident that it tastes better.

2. **Trial**. As many Belgians as possible should try the new Maes. Tasting is believing. Prejudices can best be countered by experience. Massive sampling is key. The objective is to break old habits and bring Maes back into the consideration set.

3. **Brand attitude**. Install a unique and recognisable behaviour of the brand as a real challenger. Just a good product is not sufficient. People should love the brand. Next to the strong Jupiler brand, it was necessary to build a strong and differentiated identity and attitude: no bullshit, straightforward, with guts and self-confidence, but with enough self-relativisation, a brand that does real things and not just communicates.

Firstly, brand credentials were restored, then a trial was generated. Throughout the whole campaign, attitudes were built up. The communications objectives were as follows:

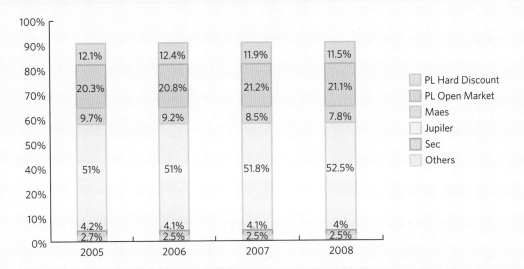

Figure 8.12 Market share of lager brands in Belgium in the off-trade channel

1. Increase spontaneous awareness, advertising awareness and product quality attributes: excellent quality and good taste, compared with the pre-test.

2. Increase trial, decrease the number of rejectors (those who do not like Maes at all) and realise a significant increase in brand adoption.

3. Install attitude on the basis of the following attributes: sympathetic, continuously does new and interesting stuff, a brand that is up to date, a brand with character, self-confident.

The focal target group of the campaign was 'entry drinkers', males between 18 and 35 who have not yet made their beer choice and are open to a different brand than the market leader. They often see Jupiler as a brand of the older generation, and want something else. These youngsters are looking for refreshingly new, challenging and modern brands with guts. For them, going out and drinking beer is no longer the exclusive territory of men and their stereotypical jokes, but also includes women.

A new beer, a new creative approach

The creative approach and the resulting campaign media and tools choice were unusual for a beer brand, and consistent with the communications strategy. The following guidelines were applied in all communication tools:

- The product is the hero; a powerful emphasis on the product, leading to an appeal in appetite.
- Blue (the Maes colour) is the differentiating colour.
- A straightforward message that can be easily decoded by all consumers.
- Self-confidence and intelligent humour.

The credentials of the campaign aimed at making the brand a hero again. The key visual introduced the new beer and new bottle in all their glory. The visual was meant to evoke pride and confidence and generate an appetite appeal. It was used in all campaign tools during the first wave. The trial campaign tried to install Maes as an active brand. Through proximity and innovative trial actions, Maes directed consumers to make them taste the new beer.

Two large-scale brand activations were rolled out, one in May and one in November. In the first one, 'Put a case in front of your window', people were asked to put an empty beercase of whatever brand in front of their window. Maes exchanged this empty case for a full one (24 bottles). During the nine-day campaign, 36 000 cases of Maes were exchanged. The campaign was intensively discussed in the (social) media. As a result of this campaign, Maes ended up in the refrigerator of many potential consumers that were up to then loyal to the market leader. They now had the opportunity to try Maes 24 times. In the second

brand activation campaign, 'A can with a message', Maes actively sought social consensus. Via the website maes.be friends could send a four-pack of Maes to their friends' homes, including a message to their friends. The 50 000 available packs were sent and delivered within days, generating 50 000 ambassadors for Maes. Both actions aimed at generating trial and sympathy in a surprising and novel way.

Consistent with the communications and creative strategy, the campaign tools were radically different from those of the competitors. Traditionally, TV has been the primary medium in a beer campaign. It allows emotions to be expressed and reaches a broad target group at the moment of consumption. Maes decided to do it differently. Outdoor was the primary medium of its campaign. This allowed the brand to be on the street, prominently and confidently talking to beer drinkers. Outdoor was complemented by radio commercials to tell the Maes story in more detail. However, traditional mass media were only a minor part of the media mix. Maes wanted to 'do' rather than 'talk'. Consequently, a large part of the budget was devoted to brand activation, to get in touch with the consumer. Brand activation was not used as a tactical tool, but as an image-building branding tool. The mass media were prominently used to announce the brand activation campaign, mixing commercials and editorial content. Next to 'paid media', 'earned media' were also used: public relations, blogs and social media. The high 'buzz potential' of the brand activation campaigns generated a lot of free media coverage and from consumers talking about the brand in blogs, on Internet forums and in social media. This resulted in the following media mix (percentages of the total budget): TV 12.8%, radio 7.8%, newspapers 0.8%, magazines 0.8%, outdoor 16.9%, brand activation 23.5%, public relations 2%, point-of-sales 9.8% and events 23.5%.

As a reaction to the Maes campaign, market leader Jupiler increased its promotional pressure by lowering its prices and increasing sales promotion activity, resulting in a substantial decrease in the average sales price and increased visibility in the shops.

Impressive results

The commercial objective was to realise a market share of 7.8% in 2009. Maes's market share in 2009 was 8.1%, substantially above the objective. Moreover, since Maes did not do well during the first three months of 2009, this had to be compensated during the campaign period. Market share during this period was 8.3% (Figure 8.13).

The evolution of awareness and image parameters was measured four times: in March (pre-test), May–June, September and December 2009. The measurements show that there was a strong and immediate impact in May–June →

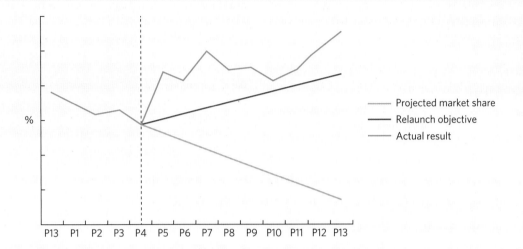

Figure 8.13 Maes market share: results versus objectives

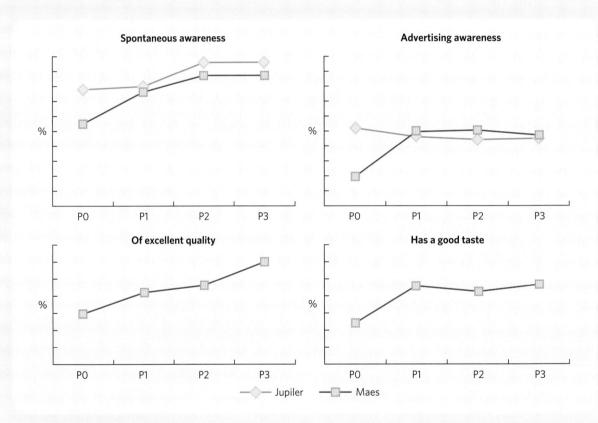

Figure 8.14 Evolution of brand credentials

that continued throughout the year (Figure 8.14). In terms of trial, the objective was to decrease the number of rejectors and to increase the number of adopters. Figure 8.15 illustrates that this objective was also reached.

The third objective of the communications strategy was to improve brand image on a number of key attributes. Figure 8.16 illustrates that brand image has substantially improved on relevant brand dimensions. These excellent

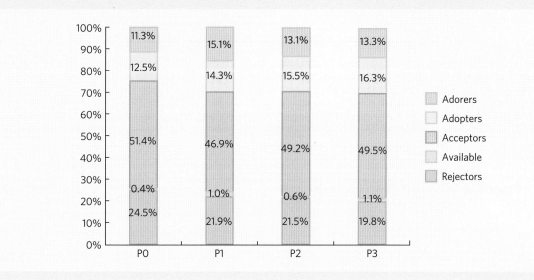

Figure 8.15 Commitment to Maes

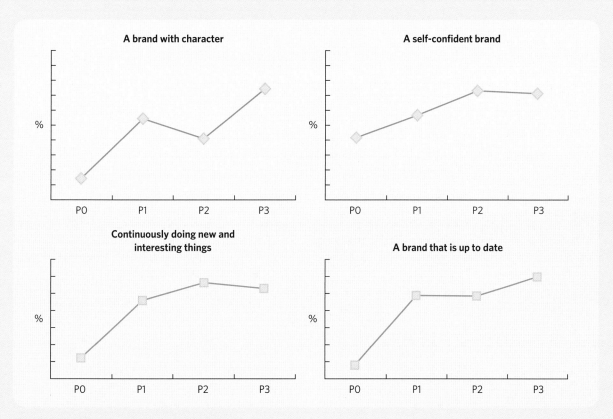

Figure 8.16 Evolution of Maes brand image

results were obtained among others because the campaign scored very well in different media, as illustrated in Figures 8.17 and 8.18.

Maes has largely reached its objectives in this successful relaunch campaign. Not only have more beer drinkers found their way to Maes and think it is a better beer and a nicer brand, but also they want to pay more for it. The combination of the market share and the 8% price increase led to a substantial increase in Maes's turnover. The Maes campaign received a Belgian Gold Effie Award in 2010.

	Maes	Average
I like it	83%	58%
Credible	92%	51%
Original	89%	61%
Informative	94%	55%
Inciting	71%	45%

Figure 8.17 Consumer evaluation outdoor campaign

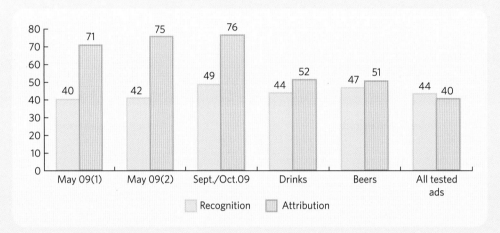

Figure 8.18 Recognition and attribution radio campaign

QUESTIONS

1. Describe and assess the problem identification by Maes and the resulting strategic communications approach and creative idea.

2. Do you think the translation of objectives into media solutions makes sense? Why or why not?

3. Assess the media mix and campaign components. Would you have used a different approach with different media and a different mix? Why or why not?

4. Assess the effectiveness of the campaign. Was it successful? Why or why not?

Sources: Maes Effie case 2010; Bert Denis, TBWA Brussels.

References

1 Donnelly, W.J. (1996), *Planning Media: Strategy and Imagination*. Upper Saddle River, NJ: Prentice Hall.
2 Donnelly, W.J. (1996), *Planning Media: Strategy and Imagination*. Upper Saddle River, NJ: Prentice Hall.
3 Donnelly, W.J. (1996), *Planning Media: Strategy and Imagination*. Upper Saddle River, NJ: Prentice Hall.
4 Nordhielm, C.L. (2002), 'The Influence of Level of Processing on Advertising Repetition Effects', *Journal of Consumer Research*, 29 (December), 371–82.
5 Pechman, C. and Stewart, D.W. (1989), 'Advertising Repetition: A Critical Review of Wearin and Wearout', *Current Issues and Research in Advertising*, 12, 285–330.

[6] MacInnis, D.J., Rao, A.G. and Weiss, A.M. (2002), 'Assessing When Increased Media Weight of Real-World Advertisements Helps Sales', *Journal of Marketing Research*, 39 (November), 391–407.

[7] Nordhielm, C.L. (2002), 'The Influence of Level of Processing on Advertising Repetition Effects', *Journal of Consumer Research*, 29 (December), 371–82.

[8] Kirmani, A. (1997), 'Advertising Repetition as a Signal of Quality: If It's Advertised so Much, Something Must Be Wrong', *Journal of Advertising*, 26(3), 77–86.

[9] Kirmani, A. (1997), 'Advertising Repetition as a Signal of Quality: If it's Advertised so Much, Something Must Be Wrong', *Journal of Advertising*, 26(3), 77–86.

[10] Kretchmer, S.B. (2005), 'Changing Views of Commercialization in Digital Games: In-Game Advertising and Advergames as Worlds in Plays', *Paper presented at DIGTAR Conference, Changing Views: Worlds in Play*, available at http://www.gamesconference.org/digra2005/overview.php (accessed June 2009).

[11] Entertainment Video Software Association (2006), 'Sales, Demografics and Usage Data 2006', http://www.theesa.com/facts/pdys/EAS_EF_2006.pdy (accessed June, 2009).

[12] Shields, M. (2006), 'In-game Ads Could Reach $2 bil,' *Mediaweek*, 12 April.

[13] Cauberghe, V. and De Pelsmacker, P. (2010), 'Advergames: The Impact of Brand Prominence and Game Repetition on Brand Responses', *Journal of Advertising*, 39(1), 5–18.

[14] Newell, S.J. and Henderson, K.V. (1998), 'Super Bowl Advertising: Field Testing the Importance of Advertisement Frequency, Length and Placement on Recall', *Journal of Marketing Communication*, 4(4), 237–48.

[15] Berger, I.E. and Mitchell, A.A. (1989), 'The Effect of Advertising on Ad Accessibility, Attitude Confidence, and the Attitude–Behavior Relationship', *Journal of Consumer Research*, 16 (December), 269–79.

[16] Hawkins, S.A. and Hoch, S.J. (1992), 'Low Involvement Learning: Memory Without Evaluation', *Journal of Consumer Research*, 19 (September), 212–25.

[17] D'Sousa, G. and Rao, R.C. (1995), 'Can Repeating an Advertisement More Frequently than the Competition Affect Brand Preference in a Mature Market?', *Journal of Marketing*, 59, 32–42.

[18] Kirmani, A. (1997), 'Advertising Repetition as a Signal of Quality: If it's Advertised so Much, Something Must Be Wrong', *Journal of Advertising*, 26(3), 77–86; Nelson, P. (1974), 'Advertising as Information', *Journal of Political Economy*, 82(4), 729–54.

[19] Donnelly, W.J. (1996), *Planning Media: Strategy and Imagination*. Upper Saddle River, NJ: Prentice Hall.

[20] Katz, H. (2003), *The Media Handbook*. Mahwah, NJ: Lawrence Erlbaum Associates.

[21] Donnelly, W.J. (1996), *Planning Media: Strategy and Imagination*. Upper Saddle River, NJ: Prentice Hall.

[22] Cheong, Y. and Leckenby, J.D. (2006), 'An Evaluation of Advertising Media Spending Efficiency Using Data Envelopment analysis', *Proceedings of the 2006 Conference of the American Academy of Advertising, Reno, NV*, 263–71.

[23] IP Peaktime (2004), *Television 2004: European Key Factors*. Neuilly-sur-Seine, Cedex, Brussels: IP.

[24] IP Peaktime (2004), *Television 2004: European Key Factors*. Neuilly-sur-Seine, Cedex, Brussels: IP; IP Peaktime (2002), *Radio 2002: European Key Factors*. Neuilly-sur-Seine, Cedex, Brussels: IP.

[25] Jones, J.P. (2002), *The Ultimate Secrets of Advertising*. Thousand Oaks, CA: Sage.

[26] Ephron, E. (1995), 'More Weeks, Less Weight: The Self-Space Model of Advertising', *Journal of Advertising Research*, 35(3), 18–23.

[27] De Pelsmacker, P., Geuens, M. and Vermeer, I. (2004), 'The Importance of Media Planning, Ad Likeability and Brand Position on Ad and Brand Recognition in Radio Spots', *International Journal of Market Research*, 46(4), 465–77.

[28] McDonald, C. (1997), 'From "Frequency" to "Continuity" – Is it a New Dawn?', *Journal of Advertising Research*, 37(4), 21–25.

[29] Newell, S.J. and Henderson, K.V. (1998), 'Super Bowl Advertising: Field-testing the Importance of Advertising Frequency, Length and Placement on Recall', *Journal of Marketing Communications*, 4(3), 237–48; D'Souza, G. and Rao, R.C. (1995), 'Can Repeating an Advertisement more Frequently than the Competition Affect Brand Preference in a Mature Market?', *Journal of Marketing*, 59 (April), 32–42.

[30] Katz, H. (2003), *The Media Handbook*. Mahwah, NJ: Lawrence Erlbaum Associates.

[31] Kamber, T. (2002), 'The Brand Manager's Dilemma: Understanding How Advertising Expenditures Affect Sales Growth during a Recession', *Brand Management*, 10(2) 106–20.

[32] Katz, H. (2003), *The Media Handbook*. Mahwah, NJ: Lawrence Erlbaum Associates.

[33] De Landtsheer, D., Van Rensbergen, N. and Van Roy, T. (2001), *Mediaplanning: Begrijpen en Benutten (Mediaplanning: Understanding and Using)*, Mechelen: Koncept.

[34] *De Morgen*, 23 September 2006.

[35] www.jcdecaux.nl (accessed 24 September 2012).

[36] *De Morgen*, 8 February 2008.

[37] Case, T. (2002), 'Media Plan of the Year', *Adweek*, 43(25), 34–36.

[38] Ritson, M. (2003), 'Marketers Need to Find a Way to Control the Contagion of Clutter', *Marketing*, 6 (March), 16.

[39] Pieters, R., Warlop, L. and Wedel, M. (2002), 'Breaking Through the Clutter: Benefits of Advertisement Originality and Familiarity for Brand Attention and Memory', *Management Science*, 48(6), 765–81.

[40] IP Peaktime (2004), *Television 2004: European Key Factors*. Neuilly-sur-Seine, Cedex, Brussels: IP.

[41] Bond, G. and Brace, I. (1997), 'Segmenting by Attitudes to TV Advertising – Eye Opener or Blind Alley?', *Journal of the Market Research Society*, 39(3), 481–508.

[42] Brace, I., Edwards, L. and Nancarrow, C. (2002), 'I Hear You Knocking . . . Can Advertising Reach Everybody in the Target Audience?', *International Journal of Market Research*, 44(2), 193–211.

43 Brace, I., Edwards, L. and Nancarrow, C. (2002), 'I Hear You Knocking . . . Can Advertising Reach Everybody in the Target Audience?', *International Journal of Market Research*, 44(2), 193–211.

44 Magiera, M. (1989), 'Advertisers Crowd onto the Big Screen', *Advertising Age*, 60(40), 14–15.

45 Van Zeebroeck, T. (1996), *Media Creativiteit (Media Creativity)*. Antwerp: MIM Standaard Uitgevery.

46 Van Zeebroeck, T. (1996), *Media Creativiteit (Media Creativity)*. Antwerp: MIM StandaardUitgevery.

47 www.afajcdecaux.dk (accessed 24 September 2012).

48 *De Morgen*, 11 May 2002.

49 White, E. (2002), 'Advertisers Hope Fragrant Posters Are Nothing to Sniff At – Firms Target UK Consumers with Ads That Sing and Spray', *Wall Street Journal*, 10 October.

50 Smets, F. (2003), 'De GeuralsWapen' ('Scent as a Weapon'), *De Morgen*, 22 March.

51 White, E. (2003), 'In-Your-Face Marketing: Ad Agency Rents Foreheads', *Wall Street Journal*, 11 February.

52 Moorman, M. (2003), 'Context Considered: The Relationship Between Media Environments and Advertising Effects', Doctoral Dissertation, University of Amsterdam.

53 De Pelsmacker, P., Geuens, M. and Anckaert, P. (2002), 'Media Context and Advertising Effectiveness: The Role of Context Appreciation and Context-Ad Similarity', *Journal of Advertising*, 31(2), 49–61.

54 Moorman, M. (2003), 'Context Considered: The Relationship Between Media Environments and Advertising Effects' Doctoral Dissertation, University of Amsterdam.

55 De Pelsmacker, P., Geuens, M. and Anckaert, P. (2002), 'Media Context and Advertising Effectiveness: The Role of Context Appreciation and Context-Ad Similarity', *Journal of Advertising*, 31(2), 49–61.

56 Bushman, B.J. and Bonacci, A.M. (2002), 'Violence and Sex Impair Memory for Television Ads', *Journal of Applied Psychology*, 87(3), 557–64.

57 Ha, L. (1996), 'Observations: Advertising Clutter in Consumer Magazines: Dimensions and Effects', *Journal of Advertising Research*, 36(4), 76–81.

58 Moorman, M. (2003), 'Context Considered: The Relationship Between Media Environments and Advertising Effects', Doctoral Dissertation, University of Amsterdam.

59 Finn, A. (1988), 'Print Ad Recognition Readership Scores: An Information Processing Perspective', *Journal of Marketing Research*, 25 (May), 168–77; Pieters, R. and de Klerk-Warmerdam, M. (1993), 'Duration, Serial Position and Competitive Clutter Effects on the Memory for Television Advertising', in Chias, I.J. and Sureda, J. (eds), *Marketing for the New Europe: Dealing with Complexity, Proceedings of the 22nd Annual Conference of the European Marketing Academy*. Barcelona: EMAC, 59–68.

60 Olson, D. (1994), 'The Sounds of Silence: Functions and Use of Silence in Television Advertising', *Journal of Advertising Research* (September/October), 89–95.

61 Janiszewski, C. (1990), 'The Influence of Print Advertisement Organization on Affect Toward a Brand Name', *Journal of Consumer Research*, 17, 53–65; Finn, A. (1988), 'Print Ad Recognition Readership Scores: An Information

Processing Perspective', *Journal of Marketing Research*, 25 (May), 168–77.

62 Reading, N., Bellman, S., Varan, D. and Winzar, H.F. (2006), 'Effectiveness of Telescopic Ads Delivered via Personal Video Recorders', *Journal of Advertising Research*, 46(2), 217–27.

63 Shrum, L.J. (ed.) (2004), *The Psychology of Entertainment Media: Blurring the Lines Between Entertainment and Persuasion*. Mahwah, NJ: Lawrence Erlbaum Associates.

64 Ruy, G., Lim, E.A., Tan, L. T.L. and Han, Y.J. (2007), 'Preattentive Processing of Banner Advertisements: The Role of Modality, Location, and Interference, *Electronic Commerce Research and Applications*, 6, 6–18.

65 Zenhui, J.J. and Bensabat, I. (2007), 'The Effects of Presentation Formats and Task Complexity on Online Consumers' Product Understanding, *MIS Quarterly 2007*, 31(3), 475–99.

66 Herr, P.M. (1989), 'Priming Price: Prior Knowledge and Context Effects', *Journal of Consumer Research*, 16 (June), 67–75.

67 Cauberghe, V., De Pelsmacker, P. and Janssens, W. (2009), 'Simultaneous Exposure to a Program and Advertising Content in an Interactive Context: Perceptual and Semantic Interference and Reinforcement, *Journal of Business Research*, 63(10), 972–8.

68 Park, C. and Young, M. (1986), 'Consumer Response to Television Commercials: The Impact of Involvement and Background Music on Brand Attitude Formation', *Journal of Marketing Research*, 23 (February), 11–24.

69 Faseur, T. and Geuens, M. (2006), 'Different Positive Feelings Leading to Different Ad Evaluations: The Case of Cosiness, Excitement and Romance', *Journal of Advertising*, 35(4), 129–420.

70 Yi, Y. (1993), 'Contextual Priming Effects in Print Advertisements: The Moderating Role of Prior Knowledge', *Journal of Advertising*, 22 (1 March), 1–10.

71 De Pelsmacker, P., Geuens, M. and Anckaert, P. (2002), 'Media Context and Advertising Effectiveness: The Role of Context Appreciation and Context-Ad Similarity', *Journal of Advertising*, 31(2), 49–61.

72 Faseur, T. and Geuens, M. (2006), 'Different Positive Feelings Leading to Different Ad Evaluations: The Case of Cosiness, Excitement and Romance', *Journal of Advertising*, 35(4), 129–420.

73 Moorman, M. (2003), 'Context Considered: The Relationship Between Media Environments and Advertising Effects', Doctoral Dissertation, University of Amsterdam.

74 De Pelsmacker, P., Geuens, M. and Anckaert, P. (2002), 'Media Context and Advertising Effectiveness: The Role of Context Appreciation and Context-Ad Similarity', *Journal of Advertising*, 31(2), 49–61.

75 Lee, A. and Sternthal, B. (1999), 'The Effects of Positive Mood on Memory', *Journal of Consumer Research*, 26, 115–27.

76 Moorman, M. (2003), 'Context Considered: The Relationship Between Media Environments and Advertising Effects', Doctoral Dissertation, University of Amsterdam.

77 Dahlén, M. (2005), 'The Medium as a Contextual Cue: Effects of Creative Media Choice', *Journal of Advertising*, 34(3), 89–98.

CHAPTER 9
Advertising research

CHAPTER OUTLINE

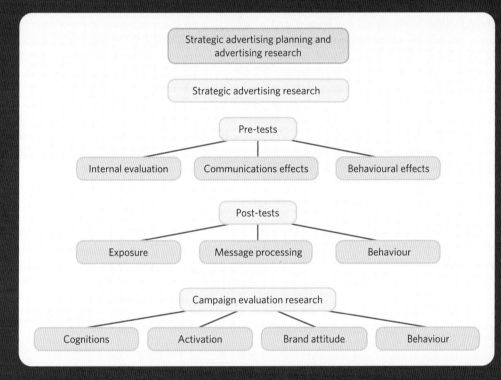

Strategic advertising planning and advertising research

Strategic advertising research

Pre-tests

Internal evaluation — Communications effects — Behavioural effects

Post-tests

Exposure — Message processing — Behaviour

Campaign evaluation research

Cognitions — Activation — Brand attitude — Behaviour

CHAPTER OBJECTIVES

This chapter will help you to:

- Carry out strategic communications research in preparation of a communications campaign
- Understand the objectives, techniques and limitations of pre-testing advertising campaigns
- Understand the objectives, techniques and limitations of post-testing advertising campaigns
- Learn the techniques and procedures of advertising campaign evaluation research

Introduction

Advertising research is not always supported by those who are involved in the communications process. Creative professionals, for instance, are inclined to perceive research efforts as a potential threat and limitation to their creativity. Moreover, many marketing managers and other communications professionals believe that research cannot replace experience and intuition, and therefore is a waste of time and money. Finally, there is a widespread belief that the effects of communications efforts cannot be measured validly, and therefore one should not even try to do so. As in all prejudices, there is a core of truth, and a lot of ego defence and/or misunderstanding.

Obviously, advertising research should not lead to a situation in which all creativity is stifled, but should lead to more relevant, functional and, therefore, more effective creativity. Furthermore, research can never replace marketing knowledge, and even intuition, but should rather serve as an eye-opener and a correction to the 'marketing myopia' that is often mistakenly called 'experience'. There is more truth in the belief about the problem of measuring the effectiveness of communications efforts. Their effect on sales, market share or profits often cannot be isolated, and the commercial pay-off of marketing communications is only visible after a certain period of time. Therefore, in advertising research, very often 'intermediate' effects, such as brand awareness, brand knowledge, attitude, preference or purchase intention, are measured, and they are assumed to be predictors of commercial success. In previous chapters it has been established, though, that positive intermediate effects are not always good predictors of commercial results. Nevertheless, the measurement of intermediate effects is frequently used in advertising research. In spite of these fundamental caveats, it is still worthwhile carrying it out. Like all research, it avoids mistakes or allows the communications manager to control the process and to adapt strategies whenever necessary.

Most of the research techniques discussed in this chapter have been developed for, and used in, an advertising context. Four basic types of advertising research will be discussed: preliminary or strategic communications research, pre-testing, post-testing and campaign evaluation research. Most of the techniques discussed can easily be transferred to other communications tools, such as public relations or in-store communications. In the chapters on specific communications instruments such as sales promotions, direct and interactive marketing and sponsorship, some specific research techniques to measure the effectiveness of these tools will be highlighted.

Strategic advertising planning and the role of research

Advertising research is used to improve decision-making in each stage of the advertising planning process. The various types of advertising research can therefore be linked to the stages in this process. This is illustrated in Figure 9.1. The starting point of a good advertising plan is a situation analysis or strategic research, on which the strategy can be built. On the basis of this research, objectives and target groups can be defined, and message and creative strategies can be developed. Following the development of an advertising strategy, a number of advertising tools (print advertisements, television spots, posters, etc.) will be developed and tested. This process is called pre-testing. After the development of the campaign, it is placed in the media. The impact of each of the tools can be assessed in post-tests. Finally, the results of the whole campaign can be compared with its objectives in campaign evaluation research. The results of the latter can serve as input for the development of subsequent advertising campaigns.

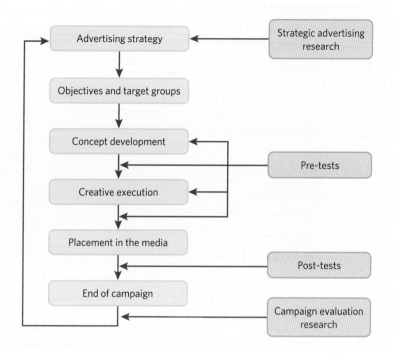

Figure 9.1 Stages in the development of an advertising campaign and the role of advertising and advertising research

Strategic advertising research

Marketing communications, as one of the instruments of the marketing mix, have to be embedded in the overall marketing strategy of the company. Therefore, it has to be consistent with the overall marketing objectives, it has to be aimed at the desired market segments and it should reflect the positioning strategy defined. Strategic communications research, and more particularly **strategic advertising research**, will therefore partially overlap with strategic marketing research. Although it is a frequently neglected research task, it is of extreme importance, since it enables the communications manager to establish a solid base on which the communications strategy can be built. Given the integrated nature of marketing communications, strategic research cannot be confined to advertising, but should cover the whole range of communications tools. Elements that have to be studied and prepared in this stage are:

- *Product.* What are its unique strengths and weaknesses, what is the unique selling proposition to be advanced, what is the advertising platform, i.e. the arguments with which to convince the target group, etc.?
- *Market.* What are the market size evolution, market shares, market segments, competitors' strategies, consumer characteristics and behaviour, etc.?
- *Environment.* What are the legal restrictions, cultural and political trends, the economic situation, etc.?

Most of these issues can be studied on the basis of desk research and/or qualitative interviews. Apart from that, more specific analyses can be carried out to prepare the communications strategy, such as the communications audit, competitor communications strategy research, communications content research and management judgement tests.

In a **communications audit** all forms of internal and external communications are studied to assess their consistency with overall strategy, as well as their internal consistency. The audit

Table 9.1 The communications audit

	Product A	Product B	Product C	Corporate
TV advertising				
Newspaper advertising				
Magazine advertising				
Sales promotions				
Direct mail				
In-store communications				
Front desk staff				
Public relations material				
Publicity				
Sponsorship				

can be carried out on the basis of an internal analysis, but should ideally be based on research with the various audiences and target groups of the company to determine the impact of all overt and non-overt communications. A framework for a communications audit is presented in Table 9.1. The consistency of the communications mix in this table should be assessed both vertically and horizontally, and the communications strategy for a number of products and/or instruments can be based on the results of this analysis.

Competitor communications strategy research is largely similar to the communications audit for the company. Competitive ads, promotions, PR material, etc., can be collected and analysed to judge competitive (communications) strategies in order to define target groups and positioning strategies more clearly for the company's own products. In addition, competitive media strategies and media mixes can be studied, not to copy them, but to get an idea of the competitors' communications budgets and shares of voice, target groups, positioning and communications strategies.

Communications content research is used to help communications creatives generate ideas about the content of new communications stimuli. When a new campaign is to be launched, brainstorming sessions can be organised, involving creatives, advertisers and consumers. Thought-starter lists, in which a multitude of potential benefits of the product is listed, may also be used to get the process underway. Finally, famous advertising gurus have issued their own sets of execution guidelines to be implemented in effective advertising. However, not only do they conflict in a number of ways, but they are also far too general to be implementable in each advertising strategy. The worst thing about these guidelines is that they lead to similar advertising executions and suffocate creative input.

If the advertising creative has too many ideas, they will have to be screened before including them in a campaign. These ideas can refer to headlines, slogans, illustrations, pictures, benefits (stated in different ways), endorsers, situations, advertising styles, etc. A sample of the target audience can be selected, and the various elements of the communications execution can be tested. The participants can be asked to order the headlines in terms of how convincing they are, the benefits in terms of their strength, the endorsers in terms of their likeability or similarity to themselves, etc., or they can be asked to rate each alternative on a scale. This a priori procedure is sometimes referred to as the Q-sort procedure.[1] It bears a lot of resemblance to the direct opinion measurement method in ad pre-testing (see below), but it is used before actual rough ad conception. Finally, in a **management judgement test** the ad execution proposals are presented to a jury of advertising managers, to check whether all the crucial elements of the strategic brief are correctly represented in the execution elements proposed. Again, this test bears a lot of resemblance to the internal analysis discussed in the pre-testing section.

Pre-testing of advertising

In a **pre-test**, advertising stimuli are tested before the ad appears in the media. The general purpose is to test an ad or different ads to assess whether or not they can achieve the purpose for which they are designed. The problems for which pre-testing can provide an answer are shown in Figure 9.2.

Often different concepts or executions of a new campaign are developed. Pre-testing helps with selecting the most effective one. As a final check, a number of characteristics of a finished stimulus can be tested before media placement. As discussed before, consumers are assumed to go through a number of persuasion stages before buying a product or becoming loyal to a brand. Advertising, and communications in general, should serve as a guide to accompany the potential consumers through these stages. To that end, communications stimuli should generate a number of intermediate processes or communications effects, such as creating attention, carrying over information, evoking acceptance of the message, credibility, positive affective reactions about the ad and the brand, and purchase intention. In a pre-test the extent to which these intermediate effects are generated can be tested. Often, a campaign consists of a number of similar ads, i.e. different executions of the same basic communications strategy. Different executions are often used to keep attention to the campaign alive by altering the format of the ad. Evidently, not all formats are equally appealing. A pre-test can help in establishing the extent to which some executions are more effective than others, and thus assist in deciding upon the frequency of placement of the various ads.

Three basic categories of ad pre-tests can be distinguished (Figure 9.3): a number of desirable characteristics can be tested internally, and samples of consumers can be used to test the communications or intermediate effects, or to test behavioural effects.

A campaign can be tested internally by the advertising agency and/or the advertiser by means of a checklist or readability analysis. **Pre-test checklists** are used to make sure that nothing important is missing, and that the ad is appealing, powerful and 'on strategy'. Table 9.2 contains an example of a checklist for internal evaluation. Every ad can be qualitatively judged on each criterion. Obviously, not every criterion will be equally important for every campaign. For instance, the number of times the brand name is mentioned may not be important at all in an image campaign, and in a provocative campaign 'likeability' may not be all that important.[2]

Another type of internal test is the **readability analysis**. Good advertising copy is simple and easy to understand, especially since members of the target group are often paying only marginal attention to the text in an ad. This implies that advertising copy should be understood 'at first glance'. Several methods have been developed to test this 'readability'. For

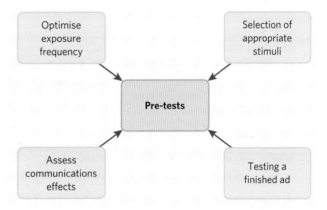

Figure 9.2 Objectives of pre-testing

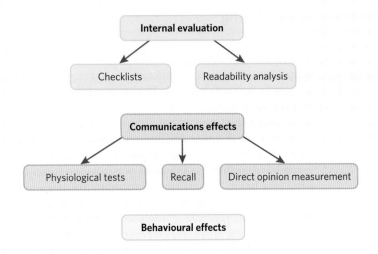

Figure 9.3 Pre-testing techniques

Table 9.2 A checklist for qualitative internal ad pre-testing

- Is the ad appealing at first sight?
- Does the ad have impact, 'standout', 'stopping power'?
- Is the ad 'on strategy', i.e. consistent with the briefing?
- Is the essential selling proposition mentioned frequently enough?
- Is there a benefit-oriented headline?
- Is the brand name mentioned often enough?
- How appropriate and credible are the images, the characters, the storyline, etc.?
- What is the visual impression: is the ad likeable, is it pleasing aesthetically?
- Are headlines, captions and body copy consistent?
- Does the text tell the same story as the visual elements: is the ad cohesive?
- Is the product shown appropriately?
- Does the relative importance of the logo, brand name, slogan, pack shot in the ad correctly reflect their relative importance?
- What seems to be the intended message of the ad, and is it consistent with the objectives of the campaign?

Source: Partly based on Pickton, D. and Broderick, A. (2001), *Integrated Marketing Communications.* Harlow: Financial Times/ Prentice Hall.

instance, a number of words in the text (e.g. every sixth word) can be removed, and a sample of consumers can be asked to fill in the missing words. The number of correctly reproduced words is an indication of the readability of the text. Another technique is the Reading Ease (RE) formula of Flesch-Douma.[3] In this formula RE is defined as depending on the length of words and sentences:

$$RE = 206.8 - 0.77wl - 0.93sl$$

where: wl = number of syllables per 100 words
sl = average number of words per sentence

A score between 0 and 30 means that the text is very difficult to read. A score close to 100 means that the text is very easy to understand. Research indicates that easy-to-read copy contains short sentences with short, concrete and familiar words, and lots of personal references.[4]

Communications or intermediate effects are measured in a sample of customers of the target group. The distinction can be made between physiological tests, recall tests, direct and indirect opinion measurement.

In a **physiological test** the reaction of the body to advertising stimuli is measured. Two types of physiological measurements can be carried out. The first involves the measurement of arousal, i.e. the activation of the nervous system, which is merely an indication of the intensity of the effect evoked by an ad. However, arousal measurement does not allow an assessment of the direction (positive or negative) of the effect, but is an indication of the primary affective reaction, which is assumed to trigger further processing of the ad.[5] Several techniques are used under very strict experimental conditions. For instance, the higher the arousal, the more the pupil of the eye dilates. Pupil dilation measurement is therefore used to assess the amount of arousal during, for instance, a TV commercial. Another measure is the galvanic skin response. In this method, the varying humidity of the skin is measured by means of an electric current, on the basis of which the amount of arousal can be assessed. Other arousal measurement techniques are heartbeat and voice pitch analysis and electro-encephalography. Most of these techniques are complicated and expensive, while the results are often difficult to interpret. Therefore, they are not frequently used.

RESEARCH INSIGHT
Measuring attitudes indirectly: The Implicit Association Test

When social desirability limits the validity of explicit attitude measurement, implicit or indirect methods can be used. They measure a person's attitude without asking him or her for an explicit opinion. Implicit attitude measurements can to a certain extent predict behaviour that is spontaneous or uncontrolled. The Implicit Association Test (IAT) is an implicit attitude measurement technique that is based on the ease with which people make associations between attributes and target concepts. Images, words, logos, colours, etc., can be used as target concepts, while adjectives and nouns can be used as attributes, for instance likeable, dirty, etc. In the IAT, people are asked to react as quickly as possible to a series of target concepts and attributes. If a person spontaneously and easily links a concept to an attribute, the speed with which he or she reacts to a combination will be higher. The opposite can be expected if the combination between the concept and attribute is less obvious or even appears contradictory to the individual. A careful analysis of reaction times provides insights into the attitude of individuals towards the concepts and characteristics of these concepts. The IAT can be used to measure the reaction of individuals towards stimuli that may contain sensitive elements, or to test ads for sensitive products or issues, such as environmentally-friendly buying behaviour, male/female stereotypes, hidden attitudes, racism, etc.[6] The results can be used to adapt elements of the creative execution of the ad, such as the models or arguments used, the combination between slogans and pictures, the type of appeal, etc.

For an ad to be effective, it has at least to be noted, and a minimum of information has to be carried over. The second type of physiological measurement tries to measure the potential of an ad to be seen. By means of a tachistoscope, print ads can be shown for a very short period of time. After exposure, the subject is asked to reproduce as many ad elements as possible. The element that is most recognised after the shortest exposure time is supposed to be the most effective one. Eye camera research[7] measures eye movements as a subject looks at a print ad or a TV commercial. This technique registers what is looked at and for how long, and can be used to improve the structure or layout of an ad. It can also be used to test in-store communications tools and sponsorship activities.

In **recall tests**, such as the portfolio test, the extent to which an individual recalls a new ad or a new execution amid existing ads is tested. The ad to be tested is put in a portfolio, together with the other ads. The subject is asked to look at the ads, and some time later (20 or 30 minutes), the recall test takes place. The subject has to name the ads and the brands, as well as the content of the ad that he or she can remember. Ads that are more frequently recognised are assumed to have drawn the attention better, and are therefore better ads.

Recall tests have a number of severe limitations. First of all, more than anything else, the memory of the individual as such is tested. People with a good memory will recall more ads and more of the content of the ads. This does not necessarily mean that the ads tested are good ones. Furthermore, product category involvement plays an important role. The more one is interested in a certain product (because one is planning to buy it in the near future, for instance), the more attention is paid to the ad, and the better it is recalled. Finally, very often the recall test is carried out very briefly after the exposure. The subject does not really have time to forget the ad. Ideally, the time between the exposure and the recall test should be as long as the time between the exposure and the buying situation in real life, but this can hardly be organised in a controlled experiment like the portfolio test.

RESEARCH INSIGHT

Attention and emotion tracking as a measure of advertising impact

Attention is the first barrier a message has to pass to make an impact, and emotion helps to create a lasting impact. The research company MediaAnalyzer, with offices in Hamburg and New York, and representatives in various other countries, developed attention tracking and emotion tracking pre-tests to provide objective measures to improve the impact of advertising.[8] Unlike traditional eye-tracking (which takes place in a laboratory situation, and is time-consuming and expensive), participants can perform the test at home, the procedure is fast and cost-efficient, large samples can be recruited and quantitative analyses can be carried out. The AttentionTracker records manual response (mouse clicks) to measure visual attention. The test ad is shown in a series of other ads in an editorial context. The respondents follow their gaze with the mouse by clicking the spot they are looking at. Comparative tests show that the correlation between eye movement measurement of attention and mouse clicks is over 90%.

The EmotionTracker measures the emotional response to the sequences of a TV commercial. An online tool makes it possible to record the emotional experience of the respondent while he or she is viewing a TV commercial. A mouse movement towards the left indicates a negative emotion and a mouse movement to the right a positive one. Through a change in the background colour to red (negative), green (positive) or white (neutral), the participants receive direct feedback on their current emotional rating of the commercial. The respondents are able to concentrate fully on the test commercial; there is no distraction through scrolling or answering questions about their feelings. The technology reveals which scenes are the central emotional contributors to the commercial, whether the commercial is able to hold the emotion or break at some point, and allows understanding of the emotionally successful elements in a TV commercial.

As in other pre-tests of this kind, the technology can be used to select the most appropriate ad and/or to optimise the structure and flow of a TV commercial or a print ad in that it can measure focal points of attention and flow of attention towards ads.

In **direct opinion measurement tests**, a jury of customers is exposed to a number of ads and asked to rate the ads on a number of characteristics. Most of the standardised ad testing procedures of advertising agencies, which enable them to compare test results over time, are of this type. Ad elements that can be tested are: clarity, novelty, evoked feelings, evoked attitude towards the ad and the brand, interest, quality of the information, the extent to which an ad induces the person to buy the product, etc.[9]

RESEARCH INSIGHT
Direct opinion measurement of the attitude towards the ad

Many ad testing scales have been developed. Most of them test at least three dimensions by means of various items: the affective reaction, the perception of informativeness and the clarity of the ad. In the following scale, for instance, all statements have to be scored on five- or seven-category scales (completely disagree–completely agree):

This ad appeals to me.	It is clear what this ad tries to say.
This ad gives useful information.	It is not immediately clear who the sender of the message is.
This ad is interesting.	The baseline is easy to understand.
This ad is beautiful.	You have to look at the ad a long time before you understand what it is about.
This ad is believable.	This ad is confusing.
This ad draws the attention.	This ad is remarkable.
This ad tells me something new.	I think this ad is well made.
This ad fits the brand.	I think this ad is original.
This ad is boring.	
This ad gives me a positive impression of the brand.	

The subject may be asked to rate each ad on a number of scales, to order them on the basis of a number of criteria or to pairwise-compare them on the basis of these criteria. The most important disadvantage of the direct rating method is that individuals are exposed to ads in a very unnatural environment. Therefore, they may be inclined to approach the ads too rationally compared with a real-life situation of ad exposure. They may even start to act and rate as 'instant experts', i.e. rating the ads from a professional advertiser's point of view, as they perceive it. This phenomenon is also known as the 'consumer jury effect'.

BUSINESS INSIGHT
A pre-test for a bank commercial

A campaign can be pre-tested and subsequently adapted to the desired profile. In the following test, this procedure is carried out for a bank commercial. A consumer jury is randomly selected and assembled in a room. A video is shown with a new commercial for the bank. After registering a number of characteristics of the respondents (age, income, gender, education, profession, clientship of banks, etc.), the following questions are asked:

'We talked to a number of people about this video. In that way we obtained a number of words by means of which they described it. We will read each pair of words. Please indicate each time which word of the pair you think adequately describes the video.'

I think this video is rather:

- dynamic – calm
- controlled – spontaneous
- boring – exciting
- mainstream – exclusive
- entertaining – informative
- conservative – new
- family-oriented – businesslike

'May we first know what your ideal bank is?'.......................

'We also talked to a number of people about banks. Again, we obtained a number of words by means of which they described banks. We will again read these words pairwise. Please indicate which one of the two is most appropriate to describe your ideal bank.'
   My ideal bank is:

- dynamic – calm
- traditional – progressive
- specialised – general
- family-oriented – businesslike
- exclusive – mainstream

On the basis of the differences in scores between the perception of the video and of the ideal bank of a particular target group, some characteristics of the campaign can be adapted and, if considered necessary, the campaign can be retested.

An example of an indirect opinion test is the **theatre test**. A group of test subjects is invited to a theatre to view a pilot programme of a new TV show. On arrival, they are invited to choose a present from a number of available items (competitive products in the same product category). If the product tested is too expensive, a lottery is organised and subjects are asked to indicate what product they would choose should they win. After viewing the programme, in which the ad to be tested is also shown, the participants are asked to make their choice again, as an extra award or because 'we made a mistake the first time'. The difference between what participants choose before and after the programme is attributed to the effect of the ad tested. Apart from being expensive, this test is potentially invalid, given the unrealistic situation of the measurement and the fact that participants know they are being tested.

Finally, behaviour tests try to measure actual behaviour, as opposed to recall, arousal or attitudes. Apart from actual buying behaviour, the response to a direct response TV commercial, to a direct mailing or to a direct response print ad can be measured. In a **trailer test** or coupon-stimulated purchasing test, respondents are randomly recruited in an experimental and a control group. The members of the first group are shown a commercial that is being tested in a trailer in a supermarket car park. The control group has to answer a number of questions without being exposed to the commercial. Several experimental groups can be formed if different commercials have to be tested. Both groups receive a number of coupons as a reward for their co-operation. An individualised store card registers the items purchased. Ad effectiveness is measured by means of differences in redemption between the various coupons. Again, the participants know that they are being tested, and this might influence their buying behaviour.

A second example of a behaviour test is the **split-scan test**, in which a split cable and scanner technology are combined to generate data on the effectiveness of advertising campaigns. In a split-scan procedure, the TV viewing behaviour of a panel of consumers is measured by means of a telemetric device. All members of the panel also receive a store card. The split-cable technology allows different random groups of panel members to be exposed to different campaigns. By means of a store card, the actual purchases of the panel members can be measured, and in that way the effectiveness of the different commercials can be assessed. The split-scan technology is very promising, because the actual behaviour of the same consumers that were exposed to the different ads can be measured in a controlled way (single-source data). Furthermore, other parameters can be manipulated or controlled, such as the frequency of exposure and the exposure of specific target groups.[10]

Although pre-testing procedures are very valuable, they have some limitations that should be taken into account when interpreting their results (Figure 9.4). A pre-test only offers the opportunity of selecting the best ad out of a series of ads tested. A pre-test will never lead to the best possible ad, but only to the best ad, given the executions tested. In that respect, pre-testing is only 'a guide to better advertising'. Pre-testing is only useful when the ads are tested in an individual interviewing procedure. Since ads are processed individually, they should also be tested individually, and not in a group setting in which the influence of the other members of the group invalidates the test rather than being synergetic. Most pre-tests take place in an experimental setting. Consumers may behave differently when exposed to an ad in a real-life situation. Some pre-test methods, especially the explicit ones such as the direct rating method, are susceptible to consumer jury effects. In most pre-tests, the influence of external factors such as competitive action on the effectiveness of the ad is not measured. Often the effectiveness of the ad is measured almost immediately after exposure. The effect of the elapse of time on ad effectiveness is not assessed. Except for procedures like the split-scan method, the effect of repetition or frequency of exposure on ad effectiveness cannot be assessed.

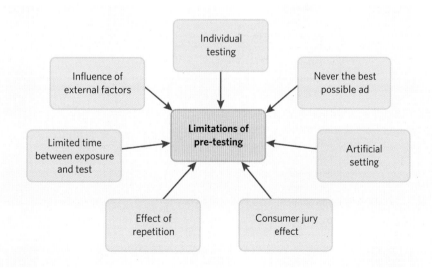

Figure 9.4 Limitations of pre-testing

BUSINESS INSIGHT
Pre-testing a new campaign for a sauce mix

In a pre-test, a number of elements can be measured that are considered to be important for the success of the campaign. However, before any judgement on the appropriateness of the campaign can be made, the results of the pre-tests should be benchmarked against other relevant campaigns. In the table below, the pre-test results of a new campaign for a prepacked sauce are given. Criteria such as attention, branding, communication, rational response and persuasion aspects are measured. The comparison is made between the new campaign and the average pre-test results of the same campaign in different countries, the average results of all other tested campaigns in the same country, and of all other food campaigns in this country. Furthermore, the pre-test results are benchmarked against normative action standards or pre-test objectives.

Pre-test scores of new campaign and benchmark campaigns for key criteria

		New campaign	Index against country average	Action standards	Country of campaign average	Country of campaign average food
Attention	Active	3.98	99	105	3.83	3.66
	Enjoyment	3.99	109	105	3.64	3.69
Branding	Brand linkage	4.18	109	110	3.90	3.88
Communication	Ease of understanding	3.73			3.65	3.70
	Specific criteria:					
	– Are practical to use	81%				
	– Have a very good taste	58%				
	– Are very good in quality	49%				
	– Are disposable in a large range of variety	71%				
	– Offer you something really new	63%				
Rational response	New information	3.15			2.59	2.67
	Different	3.23	3.15	3.30		
	Relevant	3.06			2.85	3.02
	Believable	4.05			3.66	3.79
	Didn't tell you enough	2.89			2.88	2.89
Persuasion	Persuaded me	25%	120	110	120	

Post-testing of advertising

A **post-test** is a test of the effectiveness of a single ad after placement in the media. Post-tests are only meaningful if there is a before measurement or a control measurement as a benchmark. Three types of post-tests can be distinguished (Figure 9.5): measurement of exposure, communications effect tests and measurement of behaviour.

First of all, the extent to which an ad has reached its audience can be measured. Net reach, GRP, OTS and other exposure measures can be calculated. Normally, this type of effectiveness measurement is done not only after media placement, but also as a part of the media planning effort. Similarly, the amount of publicity generated in the press or sponsorship exposure can also be measured and expressed in terms of reach or GRP.

In measuring the communications or message processing effects of an ad, two types of tests are used: recall and recognition tests. A **recognition test** is a very obvious effectiveness test. A sample of ads is presented to a consumer, who is asked to indicate whether he or she recognises the ad or not. The underlying assumption is that ads can only be effective when they are at least noted. A well-known recognition test procedure for print ads is the **Starch test**. Some 75 000 ads in 1000 issues of magazines and newspapers are assessed each year, using 100 000 personal interviews.[11] Consumers who say they have read a specific issue in a magazine are interviewed at home. The magazine is opened at a random page, and for each ad a number of questions are asked. The procedure leads to four percentage scores for each ad:

- *Non-readers*: the percentage of people who do not remember having seen the ad.
- *Noted*: the percentage of readers who claim to have seen the ad.
- *Seen/associated*: the percentage of readers who claim to have read the product and brand name.
- *Read most*: the percentage of readers who claim to have read at least half the ad.

Obviously, the Starch test is very susceptible to the test subject's honesty. However, research reveals that high 'noted' scores are positively correlated with a positive attitude towards the brand ($r = 0.43$) and a positive intention to buy ($r = 0.52$).[12]

In a **masked identification test**, part of a print ad, usually the brand name, is covered. The subject is asked if he or she recognises the ad, and if he or she knows what brand it is for. Recognition and correct attribution scores can then be calculated. Obviously, brand confusion can be measured too. The combination of recognition and correct attribution scores leads to the **useful score**: the percentage of the consumer sample that both recognised the ad and attributed it correctly to the brand advertised. In Figure 9.6, an example of the results of

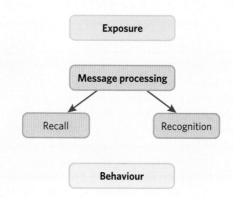

Figure 9.5 Post-testing techniques

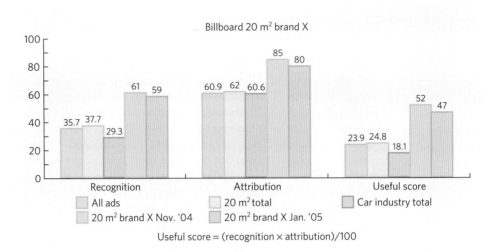

Figure 9.6 Masked identification test

a masked identification test of a billboard ad for a new car is shown, together with the results of a number of categories of control ads.

A second type of communications effect measurement is the **recall test**. In an unaided recall test, consumers have to indicate which ads they remember having seen, in a specific magazine, on TV or on billboards. In an aided recall test, the consumer's memory is helped by means of clues such as: What car ads did you see on TV yesterday? As such, the masked identification test can be regarded as an aided recall test. Unaided recall scores are usually lower than aided recall scores, which in turn are lower than recognition scores. Therefore they cannot be compared.

A well-known recall test is the **Gallup–Robinson Impact test** for print ads. Firstly, the respondents have to read a magazine at home. The following day, the respondents are called and asked to recall as many ads as they can. After that, a number of questions about the content of the ads are asked. The Gallup–Robinson procedure leads to three indicators of advertising effectiveness:[13]

- *Proved name registration*: the percentage of subjects who remember an ad without having seen it during the test.
- *Idea penetration*: the extent to which subjects have understood the main idea in the ad.
- *Conviction*: the percentage of subjects who want to buy or use the product.

Another well-known recall test, used for audio-visual ads, is the **Day After Recall (DAR) test**. In this telephone interview procedure, a number of consumers are called. They are asked to indicate which ads they saw on TV or heard on the radio the day before, within a certain product category. In the second stage, brand names are mentioned, and the respondent has to indicate if he or she remembers having seen or heard an ad for the brand. Additionally, a number of questions about the ad content are asked. The resulting percentages of correct recall are always compared with some kind of benchmark, such as all commercials within the same product category or all commercials of the day before. In the triple association test, a product category and a selling proposition are given, and the respondent has to indicate a brand name, e.g. 'What brand of petrol puts a tiger in your tank?'

Finally, the effect of an ad can be tested by means of behavioural measures. Especially in the case of direct response ads, the number of people calling a free telephone number announced in the ad, sending back a coupon or actually buying the product can be considered a measure of the effectiveness of the ad.

RESEARCH INSIGHT
Measuring website visiting behaviour

Every time a visitor clicks on a website link or interacts with a website, the web server automatically keeps track of some of the data in so-called *log files*. Most servers generate four types of log files. The *access log file* keeps track of the file names that are downloaded, the IP address of the client server that requested the file and an indication of time. The *agent log file* registers which browser is being used by which visitor's server for every visit to the site. The *referrer log file* registers the pages that were visited before the visitor landed on the web page. The *error log file* keeps track of errors that occurred during the process. The log files give information such as the number of 'hits' (downloaded files), the point in time when files were downloaded, the number of bytes transferred, the domains from which the visitor arrived (Internet service providers, proxy servers, firewalls) and the browsers used. A number of software instruments, such as Nedstat and WebTrends, have been developed to efficiently analyse and summarise this enormous data stream. Also data-mining software is used to find meaningful patterns in the large amount of data on website visiting behaviour. Log files have an important limitation. They cannot identify individual users. Therefore, log file data are often supplemented with *cookies*, a piece of software that is planted in the system of the website visitor and allows web servers to register and keep track of the revisit behaviour of visitors. The visiting of ads on websites (banners, buttons) can be assessed by means of *click-through rates*. Most click-throughs result in a transfer of the visitor to the advertiser's website. A click-through is the virtual counterpart of a response of an individual to a direct mailing.[14]

Recall and recognition tests are useful and easy to carry out, but they have a number of severe limitations (Figure 9.7). In recognition tests, consumers can say what they like, they can lie, exaggerate or guess. This makes the results of recognition tests far from reliable. An ad that is part of a campaign of similar ads will be more easily recognised or recalled. In these circumstances, it is very hard to isolate the effect of one single ad. The underlying assumption that recognition or recall of the ad eventually leads to buying the product may be erroneous. Recognising or recalling marketing communications may be a necessary condition to buy a product, but certainly not a sufficient one. Product involvement influences the results of the test. A consumer who is very interested in a certain product category will perform better in recognising ads for this product category. This does not imply anything about the effectiveness of that specific ad. Recall scores are very dependent on the time elapsed between

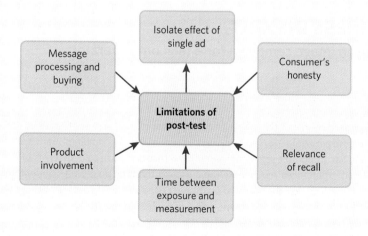

Figure 9.7 Limitations of post-testing

exposure and recall measurement. Recall scores are nearly 100% immediately after exposure, but studies indicate that they drop to about 25% the day after and to about 10% two days after exposure.[15] Rational mass appeals are recalled better than complex and/or emotional appeals, certainly after one exposure. Recall is, in a number of cases, an irrelevant indication of advertising effectiveness. The only thing recall tests measure is whether the ad has been able to draw attention. Especially in cases in which it is sufficient for a consumer to recognise a picture or a brand in a shop to be inclined to buy the product, recognition tests are a much more valid and relevant measure of ad effectiveness than recall measurements.

Advertising campaign evaluation research

Contrary to post-tests in which the effectiveness of only one ad is assessed, **campaign evaluation research** focuses on the effectiveness of a whole advertising campaign. Campaign evaluation research tends to become increasingly more relevant than post-tests. Integrated marketing communications imply that it is very difficult or even irrelevant to assess the effects of one single medium or ad. Rather, the effects of the whole communications mix should be assessed.

In campaign evaluation tests, not ad-related responses but brand-related effectiveness measures are the focus. As in post-tests, a before or control measurement is necessary to assess adequately the effect of a particular campaign. Again, communications effects as well as behaviour effects can be measured.

Communications effects measurements can be structured following the hierarchy-of-effects logic: awareness, knowledge, attitude and intention to buy. Top-of-mind awareness (TOMA) measurement is an **unaided awareness** telephone test in which the consumer is asked which brand of a specific product category is the first one that comes to mind. Subsequently, the consumer is asked if he or she can name other brands in the same product category (again unaided awareness). Finally, a number of brands are mentioned, and the consumer has to indicate the ones he or she knows (**aided awareness**). The advertising campaign is not mentioned but, by comparing the awareness before and after a campaign, its effect on brand awareness can be assessed. Furthermore, brand awareness rates of competitive products are also measured, and can serve as a control measurement or benchmark.

Attitude change or the change of the brand's image can also be measured. Often a campaign aims at changing the target group's opinion about certain aspects or attributes of a brand. Scale techniques can be used to measure this change in image components.

BUSINESS INSIGHT
Testing an image campaign for a telecoms operator

In one European country,[16] the mobile phone operator market was dominated by three competitors with a combined market share of almost 100%. The two largest companies had a combined market share of about 90%. The market was divided into two important segments, namely pre-paid and post-paid. In terms of the number of clients, the pre-paid segment had experienced much more rapid growth than the post-paid segment. Initially, 100% of the market was post-paid. By 2002, two-thirds of the customers used pre-paid cards. In 1996, the market leader had a relatively weak position in the pre-paid segment, and a very strong post-paid position. An image campaign was launched to build top-of-mind awareness, brand preference, emotional bonding and trust. Reliability and superior product quality (network, sound, number of clients, etc.) were stressed. Throughout the campaign, the results were monitored. Chart 1 shows top-of-mind brand awareness of the three competing brands. Chart 2 shows brand preference evolution.

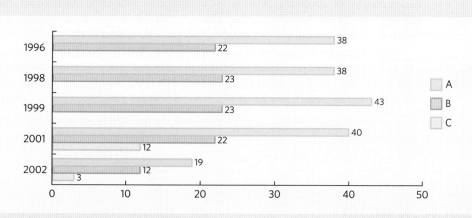

Chart 1 Top-of-mind brand awareness

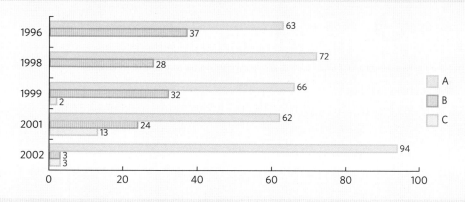

Chart 2 Brand preference

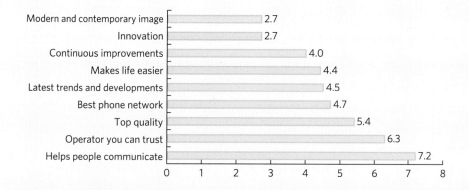

Chart 3 Relative strengths of market leader

Chart 3 gives the score of the market leader on a number of image attributes. The market leader has a better image on all the criteria measured.

Finally, the communications effect of a campaign can be measured on the basis of the intention to buy of a target group of consumers. It is important that the question on the purchase intention is related to the near future or the next purchase, e.g. 'The next time you buy coffee, what is the chance that you will buy brand X (as a percentage, or on a 10-point scale)?' An alternative measure is the **net promoter score** which is based on the question: 'To which degree would you recommend the following brand to your family or friends?', measured on a 0–10-point scale. The net promoter score is calculated by subtracting the percentage of people scoring 0–6 from the percentage of people who scored 8–10.

Besides intention to buy and to recommend, the effectiveness of an advertising campaign can also be measured by means of **activation measures**. They measure the extent to which people actively react to advertising by, for instance, looking up further information, talking to friends (buzz), and going to a store. Below are a number of examples of activation measures.

RESARCH INSIGHT
Activation measures

1. **Following the campaign you just saw, would you consider doing any of the following?**

   Please tick all options that apply.

   ☐ Search for information about the campaign online

   ☐ Search for information about the campaign in magazines or other media

   ☐ Search for information about the brand online

   ☐ Search for information about the brand in magazines or newspapers

   ☐ Search for information about other products of this brand online

   ☐ Search for information about other products of this brand in magazines or newspapers

   ☐ Visit the brand website

   ☐ Visit a store for information about the brand

   ☐ Visit a store for information about other products of this brand

2. **Following the campaign you just saw, would you consider doing any of the following?**

   Please tick all options that apply.

   ☐ Share the campaign with friends, family, colleagues or acquaintances online (e.g. through Facebook, Twitter, YouTube, blogs, etc.)

   ☐ Post something about the brand online (e.g. through Facebook, Twitter, YouTube, blogs, etc.)

   ☐ Start a conversation with friends, family, colleagues or acquaintances about the campaign

   ☐ Start a conversation with friends, family, colleagues or acquaintances about the brand

   ☐ Join a conversation with friends, family, colleagues or acquaintances about the campaign

   ☐ Join a conversation with friends, family, colleagues or acquaintances about the brand

3. **Why did you visit the brand website?**

   Please tick all answers that apply.

   ☐ See the campaign again

   ☐ Find out more about the brand and/or products

   ☐ Find price information

☐ Find a store or selling point

☐ Participate in a contest

☐ Entertain myself or relax (watch a movie, clip, etc.)

☐ Buy a product from the advertised line

☐ Buy another product of the brand

☐ Other (please specify: ....)

4. **Following the campaign you just saw, did you do any of the following?**

   Please tick all options that apply.

   ☐ Bought the brand in a store

   ☐ Bought another product of the brand in a store

   ☐ Bought the brand online

   ☐ Bought another product of the brand online

5. **How many different people would you say you talked to about this campaign in a positive way?**

   ☐ Almost everyone I know

   ☐ The majority of my friends, family and acquaintances

   ☐ Some of my friends, family and acquaintances

   ☐ One or two people

6. **How many different people would you say you talked to about the brand in a positive way?**

   ☐ Almost everyone I know

   ☐ The majority of my friends, family and acquaintances

   ☐ Some of my friends, family and acquaintances

   ☐ One or two people

Most of the communications effect measurements are frequently used in **tracking studies**, in which comparable (random) samples of consumers are asked a standardised set of questions at regular intervals (e.g. every three months). As a result, the position of a brand and competing products can be tracked over time, and effects of subsequent campaigns can be assessed. As in all before–after measurements, problems of interpretation arise. The effect of a campaign cannot always be isolated. A deteriorating image, for instance, may be the result of, among others, a bad campaign, a price increase, bad publicity, competitors' actions, an inappropriate sales promotion campaign or a bad distribution strategy. Furthermore, the effect of advertising campaigns may only become visible after some time. The performance of a brand immediately after the campaign may therefore underestimate its true impact in the long run.

Obviously, the ultimate objective of an advertising campaign is to make people buy the product and eventually to make a (better) profit. In behaviour tests the relation between advertising and buying behaviour is studied directly. Various behavioural measures of ad effectiveness can be distinguished, the most obvious ones being sales and market share evolution. Again, as in all campaign evaluation measurements, it should be noted that the evolution of market share and sales may be attributable to other marketing mix instruments than advertising. The effect of an advertising campaign cannot always be isolated easily.

BUSINESS INSIGHT
How can the effect of an advertising campaign be isolated?

Isolating the effect of an advertising campaign is not always obvious. The following two examples illustrate this.[17]

Example 1

A small bank advertised a savings account with an interest rate that was twice that of the major banks at the time. The campaign results (campaign in Year 1 and Year 2) were the following:

	Year 1	Year 2	Year 3
Spontaneous brand awareness	7%	9%	10%
Aided brand awareness	45%	47%	66%
Correct attribution of account to bank	9%	36%	55%

The following chart indicates the evolution of the number of account holders, as well as the advertising periods.

On the basis of the communications effects, the communications campaign seems to have been successful. Obviously, the number of clients increased substantially each time an advertising wave took place. The question is: Is this increase attributable to the advertising effort or to the intrinsic attractiveness of the product, i.e. the high interest rate, that is simply communicated to the target audience?

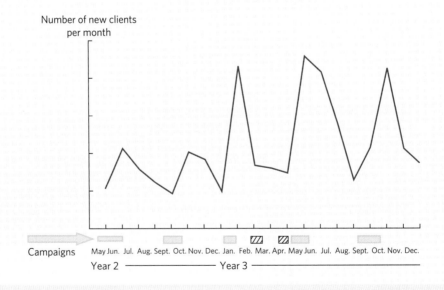

Example 2

A chain of do-it-yourself supermarkets launched a radio advertising campaign. The commercial results of the super-markets look as follows (campaign in Year 2, Year 3 and Year 4):

	Year 1	Year 2	Year 3	Year 4
Sales	100	139	188	224
Annual growth of sales		+39%	+36%	+19%
Number of transactions	100	130	171	194
Ticket size	100	107	110	116

At first sight, this seems to be an impressive result. However, when a correction is made for the expansion of the number of supermarkets that increased in the period under consideration, the following picture emerges:

	Year 1	Year 2	Year 3	Year 4
Sales	100	131	159	183
Annual growth of sales		+31%	+21%	+15%
Number of transactions	100	128	165	189
Ticket size	100	106	110	118

The result still looks impressive, but not as impressive as the first set of figures in which the effect of a larger distribution network was included.

RESEARCH INSIGHT
The 'awareness–trial–retention' framework

An analysis combining awareness and behavioural measures to assess the effectiveness of advertising campaigns is as follows. Three indicators are measured:

$AR = AW/TG$

$TR = T/AW$

$ADR = A/T$

where: AR = awareness rate
AW = number of target group members that are aware of the brand
TG = number of people in the target group
TR = trial rate
T = number of target group members that have purchased the brand at least once during a given period
ADR = adoption rate
A = number of people that have purchased the brand at least a specific number of times during the same period

Evidently, the period under study and the number of times a consumer has to have purchased the product to be called a loyal consumer have to be determined in advance, and will depend upon the product category studied.

Suppose that for two competing brands the following results have been obtained after an advertising campaign:

	Brand A	Brand B
Awareness rate	70%	20%
Trial rate	40%	20%
Adoption rate	10%	70%

Obviously, the commercial end-result is the same for both brands: 2.8% of the target group have become loyal to the brand. However, the three indicators show a more differentiated picture. Brand B was not very successful in building awareness and trial. One might say that the advertising campaign was not very effective. On the other hand, the marketing strategy seems to be on target: most people who have tried the product have become loyal to it. Brand A has had a successful advertising campaign, but something seems to be wrong with the rest of the marketing strategy. Maybe the product is of bad quality, the price too high or the distribution strategy inappropriate. It could also be that the product is a luxury item, for which in the short run trial is more important than repeat purchase.

Apart from changes in sales, more specific behavioural effects can be measured, such as trial purchases and the degree of adoption of, or loyalty to, a brand.

Most of the aforementioned measures of communications results are effectiveness measures, while marketers will also be interested in efficiency measurement, i.e. the extent to which the investment in an advertising campaign has had a commercial result. More specifically, marketers might want to know how many sales for every pound (or euro, or dollar) spent on communications has resulted. Over a longer period of time, data could be collected on advertising budgets and sales per time unit (three months, a year, etc.), and the relationship between the two may be estimated. This could result in the following:

$$S = 1.5 + 0.2 \times A$$

where: S = sales in € million
A = advertising in € million

The conclusion would be that, over time, every euro invested in advertising has resulted in €0.2 of extra sales. Additionally, the cost function of the company may be modelled, in order to be able to calculate the profitability of the advertising efforts. However, advertising efforts usually have carry-over effects: the efforts of today do not lead to extra sales during the same period only, but also to extra commercial results in future periods. This effect may be modelled as follows:

$$S(t) = 1.5 + 0.2 \times A(t) + 0.8 \times S(t - 1)$$

where: $S(t)$ = sales in period t
$A(t)$ = advertising investments in period t
$S(t - 1)$ = sales in period $t - 1$

The coefficient of $S(t - 1)$ represents the effect of advertising investments in the past on this period's sales. This effect is assumed to decrease over time. The long-term effect of advertising can in this example be calculated as: 0.2/0.8 = 0.25. This implies that, in the long run, every euro invested in advertising leads to an increase in sales of €0.25. The short-term effect of advertising on sales in the same period is only €0.20.

Evidently, life is not so simple. Firstly, sales are influenced by more than communications alone, so the model will have to be extended. Additionally, the competitors' efforts will have to be taken into consideration too. Consequently, estimating the profitability of advertising investments is a complicated task.[18]

Summary

Advertising campaigns can only be effective if they are accompanied by a well-structured research plan. Research can support the advertising activity in four stages of the advertising process. In strategic advertising research, the advertising campaign is prepared by studying the marketing strategy, the competitive situation and the competitive environment it has to be embedded in. Techniques such as the communications audit, competitor communications strategy research and communications content research are being used in this stage. During development of the advertising campaign, and before it appears in the media, the ads can be pre-tested. The major advantage of pre-testing is that it is a guide to better advertising. However, due to all kinds of limitations and the shortcomings of most of the techniques used, it can never lead to the best possible ad. Techniques used in pre-testing can be internal, such as readability analysis, or external (with consumers), such as physiological tests, recall tests and direct or indirect opinion measurement. After a specific ad has been placed in the media, post-tests can be carried out, such as exposure, recall and recognition tests, and behavioural measures. Well-known test procedures such as the Starch test, the Gallup–Robinson Impact test and the Day After Recall tests are used in post-testing. Not just a single ad can be tested, but a whole campaign. Campaign evaluation tests focus on the brand-related effects of the campaign, such as brand recall and recognition, attitude towards the brand, purchase intention and, most importantly, behavioural or commercial measures, such as trial, repeat purchase, loyalty, sales and market share.

REVIEW QUESTIONS

1. What are the major techniques used in strategic communications research?

2. Discuss ad pre-testing techniques. What are the objectives and limitations of these measurement procedures?

3. Discuss ad post-testing techniques. What are the objectives and limitations of post-testing?

4. What measures of brand-related campaign evaluation techniques can be used?

5. How can advertising efficiency be measured? Why is it so difficult to judge the effectiveness and efficiency of an advertising campaign?

Further reading

Aaker, D., Kumar, V. and Day, G.S. (2001), *Marketing Research*. New York: Wiley.

Malhotra, N. (1999), *Marketing Research: An Applied Orientation*. Upper Saddle River, NJ: Prentice Hall.

McDonald, C. and Vangelder, P. (1998), *ESOMAR Handbook of Market and Opinion Research*. Amsterdam: ESOMAR.

CASE 9:
Win for Life: reviving and repositioning a scratch game

Win for Life, a scratch product of the Belgian National Lottery

Man's natural inclination to gamble has always existed and will probably exist for all time. Any outright prohibition of gambling would inevitably have been counter-productive and would have embroiled this sphere of activity in an element of wild and therefore socially dangerous clandestinity. Being conscious of this reality, the Belgian Legislator, as early as 1851, preferred to authorise the organisation of certain games, and lotteries in particular, but under strict conditions. The National Lottery operates as a public-law limited company, and the conditions of its operation have been laid down by the Act of 19 April 2002 and, in addition, by the management contract between the public company and the Belgian State. Under these terms the National Lottery's primary mission consists of organising, in the general interest and according to commercial methods, public lotteries, betting opportunities, competitions and games of chance, but, in addition, the management contract includes a parallel mission of being a socially responsible public operator. The objective is to channel the various manifestations of gambling behaviour in Belgium, to prevent any excess, to protect vulnerable customers and to make an active and autonomous contribution to the prevention and treatment of gambling addiction. The National Lottery endeavours in addition to help limit the total size of the games of chance market in Belgium by focusing its product development and marketing policies not on the enlargement of the market, but on winning market share from private operators, whether they be Belgian or foreign, authorised or illegal. It is in this way that it has to generate, in a socially responsible manner, the funds enabling it to honour its financial obligations with respect to the Treasury and the beneficiaries of its grants.

Between 2005 and 2010, the turnover of the National Lottery ranged between €1.1 and €1.2 billion (Belgian population: 10.8 million). Around €500 million of this turnover comes from people playing Lotto, the oldest and no doubt most famous star brand of the lottery. Euromillions, a European-wide drawing game, similar to Lotto, but with much higher prizes and lower chances of winning, accounts for around €300 million. Scratch games account for around €200 million. A scratch card can be purchased in retail outlets such as newspaper or tobacco shops, supermarkets and gas stations. By scratching parts of the surface of the scratch card, one can immediately check the prize. One of the most popular scratch games of the National Lottery is Win for Life.

People can buy Win for Life scratch cards in the shop for €3 per card. They can then scratch away the zones on the card. Depending on the symbols that appear, participants can win the main prize, i.e. €2000 tax free per month for the rest of their lives, or money prizes of €2500, 250, 25, 10, 6 or 3. The chance of winning the main prize is 1 in 1 million. Overall, participants have a chance of 1 in 4 to win a prize; 62.6% of the turnover is redistributed to the players.

Win for Life was launched in 1998 but, until 2009 (with a short revival in 2006), turnover had been steadily decreasing. Based on consumer insights, the decision was taken to reposition and relaunch the product. This case describes the campaign that ran between April and December 2010, and discusses the effectiveness measures that were used to assess the success of the campaign.

Win for Life (WFL): a product in decline

After a relaunch in 2007, accompanied by a price increase of the card from €2.5 to €3, the turnover of WFL increased substantially. However, from 2008 to 2009, turnover sharply dropped by 13%, from €71.8 to 62.5 million. There were several reasons for this decline. First of all, there was a decreasing penetration of the product in the younger age groups (18–34). By contrast, the number of youngsters who know about WFL but do not buy it increased. Consequently, the conversion from 'knowing' to 'buying' drops. Additionally, the number of retail outlets that sell WFL decreased steadily, mainly because of the disappearance of many newspaper shops, in 2009 about one per day on average. WFL is primarily sold through such shops. Further, the image of WFL became more negative every year. The rational brand parameters still score high: you can win 'an extra monthly wage' for the rest of your life. This is due to the fact that earlier advertising campaigns for WFL uniquely emphasised this rational proposition. However, a number of emotional parameters of the brand score more negatively every year:

'WFL is a fun, playful brand': 45% agreed in December 2007; only 31% in December 2009.

'WFL is a modern brand': 40% agreed in December 2007; only 27% in December 2009.

WFL ran the risk of losing its attractiveness to younger people and becoming an 'old' brand. Moreover, youngsters spend more than 40% of the budget they devote to gambling on competing games, such as games in pubs, online and in casinos. These alternatives are much more geared towards the needs and motivations of this age group: an instant kick and fun and a wide availability in their living world. Moreover, draws are made on a fixed day of the week, which enables the development of a weekly routine and commitment of the players. Scratch games do not have this 'routine' element. Consequently, it is much more difficult to build commitment.

A new campaign to turn the tide

The National Lottery calculated that, without any changes, the turnover of WFL would drop by 15.6% in 2010. The aim instead was to develop an advertising campaign in the period April–December 2010 and realise an increase in turnover of 1%. The difference between the predicted drop in turnover and the 1% target increase amounts to €10.3 million. It was decided to target the campaign at 18–34 year olds to make WFL more appealing to young people and to create a new WFL generation. Four commercial objectives were advanced:

1. Increase the penetration among the target age group from 19.3% in the second half of 2009 to 22.4% in the second half of 2010.

2. Increase the conversion rate (the number of people in the target group buying WFL divided by the number of people who know about it) from 20.75 in 2009 to 23.9 in 2010.

3. Realise an immediate short-term impact on sales: 1% more sales in 2010 than in 2009.

4. WFL is an impulse product. This fourth objective of the campaign was to realise a long-term effect: sales should not drop between campaign waves.

The communication strategy was built on three angles:

1. *From a rational attribute to an emotional preference brand*. WFL wants to be more attractive to young people by positioning it as a modern and aspirational brand that perfectly understands the new generations and takes their needs into account. Instead of focusing on the rational product attribute (win €2000 per month for the rest of your life – financial security), the campaign wanted to reposition WFL on the basis of an emotional benefit: from financial to mental security. Today, people

do not just want to be rich as such. They want the security of a comfortable life and to experience it without any worries. They want to live every day in the best possible way. WFL gives them peace of mind. This insight led to the campaign promise: 'With WFL I am at ease for the rest of my life.'

2. *From accidental to conscious purchase*. WFL is an impulse product. It is therefore important to stay within the consideration set of people constantly to develop commitment and conscious purchase behaviour. WFL should have a high brand awareness based on frequent exposure.

3. *Create urgency*. Unlike the drawing games, there is no fixed 'appointment' with WFL. It was decided to make Friday 'WFL day', because retail outlets are most frequently visited on this day, and partly because it is also Euromillions playing day.

These ambitions were translated into the following communication objectives:

1. *Increase image parameters and increase motivation to buy* (Table 9.3, middle two columns). A major improvement in a number of emotional brand parameters is envisaged: exciting, sympathetic, modern, funny and playful, close to me, fits with me, like to play, etc.

2. *Increase spontaneous brand awareness and commitment*. The aim was to increase spontaneous brand awareness from 53% in 2009 to 56.8% in 2010. The percentage of committed buyers (those who have an absolute preference for the brand and for nothing else) should increase from 14.1% in 2009 to 16.8% in 2010.

3. *Increase the turnover per day, and make Friday a top-selling day*. The target group of the campaign was 18–34 year olds. The aim was to attract more of these people without losing the older age groups. In terms of motivations, most traditional WFL players are profit- and certainty-seekers. The campaign aims at convincing 'homey' people: those who are spontaneous, open, social, friendly and without worries, and are sensitive to the emotional benefit that the new campaign offers, namely peace of mind and a life without worries. All these groups strive in common for security and peace of mind. The campaign showed a happy couple with no worries. If anything minor goes wrong, WFL is there to solve it. The slogan of the campaign was: 'you may rest assured'. The tone of voice of the campaign was humorous, slightly absurd and fresh. For consistency reasons, the two main characters were the same in all creative executions, the ads on radio and TV had very similar formats, a very recognisable tune ('always look on the bright side of life') was used in all spots, and the WFL logo was prominently shown.

Table 9.3 WFL image pre-test, objectives and results

18–34 year olds	Pre-test March 2010 (%)	Objectives 2010 (%)	Results 2010 (%)
Image parameters			
Exciting	27	40.3	44
Sympathetic	18	30	41
Modern	20	32.4	41
Is a happy, fun, playful game	19	31.2	44
Is a brand that is close to me	15	26.4	30
Is a game that fits me	15	26.4	39
I want to play the game	23	35.8	45
WFL increases my peace of mind	57	68.4	73
	Dec. 2009		
Motivation to play	24	40.6	44

Source: Nationale Loterij, Belgium.

The main campaign medium was radio. Radio advertising combines image and activation, and allows the brand to be cost-efficiently omnipresent for a long period. TV spots were used to effectively demonstrate the emotional proposition, and because the core target group of WFL are frequent viewers. WFL also sponsored music festivals and in that way reached more than 1 million youngsters during the summer of 2010. The Facebook page attracted more than 5000 new fans during this festival period. This resulted in the following media mix: TV, 42%; radio, 38%; event sponsorship, 18%; point-of-sale, 2%.

A campaign with a huge impact

Despite a continuing decrease in the number of retail outlets (−240 in 2010), the campaign realised impressive commercial results.

At the end of 2010, WFL turnover increased by 7.8% compared with 2010, thereby substantially exceeding the target increase of 1%. This accounts for an extra turnover of €4.9 million. Total sales of WFL in 2010 were €67.44 million. The penetration and conversion among the young target groups increased as projected (see Table 9.3). Per campaign wave, sales increased substantially, but also, in between waves, sales remained high, a remarkable result for an impulse product (see Figure 9.8).

Table 9.3 shows the image of WFL in March 2010 (just before the campaign), the objectives with respect to a number of relevant image parameters, and the results after the campaign. The campaign has improved the key image parameters substantially, well above the objectives. Table 9.4 shows brand awareness and commitment. Also, spontaneous brand awareness and commitment have evolved

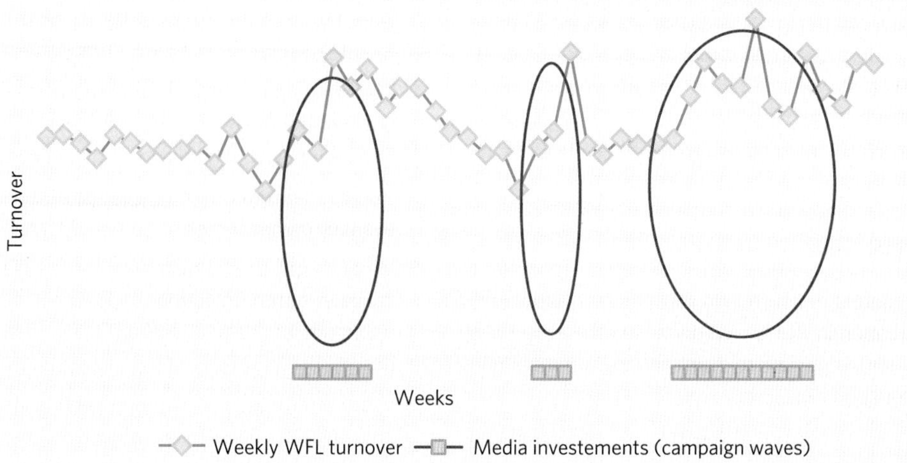

Figure 9.8 Evolution of sales during and in between campaign waves

Table 9.4 Spontaneous brand awareness and commitment: pre-test, objectives and results

18–34 year olds	End 2009	Objectives 2010	Results 2010
Spontaneous brand awareness (%)	53	56.8	60
Commitment (% committed users)	14.1	16.8	17

Table 9.5 Evolution of daily WFL sales

	Average (€)		During the campaign (index vs before the campaign)
	Before the campaign	During the campaign	
Monday	167 801	186 804	111
Tuesday	165 054	186 493	113
Wednesday	162 187	197 053	121
Thursday	198 377	226 481	114
Friday	**246 626**	**314 980**	**128**
Saturday	211 836	251 207	119

positively, well above the objectives. Table 9.5 shows the evolution of daily sales. Daily turnover has increased substantially and Friday is an even stronger selling day than before the campaign. Sales per retail outlet have increased by 13% between 2009 and 2010.

The campaign even succeeded in increasing the buying behaviour of heavy WFL users. While on average a WFL payer played 22.6 times during the last nine months of 2009 and 23.6 times during the last nine months of 2010, the heavy user segment played 61.9 times in the same months in 2009 and 82.9 times in 2010. This is a remarkable increase, given the fact that heavy users account for the vast bulk of WFL turnover. One of the aims of the campaign was to attract new younger players without losing the traditional, older customers. Also in that respect, the campaign was successful. The penetration in the 35+ segment increased from 14.7% in 2009 to 17.2% in 2010.

The return on investment (ROI) of the campaign was impressive. The campaign budget was €2.52 million. The increase in turnover between 2009 and 2010 was €4.9 million. This implies that the campaign cost was only half the sales increase. Since the gross margin on WFL is ➔

37.4%, this means an increase in margin of €1.83 million. Thus, 72% of the campaign cost was paid back by the end of the campaign. More than half a million people in Belgium played WFL in 2010, which is 22% of the 18–34 population, and 40 000 more than in 2009.

In 2011, the WFL campaign received a Belgian Gold Effie award.

QUESTIONS

1. Given the context in which Win for Life was relaunched, and the situation in 2010, would you say the objectives of the two campaigns are relevant and legitimate and in line with consumer insights?

2. Are the measurement of the results of the campaign consistent with the objectives? Why or why not?

3. Were the objectives of the campaign ambitious and were their results impressive? In other words, did Win for Life deserve to receive an effectiveness award?

4. The case does not give any information on campaign pre-testing. Design a series of relevant pre-tests for the two campaigns: what will you measure and how?

5. Can you think of other relevant post-tests and campaign evaluation measures?

6. What might be the next step for the National Lottery? A new communications approach, a new creative approach, new objectives and effectiveness measures?

7. Imagine that you had to launch Win for Life in your own country. Would your communications strategy be different? Would you set your objectives and measure your results differently? Why or why not?

Sources: www.nationale-loterij.be (accessed 15 June 2012), information provided by Marc Frederix (Nationale Loterij), Win for Life Effie case.

References

1   Rossiter, J.R. and Percy, L. (1997), *Advertising Communications and Promotion Management*. New York: McGraw-Hill.

2   Pickton, D. and Broderick, A. (2005), *Integrated Marketing Communications*. Harlow: Financial Times/Prentice Hall.

3   Ferrée, H. (1989), *Groot Inspiratieboek voor Creatieve Reclame* (*Great Inspiration Book for Creative Advertising*). Deventer: Kluwer Bedrijfswetenschappen.

4   Fill, C. (2002), *Marketing Communications: Contexts, Strategies and Applications*. Harlow: Financial Times/Prentice Hall.

5   van Raaij, F.W. (1989), 'How Consumers React to Advertising', *International Journal of Advertising*, 8(3), 261–73.

6   See also: de Houwer, J. (2001), 'A Structural and Process Analysis of the Implicit Association Test', *Journal of Experimental Social Psychology*, 37, 443–51; Maison, D. (2002), 'Using the Implicit Association Test to Study the Relation Between Consumers' Implicit Attitudes and Product Usage', *Asia Pacific Advances in Consumer Research*, 5, 650–54; Vantomme, D., Geuens, M., De Pelsmacker, P. and De Houwer, J. (2006), 'Explicit and Implicit Determinants of Fair-trade Buying Behaviour', *Advances in Consumer Research*, 33, 699–703; Vantomme, D., Geuens, M., De Houwer, J. and De Pelsmacker, P. (2005), 'Implicit Attitudes Toward Green Consumer Behaviour', *Psychologica Belgica*, 25(4), 217–239.

7   For an overview of physiological tests, see Poels, K. and De Witte, S. (2006), 'How to Capture the Heart? Reviewing 20 Years of Emotion Measurement in Advertising', *Journal of Advertising Research*, 46(1), 18–37.

8   MediaAnalyzer, 'Attention Tracking and Emotion Tracking, GRP – exploring media', September 2008, www.mediaanalyzer.com.

9   De Cock, B. and De Pelsmacker, P. (2001), 'Emotions Matter', in *ESOMAR, Excellence in International Research*. Amsterdam: ESOMAR, 63–88.

10 Aaker, D., Kumer, V. and Day, G. (2007), *Marketing Research*. New York: Wiley.

11 Aaker, D., Kumer, V. and Day, G. (2007), *Marketing Research*. New York: Wiley.

12 Zinkhan, G.M. and Gelb, B.D. (1986), 'What Starch Scores Predict', *Journal of Advertising Research*, 26(4), 23–6.

13 Duncan, T. (2008), *IMC: Using Advertising and Promotion to Build Brands*. Boston, MA: McGraw-Hill/Irwin.

14 De Pelsmacker, P. and Van Kenhove, P. (2005), *Marktonderzoek: Methoden en Toepassingen* (*Marketing Research: Methods and Applications*). Amsterdam: Pearson Education; Benelux Insites, (2002), www.insites.be; Stout, R. (1997), *Web Sites Stats: Tracking Hits and Analysing Traffic*. Berkeley, CA: McGraw-Hill.

15 Rossiter, J.R. and Percy, L. (1997), *Advertising Communications and Promotion Management*. New York: McGraw-Hill.

16 Due to confidentiality requirements, the country and companies involved are not given.

17 Due to confidentiality requirements, the names of the bank and supermarket are not given.

18 For modelling approaches in advertising research, see Leeflang, P., Wittink, D., Wedel, M. and Naert, P. (2000), *Building Models for Marketing Decisions*. Boston: Kluwer Academic; Hanssens, D.M., Parsons, L.F. and Schultz, R.L. (2001), *Market Response Models: Econometric and Time Series Analysis*. Norwell, MA: Kluwer Academic.

CHAPTER 10
Public relations

CHAPTER OUTLINE

Public relations as a communications tool

Target groups

Objectives and tasks

Instruments and channels

Budgets

Measuring effectiveness

Crisis communications

CHAPTER OBJECTIVES

This chapter will help you to:

- Understand the role of public relations in the company's communications effort
- Get an idea of the strengths and weaknesses of public relations, and the challenges it faces
- Distinguish the various target groups, objectives and tasks of public relations
- Get an overview of the instruments and channels used by public relations
- Learn about the nuts and bolts of good media relations
- Distinguish a number of public relations budgeting techniques
- Learn how to measure public relations effectiveness
- Communicate in times of crisis

Introduction

Traditionally, **public relations** (PR) is an activity which in most companies has been structurally separated from marketing communications. It originated in the function of 'press agent', the main activity of whom was to bridge the gap between the company's point of view and media coverage of the company's activities. Gradually, press agents became a vital part of the company's communications efforts targeted at various publics or stakeholders, and the activity of 'press relations' evolved into the 'public relations' function. Staying in touch and creating goodwill with all types of audiences has become an extremely sophisticated and complex task. This is illustrated by the fact that in most companies the PR function directly reports to the chief executive officer (CEO). However, not only do the type and number of target groups of PR exceed marketing communications target groups, but also the nature of the objectives is quite specific, as well as the tools and instruments used, although some of the latter are similar to those used in marketing communications. All in all, it is fair to say that PR is more complex than marketing communications, due to the variety of objectives and target groups it has to take into account.

PR also plays a vital role in integrating the company's communications efforts (see also Chapter 1). Integrated communications at the corporate level imply the creation of synergies between all communications tools, especially marketing communications and corporate communications. PR is a very important component of the latter.

Public relations as a communications tool

There are different definitions of public relations, which all stress one or more important aspects of this communications tool. Essentially, PR is a communications tool that is used to promote goodwill towards the firm as a whole.[1] It is the projection of the personality of the company, the management of reputation.[2] PR is the planned and sustained effort to establish and maintain good relationships, mutual understanding, sympathy and goodwill with **publics**, audiences or stakeholders.[3] It is those efforts that identify and close the gap between how the organisation is seen by its key publics and how it would like to be seen.[4] Publicity is the term used to describe the free media coverage of news about the company or its products, often as a result of PR efforts.

Publics are, besides customers and potential customers, groups of people that the company is not directly trying to sell products to (that is why these groups are sometimes called secondary target groups), but that are perceived as influencing opinions about the company. As such, publics can be considered as a component of the external company environment. The relations with these publics should be positive because they can be vital to the company's survival and success. Essential in most definitions of PR is that it is a two-way form of communication: the company learns from its publics and conveys information to them. Furthermore, like any other communications activity, PR should be a planned effort. It is also a major component of a successful integrated communications activity, since it covers a range of activities that can be linked to other elements of the communications mix,[5] such as the following:

- Creation and maintenance of corporate identity and image, by communicating the company's philosophy and mission through corporate advertising, open days, etc.
- Improving the company's standing as a good corporate citizen, by means of activities such as arts and sports sponsorship or community programmes.
- Maintaining good relations with the media, both for disseminating good news and in times of crisis.
- Attendance at trade exhibitions and the organisation of contacts with suppliers and intermediaries.

● Looking after internal communications, with the purpose of involving employees in the strategic priorities of the company.

PR is different from marketing communications in the strict sense of the word in a number of ways. Marketing communications tend to be commercial and short-term. Few marketers will jeopardise short-term benefits for the sake of long-term returns. Although PR executives recognise the importance of customer satisfaction and profits, and in that sense support core marketing communications efforts, their main concern is the long-term goodwill towards, and reputation of, the company as a whole. They want people to respect their organisation. As a result, marketers will always have to keep PR people focused on marketing objectives. On the other hand, PR professionals will have to challenge marketing people in terms of the effects of their actions on a broader public. The role of PR people is also to stress the importance of non-marketing audiences for the well-being of the company in the long run.[6] Good PR lays the groundwork, and creates the platform for successful marketing communications. The relation between corporate and marketing reputation is illustrated by the fact that most people seem to believe that a company that has a good reputation would not sell bad products, that old-established companies make the best products and that they would never buy products made by a company they have never heard of.

Although advertising, sales efforts and direct mailing on the one hand, and PR – more specifically the publicity generated by PR activity – on the other, can both have a similar influence on the reputation of a company and its products, there are a number of important differences between the two types of instruments. As compared with marketing communications, PR – and the resulting publicity – has a number of strengths and weaknesses. They are summarised in Figures 10.1 and 10.2.

PR targets important stakeholders and difficult-to-reach audiences such as opinion leaders, financial analysts and investors. Many of them are not interested in advertising or direct mailing, and even avoid it or are very sceptical towards it.[7] Furthermore, they are shielded from salespeople by their assistants. On the other hand, they are often interested in news and may be reached indirectly by the media exposure generated through PR activity. PR professionals can advise companies on important trends and on the consequences of corporate activities on marketing effectiveness. PR can present the company as a good citizen and, as such, contributes to the corporate image and reputation.

PR plays an important role in guiding the company through crises without too much damage to its reputation. Often, advertising and sales promotions are strictly regulated by governments. PR offers the opportunity of more message flexibility. PR is often relatively cost-effective

Figure 10.1 Strengths of public relations

Figure 10.2 Weaknesses of public relations

because the media coverage generated is free. Getting media coverage often enables the company to reach a variety of audiences and a large number of people at a fraction of the cost that would have been required in an advertising campaign.

The most important advantage of PR and the resulting media exposure over marketing communications tools may be that the former is generally considered to be more objective and therefore more believable in the perception of target groups. News is also generally more exciting, or is presented as such. Marketing communications, on the other hand, are paid for by the company, and the public are aware of that. This results in a certain cynicism about the bias in the message. As a result, PR is capable of breaking through the communications clutter more effectively.

BUSINESS INSIGHT
Hitachi: corporate compassion

Three Japanese Hitachi engineers visiting a subsidiary in the USA were killed and two were seriously injured when a truck accidentally drove into the restaurant where they were having dinner. Hitachi US responded quickly, formed a crisis management team and identified a crisis response leader. Information was released to employees and to the media as quickly as possible. The spokesman immediately expressed company concern for the victims and their families and for plant employees. He did not speculate about the causes of the accident. The company president was appropriately visible and involved. It was decided to invite all the Japanese families who wanted to come to the USA. According to Japanese tradition, they received flowers on their arrival. A day-long trip was organised to show the families where their relatives lived and where they died. They were allowed to collect the personal possessions of the victims from their rooms, which had been intentionally left untouched. A meeting was held with the lawyers investigating the cause of the accident. Internal communications were quick and overt by means of bulletin board messages, following the principle 'the more you try to hide, the worse things get'. The only false note in this otherwise well-organised and culturally fine-tuned crisis communications effort was the fact that the truck driver did not assume any responsibility for the accident, something that is, according to Japanese culture, incomprehensible.[8]

The major weakness of PR is the lack of control over the content of the press coverage of news releases. Evidently, the media have other priorities and other sources, and the published story may be quite different from the information disseminated by the PR department. The context and style of the original message may be substantially changed or completely lost. In advertising, for instance, the company has full control over the content of its communications.

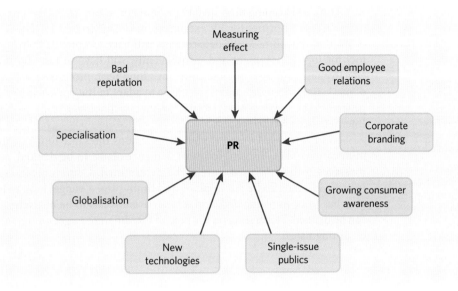

Figure 10.3 Trends and challenges in public relations

With PR, journalists act as gatekeepers: if a story is perceived as having not enough 'news value' it may not be published, especially in a period in which there is other important news to cover. The timing of ads and sales promotions is fully controlled by the company. The effectiveness of PR is hard to measure. Often, exposure measures, such as the amount of media coverage, are used, but they hardly say anything about the long-term effect of PR efforts on company goodwill or sales. Measuring the effectiveness of advertising is often more straightforward.

PR is of growing importance for companies. In the USA, three out of four companies have a PR department. The number of people working in PR is estimated to be 145 000. The growth of the PR industry is estimated to be in double digits.[9] In recent years, the UK PR market has grown by approximately 20% per year.[10] There are a number of trends that make PR an increasingly important communications tool. At the same time PR faces a number of challenges (Figure 10.3).[11]

The maintenance of good employee relations is considered to be increasingly vital. This implies effective communications between management and employees. Corporate branding is of growing importance (see also Chapter 2). PR plays a crucial role in corporate communications and, consequently, corporate brand-building. Growing consumer awareness leads to a stronger involvement of the public in the activities of companies, thereby increasing the need for proactive PR activity and crisis management. More and more 'single-issue' publics, such as animal liberation groups and consumer and environmental pressure groups, that use confrontation as a tactic, are emerging, and are seriously challenging the PR skills of companies.[12]

Events such as the opening of Eastern Europe and the former Soviet Union, as well as the globalisation of marketing activities in general, have caused substantial changes in the marketing environment. PR is an important tool in gaining an understanding of these changes, being aware of the influence of government regulations on marketing activity and laying the groundwork for effective market entry. PR departments are increasingly confronted with the need to operate globally and draw up international PR campaigns. PR activity is becoming increasingly specialised. In the past, PR firms tried to solve all the PR problems of a company. Nowadays, there is a growing trend of specialisation and niches in the PR support that companies need and, as a result, in the way in which PR companies or departments have to organise themselves.

PR suffers from a bad reputation stemming from the era in which PR activity was mainly associated with press conferences, manipulating the media and fancy parties for stakeholders. And although PR professionals view their activities as having strategic and corporate impact, many marketers classify PR as little more than a tactical ingredient of the promotional mix.[13]

Attracting and keeping high-quality personnel and improving the image of the PR profession have become priorities for PR executives and management in general. Measuring the effect of PR is a difficult task. PR departments will have to upgrade their function into a strategic tool for top management and, consequently, will have to develop the tools to prove their effectiveness in supporting the company's long-term profit base. PR, as with all other forms of marketing communications, will have to adapt to the opportunities and threats and, more generally, the environment created by new technologies such as business television, the Internet and smart telephony.

Good PR is based on a PR plan that contains the same fundamentals as any other communications plan. Target groups or audiences have to be defined, and the objectives and messages to be conveyed have to be determined. Communications channels, tools and instruments have to be put in place, and timing and a budget have to be decided on. The PR plan has to be implemented, and its effectiveness has to be measured. Different types of PR can be defined. Depending on the type of PR, different target groups, objectives and tools can be distinguished.

RESEARCH INSIGHT
Priorities for public relations research of academics and professionals

Using a Delphi research method, a 2007 study surveyed the attitudes and ideas of academic and professional PR experts and CEOs of PR companies worldwide. The study had four objectives: identify the gaps between academic research and industry needs; identify current and new trends in research from theorist and practitioner perspectives; map out the best way for knowledge to be exchanged; and define the research areas for which funding can be sought. Participants were asked to rank PR research topics in a priority order from 1 (top priority) to 10 (10th priority). The results were as follows (numbers in brackets refer to the average priority given by the respondents):[14]

1. PR's contribution to strategic decision-making, strategy development and realisation and efficient operation of organisations (2.37).
2. The value that PR creates for organisations through building social capital and managing key relationships (3.43).
3. The measurement and evaluation of PR both offline and online (4.17).
4. PR as a fundamental management function (4.35).
5. Professional skills in PR, analysis of the industry's need for education (4.68).
6. Research into standards of performance among PR professionals, the licensing of practitioners (5.90).
7. Management of corporate reputation, management of reputation (6.00).
8. Ethics in PR (6.29).
9. Integration of PR with other communications functions, the scope of PR practice, discipline boundaries (6.35).
10. Management of relationships (6.69).

Target groups, objectives and tasks

As indicated above, publics, audiences or stakeholders are groups of people or organisations to whom the company is not directly selling products, but whose favourable opinion can be vital for the company in the long run. Depending on the type of audience, different types of PR can be distinguished. They are summarised in Table 10.1.

Table 10.1 Audiences of different types of PR

Corporate				Marketing
Internal	External			
	Public affairs	Financial	Media	
Employees	General public	Investors	Television	Suppliers
Families of employees	Local community Government	Bankers Consultants	Radio Press	Distributors Competitors
Trade unions	Trade associations	Stock exchange	Trade press	Wholesalers
Shareholders	Pressure groups			Retailers

The first important distinction that can be made is between corporate and marketing PR. The main difference between the two is that **corporate PR** is mainly aimed at maintaining good relations and creating goodwill with all kinds of audiences who may be important for the company in the long run. In **marketing PR**, the direct or indirect profitability of the PR activity is more important. Marketing PR is targeted at commercial stakeholders, such as distributors, suppliers, competitors and potential customers, and is more in direct support of marketing communications. Evidently, in an environment of growing integrated communications, both types of PR will not be mutually exclusive, but will support one another.

The second important distinction is between internal and external corporate PR. **Internal PR** is aimed at internal stakeholders, such as employees and their families and shareholders. The latter could also be defined as an internal financial audience. **External PR** – the oldest form of PR activity – is directed towards various types of external target groups. Three important types of external corporate PR and PR target groups can be distinguished, namely public affairs, financial and media PR.

Apart from this typology, sometimes a distinction is made between direct and indirect PR. **Direct PR** activity is directly aimed at the stakeholders of interest, while **indirect PR** tries to reach them indirectly through other publics. In that respect, employees, consultants and especially the media can be considered as indirect PR audiences. Keeping good relations with the media, consultants and other opinion leaders is not important as such. It is because of their role as intermediate groups between the company and important 'end-audiences' that they are important PR target groups. It is no coincidence that media PR is the oldest and still a very important form of corporate PR.

BUSINESS INSIGHT
Smart Study = Money Management

A study by the Dutch National Institute for Finance Information among 2122 students revealed that the average Dutch student has a debt of €15 360 on graduation, a number that had increased by 25% over the previous four years. The study also showed that students knew surprisingly little about the consequences of borrowing money (e.g. interest rates and redemption terms) and that about 20% of Dutch students are always or regularly in the red. Building on these figures and taking into account that financial institutions in the wake of the financial crisis were pressured by governments to show responsibility, MasterCard decided to launch its 'Smart Study = Money

Management' PR campaign in order to teach students how to spend money wisely. This way, MasterCard aimed to show the authorities that it wanted to be part of the solution to mounting debt and not part of the problem.

The campaign consisted of teaching students how to spend money wisely via peer-to-peer communications. In other words, students taught other students in budget training sessions at universities across the Netherlands and spread the word further through local and student media. To avoid being accused of commercial benefit, MasterCard did not brand the campaign. MasterCard's logo, image or house style was not revealed; MasterCard was only mentioned as sponsor or facilitator. Student trainers, not MasterCard, organised and promoted the courses. They set up partnerships with the university's faculty and student organisations, and maintained local media relations. Each student gave at least one training session per month to a minimum of 15 students. Each of them also wrote a minimum of four media articles, blog posts, letters to editors or other external communications. This way, hundreds of thousands of people received budgeting tips.

Before the training started and the campaign was launched in the media, MasterCard presented the programme to different stakeholders, including MPs, civil servants at the Ministries of Finance, Social Affairs and Justice, consumer associations, the Dutch Association of Banks, the Dutch Merchants association and the Dutch Central Bank. The 'Smart Study = Money Management' campaign resonated well with students, the different stakeholders and the media. The campaign was well covered by the main Dutch newspapers, radio stations and on different websites, mentioning almost always the budgeting tips as well as MasterCard. At a cost of only €100 380, MasterCard was able to increase political goodwill enormously and the campaign opened several doors for MasterCard at a political and governmental level. The campaign received a Sabre Award for the best Benelux PR campaign in 2011. Because of its huge success, MasterCard decided to extend the campaign.[15]

Although employees can be a direct target group of PR activity, they are an important intermediate public too, because they are often in close contact with other audiences such as the general public, the local community, suppliers and distributors, etc. It is therefore vital that they should 'spread the good news' about the company. Therefore, internal PR should create goodwill with employees to motivate them to do so.

Finally, a specific type of PR activity is crisis management or crisis communications. It may involve different types of audiences, corporate and marketing, as well as internal and external ones. Crisis communications are covered in a separate section of this chapter.

Most PR objectives relate to giving information, influencing opinion and building or sustaining attitudes and feelings. Only seldom is PR directly aimed at changing behaviour. Although objectives can be similar across target groups, different emphasis can be put on different types of objectives, depending on the nature of the audience (Table 10.2).

Internal public relations

The main purpose of internal PR is to inform employees about the company's strategic priorities and the role they are playing in them, and to motivate them to carry out these objectives. Internal communications start with building a corporate identity and motivating and training the company's own personnel to behave accordingly in their contacts with external audiences. This should be a continuous concern, as discussed earlier (see Chapter 1). Additionally, employees should be informed about specific marketing actions or major decisions that affect them, to motivate them to accept the decisions and to co-operate in carrying them out. A bank that launches an advertising campaign to stress service quality should convince its own personnel to make quality of service a priority in their day-to-day contacts with customers. Otherwise the whole advertising campaign may contrast badly with the actual behaviour of the employees and may, as a result, be completely unbelievable.

Often the families of the personnel are also involved in the decisions taken, or in events that are employee-related. Organising open days and inviting friends and relatives of the personnel, for instance, may create a lot of goodwill and sympathy for the company among its employees.

Table 10.2 PR objectives and tasks

Corporate				Marketing
Internal	**External**			
	Public affairs	**Financial**	**Media**	
Information	Impact of trends	Information	Information	Support marketing agenda
Training	Public visibility	Credibility	Opinions	
Motivation	Information	Trust	Corporate image	New products
Building corporate identity	Opinions			Sponsorship
	Attitudes		Goodwill	Events
	Corporate image			
	Build goodwill			
	Influence decisions			

BUSINESS INSIGHT

KBC on-line: involving employees in an advertising campaign promoting online banking

KBC is one of the major Belgian banks. In 2000, it decided to launch an advertising campaign to stimulate online banking by switching regular customers to KBC on-line, a service that is free of charge and by which KBC customers can carry out their banking activities electronically. The online activation is done during a visit to the bank. The duration of the campaign ran from early 2000 to February 2003. During the first stage of the campaign, awareness and interest were built with the slogan 'Always your banker at hand'. The second stage focused upon the adoption of the new product: 'Don't be the last one to become a KBC on-liner.' During the last stage, the KBC on-line customer was reassured: 'Everything under control with KBC on-line'.

Especially during the early stages of the campaign, there was a risk that employees would not buy into the online idea. They may have been offended by the fact that they would be replaced by a computer, and they may have feared that, in the long run, their jobs could become redundant. Therefore, KBC involved the employees in the campaign in different ways. In the first stage of the campaign, the focus was on the importance of the availability of the personal banker. In TV spots, billboards and print ads, customers were shown in various circumstances, literally holding the hand of what appears to be their personal banker. The message is conveyed that online banking enables you to do your banking business wherever and whenever you want, but at the same time it stresses the point that human contact is indispensable. The mailings to customers were sent out from local branches to increase the link between the bank and its employees on the one hand, and the customers on the other. Each campaign stage and tool contained an opportunity (for both the employees and the customers) to engage in a personal conversation. All personnel received the campaign material six weeks before the start of the campaign so they could prepare themselves for an efficient personal follow-up to the mailing. The campaign took into account the potential negative fallout of advertising campaigns on the motivation of the employees, and tried to integrate internal PR and external communications to avoid negative side effects. The campaign was a considerable success and won a Belgian Gold Effie Award in 2003.[16]

Public affairs

Public affairs is a management function directed towards the societal and political relations of the company. It is aimed at continuously studying trends and issues related to government decision-making and opinions and attitudes of the general public. Good contacts with the general public and the local community are a part of the public affairs activity. The handling of the sinking of the Brent Spar oil platform and the *Exxon Valdez* disaster are examples of events that required consistent PR activity to restore faith and goodwill among the general public or local communities. The support of good causes by a company is aimed at restoring or maintaining goodwill with the general public. Public affairs also encompasses the relations with local, regional, national and international governments and regulatory bodies, as well as pressure groups of all kinds, such as ecological, ethnic, linguistic and consumer interest groups. It attempts to influence the decision-making of important stakeholders, or to respond to trends and changes in opinions and attitudes in such a way that the long-term goodwill of the company benefits from it. For instance, the World Federation of Advertisers (WFA) is an international lobbying group that tries to influence government regulations on promotional activity, and tries to monitor and/or counter the influence of pressure groups on behalf of the world advertising community.

Financial public relations

Financial audiences are those groups that are potential shareholders, investors or (potential) advisers to shareholders and investors, such as financial consultants and banks. They are vital for the establishment of the long-term money-raising potential of a company. A crucial objective of these audiences is to build and maintain the confidence that is necessary to give the company an image of an interesting investment. The preparation and presentation of a sound financial report, the stock exchange introduction of a company, financial communications accompanying mergers and acquisitions are all examples of **financial PR**. The European cinema group Kinepolis, for instance, was able to attract massive numbers of new shareholders as a result of a successful introduction of the company's shares on the stock exchange.

Media public relations

Since the media are the most important intermediate public, developing and maintaining good contacts with radio, TV and the (trade) press are often extremely important. All the objectives to be met by end-publics are also important in **media PR**: to inform, build favourable attitudes, create a positive image and a reservoir of goodwill, and to ensure coverage of marketing-related news (Photo 10.1). Indirectly, media PR is aimed at generating favourable publicity about the company, its products and brands and, more generally, all events and projects that support the image of the company and its marketing objectives.

Good media PR can result in positive comments during the introduction of a product, can create goodwill for the company's activities and can generate publicity for a range of organisational events, activities and sponsorship programmes. In the aftermath of the A Class moose test problems when a Mercedes A Class model overturned while undertaking a traditional moose test, Mercedes was able to neutralise the bad publicity quickly by means of careful PR campaigns directed at the specialised press. Obtaining media attention for sponsorship projects can generate publicity that is, in terms of media exposure, worth much more than the initial investment in the event. In times of crisis, the media are a crucial audience in order to avoid or neutralise negative 'fallout' from the event that caused the crisis. Bad handling of media relations caused the Perrier problem (benzene in Perrier mineral water) to evolve into a major wave of bad publicity that resulted in enormous image and commercial damage to the brand and the company.

Photo 10.1 Google creates a positive image
Source: Getty Images.

BUSINESS INSIGHT
Ariel and the Palestinians

'We cannot tolerate that, without our permission, political messages are linked with one of our products' was the official reaction of Procter & Gamble to a campaign run by the Palestine Action Platform. This pressure group launched a print advertising campaign in which a fist holds a bloodstained Palestinian shawl, accompanied by the slogan 'How will Ariel get this clean?' The purpose of the campaign was to make the public aware of the Palestinian problem and the alleged role of the former Israeli Prime Minister, Ariel Sharon, using Procter & Gamble's well-known brand of washing powder. The campaign appeared in national newspapers, and Procter & Gamble first sent friendly letters to the organisation and to the media, asking them to stop the campaign immediately. The action group was not impressed, and continued its campaign: 'It is obvious that only Mr Sharon is implied, not P&G.' Procter & Gamble then threatened to start legal action if the campaign was not stopped. The company stated that 'we as a company do not want to take a stand on the political situation in the Middle East. Therefore we do not tolerate that our brand name, for which we are responsible, is used in this manner.' By that time all major media had covered the dispute.[17] Eventually, the campaign was withdrawn. Sometimes companies are confronted with unexpected publicity that can damage their reputation or that of their brands. Fast and well-balanced PR activity is then called for.

Marketing public relations

Marketing PR is directly related to selling products and/or supporting brands. As such, it is a part of marketing communications for which often product or brand managers are responsible. Marketing PR can be used to support the launch of a new product, for instance by inviting the trade press to test-drive a new car, or to see to it that a new CD gets enough 'airplay'. It can also be used to support and revive existing products, for instance by means of creating an event when the 50th shop is opened, or after the first 100 000 cars of a certain model have been sold. Sponsorship and special events can be used as PR tools to improve the relationship with suppliers and distributors, by offering free tickets for sports or arts events. Restaurants

Photo 10.2 Longines talks to stakeholders
Source: Getty Images.

may invite journalists from the specialised press to encourage them to write a positive article and, as a result, boost sales. All these examples illustrate that marketing PR is an activity that is largely integrated with both corporate PR and other tools of the communications mix.

Depending on the problem and the objective, publics will have to be divided into primary and secondary audiences. Public relations efforts will be more intense towards primary target groups (Photo 10.2). Launching a new product, for instance, will generally imply more efforts towards the marketing PR target groups, the media and the general public than towards financial audiences or the government. Furthermore, an individual can belong to more than one public at a time. As a result, consistent PR communications across audiences is vital to avoid conveying contradictory messages to the same members of different publics.

BUSINESS INSIGHT
Sales and marketing PR

The sales team can be motivated to feed the PR department with interesting stories that can be a starting point for marketing-derived and marketing-supporting PR activity. The following sales events can be considered:[18]

- *Prestige orders*. Orders from famous companies or contracts relating to special projects that are themselves in the news.
- *Problem-solving orders*. Sales of products that have provided the solution for a particularly demanding need.
- *Added value contracts*. The product has made the lives of customers and employees more agreeable.
- *Unusual orders*. Products used at famous locations or in places of interest.
- *Sympathetic associations*. Selling products in a situation of strong human interest appeal or related to a good cause of general interest.

Instruments and channels

PR professionals use a multitude of instruments and channels to reach their objectives. The instruments used may be similar for different target groups and objectives, but some of them are specifically suited for specific target groups and objectives. Table 10.3 summarises a number of instruments and channels.

Internal public relations

A special category of PR tools and techniques is the ones used in internal PR. **Internal PR** should ideally be a two-way communications activity, in which mainly 'oral' communications techniques will be used. But other tools are of increasing importance.[19]

Personal and oral communications

Structured consultation is a crucial factor in internal PR. To count on a spontaneous and proactive attitude on the part of employees to enter a manager's office (even if the door is permanently open and the atmosphere is inviting) is insufficient. Two-way communications between managers and employees and communications among employees should be properly organised. By means of internal presentations, managers can clarify new strategic directions or important organisational changes and the role that employees play in effectuating them. Besides an obvious didactical purpose, training programmes (internally or externally) can

Table 10.3 PR instruments and channels

Corporate					Marketing
Internal	**External**				
		Public affairs	**Financial**	**Media**	
Consultation	Corporate advertising	Corporate advertising	Press kit		Product placement
Open-door policies				Press release	
Internal presentations	Annual report	Annual report	Press conference		Product events
Training programmes	Corporate events	Meetings			Sponsorship
Team projects		Newsletters	Interviews		Meetings
Team meetings	Sponsorship		Video or radio news release		Newsletters
Social activities	Lobbying				
Direct mailing	Meetings				
Bulletin boards	Newsletters				
Newsletters or video	Flyers, brochures				
Company television					
Annual reports					
Idea (suggestion) boxes					
Surveys					
House-style material					

enhance internal communications among employees because they provide the structured setting and the opportunity to communicate issues that are otherwise neglected. The same goes for team meetings, projects and social activities. An example of the latter are team-building activities, such as go-karting, paintball, exotic trips or survival weekends.

Communications through media

Direct mailing or internal e-mail can be an effective tool of internal communications. Bulletin boards, on the other hand, are not so effective. They are hardly noticed and people tend to walk past them without looking. In-house newsletters are a frequently used tool and allow the diffusion of information of a less urgent nature. Company TV narrowcast through TV sets at places in the company that are frequented by a lot of people (restaurants, halls, etc.) are excellent means of rapid diffusion of essential information. Annual reports, both financial and social, can be distributed to all personnel. Pens, noteblocks, coffee cups, placemats, mousepads, etc., can support the logos or slogans of a major internal communications campaign.

Public affairs

The purpose of corporate advertising is to reinforce the attitudes towards the company and/or its products. This type of advertising is often mainly affective, and is seldom used to convey information or to elicit sales. It is mainly targeted at the general public or broad audiences. It is a PR tool that is often used to reinforce the corporate image. Companies also use different types of publications to inform publics and/or build a favourable image with target audiences, namely newsletters, flyers, brochures and annual reports. Corporate events sponsorship is used to enhance the corporate image. The latter technique is discussed later (see Chapter 11).

Lobbying is the activity that companies undertake to influence the decisions of governmental bodies or the opinion of pressure groups in a positive direction. Lobbying implies giving information, negotiating, influencing complex decision-making units, and getting the best out of it for the company. Often, lobbying is done by specialised companies. It is an increasingly important business, in which a growing number of lobbyists are employed.

RESEARCH INSIGHT
Agenda-setting as a PR tool

Most of what consumers and stakeholders know about companies and the issues that surround them comes from the news media. There has been a tremendous growth in the volume of business news that appears in the media. The selection by journalists of the issues to cover or not to cover significantly influences the opinions and perceptions of the public. The specific ability to influence the salience of topics, attributes of these topics and images among the public by making them salient in the media is called agenda-setting. Agenda-setting theory and research lead to the following 'rules':[20]

- The amount of news about a company that appears in the news media is positively related to the public's awareness of the company.

- The amount of news coverage devoted to particular attributes of a company is positively related to the proportion of the public that defines the firm by those attributes; if a company mainly receives press coverage about its products, it will primarily be known through its products.

- The more positive (negative) that media coverage is for a particular attribute, the more positively (negatively) members of the public will perceive that attribute.

- The agenda of substantive and affective attributes associated with a company in business news coverage primes the public's attitude and opinion about the company; if the news coverage is positive (negative) about an important characteristic of the company or its activities, the whole company will benefit (suffer) from it.

- Organised efforts to communicate a corporate agenda will result in a significant degree of correspondence between the attribute agenda of the company and the news media.

The last point is particularly important for media PR. Media PR can indeed make a difference. Company news releases are estimated to influence as much as between 25% and 80% of news content. A substantial number (some say more than 50%) of the news stories in newspapers are substantially based on press releases. One study found that among the entire population of Fortune 500 companies, those with substantial press rooms on the Web were ranked much higher on the Fortune list.[21] It is also worth noting that a news story in the general news section of a newspaper is often more friendly and positive than a similar story in the business section. News media have a fascination with celebrities and elites: 45% of a company's reputation can be attributed to the CEO. Consequently, PR activity aiming at news coverage devoted to the company should be separated from PR campaigns focusing upon the CEO.

Financial public relations

Meetings, newsletters and corporate advertising can also be directed towards financial publics. But even more important are the annual and financial reports giving bankers and potential investors the necessary information on the basis of which a sound financial reputation can be developed.

Media public relations

The purpose of media PR is to generate publicity and, in that way, reach other important audiences. Publicity results from the fact that the media cover events that have some news value, or write articles on issues that are company-related. Unless something special happens – normally unexpected and not so positive for the company – the media are not going to write or report positive news about the company. Usually, professional PR activity is necessary to draw the attention of the media.

The instruments of media PR are **press kits** and **press releases**, and their audio-visual counterparts Video News Releases (VNRs) and Radio News Releases (RNRs). A press kit is a set of documents, containing photos, reports and a press release, which is sent to journalists or presented at a press conference. A press release is a document that contains the material that the company would like to see covered in the press. VNRs and RNRs are audio-visual news releases put on video or audio tape and sent to TV or radio stations free of charge for unrestricted use.[22] They are composed in such a way that excerpts can be broadcast immediately, thereby ensuring that the message reaches the audience undistorted. Many checklists have been proposed on how to write and present a good press release or a good newspaper article in general. The essentials are summarised in Table 10.4.

By means of press conferences and interviews the company can comment on the issues that it considers important and try to present them as 'news'. However, in this over-informed society, not many things are 'news'. Companies should avoid falling into the 'marketing myopia' trap concerning the news value of 'important' company events. What is news to a certain medium depends on the characteristics of the message and the medium itself, and on the way the news is presented. Table 10.5 lists some rules of good media relations.

Table 10.4 Writing a news release

- Indicate the release date
- Answer the following questions in every news story: who, what, why, where and when
- Focus and clarity: know what you want to say
- The lead paragraph: structure your story – get the main news points in the first paragraph
- News story body: flesh out the details – use short paragraphs with only one point per paragraph
- Journalistic style: use short sentences and active verbs
- Imitation: follow the style and construction of existing articles
- Completeness: document all the facts and quote from reliable sources
- Editorialising: do not give your opinion
- Names: use proper style for spelling out names
- Include illustrative materials
- Closing: add a final paragraph
- Editing: review your copy twice, then review it again
- Accuracy and simplicity: strive for a perfect news release
- Contact details: give details of the person who can be contacted

Sources: Based on Smith, J. (1995), *The New Publicity Kit*. New York: Wiley; Pickton, D. and Broderick, A. (2001), *Integrated Marketing Communications*. Harlow: Financial Times/Prentice Hall; Duncan, T. (2002), *IMC: Using Advertising and Promotion to Build Brands*. Boston, MA: McGraw-Hill.

Table 10.5 Rules of good media relations

Learn about what a medium considers newsworthy:

- Make sure the story is accurate
- Only timely stories or those on the latest developments are news – old facts are of no use
- The facts or news of an event should be perceived as important by the readers of the medium
- Everything that deviates from the ordinary is potential news – everyday events are not news
- Facts endorsed by an authority (CEO or marketing manager) are perceived as more important than facts presented by a junior employee
- Human interest is important: to whom does it happen; who is involved; how important are they; is the story fun and/or emotionally engaging and does it strike a chord?
- Tension or drama created by conflicting points of view attracts media attention
- Include the name and phone number of a contact person who can answer questions
- Do not expect a medium to copy your release as presented – it will be checked with other sources and modified

Sources: Based on Burnett, J. and Moriarty, S. (1998), *Introduction to Marketing Communication*. Upper Saddle River, NJ: Prentice Hall; Duncan, T. (2002), *IMC: Using Advertising and Promotion to Build Brands*. Boston, MA: McGraw-Hill.

Marketing public relations

Product event sponsorship, i.e. sponsoring an activity in which the product plays a major role (for instance, the Camel Trophy), is discussed later (see Chapter 11). Newsletters distributed to retailers, suppliers and other business contacts can be important instruments of PR, complementing and reinforcing salespeoples' efforts and sales promotion activity. Placing products in TV shows or movies is an increasingly popular type of communication that is at the crossroads of PR and sponsorship.

BUSINESS INSIGHT
Organising buzz to launch a film and a CD

The Da Vinci Code

Even before the movie based on Dan Brown's book was released in 2006, it succeeded in generating a lot of free publicity. The book takes the form of a mystery, and suggests that the classical Catholic interpretation of the Bible has been wrong for centuries. Religion-based films always stir up emotions, and Sony Pictures built a whole buzz marketing project to generate interest and 'rumour around the launch'. Sony set up a website (www.davincidialogue.com) on which it invited experts in Roman Catholicism to react to the criticisms voiced by the Catholic Church. In the movie trailers, some letters were brighter than others. If you collected them, you could form the words 'seek the codes', referring to a website www.seekthecodes.com. The website was a blog of a certain Lisa S. who claimed to have found many more hidden messages in the communication about the movie, and urged the visitor to participate in the game 'The Da Vinci Code Quest'. All of this was set up by Sony. Of course, Sony did not have to create a hype, it just had to support an existing one. Before the movie was released, almost 50 million people had already read the book.[23]

VantagePoint (Deus)

The new CD of the popular Belgian rock band Deus, 'Vantage Point', was released mid-April 2008. During the period before this release, a lot of publicity was generated. One week before the release, the CD could be heard in streaming on the Heineken website. This was not promoted but, as was to be expected, a music journalist picked it up and wrote about it. The publisher of the CD reacted angrily and demanded the site be closed. Many newspapers and radio stations reported this incident. Journalists were also forbidden by court order to publish interviews with Tom Barman, frontman of Deus, at a penalty of €25 000. Obviously, a lot of angry articles were written about this controversy, and it was a headline in the TV news. The newspaper *Le Soir* broke the embargo, published the interview and added three pages of comments. By the day of the release, there was probably no single Belgian who did not know the new CD was out.[24]

Budgets

PR should be operating within the same discipline that applies to other business functions. This implies that a budget has to be fixed, and that measurable objectives should be defined. Different budgeting techniques can be applied (Table 10.6).[25]

Budgets may be based on **historical comparison**, i.e. on what has been spent in previous periods, possibly adjusted as a function of changed circumstances. New product launches may result in increased budgets; less competition may imply lower budgets. Overall, this method seldom leads to sound budgeting. Maybe the historical starting figure was inappropriate, or the company is doing so well that the PR budget can easily be reduced. Most importantly, there is a lack of strategic focus: by not taking into account the changing environment, great PR opportunities or dangerous threats calling for PR action may be overlooked. In the **resources costing** method, management decides what resources are needed (an extra press officer, or an event co-ordinator) and calculates the costs implied. This method suffers from similar weaknesses to the previous one, although PR needs are to a certain extent taken into account.

In **action costing**, a PR programme or activity is planned, and the cost to carry it out is calculated. This method has the virtue of starting from the task to be accomplished, but lacks long-term perspective. The **competitive tendering** method is very similar to the previous one.

Table 10.6 PR budgeting techniques

- Historical comparison
- Resources costing
- Action costing
- Competitive tendering
- Income proportion
- Industry comparison
- Capitation rating

A PR programme is decided on and different PR agencies are requested to file a proposal and a budget. In the **income proportion** method a pre-specified proportion of margin or sales is devoted to PR. This method suffers from the same weakness as the historical comparison method. There is a lack of strategic focus, and the PR budget grows with sales – generally a situation in which less PR activity is needed. In contrast, if there is a decline in sales, PR budgets decrease at a time during which they may be needed most. In **industry comparison**, the industry average is used as a benchmark to decide the PR budget. Again, there is a lack of strategic focus, and no link with a pre-specified task.

In the **capitation rating or achievement targeting** method, audiences to be reached and objectives to be achieved are defined. For instance, a 30% awareness and a 70% favourable attitude with the general public and financial stakeholders by the end of the year may be the goals. Experience with other communications tools, such as advertising and direct mailing, may be used to calculate the budget required to achieve these objectives. This method is probably one of the most useful. However, as for all marketing communications activities, PR is not an exact science, and the objectives to be achieved are often long-term oriented. Therefore it is difficult to set a PR budget. However, PR agencies increasingly face situations in which they are paid by results rather than on a mark-up basis.[26]

Measuring public relations results

Similar to most other communications instruments, the effectiveness of a PR campaign can only be measured if clear objectives have been defined. These objectives have to be measurable and related to the PR activity. This implies that short-term or long-term awareness, opinion and/ or attitude or goodwill changes will have to be measured with the targeted publics. Evolution of sales or market share is seldom a good indicator, since they are not the main target objectives of PR activity. Furthermore, they are to a large extent influenced by other instruments of the marketing and communications mix. The result of PR activity can be assessed by means of three categories of performance measures: input, output and achievement indicators:[27]

- **Input indicators** measure PR efforts, such as the number of news stories disseminated, the number of interviews given, trade meetings organised, supermarkets visited or brochures sent. Input indicators measure efforts and not results. Therefore they are largely insufficient as measures of PR effectiveness. Nevertheless, they can be useful, since they can give a first indication of the activity undertaken.
- **Output indicators** measure the result of the PR activity in terms of media coverage or publicity. Examples of such measures are the press space or TV time devoted to the company, its events or brands, the length of the stories, the tone and news value of the headlines, readership/ viewership levels, opportunity to see, tone of coverage, etc. Again, although output measures

may be useful indicators of the result of PR activity, they do not give any information on how well the real objectives have been achieved.

- **Achievement indicators** measure the extent to which a pre-specified objective has been met with a public of interest. They are very similar to some of the measures that are being used in the assessment of advertising effectiveness. Examples include: the share of the target audience that has been reached, changes in awareness and knowledge, changes in opinions and attitudes, evolution of the image and goodwill of the company, and the extent to which behaviour has changed.

Communications in times of crisis

A special type of circumstances in which PR play an extremely important role is when the company faces an unforeseen crisis. By nature, a crisis is an event or a series of events that cannot be planned in advance. Crises can have multiple causes. A company's product may be found to contain toxic material, as in the Perrier case, a sinking ship like the *Exxon Valdez* may pollute the environment, a new car model like the Mercedes A may fail to pass the moose test, or a company executive may get involved in a personal or a financial scandal. Whether a crisis is a 'Cobra' (a sudden disaster) or a 'Python' (a slow-burning crisis or crisis creep),[28] good PR strategy should always take the possibility of a crisis into account and be prepared for it. A set of rules and procedures should be put in place well before any crisis emerges, as a result of which at least a scenario of crisis management is in place in the event of a suddenly emerging problem. Crises often turn into nightmares as a result of the lack of well-established procedures, which often have to do with the handling of external and internal communications. Crises are expected to take place more frequently than before. All kinds of audiences, like consumer interest groups and the media, watch companies more closely, and modern communications technology results in a more rapid dissemination of the news on company incidents. Therefore, preparing for crisis management is an increasingly important task for PR professionals.

An important factor in crisis management is the way in which a company behaves and communicates *in tempore non suspecto*, i.e. in the pre-crisis period. It is most important to create a reservoir of goodwill. Some rules of conduct are mentioned in Table 10.7.[29]

To know is to like. There is a strong correlation between knowing a company and liking it. Building awareness can be done most effectively by means of intensive communications with all important target groups. Target groups are not enemies or nuisances, but people who may support the company when things go wrong. Therefore, when these people have a problem or need assistance, a helping hand will not be forgotten when the company needs them. Telephone calls and letters should be responded to promptly so that audiences know that they are important to the company. Do not expect people with whom you have not communicated for a long period to remember you and offer help during a crisis.

Table 10.7 Pre-crisis communications rules

- Communicate
- Keep in touch and be responsive
- Do not act as if problems do not exist
- Build trust by communicating
- Build brand equity
- Build scenarios for the unexpected

Source: Based on Marconi, J. (1992), *Crisis Marketing: When Bad Things Happen to Good Companies.* Chicago: Probus.

The company should not pretend that problems do not exist. It has to show confidence and knowledge, but also humility. People with complaints may be disregarded, but the complaints will not go away and will rebound on the company in times of crisis. In many cases, people have only limited contact with the company, often if they have a problem or a complaint. The way in which the company responds to their problem will largely determine the way they feel about the company. Trust has to be built by communicating, being honest and being a good corporate citizen. Image-building is a long-term and sometimes expensive process, the return on which becomes visible only when the reservoir of goodwill is needed to compensate for the negative image caused by a crisis. Building brand equity is important. A positive corporate image can often be established most effectively through well-known and highly valued brands.

Finally, a company has to learn to prepare and build scenarios for the unexpected. Although many crises cannot be predicted, the likelihood of some of them can be taken into account. If you operate oil tankers, one of them may sink, causing great damage to the environment; if you operate a steel mill, a serious accident may occur; if you manufacture drugs, people may die as a result of a human error in manufacturing, as in the B Braun incident in which two babies died as a result of a lethal confusion of ingredients and labels. In the pre-crisis or scanning phase, the company should make contingency plans. In a broader context, an **issues audit** should be carried out. Issues are those potential areas that could have an important impact upon the operations of the company. The aim of an issues audit is to identify all that might be of consequence and help the company react to it and to plan ahead.[30] In general, a crisis can be prepared for by building contingency crisis management plans. Table 10.8 presents a checklist for preparing for a crisis.

In spite of all the preparations and the investment in goodwill, a crisis may occur and damage the company's image overnight as a result of mishandling the crisis. Often this counter-productive approach has to do with the way in which communications are organised – or, more often, not organised – during the impact of the crisis.

During a crisis, the following rules have to be implemented:[31]

- *Designate a single spokesperson.* Often, the damage is done during the first few hours and days of a crisis when all kinds of company executives give their – often contradictory – assessment of the facts. Every employee that comments speaks for the company.

Table 10.8 Preparing for and handling a crisis

- Prepare a list of issues, and their potential impact, to be circulated – which crises can occur?
- Identify areas of concern and of opportunity
- Monitor potential legislation that could affect markets
- Establish which publics should be taken into account
- Identify the executive responsible for leading on each issue
- Set up a crisis management team in advance
- Is the crisis management team well trained?
- Incident facilities are needed at all company locations
- Use simulations to test procedures – fine-tune all policies and procedures in 'peacetime'
- Establish a well-equipped crisis communications centre
- Develop and train your company spokespeople
- Develop policies that clarify how decisions will be made
- Provide each member of the crisis communications team with detailed background data on the company

Source: Based on Haywood, R. (1998), *Public Relations for Marketing Professionals*. London: Macmillan Business; Seymour, M. and Moore, S. (2000), *Effective Crisis Management: Worldwide Principles and Practices.* London and New York: Cassell; Anthonissen, P. (2002), *Murphy Was an Optimist.* Tielt: Lannoo.

- *Tell your story first and be honest.* It is much more difficult to neutralise rumours or to defend yourself against allegations than it is to give a clear overview of the facts first. Furthermore, it is counter-productive to lie, since pressure groups or the media will find out sooner or later, with even more consequent harm to the company's image.

- *Never go 'off the record'.* There should only be one story which is the same for everybody. Act as if all questions and answers will be made public.

- *Keep your employees informed*, to avoid rumours that take on a life of their own and that are fed by the employees' speculations. Communicate internally and externally, in parallel.

- *Position your company* or products in a larger context, stressing the positive elements, to divert attention from the element that caused the crisis.

- *Details.* Give as much information about the incident as possible.

- *Compassion.* Show understanding and regret, and make apologies.

- *Reassurance.* Everything is under control, there is no further danger.

- *What are we doing about it?* Present in-depth research by an independent organisation.

After the crisis, the company enters the readjustment phase and has to rebuild a new reservoir of goodwill, based on the same principles discussed before.

BUSINESS INSIGHT
Fortis blunders during financial crisis

On Friday afternoon, 26 September 2008, the CEO of Fortis Bank and Insurance held a press conference to state that there was nothing wrong with the bank's solvency and liquidity. A couple of hours later he had to step down, and less than 48 hours later the Belgian and Dutch governments had to intervene to prevent Fortis from going bankrupt. One week later, the French banking group Paribas stepped in to partially take over Fortis Bank. These communications mistakes undermined the credibility of Fortis with its stakeholders and destroyed its carefully built good reputation. Following this disastrous weekend, Fortis decided to withdraw its shares from the stock exchange for a couple of days. This withdrawal lasted one and a half weeks. A couple of weeks later, one of the major TV channels in Belgium aired a programme called 'The big money debate'. The CEOs of all major banks were present, but Fortis sent a lower-level manager. Crisis communications experts claim that this would have been the ideal moment for Fortis and its CEO to show that they took their responsibility seriously and were not hiding from their stakeholders. Also, in the negotiations between Paribas and the Dutch and Belgian governments, it was unclear what the role of Fortis had been. The bank did not communicate clearly about this and this deteriorated further its already tainted reputation. To add insult to injury for its shareholders, who lost a lot of money due to the Fortis crash, news got out that various top managers were granted multi-million-euro bonuses, even during the 27–28 September negotiations. Finally, in the same period, Fortis held a luxurious and expensive party in Monaco in honour of its agents. In normal circumstances this would have gone unnoticed, but at a time when many shareholders and customers of the bank felt uncertain and cheated, the party triggered a new wave of indignation and negative media stories. Fortis broke many rules of good crisis behaviour and communications in this period, even to the extent that communications experts feel that the reputation of the financial group is so damaged that it will have to be replaced by a different corporate identity altogether.[32]

IMC INSIGHT
Integrating PR in IMC

PR is most frequently used to support the corporate image. However, marketing communications can also be reinforced by PR efforts, and PR efforts can build upon other marketing communications campaigns. Publicity can be generated following sales efforts and successes: winning an important account, selling to well-known non-profit organisations or establishing links with famous organisations or events. Sponsorship efforts can be combined with PR and advertising to build powerful events that generate a lot of publicity. Sponsored celebrities can be used for corporate hospitality, reinforcing sales efforts, corporate identity and image-building, and in advertising. PR activities such as annual meetings, events and points of view can be announced through mass media advertising. Exhibitions and trade fairs can be used to hold press conferences, announcing new products, company news, etc., and to organise corporate hospitality events. Opening a new store or changing store appeal and image can be a starting point for organising events and generating publicity. In general, PR can reinforce the awareness and the corporate reputation effect of many marketing and communications activities with a variety of stakeholders.

Summary

PR is the management of reputation. It is about building and maintaining long-term goodwill vis-à-vis a large variety of audiences and stakeholders. Depending on the nature of these stakeholders, different types of PR can be distinguished. Marketing PR is directed towards marketing audiences and mainly supports marketing communications objectives. Corporate PR, such as public affairs, financial and media PR, supports corporate image and corporate reputation. A special type of PR activity is internal PR by means of which employees and shareholders are informed and/or motivated to co-operate in achieving the goals of the marketing and corporate communications plans. A broad variety of tools and media are used in PR, ranging from personal and oral communications in internal PR, to press releases, corporate advertising, direct mailing and annual reports in corporate PR. A specific task of PR is communicating in times of crisis. Building goodwill by means of pre-crisis PR is essential to limit the fallout from a crisis situation, although PR activity during the crisis is equally important.

REVIEW QUESTIONS

1. What is the role of public relations in the communications mix, and what are its strengths and weaknesses?
2. What are the trends that influence public relations?
3. Who are the target groups of public relations?
4. What are the objectives of each type of PR activity?
5. What are the tools of internal communications?
6. What are the rules and techniques of good media public relations?
7. Compare the different PR budgeting techniques and their advantages and disadvantages.
8. How can the effectiveness of PR campaigns be assessed?
9. What are the basic rules of good crisis communications?

Further reading

Anthonissen, P. (2008), *Crisis Communication: Practical PR Strategies for Reputation Management and Company Survival.* London: Kogan Page.

Meerman Scott, D. (2008), *The New Rules of Marketing and PR: How to Use News Releases, Blogs, Podcasting, Viral Marketing and Online Media to Reach Buyers Directly.* Hoboken, NJ: Wiley.

Ruff, P. and Stittle, J. (2003), *Managing Communications in a Crisis.* Aldershot and Bunlinston, VT: Gower.

Schenbler, I. and Herrling, T. (2003), *Guide to Media Relations.* Upper Saddle River, NJ: Pearson Prentice Hall.

Tench, R. and Yeomors, L. (2006), *Exploring Public Relations.* Harlow: Pearson Education.

Van Ruler, B., Vercic, T. and Vercic, B. (2008), *Public Relations Metrics: Research and Evaluation.* Mahwah, NJ: Lawrence Erlbaum Associates.

Wilcox, D. and Cameron, G.T. (2008), *Public Relations: Strategies and Tactics.* Harlow: Pearson Education.

Public Relations Review, http://www.elsevier.com.

CASE 10:
SUEZ: liquefied natural gas in New England

The liquefied natural gas (LNG) industry was developed to link gas reserves in places like Indonesia, Algeria, Equatorial Guinea, Norway, Trinidad and Venezuela with regions in need of natural gas. Japan and Korea, for example, import LNG to fulfil almost all their natural gas needs. Also, about half of Spain's natural gas needs are met by LNG imports. Like many other countries, the USA also satisfies part of its gas needs by using LNG. One of the top LNG importers to the USA is SUEZ (by means of its subsidiary SUEZ LNG NA/Distrigas). This case focuses on SUEZ and the PR activities it engages in to enhance its ability to sell LNG in Massachusetts.

Company background

SUEZ is an international industrial and services group which is active in sustainable solutions in the management of electricity, gas, energy services, water and waste management. It is the top independent producer of electricity in the world, the second buyer and the top distributor of natural gas in Europe. SUEZ employs approximately 219 000 people worldwide, earns about $90.7 billion in revenues, and invested $11 billion in 2011.

SUEZ LNG NA is the business unit of SUEZ Energy North America which manages the company's LNG activities in North America. Its Everett Terminal in New England, the first LNG import terminal in the USA, started to operate in 1971. The Everett Terminal currently provides about 20% of

New England's natural gas needs, and LNG facilities as a whole are able to meet 35% to 40% of the region's natural gas demand on peak days. SUEZ's role in the power production of New England is also critical. The Everett Terminal has connections to two interstate pipeline systems and to a local distribution company's system. Through these connections, it serves nearly all of the gas utilities in the region and key power producers, including a power plant which can generate enough electricity for about 1.5 million homes each year in Greater Boston. Since New England lacks underground natural gas storage, the terminal supplies LNG via truck to a network of local, customer-owned LNG storage tanks. SUEZ has about 40 customers who receive natural gas in vapour or liquid form, or a combination of the two.

What is LNG?

LNG is the same natural gas used by millions of people for heating and cooking, but in a different form. When natural gas is cooled to −260° Fahrenheit (−162°C), it liquefies and reduces to 1/600th of its original volume. This allows LNG to be transported and stored efficiently and economically. Moreover, LNG is neither explosive, corrosive, carcinogenic nor toxic. It does not pollute land or water resources. LNG is not transported or stored under pressure, and natural gas vapours do not catch fire as easily as those of other fuels.

All this makes LNG as safe, or even safer, to transport and store than most other fuels. To vaporise LNG, SUEZ and other LNG import terminal operators, in essence, run LNG through piping in hot water, and then use equipment to inject the natural gas into a connecting pipeline distribution system at the appropriate pressure.

SUEZ's vision of PR

PR has always been very important for SUEZ. In the beginning, when it entered the US market, it had to build trust in both the company and LNG. But even now, after more than 30 years of operations, PR is still considered business-critical. SUEZ cherishes 'local commitment and global vision'. Its business interests span much of the world, but it is eager not just to maintain but also strengthen its presence everywhere it operates. To this end, SUEZ focuses largely on personal communications since it believes that much of its success is built on the strength of its relationships. Therefore, SUEZ considers it critical that its communications lines are open, active and personal. Its CEO, senior vice president of operations, vice president of shipping, director of communications, etc., have to be familiar with, and interact with, the appropriate stakeholders. By engaging with these stakeholders, SUEZ hopes to ensure that its current business and prospects are strong in the months and years to come. The company tries to solidify its position as a credible and important player in the LNG market in North America, and hopes this reflects well on the subsidiary as well as the parent company. Having such solid relationships is indeed a necessity: if SUEZ is not considered as a credible partner in the eyes of its different stakeholders, this poses a substantial risk to its current and future business. Figure 10.4 gives an overview of the most important stakeholders SUEZ takes into account.

Government relations

SUEZ has built relationships with a variety of government officials at the federal, state and local level. Table 10.9 provides an overview of key governmental stakeholders.

SUEZ's major goal is to keep the policy-makers and elected officials informed about:

1. the need for LNG in New England and the critical role of the Everett Terminal (20% of the natural gas demand);
2. LNG's advantages as compared with other fuels (see above);
3. the safety and security records of SUEZ and the LNG industry.

Since the Everett Terminal is the only LNG import terminal that is located in an urban area in the USA (although there are several LNG storage facilities in urban areas), the latter is extremely important. The company wants to make sure that everyone realises how LNG can be handled safely and, in particular, how SUEZ has done so over the years. To this end, the company provides its own safety records and compares them with other alternatives. For example, there has never been a recorded incident of collision, grounding, fire, explosion or hull failure that has caused a breach to a cargo tank of an LNG ship. In 1979, an LNG vessel ran aground near the Rock of Gibraltar, but no cargo was spilled. The *Exxon Valdez*, on the other hand, ran aground in 1989 and caused a natural disaster by spreading 11 million gallons (50 million litres) of oil along 1300 miles (2100 km) of coastline. In 2002, a nuclear submarine surfaced beneath an LNG vessel in the Mediterranean Sea. No damage occurred to the cargo tanks. In contrast, the oil tanker *Prestige* broke in two off the coast of Spain in 2002. Moreover, in 2003, there was a fuel oil spill in Buzzards Bay and a gasoline barge fire and explosion on Staten Island. SUEZ hopes to prove with these records that LNG ships are among the best-built, most sophisticated and most robust in the world. Also, concerning LNG storage and trucking, the company can show excellent records. There has never been a report of either off-site injuries or property damage resulting from an incident at any LNG import terminal worldwide, or injuries or damage to land or water resources caused by a release of LNG from a truck.

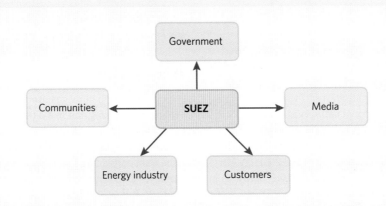

Figure 10.4 Stakeholder groups of SUEZ

Table 10.9 Key governmental stakeholders

Commonwealth of Massachusetts	• Governor and key staffers within the Economic Affairs, Consumer Affairs, Telecommunications and Energy, and Public Safety Offices • State Senators and Representatives of the district, and Senators and Representatives involved in energy, commerce and public safety • Massachusetts Port Authority • Public safety officers, including the Massachusetts State Police and State Fire Marshall
Federal	• The US Coast Guard • The Federal Energy Regulatory Commission • The US Department of Energy • The US Department of Transportation • Senators and Representatives within the Massachusetts delegation
Local	• Mayor of Everett, Everett Police and Fire Departments • Everett Common Council • Everett Board of Aldermen • Mayor of Boston, Boston Police and Fire Departments • Boston City Councillors • Chelsea City Manager, Chelsea Police and Fire Departments

With respect to security, all LNG ship officers, crew members and Everett Terminal workers are carefully trained and screened. Also, all LNG ships are boarded, inspected and escorted by the US Coast Guard through Boston Harbour. Although SUEZ has always been very committed to safety and security, this became even more so after 9/11. To counter the fear of LNG ships becoming a target for terrorists, the company used a risk-based approach focused on consequence determination, potential threats (as provided by federal authorities) and their outcomes. Several initiatives were proactively taken to address credible threats and to ensure that deliveries would continue. SUEZ introduced a detailed security plan, hired more private security personnel, increased employee awareness, installed onboard satellite tracking systems as well as cameras that monitor all areas of access, installed physical obstructions, etc. The security plan prescribes guidelines for decision-making and responses to conditions or incidents that may occur during the transit within Boston Harbour. It was developed jointly with the many stakeholders of the port of Boston, including vessel agents, docking and harbour pilots, operational Coast Guards units, port authorities, citizen action groups, federal agencies and state and local emergency response organisations. The security plan was hailed by Homeland Defense Secretary Tom Ridge as one of the best in the country and became a model for the Coast Guard's Operation Safe Commerce Project, a national effort to improve transportation safety and security. Also, several countries including Australia, Algeria, Belgium, Qatar, Trinidad, Tobago, the UK and Japan have made requests for the plan.

SUEZ's lobbyists are in constant contact with both local and national officials. More specifically, they are in contact almost daily with local officials of one type or another in the city of Everett. With state officials and other local area entities, the company has as much contact as is needed. This can vary from many times daily to weekly or bi-weekly. These contacts range from face-to-face discussions to provision of literature and reports.

Communities

SUEZ is led by the same objectives regarding community groups as with public officials: inform them on the need, the importance, the advantages and the safety and security of the product and the company. To this end, the company regularly tells the Chambers of Commerce that SUEZ is willing at any time to make a presentation to or answer questions from local groups such as neighbourhood associations and the Everett Common Council and Aldermen. In fact, about two to three times a year the latter call on the company to provide an update on its business. These Everett meetings are broadcast on local cable TV, increasing the company's reach enormously. Moreover, the company often gives guest lectures for the Everett Public High School students. Since students often talk about this at home, SUEZ reaches both students and parents in this way. Furthermore, it has also often led to favourable local press coverage.

SUEZ also demonstrates its commitment to the local community by being an active member of the Everett Chamber of Commerce, The Everett Business–Education Cooperative, the Everett Rotary Club, the Everett Kiwanis Club and the →

Table 10.10 Industry memberships

Role	Industry or trade group
Founding Management Committee member	Center for LNG (includes BG, BP, Shell, ConocoPhilips, Chevron and ExxonMobil), which is an active participant on Capitol Hill and provides information on LNG to the press
Member of the Board of Directors	Interstate Natural Gas Association of America (INGAA)
Founding member	University of Texas LNG consortium (includes BG, BP, Shell, ConocoPhilips, Chevron and ExxonMobil and the US Department of Energy), which was set up to develop public information from the basics to the safety of LNG
Member	Groupe International des Importateurs de Gaz Naturel Liquefié, an international association of LNG importers
Member	Northeast Gas Association
Member	Associated Industries of Massachusetts
Member	New England Council

Chelsea Chamber of Commerce. Finally, the company is also a major benefactor to charities and civic efforts, ranging from partial scholarships to students to sponsorship of the Little League baseball team. Moving beyond the City of Everett, SUEZ also supports the Citizens Energy/Distrigas Heat Assistance programme and the Courageous Sailing programme, which teaches inner-city kids to sail.

Energy industry

The company plays an active role in several industry and trade groups. This ensures that it is well informed on significant issues (such as legislation) that could affect the industry. Moreover, doing so allows SUEZ to have a say in the messages that the energy industry spreads to the public. Furthermore, these industry and trade groups provide excellent networking opportunities. Table 10.10 presents some of the groups SUEZ is a member of.

Customers

To cement its relationships with current and potential customers, SUEZ uses both direct and indirect means of communications. Direct communications consist of individual contacts between the SUEZ sales force and the (potential) customer. Indirect communications are obtained by:

1. participating in key industry conferences where the company affirms its plans;
2. press releases to, for example, the Northeast Gas Association, an association to which most of SUEZ's customers and prospects belong.

Media relations

LNG is a hot, but also a very sensitive, topic. SUEZ is well aware that reporters are eager to cultivate controversy on LNG. Therefore, it is important for the company to help frame the issue. To this end, the company has always responded in a very timely and helpful fashion to any requests for information and interviews, irrespective of the day (business day or weekend) and time (day or night). Besides these prompt responses, the company also behaves proactively by spreading press releases, articles and opinion pieces for various publications. For example, in February 2005 Frank Katulak, Senior Vice President of Operations for Distrigas of Massachusetts, wrote an opinion piece for a trade magazine for the chemical engineering profession on the safety of LNG and its operations to counter the rumours of LNG ships being a natural target for terrorists. Also, in the autumn of 2005 an article was published in the *Propeller Club Quarterly* on the security plan of SUEZ.

To conclude, SUEZ considers it business-critical to communicate often and well with all the stakeholders mentioned above. Remaining a credible company and partner in the eyes of all stakeholders is one of the main challenges that the SUEZ team accepts every day. As this case clearly illustrates, PR activities are exceptionally important to SUEZ. To make a comparison, advertising equals only 5% to 10% of SUEZ's PR investments.

QUESTIONS

1. What type of PR has SUEZ engaged in?
2. Is SUEZ using direct or indirect PR?
3. What other types of PR could SUEZ have used? Which specific PR activities would you recommend?
4. Which of the PR target groups discerned by SUEZ do you think is most important? Why?
5. What do you think are the main objectives of the PR activities directed at the different target groups?

6. Do you think SUEZ handled the rumours of a credible threat of terrorism in a good way? What else could it have done?

7. How can SUEZ measure the results of its PR activities?

8. Is SUEZ right in attaching so much importance to PR? Would you complement its PR activities with other MC tools? If so, which ones would you choose?

Case based on information provided by: Rick Grant, CEO SUEZ Global LNG; Julie Vitek, Director External Affairs SUEZ LNG NA; Derrick Philippe Gosselin, Executive Vice President Strategy & Portfolio Management – Chief Strategy Officer, SUEZ Energy International; and Katja Daman, SUEZ Energy International.

Katulak, F. (2005), 'LNG – A Safe Alternative Fuel', *CEP*, February 2005, www.cepmagazine.org; McKechine, J. and Skordinski, M. (2005), 'LNG Case Study: Boston Public-Private Cooperation', *Propeller Club Quarterly*, Fall, 10–13; www.gdfsuez.com (accessed 9 July 2012).

References

[1] Sirgy, J.M. (1998), *Integrated Marketing Communication: A Systems Approach*. Upper Saddle River, NJ: Prentice Hall.

[2] Haywood, R. (1998), *Public Relations for Marketing Professionals*. London: Macmillan Business.

[3] *Public Relations Practice – Its Role and Parameters* (1984), London: The Institute of Public Relations.

[4] Haywood, R. (1998), *Public Relations for Marketing Professionals*. London: Macmillan Business.

[5] Brassington, S. and Pettitt, F. (2003), *Principles of Marketing*. London: Financial Times Management.

[6] Haywood, R. (1998), *Public Relations for Marketing Professionals*. London: Macmillan Business.

[7] De Pelsmacker, P. and Van den Bergh, J. (1998), 'Advertising Content and Irritation: A Study of 226 TV Commercials', *Journal of International Consumer Marketing*, 10(4), 5–27.

[8] Bobo, C. (1997), 'Hitachi Faces Crisis with Textbook Response', *Public Relations Quarterly*, 42(2), 18–21.

[9] Burnett, J. and Moriarty, S. (1998), *Introduction to Marketing Communication*. Upper Saddle River, NJ: Prentice Hall.

[10] Lages, C. (2001), 'Dimensions of Public Relations Activity: An Exploratory Study', PhD Dissertation, University of Warwick, Warwick Business School.

[11] Dibb, S., Simkin, L. and Vancini, A. (1996), 'Competition, Strategy, Technology and People: The Challenges Facing PR', *International Journal of Advertising*, 15, 116–27; Kitchen, P.J. and White, J. (1992), 'Public Relations – Developments', *Marketing Intelligence & Planning*, 10(2), 14–17; Lages, C. (2001), 'Dimensions of Public Relations Activity: An Exploratory Study', PhD Dissertation, University of Warwick, Warwick Business School.

[12] Thomsen, S.R. (1997), 'Public Relations in the New Millennium: Understanding the Forces that are Reshaping the Profession', *Public Relations Quarterly*, 42(1), 11–17.

[13] Lages, C. and Simkin, L. (2003), 'The Dynamics of Public Relations: Key Constructs and the Drive for Professionalism at the Practitioner, Consultancy and Industry Levels', *European Journal of Marketing*, 37(1), 298–328.

[14] Watson, T. (2008), 'Priorities in Public Relations Research: An International Delphi Study Completed Research', *11th Annual International Public Relations Research Conference, University of Miami, FL, 6–9 March*.

[15] Sabre Awards (2011), *Slim-Studeren=Geld-Beheren Smart-Study=Money-Management*, http://www.holmesreport.com/casestudy-info/10776/Slim-Studeren--Geld-Beheren-Smart-Study--Money-Management.aspx; http://www.webershandwick.nl/nieuws/163/weber-shandwick-nederland-wint-sabre-award-voor-beste-pr-campagne-in-de-benelux.html (accessed July 2012).

[16] KBC On-line, Effie Award. Belgium, 2003.

[17] *De Morgen*, 3 April 2002.

[18] Haywood, R. (1991), *All About Public Relations*. London: McGraw-Hill.

[19] Albrecht, K. (1990), *Service Within*. Homewood, IL: Dow Jones-Irwin.

[20] Carroll, C. and McCombs, M. (2003), 'Agenda-setting Effects of Business News on the Public's Images and Opinions about Major Corporations', *Corporate Reputation Review*, 6(1), 36–46.

[21] Callison, C. (2003), 'Fortune 500 Company Websites and Media Relations: Corporate PR Practitioner's Use of the Internet to Assist Journalists in News Gathering', *Public Relations Review*, 29(1), 29–47.

[22] McCleneghan, J.S. (1998), 'Are VNR's all they're Cracked Up to Be?', *Public Relations Quarterly*, 42(4), 35–8.

[23] *De Morgen*, 13 May 2006.

[24] *De Morgen*, 15 April 2008.

[25] Haywood, R. (1998), *Public Relations for Marketing Professionals*. London: Macmillan Business.

[26] Gofton, K. (1997), 'Rethinking the Rules', *Public Relations – Supplement*, 6–10.

[27] Haywood, R. (1998), *Public Relations for Marketing Professionals*. London: Macmillan Business; see also Moss, D., Vercic, D. and Warnaby, G. (2003), *Perspectives on Public Relations Research*. London: Routledge.

[28] Seymour, M. and Moore, S. (2000), *Effective Crisis Management: Worldwide Principles and Practices*. London and New York: Cassell.

[29] Marconi, J. (1992), *Crisis Marketing: When Bad Things Happen to Good Companies*. Chicago: Probus.

[30] Haywood, R. (1998), *Public Relations for Marketing Professionals*. London: Macmillan Business.

[31] Lukaszewski, J.E. (1997), 'Establishing Individual and Corporate Crisis Communication Standards; The Principles and Protocols', *Public Relations Quarterly*, 42(3), 7–14.

[32] *De Morgen*, 25 October 2008.

CHAPTER 11
Sponsorship

CHAPTER OUTLINE

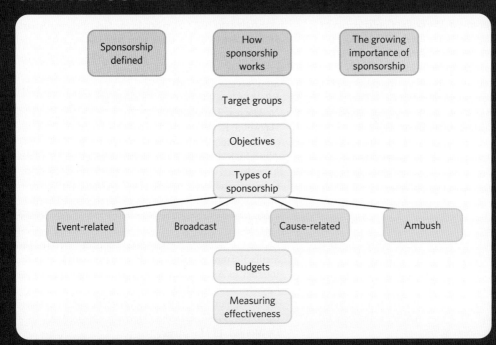

Sponsorship defined

How sponsorship works

The growing importance of sponsorship

Target groups

Objectives

Types of sponsorship

Event-related

Broadcast

Cause-related

Ambush

Budgets

Measuring effectiveness

CHAPTER OBJECTIVES

This chapter will help you to:

- Understand the difference between sponsorship and other instruments of the communications mix
- Know how sponsorship works
- Understand why sponsorship is an increasingly important instrument of the communications mix
- Distinguish the target groups and objectives of sponsorship
- Learn about the different types of sponsorship, such as event-related sponsorship, broadcast sponsorship, cause-related sponsorship and ambush marketing, and their advantages and disadvantages
- Select sponsorship proposals on the basis of a set of relevant criteria
- Measure the effectiveness of a sponsorship campaign

Introduction

Although in most companies the share of sponsorship in the communications budget is still limited, worldwide it is an increasingly important instrument of the communications mix. Not only are sponsorship budgets increasing, but also sponsored events and causes are becoming more and more diverse. Although 'spouse-driven projects' still exist, the degree of professionalism in the selection and follow-up of sponsorship projects is becoming increasingly sophisticated, and the communications effectiveness of sponsored projects has become a major concern. In contrast to advertising campaigns that are normally followed up by advertising or brand managers, sponsorship projects are often directly monitored by corporate management, illustrating the importance that is attached to this type of activity – or the lack of maturity of this particular instrument. Sponsorship is different from other communications mix instruments. It is a flexible instrument that can serve a multitude of objectives, but it is more suited for some objectives than for others. As in advertising, a number of channels – types of sponsorship – may be used, each having their own advantages and strengths and disadvantages and weaknesses. The integration of this tool in the communications mix may be an even more important condition for success than that of the other communications instruments. In any case, in an increasing number of companies sponsorship has acquired the status of one of the corner-stones of the communications and marketing strategy.

Sponsorship: what it is and what it is not

Sponsorship can be defined as an investment in cash or kind in an activity, in return for access to the exploitable commercial potential associated with this activity.[1] The company promotes its interests and brands by tying them to a specific and meaningfully related event or cause.[2] It is a thematic communications instrument with which the sponsor assists the sponsee in realising his or her project. In return the sponsee co-operates in realising the communications objectives of the sponsoring company. If the latter is not the case, the investment of the 'sponsor' is nothing more than altruism, charity, patronage or benefaction. As such, 'sponsorship' has existed for centuries. The Roman Gaius Maecenas was a great sponsor of the arts, and gave his name to the concept of Maecenatism. The De Medici family of Florence became famous as sponsors of artists such as Michelangelo. The difference between this and contemporary professional sponsorship is that sponsorship is an integrated part of the communications effort, with explicit communications and commercial objectives. The benefits of charity, on the other hand, are mainly directed towards society and/or the beneficiaries.

Generally speaking, sponsorship shares two of the fundamental objectives of advertising, i.e. the generation of awareness about the product or company, and the promotion of positive messages about the product or company.[3] However, there are a number of important differences between the two, the most important one being that advertising allows greater control over the content and the environment of the message. Advertising messages are explicit and direct, and advertisers can decide when and where to place their ads. On the other hand, although sponsorship results in a less cluttered promotion of their products, companies also have less control over sponsorship, which makes their messages more indirect and implicit. As a result, in order to make sponsorship effective, accompanying communications efforts are called for.[4] Indeed, sponsorship can be described as a 'mute non-verbal medium', as opposed to advertising, in which messages are created using visuals, vocals and context.[5]

On the other hand, sponsorship is less cluttered and financially more attractive. It can be considered a cheap form of advertising. However, sponsorship may be less effective in gaining attention as a result of the distraction factor: spectators are primarily involved with the sponsored event (a soccer game or a work of art) and pay less attention to the environment of the event, such as the sponsor.[6] Indeed, exposure to a sponsor's name or logo is not the same as sponsorship effectiveness. Furthermore, in some cases, the sponsor is closely associated with a popular sponsored event or cause, which may turn out to have a strong positive effect on corporate and brand image. Sponsorship is also easy for the consumer to understand: it essentially works on the basis of association between sponsor and sponsee. Advertising, on the other hand, often requires elaborate processing of the message.[7]

Sponsorship is different from event marketing, which, in turn, is a type of PR activity.[8] Certainly, sponsorship can be integrated into a PR campaign. During the world championship cycling in Valkenburg (1998), Rabobank was one of the structural sponsors. It invited about 5000 guests, mainly employees and customers of Rabobank in the Netherlands and elsewhere. Invitations to cultural events, for instance to see David Bowie at the Sea Beach festival in Ostend and the musical *Oliver* in one of the 12 large theatres in the Netherlands, are examples of corporate hospitality, integrating sponsorship into a PR campaign by Nashuatec.[9] **Event marketing** can be defined as using a number of elements of the promotion mix to create an event for the purpose of reaching strategic marketing objectives. An example of event marketing is the Camel Trophy.

Finally, sponsorship should be distinguished from value marketing. **Value marketing** or societal marketing can be defined as a strategy in which a company links its activities to a philosophy of general societal interest. The company positions itself on the basis of a value system that is often not product-related. For instance, the international cosmetics company The Body Shop (now part of L'Oréal) tries to combine fair business, social conscience and profitability. It produces environmentally-friendly products, based on natural ingredients, that are not tested on animals and which are sold in recycled or recyclable packaging. Raw materials are bought from Third World countries at fair prices. Sponsorship can be part of the value marketing strategy, but it is by no means its only instrument.[10]

BUSINESS INSIGHT
Corporate social responsibility campaigns in the Netherlands

Companies set up corporate social responsibility (CSR) campaigns in which they sponsor cause-related projects that improve the quality of life in society, and by means of which they can improve their own reputation. The following examples are taken from the Dutch CSR network 'Samenleving&Bedrijf' (Society and Company).

From October 2004, Microsoft Nederland co-operated with the city of Amsterdam and local non-profit organisations to establish 'Community-based Technology & Learning Centres (CTLCs)'. The project went by the name of 'Computer neighbourhood' and tried to provide computer training to people with a lack of digital skills. The purpose of the project was to prevent people from becoming isolated, and to empower less privileged inhabitants to expand their capabilities with respect to education, jobs, personal development and participation in society. The objective was to establish 16 CTCLs in which 1100 people received training. Eleven locations were set up where people from the neighbourhood could learn through short courses how to work with a computer, from chatting to e-mailing. By 2007, more than 700 inhabitants had been trained. The project was part of the global Unlimited Potential initiative launched by Microsoft Community Affairs and, by 2007, worldwide almost 30 000 CTLCs had been established in 95 countries. In these projects, Microsoft co-operated with 475 non-profit organisations.

The Shell Young Art Award project was aimed at stimulating young talent and entrepreneurship, besides acquainting youngsters with developments in modern art. Artists presented their work in three Shell locations in Amsterdam, Rotterdam and The Hague. A professional jury judged the work of the young artists and awarded prizes. The initiative started in 2000 and dozens of young artists were able to develop expertise in organising exhibitions of their works. The Shell Young Art Award was stimulating and enabled recognition and exposure with the prize-winning artists allowed to show their work in museums. In this way, the public could also get acquainted with their work. There was also an internal effect: many works of art stimulated intense discussions in the Shell offices.[11]

How sponsorship works

A number of theoretical constructs can be used to understand the effects of sponsorship. Given the fact that sponsor messages are often simple and limited to company or brand names, one could argue that the effectiveness of sponsorship is based on the exposure effect (see Chapter 3), which implies that increased familiarity with the brand as a result of exposure to a sponsor's name in the long run generates a preference for the brand. As such, the main effect of sponsorship is that the brand ends up in the evoked set or the choice set of the consumer, without attitudinal-related effects. Additionally, it could be argued that both the episodic (event-based) and the semantic (as a result of longer-term exposure) memory of spectators and participants in a sponsored event are stimulated, which could lead to higher levels of brand awareness than those resulting from advertising exposure.[12]

Congruity theory could also explain the effectiveness of sponsorship. Basically, this theory states that people best remember information that is congruent with prior expectations. As a result, sponsorships that are consistent with the expectations of the target groups about the product could be better recalled.[13] Similarly, just as there seems to be a carry-over effect between the attitude towards the ad and the attitude towards the brand, it could be argued that there is the same effect between the prior attitudes towards the sponsored event or cause and the sponsoring brand. Furthermore, it can be expected that the more a person is involved with what is being sponsored, the stronger the carry-over effect between the sponsoring brand and the sponsored event will be.[14]

Apart from these cognitively oriented theories, context effects can also partly explain how and why sponsorship works. The context of a message may be important in how a message is perceived. Since sponsorships tend to occur in positively evaluated environments, the resulting positive mood could enhance the positive image of the sponsoring brands.[15]

Finally, the behaviourist perspective may be relevant. The principles of operant conditioning posit that behaviour may be conditioned by the consequences that follow it. On the basis of this principle, it can be argued that sponsorship draws attention to a brand and in that way reinforces past favourable experience with the brand. The stimulus is being associated with a satisfactory experience and therefore reinforces it. When this point of view is accepted, it implies that sponsorship is only effective when it is directed towards consumers who are already using the brand. Another principle of conditioning is vicarious learning. By educating consumers on how a product can be used, vicarious learning increases the purchase probability. Applied to sponsorship, showing a famous and positively evaluated athlete using or endorsing a product may positively influence the target group.[16] This mechanism is very similar to the source effect in advertising: linking a relevant brand to a credible source (a bank to a classical concert, a beer to a famous entertainer) may improve its image.[17]

The growing importance of sponsorship

It is fair to conclude that sponsorship is an increasingly important instrument of marketing communications. Worldwide, the annual growth of sponsorship between 1990 and 1999 was estimated at between 10% and 15%. In the 1990s, the annual growth of advertising and sales promotion was only 6%. As a result, the relative importance of sponsorship in communications budgets has, on average, increased to 7%.[18] In some countries (Italy, South Africa and Australia), more than 13% of the advertising budget is spent on sponsorship.[19] Furthermore, part of the advertising budget is directly sponsorship-related in that it supports and leverages the sponsorship efforts (see below). According to a 2007 report,[20] the sponsoring industry was worth €7.8 billion in 2007, and the industry has grown by 37% since the year 2000. Germany is Europe's biggest sports sponsorship market with estimated expenditure of €2600 million (33% of the market). The UK is the second largest market on €1395 million (17%). Europe's biggest sponsor is Deutsche Telecom, which spends an estimated €90 million per year on sponsorship rights fees in Europe. The UK's biggest sponsor is Vodafone, which spends an estimated €45 million per year in Europe.

BUSINESS INSIGHT
UPS supports Olympic sponsorship with worldwide advertising campaign

UPS is the world's largest express carrier and largest delivery company. It entered the European market in 1988, but did not make a profit in Europe during the first ten years. In 1996, UPS made the fundamental decision to revamp its European operations. It decided to become an official partner of the 2000 Olympics in Sydney. Research identified four weaknesses: low awareness of the Olympic sponsorship; low awareness of brand and service capabilities; an undifferentiated brand position; and the fact that potential customers were unaware of UPS as an enabler of global commerce. UPS launched a global campaign to redress this situation by leveraging its association with the Olympics in a relevant way. The Olympics provided a unique opportunity to associate UPS with the core Olympic values of trust, integrity, ambition and success. The creative execution of the campaign compared UPS with the Olympics: 'If UPS are good enough to deliver for the Olympics, they must be good enough for us.' The campaign showed UPS employees demonstrating their commitment to preparing to represent their country. The advertising campaign was implemented throughout Europe and worldwide, and stretched from the national trials to the games themselves, with special focus on key business periods March–May and the weeks before and during the summer Olympics in September 2000. Fifty-four campaigns ran in the USA, Latin America, Asia and Europe, using global, pan-European and national media vehicles. Besides TV, radio spots, magazine ads and outdoor advertising, sponsorship of key news programmes was also used. Research showed that UPS awareness increased by 5% to 10% in most countries, and so did most-often usage of UPS by 3% to 20%. Year-to-year revenue growth was 4% during the first quarter of 2001. The international export volume grew by 17%, led by Europe with a 25% increase. The UPS example shows that sponsorship programmes need to be accompanied by major investments in other communications campaigns to secure maximum impact.[21]

The (perceived) importance of sponsorship is not only reflected in the increasing budgets and the diversification in sponsored causes and events, but also in the level of (top) management involvement. Studies of managerial involvement in sports and arts sponsorship campaigns in the USA and Australia show that in more than 50% of the cases senior management is involved in proposal assessment and agreement negotiations, and in about 25% of the cases in implementation and evaluation of sponsorship campaigns. Senior management is even involved in 75% of the renewal decisions.[22] This reflects the perceived importance of sponsorship, not only for marketing communications, but also for corporate communications and corporate image. The involvement of other departments mainly depends on the type of sponsorship. Sports sponsorship apparently implies the involvement of marketing or advertising departments, while art sponsorship is mostly seen as a PR matter.

There are a number of reasons why sponsorship is of increasing importance. Firstly, there is a feeling that traditional mass media advertising is becoming increasingly expensive, increasingly irritating and, as a result of communications clutter, less effective. Sponsorship is believed to have the power to escape this clutter, to isolate the brand from the competition and to get the message across at lower cost, although some predict that sponsorship clutter may become equally widespread. Furthermore, sponsored events are increasingly broadcast, thereby leveraging the initial investment of sponsorship. Overall, media, especially TV programme sponsorship (see below), are increasingly accepted, and substantially improve the levels of coverage of, and impact on, broad target groups.[23]

Due to increased leisure, sports and cultural activities, new sponsorship opportunities are emerging. Governments are less and less inclined to finance culture and other social activities, so forcing cultural and social organisations to look for financial support from private companies. Finally, legal constraints on tobacco and alcohol advertising are forcing the companies involved to look for other communications strategies to get their message across. Sponsorship is an obvious substitute to build awareness and image.

Apart from increasing expenditures, a number of other current developments in sponsorship can be discerned:[24]

- *A changing perception of sponsorship on the part of company executives.* An evolution towards more professionalism can be seen and management practice is becoming increasingly sophisticated.
- *Changing expenditure patterns.* A greater part of the budget is spent on relatively new forms of sponsorship instead of on traditional sports and the arts. Broadcast or programme sponsorship, popular music and cause-related projects are becoming increasingly important.
- *The diffusion of sponsorship to an expanding range of industries.* In the early days, sponsorship was mainly used by tobacco, alcohol and soft drinks companies, and banks and car manufacturers. Nowadays, retail groups and detergent manufacturers are joining the list.
- *The proliferation of sponsorship activity.* An increasing number of corporate sponsors, combined with a shortage of quality events, are leading to a greater exploitation of their properties by event owners.
- *Some sponsored events are evolving towards global projects.* The Olympic Games, Formula One racing and worldwide sports sponsorship by Adidas are examples of this trend.
- *Sponsorship is becoming relationship-based rather than transaction-based* (structural versus punctual sponsorship), implying a longer-term co-operation between sponsors and sponsees.
- *Sponsorship is more and more broadcast-driven.* What is not on TV is less attractive as a sponsorship project.

Target groups

Given the flexibility of sponsorship to achieve a number of objectives and the wide range of sponsorable events and causes, sponsorship audiences are very diversified. Like other instruments of the communications mix, marketing and corporate communications target groups can be distinguished. Since sponsorship is explicitly linked to an event, an extra dimension should be added. Indeed, audiences can be contacted as active participants in the event (soccer players or musicians), as live spectators who attend events (fans or visitors of a museum) and/or as media followers of the event. Figure 11.1 shows the sponsorship audience structure. In Table 11.1 the results of a study on sports sponsorship in Canada are shown, illustrating the wide range of audiences that are targeted and their relative importance.[25] Obviously,

	(Potential) customers	Financial institutions	Community leaders	Employees	Channel members
Active participants					
Live spectators					
Media followers					

Figure 11.1 Sponsorship audience structure

Table 11.1 Sports sponsorship target audiences in Canada

Audience	Mean importance (on 7-point scale)
Potential customers	5.79
Existing customers	5.62
Local community	5.60
General public	5.16
Business community	4.37
Workforce	4.33
Distributors	3.21
Shareholders	3.18
Suppliers	3.09
Ethnic groups	3.05
Government	2.74

Source: Based on Thwaites, D., Anguilar-Manjarrez, R. and Kidd, C. (1998), 'Sports Sponsorship Development in Leading Canadian Companies: Issues and Trends', *International Journal of Advertising*, 17(1), 29–50. Reproduced with permission of WARC.

depending on the objectives and the target groups of the global communications campaign, sponsorship projects will be selected that are best capable of reaching the desired target groups. For instance, products targeted at up-market demographic segments will sponsor tennis, golf and the arts, while brands targeting youngsters will focus on popular music festival or programme sponsoring.

RESEARCH INSIGHT
World Cup sponsorship and brand perception

Does major investment in sports sponsorship actually benefit brand owners? This seems to be primarily the case among young consumers. The impact of sports sponsorship on other age groups is much more limited. In 2002, NOP World questioned 1001 people from a representative sample of the UK population on behalf of the Superbrand organisation to test brand awareness and brand perception of the sponsors of World Cup soccer. Within the 15–24 year old range, 40% of people said that they would feel more confident about a brand if it sponsored high-profile sporting events such as the World Cup. Only 19% of the 25–34 year olds and 18% of the 35–44 year olds feel more confidence in a sponsoring brand. This percentage even lowers to 13% of 45–54 year olds and a mere 6% of 55–64 year olds. For the over 65s, this percentage increases slightly to 11%. The impact of high-profile sporting events appears primarily to impress the younger age groups.[26]

Objectives

Sponsorship is a very flexible communications tool that can be used to achieve both marketing (product or brand) and corporate communications objectives. Table 11.2 gives an overview of the two categories of objectives. In each of the categories a distinction can be made between the type of target group and/or the type of objective.[27]

Table 11.2 Sponsorship objectives

Corporate communications objectives	General public	Increase general public awareness of company Promote or enhance corporate image Alter public perception of company Involvement with the local community
	Channel members and trade relations	Build trade relations Corporate hospitality Demonstrate trade goodwill
	Employees	Enhance employee relations and motivations Assist staff recruitment Facilitate prospecting for the sales force
	Opinion-formers and decision-makers	Increase media attention Counter adverse publicity Build goodwill Reassure policy-holders and stockholders Personal objective of senior managers
Marketing communications objectives	Awareness building	Increase awareness with actual customers Increase awareness with potential customers Confirm market leadership Increase new product awareness
	Brand image	Alter perception of brand Identify brand with particular market segment
	Sales/market share	Induce trial of new product Increase sales/market share

Research indicates that, depending on the type of sponsorship and the type of company, different objectives are important. As far as **marketing communications** objectives are concerned, mainly awareness-building and, to a certain extent, image-building seem to be the objectives that sponsorship is most suited to achieve. These effects only become visible in the long run. Indeed, sponsorship effectiveness studies indicate that sponsors are not recognised better than their non-sponsoring competitors immediately after the sponsored event.[28] A direct increase in sales or market share is not the primary objective of sponsorship, although, for instance, a beverage supplier can obtain the sole rights for selling beverages at an event, and in this way boost sales. Linking a brand's name with a relevant event or cause is often used to improve the image with a specific target group of interest. Volvo sponsoring golf and tennis, and Adidas sponsoring, among others, soccer, are examples of this.

Equally important are the **corporate communications** objectives of sponsoring. Most studies indicate that promoting corporate image and increasing goodwill with a variety of target groups are the most important corporate communications objectives of sponsorship.[29] But internal marketing objectives and motives can be equally or even more important. The Bank of Ireland sponsors Gaelic Football and the Bank of Ireland Proms. Besides corporate image objectives, employee-related goals are equally important. The bank tries to develop a corporate identity and a corporate image by transferring the values of the sponsored events to both external publics and their own staff. In the process, staff pride is engendered. The bank is perceived as a desirable employer. Among the measurement of sponsorship effects, the attitude of the company's own staff towards the sponsored event is of primary importance.[30] Given the fact that the struggle of the future will have to be concentrated as much on attracting high-quality staff as on finding customers, the employee-related effects of sponsorship are of increasing importance.

Another important category of objectives or motives of sponsorship is corporate hospitality, which can be aimed at own staff, salespeople, distributors or any other opinion leader or decision-maker. They can be invited to attend a soccer game, to follow a cycle race, to attend a concert or to obtain backstage passes at rock concerts. Creating goodwill and establishing stronger relations in an informal context are the primary objectives.

BUSINESS INSIGHT
Corporate hospitality

Corporate hospitality is developing relationship marketing activities within the framework of a sponsorship pro-gramme. It involves, for instance, inviting employees, customers, suppliers, etc., to cultural or sports events, or the organisation of special events for these stakeholder groups at the occasion of sponsored activities. The selection of VIP events is a delicate exercise. The selection of groups requires an investigation into their interest in, and empathy towards, the sponsored event. If the managing director of one of the largest suppliers of the company is only inter-ested in opera, and not in soccer, he or she should not be invited to a soccer game. Grouping VIPs is another crucial decision. The result of the PR or relationship effort primarily depends upon the interaction between those invited. If they do not have anything to say to each other or are even hostile to one another, they should not be in the same group. Corporate hospitality can also lead to irritation, for instance if someone is invited to an event he or she does not like, or if other stakeholder groups feel discriminated against by not being invited. Therefore, it is a good idea to conduct VIP treatment at a safe distance from the event itself, away from visitors who have paid to participate in the event. If the value of the VIP treatment is substantial, this can lead to ethical problems because the expectation is raised that the 'reward' for being invited should also be significant.

Corporate hospitality can also generate negative publicity in the media. An influential sports journalist from a Dutch TV channel was interviewed in a newspaper, and was very critical about VIP events organised by sports sponsors: 'A cyclist championship for 15 000 VIPs in a concrete bunker on a car racing circuit – who was the fool who thought of that?' and 'During the final of the tennis tournament in Rotterdam, the VIP area was full of people in nice suits, talking about nothing important, while outside the world's numbers 1 and 2 were playing. No-one I asked in the VIP area knew who they were.' Needless to say, this kind of negative media publicity can destroy much of the goodwill that was built up by the sponsorship programme, and should be avoided.[31]

One of the most important motives in sponsorship is the leveraging effect of the media coverage of the event. In some cases, as in tobacco or alcohol advertising, the ban on regular advertising leads to a situation in which sponsorship is the only way to obtain mass media exposure. But a lot of other sponsorship initiatives count on the 'bullhorn effect' of media coverage too. Sponsorship is indeed becoming more and more broadcast-driven.

Although sponsorship is becoming increasingly professional, in many situations the decision to sponsor is motivated by personal interest, or 'management by hobby' of senior executives, or their husbands or wives. It goes without saying that many sports sponsorship budgets could have been spent more efficiently on other communications tools. There are many examples of sponsorships that end when the senior manager retires or gets another job. For instance, the Spanish soft drink brand KAS ended its sponsorship of a cycling team (with Sean Kelly as one of the top athletes) after its CEO retired. The sudden death in 1995 of Mr Furlan, CEO of the clothing company MG, was the cause of great concern among Italian professional cyclists, who feared that their successful team would cease to exist.

Types of sponsorship

Sponsorship budgets can be directed towards different types of projects. Figure 11.2 shows the main sponsorship types. Four basic categories can be distinguished. **Event-related sponsorship** is the best-known category. Companies may sponsor a soccer competition, a team, an athlete, shirts or even a match ball, a golf tournament, skiing or a baseball game. They can lend their

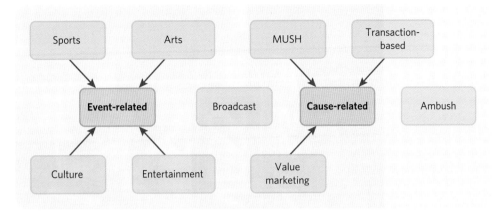

Figure 11.2 Types of sponsorship

support, in cash or kind, to an exhibition, a series of concerts, a philharmonic orchestra or an artist. Or they can sponsor a rock concert, a beach festival or an annual traditional crafts exhibition. **Broadcast or programme sponsorship** is a more recent phenomenon, at least in Europe. A brand can sponsor a sports programme, the weather forecast or a 'soap'. **Cause-related sponsorship** may be the oldest form of sponsorship, or rather charity. Rich people donating money to schools, the poor or other good causes is a phenomenon that has existed for centuries. The difference between those activities and cause-related sponsorship is that the latter is not just charity, but integrated in the company's communications strategy. **MUSH sponsorship** stands for Municipal, University, Social, Hospital sponsorship, and is a synonym for sponsorship of good causes. **Transaction-based sponsorship** (sometimes called cause-related marketing or point-of-purchase politics) is a type of sponsorship in which the company invests a pre-specified amount of money in a 'good cause' every time a consumer buys one of the company's products. Value marketing has been defined in the first section of this chapter. Sponsorship is only one aspect of value or societal marketing. Finally, **ambush or parasitic marketing** is a planned effort by a company to confuse the consumer regarding its affiliation status and to associate indirectly with an event in order to gain at least some of the recognition and benefits associated with being an official sponsor.[32] A company may be a minor sponsor of an event but, by spending considerable budgets on advertising support, it creates the impression of being an important sponsor.

Traditional event-related sponsorship still accounts for the bulk of the expenditures. Sport accounts for 86% of the expenditure (€6695 million), with arts and broadcast sponsorship taking 7% and 5% respectively (others 2%). Football is Europe's biggest recipient of sports sponsorship income on €1872 million (38%), motor sport is second on €1558 million (32%), sailing and cycling are third on €190 million and €184 million, respectively (4%), and other sports include rugby union on €161 million (3%).[33] Sports sponsoring also attracts a large variety of companies in different industries. A Dutch study found that of all sports sponsorship in the Netherlands, 18% was invested by financial institutions, 8% by consultancies, 7.5% by the automotive industry and 5.5% by the Internet/ICT industry.[34]

Event-related sponsorship

The opportunities and advantages of event-related sponsorship are multiple. Compared with advertising, it is a cost-effective instrument in terms of reaching a particular audience. Given the variety of events in terms of targeted audiences, it is an excellent tool to reach broad as well as very specific market segments in terms of demographic and psychographic characteristics. Sponsorship of opera, exhibitions or rock concerts and of cultural events in general is usually very selective in terms of the market segment reached, while some sports sponsorship is capable of exposing broad target groups to the sponsor's message (Photos 11.1 and 11.2).

Photo 11.1 Guinness sponsors football
Source: Getty Images: Guinness.

Photo 11.2 Johnnie Walker sponsors golf
Source: Getty Images.

Extensive media coverage of sports events leads to high levels of exposure of broad target groups to the sponsor's name. For instance, as far as cycling is concerned, 18.4% of managers and executives watch this sport regularly on TV, as well as 18% of farmers, 16.5% of civil servants, 16.5% of blue-collar workers, 12% of pensioners and 9% of housewives.[35] Heineken sponsored the Rugby World Cup worldwide. It was estimated that, in the UK, 83% of all men were exposed to the Heineken brand name, each of them at least 22 times.[36]

Event sponsorship is also flexible in achieving different kinds of objectives. It can increase awareness with actual and potential customers, and improve the company's image and the image of the company's products. It is a tool in relationship-building and corporate hospitality, it can be a platform for advertising campaigns, database building and sampling, and it is efficiently capable of avoiding advertising bans. For instance, as far as the latter is concerned, in a 1984 survey it was – sadly – found that the cigarette brands that were most widely recalled by children were those brands that were most commonly sponsoring televised sporting events.[37]

On the other hand, event sponsorship and, more particularly, sports sponsorship have a number of disadvantages and pose a number of threats. Spending large amounts of money on sponsorship can cause trouble with employees, especially if they are not properly informed about the relevance and economic justification of the sponsorship strategy. A company sponsoring a sportsman or woman or a team can alienate fans of the opponent.

Furthermore, unlike TV sets and newspapers, sportsmen and women lead their own lives, and sometimes attract media attention that is not always favourable to the sponsor. The drugs scandal revealed in the Tour de France of 1998 was not particularly welcomed by the teams' sponsors, although Festina, the Spanish brand of timepieces and main sponsor of one of the offending teams, did not seem to suffer too much from the negative publicity. But even without such incidents, if the team or the sportsperson does badly, this can reflect negatively on the sponsor's image. Not surprisingly, a clean image is one of the main criteria on the basis of which sports or sports teams are selected for sponsorship.[38] Finally, although sports sponsorship can be used to transcend cultural, linguistic and geographic boundaries, some sports, like bull fighting, camel wrestling and dwarf throwing, are unfit for global brand sponsorship because they are culturally unacceptable in a number of countries.

BUSINESS INSIGHT
PWC ends contract with 'unreliable' soccer coach

Georges Leekens is one of the most famous soccer coaches in Belgium. He has been a player for several top Belgian teams and, in 2012, the 62 year old coach had a track record of 20 years of coaching first division teams. From 2009 onwards, he had been coaching the national soccer team. In mid-May 2012, to everyone's surprise, he announced that he had decided to stop coaching the national team immediately because he had signed a contract with one of Belgium's top teams, Club Brugge. The Belgian Soccer Association was outraged that its national coach had 'abandoned' the national team just a few months before the qualifying campaign for the Brazil 2014 World Soccer Championships. It called his decision unethical and distrustful. The sports media eagerly reminded the public of Leekens' 'jobhopping' and 'unreliable' record.

For some time, the coach had been the endorser of PWC's recruitment campaign 'Move Forward'. In this campaign, aimed at attracting those with potential, PWC emphasises key elements such as 'trust' and 'responsibility' and 'a career is not a false promise'. Only a few days after Leekens' announcement, PWC decided to end its co-operation with him and stated: 'Following the news that Leekens resigned as the coach of the national soccer team, PWC announces that our cooperation has ended. We regret his decision to abandon the national team, but we wish to thank him for the productive cooperation and wish all the best for his further career.' Apparently, PWC judged that the behaviour of the coach was incompatible with the key message and positioning of the recruitment campaign, and therefore decided that he was no longer a suitable endorser.

Famous people can be a powerful support for a campaign, not only because they are well-known and liked, but also because of their characteristics and behaviour. However, sometimes they behave in ways that may be deemed incompatible with the companies' values, in which case they become a liability rather than an asset.[39]

Obviously, arts and cultural sponsorship is fundamentally different from sports sponsorship. First of all, arts audiences are different from sports audiences. The former are typically older and more affluent, and generally less numerous. The arts attract less media coverage and publicity, and are more suited to niche market segments than sports. However, some argue that the arts are increasingly attractive as sponsorship objects because of the increasing costs and saturation of sport sponsorship. Furthermore, a Toshiba study reveals that four times as many people visit museums and galleries as attend league football matches. Nevertheless, arts sponsors are believed to pursue corporate image and relationship and hospitality objectives rather than marketing goals. That makes arts sponsorship more of a PR tool than a marketing communications instrument.[40]

RESEARCH INSIGHT
Brand placement as effective marketing communications tool

Due to recent technological developments, the TV advertising landscape is changing rapidly. The introduction of the personal video recorder and the ongoing convergence of TV and the Internet are causing consumers to gain more and more control over which content they want to see and when they want to see it. Viewers are also becoming increasingly cynical about advertising and pay less and less attention to it.[41] Marketers increasingly consider brand placement (sometimes also called 'product placement') as an innovative new way to reach and connect with consumers. Brand placement is 'the paid inclusion of branded products or brand identifiers through audio and/or visual means within mass media programs'.[42] Brand placement is sometimes called hybrid advertising, communication in camouflage and hidden but paid for marketing communication.[43] They are paid messages that do not overly identify their commercial origins.[44] Paid brand placement spending grew 33.7% to $2.90 billion in 2007 and at a compound annual growth rate of 40.8% from 2002 to 2007, thereby significantly outpacing that of traditional advertising.[45] The European Commission has recently updated the 'Television Without Frontiers Directive', relaxing the rules of advertising to allow for brand placements. Consequently, the phenomenon is expected to grow even more.

Brand placement is a flexible tool. Brands can be placed in TV programmes, movies, books and music. Different types of programmes offer different placement opportunities. In scripted programmes, the brand can be integrated into the plot in a natural way. It can be placed prominently or subtly, and it can be shown, mentioned or both. In non-scripted programmes such as reality shows, lifestyle programmes and quizzes, brands can be used as prizes, tools or ingredients. Also non-profit issues, such as anti-smoking and anti-alcohol messages, can be placed.[46]

There are many reasons why brand placement may be an extremely effective marketing communications tool. Many TV programmes have a long shelf life, and also movies have a second life after initial release and find a new audience through DVD sales and rental.

Viewers also have a willingness to be highly involved and connected with their favourite programmes, and often have a positive affective response towards them. They are carried away in the programme. This is also referred to as narrative transportation, telepresence or flow. Consequently, they pay attention to programmes and movies and, due to meaning and affective transfer and assimilation effects, also build connections, activate positive emotions and develop favourite attitudes towards brands used in them.[47] Due to the supportive context and cognitive and affective priming, brand characteristics and attributes are better remembered and liked.[48] Later exposure to advertising will benefit from the 'truth effect' (an increased belief in a claim on account of previous exposure) and the 'mere exposure effect' (positive effect from exposure to a brief stimulus).[49] The Balance Model and the Match-up Principle imply that brand placement is most effective when there is a fit between products, characters and viewers.[50]

In brand placement, there is also an implied endorsement effect from (famous) actors, and it can therefore be at least as powerful as celebrity endorsement in advertising or sponsorship.[51] Viewers identify and build a relationship with spokespeople and learn from them ('social learning') what a brand means and how, when and by whom it is used. Actors are also trustworthy and likeable spokespeople. According to the Attribution Theory, people develop biased (positive) perceptions about brands because they are endorsed – in their perception – by trustworthy actors.[52]

In many cases, viewers are hardly aware of the placements and do not consider them as having a commercial intent. In other words, there is less 'persuasion knowledge'[53] than with advertising. Therefore, brand placement can be more convincing than traditional advertising. Brand placement combines some of the advantages of advertising and publicity.[54]

Some claim that the practice of brand placement is inherently deceptive. Audiences do not perceive it as advertising and develop no counter-arguments. Consequently, brand placement may be most effective when the distinction between advertising and programming is blurred and people are not particularly aware of its influence. Hence, there is an implicit conflict between the need to make placement effective and the need to protect consumers from being misled.[55] Explicit disclosure of brand placement may serve to increase the accessibility of the persuasive or commercial intent behind placing brands, but may at the same time produce resistance to persuasive attempts and undermine the persuasive power of brand placement.[56]

Broadcast sponsorship

Broadcast or programme sponsorship is an increasingly important phenomenon. In the UK, broadcast sponsorship is estimated to be growing by approximately 15% per year.[57] In some countries, as in Belgium, government-owned TV channels are not allowed to broadcast advertising messages, but are allowed to have their programmes sponsored, which makes broadcast sponsoring an extremely visible phenomenon. Broadcast sponsorship differs from plain advertising in a medium, in this case TV, in that the sponsor has an influence on the content of the sponsored programme. Different types of broadcast sponsorship can be distinguished. Mentioning the name of a sponsor in a TV programme is called **billboarding**: 'this programme was produced with the kind co-operation of company X'. Product or **brand placement** involves the sponsor's product being used during the programme, and it is deliberately shown to the audience. **In-script sponsoring** is a specific form of product placement. The sponsoring brand becomes part of the script of the programme. For instance, if a programme is sponsored by a telecoms company and the presenter asks the live audience to switch off their mobile phones, this establishes a connection between the sponsor and the programme. In prize sponsorship, the sponsoring company pays for awards or prizes, and is mentioned in the programme. In the case of programme participation, product placement and billboarding are combined. The TV channel produces a programme in close co-operation with a sponsor, for instance a tour operator that sponsors a travel programme, and pays for the prizes to be won in a contest during the programme.[58]

BUSINESS INSIGHT
Brand placement in movies and TV programmes

Brand placement is by no means a recent phenomenon. In the 1930s, 1940s and 1950s, tobacco companies signed contracts with movie stars to smoke in their films. Among others, in 1937–8 Gary Cooper, Joan Crawford, Clark Gable, Barbara Stanwyck and Spencer Tracy received $6800 from Lucky Strike, an amount that is the equivalent of $100 000 today. Also stars like Gloria Swanson, Bob Hope and Henry Fonda received $1500 (equivalent to about $25 000 today).[59] 'Allo 'Allo is sometimes called the mother of modern brand placement in TV programmes. There is hardly any brand of beer that did not appear in the bar behind René's back.

The champions of brand placement are the Bond movies. In *Die Another Day*, 20 brands were promoted by means of brand placement. The total value of these contracts is estimated to be $45 million. James Bond (Pierce Brosnan in this movie) is civilised, appeals to both men and women, likes luxury and technology, and is popular around the world. Halle Berry, who features as the Bond girl Jinx, appeals to youngsters. Companies try to associate their image with the attractive features of the movie characters. Bond shaves with a Philishave Sensotec, drinks Finlandia vodka, wears an Omega Seamaster watch, and again drives an Aston Martin, after a couple of BMW-dominated Bond movies. Jinx drives a Ford Thunderbird in the same colour as her bikini (a special Thunderbird 007 series is also being made), uses the new Revlon lipsticks Mission Mauve and Hot Pursuit Pink, and wears a Swatch. Other product placers are Samsonite, Sony and British Airways.[60] In the Bond movie *Quantum of Solace*, Bond is no longer 'double O seven', but 'zero zero seven', thanks to Coca-Cola, and drives his Aston Martin again, looking at his Omega watch and checking e-mails with his Sony laptop. In *Moonraker*, a cable cabin crashes into a wall with a gigantic 7UP billboard on it, and in *GoldenEye*, a tank crashes into a Perrier truck. Over the years, the champagne label Dom Pérignon featured in seven different Bond movies; in other movies James drinks Bollinger.[61]

In many cases, making movies would be impossible without brand placement contracts between companies and movie producers.

Of all sponsorship types, broadcast sponsorship is closest to advertising and, for that reason, is capable of achieving similar objectives of awareness and image-building. Furthermore, famous TV actors featuring in the sponsored programmes can be used as celebrity endorsers in subsequent advertising campaigns, thus leveraging the sponsorship effort. Nevertheless, broadcast sponsorship is perceived more positively by the public. Sponsors are closely tied to the programme itself. In fact, they are physically part of it, to the extent that viewers even believe that sponsors actively participate in making the programme. Furthermore, sometimes the endorsing brand has a better image than the programme itself. Therefore, if the sponsor fits the programme well, this can lead to very positive carry-over effects between the two. Programme sponsorship also works in a different way. The long-term association between a likeable programme and a sponsor may lead to a very strong and positive brand image. Finally, broadcast sponsorship, as opposed to advertising, is perceived to benefit everyone. This has a major positive impact on viewers' acceptance of such sponsorships.[62] Belgian research reveals that these positive effects can only be expected if there is a long-term link between an exclusive sponsor and a programme. Short-term broadcast sponsorships are usually as ineffective as ordinary advertising or sports sponsorship campaigns.[63]

BUSINESS INSIGHT
Desperate Housewives drive Ford

At the time when Ford made a brand placement contract with the producers of *Desperate Housewives*, the Ford group owned eight car makes. To reach its customers, the company increasingly relies upon product placement of its cars in movies and TV shows instead of traditional advertising, the effectiveness of which is increasingly challenged. The Ford Explorer 4×4 played a prominent role in *Jurassic Park*, and a Range Rover was prominently present in *Ocean's Twelve*, not to mention James Bond's Aston Martin. Fans of popular shows like *Desperate Housewives* now watch their favourite actresses drive car models of the Ford group: Susan drives a Volvo, and Lynette's husband goes to work in a Jaguar. Film- and programme-makers used to have to talk to each Ford brand separately, but now Ford has established 'Global Brand Entertainment', a company that supports the product placement of all Ford brands, from the Mazda Miata to the Aston Martin Vanquish.[64]

Cause-related sponsorship

Cause-related sponsorship is a combination of PR, sales promotions and corporate philanthropy, based on profit-motivated giving to good causes. MUSH sponsoring comes closest to traditional sponsoring in that money is given to good causes in return for exposure and image-building linkage with the good cause sponsored. Transaction-based sponsorship (sometimes called cause-related marketing) is different in that a company's contribution to a designated cause is linked to customers' engagement in revenue-producing exchanges with the firm.

BUSINESS INSIGHT
Cause-related sponsorship programmes as a communications tool

In October 1999, ConAgra Foods, a company owning more than 80 household brands, launched Feeding Children Better, a cause programme to stop childhood hunger. By partnering with various anti-hunger organisations and using its extensive distribution, advertising and promotion resources, the company was able to bring more food into the charity food distribution system and put child hunger on the agenda. Since the beginning of the programme, 50 Kids Cafés (places where kids can have a decent meal after school) have been funded, fresh food deliveries to relief organisations have increased dramatically and 29 trucks have been purchased for food banks with gifts from ConAgra. The programme received numerous sponsorship and non-profit awards.

Since 1995, Ford Motor Company has sponsored the Susan G. Komen's Breast Cancer Foundation. The support is not linked to Ford sales, but the company helps the organisation with donations, media support and in-kind gifts. The company also created the Ford Force, a united front of dealers, employees and the general public. More than 12 000 Ford employees and more than 3000 dealers have participated in the activities of Ford Force. The results have been impressive, both for the Komen's foundation and for Ford. Website visits and toll-free telephone calls have increased dramatically, and there is a substantial increase in breast examinations. Ford has been able to create interest and sympathy among women, previously a low-involved market segment.

Timberland, a lifestyle brand that sells footwear, apparel and accessories, and City Year, a national youth service organisation, have been partners since 1989. Timberland has donated more than $10 million in grants and in-kind gifts since the beginning of the partnership. The partnership has helped to promote a service ethic among Timberland employees, who have contributed over 170 000 hours of community service. Timberland and City Year have co-ordinated numerous other service events and campaigns. Timberland also opened a City Year office in its headquarters. As a result, the company was voted by its peers as one of the '100 best companies to work for'.[65]

These examples illustrate that cause-related programmes can enhance corporate visibility and image, involve previously uninterested market segments and improve the commitment of the employees and future employees of the organisation.

Although the objectives of cause-related sponsorship are, to a certain extent, the same as those of other sponsorship activity, more emphasis is put on the impact on corporate or brand image as a result of the link between the company or the brand and the good cause sponsored. Research has shown that effective cause-related sponsorship programmes can enhance a company's reputation and brand image and, at the same time, give customers a convenient way to contribute to non-profit organisations through their buying decisions. It is not only marketing professionals who believe that cause-related marketing can improve the image of their brands, consumers also seem to be interested. Studies indicate that as many as two-thirds of consumers are willing to take the company's contribution to good causes into account when making a decision on which brands to purchase. A 2000 survey in 12 European countries indicated that two in five consumers bought a product because of its links to good causes. Cause-related marketing allows companies to attract and retain consumers, differentiate themselves from the competition and reach niche markets. Furthermore, cause-related sponsorship can motivate and engender loyalty in employees. In a 1999 study, 87% of employees in companies with cause-related programmes indicated a strong loyalty to their employer. Gradually, for many companies, cause-related sponsorship has evolved from a short-term, one-shot activity to a long-term strategic choice. Cause programmes are selected because they fit into company competencies and long-term strategic objectives. Cause-related sponsorship places high demands on a company's strategy. A company wanting to engage in cause programmes successfully should be aware of the important principles of such activity: integrity, transparency, sincerity, mutual respect, partnership and mutual benefit. If not, the whole sponsorship programme will backfire, and the company will become known as insincere, opportunistic and lacking in credibility.[66]

A hybrid form of broadcast and cause-related sponsorship is the organised sponsorship of advocacy advertising on TV. For instance, an insurance company could sponsor TV spots in which parents are warned against situations that are potentially dangerous to children, such as water boiling on a stove, knives within reach, etc.

BUSINESS INSIGHT
Sponsors of the 2006 World Championships Football prevent ambush marketing

Twenty-one companies paid €700 million to be able to call themselves official sponsor of the 2006 World Championships Football. Fifteen major partners each paid about €40 million, smaller partners each paid €15 million. In return, they demanded exclusive publicity rights. FIFA's (the organiser) statistical handbook is sponsored by Gillette; in the press rooms only Philips video screens are installed; browsing the Internet can only be done via Deutsche Telekom; and at the bar only Coca-Cola drinks can be offered. The return on sponsorship is often substantial. For instance, Adidas sold 15 million championship footballs, as well as 3 million shirts. Of course, the competitors of these sponsors are aware of the commercial impact and, by means of ambush marketing, also try to benefit from the championships. The Dutch beer brand Bavaria launched a promotion in the Netherlands. When buying a case of Bavaria, a free pair of orange trousers with a lion's tail and the Bavaria logo was given (orange being the colour of the Dutch football team). About a thousand supporters who showed up in the orange trousers were obliged to take them off if they wanted to enter the stadium. Others got the warning not to take their wallet out of their bag, because Puma (the wallet's brand) was not an official sponsor. In the German stadiums, the name of insurance company 'Allianz' on the 'Allianz Arena' had to be covered, because the company was not a sponsor of the tournament, although it paid lots of money to link its name to the new stadium. These measures are not exceptional. Sponsors and organisers hire 'spotters' to discover and prevent all forms of ambush marketing at major events.[67]

Ambush marketing

Ambush marketing occurs when an organisation deliberately seeks an association with a particular event without being an official sponsor of the event to persuade the audience that the ambusher is a legitimate or major sponsor.[68] This can be done by sponsoring the media covering the event, by sponsoring sub-categories within the event (one team or one player), or by overstating the organisation's involvement in the event by means of supporting advertising or sales promotion activity during the event.

Ambush marketers use several techniques, some of which are illegal, most of which are at least dubious, and some of which are legitimate. Ambush sponsors can use logos and brand names in non-authorised media: they can use sports logos and sports images without permission, exploit PR opportunities, sample non-official products or brochures, or run ambiguous advertising campaigns during the time of the event. They can co-operate with sub-sponsors of the event or with the media covering the event, or they can buy advertising spots or trailers that are embedded in an event that is, as such, sponsored by another company. They can publish 'congratulation ads' for athletes that have won a match or a medal or they can sponsor non-profit projects associated with the event.[69] Not surprisingly, official sponsors try to gain exclusive sponsorship and coverage of events in the media to prevent ambushers benefiting or the effectiveness of their own sponsorship efforts diminishing as a result of competitive action.

Selection criteria

Selecting sponsorship proposals should be based on a careful comparison using appropriate selection criteria. Figure 11.3 shows a five-step multi-attribute decision procedure of sponsorship selection. Multiple criteria can be used to assess and select sponsorship proposals. They can be divided into three categories, as listed in Table 11.3.

Depending on the type of company and the type of sponsorship projects, some criteria will be more important than others. But some of them should always be assessed as important. Sponsorship budgets and supporting marketing budgets, compatibility with the company's strategic objectives, the strategic fit between the event and the company's or brand's name, image and target groups will always be important. Empirical studies show that a strong fit between company positioning and the sponsored event or organisation enhances sponsorship effectiveness.[70] This fit can be functional, i.e. the sponsor's products are used during the event by the organisation or the participants, or image-related. In the latter case, the image of the sponsor and the sponsee are congruent.[71] On the other hand, media exposure and other spin-off potential and competitive considerations may be more important in sports sponsorship, while corporate hospitality potential and the interest to employees might be more important in an arts sponsorship project. Some companies may be more concerned about their corporate image (e.g. service or business-to-business marketers), while fast-moving consumer goods companies may be more interested in the commercial spin-off potential, like sampling at the event, or organising a lottery to attend an event.

The criteria listed should be used as a starting point. However, the selection of relevant criteria and the grading of their importance will largely depend on the type of company

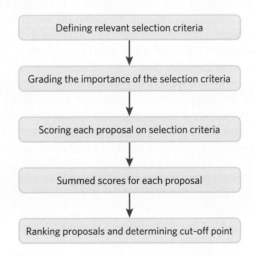

Figure 11.3 Selecting sponsorship projects

Table 11.3 Assessment criteria for sponsorship proposals

Sponsored event or cause	Potential promotional spin-off	Budget
• Type of event or cause	• Event's own communications plan	• Costs in cash or kind
• Quality level or image of the event	• Estimated media coverage	• Alternative investment for budget and expected return
• Target groups	• Quantity and quality of exposure	• Budget for supporting marketing activity
• Compatibility between sponsored event and company's promotional strategy	• Fit between company's and event's communications strategy	• Time implications for own staff
• Strategic fit between event or cause and company or brand name	• Interest with employees	
• Uniqueness of sponsorship or place of the company in the list of sponsors	• Corporate hospitality potential	
	• Sales promotion spin-off potential	
• Length of impact	• PR spin-off potential	
• Geographic scope	• Advertising spin-off potential	
• Company's role in decision-making	• Amount of supporting advertising or PR activity needed	
• Protection against ambush marketing	• Chance of negative or no media exposure	
	• Measurability and evaluation of effectiveness	

and its overall communications strategy. The eventual shortlist of potential candidates for sponsorship will ultimately depend on the relative weights of the criteria used and the available sponsorship budget.

Budgets

Obviously, it is impossible to provide detailed guidelines as to the required budgets of a sponsorship campaign. Budgets should depend on the expected effectiveness or return in terms of exposure, communications effects and sales or market share impact (see below). As in communications campaigns in general, the **objective-and-task method** is called for. Sponsorship decision-makers should decide on the objectives they want to achieve, assess to what extent a sponsorship programme can contribute to these objectives and try to calculate how large an economically meaningful sponsorship budget should be. Needless to say, in most cases this is a cumbersome task.

However, sponsorship-linked budgets are not limited to the expenditures directly related to the sponsored event or cause, but also encompass all communications efforts and budgets that are spent leveraging the investments in the activity or cause. Buying the sponsorship rights is indeed 'just a licence to spend more money to leverage the initial investment'. For instance, Coca-Cola spent $40 million to become an official sponsor of the 1996 Olympics, and an estimated $500 million to leverage this status.[72] A Canadian study revealed that only 37% of sports sponsors do not provide an additional support budget. But almost 20% allocate an additional budget of 50% of the sponsoring budget or more to communications support activities.

Indeed, there are different reasons why sponsorship should be supported by other media efforts. Firstly, as has already been mentioned, sponsorship has its limitations. Very often brand awareness and brand image are supported, but other necessary communications and commercial objectives, like building knowledge about the brand and generating sales, will have to be achieved by means of additional communications support. But most importantly, the general principle of integrated communications also applies to sponsorship: the more it is supported by, and integrated in, the rest of the communications mix, the more effective it will be. For instance, among the sponsoring companies of the 1996 Olympics that also ran advertising on the events, 64% succeeded in creating the link. On the other hand, of the official sponsors that did not run advertising, only 4% created the link.[73]

Measuring sponsorship effectiveness

Similar to the measurement of the effectiveness of other communications tools, isolating the effect of sponsorship is complicated by a number of factors, such as the simultaneous use of instruments of the marketing and communications mix, the carry-over effect of earlier activities, creative management issues, the pursuit of multiple objectives and the discretionary nature of media coverage.

Sponsorship is to a certain extent similar to advertising in that one of its main objectives is to build brand awareness with specific target groups. Additionally, and equally important, brands try to improve their image by linking their name to the event sponsored. Furthermore, in a number of sponsorship projects, communications results are not only obtained during the sponsored event, but also as a result of their media coverage. Sponsorship research reflects these objectives and characteristics of this communications mix instrument.

Four types of sponsorship effectiveness can be distinguished (Figure 11.4). Two types of exposure can be distinguished: the number of people attending the event and the exposure resulting from the media coverage of the event. By counting the number of attendees at a sponsored event and/or studying the composition of the audience present, the number of consumers reached and the frequency of their exposure to the brand name can be estimated. If the sponsored event is covered by the media, the number of lines, pages or times the brand name is mentioned, or the number of seconds it is shown on TV or heard on the radio, can be calculated. On this basis, reach and frequency of exposure can also be estimated, as well as the monetary value of the exposure obtained. Evidently, frequency of exposure and reach only give an indication of the probability of having contacted parts of the target group, but nothing about the actual number of contacts, let alone of their quality or impact.

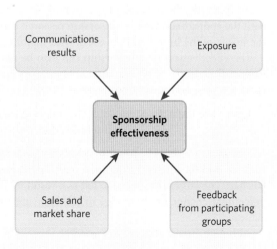

Figure 11.4 Types of sponsorship effectiveness measures

Communications results can also be measured. In this respect, sponsorship campaign effectiveness measurements are very similar to the advertising campaign tests discussed (see Chapter 9) on advertising research: brand awareness, correct sponsor attribution and the effect on the image of the sponsored event and the sponsoring brand can be measured. Besides increasing brand awareness, associating the brand with the sponsored event is the most important objective of a sponsorship campaign. As a result, measuring the percentage of the target group able to attribute correctly the name of the sponsoring brand(s) to an event is one of the most important measures of sponsorship effectiveness. In this type of test, a list of sponsored events is presented to a sample of consumers, who have to attribute (aided or unaided) the sponsors of the event. This results in an indication of the percentage of the target group that can correctly attribute sponsors to events, as well as measures of 'sponsor confusion'. Correct (aided and unaided) sponsorship attribution can be very low, while sponsorship confusion is in some cases stunningly high.

BUSINESS INSIGHT
Virgin's Festival buddy

The airline company Virgin Express sponsors several music festivals. To counter the problem of festival visitors not knowing/remembering who actually sponsored the festival, Virgin decided to move from just being present during the festivals to involving festival visitors before and during the festival. To this end, Virgin launched the Festival buddy campaign. Festival lovers could register by means of SMS or on the festival buddy website. Afterwards, Virgin sent them a 'buddyword' by SMS. The challenge for the registered persons was to find another person with the same buddyword. Everyone who succeeded in this and presented themselves with their buddy at a Virgin stand on one of the festivals won a free Virgin flight. The campaign created an enormous viral effect and was a real hype for several months in many communities. A Google search on the word 'festivalbuddy' delivered about 80 000 results. Someone created a special 'festivalbuddy-matching' site and during the festivals several people wore a T-shirt on which their buddy word was printed in the hope of finding their buddy. No doubt, Virgin succeeded in its objective of being linked to the sponsored festivals.[74]

Additionally, the purpose of sponsorship is to associate the sponsoring brand or company with the sponsored event. Sponsorship research can therefore also focus on the link between the image of the brand and the event with members of the target group.

The effectiveness of sponsorship can also be conceptualised by means of the 'Persuasive Impact Equation'.[75] This equation integrates a number of important sponsorship impact factors at the communications level:

Persuasive impact = Strength of the link × Duration of the link
× (Gratitude felt due to the link + Perceptual change due to the link)

The more the target group members are aware of the link between the sponsor and the sponsee, and the longer the duration of this perceived link, the more the impact a sponsorship has had. The larger the gratitude felt as a result of the sponsorship, and the more positive the perceptual change of the image of the sponsor, the more the impact the sponsorship has achieved.

Although increasing sales or market share is not the primary objective of sponsorship, its long-term effectiveness can also be assessed by estimating the sponsorship's commercial impact.

Finally, sponsorship effectiveness can also be measured on the basis of feedback from participating groups. Given the nature of some types of sponsorship, its effectiveness primarily lies in the reaction of participants to corporate hospitality sponsorship projects or the opinion of employees about sponsorship programmes. This will particularly – but not exclusively – be the case in cultural or cause-related sponsorship.

IMC INSIGHT
Integrating sponsorship in IMC

Sponsorship is probably one of the marketing communications tools that requires most support from other tools to be effective and, at the same time, offers ample opportunities for marketing communications spin-off activities. Sponsorship of events, teams and organisations can be referred to in TV advertising during the event or in the ads of sponsored partners, by means of cross-reference to teams, celebrities, events, etc. TV coverage of events can be used as an opportunity for programme sponsorship or product placement. Events can be an opportunity for couponing or sampling, but also for corporate hospitality. Cause-related sponsorship can be part of a PR campaign aimed at building a good reputation for the company and its brands. It can enhance corporate identity building by means of the opportunities it offers to motivate and reward employees. During the sponsored event, a microsite can be set up on which games, promotions and other customer contact opportunities are offered, which can subsequently be used for customer relationship marketing and direct communications. In-store merchandising can hook up to the sponsorship campaign by drawing attention to the sponsored event and by offering special promotions connected with the sponsorship campaign.

Summary

Sponsorship is an increasingly important instrument of the marketing communications mix. This becomes clear not only from the increasing budgets spent on sponsoring, but also from the fact that the key roles in sponsorship decisions are often played by members of top management. Sponsors often try to escape the advertising clutter by linking their name to an event, and hope for beneficial carry-over effects from the event on company and brand awareness and image. Target groups for sponsorship not only are those that visit or participate in the event, but can also be any of the other marketing and corporate audiences of a company. Four basic types of sponsorship can be distinguished. Event-related (culture and sports) sponsorship is best known. Cause-related sponsorship, or sponsoring good causes, is the oldest form. Broadcast sponsorship is a more recent phenomenon, but is growing fast. The youngest type is ambush marketing, whereby a company tries to benefit from an event it does not sponsor. To integrate sponsorship effectively into the marketing communications mix, it is crucial to select the right sponsorship projects and to manage them at close range. Criteria that can be used to select projects can be event-related (type of event, quality level, target groups, uniqueness of sponsorship, fit with strategic objectives, etc.), spin-off-related (indirect communications effects, media coverage, interest with employees, advertising and PR spin-off, etc.) and budget-related (cost in cash or in kind, time implications for staff, etc.). Sponsorship effectiveness can be measured on the basis of exposure, communications results, commercial results or on the basis of feedback from participating groups.

REVIEW QUESTIONS

1. What is the difference between sponsorship and advertising, public relations and value marketing?

2. How can the mere exposure effect, congruence theory and operant conditioning explain how sponsorship works?

3. What are the most important current developments in sponsorship?

4. How can sponsorship be used to reach a variety of objectives in different target groups?

5. What are the advantages and disadvantages of the various types of event-related sponsorship?

6. How can cause-related sponsorship contribute to a company's communications strategy?

7. What criteria can be used to select sponsorship proposals?

8. How can the effectiveness of a sponsorship campaign be measured?

Further reading

Adkins, S. (1999), *Cause-related Marketing: Who Cares Wins*. Oxford: Butterworth–Heinemann.

Duffy, N. and Hooper, J. (2003), *Branding: Harnessing the Power of Emotion to Build Strong Brands*. Chichester: Wiley.

Grey, A.M. and Skildum-Reid, K. (2008), *The Sponsorship Seeker's Toolkit*. Sydney: McGraw-Hill.

Lagae, W. (2005), *Sports Sponsorship and Marketing Communications*. Harlow: Prentice Hall.

Lehu, J.-M. (2009), *Branded Entertainment: Product Placement and Brand Strategy in the Entertainment Business*. London: Kogan Page.

International Journal of Sports Marketing & Sponsorship, http://www.imrpublications.com/JSMS/.

CASE 11:
Carrefour: setting up convenience stores at music festivals

Carrefour: a world leader in distribution

The Carrefour Group is one of the world's leading distribution groups. It is the world's second-largest retailer and the largest in Europe. The group currently operates four main grocery store formats: hypermarkets, supermarkets, cash & carry and convenience stores. The Carrefour Group currently has over 9500 stores, either company-operated or franchises. It operates in three major markets: Europe, Latin America and Asia. With a presence in 32 countries, over 57% of group turnover derives from outside France. The group sees strong potential for further international growth in the future, particularly in such large national markets as China, Brazil, Indonesia, Poland and Turkey. In 2009, Carrefour had a turnover of €112 245 million and 471 000 employees. Wherever it has a presence, Carrefour is actively committed to promoting local economic development. The group consistently emphasises local recruitment plus management and staff training on the job wherever they work. Typically, the Carrefour Group will be one of the leading private employers in any country where it operates. Naturally, this is the case for France, where the group was originally founded, but it is also true of such countries as Brazil, Argentina, Colombia,

Italy and Greece. The group also seeks to support local suppliers, with some 90% to 95% of the products on its shelves sourced locally, depending on the country.

Faithful to the concept of 'everything-under-one-roof', Carrefour hypermarkets offer an average surface area of 8400 m^2 filled with a range of between 20 000 and 80 000 food and non-food items, all at attractive prices. With over 1100 hypermarkets in 32 countries, the Carrefour Group is consolidating its number one global position in this format. In 2007, expansion accelerated with 123 new hypermarkets, particularly in Asia, with the building of 36 new hypermarkets, including 22 in China – where the group broke its record for store openings in a one-year period. In Europe, 51 new hypermarkets came on board, including the 160th in Spain and the 71st in Poland following integration of the 15 AholdPolska hypermarkets. In Latin America, the group became the number one food retailer in Brazil after acquiring the 34 Atacadao discount hypermarkets and inaugurating 62 new hypermarkets. Hypermarkets account for almost 60% of Carrefour sales and employ more than 300 000 people.

Carrefour supermarkets, with surface areas ranging from 1000 to over 2000 m^2, offer a range of some 10 000 listings, most of them food. Rural stores are currently developing a broader offering of non-food products, such as clothing and household goods. In 2007, the Carrefour Group opened 326 new supermarkets, mainly in Europe. At year end 2007, the Carrefour Group had 2708 supermarkets in 10 countries, accounting for 23.5% of sales and employing almost 85 000 people.

Carrefour's cash & carry stores offer a reduced product range at discount prices – around 20% lower than major brands – in surface areas ranging from 200 to 1000 m^2 for Dia stores with a parking lot. The range mainly comprises Dia-branded food products plus a small selection of established, major brand items. The group's cash & carry stores offer a range of quality fresh products at attractive prices. In France, they offer everything a family needs, with between 1500 and 1800 food listings plus a limited number of essential personal care and cleaning products. At the end of 2007, there were 897 discount stores with more than 6000 employees, accounting for almost 10% of sales.

A key element in the group's multi-format policy is the convenience stores. They offer a complementary outlet to urban and rural customers. Each of the group's convenience store banners stands out for the way it tailors its offering to the needs of its customer base. In France, the convenience stores offer a range of products and services (e.g. home delivery, dry cleaning, 48-hour photo development, ticket distribution, photocopying, stamps, newspapers and more). With surface areas that range between 50 and 900 m^2, convenience stores can be adapted to suit any situation, from urban sites to the most rural location, where they help to counteract the trend of disappearing services. Worldwide,

Carrefour operates 4800 stores in seven countries, mainly under franchising agreements.

Carrefour is the largest retailer in Belgium. In 2007, it operated 626 shops, 57 of which are hypermarkets, 378 supermarkets and 191 Express convenience stores. It employs 15 500 people and has a turnover of €5.27 billion.

Music festivals: a large and unserved audience

As in many other countries, in Belgium during the summer season there is a music festival nearly every weekend. The three largest ones are Graspop, Pukkelpop and Rock Werchter.

The first Graspop festival was held in 1986 as a family music festival with mainly local acts. After ten years, in 1995, the festival faced a sharply decreasing audience, despite international top acts such as Joe Cocker and Simple Minds. The 1993 and 1994 festivals were, however, very successful, featuring heavy-metal bands such as Motörhead, the Ramones, Paradise Lost and Biohazard. The management therefore decided to reposition the festival as an international open-air metal music festival, the Graspop Metal Meeting, on the last weekend of June. The first festival in 1996 was a big success. Ten thousand metal heads enjoyed the music of 15 bands, featuring Iron Maiden and Type O Negative as top acts. By 1998, the metal crowd increased to 20 000, a loyal group of fans that in subsequent years turned out for top acts such as Black Sabbath, Judas Priest, Agnostic Front, Slayer, Sepultura and Alice Cooper. The 10th anniversary in 2005 was celebrated with 80 000 visitors, offering a three-day festival on four different podiums featuring over 60 bands. In 2007, the festival welcomed 100 000 visitors (calculated as the sum of all visitors per festival day, or 48 000 'unique' visitors), about 30 000 of whom stayed on the camping ground. In total, Graspop has featured over 350 bands. It is one of the major festival events in Belgium.

Pukkelpop is a three-day music festival which celebrated its 23rd anniversary in 2009. It is internationally renowned for its focus on alternative, progressive and underground music. In 2007, 152 000 visitors (77 000 unique) came to Pukkelpop, to experience more than 210 acts. Fifty thousand visitors spent the night on the camping ground.

The history of Rock Werchter dates back to 1967, when a so-called beat happening was organised long before Woodstock in the USA and the Isle of Wight in the UK. At its height in 1978, this Jazz Bilzen event, back then a four-day festival, drew 15 000 festival-goers on its main day. Three years later, only 6000 people showed up and the festival stopped. From 1981 the festival was held in two places (Torhout and Werchter), when about 20 000 and 27 000 spectators showed up. Things really 'exploded' in Werchter in 1982, when about 40 000 people were standing at the festival gates. In 1998, the festival presented 23 acts. In 2008, there were 60, on two stages. Rock Werchter has turned into one of the most important and – according to its fans – best festivals in the world. It receives 107 000 unique visitors, 60 000 of whom stay on the camping grounds.

All these visitors have to eat, drink and camp, and thus form a gigantic and largely unserved audience for a convenience store with a well-adapted product mix. In 2008, Carrefour decided to develop tailor-made points-of-sales at these festivals.

Carrefour festival shops: tapping into a unique point-of-sales opportunity

The Belgian fast-moving consumer goods retailing industry is dominated by three major players with nearly equal market shares: Delhaize, Colruyt and Carrefour. Carrefour was perceived as stuck in the middle: its image was unclear if not negative. At the end of 2006, it was apparent to Carrefour that it had an image problem. Delhaize was known for its quality products, Colruyt was the cheapest retailer for manufacturer-branded products and Carrefour was big, cold, distant and very French. In terms of communications mix, the company used advertising campaigns and sales promotion brochures, but very little, if any, PR and sponsorship. In 2007, the whole marketing management was changed and, by the end of 2008, it was decided to reposition Carrefour using the slogan 'The power to choose'. It was also decided to use sponsorship and PR more intensively to carry over an image of warmth, cosiness and 'close to the people'.

One of the first ideas that came to mind was to be present at one or more of the many music festivals that take place annually in Belgium. However, the management felt that it would not be sufficient to have a logo on the festival billboard or to be visually present at the festival venue, but better to link its presence to a cost-efficient, innovative and fun experience in a way that could generate many contacts with young customers and potential customers, not so much to build brand image, but to build experiences that would enhance brand image. The idea arose to install a shop at selected festival camping grounds. The weak point of music festival camping lots is that people have to survive in basic conditions and accommodation is not very sophisticated. Of course, people can buy beer, soft drinks, hamburgers and sausages, usually at high prices, but festival attendees want more. Providing a shop would give them the opportunity to buy food and other convenient products at fair prices, consistent with the slogan of 'The power to choose'.

The selection of music festivals was based on two criteria. First of all, the festival should be large enough and enough people should stay for a number of days on the camping ground to make it worthwhile. Secondly, there should be enough variation in the public to reach customers and potential customers. Eventually, three 2008 festivals were selected: Graspop (25–28 June), Rock Werchter (2–5 July) and Pukkelpop (19–22 August).

At each of the festival camping grounds a 100 m^2 (10 m × 10 m) convenience shop was set up with two checkout counters each with a capacity of 1000 checkouts per day. The shops were open the evening before the start of the festivals, and during the festivals every day from 8 a.m. to 10 p.m., and the morning after the festival. The shops were positioned as 'Express festival shops', Carrefour's convenience store label. Conventional Express shops are open on Sundays and offer mainly an assortment of food products. It was decided to apply normal shop prices and not add a 'festival premium' like most other drink and food stands usually do. Also, private labels are becoming increasingly popular. The company therefore decided to use the opportunity to promote its own private label 'Carrefour' under which a wide assortment of about 3000 products are sold, and to offer as many Carrefour products as possible. The assortment of 280 products was adapted to what camping goers need: tents, batteries, toilet paper, tape, toothbrushes, sleeping bags, camping gas, deodorant, shaving cream, sun block, condoms, tooth picks, disinfectant, bottle openers and food and drink items such as rice, spaghetti, ketchup, fruit, vegetables, yoghurt, milk, mineral water and, every morning, freshly baked bread. Express shops are renowned for their fresh products. Baking fresh bread in the shop creates a more genuine real shopping experience. At Graspop, barbecuing is allowed, so barbecue material was also sold. Pack sizes were small and adapted to what people would need for one weekend. No alcohol, soft drinks and cigarettes were sold, because a substantial part of the festival's profit comes from selling these products. Festival organisers are very wary about guerrilla marketing, and they see to it that if, for instance, Coca-Cola is an official sponsor, no Pepsi is sold on the festival grounds. Where Coca-Cola was an official festival sponsor, Carrefour sold only Chaudfontaine water, a Coca-Cola company brand, in order to blend in with other festival sponsors. The shops were operated by students, but shop management was entrusted to Carrefour staff, selected after an internal call for candidates. The response, both from its own employees and from external people interested in shop keeping at the festivals, was massive. Also internally, the initiative led to a lot of 'rumour around the brand'. The cost of setting up these stores at festivals, including the festival sponsorship fee, logistics, shop keepers' salaries, stands and transportation, was significantly lower than that of a main festival sponsor, and in the latter case no real experience is provided and main sponsors still have to provide sampling and animation at an extra cost.

A cost-effective marketing communications project

Obviously, there was a direct return on investment. The festival shops realised a significant turnover. Sales per customer per purchase were similar to what is sold in an average regular Express shop. To Carrefour's own surprise, during the first business hour at Rock Werchter 40 tents were sold. In total, about 4000 chocolate cakes, over 6000 croissants, more than 5000 breads and sandwiches and over 2000 doughnuts were sold, but also 3000 bottles of milk, 400 raincoats, 300 toothbrushes, hundreds of plastic spoons, forks, knives and plates, 1500 apples and 1000 nectarines, and 3000 packets of crisps.

Of course, image-building was at least as important. Festival attendees were all very positive. After the festivals, various blogs were screened; no single negative remark was found and people remarked: 'if I would have known there was going to be a shop, I would not have brought so much stuff'. Many people appreciated the fair, 'normal' prices, and nobody complained about the long queues.

Also festival organisers were very enthusiastic. They consider it a very cost-effective way of offering added value on their festivals, and they urged Carrefour to set up shops at other camping grounds too. Most festival organisers announced the presence of the shop on their websites and issued press releases. Rock Werchter announced the presence of the Express shop explicitly on its 2009 festival website. Competitors of Carrefour have also shown their interest in being present at the festivals, a move that Carrefour blocked by negotiating a right of first refusal. Also, other festivals have asked Carrefour to set up a store at their venues.

At Rock Werchter, the shop was set up along a major road. Many people other than festival attendees have therefore been exposed to this new initiative.

The shops also led to massive amounts of free publicity in almost every Belgian newspaper, featuring extensive coverage with headlines such as: 'Festival shops: bull's eye', 'Carrefour finds hole in festival market', 'Supermarket on festival camping ground'.

Due to the short planning cycle, Carrefour itself did not support its initiative by means of other communications efforts.

Adapting and extending the project in 2009

After a thorough evaluation, the market team decided to extend the initiative and to make some adaptations. In 2009, shops were set up at the same three festivals, and a fourth festival, Dranouter Folk (6–9 August), was added. Shop floor surface was slightly enlarged, and a third check-out was provided. The shops would no longer be open the day after the festival – attendees pack and leave as soon as they can. However, opening hours during the festival were extended, based on the 2008 experience. On the evening before the start of the festival, the shops were open until 2 a.m., and on festival days between 7 a.m. and 11 p.m. The assortment only required minor modifications since it appeared to be well adapted to festival attendees' needs. Even more Carrefour private label products were offered instead of A-brands. Price-level policy was the same. Although the branding of the shops on the outside was OK, inside branding was improved. Also some fine-tuning was called for. For instance, at Pukkelpop, coffee brand Douwe Egberts organised a 'breakfast action' with coffee and croissants. Therefore, these products were not part of the assortment at this festival.

QUESTIONS

1. Do you think that setting up a point-of-sales at music festivals was a good idea? Does it focus on the right target groups? Is it meaningful in terms of image-building for Carrefour?

2. Did Carrefour take the right decision in terms of festival selection, pricing strategy, assortment and shop layout? Why or why not? What would you do differently?

3. If a retailer in your own country were to think of doing a similar project, which festivals could they select and why? Would the retailer have to organise its shops in a different way than Carrefour? Why or why not?

4. At the 2008 festival, Carrefour did not support the initiative by means of other marketing communications activities. Build a supporting Carrefour communications plan for the next festival.

5. In what way could Carrefour measure the success and effectiveness of this project?

Sources: www.carrefour.com; www.carrefour.eu; www.graspop.be; www.pukkelpop.be; www.rockwerchter.be.

Information provided by Lars Vervoort, Corporate Communication Manager, and Tine Nelissen, PR & Communication Coordinator.

References

[1] Meenaghan, T. (1991), 'The Role of Sponsorship in the Marketing Communication Mix', *International Journal of Advertising*, 10(1), 35–48; Lagae, W. (2006), *Marketingcommunicatie in de Sport*. Amsterdam, Pearson Education Benelux.

[2] Erdogan, Z.B. and Kitchen, P.J. (1998), 'The Interaction Between Advertising and Sponsorship: Uneasy Alliance or Strategic Symbiosis', in Kitchen, P.J. (ed.), *The Changing World of Corporate and Marketing Communication: Towards the Next Millennia, Proceedings of the 3rd Annual Conference of the Global Institute for Corporate and Marketing Communication*. Glasgow: Strathclyde Graduate Business School, 144–55.

[3] Hastings, G.B. (1984), 'Sponsorship Works Differently from Advertising', *International Journal of Advertising*, 3(2), 171–8.

[4] Erdogan, Z.B. and Kitchen, P.J. (1998), 'The Interaction Between Advertising and Sponsorship: Uneasy Alliance or Strategic Symbiosis', in Kitchen, P.J. (ed.), *The Changing World of Corporate and Marketing Communication: Towards the Next Millennia, Proceedings of the 3rd Annual Conference of the Global Institute for Corporate and Marketing Communication*. Glasgow: Strathclyde Graduate Business School, 144–55.

[5] Meenaghan, T. (1983), 'Commercial Sponsorship', *European Journal of Marketing*, 7(7), 5–71.

[6] Marshall, D.W. and Cook, G. (1992), 'The Corporate (Sports) Sponsor', *International Journal of Advertising*, 11(3), 307–24.

[7] Bloxham, M. (1998), 'Brand Affinity and Television Programme Sponsorship', *International Journal of Advertising*, 17(1), 89–98.

[8] Cornwell, T.B. and Maignan, I. (1998), 'An International Review of Sponsorship Research', *Journal of Advertising*, 27(1), 1–21.

[9] Adfo Specialist Group (1999), *Rabobank Wielerplan (Rabobank Cycling Plan)*, Adfo Sponsoring Cases no. 2, Alphen aan den Rijn: Samson; Adfo Specialist Group (2000), *Nashuatec en Oliver (Nashuatec and Oliver)*, Adfo Sponsoring Cases no. 5, Alphen aan den Rijn: Samson.

[10] See also: Abshire, M. (2002), 'Consumer Product Manufacturers: Maintain Giving in Uncertain Times', *Corporate Philanthropy Report*, 17 (March), 1–11; Polonsky, M. and Macdonald, E. (2000), 'Exploring the Link Between Cause-related Marketing and Brand Building', *International Journal of Nonprofit and Voluntary Sector Marketing*, 5 (February), 46–57.

[11] www.samen.nl.

[12] Cornwell, T.B. and Maignan, I. (1998), 'An International Review of Sponsorship Research', *Journal of Advertising*, 27(1), 1–21.

[13] Watson, J. and Watson, J. (2001), 'Sponsorship and Congruity Theory: A Theoretical Framework for Explaining Consumer Attitude and Recall of Event Sponsorship', *Advances in Consumer Research*, 28, 439–45.

[14] Hansen, F. and Scotwin, L. (1995), 'An Experimental Enquiry into Sponsorship: What Effects Can Be Measured?', *Marketing and Research Today*, 23(3), 173–81.

[15] De Pelsmacker, P., Geuens, M. and Anckaert, P. (2002), 'Media Context and Advertising Effectiveness: The Role of Context Appreciation and Context–Ad Similarity', *Journal of Advertising*, 31(2), 49–61.

[16] Hoek, J., Gendall, P., Jeffcoat, M. and Orsman, D. (1997), 'Sponsorship and Advertising: A Comparison of Their Effects', *Journal of Marketing Communication*, 3(1), 21–32.

[17] Hansen, F. and Scotwin, L. (1995), 'An Experimental Enquiry into Sponsorship: What Effects Can Be Measured?', *Marketing and Research Today*, 23(3), 173–81.

[18] Irwin, R., Sutton, W. and McCarthy, L. (2002), *Sport Promotion and Sales Management*. Champaign, IL. Human Kinetics.

[19] Meenaghan, T. (1998), 'Current Developments and Future Directions in Sponsorship', *International Journal of Advertising*, 17(1), 3–28.

[20] http://www.imrpublications.com/imr_product.php?dwagu_product_id=1&dwagu_product_data_id=9 (accessed June 2009).

[21] Euro Effie (2002), Berlin: Gesamptverbrand Werbeagenturne GWA eV, http://www.euro-effie.com.

[22] Quester, P.G., Farrelly, F.J. and Burton, R. (1998), 'Sports Sponsorship Management: A Multinational Comparative Study', *Journal of Marketing Communication*, 4(2), 115–28; Farrelly, F.J. and Quester, P.G. (1997), 'Sports and Arts Sponsors: Investigating the Similarities and Differences in Management Practices', in Meenaghan, T. (ed.), *New and Evolving Paradigms: The Emerging Future of Marketing*, American Marketing Association Special Conference Proceedings. Dublin: University College, 874–86.

[23] Quester, P. (1997), 'Awareness as a Measure of Sponsorship Effectiveness: The Adelaide Formula One Grand Prix and Evidence of Incidental Ambush Effects', *Journal of Marketing Communications*, 3(1), 1–20.

[24] Meenaghan, T. (1998), 'Current Developments and Future Directions in Sponsorship', *International Journal of Advertising*, 17(1), 3–28.

[25] Thwaites, D., Anguilar-Manjarrez, R. and Kidd, C. (1998), 'Sports Sponsorship Development in Leading Canadian Companies: Issues and Trends', *International Journal of Advertising*, 17(1), 29–50.

[26] www.nop.co.uk/news, 23 May 2003.

[27] Thwaites, D., Anguilar-Manjarrez, R. and Kidd, C. (1998), 'Sports Sponsorship Development in Leading Canadian Companies: Issues and Trends', *International Journal of Advertising*, 17(1), 29–50; Abratt, R., Clayton, B.C. and Pitt, L.F. (1987), 'Corporate Objectives in Sports Sponsorship', *International Journal of Advertising*, 8(2), 299–311; Hansen, F. and Scotwin, L. (1995), 'An Experimental Enquiry into Sponsorship: What Effects Can Be Measured?', *Marketing and Research Today*, 23(3), 173–81.

28 Quester, P. (1997), 'Sponsoring Returns: Unexpected Results and the Value of Naming Rights', in Meenaghan, T. (ed.), *New and Evolving Paradigms: The Emerging Future of Marketing, American Marketing Association Special Conference Proceedings*. Dublin: University College, 692–4.

29 Cornwell, T.B. and Maignan, I. (1998), 'An International Review of Sponsorship Research', *Journal of Advertising*, 27(1), 1–21.

30 Grimes, E. and Meenaghan, T. (1998), 'Focusing Commercial Sponsorship on the Internal Corporate Audience', *International Journal of Advertising*, 17(1), 51–74.

31 Lagae, W. (2005), *Sports Sponsorship and Marketing Communications*. Harlow: Prentice Hall.

32 Irwin, R., Sutton, W. and McCarthy, L. (2002), *Sport Promotion and Sales Management*. Champaign, IL: Human Kinetics.

33 http://www.imrpublications.com/imr_product.php?dwagu_product_id=1&dwagu_product_data_id=9 (accessed June 2009).

34 Westerbeek, H., Shilbury, D. and Quick, S. (2007), *Strategischesportmarketing (Strategic sports marketing)*. Nieuwegein: Arko Sports Media.

35 Lagae, W. (1997), 'Het Pokerspel van de Professionele Wielersponsoring' ('The Poker Game of Professional Cycling Sponsorship'), in Duyck, R. and Van Tilborgh, C. (eds), *Aan Marketing Denken en Doen. Marketing Jaarboek (Thinking of and Doing Marketing. Marketing Yearbook)*. Zellick: Roularta Books, 86–94.

36 Brassington, F. and Pettitt, S. (2003), *Principles of Marketing*. London: Pitman.

37 Cornwell, T.B. and Maignan, I. (1998), 'An International Review of Sponsorship Research', *Journal of Advertising*, 27(1), 1–21.

38 Thwaites, D., Anguilar-Manjarrez, R. and Kidd, C. (1998), 'Sports Sponsorship Development in Leading Canadian Companies: Issues and Trends', *International Journal of Advertising*, 17(1), 29–50.

39 *De Morgen*, 16 May 2012.

40 Farrelly, F.J. and Quester, P.G. (1997), 'Sports and Arts Sponsors: Investigating the Similarities and Differences in Management Practices', in Meenaghan, T. (ed.), *New and Evolving Paradigms: The Emerging Future of Marketing, American Marketing Association Special Conference Proceedings*. Dublin: University College, 874–86.

41 Balasubramanian, S.K., Karrh, J.A. and Patwardhan, H. (2006), 'Audience Response to Product Placement: An Integrative Framework and Future Research Agenda', *Journal of Advertising*, 35(3), 115–41.

42 Karrh, J.A. (1998), 'Brand Placements: A Review', *Journal of Current Issues and Research in Advertising*, 20(2), 31–49.

43 Balasubramanian, S.K., Karrh, J.A. and Patwardhan, H. (2006), 'Audience Response to Product Placement: An Integrative Framework and Future Research Agenda', *Journal of Advertising*, 35(3), 115–41.

44 Gupta, P.B. and Lord, K.R. (1998), 'Product Placement in Movies: The Effect of Prominence and Mode on Audience Recall', *Journal of Current Issues in Advertising*, 20(1), 47–59.

45 PQ Media (2008), 'Exclusive PQ Media Research: Branded Entertainment Market Defies Slowing Economy, Expands 14.7% to $22.3 bil. in 2007', http://www.pqmedia.com/about-press-20080212-bemf.html (accessed June 2009).

46 Russell, D.W. and Russell, C.A. (2008), 'Embedded Alcohol Messages in Television Series: The Interactive Effect of Warnings and Audience Connectedness on Viewers' Alcohol Beliefs', *Journal of Studies on Alcohol and Drugs*, 69(3), 459–71; Russell, C.A. and Stern, B.B. (2006), 'Consumers, Characters and Products: A Balance Model of Sitcom Product Placement Effects', *Journal of Advertising*, 35(1), 7–21; Gupta, P.B. and Gould, S.J. (2007), 'Recall of Products Placed as Prizes Versus Commercials in Game Shows', *Journal of Current Issues and Research in Advertising*, 29(1), 43–53.

47 Karrh, J.A. (1998), 'Brand Placements: A Review', *Journal of Current Issues and Research in Advertising*, 20(2), 31–49.

48 McCracken, G. (1989), 'Who is the Celebrity Endorser? Cultural Foundations of the Endorsement Process', *Journal of Consumer Research*, 16, 310–22; Balasubramanian, S.K., Karrh, J.A. and Patwardhan, H. (2006), 'Audience Response to Product Placement: An Integrative Framework and Future Research Agenda', *Journal of Advertising*, 35(3), 115–41.

49 Law, S. and Braun, K.A. (2000), 'I'll Have What She's Having: Gauging the Impact of Product Placements on Viewers', *Psychology & Marketing*, 17(12), 1059–75.

50 Russell, C.A. and Stern, B.B. (2006), 'Consumers, Characters and Products: A Balance Model of Sitcom Product Placement Effects', *Journal of Advertising*, 35(1), 7–21.

51 Yang, M., Roskos-Ewoldsen, B. and Roskos-Ewoldsen, D.R. (2004), 'Mental Models for Brand Placement', in Shrum, L.J. (ed.), *Psychology of Entertainment Media: Blurring the Lines Between Entertainment and Persuasion*. Mahwah, NJ: Lawrence Erlbaum Associates, 79–98.

52 Balasubramanian, S.K., Karrh, JA. and Patwardhan, H. (2006), 'Audience Response to Product Placement: An Integrative Framework and Future Research Agenda', *Journal of Advertising*, 35(3), 115–41; La Ferle, C. and Edwards, S.M. (2006), 'Product Placement: How Brands Appear on Television', *Journal of Advertising*, 35(4), 65–86.

53 Friestad, M. and Wright, P. (1994), 'The Persuasion Knowledge Model: How People Cope with Persuasion Attempts', *Journal of Consumer Research*, 21 (June), 1–31.

54 McCarthy, J.A. (2004), 'Product Placement: The Nature of the Practice and Potential Avenues of Inquiry', in Shrum, L.J. (ed.), *Psychology of Entertainment Media: Blurring the Lines Between Entertainment and Persuasion*. Mahwah, NJ: Lawrence Erlbaum Associates, 45–62.

55 Bhatnagar, N., Aksoy, L. and Malkoc, S.A. (2004), 'Embedding Brands Within Media Content: The Impact of Message, Media and Consumer Characteristics on Placement Efficacy', in Shrum, L.J. (ed.), *Psychology of Entertainment Media: Blurring the Lines Between Entertainment and Persuasion*. Mahwah, NJ: Lawrence Erlbaum Associates, 99–116; Law, S. and Braun-LaTour, K.A. (2004), 'Product Placements: How to Measure their Impact', in Shrum, L.J. (ed.), *Psychology of Entertainment Media: Blurring the Lines Between Entertainment and Persuasion*.

Mahwah, NJ: Lawrence Erlbaum Associates, 63–78; Avery, R.J. and Ferraro, R. (2000), 'Verisimilitude or Advertising? Brand Appearances on Prime-time Television', *Journal of Consumer Affairs*, 34(2), 217–44.

56   Russell, D.W. and Russell, C.A. (2008), 'Embedded Alcohol Messages in Television Series: The Interactive Effect of Warnings and Audience Connectedness on Viewers' Alcohol Beliefs', *Journal of Studies on Alcohol and Drugs*, 69(3), 459–71; Campbell, M.C., Mohr, G.S. and Verlegh, P.W.J. (2007), 'Effects of Product Placement and Sponsorship Disclosure: A Flexible Correction Approach', *Proceedings of the ICORIA Conference, Lisbon*, CD-ROM.

57   Brassington, F. and Pettitt, S. (2003), *Principles of Marketing*. London: Pitman.

58   Floor, J.M. and van Raaij, W.F. (2002), *Marketing-communicatiestrategie* (*Marketing Communication Strategy*). Groningen: Wolters-Noordhoff.

59   *De Morgen*, 26 September 2008.

60   *De Morgen*, 16 November 2002.

61   *De Morgen*, 3 October 2008.

62   Bloxham, M. (1998), 'Brand Affinity and Television Programme Sponsorship', *International Journal of Advertising*, 17(1), 89–98.

63   De Pelsmacker, P., Van den Bergh, J. and Anckaert, P. (1998), *De Effectiviteit van Sponsoring* (*The Effectiveness of Sponsorship*), Marketing Communication Research Centre, Research report no. 8. Ghent: De Vlerick School voor Management.

64   *De Morgen*, 4 May 2005.

65   http://community.timberland.com, http://company.conagrafoods.com/phoenix.zhtml?c=202310&p=foundation, http://ww5.komen.org (accessed 26 September 2012).

66   www.bsr.org, 23 May 2003.

67   *De Morgen*, 29 June 2006.

68   Westerbeek, H., Shilbury, D. and Quick, S. (2007), *Strategischesportmarketing* (*Strategic sports marketing*). Nieuwegein: Arko Sports Media.

69   Lagae, W. (2005), *Sports Sponsorship and Marketing Communications*. Harlow: Prentice Hall.

70   Simmons, C.J. and Becker-Olsen, K.L. (2006), 'Achieving Marketing Objectives Through Social Sponsorships', *Journal of Marketing*, 70(4), 154–69.

71   Poon, D.T.Y and Prendergast, G. (2006), 'A New Framework for Evaluating Sponsorship Opportunities', *International Journal of Advertising*, 25(4), 471–88.

72   Sandler, D.M., Shani, D. and Lee, M.S. (1998), 'How Consumers Learn About Sponsors: The Impact of Information Sources on Sponsorship', in Meenaghan, T. (ed.), *New and Evolving Paradigms: The Emerging Future of Marketing, American Marketing Association Special Conference Proceedings*. Dublin: University College, 869–71.

73   Erdogan, Z.B. and Kitchen, P.J. (1998), 'The Interaction Between Advertising and Sponsorship: Uneasy Alliance or Strategic Symbiosis?', in Kitchen, P.J. (ed.), *The Changing World of Corporate and Marketing Communication: Towards the Next Millennia. Proceedings of the 3rd Annual Conference of the Global Institute for Corporate and Marketing Communication*. Glasgow: Strathclyde Graduate Business School, 144–55.

74   Cuckoo Awards 2006.

75   Crimmins, J. and Horn, M. (1996), 'Sponsorship: From Management Ego Trip to Marketing Success', *Journal of Advertising Research*, 36(4), 11–21.

CHAPTER 12
Brand activation

CHAPTER OUTLINE

Importance of sales promotions	Objectives and target groups

Consumer promotions
- monetary incentives
- prizes
- product promotions

Trade promotions

Sales promotions research

Point-of-purchase communications

Brand experience

Objectives and dimensions of experiential marketing	Sense Feel/Relate Think Act	Brand experience research

CHAPTER OBJECTIVES

This chapter will help you to:

- Understand why brand activation is increasingly important
- Learn about the various types of brand activation (sales promotions, point-of-purchase communication and experiential approaches) and their objectives
- Understand to what extent the various types of brand activation are effective
- Learn about the techniques to measure brand activation effectiveness

Introduction

Consumers have an abundance of choice. They can quickly compare alternatives on the Internet or solicit other consumers' opinions. Products are available anywhere and anytime. Further, competition in many markets has become fierce as product categories moved in their maturity stage. In such environments, passive communications are not enough. Advertising, PR and sponsorship can help build awareness, brand knowledge and brand image, but ultimately companies need sales. In that respect brand activation plays an important role. Brand activation shifts the focus of marketing communications to the heart of marketing: stimulating the purchase process.[1] Brand activation means bringing consumers from a passive to an active state, to a state where they are ready to purchase and repurchase. This chapter discusses three important tools by which brand activation can occur: sales promotions, point-of-purchase communications and brand experiences.

Sales promotions

Unlike many other instruments in the communications mix, sales promotions are a category of techniques aimed at increasing sales in the short run, and therefore mostly used for a short period of time.[2] Essentially, sales promotions are 'action communications' to generate extra sales, both from existing customers purchasing more products and by (temporarily) attracting new customers, on the basis of a temporary incentive or deal. The main characteristics of promotions are that they are limited in time and space, they offer better value for money and they attempt to provoke an immediate behavioural response.

The effectiveness of promotions is often attributed to the operant conditioning mechanism: behaviour that is rewarded serves to reinforce future behaviour. Sales promotions are, as a result of this type of conditioning, quickly recognised by consumers as a reinforcer, a reward, based on their past experience. For this mechanism to take place, the incentive has to be important enough for a consumer to notice a relevant difference from his or her anchorpoint, i.e. the 'normal' price quality expectation. In other words, the incentive has to exceed the 'just noticeable difference threshold'.[3] Promotions have to be substantial enough to trigger a behavioural response.

The growing importance of sales promotions

Sales promotions are a very important instrument of the communications mix. In 1980, American companies spent 44% of their advertising and promotions budget on advertising.[4] Since then, sales promotion expenditures have constantly increased, outweighing advertising expenditures.[5] Now, about one-third of UK and Chinese grocery sales and more than 40% of US grocery sales come from products on promotion.[6] This evolution can be attributed to a number of factors (Figure 12.1).

In an increasing number of product categories, more and more brands and product lines are offered and differences in intrinsic qualities between brands have become smaller. Therefore, brand differentiation on the basis of advertising becomes increasingly difficult. Promotion is seen as a useful tool to attract the attention of target groups and to 'seduce' them into buying their brands. Traditional advertising has also become less effective due to communications clutter and ad avoidance. Therefore, marketers are looking for other tools to attract consumers' attention to their brands.

Consumers, at least for certain fast-moving consumer product categories, are less brand loyal, and are becoming increasingly price-conscious, a trend which the recent worldwide crisis only increased.[7] This results in an increased response to material incentives, such as

Source: Alamy Images: Anthony Hatley.

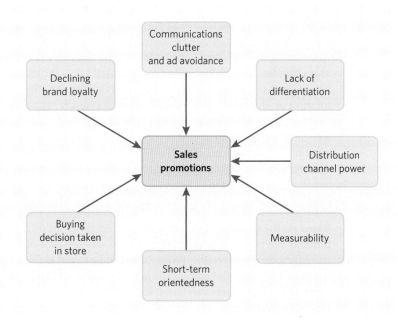

Figure 12.1 Factors affecting the increasing use of sales promotions

Figure 12.2 Saving strategies adopted worldwide by households in response to the crisis

Source: from Shopping and saving strategies around the world, The Nielsen Company (2011), http://www.nielsen.com/content/corporate/us/en/insights/reports-downloads/2011/global-shopping-survey-oct-2011.html.

promotions. In a 2011 online survey of more than 25 000 Internet respondents across 51 countries, only 9% appeared to have taken no particular actions to save on household expenses as compared with the year before. The most popular actions undertaken by the other respondents were looking out for sales, using coupons, shopping at value retailers and looking for large value packs (Figure 12.2).[8]

The majority of buying decisions take place within the retail outlet. An increasing number of product or brand purchasing decisions are essentially impulse-buying decisions. Since communications efforts are most effective at the time and place when and where the consumer makes his or her decision, in-store communications elements and incentives become more attractive tools of persuasion.

Companies are becoming increasingly short-term oriented. However, the effects of traditional advertising campaigns only become visible in the long run. Product managers who want to see immediate results from their communications efforts will therefore be tempted to use promotion tools rather than long-term thematic advertising campaigns. Moreover, also management appears to stimulate the use of sales promotions at fiscal quarter ends to boost earnings in order to meet key benchmarks. Research shows that the quarterly net income can be boosted up to 5% depending on the depth and the duration of the promotion, although it comes at a cost in the following period of about 7.5% of quarterly net income.[9] The result of a promotion campaign can be more easily measured than that of an advertising campaign. Advertising is often aimed at obtaining intermediate effects, such as awareness and favourable attitudes, eventually leading to increased sales. Promotions are aimed at an immediate behavioural response, which can be readily measured. The immediate availability of results for most product managers is a very welcome characteristic of promotions. Finally, distribution channels are becoming increasingly powerful. Many brands are jostling for shelf space and, as a result, retailers are in a position to decide which brands will obtain shelf space under which conditions. Often, promotional tools are used to persuade the trade channel. Furthermore, the distribution channel is taking an increasing part of the promotional activity of manufacturers.

Objectives and target groups of sales promotions

Based on the initiator of the promotions and the chosen target groups, several types of promotions can be distinguished (Figure 12.3). The initiator of the promotions can be either the manufacturer or the retailer. Promotions can be aimed at three types of audiences: distributors, the sales force and the end-consumer. Normally, retailers only promote to end-consumers, whereas manufacturers can target their efforts at all three target groups. This results in four types of promotions:

- consumer promotions by manufacturers;
- consumer promotions by retailers;

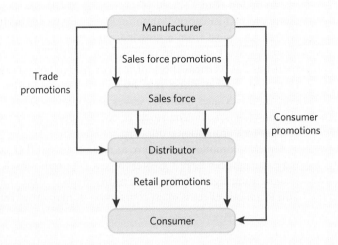

Figure 12.3 Basic types of sales promotions

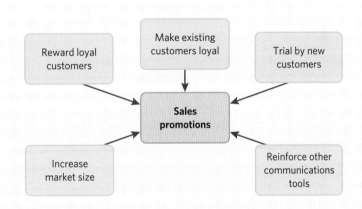

Figure 12.4 Objectives and target groups of consumer promotions

- trade promotions by manufacturers, aimed at distributors;
- sales force promotions by manufacturers.

The first two types are essentially similar in nature, since they are aimed at the end-consumer.

Consumer promotions can have several objectives and target groups[10] (Figure 12.4). Potential new customers can be attracted to try the product. Inducing trial by new customers is one of the most important objectives of a promotion campaign. This 'horizontal' effect results from brand-switching (i.e. consumers of competing brands purchase the promoted brand), or from attracting consumers who have never tried the product category before. Trial promotions are particularly important when launching a new brand or a new item in a product line. When a retailer opens a new store, trial promotions (in this case by the retailer) can be an important tool to generate store traffic, in other words to make consumers enter the store.

Existing customers can be made loyal, and loyal customers can be rewarded for their loyalty. For a marketer it may be more important (and certainly less expensive) to retain a (loyal) customer than to convince a competitor's client to switch brands. Therefore, promotions are frequently aimed at inducing repeat purchase or rewarding loyal customers to stop them trying a competitor's product on promotion.

Promotions can be used to increase market size, as such, by stimulating the use of an entire product category. Promotions of this type are particularly suitable for market leaders who benefit most from a growing market or from a market without seasonal fluctuations. Examples are last-minute offerings, or selling ice cream during winter. Another way of inducing this 'vertical effect' of market growth is to increase sales with existing consumers. Consumer 'basket-filling' (e.g. by giving discounts when large volumes are purchased) not only increases sales, but also serves as a buffer against competitors' actions. As long as the consumer has sufficient stock of the product, he or she may be less inclined to try a competitor's promotional offerings.

Finally, promotions can serve as reinforcers of other communications tools. An advertising campaign can have a greater impact if a promotion is included. The response to a direct mailing campaign may be much more effective if the mail is linked to a promotional offer. This symbiotic effect is often counted on in mail order catalogue selling.

BUSINESS INSIGHT
Bluetooth changes the world of promotions

You are walking through your supermarket on an ordinary weekday. In the wine department, there is a flat-screen TV telling you that during the weekend there will be a 30% discount on your favourite wine. You take your mobile phone, use it to locate the flat-screen via Bluetooth, which, in turn, sends a code to your phone. The next weekend you buy the bottles of wine, show the code on your phone at the checkout, and get the discount. You are satisfied because you don't need to clip coupons from your newspaper or supermarket brochure. And the supermarket is happy because you returned over the weekend, probably spending more money than just on the wine, and you may have told your friends who may normally go to a different supermarket. You can even forward the electronic coupon to them.

The new technology is called BluPull and was developed with partners such as Panasonic, JVC, Coca-Cola, Volvo and Carlsberg. The application also allows for video to be downloaded. For instance, you can record a promotional film on how to operate a piece of equipment, shown in a do-it-yourself store, on your mobile phone, and upload it to your computer to have a closer look at it at home. The system is useful not only for consumers and shops, but also for advertisers. The latter can keep track of the number of consumers who downloaded the promotion or the video, which enables them to assess the return on investment of their promotions even better.[11]

The effect of marketing efforts is increasingly dependent on the co-operation of the distribution channel. To that end, **trade promotions** are used to persuade channel members to include the product in their mix, to give it appropriate shelf space and to assist in promoting the product to the end-consumer. One of the most important objectives of trade promotions is to gain the support of the distribution channel, both wholesaler and retailer, when launching a new product. In order for an end-consumer to be able to buy the product, it has to be on the shelves in sufficient quantities and in a sufficiently large number of retail stores. Since the number of new products is increasing steadily, the trade channel has to choose which ones to carry in its assortment and to promote. In that case, trade promotions precede consumer promotions, and successful trade promotion is a prerequisite for an effective new product launch. In that respect, trade promotion is also 'trial' promotion in the sense that the distribution channel has to be persuaded to include the new product in its assortment. Furthermore, the success of a new product often depends on the number of retail outlets in which the product is on the shelf. Therefore, trade promotions are often aimed at intensifying distribution in terms of the number of outlets in which the product is available.

For existing products, it is useful to keep the trade channel motivated to sell the brand. Trade promotions are aimed at maintaining shelf space or at inducing the retailer to promote the product by means of retailer promotions. One way to motivate the trade channel to push the product is by increasing its stock. Full warehouses induce the trade to pay more attention to selling the products in stock, i.e. to give them more shelf space and to promote the products actively themselves. On the other hand, trade promotions can be used to decrease the stock of a product in the trade channel rapidly, e.g. when a new product launch is being prepared. In a more general sense, trade promotions are used to keep the distribution channel loyal to a product (category). Much as in the case of 'rewarding' the consumer for loyalty to a brand by means of consumer promotions, the distribution channel may be rewarded for its loyalty in giving shelf space to a product by means of trade promotions.

The sales force are an integral part of the distribution effort, since they are the first link in the distribution channel. As a result, offering them incentives to market the product well is a vital first step in any marketing strategy. The most important objectives of **sales force promotion** are to induce the sales force to approach new customers, more specifically members of the trade channel, to try the product, or to increase the volume purchased by existing customers. In industrial marketing situations, new final customers can be the target. The sales force can also be encouraged to push new or existing brands as part of an integrated short-term sales promotions effort, or in support of an advertising campaign. As in consumer promotions, a synergetic effect between sales force promotions and other communications tools, such as advertising, can be established. Finally, the sales force can be motivated to help the distribution channel to improve exposure of the brand, by giving it more and better shelf space, keeping the shelves filled, checking stocks, and pushing and improving the use of displays and other in-store communications material.

Depending on the objective of the promotions, a number of specific tools can be used. An overview of consumer and trade promotion techniques is given in the following sections.

Consumer promotions

Depending on the type of incentive, we distinguish three categories of consumer promotions: monetary incentives, product promotions and the chance to win a prize (Table 12.1).

Monetary incentives

Different types of monetary incentives can be used, but they all lead to an improved price/quality perception by the consumer by lowering the price of the product (Photo 12.1).

The most direct and simple monetary incentive is the **price cut on the shelf** in which the consumer gets an immediate discount when buying the product. It can be used to generate trial, stimulate repeat purchase behaviour and for 'basket-filling' purposes. The advantage for

Table 12.1 Consumer promotion tools

Monetary incentives	Chance to win a prize	Product promotions
• Price cut on the shelf	• Contests	• Sampling
• Coupons	• Sweepstakes and lotteries	• Extra volume
• Cash refunds		• Free in mail
• Savings cards		• Premiums
		• Self-liquidators

Photo 12.1 Sampling brochures from Debenhams
Source: Getty Images.

the consumer is that the price cut is immediate and unconditional. The manufacturer can easily and quickly organise sales promotions of this type, and it does not lead to extra workload for the retailer. Furthermore, price cuts on the shelf almost invariably lead to additional turnover, especially when competing brands offer their promotions in different time periods.[12]

BUSINESS INSIGHT
Price cuts are not always profitable

For a price cut to be profitable, certain – sometimes unrealistic – conditions have to be met. Suppose a six-pack of chocolate bars costs €2. The manufacturer's margin is €0.4. A price cut of 10% means that the chocolate bars are now sold at €1.8. If the price cut is fully absorbed by the manufacturer, this means that half (€0.2/0.4) of the profit margin per chocolate bar pack is being given away. To enable the manufacturer to earn as much total profit as before, twice as many chocolate bars will have to be sold; that is, the sales volume will have to increase by 100%. Hence, a status quo in profitability implies a price elasticity of demand of 10, i.e. a price cut of 10% should lead to an increase in demand of 100%.

On the other hand, there are a number of disadvantages, the most important being the potential damage to the image of the product and the store. Although promotions always run the risk of damaging a brand's high-quality image, this is more the case with immediate and directly visible price cuts. When price cuts are used too frequently, the company runs the risk of selling discounts rather than products. Furthermore, too frequent price cuts influence the consumers' expectations of the normal price: no price cuts may be perceived as price increases. Price cuts can be very expensive for both the manufacturer and the retailer. Large extra volumes may be required to compensate for the loss of margin per unit. Therefore, although the promotion campaign may be successful in terms of extra volume or extra trial, its profitability may be far from impressive.

Coupons are vouchers representing a monetary value and with which the consumer can get a discount on a specific product. Coupons may be inserted in print ads, in direct mailings or in newspapers and/or magazines. They can also be offered online, on mobile phones, on-pack, in-pack or near-pack, or be distributed after a previous purchase. AMEX cardholders can get targeted deals within their Facebook account. The deals are based on their own and their friends' likes and interests. If the consumer accepts the promotional offer, it is automatically added to his or her AMEX credit card. When shopping in a store later on, the coupon can be redeemed when the AMEX card is used.[13] The percentage of coupons distributed that are used when buying a product is called the redemption rate. Coupons are popular worldwide although huge variations between countries exist. North American and Asia-Pacific consumers heavily used coupons in 2011 (used by 65% and 55% of the citizens respectively). In Europe the average percentage of people using coupons is 38%, with huge differences between Belgium and Portugal (63%), Greece (55%), France (53%) and Spain (50%) on the one hand, and Northern and Eastern European countries on the other hand in which coupon usage is rather marginal.[14]

As a promotional tool, coupons can serve a number of objectives, of which stimulating trial is a very important one. Couponing has the advantage that the consumer gets an immediate discount, provided that he or she has noticed and is prepared to use the coupon. The consumer does not have to do much to enjoy the promotion. Manufacturers can target a couponing campaign very well, in specific media and/or retail outlets, and for specific product categories and towards well-defined target groups. The retailer also benefits from couponing in the sense that it often generates extra sales. A problem with couponing is that it is often difficult to predict the redemption rate, and thus the couponing budget. Furthermore, instead of inducing trial, couponing may only have the effect of 'subsidising' already loyal customers. The latter is not necessarily a disadvantage, since 'basket-filling' by existing customers may be

Michaels

LIMITED-TIME SAVINGS

50%OFF

ANY ONE REGULAR PRICED ITEM

**STORE COUPON VALID MONDAY, SEPTEMBER 22, 2008
THROUGH SATURDAY, SEPTEMBER 27, 2008**

One coupon per customer per day. Coupon must be surrendered at time of purchase. May not be used for prior purchases or sale price items or combined with any other coupon, offer, sale or discount. May not be used to purchase shopping cards, gift cards, gift certificates, class fees, in-store activities or The Knack Saturdays kits. Excludes special order custom floral arrangements, special order custom frames and materials, books and magazines and all Cricut products. Valid at Michaels stores only. Limited to stock on hand. Reproductions not accepted. Void where prohibited.

the primary objective of a couponing action. If the consumer is not price-sensitive, he or she will probably not notice the coupon or not use it, in which case the promotion action will be ineffective. Finally, the co-operation of the retailer is necessary since couponing means more work at the checkout.

BUSINESS INSIGHT
The Procter & Gamble zero-couponing strategy

Procter & Gamble is one of the largest coupon distributors. In 1992, the company announced a new strategy. It decided to spend 50% less on couponing, and to adopt an EDLP (Every Day Low Prices) strategy, dropping retail prices by $2 billion. In January 1996, the company launched an 18-month no-coupon test in a carefully chosen part of the State of New York, where 90% of the shoppers were known to use coupons. The vast majority of other manufacturers, retailers and wholesalers believed that this was a viable strategy, and some of them followed Procter & Gamble's lead. However, the no-coupon strategy was very unpopular among consumers. Many consumers considered coupons as 'an inalienable right'. Consumers in the test region started boycotts, public hearings and petition drives. Signs saying 'save our coupons' appeared in front gardens, and the local media were flooded with letters of complaint to editors. The protests even made it into the national media. Public officials joined the protests, claiming that Procter & Gamble was the company of 'profit and greed' that hurt 'average Joe'. A resolution was voted to ask Procter & Gamble to abandon its strategy. Petitions with more than 20 000 signatures were sent to the company. After only 14 months, the company pulled the plug on its no-coupon test in April 1997. A settlement was agreed upon whereby $4.2 billion worth of coupons was distributed that could be redeemed at any supermarket in the region by any consumer or for any food item. However, Procter & Gamble did not admit any wrongdoing. It still claimed that during the test period consumers received at least equally good value for money, without the cost and inconvenience of coupons. Nevertheless, the sales of Procter & Gamble were flat during the test period, while on average the use of coupons of competitors of Procter & Gamble and different product categories increased substantially. The company's experience has triggered new methods to distribute coupons. Instead of inserting them in media, more and more coupons are made available through shelf dispensers at the point-of-sale, in frequent buyer and loyalty programmes, in combination with free samples at the store, through direct mailings, the Internet, or electronically at the checkout.[15]

Cash refunds are discounts offered to the consumer by means of refunding part of the purchase price after sending a proof of purchase. The refund is transferred to the customer's bank account. A cash refund is very similar to couponing in that it is mainly a trial-inducing promotion technique in which the consumer receives a price discount. Normally, cash refunds result in a more substantial discount than coupons. Therefore, the resulting trial purchases tend to be higher. Furthermore, in contrast to direct price cuts and couponing, the consumer has to pay the full price at the checkout. As a result, the consumer is less easily conditioned to expect lower prices, and price expectations are less easily adjusted. As in the case of coupons, cash refund actions can be put in place very rapidly. The main advantage for manufacturers is that the redemption of proofs of purchase enables them to build up a customer database. An advantage for the retailer is that refunds do not result in extra work at the checkout.

Similar to couponing, it is difficult for the manufacturer to predict the success of a refund action, and hence the budget required. Again, there is the risk that existing customers will be subsidised instead of new customers being attracted. The main disadvantage for the consumer is that it takes more trouble to get the discount, especially if it means saving a number of proofs of purchase before part of the price is refunded. Misunderstandings may occur if the consumer expects an immediate discount at the checkout or if it is not clear what part of the package the consumer has to send back to obtain the refund. The retailer may run the risk that the 'old' packages, of which no part of the price is refunded, are difficult to sell.

Monetary incentives may also be offered on the basis of repeat purchases. **Savings cards**, possibly combined with trading stamps, are promotion techniques on the basis of which customers receive a discount provided they have bought a number of units of the brand during a specific period of time, e.g. 'buy 10 items during one year, and you get a 20% discount when you buy the 11th item', or when trading stamps are handed in at the moment of purchase. This tool is often used by shops to stimulate store loyalty. A disadvantage for the consumer is that it may take a long time before the consumer experiences the benefits of loyalty. An advantage of the system is that the consumer is not conditioned to an immediate lower price. Moreover, promotions of this type (retention promotions) are very suitable for generating brand or store loyalty. A final advantage is that the retailer can build a consumer database. Store cards, combined with scanning of barcodes of goods purchased, lead to powerful databases which improve the ability of the retailer to understand consumer behaviour.

Contests, sweepstakes and lotteries

Contests differ from sweepstakes and lotteries in that in the former the participant can influence the outcome of the game. Creating a slogan or an advertising headline, recognising a voice or a piece of music, estimating how many people will send back a coupon, etc., are examples of contests. Lotteries and sweepstakes are based purely on chance. In a sweepstake, consumers receive a (set of) number(s), the winning ones of which are decided on in advance. This means that, if only 10% of the customers having received a set of numbers participate by buying a product, only 10% of the prizes have to be awarded.

Chance games are easy to organise and relatively cheap. However, the benefit for the consumers is not unconditional or immediate. They have to participate actively to have a chance of winning. Chance games and lotteries are also plagued by 'professional players', a group of consumers obsessed by the possibility of winning something, and who therefore participate in all campaigns. There is only a very slim chance that this type of consumer will ever become loyal to the promoted brand. Furthermore, contests and lotteries are seldom capable of generating trial purchases. Retailers are not particularly inclined to co-operate in promotions of this type since they do not generate long-term benefits for the store either. Finally, in most countries legal restrictions on contests and gambling exist, which result in either straightforward, and thus not so creative, contests or near-illegal situations.

Source: Alamy Images: Alex Segre

Product promotions

In product promotions the consumer is offered products free, either as an incentive to buy a product, or as a reward for having purchased it.

Sampling is a promotion technique that consists of distributing small samples of a product, sometimes in a specially designed package free of charge or at a very low cost. This technique can be used in a very general way for a broad target group as well as in a very targeted way (see Photo 12.1). Sampling is the ideal promotion tool for generating trial, especially in those cases in which the product characteristics cannot be communicated very convincingly by means of advertising, and/or in those cases in which it is possible for a potential customer to get an idea of the product's benefits on the basis of trying it in small quantities. A possible disadvantage is that manufacturing and distributing small samples in large quantities, or demonstrations at supermarkets, may be quite expensive, and may lead to logistical problems for both the manufacturer and the retailer.

In **extra volume or BOGOF (buy one get one free) promotions** an extra quantity of the product is temporarily offered at the same price (Photo 12.2). Promotions of this type are mainly used to induce 'basket-filling' by regular users. Consumers are not tempted to try a product for the first time if it is offered in larger volumes – quite the contrary. On the other hand, regular users may be attracted by the extra free volume, and therefore buy more of the product. Especially larger families are very much in favour of this type of promotion.[16]

Promotions of this type are very attractive for consumers since the advantage is immediate and unconditional. It does not result in extra workload or costs for the retailer, except the problem of fitting larger pack sizes onto the shelves. In terms of organisation, the extra volume promotion is a very simple tool for the manufacturer. The promotion can easily be communicated on-pack or via an advertising campaign. The disadvantage is that extra volume promotions tend to be quite expensive. Special packages have to be designed, logistical problems may arise and the extra volume sold does not always compensate for the implicit price cut. Retailers may experience logistical problems too, and may find it difficult to sell old stock without product plus promotion. Furthermore, as a result of the basket-filling, retailers may see a fall in sales after the promotion, since consumers have all the product they need for a while. If this promotional tool is used too often or for too long, consumers' expectations as to the normal price/quantity rate may be conditioned in the wrong direction.

Photo 12.2 Buy one, get one free
Source: Corbis: Richard Cummins.

RESEARCH INSIGHT
Different promotional techniques for 'vices' and 'virtues'

Although consumers prefer promotions to the regular offering, not all promotions are equally liked. Research shows, for example, that bonus packs are generally liked better than price cuts. The reason for this is that bonus packs are perceived as 'gains', as 'getting something for free for the same price', whereas price discounts are interpreted as a 'reduced loss'. Also in the longer term, bonus packs lead to less harm for the brand as the focus is on the 'bonus part' and not on the 'monetary value'.[17] The foregoing may hold true in general, but there appears to be a difference according to the product type that is in promotion. Recent research, for example, shows that people react differently to promotions for healthy food as compared with promotions for unhealthy food (also referred to as 'vices' and 'virtues'). Apparently, bonus packs score poorer than price cuts when promoting unhealthy food. The reason for this is that it is much harder for consumers to justify why they responded to a bonus pack promotion as it would mean consuming even more of something they should actually avoid. A price cut, on the other hand, can function as a guilt-mitigating mechanism as it gives a better reason to buy the unhealthy food. For healthy food, neither justification nor guilt applies, and consequently for these types of products, the main effect of bonus packs being preferred to price cuts holds.[18]

With **free in-mail promotions**, the customer receives a (nearly) free gift in return for a proof of purchase which has to be sent to the manufacturer. In that sense, promotions of this type are very similar to the cash refund, the only difference being that the consumer receives a gift instead of money. The main purpose of this type of promotion is not to generate trial, but to reward loyal customers, or to improve the link between the consumer and the brand. Moreover, such promotions can generate a lot of valuable information for the construction of a database on the interests and consuming habits of (potential) customers. This information can be used for future marketing action, and is one of the major advantages of this type of promotion. The disadvantages are that the consumer does not derive an immediate benefit, the logistics may be very expensive and time-consuming, and there is not much of a benefit for the retailer.

Premiums may be offered in-, on- or near-pack. They are small gifts that come with a product, e.g. a free glass when buying a bottle of cognac, or a pair of sunglasses when buying two bottles of sun lotion. Sometimes the package itself is a premium, like marmalade in a glass that can be used afterwards. Premiums tend to be successful, since for most consumers getting something for free is a powerful incentive. Such promotions can be used to generate impulse buying and trial, to reward existing customers and to stimulate repeat buying by offering a series of premiums that can be collected, like a set of glasses or stickers. Consumers like this type of promotion because the benefits are immediately visible and easy to obtain. The budgetary implications for the manufacturer are clear in advance, and a premium can be easily combined with other types of promotions. Furthermore, there are no extra handling costs after the promotion campaign. The advantage for the retailer is that a premium campaign can generate extra store traffic and extra sales.

BUSINESS INSIGHT
DutchDress and V-dress

The relatively small Dutch beer brand Bavaria managed to attract quite some attention during the soccer World Cup in South Africa. Whereas most brands targeted male soccer fans, Bavaria developed a sexy, orange dress, the DutchDress, for female soccer fans. Sixty singing and dancing Bavaria models did not go unnoticed during the game between The Netherlands and Mexico, resulting in a rush to the store. In no time 160 000 DutchDresses were sold and Bavaria ran out of stock. Bavaria had clearly chosen the right sales promotion premium. For its effective campaign, Bavaria received a Gold Esprix Award in 2011. Needless to say, Heineken, as the main sponsor of the tournament, was not amused by Bavaria's hijacking. . . .

Inspired by its previous success, Bavaria developed a new dress for the European soccer championship, the V-dress. The 'V' stands for the V-shape at the neck, for Victory and for *vrouwelijkesteun* ('female support'). The V-dress is offered as a premium in a pack of six Bavaria bottles for €9.99. Fortunately, the campaign was a bigger success than the results of the Dutch soccer team.[19]

A disadvantage is that the wrong kind of premium may damage the long-term image of the brand. Finally, there is always the risk that only existing customers are subsidised, and that no extra trial or basket-filling results. The disadvantage for the manufacturer is that the production, handling and logistics costs may be quite substantial. The retailer may experience difficulties in displaying the product with the premium. Especially with near-pack premiums, shelf space has to be provided, and the retailer has to check for consumer fraud. The old stock of the product may also be difficult to sell. Moreover, if the premium is a product that is also being sold by the same retailer (a glass, sunglasses, etc.), sales of these items may fall.

RESEARCH INSIGHT
Magazine sales promotions

When a new magazine comes onto the market, its sales usually climb to their potential in a short period of time. Next, a slow but steady decline follows. A traditional strategy to counter this sales decline is to develop advertising campaigns to strengthen brand awareness and reinforce brand loyalty, or to offer non-price promotions. A new type of sales promotion in the magazine industry is a value pack containing the magazine plus another product. The magazine is sold at the same time with and without the promotion at different prices. For example, a value pack can consist of the magazine and a dictionary. Promotions are serialised by fractioning the different CDs of the dictionary across different magazines. The objectives of this new type of promotion are (1) acquiring new customers and (2) increasing the loyalty of current customers. A recent study investigated whether such promotions are effective in slowing down the long-term decrease of sales. This indeed proved to be the case. Although temporarily offering the magazine with and without promotion cannibalises sales of the magazine without promotion, this loss seems to be offset by a long-term increase in non-promoted sales induced by product awareness and loyalty enhancement.[20]

Finally, **self-liquidators or self-liquidating premiums** are presents that can be obtained in exchange for a number of proofs of purchase, and an extra amount of money. Sometimes self-liquidators can be obtained in the store, but more frequently they have to be ordered by mail. Similar to free in-mail promotions, self-liquidators are mainly used to stimulate repeat purchase and brand loyalty, rather than to generate trial. The advantage for consumers is that they can obtain products of relatively high quality at a minimum cost. On the other hand, they have to go to some trouble to obtain a product, the quality of which is unknown. For the manufacturer, following up the campaign may be cumbersome, but valuable information about the consumer is obtained. If well communicated in-store, the campaign generates attention, to the benefit of both the manufacturer and the retailer.

Different manufacturers may also co-operate to generate synergies between their promotional efforts (joint promotions). Similarly, a single manufacturer can offer a joint promotion for two different own brands. One item may be offered as a premium for the other, purchase proofs of different products may be requested to obtain a self-liquidator or a free in-mail present, and discounts may be made contingent on the purchase of different items at the same time. To increase the benefits for both the manufacturer and the retailer, they can co-operate in the organisation of promotion campaigns. Retailers can pay part of the manufacturer's promotion budget, perhaps in return for exclusiveness of the campaign in their stores, or they can provide the necessary in-store communications to draw attention to a promotion campaign.

In Table 12.2, an overview is given of the different consumer promotions techniques, together with their main objectives, advantages and disadvantages.[21]

Table 12.2 Objectives, advantages and disadvantages of consumer promotions

	A	B	C	D	E	F	G	H	I	J
Promotion objectives										
Generate trial	+	++	++	––	––	++	––	––	––	––
Induce repeat purchase	+	+	++	++	––	––		––	––	++
Basket-filling	++	+	+	+		––	––		+	
(Dis)advantages										
Direct consumer benefit	++	++	––	––	––	+	++	––	++	––
Ease of obtaining benefit	++	+	––	––	–	++	++	––	++	––
Impact on brand image and brand loyalty	––	–		++	–			+		+
Manufacturer's workload and problems	++	+	–	+	––	–	–	––	–	––
Impact on consumer's price perception	––	–	+	––	+		–			+
Ease of targeting	––	++	++	++		+	––	++	–	––
Ease of budget planning	––	––	––	–	+	++	++	++	++	–
Database support	––	––	++	++	++	––	––	++	––	++
Immediate increase in sales	++	+		–			++		+	
Impact on store image and store loyalty	–			++	––				+	
Retailer's workload	++	–	+	–			–		––	–

++ very positive   + positive   – negative   –– very negative
A price cut on shelf   **C** cash refunds   **E** contests, sweepstakes and lotteries   **G** extra volume   **I** premiums
B coupons   **D** savings cards   **F** sampling   **H** free in-mail   **J** self-liquidators

Trade promotions

Different promotion tools can be used to motivate the trade. They are summarised in Table 12.3.[22] **Off-invoice allowances** are direct price reductions to the trade during a limited period of time. They are the simplest form of trade promotions. The trade may receive a discount per unit purchased or a discount after selling a certain volume of the product. Discounts may also be given after a longer period of time, when a certain volume of sales has been reached (discount overriders). Also, the count–recount method is retrospective in that the stock of the manufacturer's brand is counted at the beginning and at the end of a period, and a discount, for instance per case sold, is given. A **slotting allowance** is a one-time, up front fee that is charged by retailers before they allow a new product on their shelves to cover the start-up costs of entering a new product into their system. Manufacturers often contest these allowances because they feel that they are subsidising the retailer's business. **Advertising/performance allowances** are monetary incentives aimed at encouraging the retailer to advertise the manufacturer's brand and are provided when proof of the ad is produced. In fact, the manufacturer pays part of the advertising campaign of the retailer. In some cases, a percentage of everything the retailer buys from a manufacturer is put into a **co-operative advertising** fund.

Table 12.3 Trade promotion tools

- Off-invoice allowances
  - Individual case bonus   – Count and recount
  - Volume allowance   – Free merchandise
  - Discount overriders
- Slotting allowances
- Advertising/performance allowances
- Co-operative advertising allowances
- Buy-back allowances
- Dealer contests
- Dealer loaders

The dealer adds an agreed-upon percentage to the fund, and uses it to advertise the brands of the manufacturer. To stimulate the retailer to put a new brand or a renewed version of the product on the shelves, the manufacturer sometimes offers to buy back the 'old' product, or commits to buying back the stock of the new product that is not sold during a specific period of time. This is called a **buy-back allowance**. To motivate retailers to sell more of the manufacturer's product, a contest among them may be organised in which, for instance, trips or other prizes can be won. In some cases, additional materials (**dealer loaders**) are offered during a promotional campaign, for instance a refrigerator during a soft drink promotion. After the promotion, the retailer can keep the extra equipment.

Trade allowances result in a higher profit margin for the wholesaler or the retailer. This higher margin can (partly) be used to offer a discount to the end-consumer by means of retail promotions, or to stimulate sales by means of more shelf space or other in-store communications tools. In those cases, the trade promotions can eventually result in a favourable effect on end-consumer purchases. If the (volume-based) trade allowance is used by the retailer only to increase inventory temporarily, the trade promotions will not result in an increase in sales to the end-consumer. Although trade promotions have become increasingly important as a result of the growing power of the distribution channel, their effectiveness largely depends on the incentives given to the retailer to pass on the benefits to the end-consumers and to stimulate short-term sales in-store.

RESEARCH INSIGHT
Are sales promotions effective?

Although some recent studies[23] find a (small) positive long-term sales evolution from promotional efforts, most studies lead to the conclusion that, although promotions may be effective in the short run, they result in negative effects in the long run. Competitive campaigns neutralise the effects, and the only result is an increase in promotion costs for the same amount of sales, and stable, long-term market shares. Furthermore, promotions may undermine the effect of more strategic marketing instruments, such as advertising and sponsorship, which try to build brand image in the long run. Therefore, some manufacturers increasingly rely on the EDLP strategy, aimed at maintaining a relatively low stable price, as opposed to the 'high–low' (HILO) strategy in which frequent promotions are used. The potential effects of sales promotions are summarised below.

In the *short term* most promotion campaigns lead to an increase in sales and market share.[24] Reported promotional price elasticities range between 4 and 10, but do not always exceed short-term advertising elasticity.[25] The effect of promotions on short-term profitability is unclear, though. Some studies indicate that promotions lead to higher profits, whereas others warn of pressured margins.[26] Furthermore, various studies indicate that 80% of the sales increase as a result of promotions is attributable to attracting buyers of competitive products.[27] However, a retailer does not benefit much from brand-switching within the store. Retailers are more interested in the extent to which sales promotions stimulate store-switching or increase category demand in the focal category as well as in other categories (cross-promotion effects). Research shows that sales promotions indeed attract new customers to the store leading to an increase in the retailers' market share.[28] Increased store traffic also leads to additional sales in other product categories.[29] According to a recent study, one in two price promotions expand own-category revenues with a probability of 61% that at least one other category is positively affected. These cross-promotional effects seem more likely to occur between the categories more closely located to one another in the store.[30]

In the *medium term* (4–6 weeks after the promotion), the effect of the campaign on repeat purchase and the lack of a 'post-promotion dip' become important indicators of effectiveness. When not only new customers are attracted by the promotions, but also existing customers buy more of the product during the promotion campaign, a 'post-promotion dip' in sales can result. Therefore, to assess the effectiveness of a promotion campaign, both the sales during the campaign and after the campaign have to be measured. If the product is frequently on promotion, also a pre-promotion dip may occur: consumers anticipate the campaign and postpone their purchase.[31] Further,

promotions can have a negative effect on the medium-term image of the brand because consumers remember afterwards to have chosen the brand because of the promotion rather than the intrinsic value of the product. They may then see less reason to buy the product again when it is not on promotion.[32] According to the 'Mental Accounting Theory' and the 'Prospect Theory', consumers base their decisions on the difference between the actual stimulus and a stimulus of reference. Promotions can result in a decrease in 'reference price'; in other words, consumers get used to promotions and they adjust their price expectations as a result of frequent promotions. Consequently, the normal price becomes expensive and a future promotion will have to be more 'impressive' to be perceived as a promotion.[33] Promotions may also influence repeat-buying decisions adversely because the long-term attitude towards the brand is being damaged.[34] In this sense, repeated monetary promotions have been shown to be more likely to harm brand attitudes than repeated non-monetary promotions.[35] However, if the consumer is already a loyal customer before the campaign, and has already developed a clear attitude towards the brand, the effect of promotions on his or her long-term attitude towards the brand will not be affected. Similarly, in markets in which promotion campaigns are frequently used, and in markets in which most consumers are brand-switching anyway, the effect of promotions on brand attitude and thus repeat purchase will be limited.[36]

Frequent promotions may lead to 'deal-proneness', with adverse effects on brand attitudes, market shares and sales in the *long term*. Research even indicates that frequent use of promotions leads to a 'prisoner's dilemma' as a result of which competitors retaliate in order not to lose market share, and long-term market shares are not affected. In a long-term market share analysis of 341 products, it was shown that 60% of all market shares remained stable over a period of nine years. Only in 24% of the cases was a significant effect of promotions on market share evolution found.[37] Similarly, in a study of 400 products, 78% of market share appeared to be stable in the long run, which means that a maximum of 22% of the market share could have been affected by promotion campaigns (or by other marketing mix instruments, for that matter).[38]

Promotions will have a stronger effect on products that the consumer can easily hold in stock, and on products that are bought by large numbers of consumers and for which supporting communications campaigns are organised. A recent study by Nielsen shows that consumers are 32% more responsive to a sales promotion campaign of brands that also used above-the-line advertising.[39] Promotions will be less effective in very competitive markets and when the campaign is preceded by a competitor's promotion.[40] Furthermore, promotions seem to be more effective for brands with a small market share than for major market players.[41] Variety-seeking consumers and consumer segments with high 'deal-proneness' (such as young families) are more influenced by promotions than others.[42] The risk of 'deal-to-deal buying', i.e. postponing purchases until the next promotion campaign, is somewhat higher in those segments, and less frequent use of promotion campaigns is advised.[43]

Sales promotions research

Sales promotions can be pre- and post-tested. Sales promotions pre-testing is very similar to advertising pre-testing. Consumers may be exposed to sales promotions ideas, in a focus group setting or elsewhere, and may be invited to express their opinion about them. However, since the objective of most sales promotions campaigns is to provoke immediate buying behaviour, most promotions research will focus on behavioural response measures. Promotions are essentially aimed at stimulating trial purchase and at increasing sales with existing consumers. Therefore, effectiveness measures will focus on the evolution of sales compared with non-promotion periods, or on the comparison of different types of promotions as to their ability to generate extra sales.

When launching a new brand, or monitoring the sales evolution of an existing brand for which sales promotions campaigns are being used, the following analysis using consumer panel data can be carried out.[44] It is based on a decomposition of the market share of the brand as follows:

Market share = (Attraction × Conviction × Domination × Intensity)/Shock absorption

Where: Attraction = Number of buyers of our brand/total number of buyers of the product category.

Conviction = Number of loyal customers of our brand/number of buyers of our brand.

Domination = Average volume of our brand purchased per loyal customer of our brand/average volume of the product category purchased per loyal customer of our brand.

Intensity = Average volume of the product category purchased per loyal customer of our brand/average volume of the product category purchased per buyer of the product category. If the intensity rate equals 1, the loyal customers of our brand are buying the same amounts of the product category as the average buyer of the product category.

Shock absorption = Total purchases in volume of our brand by loyal customers/ total purchases in volume of our brand.

The definition of a 'loyal customer' is based on repeat purchase within a specified period of time. All indicators are measured per period (monthly, bi-monthly, etc.). All measures are volume-based. The attraction rate measures the penetration of the brand and is a measure of the effectiveness of trial promotions. The conviction rate gives an indication of loyalty promotions effectiveness, more specifically the success of repeat-buying promotion campaigns. The domination rate indicates to what extent loyal customers are truly loyal. The higher the domination index, the more exclusively loyal customers are loyal to a brand. It is an indication of the effectiveness of loyalty and basket-filling promotions. The intensity rate indicates the extent to which the brand is capable of attracting heavy users of the product category. If this indicator is larger than 1, the brand is capable of attracting a more than proportional amount of heavy users. As such, it is also an indication of the basket-filling capacity of promotional campaigns. The shock absorption index indicates to what extent the brand is vulnerable to competitive campaigns. The higher the shock absorption rate, the more the sales are based on loyal consumers, and the less vulnerable the brand is to switching behaviour caused by competitive actions. In Figure 12.5, an example is given of the launch of a new brand of detergent.

The effectiveness of promotions is often assessed by studying the evolution of sales over a period of time during which several types of promotions have been implemented. By studying the evolution of sales during the campaign, and comparing it with the sales level before and after the campaign, the extra sales volume generated by the campaign can be calculated.

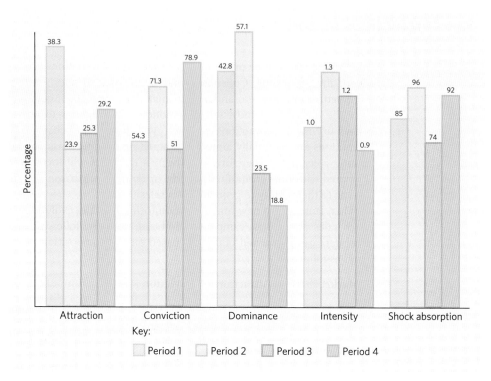

Figure 12.5 Monitoring the effectiveness of sales promotions campaigns: the launch of a new detergent

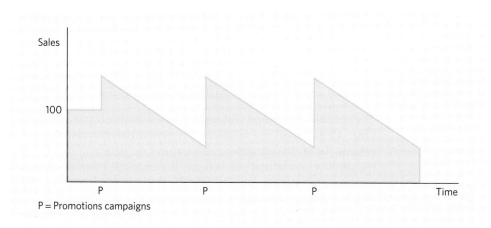

Figure 12.6 The sawtooth effect of sales promotions campaigns

This type of analysis will also reveal potential 'sawtooth' effects, which follow the 'post-promotion dip' which is often the result of some types of promotions. Basket-filling promotions may induce consumers to buy large quantities of the product on promotion, after which they have enough stock for a number of weeks or months, and sales drop sharply in the post-promotion period. This phenomenon is illustrated in Figure 12.6. Obviously, if the only net result of promotion campaigns is that the post-promotion dip entirely compensates for the extra sales during the promotional period, the only thing that has happened is that the company has given up part of its profit margin. The success of a promotion campaign can be

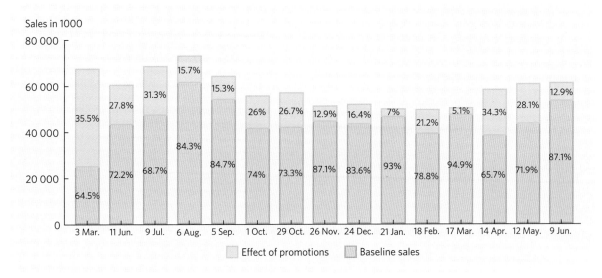

Figure 12.7 Baseline sales and the sales effect of promotion campaigns

judged on the basis of the size of the positive difference between the extra sales during the promotional period and the drop in sales during the post-promotion dip.

Figure 12.7 shows another example, based on retail panel data, of the baseline sales of a product, calculated on the basis of medium-term 'normal' sales, and the sales effect of promotion campaigns in subsequent months.

Obviously, the only relevant measure of promotions effectiveness is its long-term profitability. Sales volumes, sales prices and promotion costs will have to be combined into an economic analysis of the profitability of promotion campaigns.

Point-of-purchase communications

Point-of-purchase communications or POP communications, also called in-store, point-of-sales or POS communications, are another powerful tool to activate a brand as they – as is the case for sales promotions – reach consumers at the point when they are making the decision about which product or brand to buy. As indicated earlier (see Chapter 5), purchase intentions often do not result in an actual purchase because of situational factors such as out-of-stocks, competitive brands that are on promotion and attention-grabbing displays. Besides altering purchase intentions, the store environment also significantly influences consumer behaviour in the sense that about one-third of unplanned purchases can be attributed to the fact that the point-of-sales environment makes consumers aware of new needs while they are shopping.[45] According to a global study, nearly 30% of shoppers make up their mind at the point of purchase and do not know in advance what brand they are going to buy. One in ten shoppers change their minds in store and buy a different brand than they had planned upfront. Almost 15% buy a product from a product category they did not intend to buy before entering the store, and 1 in 10 shoppers leave the store without buying a product they planned to buy. Although there are huge differences across countries, Figure 12.8 shows that many consumers make at least one decision at the point of purchase.[46] Furthermore, consumers spend more and more time on the road away from home, which makes it harder for traditional media to reach them.[47] No wonder that managers invest considerable resources in point-of-purchase communications to influence shoppers.[48]

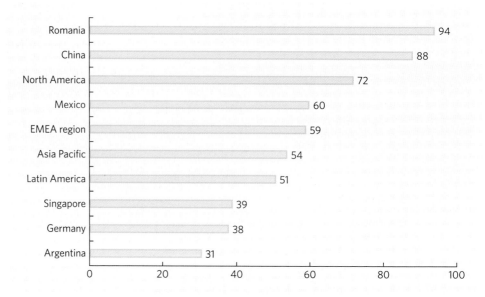

Figure 12.8 Percentage of people making at least one decision in-store

Source: Based on Ogilvy & Mather (2008), 'Turning Shoppers into Buyers: The Truth Behind Shopper Decisions Made in Store', http://www.scribd.com/doc/11302909/Turning-Shoppers-Into-Buyers#wordpress (accessed July 2012).

RESEARCH INSIGHT
Factors driving up unplanned buying

It is well known that POP communications attract a shopper's attention and drive up unplanned purchases. The extent to which unplanned purchases are influenced depends on several factors. For example, shoppers appear to do most unplanned buying when they shop in unfamiliar stores and have a lot of time available.[49] Unplanned purchases are also more likely to occur for hedonic product categories and increase with the number of aisles the shopper visits.[50] Further, recent research shows that consumers' shopping goals also impact the extent to which they are seduced to do unplanned purchases. Shoppers may go to the store holding a goal that can range from very specific and concrete (e.g. to redeem a specific coupon) to very general and abstract (e.g. to fill up on weekly needs). Consumers in an abstract state of mind are more flexible and receptive to their environment, whereas consumers in a concrete mindset are more focused on their specific goal. Not surprisingly then, consumers with an abstract (vs concrete) shopping trip goal appear to engage more in unplanned buying. The expected percentage change in unplanned buying amounts to about −25% for a very concrete shopping goal (such as shopping for special offers and promotions), to about +2% for a less concrete shopping goal (such as shopping for immediate consumption), to 27% for a rather abstract goal (such as a fill-in trip to get daily essentials) and to almost +60% (or an increase of 10% on the total amount spent) for a very abstract shopping goal (such as weekly fill-ups). If a consumer decides to shop in a store because of its low prices, unplanned purchases increase from 12% to 13% (these additional purchases can be easily justified on the basis of the low prices), whereas shopping in a store because of the image or higher-quality products is less likely to stimulate unplanned purchases. One-stop shopping, in contrast to shopping in multiple stores, also drives up unplanned purchases, more specifically with an average of 12%.[51]

POP communications are most effective when they form part of an integrated communications plan, which means that, for instance, they reflect what consumers have seen on TV or billboard ads, and correspond with PR efforts or sponsorships.[52] Indeed, it has been shown that, for instance, when advertising and POP communications are combined, as compared with using advertising only, sales increase by more than 100%.[53] Also, the combination of POP and sales promotions appears to have enormous advantages over and above the use of POP or sales promotions only.[54]

Point-of-purchase as a communications tool

POP communications can be defined as any promotional material placed at the POP, such as interior displays, printed material at shop counters or window displays (Photo 12.3).[55] However, it also includes in-store broadcasts, video screen demonstrations, shopping-trolley advertising, shelf talkers, coupon dispensers, wastepaper baskets and interactive kiosks (devices by means of which the consumer can interactively retrieve information about the shop and the products in the shop). POP communications are not only concerned with POP advertising. Also, the way the products are placed on the shelves, the store image and store atmospherics (e.g. the scent and the music in the store) form an integral part of POP communications. In short, POP communications involve all aspects of the store and the store environment that can signal something to customers about the quality, price or product assortment, whether it is initiated by the retailer or by the manufacturer.

Photo 12.3 Red Bull: in-pub communication on Table Mountain (Cape Town)

BUSINESS INSIGHT
No hot Nikes at Foot Locker any more

Nike was founded in 1972 and Foot Locker in 1975. Foot Locker started with a new concept: a store devoted to athletic shoes only. This aroused Nike's interest, and Nike wanted very badly to get into the area. Selling its shoes in an athletic shoe store would rub off on its own image. In the beginning, Foot Locker was hesitant since it did not want to sell 'unbranded footwear' and Nike was still unknown at that time. Over the years, the two companies grew together and were able to benefit from each other's strengths. Nike's ad campaigns triggered demand for its shoes, and Foot Locker's extensive network of stores made the shoes available everywhere for the consumers. Nike got prominent displays in Foot Locker stores and Foot Locker got Nike's newest models. This allowed Foot Locker to grow five times as fast as its competitors. To drive sales, Foot Locker began to aggressively discount its products over the last few years. Nike, on the other hand, wanted to preserve its image of cutting-edge fashion king. This led to a dispute between the two companies that started in the beginning of 2002. When Nike posed rigid terms on the selection and price of shoes it would sell to Foot Locker, Foot Locker announced a cut in its Nike order by 15% to 25% in the hope that Nike would reconsider its terms. Nike responded in the opposite way: it slashed its planned shipments to Foot Locker by 40%, withholding its most popular and newest sneakers. Consumers could no longer find Nike's hottest shoes at Foot Locker, shoes that Nike began selling to Foot Locker's competitors. Moreover, Nike's campaigns were no longer driving consumers to Foot Locker's stores. All this induced a serious drop in sales, a negative impact on its image and an enormous marketing challenge for Foot Locker.[56]

Objectives and target groups of POP communications

POP communications can serve several objectives or functions (Figure 12.9). An eye-catching exterior store design may attract the consumer's attention and may differentiate the store from its competitors, in that way increasing the likelihood that the consumer will enter the store. Think of the flagship stores of Apple, Nike, and Prada, for example, which clearly stand out in the shopping street. In supermarkets, eye-catching displays or funny floor ads may draw attention to specific products and may induce the consumers to buy a product they did not intend to buy before entering the store. Effective POP material should remind consumers of ongoing or previous advertising, PR, sales promotion or other campaigns, reinforcing the communications message. Because of the high amount of communications clutter today, consumers have difficulty remembering the different messages and often confuse brands. POP material is a good tool to aid consumers in this. Besides reminding, POP

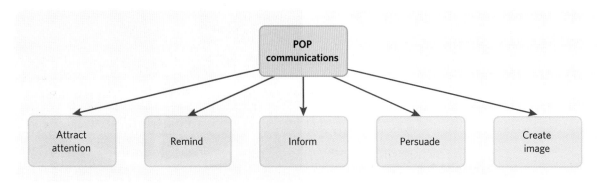

Figure 12.9 Point-of-purchase communications objectives

material can also inform consumers. Detailed information on a DVD recorder or a computer can be shown on large displays, the store's design may signal the intended target groups, or an interactive display may help consumers decide on what kind of wine is best served with certain meals.

BUSINESS INSIGHT
Augmented reality in the store

In 2010 Shiseido installed an interactive terminal, the Digital Cosmetic Mirror, at the Takashimaya department store in Shinjuku. The terminal instantly became world news as it was one of the first applications of augmented reality. The mirror, which functions as a monitor, first scans a customer's face and then shows the customer how colours and shades of make-up would look on the customer. Thus, there is no longer any need to actually try the make-up on. This not only saves the company a lot of money on samples, but also it is more convenient for the customer as many more different shades can be tried on. Further, unlike other interactive tools, the Cosmetic Mirror gives consumers also tailored recommendations.[57]

Meanwhile, several companies have made use of augmented reality to facilitate consumers' choice. IKEA, for example, uses augmented reality codes on its flyers. Consumers often do not have a clue about how a certain piece of furniture would fit into their home. The augmented reality codes on the flyers make it possible to embed life-size 3-D models of furniture onto a piece of paper, which could be envisaged through a digital or mobile phone camera. Thus, the technique allows customers to literally bring the furniture into their home and to get a clear idea of which model and which colour would result in a nice fit.[58]

Another objective of POP communications is to persuade consumers, to influence their decision-making at the point of sale and to trigger impulse purchases. Finally, POP communications serve to help with building an image, both of the retailer and the products sold.

In order to be able effectively to communicate the store, the products and the brands offered, market segmentation and a clear understanding of the characteristics of target groups are essential components of a marketing communications strategy. For example, with fashion clothing the most important attributes seem to be price, quality, product selection and service offered by the personnel.[59] However, different target groups will prefer different levels of these characteristics. Knowing the exact preferences of the target groups is essential to fine-tune the interior and exterior design of the store, the POP material present in the store, the product assortment and the overall image of the store. For example, the fashion retailer catering to wealthy women must design the store in a way that looks exclusive and expensive. On the other hand, if you want to communicate that you have low prices and that consumers can get bargains, it may not be a good strategy to have the products neatly arranged by size or colour. A chaotic mélange and large price displays attracting bargain hunters like a magnet seem to be a better strategy to communicate the bargain possibilities.[60]

POP communications tools

In-store communications have an enormous potential impact on the consumer. Several studies show that displays and shelf talkers are able to trigger purchase responses, sometimes even when the price reduction is negligible.[61] Therefore, POP material is receiving growing interest and is used more and more often. Special product presentations on existing shelves, displays, billboards and pallets are most often used, although also more sophisticated tools are becoming popular (see below).

BUSINESS INSIGHT
The shop of the future

In Philips' ShopLab project in Eindhoven, the Netherlands, the shop of the future is being developed. One of its novelties is the intelligent shop show-window. When somebody passes a shoe store, for instance, an ad is projected onto the window. When this person looks at a specific pair of shoes, seconds later the sizes, materials and prices appear. With a couple of simple touches on the window, the shoes can be reserved. This is especially handy when people walk along a shopping street at night, when the shops are closed. In the shop itself, LED cubicle displays can be placed that, chameleon-like, perfectly adapt to the colour of the item displayed, or take on the most contrasting colour, as the shopkeeper wishes. Spotlights focus on a specific item as soon as someone approaches within half a metre. In that way, each product in the store attracts attention in turn. People who are manifestly bored and do not show any interest in the products in the shop are also spotted. They are accompanied to a cosy armchair with interesting magazines available. The absolute favourite of retailers is the Lightwand behind the checkout counter. Fashion colours change every season. A shopkeeper who wants to reflect this in the shop or at the checkout has to repaint several times a year. With the Lightwall technology, a colour sensor pen can measure the exact colours of a piece of clothing, and exactly replicate them on the LED wall. Porsche is one company that has invested in this new Ambiscene technology. The interior of the dealer room changes to match the colour of the car that is in it. In that way, shopping becomes a much more entertaining experience. Retailers of luxury products are especially interested in the concept of individualising the look and feel of each store. For instance, no two Prada stores are the same. Why would you visit a Prada store in London if it is the same as one in Paris? New in-store light technologies can give a shop an exclusive and dynamic look and feel.[62]

Window shopping is literally possible at Ralph Lauren in New York and Chicago. Inspired by the movie *Minority Report* in which advanced touchscreen technology plays an important role, the company wanted to create a promotion stunt alongside its role as one of the main sponsors of the US Open tennis tournament. In the show-windows of the shop in New York, touchscreens were installed by means of which passers-by could buy Ralph Lauren products. As soon as they made their choice, they could pay by credit card and the item would be delivered at home. A projector in the shop streamed the information to the touch-sensitive window. Almost half of the passers-by stopped to have a look at what was happening. Soon, another store in Chicago was equipped with the new technology. The latter store specialised in skiing. Shoppers were virtually taken to the ski slopes in Aspen, received information about Ralph Lauren products, fashion and weather and snow conditions, and could even get virtual skiing lessons.

The Adidas flagship store in Paris is equipped with a window screen that reacts to gestures. Pointing at a product is enough; the window no longer needs to be touched. Top of the bill is the virtual mirror. Customers try on a pair of shoes, and then choose other models and colours on-screen. The virtual mirror shows the shoes on their feet without actually trying on the real shoe. Customers can also design a customised shoe. Via the screen, colours, design and decorations can be changed. The shoes are then manufactured and shipped to the customer.[63]

In a US study, about 1000 shoppers were asked to indicate the POP elements to which they pay particular attention when grocery shopping and the POP elements that have motivated them in the past to buy a product or brand they had not planned to purchase beforehand.[64] Figure 12.10 summarises the results.

According to the consumers, in-store samples seem to be particularly effective. More than two in three respondents claim that these attract attention and have in the past persuaded them to buy the product or brand. Moreover, 68.3% say they try in-store samples almost every time they are available, while 26.3% say they do this occasionally. Of course, trying a sample is not the same as buying a product. Some 13% admit buying the product or brand almost every time they try a sample, while about 73% claim to buy the tried product occasionally. Besides in-store samples, coupons, on-pack promotions and displays are also

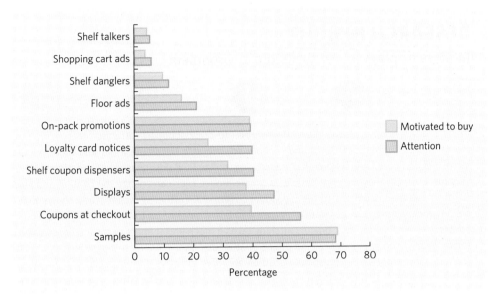

Figure 12.10 Attention and purchase motivation of different POP elements
Source: Grocery Incentive Study 2002 (http://www.pmalink.org/research/CDPgrocery_F.asp). © Copyright 2003.

deemed very effective. Interestingly, according to this study, 50% of the grocery shoppers who use shelf coupon dispensers most frequently use the coupons for brands they have not tried before, while a quarter of them use the coupon only if it is for the brand they intended to buy.[65] Other studies have also demonstrated the effectiveness of shelf coupon dispensers. It has been found, for example, that consumers tend to respond even more easily to shelf coupons than to price reductions of the same amount.[66] Floor ads or floor graphics and shopping cart ads also appear to work, sometimes even better than assumed by the respondents of the US study above. Nestlé, for example, tested its floor graphics in Germany. To this end, floor graphics were placed in aisles of six test stores and compared with six similar control stores without floor graphics. According to 3M, the developer of Nestlé's floor graphics, sales were 23% higher in the test as compared with the control stores. Furthermore, brand recall of products advertised by means of floor graphics amounted to 47%, as compared with 19% for wall posters and 10% for shelf stickers.[67] Walls promoted its Solero ice cream by means of shopping cart ads in 100 Asda supermarkets. The most memorable image from a recent TV ad was used as the basis for the poster. It featured a man with an iceberg capping his head eating a Solero ice cream. The baseline read 'the mind cooler'. One in four trollies were decorated with a poster on the outside, as well as on the inside, so that both the trolley pusher and other shoppers could see the message. The cost of the campaign was estimated at 63 pence per 1000 exposures. Sales of Solero were monitored in 32 Asda stores, half of which ran the trolley advertising campaign. The results showed a sales increase of over 20% in the test as compared with the control stores.[68]

Although more difficult and more expensive to install – and therefore only rarely used – POP advertising messages can also be customized. The Cyber Solution Laboratory of the Japanese telecoms company NTT developed a system called 'information rain'. Cameras observe the customers and, based upon the information that is generated in this way (for instance, the amount of time the customer looks at a certain shelf), advertising messages are generated and projected on the body of that customer. Obviously, customised POP may drive consumer responses even more.[69]

The spot where POP material is installed also exerts an influence on purchase behaviour. In a US study, in-aisle displays resulted in 58% unplanned purchases, as compared with 61% for displays at the end of aisles and 64% for displays placed at the checkout.[70]

RESEARCH INSIGHT
In-store displays in a virtual store environment

In-store displays have proven their effectiveness to draw shoppers' attention to specific products in brick-and-mortar stores. Promotional signs and in-store ads are also becoming more and more popular in online grocery stores. As compared with offline POP advertising, online POP ads have several additional advantages: (1) they are very low cost; (2) they are very flexible (a simple mouse click can change the content and place of a display); and (3) they can be customised to the individual customer.[71] Further, a recent study shows that in-store displays in online grocery stores can generate an increase in brand sales of up to 106%. Comparing brand and category-level effects, the results show that brand-switching takes a much bigger share of the increased sales than new comers to the category. In correspondence with offline in-store displays, in online settings the location also matters. Displays that are shown first and in an isolated position are more effective. More specifically, the effect of a display shown on the first screen is twice as large as the one for an aisle display. The latter in turn enhances brand sales to a larger extent than shelf tag displays.[72]

Store atmospherics

Besides the POP communications tools discussed above, **store atmospherics** need to be mentioned as a specific aspect of POP communications. Atmospherics can be defined as the effort to design buying environments to produce specific emotional effects in the buyers that enhance their purchase probability.[73] As a store's atmosphere is appreciated through the senses, sensory aspects are considered the typical dimensions of store atmosphere (see Figure 12.11). Taste is not usually considered a meaningful dimension of the store atmosphere since one cannot taste an atmosphere. However, some food stores are renowned for their in-store 'degustations', which may in that case be regarded as an atmospheric dimension for these food retailers.

The atmosphere adds a valuable characteristic to the product and serves three main functions.[74] Firstly, the atmosphere can generate attention by using specific colours, music, etc., which make a store stand out. Secondly, the atmosphere creates a message by using the atmospheric characteristics in such a way that they express, for example, the intended store audience. Thirdly, the atmosphere arouses people, which may tip the scale in favour of buying certain products or brands (Figure 12.12).[75]

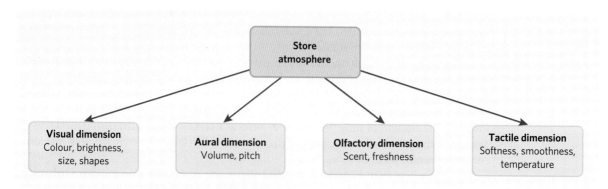

Figure 12.11 Dimensions of store atmosphere

BUSINESS INSIGHT
Seducing consumers on the shop floor

Music is an important in-store marketing tool. According to the Canadian marketing expert Jean-Charles Chebat, the best music is original songs, not 'easy listening' versions of songs. Nor is it a good idea to turn on a radio channel, or to buy a couple of CDs and play the same songs all the time. The latter irritates the staff who, in turn, project their irritation on the customers. The choice of the type of music can be adapted to specific target groups that shop at different times of the day: older consumers shop during the day (play their hits); at noon, mostly hurried and/or stressed people pop in (calm music is called for); after four o'clock teenagers take over (a bit louder and modern); and during weekends it is mostly families who do their shopping. They want to shop efficiently and need fast music to create the illusion of a 'blitz visit'. At the checkout they need slow music to create the perception of shorter queuing times. The customers do not need to know the music. They just need to recognise it, and feel that the shop atmosphere fits in with their lifestyle. Combining smell and music is even more effective. Fast music calls for citrus odours; slow music connects with lavender. Supermarkets creating the right atmosphere using music and smell have seen their turnover increase by as much as 40%.

Several marketers understood the previous message well. The luxury brand Delvaux decided to play more jazz and pop-electro music in its shops, instead of classical music, because it wanted to attract younger people. The British clothing retailer Donaldson plays 1960s' hits, because its public mainly consists of baby boomers. The Swiss Chocolate chain Galler discovered the positive impact on its clients of the smell of vanilla, and artificially creates it in all its shops. People with a sweet tooth cannot resist the smell of burned nuts or cacao beans. In shops where Galler operates cacao burners, turnover increased by 20%.[76]

Although empirical research in this field has been scarce, the few studies to date seem to support the idea that physical attributes in the store induce emotional states, which in turn affect consumer behaviour.[77] An experiment in a British supermarket revealed the following.[78] Four French and four German wines were put on the supermarket's wine shelves. On days when French accordion or Gallic favourites such as the 'Marseillaise' or can-can music was played, Beaujolais and Côtes du Rhône sold extremely well (40 French versus 8 German bottles), while on the days when German, side-splitting Keller music was played, the German wine sales rose (12 French versus 22 German bottles). Interviews revealed that consumers were certain that the kind of music did not influence their purchase. Also, in a restaurant setting, it has been shown that when visitors' preferred music is playing they stay significantly longer in the restaurant and spend significantly more on both drinks and food.[79] Another study investigated an ambient effect, consisting of specific combinations of music and lighting, and a social effect consisting of the number and the friendliness of the personnel. Background classical music with soft lighting as compared with foreground top 40 music with bright lighting induced a significantly more pleasurable feeling, except when the less attractive ambient environment was offset by very friendly personnel. Feelings of pleasure and arousal were found to increase the customers' willingness to buy (Figure 12.12).[80] In a store setting in which the visual dimension or store design factor (colour, layout and displays), the store social factor (number of employees, the outfit of the employees) and the store ambient factor or aural dimension (music) were manipulated, it was found that all three factors had a significant direct impact on store perceptions (such as merchandise quality perceptions, price perceptions, etc.) and an indirect impact on store patronage intentions via the evoked perceptions. The impact of the design factor appeared to be much stronger than that of the social and ambient factors, though.[81] With regard to aroma, the link between aroma

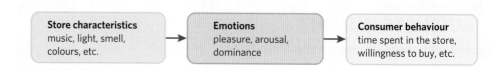

Figure 12.12 Relation between store environment and consumer behaviour

Source: Based on Mehrabian, A. and Russell, J.A. (1974), *An Approach to Environmental Psychology.* Cambridge, MA: MIT Press.

advertising and increased sales still has to be proved. However, according to the experience of Simon Harrop of the The Aroma Company, a pleasant aroma induces a better response than no aroma or, worse, an unpleasant smell.[82] One study[83] showed that products in a scented shop were perceived to be better than identical goods in an unscented shop, while another study found that a scented versus an otherwise identical unscented store induced more positive evaluations of the store and of the merchandise, increased the intention to visit the store, increased the intention to purchase some of the products and lowered the perception of the time that consumers had spent in the store.[84]

RESEARCH INSIGHT
The impact of colour on consumers' approach-avoidance behaviour

In an experimental study involving almost 800 respondents, the Mehrabian and Russell framework shown in Figure 12.12 was applied to store environmental colour. In total, 32 different colours were tested for a hypothetical design store: eight different hues or pigments (green–yellow, red, blue–green, purple–blue, green, yellow–red, yellow and blue), each at two different brightness levels (a bright and dark version of the colour) and at two different saturation levels (saturated version containing a large proportion of the pigment versus an unsaturated version containing a large proportion of grey). The results revealed that for two of the eight hues a significant difference in evoked feelings could be found. Blue elicited significantly more pleasure and less tension in consumers than green–yellow. Moreover, brighter colours induced significantly more pleasurable feelings and less tension than darker colours, while more saturated coloured stores were judged by the respondents as significantly less tense. These results show that the first part of the model in Figure 12.12 is confirmed: store colour has a significant impact on consumers' feelings. Furthermore, evidence was also found for the second part of the model in Figure 12.12: the pleasure evoked by the store colour was positively related to respondents' approach behaviour towards the store (i.e. willingness to spend time in the store, to spend money in the store, etc.), while colour-evoked tension had a negative impact on approach behaviour. The conclusion of this study seems to be that storekeepers had better avoid painting the store walls in green–yellow and rather choose a (bright version of) blue instead. If blue does not fit the rest of the interior, yellow–red or yellow are also good alternatives.[85]

Besides affecting the time that consumers spend in the store or their willingness to buy, high pleasure feelings seem to be related to high customer satisfaction levels.[86] This is important since customer satisfaction seems to be the driving force of customer loyalty.[87]

In conclusion, the majority of the atmospherics research seems to support the relationship between store atmospherics, emotions and consumer behaviour. Some practitioners even say that '50% of consumers' decisions are made because of the environment they are in'.[88] Therefore, a good understanding of store atmospherics and store dynamics is very important, both for the manufacturer and the retailer.

POP communications research

POP communications should be pre- and post-tested. In a pre-test, the attention-grabbing character of different displays, floor ads, wobblers, shelf tags, etc., can be assessed. If informing consumers is an objective of the POP communications, also the extent to which the information is easy to understand, believable, useful, etc., should be pre-tested. To get an idea of what the POP communications mean in terms of brand image, consumers' opinions may be solicited. This type of research is very similar to advertising research. However, since the objective of most POP campaigns is to stimulate immediate sales, most POP communications research will focus on behavioural response measures. Therefore, as is the case for sales promotions research, effectiveness measures will concentrate on the evolution of sales compared with (comparable) previous periods, or on the comparison of different types of POP communications as to their ability to generate extra sales.

Brand experience

The most powerful instrument to activate consumers is a positive brand experience. A **brand experience** can be defined as 'sensations, feelings, cognitions, and behavioral responses evoked by brand-related stimuli that are part of a brand's design and identity, packaging, communications, and environments'.[89] Just the product itself or any single communications tool can deliver a brand experience. However, as most of the following examples will show, strong results are more likely when an integrated approach is used and the brand experience is related to the brand promise. Brand activation by means of creating brand experiences should bring the spirit of the brand to life. By doing so, the brand's promise becomes more credible and acceptable. In addition, stimulating brand interactions (both between the consumer and the company and among consumers) enhances consumers' engagement, making brand purchase and repurchase more likely. Recent academic research indeed shows that brand experiences have a direct effect on consumer satisfaction and loyalty, as well as an indirect effect via a change in brand personality associations.[90] Consumers also appear to use their experienced emotions (sometimes even more than product characteristics) to evaluate brands. Consequently, next to brand awareness and cognitive associations, brand experiences should also be considered as key drivers of **brand equity**.[91]

Objectives and dimensions of experiential marketing

Brand experiences serve diverse objectives and functions (Figure 12.13). A first objective of experiential marketing is to attract attention to the brand. As experiences form stronger traces in consumers' memory and a brand experience makes sure the experience is closely linked to the brand, a strong brand experience normally results in increased brand awareness and brand recall. By making a brand's promise more tangible and making a brand alive, brand experiences can also aim to increase brand comprehension. By relating useful and/or pleasuring experiences to the brand, a third objective – a more positive brand image – can be reached. Clever activation campaigns can make the brand stand out and/or make the brand contemporary again. As experiential marketing can be used in a very targeted way, it can also be used to enhance the brand image in specific target groups. If carried out in a proper way, experiential marketing is more involving than traditional campaigns, increasing customers' engagement. As a consequence, customer loyalty and strong brand relationships may be formed. Finally, as is the case for all activation campaigns, the main goal of creating brand experiences remains to increase sales in the short term.

In order to reach these objectives, marketers should tap into one or more experiential dimensions. Schmitt distinguishes the following experiential modules or dimensions: sense,

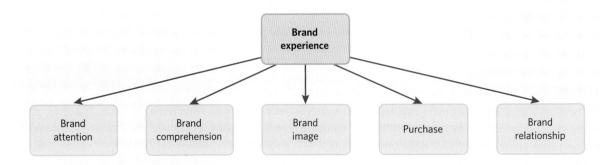

Figure 12.13 Objectives of brand experiences

feel, think, act and relate.[92] More recent research points out that the feel and relate dimensions converge as the relate dimension usually goes together with strong emotions.[93] Ideally, marketers should try to create holistic brand experiences evoking at the same time sensory, affective, intellectual and behavioural experiences. Table 12.4 describes the different experiential dimensions, which we will discuss in more detail below.[94]

Sense

Consumers become conscious of products, brands and marketing actions by their senses. Unlike store atmospherics, the importance of which was laid out a few decades ago,[95] sensory

Table 12.4 Decomposing brand experience in different experiential dimensions

Experiential dimension	Description of the experiential dimension	Examples of brands scoring high on the dimension
Sense	Creating sensory experiences through the senses of sight, sound, touch, taste and smell. Ideally marketers follow the principle of 'cognitive consistency/ sensory variety' by sticking to a clear, consistent underlying concept combined with fresh and new elements	Ferrari, Victoria's Secret, Disney, Apple, Starbucks, Lego, Puma, Toys 'R' Us, The Body Shop, Abercrombie & Fitch, BMW
Feel/Relate	Creating affective experiences by appealing to customers' inner feelings and emotions and/or by relating the customer to a broader social system. Affective experiences can range from mildly positive moods to strong emotions of joy and pride	Disney, Victoria's Secret, Hallmark, Starbucks, Harley-Davidson, BMW
Think	Appealing to the intellect by engaging consumers in convergent/analytical and/or divergent/imaginative thinking experiences	Lego, Sudoku, Apple, Fair Trade, The Body Shop
Act	Enriching customers' lives by stimulating motor actions and behavioural experiences and showing them alternative ways of doing things	Adidas, Gatorade, Puma, Nike

Source: Based upon Schmitt, B. (1999), *Experiential Marketing*, New York: Free Press; Schmitt, B. (1999), 'Experiential Marketing', *Journal of Marketing Management*, 15, 53–67; and Brakus, J.J., Schmitt, B.H. and Zarantonello, L. (2009), 'Brand Experience: What Is it? How Is it Measured? Does it Affect Loyalty?', *Journal of Marketing*, 73 (May), 52–68.

marketing (meant to activate a specific brand instead of to make a store in general stand out or to stimulate the general budget spent in the store) has been ignored for a long time. However, now the importance of sensorial marketing is generally acknowledged.[96] Aesthetic products and aesthetic packaging are exciting and appealing, increase our affective involvement and even make us prefer an unknown, more expensive brand above a known, cheaper-priced brand in a standard packaging.[97] Smelling freshly baked waffles makes us feel like buying one even though we are not hungry. Crisps should make the right sound or we do not believe they are fresh. We often cannot resist tasty food even if we know this type of food is not healthy. And we first want to touch products to avoid buying something that does not feel right. Importantly, how a product is perceived by one of our senses can impact or bias our perception of the pleasantness of the product derived from our other senses, influencing an overall, multisensory product experience.[98] Therefore, delivering a consistent multisensory experience can positively influence brand evaluations.[99] Abercrombie & Fitch understands this well. In line with an image of a sexy, near-luxury brand, it makes sure to use half-naked, good-looking models, and have stylish clothing consisting of high-grade materials such as cashmere, pima cottons and high-quality leather. The music in its stores puts consumers in the appropriate mood, and its stores as well as its clothes are scented with a nice, distinct smell. Even after having bought Abercrombie & Fitch merchandise, consumers can still smell the distinctive scent, reinforcing the experience one got in the store. In short, sight, touch, sound and smell are nicely aligned to create a near-luxury, movie-like brand experience.[100]

Academic research stresses the importance of aligning the different senses to create a powerful multisensory experience. For instance, research shows that in people's minds sourness, bitterness, crunchiness and carbonation correspond cross-modally with angular shapes and sharper, plosive stop consonants (e.g. marketers are advised to pack crisps in an angular pack and use 'c', 'd', 'g', 'k', 'p', 'q' or 't' in its brand name, such as Croky), whereas sweet, still and creamy food and beverage products benefit more from rounder shapes and back vowel brand names (e.g. yoghurt is better packed in a round packaging using an 'o' rather than an 'i' in the brand name, such as in Yoplait).[101]

To activate a brand by means of sensory marketing, marketers should reach the consumers' five senses on a deeper level than mass communications or store atmospherics in general do. It should be done in a personal, preferably interactive way.[102] Ideally, the brand experience provides proof of a brand claim. Gillette, for example, can claim in a TV spot that Gillette Fusion gives a smooth shave, but consumers automatically activate their persuasion knowledge when confronted with advertising and will question the message. However, when Gillette gives them a free shave and lets them experience the smoothness, the message becomes credible because the claim has been prooved.[103]

BUSINESS INSIGHT
What about facial hair?

Philips proved its 'sense and simplicity' slogan in Taiwan with a simple campaign. To promote its grooming kits in a country in which men are not really interested in facial hair, Philips did not make use of an app or other digital gimmick to convince men to grow a beard or stubbles. They just distributed transparent mugs with a translucent beverage to hairdressers. Hairdressers were chosen because people are very receptive to hairdressers' advice on their looks. On the mugs, one of thousands of varieties of a facial hair pattern was printed. On some there was only a moustache, on others only a beard or both a moustache and beard. When the hairdressers brought a drink (as usual), the Taiwanese men were surprised by seeing in the mirror how they looked like with facial hair. Besides advice, the hairdressers also distributed coupons for the Philips grooming kit (50% off). Of all Taiwanese men visiting a hairdresser during the campaign, 95% changed their minds about facial hair, and 25% redeemed the coupon. With a simple campaign, built on the 'sight' sense, Philips proved its 'sense and simplicity' slogan for a cost of per $2 contact.[104]

Feel/Relate

The power of emotions has already been described (see Chapter 3). Experiential marketing builds on this power but goes one step further than emotional advertising does. It tries to bring the brand to life by brand interactions. For example, a brand activation programme often makes use of a website that enables consumers to contact the company easily and exchange information with other consumers.[105] Moreover, effective brand activation campaigns stimulate not only brand–consumer interactions, but also consumer–consumer interactions, to have joint brand experiences. The Rugbeer campaign of Salta Cerveza (see below) is a good example of how friends interact together with the brand. This way, a deeper emotional engagement can be reached making brand loyalty more likely.

BUSINESS INSIGHT
Rugbeer

Argentina is the country with the most soccer fans in the world, but in the Salta Province people are more into rugby. To tap into these feelings and give the rugby fans a special experience, Salta Cerveza came up with a Rugbeer vending machine that needed to be 'tackled' to get a beer. The Rugbeer vending machine was equipped with a so-called 'pussy meter', going from 'chicken' to 'bull'. Only if the machine were tackled hard enough would a can of beer come out. On the first night, the vending machine was tackled 332 times. People interacted not only with the brand, but also with each other. Indeed, many youngsters made a kind of game out of it: who could tackle the machine the hardest? Next, the machine went on tour around several pubs. Besides delivering funny and painful brand interactions, the campaign also increased sales of Salta Cerveza by 25%.[106]

As also outlined earlier (see Chapter 2), going a step further in emotional engagement stimulates brand communities. For instance, during the Jeep jamborees, Harley-Davidson brand fests and the Vespa community rides, really strong emotional experiences can be jointly built in a group of very passionate brand lovers. Also members of online communities – such as those of Nutella, Nike, Audi and Ducati – exchange all kinds of strong brand experiences. Importantly, research has shown that brand communities strengthen loyalty and long-term brand relations.[107]

Think

Brand experiences can also be built by having consumers think. Think campaigns are common for new technology products and have been used for such product categories for ages. Examples are Apple's 'Think Differently' campaign or Microsoft's 'Where Do You Want to Go Today?' campaign.[108] However, in other industries experiences can also be built on the think dimension and customers can be engaged creatively. Lego, for example, stimulates not only kids to think creatively with their hands, but also grown-ups. Lego invented LEGO® Serious Play®, a thinking, communicating and problem-solving technique that helps companies make better decisions through structured play activities using Lego toys. In a three-hour workshop, every person at the table is asked to build a model of leadership, a new product innovation, a model for future growth or a model of corporate culture. Next, participants tell a story about what they have built. Everybody is engaged and actively participates in the discussion. LEGO Serious Play has been successfully employed for team-building and problem-solving purposes in several organisations such as NASA, Royal Bank of Canada, and in academic and public settings.[109]

Think campaigns can also be used to activate consumers' conscience, to make them rethink common practices and old assumptions.[110] The Fair Trade brand, for example, makes people reconsider current prices and makes them realise that farmers of Third World countries need a fair wage for their crops. As another example, the Flemish radio channel Studio Brussels launched the 'we do give a shit' campaign to make people aware of the silent disaster of diarrhoea worldwide. Besides educating people about the problem, Studio Brussels was able to engage the Flemish population to raise money in crazy ways: by playing music, weight-loss contests, making calendars, study marathons, etc. Despite the financial crisis, more than €7 million was raised.[111] In conclusion, making people think can be very beneficial for many brands as thinking leads to stronger brand traces in memory, making it more likely that the brand will be recalled and chosen in a future purchase situation (see also Chapter 2).

BUSINESS INSIGHT
Don't mess with the crime scene

More and more criminals escape conviction in South Africa because citizens disturb crime scene evidence. To make people aware of the problem and to educate the public that they should never interfere with a crime scene, an interactive DNA project was launched. A large floor board was installed in Cape Town train station featuring the face of a criminal and underneath the picture the slogan 'Disturbing a crime scene makes it impossible to identify the criminal'. The floor board was made of short-lasting material. Therefore, after a couple of hours of people walking across it, the criminal's identity disappeared. The activation engaged thousands of people. Many of them asked the DNA project representatives questions about the project while others took pictures. To all, the message was clear: 'never disturb a crime scene'. The project was also largely covered by the press so that a wide audience were reached.[112]

Act

Act campaigns aim to create physical experiences and/or stimulate changes in longer-term patterns of behaviour or lifestyles.[113] Whereas behavioural change can be rational in nature such as proposed by the Theory of Planned Behaviour ('Public transportation is environmental friendly', 'My peers have a positive attitude towards public transportation' and 'I know it is easy for me to take public transportation', so 'from now on, I'm going to my work by public transportation'), lifestyle and behavioural changes are often more motivational and emotional in nature.[114] Therefore, brand experiences could be more successful in engendering such changes than non-interactive, mass communications. In its Climacool campaign, Adidas provided youngsters with such a behavioural experience, trying to increase their interest in running and make them more sportive (see below).

BUSINESS INSIGHT
Ready to run?

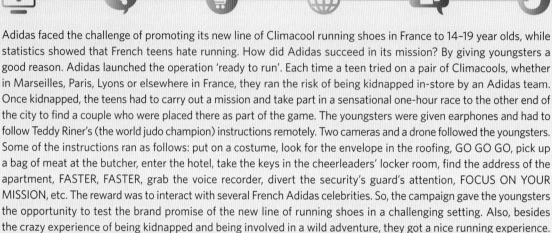

Adidas faced the challenge of promoting its new line of Climacool running shoes in France to 14–19 year olds, while statistics showed that French teens hate running. How did Adidas succeed in its mission? By giving youngsters a good reason. Adidas launched the operation 'ready to run'. Each time a teen tried on a pair of Climacools, whether in Marseilles, Paris, Lyons or elsewhere in France, they ran the risk of being kidnapped in-store by an Adidas team. Once kidnapped, the teens had to carry out a mission and take part in a sensational one-hour race to the other end of the city to find a couple who were placed there as part of the game. The youngsters were given earphones and had to follow Teddy Riner's (the world judo champion) instructions remotely. Two cameras and a drone followed the youngsters. Some of the instructions ran as follows: put on a costume, look for the envelope in the roofing, GO GO GO, pick up a bag of meat at the butcher, enter the hotel, take the keys in the cheerleaders' locker room, find the address of the apartment, FASTER, FASTER, grab the voice recorder, divert the security's guard's attention, FOCUS ON YOUR MISSION, etc. The reward was to interact with several French Adidas celebrities. So, the campaign gave the youngsters the opportunity to test the brand promise of the new line of running shoes in a challenging setting. Also, besides the crazy experience of being kidnapped and being involved in a wild adventure, they got a nice running experience. But most importantly, they could meet their heroes, whom Adidas hopes are influential enough to motivate the youngsters to take on a more active lifestyle. Needless to say, the youngsters were really wild about the operation. During the campaign, the number of youngsters trying on Climacool running shoes increased by more than 500%. The campaign also got a lot of media coverage and was widely adopted by the most influential French blogs.[115]

A special and very involving case of brand activation campaign that relies on the act dimension (and also largely on the think dimension) is the co-creation campaign. **Co-creation** or soliciting input from customers for new products is being used increasingly by companies.[116] For example, of the high-tech firms listed in the S&P 500 index, more than 80% indicate that they have established virtual user communities to generate users' input.[117] This is not surprising as it is generally acknowledged that a company's competence in identifying and integrating knowledgeable users in the new product development process represents a major competitive advantage.[118] But how to get the most out of co-creation? Who should be attracted and what should be the incentive? Firstly, the right consumers should be involved. Whereas for technological products, lead users are often considered most effective, this does not need to be the case for non-technological products. In the latter case, crowd sourcing (i.e. making use of a group of consumers on the Internet) is being used increasingly.[119] In order to know which incentive should be provided, it is important to realise that consumers participate in co-creation for a variety of reasons.[120] Some are motivated by an intrinsic interest in innovation, others by general curiosity, dissatisfaction with current alternatives, to gain knowledge, to show ideas, or to receive monetary rewards. Generally, four consumer types can be distinguished based on their pattern of motivation: reward-oriented, need-driven, curiosity-driven and intrinsically interested consumers. Reward-oriented people are in co-creation for the money and need-driven consumers to find a solution for their current problems. Curiosity-driven and intrinsically interested consumers, on the other hand, are seeking a compelling experience. They are interested in getting feedback, being part of a community with a lot of interaction and discussion of ideas, the possibility to collaborate and vote for their favourite idea. Being officially recognised as a co-developer is also attractive to these latter types of co-creation consumers.[121] So, to encourage participation in co-creation, marketers best follow a balanced strategy: (1) using a platform that allows consumer interaction and community-building, and (2) providing an attractive but not too attractive incentive. Firstly, providing the possibilities for social interaction is crucial. Research has shown that more intrinsically motivated consumers value the interaction with like-minded consumers and it increases their co-creation experience. This co-creation experience in turn has a positive effect on the quality and number of submitted ideas, and increases consumers' participation frequency and consumers' interest in future participation.[122] Secondly, an incentive should be offered to avoid being accused of taking advantage of consumers. Research shows that the higher the reward, the higher the number of ideas that are submitted.[123] However, the incentive should not be too attractive because it could stimulate consumers to adopt a minimax strategy (i.e. do the least possible for the most possible reward), and crowd out consumers' intrinsic motivation.[124]

BUSINESS INSIGHT
Create your own flavour

Although Lay's was market leader in the salted snacks category in Belgium, its market share was under pressure because of the rise of private labels. To stop its loss in market volume and value, Lay's decided to activate its brand by focusing on its core value: taste. Lay's also aimed to involve its (potential) customers to the maximum. Building on the increasing popularity of cooking and experimenting with flavours, Lay's came up with a 'create your own flavour' campaign. The purpose was to launch a limited edition of the flavour created by one of the consumers. In a first stage, consumers were encouraged to submit their own flavour. The incentive was €25,000 in cash and 1% of the turnover of the limited edition sales. TV commercials made sure the general public were aware of the campaign. Packaging and in-store communications pushed sales, Facebook increased brand conversations (with messages like 'I'm actually more looking forward to the launch of the new Lay's flavour than to the launch of the new iPhone'), and a good PR plan made sure the campaign was covered in the general press. Almost 246 000 flavours were submitted. A jury consisting of two chefs and one consumer selected two flavours that were developed and launched: Lay's Bicky Crisp and Lay's Indian Curry Style. An ad thanked all consumers for submitting their taste and announced the two selected flavours that were from then onwards for sale. Next, it was up to the consumers again to select their favourite. Over eight weeks there was a big contest between both flavours with Bicky Crisp coming out as the winner. Again Facebook, point-of-sales, packaging and advertising played important roles. The campaign was a big success: (1) 134 581 people voted on the website for their favourite flavour; (2) 1.2 million people visited the Facebook page; (3) Lay's saw an increase of more than 10% on image parameters like 'great taste', 'high quality', 'contemporary' and 'for someone like me'; (4) Lay's Brand Engagement Index increased significantly; (5) more than 1.56 million Lay's Limited Edition Bicky Crisp and Indian Curry Style were sold; and (6) Lay's market share increased, whereas that of private labels decreased. The campaign won a Gold Activation Award. A similar campaign ran in several other European countries, with great results there as well. For example, in the Netherlands 678 682 flavours were submitted, 6 million Lay's Limited Edition 'PatatjeJoppie' were sold and 216 739 people voted for their favourite flavour.[125]

Brand experience research

Brand experience communications can be pre-tested and post-tested. Many of the objectives of experiential marketing are the same as for a traditional advertising campaign (i.e. attracting attention, brand comprehension, brand image). Therefore, very similar methods as for advertising research can be used, such as recall tests and direct opinion tests. As for the sales response, the methods discussed for sales promotions research can be used. The latter are also valuable to get an idea of the evolution in loyal customers. The extent to which the campaign induced sensory and feelings responses can be probed with physiological tests and feeling-oriented direct opinion tests. Finally, the extent to which the campaign also elicited word-of-mouth and word-of-mouse should be assessed. Such methods will be tackled later (see Chapter 15).

IMC INSIGHT
Integrating brand activation in IMC

Brand activation is most effective when the instruments used – sales promotions, point-of-purchase communications or brand experiences – are integrated in the overall marketing communications efforts. First of all, the effectiveness of trade promotions can be enhanced by supplementing them with consumer promotions. Promotions can be announced via commercials in the mass media and reinforced by point-of-purchase communications. Public relations can be combined with sales promotions to create events and specific brand experiences in which, for instance, samples and/or coupons can be distributed, or prizes can be won. Advertising and POP communications can use images of these events to remind consumers of their brand experiences. Within the framework of sponsorship of events, team sampling, couponing and demonstrations can be used to acquaint the public with the product and to stimulate trial. Consumers can also be involved by getting them to vote for their favourite versions, come up with original ideas for product innovation or marketing communications, etc. Press releases on brand experience programmes and specific customer responses to these programmes can be developed in an effort to get free publicity. Coupons can be inserted in direct mailings, or e-coupons can be distributed through the company's website or Facebook page or via interactive advertising on interactive digital TV commercials. Product placement can be used to stir up interest in a company's offerings via interactive promotional offers during product use in the TV programme. Brand experience programmes can deliver proof of the brand promise promoted in mass ads. Customer engagement and loyalty that result from brand experience programmes can be reinforced by customer relationship programmes, which in turn can be enhanced by linking them to various types of loyalty promotions: contests, saving cards, self-liquidators, etc. Promotions may also serve as a traffic-building device for stands at exhibitions and trade fairs, and exhibitions and trade fairs can be used as venues to build specific brand experiences.

Summary

Brand activation plays a crucial role in stimulating brand purchases in the short term. Brand activation programmes have become increasingly important as a result of communications clutter, less brand loyalty, and the lack of differentiation between brands. Three important tools to activate a brand are sales promotions, point-of-purchase communications and creating brand experiences. Sales promotions can be targeted at retailers, the sales force or end-consumers. Consumer promotions include monetary incentives (price cuts, coupons, savings cards), prizes (competitions, sweepstakes and lotteries) and product promotions (sampling, extra volume, free in-mail, premiums). By means of sales promotions, various objectives can be pursued: attracting new customers, making existing ones loyal, increasing market size, reinforcing other communications tools and rewarding loyal customers. Although in the short run promotions can increase trial, loyalty and profitability, they can also lead to deal-proneness, brand-switching, a post-promotion dip and negative effects on profitability. In the medium and long run, the effects are unclear, but a potential negative effect on brand image should be taken into account.

As is the case for sales promotions, point-of-purchase communications enjoy the advantage that they reach consumers at the moment when, and the place where, they are making decisions. The objectives of in-store communications are to attract the consumer's attention, to remind him or her of ongoing or previous advertising, to inform, to persuade and to build an image of the brands on shelves. Several instruments of in-store communications can be used, such as shelf displays, floor graphics, trolley advertising, moving displays and interactive kiosks. Besides these specific communications instruments, store atmospherics are also important. Most POP communications appear to be effective.

Brand activation by means of creating brand experiences is an especially powerful communications tools. Besides stimulating sales, objectives like attention tracking, stimulating brand comprehension and brand image, and creating strong relationships can be pursued. Brand experiences try to bring the brand alive by tapping into one or more of the following experiential dimensions: sense, feel/relate, think and act. Creating a holistic, interactive experience that is built on the brand's values and is smoothly integrated with other communications tools is key.

REVIEW QUESTIONS

1. Why is brand activation becoming increasingly important?
2. What are the objectives and target groups of sales promotions?
3. Discuss the various tools of consumer promotions, their objectives, their advantages and disadvantages for both the manufacturer and the retailer.
4. To what extent are sales promotions effective in the short and the long run?
5. What are the tools and objectives of point-of-purchase communications?
6. How effective are the various point-of-purchase tools?
7. What are the objectives of experiential marketing programmes?
8. Discuss the different experiential dimensions that marketers should try to activate to create a strong brand experience.
9. How can you explain the effectiveness of brand experiences?

Further reading

Hultén, B., Broweus, N. and van Dijk, M. (2009), *Sensory Marketing*. London: Palgrave Macmillan.

Lindstrom, M. and Kotler, P. (2010), *Brand Sense: Sensory Secrets Behind the Stuff We Buy*. New York: Free Press.

Mullin, R. (2010), *Sales Promotion: How to Create, Implement and Integrate Campaigns that Really Work*. London: Kogan Page.

Stahlberg, M. and Ville, M. (2012), *Shopper Marketing: How to Increase Purchase Decisions at the Point of Sale?* London: Kogan Page.

Shopper marketing: http://shoppermarketing.com/home/.

Journal of Promotion Management, http://www.tandfonline.com/toc/wjpm20/current.

CASE 12:

'The Perfect Size': for every moment, there is a Mars bar

Introduction

Frank Mars was born in 1882 in Hancock, Minnesota. Since he suffered from a mild form of polio, his mother taught him at an early age to make chocolate dips to keep him entertained. From 1911 onwards, Frank Mars started making and selling candy to small stores. Being successful in this business, he founded the Mars Candy Factory in Tacoma, Washington. The first big breakthrough came in 1923 with the introduction of the first Milky Way®. Milky Way was an instant success and sales rocketed to $800 000. In 1925, Frank's son, Forrest, joined the company and added pet care and food to Mars' portfolio. Now, Mars Inc. is one of the largest family businesses worldwide with more than 70 000 employees in 73 countries. Holding a leading position in each of the six different segments it serves, namely Petcare, Chocolate, Wrigley, Food, Drinks and Symbioscience, Mars Inc. realises a turnover of more than $30 billion. Mars Inc. owns 52 A brands, several of which are real global favourites. Think of M&M's®, Snickers®, Twix®, Mars®, Uncle Ben's® rice, Pedigree® and Cesar® dog food, and Whiskas® and Sheba® cat food. The global appeal of Mars' products is underscored by the fact that the products are sold and enjoy a high popularity in about 180 different countries. For example, Mars Inc. makes 7 of the world's 20 best-selling chocolate snacks.

Changing consumer needs in Belgium

Long-run success goes together with excellent products and a profound insight into customer needs. To this end, all Mars subsidiaries carefully monitor the trends in the environment and regularly conduct consumer research. As is the case for Mars Belgium, AC Nielsen data from 2006 showed that chocolate is an important category in the Belgian snack market, holding a share of 28% as compared with 33% for biscuits, 15% for crisps, 4.9% for candy and 6.7% for ice. However, the growth rate for chocolate (+3.3%) was markedly smaller than for the other categories (+4.7% for biscuits, +6.8% for crisps, +4.9% for candy and +6.7% for ice). A closer look at the specific chocolate varieties revealed that all varieties were growing, except for a decline of 2.2% in volume for chocolate bars. Making a distinction between biscuit, hunger and indulgent chocolate bars, the AC Nielsen data revealed that the problems were situated in the biscuit and hunger bars (see Figure 12.14).

Although the general trend for biscuit and hunger bars was negative, this was not the case for the Mars brands in these categories (see Figure 12.15). Nevertheless, Mars Belgium felt it had to secure its future, especially because its core brands were situated in these categories and because other sources confirmed the negative trend in the category. Panel data from GFK, for example, indicated that

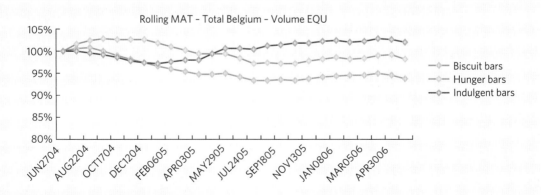

Figure 12.14 Moving annual turnover for the total category

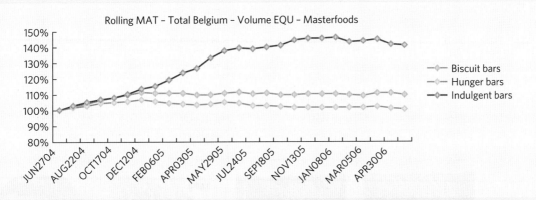

Figure 12.15 Moving annual turnover for Mars' products
Source: NV Mars Belgium SA

Table 12.5 Consumption trend for candy bars

	Dec. 04	Mar. 05	Jun. 05	Sep. 05	Dec. 05	Mar. 06
Occasions per buyer	10.29	9.91	9.59	9.30	9.12	9.18
Kg per occasion	0.538	0.534	0.530	0.525	0.525	0.524

consumers bought candy bars fewer times per year and less volume per purchase (see Table 12.5).

Combined with Mars Belgium's own research, two important consumer insights were generated. Firstly, consumers in general, but also youngsters in particular, focus increasingly on a good balance between eating and exercising. At certain moments (e.g. just before exercising, at moments when they are hungry) they want products to fulfil their energy needs but, in general, they are looking for healthier and less heavy snacks.

Secondly, the persons in the household responsible for shopping want both lighter snacks and greater value for money. Mothers especially prefer a greater number of smaller portions in a pack. Children do not notice the difference, but mothers feel less guilty if they can give their children a lighter snack. Moreover, more portions in a pack means they last longer.

The Perfect Size concept

To activate chocolate bar consumption and to regain gatekeeper acceptance on its core brands (Mars, Twix and Snickers), Mars Belgium introduced its Perfect Size concept. More specifically, Mars Belgium differentiated the bar weight according to consumption moments (see Table 12.6). When consumers buy a bar in the out-of-home (OOH) channel (e.g. from a vending machine, at a petrol station, at the cinema, in an amusement park, etc.),

they are often driven by impulse and looking for energy. At these moments, concern about calorie intake is low and a larger bar is preferred. Therefore, for the 'buy now, eat now' moments, Mars Belgium provides the regular, single bars in OOH outlets. Consumers also like to eat bars during a break or for pleasure at work, in school or at home. This consumption is usually planned in advance and the shoppers' (i.e. parents as 'gatekeepers') concerns of less weight per bar and more bars per pack play an important role here. For these 'buy now, eat later' situations, Mars Belgium replaced its three-pack with a four-pack, its six-pack with a seven-pack and its ten-pack with a twelve-pack. The weight per portion went down from 54 to 45 g for a Mars bar, from 58 to 50 g for a Twix and from 60 to 50 g for a Snickers. For consumers who like to indulge themselves once in a while at home, minis varying in weight from about 15 to 20 g are ideal. Finally, for social sharing and gift-giving, miniatures are offered, such as in the Celebrations box. The latter buying acts are assumed to be more conscious and planned in advance, and are more likely to take place at retailers.

Early qualitative research results indicated that consumers really liked the concept. Comments from consumers included: 'with smaller bars, I can eat more often a snack to keep me going'; 'a smaller bar gives me the opportunity to control the balance for me and my family'; and 'the larger the pack size, the more value for money we get, and the more snack times I get with my family'.

Table 12.6 Every bar has its own moment

Bar moments	Energy	Break, pleasure	Indulgence	Social Sharing
Buy where?	Out-of-home	Retail	Retail	Retail
Eat where?	Out-of-home	Out-of-home or In home	In home	In home
Eat when?	Buy now, eat now	Buy now, eat later	Buy now, eat later	Buy now, eat later
Offer	Single	Multis	Minis	Miniatures
Example				

Launch and communications support of the differentiated weight bars

To launch the Perfect Size concept, Mars Belgium went for an integrated communications approach. Firstly, timing was important to avoid having communications without products, or having the new products without any accompanying communications. In less than three weeks, the new Perfect Size products were transferred from Mars Belgium's warehouse through the retail warehouse to the points-of-sale, and all old products were replaced with new ones. Secondly, the concept was explained to the retail partners. Account managers explained the consumer insights and indicated why this new concept showed a better fit with contemporary consumer needs. They also mentioned the positive response that the concept had received in qualitative research. Further, they stressed what the new concept would mean for the distributor in terms of activation of the category and in terms of how the shelves should look. Mars Belgium, for example, advised the distributors to reorder their chocolate products according to consumption moment.

Thirdly, the launch of the Perfect Size concept and the new planogram was accompanied by wobblers to attract consumers' attention to the new package formats. Both the pack and the wobbler looked like a promotion offer (red with white font), which underscored the value-for-money aspect of the multipacks. Fourthly, three months later a big bang was created with: (1) massive TV advertising and outdoor support; (2) sales activation by means of the distribution of free coupons door-to-door to 2 million Belgian households (i.e. about 50% coverage of the Belgian population) and free coupons on the shelves offering a discount of 50 cents on a family pack; and (3) maximum in-store visibility by having large branded displays, explanatory leaflets, in-store tasting and an in-store event by means of which each store could elect a 'winner'. Sales promotions performed a crucial role in the campaign. It was the communications tool that best covered the total target group. Not only did the sales promotions reach shoppers in the store, but they also reached most of the Belgian households at home. One in two households received a separate coupon. Moreover, the sales promotions made it possible to be listed in the retailers' promo pages, by means of which a large part of the remaining households could be reached.

Source: NV Mars Belgium SA.

Results

The integrated campaign helped to increase the sales value of Mars by 22%, of Snickers by 19% and of Twix by 17%. These numbers do not reflect a promotion versus a non-promotion peak, but a comparison between a four-month period during and after the promotion period with the same four months a year earlier (see Figure 12.16). The best results were obtained during the periods when above- and below-the-line support were combined. Importantly, not only were the short-term results positive, but a long-term positive evolution can be seen on all multipacks (see Figure 12.17). This means that it is not just the campaign that increased sales, but the concept itself seems to be accepted as well.

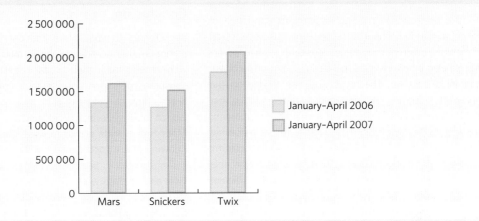

Figure 12.16 Sales value of multipacks before and after the introduction of the differentiated weight bars

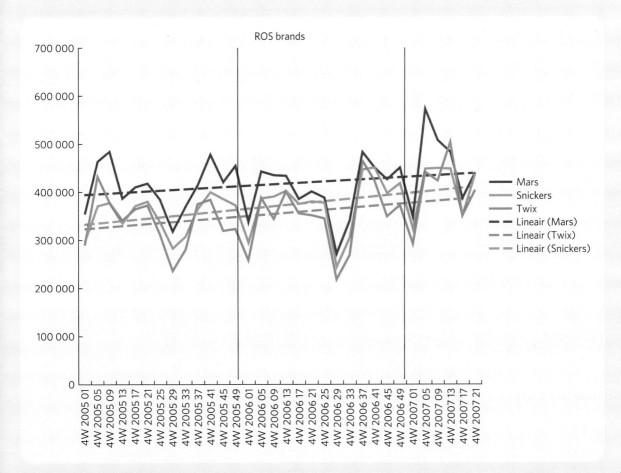

Figure 12.17 Long-term trend in sales value of Mars, Snickers and Twix

Perfect Size also in the Netherlands

Mars Netherlands was confronted with the same trends and problems as Mars Belgium. Therefore, the Perfect Size concept was also launched in the Netherlands. The approach was more or less the same, although small differences did exist. For example, Mars Netherlands did not have a six-pack in the past, but a five-pack. With the new concept it moved from a five- to a seven-pack. It did not move from a ten- to a twelve-pack, but kept a ten-pack consisting of smaller bars. As in Belgium, the supporting campaign mixed and matched different communications tools such as advertising, sales promotions, personal selling, point-of-purchase communications, etc. The focus was also largely on the seven-pack. Also in the Netherlands, differentiating bar weight according to consumption and purchase moment turned out to be a good move. Qualitative research pointed to the same positive consumer reactions as in Belgium. Consumers mentioned among others: 'I want to be able to snack in between; three meals a day is not sufficient anymore'; 'With smaller bars, I can more easily keep my weight in balance'; and 'The new pack format increases my value for money perception'.

Also, quantitative results were very positive. The Perfect Size concept led to a total sales increase of 6%. Mars Netherlands lost two-person households (probably because of the larger pack formats), but this was more than offset by an increase in households with children. Indeed, total penetration increased from 14.7% in period 3 of 2006 to 16.1% in period 3 of 2007. Further, both 'promotion sales

value' and 'neutral sales value' increased. Figure 12.18 shows the sales value that was realised with and without sales promotion support. As in Belgium, the seven-packs especially were very successful (see Table 12.7 for general results for all three brands and Figure 12.19 for period-by-period results for Twix). This is not surprising in view of the fact that the campaign focused on this pack format.

Conclusion

By listening to consumers and carefully watching consumption trends, Mars Belgium and Mars Netherlands were able to tailor their products better to contemporary consumer needs. According to a company official, 'Big brands have to progress with their consumers.' With the launch of the Perfect Size concept, Mars Belgium and Mars Netherlands practised what the company preaches. Knowing that a good concept will not sell itself, a massive communications campaign helped activate the Mars, Twix and Snickers bars. The campaign cleverly mixed and matched different communications elements. Indeed, at Mars Belgium and Mars Netherlands it is also common knowledge that a full focus, or a 360° approach, combining among other things advertising and sales promotions, is much stronger than either advertising or sales promotions alone. Tailoring bar weight to consumption moments resulted in smaller bars, but larger bottom lines for both subsidiaries. Most importantly, this was the case not only during the marketing communications campaign, but also in the longer term.

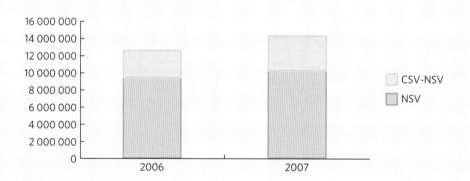

Figure 12.18 Customer sales value increases after launch of Perfect Size concept

Table 12.7 Positive results during non-promotion period for new pack formats in the Netherlands

	Mars 7- vs 5-packs	Snickers 7- vs 5-packs	Twix 7- vs 5-packs
Sales in euros	15.00%	20.00%	27.00%
Sales in volume	4.30%	10.00%	8.30%

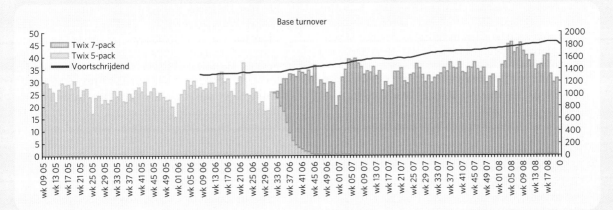

Figure 12.19 Detailed results for Twix comparing sales before and after resize

QUESTIONS

1. What are the advantages and disadvantages of the Perfect Size concept for (a) Mars Belgium and Mars Netherlands, (b) the consumers, (c) the trade partners?

2. What do you think was the main objective of the 'big bang' communications programme that supported the launch of the Perfect Size concept?

3. Mars Belgium used coupons. Would you have chosen another type of promotion? If so, which one and why?

4. Looking at the integrated campaign, would you have mixed and matched different communications tools? Why (not)?

5. How important do you think trade promotions versus consumer promotions were for introducing the new pack formats?

6. Would you advise Mars Belgium and Mars Netherlands to continue to use sales promotions after the introductory period? Which ones?

7. How would you advise Mars Belgium and Mars Netherlands to test the effectiveness of their sales promotions?

Source: Based on Information provided by Chantal Hendrickx, Trade Marketing Manager, Mars Belgium; www.mars.be; www.mars.nl; www.mars.com.

References

1 Alberts, P.G., 'Theory of Brand Activation', www.brandactivation.nl (accessed July 2012).

2 Felgate, M., Fearne, A., DiFalco, S. and Garcia-Martinez, M. (2012), 'Using Supermarket Loyalty Card Data to Analyse the Impact of Promotions', *International Journal of Market Research*, 54(2), 221–40.

3 Kardes, F.R., Cline, T.W. and Cronley, M.L. (2011), *Consumer Behavior: Science and Practice*. Mason, OH: South-Western Cengage Learning.

4 Duncan, T. (2002), *IMC: Using Advertising and Promotion to Build Brands*. Boston, MA: McGraw-Hill/Irwin.

5 Felgate, M., Fearne, A., DiFalco, S. and Garcia-Martinez, M. (2012), 'Using Supermarket Loyalty Card Data to Analyse the Impact of Promotions', *International Journal of Market Research*, 54(2), 221–40; Briggs, F. (2011), 'Promotions Fuel Supermarket Sales Lifts, Reports Nielsen', http://retailtimes.co.uk/promotions-fuel-supermarket-sales-lifts-reports-nielsen/ (accessed July 2012); Raghubir,

P., Inman, J.J. and Grande, H. (2004), 'The Three Faces of Consumer Promotions', *California Management Review*, 46, 23–41; Del Vecchio, D. (2005), 'Deal-Prone Consumers' Response to Promotion: The Effects of Relative and Absolute Promotions Value', *Psychology & Marketing*, 22, 373–91.

6 The Nielsen Company (2012), 'Marketing Effectiveness: Getting the Right Returns from Brand Investments', http://www.nielsen.com/us/en/insights/reports-downloads/2012/marketing-effectiveness.html (accessed July 2012); Briggs, F. (2011), 'Promotions Fuel Supermarket Sales Lifts, Reports Nielsen', http://retailtimes.co.uk/promotions-fuel-supermarket-sales-lifts-reports-nielsen/ (accessed July 2012).

7 McDonald, C. (1992), 'Finding Out How – Unleashing the Power of Single-Source Data to Explain the Marketing Mix', *Admap* (December), 21–5; Pickton, D. and Broderick, A. (2001), *Integrated Marketing Communications*. Harlow: Financial Times/Prentice Hall.

8 The Nielsen Company (2011), 'Shopping & Saving Strategies Around the World', http://www.nielsen.com/content/corporate/us/en/insights/reports-downloads/2011/global-shopping-survey-oct-2011.html (accessed July 2012).

9 Chapman, C.J. and Steenburgh, T.J. (2011), 'An Investigation of Earnings Management Through Marketing Actions', *Management Science*, 57(1), 72–92.

10 See also www.incentivesatwork.com (accessed 27 September 2012).

11 *De Morgen*, 12 October 2007.

12 Freimer, M. and Horsky, D. (2008), 'Try It, You Will Like It – Does Consumer Learning Lead to Competitive Price Promotions?', *Marketing Science*, 27(5), 796–810.

13 Riedall, K. (2011), 'Linkable Offers – A Redemption Revolution', http://www.brandchannel.com/brand_speak.asp?bs_id=302 (accessed July 2012).

14 The Nielsen Company (2011), 'Shopping & Saving Strategies Around the World', http://www.nielsen.com/content/corporate/us/en/insights/reports-downloads/2011/global-shopping-survey-oct-2011.html (accessed July 2012).

15 Slater, J. (2001), 'Is Couponing an Effective Promotional Strategy? An Examination of the Procter & Gamble Zero-couponing Test', *Journal of Marketing Communications*, 7(1), 3–10.

16 Felgate, M., Fearne, A., DiFalco, S. and Garcia-Martinez, M. (2012), 'Using Supermarket Loyalty Card Data to Analyse the Impact of Promotions', *International Journal of Market Research*, 54(2), 221–40.

17 Chandran, S. and Morwitz, V.G. (2006), 'The Price of "Free"-dom: Consumer Sensitivity to Promotions with Negative Contextual Influences', *Journal of Consumer Research*, 33(3), 384–92.

18 Mishra, A. and Mishra, H. (2011), 'The Influence of Price Discount Versus Bonus Pack on the Preference for Virtue and Vice Foods', *Journal of Marketing Research*, 68 (February), 196–206.

19 http://www.esprix.nl/core/winnaars_esprix_2011#!pretty Photo[bavaria]/0/, http://www.versereclame.nl/2012/04/18/de-ek-gadget-van-bavaria-de-v-dress/ (accessed July 2012).

20 Esteban-Bravo, M., Múgica, J.M. and Vidal-Sanz, J.M. (2009), 'Magazine Sales Promotion: A Dynamic Response Analysis', *Journal of Advertising*, 38(1), 137–46.

21 See also www.incentivesatwork.com (accessed 27 September 2012).

22 Duncan, T. (2002), *IMC: Using Advertising and Promotion to Build Brands*. Boston, MA: McGraw-Hill/Irwin; Brassington, F. and Pettitt, S. (2003), *Principles of Marketing*. Harlow: Financial Times/Prentice Hall.

23 Ataman, M.B., Van Heerde, H.J. and Mela, C.E. (2010), 'The Long-Term Effect of Marketing Strategy on Brand Sales', *Journal of Marketing Research*, 47(5), 866–82; Slotegraaf, R.J. and Pauwels, K. (2008), 'The Impact of Brand Equity and Innovation on the Long-Term Effectiveness of Promotions', *Journal of Marketing Research*, 45 (June), 293–306.

24 Zhang, Q., Seetharaman, P.B. and Narasimhan, C. (2012), 'The Indirect Impact of Price Deals on Households' Purchase Decisions Through the Formation of Expected Future Prices', *Journal of Retailing*, 88(1), 88–101; Chapman, C.J. and Steenburgh, T.J. (2011), 'An Investigation of Earnings Management Through Marketing Actions', *Management Science*, 57(1), 72–92; Felgate, M., Fearne, A., DiFalco, S. and Garcia-Martinez, M. (2012), 'Using Supermarket Loyalty Card Data to Analyse the Impact of Promotions', *International Journal of Market Research*, 54(2), 221–40; Allenby, G.M. and Lenk, P.J. (1995), 'Reassessing Brand Loyalty, Price Sensitivity and Merchandising Effects on Consumer Brand Choice', *Journal of Business and Economic Statistics*, 13(3), 281–9; Leone, R.P. and Srinivasan, S.S. (1996), 'Coupon Face Value: Its Impact on Coupon Redemptions, Brand Sales, and Brand Profitability', *Journal of Retailing*, 72(3), 273–89.

25 Chapman, C.J. and Steenburgh, T.J. (2011), 'An Investigation of Earnings Management Through Marketing Actions', *Management Science*, 57(1), 72–92; Ataman, M.B., Van Heerde, H.J. and Mela, C.E. (2010), 'The Long-Term Effect of Marketing Strategy on Brand Sales', *Journal of Marketing Research*, 47(5), 866–82; Sethuraman, R. and Tellis, G.J. (1991), 'An Analysis of the Trade off Between Advertising and Price Discounting', *Journal of Marketing Research*, 28 (May), 160–74.

26 For instance, Dhar and Hoch report profit increase between 113% and 235%: Dhar, S.K. and Hoch, S.J. (1996), 'Price Discrimination Using In-Store Merchandising', *Journal of Marketing*, 60 (January), 17–30, while Nielsen warns for margins being hurt: The Nielsen Company (2012), 'Marketing Effectiveness: Getting the Right Returns from Brand Investments', http://www.nielsen.com/us/en/insights/reports-downloads/2012/marketing-effectiveness.html (accessed July 2012).

27 Gupta, S. (1988), 'Impact of Sales Promotions on When, What and How Much to Buy', *Journal of Marketing Research*, 25 (November), 342–55; Blattberg, R.C. and Neslin, S.A. (1989), 'Sales Promotion: The Long and the Short of It', *Marketing Letters*, 81–97.

28 Grover, R. and Srinivasan, V. (1992), 'Evaluating the Multiple Effects of Retail Promotions on Brand Loyalty and Brand Switching Segments', *Journal of Marketing Research*, 29 (February), 76–89.

29 Mulhern, F.J. and Padgett, D.T. (1995), 'The Relationship Between Retail Price Promotions and Regular Price Purchases', *Journal of Marketing*, 59 (October), 83–90.

30 Leeflang, P.S.H. and Parreno-Selva, J. (2012), 'Cross-Category Demand Effects of Price Promotions', *Journal of the Academy of Marketing Science*, 40, 572–86.

31 Grover, R. and Srinivasan, V. (1992), 'Evaluating the Multiple Effects of Retail Promotions on Brand Loyalty and Brand Switching Segments', *Journal of Marketing Research*, 29 (February), 76–89; Neslin, S.A., Henderson, C. and Quelch, J. (1985), 'Consumer Promotions and the Acceleration of Product Purchases', *Marketing Science*, 4(2), 125–45.

32 Rothschild, M.L. (1987), 'A Behavioral View of Promotion Effects on Brand Loyalty', *Advances in Consumer Research*, 14, 119–20.

33 Kardes, F.R., Cline, T.W. and Cronley, M.L. (2011), *Consumer Behavior: Science and Practice*. Mason, OH: South-Western Cengage Learning; Mayhew, G.E. and Winer, R. (1992), 'An Empirical Analysis of Internal and External Reference Prices Using Scanner Data', *Journal of Consumer Research*, 19 (June), 62–70.

34 Valette-Florence, P., Guizani, H. and Merunka, D. (2011), 'The Impact of Brand Personality and Sales Promotions on Brand Equity', *Journal of Business Research*, 64, 24–8.

35 Yi, Y. and Yoo, J. (2011), 'The Long-Term Effects of Sales Promotions on Brand Attitude Across Monetary and Non-Monetary Promotions', *Psychology & Marketing*, 28(9), 879–96.

36 Kahn, B.E. and Louie, T.A. (1990), 'Effects of Retraction of Price Promotions on Brand Choice Behavior for Variety-Seeking and Last-Purchase-Loyal Consumers', *Journal of Marketing Research*, 27 (August), 279–89.

37 Lal, R. and Padmanabhan, V. (1995), 'Competitive Response and Equilibria', *Marketing Science*, 14(3), 101–8.

38 Dekimpe, M.G. and Hanssens, D.M. (1995), 'Empirical Generalizations about Market Evolution and Stationarity', *Marketing Science*, 14(3), 109–21.

39 The Nielsen Company (2012), 'Marketing Effectiveness: Getting the Right Returns from Brand Investments', http://www.nielsen.com/us/en/insights/reports-downloads/2012/marketing-effectiveness.html (accessed July 2012).

40 Kumar, V. and Pereira, A. (1995), 'Explaining the Variation in Short-Term Sales Response to Retail Price Promotions', *Journal of the Academy of Marketing Science*, 23(3), 155–69.

41 Slotegraaf, R.J. and Pauwels, K. (2008), 'The Impact of Brand Equity and Innovation on the Long-Term Effectiveness of Promotions', *Journal of Marketing Research*, 45 (June), 293–306; Tellis, G.J. and Zufryden, F. (1995), 'Tackling the Retailer Decision Maze: Which Brands to Discount, How Much, When and Why?', *Marketing Science*, 14(3), 271–99.

42 Felgate, M., Fearne, A., DiFalco, S. and Garcia-Martinez, M. (2012), 'Using Supermarket Loyalty Card Data to analyse the Impact of Promotions', *International Journal of Market Research*, 54(2), 221–40; D'Astous, A. and Jacob, I. (2002), 'Understanding Consumer Reactions to Premium-based Promotional Offers', *European Journal of Marketing*, 36(11), 1270–86.

43 Simester, D. (1997), 'Optimal Promotion Strategies: A Demand-Sided Characterization', *Management Science*, 43(2), 251–6.

44 GfK Belgium.

45 Park, C.W., Iyer, E. and Smith, D.C. (1989), 'The Effects of Situational Factors on In-Store Grocery Shopping Behavior: The Role of Store Environment and Time Available for Shopping', *Journal of Consumer Research*, 15, 422–32.

46 Neff, J. (2008), 'Pick a Product: 40% of Public Decide in Store', *Advertising Age* (July 28), http://adage.com/article/news/pick-a-product-40-public-decide-store/129924/ (accessed July 2012); PRNewswire (2008), 'When Shoppers Become Buyers', http://www.prnewswire.co.uk/news-releases/when-shoppers-become-buyers-152985515.html (accessed July 2012); Ogilvy & Mather (2008), 'Turning Shoppers into Buyers: The Truth Behind Shopper Decisions Made in Store', http://www.scribd.com/doc/11302909/Turning-Shoppers-Into-Buyers#wordpress (accessed July 2012).

47 Liljenwall, R. and Maskulka, J. (2002), *Marketing's Powerful Weapon: Point-Of-Purchase Advertising*, Washington, DC: Point-Of-Purchase Advertising International.

48 Bell, D.R., Corsten, D. and Knox , G. (2011), 'From Point of Purchase to Path to Purchase: How Preshopping Factors Drive Unplanned Buying', *Journal of Marketing*, 75 (January), 31–45; Parmar, A. (2002), 'POP Goes the World', *Marketing News*, 11 November, 13.

49 Park, C.W., Iyer, E.S. and Smith, D.C. (1989), 'The Effects of Situational Factors on In-Store Grocery Shopping Behavior: The Role of Store Environment and Time Available for Shopping', *Journal of Consumer Research*, 15(4), 422–33.

50 Inman, J., Winer, R.S. and Ferraro, R. (2009), 'The Interplay Among Category Characteristics, Customer Characteristics, and Customer Activities on In-Store Decision Making', *Journal of Marketing*, 73 (September), 19–29.

51 Bell, D.R., Corsten, D. and Knox, G. (2011), 'From Point of Purchase to Path to Purchase: How Preshopping Factors Drive Unplanned Buying', *Journal of Marketing*, 75 (January), 31–45.

52 Chadwick, P. (2003), 'POP Dos and Don'ts', *Promotions & Incentives*, April, 45–7.

53 Leeds, D. (1994), 'Accountability Is In-Store for Marketeers in '94', *Brandweek* 14 March, 17.

54 Tellis, G.J. (1998), *Advertising and Sales Promotion Strategy*, Reading, MA: Addison-Wesley.

55 Rosenberg, J.M. (1995), *Dictionary of Retailing and Merchandising*. New York: Wiley.

56 Tkacik, M. (2003), 'Rubber Match: In a Clash of Sneaker Titans, Nike Gets Leg Up on Foot Locker', *Wall Street Journal*, 13 May.

57 William (2010), 'Augmented Reality Cosmetic Mirror in Tokyo', http://www.japantrends.com/augmented-reality-cosmetic-mirror-in-tokyo/ (accessed July 2012).

58 See http://issuu.com/mkparsley/docs/ikea (accessed July 2012).

59 Birtwistle, G., Clarke, I. and Freathy, P. (1998), 'Customer Decision Making in Fashion Retailing: A Segmentation Analysis', *International Journal of Retail & Distribution Management*, 26(4), 147–54.

60 Kotler, P. (1973), 'Atmospherics as a Marketing Tool', *Journal of Retailing*, 49(4), 48–64.

61 Inman, J.J. and McAlister, L. (1993), 'A Retailer Promotion Policy Model Considering Promotion Signal Sensitivity', *Marketing Science*, 12, 339–56; Inman, J.J. and Winer, R.S. (1998), *Where the Rubber Meets the Road: A Model of In-Store Consumer Decision Making*, Working Paper, Report no. 98–122. Cambridge, MA: Marketing Science Institute.

62 *De Morgen*, 13 January 2007.

63 *De Morgen*, 21 April 2007.

64 *Grocery Incentive Study 2002*. New York: The Promotion Marketing Association, http://www.pmalink.org (accessed July 2005).

[65] *Grocery Incentive Study 2002.* New York: The Promotion Marketing Association, http://www.pmalink.org.

[66] Dhar, S.K. and Hoch, S.J. (1996), 'Price Discrimination Using In-Store Merchandising', *Journal of Marketing*, 60, 17–30.

[67] 'Building the Nesquik Brand' (1998), *In-Store Marketing* (March), 28.

[68] 'Special Report: Ambient Media Is Providing Retailers and Suppliers with Yet Another Way of Advertising Their Products in Store and Influencing Consumers' Buying Decisions' (1998), *In-Store Marketing*, (January), 32–3.

[69] *De Morgen*, 15 October 2004, 25 July 2005.

[70] Inman, J.J. and Winer, R.S. (1998), *Where the Rubber Meets the Road: A Model of In-store Consumer Decision Making*, Working Paper, Report no. 98–122. Cambridge, MA: Marketing Science Institute.

[71] Breugelmans, E. and Campo, K. (2011), 'Effectiveness of In-Store Displays in a Virtual Store Environment', *Journal of Retailing*, 87(1), 75–89; Zhang, J. and Krishnamurthi, L. (2004), 'Customizing Promotions in Online Stores', *Marketing Science*, 23(4), 561–78; Bakos, Y. (2001), 'The Emerging Landscape for Retail E-Commerce', *Journal of Economic Perspectives*, 15(1), 69–80.

[72] Breugelmans, E. and Campo, K. (2011), 'Effectiveness of In-Store Displays in a Virtual Store Environment', *Journal of Retailing*, 87(1), 75–89.

[73] Kotler, P. (1973), 'Atmospherics as a Marketing Tool', *Journal of Retailing*, 49(4), 48–64.

[74] Kotler, P. (1973), 'Atmospherics as a Marketing Tool', *Journal of Retailing*, 49(4), 48–64.

[75] Mehrabian, A. and Russell, J.A. (1974), *An Approach to Environmental Psychology.* Cambridge, MA: MIT Press.

[76] *De Morgen*, 15 October 2004, 25 July 2005.

[77] For example, Donovan, R.J. and Rossiter, J.R. (1982), 'Store Atmosphere: An Environmental Psychology Approach', *Journal of Retailing*, 58 (Spring), 34–57.

[78] North, A.C., Hargreaves, D.J. and McKendrick, J. (1999), 'The Influence of In-Store Music on Wine Selections', *Journal of Applied Psychology*, 84(2), 271–6.

[79] Caldwell, C. and Hibbert, S.A. (2002), 'The Influence of Music Tempo and Musical Preferences on Restaurant Patrons' Behavior', *Psychology & Marketing*, 19(11), 895–918.

[80] Baker, J. and Levy, M. (1993), 'An Experimental Approach to Making Retail Store Environmental Decisions', *Journal of Retailing*, 68(4), 445–60.

[81] Baker, J., Parasuraman, A., Grewal, D. and Voss, G.B. (2002), 'The Influence of Multiple Store Environment Cues on Perceived Merchandise Value and Patronage Intentions', *Journal of Marketing*, 66, 120–41.

[82] 'Special Report: Ambient Media Is Providing Retailers and Suppliers with Yet Another Way of Advertising their Products in Store and Influencing Consumers' Buying Decisions' (1998), *In-store Marketing* (January), 29–33.

[83] Ethridge, M. (1996), 'We Follow Our Noses to Stores', *Akron Beacon Journal*, 20 January, B1.

[84] Spangenberg, E.R., Crowley, A.E. and Henderson, P.W. (1996), 'Improving the Store Environment: Do Olfactory Cues Affect Evaluations and Behaviors?', *Journal of Marketing*, 60 (April), 67–80.

[85] Brengman, M. (2002), 'The Impact of Colour in the Store Environment: An Environmental Psychology Approach', Doctoral Dissertation, Ghent University.

[86] Dawson, S., Bloch, P.H. and Ridgway, N.M. (1990), 'Shopping Motives, Emotional States, and Retail Outcomes', *Journal of Retailing*, 66 (Winter), 408–27.

[87] Bloemer, J. and de Ruyter, K. (1998), 'On the Relationship Between Store Image, Store Satisfaction and Store Loyalty', *European Journal of Marketing*, 32(5/6), 499–513.

[88] Miller, R. (2002), 'How to Exploit POP Around the Globe', *Marketing* (August), 27.

[89] Brakus, J.J., Schmitt, B.H. and Zarantonello, L. (2009), 'Brand Experience: What is it? How is it Measured? Does it Affect Loyalty?', *Journal of Marketing*, 73 (May), 52–68.

[90] Brakus, J.J., Schmitt, B.H. and Zarantonello, L. (2009), 'Brand Experience: What Is it? How Is it Measured? Does it Affect Loyalty?', *Journal of Marketing*, 73 (May), 52–68.

[91] Esch, F.-R., Möll, T., Schmitt, B., Elger, C.E., Neuhaus, C. and Weber, B. (2012), 'Brands on the Brain: Do Consumers Use Declaritive Information or Experienced Emotions to Evaluate Brands?', *Journal of Consumer Psychology*, 22, 75–85.

[92] Schmitt, B. (1999), *Experiential Marketing.* New York: Free Press; Schmitt, B. (1999), 'Experiential Marketing', *Journal of Marketing Management*, 15, 53–67.

[93] Brakus, J.J., Schmitt, B.H. and Zarantonello, L. (2009), 'Brand Experience: What Is it? How Is it Measured? Does it Affect Loyalty?', *Journal of Marketing*, 73 (May), 52–68.

[94] Schmitt, B. (1999), *Experiential Marketing.* New York: Free Press; Schmitt, B. (1999), 'Experiential Marketing', *Journal of Marketing Management*, 15, 53–67.

[95] Kotler, P. (1973), 'Atmospherics as a Marketing Tool', *Journal of Retailing*, 49(4), 48–64.

[96] Hultén, B., Broweus, N. and van Dijk, M. (2009), *Sensory Marketing.* London: Palgrave Macmillan.

[97] Reimann, M., Zaichkowsky, J., Neuhaus, C., Bender, T. and Weber, B. (2010), 'Aesthetic Package Design: A Behavioral, Neural, and Psychological Investigation,' *Journal of Consumer Psychology*, 20, 431–41.

[98] Spence, C. (2012), 'Managing Sensory Expectations Concerning Products and Brands: Capitalizing on the Potential of Sound and Shape Symbolism', *Journal of Consumer Psychology*, 22, 37–54; Spence, C. and Gallace, A. (2011), 'Multisensory Design: Reaching Out to Touch the Consumer', *Psychology & Marketing*, 28(3), 267–308; Hultén, B. (2011), 'Sensory Marketing: The Multi-Sensory Brand-Experience Concept', *European Business Review*, 23, 256–73.

[99] Spence, C. (2012), 'Managing Sensory Expectations Concerning Products and Brands: Capitalizing on the Potential of Sound and Shape Symbolism', *Journal of Consumer Psychology*, 22, 37–54.

[100] http://en.wikipedia.org/wiki/Abercrombie_%26_Fitch (accessed July 2012).

[101] Spence, C. (2012), 'Managing Sensory Expectations Concerning Products and Brands: Capitalizing on the Potential of Sound and Shape Symbolism', *Journal of Consumer Psychology*, 22, 37–54.

102 Hultén, B., Broweus, N. and van Dijk, M. (2009), *Sensory Marketing*. London: Palgrave Macmillan.

103 www.brandstreet.wordpress.com/2007/02/13/brand-activation-bringing-your-brand-to-life (accessed July 2012); Alberts, P.G., 'Theory of Brand Activation', www.brandactivation.nl (accessed July 2012).

104 Philips June 2012 campaign in Taiwan described on: www.brandactivation.nl/en; http://www.youtube.com/watch?v=5eErLNDmdoo&feature=player_embedded (accessed on July 2012).

105 Alberts, P.G., 'Theory of Brand Activation', www.brandactivation.nl (accessed July 2012).

106 Salta Cerveza June 2012 campaign, www.brandactivation.nl/en, http://www.youtube.com/watch?v=T67EncQPwNk&feature=player_embedded (accessed July 2012).

107 Hur, W.-M., Ahn, K.-H. and Kim, M. (2011), 'Building Brand Loyalty Through Managing Brand Community Commitment', *Management Decision*, 49(7–8), 1194–1213; Stokburger-Sauer, N. (2010), 'Brand Community: Drivers and Outcomes', *Psychology and Marketing*, 27(4), 347–68; Jang, H., Olfman, L., Ko, I., Koh, J. and Kim, K. (2008), 'The Influence of Online Brand Community Characteristics on Community Commitment and Brand Loyalty', *International Journal of Electronic Commerce*, 12(3), 57–80; Füller, J., Matzler, K. and Hoppe, M. (2008), 'Brand Community Members as a Source of Innovation', *Journal of Product Innovation and Management*, 25(6), 608–19.

108 Schmitt, B. (1999), 'Experiential Marketing', *Journal of Marketing Management*, 15, 53–67.

109 http://www.youtube.com/watch?v=k4VZ8xnJn2I (accessed July 2012).

110 Schmitt, B. (1999), *Experiential Marketing*. New York: Free Press.

111 http://www.unric.org/en/sanitation/27276-citizens-of-flanders-collected-over-7-million-euros-to-fight-diarrhea-worldwide (accessed July 2012).

112 DNA June 2012 campaign in South Africa, www.brandactivation.nl/en, http://www.youtube.com/watch?v=8jM08SYzvjo&feature=player_embedded (accessed July 2012).

113 Schmitt, B. (1999), *Experiential Marketing*. New York: Free Press.

114 Schmitt, B. (1999), 'Experiential Marketing', *Journal of Marketing Management*, 15, 53–67.

115 Adidas June 2012 campaign in France www.brandactivation.nl/en, http://vimeo.com/44039499# (accessed July 2012).

116 Howe, J. (2008), *Crowdsourcing: Why the Power of the Crowd Is Driving the Future of Business*. New York: Crown Business.

117 Mahr, D. and Lievens, A. (2012), 'Virtual Lead User Communities: Drivers of Knowledge Creation for Innovation', *Research Policy*, 41(1), 167–77.

118 Prahalad, C.K. and Ramaswamy, V. (2004), *The Future of Competition: Co-creating Unique Value with Customers*. Boston, MA: Harvard Business School Press.

119 Zheng, H., Li, D. and Hou, W. (2011), 'Task Design, Motivation, and Participation in Crowdsourcing Contests', *International Journal of Electronic Commerce*, 15(4), 57–88.

120 Zheng, H., Li, D. and Hou, W. (2011), 'Task Design, Motivation, and Participation in Crowdsourcing Contests', *International Journal of Electronic Commerce*, 15(4), 57–88; Füller, J. (2010), 'Refining Virtual Co-creation from a Consumer Perspective', *California Management Review*, 52(2), 98–122.

121 Füller, J. (2010), 'Refining Virtual Co-creation from a Consumer Perspective', *California Management Review*, 52(2), 98–122.

122 Füller, J., Hutter, K. and Faullant, R. (2011), 'Why Co-Creation Experience Matters? Creative Experience and Its Impact on the Quantity and Quality of Creative Contributions', *R&D Management*, 41(3), 259–73.

123 Terwiesch, C. and Xu, Y. (2008), 'Innovation Contests, Open Innovation, and Multiagent Problem Solving', *Management Science*, 54(9), 1529–43.

124 Füller, J. (2010), 'Refining Virtual Co-creation from a Consumer Perspective', *California Management Review*, 52(2), 98–122; Kruglanski, A.W., Stein, C. and Riter, A. (1977), 'Contingencies of Exogenous Rewards and Task Performance: On the "Minimax" Principle in Instrumental Behavior', *Journal of Applied Social Psychology*, 7(2), 141–8.

125 Best of Activation Awards 2012, www.pub.be (accessed July 2012).

CHAPTER 13
Direct marketing

CHAPTER OUTLINE

Direct marketing as a marketing communications technique

Direct marketing objectives and target groups

Direct marketing media and tools

Relationship marketing

Measuring direct marketing effectiveness

CHAPTER OBJECTIVES

This chapter will help you to:

- Understand what direct marketing communications are, and why they are important in marketing communications
- Get an overview of the objectives and target groups of direct marketing communications
- Acquaint yourself with the direct marketing media, tools and techniques
- Understand why database marketing is so important, and how a database should be managed
- See how direct marketing communications can contribute to relationship marketing
- Measure the effectiveness of a direct marketing communications campaign

Introduction

The success of direct marketing originates from the corner shopkeeper's philosophy of having close and personal contact with customers, knowing everyone's needs and wants, providing them with the best solutions to their problems and giving them excellent after-sales service. This makes them happy and loyal customers. The growing opportunities offered by technology, automation and database-supported marketing intelligence systems, and the reductions in computer hard- and software prices, have encouraged marketers to execute their marketing activities with an emphasis on efficiency and quantifiable objectives. Advertising budgets are being cut and the cost-effectiveness of communications media becomes crucial.[1] Direct marketing activities do not require huge production costs like, for instance, TV commercials and, consequently, are more accessible to all kinds and sizes of companies. They are also very flexible, highly selective (easy to target) media. Knowledge of customer habits and needs and other detailed market information are considered to be highly valuable tools for marketing strategy development. This is due to fundamental changes in the marketplace in the 1990s. The threat of high-quality/low-price private label brands has changed consumers' attitudes towards brands. As there is less and less difference between products, consumers are finding brand loyalty increasingly irrelevant. Manufacturers have to look for communications tools that motivate consumers to try products and give them incentives to keep using their brands. These changes have led to the growing importance of one-to-one communications and relationship marketing, based on lifetime bonding of customers. Direct marketing has given added value to this kind of marketing activity in comparison with traditional mass marketing.

With a high Internet penetration the number of e-mail addresses has been increasing at a fast pace, allowing direct marketers to develop e-mailing campaigns that are more flexible and much cheaper than traditional direct marketing media. E-marketing and e-mailings will be discussed later (see Chapter 15) under e-communications.

Direct marketing as a marketing communications technique

The definition of direct marketing has undergone various changes. In the beginning (the 1960s), it was considered as a type of distribution (direct selling through a different channel), as used by mail order companies. In the 1970s, direct marketing became a marketing communications tool with emphasis on feedback and optimising response rates on mailings and other direct marketing tools. From the 1990s onwards, long-term relationship-building and increasing customer loyalty ('retention marketing') became the main issues in direct marketing.[2] These different views on direct marketing are reflected in the quite diverse definitions of direct marketing found in the literature. Hughes defines direct marketing as 'any marketing activity in which you attempt to reach the consumers directly, or have them reach you'.[3] Kobs stresses the importance of a database as a basic tool for direct marketing activities (a communications tool according to him) in his definition: 'Direct marketing gets your ad message direct to the customer or prospect to produce some type of immediate action. It usually involves creating a database of respondents.'[4]

In general, direct marketing means contacting customers and prospects in a direct way with the intention of generating an immediate and measurable response or reaction. 'Direct' means using direct media such as mailings (including e-mailings), catalogues, telephone or brochures, and not through intermediaries such as dealers, retailers or sales staff. An immediate response is possible via the Internet (e-mail/website/social media), answering coupons, phone or a personal visit by the customer to the store or retailer. In order to make direct contact with customers and prospects, a database is required. Databases can be considered as the heart of direct marketing. Some issues on database marketing are explored below.

Table 13.1 The difference between mass and direct media

Mass media	Direct media
• Segmenting	• Individualising
• Recall, recognition and image measurement	• Response measurement (per client)
• Mass one-way communications	• Targeted two-way communications
• Market share	• Customer share

There are a number of fundamental differences between direct marketing media communications and traditional mass media communications. They are given in Table 13.1. The basic philosophy of direct marketing is to consider each customer as an investment. Identification of each customer means that the most appropriate communications can be targeted in an interactive way. Customers are personally addressed and are able to respond. Data involved with these transactions are stored in the database and may be used to establish long-term relationships by adapting a company's offer to the needs of the customer. Consequently the main goal of a direct marketer is to increase customer share (i.e. the quantity and frequency of purchases of each individual customer) rather than market share.

The importance of direct marketing in European countries has been increasing consistently since the late 1990s. Even during years of economic recession, direct marketing expenditures kept rising. In October 2011, the Direct Marketing Association (DMA) released *The Power of Direct Marketing*, a biennial forecast of direct marketing's economic impact on the US economy. Direct marketing continues to grow faster than the US economy. In 2012, sales as a result of direct marketing activities grew 7.1% to nearly $2 trillion, while overall sales in the USA only grew by 5.1%. Direct marketing spending grew by 5.6% to $163 billion in 2011 and in the USA accounts for 52.1% of total advertising spending. Over the past five years this share has increased year by year, a trend expected to continue through to 2016. A parallel trend may explain this: in 2011 the ROI of direct marketing was projected at $12.03, compared with $5.24 for general advertising. Much of the spending growth is led by digital channels, which continue to outpace other channels in expenditure growth. It is expected that their share of the marketing budget will increase from 19% in 2011 to 21% in 2012. The total spend on digital marketing (mobile, social network, search engine, display, advergaming, blogs, etc.) has grown by $14.5 billion since 2006. Digital marketing is widely covered later under e-communications. *Direct mail* (+4.6%) and *DRTV* (+6.1%) both bounced back strongly in 2011. Direct response magazine ads, direct response radio commercials, inserts and telephone marketing will all experience negligible growth. Spending on direct response newspapers will continue to fall.[5]

In the UK, a recent IPA Bellwether study revealed that there is a trend in marketing communications spend towards online advertising, direct marketing and sales promotions, while spend on traditional media (broadcast and print advertising) is going down.[6] According to the predictions of Advertising Association/WARC, spending on *direct mail* in the UK will fall 1% to £1.71 billion in 2012, after growing 1.5% in the previous year. Royal Mail has claimed that in the half year ended 25 September 2011 its UK letter volumes dropped 6%.[7] However, in the UK, the *e-mail marketing* industry recorded in 2010 its most successful half-year to date, due to an increase in website traffic generated by e-mail, an increasing number of e-mail addresses (90.2 million in Q1 2010 to 101.7 million in Q4 2010) and a rise in the number of campaigns being run. The volume of e-mails being sent during the second half-year of 2010 grew by 35%. The DMA's e-mail tracking study in early 2011 showed that consumers are receiving more e-mails of interest to them. E-mail is driving more traffic to websites than ever before.[8]

During the last decade direct marketing has moved from a typical and traditional mail order company activity to an important communications tool for many other company types.

Martin Hayward, former Director of Strategy and Futures at Dunnhumby UK, formulated it as follows in his report 'Marketing Communications towards 2020: Looking for meaning in a land of plenty':

> This new and plentiful data and insight is important because it is transforming the timescale and analysis of marketing communications to the extent that in reality, all marketing is becoming direct marketing. It will take the industry a little while to get over this – many marketers have still not come to terms with the new reality – that their actions will lead to rapidly measurable responses that will often need to be acted upon equally rapidly. Direct marketing has always been seen as the rather unglamorous tactical cousin of the real business of marketing, but the reality today is that all marketers will now need to embrace the targeting, measurement and rapid response skills pioneered in this discipline. There is no shame in knowing who you want to talk to, getting the right message efficiently to them and accurately measuring the result.[9]

Erik Van Vooren, Chairman of the Direct Marketing Institute, sees the following challenges for the direct marketing marketers. First, one-to-one communications have a new meaning. Previously, a marketer was the 'one' who could control the message that was sent to the other 'one', the consumer. Today this model has completely altered. Now the consumer is as much the 'one' that sends the message, and, due to the leverage of social media, the message is received in seconds by 'many' others. The marketers have lost control of the communications flow and need to become real conversation managers. Secondly, customer data are changing. Initially, databases were no more than directories where some criteria were added. Later came the customer relationship marketing (CRM) solutions with the promise to have a 360° view of the relationship with the customer. Because the various data systems were not linked to each other or because the discipline did not keep the systems up to date, many of these projects failed. **Social media**, however, have dynamic databases. These are maintained by the customer in real time and have a content that covers the social and professional lives of consumers. Static databases are completely out of date. Finally, customer loyalty is put under pressure. Good customer service and high customer satisfaction are no longer a guarantee of customer loyalty. Companies may invest in great efforts to improve basic services; the customers' expectations rise much faster.[10]

Objectives and target groups

Direct marketing may be the appropriate communications tool for different purposes.

Direct sales

Direct marketing communications may be used as a direct sales channel or distribution technique: selling products and services without face-to-face contact with intermediaries (salespeople, dealers or retailers). The best example is the mail order business. Catalogues are mailed to prospects and orders are taken by phone or by mail. With the increased Internet usage, fixed and mobile broadband penetration, and innovations in easy online payment systems, online shopping has now been largely adopted. A large number of retailers are using more than one retailing format. Multi-channel marketing is the new growth strategy among retailers to enhance their sales volume. The Internet and catalogues are used simultaneously. Retailers are employing several marketing strategies, including in-store catalogue kiosks, online catalogues, e-mail promotions, sales associate referrals and sales circulars to reach more customers. Subsequently, the emergence of e-marketing initiatives such as e-mailing have augmented sales in the mail order industry.[11]

As the roots of direct marketing lie in the mail order industry, many authors argue that the real strength of direct marketing, as illustrated by mail order success stories, still relates to what is called 'transactional direct marketing' or selling. The database compiled by companies allows them to segment their target groups by needs and values and to maximise the probability of response. It also allows marketers to develop profiles of the most profitable customers, and hence target new prospects more efficiently. This efficiency at transaction marketing is what has driven marketing's growth, and many marketers leave direct marketing at that 'direct sales level'.[12]

New financial services organisations and brands such as the European online bank Egg (www.egg.co.uk) have been developed to function as direct sales businesses. Egg initially started in the UK in 1998 and grew into the world's largest pure online bank. Egg offers a range of direct banking services including credit cards (bought by Barclays Bank in 2011), savings, loans and mortgages. It also provides its customers with top-of-the-range online banking facilities. Its products and services are specifically tailored to fit the direct marketing medium, and they are simplified so that customers require less advice as part of the decision-making process. This considerably improves response and conversion rates through building consumer confidence. On the other hand, the new brand had to be independent and therefore could not leverage the heritage or awareness of its parent company. It had to build its own customer base and generate awareness and trust on its own terms.[13] Egg won several awards with its 'What's in it for me?' campaign.[14]

Sales or distribution support

Direct marketing can also be used to support the activities of the sales team, dealers or retailers. Although the actual selling is done by intermediaries, direct marketing tries to prepare, stimulate and facilitate sales. It can also be used to follow up sales. Direct marketing is also often used to support personal sales. Sales visits are rather expensive, but a high frequency of contacts has to be maintained or even increased because of the highly competitive market environment. In this case direct marketing has a funnel function (see Figure 13.1). Reducing a high number of potentials to a limited number of qualified prospects (to be visited by the sales representative) is the main objective. Direct marketing will take over some of the sales team's tasks to reduce costs.[15]

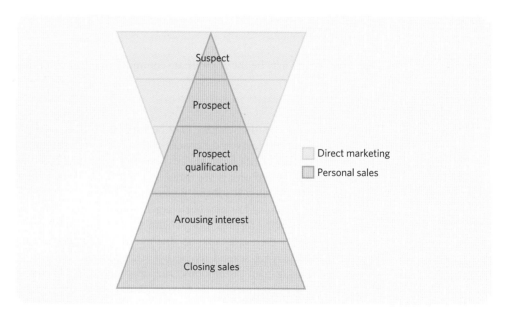

Figure 13.1 Direct marketing as a sales supporting tool

Caja Madrid, one of the oldest Spanish Saving Banks, launched a new investment management portfolio, offering its wealthy private banking customers a personalised service based on their individual investor profile. An impressive campaign was set up to communicate to high-net-worth clients that its first-class fund managers could offer superior advice, using all the advanced technology at their disposal to buy and sell astutely. This financial service was called La Dolce Vita – or the good life – which summarised in three little words the benefit of the scheme. The idea behind the mailing was based on an analogy with fine dining: give a chef all the best ingredients and he will create an exceptional dish like the Caja Madrid advisers can create exceptional results. All the ingredients needed to make a gold risotto were sent by mail, including a 22-carat golden sheet. The results were astounding: 43% of the high-value names on the database who received the mailing called their Caja Madrid personal account manager. The expected response was 15%.[16]

Customer retention and loyalty

Direct marketing is also the appropriate tool to improve relations with customers and increase their satisfaction and loyalty. Customer loyalty is important for different reasons. One study involving 27 brands showed that the most loyal customers (12%) are responsible for 69% of the sales figure of a brand.[17] Others claim that lack of loyalty slows company performance by 25% to 50%. Relationship marketing has two positive effects: firstly, customer retention, in combination with gaining new customers, leads to a higher number of customers; secondly, the longer they stay, the more profitable they become. The return per customer will increase, operational costs will decrease, positive word of mouth will lead to new customers and loyal customers are less price sensitive. Figure 13.2 shows how profits increase year on year due to the different effects of customer loyalty.[18]

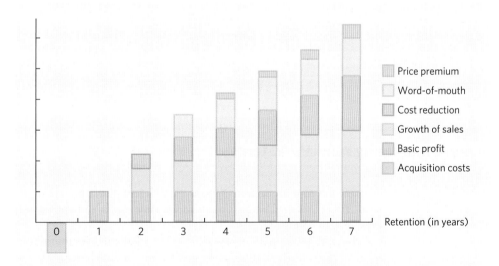

Figure 13.2 Profit per client as a function of customer retention

The role of direct and database marketing in achieving higher levels of customer loyalty is not undisputed. A fair amount of academic research seriously doubts that loyalty schemes, magazines or other tactical initiatives make much difference. Emotional loyalty is said to be only a reality when personal interactions take place.[19] Moreover, large-scale and longitudinal studies have found that the relationship between loyalty and profitability is much weaker than proponents of CRM and loyalty programmes claim. One study discovered little or no evidence to support Reichheld's hypothesis that customers who purchase steadily from a company over time are cheaper to serve, less price sensitive or effective at bringing in new business by positive word-of-mouth advertising. Instead of focusing on loyalty alone, a trend among many marketers, companies will have to measure the relationship between loyalty and profitability in order to identify the really interesting consumers. To track the performance of its loyalty programme, one US high-tech corporate service provider set up a costing scheme to measure all costs for each customer over five years. The results took it by surprise. Half of the customers who had regularly been buying for at least two years (the company thought these could be called 'loyal' customers) barely generated profit, while about half of the most profitable customers were buying high-margin products in a short time, before completely disappearing.[20]

BUSINESS INSIGHT
Belgian Post's 'Love Letters' direct mail and online campaign

In this world of the Internet and e-mails, the sending of actual letters has been declining. The Belgian Post wanted to retain the loyalty of its consumers following the mail service organisation's rebranding exercise. It ran a campaign aimed at intensifying the emotion of receiving a letter while promoting a tagline: 'The Post takes care of it'. The campaign was based on the idea that it would be great if a famous writer could help you compose a declaration of love. The Belgian Post hired four celebrities to act as love letter ghost writers for ordinary Belgians. The campaign immediately received wide media attention, which boosted traffic to the 'Love Letters' website. Online you needed to fill in the name and address of your loved one. Then you saw how the famous writer wrote down the name of your darling, and you watched the letter being posted and, on Google Maps, winged its way to the address of that very special person. The next day, the loved one would receive your handwritten letter with a unique URL that persuaded him or her to watch a video of how the letter came to be. In one month, 22 000 letters were sent. The 'Love Letters' website received more than 100 000 unique visitors. This campaign won the Silver John Caples International Award.[21]

Direct marketing media and tools

To meet the communications objectives, different direct marketing media and tools can be used. Two types may be discerned: **addressable media** and **non-addressable media**. They are presented in Figure 13.3.

Although it may seem paradoxical, direct marketing communications can also make use of mass media or non-addressable media, but the difference with mass communications is that they are used to generate a direct response among receivers of the message. Direct response advertising (print, radio, TV, online) makes up an important part of the advertising activity. Direct response advertising has dominated the online ad business, although in 2012 a shift towards more online branding ads was predicted. A new report from the advertising-

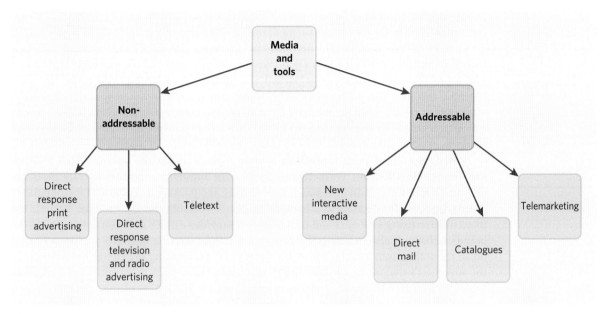

Figure 13.3 Direct marketing media and tools

focused website Digiday found that marketers will spend some 60% of their online budgets on brand ads this year, potentially more than direct response ads for the first time in history. On the other hand, 56% of marketers plan to raise online direct response advertising budgets, but only 15% will do so by more than 20%.[22]

Non-addressable media

BUSINESS INSIGHT
Coop generating traffic via unaddressed mail-only

Coop, a Swiss food retail chain, wanted to generate new customers and new sales in four retail outlets in Switzerland. People living in the neighbourhood of these locations received an unaddressed mail. The mail, attached to the edge of the letterbox, contained a coupon that was instantly visible together with the central message. Coop obtained 2.5% coupon redemption and the sales revenue was 30% higher than the year before.[23]

Direct response print advertising

Direct response print advertising or **coupon advertising** means placing an ad in a newspaper or a magazine with the following characteristics:

- direct feedback from the reader (respondent) to the advertiser by returning a coupon, calling a phone number, visiting a website, participating in a contest;
- a clear link between the response (feedback) and the message advertised;
- identification of the respondent.

Direct response print advertising is not addressable and not individually targeted at one single consumer. The ad is placed in a mass medium (newspaper or magazine). The primary goal of direct response ads is to select interested consumers or companies from a large audience. Direct response advertising is also a good way to provide interested consumers and prospects with more information than can be 'packed' in a traditional ad. By responding, the interested potential customer can obtain more detailed information, for instance by mail (receiving a catalogue) or online when the reader is directed to the company's or brand's website. Ads with a coupon seem to be quite effective in that they are able to produce up to 20% better attention scores than other ads.

Nowadays a lot of print campaigns contain a black and white square, called a Quick Response Code (**QR-code**). Formerly designed for the automotive industry to track parts, the QR-code became common in consumer advertising and packaging, because of the popularity of smart phones functioning as a barcode reader. As a result, the QR-code has become the focus in advertising strategies and tactics since it provides a quick and effortless access to the brand's website. It also increases the conversion rate by coaxing qualified prospects further down the conversion funnel without any delay or effort, bringing the viewer immediately to the advertiser's site, where a longer and more targeted sales pitch may continue.[24] According to the Multichannel Merchant survey released in June 2012, 47% of the respondents said they are using QR-codes, an increase from just 8% the year before; 63.2% are using them in their print catalogues, while 47.4% are using them in postcards and/or other non-catalogue mail pieces.[25]

A recent report from ScanLife found that consumers scanned 13 million QR-codes, an increase of 157% year on year in the first quarter of 2012. The most popular QR-code marketing campaigns are delivering video, app downloads and product details.[26] An online study by SKOPOS revealed that 24% of Germans had used a QR-code, citing the ability to retrieve information quickly without the need to input a web address. However, only 4% of Germans are regular users of QR-codes. In the UK the QR-code usage is 12%. But no less than 74% of QR-code users in the UK said they had had a bad experience with it.[27]

QR-codes can also be used to build an e-mail subscriber list. If a company uses a QR-code to send people to an e-mail signup, the company should make sure to give them a good reason to subscribe to the list. A QR-code can even be integrated automatically to make a phone call or generate a short text message.[28]

BUSINESS INSIGHT
Speedo puts QR-codes in its catalogue

In the summer of 2011, Speedo launched 'The Speedo Pace Club', a new website and mobile application that uses video, informative editorial, social activation and training modules to empower swimmers. To support this launch, an integrated consumer and new media campaign was designed to enhance traffic to the site, using Facebook, Twitter and YouTube. Also, mobile was incorporated into the new Speedo 2012 Racing Catalogue, which features Speedo's first ever QR-codes, providing new and relevant content to Speedo customers. Catalogue readers who scan a QR-code can view video interviews with competitive swimmers talking about how they use a particular item.[29]

Speedo largely used the codes in its 2012 Spring Performance catalogue. The company is not using the sponsored athletes in mass media to state that these athletes are using a certain Speedo product and praise its benefits. Instead the company did this with the QR-code videos in order to convince the consumer to buy this product in the last phase of the buying cycle.[30]

Direct response television advertising

Direct response television (DRTV) uses TV as a medium to generate reactions. Quite often, different direct response propositions are combined in one commercial or DRTV is integrated in a multi-step strategy to generate extra sales. The power of DRTV as a sales tool is proved by the success of teleshopping programmes or even teleshopping channels.

DRTV commercials are different from traditional TV advertising or direct response ads in a number of ways. The first is the choice of a response method. Providing the possibility to react by phone will create more response than a simple mail-answering method. The phone number will have to stay long enough on-screen (11 seconds) to allow viewers to memorise the number. Visual and auditory support and repeating the phone number will also increase response. Today the 'red button' on the remote control is also used to encourage the viewer to take action: participate in a contest, look for more information, receive coupons or samples. Studies in Europe reveal that there are different factors influencing click behaviour (the red button) in interactive ads. If the visual call to action is supported by an audio message, the click rate is higher. Announcing the interactive spot previously seems to be more efficient. A clear, simple, call to action is needed, and it is good to avoid call to actions that are only targeting viewers looking for price reductions.[31]

BUSINESS INSIGHT
'Helping Hands' Telenet

The Belgian market for fast Internet access is becoming more and more saturated. A price war is not far away. The growing potential Internet use by the over 50s was the starting point for the launch of the 'Helping Hands' campaign in 2007 for Telenet, a Belgian Internet provider. Young and old can learn from each other. This truth also works for the Internet, but who is learning from whom may change. Where the grandfather used to teach his grandson how to ride a bike, today the grandson teaches his grandfather how to use a computer and about the complex world of the Internet. Telenet's campaign was developed based on this insight. A DRTV spot was created with a clear call to action, next to a direct mail action targeted at the 50+ age group. The campaign generated a clear increase in Telenet results and had a high score on conversion and likeability by Telenet wholesalers.[32]

Direct response radio advertising

Similar to DRTV advertising, direct response radio advertising is an interactive form of radio advertising, aimed at generating direct behavioural responses from the listening audience using the phone, post or the Internet. Although direct response radio advertising can be used both for mass and niche markets in a consumer or business-to-business environment, content analysis of broadcast commercials has shown that services like banking and insurance and the tourism industry in particular use this kind of advertising. Compared with other advertising media, radio suffers from characteristics such as external pacing, volatility and lack of attention. However, it also has some advantages. It is relatively cheap in both renting and production costs as the average costs of radio GRP tend to be five to ten times lower than the average costs of TV GRP. Radio advertising is also a selective medium, allowing advertisers to limit reach to certain geographic areas or demographic and lifestyle groups, as the specialised music and news programming of radio stations usually attracts specific audiences. Radio is also a very flexible medium to advertisers as commercials can be delivered shortly before the first broadcast. The last advantage is its availability to a broad public in any place, at any time. The growing penetration and use of mobile phones is facilitating response to advertising in cars and other places where a fixed phone line is not available.

Addressable media

Addressable media are media by means of which it is possible to communicate individually with each customer or prospect. The most important addressable media are e-mail, direct mail, telemarketing and catalogues.

Direct mail

Direct mail includes written commercial messages, personally addressed and sent by mail. A direct mailing usually consists of an envelope, a sales letter accompanying a brochure and an answering card. The pros of direct mail are the selectivity, the opportunity to personalise messages, flexibility in the use of very creative ideas, and the ability to communicate fast, target specific groups and customise messages and offers. The con is that the response to mailings is usually rather low. This is due to the 'clutter' and the resulting 'junk mail' image of direct mail.

Postal companies are facing major challenges[33] with the increasing digitisation of communications and business processes, the liberalisation of the letter mail market and the global economic crisis. At the same time these represent opportunities to grow and develop the business successfully:

- *Substitution of letters by e-mail.* With the increased use of electronic media, accelerated by the intensified cost pressure, the volumes for traditional letter mail products around the world have been stagnating and even decreasing. A study carried out on behalf of the European Commission concludes that the trend towards declining postal volumes will continue, especially in Western European markets. On the other hand, the market for direct marketing and the continuous increase in the number of households tend to provide a positive impetus for growth (Figure 13.4).

- *Full liberalisation of the European letter mail market as of 2011.* The liberalisation process in other industries (e.g. telecommunications or utilities) has taught us that former monopolies generally lose market share. In the postal sector, market share losses strongly depend on the particular regulatory environment and competitive market situation. Usually, the national postal providers maintain a high market share in their respective domestic markets (about 90% in Germany and Sweden). This is due to the high fixed costs (investments and operating expenses) when entering a new postal market.

- *Ongoing boom in online shopping.* In particular, the B2C parcels business has posted ongoing growth due to the boom in online shopping.

- *Customers demand enhanced convenience.* E-commerce has high demands on availability and service and on delivery speed and precision. The key issues for logistics are now reliability, efficiency and customer-friendly services.

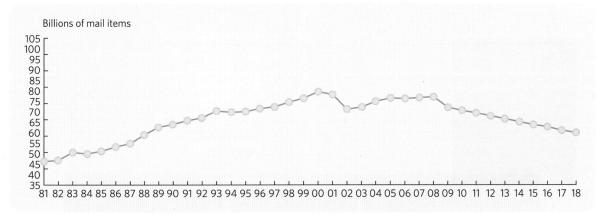

Figure 13.4 Development of addressed mail items in the five largest European markets
Source: The Boston Consulting Group.

RESEARCH INSIGHTS
Direct mail response rates beat digital

The perception exists that digital channels outperform traditional direct mail and telemarketing. However, the Direct Marketing Association (DMA) tracked consumer behavior, following almost 30 billion e-mails and 2 billion online display views in the days and weeks following the exposure to an online ad, and found that direct mail had a higher response rate than e-mail and a much higher response rate than online ads. E-mail has a response rate of a mere 0.12%, while direct mail generates a 4.4% response rate. The latter has decreased by 25% overall, but still does better than digital channels.

For direct mail items of normal size, response rates are between 1.3 and 3.4%. Oversized mail does slightly better with response rates between 1.5 and 4%. Postcards generate response rates of between 1.2 and 2.5%, and catalogues between 1 and 4.2%. Telephone direct marketing is most effective, with response rates between 8.2 and 13%. On the contrary, electronic direct marketing is far less effective. E-mail response rates are between 0.03 and 0.12%. Display ads only generate a 0.04% response, and paid search 0.22%.

Online ads lead to only 6% immediate conversion after the click, which means that 94% of the conversion takes place later on. Due to lower costs of e-mailing, the Return on Investment of e-mail campaigns is four times higher than that of traditional mailings: $28.50 versus $7. Consumers are constantly receiving digital messages that they often perceive as irrelevant and irritating. This may be the reason for the low conversion and for the fact that traditional mailing remains a very strong marketing communications tool.

BUSINESS INSIGHT
Lotus Bakeries switches to online direct marketing

Lotus Bakeries, with headquarters in Belgium, is selling authentic specialties like biscuits and cakes throughout Europe and the USA. Over the past three years the Lotus CRM programme has been optimised by maximising readers' participation in the *Lekkers* magazine and coupon usage. In 2011, Lotus Bakeries wanted to increase its frequency (10 to 365 contacts per year) and interactivity with consumers. It decided to switch to a 100% online

CRM platform called 'Lotus Friends', based on tasting and sharing. This was quite a risky move and a huge challenge. The aim was to merge the 300 000 offline fans with the 29 000 e-mails opt-ins into one big online family before December 2011. Therefore a final paper mailing was sent to the offline fans with an invitation to join 'Lotus Friends' online. The incentive was an e-coupon for free tasting. The online family needed to start sharing. A conversation about the ultimate cookie taboo 'do you dunk your cookie in your coffee or not' was started. Via a Facebook game, the Lotus Friends needed to guess if their friends were dunking or not. The incentive was a trip to New York.

In all, 16 875 participants played the Facebook game immediately. The yearly target was achieved in April: 8500 registrations came directly via the Facebook game and 300 000 e-coupons were printed. The monthly e-newsletter had an open rate of 2.75 times the IAB benchmark and a click-through rate of twice the IAB benchmark.[34]

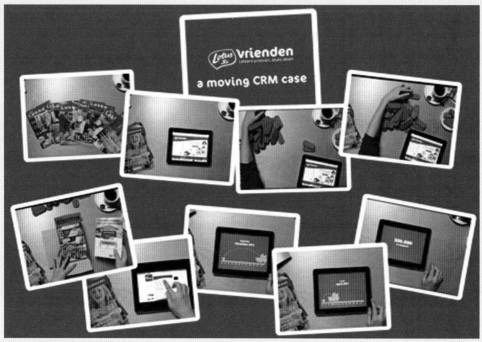

Source: Lotus Bakeries.

BUSINESS INSIGHT
Ten-year Nivea CRM (1998–2008)

Nivea has more than 15 sub-brands, four of which are very important: Nivea Visage, Nivea Vital, Nivea Beauté and Nivea Baby. Although the Nivea brand has a penetration of 60%, consumers typically use no more than one or two sub-brands. The CRM programme needed to recruit Nivea consumers and turn them into real brand ambassadors by giving them exclusive information tailored to their specific profiles. Further, medium/high users were recruited and stimulated to use the other sub-brands of the Nivea brand.

In the first phase of the CRM strategy, an extensive user survey was conducted to make sure only consumers with a real interest in Nivea would subscribe to the CRM programme. The interested consumers were then grouped via a scoring model into nine segments, based upon the usage and the usage frequency of the Nivea brand. The members received well-targeted mailings with specific offers according to their profiling in the scoring model. New Nivea product launches were communicated in a consistent and recognisable look and feel ('Natural Beauty' concept), in line with the above campaign, through three contact moments per year. Every mailing grouped information, a present, coupons or a contest. The tone of voice was familiar and friendly. Each year the user survey is updated and a yearly report informs marketers about progress.

There are about 400 000 members in the programme: 88% of them are part of the three highest segments; 47% are in the highest two and use at least two of the four main sub-brands. Members use up to 30% more Nivea products than non-members. Coupon redemption is responsible for 40% to 60% of sales of new products in the two months following a mail drop.[35] In 2008, the 'Nivea Awards' were born. With the pay-off 'Beauty is . . . to be inspiring', Nivea Belgium initiated several awards for women dedicated to making the world a better place. A national campaign invited Belgians to nominate women who are truly inspiring because of their inner beauty and put them into four categories: 'family', 'society', 'culture' and 'women of the hearts'. Again in this case, the Nivea brand ambassadors were the most active: 22.5% click-through on opened e-newsletters; 5250 dossiers sent in, generating more than 105 000 votes with more than 1 million views. The participants acting as brand ambassadors started a virtual buzz. The social media widget was installed 1049 times with 270 000 views. The PR effect was very visible on blogs, forums, Facebook, etc. The campaign ended in an Award-gala show.[36]

BUSINESS INSIGHT
The power of a PURL in direct mail

A PURL is a personalised website (URL), customised to the person visiting the website. It is often used in combination with direct mail campaigns to increase the response. When a direct mail recipient receives his or her PURL (for instance, in a postcard mailing) and logs onto the PURL, the information from the database is used to tailor the web page experience to that person. Moreover, once logged in, the website can track the respondent's activity and continue to tailor the information based on his or her behaviour to improve understanding of the customer. By combining both media, marketers can take advantage of the comfort, tangible appeal and quality of commercial print on the one hand, and the immediacy, tracking and instant response of the Internet on the other hand.

A bank that was not succeeding well in getting clients to switch to electronic banking with its direct marketing approach used variable data printing combined with the PURL method. The bank increased registrations from 0.4% to 2.5% (an increase of 625%). Of all people who actually visited the personalised site, 8 out of 10 enrolled.[37]

Telemarketing

Telemarketing is any measurable activity using the phone to help find, get, keep and develop customers.[38] Telemarketing may be considered as a number of different activities that can be defined on the basis of two dimensions, i.e. the party taking the initiative (inbound versus outbound telemarketing), and the extent to which it is used as a sales-generating versus a sales-supporting direct marketing tool (Table 13.2).[39]

Outbound telemarketing means that the marketer is taking the initiative to call clients or prospects (outgoing calls); **inbound telemarketing** implies that interested customers or prospects are using the phone to contact the company and ask for product information, order a product, ask for help with a problem or file a complaint (incoming calls). Using telemarketing to take orders is especially common in mail order companies or for direct response advertisers. **Telesales** involve actively calling consumers or companies with the purpose of selling products or services. **Teleprospecting** is searching for prospects by phone. Two other uses are controlling and actualising databases and settling dates for the sales team. Telemarketing might also be a good way of creating synergetic media effects when it is used together with other marketing

Table 13.2 The different functions of telemarketing

	Sales generating	Sales supporting
Inbound telemarketing	Taking orders	Product and company information Customer service, helpdesk Complaints service
Outbound telemarketing	Telesales	Organising meetings/dates for salespeople Teleprospecting Updating commercial databases Supporting other marketing communications Generating traffic Telefactoring

Source: Based on Walrave, M. (1995), *Telemarketing: Storing op de Lijn?* (*Telemarketing: Badly Connected?*). Leuven/Amersfoort: Acco.

communications activities. For instance, the response to a direct mailing might be increased by calling to announce the arrival of the mailing. Telemarketing can be used to generate more traffic at the point-of-sales or to collect debts (telefactoring).

The phone is the most direct of all direct media tools and has some advantages. It is a flexible, interactive and quick medium, the effectiveness of which can be tracked immediately. On the other hand, it is quite a hard-selling and intrusive medium and, with its costs being 10–20 times higher than a mailing, it is a rather expensive tool. However, costs should be gauged against response figures to make a correct evaluation.

In its April 28 issue of 2011, *Time* magazine explored telemarketing in the USA.[40] According to *Time*, calls and sales are on the rise. It reported that revenue from telemarketing pitches increased 250% from 1990 to 2002, to $295 billion, and is still growing. Approximately 100 million calls are placed daily in the USA to homes and businesses. Telemarketers moved the call centres to countries where more pliant employees line up for such work, taking into account the falling prices of international phone calls. Over the past 15 years, telemarketing has grown very rapidly. As the economy is moving from a manufacturing to a service base, many people believe that telemarketing is the perfect growth tool. Telemarketing is in fact all about customer contact, dealing with the public. One trend that will affect the telemarketing industry is the increasing demand for privacy regulation.

The following driving forces will continue the expansion of telemarketing:

- Increasing demand for convenience and speed in the transaction of business.
- The improvement in the capabilities and the price performance of computer technologies and telecommunications.
- The abundance of software that facilitates the development of more extensive and more creative databases.
- Increase in the knowledge of how to develop and operate successful telemarketing programmes.

Catalogues

A **catalogue** is a list of products or services presented in a visual and/or verbal way. It may be printed or electronically stored on a disk, a CD-ROM or in a database, or even visualised on a website, where one can virtually turn the pages. Catalogues are, of course, mostly used by mail order companies. Although customers are not able to feel, try, smell, taste, etc., the product in a catalogue, it does give them the freedom to go through it, choose from a wide range of products and save time.

There are different types of catalogues.[41] *Reference* catalogues are an extensive overview of all products with their characteristics, references and prices. This kind of catalogue is typically nothing more than a purely technical description and therefore more used in industrial markets.

The hard-selling catalogue is a sales-generating tool that should be able to sell without further involvement of a salesperson, a dealer or distributor. These catalogues are used by clothing, soft- and hardware, books and CD mail order companies. Other types of catalogues are more to support sales and used as guidelines during a sales conversation or during a shop visit to stimulate customers to visit the store, like the IKEA catalogue. This catalogue is the main marketing tool of IKEA and gets around 70% of the annual marketing budget. It is printed in 38 different editions, in 17 languages for 28 countries; 110 million catalogues were circulated last year – three times higher than that of the Bible – with 13 million of these being available in the UK.[42] In 2010 IKEA took its catalogue mobile and launched an augmented reality application for Apple's iPhone. After selecting a piece of furniture from the catalogue, users can place it any- where inside the room around them, changing its size to fit the perspective by using the phone's camera. In July 2010, hundreds of thousand applications were downloaded across Europe.[43]

Because catalogues have been around for so long, they have become very sophisticated, strategic vehicles. Still, the increasing cost of postage has made catalogues a challenging choice for investment. Today, the role of catalogues is changing. The catalogue is no longer just a direct selling tool. It drives web and store traffic, it is a channel between technologies and it communicates and builds brands. These catalogues with their expanded roles are sometimes referred to as 'Megalogues'. Megalogues are much more strategic than the catalogues of the past.

As selling is the primary objective of many companies, the catalogues that drive sales must make purchasing easy and must create an effortless buying environment. The product selec- tion and the applications (photography, copy, illustrations, etc.) need to present the products in an easily digestible, quickly understandable manner. Catalogues focusing on generating a direct response must offer a broader selection of merchandise and provide adequate informa- tion for product purchase.

Many companies have been driving business to the Web for quicker, less expensive fulfill- ment. Catalogues did a good job in driving consumers to the Internet, although there is still the opportunity to connect better with consumers resulting in improved service, branding and sales. The customer wants to have an easy transition from print, web, e-mail and mobile. Driving traffic to the Internet is only the starting point for catalogues. Tablet commerce and mobile commerce represent the fastest-growing commercial opportunities. The focus on multimedia becomes all the more important as catalogue pages reduce in number.[44] Royal Mail in the UK reported that 45% of social net workers say they have used a catalogue in the past six months, which proves that catalogue users are getting younger and more web-savvy.[45]

Drama is the new technique used to motivate a retail-friendly audience to take action. There is less emphasis on the product and related copy. Stronger luxury companies like Godiva place greater focus on brand development and imagery. A traffic-generating catalogue must be less about product copy and more about drama and promotional messaging that generates action.[46]

New interactive media

New media are often a combination of existing media such as phone, cable, TV and computers in new applications. That is why they are also called multimedia. Interactive media are characterised by the fact that they deliver tailor-made information to the users at the moment when the user wants to have this kind of information. In other words, the user is directing the information process. Media such as the Internet, websites and e-mail are the most important new interactive media. These techniques will be explored in more depth later (see Chapter 15).

Database marketing

A **database** is a collection of interrelated data of customers and prospects which can be used for different applications such as analysis, individual selection, segmentation and customer retention, loyalty and service support.[47] The minimum requirements of a good marketing

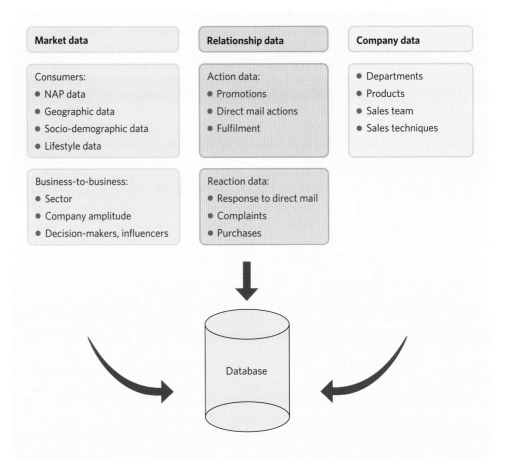

Figure 13.5 The marketing database

database are personal data, including NAP (name, address, phone and e-mail, age), transaction (purchase history) data and communications (received mailings, incentives, marketing actions and reactions) data. The database could also indicate which products, company departments and salespeople are involved with a certain marketing action. In fact, a database stores three kinds of data: market information, relationship data and company data (Figure 13.5).

There are two possible sources of data:[48] internal and external. Most companies already have the basic information needed to start a database:[49] order and invoice information, such as customer names, addresses, account numbers, purchase data, method of payment, etc. These customer files are internal data which may be the first basis to start up a database. External data are all types of lists compiled outside the company which can be bought or hired for direct marketing purposes. Examples are subscriber lists of newspapers and magazines, or databases segmented on lifestyle and consumption habits.

In the UK, Intelligent Lemon, a creative and design company, released early in 2009 two new consumer databases through Wyvern Direct Response, a direct marketing services company. Travellers Content and Ladies Gossip are two fast-growing member websites. They attract over 2000 new members per month. Both have postal, e-mail, landline and mobile data available as well as date of birth, gender, number of children and segmentation levels. All data are fully opted in with third-party permissions for each data item. In total, 100 000 Travellers Content members and 61 000 Ladies Gossip members are being released.[50,51]

The success of any direct marketing campaign depends heavily on the quality and structure of the database used. The effectiveness of direct marketing campaigns will increase with improved targeting. The latter means that individuals may be reached with a relevant message improving response and reducing irritation levels. Repeat business and new business are the key factors to company growth. The former will need communications with the current loyal customers. Those heavy users are often small in number and thus only accessible through direct marketing targeting. Strategic use of the database and accurate segmentation based on the registered consumer profiles will be crucial for these goals. New business success depends on the ability to identify potential customers with the correct profile as good prospects for the kind of products or services the company has to offer. Learning from the current customers and keeping all kinds of useful information about these customers in a database will make it easier to develop a good list of prospects.

As the marketing database is a crucial instrument of direct marketing communications, it is important that it is correctly managed. Most of the data will expire quickly, and frequent updates are required to prevent the database from losing its value. There are five potential pitfalls for a marketing database:

- *Incompleteness.* Some data are not collected for all records in the database.
- *Data expiration.* Some data expire quickly, for instance function (job title) and home address.
- *Unreliability.* Some data might be false because the source is not trustworthy.
- *Inconsistency.* Some data are not changed automatically.
- *Duplications.* Two or more identical records may be stored due to different spellings, resulting in two or more of the same mailings.

BUSINESS INSIGHT
Mamas & Papas' customer relationships

Nursery brand Mamas & Papas offers a range of high-quality prams, pushchairs, nursery furniture, clothes and toys through its website and over 60 stores across the UK.

Because of the limited purchasing period (from early pregnancy to the toddler years of the child), the opportunity for customer engagement is time-limited. The company wanted to create relationships that are more fruitful with its customers and generate more value from its customer life cycle. Together with a specialised agency, Mamas & Papas has been able to analyse its customer data and map the ideal purchasing journey by identifying key customer touchpoints. It has built an accurate picture of every customer, understanding their purchasing behaviour and segment. Well-targeted marketing communications allow the brand to engage on a consistent basis with parents and grandparents: namely, e-mail marketing campaigns based on different three-month periods and targeting special offers at specific groups.

As a result, the value derived from its customer database increased significantly. Customers opted into marketing communications are worth 50% more than those who are not opted in. Knowledge of the due date of the child allows even more relevant and accurate communications. Mamas & Papas has found that these customers are worth 130% more in terms of spend than non-opted-in customers and transact twice as many times. Repeat customers online have also increased by 27% year on year.

Mamas & Papas also mapped the ideal customer purchasing journey for expectant and new parents. It can tailor communications to that journey, enhancing the customer experience by pre-empting their needs and deploying reactive communications whenever a customer deviates from that path in order to extend and enhance the value of each customer. This was just the first phase of a longer process in extending the relationship with customers. It is based on more cross-channel data from in-store and mobile activity to build a consistent view of individual customers, to create more effective customer segmentation and to deliver more relevant communications and a better customer experience.[52]

Figure 13.6 Five stages in the use of database marketing

Source: Based on Bügel, M.S. (1997), 'Van Direct Mail naar Event-Driven Marketing' (From Direct Mail to Event-Driven Marketing), *Tijdschrift voor Strategische bedrijfs communicatie*, 3(2), 98–106.

The growing importance of **one-to-one marketing**[53] has made it clear that generating and managing customer information has moved from a strategic opportunity to a strategic necessity. Companies that are first to detect and answer customer needs with the right product or service at the right moment, offered through the right channel, have a substantial competitive advantage. A file with address data is not enough to support marketing decisions and drive customer loyalty programmes. More sophisticated database techniques have to be used. Figure 13.6 shows five stages in the use of database marketing:[54] from the use of the database as a file with addresses (untargeted approach) to the use of database marketing to get the right product through the right channel at the right moment to the customers (event-driven database marketing).

Stage 1: Untargeted marketing

Often, the starting point of database marketing in a company is the phase in which a company uses a database of prospects. They are selected on certain criteria to fit with the target group of the product or service that the direct marketer will promote in the mailing sent to this broad group of potential customers.

Stage 2: Product-driven mailings

The disadvantage of the first step in database marketing is that the criteria to determine who will be addressed are compiled by the marketer. Sometimes, when the wrong criteria are chosen, the mailing can be ineffective. The second step in database marketing is to choose the target group on the basis of a test action instead of mailing a predetermined target group. This second step is based on response scoring models. A sample of potential prospects is mailed, and response profiles are compared with non-response patterns. The result of this comparison is a model of customer characteristics with a predictive value for response. This model is then used to give a score (the likelihood of response or, in other words, the need of every customer for the product or service offered in the mailing) to every potential prospect. Those prospects for whom the estimated returns (based on response chance) would be higher than the mailing cost are then selected for mailing. Product-driven database marketing uses customer information to select the right customers for a certain product or service. This is a more targeted form of direct marketing offering more relevant propositions to consumers and lowering mailing costs for the direct marketer.

The disadvantages of this strategy are that too great a focus on action-driven mailings could lead to cannibalisation, i.e. stealing sales from some of the other products of the company, and incentives and loyalty systems could subsidise consumers who would have bought the products without these incentives. This has a negative influence on profits.

Stage 3: Client-driven mailings

To take the negative aspects of product-driven database marketing into account, a measure for individual client relationship value can be developed. The decision to contact certain customers will depend on the change in this relationship value rather than the profits on individual actions. Only customers who increase their relationship after a certain action are targeted. This introduces the concept of lifetime value[55] or the expected return a certain customer will deliver during the years that he or she has a relationship with the company. This implies an estimation of the lifetime of a client as well as the profitability of every individual customer (share of wallet).[56] In this stage, the direct marketer tries to target the right customers with the right products.

Stage 4: Multi-channel database marketing

This database marketing technique integrates the knowledge on channel sensitivity into marketing activities. Some prospects are more open to direct mail than others. In this approach, actions to sell the same kind of products or services are sent through different sales channels (direct sales, personal selling, etc.). Which combination of sales channels will be used depends on the sensitivity of every individual customer and the costs of each channel. Both types of data are stored in the marketing database. Multi-channel marketing uses the database to offer the right product to the right client through the best channel.

Stage 5: Event-driven database marketing

In stage 4, products and services are promoted and proposed during the action period. But consumers' needs are not always met during this action period. The chance of a mailing arriving just in time, i.e. when the consumers are actually considering a certain purchase, is slim. By the time they are planning the purchase, there is only a slight chance that they will remember the mailing, and the action of competitors could get more attention. To avoid this, it is necessary to adjust the timing of mailings and other marketing actions to the moment when customers' needs become prevalent. Needs often arise as a consequence of certain events in the life of a customer (marriage, buying a house, birth of a child, moving, etc.), or they are related to the relation between the client and the company (e.g. an information request two weeks ago, €2500 in a customer's bank account, etc.). In event-driven database marketing, customers are actively followed to detect changes in needs and to offer them the right products at the right moment (through the right channel). Smart chip cards, Internet and call centres may be used to keep track of these changes. Instead of traditional promotion planning done by a marketer, all actions take place at the most effective moment for each individual client.

BUSINESS INSIGHTS
AS Adventure's mails winter sports fans

In March 2010, AS Adventure (a retail chain of sports garments and equipment) opened a new store in the heart of Brussels. The store is a combination of a normal AS Adventure shop combined with a specialised ski store. The direct mailing communicating the opening aimed to increase traffic to the shop, raise awareness of the specialised ski shop and boost sales by stressing the promotional offers. It was targeted at young families and winter sports fans living in the Brussels area. The creative concept was based on famous ski resorts, turning Brussels into Belgium's newest winter sports area. The envelope featured a teaser 'new winter sport resort in Brussels'. It had a ski pass inside offering discounts on winter sports material and a folded map displaying the ski collection and with the newest shop featured as the central spot of Brussels' newest sport area. The mailing was sent in November 2010 to a carefully targeted 16 000 families. December resulted in the peak month for this AS Adventure store, recording 7239 individual sales visits (more than in November, the traditional peak month) and sales of winter sports items increased 403%.[57]

Privacy concerns

With the rising use of databases linked to the growing desire to get to know individual customers, consumers are concerned about what companies know about them and how those companies obtain and use personal information. The primary source of consumer privacy concerns revolves around personal or individual-specific data such as names, addresses, demographic characteristics, lifestyle interests, shopping preferences and purchase histories. Growing numbers of marketers are assimilating and using information from (and about) individual consumers and renting or exchanging data or lists describing the habits and characteristics of individual consumers. The privacy literature suggests that most of the individual-specific consumer information used for marketing purposes falls into five broad categories: demographic characteristics, lifestyle characteristics (including media habits), shopping or purchase habits, financial data, and personal identifiers such as names, addresses, social security numbers. A survey has found that consumers are most willing to provide marketers with demographic and lifestyle information and least willing to provide financial information (such as annual household income, the kind of credit cards they possess and the two most recent credit card purchases) and personal identifiers. On the other hand, the majority of respondents were always willing to share their two favourite hobbies, age, marital status, occupation or type of job and education. Although most consumers understand the need for financial information when purchasing on credit, a request for income information, particularly from a non-financial or non-insurance service marketer, has a profound negative effect on purchase intentions. Most consumers desire more control over the collection and use of information. They want to control what companies do with their information as well as control the number of catalogues and the amount of advertising material they receive. The DMA strongly recommends an opt-out format (allowing consumers to remove their names from a list by checking a box on a form). Apart from the control of information disclosure, privacy also has to do with control over unwanted intrusions such as telemarketing, unwanted direct mail or unsolicited commercial e-mail (spam). The Internet channel in particular has fostered a new set of privacy concerns resulting from the ease with which data in this channel can be collected, stored and exchanged. Additional consumer concern results from the volume of spam due to the low absolute cost and waste inherent in sending commercial e-mails.[58] In some countries people can add their address and/or phone number to a blacklist. Once they are on the list, no marketing activities can be done via mail or phone at that address. The Advertising Standards Authority and the Code of Practice of the DMA govern the list. In countries such as Belgium, Spain, Germany and the UK this list is called the Robinson list. In other countries like the Netherlands, New Zealand, Canada and the USA this list is the 'Do not call' or 'Do not mail' list.[59] Nevertheless, research has shown that consumers are more likely to request name removal from phone lists than e-mail lists. But on the other hand, removal from e-mail lists was more desired than postal mail lists.[60]

Relationship marketing[61]

Marketers still tend to spend more and exert more effort on gaining new customers than on keeping current customers satisfied and loyal. Marketing budgets assigned to promotional activities aimed at attracting new customers are five times bigger than the part spent on current customers.[62] But the efforts involved in attracting new customers are much higher than those required to keep current customers loyal. In fact, some claim that companies can realise profit increases of 35% to 85% just by decreasing customer loss by 5%. Moreover, as mentioned above, the profit per customer can also be assumed to increase, the longer a customer stays with the company. This is the result of diminishing acquisition costs, lower operational and service costs per client per year, combined with a rise in the average yearly purchases per loyal client, declining price sensitivity and, last but not least, positive word of mouth (more referrals) attracting new customers in a cost-effective manner.[63]

In **relationship marketing**, a marketer's challenge is to bring quality, customer service and marketing into close alignment, leading to long-term and mutually beneficial customer relationships.[64] In other words, the direct marketer tries to create and maintain relationships of value. For example, Harley-Davidson created the Harley Owners Club, which has about 1 million members worldwide. Besides motorbikes, Harley-Davidson offers its members an insurance programme, a travel agency, an emergency roadside service, two magazines, member competitions and more than 1200 local chapters.[65]

BUSINESS INSIGHT
Heinz's baby club

Heinz is a long-established food brand that sells thousands of food products in over 200 countries. One of its product ranges is specifically designed for infants. Because of legal restrictions in the UK, Heinz could not talk to new mothers about moving from Heinz milks to its wet foods and snacks for babies. Nevertheless, Heinz wanted to engage with parents to increase awareness of these specific products. So the Heinz Baby Club was born – a club, sufficiently different from other clubs, that aimed to become a favourite source of information about nutrition and baby care for parents. The campaign, targeted at new parents and expectant mothers, was a cross-media campaign including direct mail and digital marketing. Because learning to be a mother is a journey of discovery, every pack looked like an explorer's backpack containing relevant content, offers, vouchers, each reflecting a phase of the journey. Different packs were developed: a Birth Pack, a Weaning Pack and a Feeding Textures Pack. Twenty-three e-mails were sent over a period of 21 months. After 6 months, around 24 000 mums had registered with the club. The opening rate of the e-mails was 39% with an average click-through rate of 6.3%.[66]

The fundamental importance of relationship marketing is related to the principle that customer satisfaction, loyalty and profitability are correlated. **Lifetime value of a customer**, or the net present value of the profits a company will generate from a customer over a period of time (usually 4–5 years), is an important concept for the direct marketer involved with relationship or retention marketing. By computing the average lifetime value of its customers, the company will be able to determine how much it can invest in attracting and making loyal potential new customers. Not all customers should be made loyal.[67] It makes no sense to build up a loyal but unprofitable relationship. With the Pareto principle in mind, 80% of time and promotional efforts should be allocated to 20% of customers. To identify these customers the information assembled about their past behaviour will help the direct marketer select the right customers for further loyalty development. Apart from traditional socio-demographic and psychographic segmentations, customer portfolio segments can be measured in terms of number of customers, number of purchases (frequency of purchase), recency of purchases and contribution to sales and profits (monetary value).[68]

During a relationship, customers can progress from being a prospect to being a customer, client, supporter and, at the top of the loyalty ladder, an advocate. The latter are so involved with the organisation that they are very loyal and influence others by positive word of mouth (WOM), which is of high value for a brand knowing that WOM is one of the main credible information sources for consumers today. The relationship direct marketer wants to encourage customers as far up the loyalty ladder as possible.

Customer loyalty will be won by being better than competitors (offering superior products and services) or by loyalty strategies. There are two strategies to stimulate customer loyalty: a rewarding strategy and a relationship strategy. The former implies rewarding loyal behaviour by giving 'hard' advantages to reinforce and maintain customer loyalty. Examples are frequent flyer programmes, gifts, prizes or money. Rewarding strategies are targeted at rational calculating customers. But, as these rewards are easy to copy or exceed by competitors, they are rarely the best strategy when they are not used in combination with a relationship strategy. The latter consists of creating tight relations with customers by gathering information about each individual customer and using it intelligently by providing soft, personalised and customised advantages. Examples are sending targeted and relevant messages, special events for customers, etc. These relationship strategies are targeted at affective-oriented customers. For instance, someone calls a local florist and orders a bouquet for their mother's birthday; the next year they get a postcard from the florist three weeks before their mother's birthday, which reflects the number and type of flowers ordered last year, accompanied by the message that it only takes one phone call to send her flowers again. Which of the strategies should a direct marketer choose? Rewarding programmes are effective to use as a first step in the process of building a close relationship. They will bring customers into the programme. However, this will not be enough to keep customers loyal.

A marketer introducing a loyalty programme should consider the following strategic points involved in sharing value with customers.[69] To profit from loyal customers, marketers should offer the best value to the best customers: those clients creating most profit should benefit from this situation, which will make them even more loyal and profitable. For instance, a company could consider offering lower prices to its loyal customers. Unfortunately, most companies forget this and deliver products or services of the same quality to all customers. The value created by a customer loyalty programme should lead to higher returns than costs. A reward programme may never be a cost and should not attract price- or promotion-sensitive customers of competitors instead of rewarding loyal clients. Rewards should concentrate on stimulating desired behaviour (loyalty, WOM) and discourage unwanted, unprofitable behaviour (customer defection). Loyalty programmes are long-term actions and not short-term promotions, and long-term advantages should be communicated rather than promoting switching behaviour. Loyalty programmes should attract valuable customer segments and discourage less valuable segments by being self-selective and individually correcting. For example, MCI's Friends and Family loyalty programme offered 20% to 50% discount on calls to a specified network of friends and family. The proposition is most attractive to heavy users of long-distance calls, a core segment for MCI.

In the customer's mind, five elements determine the value of a loyalty programme: cash value, the number of options, aspiring value, relevance and convenience. The value should be calculated as a percentage discount on the amount a consumer has to spend to be able to get the reward. A free trip to a Caribbean island or a new car has a higher aspiring value than a discount on a phone bill. Customers should also be able to choose from different benefits. A programme is only relevant if the aspired benefit is within reach; if it takes years to collect the necessary air miles to make a free trip it will not be of any relevance to a customer. If it takes a lot of administration, whether for the customer or the retailer, a loyalty programme has a small chance of success. This is what is meant by 'convenience'.

Measuring direct marketing effectiveness

Direct marketing and interactive marketing are behaviour-oriented in nature, and therefore research into the effectiveness of direct and interactive marketing campaigns will invariably be tests of 'counting' behavioural response, e.g. the number of people responding to a free phone number in a DRTV commercial.

Evidently, all communications effectiveness tests are aimed at subsequently improving the communications effort. In direct marketing, which is essentially database-driven, the optimisation of a direct mailing campaign can be based on response scoring models, i.e. a procedure in which a number of indicators of behavioural response in the past are combined. A well-known response scoring model is the **RFM-model**. For all customers in a database, three behavioural response parameters are measured:

- *Recency*: the time elapsed since the last purchase.
- *Frequency*: the frequency with which a customer places an order.
- *Monetary value*: the average amount of money a customer spends per purchase.

Obviously, the shorter the time elapsed since a customer placed an order, the more frequently he or she buys something; and the higher the average amount of money spent, the more positive the expected response is following the next mailing campaign.[70] For each of the three variables, a number of categories can be defined, and each category can be given a 'value' or score representing the importance of each category for future response. This is illustrated in Table 13.3.

Evidently, the values attached to each category are, to a certain extent, arbitrary, but they can also be derived from the analysis of past response behaviour. The RFM values can now be used selectively to mail those members of the target group that have the highest score on one or two of the three factors, or on a combination of all three. It can, for instance, be decided to mail only those customers that have a score of at least 80 on the recency value, as well as a score of 30 on the frequency factor. Response scoring models can improve the effectiveness of mailing or e-mailing campaigns. It is advisable, however, to pre-test a campaign before sending it out to a sample of target group members.

Table 13.3 The RFM-model

Recency	Score	Frequency	Score	Monetary value	Score
Last 6 months	100	Once a year	0	Less than €100	0
7–12 months	80	Between 2 and 4 times a year	30	More than €100	20
13–24 months	60	More than 4 times a year	70		
25–36 months	30				
37 months or more	0				

Some publications have criticised the RFM score model as a poor way to measure loyalty. One problem is that patterns of buying behaviour for frequently purchased goods are different than those for infrequently bought goods. RFM ignores the average time between purchases as a key variable, while the probability that someone who is within historic range of buying frequency will buy again in the future is higher than for someone who is way past the average time between two purchases. RFM analysis would determine that someone who buys more frequently and has bought recently is more loyal, and therefore direct marketing activities and investments would be targeted at the wrong profile of customers. Take, for instance, two customers, Mr Smith and Ms Jones, who both start to buy goods from a company in month 1. During the first year they purchase at different rates: Smith buys again in the second, sixth and eighth months, whereas Jones purchases again in the eighth month. A simple RFM analysis suggests that Smith is more loyal and thus more interesting for direct marketing investments than Jones because his purchases are more frequent and recent. But Smith usually buys every 2.3 months and yet by month 12 he has not bought anything for four months. Jones, too, has not bought anything since month 8, but she normally does not purchase anything for seven months. On this basis, the chance that she will buy again in the future is higher than for Smith. This is a case of *event-history modelling*. In its simplest form, the formula to calculate the probability that a customer will keep on buying is t^n, with n the number of purchases that the customer made during a period (in this case a year) and t the fraction of the period represented by the time between the customers' first and last purchase. Unlike RFM, this model is particularly good at predicting how soon a customer's buying activity will drop off and might prevent heavy over investment in profitable but disloyal customers.

The second main disadvantage of a scoring model such as RFM is that the monetary value is mostly based on revenue rather than profitability. By multiplying the probability figure for each period (e.g. a quarter) by the historical average profit number, the sum will be the estimated profit for each customer over the next year.

After analysing the customers' profitability and the projected duration of the customer relationship, all customers can be placed into one of the four categories in the matrix shown in Figure 13.7.

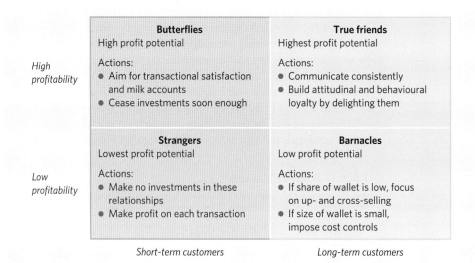

Figure 13.7 Reinartz and Kumar's matrix for categorising customers and relationships

Source: Reprinted by permission of *Harvard Business Review*. From 'The Mismanagement of Customer Loyalty' by Reinartz, W. and Kumar, V., July, 2002, pp. 86–94. Copyright © 2002 by the Harvard Business School Publishing Corporation; all rights reserved.

BUSINESS INSIGHT

A 208% higher conversion rate for targeted e-mails over general e-mails to entire database using the RFM-model

The beads and jewellery-making supply retailer Artbeads.com sends marketing e-mails each week. It used to send one single version for everyone on its list, often including discounts. To prevent customers from getting hooked on the discounts, the marketing team identified valuable segments. This allowed the team to send targeted e-mails and increase results, all on a small budget.

1. Target a high-value segment

Using the RFM-model is a good way to detect a valuable segment. E-mail subscribers are looked at according to one of three factors:

Recency. How recently has the subscriber made a purchase? For example, subscribers who have purchased in the last 72 hours may be more willing to respond to a targeted e-mail campaign than others.

Frequency. How often does the subscriber purchase? For example, subscribers who purchased three or more times in the last six months might be more willing to respond than others.

Monetary. How much does the subscriber spend? For example, subscribers who spent 50% more than the average lifetime customer value last year might be more willing to respond than others.

Target one-time big spenders

For these, Artbeads.com looked to the 'monetary' factor. The campaign targeted people who had all the following characteristics:

- current e-mail subscriber;
- made only one purchase in the last 18 months;
- purchase amount ranked in the top 25% of all orders placed in that period.

This amounted to less than 10% of the database but still to more than 6000 subscribers.

2. Craft e-mail design and copy

Artbeads.com planned to send a one-time promotion with a personal touch to this audience in order to generate revenue and at the same time test the viability of the audience as an e-mail segment.

The key design and copy features of the e-mail for this campaign were:

Personal tone. The e-mail was written as a letter from the CEO, thanking the customer for his or her latest purchase. The only image was a large picture of the CEO smiling.

Make the customer feel special. The first name of the subscriber was used in the e-mail subject line and greeting. Then Artbeads.com went a step further in the personalisation of the e-mail by adding that the placed order was among the larger orders placed in the last 18 months.

Give an exclusive discount. The e-mail had only one single call to action embodied in a large button that linked to the homepage, which included a coupon code for an exclusive 20% discount.

Add urgency to offer. The receiver had only three days to take advantage of the offer.

3. Send and track results

This targeted, segmented e-mail campaign achieved the following:

Open rate: 20.25%
Click-through: 4.36%
Conversion rate: 0.71% (conversion defined as 'purchase'), which was 208% higher than all other rates obtained before, having a range from 0.04% to 0.23% for conversions.

Keep the list strong

Sending this kind of e-mail to the entire list would have encouraged a large number of subscribers to start ignoring the company's e-mails (or even mark them as spam).[71]

IMC INSIGHT
Integrating direct marketing communications in IMC

Direct marketing communications should be well integrated into the IMC mix. First of all, different forms of direct marketing can be combined. For instance, a telemarketing campaign can serve as input for a better targeted direct mail shot. Direct marketing communications and CRM can support personal selling by generating leads, collecting information and identifying prospects, thus making sales calls more effective. Sales call results can be ploughed back into the CRM system, and can be used for follow-up. Database enrichment as a result of direct mailing or telemarketing can also be used for handling requests and complaints, cross-selling and generating traffic to exhibitions and trade fairs, and it can provide important information about customer characteristics, attitudes, preferences and buying behaviour. Results of sales promotion and advertising campaigns can be integrated into the customer database and used to find out which advertising appeals worked and which promotion campaigns were effective. These impact analyses can be used to generate more impact with future direct marketing, promotion and advertising efforts. Direct marketing communications can also be used for direct (potential) customers to a website, and to register and react to in-bound calls resulting from a direct response advertising campaign, or to contacts generated through the company website.

Summary

Direct marketing communications are an increasingly important instrument of the communications mix, and have the unique characteristics of being able to reach the consumer personally and directly, and immediately measure the effects. Direct marketing can serve a number of objectives, such as direct sales, sales and distribution support, and customer retention and loyalty enhancement. Direct marketing uses a multitude of tools and media. Some of them are non-addressable mass media instruments, such as direct response print and TV ads and teletext. Others are addressable or personalised, such as direct mail, telemarketing and catalogues. A prerequisite for successful direct marketing communications is building, maintaining and managing a marketing database which enables the company to collect individualised information on all its customers and prospects, and use it in one-to-one marketing communications campaigns. Depending on the sophistication of data collection and data use, five types of databases and direct marketing techniques can be distinguished. Given the fact that keeping existing customers loyal is far less expensive than gaining new customers, relationship marketing, using databases and direct marketing techniques, becomes increasingly important. Based on database information on customer response to previous campaigns, several techniques, such as the RFM-model, have been developed to assess the effectiveness of direct marketing communications campaigns.

REVIEW QUESTIONS

1. What is direct marketing?
2. What are the typical characteristics of direct marketing communications, and to what extent do they differ from mass marketing communications?
3. What are the main challenges that direct marketers will face in the near future?
4. What are the objectives and tasks of direct marketing communications?
5. How can mass media advertising be used in a direct marketing communications campaign?
6. Compare the various media and tools of addressable direct marketing communications. What are the advantages and disadvantages of each tool?
7. What are QR-codes and how can they be integrated into the different direct marketing tools?
8. What is the 'new' role of catalogues?
9. How important is a database for direct marketing communications and how can it be managed?
10. What are the stages in the evolution of database marketing use?
11. What is the importance of relationship marketing and how can direct marketing communications techniques contribute to customer loyalty?
12. How can the RFM-model be used to measure the effectiveness of a direct marketing campaign?

Further reading

Alpert, J. (2012), *The Mobile Marketing Revolution: How Your Brand Can Have a One-to-One Conversation with Everyone*. New York: McGraw-Hill Professional.

Bird, D. (2007), *Common Sense Direct Marketing and Digital*, 5th edition. London: Kogan Page.

Peppers, D. and Rogers, M. (2011), *Managing Customer Relationships: A Strategic Framework*. Hoboken, NJ: Wiley.

Spiller, L., and Baier, M. (2012), *Contemporary Direct and Interactive Marketing*, 3rd edition. Chicago: Racom Communications.

Tapp, A. (2008), *Principles of Direct and Database Marketing*, 4th edition. Harlom: Financial Times/Prentice Hall.

Thomas, B. and Housden, M. (2011), *Direct and Digital Marketing in Practice*, 2nd edition. London: A&C Black.

Zoratti, S. and Gallagher, L. (2012), *Precision Marketing: Maximizing Revenue Through Relevance*. London: Kogan Page.

CASE 13:
Lotus Bakeries and LotusFriends: applying e-CRM in an FMCG market

Lotus Bakeries

Lotus was founded in Belgium in 1932 by three Boone brothers. The company specialised in caramelised biscuits, an original Belgian specialty. The typical taste – which is due to the caramelisation of the sugar during the baking process – quickly made caramelised biscuits a top product in the Belgian biscuit market. A merger in 1974 with the Belgian company Corona added cakes (pastry), waffles and galettes to Lotus's product portfolio. As internationalisation became important and the cakes and pastry market is character-ised by huge regional differences in taste and consumption, several acquisitions of Belgian, Dutch, French, German, etc., companies soon followed to build a stronger, international position. For caramelised biscuits no acquisitions took place as this product is a Belgian specialty and was appreciated internationally as it was. As of 2001, all the regional brands (like Suzy, De Bruin, Cremers, Corona, Le Glazik, etc.) were branded under the single brand Lotus, and the names of the subsidiaries in the Netherlands, France, Luxembourg, Germany and Switzerland were all changed to Lotus Bakeries. In line with the company's objective to become recognised as a leading manufacturer of authentic, high-quality specialties, Lotus Bakeries took over Peijnenburg, the Dutch market leader in gingerbread, in 2006 and Anna's, the Swedish market leader of peparkakor (a thin and crispy biscuit enriched with cinnamon and ginger spices), in 2008. Thus, currently Lotus Bakeries produces and sells specialty products under three strong brands: Lotus, Peijnenburg and Anna's.

With a strong focus on the best-performing products within each brand, Lotus Bakeries has seen a steady growth in both traditional markets and in new growth markets over the past few years (see Figure 13.8 and Figure 13.9).

How did it succeed in making its authentic, yet contem-porary specialties increasingly popular? First of all, it was able to start from a high-quality product with a distinctive taste. Such a distinctive product is crucially important. Secondly, the company relied on focused product innova-tions, aimed partly at format innovation (e.g. mini-variants) and partly at introducing products for new consumption moments (e.g. caramelised biscuit spread and caramelised biscuit ice cream). Thirdly, the company invested more resources in marketing communications. Not only did it spend more above the line (featuring ads that stressed the

fact that coffee moments need Lotus, see Photo 13.1), but also it created a stronger bond with the customers, among other things, by installing the 'LotusFriends' site (see below).

Importantly, to implement its strategy and meet the challenging international objectives, Lotus Bakeries' group policy is set by the Executive Committee, but then passed

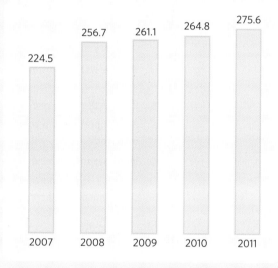

Figure 13.8 Evolution of turnover (€ millions)

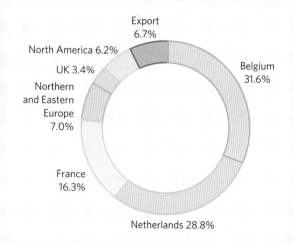

Figure 13.9 Turnover in different markets

Photo 13.1 Ads that emphasise the fact that coffee moments need Lotus
Source: Lotus Bakeries.

on to the various corporate departments, country and regional organisations (see Figure 13.10). The company has sales organisations in nine European countries and in the USA/Canada, and an export department for the other countries. A major goal of the country and regional organisations is to adapt Lotus Bakeries' commercial policy in a market-oriented way and to make sure that the policy reflects the particular, local market. Such an organisational structure helps to bring the company's brands closer to the local customers.

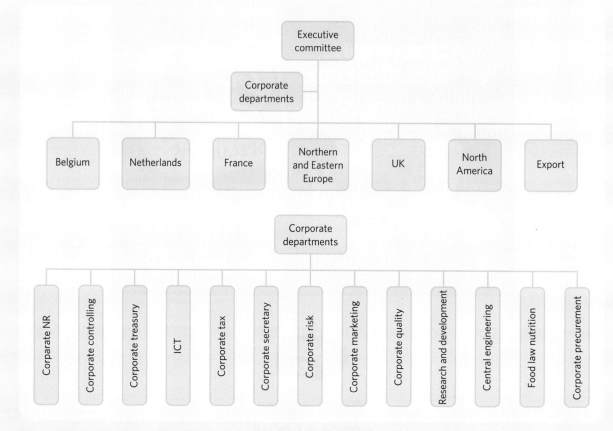

Figure 13.10 Lotus Bakeries' organisational structure

Changes to the CRM programme

As Figure 13.9 shows, Belgium is still the most important market for Lotus Bakeries. The company is well known and has built a strong reputation in Belgium over the past few decades. Nevertheless, company–customer relations began to sour during recent years, mainly due to pressure from private labels. Building a stronger bond with the customers became crucially important. Further, as the company had gradually diversified, several customers – even in Belgium – were unaware of the fact that the company has much more to offer besides caramelised biscuits and waffles. Lotus Bakeries recognised that this was actually a good opportunity for cross-selling. Thus, in order to remain strong in its home country, the question was: How can the company build a stronger relation with its Belgian customers and at the same time stimulate these customers' interest in the company's full product portfolio?

Besides an above-the-line image campaign which ran in most countries served by Lotus Bakeries, the company decided to launch a new direct marketing programme. In 2007, the direct marketing programme of Lotus Bakeries consisted of sending direct mailings to 300 000 consumers, and this not more than four times a year. The direct mailing contained coupons for Lotus Bakeries' products to activate the brand. However, an analysis of the redemption numbers and the results of a telephone survey amongst Lotus's customers revealed that customers did not have a strong bond with the brand. The presence of strong competitors, both other A-brands and private labels, made clear to Lotus Bakeries that the company needed to strengthen its relationship with its customers. To this end, it created a new CRM platform. The objectives of this new platform were:

1. To link the brand with the communications campaign.

2. To stimulate cross-selling.

3. To identify and to involve important customers in the CRM platform.

4. To qualify Lotus consumers with a strong brand relationship.

In order to meet these objectives, several tactical short- and long-term changes to the CRM platform were effectuated. The slogan '*Lotus – daar zit liefde in*' ('Lotus – there is love in it') was internally translated to a platform carrying a name that reflected the brand essence and the shift from a product to a consumer focus: the Lotus Family. The transformation process consisted of the following steps:

Step 1: Database

It was first of all necessary to contact only the right consumers. Therefore, Lotus Bakeries installed an ongoing selection of all identified consumers in its database to filter out those consumers who had not interacted with the company over the past two years. This meant that if a consumer did not interact with Lotus Bakeries, for example by using a coupon from a direct mailing sent to them, or by participating in a contest or submitting a savings card during the preceding two years, then this consumer was characterised as 'non-active' and would no longer receive any direct mail. Tequila, the CRM advisory agency of Lotus Bakeries, developed an additional database cell (which meanwhile has developed into a separate company, SPICE), to be able to better identify customers and link their redemption history. SPICE enables Lotus Bakeries to regularly measure and analyse the impact of CRM actions. It also allows the company to keep track of its customers' history, preferences and participation in the different direct marketing actions.

Step 2: Content and tone of voice of the CRM programme

The new CRM platform also entailed a clear choice to pro-vide less product information. Lotus Bakeries purposefully evolved from a product-centric to a consumer-centric company in order to better reflect its brand essence and to create more intense brand experiences. This approach paid off. Consumers started to read the contents of the magazine more thoroughly, which enabled them to develop a stronger bond with Lotus.

Step 3: Coupons

Personalised coupons were added to each direct mailing to encourage consumers to try out new or other Lotus Bakeries' products and to get a deeper penetration in each of its pro-duct categories. By means of highlighting specific products not only in the editorial, but also by means of coupons, Lotus Bakeries hoped in the long term to stimulate families to use the coupons in order to keep the brand top-of-mind and especially to boost short-term sales.

Step 4: Extension to online media

To bring the company more in line with the growing import-ance of digitisation, the corporate website was addressed in 2009. Besides a pure corporate website featuring facts and figures such as the annual report and the company's stock price, a separate consumer website was developed which allowed interactivity and enhanced consumers' brand experience. The consumer website contains, for example, a recipes module where consumers can suggest ideas for starters, main courses and desserts for which Lotus Bakeries' products are used as an ingredient. Further, online contests

running jointly with offline CRM contact moments and an archive of all mini consumer magazines deliver a strong brand experience and give consumers a reason to visit the site. This way, also in the absence of an extra recruitment campaign, traffic to the site is high. This classic CRM approach worked very well: within the active group of 300 000 families, the number of coupon users showed a growth of 500% while the redemption rate almost doubled.

Applying e-CRM: LotusFriends

After three years of classic CRM, Lotus Bakeries took up the next challenge: How to improve even further? Lotus Bakeries wanted to rejuvenate and energise the brand to be able continuously to attract new customers. Therefore, Lotus Bakeries decided to take into account the current media consumption behaviour of consumers. Realising that the media behaviour of consumers was shifting to the online world, the company changed its approach drastically. Lotus Bakeries wanted to follow its customers in the online world in order to communicate with them on a more frequent basis and in a more interactive way. To this end, in 2010 the company launched 'LotusFriends' (in Dutch, 'LotusVrienden'; and in French, 'LesAmisLotus'), an online platform based on two pillars: 'taste goodies' and 'share pleasures' (in Dutch, 'lekkers proeven' and 'leuks delen'; and in French, 'goûtez à nos délices' and 'partagez les plaisirs') (see Photo 13.2). This platform was again based on the fact that the company wanted to enhance brand bonding as well as to stimulate cross-selling.

Lotus Bakeries had the postal addresses of 300 000 families, but unfortunately close to zero e-mail addresses. Therefore, the company set a target of collecting 100 000 e-mail addresses from the active Lotus families in its data-base by the end of 2011. Lotus Bakeries sent out a final mailing. The mailing consisted of a movers box containing the request to visit Lotus on the LotusFriends website and providing two reasons to comply with this request: (1) a coupon that could be downloaded online; and (2) a contest to win a trip to New York by guessing how many of the consumer's Facebook friends dips their caramelised biscuit in their coffee. After a single month (and not at the end of the year), the company met its target of 100 000 e-mail addresses. All these people became LotusFriends and several indicated how often they used products from Lotus Bakeries and from its competitors. This was perfect information to start a segmented e-coupon approach via the new LotusFriends platform.

LotusFriends is conceptualised as an interactive plat-form with a clear focus on the consumer and his or her opinion. Consumers can download coupons, every month, to dis-cover new products and provide honest feedback. But Lotus Bakeries goes a step further than merely asking for scoring of its products. LotusFriends actually involves consumers

Photo 13.2 The LotusFriends CRM website
Source: Lotus Bakeries.

with the brand: 'Do you know a tasty recipe?', 'Could you come up with a catchy name for our new biscuit?', 'Lotus is interested in your opinion!' Lotus stimulates interactions not only between the company and its customers, but also among its customers. By being so close to its customers, Lotus Bakeries is able to create additional brand value.

Results of the new (e-)CRM approach

Could Lotus Bakeries meet its objectives with the new direct marketing and CRM approach? Let us take a look at each of the objectives separately.

1. *Link the brand with the communications campaign*. Due to the relevant content of the CRM programme, the link between the brand and its campaign has become stronger. This is clearly illustrated by the results of a study investigating to what extent consumers recall having received a mailing from Lotus Bakeries and to what extent consumers recall the content of the mailing. Specifically, more than 90% of the consumers recall having received a Lotus mailing and more than 80% (this number quadrupled since the null measure) know what the mailing was about.

2. *Stimulate cross-selling*. The recurring coupons at each contact – whether by means of the classic direct mailing or by e-mail – focus each time on another product and helps the consumer to become acquainted with the full Lotus Bakeries' assortment. In two years, the average redemption rate has almost doubled. However, cross-selling is only possible if as many families as possible use the coupons. With the new direct marketing approach, Lotus Bakeries has managed to get five times more families to redeem a trial coupon.

3. *Identify and involve important customers in the CRM platform*. The company has succeeded in a very short time in registering more than 100 000 consumers in the new database. For all these consumers, Lotus Bakeries now has the e-mail as well as the postal addresses.

4. *Qualify Lotus consumers with a strong brand relationship*. Lotus Bakeries offers a qualification questionnaire to the customers in its database. As the company offers neither an incentive nor a punishment to fill out the questionnaire, it can be assumed that only consumers with a strong brand relationship are willing to invest time in this. Subsequently, more than 40% of the active

consumers in the database have voluntarily qualified themselves. For these consumers, Lotus Bakeries now has information on which products they buy, how often they eat which products, and where they buy these products.

As well as these results, it also became clear that the contact moments effectively drove website visits. Without any call to action in above-the-line media, more than 60% of the active consumers in Lotus's database have visited the website. Further, the strong bond with the brand is also evidenced by the fact that Lotus Bakeries' e-mail campaigns result in click-through rates of up to 45%, which is way above the benchmark of 25% put forward by the Interactive Advertising Bureau (LAB).

In sum, the CRM platform 'LotusFriends' turned out to be a real success. By making the content more relevant for consumers, the average consumer visits three times more pages than before.

Every month, LotusFriends spend about four minutes on the site sharing their opinions with other LotusFriends. And more than half of the registered consumers that print an e-coupon use it every month to try out another Lotus Bakeries' product.

QUESTIONS

1. What are the main objectives of Lotus Bakeries with its LotusFriends site?

2. How can Lotus Bakeries differentiate between its customers? Would you advise it to take on a segment approach or a one-to-one approach? And what exactly would you advise it to do?

3. Does LotusFriends help Lotus Bakeries to communicate more effectively and more efficiently with its customers?

4. What methods are available to measure the effectiveness of Lotus Bakeries' latest e-mailing campaigns?

5. Do you think Lotus Bakeries' CRM programme is a good means for creating loyalty?

6. What is the challenge that Lotus Bakeries is currently facing and what can it do to stay ahead?

Sources: Case prepared by Christoph Vandewiele, Marketing Strategist, TBWA, Brussels. Based on: http://www.lotusbakeries.com/corporate/; http://www.lotusbakeries.be/; Lotus Bakeries' annual report 2011 and internal reports.

References

[1] Bell, F. and Francis, N. (1995), 'Consumer Direct Mail – Just How Effective Is It?', *Seminar on Advertising, Sponsorship and Promotions: Understanding and Measuring the Effectiveness of Commercial Communication*. Madrid: ESOMAR.

[2] Hoekstra, J.C. (2002), *Direct Marketing: Van Respons tot Relatie (Direct Marketing: From Response to Relationship)*. Groningen: Wolters-Noordhoff.

[3] Hughes, A.M. (1995), *Second Generation Strategies and Techniques for Tapping the Power of your Customer Database*. Maidenhead: McGraw-Hill Trade.

[4] Kobs, J. (2001), *Profitable Direct Marketing: A Strategic Guide to Starting, Improving and Expanding any Direct Marketing Operation*. Chicago: McGraw-Hill/Contemporary Books.

[5] http://www.the-dma.org/cgi/disppressrelease?article=1513 (accessed 28 September 2012).

[6] http://www.dma.org.uk/news/marketing-spend-confidence-low (accessed 28 September 2012).

[7] http://www.brandrepublic.com/news/1126727/Direct-mail-spend-predicted-fall-1-year/ (accessed 28 September 2012).

[8] http://www.dma.org.uk/news/email-marketing-hits-new-highs-most-successful-halfyear (accessed 28 September 2012).

[9] http://www.mmc.co.uk/Knowledge-centre/Research/How-the-future-of-marketing-will-look/ (accessed 28 September 2012).

[10] http://www.vanvooren.be/content/user/File/public/15_DM_experts_delen_hun_visie.pdf (accessed 28 September 2012).

[11] http://www.prweb.com/releases/mail_order_online_catalog/online_shopping/prweb9116967.htm

[12] Tapp, A. (2001), 'The Strategic Value of Direct Marketing: What Are We Good At? Part 1', *Journal of Database Marketing*, 9(1), 9–15.

[13] Shannon, R. (2002), 'Grasping the Direct Marketing Advantage', *Journal of Financial Services Marketing*, 7(1), 75–9.

[14] http://new.egg.com.

[15] Goldberg, B.A. and Emerick, T. (1999), *Business-to-Business Direct Marketing*. Yardley, PA: Direct Marketing Publishers.

[16] http://www.mmc.co.uk/Knowledge-centre/Case-Studies/Caja-Madrid-La-Dolce-Vita-direct-mail-case-study/ (accessed 28 September 2012).

[17] Baldinger, A.L. and Rubinson, J. (1996), 'Brand Loyalty: The Link Between Attitude and Behavior', *Journal of Advertising Research*, 36(6), 22–34.

[18] Reicheld, F.F. (2001), *The Loyalty Effect: The Hidden Force Behind Growth, Profits and Lasting Value*. Boston, MA: Harvard Business School Press.

[19] Tapp, A. (2001), 'The Strategic Value of Direct Marketing: What Are We Good At? Part 1', *Journal of Database Marketing*, 9(1), 9–15.

[20] Reinartz, W. and Kumar, V. (2002), 'The Mismanagement of Customer Loyalty', *Harvard Business Review* (July), 86–94.

[21] http://www.caples.org/love-letters-belgian-post, http://www.mmc.co.uk/Knowledge-centre/Case-Studies/Belgian-Post-Love-letters-direct-mail-and-online-campaign/ (accessed 28 September 2012).

[22] http://www.forbes.com/sites/roberthof/2012/01/09/look-out-google-online-brand-ad-spending-may-pass-search-in-2012/ (accessed 28 September 2012).

[23] http://www.ipc.be/en/Intelligence/Direct_Marketing/~/media/Documents/PUBLIC/Markets/Case_Studies/COOP.ashx (accessed 28 September 2012).

[24] http://en.wikipedia.org/wiki/QR_code (accessed 28 September 2012).

[25] http://www.marketingcharts.com/direct/qr-code-adoption-by-merchants-booms-22306/ (accessed 28 September 2012).

[26] http://www.marketingcharts.com/topics/demographics/consumer-qr-code-scans-up-157-22145/ (accessed 28 September 2012).

[27] http://www.bizreport.com/2012/05/mobile-quarter-of-germans-have-used-qr-codes.html (accessed 28 September 2012).

[28] http://www.fastcompany.com/1720193/13-creative-ways-to-use-qr-codes-for-marketing (accessed 28 September 2012).

[29] http://www.mobilemarketer.com/cms/news/content/10579.html (accessed 28 September 2012).

[30] http://www.delivermagazine.com/2012/01/qr-codes-generate-catalog-of-success/ (accessed 28 September 2012).

[31] http://www.slideshare.net/cleverwood/cleverwood-i-dtvpresentation (accessed 28 September 2012).

[32] Cuckoo Awards 2008, *Pub magazine* nr 7, 15 May 2008, Wolters Kluwer.

[33] http://www.post.at/gb2009/en/Postmarkt_Europa.php (accessed 28 September 2012).

[34] http://www.youtube.com/watch?v=lIoEux3pjtM, http://go.eventdrive.be/cuckoos (accessed 28 September 2012).

[35] Cuckoo Awards 2008, *Pub magazine* nr 7, 15 May 2008, Wolters Kluwer.

[36] http://www.slideshare.net/DePostLaPoste/tequila-3414096, http://www.betterfutureindia.com/grow-business/csr-concepts--branding/the-nivea-awards (accessed June 2009).

[37] http://ezinearticles.com/?The-Power-of-PURLs&id=816064 (accessed April 2012)

[38] Liederman, R. (1990), *The Telephone Book: How to Find, Get, Keep and Develop Customers*. London: McGraw-Hill.

[39] Walrave, M. (1995), *Telemarketing: Storing op de Lijn?* (*Telemarketing: Badly Connected?*). Leuven/Amersfoort: Acco.

[40] http://www.themarketingsite.com/live/content.php?Item_ID=3351 (accessed 28 September 2012).

[41] Van Vooren, E. (1994), *Direct Marketing Actieboek: Bondige Tips voor Business-to-Business Marketers* (*Direct Marketing Action Book: Shorthand Tips for Business-to-Business Marketers*). Zellik: Roularta Books.

[42] http://www.ikea.com/gb/en/about_ikea/newsroom/ (accessed 28 September 2012).

[43] http://www.mobilecommercedaily.com/2010/07/02/ikea-takes-its-product-catalog-mobile-with-augmented-reality-app (accessed 28 September 2012).

[44] http://www.mmc.co.uk/News/Why-catalogues-are-morphing-into-megalogues/ (accessed 28 September 2012).

[45] http://www.themarketer.co.uk/trends/all-trivia-articles/catalogue-marketing/ (accessed 28 September 2012).

[46] http://www.mmc.co.uk/News/Why-catalogues-are-morphing-into-megalogues/ (accessed 28 September 2012).

[47] Tapp, A. (2008), *Principles of Direct and Database Marketing*. Harlow: Financial Times/Prentice Hall.

[48] Tapp, A. (2008), *Principles of Direct and Database Marketing*. Harlow: Financial Times/Prentice Hall.

[49] Katzenstein, H. and Sachs, W.S. (1992), *Direct Marketing*. New York: Macmillan.

[50] www.dmarket.co.uk (accessed 28 September 2012).

[51] www.wyverndm.co.uk (accessed 28 September 2012).

[52] http://www.dmarket.co.uk/a/mamas-and-papas-blooms-with-experian (accessed 28 September 2012).

[53] Peppers, D. and Rogers, M. (1996), *The One-to-One Future: Building Relationships One Customer at a Time*. London: Piatkus Books.

[54] Bügel, M.S. (1997), 'Van Direct Mail naar Event-Driven Marketing' ('From Direct Mail to Event-Driven Marketing'), *Tijdschrift voor Strategische Bedrijfs-communicatie*, 3(2), 98–106.

[55] Hughes, A. (2005), *Strategic Database Marketing: The Masterplan for Starting and Managing a Profitable Customer-based Marketing Program*. Hightstown, NJ: McGraw-Hill.

[56] Peppers, D. and Rogers, M. (1996), *The One-to-One Future: Building Relationships One Customer at a Time*. London: Piatkus Books.

[57] http://www.dmplaza.be/2011/03/18/agency-of-the-month-head-office-as-adventure/ (accessed 28 September 2012).

[58] Phelps, J., Nowak, G. and Ferrell, E. (2000), 'Privacy Concerns and Consumer Willingness to Provide Personal Information', *Journal of Public Policy & Marketing*, 19(1), 27–41; Milne, G. and Rohm, A. (2000), 'Consumer Privacy and Name Removal across Direct Marketing Channels: Exploring Opt-in and Opt-out Alternatives', *Journal of Public Policy & Marketing*, 19(2), 238–49.

[59] http://en.wikipedia.org/wiki/Robinson_list (accessed 28 September 2012).

[60] Phelps, J., Nowak, G. and Ferrell, E. (2000), 'Privacy Concerns and Consumer Willingness to Provide Personal Information', *Journal of Public Policy & Marketing*, 19(1), 27–41; Milne, G. and Rohm, A. (2000), 'Consumer Privacy and Name Removal across Direct Marketing Channels: Exploring Opt-in and Opt-out Alternatives', *Journal of Public Policy & Marketing*, 19(2), 238–49.

[61] De Wulf, K. (1998), 'Relationship Marketing', in Van Looy, B., Van Dierdonck, R. and Gemmel, P. (1998), *Services Management: An Integrated Approach*. London: Financial Times Pitman, 210–43.

[62] Bunk, R. (1992), 'FluktuationMinimieren: Was Kunden-Bindet' ('Minimise Fluctuations: It Keeps Customers Loyal'), *Absatzwirtschaft*, 4, 36–47.

63 Riechheld, F.F. and Sasser, W.E. (1990), 'Zero Defections: Quality Comes to Services', *Harvard Business Review* (September/October), 105–11.

64 Christopher, M., Payne, A. and Ballantine, D. (1994), *Relationship Marketing: Bringing Quality, Customer Service and Marketing Together*. Oxford: Butterworth–Heinemann.

65 www.harley-davidson.com (accessed 28 September 2012).

66 http://www.mmc.co.uk/Creative-Showreel/NoFlash/Campaign/?campaign=938743b0-5675-454a-8230-92d2b6d32d28, http://www.ipc.be/en/Intelligence/Direct_Marketing/~/media/Documents/PUBLIC/Markets/Case_Studies/Best%20Practice%20-%20Heinz%20-%20Baby%20Club.ashx (accessed 28 September 2012).

67 Reichheld, F.F. (2001), *The Loyalty Effect: The Hidden Force Behind Growth, Profits and Lasting Value*. Boston, MA: Harvard Business School Press.

68 Curry, A. and Curry, J. (2002), *The Customer Marketing Method: How to Implement and Profit From Customer Relationship Management*. Riverside, NJ: Simon & Schuster.

69 O'Brien, L. and Jones, C. (1995), 'Do Rewards Really Create Loyalty?', *Harvard Business Review*, 73(3), 75–82.

70 David Sheppard Association (1999), *The New Direct Marketing: How to Implement a Profit-Driven Data-base Marketing Strategy*. Maidenhead: McGraw-Hill Education.

71 http://www.marketingsherpa.com/article.php?ident=32173 (accessed 28 September 2012).

CHAPTER 14
Exhibitions and trade fairs

CHAPTER OUTLINE

Types of exhibition

The role of exhibitions in marketing communications

Objectives and target groups

Planning an exhibition

Assessing effectiveness

CHAPTER OBJECTIVES

This chapter will help you to:

- Understand the role of exhibitions and trade fairs in marketing communications
- Learn about the objectives and target groups of trade fairs and exhibitions
- Plan an exhibition
- Assess the effectiveness of exhibition participation
- Understand the limitations and drawbacks of exhibitions as a marketing communications tool

Introduction

An exhibition or trade fair is a place where manufacturers and retailers of a certain product category or sector meet each other to talk about trade, to present and demonstrate their products and services, to exchange ideas and network and actually to buy and sell products.

Exhibitions and trade fairs are one of the oldest communications tools. They originate from the Roman period when merchants traded at fixed places called 'Collegia Mercatorum'. At trade fairs, goods were exchanged for other goods until coinage became more widespread in the sixteenth century. Value was defined by supply and demand. Most trade fair and exchange buildings were built during the Middle Ages. The invention of the car in the late nineteenth century made some people predict that exhibitions and fairs would disappear because merchants would travel to meet buyers for personal selling. However, exhibitions have proved their added value to other communications mix elements and are an important part of the communications mix. Several studies have proved that there is a complementary effect of trade shows on personal selling. Trade show exposure significantly reduces the cost of follow-up sales efforts to close the sale. This cost reduction exceeds the breakeven, and return-on-sales figures are higher among show attendees than non-attendees. Trade shows also generate positive effects on customer purchase intentions.[1]

This chapter discusses the place of trade fairs and exhibitions in the marketing communications mix and the objectives and target groups for which trade fairs and exhibitions may be used, and provides a framework for how to use this communications tool in an effective way.

Types of exhibitions and trade fairs

Exhibitions can be broadly divided into public fairs and trade fairs (Table 14.1).

Public or general fairs are open to the general public. There are two kinds of public fairs: general interest fairs and special interest fairs. The former target a broad audience and often exhibit a wide and diverse range of products and services. They are strongly promoted and aim to attract as many visitors as possible, especially buying visitors. For instance, The France Show in January 2012 attracted more than 17 800 visitors over three days. The France Show is the UK's largest event dedicated to France for lovers of French culture, cuisine, wine and way of life. The show also incorporates the largest French Property Exhibition in the UK. In two seminar theatres expert advice is offered to all those planning to move to France. The France Show is organised by the publishers of French magazines (*French Property News*, *Living France* and *France* magazine) and the French property portal.[2] Special interest fairs are fairs targeted at certain segments of the general public. They often place emphasis on informing visitors rather than making them buy. For instance, Adventure Affair is a fair for exciting and active leisure activities such as bungee jumping, mountain climbing, survival trips, etc.

Trade fairs are open to people working in a certain field of activity or industry. There are four kinds of trade fairs. In **horizontal trade fairs**, exhibitors from one single industry exhibit their products and services to professional target groups, such as sales agents or distributors,

Table 14.1 Types of exhibition

Public fairs	Trade fairs
General interest	Horizontal
Special interest	Vertical
	Conference-bound
	Trade mart

from different industries. Companies selling chemical components may participate in that type of exhibition to market their products to buyers from different industries (food, detergents, etc.). In **vertical trade fairs**, different industries present their goods and services to target groups belonging to one single field of activity. Various marketers of building materials, wooden doors, plumbing equipment, etc., may participate in trade fairs aimed at construction companies.

BUSINESS INSIGHT
RFID: establishing a fair

RFID 2007 is an event organised by Fairtec. Fairtec is a Belgian organiser of technical fairs in the Benelux countries. RFID was organised for the first time in Belgium on 7 July 2007 in the Metropolis Business Center in Antwerp. RFID (Radio Frequency Identification) technology has been around for many years and is used in applications such as access control, animal tagging and electronic payment. The technology consists of two elements that communicate via radio waves: a tag (or transponder) and a reader. It is a promising and upcoming technology in various industries for many different applications. RFID 2007 offered an opportunity for companies to expand their network in the Benelux countries. RFID focuses on three domains: logistics and distribution, control and sensors, and supply management.

The problem for RFID was who to communicate with. Fairtec was sure that many companies could be interested in this technique, but they did not know which specific persons to communicate with. Therefore, at the beginning, Fairtec decided to communicate broadly. A website where people could register was very helpful in making communications easier. Another way to communicate RFID was to have contacts with the Flemish engineering federation. This federation could help communicate the existence of RFID to possible visitors. Communications in foreign countries for RFID were done via trade magazines. For the RFID event, a special English-language website was developed for the visitors as well as for the exhibitors. Fairtec also tried to give incentives to exhibitors who made the databases of their clients available. It made use of all the existing databases from former years, and every visitor who had expressed an interest in the automation industry got an invitation to the RFID fair. RFID is an international event. Therefore, the location and the date when the fair is being organised are essential. It is very important to organise a certain fair by taking the other international fairs into account. The big fairs are normally organised every two or four years in May or June, and all other fair organisers follow these dates. Fairtec organised its RFID fair in July in Brussels, a well-known international city.[3]

Conference-bound exhibitions[4] are small exhibitions linked to a conference. They have a low reach, but may be highly effective as a result of their high selectivity on the target group. This kind of exhibition, in combination with a conference or symposium, has become very popular both because it is financially attractive to conference organisers and because they offer an effective way to reach target groups that are hard to reach through other communications media. The fair conference formula is very popular in the USA, as opposed to exhibitions which are more explicitly aimed at buying and selling. Unlike their European counterparts, American companies do not enjoy buying and selling in the open. In Europe the concept of a 'market', where sellers and buyers of competing products stand next to each other and try to out-shout each other, has always existed.

A **trade mart** is a hybrid kind of exhibition, i.e. half-exhibition, half-display, with a high frequency. Participants rent a permanent stand and aim to sell. Participants in trade marts have samples permanently on display.

In Table 14.2, an alternative classification of exhibitions is presented, based on types of visitors and exhibitors.[5] Other classifications include: public versus private fairs, indoor versus outdoor exhibitions and static versus mobile exhibitions.

Table 14.2 Types of exhibition based on the type of visitors and exhibitors

	Visitors	Vertical	Horizontal
Exhibitors	*Vertical*	**Focused shows** Reserved for companies and clients from a specific industry	**Multi-industry visitors** Companies from a specific industry exhibit to a diverse public
	Horizontal	**Multi-industry exhibitors** Different companies exhibit to a specific public	**Diversified trade shows** Different companies exhibit to a diverse public

Source: Based on Shoham, A. (1992), 'Selecting and Evaluating Trade Shows', *Industrial Marketing Management*, 21, 335–41.

The role of exhibitions in marketing communications

Like direct marketing and personal selling, exhibitions and trade fairs are considered to be a more personal and thus a 'below-the-line' communications tool. Demonstrations, one-to-one contacts with customers and prospects, direct selling and public relations are combined in this medium. Exhibitions have the advantage that all the senses (listening, watching, feeling, tasting and smelling) can be stimulated. The Index study of the CEIR (Center for Exhibition Industry Research) reported an increase in the overall trade show industry of 15% in 2011, compared with 2010. The positive growth brought an end to three consecutive years of decline. The growth is reflected in all four metrics of measurement (real revenues, net square feet, attendees and exhibitors). Additionally, the index forecasts increases for the upcoming years (3.2% in 2013 and 3.4% in 2014).[6]

Table 14.3 shows the result of a study among 311 Belgian companies that were asked to rank their most important promotional tools.[7] A comparison was made between rarely exhibiting companies and frequently participating companies.

Personal selling and direct marketing are most frequently cited as important communications tools. For exhibitors, trade fairs take third place, but non-exhibitors think that advertising, own events and PR are far more important. The same study concluded that, for investment goods, personal selling was significantly more important than for consumer goods and services. Trade fairs and exhibitions proved to be of little importance for services. On average, only 8% of the communications budgets in these industries was spent on trade fairs, compared with 15% in investment and consumer goods.

Table 14.3 The place of exhibitions in the communications mix

Exhibiting companies		Non-exhibitors	
Tool	Score/5	Tool	Score/5
1. Personal selling	4.09	**1.** Personal selling	3.51
2. Direct marketing	3.48	**2.** Direct marketing	3.13
3. Own events	3.36	**3.** Ads in professional magazines	2.99
4. Exhibitions	3.35	**4.** Own events	2.83
5. PR	3.34	**5.** PR	2.82
6. Ads in professional magazines	3.19	**6.** Exhibitions	2.23
7. Sponsorship	2.33	**7.** Sponsoring	2.03

Source: De Pelsmacker, P., Van den Bergh, J. and De Schepper, W. (1997), *Febelux Research on the Image of Exhibitions and Trade Fairs Among Companies and Communication Agencies.* Ghent, Belgium: De Vlerick School voor Management.

In business-to-business markets, trade shows represent a large part of the marketing spending. According to a CEIR survey in February 2012, B2B exhibitions received an average of 39.2% of respondents' marketing dollars in 2011, with those allocating on average 64% of their budgets to this channel. The survey required marketers to have participated in at least one B2B exhibition in the past two years.[8]

Objectives and target groups

A company should first focus on the objectives it wants to achieve by participating in an exhibition or trade fair. Exhibition goals vis-à-vis the overall communications and marketing objectives should be formulated, often integrating specific goals of sales and marketing departments. Figure 14.1, displays a number of objectives which may positively influence the decision to participate in exhibitions and trade fairs.[9]

Selling products is especially important for companies in markets in which an important proportion of the annual sales is done in trade fairs. Examples are cars, clothing and china-ware. Trade fairs and exhibitions are important to make the first contacts with prospects and to generate leads that could eventually lead to sales. On the other hand, they are also meeting places where clients are met and contacts are reinforced. Moreover, the public of exhibitions are highly selective since they would not come to the fair if they were not interested in the exhibited products or services. A research report from the CEIR says it costs 56% less to close a lead generated at an exhibition than a lead generated in-field ($625 versus $1117). Booths at exhibitions lead to hundreds or thousands of face-to-face interactions with highly targeted individuals.[10] Launching and/or testing a new product can be another important objective of trade fair participation. Visitors and other participants of exhibitions learn about new products. A company can use trade fairs as a 'test market' for new products by observing visitor interest, reactions and intentions to buy certain innovations.[11] Possible improvements

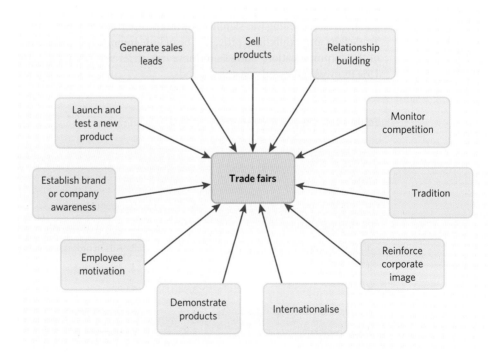

Figure 14.1 Marketing communications objectives and trade fair participation

and new applications may be discovered in that way. For instance, Nivea for Men used an exhibition to launch its range of grooming products under the 'for men who dare to care' theme. Pre-show mailings, tube posters and show sponsorship drove people to the stand where sampling, interactivity and a competition took place. Nivea supported its product launch with media coverage as a result of the exhibition and gave out thousands of free samples to its target group. Another example is Procter & Gamble launching Sunny Delight, a range of fruit drinks, at a top retailing trade show. In this case, the objectives were push marketing to get the new drinks noticed among the distribution as well as to earn shelf space. P&G attracted 35% to 40% of the entire exhibition audience to its colourful stand with free prize draws and product sampling, generating thousands of leads for sales call follow-up. Within a few months of its launch, Sunny Delight was rivalling the sales figures of Coca-Cola and Pepsi in the UK.[12]

BUSINESS INSIGHT
M+R: repositioning an existing fair

M+R is a trade fair organised by Fairtec. M+R Antwerp and M+R Brussels are one-day trade fairs for measuring and regulation instrumentation in the process industry. The M+R programme gives visitors the opportunity to experience the whole range of products and services for the process industry. There are exhibitors from many different industries (batch systems, embedded systems, factory automation, identification systems, intelligent instrumentation, PLC, test and measurement, automatisation, digital data transmission, operating panels, sensors, etc.). At the M+R fair in Antwerp, 25% of the visitors had come to the fair for the first time, meaning that every fair brings a pool of potential new clients to reach. Fairtec focuses on organising smaller specialised fairs to compete with the large, international, broader-scoped fairs in Germany and France. Its position is complementary to those large fairs. In Europe, every country has its own large fairs because every national headquarters of a big international company still keeps its proper national identity. M+R is a flexible concept. Companies can decide to participate every six months, every year or on a two-year basis.

In 2002, Fairtec decided to diversify geographically by organising the same fair concept in the Netherlands. Fairtec noticed that a lot of exhibitors at the Belgian fairs also had sister companies in the Netherlands. So it concluded that, instead of opening its doors to Dutch exhibitors, it should implement the concept in the Netherlands for Dutch exhibitors and visitors. So Fairtec went with M+R to, among other places, Rotterdam, Amsterdam and Eindhoven. The one-day regional fair formula was intended to be a flexible alternative to the traditional four-day *Het instrument* fair that takes place in the Netherlands every second year. The Dutch venture started in 2002, but in 2004 it had already come to an end. The fair had only 65 exhibitors and 600 visitors in Rotterdam, which was not enough for such a large port city. For instance, in Antwerp there were 100 exhibitors and around 1500 visitors. Apparently, diversifying by entering a larger geographical market did not work, because the Dutch fair *Het instrument* ('The instrument') proved to be too strong a competitor for M+R in the Netherlands. Having lost its place as an organiser on the Dutch market, Fairtec moved to reposition its marketing approach to attract Dutch companies and visitors to the M+R fair in Antwerp.

In 2007, Fairtec thought about making changes to the M+R formula. A lot of exhibitors felt that the fair was too crowded, and exhibitors complained that not all interested visitors could be contacted. One possible solution was to organise a two-day fair instead of a one-day fair, in one place. At the time, M+R attracted 1500 visitors on one day. If the fair were expanded over two days, only 750 visitors a day would attend, which is not enough. So, making M+R a two-day fair is a possible risk for the organiser. Another question was: Would exhibitors be happy? They would incur more costs because they would have to rent the space and the stand for one more day. The result of a survey showed that exhibitors did not want to change the current format of short, relatively small fairs in two cities.[13] In 2012, the fair was still organised in Ghent and Antwerp for one day.

New companies can take off quickly in a market by immediately marketing their products and services to the target market in a direct way. Trade fairs may help to increase brand and company awareness rapidly within the target market, and to make deals with customers whom they would not have met as quickly using other communications tools. One of the major strengths of trade fairs is that products and services can be demonstrated and potential buyers may experience the value of products by trying them out, looking at them, touching them, etc. Potential customers can have all the technical details they want and the products' features and unique selling points can be demonstrated.

In an era when food retailers are seeking to differentiate themselves, the SIAL show in Paris, an international food, beverage, wine and spirits exhibition, provides a showcase of innovative products in three ways. The exhibition floor offers a range of products divided into product areas, then subdivided by country of origin. A trend showcase provides a specific array of products that are among the most outstanding of the new products. The show's own SIAL d'Or Awards spotlight items that are distinguished as fresh, inventive and trendy by a panel of judges. In the category 'Savory Frozen Products' the Italian company Agrifood Abruzzo won the award in 2012 with its 'Foglia a Foglia' product. Foglia a Foglia is a dish made from layers of leaves of frozen spinach, beet, savoy cabbage and chicory. The innovative technology keeps the leaves intact, and preserves the flavour, colour and tenderness of the fresh vegetables. Since 2010, SIAL has also rewarded innovative products aimed at children aged 3 to 12 via the Disney-SIAL Award. These products must combine the nutritional value required for a balanced diet with taste and fun so that they satisfy both parents and children. The biennial SIAL exhibition in Paris attracts more than 136 400 delegates from 200 countries and is one of the biggest events in the world for the food industry. It offers foreign and small companies the opportunity to demonstrate their innovative products to the world's biggest retailers.[14]

BUSINESS INSIGHT
Repositioning the Adventure Affair

'Adventure Affair' is a public fair for adventurous travellers with a global passion organised by Flanders Expo. There are more than 100 exhibitors who give people a look at all the adventurous and sport-oriented vacations, specialised tour operators, new discoveries and destinations. The fair is also for active and extreme sports fans (diving, mountainbiking, wildwater rafting, etc.). At the 2007 fair, around 12 000 visitors were registered. The fair is composed of different sections: 'Far away', 'Near home', 'Material', 'Bikes', 'Big kick', 'Non-profit', 'Four-wheel drive' and 'Living abroad'.

In 2003, the organisation realised that there was a problem. Adventure Affair was overly focused on a niche. The fair had been in existence since 1996. But, at that time, adventure travel was, for example, backpacking in Vietnam. Nowadays people think differently about adventure travel: everyone is going to Vietnam. The concept of adventure travel has acquired a new connotation. There were few young people at the fair. The young public did not seem to be interested anymore, and they did not find what they were looking for at the fair. The organisation realised that the market for adventure travel had changed in such a substantial way that a repositioning of the fair was more than necessary to keep it alive. A SWOT analysis showed that the fair was still well known and that the market for adventure was still rising. Other strengths were the fact that the fair received a lot of media attention and that it attracted a qualitatively high visitor public. A major weakness was the fact that the fair for adventure travel was no longer perceived as adventurous enough. Every year fewer people visited the fair. There were also many opportunities, though. Adventure Affair could diversify into the more exciting side of adventure and travelling and could focus on a younger public without neglecting the older public. On the basis of the results of the SWOT analysis and brainstorming, the organisation found out that there had to be more modern kicks at the fair. So it decided to reposition the fair for a younger public by changing the activities and offerings at the fair and by branding and communicating it differently.

Flanders Expo felt that the fair needed more short adventure vacations on offer and decided to work more on excitement, kicks and adrenaline. It implemented new activities at the fair, such as a four-wheel drive section, an outdoor bungee jump, an evening event where visitors could watch travel movies and listen to traditional music from abroad, a rope and obstacle course, etc. The fair now offers adventure to the elderly but also to the young public looking for kicks. In order to reposition the fair, the organisation has chosen to strengthen the brand in the consumers' minds but also to take in a new, unoccupied position that consumers could value and appreciate. The fair is still the fair it was before, but the organisation has extended and renewed it. The limitation of the first positioning was that the organisation over-positioned the fair, installing too narrow an image. The repositioned Adventure Affair is now a concept that attracts a young as well as an older public.

The organisation has changed the fair and communicated its repositioning by means of a new media campaign. First of all, the organisation worked together with two radio stations, Studio Brussel and Q Music. Studio Brussel is an alternative rock radio for younger people. Q music is a more general radio station but also attracts a younger public. A print campaign was also developed in an innovative and attractive way: a woman was pictured in the mouth of a shark. All the communications tools conveyed the message that the fair was an event where people could find extreme kicks, and that it was not just a fair for adventurous travelling. Another marketing tool used by the organisation was to co-operate with a popular adventure-type TV programme in Belgium, *Expedition Robinson*. In this programme 15 people go to live on an uninhabited island. They have to survive by searching for their own food, and the contestants also have to do tests. The person who can stay the longest on the island becomes the Robinson. In 2005, the selection for the candidates who wanted to participate in the programme took place at Adventure Affair. Applicants could register their interest in advance on the website and then had to take part in an adventurous activity while at the fair. The organisers also actively encouraged visitors to register via the website. While doing this, they could indicate what their interests were, meaning that they could receive relevant newsletters during the year.

The repositioning was a success. The level of appreciation from the visitors as well as from the exhibitors was higher after the repositioning than before it. In 2003, the number of fair visitors was 15 239; in 2006, there were 17 066 visitors. The number of exhibitors increased from 96 in 2003 to 112 in 2006. The surface area of the fair increased from 2559 m² in 2003 to 5153 m² in 2006.[15]

Exhibitions are a part of a company's relationship marketing programme with its customers and are also a PR tool to support the corporate image of the company and the quality and fame of its brands. Companies not participating in certain exhibitions or trade fairs may send out negative signals to the market. Customers and prospects will have questions about the absence of a company at a trade fair, and competitors will try to profit from its absence. Multinational companies may increase their international brand awareness and sales by participating in foreign trade fairs. This could lead to new contacts and sales contracts in new foreign markets. For instance, Russian and Asian trade fairs may help European companies develop markets outside Europe. Often they will be able to enjoy financial and organisational support from governmental export departments. Overseas trade shows are the least costly and most efficient way to check out international opportunities for franchisers with expansion plans who want to determine interest in their concept before making further investments. National franchise exhibitions in Birmingham, Valencia, Brazil, Hong Kong, Singapore and Milan have all averaged between 15 000 and 30 000 attendees.[16]

There is no quicker way to learn about the new products and policies of competitors than by participating in exhibitions and trade fairs. Competitor analysis and comparing own products and prices with those of competitors could also be an objective for participating in an exhibition. Trade fairs often offer the opportunity to build relationships with customers. Clients feel important if they are treated as VIPs (champagne, food, personal demonstrations of novelties, etc.) at fairs and exhibitions. Companies often have special guest suites and activities reserved for their best customers. Sometimes, exhibitions and VIP arrangements for

Table 14.4 Objectives of trade fair participation in the UK and Belgium

Objective	UK (N = 104)		Belgium (N = 311)	
	Mean (10 points)	Rank	Mean (5 points)	Rank
Meeting new customers	8.87	1	4.25	1
Launching new products	8.68	2	3.86	4
Taking sales orders	7.69	3	2.82	23
Enhancing company image	7.52	6	3.89	3
Interacting with existing customers	7.67	4	3.73	7
Promoting existing products	7.53	5	3.82	5
Getting information about competitors	4.84	10	3.66	8
Getting an edge on non-exhibitors	4.57	12	–	–
Keeping up with competitors	4.86	9	–	–
Enhancing staff morale	3.90	13	1.72	26
Interacting with distributors	4.80	11	–	–
Doing market research	5.77	7	–	–
Meeting new distributors	5.01	8	–	–
Increasing company awareness	–		3.93	2
Reaching as many people as possible	–		3.76	6
Increasing brand awareness	–		3.63	9
Reaching people in an effective way	–		3.60	10

Source: Based on Blythe, J. (2002), 'Using Trade Fairs in Key Account Management', *Industrial Marketing Management*, 31, 627–35; De Pelsmacker, P., Van den Bergh, J. and De Schepper, W. (1997), *Febelux Research in the Image of Exhibitions and Trade Fairs among Companies and Communication Agencies*. Ghent, Belgium: De Vlerick Leuven Gent Management School.

salespeople in luxury hotels etc. are used as an incentive to enhance personnel morale and to motivate employees. Further, new salespeople may be recruited at exhibitions and trade fairs. Finally, some companies stick to their tradition of participating in certain exhibitions and do not consider other communications objectives because 'we do it every year, it is a tradition'.

In Table 14.4, the results of a study of exhibition objectives among 104 UK companies[17] are compared with a study among 311 Belgian firms.[18] As this table shows, the six most frequently formulated goals are similar for both countries: interaction with new and existing customers, promoting existing and new products, learning about competitors' new products and enhancing the corporate image are the most important reasons why companies choose to participate in exhibitions or trade fairs. Taking sales orders seems more important in the UK, whereas brand and company awareness are more frequently formulated goals in Belgium.

Overall, an exhibition or trade fair combines a number of the following functions: sales generation, promotion, contact generation, demonstration, research, promotion of the company and its image, and PR.

For a stand to be successful, both sales teams and marketing must work in tandem. An exhibition should be as much about customer relationships as about sales. Quantel, a manufacturer of high-end creative software for the film and TV industry, regularly exhibits at the National Association of Broadcasters show in Las Vegas and at the International Broadcasting Convention in Amsterdam. Its goal is to generate more sales leads but not at the risk of diluting the brand equity. At the same convention, Microsoft TV wanted to make visitors aware of its name in the broadcasting marketplace while ensuring that the sales force could engage visitors with the product in a suitable environment. At the stand, physical barriers

Table 14.5 Trade fairs as instruments to reach specific marketing communications objectives

For objective X	Competing medium Y is	Worse	Equal	Better
Meeting new customers	Direct marketing	12.7%	32.9%	54.4%
Enhancing company image	Magazines	6.8%	52.7%	40.6%
Interacting with customers	Personal selling	2.9%	20.2%	76.9%
Promoting existing products	Personal selling	15.5%	24.1%	60.3%
Launching new products	Own events	3.7%	14.3%	82.5%
Getting competitor intelligence	Magazines	29.9%	46.4%	23.7%
Discovering market trends	Magazines	19.7%	37.6%	42.7%
Increasing company awareness	Magazines	7.4%	58.8%	33.7%
Reaching as many people as possible	Magazines	17.9%	32.8%	49.3%
Increasing brand awareness	Magazines	5.3%	44.2%	50.4%
Reaching people in an effective way	Personal selling	15.5%	24.1%	60.3%

Source: Based on Shipley, D. and Wong, K.S. (1993), 'Exhibiting Strategy and Implementation', *International Journal of Advertising*, 12, 117–30.

were discarded and the stand was divided into zones by changes in colour, furniture, textures and materials. Large screens and chill-out areas enabled visitors to see the message.[19]

What is the perception of marketing managers as to the suitability of exhibitions to reach these objectives, compared with other communications mix instruments? This is illustrated in Table 14.5, which shows that exhibitions only score higher than competing media on competitor intelligence goals (observing the competition). To support company awareness and image, trade fairs also get high scores; nevertheless, half of the surveyed companies stated that advertising in specialist magazines is equally valuable in reaching that specific objective. The results of this study suggest that exhibitions tend to be weaker in attaining the formulated goals, even in those that were regarded as particular strengths of exhibitions, than other marketing communications instruments.

Exhibitions and trade fairs can be directed at a number of quite different target groups, each having its own expectations and information needs. This will have an influence on designing the stand and choosing what kind of information is presented in what way. Target groups include customers, prospects, competitors, suppliers, own personnel and journalists (media). All this depends on the type of exhibition.

Visitors may have a number of reasons for attending an exhibition. They may want to increase their knowledge about products, services and companies, discover novelties and evolutions, contact other people working in the same area and prepare specific purchases.

As a result, areas of interest and typical questions of exhibition visitors are:[20]

- comparing different suppliers and having an overview of supply;
- technical novelties and trends;
- scientific information;
- product and system information;
- technical information;
- user conditions;
- prices and sales conditions;
- competitor analysis;
- who the preferred supplier is;
- who may be potential partners;
- training.

The more heterogeneous the target groups of the exhibition, the simpler the stand concept will have to be.

Planning an exhibition

The success of participating in an exhibition is highly determined by the preparation. As planning and implementing exhibitions is a labour-intensive and long-term process, a checklist should be used throughout the entire procedure. Most projects start one year in advance of the actual exhibition. The logical steps one should follow when planning an exhibition are shown in Figure 14.2.[21]

In the first stage of this process, exhibitions are considered as a medium or communications tool and compared with other media to reach the communications goals as stated in the communications plan of the marketing strategy. A company should also choose an exhibition that is most representative for the communications objectives it has planned. A number of selection criteria will help marketers to make the right choice:

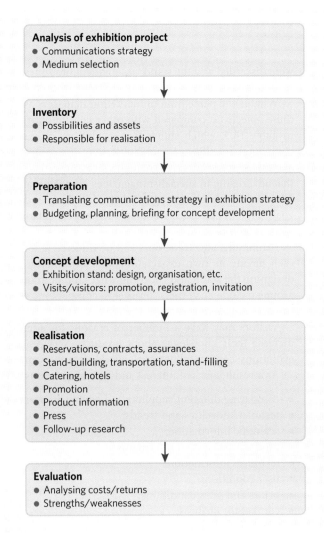

Figure 14.2 The exhibition planning process

Source: Based on Van Den Tempel, W. (1985), 'Beursdeelneming en Return on Investment' (Trade Fair Participation and Return on Investment), in *Beurzen en Tentoonstellingen: Praktijk Handboek voor Communicatief Exposeren* (*Trade Fairs and Exhibitions: A Practical Guide to Expose and Communicate*). Deventer: Kluwer.

- *Reach of the exhibition or trade fairs*: both quantitatively (number of visitors) and qualitatively (profile of visitors).
- *Costs and estimated return* of fair participation.
- *Programme of the exhibition*: the subject of the exhibition should correspond to the characteristics of the products or services a company is selling.
- *Presence of competitors*: not participating could send negative signals to the market of buyers, and competitors may use your absence as a strategic tool in negotiations with your (ex-)clients.
- *Reputation and fame* of an exhibition and its organiser.
- *Number of participants.*
- *Media attention* for former exhibitions.
- *Own experiences* with previous exhibitions.
- *Supporting activities*, such as workshops, readings, conferences.
- *Timing of a trade fair*: fairs should be scheduled into the planning of a company and sales leads generated at a fair need sales capacity immediately after the fair.

Types of visitors and the types of products or services presented at trade fairs are the most important selection criteria. Other important criteria include estimated numbers of leads, numbers of visitors, costs and publicity. Date and duration of the event and reputation of the organiser are the least important criteria. For instance, for financial advisers, fairs for senior citizens can draw big crowds of retirees looking for financial information, but there is a good chance that every broker and insurance agent will be present at the fair as well. The same can be said for specific financial expositions. Therefore financial advisers should be more creative in their choice of public fairs. For instance, expositions for expectant parents might be interesting to reach parents and grandparents. Health fairs can also be interesting. Even boat shows or construction equipment trade shows could be important fairs for the financial adviser. The former attracts people with enough money for boats, who will certainly also have funds to invest. The attendees of the latter are owners of, or upper management in, companies that could need retirement plans and other financial advice.[22]

BUSINESS INSIGHT

Infratech: evaluation of the market potential for a new trade show concept by analysing exhibitor markets

Infratech is a Dutch trade fair for civil engineering, ground, water and road construction that takes place in the Ahoy in Rotterdam. In 2008, the Belgian fair organiser Flanders Expo decided to organise 'Infratech Belgium'. The first version of the new trade fair was held in Flanders Expo on 12–15 February 2008. The dynamic world of the civil engineering, hydraulic engineering, road construction and traffic engineering industry demands up-to-date knowledge and excellent contacts. The pace of technological development is fast and working conditions are becoming increasingly complicated and, consequently, there is an increasingly urgent need for fast, effective collaboration and tailored solutions for implementation of infrastructure projects. The exhibitors are companies working in general construction (manufacturers and distributors of construction machinery and materials, concrete construction, groundwork, soil surveys, etc.), road construction (road construction work, bridge construction, tunnel construction, paving, sewer work, etc.), hydraulic engineering (dredging, water treatment plants, water barrier and water barrier products, underwater work, hydrological construction, harbour construction, etc.), railway engineering (railway construction, manufacturers of railway machinery, etc.), drilling (drilling and sounding work, horizontal drilling and well drilling, etc.), traffic engineering (signage and signalling systems, mobility and traffic management, traffic signs and signals, road and yard signage and signalling systems, building signs and signalling systems, traffic signs along connecting roads, etc.) and energy (energy supply, renewable energy, energy saving and recovery). Also, suppliers of pumps and compressors, transmission components, crane and lifting equipment cables, pipes and tubes, pipeline systems, mains networks, and so on, are invited.

In preparing the new fair, the organisation found out that the number of contracts awarded by public tender is increasing. In recent years, the Belgian government has started making major investments in road construction and public transport. There have also been investments for expanding regional airports and investments in water management. The total volume of contracts awarded in 2007 reached €50 billion. This information shows that the market is increasing. A booming market is necessary to start up a fair. The next step is to analyse the exhibitor market to see if there is a good market potential. For Infratech Belgium, Flanders Expo hired a market research agency that carried out an analysis of the Belgian market. The market research is based on surveys with different companies which could be potential exhibitors or visitors to the Infratech fair. The organisation explains the concept of the fair to the companies and does the survey afterwards. The organisation has also done a SWOT analysis on the market situation before launching the Infratech fair concept. Based on this information, the organisation saw that there was a place for Infratech on the fair market.

Flanders Expo also studied the match between the Infratech offer and market structure and demand. A successful fair has to correspond with the existing market. This means that a fair has to show a good balance between all the market players and all the products of a certain industry, in this case civil engineering, hydraulic engineering, road construction and traffic engineering. The organisation defined a typology for the different potential exhibitors. This typology is based on the different positions of the exhibitors in the market and their individual developments. According to a market study, the organiser reaches an ideal mix of exhibitors: trendsetters/market leaders (8%), international and national brand companies (27%), competitive compulsory exhibitors (41%), hangers-on (17%) and newcomers (7%). Infratech is especially aware of the importance of newcomers and market leaders at the fair. Newcomers are very important to keep the fair innovative, and market leaders are very important to attract the national market industry. If the market leaders are not present at Infratech, other exhibitors will evaluate the fair as less important. Internationalisation is important because more management decisions are being taken in foreign countries. Potential exhibitors should be aware of this. On the other hand, many visitors take local decisions. Visitors detect trends in foreign countries, but they will order similar products and technologies in Belgium. Therefore, a local Belgian fair such as Infratech is useful.[23]

In the next phase, budgets, time and capacity are checked and one person is made responsible for the planning and implementation of the trade fair. Then, a strategy and exhibition goals are defined, together with the budget, back-timing and briefing for the development of stands, animation, etc. This is developed further in the next steps. Later, the participation is evaluated through the tools discussed in the next paragraph.

The promotion stage is one of the more important exhibition-supporting activities of the planning process. A direct mailing or e-mailing to invite clients and prospects (with free entrance tickets) is often employed. Advertising on radio and TV may be used to bring the exhibition and stand to the attention of the public. Ads in the exhibition catalogue and on its website will help visitors find a stand and have an important after-fair promotion effect. Free entrance tickets, direct mails and ads in the catalogue are frequently used as pre-promotion tools. Press releases and ads in above-the-line media are also used.

Companies which successfully develop integrated marketing communications programmes emphasising trade shows do so because these trade fairs create sales for them. These companies create a competitive advantage through their use of shows in two ways: they are twice as likely to close sales from their trade show exposure; and they are able to gain these sales more efficiently, at a lower cost per sale. They also obtain up to three times more exposure because they can exhibit in more shows at the same cost. These companies have additional expertise, enabling them to make better use of trade shows. In addition, responsibility and authority for the show operations and success lie with someone who has and can develop expertise. A study clearly indicates that success is not based on preference for shows but rather on the performance of activities that lead to success. Less successful companies can increase success by identifying someone in the organisation to take the exhibition marketing responsibility.[24]

Assessing effectiveness

After participating in an exhibition, a company should evaluate the effectiveness of its efforts. There are four major reasons for measuring the results of every exhibition:[25]

- To justify investments (by calculating return on investments, just like for any other item in the marketing budget).
- To help choose the right exhibitions.
- To improve trade show activities (before, during and after the show).
- To encourage goal-driven activities.

This means that results should be compared with the objectives. Sales figures from current clients as well as new customers, and market and competitive information gathered at the fair, are criteria to evaluate whether the exhibition brought value for money.[26] Sometimes exhibiting companies evaluate a fair by asking their sales reps about the contacts they made during the fair. Often this leads to stories about jealous competitors or first contacts with important new customers 'in the near future'. This is not the most objective or appropriate tool for analysing exhibition success. Others look at increases in sales returns after a fair, but this would only be a good evaluation if direct selling were the main goal of participating. Future sales returns cannot be predicted as many contracts have not yet been signed.

The coverage or reach of exhibitions and trade fairs differs from that of traditional print or other media. Gross reach has to do with the number of exhibition visitors, net reach could be the number of stand visitors. But effectiveness does not depend on the number of visitors only, but also on the quality of visits. Since 2000 the Audit Bureau of Circulations (ABC) has provided an independent 'currency' by which the success of exhibitions and trade shows can be compared. The two types of certificates issued are 'standard', which amounts to a number count only, and 'profile', which has audited demographics of the visitors. International Confex, for example, a trade fair targeting the travel industry and held every spring, has a profile certificate.[27]

BUSINESS INSIGHT
Measuring the return on investment of trade shows

In many companies, decisions on trade fair participation are largely uncontrolled and based on tradition, emotions and local habits. In an international industrial marketing company,[28] the management considered better planning and decision-making for trade shows and events based on formal ROI measurement to be a priority. The problem was that the customer relations management database only provided an incomplete picture of the selling cycle. Some data were available on lead intake (including the source: web, mailing, trade show), quotations and invoicing, but there were no other systematic data. The company had some idea, though, of the length of typical selling cycles for different product types: product C, twelve months; product B, nine months; and product A, six months (true product names disguised for confidentiality reasons). Other useful available metrics were the ratio of new versus existing contacts, the spread over different product groups and direct and indirect budgets allocated. Based on these limited data, the company built and tested an ROI calculation model based on the best available data and accepted by the sales division, and easy to implement and maintain without any new software or systems. This model was intended to allow for better decisions and planning with respect to the function of targets, budgets and, based on ROI measurement, smaller and more focused stands, and the consideration of alternatives such as road shows, master classes, webinars, better trade shows and events results, target-setting and show preparation, management and follow-up. The basic logic of this ROI model is given in the figure below.

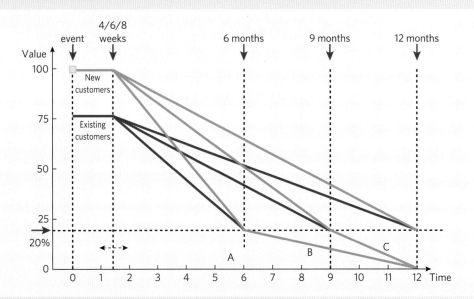

Trade shows and events ROI model

At most trade shows, the three product types A, B and C are presented. They are shown on the horizontal axis. As mentioned above, the average time between a first contact and a sale is on average six months for product A, nine months for product B and twelve months for product C. This is also marked on the horizontal axis. The logic of the system is that any effect a trade show can have would end after these time periods. However, the model allows for an 'after effect' of an extra 20% of sales after these periods. All 'after effects' are assumed to end after one year. The ROI measurement of trade show effectiveness is thus limited to a measurement cycle of 12 months. The vertical axis shows which percentage of sales of each type of product that was realised after the show can be attributed to show participation. Orders taken at the fair itself are not taken into account, because it is assumed that they are not the result of trade show participation and buyers at the show had already decided to place an order before the start of the fair.

At the show, a number of leads are explored (e.g. business cards, sales conversations). For new customers, it is assumed that 100% of these can be attributed to the fair. Based on previous experience and historical data, for existing customers, it is assumed that only 75% of the new orders are fair-related. After 4–8 weeks, mainly depending on the size of the fair, return on fair participation begins to be measured. A sale made to a new customer immediately after this period is 100% attributed to fair participation. This percentage declines linearly as time goes by and, for product A for example, only 20% is attributed to the fair after six months. Between six and twelve months, sales of product A are linearly decreasingly attributed to the fair, until the percentage reaches zero after twelve months. The same basic mechanism with different time intervals is used for the other two products, and for existing customers (starting at 75%). The percentage of sales attributed to the fair decreases over time. The logic behind this is that, as time passes after fair participation, the impact of other marketing efforts on sales becomes more important. Finally, the total impact of the fair is calculated as a weighted average of sales in the period following fair participation. The weights are the percentage for each point in time that can be found on the vertical axis. The impact of the fair on sales is separately calculated for new and existing customers and for the three types of products.

In order to be able to assess the effectiveness of trade fair participation, a number of research methods can be applied.[29] During the course of the fair, the following research can be carried out:

- *Counting the distributed information material* (brochures etc.). This is a way to estimate the interest in the company and its products and services, and is also a technique to evaluate image-building objectives.

- *Counting the number of passers-by and stand visitors.* This may be used for different objectives. Possible counting mistakes may occur when certain people visit the stand more than once to ask for additional information or after comparing other stands.

- *Counting the number of personal contacts.* This is especially appropriate when objectives include sales leads and supporting new and current trade relations. The number of contacts and the quality of those contacts (hot/medium/cold prospects) should be distinguished.

- *Analysis of visitor flows to the stand.* Through time-lapse video registration it is possible to observe and analyse behaviour and walk patterns of visitors during an entire exhibition day.

- *Observing visitor behaviour.* By observing stand visitors (where do they stop, what are they looking at, etc?) it is possible to detect what visitors find important and what is catching their attention. Eye-camera tests and tachistoscope tests (described in Chapter 9 on advertising research) are tools that are used for this kind of observational research.

- *Questionnaires for stand visitors.* This offers all possible ways of measuring the effectiveness for different objectives such as evaluating pre-exhibition communications impact, stand concept and response to informational and other needs, company image testing, etc. However, on-stand face-to-face interviewing could be quite annoying for visitors (taking up their time).

Other analytical tools can be used to measure the effectiveness of an exhibition after the fair:

- *Questionnaires for stand visitors.* Strengths and weaknesses, awareness and recall can be tested, and suggestions for further exhibitions may result from this kind of research. This implies that visitors' personal data have been stored.

- *Surveying stand personnel.* Stand personnel can be interviewed about their perceptions of the contacts with visitors. However, it is not easy to filter out their subjective assessments of these contacts.

- *Response analysis of sent invitations.* How many of the invited people have visited the stand? What were the reasons why invited people did not come to the stand?

- *Sales returns.* What are the sales results of the fair? Is the increase in return large enough, compared with the objectives?

- *Ratio analysis.* Some ratios help to measure effectiveness of exhibitions:[30]
  - Exhibition coefficient I = Value of transactions generated at the fair/Total fair costs
  - Exhibition coefficient II = Yearly sales of the company/Yearly fair costs
  - Visitor price = (Trade fair costs/Number of fair visitors) × 1000
  - Stand contact price = Trade fair costs/Number of stand contacts
  - Costs per stand worker[31] = Trade fair costs/Number of stand personnel
  - Costs per m^2 = Trade fair costs/Amount of m^2

When an exhibitor wants to make comparisons with other marketing and communications instruments over time, the next ratio[32] may be helpful:

$$\text{Sales efficiency quotient} = \frac{\text{Order administration costs on the trade fair}}{\text{Order administration cost through other sales channels or media}}$$

The first condition to be able to measure effectiveness is the presence of quantitatively defined concrete objectives. A study of 311 Belgian companies revealed that 27% of the exhibition participants always set objectives before participating in exhibitions and trade fairs; 29% hardly ever sets objectives; and 57% of all surveyed companies claim that they track the effectiveness of the exhibitions in which they participate.[33]

To conclude, trade show performance has traditionally been evaluated by outcome-based measures such as different sales-related activities (for instance, on-site sales and sales immediately after the trade show). But, on the other hand, behaviour-based control systems can also be used to evaluate participation in a trade fair. In a behaviour-based control system, the process rather than simply the outcome is addressed. In this system, the stand personnel are directed to perform behaviours that are part of the marketing strategy. Four behaviour-based dimensions can be identified:[34]

- *Information-gathering activities* including all activities related to the collection of information about competitors, customers, industry trends and new products at the trade show.
- *Image-building activities* related to building corporate image and reputation at the trade show.
- *Motivation activities* directed at the motivation of company employees and customers.
- *Relationship-building activities* with established customers as well as new customers.

Limitations of fairs and exhibitions

There are a number of reasons why companies could have a negative attitude to participating in trade fairs and exhibitions. Visitors are overwhelmed with lots of information during a short period of time, and it is likely that communicating a message in this clutter will be ineffective. Competitors are easy to contact and comparisons are possible. It is likely that a client will find a better offer for his or her preferences at the fair; on the other hand, it is also possible to gain new customers (ex-clients of competitors). Trade fairs are often hectic and exhibitions with a high visitor number will only lead to very superficial contacts. Exhibitions are exhausting. Weary visitors are difficult to contact and will not be very willing to buy. Half of the visitors spend a maximum of 3–4 hours at an exhibition. The most frequently mentioned reason why trade fairs are not chosen as a communications tool is the high cost. Low sales responses and satisfaction about the current communications mix are also high-scoring reasons.[35]

Online trade shows

Although traditional trade shows still have advantages for companies that want to showcase their products, online shows have emerged as an attractive option for those with audiences that are too focused to justify the expenses of a real-world show. Recession, tight corporate travel and marketing budgets, and terrorism have taken their toll on traditional exhibitions. For instance, in 2002 attendance at trade shows fell by 2% and sales of exhibition space declined by 5%. Meanwhile the popularity of online shows has been growing. Most of those budgets would be spent on more specialised exhibits, smaller shows with targeted audiences and refined messages. For instance, *EE Times* magazine was targeted at such an audience of electronic engineers. In November 2002, the magazine moved its IP/System on Chip conference to cyberspace for the first time. Using software from the Israeli firm Unisfair, *EE Times* created a website depicting a conference centre, complete with virtual visitors walking along paths to the conference hall and an exhibition space. A click on the conference hall took the visitors, paying nothing for the two-day event, into a virtual auditorium where presenters' slides filled the screen while their speeches were broadcast via streaming audio. In the exhibition hall, attendees could view exhibitors' displays and chat with sales reps. Exhibitors such as IBM, Intel and Motorola could get details on who viewed products and contact visitors in real time. The online trade show drew about 600 live attendees, with another 1100 viewing an archive of the event. Due to its success, the show was immediately rescheduled.

However, virtual shows have one big disadvantage when compared with their real-world counterparts: the lack of personal face-to-face contact. Virtual exhibition halls and online chat might be successful but cannot beat the ability to see, touch and play with a product or shake hands with a potential business partner. As traditional shows involve more effort from, and higher costs for, attendees, leads generated are more likely to turn into actual sales as less serious shoppers are weeded out. Some virtual trade shows are trying to make their events more realistic by using technologies that allow individuals to be represented by lifelike avatars who can move and interact in a simulated world online. Another standard feature of traditional exhibitions, the goodie bag of promotional items given out by exhibitors and organisers, is also very important. DataWarehouse.com sends out gifts to a random sample of about two-thirds of visitors half-way through each show.[36]

In May 2012, the Belgian city of Ghent held its first digital job exhibition. Thirty-three companies with local plants or offices, such as Coca-Cola, Eandis, Volvo Group Belgium, Innogenetics, attended this virtual experiment. On the website www.gentwerkt.be ('Ghent works'), a person looking for a new job could see three different screens, representing three halls, with the logos of the participating companies. By clicking on the logo, the visitor entered the virtual stand. Via Skype and chat sessions the job hunter could have live contact with the recruiter representing the company. After one day, the fair had nearly 4000 virtual visitors and more than 1000 CVs were posted.[37]

IMC INSIGHT
Integrating exhibitions and trade fairs in IMC

Obviously, exhibitions and trade fairs can be announced in advertising campaigns and on websites, or awareness and interest can be created through press conferences, but, in the first place, exhibition and trade fair activities should be well integrated into the direct marketing and personal selling efforts. Direct marketing can be used to announce the fair to customers and stakeholders. Information collected at the fair can be ploughed into the customer database and be used for more effective mailing campaigns or for better advertising and promotion. At the trade fair, prospects can be identified and deals can be closed. It is an opportunity to invite loyal customers and to build a stronger relationship with them. Exhibitions and fairs are also opportunities to hold press conferences and organise corporate hospitality events. Prospects, identified through sales efforts and direct marketing campaigns, can be invited to the fair for a more personal approach. In general, fairs and exhibitions can make direct marketing and sales efforts more effective, and the latter can turn fairs and exhibitions into powerful tools by adequately preparing for them.

Summary

Exhibitions and trade fairs are mainly, but not exclusively, used in business-to-business marketing as places for merchants of a certain product category or industry to meet and talk. Different types of exhibitions can be distinguished, such as public fairs, horizontal and vertical trade fairs, conference-bound exhibitions and trade marts. The place of exhibitions, especially in business marketing communications, is considered to be almost as important as direct marketing and personal selling. The objectives of exhibitions can be very diverse: to launch and test new products, establish brand or company awareness, demonstrate products, reinforce corporate image, monitor the competition, build relationships, generate sales leads and sell products. Exhibitions and trade fairs have to be planned carefully. After an analysis of the exhibition project, and making an inventory of what is needed, the actual exhibition has to be prepared, a concept for a stand has to be developed and the exhibition has to be realised (reservations, stand-building, catering, press, etc.). After the exhibition, the results have to be evaluated. This can be done by counting the distributed information and the numbers of passers-by and personal contacts, by analysing the flow of visitors and observing visitors' behaviour, or by surveying them. Sales returns can be measured.

REVIEW QUESTIONS

1. What is the importance of trade fairs and exhibitions in the marketing communications mix?

2. What are the main objectives of trade fair participation, and for which objectives are exhibitions and trade fairs most suited?

3. What are the basic steps and considerations in the development of an exhibition participation plan?

4. How can the effectiveness of exhibitions and trade fairs be assessed?

5. What are the limitations of trade fair participation?

Further reading

Kirchgeorg, M., Dornscheidt, W.M., Giese, W. and Stoeck, N. (2006), *Trade Show Management.* Wiesbaden: Gabler.

Krauel, J. (2008), *New Trade Show Design.* Barcelona: Links International.

Raj, R., Walters, P. and Rashid, T. (2008), *Events Management: An Integrated and Practical Approach.* London: Sage.

Siskind, B. (2005), *Powerful Exhibit Marketing: The Complete Guide to Successful Trade Shows, Conferences, and Consumer Shows.* Mississanga, ON: Wiley.

Stevens, R. (2005), *Trade Show & Event Marketing: Plan, Promote & Profit.* Andover; Thompson Learning.

CASE 14:
FISA – Batibouw: how to calculate the effectiveness of a trade show

Company profile

FISA is a company of 14 employees that came into being at the first Brussels Building Fair in 1960, and got its actual name Batibouw in 1973 (Photo 14.1). Batibouw is the core business of FISA, but also a number of spin-off activities are organised, such as 'Red Turtle Art', an art contest open to all amateur artists. Batibouw supports novice or experienced artists and, in that way, proves that the building trade and a sense of beauty can go hand in hand. A 'Public Award', 'Artist Award' and 'Press Award' are presented to the winners in the categories of painting, sculpture and photography. Another activity of FISA is the casius.be and casius.nl websites that help people to find a good specialist quickly and free of charge. Finding a reliable builder, architect, decorator, plumber, electrician and other specialist contractors in the home improvement market is sometimes difficult. The database of Casius contains details of thousands of home builders and improvement professionals throughout Belgium and the Netherlands. Casius was founded in 1999 and quickly became a successful Internet company in the Benelux countries. FISA also organises 'Second Place', the first Belgian fair for second homes. The first fair took place in 2006. For the first time, everything that interests people looking for a second home was gathered together under one roof. FISA also organises, together with the architect organisation NAV and Media Office, the event 'My house, my architect'. This is an initiative of the organisation of architects to exhibit 220 recently built or recently renovated houses. These houses can be visited for an entire weekend. The purpose is to put future builders or renovators into contact with the architect and his or her

Photo 14.1 Batibouw, the Belgian building and construction fair
Source: Reproduced with permission of FISA, Belgium

work. The strategy of FISA is to engage in new ventures, but the core business of Fisa is still Batibouw.

In total there are around 232 fair and event locations in Belgium, which might seem a lot for a small country. Many of them, though, are small. The biggest in Belgium is Brussels Expo at 140 000 m², where Batibouw takes place. Batibouw is one of the largest and most visited fairs in Belgium. It attracts around 1000 exhibitors and 370 000 visitors each year. Compared with other fairs, this is large: Agriflanders (350 exhibitors and 86 000 visitors); Bois & Habitat (250 exhibitors and 86 000 visitors); Furniture Fair (189 exhibitors and 9532 visitors); Accenta (400 exhibitors and 85 000 visitors); Febiacvzw – Autosalon (300 exhibitors and 349 000 visitors).

Batibouw is the largest building fair in Belgium, although there are other smaller, regional fairs that are also dedicated to building or related subjects and can also be found at Batibouw. These include BIS fair ((a building and real estate fair in Flanders Expo with 350 exhibitors); Hout, Energie en Wonen ('Wood, Energy and Living' at Antwerp Expo); Vlaanderenverbouwbeurs (a renovating fair at Waregern Expo); Bois et Habitat Namur ('Wood and Living Namur'); Salonenergie et Habitat ('Energy and Living' at Namur Expo); Domotix Forum (Domotica Fair at Brabanthal); Architect at work (a fair for architects at Kortrijk Xpo); Batireno (a construction and renovation fair at Namur Expo); and Bouwinnovaitie (building innovation at Grenslandhallen).

Batibouw's history

The 'Bouwsalon van Brussel' ('Brussels Building Fair') was launched by Georges de Vestel in 1960. Until then, smaller regional building fairs were open to the general public. Georges de Vestel's dream was to set up a trade fair in Brussels, not only for professionals but also for the public at large. In 1967 the fair – which was still called the Brussels Building Fair – launched its new logo: a turtle in blue, green and orange. The red and green turtle, which is still used today, was developed in 1976 by the renowned graphic designer Julian Key. Until 1968, the fair had its base in the Rogier Centre in the city centre. However, its increasing success forced the organisation to find another venue and the fair moved to the Heysel Expo exhibition centre. By its tenth birthday in 1970, the fair covered Halls 2, 3, 8 and the Patio of this huge exhibition complex. In 1973, a new name was chosen: 'BATIBOUW', a typically Belgian combination of two words – the French *batir* and the Dutch *bouwen* (both meaning 'to build'). Due to its growing support among the general public and professionals, Batibouw became an increasingly international building, renovation and decoration fair.

The fair attracted more and more visitors, but also exhibitors' interest and booth surface area continued to

grow. Since 1993, all 13 halls of the Brussels Expo exhibition centre, covering a gross surface area of some 140 000 m², have been completely filled. Each year for the past 48 years, countless products and services have been introduced and presented at Batibouw. For 11 days the entire building industry is the centre of attention. The event receives extensive media coverage. Batibouw is also strongly supported by policy-makers, who implement special measures to enhance this key economic sector's resilience. Today, Batibouw has become the flagship of an industry that every Belgian holds dear. So, now, Batibouw is a fair that does not really have to be marketed, with 85% of exhibitors registering automatically again for the next fair. The other 15% are companies that have ceased to exist or think that participation is too expensive. In 2007, the rent for a stand at Batibouw was €120.96/m². Normally for Batibouw, every sub-industry (kitchen, bathroom, etc.) occupies a full hall. Every hall is full, and there is always a waiting list for potential new exhibitors. Demand for exhibition space outstrips supply. For Batibouw, there are no problems finding sufficient exhibitors. There is no need to convince people to participate at Batibouw. The fair is so popular and visible that companies just want to be there.

How to increase the effectiveness of the fair for the organiser and the visitors

FISA always tries to organise the fair from the perspective of the visitor. A fair can only survive if it attracts enough visitors. Therefore, the organisation invests in finding out what the public need and want and how it can generate visibility and media interest to attract the public. For instance, Batibouw is a big fair, there are a lot of people and it can be an exhausting experience for the visitor. Therefore it is necessary to segment the fair. The first focal point in the communication strategy is to clearly communicate where visitors can find products and stands. A second focal point is identifying new trends. Every year, there are hundreds of new innovations at Batibouw. But one innovation is more spectacular than another. Therefore, Batibouw always works with three themes for the fair. These themes are artificially created, but they always attract a lot of media attention, and articles appear in the press about the fair and building in general. For instance, the first theme in the 2007 fair was lifestyle, which put the kitchen in the spotlight. The second theme was technical, 'the acoustic norm'. The third and last theme concerned saving energy. If these three themes are well chosen, success is guaranteed.

Exit polls of exhibitors and visitors are very important to learn more about client satisfaction and, perhaps, to improve some elements in the future. The exit polls of visitors of Batibouw 2007 revealed the following. Batibouw had 361 644 visitors, of whom 290 159 were private individuals and 71 485 professionals. Of the professionals, 62% came on the first two days that are limited to professional visitors and 38% came on the other days. As a comparison, in 2006 there were 369 178 visitors (Figure 14.3).

All professional visitors wear a name badge so that they are easily recognisable to exhibitors. Professionals are registered in advance so the organisation has information about them. At the end of every day, it can see if the professionals have been at the fair and then send them an e-mail to thank them for their visit and ask if they want to fill in a questionnaire. In 2007 forty-two per cent of the professional visitors came to Batibouw to get in touch with the market, 25% to learn about new products, 13% to look for concrete solutions for specific problems, 9% to discover existing suppliers and 5% to discover new suppliers. Fifty-four per cent of the professionals said they were prepared when coming to the fair and 46% said they were not prepared. From the 54% who came prepared for the fair, 41% informed themselves on the Batibouw website, 16% read articles in the press, 3% read the Batibouw catalogue and 40% had other ways of preparing. Seventeen per cent of the professional visitors found exactly what they expected at the fair, 69% for the most part, 12% not really, 1% not at all and 1% had no opinion. When FISA asked the professional visitors if they were attending to buy from an exhibitor because they met it at the fair, 21% were sure, 51% said maybe, 15% thought not and 13% had no opinion. Seventy-eight per cent of the professionals said that

they had discovered a few companies at the fair that they did not know before, 8% said that they had discovered a lot of new companies and 14% said that they had not discovered any.

FISA also surveys the private (non-professional) visitors. Twenty-six per cent of the general public visited the fair in 2007 because they were building a new house, 39% were renovating, 19% were redecorating, 12% had no specific reason and 4% had another reason not mentioned. Sixty-three per cent of the private visitors prepared for their visit and 37% did not. Half of them prepared themselves by using the website, 17% by reading articles, 5% by reading the catalogue and 28% used other ways to prepare themselves. Thirteen per cent saw totally what they had expected on the fair, 70% for the most part, 14% not really, 2% not at all and 1% had no opinion. Eighteen per cent of the public visitors thought about placing an order with an exhibitor they had seen at the fair, 60% thought there was a possibility, 16% thought they would not and 6% had no opinion. Seventy per cent of the public visitors said they had discovered a few companies they did not know before visiting the fair, 25% said they had discovered a lot of new companies and 5% said they had not discovered any.

Batibouw is a strongly segmented fair, so every segment of the building industry is located in a different hall. In the survey, the organisation asks visitors which hall they came to visit. Based on those answers, the organisation learns more about what people are looking for in their homes or what are they are interested in. Once FISA has gathered all the information, it shares it with exhibitors. It is important

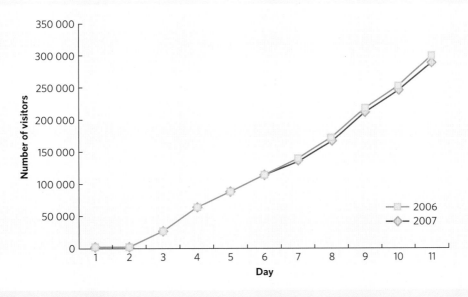

Figure 14.3 Daily visitors at Batibouw, 2006 and 2007
Source: Geert Maes, CEO, FISA.

that they know about the profile of the visitors. The organisation does not give names or addresses to the exhibitors, though.

Batibouw's website had 284 246 visitors in 2006 and 445 688 in 2007 during the fair. Over the whole year of 2006, the website received almost a million visitors. FISA also sells tickets online. A visitor who buys a ticket at the entrance pays €12, a visitor who buys tickets online only pays €10. In that way, FISA has the names and addresses of buyers who buy tickets online. During the year FISA sends four or five newsletters to visitors of previous fairs. The newsletters are about building and construction but also about the other activities of the organisation.

Exhibitors are also surveyed. Eighty-four per cent of them in 2007 intended to participate at Batibouw 2008, 14% had doubts and 2% said they would not participate. More than 83% of exhibitors gave a participation satisfaction score of more than 7 on a 10-point scale (Figure 14.4). The exhibitors are satisfied with the number of professional visitors and even more satisfied about the quality of the professional visitors. Almost all exhibitors are also satisfied about the quality of the public visitors.

How to increase the effectiveness of a fair for the exhibitors

Batibouw goes to great trouble to make fair participation for the exhibitors more effective.

Helping the exhibitors to create fair participation awareness and traffic

The duty of a fair organiser is to get people into the fair. The priority of an exhibitor is its place at the fair. Batibouw offers a whole range of cost-efficient options to exhibitors so that they can promote both themselves and Batibouw on a scale that is not too expensive. For instance, FISA hands out stickers to exhibitors that they can use in their mails to clients, and posters that they can hang up in their exposition halls. Exhibitors can use the Batibouw logo – the turtle – on their mail and their invoices.

Further, FISA has a deal with most Belgian media groups, both general and specialised. The media give exhibitors a discount in the months before the fair, if they put an ad with the red turtle logo in their magazines and newspapers. Sixty-three per cent of exhibitors made use of the Batibouw ad material to announce their fair participation. Seventy-one per cent sent personal invitations, 48% wrote e-mails, 62% did a classic mailing, 31% announced it in the professional press, 30% announced their participation in the consumer press, 13% did a poster campaign, 6% advertised on TV and 3% on radio.

Batibouw also gives exhibitors the opportunity to rent a manual scanner for about €100. This allows them to quickly register information about visitors. Every evening, the organisation gives exhibitors a USB stick or a disk with all the information about the visitors to their stand on that day.

In order to raise awareness about and make visible examples of 'good practice', Batibouw issues communications awards. One award concerns the best reception. How are people received? Do the sales representatives feel what the customer needs and wants? Is the reception friendly? Another award goes to the best product presentation. The third award goes to the best communications strategy, before as well as during the fair. Awards are given to exhibitors who rent less than 70 m^2 and to exhibitors who

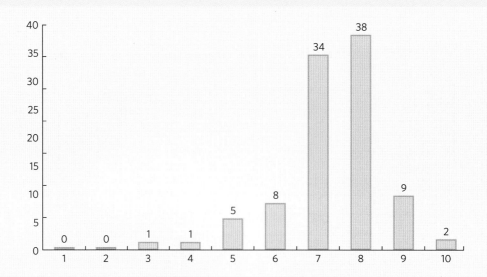

Figure 14.4 Exhibitors' satisfaction score at Batibouw 2007
Source: Geert Maes, CEO, FISA.

rent more than 70 m², so that small and large exhibitors have equal chances.

Finally, every year Batibouw organises an information day dedicated to inform exhibitors. Also, during the year, Batibouw organises two lunches. At these lunches, a guest speaker connected to the building industry is invited, for instance the renovators of the Atomium Monument in Brussels or the company building the highest towers in Dubai.

FISA devotes a lot of effort to generating publicity and media exposure for Batibouw. The value of media exposure of the fair was estimated to be around €175 000. Batibouw organises a press conference every year, where there are about 120 visitors.

Good organisation

The logistics of a fair are very complex. Therefore every year, the organisation produces a toolkit. This toolkit contains the regulations of the fair and a checklist for exhibitors on security, water, electricity, parking subscriptions, etc. Most exhibitors do not need the organisation to help set up their stand; they hire a stand building company. Some exhibitors create their own stand. They can ask the Batibouw organisation to supply what they need to build their stand. Also, during the fair logistical problems require fast and effective solutions. If there are any disturbances at the fair, the organisation tries to take care of them quickly. For example, at one time in one of the halls there were companies which were exhibiting tools that made a lot of noise. The exhibitors wanted to show their tools and used them in the halls. However, the noise was very disturbing for other exhibitors. So the organisation parsed a new regulation where exhibitors can demonstrate their tools, but they can do so only in a sound-proof cage.

The organisation is aware that some stands will have more traffic than others, depending on where they are situated. Some exhibitors explicitly ask to have a specific position in the hall. The organisation, however, works as follows: the companies that have been exhibiting for the longest time at the fair get first choice. Eighty-five per cent of the exhibitors immediately register for the following year, and 99% of them want to have the same place as the year before.

Controlling the profile of Batibouw's exhibitors

Of course, exhibitors have to be part of the building industry. Batibouw only accepts manufacturers, exclusive importers or agents at the fair. When the organisation receives a new request from a company that wants to exhibit at the fair, it always checks out the company first. FISA also looks at the promotional materials of the company and visits its showrooms. The organisation can refuse to allow a company to participate, if it believes that the company is bad for the image of the fair or if it does not comply with the fair regulations.

How exhibitors can improve the effectiveness of their fair participation

Professional exhibitors know their objectives before participation and work towards these. When the organisation asks exhibitors why they participate at a fair, the reply is often: 'Because our direct competitors are there too.' This is the wrong motivation. Other exhibitors say that they are participating because, if they do not, people will think that their company is not doing very well. There are not many exhibitors who come to the fair with real objectives like a clear view of the products to exhibit, the costs, the market potential and the number of contacts to be reached.

The return on investment of trade fair participation is often hard to measure. Some exhibitors measure their contacts by counting the number of brochures distributed. That is only a start because an exhibitor does not know what happens to those brochures afterwards. Some fairs are real selling fairs. However, Batibouw is less of a selling fair.

Exhibitors sometimes evaluate the success of fair participation by the number of visitors to the stand. Exhibitors can also count the personal contacts. However, it is more relevant to measure the cost per useful contact at the fair. Based on a FISA study, the price per contact (based on stand prices and number of visitors) for Batibouw is less than €10. There are lots of magazines on building houses. Advertising in these media results in a certain cost per person reached. In terms of the cost per contact, to participate at Batibouw is less expensive than to advertise in a building magazine, and the exhibitor reaches the same target group. In any case, every exhibitor should work this out according to their particular situation, based on the full cost of fair participation and the number of useful contacts or sales leads made. Since the cost of fair participation is known to the exhibitors, the cost per contact is easy to calculate.

The fair can have a strong impact on company and product image, customer activation, brand awareness and creating an emotional link with the brand that an exhibitor can set up due to fair participation. Some people call Batibouw the biggest bar in the country. Professional visitors especially try to treat their potential clients in such a way that a positive impression of their company is created. However, it is difficult to isolate the effect of fair participation on these perception- and image-related indicators. The most important indication of fair participation ROI for an exhibitor is the profits as a result of participation in the fair.

Exhibitors can also think of brand activation and CRM at their stand. For instance, an exhibitor for a brick company promised a cheque for €100 if a stand visitor promised to buy bricks from the company in the year to come. The company asked clients which bricks they preferred and also asked for their address. The cheques were an instrument to measure the number of people who came to their stand. It also allowed the company to set up a database of potential prospects, with whom they could communicate all year long. But the cheques were more than that. They were also an instrument for scheduling production. Based on the questions and answers about brick preferences, the marketing department at the fair could tell the production division which bricks had the most success, and thus which bricks should be produced more. These are techniques that do not cost a company a lot, but they are very valuable because they enable the company to obtain the addresses of potential future clients.

QUESTIONS

1. Give a short description of Batibouw, and the market and competitive situation it operates in.

2. Which fairs in the building industry could pose a new challenge for FISA and why?

3. What would be other good ideas, besides the Batibouw building lunches, the 'Red Turtle Art' and the awards, to create a stronger link between Batibouw and its visitors?

4. How does Batibouw assist exhibitors to make their fair participation more effective? What do you think of these efforts? Try to come up with other activities or techniques to help exhibitors.

5. How do exhibitors measure the effectiveness of their participation? What do you think of the way they do it? Try to come up with other measurement techniques.

6. A brick exhibitor gave cheques for €100 to stand visitors who promised to buy bricks from the company in the following year. What are the three functions of this promotion campaign? Think of other CRM actions for different building companies that should have similar effects.

Sources: Kirchgeorg, M., Dornscheidt, W.M., Giese, W. and Stoeck, N. (2005), *Trade Show Management*. Wiesbaden: Gabler; Geert Maes, CEO FISA; www.batibouw.com June 2009; www.beurskalender.be June 2009; www.casius.be June 2009; www.exhibitions.be June 2009.

This case was prepared with the collaboration of Lien Standaert.

References

[1] Smith, T., Gopalakrishna, S. and Smith, P. (1999), *Trade Show Synergy: Enhancing Sales Force Efficiency*. ISBM report 24-1999. Institute for the Study of Business Markets, Pennsylvania State University.

[2] http://www.thefranceshow.com (accessed 1 October 2012).

[3] Interview with CEO of Fairtec, KoenDamman, 9 May 2007, www.fairtec.com.

[4] Groenendijk, J.N.A., Hazekamp, G.A.Th. and Mastenbroek, J. (1992), *Public Relations & Voorlichting: Beleid, Organisatie en Uitvoering (Public Relations and Press Relations: Management, Organisation and Implementation)*. Zaventem: Samson bedrijfsinformatie.

[5] Shoham, A. (1992), 'Selecting and Evaluating Trade Shows', *Industrial Marketing Management*, 21, 335–41.

[6] http://www.marketingcharts.com/direct/exhibition-industry-rebounds-strongly-in-2011-21621/ (accessed 1 October 2012).

[7] De Pelsmacker, P., Van den Bergh, J. and De Schepper, W. (1997), *Febelux Research on the Image of Exhibitions and Trade Fairs among Companies and Communication Agencies*. Ghent: De Vlerick School voor Management.

[8] http://www.marketingcharts.com/direct/exhibition-industry-rebounds-strongly-in-2011-21621/ (accessed 1 October 2012).

[9] Anderson, A.H. and Kleiner, D. (1995), *Effective Marketing Communication: A Skills and Activity-Based Approach*. Oxford: Blackwell Business.

[10] Chapman, B. (2001), 'The Trade Show Must Go On', *Sales and Marketing Management*, 153(6), 22.

[11] Kotler, P. (1984), *Marketing Management: Analysis, Planning and Control*. London: Prentice Hall.

[12] *How to Exhibit: Maximising the Power of Exhibitions*. The Association of Exhibition Organisers (AEO) (2002), www.exhibitionswork.co.uk.

[13] Interview with CEO of Fairtec, KoenDamman, 9 May 2007, www.fairtec.com.

[14] Duff, M. (2002), 'European Food Expo Beckons U.S. with Trends not Found at Home', *DNS Retailing Today*, 41(21), 8–48. Also, http://www.sialparis.com/ (accessed 1 October 2012).

[15] Interview with CEO of Flanders Expo John Buyckx, 20 April 2007; www.adventureaffair.be, www.flexpo.be (accessed 1 October 2012).

[16] Fishman, B. (2003), 'International Trade Shows: The Smartest Ticket for Overseas Research', *Franchising World*, 35(3), 25–8.

[17] Shipley, D. and Wong, K.S. (1993), 'Exhibiting Strategy and Implementation', *International Journal of Advertising*, 12, 117–30.

[18] De Pelsmacker, P., Van den Bergh, J. and De Schepper, W. (1997), *Febelux Research on the Image of Exhibitions and Trade Fairs among Companies and Communication Agencies*. Ghent: De Vlerick School voor Management.

[19] Greaves, S. (2002), 'Unifying Sales and Branding at Events', *Marketing* (November), 25.

20 Wenz-Gahler, I. (1995), *Messenstand-Design* (*Trade Fair Stand Design*). Leinfelden-Echterding: Alexander Koch.

21 Van Den Tempel, W. (1985), 'Beursdeelneming en Return on Investment' (Trade Fair Participation and Return on Investment), in *Beurzen en Tentoonstellingen: Praktijk Handboek voor Communicati Fxposeren* (*Trade Fairs and Exhibitions: A Practical Guide to Expose and Communicate*). Deventer: Kluwer.

22 Klein, L. (2003), 'How to Make Trade Shows Work for You', *National Underwriter*, 107(1), 11.

23 Kirchgeorg, M., Dornscheidt, W.M., Giese, W. and Stoeck, N. (2005), *Trade Show Management*, Gabler. Interview with CEO of Flanders Expo John Buyckx, 20 April 2007; www.exhibitions.be; www.flexpo.be (accessed 1 October 2012).

24 Tanner, J. (2002), 'Leveling of the Playing Field: Factors Influencing Trade Show Success for Small Companies', *Industrial Marketing Management*, 31, 229–39.

25 *How to Measure Exhibition Success: A Workbook for Marketers.* The Association of Exhibition Organisers (AEO) (2002), www.exhibitionswork.co.uk (accessed May 2007).

26 Anderson, A.H. and Kleiner, D. (1995), *Effective Marketing Communication: A Skills and Activity-Based Approach.* Oxford: Blackwell Business.

27 Greaves, S. (2003), 'Events Answer Industry Needs', *Marketing* (February), 27; Benady, D. (2003), 'Show You Count', *Marketing Week* (February), 41–4.

28 Due to a confidentiality agreement, the company name is not given.

29 Meffert, H. and Ueding, R. (1996), *Ziele und Nutzen von Messebeteiligungen: Zusammenfassung einer Empirisch Gestützten Untersuchung auf der Grundlage einer Befragung Deutscher Aussteller* (*Objectives and Usefulness of Trade Fair Participation: Summary of an Empirical Study Amongst Trade Fair Participants*). Cologne: Institütfür Marketing-Universität, Ausstellungs- und Messe-Ausschus der Deutschen Wirtschaft (AUMA).

30 Postma, P. (1986), *Marketing voor Iedereen* (*Marketing for Everyone*). Amsterdam: Omega Books.

31 Deelen, M. and Muys, W. (1991), *Verkoopactief Deelnemene aan Beurzen* (*Sales-Active Trade Fair Participation*). Deventer: Kluwer Bedrijfswetenschappen.

32 Meffert, H. and Ueding, R. (1996), *Ziele und Nutzen von Messebeteiligungen: Zusammenfassung einer Empirisch Gestützten Untersuchung auf der Grundlage einer Befragung Deutscher Aussteller* (*Objectives and Usefulness of Trade Fair Participation: Summary of an Empirical Study Amongst Trade Fair Participants*). Cologne: Institütfür Marketing-Universität, Ausstellungs- und Messe-Ausschus der Deutschen Wirtschaft (AUMA).

33 De Pelsmacker, P., Van den Bergh, J. and De Schepper, W. (1997), *Febelux Research on the Image of Exhibitions and Trade Fairs among Companies and Communication Agencies.* Ghent: De Vlerick School voor Management.

34 Hansen, K. (1999), 'Trade Show Performance: A Conceptual Framework and Its Implications for Future Research', *Academy of Marketing Science Review*, 1999(8), 135–50.

35 Shipley, D. and Wong, K.S. (1993), 'Exhibiting Strategy and Implementation', *International Journal of Advertising*, 12, 117–30.

36 Saranow, J. (2003), 'The Show Goes On: Online Trade Shows Offer a Low-cost, Flexible Alternative for Organizers – Especially in These Days of Tight Travel Budgets', *Wall Street Journal*, 28 April, R.4.

37 http://www.nieuwsblad.be/article/detail.aspx?articleid=NL3PHU6K, http://www.nieuwsblad.be/article/detail.aspx?articleid=BLRTO_20120511_002 (accessed 1 October 2012).

CHAPTER 15
E-communication

CHAPTER OUTLINE

The growing importance of e-media

E-communication objectives

E-marketing tools

Mobile marketing

Interactive television

The social media revolution

Relationship marketing and the Internet

Tracking the effectiveness of e-communications

CHAPTER OBJECTIVES

This chapter will help you to:

- Assess the importance of the Internet and other new media as interactive communications tools
- Distinguish the different types of e-marketing tools related to different communications objectives
- Understand the Internet as an advertising medium, its success factors, and the different types of Internet advertising
- Learn about the new evolutions in social media platforms such as Facebook, Twitter and Pinterest, mobile marketing, interactive television, blogging and podcasts
- Understand how the Internet contributes to relationship marketing
- Learn how the effectiveness of e-communications can be measured

Introduction

Mass marketing communications techniques have dominated communications strategies for decades. Gradually, direct marketing principles have been adopted that allow access to each member of the target group on an individual basis. The current stage in this evolution is the trend towards real interactivity, i.e. not only is the marketer capable of communicating with his or her target group on a one-to-one basis, but also individual members of the target group are capable of responding to, and interacting with, the sender of the message. Moreover, they often start the conversation themselves. Although some direct marketing communication techniques also allow a certain degree of interactivity, the increasing penetration of the Internet and mobile phones and the popularity of new interactive media such as interactive TV and social media are changing the nature of marketing communications interactivity. Today people's media attention is fragmenting. At the end of 2011, mobile phone penetration in Europe exceeded 100% with an average of 120%. Country figures of 2010 reveal that Finland (156%), Italy (150%), Lithuania (147%), Austria (146%), Croatia (145%) and the UK (131%) have the highest penetration, while the following European countries are performing at less than the EU average: Ukraine (119%), Norway (116%), Sweden (116%), the Netherlands (115%), Romania (115%), Belgium (113%), Spain (112%), Malta (109%), Greece, Slovak Republic and Iceland (108%), Ireland (105%), Latvia (102%) and France (101%). The rest of the European countries have a penetration less than 100%.[1] So, marketers have to follow them into the new media they are consuming. The Internet is fundamentally different from traditional, and even direct, marketing communications tools: consumers can go all the way from awareness to interest to desire to action, all within the same medium and within the same session.[1] Its unique characteristics and current evolutions are further explored in the first section of this chapter. The next sections focus on the different interactive media that a marketer can use for different communications objectives, with specific sections dedicated to interactive TV, mobile marketing and the recent evolutions in social media. Related topics such as relationship marketing and loyalty marketing using the Internet are also considered. Specific ways to measure the effectiveness of Internet presence are discussed in the last section. Although the Internet has the capability to support all aspects of company processes (including logistics, e-commerce, e-procurement, etc.), this chapter will specifically focus on the use of new media for marketing communications purposes.

The growing importance of e-media

The **Internet** refers to the computer network infrastructure that enables the exchange of digital data on a global scale. Worldwide, 888 million hosts[2] are interconnected through cable and telephone networks. Through historical developments (the Internet was first a military tool developed to make communication possible in case of nuclear war and was later adapted by academics to share and exchange information) and intentional efforts, nowadays the Internet is a unique, independent medium that is not owned or operated by a commercial or government body. Although the Internet is also the network serving e-mail applications, news servers (newsgroups), ftp (file transfer), gopher (pure text-based information exchange), etc., it is often used as a synonym for the **World Wide Web (WWW)**, the interactive and graphical communications medium invented by Tim Berners-Lee, a physicist at the European Centre for Nuclear Research (Cern).[3] The Web is characterised by the use of hypertext mark-up language (HTML) that allows documents consisting of text, icons, sounds or images to be shared by different users, regardless of the computer operating system they use. The hyperlinks (text- or image-based) make it possible to navigate quickly through documents and pages by simple mouse clicks. The growth of the WWW can be attributed to the user-friendly, consumer-operated pages utilising this hypertext capability.[4]

At the end of 2011, there were, on a global scale, 225 million domain names[5] (an indication of the number of websites). Worldwide, 2.3 billion people (501 million of whom are in Europe) are connected to the Internet, which is a global penetration (i.e. the number and percentage of people that have access to the Net) of 32.7% and an average European penetration of 61.3%. Within the European Union (EU27: 71.5%), Sweden has the highest penetration figure of 92.9%, followed by Luxembourg (91.4%), the Netherlands (89.5%), Denmark (89%), Finland (88.6%), Germany (82.7%) and Belgium (81.4%). Greece (46.9%), Bulgaria (48.8%) and Romania (39.2%) have the lowest Internet penetration in the EU27.[6]

In Europe, 1 in 5 advertising euros is now spent online. The big switch to bringing online advertising into the mainstream media mix continues across Europe. Online advertising has already crossed into the mainstream of media in several European markets. The latest IAB market tracking study – which collates online adspend from 26 countries – indicates that total online advertising broke €20.9 billion in 2011, confirming the consistently steep growth. The European growth in 2011 was 14.5%, which is lower than the 22% growth in the USA. The top five markets in Europe (UK, Germany, France, Italy, Netherlands) account for 68% of the total online advertising market, down slightly from 69.2% in 2010.[7] Advertisers increasingly recognise online as a branding medium; video commands a significant and growing share of spend, and search continues to deliver good and measurable results. The explosion of 'big data' has delivered enhanced targeting capabilities, improving monetisation of publishers' inventory. There is a trend for advertisers to shift ad budgets from mature to emerging markets, which is fuelling their online economy. An expanding broadband infrastructure adds to the attractiveness of those markets.[8] There is a new generation of marketing practices that are using sophisticated 'behavioural advertising' techniques to learn about the viewer's interest and provide tailored messaging. TV-like commercials can now be easily produced, allowing TV assets to be rebroadcast online and the campaign stretched further. The creative power of the engaging 'rich media' formats that take commercial messages across the whole web page has given creative directors a new freedom in design. And the standardisation of advertising formats and some of the workflow processes has removed a barrier that long held agencies back from recommending the Web. There are other compelling reasons to use the Internet as a marketing communications medium. Daytime is prime time – audiences that could never be reached before are now available and attentive. The Internet is a medium of a thousand niches – it combines exceptional lifestyle targeting with a mass reach. Accountability and making budgets stretch further are a strategic advantage of digital channels.

As online's share of the market has grown, spend is being drawn from other channels. Although some of this spend is migrating from the print editions of publications – particularly consumer magazines and directories – much is moving to the Internet pure play firms, in whose hands the market remains highly concentrated.

Direct mail is suffering as customer acquisition budgets move to search, and retention budgets move to e-mail marketing. Classified advertising in newspapers and magazines is finally migrating to the Web, with recruitment the largest single advertising sector online in several markets, and much of the advertising spend evaporating in favour of free-to-air models or disinter mediation as consumers access company websites directly.[9]

E-communications objectives

While we are witnessing more enthusiasm for the integration of Internet marketing tactics in today's marketing plans, few brand managers have a clear idea of which of these tactics are most appropriate for accomplishing various marketing objectives. In many cases, a trial and error process is undertaken, often heavily influenced and stimulated by whichever tactic the Internet or advertising agency is trying to sell to the brand manager. Because this calls for the development of an overall framework that allows marketers to categorise the different digital marketing tactics, InSites Consulting has developed such a framework, on which the following is based.[10]

Basically, the e-marketer can focus on four specific marketing goals when turning to digital tools:

- *Generating brand awareness*: putting or reinforcing the brand in the evoked set (i.e. the set of brands that is considered when the need or desire for the product or service arises) of consumers. In line with most research and cases found on this subject, stimulating brand awareness is ideally achieved via online advertising, content sponsorship, advergames and viral and social media marketing.

- *Shaping brand image and brand attitudes*: defining, reinforcing or changing the set of associations that differentiate the brand from competing products and improve consumers' knowledge and judgement about a brand. According to the literature on the subject, shaping brand attitude is best achieved by brand sites, online advertising, anchor deals, e-mail marketing, mobile marketing, online contests and peer-to-peer games.

- *Generating trial*: attracting new buyers to the brand by attracting brand-switchers (i.e. consumers of competing brands) or consumers who have never tried the product category before. Trial stimulation implies an increase in the brand penetration rate in a certain market. Mobile marketing, e-mail marketing, online contests, e-couponing and e-sampling are the best online marketing instruments to attain this objective.

- *Creating loyalty*: influencing consumers' buying behaviour in the sense of increasing the number of satisfied and committed buyers. Striving for customer loyalty is also a cost-saving strategy as research indicates that the cost of attracting new customers can be as much as six times greater than the cost of retaining customers. E-mail marketing, brand websites, virtual communities and certain e-rewarding games and online loyalty promotions contribute to the objective of generating and sustaining brand loyalty.

Generating traffic to a website or social media page is often emphasised in publications but is not actually a marketing communications end-goal, except for e-commerce sites for which traffic is essential. Of course it is important to engage customers by the e-marketing actions that a company undertakes but, in the end, site traffic will have to lead to one of the four objectives defined above. This is also the case for increasing market and consumer knowledge through employing e-direct marketing and database programs. In the next section each type of e-marketing tactic is described and illustrated with examples.

E-marketing tools

Marketers have a large number of different e-marketing communications tools at their disposal. In this section, we describe each instrument of the e-communications mix. The multimedia capabilities of the Net allow advertisers to use content, graphics, movement, audio and video. Almost every traditional communications tool has an online twin, e.g. e-coupons or online contests and seminars. Since almost every Internet user has his or her own e-mail address and social profile, marketers can build a direct communications line with customers and prospects at lower costs than traditional direct marketing. The huge success of mobile telecommunications and the increasing penetration of smart phones in Europe are opening new opportunities for companies to use wireless advertising and apps to reach their target groups.

Brand websites

Brand websites are sites with specific brand-related information and/or services. A brand site can be used to communicate with the target groups and also as a platform that enables interaction with, or between, customers or the collection of individual customer data, for instance by letting them subscribe to receive e-newsletters. Coca-Cola encourages site visitors to register and leave their personal data in exchange for 'goodies' like games, downloads (screensavers) etc. On the one hand, evidence has been found for the brand attitude-forming capabilities of a brand website that delivers information and applications that reinforce the positioning of the brand.

BUSINESS INSIGHT
O'Neill's state-of-the-art website

Early in 2009, O'Neill launched a new global website, providing visitors with fast and super-easy access to the world of O'Neill, and featuring the latest in functionality and design. The site stands out from the crowd by featuring large-format, mind-blowing imagery. Along with a show case of the latest O'Neill's collections, international events and team riders, the site also provides direct access to O'Neill TV. Another new feature is the separate dedicated areas for men and women. From the first click, the visitor has to decide whether he or she wants to discover the male or female version. Each site has its own unique design and content. The site showcases all the latest team-rider news and blogs, as well as new collections and trends, but with a different look and feel. There is also a 'heritage' section, giving information on Jack O'Neill – the man who founded O'Neill back in 1952 and who is responsible for some of the industry's most groundbreaking inventions and innovations, including the wetsuit.

In 2012, O'Neill celebrated its 60th anniversary. The site is still using the gender split approach, featuring access to O'Neill's social media pages, such as Facebook, Twitter and YouTube. Over 90 000 fans like the O'Neill girls' Facebook page, whereas the male page has more than 350 000 fans; 2324 people are following the Twitter O'Neill girls' account versus 14 000 followers for the general O'Neill account. O'Neill has 2212 subscribers on its YouTube channel and 1.7 million views.[11]

Brand websites are also essential for effectively sustaining or increasing the loyalty of user groups. A brand website is necessary for 'maintenance communication' all year round, 24 hours a day, with loyal customers and brand-lovers. If heavy users of a brand bond with the brand and the company, they will also expect to find more product information on the Internet and might even want to contact the people behind their favourite product. However, merely having a website is, in most cases, a waste of budget since only the leading brands supposedly benefit from spontaneous traffic towards their brand sites. Brands with a moderate or low unaided brand awareness are likely to be disillusioned by the reach of their website. Hence, websites need continuous traffic-generating efforts. Successful traffic generators are online advertising, search engine optimisation and including the URL on corporate media (stationery such as business cards, letter headings and brochures), on packaging and in offline advertising. The way a site is marketed has a substantial impact on the types of customers it attracts. Loyal customers are attracted by referrals, whereas promotional discounts and general untargeted banner advertising attract 'butterflies'.[12]

BUSINESS INSIGHT
Kaiser Chiefs release more than 600 000 versions of their new album

Instead of releasing their fourth CD in the traditional way, the British band Kaiser Chiefs posted the 20 songs on their new album 'The future is medieval' on a dedicated Internet site. For €8.50 fans could download a selection of ten songs in their own preferred order, along with a cover. In that way, more than 600 000 versions of a ten song album could be composed. Further, you could put your version up for sale, and earn £1 per unit sold.

The band claim that they 'wanted to do something new'. They acknowledged that the Internet is the future of music distribution. The unique selling idea is that fans can also earn some money on the release of the new album. Nevertheless, the whole idea is controversial. Traditionally, all songs on a new album are combined in a certain order on a fixed medium (a CD) that, together with the artwork, reflect an artistic project and vision. This concept is lost in the online project.

The team had to develop new website technology to accommodate the new business model. PayPal assisted in organising the payment flows, to learn more about this new model. Universal, the distributor of the Kaiser Chief albums, was enthusiastic because of the huge free publicity that the project generated. The money that went into developing the technology was easily earned back because marketing costs were drastically cut. As expected, the initiative drew so much media attention that any extra promotion efforts were not needed.

In spite of the success of the initiative, in mid-2011 the album was also released on a traditional CD, although the band acknowledged that this was done 'for old times' sake'. However, young people do not associate music with disks. Today music is something that is available on the Internet and that you listen to on your iPod.[13]

A brand site does not have to be hosted continuously but can be used for a short period during a product launch. These temporary sites are also called **micro-sites**. The growing complexity of corporate sites and the limitations of banner advertising have induced advertisers to develop this new way of providing richer online experiences with more complex messages (than traditional media). A micro-site is a small website that exists for a specific purpose, and often does not contain more than five or six pages. Companies often buy a specific URL related to the launch or promotion of a new product or service and then use the micro-site to enhance brand experience and to create brand/product excitement without revamping the existing website. It is a good way to isolate a user and maintain his or her attention to one product or a specific range of products. This is exactly what the Belgian band Absyn the Minded did when they created www.mostexclusivevideoever.com. On this micro-site the video clip of their new song 'Space' was only displayed each time a music station actually played their song. The video was exclusively available on this site, not on TV, nor via YouTube or any other music site.[14]

Retailers frequently use micro-sites to highlight certain goods out of their massive assortment. Because of the many possibilities of adding content, audio, video and interaction, micro-sites have many advantages over banners and other standardised ad formats. But, just like a standard brand or company site, micro-sites need promotion to be found and noticed by the target group. Micro-site-based campaigns have a limited shelf life that is comparable with any other advertising campaign. For companies selling low-interest or impulse-buy products, such as insurance companies or fast-moving consumer packaged goods such as soft drinks and candy bars, micro-sites are an interesting alternative to large and expensive websites that often demand enormous efforts to generate traffic to them. Direct and/or mass marketing can drive an audience directly to the specific URL, so that the pertinent information is only a few clicks away, ideal for search engine optimisation. Besides being easy to remember, a specific URL can help increase a brand's micro-site's presence in organic search engine results, driving more traffic and elevating perceived expertise.

BUSINESS INSIGHT
French wines: a touch of magic

To promote French wines to the UK, a campaign wanted to prove that there really is a French wine for every occasion. In addition, the agency wanted to recommend specific wines to accompany local dishes by region, while simultaneously promoting tourism in France. To meet the above challenge a micro-site was set up. Traffic towards this specific site was effectuated via a partnership with BBC Good Food. Display ads on the homepage bbcgoodfood.com directed users to the micro-site. In addition, users could click on a feature in the wine section of the website. This took them to a bespoke micro-site, where the client's branding dominated. By exploring this micro-site visitors could discover the climate of the region, and the resulting obstacles that vineyards encounter when growing grapes there. On further discovery, they could find historic facts about the region, must-see travel destinations to visit and recommended recipes to go with each type of wine. A separate section of the website featured a competition, allowing users to win a two-night trip to the French wine region of their choice by answering a question on the content.

After being exposed to the display advertising, over a third of the respondents said they would benefit in some way from seeing the ad, and 27% pretended to look for more information. Respondents were also more likely to visit the website, visit in-store and buy something after seeing display ads on the site.[15]

Search engine optimisation

The biggest issue with having a brand or company website is to attract visitors to the site. Unlike traditional advertising with its interruptive nature, online marketing communications often require an action from the consumer as the Internet is a pull medium. To find this, traffic marketers use a combination of offline and online marketing communications techniques. One specific online technique is **search engine optimisation (SEO)**, improving the listing in search engines. A survey conducted by PEW Internet in May 2011 revealed that 92% of the online adults use search engines to find information on the Web. This places search at the top of the list of most often used online activities among US adults.[16] The search engine is the new homepage for brands and businesses.

Search engine optimisation is important to many companies, not least to online stores and e-commerce sites. Some web agencies are specialists in registering sites in top and niche search engines and in improving their rankings on the engine. For this purpose, they use specific metatags, page titles, reciprocal linking, hidden keywords and multiple domain names as these are the factors that influence search engine robots' behaviour. Today the dynamics (frequency of changing content, links towards the site, likes/shares of site content via social media such as Facebook and Twitter, etc.) on the site are also taken in consideration to rank the site in the result list.

Another way of increasing search engine share-of-voice is **keyword buying**, one of the online advertising techniques explained below.[17]

Online advertising

Online advertising can be defined as commercial messages on specific rented spaces on websites of other companies. Whereas global advertising spending is growing by nearly 4%, global *online* ad spending is expected to grow by another 16% year on year up to nearly €76 billion by the end of 2012. By the end of the same year US online ad spending is expected to surpass print spending in newspapers and magazines. The current share of online ad spending of 19% of global ad spending is forecast to make 22% worldwide in 2015.[18] In the UK, online advertising is likely to grow by around 11% to €5.9 billion in 2012, whereas TV is set to increase by just 0.7%. Print will also increase by only 0.3%, with other traditional methods of advertising, mostly radio, increasing by 2.6%. Europe solidifies its online advertising position even further with an 11.7% increase in online ad spending predicted against 3.4% for TV. Already in 2011 video was the fastest-growing form of online advertising and will continue to be in 2012. Banner ads also play a key role in the advertising campaigns of online marketers, due to their ability to be adapted for both desktop and mobile devices, the latter of which is set to become a major advertising platform as smart phone penetration increases.[19] **Banner ads** are graphic images (animated gifs or Java applets) used as ads. Several formats (defined by number of pixels) exist: some are known as **buttons** (very small rectangles or squares), rectangles and **skyscrapers** (a thin and small format, typically along the right side of a web page). These are a popular choice as they remain in view as the reader scrolls down the page. A good banner ad campaign might include a mixture of different sizes and positions for banner ads. Next to the size, the choice needs to be made whether the banner ad needs to be static or animated or even incorporate sound. Apart from banners and their variants, other forms such as pop-ups and interstitials exist. **Pop-ups** are banners that appear in a separate window on top of or beneath (in which case they are called **pop-unders**) the visited website. **Interstitials** are ads that appear temporarily when loading a new web page. Sometimes they cover part of the browser; sometimes they take over the entire screen. **Superstitials** are additional pop-up browser windows that are opened when a new web page is opened; they are very intrusive and irritating. Interstitials can be static (an image file) or dynamic. In the latter case, they often consist of a so-called **rich media ad**, i.e. an ad using animated content such as audio/video, Flash, Java, etc., to create special effects, interaction, or moving or floating ads. The floating ad that moves over the browser in an animated way and is usually very effective in getting the attention of the website visitor is also called '**shoskele**' or overt. Some newer and popular types of online ads are wallpaper, where an ad appears and changes the background of the website, and billboards.

RESEARCH INSIGHT

Size matters: large ads boost brand awareness

According to new research conducted by Millward Brown, the new large-display ad formats such as 'Billboard' and 'Wallpaper' are outperforming standard banners such as Mid-Page Unit (MPU) banner (flash or movie banner) against key brand metrics, especially at the start of the purchase funnel.

The study was based on 940 campaigns over a two-year period across the UK, USA, Europe, South America and Australasia and examined the performance of formats on the following key brand metrics: aided brand awareness, online ad awareness, message association, brand favourability and purchase intent.

Six formats were analysed, three new (billboard, wallpaper and half-page) and three already-established formats (skyscraper, MPU and banner). The results highlight the performance of the different ad formats against brand metrics by showing the average uplift achieved by exposure to each format:

- The billboard outperformed the other formats analysed. It offered three times better ad awareness levels and double the level of brand favourability uplift than the next best-performing format (wallpaper).
- The wallpaper format provided five times the level of message association and the highest level of brand awareness.
- The skyscraper outperformed other formats at the end of the purchase funnel, achieving an uplift of 1.4 percentage points for purchase intent.[20]
- The Thomas Cook travel group is offering different banner ad possibilities for third parties on its websites.[21]

A specific type of targeted online advertising is **keyword buying**, also known as **search engine advertising (SEA)**. This is advertising on large search engines such as Google, Yahoo!, Bing, etc., that is triggered by specific keywords and search terms and which appears alongside and sometimes above or below the search results. Keyword buying is all about placing a catchy ad on several relevant websites, blogs and social media to bring more visitors to the target website if the user clicks on the ad. These 'smart ads' ensure higher impact and low waste for advertisers looking to target genuine potential customers. This type of advertising uses the unique benefits of the Web as a pull medium.[22] Unlike the other types of online advertising that are CPM-based (cost per thousand) ad formats, keyword buying uses a **pay per click model**. This means that advertisers only pay for each click-through on their sponsored link. The prices per click vary and are set by bidding on keyword combinations. The more popular the keyword, the more expensive it is. Search engine marketing (SEM) is one of the fastest-growing online advertising businesses.

BUSINESS INSIGHT
Gulf Stream keyword advertising campaign

Gulf Stream Gear sells custom boat lettering and apparel online through nationally targeted campaigns. Over 11 months, 127 403 visits were driven to the site of which 1594 produced sales. As the average cost per sale is $37.78 and the average basket is $175 and up, the Adwords campaign turns out to be very profitable. The sales tend to slow during winter. Therefore a special holiday season campaign was created. To increase sales the focus was on boating, yachting and fishing gifts tailoring keyword and ad text to holiday sales. During December 2009, there were 10 068 visits, 162 of which made a purchase at an average of $31.98 per sale. During winter, the focus was on the trade shows to drive traffic and sales at these trade shows. Advertising is responsible for over 80% of the site's overall traffic.[23]

Another smart way of linking is **affiliate marketing** or **affiliate networking**. Online retailers often use this performance-based marketing in which a business rewards one or more affiliates for each visitor brought about by the affiliate's own marketing efforts. Affiliates often use regular advertising methods such as organic search engine optimisation (SEO), paid search engine marketing, e-mail marketing and display advertising.[24] There are several options for affiliate compensation: commission (for every sale which is a direct result of click-through traffic from the affiliate's website), pay per click, pay per lead (for every person who signs up for something), residual income (for every time a customer renews a service or purchases additional products after initial click-through from an affiliate's website) or pay per sale (for every time a person purchases a product or service after clicking through an affiliate's website).[25]

Amazon.com, the online book and CD shop, does not use an affiliate network which would take commissions from sales, but has developed its own affiliate programme and offers a wide range of methods of linking to its site to help improve conversion. For example, affiliates can use straight text links leading direct to a product page, or they can use dynamic banners that feature different content such as books about Internet marketing or a search box. Amazon created tiered performance-based incentives to encourage affiliates to sell more Amazon products.[26] For Amazon, this affiliate network accounts for a quarter of its revenue.[27] For its part, Amazon displays relevant Google text ads and banner ads from brands. In 2011, Amazon revealed that worldwide media sales accounted for 17% of its total revenue. As for the rest of its marketing approach, Amazon does not reveal much in its annual reports, but it is clear that there is a focus on targeted online marketing, sponsored search, interactive portal advertising, e-mail campaigns and search engine optimisation.[28]

RESEARCH INSIGHT
Impact measurement of online campaigns[29]

Online advertising formats are more developed, videos are more sophisticated, targeting tools are more focused and advertisers are gradually directing their communications budgets towards online advertising. It is clear that measuring online performance has become critical. A study conducted in 2010 by PWC for IAB France highlighted some interesting insights. For display advertising campaigns, the click-through rate remains the most widely used indicator. But this rate says nothing about the impact of a campaign on a brand's image or on the browsing or purchasing behaviour. Several studies demonstrate the impact that the Web has on a brand. For example, an analysis conducted on a campaign run by a catering firm reveals that brand identification improved by 10%. By studying display advertising campaigns run by four advertisers from different industries, Médiamétrie Net Ratings indicated that the purchase intent of Internet users who were exposed to these campaigns increased by 11%. In a study of 73 display advertising campaigns reaching 100 000 Internet users, United Internet Media found that the Internet enabled the rate of aided brand awareness to jump by 26%.

Indicators other than the click-through rate can help determine the impact that online advertising has on branding: for example, indicators such as exposure (the actual visibility of a display ad and the average time during which Internet users are exposed to the ad) and interaction. Several studies have revealed a close correlation between interaction and impact on a brand's reputation and image. By assessing the Internet users' engagement (browsing behaviour, depth, duration and actions) on a website, advertisers can measure the impact of their online branding campaigns. In 2010, 8 out of 10 Internet users interviewed by Médiamétrie reported consulting a website before purchasing a product. This behaviour is confirmed in a study conducted by comScore. The exposure to display advertising campaigns resulted in a 10% increase in shop sales. Exposure to advertising also has an impact on the behaviour of Internet users on the brand website. A 2009 study by the Online Publishers Association reports that the time spent by Internet users on websites is on average 50% higher following exposure to a display advertising campaign. The PWC study, based on experts' interviews and desk research, indicates five levels for effectively measuring online advertising and nine categories of indicators for measuring online performance. The study also reveals that with the growing online advertising possibilities, the use of some measuring methods is still developing.

Five levels for effectively measuring online advertising

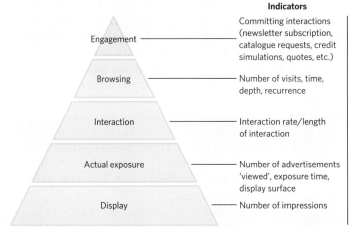

	Indicators	Level of maturity and trend in use
Engagement	Committing interactions (newsletter subscription, catalogue requests, credit simulations, quotes, etc.)	Developing, depending on advertisers Often associated with purchases Through recommendations Still not widely used for measuring branding
Browsing	Number of visits, time, depth, recurrence	Mature and fundamental for online retailers Developing for brand-focused Advertisers
Interaction	Interaction rate/length of interaction	Developing rapidly, in line with Growth in rich media and video Often only partially exploited
Actual exposure	Number of advertisements 'viewed', exposure time, display surface	On the rise, being trialled By many advertisers Not yet fully available
Display	Number of impressions	Mature, minimum indicator

Nine categories of indicators for measuring online performance

Display
- Number of impressions
- Number of 'visible' advertisements
- Number of advertisements viewed
- Exposure time

Conversion
- Clickthrough rate
- Conversion rate
- Post-view conversion rate
- Post-click conversion rate

Traffic
- Number of visits generated
- Number of pages viewed
- Lengh of visit
- Abandon rate

Interaction
- Interaction rate
- Interaction time
- Expansion rate
- Rate of videos viewed
- Rate of videos viewed in full
- Video viewing time
- Activity on social networks

Subscription
- Number of subscriptions (requests for information, games, newsletters, etc.)
- Subscription rate
- Recommendation rate (social networks, viral e-marketing campaigns)

Media
- Gross rating point (GRP)
- Memorised coverage
- Coverage rate
- Message repetition rate

Distribution
- Additional sales generated
- Revenue generated
- Lead conversion rate
- Impact on the frequency and volume of purchases
- Retail outlet traffic generated by the Web

ROI
- Acquisition cost (offline vs online)
- ROI (revenue generated/advertising expenditure)

Post-tests
- Impact on awareness
- Impact on advertisement recall
- Impact on brand image
- Impact on purchase intentions
- Impact on recommendations

Source: From *Measuring the effectiveness of online advertising: Study conducted by PwC for IAB France and the SRI* (2010).

Less standard advertising formats are advertorials, content sponsorship and anchor deals. These three formats are not supported by media sellers and so result from direct negotiations with each specific website owner. **Advertorials** are informative ads with an editorial approach but also a clearly identified advertiser. They can be used to communicate product and services news or attributes, third-party endorsements, research or trends and can include visuals and links to the site of the advertising company. The content of the advertorial should be informative and engaging. Advertorials improve the opinion about the sponsoring company and increase awareness, influence image and encourage interest.

Content sponsorship consists of placing an advertiser's message in an area on a website that stands out from other ads, for instance a fixed and exclusive presence in a chosen section that is relevant to the advertiser's brand. Area and topic sponsorships are the two most common types. Homepage restyling, an adaptation of the look and feel of a web page using the colours, corporate style and images of the advertisers, is another popular form. Many consumer product companies are moving towards this kind of online alliance strategy after being confronted with the long development timeframes and the high costs involved with building, maintaining and driving traffic towards an own-brand site.

BUSINESS INSIGHT
Using the Internet to launch brands

In March 2011, Johnson & Johnson introduced Listerine Zero (a new mouthwash product) onto the Australian market. In June, an online-only test campaign (among others, on Facebook and different search engine sites) was set up for the purpose of evaluating the impact of online advertising on sales and the brand. No media activity or POS occurred prior to this test, conducted by Nielsen. The test campaign managed to reach a wide audience: 44% of the target of 25–54 year olds. Exposure to the campaign significantly increased a number of brand equity measures for Listerine Zero: awareness (from 5% to 11%), consideration (from 3% to 6%), recommendation (from 14% to 35%) and purchase intention (from 13% to 43%). Sales increased by 11% across the market.[30]

The IAB UK conducted a study on the effectiveness of the online launch campaign of Starbucks VIA, a new instant premium coffee brand. For the launch, display ads were shown at portals sites (such as Yahoo!), lifestyle sites (such as InStyle.co.uk and Marieclaire.co.uk) and social sites (such as Facebook). The online campaign reached 52% of the online population. Online delivered substantial incremental reach as 65% of those exposed to online ads did not see the print ad; 55% of those exposed to online ads did not see the outdoor activity. When compared with other media, online was the biggest driver of reach – and the most cost-effective. The online campaign was seen to deliver this audience at a fifth of the cost of the press campaign, which illustrates that digital advertising delivers strong results at a competitive price. A major strength of online is its ability to drive awareness, making it a strong tool for launching new brands.

Product awareness grew by 19% between the control group and the exposed group. Among heavy Internet users (usage of over 21 hours per week), product awareness increased by 77%. Meanwhile, ad awareness rose by 41% between the two groups.

Women's purchase intent increased sharply across age groups (+40% in women aged between 35–44 and 55+). Online was found to deliver the increase in product awareness at 80% the cost of press and half the cost of outdoors.[31]

Anchor deals represent the presence of a brand on certain content sites and portals as a supplier of brand-related content continuously for a long period. In exchange for co-branding on all Pepsi bottles, in-store displays and so on, Yahoo! handled all the technical assistance for the Pepsistuff.com website. The site became the centrepiece of the most successful campaign Pepsi ever ran. Consumers logged on to the site by entering a code found under the caps of

Pepsi bottles. Each code was worth 100 points and could be redeemed for prizes such as DVDs and digital rewards (music downloads, credits at Yahoo! auctions, etc.). More than 50% of redeemed prizes were digital, saving Pepsi lots of money. Pepsi also saved $10 million by not having to print prize catalogues, and the anchor deal with Yahoo! resulted in 2.9 million people providing their name, e-mail address, zip code and date of birth, a valuable database for organising polls, launching new products such as Pepsi Blue (the Pepsi-with-berries fusion launched in Spring 2003) and promoting the music celebrity endorsement with Britney Spears and Shakira.

Targeting online advertising

Online advertising is most effective when it is well-targeted. Marketers can target broadly using content targeting or specifically using several criteria:

- *Context/content targeting.* Web page content and context can be used to target online ads. For example, Unilever targeted people interested in cooking and lifestyle (predominantly women aged between 20 and 49) for its brands Hertog, Knorr, Maggi and Blue Band by using advertorials and content sponsoring on the website of *Life & Cooking*, a TV cookery programme in the Netherlands.[32]
- *Web server/browser.* A web server or ad server can deliver ads based on the profile of the user connected to the site, including IP (Internet Protocol) address, browser, operating system and the date and time of the server request. A marketer can display targeted ads based on these simple characteristics, for instance IP addresses reveal the geographic location of the user.
- *Registration/customer data.* A website or ad network can show targeted ads based on user registration data (obtained from memberships, participating in contests, purchases, etc.).
- *Clickstream/behavioural data.* As visitors click through a site or different sites, ad networks and sites can show ads that are related to the kind of content the Internet user is viewing. A study from the Network Advertising Initiative found that the conversion rate for behavioural targeted ads was 6.8% while non-targeted ads performed comparatively poorly with 2.8%.[33]
- *Collaborative filtering.* Online ads can be shown to a particular user based on matching his or her profile with other users that share common interests.[34]

Online events and web(sem)inars

Even face-to-face communications tactics such as exhibitions, trade shows and events have been translated to an online environment. Victoria's Secret, the American undergarment brand, introduced one of the first commercial online events in 1999 when it held its Web-based fashion show. It was announced in ads in the *New York Times*, TV commercials during the Super Bowl football game and other traditional advertising media. The online event drew 1.2 million visitors, an 82% increase in web traffic. In subsequent years the online fashion shows were continued. Web(sem)inars, with experts that first give an exposition and after-wards participate in chat sessions, are also becoming more common in business-to-business markets and professional segments, as discussed previously on exhibitions and trade fairs and on online trade fairs. An interesting Web 2.0. online service is SlideShare, the world's largest community for sharing presentations. It has 58 million monthly visitors and 16 million registered users. Besides presentations, SlideShare also supports documents, PDFs, videos and webinars. Launched in October 2006, SlideShare was voted among the world's top 10 tools for education and e-learning in 2010.[35]

Advergames and online games

Advergames are a rich media type of brand-related online entertainment used as a tool for brand interaction and experience. In other words, advergames use interactive game technology to deliver embedded messages to consumers. The advertising message can then become an integral part of playing the game. Advergames are often used in combination with e-mail and viral marketing campaigns as their entertainment value increases the value perception of the mail receivers and tends to evoke consumer responses beyond their own personal interaction, such as forwarding the message to friends and relatives. In this way, advergames can reach up to four times the initial number of gamers through referrals. Gaming is getting more and more attention. In June 2011, 25.2 million Germans visited online gaming sites, an increase of 8% compared with the previous year. Online gaming now reaches 46% of German Internet users. In addition to online gaming on computers, mobile gaming is on the up: 14.1 million mobile phone users have played at least one game on their mobile device during a three-month average ending June 2011.[36]

Game advertising can have the following objectives:

- *Building brand/product awareness.* The ultimate way to succeed in this is to build a game or game portal around your own brand or products. As the awareness objective is mostly linked to the ambition of reaching a great part of your target group, this might not be the right option to take unless enough media support can be given. Using existing game traffic could be another strategy to take into consideration.

- *Driving traffic.* Using the enormous number of gamers visiting games, game portals, virtual worlds or online games are among the possibilities. Another can be to add a viral marketing element to your campaign, so users can invite other gamers.

- *Conversion/sales.* For many campaigns this is the ultimate goal. Because more and more e-commerce is taking place, the conversion of the visitor into buying behaviour can be better monitored. The biggest sales impact is seen when games are used as premiums or as co-brands.

- *Collecting data.* Games are also often used to build up a database for direct marketing/mailing purposes by returning a free (branded) game as a counterpart for personal information given by the surfer.

- *Education.* This can be the main goal in the case of 'serious games'. Games can tackle serious topics in a more accessible way. Games for kids are often used to teach them certain capabilities and knowledge in a playful way. Management issues can also be tackled in games.[37]

BUSINESS INSIGHT
Using online games as marketing communications tools

Candy producer Nabisco launched its own game portal site Candystand.com in 1997. Each month, this portal site attracts 3.5 million visits, with each visit lasting on average half an hour. In February 2007, Candystand.com became one of the first free game portals to offer an interface for the Wii at wii.candystand.com. Today the site is owned by Funtank.[38] Since the end of 2010, this game has also been available as an iPad app.

In April 2011, Unilever launched 'The Magnum Pleasure Hunt (across the Internet)' to market the new Magnum ice cream Temptation Fruit. It was the most tweeted web address in the world within just one week of launch. At first, when visiting the site, you are guided how to move a Magnum girl with the arrow keys, as in a computer game. Then the action takes off. The girl runs along different websites and brand pages (Samsung, Dove, some touristic sites, jewellery, Bed Head hair products, Spotify, Saab, etc.) where she is interacting with things on the pages while you have to get her to collect cranberries. According to Adverblog, a professional ballet dancer was chosen to get all the moves right.[39]

Following this success, where an impressive 7 million players took part, Unilever launched a follow-up in April 2012, 'Magnum Pleasure Hunt 2 across the globe' to support the launch of its new variety Magnum Infinity. Again, you have to control the female character but this time the journey travels through New York, Paris and Rio – collecting 'bonbons' and cocoa nibs along the way using Bing maps Streetside view interface. She passes famous brands such as luxury Italian jeweller Bvlgari, on-trend surf manufacturer Quicksilver, KLM Royal Dutch Airlines and the exclusive Hotel Fasano in Rio de Janeiro. From street lamps to road signs, each backdrop featured within the game was built to perfection from a staggering 6500 photographs and 3-D recreation, ensuring the game boasts an astoundingly life-like look and feel.[40]

In Amsterdam, this campaign was taken a little further and extended it into a real-time mobile augmented reality game for one day. There were 150 chocolate bonbons hidden across the '9 straatjes' (a trendy district) of Amsterdam. The aim was to collect them at first through the augmented reality app, and win a trip to New York.[41]

Source: GAIA.

In April 2011, the Mobile operator Sonera was the first to open 4G, the world's fastest mobile connection, in Finland. Since 4G is all about speed, Sonera created a game – a reaction speed test. The communication was done via a communications campaign in print magazines adding a QR-code. By scanning this code with a mobile phone, one could challenge oneself and a friend and win a Sonera 4G connection.[42]

Belgian animal rights organisation GAIA developed an online Facebook game as part of its annual 'Boycott-cot!' campaign in 2012. 'Chicken Squeeze' is a new 'Tetris-like' online game that challenges players to earn eggs (points) by putting as many hens as possible in ridiculously small spaces. At the end of the game, (battery) cages appear. Once the game is played, with a simple click players can participate in an online petition action against battery cage eggs. An e-mail with the demand to stop using battery cage eggs is sent to the Belgian supermarkets which are still using eggs of millions of (battery) chickens in all sorts of products such as mayonnaise, pasta and biscuits.[43]

There are three main types of advergames:[44]

- *Sponsored games.* Apart from the audience fit, there is no direct link to the advertiser. The brand simply pays to have its name on an existing game.

- *A game specially created to promote a brand or product.* Barclaycard's Waterslide TV advert tie-in iPhone game became the most popular free branded advertising game in the history of the iTunes app store within 13 days of its release back in 2009.

- *A game created around a business or product function.* This is done in order to increase user engagement and purchase frequency by demonstrating brand attributes.

Qantas has a frequent flyer app that encourages both engagement and purchase. This is known as gamification (the use of game design techniques, game thinking and game mechanics to enhance non-game contexts).[45] Another popular example is 'Foursquare' which is a web and mobile application that allows registered users to post their location at a venue ('check-in'), and connect with friends and share experiences. Every check-in (shops, hotels, restaurants, etc.) is awarded with points to unlock badges for the things members do in the real world and compete with their friends. As of April 2012, there were more than 2 billion check-ins with Foursquare. Users can choose to have their check-ins posted on their accounts on Twitter, Facebook, or both.[46]

Applying this kind of game thinking is having a profound effect across business, government and even the sciences. The 'Fold It' project, for example, aims to find cures for diseases such as AIDS, cancer and Alzheimer's through puzzle-solving. In September 2011 the Fold It players used human intuition to solve in a few days an enzyme structure problem which had been befuddling researchers for years. This has potential, as reported on the BBC, to pave the way for the development of anti-AIDS drugs.[47]

Although the costs of creating an advergame clearly exceed those of rich-media banners, interaction time and brand immersion should be considered as well. Online games and advergames are tools that permit the online marketer to build brand awareness and brand image through a more interactive user experience.[48] For example, players of the 'Jurassic Park III' game played for an average of 19 minutes, which is obviously a guarantee of a bigger mind-share among the target groups. The retention value of advergames is said to be ten times higher than the retention value of traditional broadcast commercials. They allow voluntary self-induced exposure to brand communications and are a non-intrusive and non-interruptive means of internet advertising.[49]

RESEARCH INSIGHT

Children in a changing media environment: persuasion knowledge for integrated advertising formats

Compared with earlier generations, today's children are overwhelmed by an increasing amount of commercial messages. As a result, advertisers are adopting alternative advertising techniques in order to break through this ad clutter and capture their attention.[50] One of these techniques is the integration of the persuasive message *into* the media content itself. By doing so, the involved audience are exposed to the ad during the natural process of watching a movie or programme, playing a game etc.[51] The integrated nature of this technique not only makes it impossible for viewers to skip the ads, but also implies that they are exposed to the commercial message and the media content at the same time. This results in blurred boundaries between advertising, entertainment and information.[52]

One of the most common theoretical explanations to describe children's understanding of the persuasive intention of commercial messages is the Persuasion Knowledge Model (PKM).[53] According to the PKM, persuasion knowledge is the knowledge that consumers develop about marketers' motives and tactics. This knowledge helps them to identify how, when and why marketers are trying to influence them. As a result, people are able to critically process the ad and 'cognitively defend' themselves against its persuasive influences. With young children, however, this knowledge is not yet fully developed. Since the traditional, linear advertising formats no longer dominate the media environment that children live in, today's media environment is characterised by integrated advertising formats. This trend demands a re-evaluation of the insights concerning the development of children's persuasion knowledge.

An exploratory qualitative study set out to investigate the persuasion knowledge of children when exposed to various new advertising formats which are embedded into different media contents. Three different advertising formats, namely product placement in a TV programme, an advertiser-funded TV programme and an advergame, were tested. Children from three different age groups (4–6, 7–8, 9–12 years) participated in this qualitative study to investigate at which age persuasion knowledge is developed for each of these formats. The results of this study were obtained from 30 in-depth interviews with children between 4 and 12 years old. To further elaborate on these findings, nine additional focus groups were conducted. In both the interviews and the focus groups, children were confronted with several advertising formats. The stimuli consisted of an advergame for McDonald's, a fragment from a TV programme (a craft programme for children) containing product placement ('Pritt' a glue stick often used by children) and a fragment of an AFP (a TV show set in a popular amusement park, with the park being an important part of the storyline). After each exposure to an advertising format, the children were asked several questions in order to measure their level of persuasion knowledge with respect to that specific advertising format. Each interview was recorded and transcribed for later analyses.

Only 4 out of 30 children recognised the brand correctly after seeing the product placement fragment, while 25 out of 30 children recognised the brand correctly after seeing the AFP and 19 out of 30 children recognised the correct brand after seeing the advergame. This implies that the children had most difficulty spotting the brand when it is integrated into a TV programme. Brand recognition in the product placement format is low in all age groups. The brand in the advergame is better recognised when children grow older. As such, the youngest respondents had trouble recognising the brand, although it was prominently placed in the advergame. The older respondents recognised the brand immediately, even the more subtle brand connections. Finally, brand recognition within AFP is highest for the youngest and oldest respondents.

In general, it was difficult for the children to understand the commercial intent of the persuasive message. The answers concerning the commercial intent of each format differ considerably between the three formats. In particular, while 15 out of 30 children think that playing a funny game is the main purpose of the advergame, and 20 out of 30 children think that watching a nice TV programme is the main purpose of the product placement fragment, only 9 out of 30 children think that watching a nice TV programme is the main purpose of AFP. Accordingly, 17 out of 30 children figured out correctly that the commercial intent of the AFP is to buy or like the integrated products. However, while the oldest children knew the programme was made to make them buy something, younger children replied that the programme was made 'so that they would have something to watch'. Also, the two youngest groups were convinced that the TV programme was made by the researchers or a camera man, while the oldest children knew this was made by the advertiser. Only in 4 of the 30 cases did children correctly understand the commercial intent of the product placement fragment. Children from the first and second age group did not notice the commercial message. They did not mention the brand and when asked if the programme wants to sell them something, they all answered that this is not the case. In the oldest group, some children indicated that they saw a brand. They mentioned that the TV channel probably 'works together' with that brand, and that it was paid to show the brand. Although not all the children recognised the placement, most of them seemed to know that this is a common practice in TV programmes. The commercial intent of the advergame is correctly understood in 8 of the 30 cases. When asked why the game was made, the two youngest groups mainly replied that it was made so that they could play a funny game on the Internet, while the oldest group indicated that it is to convince them to visit McDonald's and spend money there. Accordingly, when asked who made the game, the youngest children replied 'you' meaning the researcher or 'the computer man'. Some children from the second age group replied 'McDonald's' but they were not sure. The oldest children, on the other hand, all answered 'McDonald's' right away. This implies that the youngest groups had no idea of the commercial intent of the game. When asked if the game tries to sell them something, they were all convinced that this is not the case. One respondent from the second age group replied 'I don't understand why McDonald's is pictured in that game. That's for eating, why is it in a game? That is strange.'

In general, children have difficulties recognising and understanding the persuasive intention of the integrated commercial content. Especially for product placement, this seemed to be hard for all age groups. The ad recognition and understanding of AFP was highest. For advergames the results show that children could recognise the ad embedded in the game, but had problems in understanding its underlying commercial intent.

Example of the questionnaire used for each of the advertising formats

Format 1: McDonald's Advergame

1. Did you see one of these things in the game?

Pritt logo	McDonald's logo	OLA logo	KZOOM logo	Efteling logo
Delhaize logo	K3 logo	Kellogg's logo	'Rocket' ice logo	Ketnet logo

2. Who do you think made this game?

| Ketnet (TV channel) | McDonald's | The teacher | The researcher | Someone else |

3. What is the purpose of this game? Choose the answer that you think is correct:

| Teach me how to use the computer | To play a fun game | To make me like McDonald's | To make me happy | To visit McDonald's or ask mum or dad to go there |

As the penetration of smart phones is growing, European gaming gets more social (connect, compete and socialise with friends and others). According to a study conducted by comScore, 42% of people in the EU5 countries played a game on their mobile device during February 2012, with the UK leading the way. In the same period, 6.1 million EU5 smart-phone gamers logged into a social game on their devices, an increase of 42% in the past six months, representing 13.2% of smart-phone gamers overall.[54]

Viral marketing

Quite often the success of advergames and online games depends strongly on the strength of online word-of-mouth advertising, also called 'word-of-mouse' advertising. **Viral marketing** is a set of techniques that is used to spur brand users and lovers, game participants or advocate consumers among the target group to promote their favourite brand to friends and relatives. They are put to work to spread the word about the brand or product by using e-mail, SMS, 'tell or send to a friend' buttons or via different social media sites as Facebook, Google+, YouTube, review sites and influential blogs. Viral marketing attempts to harness the strongest of all consumer triggers: namely, personal recommendation. Viral marketing uses the snowball principle, and the typical network nature of the Internet strongly supports rapid exponential growth in the message's exposure and its influence in a relatively effortless manner. Just like viruses, viral marketing strategies take advantage of rapid multiplication to explode the message to thousands or millions of 'victims'. One of the first viral campaigns was set up by Hotmail. By simply using the free Web-based e-mail package, consumers hawked the message as every message they sent contained a Hotmail ad ('Get your own private free e-mail at http://www.hotmail.com'). Hotmail grew to 12 million accounts in its first year, 1996. Compared with the results of its print campaigns (100 000 new subscribers), this result was impressive.[55]

BUSINESS INSIGHT
Successful viral marketing campaigns

Two of the most shared videos on YouTube use humour. In February 2011, Volkswagen launched the viral marketing campaign 'The Force', featuring a pint-sized Darth Vader, to introduce the new 2012 Passat. A week before the Super Bowl, teaser videos and eventually the full video were seeded. This effort received a major buzz with 13.7 million views prior to the game. Volkswagen used its own social channels as an integral part of its digital activation, Facebook, Twitter and YouTube, next to featuring the Passat spot on the homepages of MSN and Yahoo!. As a result over 120 blogs and media outlets mentioned the spots, including *Perez Hilton*, *AdWeek*, *New York Times*, *MotorTrend*, *BrandWeek* and *Jalopnik*. During Super Bowl Sunday Volkswagen secured exclusive ownership of ESPN's mobile site to be part of the conversation that day. The day after the big game the homepage of YouTube was secured to capitalise on the post-game buzz. To further sustain the buzz, additional video content (like behind the scenes, bloopers, etc.) was released. On YouTube, the award winning 'The Force' commercial received over 53 million views and 203 000 likes by mid-May 2012. During the week of the Super Bowl, daily Facebook interaction rates (likes and comments) were up 214%, and VW added over 12 000 fans in just one week. On Twitter, the average click-through per tweet was 820, an increase of 925%. During this same time period, VW added more than 500 followers.[56]

The second most shared ad of all time is a promotional video posted by the American TV channel TNT for its launch in Belgium. The flash mob-style PR stunt was launched exclusively via social media and on the TNT website, though there was also a short trailer in cinemas on the continent for two weeks. It has taken YouTube by storm, getting 10 million views in 24 hours, and 23 million views and 214 896 likes in just one week. TNT placed a large red button in the middle of a quiet square in a Belgian town along with a 'push to add drama' sign hanging near it. It then captured the reaction of the bemused, astounded crowd when one of them actually pushed the button. A series of dramatic events followed: the arrival of an ambulance with attendants dropping the 'patient' from the stretcher several times, a cyclist ramming into the ambulance's open door, and a fist fight between the cyclist and the burly ambulance driver. Including a scantily dressed woman on a motorbike being chased by a car, a fake encounter that left a person 'dead' and the bizarre arrival of a team of rugby players, led to a video that was dramatic in the true sense of the word. At the end of June 2012, the video had reached over 35 million views and 280 000 likes.[57] The ad has clearly been very successful at driving exposure for the brand. WaveMetrix analysed the nature of discussion around the video, to investigate how exactly it affected consumers' perceptions of TNT. The analysis reveals that consumers discuss the effectiveness of the video as an ad more than anything else: a great deal of comments praised the video as great advertising and said that they wish more ads were like this. However, only a small proportion of those comments discuss the TNT channel itself, a few saying they 'want to watch' because of the ad. The ad drives consumers to perceive TNT as a unique, clever brand.[58]

Viral marketing campaigns work best between groups with strong common interests. This implies that they allow marketers to spread selective messages to selective groups. By using viral marketing tactics carefully, marketers may avoid negative reactions and gain an excellent return on investment by increasing the reach of a marketing message to a targeted group that is much larger than the audience originally covered. Viral marketing is increasingly popular for three reasons. Firstly, entire social networks are online today as a large number of everybody's friends and family members are using social media. Secondly, contacting individuals online is virtually cost-free, and it is possible for each individual to contact hundreds more without much effort or cost.[59] According to a survey, 81% of those who receive viral messages pass them on to at least one other person, and almost half of those receivers are likely to pass the message along to two or three other people.[60]

Finally, for 68% of surfers, word of mouth is the top source for learning about new websites, which puts referrals and viral marketing in second place after search engines (74%) and above links on other sites (65%), ads (46%) and online advertising (45%).[61] Several studies prove the power of word of mouth: 90% of the consumers trust recommendations from people they know; even 70% trust unknown users; 14% trust advertising while only 8% trust celebrities; 92% have more confidence in information found online than they do in anything from a salesperson or other source; 70% consult reviews or ratings before purchasing. The peer consumer has the power today.[62]

Just as with off line word-of-mouth advertising, word of mouse is not driven by marketers and it is hard to keep control over the messages. This could imply negative associations with the brand and a dilution of brand assets as the same strengths could work against a company if dissatisfied customers share their anger with their contacts. Therefore, marketers should consider pre-testing viral marketing campaigns on a small scale. If viral messages contain audio or video components, some Internet users might consider them as bandwidth and mailbox space-consuming 'spam' (unwanted and unsolicited e-mails).

RESEARCH INSIGHT

Balance and sequence in online reviews: how perceived usefulness affects attitudes and intentions

Traditional word-of-mouth (WOM) communications have been proven to influence both pre-purchase decisions as well as post-purchase product perceptions.[63] With the increasing use of the Internet and advancing information technology, this face-to-face or offline communications form now also takes place on various types of electronic word-of-mouth (eWOM) platforms, such as social and professional networking sites (Facebook, LinkedIn), consumer review websites (CNet, Epinions), online communities (fan sites), etc. In general, eWOM has been shown to affect consumers' attitudes and behaviours toward products and brands.[64]

More and more people exchange or share product information on the Internet and this available information allows other consumers to deliberate their purchase decision. Most consumers consider user-generated content such as online reviews as less intrusive than producer-generated content (e.g. advertising), because they actively search for the information themselves.[65] Information retrieved from user-generated sources is also generally perceived as more credible, and consequently more useful, than information generated by marketers. This is especially true for experience products, such as hotels and restaurants.[66] Assuming that consumers are consulting online reviews because they intend to buy a certain product or service, some reviews will be categorised as useful (i.e. helpful in making a decision about whether or not to buy or use the reviewed product or service), and others less so.[67]

A study of 413 respondents (M_{age} = 39 years, 38% male) investigated how the balance (the ratio of positive and negative reviews) and sequence (the order in which the reviews are presented) of a set of online reviews impact the perceived usefulness of these reviews as a set. In a second analysis of the study, it was investigated how the perceived usefulness of a review set moderates the relationship between readers' recall of review information, their impression about the reviews and their attitude and behavioural intention towards a reviewed hotel.[68] The main experiment was a 3 (balance: positive, neutral, negative) × 4 (sequence: positive/negative, negative/positive, positive/negative/positive, negative/positive/negative) full factorial between-subjects design. Each respondent read the same eight reviews as developed in a pre-test, but, depending on the condition, these were framed either positively or negatively, and were presented in a different order. Balance was manipulated by varying the proportion of positive and negative reviews presented in each set. For a positive balance, six out of eight reviews were positive, while the other two were negative. With a neutral balance, four positive and four negative reviews appeared. The negative balance consisted of six negative reviews and two positive reviews. Sequence was manipulated by altering the position of the negative and positive reviews within the set. One sequence presented the positive statements grouped together first, followed by all the negative statements in a set. The second sequence condition was the reverse of the first (negative first, followed by positive). The 'wrapped' conditions started with half of the positive (negative) reviews, followed by all the negative (positive) reviews, again followed by half of the positive (negative) reviews.

The results show that the perceived usefulness of an online review set is affected by its balance and sequence. Unbalanced (positive or negative) review sets are considered more useful than those that are balanced (neutral). Compared with balanced sets, unbalanced sets provide the reader with a clear general direction and therefore, consistent with the diagnosticity principle,[69] the balance of a set of reviews is accountable in determining whether or not the reviews are useful. As there are more individuals agreeing that the hotel is good (in case of positive balance) or bad (in case of negative balance) compared with the neutral conditions, the reader may have more confidence that the information is true. When there are too many conflicting opinions, and half of the group express a positive judgement while the other half pronounce a negative evaluation (i.e. in a neutral balance), this contradictory information leaves the reader at a loss about whether or not to buy this product, and this should be perceived as less useful than when the group utters a more straightforward opinion and the balance is clearly positive (negative).[70] As a result, such consistent information in the positive and negative balance is perceived as more useful than the relatively inconsistent information in the neutral balance.

There is also a sequence effect. When the balance of a set of reviews is clearly positive or negative, wrapping negative reviews in positive ones or vice versa significantly increases the perceived usefulness of the reviews. This is in line with the reinforcement of primacy and recency effects principle: both the first and the last elements in a list result in a higher impact in comparison with all other elements in the list. Other studies on sequence bias in an online environment have found evidence for primacy effects,[71] recency effects,[72] and primacy and recency effects reinforcement.[73]

After reading the reviews, potential buyers retain some of the review information in their short-term memory. This recalled information forms the basis of their attitudes and behavioural intention towards the reviewed object. When people perceive the reviews to be more useful, their impression towards the reviewed object becomes a stronger predictor of their attitude and behaviour than when they perceive the reviews to be less useful. These findings are also consistent with the accessibility–diagnosticity framework.

Online contests and sweepstakes

Related to online games are the Internet versions of contests and sweepstakes. They are particularly effective for generating enthusiasm, building brand recognition and rewarding long-time customers. Online contests often have an offline component, for instance in TV or radio ads to get attention, or on packaging, leaflets, etc., to communicate the contest. For easy access to the brand's website a QR-code can be added. Scanned via a smart phone it leads the consumer directly to the site. Sometimes other codes such as access codes or lottery numbers are distributed either in or on packaging but relate to the brand's (promotional contest) website. A contest should arouse a customer's interest and demand interaction. E-contests can just draw winners at random (sweepstake) or ask for a certain skill or creative involvement (contest).[74] For example, Heineken celebrated its 140th birthday by offering the design community the chance to create a limited edition bottle via Facebook. Part of the competition required the designer to pair up his or her design with another designer through Facebook.

Heineken received over 30 000 entries across 100 countries. The top 100 designs were presented to a jury in New York where they were judged on their creativity and also their complementary pairing. Heineken produced 1 million bottles of the winning design for worldwide sale.[75] Just like advergames, online contests seem to be growing in popularity. Keys to success are an appropriate play value of the contest and appropriate incentives to participate. The latter is determined by the business a company is involved in and the goal of the contest. For instance, if the objective of the contest is to create a customer database, a company should offer one of its products as a prize. This relevancy will attract the right entrants, since providing an incentive to people who can and will buy your products and services should be the goal. A contest or sweepstake with a high number of participants might look successful at first sight but, if it attracts the wrong people, namely those who enter any contest just to win something, the campaign will not be effective and customer acquisition costs will rise. Prizes should also create a sense of value, uniqueness and emotional appeal to winners. If the prize is large enough or attractive enough, people will take the time to enter and fulfil requirements such as registration and they will even share the contest with their friends and colleagues. Of course, contests and sweepstakes will only work if people know about them, and if you want people to come back regularly, it will be necessary to award prizes on a daily or weekly basis.[76]

E-sampling and e-couponing

Companies (especially those in the consumer packaged goods business) can use the Internet as a means of promoting their products by sampling or couponing, for instance banner advertising leads consumers to a data-capture page where they leave their details to receive samples or coupons. Traditionally, brands had few options for reaching consumers with a sample: sampling at events, on street corners, in the mailbox, with newspapers or magazines, on door hangers and in-store sampling. The Internet adds a new way of sampling (combined with mail addresses) at a lower cost per converted person because of the opt-in request.

E-sampling gives marketers the option to carry out extremely accurate one-to-one demographic, geographic and psychographic targeting, whereas traditional sampling is often based on convenience targeting (street corners, shop) or neighbourhood clusters (mailbox sampling). There is also less waste or duplication as 'one sample item per household' can be controlled and consumers make a conscious choice to request a sample themselves. As targeted users can be part of a marketing database that tracks their behaviour and engages them over time, e-sampling is less of a one-shot and more part of a CRM campaign. Companies can also get real-time, instant consumer feedback on usage and likeability of the sample without high costs or much effort.[77] For some businesses, e-sampling can be completely handled online, for instance software companies providing free downloads or demo versions of their software, often with an expiration time of 30–60 days. Online music and book stores like Amazon allow their customers to sample 30-second clips of music or fragments of books before ordering.[78]

E-coupons are the online equivalent of print coupons and can be redeemed online (on e-commerce sites) or printed. They can be delivered via e-mails or via a website. Just as with e-sampling, they offer the ability to monitor the user's online shopping behaviour (if redeemed online) and can reach an audience that would not bother to cut out print coupons in newspaper or magazine ads. Apart from these advantages, online couponing can also save money compared with offline printing costs and advertising costs. E-couponing also makes it possible for the advertiser to experiment with split-run tests (choosing which offer/design combination has the best response results and then quickly adapting the coupon's value or message) and to make immediate and automatic responses by tailoring the coupons to the demographic profile of the consumer. Research has found that about 48% of the web population uses online coupons.[79] In 2010, online coupon sites emerged as an important channel in driving consumer behaviour in Europe. This growth was the highest seen in any region in 2010, bringing the reach of coupon sites in Europe to 9.6% of all Internet users. The sizeable growth can largely be attributed to Groupon, which was not a significant player in Europe in 2009. Groupon, a deal-of-the-day website that features discounted gift certificates usable at local or national companies, was able to establish a presence in more than a hundred European cities in 2010 and now reaches more than 12 million visitors a month, approximately one-third of the total market.[80] Google reports that 95% of smart-phone users have searched for local information, proving that location-based, deal searching is vital to digital couponing.[81]

E-mail marketing

E-mail marketing is basically not much more than using the Internet and e-mail for direct marketing practices. There are different types of e-mail:[83]

- *Direct e-mail.* The one 'killer' application that is most used by Internet users is e-mail. Just as in traditional direct marketing, e-mail marketing can be used inbound and outbound.[84] Most of the time it is used to send a promotional offer and push the consumer into a certain action.

- *Retention e-mail.* These mails are sent with the purpose of strengthening the brand attitude and experience. A popular example of retention e-mails is the e-newsletter. These online newsletters can contain ads, but the main purpose is to create an impact in the longer term by engaging consumers with the brand. They offer the reader a certain added value such as informative content.

- *Ads in e-mails of third parties.* Instead of issuing a newsletter of their own, advertisers can select newsletters of third parties and 'buy' some advertising or content space.

The net provides speed, flexibility and low costs compared with traditional direct marketing media, and customisation and full individualisation are much easier and cheaper. With these features, e-mail marketing usage has grown significantly during the last five years. One of the clear reasons for this surge in volume and spending is that e-mail marketing is more effective in terms of response than traditional direct mail or other web campaigns such as banners or interstitials. Click-through rates (CTRs) of B2B e-mail newsletters range from 5% to 15%. For B2C promotional e-mail marketing campaigns this ranges from 2% to 12%. B2C promotional e-mail marketing campaigns often range from about 2% to 12%. E-mail campaigns with less than a 2% CTR may be a result of over-mailing and questionable e-mail opt-in processes. Highly segmented and personalised e-mail lists (B2B and B2C) are often in the 10% to 20% CTR range. E-mail messages with very strong content but sent to unsegmented lists (for instance, news or trend-type e-newsletters) often have CTRs in the 10% to 15% range. Trigger or behaviour-based e-mail campaigns (sent to recipients based on some behaviour they showed, such as clicking on a product link, visiting a specific web page, etc.) are often in the 15% to 50% range.[85]

Banner CTRs are still far below 1%, and a traditional average direct marketing response rate is 2%.[86] Moreover, it is estimated that an e-mail marketing campaign costs between 60% and 65% less than a traditional postal direct marketing campaign by eliminating postage, paper and printing expenses. This also implies that e-mail made it possible to start using direct marketing for lower-cost items and that communicating with less frequent buyers is now profitable.[87] E-mails reach their destination within a few seconds of sending, and responses will also typically arrive within 48 hours of a communication. Compared with the usual six weeks response time for a traditional direct mail campaign, this speed of delivery and response is clearly another advantage of e-mail marketing.[88]

Marketers also appreciate the easy and inexpensive way of tailoring messages to groups of customers or even individuals. Content of e-mails and newsletters can be customised to specific customer interests and needs, and running tests on small samples to refine messages before finally mailing them to the entire target market is cheap. Research has shown that personalisation has profound effects on results. The average CTRs can be expected to double when messages are fully personalised. Personalisation effects grow over time: where impersonal e-zines (electronic magazines sent by e-mail or e-newsletters) are still able to reach curious people, only the personalised ones seem to be able to continue attracting the attention of readers.[89]

Measurement and tracking of e-mail marketing effectiveness can be carried out automatically even at a detailed level. There is also a link with viral marketing as it is easy for receivers of a promotional e-mail message to pass it along to other readers simply by forwarding it to them.

Privacy and legal issues were once a hot and controversial issue in the e-mail marketing industry, but now most markets have restricted and regulated the use of commercial e-mails. Spam (unsolicited e-mails) is forbidden in Europe and opt-out possibilities should be offered in each message sent, creating a good environment for permission-based programmes. Permission and privacy must be cornerstones of every e-mail marketing programme. Successful e-mail campaigns are based on trust. **Opt-in** means that users have voluntarily agreed to receive commercial e-mails about topics that they find interesting. They do so by subscribing on websites and checking a box. **Opt-out** means that users have to uncheck the box on a web page to prevent being put on an e-mail list. 'Opt-in' is better than 'opt-out' as the quality of the database or list will be better.[90] Companies should always stress the purpose of collecting addresses and guarantee that the information will not be disclosed to third parties or misused. However, the real threat for e-mail marketing is overuse due to its low cost and reputation for outperforming other online actions and traditional direct marketing. Some analysts predict that response rates will seriously be driven down due to each consumer's inbox being flooded by thousands of commercial messages and massive opting out. Another limitation is the lack of good opt-in e-mail databases. Supply is limited, which results in companies renting the same lists, with bombarded and tired consumers as a consequence. Often the first and most difficult challenge for marketers who want to launch an e-mail campaign is to create a good target database of prospects and customers.[91] The second challenge is then to deliver the right content as low relevance of content and high mailing frequency both incite consumers to unsubscribe from a mailing list. A survey among 1000 e-mail users concluded that the preference in e-mail content differs between males and females. Men are more interested in thematic content such as compelling news and information while for women promotional content like discount offers and samples are welcome.[92]

BUSINESS INSIGHT
Argos's winning e-mail campaign

Argos, a UK-based online retailer, wanted to introduce a product review section on its website. E-mail was identified as the best channel in achieving this goal. Two weeks after the purchase of a product on the Argos website, the customer was sent an e-mail, ensuring that he or she had time to use the product and that the experience was still fresh in his or her mind. In a bid to increase the sales of the reviewed products online, the e-mail thanked the shopper for his or her purchase and offered the opportunity to write a review. Instead of sending generic e-mails, Argos personalises its messages depending on what products the recipient has purchased. This approach resulted in a CTR of more than 42% and open rates of more than 30%, as well as low unsubscribe rates. The target was to generate 209 000 reviews in six months. In only four months, Argos received 203 095 reviews. The communications agency of Argos received the Revolution Award 2009 in the category 'Best use of e-mail' for this campaign.[93]

Mobile marketing

Mobile marketing or **wireless advertising** consists of all the activities undertaken to communicate with customers through the use of mobile devices to promote products and services by providing information or offers. In 2008, mobile media began to catch up with the hype, as both consumers and advertisers embraced mobile technologies like never before. The introduction

Table 15.1 Smart-phone penetration and mobile Internet use in Europe

	Smart-phone penetration Base: total population	Daily Internet access Base: smart-phone users
United Kingdom	51%	64%
Sweden	51%	75%
Denmark	45%	39%
Spain	44%	56%
The Netherlands	43%	64%
France	38%	55%
Germany	29%	53%
Italy	28%	50%
Belgium	22%	46%

of the smart phone, heightened by Apple's iPhone launch in mid-2007, was the true turning point for the industry.[94] Due to 3G technology, mobile marketing is more productive and useful to marketers as it provides new opportunities such as video calls (see who you are talking to in real time), mobile TV (watch TV directly on your mobile phone), music/video download (use of mobile phone as an MP3 player) and mobile Internet (surf via your laptop or smart phone, while on the move). In global and regional mobile advertising spending was analysed. An IAB study valued global mobile advertising at €3.8 billion, with regional shares of: Europe 25.9%, North America 31.4%, Latin America 3.5%, Asia Pacific 35.9%, Middle East and Africa 3.2%.[95]

In 2011, global smart-phone penetration was 27%. In North America and Europe, smart-phone penetration is highest, with 63% and 51% market shareres pectively.[96] Table 15.1 gives an overview of the penetration of smart phones in some European countries and their daily Internet access, based on a study conducted by Ipsos for Google in May 2012.[97]

Sweden and the UK are the leading countries in Western Europe when it comes to smart-phone penetration. Mobile research company mobile SQUARED estimated that in 2011 in the UK there were more than 32 million smart phones and expected that figure to double by 2015. eMarketer estimates that more than 17 million of UK inhabitants will go online via mobile in 2012, and that number will rise to more than 20 million by 2015.[98] With a daily Internet access via smart phones from 39% in Denmark up to 75% in Sweden, the mobile experience is shifting closer to the online experience. For marketers, increased mobile Internet will drive them towards creative strategies that make the best use of multiple platforms, without irritating consumers with too many marketing messages. They should be aware that their message (e-mailings and website) is 'mobile-proof': readable on smaller screens and the 'call-to-action' link is clickable by thumb. They should make sure the content can be shared through different social media such as Facebook, Twitter, Google+, etc. According to the same Ipsos study, the smart-phone users have an average of 19 applications on their phones in Spain and Belgium, up to an average of 30 apps in Sweden and France.[99] **Apps or mobile applications** are software applications, usually designed to run on smart phones and tablet computers. They are available through application distribution platforms, which are typically operated by the owner of the mobile operating system.[100] In the USA the average smart-phone user has 41 apps and is spending an average of 39 minutes per day in using them. The top five apps are Facebook, YouTube, Android market, Google Search and Gmail.[101]

An InSites Consulting study revealed that 10% of smart-phone users participated in a mobile marketing campaign. Most of them via SMS and about 20% of them by downloading a branded app. Mobile couponing is not gaining a high acceptance. The overall penetration of branded apps/games is very low and improvement in this domain is needed. A branded app should add value for consumers, and help them do things better. 'What's in it for me?' is key for the app user.[102]

BUSINESS INSIGHT
Mobile marketing by Cornetto

During the summer of 2010, Unilever's Cornetto brand ran an innovative mobile marketing campaign that brought together a brand message of love and fun with leading-edge mobile technology. Cornetto is Unilever's very popular ice cream brand all across Europe and the market leader in Turkey. Cornetto has traditionally been a youth-focused brand (the median age in Turkey is 28 years) and the brand messaging is that Cornetto helps you reach out to people that you want to be with. Cornetto ice creams can act as an icebreaker and overcome shyness. The millions who pass through the Beyoglu district, the heart of Istanbul, were invited to participate in a multi-player mobile game. A 'pac man' type of game was projected on the windows of a large building so that almost everyone walking down the street saw it straight away. A special phone number was also projected onto the wall. Once that number was dialled, the game was explained to consumers via their mobile phones. Each player got a different coloured character that they could move around by using their phone keys in order to catch three Cornetto ice creams cones in less than 45 seconds. If successful, the player received a big heart on the mobile screen as well as an SMS coupon for a free Cornetto at the event bar. The game was announced through leaflets and interactive screens. On the night of action there was an event area enriched with live shows and musical entertainment. The game itself ran for 15 evenings, for two hours per evening. On average 100 people per hour played the game; nearly 3 million saw the project in action. The Cornetto mobile game campaign in Turkey won the 2011 GSMA Award for 'Best Mobile Advertising & Marketing Campaign'.[103]

In April 2012, the Belgian supermarket chain Delhaize launched Europe's first virtual store at the central railway station of Brussels. The virtual supermarket, named 'Delhaize Direct Cube', consisted of four panels containing 300 photos of popular items, where customers could scan the desired ones via their smart phone (an app is needed) and get them delivered later to one of the 100 pick-up points. A mobile Internet connection was not needed because the cube also featured a Wi-Fi hotspot. In total Delhaize had seven cubes moved across the country during a test period of two months.[104]

In Germany, the bank ING-DiBa wanted to connect its offering to a younger audience. During the Basketball League the bank aimed to leverage smart phones to create an interactive experience that anyone could play: 'Free Throw Billboards' were born. Users could connect their phone directly to a billboard, turning it into a virtual basketball, and take three 'Free Throws' in the competition. The installation required Facebook Connect, powering a live broadcast to friends and family, along with a wall post of the person in action shooting virtual basketballs.[105] This campaign resulted in 21 493 passers-by during the event, 2823 actual players and 7981 likes.[106]

With the increase of smart-phone (and tablet) penetration, the audience for mobile advertising has got bigger and become easier to segment and target. It is time for marketers who want to include mobile in their advertising initiatives to do trials and take advantage of mass consumer adoption of smart phones. Worldwide mobile advertising revenue was forecast to reach $3.3 billion in 2011, which is more than double the spending of 2010, and according to Gartner revenue is expected to reach $20.6 billion by 2015. In North America and Western Europe mobile advertising budgets will grow most, representing 28% and 25% of the global market by 2015.[107] Mobile SQUARED predicts that the five main European markets (France, Germany, Italy, Spain and the UK) will reach a mobile advertising spend of $1 billion in 2014, which is a year earlier than was previously expected and another strong indication that the momentum for mobile marketing is there. At present, the UK has a share of 47% in these spendings, followed by France and Italy, but is expected to fall back to 40% by 2016. Overall, Germany's mobile market is likely to grow fastest.[108] Not all types of mobile advertising will generate the same opportunity. Search and maps will take the highest share, while video/audio ads will see the fastest growth through 2015.[109]

Wireless advertising can be broken into two categories: push and pull. **Push advertising** is categorised as messages that are proactively sent out to wireless users and devices like alerts, SMS messages or even voice calls. It should be reserved for companies that have established a relationship and obtained permission to push communications to wireless users. Due to privacy issues and user backlash, pushed mobile advertising will seldom be used for new customer acquisition. **Pull advertisements** are messages shown to users as they are navigating WAP or wireless sites and properties. Both push and pull advertising should be carefully targeted and of relevance to the viewer to improve customer response and acceptance. Users should never feel that viewing the advertiser's message is costing them airtime.

Often, mobile marketing is aimed at young consumers, because they have an intimate relationship with their mobile phones. Mobile phones have become the focal point of technology conversion. As their possibilities expand, their importance to young consumers will continue to increase. It is likely that mobile phones will surpass the personal computer as the most important single piece of technology in young consumers' lives. Texting is as natural to youth as picking up a phone. Texting is even overtaking speaking, particularly for girls. Teen females are sending and receiving 3952 messages per month versus 2815 for males.[110] Marketing via mobile to young consumers is understanding that their use of mobiles differs from the use by adults. Texting has created a whole new language, with different syntax and grammar. Young people want to be entertained, e.g. gaming, contests, etc., and they want two-way interaction on their mobiles because they welcome dialogue.

Simple push SMS does not take full advantage of the medium. Research and practical experience have demonstrated that youngsters love to talk back. They experience brands in a new and more fundamental way. They love to display commercial logos on their personal devices as well as expecting brands to listen to them. Young consumers do not hate advertising, but they dislike advertising that is irrelevant or even unwanted. Therefore, permission is key in connecting with millennials in an interactive way.[111] SMS has many advantages as a marketing tool. SMS is instantaneous, but it has an even faster and wider reach than e-mail as the mobile device usually accompanies the user and SMS can be received anywhere, at any time. It also allows for more precise targeting as every mobile phone has one single user.

Over 90% of SMS campaigns are read by the receiver, generating average response rates of 15% to 30% or even as much as 45%, while marketing e-mails have a response rate of only 6%. These rates are reached due to the ease and speed by which users can reply, with relatively little effort. Another important element is that SMS messages are cheap. With a cost of $0.05 per message, there are few other methods that provide such a strong ROI.[112] As SMS actions are quite intrusive, they should always be launched on an opt-in basis, which implies that they should be regarded as a complement to other marketing communications. An SMS message is most appreciated when the content is appealing (an offer, a game, an incentive, a contest) and attractive. The most effective wireless campaigns are sweepstakes. An instant-win contest is a good way to acquire a database of consumers.

Mobile phones can do more than just listen. They can also create. The texting, imaging, audio and video capabilities of mobile phones can be used to create near-real-time content, known as mobcasting. Mobcasters upload their content directly from their phones to the Internet where it can be downloaded/viewed by others. Mobile is certainly not a medium in isolation. Therefore all mobile marketing campaigns should be integrated into the overall marketing and media mix.[113]

BUSINESS INSIGHT
Mobile marketing at work

The D'Ieteren Group sells cars in Belgium for the Volkswagen, Audi, Skoda and Porsche brands. For car dealers, making appointments with customers increases the workload greatly. Sending out messages via e-mail didn't work as customers often read their e-mails too late or did not have the opportunity to connect online. Using an SMS communication platform was the solution for D'Ieteren's problem. Once a car is ready, the owner receives an automatically generated SMS; there is also the option for the dealer to add a personal message such as opening hours or other important details. In order to increase the innovative image of D'Ieteren, a mobile website and dealer locator are also offered. With this mobile approach, D'Ieteren is able to reach 50 new dealer appointments per month.[114]

In June 2011, Bacardi partnered with Live Nation in a summer promotion using mobile marketing to strengthen brand awareness, drive engagement and provide a deeper connection with fans whenever they seek music information. Live Nation launched advertising on its Live Nation mobile website with Bacardi as the first big advertiser. The campaign used Bacardi's 'Best Shared Live' tagline to build customer engagement via mobile, online and in-store elements and had as a goal to bring people together (in line with Bacardi's together advertising campaign) and strengthen brand awareness by integrating live music into their daily lives. When consumers click on an ad for Bacardi on the Live Nation mobile site, they have three different options. They can link to a mobile page with cocktail recipes, they can enter sweepstakes with a chance to win a trip to any Live Nation concert in the USA or they can link to the Bacardi Facebook page. Bacardi also participated in a new SMS share functionality: anyone searching on the mobile site for a venue or band can send an SMS message to a friend with all the details of this band. Bacardi sponsored these messages.[115]

AMF Pension wanted to encourage people to start thinking about their pension while they were still relatively young. Outdoor advertising was used to invite passers-by to take a picture of themselves with their mobile phones and send it to the pension-provider. A few minutes later, AMF sent back a picture showing how the person might look when they are 70 years old. The campaign is a smart use of mobile media to create an interaction with the end-user.[116]

In a recent fundraising campaign the Red Cross was able to collect $5 000 000 for Haiti. This was done by making use of text messaging. Giving a contribution was very simple. All people had to do to help out was text the word Haiti to a certain number and a $10 donation was automatically made. This was very simple and yet effective marketing campaign, since nobody had to go out to make a donation. To date this has been the most effective SMS campaign done by any charity organisation.[117]

British Airways wanted to promote its Executive Club mobile application. This app allows members to manage their account, reservations, and access real-time flight information via their mobile phones. British Airways decided to run a mobile e-mail campaign to reach its members after research had shown that this was the preferred way for travellers to receive information. To be successful, the e-mail had to be optimised so it was viewable on a small screen and it also needed to suit the users' commonest devices. The mobile e-mail allowed users to access their inbox no matter where they were travelling on any given day. The e-mail was targeted and to the point. Someone with an iPhone would receive information about a new app that allows him or her to scan the ticket instead of printing it out. The mail showed examples of what the app could do. The campaign resulted in 250 000 downloads.[118]

Kraft Foods wanted to promote the launch of new instant coffee products, Jacobs 3in1 and Jacobs 2in1. The main objective was to place product samples among early adopters and opinion leaders and build a customer database for future CRM. The call to action invited consumers to request a product sample by texting a keyword. The campaign was promoted in print and TV ads as well as with online and mobile banner ads. A targeted list of opted-in consumers also received push SMS messages inviting them to text in for the sample. The consumers who responded were sent a link to the mobile sampling portal. Over 400 000 samples were requested, and more than 80 000 users opted in for future messaging. Because the keyword was specific for each medium, results could easily be broken down over the different media: the 650 banner ads on selected portals had a CTR of 3%, compared with 10.6% of the targeted list who responded to the push text messages, and only 0.4% responded to the TV ad.[119]

When using mobile marketing techniques, a lot of legal and moral implications have to be taken into account. The Mobile Marketing Association (MMA), which represents more than 700 companies worldwide, is the key institute regulating the mobile industry. The MMA has released its Global Code of Conduct, designed to provide guidelines that all mobile marketers should consider and build their mobile marketing initiatives around. This code has five categories:[120]

1. *Notice: the fundamental principle.* Informing users of the marketers' identity or products and services offered, as well as the key terms and conditions that govern an interaction between the marketer and the user's mobile device.

2. *Choice & Consent.* Respecting the right of the user to control which mobile messages he or she wants to receive by obtaining consent (opt-in) and implementing a simple termination (opt-out) process.

3. *Customisation & Constraint.* Ensuring that collected information is used to tailor communication to the interests of the recipient and is handled responsibly, sensitively and in compliance with applicable law.

4. *Security.* The implementation of reasonable procedures to protect user information from unauthorised use, alteration, disclosure, distribution or access.

5. *Enforcement & Accountability.* The MMA expects its members to comply with the MMA Privacy Code of Conduct and has incorporated the code into applicable MMA Guidelines.

Interactive television

Interactive (digital) television, or **i(D)TV**, is television content that gives viewers the ability to interact with programmes and to use a number of interactive services such as t-government, t-banking, t-commerce, t-learning information, games, video-on-demand and communication (t-mail), all supported by a set-top box.[121] This relatively new medium offers new possibilities for marketers as they are now able to move buyers through the complete buying process. Traditional TV is still doing its job in reaching and attracting people, while the power of SMS and mobile is to convert and support. Interactive TV has many characteristics of the Internet (attract, engage and convert) and can empower TV as a medium. Viewers can choose among many more channels and watch content on demand. The viewer is in control. Interactive TV can elaborate a brand with the possibility of giving more in-depth information, generating leads and stimulating trial. Viewers can ask for extra information about products and services, receive coupons or samples and even buy a product, all with one push of a (mostly red) button. Western Europe will not reach full digital TV penetration until 2017, despite a penetration of 85% by the end of 2011. Only Finland and Spain had fully converted to digital TV services by the end of 2011. Another two countries are expected to have joined them by the end of 2012 – Italy (currently on 87% penetration) and the UK (currently on 95% penetration). Switzerland, with the lowest digital penetration rate in Western Europe, will rapidly convert from the 56% penetration it recorded at the end of 2011.[122] In the Netherlands, digital TV penetration rose from 69% in the first half of 2011 to 73% at the end of 2011.[123]

iDTV will also enhance the possibilities of understanding the viewing behaviour of the target group as well as developing personal relationships with viewers and making tailored interactive advertising content adapted to the needs of the viewers.[124] Apart from interactive commercials, the iDTV medium provides advertisers with other possibilities:

- *Programmercials or programme sponsoring*, for instance a tour operator sponsors a travel programme on iDTV that gives viewers the opportunity to receive more information about a destination, order a catalogue or book a holiday.

- *Advertising messages or logos on the electronic programme guide*, visited on average 5–10 times by the iDTV viewer.

- *Linking with certain t-services*, for instance the *Financial Times* sponsoring the t-banking application on iDTV.

- *Bannering during programmes*.

- *Walled gardens*, a kind of website created specifically for iDTV, and linked with an interactive commercial or an iDTV programme, for instance through product placement.[125]

BUSINESS INSIGHT

Interactive TV campaigns: Burger King's Whopperlust and Yeo Valley

In June 2011, Burger King started a new interactive TV campaign 'The Whopperlust' on Direct TV channel 111. Burger King wanted to challenge people and do something beyond just a Facebook like. The longer you stare, the more free Whoppers you get. If you stare for five minutes, at some point there will be an on-screen prompt to press an arrow button on your remote. After that, you can go double or nothing and stare for ten additional minutes to win two Whoppers. If you stay on for another 15 minutes, you can even win three Whoppers. To win the three Whoppers, you have to spend a total of about 30 minutes staring. Burger King mailed coupons to those winning households. After a couple of days Burger King had given away 50 000 Whopper scoupons.[126]

Yeo Valley is the UK's leading organic brand. To achieve growth during recession, it had to break out of its declining niche and appeal to the everyday families of the UK. The goal of the marketing campaign was clear: take the Yeo Valley brand into the mainstream. In essence, the strategy was to take a focused approach to media through the popular TV programme *X-Factor* that in return delivered increased engagement with its viewers and results for Yeo

Valley. A two-minute spot was broadcast in the first live final to get the viewers talking about Yeo Valley and their rapping farmers. This was followed by a spot campaign for ten weeks delivering about 14 million viewers a week. Secondly, The *X-Factor* licence was used for the creation of a competition to win tickets to attend the live finals. This was promoted through clickable VoD and display ads across The *X-Factor* pages on ITV.com, as well as in-store through on-pack branding. All media directed viewers to visit the Yeo Valley farm online to enter the competition. Thirdly, there was an integration into The *X-Factor* 'live chat' function on ITV.com, promoting the competition and starting the conversations about Yeo Valley, which went live across the multiple social media platforms. These were the results:

- 1.8 million YouTube views
- No. 1 trending Twitter topic worldwide
- 35 million Tweet impressions
- 35 000 Facebook fans
- 400% increase to the online farm
- 30 000 competition entries
- 30 000 single downloads, with seven weeks in the top 100
- 71% increase in brand awareness
- 15% increase in sales value
- half a million new households to the brand.[127]

The following trends are emerging in different European countries:[128]

1. *From broadcast towards on demand.* In many countries **video-on-demand (VoD)** entered the top five TV channel charts, and the service to review missed programmes that many channels offer is increasingly popular. Transactional VoD services include the online retail and rental of audio-visual works, primarily feature films, audio-visual fiction, documentaries, educational programmes, cartoons, etc. The market for VoD services in Europe is dynamic, diverse and growing rapidly, though nevertheless lagging behind the USA. More than 500 on-demand audio-visual services were available in Europe in 2008 and VoD generated turnover of €544 million. It is predicted that VoD turnover in Europe will increase dramatically over the next few years and thus will represent a more significant aspect of the audio-visual markets.[129]

2. *Fragmentation.* Previously, a household had one TV; now different TVs are available within one household, and people are even watching TV via the computer or mobile devices. TV broadcast distribution is increasingly diversified. In 2009, satellite broadcast accounted for 31% of the EU TV market, cable for 30%, digital terrestrial TV for 25% and IPTV (digital TV over the Internet) for 5%. Western Europe is the largest IPTV market, accounting for 40% of global subscribers in 2010. France is the leading country in the world for IPTV (23% of the global total), followed by China (16%) and the USA (16%).[130]

3. *The quality of digital TV and digital broadcasting is improving day by day.*

4. *Personalisation in terms of both offers and ads.* More suggestions will be offered by advertisers in the way that Amazon has been doing for years on the Internet. ('Other buyers also bought the following titles' (based on collaborative filtering).

5. *User-generated content.* More and more user-generated TVs, videos and channels that can even be shared.

6. *Connected TV.* The sales of Internet-connected TV are booming across Europe. Reports from both the Netherlands and Germany show that more than half of all sets sold in 2011 are connected. GfK claimed that in 2012 around two-thirds of TV sets in the Netherlands will be able to connect to the Web. This growth will lead to 56% connected TV penetration in three years' time in the Netherlands. These figures only reflect pure connected TV sets, not those connected to the Web by using a separate set-top box or games console. GfK's figures for the Dutch market are in line with those for the German market, where every other TV sold in Germany will be connected according to figures from the German industry association BITKOM. The figures show an impressive growth of 1000% from just two years ago. And the Germans are actively seeking these sets rather than just buying sets that happen to be connected: 46% of Germans really want web content on their TV.[131] According to a report from Digital TV Research, the number of TV sets connected to the Internet will reach 551 million by 2016 for the 40 countries covered in this report, up from 124 million at the end of 2010. The Connected TV Forecasts Report states that this translates to 20% of global TV sets by 2016, up from only 6% of the end of 2010.[132]

7. *Dual screening or second screening.* This is rather new consumer behaviour. Back in 1999, the future of interactive TV was what is now called **dual or second screening**, with people interacting with their TV via their PC. The idea was soon overtaken by the use of the 'red button interactive TV'. But now, with cheap laptops, the increasing penetration of smart phones and the rise of social media, dual screening is back on the agenda: 60% of people claim to watch TV and go online simultaneously two or three times a week, while 37% claim to do so every day. There are roughly three ways in which people use TV and the Internet together. There is co-incident usage, where people are looking at something on their laptop that is not related to what is on TV. To advertisers this is the same as someone reading the newspaper. Secondly there are people using the PC/smart phone or tablet for something related to the TV show but not in sync with it, such as visiting a brand's social media site. And then there is the group of people who are deeply synchronising with the programme, e.g. playing along with a TV game, twittering about the TV show, etc. This synchronous use is of big interest to advertisers.[133]

   Mediascope Europe 2012 revealed that 48% of Europeans are using the Internet while they are watching TV and 16% of the time spent watching TV is done while using the Internet. The heaviest Europeans online/TV multitaskers are the Norwegians at 70%, followed by the French at 68% and 62% of those watching TV in the UK; 33% of all European TV and online multitaskers claimed synchronous use. This means there is a significant opportunity for brands to engage the consumer via both platforms.[134]

   Connected TV offerings tend to fall into two camps: closed and applications-based versus open and browser-based. Both closed and open systems vary widely in the content and services they offer. A connected TV set or device may have all or only some of these.[135]

8. *Social TV.* Connected TV creates **social TV**. The fact that TV is connected with the Internet fundamentally changes the nature of TV by giving viewers access to VoD, web video and new online services, such as social networking. Facebook is so large that it has a user base in some countries equal to or even larger than the audience for the most popular broadcast TV programming. Given the popularity of social networks, people are frequently talking about TV shows at the same time as they are watching them. A September 2010 survey conducted in the UK for Intel found 45% of individuals use social networking services such as Twitter and Facebook to discuss a programme while it is being shown. Second-screen devices used when viewing TV include a laptop (57%), a desktop computer (23%) and an Internet-enabled smart phone (19%). The MTV Video Music Awards in September 2010 featured extensive Twitter integration so that music fans could respond to the live show in real time. This show attracted its highest viewing figures since 2002, with 11.4 million people watching and simultaneously sending 2.3 million tweets during the broadcast.

Tweets about Lady Gaga peaked at 9200 per minute. Tweets were appearing on stage during the show, via a screen 95 feet (29 m)wide.[136]

Social TV is gaining relevance:[137]

- Fox's *Family Guy* has 41.5 million Facebook 'likes';

- ITV's *X-Factor* attracted more than 58 000 tweets per day during the last series;

- BBC's *Top Gear* has 10.2 million Facebook 'likes';

- *Glee* accounted for 16% of all social media activity among the major US networks' shows;

- 275 million Facebook users have 'liked' a TV show, and on average they like six;

- Twitter has more than 100 million active users.

BUSINESS INSIGHT
How social TV influences the rules of TV advertising

Because of the existence of on-screen applications, TV advertising needs to be seen in another, more social, perspective. Through these applications the consumers can discuss and appraise commercials at the same time as they are watching them. Viewers will increasingly rely on the opinions of others before they discover for themselves advertiser funded programming, sponsored web shows and branded online video, all accessible through their connected TV. Therefore advertisers need to rethink the content of their campaigns and run social ads.

For social networks such as Facebook and Twitter, advertising is their main revenue source. Facebook aims to tap the $180 billion worldwide TV advertising spend. Once Facebook users are 'liking' a brand's Facebook page, they can then opt in to get commercial messages from this company, such as brand status updates, along with HD video commercials.

Twitter focuses on brand communications via its sponsored messages (promoted tweets). These tweets, clearly labelled 'promoted', are seen in the 'Trends' section of the Twitter site and can be passed on to followers. Via connected TV apps for Facebook or Twitter, viewers see the status updates or tweets, so also brand updates or promoted tweets, on their TV screen, directly alongside TV programming and commercials.

A logical future development are apps that display whole Facebook pages, personally targeted display ads or leads to video for TV shows and brands incorporating video. The screen space of connected TVs with browsers will be divided between the broadcast commercials and sponsored programming, and compete for viewer attention with socially targeted advertising. This new more social way of advertising will transform the TV ad market completely.[138]

The social media revolution

With technology-fuelled changes in recent years, marketing is increasingly about two-way mass conversations between Internet users. As **Web 1.0** was the web-as-information-source with static websites, **Web 2.0** (aka **social media (networks)**) is a concept of web-as-participation-platform in which users participate and connect to each other using services as opposed to sites.[139] It can be seen as a collection of emerging technologies enabling social networking by offering Internet users the ability to collaborate, add, edit, share and tag content of different kinds (text, sound, video, images). This so-called 'consumer-generated content' includes **weblogs** (or **blogs**), video blogs (vlogs), podcasts, wikis, mobile phone photography and RSS feeds. One of the earliest Web 2.0 applications was Napster, a peer-to-peer file-swapping tool that leveraged personal music catalogues across its user base and facilitated music sharing. According to Kaplan and Haenlein[140] (who applied a set of theories in the field of media research), there are six different types of social media (Table 15.2).

Collaborative projects

The main idea underlying **collaborative projects** is that the joint effort of many actors leads to a better outcome than any actor could achieve individually, also referred to as 'the wisdom of crowds'. Examples within this category include the online encyclopaedia Wikipedia and the social bookmarking web service Delicious, which allows the storage and sharing of web book-marks. Companies must be aware that collaborative projects are becoming a very important source of information for many consumers. Although not everything written on Wikipedia may actually be true, it is believed to be true by more and more surfers. Adobe Systems main-tains a list of bookmarks to company-related websites and conversations on Delicious.

Blogs and microblogs

Weblogs, or contracted 'blogs', are frequently updated personal web journals that allow owners to publish ideas and information. Blogs are usually managed by one person only, but provide the possibility of interaction with others through the addition of comments. Some blogs are just expressions of individual opinions and analysis, while others aggregate infor-mation or serve mainly to direct readers to other blogs, websites or other sources. Some are company-internal and only accessible to employees or departments within a company. Others are posted on public websites and available for anyone to see and react. The earliest

Table 15.2 Classification of social media by social presence/media richness and self-presentation/self-disclosure

		Social presence/Media richness		
		Low	Medium	High
Self-presentation/ self-disclosure	**High**	Blogs	Social networking sites (e.g. Facebook)	Virtual social worlds (e.g. Second Life)
	Low	Collaborative projects (e.g. Wikipedia)	Content communities (e.g. YouTube)	Virtual game worlds (e.g. 'World of Warcraft')

Source: Users of the world, unite! The challenges and opportunities of social media, *Business Horizons*, Vol. 53 (1), pp. 59–68 (Kaplan, A.M. and Haenlein, M. 2010), p. 62, Copyright © 2010, with permission from Elsevier.

blogs were started in the late 1990s, but real interest has skyrocketed over the past few years. By the end of 2011, Nielsen tracked over 181 million blogs around the world, up from 36 million in 2006. Women make up the majority of bloggers, and half of bloggers are aged 18–34; about 1 in 3 bloggers are mums.[141]

BUSINESS INSIGHT
Belgian blogger launches successful book

The Belgian Mme Zsazsa (32) is one of the leading ladies in the blogosphere in Belgium and the Netherlands. What started in 2006 as a result of a new job search ended – via lessons in pattern design – in a blog that won the prestigious *Weekend Knack* (Belgian lifestyle magazine) Blog Award in the category 'personal' blogs. As creative mother of two boys, she posts articles on making clothes, gardening, vegetarianism, recipes, trips with the kids, etc., always with a slice of humour written in her own typical way and decorated with stylish pictures. Over 110 000 surfers a month read her blog. Nearly 6000 followers are fans of her Facebook page. Last year she started to allow advertising on her blog, mainly from web shops selling fabrics, clothes and other items aimed at families with kids. In April 2012, she released her first book on making skirts, which in no time became the best-selling non-fiction book in Belgium with 38 000 copies sold by June 2012. She now has her own newspaper column.[142]

Bloggers are active across social media: they are twice as likely to comment on consumer-generated video sites like YouTube, and nearly three times more likely to post on message boards/forums.[143] According to the blogosphere study of Technorati, the leading search engine for blogs, 38% of bloggers are writing about brands that they love or hate; 65% of bloggers use social media to follow brands and blogging on these brands is a common activity.[144] Blogs take the pulse of consumer trends and can build relationships. One of Kryptonite's popular U-shaped bike locks had to be recalled and exchanged after a blog posting on bikerforum.net said it could be picked with a Bic pen. The story raced through the blogosphere and was picked up by the *New York Times* and other big media. The product exchange implied a cost of $10 million for Kryptonite. A South African winery, Stormhoek, made use of blogs to enter the UK market. The founder sent sample bottles to 150 bloggers in the UK with no obligation to say anything about the wine, but a lot of them ended up writing about it. By interfacing with the blogosphere, Stormhoek changed the way it looked at its primary customers (supermarket chains) and end-users (the supermarket's customers). Simply telling the blog story to supermarket buyers and importers made the sales process easier and, as a result, the wine got a 19% share of its category in the UK market and sales doubled from 50 000 cases in 2004 to 100 000 in 2005.[145]

Twitter can be considered as a micro-blog but is at the same time a free social network service. Twitter enables users to send and read users' updates known as tweets. These are text-based posts of at most 140 characters that are displayed on the user's profile page and delivered to other users (called followers) who subscribe to it. Tweets can be sent and received via the Twitter site, via SMS or external applications. On 21 March 2012, Twitter celebrated its sixth birthday and announced that it had 140 million users and 340 million tweets per day. In April 2012, Twitter opened offices in Detroit aimed at working with automotive brands and advertising agencies.[146]

BUSINESS INSIGHT
Your tweet on Times Square

Taco Bell is an American chain of fast food restaurants serving more than 2 billion consumers each year in more than 5800 restaurants in the USA. In the spring of 2012, Taco Bell teamed up with Frito Lay and created the Doritos Locos Tacos. To draw attention to this novelty, Taco Bell used social media to push out live tweets to Taco Bell micro-sites. Once a Doritos Locos Taco was experienced, the consumers were encouraged to tweet their excitement using both #DoritosLacosTacos and #Contest. The tweet that got the most retweets could win a truck full of Doritos Locos Tacos or one of the other prizes. Next to the prizes, the tweets (after user permission) could also be seen on digital billboards located in Times Square and on Sunset Boulevard. A streaming camera allowed the action on each billboard to be viewed on the Taco Bell website. Another set of cameras was co-ordinated to take pictures of tweets on the billboards that were sent back to individual users. The positive user response of the campaign influenced the targeted group who is very social-media-savvy and took special interest in seeing their tweets on digital billboards, said the company.[147, 148]

BUSINESS INSIGHT
Fundraising using Twitter to make a Dutch movie

Dutch film director Eddy Terstall needed funding (€18 000) for his new short film. With budgets being cut, the usual channels of fundraising had to be replaced with a more creative approach. He came up with an idea that would engage film fans and involve them in the process. The PR campaign was built around a single premise – personalised content in return for donations. Eddy's Twitter followers were invited to tweet a message and make a donation. Every €10 donated resulted in 10 seconds of film directed by Eddy, based upon the donor's own idea and posted on their Facebook wall. For €60 or more, donors received a film of one minute to share with friends and family. The single message was a tweet by Eddy to his followers. The single medium was the micro-site of the campaign.

The main objective was obviously to generate publicity to reach serious investors. The tweets were attention-seeking tools to get to the real investors. The results were as follows:

- Earned media: 47 tweets leading to films, 37 articles in Dutch media, 1 print, 32 online magazines, 4 blogs, worth €11 806.

- Commercial result: €20 000 was raised before the deadline, another €120 000 was raised in the six weeks following the deadline. Because of this, Eddy decided to turn his short movie into a full length feature film.[149]

A **podcast** is a sound file with an RSS feed that can be listened to by any MP3 or audio player (not only iPods as the name would suggest). This technology makes it easy for people to create their own audio recordings and post them on the Web. The new Edison Media Research done in 2012 revealed that 29% of Americans listened to an audio podcast and 26% of Americans even viewed a video podcast. Furthermore, 17% of Americans had downloaded and listened to an audio podcast during the last month. People consuming audio podcasts are spending 70 minutes more online than the average American is doing. For people consuming video podcasts this extra time is 93 minutes. Podcast consumers are extremely attractive advertising targets as they are well educated and earn good money. Podcast consumers are watching TV in non-traditional ways: 41% do it via their computer and about 20% smart-phone users are podcast consumers. They are also Internet social, as 74% of them are using Facebook, 28% use LinkedIn and 21% are using Twitter. Podcast consumers are heavy YouTube users.[150]

Content communities

The main objective of content communities is sharing content between users. Content communities share different media types, such as text (e.g. BookCrossing, via which more than 1 million people from over 132 countries share 9 122 677 books),[151] photos, videos and presentations (e.g. SlideShare, which has 60 million monthly visitors and 130 million page views, and is among the most visited 200 websites in the world. Besides presentations, SlideShare also supports documents, PDFs, videos and webinars).[152]

The most important photos communities are Flickr (owned by Yahoo!) with about 51 million registered users uploading 4.5 million pictures per day[153] and Instagram, launched in 2010 and bought in April 2012 by Facebook. Instagram is a free photosharing program that allow users to take a photo (with their mobile phone), apply different digital filters to it, and then share it on a variety of social networking sites, including Instagram's own. Initially, Instagram was only supported on iPhone, iPad and iPod Touch. In April 2012, Instagram for Android camera phones was launched via the Apple Store and Google Play Store, where it had more than 1 million downloads within 12 hours. In April 2012, over 30 million accounts were set up on Instagram.[154] According to the statistics from Instagram, the average number of photos uploaded per second at the end of 2011 was 60, which is about 5.2 million per day. Instagram is growing faster than Flickr.[155]

Some brands are still using Instagram in the same way brands used the Internet in 1999, as a way of 'digitising' their existing marketing materials. Other brands using Instagram in a better way are fashion brands such as Bergdorfs, Burberry, Gucci and Threadless. Their photo streams are more than just product shots: they offer the viewer interesting content (employees, old ads, fashion show backstage shots, piles of T-shirts) captured from a specific point of view and an editorial eye. They have learned that it is about being interesting, not about pushing products.[156] Burberry adopted Instagram very early on and has developed a followers base of over 356 000 people. The fashion company is displaying not only clothing and ads with unique filters, but also snapshots of London supporting its British roots. During its September London runway shows, Burberry fans got real-time photos of the show on Instagram before they were available anywhere else.[157,158]

Content communities carry the risk of being used as platforms for the sharing of copyright-protected materials. While most of them have rules in place to ban and remove such illegal content, it is difficult to avoid popular videos (like episodes of comedy dramas) being uploaded to YouTube only hours after they have been broadcast on TV. On the other hand, the high popularity of content communities makes them a very attractive contact channel for many companies, including TV channels.

YouTube and Vimeo are two examples of video content communities. YouTube, started in 2005 and bought by Google in October 2006, is big, very big. It gets 4 billion page views a day, which adds up to a trillion a year. It has 800 million users who watch 3 billion hours of video a month (i.e. 340 000 years).[159] Every second one hour of video is uploaded to YouTube.[160] Individuals have uploaded most of the content, although media corporations such as CBS, the BBC and other companies offer some of their material via the site. YouTube is structured by channels. These are places where an individual user can group a bunch of videos together onto one page. The most popular channels are those of celebrities such as Justin Bieber (1.5 million subscribers and 51 million views), Rihanna (2.3 million subscribers and 24 million views) and Lady Gaga (1.6 million subscribers and 30.6 million views).[161] Even the British Royal Family had their own Royal Channel reporting in June 2012 on the Queen's Diamonds Jubilee.

BUSINESS INSIGHT
Creative use of YouTube by Tipp-Ex

Tipp-Ex, European leader in correction products, wanted to promote its whiteout Pocket Mouse in the back-to-school period. Tipp-Ex released an interactive product demonstration on YouTube allowing viewers to rewrite the story. It created the first Tippexperience, 'A hunter shoots a bear', in August 2010. This video featured a hunter camped out in the woods who was suddenly facing a bear. At the end of the video the viewer could decide whether the hunter should shoot the bear or not. Whatever the choice, the hunter took the Tipp-Ex Pocket Mouse displayed on the banner next to the video, whited out the word 'shoot' in the title of the video and invited the viewers to write another word on the blank space; 42 alternative scenes where shot. The video became a viral hit. In the first 36 hours, it got 1 million views, was shared 100 000 times on Facebook and received one tweet per second. It was even twittered by Ricky Martin and Alissa Milano. It got a lot of international attention both on- and offline. After 100 days, it attained 35.5 million views on YouTube with an average brand exposure of five minutes. Each user typed on average 15 words. It was shared 318 000 times via Facebook and Twitter. This campaign increased the purchase intention in Europe by 100% and the sales went up by 30%.[162]

After the worldwide success of the 'Hunter shoots a bear' campaign of 2010, Tipp-Ex returned by giving the viewer the possibility of rewriting history with 'Hunter and bear's 2012 Birthday Party'. By entering a new date instead of 2012, when a meteorite is ruining the party, the viewer can enjoy the party in another year. There were 46 different scenes available and 8 scenes that required interactions.[163]

Vimeo, founded in November 2004, is another video-sharing website on which users can upload, share and view videos. Seven years later Vimeo had 64 million unique visitors, which is an increase of 82%. Its membership increased by 48% up to 9 million by November 2011; 15% of Vimeo's traffic comes from mobile devices.[164]

Social networking sites

Social networking sites enable users to connect by creating personal profiles, inviting friends to access those profiles, sending e-mails and instant messages between each other. These personal profiles can include photos, video, audio files, blogs, link to websites, in fact any type of information.

RESEARCH INSIGHT:
Consumers' reactions to brands placed in user-generated content: the effect of prominence and endorser expertise

Brand placement, the (paid) inclusion of branded products or brand identifiers in mass media productions, is rapidly gaining in popularity as an alternative to traditional advertising. Through integration of the brand in media content, advertisers have a unique opportunity to append favourable associations to their brand.[165] The global spending on brand placement amounted up to $6.25 billion in 2009, the vast majority of which was spent on traditional advertising media (e.g. TV, radio, feature films, etc.).[166] With the growing shift of both consumers and marketers to online media, brand placements in new and online media are expected to rise. User-generated content (UGC) is omnipresent in online environments and its rapid growth has created some of the most successful digital brands, such as YouTube and Wikipedia.[167] UGC-sharing websites are just one of the ways that brands can now interact with consumers.[168]

Previous research in traditional media points out that not all brand placements are equally effective,[169] and that the outcome varies depending on the characteristics of the placement and the consumer.[170] In a sample of 259 participants aged between 15 and 79 (mean age of 28), in which 41.9% were male, the effect is studied of two placement characteristics, namely brand placement prominence and endorser expertise on brand recognition and purchase intention. In addition, the moderating role of UGC liking was explored. The second purpose of the study was to investigate the effects of multiple brand placements.

A 2 (prominent vs subtle placement of one brand) × 2 (expert vs amateur endorser) full factorial between-subjects experimental design was set up. The authors shot four videos of a cooking tutorial ('how to bake pancakes'). These videos were identical in script and placed brands, and only differed in the intended manipulations. Expertise was manipulated by using two different endorsers. The expert was a celebrity TV chef who was willing to participate. The non-expert endorser was a student. Prominence was manipulated by explicitly pronouncing the brand name and simultaneously taking a two-second close-up of the product. In the 'subtle placement' condition, the endorser was merely shown using the product, without mentioning the brand name and without a close-up. The manipulated brand was Solo, a well-known Belgian brand of butter. Five other brands were subtly visually incorporated in the videos: Coca-Cola (soft drink), Whirlpool (kitchen equipment), Inza (milk), Tiense Suiker (sugar) and Tefal (frying pans). These other brands were placed in the same fashion in all videos. The videos were posted on YouTube. The video included a link to an online questionnaire.

While prominence exerted a significant effect on recognition (80.4% vs 93.9%), endorser expertise had no significant effect (87.9% vs 87.5%). The highest level of brand recognition was achieved when the (Solo) brand was prominently placed through an expert endorser (95.5%). This resulted in a significantly higher brand recognition than a subtle placement with an expert endorser (77.4%). However, the difference between a prominent placement by an expert and the prominent placement by an amateur (92.3%) was not significant. An amateur endorser and a subtle placement resulted in a brand recognition of 83.1%. UGC liking did not moderate the effect of endorser expertise on brand recognition of Solo. However, the effect of prominence on recognition was moderated by UGC liking. Prominent placements generated a significantly higher brand recognition than subtle placements, only for viewers with a high UGC liking (93.3% vs 72.0%). This difference was not significant for low UGC likers (91.5% vs 88.6%). For 4 out of 5 of the non-manipulated other brands that were placed in the videos, the manipulation of the prominence level of the Solo brand did not have an effect on the recognition of these brands. There was one interesting exception, namely Tefal, a brand of frying pans. When Solo was placed prominently, the brand recognition of Tefal (91.7%) also significantly increased compared with when Solo was placed subtly (58%), even though the prominence level of Tefal remained constant. This could be due to the fact that Tefal is the brand most closely associated with the manipulated Solo brand, because Solo butter is used in the Tefal frying pan. The degree of endorser expertise did not have a significant main effect on the brand recognition of any of the five non-manipulated placed brands. There was also no significant interaction effect between endorser expertise and Solo prominence on the brand recognition for Tefal. The positive effect of Solo prominence on brand recognition for Tefal was significant for both the amateur (92.3% vs 62.7%) and the expert condition (91% vs 52.8%).

Although placement prominence has consistently been found to positively influence brand recognition in traditional media,[171] in the present study, a prominent placement only has a significant effect on recognition when combined with an expert endorser. Endorser expertise seems to reinforce the effect of prominence on recognition. This might be caused by an incongruency effect, caused by the appearance of a known expert in an online format usually featuring unfamiliar amateurs. Prominence and endorser expertise also exert a reinforcing effect on purchase intention. Prominent placement causes significantly higher purchase intention than subtle placement when the brand is used by an expert. People who are fond of UGC content have better recognition scores when the brand is prominently placed, and report a greater purchase intention when the brand is used by an amateur than by an expert. Most UGC videos are acted out by hobbyists without professional training and the appearance of a celebrity expert disrupts this pattern. This may cause dissonant feelings on behalf of the experienced viewer, which in turn activates persuasion knowledge. This effect is not present with less experienced users. Marketers should be cautious when placing their brands in UGC videos featuring celebrity experts, especially when these are targeted at people who are fond of UGC videos. These consumers prefer an amateur endorser.

MySpace was launched as a social networking site with 250 million registered users in 2012. It had enormous success during the period of 2005–8, after which the decline started. Specific Media and Justin Timberlake bought it in June 2011. Since MySpace introduced new ties with rival social networks Twitter and Facebook, its popularity is again rising with more than 1 million new users within the first 30 days signing up to MySpace. The new owner promised to reposition the social network to focus on music. MySpace has a music catalogue of more than 42 million songs whereas Spotify (with 10 million users)[172] has about 15 million songs in the USA.[173]

The largest social networking site is Facebook, launched in 2004 and with 900 million monthly active users in May 2012. It was initially founded by Mark Zuckerberg to stay in touch with his fellow students from Harvard University. Social networking sites are of such high popularity, specifically among younger Internet users, that the term 'Facebook addict' is included in the *Urban Dictionary* (www.urbandictionary.com), a collaborative project of the development of a slang dictionary for the English language.

In September 2011, InSites Consulting conducted an overall study of social media. Awareness and usage of social networks are high. In Europe, 98% of people know at least one social network and 73% are members of at least one network, mostly Facebook. Social networkers are members of 1.9 networks on average. Current social networkers have no intention of stopping their membership, nor do they feel the need to further expand their membership on social network sites. Facebook rules, at least in Europe, the USA and Australia, but is having a hard time in China and Japan. No other network reaches its 96% awareness and 62% usage level among Internet users. In Russia and Ukraine, Vkontakte (a Facebook look-alike) is big with a penetration of 39% and an awareness of 55%.[174] In the Netherlands, Facebook recently surpassed Hyves as being the biggest social media platform with 6.5 million active users versus 4.4 million for Hyves. Only 20% of the Dutch people log in daily to their Hyves account, whereas this figure is 60% for Facebook.[175]

Twitter and MySpace are the second and third most popular social media in Europe in terms of both awareness and membership. Although Twitter has a high awareness (80%), there seems to be a Twitter paradox since only 16% are using it. Compared with Facebook, Twitter is still a rather small network of people. The future looks promising, but there is still a long way to go. Facebook and Twitter are a perfect couple as they are serving different needs. When people join Twitter, their Facebook usage does not decrease. Twitter users are typically using more social media than non-Twitter users. Given the fact that LinkedIn is a professional network, it is worth pointing out that this network ranks fourth, in terms of both awareness and membership (Table 15.3).[176]

Table 15.3 Overview of the penetration of social media platforms in Europe

Country % of total population	Facebook[177]	Twitter[178]	LinkedIn[179]	Google+[180,181]
Europe	28.7%		4.6%[181]	
Norway	56.9%		11.6%	
Denmark	51.67%		14.9%	10.5%
Sweden	51.4%		9.8%	9.3%
UK	49.9%	38%	13.4%	7.4%
Ireland	46%		13.3%	10.6%
Belgium	45.1%		10%	5.9%
Finland	40.8%		6.5%	10.7%
Portugal	40.7%		7.3%	8.3%
Hungary	39.8%		1.9%	
Turkey	39.4%	10%	1.3%	
The Netherlands	38.9%	33%	18.7%	5.9%
Switzerland	38.3%		8.1%	5.9%
France	37.7%	8%	5%	
Italy	37.3%		4.9%	
Spain	35.3%	17%	5.7%	
Germany	28.8%	6%	1.8%	

BUSINESS INSIGHT
Pinterest, the new hype in social networking

Pinterest is a content curation platform which allows users to organise and share interesting content that they find on the Web, that they upload themselves or that they see with other users. It is a pinboard-style/bookmarking site, a social network, a gift finder and a platform for collaboration all in one. Pinterest was founded in March 2010 and by the end of May 2012 it had become the third most visited social network in the USA after Facebook and Twitter. In January 2012 an average Pinterest user spent 89 minutes on the site.[182]

The content (such as links, images, videos) is organised on different 'Boards', created and named by the user him- or herself. Popular categories are travel, cars, film, humour, home design, sports, fashion and art. Users can browse other pinboards for inspiration, they can 're-pin' (over 80% of the pins are 're-pins' of other users) images to their own collections and they can 'like' photos and comment on them. Other users or a selection of other users' boards can be followed. You and your friends can even start up a collaborative board where all the invitees can pin/re-pin interesting stuff.

Pinterest allows its users to share 'pins' on both Twitter and Facebook. This integration allows users to share and interact with a broad community. More than 20% of Facebook users are using Pinterest on a daily basis. Apps for the iPhone (March 2011) and iPad (May 2012) brought in a greater than expected number of downloads. Pinterest Mobile (for non-iPhone users) was launched in September 2011. In August 2011, *Time* magazine listed Pinterest in its article on 'The 50 Best Websites of 2011'.

According to Hitwise data, the site became one of the top 10 largest social network services in December 2011 with 11 million total visits per week. In January 2012, the company was named the 'Best new startup of 2011' by TechCrunch. ComScore reported the site had 11.7 million unique users in January 2012, making it the fastest site in history to break through the 10 million unique visitor mark, even with an invite-only policy.[183]

For a retailer Pinterest is interesting as a showcase for its products (and prices). A user can even browse for gifts by clicking on the homepage on 'gifts' and filtering a price range. Pinterest is establishing itself as a huge traffic driver for online retail. Also, online publishers are receiving a lot of traffic generated via Pinterest, even more than Twitter did in February 2012. Content from magazine websites and blogs that focus on home décor, arts and crafts, style and food are among the most frequently 'pinned' subjects on Pinterest. It is no surprise that those sites are reporting significant traffic growth from Pinterest.[184]

Pinterest in Europe

In January 2012, the most important European market for Pinterest was the UK with 245 000 unique visitors, followed by Germany with 67 000 unique visitors and Spain with 62 000 unique visitors. In the USA 83% of its users are female, whereas the opposite is true for the UK, where 56% of users are male. In the USA the largest group (28%) is aged 35–44 years; 42% of users in the UK are aged between 25 and 34. In the USA most of the pins are design-related. In the UK the site is more business-related.[185]

Brands using Pinterest

As Pinterest is one of the fastest-growing social sites of the moment with a large user base, the site is becoming more and more interesting for brands. It should not take too long before brands start integrating Pinterest in their social media approach.

Kotex claims to be the very first, although Peugeot did organise a Pinterest Puzzle previously. The 'Womens Inspiration Day by Kotex' is a sort of influencer campaign. By analysing individual pins, Kotex identified 50 influential women in Israel. Based on their individual interests, Kotex made up a box full of individual gifts. To receive their gift box, all they needed to do was to 're-pin' the Kotex gift. The women received their gifts and posted comments about them on their social pages, blogs and of course their Pinterest page. The campaign resulted in 2284 interactions and almost 695 000 impressions.[186,187]

Etsy, an e-commerce website with handmade, vintage, art and craft items is one of the most followed brands (94 250 followers in June 2012) and displays a huge variety of boards conveying its personality.

Different travel agencies, such as Travel Channel with 17 156 followers and Thomas Cook (organised per country), are providing visual inspiration on where to book your next holiday.

GAP (8610 followers) is showcasing popular products, gift guides, new collections, icons and inspirations for using old T-shirts for DIY projects, as well as specific pinboards of its major designers.

British brands are starting experiments with Pinterest. In April 2012, Harrods invited customers to create a mood board, which was the inspiration for a 'Queen's Diamond Jubilee Street Party' window. To take part in this Pinterest competition your board had to be titled 'Harrods Street Party Window' and, once completed, a tweet needed to be sent to Harrods containing a link to your board including the hashtag #HarrodsWindows. Harrods promoted the competition on its Facebook page (202 000 fans) and via its Twitter account (101 000 followers). The competition drew on people's love of taking pictures and intersected well with what Pinterest can deliver. On its own Pinterest page Harrods also created a themed board including images of past Harrods window displays to inspire potential competition participants. The winner was brought to London and put up in a top hotel in advance of the official unveiling of the window.[188]

The popularity of Pinterest is a consequence of consumers feeling increasingly more comfortable with recommendations from friends or other users when they come through social personalisation.[189] Pinterest is more trusted as an information source than Facebook and Twitter by general Internet users. But Pinterest is also seen as a place 'to have fun', as well as 'get product information' and 'find out about new products'.[190]

Communities on Pinterest are less about friends and more about common interests. The Liverpool Football Club was the first Premier League club to launch Pinterest boards aiming to appeal to a broad cross-section of its supporter base. Boards include among others 'Liverpool Legends' to track some of the greatest players and managers in Liverpool Football Club's history, 'The Greatest Fans in the World', a photo tribute to the supporters who follow Liverpool, and even 'LFC Cakes', a collection of club-themed cakes and cupcakes.[191]

While the USA leads with the highest number of Twitter accounts, 107.7 million by the end of 2011, the Netherlands has the most active users. While many statistics are about the number of users on Twitter, and the social network's growth in general, it is more interesting to see how active those users actually are. Globally, the percentage of accounts posting a tweet during a three-month period remains at 27%. This means that at least 73% of those millions of accounts were dormant for at least three months. The Netherlands has the most active accounts with 33% of them posting a tweet in the three-month period. Other active countries are Japan, Spain, the USA and Indonesia. This low percentage of active users highlights the fact that a vast number of Twitter users are choosing to use the social network to consume information, rather than share it. This reinforces the idea that only a small percentage of Twitter users are producing most of the shared content.[192] In October 2011, Yahoo Research revealed that 50% of the most influential tweets consumed are generated from just 20 000 elite users. The remaining Twitter users merely retweet or rebroadcast the highly influential content. Media present the bulk of the information, and celebrities are the most followed.[193] When we look at the global ranking of the accounts having the largest group of followers, we see that indeed celebrities take the lead: Lady Gaga with 25 million followers (her Facebook account has 51.5 million fans) followed by Justin Bieber with 22.6 million followers (Facebook page with 43.8 million fans) and Katy Perry with 20.4 million followers (Facebook page with 43.5 million fans). The first international brand in the Twitter ranking is Starbucks Coffee with 2.6 million followers, whereas its Facebook page has 30.2 million fans.[194] JetBlue Airways, now ranked in seventh place in the Twitter Brands charts with 1.7 million followers, was among the first corporate companies to join Twitter in 2007. JetBlue is often cited as an example of small corporate twittering. It joined Twitter to help its customers. By simply asking, it found out what the customers wanted. The company found that customer service tweets generated more followers and replies, and tweets about press releases got no response. This approach has made it quite successful. JetBlue tore down the wall between the customer and the brand by implementing Twitter.[195] Google reported in April 2012 that Google+ boasted over 170 million members globally vs nearly 900 million users for Facebook.

BUSINESS INSIGHT
KLM launches Meet & Seat on Facebook and LinkedIn

If you want to find out who is taking the same flight as you, you have to fly KLM. With 'Meet & Seat' you can view other passengers' Facebook or LinkedIn profile details and see where they will be sitting – long before your flight takes off. This new KLM Airlines' service lets you find out about interesting people who will be on board the same KLM flight, such as other passengers attending the same event as you at your destination. In February 2012, KLM 'Meet & Seat' was piloted for bookings with one passenger and for KLM flights between Amsterdam and New York, San Francisco and Sao Paulo from 90 days until 48 hours before departure. Based on social media profiles, passengers can choose seat partners. KLM has been experimenting with social media since the volcanic ash cloud in 2010. On Facebook, KLM has more than 1 million followers, which makes it the third most followed airline in the world. KLM wants to integrate social media throughout its entire flight operations so passengers can get quick answers to questions and complaints, and so that they can easily rebook online for a later flight. At the headquarters in Amstelveen, KLM has set up a permanent 'Social Media Hub', where dozens of employees are active 24 hours a day.[196]

Demographics and usage

When it comes to demographics, women outnumber men on some social networks – women make up 53% of Facebook users and 49% of MySpace users. LinkedIn and Twitter have a more male profile: a majority of LinkedIn members (56%) and Twitter users (55%) are men. People link online with their offline friends. Social networking is a way for people to meet up with others. On average a Facebook account has 133 friends; a Twitter account has 59 followers. Checking the status of others, chatting and messaging are the main activities on social networks, all two-way communications streams. An average Facebook session lasts 37 minutes, compared with a Twitter session of 23 minutes.[197] Dutch people spend an average of 5 to 10 minutes on LinkedIn.[198] A study conducted in Sweden revealed that an average Facebook user spends 75 minutes a day on Facebook and logs on 6.1 times a day. Women spend more time on Facebook, 81 minutes, versus men, 64 minutes, and write more about their relationships and emotions than men do. In general, 38% share negative information on their status.[199]

Although there are age restrictions on most social network sites, for instance Facebook is for 13+, millions of pre-teens use these sites anyway. Some get permission from their parents to create an account. Others lie about their age to get past the sign-up restrictions. According to a study conducted by EU Kids Online, 38% of 9 to 12 year olds have a social networking profile. This percentage grows to 77% with the group of 13–16 year olds. The main social network site for 9–12 year olds is Facebook with a penetration of 20%. Among 13–16 year olds, 46% use Facebook as their main social network site.[200] Facebook is planning to abandon the restriction of 13+ by linking the kids' pages to that of the parents. The parents can keep an eye on the applications used and to give their approval on friends requests.

Opportunities for brands

People join social networks to learn about their friends, but also to get information about (new) products and brands. However, they do not like the traditional marketing messages. People prefer people above brands. This implies that companies and brands should use their social media differently. It is about being human and putting personal identity above an institutional identity. About half of the European social networkers follow brands or companies on social media. They connect to brand pages because of personal brand experiences and conversations about brands by peers. They seldom connect because brands or companies ask them to. People in the south of Europe follow more brands (17.3 on average) than those in other regions. Social networkers expect some sort of benefit from companies on social networks, such as product information, promotions and event announcements. There is still a huge opportunity for companies to get in touch with their customers: 58% have never experienced any action by a company or brand on social network sites; 36% of the social networkers in Europe post information about brands; 53% react to comments; and 51% ask for information. Consumers prefer to react on brand updates rather than get into a dialogue with a brand. Content planning and regular content updates are one way to increase the engagement with fans. If people share information about a brand, company or product, it is often about the product or brand experience they have recently had. Recall that positive experiences dominate negative ones. One-third of European social networkers share much more than they did in the previous year. Again, the credibility of word of mouth is important. Consumers trust each other most. When people look for information on products, companies or brands, they tend to look for information coming from their peers. Positive brand experiences have the highest impact on brand perception and buying intention. Use your own employees as brand ambassadors.[201]

Social networkers with a smart phone follow brands on social media more often: 56% of connected smart phone users follow a brand on social media. On the one hand, marketers can expect more impact from reaching social networkers through smart phones, but on the other hand mobile social networkers also expect more from companies and brands. They want to be more involved – almost half of them are interested in co-creating products, packaging, campaigns – and they expect companies and brands to start conversations with them.[202]

BUSINESS INSIGHT
Sainsbury's listened to 3 year old kid and rebranded its Tiger bread

The power of people using social network sites towards brands is big. What started with a letter from a 3 year old toddler over a Facebook page set up by the mother ended in a rebranding of Sainsbury's Tiger bread towards Giraffe bread. The new Giraffe loaves went on sale eight months after toddler Lily Robinson sent a letter to the supermarket suggesting the splotches on the bloomer's crust resemble more a giraffe's pelt than that of a tiger. Sainsbury's customer manager agreed, explained to her the origins of the bread's name and questioned the zoological skills of the baker who came up with it. He also gave Lily a gift voucher to spend in the supermarket, which she could use 'to buy some tiger bread (and maybe if mum and dad say it is OK you can get some sweeties too!)'. Further on, Lily's mother used the social media and started a Facebook page called 'Campaign to change Tiger Bread to Giraffe Bread at Sainsbury's' with 1000 'likes' and comments, and nudging Sainsbury's into action. Eight months later Tiger bread received its new name.[203]

Source: Copyright © Telegraph Media Group Limited 2012.

In May 2012, 64 of the world's 100 most valuable brands, as identified by Interbrand, had an official presence on Google+, the social network of Google launched in September 2011. The scale of brand activity on Google+ still pales in comparison with Facebook and Twitter.

Commercial videos to the site typically receive the best reaction, ahead of text updates, photos and then articles. Marketers also seem to be making more regular efforts to refresh their pages, with 43 brands now posting at least three times a week.[204] Cadbury UK is the first brand in the Google+ ranking with 1.36 million followers, followed by Ferrari (0.90 million), H&M (0.86 million), Virgin (0.85 million) and Red Bull (0.76 million) completing the top five.[205] In the global charts of 'branded' Facebook pages, Coca-Cola takes first position having 42.3 million fans in May 2012. This FMCG brand is followed by Disney (36 million), Converse (30.8 million) and Starbucks (30.2 million). Red Bull completes the top five with 28.3 million fans.[206]

BUSINESS INSIGHT
The Coca-Cola Facebook page

One of the most inspiring stories about social media is the Coca-Cola Facebook page. The timeline starts with the real beginning of the brand in May 1886.[207] This fan page was initially not even created by Coca-Cola itself but by two brand fans, Dusty and Michael. They were searching for The Coca-Cola Fan Page on Facebook, but because they could not find one that felt official enough, they decided to create one themselves. This page turned out to be the largest product fan page on Facebook. Coca-Cola rewarded the two creators by bringing them to Atlanta and giving them a tour of the Coke facility. The fan page remains theirs, but now they have the blessing and help of Coca-Cola. The Coca-Cola marketing team are still involving Dusty and Michael in many activities: they made a video of the history behind the fan page, they baked a big celebration cake for the 25 million fans, etc. By empowering the fans to keep their Facebook page, Coke ensured passionate page owners.[208]

At first glance, the Coca-Cola fan page seems generic, but on taking a closer look, this page is really a testament to the brand's commitment to user participation. Firstly, Coca-Cola is displaying user-created content in its main page wall feed by default, which means that the page is really powered by user-generated content, good and bad. Another way that Coca-Cola stands out is in its approach to photo albums. It has a number of albums showing off the product, workers at the company, pictures of Coke fans, Coke products from all around the world and pictures of old Coke nostalgia. The photo albums reflect that Coca-Cola is also a collector's item.

When Facebook introduced its Timeline format for brand pages in December 2011, it gave marketers additional opportunities on their pages for more emphasis on images and engagement on the wall. On the first page a wide-open space was created that can be filled with a unique image representing the brand at its best or even a banner ad or the announcement of a promotion or event. It is the first thing people see when they visit a Facebook page. Filling out the timeline shows a more human side of the brand: the history of the brand, most memorable events, packaging changes, marketing campaigns, information about the people working for the brand, etc., can all be plotted on the timeline. Another feature that came with the introduction of the Timeline layout is the possibility of highlighting posts by displaying the update across the width of the page, giving more weight to key news. Another new option is the 'Pin to Top', which extends the life of the content. When Red Bull pinned a month-old video of its sponsored skier Bobby Brown to its Facebook brand page, the post received 2000 more 'Likes'. Social media users are continuously bombarded with information, so pinning helps to cut through the noise and ensure that fans will see the best posts.[209]

BRAND INSIGHT
Creative usage of Facebook's Timeline

Quechua has used the opportunities of the Timeline in a creative way. Quechua creates eco-friendly apparel, accessories and gear for mountain hiking. It is well represented in Europe. Each of the 300 photos posted on the Timeline shows the successive movements of a man hiking through the mountains. Based on the old process of making cartoons, the viewer needs to flip through the photos and get the illusion that the man is actually climbing. To achieve this effect the viewer needs to scroll down towards the first picture. Once the photos are loaded the viewer presses Shift + space and the action takes place. The 'movie' captures the tonality of the brand, not in a rough way, but in a way that is all about the peace that nature brings.[210]

Saying thanks to fans can also be done in a very creative and entertaining way. In April 2012, Kraft Mac & Cheese thanked 4800 fans that 'liked' a Facebook post with a seven-minute song called 'Likeapella'. The song namechecked every single one of them and was posted as video content on Kraft's Mac & Cheese wall.[211]

To conclude, there are five key success factors for a company or brand to be social:[212]

1. *Be active*. Social media are about sharing, interaction and engaging. If you want to develop a relationship with consumers, it is advisable to take the lead and to be active.

2. *Be interesting*. If you would like your customers to engage with you, you need to give them a reason for doing so. You must do better than just saying you are the best. An important start is to listen to what your consumers want to hear and what they want to talk about. What topics or approach would be interesting for your consumers?

3. *Be humble*. Before entering into social media you have to take some time to discover them and learn about their history and basic rules.

4. *Be unprofessional*. Avoid over-professional content and behave as a friend, not as a brand or a company.

5. *Be honest*. Respect the rules of the game. If companies are not allowed to participate (as on Wikipedia) do not force your way in.

BUSINESS INSIGHT
Britneys Spears' use of social media[213]

Britney Spears is one of the most successful female recording artists in contemporary music worldwide. She relies on social media applications to maintain her celebrity brand image. The use of social media during the launch of her single 'Hold It Against Me' in 2011, combined with her own webpage BritneySpears.com, can be seen as a prime example of social media usage to support new product introductions.

In 2010, Britney Spears was the first Twitter account holder to exceed 5 million followers, leaving actor Ashton Kutcher and pop stars Justin Bieber and Lady Gaga far behind. She, and of course her employees, rely in a close to near-perfect way on social media to build and strengthen her celebrity brand image. They maintain her webpage/blog (www.BritneySpears.com, new version since October 2008), two YouTube channels (Britney Spears and

Britney TV, since October 2005 and December 2006), a Twitter account and a Facebook profile (both since August 2008).

In June 2012, Britney Spears had around 1.2 million subscribers on YouTube, 17.4 million followers on Twitter and 19.5 million fans on Facebook. In addition to these primary activities, Britney Spears also maintains a profile on MySpace (created in October 2003) and on Google+ (since its launch in September 2011) with 3.4 million followers. Her iPhone application 'It's Britney' provides official news and exclusive messages, and allows users to assemble digital images of Britney and themselves. All these platforms allow Miss Spears and her team to be in close contact with her fan base and interact with them on a daily basis. Important messages are communicated via her social media tools instead of via press interviews. This approach generates a feeling of privilege and appreciation with the fans. In responding to the questions of her fans, the Britney Spears team pay close attention to ensuring that it is absolutely clear who is providing the responses. Posts made by Britney Spears are marked using the '~Brit' signature.

Two weeks prior to the launch of her new 'Radiance' fragrance, she posted on her webpage, Facebook and Twitter: 'Happy Friday people! Am I part of your future?' followed by a link to her Facebook presence, through which readers could launch an application related to the Radiance advertising spot. The app used a fortune teller, and showed users different pictures of themselves and their friends in the form of a crystal ball. These pictures, captured from the respective user's Facebook photo albums, were followed by a video of the Radiance spot itself. On Twitter, this post received 1052 replies and 666 retweets from 1516 users and was read by about 500 000 people. In total, 43 000 people clicked on the link and used the 'crystal ball' application on Facebook.

Britney Spears and her team also collaborate with social media pages owned by third parties such as fan blogs in order to make sure that the posts are consistent with the messages on the channels 'owned' by Spears' team.

The launch of 'Hold It Against Me'

Prior to the official release of the single 'Hold It Against Me' a demo tape was 'leaked' on YouTube. That day Britney Spears posted on Twitter: 'Heard an early demo of my new single leaked. If u think that's good, wait til you hear the real one Tuesday. ~Brit'. This post, combined with the demo tape, resulted in substantial press coverage of the single even before its release on 10 January 2011. A similar strategy was used to launch the video of the single. Historically, music videos were released simultaneously with their respective single in order to increase sales. Yet, in the case of 'Hold It Against Me', the video was not even produced by the single release. It was shot two weeks later. During the shooting, Twitter followers could read about the progress of the video shoot.

Two weeks before the release date of the video, 14 teasers were shown on YouTube on a daily basis under the motto '14 Days, 14 Teasers, 1 World Premiere'. Each clip generated between 1 and 5 million views. The grand premiere of the entire video was accompanied by a live discussion on MTV.com. In parallel, Britney Spears commented on Facebook and Twitter. In addition to its unique release strategy, the 'Hold It Against Me' video relied heavily on product placement. The video included sequences during which four products and logos were displayed prominently: the women's fragrance Radiance produced by Britney Spears for Elizabeth Arden; an eye shadow from the company Makeup Forever; the logo of Sony (owner of the music label of Britney Spears); and the online dating site PlentyOfFish.com. The product placement received negative comments from many critics and journalists but was perceived rather positively by fan groups.

Prior to the 'Hold It Against Me' video release, over 400 fan clips with potential choreography for the new song were posted on YouTube. Some clips received more than 100 000 views. Britney Spears encouraged the development of user-generated content by including links to some of these videos on BritneySpears.com.

The results

During its first week, the single was downloaded 411 000 times from iTunes, which was the best sales week for a digital song in the history of Britney Spears and the most successful debut of a single with a woman as lead artist. Unsurprisingly, the song jumped to the top of the iTunes charts in 16 countries and the USA. On top of this the site PlentyOfFish.com increased its traffic by 20% and product placements in the video generated $500 000 of profit for Britney Spears.

Learnings

The launch of Britney Spears' 'Hold It Against Me' is a good example of how companies can use social media to support the introduction of new products through viral marketing. First of all, Britney Spears and her social media manager choose carefully the platforms they are concentrating their efforts on (YouTube, Facebook and Twitter) in addition to her own webpage. Social media are a toolset, not a list of sites you have to have a presence on. Firms that have a lot of information to share might prefer the interactivity of Twitter, others probably see a better fit in Facebook, where infrequent postings are less of an issue, or in a personal blog that allows better control of the information flow and resulting comments. You can pick an existing platform or make your own. Britney Spears used a combination of platforms of third parties (Facebook/YouTube/Twitter) with her own webpage/blog. Although she is still present on MySpace she did not use it because of the decreasing relevance. Google+ did not exist at that time and her followers today on Google+ are still far below her presence on Facebook and Twitter.

Using different social media platforms needs co-ordination and substantial effort in order to ensure activity alignment and consistency. Such activity alignment and media plan integration is an important cornerstone of any social media strategy.

Britney Spears does not issue press releases. Instead, she communicates all information through her chosen social media applications. This ensures consistency between data available both online and via traditional media. The media team even collaborate closely with third-party applications to ensure this consistency. Being important and being active are essential. By leaking demo tapes, posting teasers and spreading the product launch over a period of several weeks this advice was put into practice by Britney Spears and her team. The Britney Spears media team pay close attention to how they communicate with fans. The language they use for updates on Facebook and Twitter is colloquial, and therefore consistent with the way friends would speak to each other without being over-professional. In addition, they are honest with the fans by making it explicit that only messages signed with '~Brit' are actually posted by Britney Spears herself. In the early days of her Twitter account, this was not the case and it was heavily criticised by fans. So she listened and adopted her strategy accordingly.

Media investments

More businesses are investing in social media. During February 2012, 27.5% of the 73.7 billion UK ad impressions were display ads on social networking sites. The category with the highest share of these kinds of ads was consumer goods with 40% of their total display ad impressions being socially published, followed by media and entertainment, with 35.7%. One of the advertisers placing the highest share of ads in the UK was KX Energy Drink with 89.3% of its total impressions being published on sites like Facebook and LinkedIn.[214]

In the USA social media advertising spending may rise to $9.8 billion in 2016. In 2012 the spending on social media was predicted to be $4.8 billion. The drivers for this increase are better performance, richer formats and creative elements, like video.[215] Over the next five years, social media ad spend is expected to have a share of 19.5% of the total marketing budget. At the start of 2012, this was 7.4% (Table 15.4).[216]

Table 15.4 Ad revenue of social networking sites

	Ad revenue 2011 ($)	Change vs 2010
Facebook[217]	2.6 billion (85%[218] of 3.1 billion annual revenue)	+69%
YouTube[219]	1.6 billion	+60%
LinkedIn[220]	226 million	+46,1%
Twitter[221]	139.5 million	+213%

With 900 million users, and nearly 500 daily active users, Facebook takes the major part of the online social media advertising budget. This is comprehensible seeing the opportunities that Facebook gives to marketers to advertise:[222]

- 900 million potential customers;
- targeting possibilities by location, age and interest;
- simple image, text-based and even video ads;
- ads to mobile devices (425 million users are using Facebook on their mobiles);
- larger ads on the side of the homepage that users see when they first log in;
- ads that run inside the Facebook Newsfeed;
- ads that appear when a user logs out of Facebook.[223]

Referring back to the Kaplan and Haenleins classification[224] of social media, there are still two boxes that need clarification: **virtual game worlds** and **virtual social worlds.**

Virtual worlds

Virtual worlds are platforms that replicate a 3-D environment in which users can appear in the form of personalised avatars and interact with each other as they would in real life. In this sense, virtual worlds are probably the ultimate manifestation of social media, as they provide the highest level of social presence and media richness. Virtual worlds come in two forms: gaming and social.

Virtual game worlds

These require their users to behave according to strict rules in the context of a massively multiplayer online role-playing game (MMORPG). Since standard game consoles like Microsoft's X-Box and Sony's PlayStation allow simultaneous play among a multitude of users around the globe, in recent years these virtual game worlds have gained popularity. The world's most subscribed MMORPG is the cod-medieval 'World of Warcraft', which had around 10.2 million subscribers in December 2011 but peaked around 12 million back in late 2010.[225] The rules of such games are very strict, which limits the degree of self-presentation and self-disclosure. Similar to the idea of product placement in movies, brands can have in-game advertising as well as leverage the high popularity of virtual game worlds in more traditional communications campaigns. Japanese automotive giant Toyota used pictures and mechanics from the 'World of Warcraft' application in its Tundra commercial to reach the 2.5 million players in the USA alone.[226]

Virtual social worlds

This second group of virtual worlds allows inhabitants to choose their behaviour more freely and essentially live a virtual life similar to their real life. Again, virtual social world users appear in the form of avatars and interact in a 3-D virtual environment. A good example of such a virtual world is the Second Life application, founded in 2003. Besides doing everything that is possible in real life (speaking, walking, sunbathing, etc.) Second Life also allows users to create content (such as design virtual clothing or furniture items) and to sell this content to others in exchange for 'local' currencies. Since 2010 Second Life saw a drastic decline in the number of concurrent active users and had to lay off a substantial number of its staff. Other virtual social worlds like The Sims Online (owned by Electronic Arts) still seem to be quite popular among teens with many opportunities for marketers to include branded items. In the past H&M had a shop with a virtual 3-D clothes collection and, in May 2012, Diesel announced the launch of The Sims 3 Diesel pack stuff full of Diesel-branded apparel, accessories and furniture.

Relationship marketing and the Internet

The basis of loyalty programmes consists of collecting data that are related to the customers' behaviour. What kind of customers are they? What do they ask for? What do they buy? What interests do they have and how can e-communications to be tailored their wants? Customer profiles drive what the website looks like, which e-mails customers receive, what kind of offers they receive, etc. The Web is not about fragmenting audiences but about creating one-to-one relationships for marketers and increasing the bond between consumers and producers. Database applications, like collaborative filtering used by Amazon.com, focus on customer retention rather than acquisition. The Internet is well suited for the evolution towards an individualised, tailored value proposition. It offers addressability, two-way continuous inter-activity, customisation capabilities, on-demand availability and seamless transactions. Marketers can leverage interactive media to identify self-selected users, enhance loyalty by providing value-added services, use what they learn about their customers to customise existing products or create new products and services, and start an ongoing online communication with customers. E-mail communications with customers are more personal and intimate than the traditional letter with glossy brochure. When a customer sends an e-mail to a company, the person who replies to the e-mail suddenly becomes the representative for the whole company.[227]

Relationship marketing is all about building confidence and growing the relationship. Make your consumers 'feel' they can count on you, and then deliver. Because we live in a digital world this relationship is more and more created and supported via the tools provided by social media. A formula for success includes building a quality online community. Use and select carefully social media platforms such as Facebook, Twitter, Pinterest, LinkedIn, Google+, etc., as they will help in promoting your brand. Offer quality content on blog posts. Above all be consistent in your brand message and offer value. Be honest and passionate about your brand and care about your fans and followers. Listen to your current and potential customers and offer solutions to their problems, needs or interests. Once the relationship is solid you can reach out to your friends, followers and fans by giving them clear offers or calls to action. Maintain a consistent style, using personal and promotional content. Integrate offline activities to optimise online, like networking, joining relevant groups, and be accessible.

The use of loyalty programmes can be very successful. Identify advocates of your brand and get them to help in promoting your products and services. Encourage them to share their product experiences with their networks, interact with them regularly, swap tips and ask for their advice. This is again a form of relationship-based marketing. And do not forget to reward your brand advocates even if it is simply thanking them publicly with a Tweet or Facebook post. Relationship marketing is the new currency of business but also via the Internet it takes time and effort.[228]

BUSINESS INSIGHT
Dunkin' Donuts builds relationships online

Based on purchase data - collected through the Dunkin' Donuts Perks Card (DD Perks), their own loyalty card – Dunkin' Donuts found out that the heavy Dunkin' Donuts customers visit the store several times a week while spending twice as much as the average customer. The light customer however spends less than 25% of the average amount. Next to the increase of in-store sales, Dunkin' Donuts wanted to quintuple its customer database, leading them to run a national online campaign with Yahoo!, after a long history of using traditional media channels such as TV and print. The reasons behind this choice were the higher levels of accountability and engagement associated with online campaigns.

Yahoo! ran a 41-day display campaign with promotions to encourage customers to register with the Dunkin' Donuts loyalty programme. To increase campaign performance, behavioural targeting and continual optimisation were implemented.

The campaign resulted in more than 16 000 sign-ups, and enrolment increased by 300% between the first 14 days and the last 14 days of the campaign.[229]

The essence of CRM is to have a single comprehensive database with a complete history of the prospect or customer that can be accessed from any of the customer touchpoints (sales, call centre, personalised website and customer service).[230] Dell provides a Premier Pages service for its corporate clients. Premier Pages are sites dedicated to a particular customer and only accessible to that customer. Each dedicated site holds a record of all previous interactions between the customer and Dell and can be used to communicate with the customer and inform him or her about exclusive offers. The collaborative software that Amazon.com, the online book and CD retailer, uses allows communication of personalised advice on products that the software predicts to be interesting for a certain customer.[231] LivePerson software (www.liveperson.com) offers website integration with live customer service representatives in real time.[232]

Tracking the effectiveness of e-communications

The company website is a way to reach customers directly and deliver information to them, take their orders and build relationships. The Net is also a medium used to place advertising and to create a direct communications line with customers and prospects. For these reasons, it is important for marketers to know how their website and online marketing campaigns are performing and how they can improve the effectiveness and efficiency of their site and digital strategy. As the Internet is an interactive and computer-supported medium, all information about site traffic is stored on the net server in server log files. Analysing these files is one way of tracking website performance. About half of Belgian and Dutch marketers feel that the results of online marketing actions are more measurable than those of most other traditional marketing actions. The only other technique whose effectiveness is even easier to measure, in their view, is direct marketing.[233]

Assessing the effectiveness of e-marketing involves finding answers to questions like:

- Are the corporate and marketing objectives identified in the e-marketing strategy being met?
- Are the marketing communications objectives identified in the e-marketing plan achieved?
- How effective are the different promotional tactics used?[234]

Measuring website effectiveness

The most basic method to measure site effectiveness is by asking for feedback on the website. This can be done by asking visitors to leave a contact e-mail address or by inserting a feedback form on one of the web pages. Both methods will only elicit the most extreme (negative and positive) reactions, and are not representative of the site audience. Moreover, little feedback

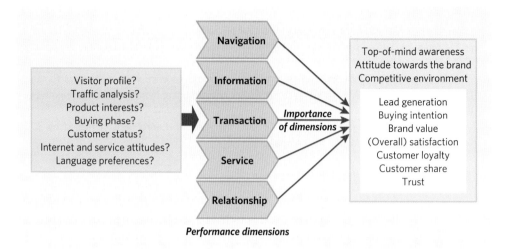

Figure 15.1 Assessing website marketing performance: the InSites Consulting model
Source: Developed by InSites, www.insites-consulting.com.

may be expected. Including a feedback form may provide more detailed feedback and more direction as specific questions and categories of information can be included in the feedback form.

To find out who really visits a website and what his or her evaluation of the site, the brand and the sales effects are, visitor surveys (online or offline) are necessary. Surveys may give socio-demographic, psychographic and webographic (with regard to the use of the Internet) profiles of visitors. They can also measure attitudes, satisfaction and intentions, and are a good way of tracking the effectiveness and success of a website. InSites Consulting (www.insites-consulting.com), a leading European Internet research agency, developed a model to evaluate the performance of a website using scientifically tested questionnaires and constructs, adaptable to specific research questions and needs (see Figure 15.1). In pre-testing, usability testing and post-testing of websites, qualitative market research techniques such as focus groups and in-depth interviewing can be used in conjunction with quantitative Internet panel surveys to add research insights to the website visitor surveys. Website users' input should be integrated with the design process to ensure targeted and effective website building.

Even without any research budget there is a possibility to gain insights into how many (unique) visitors your site has per day/week/month/etc., how visitors use your site, how they arrived on your site (from which site, using which searching words, etc.), from which countries, how you can keep them coming back by using Google Analytics. Google Analytics is a reporting platform where the user can decide which parameters are of interest. Content reports give insights into which parts of the website are performing well, which pages are most popular, how much time the surfer is spending on these pages, in order to create a better experience for the visitor, your prospect or customer. Even social media (what your visitors are sharing and where) and mobile (know which mobile platforms work best, see where mobile traffic comes from) are now incorporated. You can analyse how visitors interact with sharing features on your site. Conversion parameters give insights into the number of customers that the brand or the company attracts, how much it sells and how users are engaging with the site.[235]

Also, Google Analytics can be used for analysing an online advertising campaign. Advertising Analytics is providing detailed insights to know if the advertising programme is working. All digital channels such as search, display, social, affiliate and e-mail can be included to see the effect on conversion rates and return.[236]

Apart from these measures, the most important issue for marketers is what happens after users click through an online ad or visit a website. Does the online marketing strategy lead to conversion? What is the effect of the e-marketing campaign on brand equity and purchase intention? For e-commerce sites, purchase behaviour is easy to link to e-marketing tactics but, for most companies and businesses, the effects on sales are difficult to trace as they often take place in the offline distribution system. Using post-campaign research that consists of an initial tracking of brand awareness, brand image and intention to buy before the campaign and a post-campaign survey tracking the same metrics can deliver this kind of information. InSites Consulting also offers an e-ROI methodology that tracks the behaviour of customers and prospects after they have visited a company's website, by using a recontact survey. In this way, InSites is able to calculate the ROI of a website and online advertising campaign.

BUSINESS INSIGHT
Measuring social media[237]

There is a lot of discussion on how to measure social media performances and how marketers can calculate their ROI. Most social media experts agree that there is not one established framework to measure social media success. Nevertheless there are some tactics that a marketer can adjust and apply to his or her social media strategy to help create a framework that works.

Step 1: Set the goals

Marketers need to know upfront what their goals (quantitative and qualitative) are before they can measure how successful the efforts have been in achieving them.

What do you want to accomplish through your social media efforts? Is it selling more products, getting more reviews, driving more traffic to the website, establishing the brand or company as a leader, generating leads, increasing the fan base, reaching specific target groups, increasing brand awareness, etc.?

Step 2: Establish the baselines

Based on the goals from step 1, establish measurable baselines for comparison later.

Create an overview that includes several parameters like current sales figures, review counts, number of hits in Google, statistics of the website stats, customer satisfaction and others depending on the goals. Some are easier to measure than others.

Step 3: Track the efforts

Plenty of tools are available to measure social media efforts. Some are (freely) provided by the social media platform itself (e.g. Facebook and WordPress), some are paid services. It is important to use more than one tool to track the efforts, as each individual tool gives specific insight into one or more aspects of your social media presence. Be aware that you should stick to the ones relevant for the goals that were set. If well selected a complete picture is given.

Facebook's statistics tool, Insights, tracks and analyses demographics, engagement, referrals, click-throughs, and more for Facebook pages. Facebook Insights breaks down the demographics and activities of a page's fans. This also allows the company to gain insight into how users engage with a specific post, where referrals are coming from, how well individual posts are doing and how content is shared.

For websites or blogs that are powered by WordPress, there are a number of good plug-ins that help in analysing, e.g. WordPress.com Stats. They provide insights on how visitors are interacting with a site: which posts are the most popular, where incoming referrals are coming from, which key terms visitors are using to find a site, which outgoing links are clicked, and more.

Twitter accounts can be managed and analysed via HootSuite, which has some nice analysis tools. The pro version allows an integration of Facebook Insights and Google Analytics. This tool helps in seeing which of the tweets is getting the most engagement, and even attempts to calculate the 'sentiment' of your Twitter followers towards your tweets.

Klout, a free external tool, uses an interesting set of criteria to determine what it refers to as a 'Klout Score'. The scores range from 1 to 100 with higher scores representing a wider and stronger sphere of influence. Therefore Klout uses variables on Facebook, Twitter, LinkedIn and Google+ to measure what it calls 'True Reach' (size of your engaged audience), 'Amplification Probability' (the likelihood that your messages will generate action as retweets, @messages, likes, comments) and 'Network Influence' (how engaged your audience are). An overall score over 30 is considered good. If your goal is to increase virality and your posts are neither shared nor retweeted, nor get likes or comments, you have to take action.

Google has different analytical tools that give very good insights. Next to Google Analytics, which tracks and analyses website and social media visitors, there is Google Webmaster Tools that gives insight into how Google indexes a site, which search terms are used to find a site, errors on a site, and more. You can get advanced metrics on specific search terms with Google Trends, and Google Alerts can keep you informed when certain terms (e.g. your brand, company, website name, or your book title) land high in search results.

Real-time search engines and analytical tools like Socialmention give good insights into the kind of attention that posts and updates are getting. In addition, Socialmention shows the reach, sentiment and passion that followers have for a name or brand. These search engines also give insights into the key terms that are typically associated with a brand.

Next to the free services, a lot of paid social media metric services are popping up (e.g. PostRank, Radian 6, JitterJam). When choosing one, be aware that they integrate social accounts, that they measure RSS feeds, website, other documents, interactions across other social sites, etc.

Step 4: Stay informed, but trust your instincts

You know your business better than anyone, so be careful in following advice that does not apply to your goals. Since the social media environment is changing so rapidly, marketers need to stay informed about the latest trends.

Summary

In large parts of Europe, the Internet reaches more than 80% of the population. Mobile and smart-phone penetration is increasing month after month, and connected TV is expected to penetrate further within a few years. As a consequence, consumers' media attention is fragmenting and marketers will have to follow them into the new digital media. They therefore employ a number of e-marketing tactics that all contribute to the communications objectives: creating brand awareness, shaping brand attitudes, generating trial and sustaining loyalty. Brand websites are essential for most brands to support brand image and communicate with customers. Merely having a website is not enough, and other offline and online advertising tools such as search engine optimisation will be required to drive traffic to the site. Because of the time and budget involved, more and more companies tend to create temporary mini-sites called micro-sites to draw users and bring a new product or service to their attention. Online advertising is on the rise in Europe with video and mobile as the segments that are increasing the most, and new ad formats regularly see the light. Keyword buying and content sponsorship are formats that are known to work on their strengths: namely, relevance to the target group. Ad types that are very popular due to their customer engagement and impact are advergames or online games. Although the cost of this kind of interactive advertising tends to be much higher than for other ad formats, the interaction time leads to a higher brand immersion. Related to these games are viral marketing actions, which make good use of the network characteristics of the net community, online contests, and e-sampling and e-couponing, which have a number of advantages over their offline counterparts. The same is true for e-mail marketing, the digital form of direct marketing communications, which has recently been joined by action-driven mobile marketing communications to the cell phones of consumers. The rise in social digital TV is giving marketers new opportunities. Finally, the Internet, as an intrinsically interactive medium, can also be used to develop and sustain customer relationships, for instance via customer service pages on the Net or virtual communities. The participation of the consumer in the dialogue between brand or company and consumers via the different social media networks such as Facebook and Twitter is of massive importance to the marketer. Marketers need to become conversation managers.

The effectiveness of e-communications can be assessed by the use of free research platforms such as Google Analytics or via ad hoc research using visitor surveys.

REVIEW QUESTIONS

1. How is the Internet and online advertising market in Europe evolving?
2. How can a brand or company website contribute to a marketing plan?
3. Discuss the different kinds of online advertising and compare them in terms of performance.
4. What other e-marketing tools are available? For which communications objective would you choose them?
5. What is meant by 'viral marketing'?
6. What are the dos and don'ts of e-mail marketing?
7. Explain the added value of mobile marketing to an e-marketing plan.
8. How can marketers benefit from a new evolution such as social television?
9. How can social media help to build a relationship with customers?
10. How can the effectiveness of e-marketing tactics be tracked?

Further reading

Burger, N. (2012), *Paid. Owned. Earned. Maximizing Marketing Returns in a Socially Connected World*. London: Kogan Page.

Metz, A. (2012), *The Social Customer: How Brands Can Use Social CRM to Acquire, Monetize, and Retain Fans, Friends and Followers*. New York: McGraw-Hill.

Proulx, M. and Shepatin, S. (2012), *Social TV: How Marketers Can Reach and Engage Audiences by Connecting Television to the Web, Social Media, and Mobile*. Hoboken, NJ: Wiley.

Zicherman, G. and Linder, J. (2010), *Game-based Marketing: Inspire Customer Loyalty Through Rewards, Challenges and Contests*. Hoboken, NJ: Wiley.

CASE 15:
The Global Fund's Born HIV Free campaign

The Global Fund in need of a different communications strategy

In 2002, at the directive of the G8, the Global Fund to Fight AIDS, Tuberculosis and Malaria was created as a rapid response mechanism to dramatically increase resources to fight three of the world's most devastating diseases, and to direct those resources to areas of greatest need. The Global Fund operates as an international financing institution. Its purpose is to attract, manage and disburse resources to fight AIDS, TB and malaria. It does not implement programmes directly, relying instead on a broad network of partnerships with other development organisations on the ground to supply local knowledge and technical assistance where most needed. It addresses gaps in country efforts to fight the three diseases and strengthen underlying health systems by financing programmes that complement those of other donors, and seeks to use its own grants to stimulate further investment by both donors and recipients. To date, it has committed $22.6 billion in 150 countries to support large-scale prevention, treatment and care programmes against the three diseases. In just ten years, programmes financed by the Global Fund have saved 7.7 million lives.

Like many of its counterparts in the development community, the Global Fund began facing difficult circumstances in 2010 in securing funding to both maintain and expand its life-saving programmes. Until that time, the Global Fund's communications strategy was much focused on a few thousand thought-leaders and policy-makers in donor countries. But around 2010, they started to receive strong signals from government donors that they could not simply continue to tell their constituents that they were giving the Global Fund so much money because it was the right thing to do, and that they had to make some real efforts to make themselves better known to their voters. The lack of public awareness about the Global Fund's successes, or even its existence, was also a consequence of its communications strategy prior to the difficult global economic circumstances that came to a head in 2010.

In May 2010, the Global Fund began talking to the general public with the launch of the Born HIV Free campaign, a six-month awareness and advocacy campaign that ran until 5 October, the day when donors made their three-year (2011–13) contribution pledge to the Global Fund. The cam-

paign narrative and call to action was focused on the goal of virtually ending the transmission of HIV from mother to child by 2015. The Born HIV Free campaign was created to put the issue of preventing mother-to-child transmission (PMTCT) of HIV on the global agenda, get taxpayer support for the work of the Global Fund and expose the Global Fund to the general public in the context of the replenishment and pledges for 2011–13. The campaign 'ask' was simple – add your name to the digital petition that states your belief in that goal, and affirm your support for your government's contribution to the Global Fund.

Source: The Global Fund.

The Born HIV Free campaign communications plan

The Born HIV Free campaign was set up as a multi-stage, multimedia communications campaign targeting the general public from Spain, France, UK, the Netherlands, Italy, Germany, Nordic countries and Ireland. It ran from April to October 2010 and consisted of a series of vivid and imaginative animated films, social marketing tools, the campaign website, and offline campaign events and products. The campaign used solely positive messages, calling upon Europeans to help end mother-to-child transmission of HIV – and to express to their governments that they have public support to continue and increase their funding to the Global Fund. The continued ambassadorship and 'voice' of the Global Fund's Ambassador, Carla Bruni-Sarkozy, was central to the Born HIV Free campaign. The campaign draws on extraordinary assets from partners – corporate and individuals – and the communications plan aims to maximise their visibility for the purpose of recognition of their contribution and to ensure the success of the campaign.

The campaign rested on three pillars: (1) online visibility; (2) social media outreach; and (3) offline events. It was organised in four phases. To leverage the content and spread the word, discussions and word of mouth are vital. The campaign activated and nurtured relationships with a number of multipliers including:

- 100 top digital influencers (including bloggers) from a number of European countries. Material was developed for them to spread the word in three languages (Spanish, English, French).

- 200 high-profile personalities from all walks of life, including celebrities, politicians, the media. The 'messengers' were requested to promote the campaign in their sphere of influence. They were provided with marketing material and specific requests for them to be able to act on behalf of the campaign.

- A dozen partners of the Global Fund were activated to spread the word among their constituencies and employees. These groups include health-based communities, NGOs, implementing partners, Product (RED), One, etc.

- Social networking and community management. The campaign established communities in international and national social platforms and had dedicated staff to ensure a two-way conversation with the communities.

> Phase 1: Start online (2–4 weeks prior to launch)

Community growth – bottom-up grassroots endorsement Trigger interest without revealing too many elements

Social media platforms and website

- Opening and launch of campaign through social media platforms (Facebook, Causes, Twitter, LinkedIn, and national site key markets when possible; YouTube should open only at launch day). Basic information about the campaign is provided, along with teasers, a trailer of one film, etc.

- Holding page on campaign website to go live. Minimum and basic information is exposed, including launch date and e-mail subscribe function. Mirror content exposed on social media platforms and encourage Facebook sign up.

Partner activation

- Roadshow of spokespeople of the campaign to capitals of target countries to create excitement and seed stories among selected media and selected bloggers.

- Partners and their employees are invited to join the social media groups (NGOs, media and offline partners, the Global Fund, etc.).

- Spread kit is sent to trusted partners (embargoed) in advance, for planning purposes. The owner of each relationship sent material to their own contacts.

- Spread kit for influencers, bloggers and further related partners sent one week prior to launch.

- T-shirts sent to 200 'messengers' to wear and trigger interest from media.

Media (offline/online)

- *Madame Figaro* magazine hits news stands on 26 March. Mentions the name of the campaign and its purpose without revealing further details.

- Spread kit is sent to media contacts, embedding the campaign into its context without going into details of activities but referring to the countdown so as to enable feature coverage.

- Spread kits for a wider group of mainstream media and bloggers with a minimal amount of information about the campaign sent a couple of days before the campaign launch.

- A small number of interviews with selected print and TV media, featuring Mme Bruni-Sarkozy, are recorded. Embargoed interviews to appear on launch day.

> Phase 2: Launch (one day)

Big European launch – press and bloggers outreach with all partners

The Global Fund launched the Born HIV Free campaign on 19 May 2010 in Paris. The launch event created pan-European visibility and was the main vehicle to acknowledge the contributions of the main partners. Partnerships, substantial donations and *pro bono* support by Google, YouTube and international health organisations (WHO, UNAIDS) were highlighted.

Digital

- Launch of banner campaign in ten countries (TV, Internet, print).

- Launch of campaign website.

- Launch of YouTube channel with first video featured on the YouTube Homepage. YouTube functionalities activated.

- Wikipedia page on the campaign is launched. Mentions objectives, data, facts and figures and ambassadorship. Links to CBS's website, the Global Fund's pages and related articles.
- Launch of partners' spreading efforts.
- Frequent updates on all social media platforms.
- Michel Kazatchkine to tweet on the campaign Twitter account.
- Partners (media, sponsors and offline) are acknowledged on website, media releases and social media.

Media

A global press conference was held on the day of the launch. The conference was broadcast on the Web. A press release was issued to accompany a Video News Release (VNR) with quotes from Carla Bruni-Sarkozy and other partners. The VNR was sent to the main evening news broadcast of the ten target countries and was highlighted on all social media platforms and the YouTube channel. Targeted journalists were selected from a wide range of media.

> Phase 3: Rollout (5–6 months – launch to end September)

Constant presence, sustainable communication

The rollout from the launch to the end of September involved a mix of online and offline operations that jointly created a European movement through an online video campaign and messenger, fashion, music and urban events.

Social media platforms and website

- Launch incentive programme (competition included) on social media platforms. Competition prize includes field trip to South Africa in August for one person from each of the target countries.
- Second film on YouTube 2–3 weeks after launch.
- YouTube competition to create third film.
- T-shirt: online distribution.
- Facebook users' and selected bloggers' trip to Africa, together with African journalists.
- Launch online goodies collector (May).

Media opportunities

- Mother's Day (May): Lifestyle media/radio double-ribbon brooch competition; interviews with media on markets where Mother's Day is strong; talkshows on chosen markets.
- Cannes Film Festival (May): T-shirt distribution at the Cannes Film Festival; capture photos of celebrities with T-shirt.

- Vienna's International AIDS Conference (July): Ambassador participation and visit to campaign's interactive stand and sign up for the campaign.
- Concerts: Paul McCartney's 'Hard Rock Calling' concert on 27 June 2010 became the first European performance to be streamed via YouTube. This live stream was dedicated to the Born HIV Free campaign with campaign messages (show your support and sign up now) on YouTube at the beginning, end and during short breaks. The concert was promoted on the Born HIV Free website, Facebook, Twitter and Flickr.
- Solidays, the annual three-day music festival in Paris, 25–27 June 2010, organised by Solidarité SIDA.

Offline operations

Special issues were featured in magazines, a 'double-ribbon' brooch was sent to 200 high-profile personalities from all walks of life (messengers), and video interviews and talkshows were organised for messengers.

> Phase 4: Wrap-up (3 weeks)

Strong finish – event

From the last week of September to 5 October, the day of the Replenishment meeting (the meeting at which the funding of the Global fund is decided upon). The campaign continued to provide reports and updates to followers also in the weeks and months after 5 October.

Social media platforms, website and offline

- Digital campaign to have online users take one single action on one specific day.
- Offline event – display of support.

The event tried to take advantage of the gathering of Heads of State and Ministers of Health in New York for the Clinton Global Initiative, the General Assembly and the Millennium Development Goals Summits in New York City at the end of September. A video press release was issued of the ambassadors talking about the support already given and thanking the European population for its engagement. A global press conference was held to wrap up the campaign. It showcased the outcome of the campaign and ensured press coverage in mid-September. The conference was broadcast on the Web.

Campaign results

According to a tracking survey conducted in November 2010 in a sample of 1404 Broad Elites/'Chattering Classes' (university-educated, higher-income people with an active interest in national and international economic/political affairs – whose opinions and views both reflect and help to shape those of policy decision-makers, influencers and commentators) in seven countries (France, Germany, Italy, the Netherlands, Spain, UK, USA), more than 25% of these opinion-makers and chattering classes recognised the campaign. When prompted (aided awareness), 25% were aware of the Global Fund, 22% of the product associated with the campaign (RED) and 12% of the Born HIV Free campaign. When prompted, 22% recognised the logo of the campaign; 16% of those aware of the campaign associated Carla Bruni-Sarkozy with it, while 25% associated it with Bono or Angelina Jolie. The highest awareness was reached on TV (24%) and Facebook (23%). About a fifth heard about the campaign on YouTube (19%). The campaign raised prevention of mother-to-child transmission of HIV awareness significantly with a 21% increase in awareness and understanding of the issue in those aware of the campaign. Those aware of the campaign had a better understanding that mother-to-child transmission of HIV is preventable (73%), while only 52% of those unaware of the campaign believed it is possible to prevent it.

Between its launch on 19 May 2010 and its formal closing on 5 October 2010, the campaign was viewed more than 250 million times, with over 20 million actions (people engaged) and more than 700 000 signatures for the campaign petition. Current social media presence is higher than 500 000 (Facebook, Global Fund & Born HIV Free, Causes, Causes petition-signers, Twitter). The overall campaign cost was $23.2 million, $2.8 million of which was paid by the Global Fund and $20.4 million was *pro bono* support. Consequently, the cost per signature was $4 and the cost per engagement was $0.14. Besides these concrete results, the campaign also served as a tool to kick off communications with the general public and built foundations of relationships with companies, the general public and celebrities. It received widespread coverage online.

During the first week after the launch day, 4200 signatures were collected, media coverage was 222 articles and 312 blogs, mainly in Europe, and some radio and TV coverage in France, due to the fact that the launch event was in Paris and attended by the ambassador of the campaign, Carla Bruni-Sarkozy. According to the comments received, she has a controversial image. She has both fans and critics who object to her past provocative behaviour, morality and glamorous and controversial conquests. Nevertheless, nearly half think Carla Bruni-Sarkozy is an appropriate spokesperson for the campaign – with 1 in 5 saying she is inappropriate. She was also instrumental in attracting celebrities (Jean-Paul Gaultier, Paul McCartney and others) and was influential in getting partnership deals (Orange, Google, ad space, etc.).

Several channels and tools were used throughout the campaign: classical mass media advertising (e.g. the 'Baby in the sky spot'), a launch event, guerrilla (street) marketing, presence at music festivals (e.g. Solidays), partnerships (among others, with Tiffany), celebrity advocacy (e.g. Paul McCartney concert in support of the campaign), 'saving lives' videos with testimonials. Figure 15.2 gives an impression of the cost and relative impact of each of these tools (not all tools mentioned in the figure were discussed in the text). The cheapest and most effective ones in terms of achieving the goals of petition signatures and active engagement were social media, Thank you and Euronews ads, street marketing, the Paul McCartney concert and the bloggers' trip. Selected results for some of these tools are given below.

Traditional mass media advertising

Euronews started to broadcast the 'Baby in the Sky' spot three times per day as of 20 June in 155 countries. Firstly, the 30-second version as of July 13, then the 73-second version. Total exposure to the spot was 40 million. The spot worked well as an awareness tool, generating increased visits to the Born HIV Free campaign website. The public space company J.C. Decaux donated advertising space in eight European capital cities in August and September. A series of large posters and advertising billboards featured Carla Bruni-Sarkozy wearing the Born HIV Free campaign T-shirt and inviting the public to join the campaign by signing up via the YouTube channel. Exposure was 80 million. The budget was $2800.

On 6 October, the day after the Replenishment Conference, Thank You ads appeared in five major European newspapers (*El Pais*, *Le Figaro*, *FT*, *Independent*, *Bild*). The Italian monthlies *Progress* and *Progress Viaggi* ran the same ad in November and put a banner on their websites. The ads thanked people and governments for supporting the campaign and the Global Fund. Total readership was 19.2 million. The budget was $6000.

Paul McCartney concert on YouTube

The live streaming of the Paul McCartney concert on YouTube was a huge success. It generated 41 000 signatures, 27 000 of which through the campaign website (the highest increase in signatures in a one-week period), 2 million YouTube channel visitors from all over the world, and 7000 tweets. The event resulted in media coverage of 68 articles. The budget was $16 600.

Street marketing

The Born HIV Free campaign took to the streets of New York and, via social networks, to everyone's computer screens on 21 September during the Millennium Development Goals summit in an initiative aimed at signposting world leaders in the direction of decisive backing for the Global Fund and its work. In partnership with Google and YouTube, the initiative saw campaign envoys taking up positions on the corners of strategic Manhattan Road intersections holding signs with compelling HIV facts and urging that we free future generations from HIV by 2015. Also, 3000 flyers were distributed in New York and 2268 people viewed Google Maps online. The budget was $65 000, part of which was covered by YouTube. A bubble effect was created to make decision-makers become aware of the Global Fund. This initiative was timed with a *New York Times* ad to create a maximum impact. →

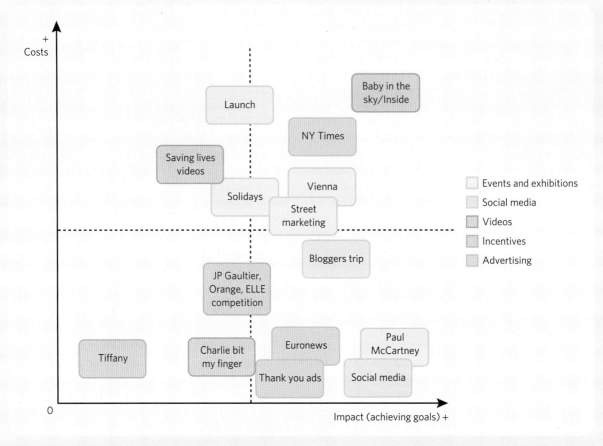

Figure 15.2 Costs vs impact matrix of campaign tools
Source: From InSites Consulting.

Source: The Global Fund.

Born HIV Free YouTube channel

The Global Fund, in partnership with RED Design, launched a custom-designed YouTube channel for the Born HIV Free campaign. The YouTube channel hosted the videos for the campaign, live streams of events, and allowed people to sign up directly through the channel. This resulted in 17.9 million channel visits, 13.5 million channel visitors, 2.75 million video views and 70 000 signatures. The YouTube channel generated considerably higher traffic on the campaign website than any other platform during the campaign.

The Born HIV Free campaign website

The Global Fund, in partnership with RED Design, launched a unique flash-based website for the Born HIV Free campaign. This website provided information about the campaign, Carla Bruni-Sarkozy and mother-to-child transmission of HIV. During the campaign, the website was visited 135 975 times by 118 906 unique visitors. The website collected 70 000 signatures. These visitors spent an average of three minutes on the website. The website had approximately a 60% visitor-to-signature conversion ratio. The majority of visitors to the campaign were from France, which had twice the number of visitors as the USA and the UK, both of which in turn had twice the number of visitors as the following group of Italy, Germany, German Switzerland, Brazil, Canada and the Netherlands.

The majority of the traffic on the site originated from search engines, referral sites, advertising and direct (inconclusive) traffic (Figure 15.3); 61% of visits originated from users searching for 'YouTube' on the Google search engine and clicking on the first sponsored result. This traffic remained on the website for an average of 26 seconds and viewed an average of 1.11 pages. 21.18% of visits originated from within YouTube itself, and 97% of these visits were referred from the Born HIV Free channel. This traffic remained for approximately 2:35 minutes before leaving the page; 11.29% of visits have no clear source. 1.2 million visits occurred during the Paul McCartney concert. In addition, the Twitter integration during the event generated a huge number of tweets, which (owing to widespread use of applications to access Twitter), appear as direct traffic. Hence, the majority of this traffic is likely to have originated from Twitter referrals during the concert. Visits from the Twitter website itself had a similar spike during the concert. Visitors from the Paul McCartney concert stayed on the website for approximately 2:45 minutes. Visitors from YouTube (outside of Paul McCartney) stayed for 1:50 minutes. 2.6% of visits originated from banner advertising. This traffic remained on the page for 24 seconds and rarely visited another page. 0.38% of visits originated from Facebook. Visitors from Facebook spent over four minutes on the website.

Social media

The Global Fund launched a Facebook fan page for the Born HIV Free campaign to increase the level of engagement from supporters. During the campaign period the page resulted in 19 583 members and 70 291 visits which on average lasted 1.15 minutes, and 6509 interactions. The audience were 57% female, 40% male; 56% of the audience were aged 18–34 and 32% aged 35+. Most of the likes and interactions were driven by a small number of highly engaged people. The growth of the Facebook channel was initially slow and needed promotion from other sources to gain initial momentum. Once that momentum was established, the channel was

	Source/Medium	None ∨	Visits ↓	Pages/Visit	Avg. Time on Site
1.	google/organic		10 893 312	1.11	00:00:26
2.	youtube.com/referral		3 783 761	1.16	00:02:35
3.	(direct)/(none)		2 004 449	1.15	00:00:45
4.	ad-emea.doubleclick.net/referral		469 365	1.12	00:00:24
5.	search/organic		184 398	1.12	00:00:32
6.	facebook.com/referral		67 184	1.20	00:01:07
7.	voila/organic		45 729	1.24	00:00:53
8.	twitter.com/referral		41 605	1.23	00:01:35
9.	upload.youtube.com/referral		26 226	1.20	00:01:14
10.	s0.2mdn.net/referral		21 673	1.16	00:00:35

Figure 15.3 Traffic analysis on the Born HIV Free website

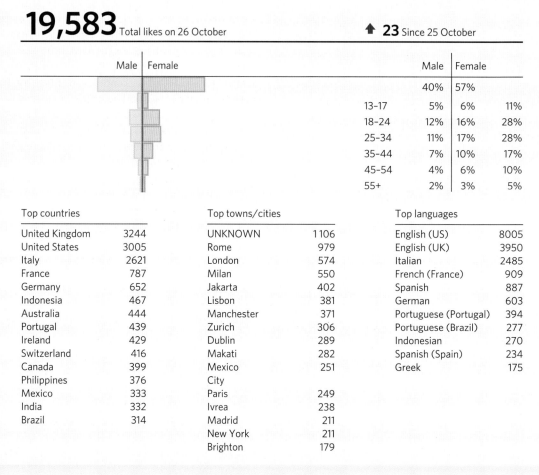

19,583 Total likes on 26 October   ↑ **23** Since 25 October

	Male	Female	
	40%	57%	
13–17	5%	6%	11%
18–24	12%	16%	28%
25–34	11%	17%	28%
35–44	7%	10%	17%
45–54	4%	6%	10%
55+	2%	3%	5%

Top countries		Top towns/cities		Top languages	
United Kingdom	3244	UNKNOWN	1106	English (US)	8005
United States	3005	Rome	979	English (UK)	3950
Italy	2621	London	574	Italian	2485
France	787	Milan	550	French (France)	909
Germany	652	Jakarta	402	Spanish	887
Indonesia	467	Lisbon	381	German	603
Australia	444	Manchester	371	Portuguese (Portugal)	394
Portugal	439	Zurich	306	Portuguese (Brazil)	277
Ireland	429	Dublin	289	Indonesian	270
Switzerland	416	Makati	282	Spanish (Spain)	234
Canada	399	Mexico	251	Greek	175
Philippines	376	City			
Mexico	333	Paris	249		
India	332	Ivrea	238		
Brazil	314	Madrid	211		
		New York	211		
		Brighton	179		

Figure 15.4 Geographic, gender and age spread of the Facebook audience

effective at achieving a steady level of growth from 5000 to 19 000. Figure 15.4 shows the gender, age and geographic spread of the Facebook audience. Facebook cultivated an engaged audience with a deeper interest in the subject than other platforms. It might be assumed that the best supporters of a campaign were those on Facebook. To actively engage members, it was important to provide interactive content.

The Global Fund launched a Causes page and petition to increase referrals to the Born HIV Free campaign and provide a means through which people could sign up without leaving the Facebook platform. Causes is the world's largest platform for activism and philanthropy. The platform empowers individuals to create grassroots communities called 'causes' that take action on behalf of a specific issue or non-profit organisation. In addition, through associated Causes to the Global Fund, over 100 000 supporters in related Causes (namely, Product RED and Join RED) were messaged at various times during the campaign. The total reach of this tool was 129 000 members in 22 affiliate

causes and 48 662 members of the Born HIV Free cause were created, resulting in 143 858 signatures and more than 10 000 video views. Causes was a very effective platform for raising awareness of the campaign and collecting signatures. The Born HIV Free campaign benefited from a close relationship with the staff of Causes who helped to promote the campaign to huge existing groups. In addition, the platform provided the means to message an engaged audience of almost 250 000 members. During the campaign the Causes platform became increasingly popular with members sharing videos with each other. Many videos gained the majority of their views through this platform. Causes recently became the first platform to have application news contents included in the news feeds of the members. This represents further opportunities in the future to grow the audience and spread campaign messages further than before.

By working with Twitter the campaign team wanted to persuade millions of members, many of whom would not be aware of the Global Fund mission, to run the largest digital petition ever undertaken on Twitter. To achieve this, Twitter's support was gained by means of promoted tweets, free media space on Twitter profiles, consultancy (using Twitter's expertise and advice to mobilise an audience around emotive causes), suggested User List (to be added to the Suggested User List for Twitter under charities and under staff picks), promotion on Twitter.com/blog, coverage in the monthly newsletter, outreach to top Twitter members, staff champions of the cause, etc. Twitter appeared to be not the appropriate tool for engagement and it quickly became evident that it would not be a major online communications channel. Therefore, only limited resources and efforts were allocated to Twitter after the launch.

Bloggers

Bloggers are hugely influential and command large audiences. These audiences are usually more engaged and feel more connected with a blogger than with a traditional journalist. The endorsement of popular bloggers can start an avalanche of attention and build momentum for campaign efforts. The Global Fund organised a Born HIV Free competition for bloggers with the possibility for the winner to visit Global-Fund-supported programmes with the objective of bringing the blogger closer to the organisation. The more a blogger feels influenced by a campaign and likes the people involved, the more likely the blogger will post positively about the event.

Seven bloggers from the USA, Canada, Spain, Germany and France came to Lesotho for a three-day trip, visiting hospitals and interviewing pregnant women on PMTCT treatment and HIV-positive mothers having HIV negative children. The number of posts related to the trip was 38 (10 German, 10 Spanish, 9 French, 7 Canadia, 2 American). Most bloggers wrote and posted a story almost every day, which ensured transparency and continuous follow-up for the readers. The invited bloggers felt part of the campaign and became its ambassadors.

Conclusions

In terms of the main objectives of the campaign, i.e. increase public awareness, traffic and petition-signing, the Born HIV Free campaign was a success. However, the campaign failed to enhance the Global Fund brand.

One of the biggest challenges of running a digital-based campaign with media vehicles and social media platforms as stakeholders is to decide what to do with traffic: that is, either to drive campaign traffic to one central place or to diversify and have many hubs; to drive traffic to your site, or to go where the traffic is. The campaign officially had three online hubs to gather signatures of support: the campaign website, the campaign YouTube channel, and the campaign Causes page on Facebook. Each proved to be useful in helping to achieve the Global Fund's campaign objectives, but in a segmented way. The campaign website kept users on it the longest and converted the highest rate of petition-signers, while the YouTube channel enjoyed the highest amount of traffic (around 20 million visits) and therefore brand exposure, but did not convert visitors to petition-signers at a high rate (0.001%). The campaign Causes page on Facebook collected the most petition signatures, but did much more to expose the issue of prevention of HIV from mother to child than the Global Fund brand.

With the Born HIV Free campaign, the Global Fund made a conscious choice to push an issue rather than its brand in the campaign's core DNA. More than anything, the Born HIV Free campaign was about putting the attainable goal of an HIV-free generation by 2015 on the agenda. The downside to this is that the Global Fund was not able to create the same impact on raising its brand awareness. Only a few of the campaign aware spontaneously made the connection between the Global Fund and Born HIV Free. The campaign was huge and complex due to its length, the large number of partners, and different goals: signatures vs traffic. The Global Fund brand did not benefit from the campaign. This was mainly due to the incredibly complicated brand landscape of the campaign. During the most highly publicised moments of the campaign, the Global Fund essentially squared itself off against the campaign brand – Born HIV Free, the brand of its spokesperson, Carla Bruni-Sarkozy – and its committed commercial partner, YouTube. This crowded and complicated brand architecture of the campaign proved to be a diluting factor for the Global Fund brand, and made it difficult for even the campaign aware to connect the dots. The most obvious conclusion one would likely draw from the results of the survey with 'chattering classes', shown in Figures 15.5 and 15.6, is that the Global Fund simply did not create a strong enough connection between its brand and the campaign.

After the Born HIV Free campaign, the conclusion is that driving traffic to a controlled own platform like a website, while promoting on the platforms where the traffic is, like Facebook or YouTube, is the formula that will help achieve the campaign's goals, while creating maximum brand impact. The segmentation of web traffic for the Born HIV Free campaign was accepted by the Global Fund as an inherent compromise to be able to engage as many partners as possible. But the Global Fund is using this as a lesson-learned after seeing the impact that Born HIV Free had on raising awareness for an issue, while leaving the brand of the organization as an afterthought. At the moment with their current digital-based campaign, 'One Million Lives', the Global Fund is being disciplined about driving traffic to one central place, the campaign website, where they can have complete control over their brand exposure to users, even though it means not being able engage with partners in the same capacity that they did with Born HIV Free.

Achieving public adoption requires each of the following steps:		Questions asked:
Awareness – spontaneous	Is your organisation top of mind in the field of international aid?	Thinking about large global organisations that provide aid, such as NGOs, what organisations come to mind? (% mentions)
Awareness – aided	Are consumers aware of the organisation?	Which of the following international aid organisations are you aware of? (% mentions)
Familiarity	Are broad elites familiar with the organisation and its programmes?	How familiar are you with each of the following organisations? (% Very – somewhat familiar)
Favourability	Are broad elites favourable to not only the cause, but the organisation itself?	How favourable are you towards each of the following organisations? (% Very favourable)
Agree with cause	Do broad elites agree with the issues the organisation deals with?	To what extent would you agree that the following organisations deal with issues that are important to you? (% Agree strongly)
Action	Are broad elites likely to support the organisation and its cause?	How likely would you be to support funding for each of the following organisations? (% Very likely to support)

Wave 2: November 2010	The Global Fund	UNICEF	Int. Red Cross	WHO	MSF	World Bank	OXFAM
Awareness – spontaneous	0%	26%	28%	4%	25%	2%	11%
Awareness – aided	25%	89%	71%	70%	63%	57%	46%
Familiarity	11%	51%	40%	34%	35%	22%	21%
Favourability	10%	41%	35%	27%	36%	12%	16%
Agree with cause	9%	38%	31%	24%	30%	11%	15%
Action	6%	28%	21%	13%	22%	6%	12%

Figure 15.5 Awareness of the Global Fund and other international organisations

	Total sample studied		
	Mar. 2010	Nov. 2010	Shift
Awareness – spontaneous	0%	0%	0
Awareness – aided	23%	24%	+1
Familiarity	10%	9%	−1
Favourability	9%	9%	0
Agree with cause	10%	8%	−2
Action	8%	6%	−2

Figure 15.6 Awareness of the Global Fund before and after the Born HIV Free campaign

QUESTIONS

1. Assess the approach of the Global Fund.

2. What did it do well and why?

3. What could have been done differently and why?

4. Did it use online channels and social media well? Why or why not?

5. How could it build a new campaign upon this one in the future?

6. Which media should be used more intensively? Which ones can be dropped?

7. Should it keep on using celebrity endorsement? Why or why not? What type of celebrity?

8. How could it alter its campaign to support the brand equity of the Global Fund better than in the previous campaign?

Sources: http://www.causes.com; http://www.youtube.com/bornhivfree?x=support; http://www.youtube.com/watch?v=tkrG9voS24c; www.theglobalfund.org. All information and documentation provided by Claudia Gonzalez, Head of Marketing, The Global Fund to fight AIDS, TB and Malaria.

References

1 Butterfield, L. (2003), *AdValue: Twenty Ways Advertising Works for Business.* Oxford: Butterworth–Heinemann.

2 Based on Internet Domain Survey Host Count (January 2012), https://www.isc.org/solutions/survey (accessed May 2012).

3 Samiee, S. (1998), 'The Internet and International Marketing: Is there a Fit?', *Journal of Interactive Marketing*, 12(4), 5–21.

4 Peters, L. (1998), 'The New Interactive Media: One-to-one, but Who to Whom?', *Marketing Intelligence & Planning*, 16(1), 22–30.

5 http://www.verisigninc.com/en_US/news-events/press-room/index.xhtml (press release accessed 8 March 2012).

6 Based on www.internetworldstats.com/stats.htm (accessed May 2012).

7 http://www.iabeurope.eu/news/europe's-online-ad-market-tops-€20bn-despite-economy.aspx (accessed 2 October 2012).

8 http://www.iabeurope.eu/news/europe's-online-ad-market-tops-€20bn-despite-economy.aspx (accessed 2 October 2012).

9 www.iabeurope.eu (accessed 2 October 2012).

10 De Wulf, K., Van den Bergh, J., Vergult, C. and De Boek, F. (2003), 'Using Internet Marketing Tactics to Support FMCG Brands: An Overview of Lessons Learned', *White Paper published by InSites Consulting*, http://www.insites-consulting.com.

11 http://www.oneill.com (social media figures accessed May 2012).

12 Reicheld, F. and Schefter, P. (2000), 'E-loyalty, Your Secret Weapon on the Web', *Harvard Business Review*, July/August, 105–13.

13 *De Morgen*, 18 June 2011

14 http://www.rambla.be/absynthe-minded-launches-most-exclusive-video-ever (accessed 2 October 2012).

15 http://www.immediatemedia.co.uk/advertising/case_studies.html (accessed 2 October 2012).

16 www.pewinternet.org/Reports/2011/search-and-email/report.aspx (accessed 2 October 2012).

17 Strauss, J., El-Ansary, A. and Frost, R. (2008), *E-Marketing*, 5th edition. Englewood Cliffs, NJ: Prentice Hall.

18 www.groupm.com and www.emarketer.com (accessed 2 October 2012).

19 http://www.seotops.com/ad-spending-online-set-to-increase_2457/ (accessed 29 February 2012).

20 http://www.digitalstrategyconsulting.com/intelligence/2012/04/size_matters_large_ads_boost_b.php (accessed 2 October 2012).

21 http://www.thomascookmedia.be/web/tcmedia/hotels/online-advertising/formats (accessed 2 October 2012).

22 Adams, R. (2003), www.advertising. *Advertising and Marketing on the World Wide Web.* Cambridge: Ilex Press.

23 http://www.gazelleinteractive.com/gulf-stream-gear-case-study/ (accessed 2 October 2012).

24 http://en.wikipedia.org/wiki/Affiliate_marketing (accessed 2 October 2012).

25 http://david-r-wetzel.suite101.com/best-affiliate-marketing-networks-a58383 (accessed June 2009).

26 http://www.smartinsights.com/digital-marketing-strategy/online-business-revenue-models/amazon-case-study/ (accessed 2 October 2012).

27 Strauss, J., El-Ansary, A. and Frost, R. (2008), *E-Marketing*, 5th edition. Englewood Cliffs, NJ: Prentice Hall.

28 http://www.smartinsights.com/digital-marketing-strategy/online-business-revenue-models/amazon-case-study/ (accessed 2 October 2012).

29 http://www.pwc.com/en_GX/gx/entertainment-media/pdf/IAB_SRI_Online_Advertising_Effectiveness_v3.pdf (accessed 2 October 2012).

30 http://www.aimia.com.au/enews/IAB/IAB%20Retail%20Study%20-%20Finalv3.pdf (accessed 2 October 2012).

31 http://www.iabuk.net/video/starbucks-building-brands-online-trilogy, http://www.iabuk.net/sites/default/files/

research-docs/research_starbucksresultssummary_8217. pdf (accessed 2 October 2012).

[32] Weima, K.W. (2002), *Webvertising: Tools voor een Effectieve Campagne* (*Tools for an Effective Campaign*), Alphen aan den Rijn: Kluwer.

[33] http://www.bizreport.com/2010/03/nai_behaviorally-targeted_online_ads_twice_as_effective.html (accessed 2 October 2012).

[34] Allen, C., Kania, D. and Yaeckel, B. (2001), *One-to-One Web Marketing: Build a Relationship Marketing Strategy One Customer at a Time.* New York: Wiley Computer Publications.

[35] http://en.wikipedia.org/wiki/SlideShare (accessed 2 October 2012).

[36] http://www.comscore.com/Press_Events/Press_Releases/2011/8/Nearly_1_out_of_2_Germans_Visits_Online_Gaming_Sites (accessed 2 October 2012).

[37] www.newzoo.nl (accessed 2 October 2012).

[38] Interactive News, August 2002, and www.forbes.com. (accessed 2 October 2012).

[39] http://www.mindjumpers.com/blog/2011/04/magnum-pleasure-hunt/ (accessed 2 October 2012).

[40] http://www.tracyandmatt.co.uk/blogs/index.php/magnum-pleasure-hunt-2-play-across-the-g (accessed 2 October 2012).

[41] http://www.digitalbuzzblog.com/magnum-pleasure-hunt-across-amsterdam-arg/ (accessed 2 October 2012).

[42] http://www.adverblog.com/2011/10/24/the-paper-adver game/#more-9186 (accessed 2 October 2012).

[43] http://www.gaia.be/nl/nieuws/gaia-lanceert-chicken-squeeze- (accessed 2 October 2012).

[44] http://www.digitalstrategyconsulting.com/netimperative/news/2012/05/guest_comment_lifes_a_game_and_1.php (accessed 2 October 2012).

[45] http://en.wikipedia.org/wiki/Gamification (accessed 2 October 2012).

[46] http://en.wikipedia.org/wiki/Foursquare, https://four square.com/ (accessed 2 October 2012).

[47] http://www.digitalstrategyconsulting.com/netimperative/news/2012/05/guest_comment_lifes_a_game_and_1.php (accessed 2 October 2012).

[48] Abcnews.com, November 2002.

[49] Kretchmer, S.B. (2001), 'The Emergent Advergames Industry: Developments, Impact, and Direction', http://www.cric.ac.uk/cric/events/dgi/abstracts/kretchmer.htm (accessed July 2009).

[50] Calvert, S.L. (2008), 'Children as Consumers: Advertising and Marketing', *The Future of Children*, 18(1), 205–34.

[51] Cebrzynski, G. (2006), 'Lights! Camera! Product Place-ment!', *Nation's Restaurant News*, 40(49), 1–5.

[52] Raney, A.A., Arpan, L.M., Pashupati, K. and Brill, D.A. (2003), 'At the Movies, on the Web: An Investigation of the Effects of Entertaining and Interactive Web Content on Site and Brand Evaluations', *Journal of Interactive Market-ing*, 17(4), 38–53.

[53] Friestad, M. and Wright, P. (1995), 'Persuasion Knowledge – Lay Peoples and Researchers Beliefs about the Psychology of Advertising', *Journal of Consumer Research*, 22(1), 62–74.

[54] http://www.digitalstrategyconsulting.com/intelligence/2012/05/european_mobile_gaming_gets_so.php (accessed 2 October 2012).

[55] Neuborne, E. (2001), 'Viral Marketing Alert!', *Business Week*, 19 March.

[56] http://www.mediacom.com/en/news--insights/blink/issues/edition-2-2011/case-study-vw---setting-the-stage-for-success.aspx (accessed 2 October 2012).

[57] http://www.digitalstrategyconsulting.com/intelligence/2012/04/video_viral_of_the_week_tnts_d.php#more (accessed 2 October 2012).

[58] http://wave.wavemetrix.com/content/consumer-reactions-tnt-s-hugely-viral-dramatic-surprise-video-demonstrate-effect-00917 (accessed 2 October 2012).

[59] Krishnamurthy, S. (2000), 'Is Viral Marketing All It's Cracked Up to Be?', Clickz.com, www.clickz.com/mkt/onl_mkt_comm/article.php/823941 (accessed June 2009).

[60] Jupiter MMX, 2002.

[61] DBT Database & Internet Solutions (2001), 'Viral Market-ing', December, www.dbt.co.uk (accessed July 2003).

[62] http://www.slideshare.net/MichaelBouchier/wom-power (accessed 2 October 2012).

[63] Matos, C.A. and Rossi, C.A.V. (2008), 'Word-of-Mouth Communications in Marketing: A Meta-Analytic Review of the Antecedents and Moderators', *Journal of the Academy of Marketing Science*, 36(4), 578–96; Sweeney, J.C., Soutar, G.N. and Mazzarol, T. (2008), 'Factors Influencing Word of Mouth Effectiveness: Receiver Perspectives', *European Journal of Marketing*, 42(3/4), 344–64.

[64] Lee, J., Park, D.H. and Han, I. (2008), 'The Effect of Negative Online Consumer Reviews on Product Attitude: An Infor-mation Processing View', *Electronic Commerce Research and Applications*, 7(3) 341–52; Park, C. and Lee, T.M. (2009), 'Antecedents of Online Reviews' Usage and Purchase Influence: An Empirical Comparison of US and Korean Consumers', *Journal of Interactive Marketing*, 23(4), 332–40.

[65] Winer, R.S. (2009), 'New Communications Approaches in Marketing: Issues and Research Directions', *Journal of Interactive Marketing*, 23(2), 108–17.

[66] Bronner, F. and de Hoog, R. (2010), 'Consumer–Generated Versus Marketer-Generated Websites in Consumer Decision Making', *International Journal of Market Research*, 52(2), 231–48.

[67] Cheung, C.M.K., Lee, M.K.O. and Rabjohn, N. (2008), 'The Impact of Electronic Word-of-Mouth – The Adoption of Online Opinions in Online Customer Communities', *Internet Research*, 18(3), 229–47.

[68] Purnawirawan, N., De Pelsmacker, P. and Dens, N. (2012), 'Balance and Sequence in Online Reviews: How Perceived Usefulness Affects Attitudes and Intentions', *Journal of Interactive Marketing*, 26(4), 244–55.

[69] Ahluwalia, R. and Gürhan-Canli, Z. (2000), 'The Effects of Extensions on the Family Brand Name: An Accessibility-Diagnosticity Perspective', *Journal of Consumer Research*, 27(3), 371–81.

[70] Forman, C., Ghose, A. and Wiesenfeld, B. (2008), 'Examining the Relationship between Reviews and Sales: The Role of Reviewer Identity Disclosure in Electronic Markets', *SSRN eLibrary*.

71 Drèze, X. and Zufryden, F. (2004), 'The Measurement of Online Visibility and Its Impact on Internet Traffic', *Journal of Interactive Marketing*, 18(1), 20–37.

72 Buda, R. and Zhang, Y. (2000), 'Consumer Product Evaluation: The Interactive Effect of Message Framing, Presentation Order, and Source Credibility', *Journal of Product and Brand Management*, 9(4), 229–42.

73 Purnawirawan, N.A., De Pelsmacker, P. and Dens, N. (2010), 'Balance and Sequence in Online Reviews: The Wrap Effect', *9th International Conference on Research in Advertising (Icoria) Proceedings, Madrid*.

74 Strauss, J., El-Ansary, A. and Frost, R. (2003), *E-Marketing*, 3rd edition. Englewood Cliffs, NJ: Prentice Hall.

75 http://www.digitalbuzzblog.com/heineken-limited-edition-bottles-via-facebook/ (accessed 2 October 2012).

76 'Supermarket Sweep', *Advertising Age, Direct & Database Supplement*, 16 October 2000.

77 *Internet Sampling: Reaching Consumers* (2001), Congress Presentation, *10th Annual Conference on Global Electronic Marketing (GEM), San Diego, CA*.

78 Strauss, J., El-Ansary, A. and Frost, R. (2008), *E-Marketing*, 5th edition. Englewood Cliffs, NJ: Prentice Hall.

79 http://blog.nielsen.com/nielsenwire/consumer/global-consumers-go-sale-searching-and-coupon-clipping/ (accessed 2 October 2012).

80 http://www.onlinemarketing-trends.com/2011/04/rise-of-e-coupons-in-europe.html (accessed 2 October 2012).

81 http://mashable.com/2012/01/19/digital-coupon-trends/ (accessed 2 October 2012).

82 http://adage.com/article/news/social-sampling-scores-big-kleenex/149272/ (accessed 2 October 2012).

83 IAB Belgium (2006), *Email Marketing Cookbook*. Zellik: Interactive Advertising Bureau.

84 Chaffey, D., Ellis-Chadwick, F., Johnston, K. and Mayer R. (2008), *Internet Marketing: Strategy, Implementation and Practice*. Harlow: Financial Times/Prentice Hall.

85 http://www.lyris.com/email-marketing/85-Average-Email-Click-Through-Rate (accessed June 2009).

86 Waring, T. and Martinez, A. (2002), 'Ethical Customer Relationships: A Comparative Analysis of US and French Organizations Using Permission-based E-mail Marketing', *Journal of Database Marketing*, 10(1), 53–69.

87 Rapp, S. and Martin, C. (2001), *Max-e-marketing in the Net Future: The Seven Imperatives for Outsmarting the Competition in the Net Economy*. New York: McGraw-Hill.

88 Furger, R. (2000), 'E-mail's Second Shot', *Upside*, 12(4), 160–8.

89 Postma, O. and Brokke, M. (2002), 'Personalisation in Practice: The Proven Effects of Personalisation', *Journal of Database Marketing*, 9(2), 137–42.

90 Strauss, J., El-Ansary, A. and Frost, R. (2008), *E-Marketing*, 5th edition. Englewood Cliffs, NJ: Prentice Hall.

91 Khera, R. (2002), 'E-mail Marketing Primer: 12 Tips for Successful Campaigns', *The Magazine for Magazine Management*, 30(9), 53.

92 EMarketer (2002), 'Does Permission E-mail Marketing Push Consumers to Purchase?', *eMarketer e-zine*, October, 28.

93 www.revolutionawards.com (accessed 2 October 2012).

94 www.emarketer.com (accessed 2 October 2012).

95 http://www.iabeurope.eu/news/global-mobile-advertising-market-valued-at-$53-billion-(€38-billion)-in-2011.aspx (accessed 2 October 2012).

96 http://techcrunch.com/2011/11/28/its-still-a-feature-phone-world-global-smartphone-penetration-at-27/ (accessed 2 October 2012).

97 http://www.ourmobileplanet.com/en-gb/downloads/ (accessed 2 October 2012).

98 http://www.emarketer.com/Article.aspx?R=1008983 (accessed 2 October 2012).

99 http://www.ourmobileplanet.com/en-gb/downloads/ (accessed 2 October 2012).

100 http://en.wikipedia.org/wiki/Mobile_apps (accessed 2 October 2012).

101 http://blog.nielsen.com/nielsenwire/online_mobile/state-of-the-appnation---a-year-of-change-and-growth-in-u-s-smartphones/ (accessed 2 October 2012).

102 http://www.slideshare.net/InSitesConsulting/mobile-mindset-report-by-insites-consulting (accessed 2 October 2012).

103 http://www.mobiadnews.com/?p=5165 (accessed 2 October 2012).

104 http://blogs.thisplays2.com/narrowcasting/, http://www.yourdailymac.net/2012/04/delhaize-launches-virtual-shopping-concept-direct-cube/ (accessed 2 October 2012).

105 http://www.digitalbuzzblog.com/ing-the-free-throw-challenge-digital-billboards/ (accessed 2 October 2012).

106 http://www.brandactivation.nl/node/1286 (accessed 2 October 2012).

107 http://www.gartner.com/it/page.jsp?id=1726614 (accessed 2 October 2012).

108 http://www.warc.com/LatestNews/News/Mobile_adspend_to_surge_in_Europe.news?ID=28820 (accessed 2 October 2012).

109 http://www.gartner.com/it/page.jsp?id=1726614 (accessed 2 October 2012).

110 http://blog.nielsen.com/nielsenwire/online_mobile/new-mobile-obsession-u-s-teens-triple-data-usage/ (accessed 2 October 2012).

111 Based on: de Kerckhoven A. (July–September 2002), 'Building Brand Dialogue with Mobile Marketing', *Advertising & Marketing to Children*, World Advertising Research Center; Jones, A. (2002), 'Wireless Marketing: The Linking Value of Text Messaging', *Young Consumers*, 3(2), 39–44.

112 http://www.techipedia.com/2011/sms-marketing/, http://www.punchkickinteractive.com/services/sms-text-messaging-campaigns/ (accessed 2 October 2012).

113 Based on: de Kerckhoven A. (July–September 2002), 'Building Brand Dialogue with Mobile Marketing', *Advertising & Marketing to Children*, World Advertising Research Center; and on Jones, A. (January–March 2002), 'Wireless Marketing: The Linking Value of Text Messaging', *Advertising & Marketing to Children*, World Advertising Research Center.

114 http://www.mobileweb.be/nl/connectiviteit-sms-mms/dieteren-sms-dienst.asp (accessed 2 October 2012).

115 http://www.mobilemarketer.com/cms/news/advertising/10311.html (accessed 2 October 2012).

116 www.adverblog.com (accessed January 2009).

117 http://www.slideshare.net/bigsplashweb/mobile-marketing-case-studies-10746522 (accessed 2 October 2012).

118 http://www.slideshare.net/bigsplashweb/mobile-marketing-case-studies-10746522 (accessed 2 October 2012).

119 http://www.text-board.com/marketing/sms-marketing-examples/ (accessed 2 October 2012).

120 MMA (2008), 'Global Code of Conduct', http://www.mmaglobal.com/codeofconduct.pdf (accessed May 2012).

121 Wise, T. and Hall, D. (2002), 'Pause or Play? The Future of Interactive Services for Television', Accenture.

122 http://archive.iptv-news.com/iptv_news/april_2012/western_europes_digital_switchover_slows_down (accessed 2 October 2012).

123 http://www.i-policy.org/2012/02/dutch-digital-tv-penetration-reaches-729.html (accessed 2 October 2012).

124 Lekakos, G. (2002), *An Integrated Approach to Interactive and Personalized TV Advertising*. Athens: University of Economics and Business.

125 Bernoff, J. (2002), 'Smarter Television', *The Forrester Report* (July).

126 http://mashable.com/2011/06/15/free-whopper-tv-campaign/ (accessed 2 October 2012).

127 http://www.itvmedia.co.uk/insights-and-effectiveness/case-studies/building-awareness/yeo-valley-case-study (accessed 2 October 2012).

128 www.frankwatching.com, 'Cross Media Café Digital TV The Netherlands' (March 2009).

129 http://ec.europa.eu/internal_market/consultations/docs/2011/audiovisual/green_paper_COM2011_427_en.pdf (accessed 2 October 2012).

130 http://ec.europa.eu/internal_market/consultations/docs/2011/audiovisual/green_paper_COM2011_427_en.pdf (accessed 2 October 2012).

131 http://www.worldtvpc.com/blog/connected-tv-sales-europe-booming/ (accessed 2 October 2012).

132 http://www.broadbandtvnews.com/2011/11/01/connected-tvs-will-reach-20-penetra/ (accessed 2 October 2012).

133 http://www.marketingweek.co.uk/double-your-impact-with-two-screens/3030126.article (accessed 2 October 2012).

134 http://www.iabeurope.eu/research/mediascope-europe/mediascope-key-findings-2012.aspx (accessed 2 October 2012).

135 http://www.brandchannel.com/images/papers/530_futurescape_wp_connected_tv_0911.pdf (accessed 2 October 2012).

136 http://www.brandchannel.com/images/papers/530_futurescape_wp_connected_tv_0911.pdf (accessed 2 October 2012).

137 http://socialtvworldsummit.com/social-tv-gaining-relevance/ (accessed 2 October 2012).

138 http://www.brandchannel.com/images/papers/530_futurescape_wp_connected_tv_0911.pdf (accessed 2 October 2012).

139 Decrem, B. (2006), 'Introducing Flock Beta 1', Flock official blog, http://www.flock.com/node/4500 (accessed June 2009).

140 http://michaelhaenlein.com/Publications/Kaplan,%20Andreas%20-%20Users%20of%20the%20world,%20unite.pdf (accessed 2 October 2012).

141 http://blog.nielsen.com/nielsenwire/online_mobile/buzz-in-the-blogosphere-millions-more-bloggers-and-blog-readers/ (accessed 2 October 2012).

142 http://www.suikerkrant.be/interview/1870-blogito-ergo-sum-ik-blog-dus-ik-ben, http://madamezsazsa.blogspot.be/ (accessed 2 October 2012)

143 http://blog.nielsen.com/nielsenwire/online_mobile/buzz-in-the-blogosphere-millions-more-bloggers-and-blog-readers/ (accessed 2 October 2012).

144 http://technorati.com/social-media/article/state-of-the-blogosphere-2011-part1/page-2/#ixzz1wpZSNBEO (accessed 2 October 2012).

145 'Invisible Marketing: What Every Organization Needs to Know in the Era of Blogs, Social Networks and Web 2.0', *White Paper*, www.marqui.com/resources/whitepapers.

146 http://en.wikipedia.org/wiki/Twitter (accessed 2 October 2012).

147 http://en.wikipedia.org/wiki/Taco_Bell, http://www.digitalsignageconnection.com/taco-bell-builds-buzz-doritos-locos-tacos-dooh-campaign (accessed 2 October 2012).

148 http://snapshot.doritoslocostacos.com/dlt/snapshot.html?guid=dc7402bb-42ec-4bd0-b81d-c3b7ad8e7b64 (accessed June 2012).

149 http://www.eurobest.com/winners/2011/pr/entry.cfm?entryid=2557&award=101 (accessed June 2012).

150 http://www.edisonresearch.com/home/archive/2008/04/the_podcast_con_1.php (accessed June 2009); http://www.edisonresearch.com/home/archives/2012/05/the-podcast-consumer-2012.php?utm_source=feedburner&utm_medium=feed&utm_campaign=Feed%3A+edisonresearch%2FTZWb+%28Edison+Research%29 (accessed 2 October 2012).

151 http://www.bookcrossing.com/about (accessed 2 October 2012).

152 http://www.slideshare.net/about (accessed 2 October 2012).

153 http://advertising.yahoo.com/article/flickr.html (accessed 2 October 2012).

154 http://en.wikipedia.org/wiki/Instagram (accessed 2 October 2012).

155 http://www.kullin.net/2012/01/instagram-now-growing-faster-than-flickr/ (accessed 2 October 2012).

156 http://brandisaction.com/ (accessed 2 October 2012).

157 http://www.businessinsider.com/these-brands-are-doing-amazing-things-with-instagram-2012-6#burberry-5 (accessed 2 October 2012).

158 http://web.stagram.com/n/burberry/ (accessed 2 October 2012).

159 http://www.time.com/time/magazine/article/0,9171,2104815-8,00.html (accessed 2 October 2012).

160 http://www.onehourpersecond.com/ (accessed 2 October 2012).

161 http://www.socialbakers.com/youtube-statistics/ (accessed 2 October 2012).

162 http://www.youtube.com/watch?v=PkJSw-SMZVE (accessed 2 October 2012).

163 http://www.adverblog.com/2012/04/11/tippexperience-2-the-hunter-and-the-bear-are-back/ (accessed 2 October 2012).

164 http://vimeo.com/blog/post:468, http://en.wikipedia.org/wiki/Vimeo (accessed 2 October 2012).

165 Roehm, M.L., Roehm, H.A., Jr and Boone, D.S. (2004), 'Plugs versus Placements: A Comparison of Alternatives for Within-program Brand Exposure', *Psychology & Marketing*, 21(1), 17–28.

166 PQMedia (2010), 'Global Branded Entertainment Marketing Forecast 2010–2014', http://www.pqmedia.com/brandedentertainmentforecast2010-read.html (accessed 2 October 2012).

167 Krishnamurthy, S. and Dou, W. (2008), 'Advertising with User-generated Content: A Framework and Research Agenda', *Journal of Interactive Advertising*, 8(2), 1–4.

168 Winer, R. (2009), 'New Communications Approaches in Marketing: Issues and Research Directions', *Journal of Interactive Marketing*, 23, 108–17.

169 McCarty, J.A. (2004), 'Product Placement: The Nature of the Practice and Potential Avenues for Inquiry', in Shrum, L.J. (ed.), *The Psychology of Entertainment Media: Blurring the Lines between Entertainment and Persuasion*. Mahwah, NJ: Lawrence Erlbaum Associates, 45–61.

170 Balasubramanian, S.K., Karrh, J.A. and Patwardhan, H. (2006), 'Audience Response to Product Placements: An Integrative Framework and Future Research Agenda', *Journal of Advertising*, 35(3), 115–41.

171 De Pelsmacker, P., Wouters, M., Purnawirawan, N. and Dens, N. (2011), 'I See You, but I Don't Like You: Consumer Responses to Prominence and Plot Connection for Brands Placed in Movies', *Proceedings of the 40th European Marketing Academy Conference, Ljubljana*.

172 http://statspotting.com/2012/03/1500-years-the-time-spotify-users-have-spent-on-spotifys-desktop-apps/ (accessed 2 October 2012).

173 http://www.guardian.co.uk/technology/2012/feb/14/myspace-one-million-users (accessed 2 October 2012).

174 http://www.slideshare.net/stevenvanbelleghem/social-media-around-the-world-2011 (accessed 2 October 2012).

175 http://www.marketingfacts.nl/berichten/de-laatste-social-media-cijfers-van-nederland/ (accessed 2 October 2012).

176 http://www.slideshare.net/stevenvanbelleghem/social-media-around-the-world-2011 (accessed 2 October 2012).

177 http://www.socialbakers.com/facebook-statistics/ (accessed 2 October 2012).

178 http://rossdawsonblog.com/weblog/archives/2012/02/which-countries-have-the-most-twitter-users-per-capita.html (accessed 2 October 2012).

179 http://www.socialbakers.com/linkedin-statistics (accessed 2 October 2012).

180 http://www.socialbakers.com/linkedin-statistics (accessed 2 October 2012).

181 http://press.linkedin.com/about (accessed 2 October 2012).

182 http://www.vabsite.com/2012/02/pinterest-users-usage-trends-statistics.html (accessed 2 October 2012).

183 http://www.slideshare.net/litmanlive/the-ultimate-guide-to-pinterest-11613788, http://en.wikipedia.org/wiki/Pinterest (accessed 2 October 2012).

184 http://mashable.com/2012/03/08/pinterest-more-traffic-twitter-study/ (accessed 2 October 2012).

185 http://www.comscoredatamine.com/2012/02/is-pinterest-the-next-big-social-network-in-europe/ (accessed 2 October 2012).

186 http://www.viralblog.com/social-media/kotex-launches-worlds-first-pinterest-campaign/ (accessed 2 October 2012).

187 http://www.youtube.com/watch?v=UVCoM4ao2Tw (accessed 2 October 2012).

188 http://wallblog.co.uk/2012/04/11/harrods-and-confused-com-launch-pinterest-campaigns/#ixzz1xTbXQ2AZ (accessed 2 October 2012).

189 http://brand-e.biz/brands-need-to-take-note-of-pinterest-traffic_21308.html (accessed 2 October 2012).

190 http://marketingland.com/study-says-pinterest-more-trusted-by-women-than-facebook-twitter-8021?utm_source=pluspost&utm_medium=plus&utm_campaign=stream (accessed 2 October 2012).

191 http://brand-e.biz/brands-need-to-take-note-of-pinterest-traffic_21308.html (accessed 2 October 2012).

192 http://thenextweb.com/socialmedia/2012/01/31/study-shows-that-only-27-of-twitter-users-tweeted-during-a-3-month-period/ (accessed 2 October 2012).

193 http://thenextweb.com/twitter/2011/10/03/study-from-yahoo-shows-that-50-percent-of-all-tweets-come-from-just-20000-users/ (accessed 2 October 2012).

194 http://www.socialbakers.com/twitter/, http://www.socialbakers.com/facebook-pages/ (accessed 2 October 2012).

195 http://kylelacy.com/25-case-studies-using-twitter-to-increase-business-and-sales/ (accessed 2 October 2012).

196 http://www.dutchdailynews.com/klm-launches-meet-seat-on-facebook-and-linkedin/ (accessed 2 October 2012).

197 http://www.slideshare.net/stevenvanbelleghem/social-media-around-the-world-2011 (accessed 2 October 2012).

198 http://www.marketingfacts.nl/berichten/hoe-gebruiken-wij-in-nederland-linkedin/ (accessed 2 October 2012).

199 http://www.infodocket.com/2012/04/02/social-media-in-europe-survey-of-1000-swedish-facebook-users-released/ (accessed 2 October 2012).

200 http://www2.lse.ac.uk/media@lse/research/EUKidsOnline/EU%20Kids%20II%20(2009-11)/EUKidsOnline IIReports/Final%20report.pdf (accessed 2 October 2012).

201 http://www.slideshare.net/stevenvanbelleghem/social-media-around-the-world-2011 (accessed 2 October 2012).

202 http://www.slideshare.net/stevenvanbelleghem/social-media-around-the-world-2011 (accessed 2 October 2012).

203 http://www.telegraph.co.uk/news/newstopics/howaboutthat/9053800/Sainsburys-changes-Tiger-Bread-to-Giraffe-Bread-following-advice-from-3-year-old.html# (accessed 2 October 2012).

204 http://www.warc.com/LatestNews/News/EmailNews.news?ID=29840&Origin=WARCNewsEmail (accessed 2 October 2012).

205 http://socialstatistics.com/?number=100&kind=user-circles (accessed 2 October 2012).

206 http://www.socialbakers.com/facebook-pages/brands/ (accessed 2 October 2012).

207 http://mashable.com/2009/06/16/killer-facebook-fan-pages/ (accessed 2 October 2012).

208 http://mashable.com/2009/03/30/successful-facebook-fan-page/ (accessed 2 October 2012).

[209] http://mashable.com/2012/05/17/facebook-timeline-brand-tips/ (accessed 2 October 2012).

[210] http://www.creativeguerrillamarketing.com/social-media-marketing/quechua-facebook-timeline-flipbook-campaign/ (accessed 2 October 2012).

[211] http://mashable.com/2012/05/31/facebook-marketing-trends/ (accessed 2 October 2012).

[212] http://michaelhaenlein.com/Publications/Kaplan,%20Andreas%20-%20Users%20of%20the%20world,%20unite.pdf (accessed 2 October 2012).

[213] 'The Britney Spears Universe: Social Media and Viral Marketing at its Best', Andreas M. Kaplan and Michael Haenlein, ESCP Europe, 79 Avenue de la République, F-75011 Paris, France.

[214] http://www.comscoredatamine.com/2012/03/social-networks-the-place-to-advertise-consumer-goods/ (accessed 2 October 2012).

[215] http://www.bloomberg.com/news/2012-05-15/social-media-ad-spending-to-jump-to-9-8-billion-in-2016.html (accessed 2 October 2012).

[216] http://www.simplyzesty.com/social-media/social-media-ad-spend-to-hit-19-5-of-total-marketing-budget-in-five-years/ (accessed 2 October 2012).

[217] http://searchenginewatch.com/article/2143126/Facebook-IPO-Show-Ad-Revenue-Increased-69-in-2011 (accessed 2 October 2012).

[218] http://blogs.reuters.com/anthony-derosa/2012/02/01/the-most-interesting-data-points-in-facebooks-ipo/ (accessed 2 October 2012).

[219] http://finance.yahoo.com/news/YouTube-Will-Generate-Ad-wscheats-3715219348.html, http://gigaom.com/video/youtube-revenues-doubled/ (accessed 2 October 2012).

[220] http://www.emarketer.com/PressRelease.aspx?R=1008806 (accessed 2 October 2012).

[221] http://www.emarketer.com/PressRelease.aspx?R=1008806 (accessed 2 October 2012).

[222] http://blogs.reuters.com/anthony-derosa/2012/02/29/facebook-brings-new-ad-opportunities-to-brands/ (accessed 2 October 2012).

[223] http://blogs.reuters.com/anthony-derosa/2012/02/29/facebook-brings-new-ad-opportunities-to-brands/ (accessed 2 October 2012).

[224] http://michaelhaenlein.com/Publications/Kaplan,%20Andreas%20-%20Users%20of%20the%20world,%20unite.pdf (accessed 2 October 2012).

[225] http://wow.joystiq.com/2012/02/09/world-of-warcraft-subscriber-numbers/ (accessed 2 October 2012).

[226] http://www.youtube.com/watch?v=viR_RlMOsds&feature=related (accessed 2 October 2012).

[227] Smith, P.R. and Chaffey, D. (2002), *eMarketing Excellence: The Heart of eBusiness*. Oxford: Butterworth–Heinemann.

[228] http://www.websuccessteam.com/WSTblog/2011/12/relationship-marketing-2012/ (accessed 2 October 2012).

[229] http://advertising.yahoo.com/article/case-study-going-online-to-strengthen-customer-relationships.html (accessed 2 October 2012).

[230] Allen, C., Kania, D. and Yaeckel, B. (2001), *One-to-One Web Marketing: Build a Relationship Marketing Strategy One Customer at a Time*. New York: Wiley Computer Publications.

[231] Jobber, D. and Fahy, J. (2003), *Foundations of Marketing*. Maidenhead: McGraw-Hill.

[232] Strauss, J., El-Ansary, A. and Frost, R. (2003), *E-Marketing*, 3rd edition. Englewood Cliffs, NJ: Prentice Hall.

[233] Van den Bergh, J. (2002), '45% of Belgian Marketers Actively Set Up Internet Actions', Press release of the *eBenchmark Survey* of InSites Consulting, 9 December, www.insites-consulting.com.

[234] Chaffey, D., Mayer, R., Johnston, K. and Ellis-Chadwick, F. (2003), *Internet Marketing: Strategy, Implementation and Practice*. Harlow: Financial Times/Prentice Hall.

[235] http://www.google.com/analytics/features/index.html (accessed 2 October 2012).

[236] http://www.google.com/analytics/features/advertising.html (accessed 2 October 2012).

[237] http://www.socialmedia.biz/2012/03/19/4-steps-to-measuring-social-media-success/ (accessed 2 October 2012).

CHAPTER 16
Ethical issues in marketing communications

CHAPTER OUTLINE

Ethics and marketing communications	Ethical decision-making models and rules
Unethical marketing communication practices	Unethical use of marketing communication instruments
Stereotyping	Advertising
Controversial messages	Public relations
Covert marketing	Personal selling and direct marketing
Targeting vulnerable groups	Packaging
	Sales promotion
Regulation of marketing communication practices	Self-regulation of marketing communication practices
Corporate social responsibility	

CHAPTER OBJECTIVES

This chapter will help you to:

● Understand what morals and ethics mean both in general and in marketing communications practice

● Distinguish the different points of view with respect to ethics and the rules that marketing communications professionals may follow in order to behave in an ethical way

● Learn about the major ethical issues in marketing communications: stereotyping, controversial messages, targeting vulnerable groups such as children, and using covert marketing techniques such as stealth marketing and buzz marketing

● Understand how marketing communications tools such as advertising, public relations, selling, promotions and packaging can be used in an unethical way

● Get an idea about regulation and self-regulation principles and organisations with respect to marketing communications

● Understand how companies may benefit from corporate social responsibility programmes

Introduction

Marketing communications professionals are often accused of unethical behaviour. Business practice and societal concerns sometimes clash, and certain marketing communications practices are therefore perceived as 'wrong'. In order to behave well and be perceived as a 'good citizen', and in their own long-term business interest, companies should follow ethical standards and rules and apply them to their marketing communications practice. Among the most debated ethical issues are stereotyping, targeting vulnerable groups, using controversial messages and covert marketing. Indeed, marketing communications are often accused of building and maintaining stereotypical gender roles, of deliberately using shocking images, of relentlessly and inappropriately targeting children and of using techniques such as stealth marketing, buzz marketing and brand placement that can be regarded as intrinsically deceptive or misleading. Unethical practices can be found in many marketing communications tools: deceptive advertising, dishonest public relations, fraud in sales promotions, misleading packaging and privacy-invading direct marketing and selling. To avoid negative consequences for customers, laws and regulations have been formulated, and many countries and industries have established self-regulation procedures and organisations to improve the ethical standards of marketing communications practice. Companies themselves may go beyond that and engage in corporate social responsibility programmes to position themselves as ethical and as good citizens.

Ethics and marketing communications

Every society has certain moral and value standards that act as behavioural guidelines for citizens: what is right and wrong in different situations? A distinction should be made between morals and ethics. **Morals** are beliefs or principles that individuals hold concerning what is right and what is wrong. Morals direct people as they make decisions. **Ethics** are principles that serve as operational guidelines for both individuals and organisations. They are related to moral feelings of right and wrong.[1] Ethics are generally not written down but rather held in the social consciousness (attitudes and feelings) of an organisation or a population.[2] Ethics is thus the study and application of morality: those practices and activities that are importantly right or wrong.

With respect to what is ethical or not, several approaches can be discerned.[3] A classical distinction is the one between the deontological and the teleological approaches. The **deontological approach** focuses upon duties. Some actions are intrinsically right or wrong. The **teleological approach** focuses on consequences. Good or bad depends on what happens as a result of the action. This is very much an 'end justifies the means' approach and will lead to utilitarian points of view such as selecting actions that can be expected to result in the greatest good to the greatest number. The problem with a deontological approach is that it cannot handle conflicts of duty. For instance, in wartime, an individual may have the duty to hide another person from a hostile invader. At the same time, he or she has the duty to tell the truth about it. On the other hand, a teleological approach cannot handle considerations of justice, i.e. treating people as being of equal worth. McIntyre *et al.* developed a four-cell taxonomy based on the deontological (idealism) and the teleological (relativism) principle. Situationists score high in both relativism and idealism. Absolutists score low in relativism but high in idealism. Subjectivists score high in relativism but low in idealism. Exceptionists score low in both dimensions.[4]

Other ethical principles are distributive justice and ordinary decency. According to **distributive justice**, rewards are allocated in proportion to the contribution made to organisational ends. **Ordinary decency** means that, for instance, lying, cheating and coercion are always considered unethical. Still others distinguish three basic dimensions of ethical decision-making: moral equity (perceived fairness, justice, acceptability), relativism (guidelines, requirements of the social/cultural system) and **contractualism** (implied obligation, contracts, duties, rules).[5]

Ethical issues in marketing communications originate from the clash between business practice and social concerns, such as environmental and social values and societal notions about honesty, honour, virtue and integrity.[6] Marketing and marketing communications have often been accused of creating a materialistic culture of conspicuous consumption, playing on emotions, simplifying real human situations into stereotypes, exploiting anxieties, employing techniques of intensive persuasion that amount to (hidden) manipulation, maximising appeal and minimising information, trivialising, and generally reducing men, women and children to the role of irrational consumer (Photo 16.1).[7]

Photo 16.1 Stereotyping?
Source: Getty Images.

There is a decades-old debate concerning whether marketing communications mirror or shape society and whether the alleged criticisms are warranted. Those who claim that marketing communications shape society argue that, through marketing's persuasiveness and creativity, it creates a culture of consumption and materialism and overspending. It drives up the cost of products; it is used to sell inferior products and products that are not good for us (such as alcohol and tobacco); it sets unrealistic expectations, is done in bad taste and creates visual pollution (e.g. sex and violence used to gain attention to the message). Finally, it imposes American culture on other cultures. Those who say marketing communications mirror society claim that marketing's persuasiveness is largely overestimated. Some claim that overspending is endemic in many societies and not just because of marketing. Also banks and consumer credit practices are to blame. Marketing may well emphasise materialism, but is materialism necessarily wrong? Moreover, out of the thousands of messages that people see, only a few are remembered; nine out of ten new product introductions fail; companies spend a lot of money on marketing research to find out what consumers want, and then make and offer it. Most companies want loyal customers, and selling an inferior product is the best way to lose customers. Emerging social consciousness about the environment has led marketing communications to integrate this issue and argument into marketing campaigns and not vice versa. Marketing communications professionals go to a great deal of effort to reach only those consumers that they expect will be interested in the product and the message. 'Freedom of speech' advocates will argue that there is no need to establish standards of good taste and morality in marketing communications. Most of the time, marketing costs are only a small percentage of the selling price, and marketing increases competition which, in turn, lowers prices. Furthermore, for many people a product has an objective and a psychological value (for instance, a shirt of a famous soccer player is expensive, but some people like to pay extra money for the additional psychological benefit). On the other hand, people are free to choose not to pay the extra money for psychological value. Probably, the truth is between these extremes: if marketing communications do not work, that would imply that all marketing investments are useless; if marketing communications work all the time with everyone, it means consumers do not have a conscious will.[8]

The notion of social acceptability changes over time and varies from one culture or country to another. For instance, a US study among college students in 2003 showed that they had less salient ethical concerns about advertising than in a similar study 25 years previously. This could be due to increased cynicism and scepticism on the part of the generation Y consumers that leads to lower expectations about ethicality in advertising. However, students still seemed to be equally critical, and questioned advertising and its truthfulness: 65% believed that advertising does not present a true picture of products, 45% said that advertising is too misleading and 57% that it was too exaggerated.[9] Fam and Waller interviewed 1014 students in four Asian countries about the deliberate use of controversial and offensive images in advertising that may offend some people and studied what makes ads controversial. They found that what makes people find images offensive is related to cultural characteristics. For instance, in collectivistic cultures, what could disrupt the harmony of society is considered to be very unethical. In more religious cultures or cultures that adhere to Confucian dynamism, higher ethical and moral standards are upheld.[10] A US study among 235 marketing professionals revealed that several cultural characteristics determined marketers' perceptions of the role of ethics and social responsibility in the overall success of the firm. Idealism, the presence of corporate ethical values, uncertainty avoidance and Confucian dynamism had a positive effect on the perceived role of ethics, while relativism and power distance had a negative impact.[11] Not all individuals can even agree on what might create offence. It is in the areas of taste and decency that most difficulty arises in defining ethical marketing communications.[12]

BUSINESS INSIGHT
Durex TV and print campaign

Durex ran a TV campaign on MTV across Europe in 2001. One of the ads featured an enormous sperm-like crowd following a man walking down the street to meet his girlfriend. When the couple meet, the sperm crowd gets blocked by a huge latex wall. The sperm get trapped in a huge condom, after which the baseline 'Durex: For a Hundred Million Reasons' appears. Since most US TV channels do not permit condom advertising, Durex ran a radio campaign in the USA instead. The ads were made up of playful interviews with couples who talked about their sexual experiences. For example, in one ad a girl giggled, 'We were on vacation and I lifted my skirt', to which her boyfriend responds, 'Yeah, I think she was in her exhibitionist phase then.' Due to media availability, ad theme and ad execution were completely different for Europe and the USA.[13]

Ethical decision-making models and rules

Different views can be held on how to apply ethical decision-making in marketing (communications).[14] Under the **caveat emptor** rule, anything is allowed that maximises profits within the law. This view implies that the law is the only benchmark for ethical behaviour, and that what is legal must therefore also be ethical. The **ethics code** view strives for standards on the basis of which companies' and industries' ethical performance is judged, or at least to which they aspire. This set of standards often contains ethical guidelines that go further than the law. In the **consumer sovereignty** approach, ethical marketing decisions are determined by the answer to three important questions. Is the target market vulnerable in ways that limit consumer decision-making (consumer capability) and are consumers' expectations at purchase likely to be realised? Do consumers have sufficient information to judge (consumer information) and can consumers go elsewhere? Would they incur substantial costs or inconvenience by transferring their loyalty (consumer choice)? Finally, there is the **caveat venditor** principle which implies that the maximisation of consumer satisfaction or well-being should be the ultimate aim of marketing action. This point of view is the most ethical one in that its ultimate benchmark is doing everything in the best interest of the consumers.

A survey of 206 US advertising professionals studied the relative influence of four factors on decision-making about advertising content and policy. In general, legal considerations were found to be the most important. Overall, ethical issues appeared to be of minor importance, except for the oldest age group, for which they were the most important. Approval of management and peers and business considerations appeared to be moderately important, except for the youngest age group, who felt that the latter was the most important.[15] A multi-country study of the opinion of advertising professionals about ethics in advertising revealed that ethical limits seem to be restricted to the codes of ethics, legislation, habits and customs, but not to natural law (common sense) or people's values and beliefs.[16]

Others hold that any marketing communications decision should in any case be legal, decent, honest and truthful. **Legal** means that it should be allowed under the current regulations and laws of the country in which the company operates. **Decent** means that it should not contain anything that is likely to cause widespread offence, fear or distress; for instance, the use of shocking claims or images for the sake of creating attention should be avoided, unless a valid and acceptable reason is given. **Honest and truthful** implies that it should not exploit inexperience or lack of knowledge of consumers; no claims should be made which are inaccurate, ambiguous or intended to mislead whether through explicit statement or through

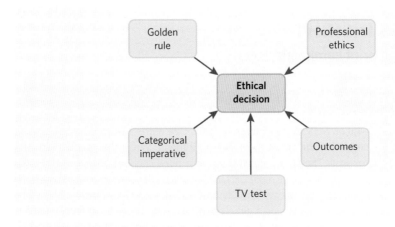

Figure 16.1 Rules of thumb when facing an ethical dilemma

omission. Although this principle seems obvious, it may be interpreted in a not so obvious way. For instance, UK law allows for obvious untruths or exaggerations that are unlikely to mislead because the audience would consider them as acceptable exaggerations.[17]

In Figure 16.1 an overview is given of a number of rules of thumb for marketers facing what appears to be an ethical dilemma.[18] The **golden rule** states that, when faced with a decision that appears to have ethical implications, act in a way that you would expect others to act towards you. The **professional ethics** rule states that you should take only actions that would be viewed as proper by an objective panel of your professional colleagues. The philosopher Kant's **categorical imperative** means one should act in such a way that the action taken under the circumstances could be a universal law of behaviour for everyone facing those same circumstances. This rule is very similar to the deontological stance discussed above. The **TV test** means that a manager should always ask if he or she would feel comfortable explaining this action on TV to the general public. Finally, the **outcomes rule** judges the ethical quality of a decision in terms of performance, rewards, satisfaction and feedback. This is a relativistic point of view that is consistent with the teleological principle discussed above.

Several ethical issues in marketing communications warrant further discussion. They can be divided on the basis of marketing communications practices or for a number of marketing communications instruments.[19]

Unethical marketing communications practices

Among commonly cited unethical communications practices are stereotyping, targeting vulnerable groups, covert marketing and controversial marketing communications messages.

Stereotyping

Stereotyping is an automatic perceptual bias enabling people to construct simplified images of reality. Men and women are often depicted in a stereotypical way, and therefore marketing communications are often accused of proclaiming and supporting conservative gender roles in society. Also, the elderly are often depicted as ignorant and helpless, and other cultures and/or ethnic groups are often portrayed in a stereotypical way that may offend them and stimulate prejudices in society. But stereotyping can also be more subtle. For instance, childless women may be offended by ads directed to mothers. In one of the cases that was brought before the Jury of Ethical Practices (JEP) in advertising in Belgium, a woman complained

Source: Image courtesy of The Advertising Archives.

about a government campaign promoting a healthy lifestyle using the slogan 'a healthy person is worth two'. She claimed that she had been unhealthy for all her life and that she felt stigmatised by the slogan and the campaign. The jury expressed its sympathy with the lady's health problems but ruled that the government used a perfectly acceptable metaphor and dismissed the complaint.

A recent study of 600 female role portrayals in online ads for global products concluded that women are generally portrayed in a stereotypical or decorative way and that sexism is prevalent in online ads worldwide. On websites directed at women, females were generally portrayed as decorative. Websites directed at men mostly showed women in a dependent or a traditional role. General-audience websites featured women mostly as housewives or equal to men.[20] Lin studied stereotyping (role portraying) in Taiwanese ads featuring female models. The results showed that in domestic magazines the classical 'girl next door' role appeared to be very acceptable. This can be attributed to conservative Confucian beliefs about women's role in society. However, trendy role models resulted in the highest preference in foreign magazines. This can be explained by the fact that these magazines are read by women with higher levels of education and by women's increasing participation in the labour force. These results indicate that stereotyping is perceived differently by different consumers. It also suggests that advertising both reflects and determines and shapes culture.[21]

RESEARCH INSIGHT
Gender role stereotypes in Belgian TV advertising

Advertising practitioners make use of stereotyping to quickly transfer the essential meaning of their messages. One of the stereotypes frequently used in advertising is gender stereotyping. 'Gender' refers to the personal appearance, personality attributes and socio-sexual roles that society understands to be 'masculine' or 'feminine'.[22] For example, women are often stereotyped as dependent on or subservient to men, as preoccupied with physical attractiveness, as sex objects, etc.[23] Women are generally depicted as younger and thinner than men, and they are often represented as caretaking mothers or housewives.[24] Women act as product users rather than experts and are often portrayed as passive and dependent on their male counterparts.[25] Female characters occupy a more inactive, decorative role that is subordinate to that of the male character or voice.[26] They are also more likely to be portrayed in sexually appealing roles than men[27] and even serve as rewards to men for using a certain product.[28] Men, on the other hand, are portrayed as older, less often married and more experienced. They are more often represented as spokespeople or experts, meaning advertisers tend to put men in an autonomous, authoritarian and independent role.[29]

A Belgian study[30] set out to see whether gender role depiction in Belgian TV advertising has evolved over time, in accordance with prevailing regulation. The largest commercial TV network in Belgium provided a database containing all televised ads broadcast on Belgian commercial TV since 2002. From this database, commercials from two periods (i.e. January 2002 to April 2003 and January 2009 to April 2010) were randomly selected. Commercials of less than 15 seconds, commercials containing no adult characters, and movie trailers were omitted. Only characters playing a prominent role (being shown for at least three seconds) were coded. The total sample resulting from this procedure consisted of 493 TV commercials, 250 from the first period and 243 from the second period. In these commercials, 907 main characters were coded for analyses.

Of the 907 coded models, 47% were female and 53% were male. Both men (50%) and especially women (71%) were mostly presented as young and least in the older age category (11% of men, 8% of woman). Men (39%) appeared more frequently as middle-aged than women (21%). Women (19%) were depicted significantly more often as using the product than men (11%). Women (20%) are significantly more frequently depicted as sexual objects than men (5%). Almost half (44%) of the women in the ads were shown in a domestic setting, while this occurred significantly less frequently for men (30%). Men (27%), by contrast, are proportionally more frequently portrayed in a professional context than women (9%). Out of the 907 registered models a total of 129 were depicted in a working situation. This total entails 97 male characters and 32 female characters. Within the workplace, the majority of men (55%) are shown as interpreting a superior role, while women are most often shown in a subordinate role (57%). Men and women are also portrayed significantly differently in their roles within a family setting. Women (17%) are also more often depicted in a parental role than men (11%). Only 1% of the men in the ads are performing household chores, while this percentage is significantly higher for women (12%). When women are shown in a family context, they are vastly portrayed as dominant within the family (90%), while this is only the case for 25% of the men shown in a family context. Almost all (99%) women and the majority of men (66%) were rated as 'not muscular'. Men were coded significantly more often as 'slightly muscular' (27%) or 'strongly muscular'

(5%) than women, though. While 89% of women in the ads were judged to be underweight (versus 27% of men), men were most likely to be shown in a 'normal' weight class (66%, versus 9% of women). Overweight men (5%) and women (2%) were rare.

In comparison with the first period (2002–3), gender portrayal did not fundamentally change in the second period (2009–10). The study demonstrates that advertising on Belgian TV today is permeated by gender stereotypes. Notwithstanding societal and regulatory changes, advertisers still use stereotypical gender roles to convey their messages, and we see little decrease from the 2002 situation.

The use of models in marketing communications often supports the stereotype that happiness depends on physical attractiveness, for instance by showing 'before–after' pictures for slimming and beauty products. Advertising to men often appeals to worries about virility (Viagra, hair transplants, hair colouring products). Idealised advertising and media images have been shown to affect how individuals think about themselves.[31] In previous studies, images of thin women and buff men negatively impacted on mood and bodily perceptions of respectively women and men, through the process of social comparison.[32] Models being Photoshopped to make them look more 'ideal' than they are is a common practice in advertising (see, for instance, the Dove ad at http://www.youtube.com/watch?v=T4y5b7INvqE). According to Spurgin, advertisers are ethically obliged to avoid certain aesthetic results that are produced by computer-generated images of perfection because this is misleading. Most people are not aware of the fact that the picture only exists virtually. The author claims that this type of advertising is deceptive and violates the autonomy of those subjected to it.[33]

Controversial messages

Controversial or 'shock advertising' can be defined as advertising that deliberately rather than inadvertently startles and offends its audience, by means of deliberate norm violation – transgression of law or custom (obscenity) or moral/social code (vulgarity) – or by showing things that outrage the moral or physical senses (e.g. provocative or disgusting images).[34] Controversial advertising appeals, appeals that evoke negative emotions, or shock tactics are widely used as a creative technique to grab the attention of the public or to bring shock values to the brand.[35] The whole point of using controversial ads is to break through the clutter, facilitate recall and have a positive (or at least not a negative) impact on advertising and brand attitudes. Controversial advertising can be divided into two broad categories: advertising for offensive products or ideas (e.g. politics, female hygiene products and alcohol; some may even say professional services like dentists, lawyers and doctors),[36] and controversial advertising executions (e.g. sexual appeals). Several authors defined various categories of controversial ads, in terms of ads for both controversial products and controversial imagery: unmentionables, socially sensitive or indecent, unethical advertising and unacceptable advertising (causing offence).[37] Waller found six reasons for advertising to be seen as offensive: racist, anti-social behaviour, sexist, too personal a subject, indecent language and nudity.[38] Shimp and Stuart used a panel of 25 college students to establish six categories of disgusting advertising: gross depiction, indecent, sexually oriented, gross animal and human waste scenes, associational disgust presentation, disgusting political ads and miscellaneous.[39] Several well-known brands are known to have used controversial appeals, the most frequently cited being Benetton, but also Calvin Klein, Citroën, Moschino, Esprit, Gucci, Sony PlayStation and Reebok.[40] Disgust appeals are sometimes used in public service announcements, for instance AIDS awareness campaigns, in which case they can generate a lot of attention to and memory of the message.[41] However, using disgust in a less congruent commercial setting does not necessarily lead to increased brand recall, but has been shown to have a negative effect on ad and brand attitudes, especially with high-affect intense and high-involvement consumers.[42]

BUSINESS INSIGHT
UNICEF: Don't let war affect the lives of children

In 2006, UNICEF in Belgium created a unique, but shocking TV commercial about the impact of war on children. The ad features the blue Smurf cartoon characters in a war setting. The ad starts out on a nice sunny day with the traditional Smurf song: 'Hey, come to Smurf country, welcome to all. Yes, come to Smurf country, the country of pomp and circumstance'. Immediately after, the Smurf village is annihilated by warplanes. Smurfs are lying dead all over the street, a baby is crying without its mum or dad being around . . . The tagline of the spot reads 'Don't let war affect the lives of children.' The ad was meant for the adult population and was aired only after 9 p.m. The objective of the campaign was to raise awareness about the many ways in which conflict destroys children's lives in general, and to raise money for the rehabilitation of former child soldiers in Burundi in particular. Currently, about 300 000 children are being used as child soldiers worldwide. Moreover, almost one in two of the 3.6 million humans killed in conflicts since 1990 are children. The campaign showed what many children are experiencing in real life. The ad featured Smurfs because Smurfs have been part of Belgian culture since 1958. Adult viewers immediately recognise the blue cartoon figures which make them think back to their youth. The emotional bond they have with the Smurfs made the ad more shocking. Smurfs were deliberately used here to enhance the impact and awareness of the campaign. The campaign has been in the news worldwide, receiving both positive and negative comments. Some think the ad featured unnecessary violence, others praised the creative approach to draw attention to the problem. One way or another, the campaign worked and received an award for its effectiveness.[43]

Sex and nudity appeals are frequently used in advertising as a means to attract attention to the ad (Photo 16.2). Today, up to 38% of ads using men show the model in a sexual context.[44] Women, however, are even more likely to be portrayed in sexually appealing roles. Most previous research has concluded that scantily dressed or erotic appeals elicit a negative affective reaction of the public and result in decreased brand recall.[45] Two experimental studies involving Belgian men and women explored how more revealing displays of a model's body in advertising messages can impact on individuals' body esteem. Samples of Belgian men and women were exposed to an advertising image containing a male or female model in either pyjamas or just underwear. The results showed that scantily dressed models had a negative effect on individuals' body esteem compared with dressed models. When the models were dressed more revealingly, it was the opposite-sex model that had the most negative effect on participants' body esteem, possibly due to an increased sexual salience. Scantily dressed models in advertising appear to affect the body esteem of both men and women.[46] Some would deem this effect to be undesirable and thus unethical.

Covert marketing

Covert marketing is a firm's marketing actions whereby consumers believe that the activities are not those of the firm. It exists in many forms, and is sometimes referred to as stealth marketing, buzz marketing, masked marketing or word-of-mouth marketing. **Stealth marketing** is formally defined as the use of marketing practices that fail to disclose or reveal the true relationship with the company that produces or sponsors the marketing message. **Buzz marketing** is giving people a reason to talk about the company's products or services and making it easier for that conversation to take place.[47] Also, covert forms of information gathering, such as placing 'cookies' on a person's computer system to enable identification of this person when he or she next visits the website, are a form of covert marketing. Another example is a **flog** (fake weblog), when firms develop a fake consumer blog about the consumption of some

Photo 16.2 Using a controversial picture of a celebrity to support a 'good cause'
Source: Getty Images.

product or service without stating the company's role in the communication. These tactics are inherently deceptive and thus unethical because they are likely to mislead a reasonable consumer on material aspects of a company's marketing efforts, and because they are intrusive or exploitative of social relationships or the kindness of strangers.[48]

BUSINESS INSIGHT
Stealth marketing

In 2002, Sony Ericsson's communications agencies hired 60 actors to pose as tourists in ten cities across the USA. Unsuspecting people were asked to take a picture of the fake tourists with the new T68i camera phone. After the person agreed, the actor demonstrated the use of the camera and began talking up its benefits and features. The actors did not identify themselves as being paid by Sony Ericsson. Other initiatives included actresses talking to strangers in trendy bars while using the phone and pairs of actresses playing an interactive version of the game 'Battleship' at either end of a bar. In this way, many people got direct experience with the phone or learned about it through word of mouth. When exposed, the company did not apologise. It claimed that talking to strangers is not an offence, and the campaign was very effective.

In 2006, the US retailer Wal-Mart's communications agency launched a blog sponsored by Wal-Mart called 'Working families for Wal-Mart'. The blog described the adventures of Laura and Jim, two ordinary people who travelled across the USA in a recreational vehicle, stopping at Wal-Mart locations, camping out in Wal-Mart parking lots and talking to Wal-Mart staff who were, of course, all very positive about various aspects of Wal-Mart's business behaviour (social contribution, environmental policy, etc.). Upon exposure, Laura and Jim claimed that they came up with the idea themselves, contacted 'Working families for Wal-Mart' and were then offered support for their trip (the vehicle, fuel, writing the blog, etc.). This is a typical example of a 'flog'.

The most powerful form of marketing is an advocacy message from a trusted friend. In 2001, Procter & Gamble founded a teen network called Tremor. The network has 250 000 members who are considered to be 'connectors' in their social network of friends. Connectors are early adopters who have an extensive social network. P&G sends them samples and encourages them to promote them with friends, family and strangers. Tremor was so successful that P&G decided also to launch Vocalpoint, a network of 450 000 mothers that has actively supported campaigns for more than 10 P&G brands. Buzz marketing initiatives like Tremor and Vocalpoint successfully use word of mouth by giving products to consumers who, in turn, strongly advocate these products in their daily interpersonal reactions. P&G claims that this does not prevent members from disclosing P&G's support, and that therefore these actions are not unethical.[49]

Due to recent technological developments, the TV advertising landscape is changing rapidly. The introduction of the personal video recorder and the ongoing convergence of TV and the Internet are causing consumers to gain more and more control over which content they want to see and when they want to see it. Marketers increasingly look at brand placement (sometimes called 'product placement') as a powerful way to connect with consumers. **Brand placement** is the paid inclusion of branded products or brand identifiers through audio and/or visual means within mass media programmes.[50] Paid brand placement spending grew 33.7% to $2.90 billion in 2007 and at a compound annual growth rate of 40.8% from 2002 to 2007, thereby significantly outpacing that of traditional advertising.[51] The global spending on brand placement amounted to $6.25 billion in 2009, the vast majority of which is spent on traditional advertising media (e.g. TV, radio, feature films, etc.).[52] The European Commission has updated the 'Television Without Frontiers Directive', relaxing the rules of advertising to allow for brand placements. Consequently, the phenomenon is expected to grow even more. Brand placement can be considered a covert technique. According to Nebenzahl and Jaffe, brand placement is the ultimate example of unethical, inherently deceptive advertising, since it is both disguised and obtrusive. Often viewers are not aware of the fact that brands are intentionally placed in TV programmes or movies, and they often do not pay conscious attention to them. Placement works best if audiences do not perceive it as advertising, are not particularly aware of its influence and do not develop defence mechanisms and counter-arguments as a result of persuasion knowledge.[53] Therefore, there may be an implicit conflict between the need to make a placement effective and the need to protect consumers from being misled.[54] Brand placement disclosure, i.e. communicating to the viewers that brands are placed in media content, may serve to increase the accessibility of the persuasive or commercial intent behind placed brands, but may produce resistance to persuasive attempts and lead to counter-arguments undermining persuasive power.

Targeting vulnerable groups

One of the most debated ethical issues is marketing to children. Estimates suggest that children in the USA spend on average four hours per day watching TV and are exposed to about 25 000 commercials per year. The Internet has further expanded the exposure of children to advertising. In 2002, approximately $15 billion was spent in the USA on marketing communications directed at children, including TV and print ads, sales promotions, brand placement in movies and integrated merchandising plans, and in-school marketing. Sometimes adult products are also targeted at pre-adults (for instance, so-called 'alcopops'). 'Old Joe', 'Smooth Joe' (Camel) allegedly induced many teenagers to smoke. Breweries promote their beer brands to college students during spring breaks, festivals, etc. A study in seven countries revealed that 'tweens' (ages 9–14) consider TV as the single most important source of product information.[55] Companies advertise in and around schools, air commercials during children's programmes, target children on product packaging, on point-of-purchase displays and during sporting events, and place brands in programmes targeted at children. Schools accept and display brand messages, disguised as educational materials, in exchange for money, free equipment, curriculum materials, classroom videos, etc., that may contain biased or incomplete information that favours the company or its economic agenda.

Source: Image courtesy of The Advertising Archives.

RESEARCH INSIGHT
Advertising to children: the call for regulation

Many countries have strict rules and legislation about advertising to children.[56] The negative social consequences of advertising to children underpin the rationale for advertising restrictions, and the debate has mainly focused on food products.[57] Notwithstanding this extensive regulation, there is no strong consensus that advertising directed at children should be banned.[58] In the context of the obesity debate, Berman[59] states that there is no reason to believe that a complete ban on advertising would have any impact on childhood obesity rates, and Eagle *et al.*[60] also conclude that there is a growing body of evidence that banning food ads targeted at children would be both inequitable and ineffective. Nevertheless, many parents seem to be in favour of stricter legislation on and control of (food) advertising directed at children. Burr and Burr,[61] in their study of 400 US parents, had already noticed a call for greater federal legislation. And Chan and McNeal[62] also concluded that parents feel strongly that advertising should be banned on children's programming. On the other hand, Spungin[63] wonders whether, without food advertising, parents would buy better food. In this study, 40% of parents thought they did not have enough information about providing their children with a healthy diet, and they did not particularly like advertising bans. In any case, Nathanson *et al.*[64] concluded that a high perceived threat and concern about TV content lead to more support for censorship.

Besides these 'hard' regulations, there are also 'soft' measures. The most widely known are self-regulatory initiatives by the advertising industry. Gray[65] states that advertising self-regulation is the best way to control advertising, and refers to the 'International Code of Advertising Practices' of the International Chamber of Commerce (ICC). The CARU (Children's Advertising Review Unit), a self-regulatory body in the USA, claims to ensure that advertising directed at children is truthful, accurate and appropriate.[66] However, in the 1970s, it had already been found that there is a great deal of cynicism about self-regulation and, as long as there are concerned parents who question the efficacy of industry self-regulation efforts, children's advertising is likely to remain a controversial issue.[67] Soft measures refer not only to self-regulation by the industry, but also to initiatives such as the formation of parent monitor groups, independent organisations or multi-party bodies (consisting of parents, educators, broadcasters, etc.).[68]

As far as the support for hard or soft measures is concerned, Walsh *et al.*[69] concluded that many options on regulations and control had been offered, but that mothers were inconsistent in their views and preferences.

Some say that advertising to children is inherently unfair and deceptive because children lack the cognitive skills and life experiences needed to resist persuasive claims and because marketers take advantage of a child's inability to weigh evidence and make an informed decision. A counter-argument is that ads can help parents and children to make informed choices. In any case, children have a number of unique vulnerabilities. It is only by the age of five that they are able to distinguish between commercial and non-commercial content. By approximately eight years they are able to recognise the persuasive intent of advertising and to use this knowledge to interpret selling messages. It is only when children are aged 10–12 that they acknowledge that advertising does not always tell the truth and that they become sceptical about advertising; in other words, they actively use their defence mechanism. A new challenge is the blurring of advertising and entertainment. TV commercials focus on entertainment and image creation and are often linked to exciting website games (advergames) and brand characters. Brands targeted at children are placed in movies. Commercially sponsored websites contain games and promotions designed for children. Research indicates that more than two-thirds of websites designed for children rely on advertising as their primary source of income. Research also reveals that primarily older children (11–12) are more likely to shape their product usage as a result of this banded entertainment or 'advertainment'.

Disguising promotions as entertainment makes it harder for children to deploy defence mechanisms. This new evolution is an ethical issue because it is potentially misleading by concealing the true nature of the materials and omitting to disclose its commercial intent.[70] Children have not yet developed sensitivity to this type of promotional tool and they are more susceptible to placements than adults. A study in Canada and the USA revealed that parents in both countries consider the explicit plot-connected placement of ethically charged products such as alcohol, tobacco and fast food as the most unethical, and believe it should be subject to more regulation.[71]

RESEARCH INSIGHT
Parental views about advertising to children

Advertising to children has long had a bad reputation and parents are concerned about it.[72] Burr and Burr[73] have already reported that parents had strong doubts about the honesty of advertising to children and that they displayed a strong degree of cynicism about TV advertising to children and its apparently misleading aspects. TV advertising has been described as manipulative, promoting materialism, stifling creativity and disrupting parent–child relationships.[74] Burr and Burr[75] state that some abuses of advertising are perceived to be unique to child-centred advertising: it manipulates the child, imposes stress and strain on low-income parents, and arouses desires which would not otherwise be salient. A particularly negative potential effect of children's advertising is the 'pester power' or 'nag factor'.[76] This means that 'advertising encourages children to nag their parents into something that is not good for them, they don't need or the parent cannot afford'.[77] Although in one study 86% of parents say they do not concede to children's demands,[78] it may be a major factor in conflicts between parents and children caused by advertising.

Many food ads in children's programmes are perceived to promote unhealthy products (containing too much sugar, fat or salt). The amount of advertising to which children are exposed has the potential to influence children's health attitudes and behaviours.[79] Therefore, besides children's advertising in general, many parents also have negative attitudes towards food advertising in particular. Positive nutritional tendencies lead to objections to TV food advertising aimed at children and, for instance, Chan and McNeal[80] concluded that Chinese parents held negative attitudes towards TV advertising in general and children's advertising, and food advertising to children in particular, because, according to them, it encourages bad eating habits.

A particular reason for parental concern is that children are regarded as vulnerable and as not having the cognitive abilities to understand advertising, as well as not being mature enough to make choices that affect them or their health.[81] Although it is widely accepted that children of five can understand the difference between a programme and an ad and that, from eight years onwards, they also understand the commercial intent of advertising,[82] this does not mean they are not influenced by advertising, just like anyone else, and it certainly does not mean that parents feel the same way.

These perceived negative characteristics of children's (food) advertising may only worry parents in so far as they perceive that this advertising has an influence on children. In one study, obese children recognised more of the food ads, and there was also a correlation with the amount of food eaten after exposure to ads. The author concluded that exposure to food ads promoted consumption.[83] Others claim that advertising is aimed at brand sales, not category sales, and category sales are mostly established long before exposure to ads.[84] Furthermore, 90% of the food is bought by parents, so they control the diet.[85] This leads Young to conclude that 'the route from advertising to obesity is a long and tortuous one'.[86] Although the link between food advertising, eating habits and obesity is unclear, a lot of it promotes (unhealthy) food products, is claimed to blur the line between diet and nutrition,[87] and is perceived to have the potential to influence children's health attitudes and behaviours.[88] To what extent does this worry parents? Grossbart and Crosby[89] found conflicting evidence on parents' perception of the influence of TV advertising on their children. And 20 years later, a UK study involving 1530 parents also concluded that parents believed children were influenced by advertising, but that they thought that they (the parents) had more influence than ads and that there was a high level of acceptance (as part of modern life).[90] Nevertheless, many parents appear to be actively mediating their children's TV viewing behaviour. Many researchers, e.g. Grossbart and Crosby, Nathanson, and Nathanson *et al.*, have already concluded that parents with negative attitudes towards TV advertising more strictly control their child's viewing behaviour, indicating that they perceive these negative characteristics as influencing children.[91] For instance, Chan and McNeal found that 89% of parents exercise some control over the contents and time of TV viewing.[92]

Not only children, but also the elderly are sometimes victims of (tele)marketing fraud or hard-sell pitches with puzzling details, e.g. lotteries, investment offers and prize promotions. Moreover, people in developing countries can be treated in an unethical way, for instance in countries where there are fewer trade and product restrictions (e.g. tobacco, unsafe drugs).

Unethical use of marketing communications instruments

All marketing instruments can be used in a decent, ethical way, but some practices concerning these instruments receive criticism because they are (deemed to be) unethical.

Advertising

Of all the marketing communications instruments, advertising is the one that receives most criticism because of its alleged untruthful, deceptive and manipulative nature. For instance, Sneddon argues that advertising as a whole spreads values that compromise both 'deep' autonomy (being an autonomous person) and 'shallow' autonomy (taking autonomous decisions).[93] On the other hand, what psychological principle would explain that advertising makes people do things against their will? Persuasion is a legitimate form of human interaction that all individuals and institutions perform and, as such, there is nothing unethical in trying to persuade a person to buy a product or a service or to engage in a certain (buying) behaviour. As already mentioned in one of the previous sections, advertising is often accused of being offensive and in bad taste, creating and perpetuating stereotypes, making people buy things they do not really need (but who is to decide what people need?), and playing upon people's fears and insecurities, as in fear appeals.

RESEARCH INSIGHT
Advertising to children and obesity

It is estimated that in the USA the average child sees more than 40 000 TV commercials a year and that advertisers spend more than $12 billion per year to target the youth market.[94] This is attributed to the strong contribution of children to the consumer economy. McNeal[95] estimated that children aged 14 years old and under make $24 billion in direct purchases and influence $190 billion in family purchases. Ads for food during children programmes are estimated to be 37% of all ads in the USA and 49% in the UK.[96] Furthermore, Lyna[97] claims that 97.5% of all food commercials appearing on weekend morning TV and 78.3% of weekend programming are for unhealthy foods.

There is widespread criticism that kids are targeted in relentless ways by food and drinks companies.[98] Therefore, food advertising to children may be contributing to the increase in childhood obesity by promoting unhealthy foods (especially sugary cereals, sweets, fast food restaurants). In many countries obesity is a serious and increasing health problem. It is estimated that obesity accounts for $40 billion of treatment costs a year.[99] However, obesity is a multifactor phenomenon. A sedentary lifestyle and lack of physical activity (the 'couch potato' effect), family eating habits and attitudes towards (fat) food, genetic predisposition, peer pressure, quality of life, in-school food service, nearby retail outlets, socio-economic status, TV viewing and advertising have all been suggested to be determining factors of obesity.[100] The empirical evidence for the link between obesity and TV viewing and advertising is mixed at best.[101] Eagle *et al.*[102] state that TV viewing is correlated with obesity only to the extent that viewing may replace more active pastimes. Vandewater *et al.*[103] in their study of 2831 children aged 1–12 concluded that TV viewing had no effect on obesity (measured as Body Mass Index), and other studies also found only a weak link between TV viewing and obesity.[104] However, food advertising on TV has been partially held responsible for what has been called the 'obesity epidemic'.

Threat-based ads, commonly known as 'fear appeals', are often used in social marketing campaigns (traffic safety, AIDS campaigns, etc.). However, Hastings *et al.* state that any deliberate fostering of anxiety by marketing communications has ethical implications. Indeed, like any other ad that exerts emotional pressure, fear appeals can be regarded as manipulative. Further, fear appeals expose a person against his or her will to harmful or seriously offensive images. Any fear appeal that is not psychologically comfortable may be considered unethical. Moreover, fear may induce reactance, defensive avoidance and fatalism. Research has also shown that fear appeals may lead to maladaptive social responses, for instance heightened anxiety among those most at risk and complacency among those not directly targeted. This may lead to fear control (i.e. ignoring or avoiding the message to avoid fear) instead of danger control (following the advice in the message). Finally, fear appeals may lead to increased social inequity between those who respond to fear campaigns and those who do not. Research has shown that the latter are more often better off than the former.[105] On the other hand, the use of strong fear appeals may not be perceived as unethical if consumers feel they can use the recommended product or adopt the recommended behaviour to effectively eliminate the threat posed by the message (teleological view). Research shows that perceived efficacy to cope with the threat leads to an increase in perceived ethicality and to a better attitude towards the message and the product.[106]

Another ethically charged practice is subliminal or supraliminal advertising. Subliminal messages are received subconsciously, below a person's perceptual threshold, while supraliminal messages are above the noticeable perceptual threshold, but consumers are often unaware of their presence. An example would be subliminally or supraliminally inserting the word 'sex' or a naked person into an advertising message in an attempt to influence a person to buy a product. Although there is little or no proof that such messages work, they are often considered to be unethical. Subliminal and supraliminal presentations of stimuli are untruthful by omission: either people cannot observe what you are doing, or they can observe but they do not know what the persuasion process is.[107]

In general, advertising is expected not to be deceptive or misleading, exploit fear or superstition, further violence or discrimination, plagiarise, misuse quotations, statistics or research, or omit material facts (for instance, the health side effects of medication). A special category of potentially misleading advertising is **puffery**, the use of hyperbole or exaggeration of attribute and benefit claims to promote a brand. Calling a product 'the best' is hard to prove, but rarely challenged. Puffery is sometimes called 'soft-core deception'. On the other hand, puffery, just like metaphors, may be seen as a legitimate creative technique that is not misleading because any 'reasonable' consumer knows what is going on.

Attas explored the ethical quality of deceptive advertising. He claims that 'deceptive' is the wrong term. First of all, if no harmful behaviour follows from an ad, nothing blameworthy has happened. In other words, deception is not a normative concept; advertising should be judged by its consequences (i.e. teleologically). Some ads are indeed (un)intentionally misleading in the sense that they lead to false beliefs and material harm. However, sometimes advertising is just miscomprehended, in which case this is a responsibility of both advertisers and consumers. The legal notion of deception ignores intention and focuses upon the consumer's perception. The line between miscomprehension and misleadingness (an ethical problem) rests upon the 'reasonable person standard'. In other words, an ad cannot be considered to be ethically wrong if a 'reasonable person' comprehends it correctly. The author claims that, for that reason, misleadingness is a normative issue and cannot be determined empirically. Who is going to decide on who is a 'reasonable person'?[108] Further, Koslow argues that consumers are sometimes sceptical about honest claims that they find hard to believe, even if they have no rational reason for doing so. Consumers are often too vigilant against potentially misleading advertisers. This is due to reactance and defensive avoidance ('this message has a commercial intent; I will not be persuaded just like that; they shouldn't think I am so easily convinced').[109]

Public relations

Stakeholders expect companies to be open, loyal and credible and to have integrity. The term public relations sometimes seems to be used in a way that is almost synonymous with half-truth, insincerity and manipulation, and PR communications often seem to distract and obfuscate rather than inform. Often, the most ethically sensitive situation is when companies are faced with a crisis. How do companies react to negative publicity? Do they acknowledge problems, for instance with respect to unsafe products? No company should do things that harm its long-term reputation with its stakeholders. Firms that make a habit of using PR techniques to mislead stakeholder groups are in effect consuming in the short term the trust upon which their long-term profitable existence may depend.[110]

Another PR-related instrument that is ethically sensitive is corporate hospitality – entertainment and hospitality offered by the selling organisation to the buying organisation. Where does building closer relationships with stakeholders end and bribery begin? Some would say that corporate hospitality is far less serious than bribery, but on the same continuum.

Direct marketing

Direct marketing, and especially teleselling, is often accused of high-pressure sales techniques, particularly when applied to vulnerable groups. Telesales calls sometimes intrude on personal privacy (e.g. unsolicited direct mails or calls, unwelcome sales approaches), and there is a general concern about the large amounts of personal data being collected and ending up in databases for (direct) marketing purposes. Also in these cases, respect for individuals, e.g. refraining from causing unwarranted distress or shock, ensures that marketing communications remain within generally accepted boundaries of taste and decency.

BUSINESS INSIGHT
The privacy issue and two big brands

In March 2003, Benetton and Philips announced that Philips was going to help Benetton embed computer chips in the clothes it sells, enabling individual garments to be tracked, potentially beyond the point-of-sale. This initiative was announced at a time when the following things also happened:

- The US government confirmed that it was going to mine commercial databases for clues about terrorist organisations.

- The movie *Minority Report* with Tom Cruise featured talking billboards that track wherever you go.

- The US government threatened to block flights to America by European airlines that refuse to give the US government access to passenger lists.

- Surveys indicated that a majority of consumers do not believe commercial companies are handling personal information about their customers in a confidential way.

Within two days, a consumer privacy group was calling for an immediate worldwide boycott of Benetton. CASPIAN, Consumers Against Supermarket Privacy Invasion and Numbering, warned the public that Benetton could easily link the serial number in a sweater to credit card information, and that this information would be available to anyone with access to the Benetton database. A number of consumers expressed their concern about the initiative. A website calling for a Benetton boycott and posters featuring messages such as 'I'd rather go naked' quickly appeared. Less than three weeks later, Benetton announced that it was 'reconsidering', and no chips were currently present in the garments produced. Philips removed all traces of the press release from its website. Companies should be increasingly aware of the perceptions of the general public, pressure group activities and the potential damage to the image of the company that occurs as a result of PR initiatives that do not take major concerns of these publics into account.[111]

Packaging

Packaging can be deceptive or misleading because label information suggests either desirable ingredients or attributes or less undesirable ingredients (low cholesterol). Usually, packaging graphics show the product as appealingly as possible, but sometimes this is not a true representation of the product (for instance, a children's toy seems larger than it is, the picture contains features that are not part of the product). Some packaging is unsafe for children or can be tampered with. Also, the environmental implications of some types of packaging may be considered as unethical. According to a US study, professionals judge packaging as unethical when using the word 'light' relating to texture and not to calorie content, packaging store brands to mimic manufacturer-brand packaging, being aware of safety hazards and not doing anything about them, charging more per unit for a large package than a small package, and not attending to environmental problems when packaging materials are available to do so.[112]

Sales promotion

Failing to mail a free premium object or to provide a rebate cheque, making consumers believe that their odds of winning a prize in a contest are much greater than they actually are and advertising a promotion that is not sufficiently available are unethical practices. Connections, a tour operator that sells low-prize long-distance flights, was faced with a consumer complaint because it was felt that the low-cost flights to Thailand as advertised were available only in small quantities and the other available tickets were substantially more expensive.

Regulation of marketing communications practices

Regulation of marketing communications is called for when the expectation is that, without regulation, consumer decisions would be based on false or limited information. The advantages of regulation are that consumer choice is improved, product quality is improved (e.g. information on health issues has led to more healthy food) and prices are reduced (due to a reduction in a seller's informational market power). Sometimes the distinction is made between regulation of **deceptive marketing communications** and regulation of unfair practices. Consumers are deceived when there is a claim–fact discrepancy and the false claim is believed by customers. Moreover, the message must be misleading, i.e. representation, omission or practice that is likely to mislead the customer, from the perspective of a reasonable consumer, i.e. by a reasonable number of the group to which the practice is targeted, and the deceptive practice must be material, i.e. important and likely to impact on consumers' choice or conduct regarding the product and thus relate to a central characteristic. **Unfair marketing communications** are acts or practices that cause or are likely to cause substantial injury to consumers, which are not reasonably avoidable by consumers themselves and not outweighed by countervailing benefits to consumers or competitors. They may go beyond questions of fact and relate merely to public values, e.g. offends public policy as it has been established by statutes, is immoral, unethical, oppressive or unscrupulous, or causes substantial injury to consumers, competitors or other business.[113] Each country has its own laws and regulations. A detailed discussion is beyond the scope of this book.

Self-regulation of marketing communications practices

In order to retain trust and credibility, advertising needs to meet high ethical standards. The advertising industry in many countries has recognised this fact and has started to regulate its industry by establishing codes of practice or sets of guiding principles, a process called **self-regulation**. On top of legislation and government regulation, in many countries organisations or systems of self-regulation are in place. Table 16.1 summarises the pros and cons of self-regulation. Although the features and operation of the self-regulatory systems may be quite different in different countries, they all share the same goal: 'ensuring legal, decent, honest and truthful advertising, prepared with a sense of social responsibility to the consumer and society and with proper respect for the rules of fair competition'.[114] The ICC was the first to publish its International Code of Advertising Practice (ICC code) in 1937. All the codes in use today, all around the world, are based on this code. Self-regulatory organisations (SROs), which are funded by the advertising industry, ensure that the rules are applied. If an advertiser is not willing to comply voluntarily with the decision of the SRO, media may be refused for future advertising, negative publicity may be used or the case can be referred to the appropriate statutory authority. Due to its flexibility, speed and low cost, self-regulation makes an ideal complement to the law.[115]

Table 16.1 Pros and cons of self-regulation

Pros	Cons
• Usually faster and less expensive, more flexible and up to date	• Business competition and innovation are impaired by restrictions
• Does not require 'injury' to be proven as in law	• Voluntary regulations may only impose minimum standards and enforcement may be lax
• Assists and complements statutory regulation	• Lacks effective judicial and sanction tools
• Generates greater moral cohesion than the law – whole industry co-operates to reflect current values and norms	• System may lack too few lay people and involve too many industry representatives with the potential of over-indulgent self-interest
• Helps minimise friction between consumers and businesses	
• Media voluntarily participate in enforcing self-regulation	

ICC codes

The ICC has issued several codes, including an International Code of Advertising Practice (1997), Sales Promotion (2002), Direct Marketing (2001), Sponsorship (2003), Children and Young People (2003), electronic media (2004), etc.[116] According to these codes, marketing communications should not contain statements or visuals which offend, denigrate, mislead or abuse the trust of consumers or another party. Consumers should be able to recognise the communication as a marketing tool. No testimonials should be used 'unless they are genuine, verifiable, relevant and based on personal experience or knowledge'. All marketing communications tools should avoid imitation of competitive and non-competitive actions in case this imitation might mislead or confuse consumers. For sales promotions, it should be clear to consumers how they can obtain the promotional offer (i.e. what the exact conditions are), the value and nature of the promotion should not be misrepresented, and any geographic, age, quantity or other restrictions should be clearly indicated. Concerning children and young people, marketing communications may not be framed in a way that takes advantage of their youth or lack of experience or that strains their loyalty towards their parents or guardians. In the case of direct marketing or sales promotions, no products should be delivered for which consumers have to pay unless consumers have requested the supply of these products. Also, no offers that could be perceived as bills or invoices for unordered products should be made. Moreover, data can be collected 'for specified, explicit and legitimate purposes only' and consumers should be provided with the opportunity to 'opt out' from marketing lists or to require that their data cannot be handed over to third parties. This has a serious impact on the possibilities of creating or buying databases with the intent to use them for direct marketing purposes.

European Advertising Standards Alliance (EASA)

EASA,[117] created in 1992, is Europe's single voice for the advertising industry and acts as a co-ordination point for the self-regulatory bodies of the respective European countries. The latter should not imply that Europe will come under one general system for all its Member States, but rather that all main principles will be adopted. As the director-general of EASA puts it: 'We must be careful of a one size fits all approach and allow markets the freedom to develop a system which responds to the EASA's Common Principles as well as the needs of that particular country, its advertising concerns and consumers.'[118] The EASA principles exist in addition to other European (and national) laws such as the prohibition of having more than 12 minutes of commercial messages an hour, the prohibition on tobacco advertising and the prohibition of associating alcohol consumption in advertising with driving, physical performance, social or sexual success or therapeutic qualities.

EASA has three major goals: to promote self-regulation; to support existing self-regulatory systems; to ensure that cross-border complaints are resolved speedily and effectively. For example, the Italian self-regulatory office ran an advertising campaign on TV, radio, press and poster sites with the tagline 'We love advertising so much that sometimes we have to restrict it.' The ads featured a heart covered by a seatbelt and had the purpose of informing Italian consumers of the role of the Istituto Autodisciplina Pubblicitaria. In Belgium, a website was launched inviting consumers to fill in an online complaint form.

In 2010, the 26 self-regulatory bodies, members of EASA, received over 53 000 complaints. The number of complaints remains relatively stable over the years (Figure 16.2). The countries with the highest adspend also received most complaints: the UK and Germany account for 73% of all complaints. In 2010, one-third were based upon the alleged misleading character of the ads, and another 25% were deemed to be offensive (taste and decency). Nine per cent of the complaints were based on the inappropriateness for children, and another 9% had to do with discrimination and denigration. Seven per cent were related to gender portrayal. In the category 'taste and decency', the majority of the complaints were related to ads being offensive (61%), 19% on the basis of the alleged inappropriateness for children, and

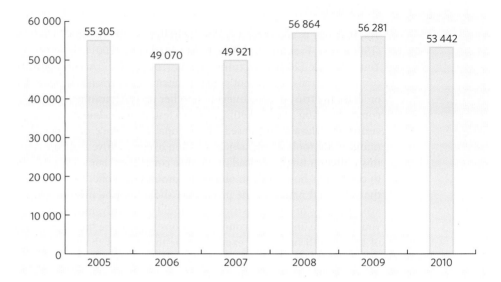

Figure 16.2 Evolution of complaints received by EASA members, 2005–10

Source: from *Statistics Report 2010: European trends in advertising complaints, copy advice and pre-clearance*, European Advertising Standards Alliance (EASA) (2010).

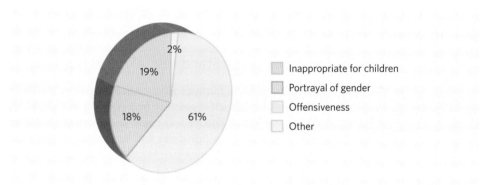

Figure 16.3 Percentage of complaints received by EASA members in the 'taste and decency' category, 2010

Source: from *Statistics Report 2010: European trends in advertising complaints, copy advice and pre-clearance*, European Advertising Standards Alliance (EASA) (2010).

18% because of gender issues (Figure 16.3). On average, at a European level, the electronic and information communications technology sector, the food and non-alcoholic beverages sector and the leisure and entertainment sector were the most complained about products/services sectors. Audio-visual media services were the most complained about medium. Slightly more than one-third of the complaints were upheld (Figure 16.4).[119]

Although all codes and most national laws are based on the ICC code, regulations may differ greatly from one country to another, even within the EU. As a consequence, an ad or a communications practice such as direct marketing or sales promotions may be acceptable in one country, but may be prohibited elsewhere. Therefore, it is advisable for a company to be well briefed on local regulations.

The UK system of self-regulation has been called the most developed and effective self-regulation system in the world. It results in about 12 000 cases a year being investigated. Of these, about 1000 have to be withdrawn or modified. In the USA, the combined actions of the Federal Trade Commission, the National Advertising Division, the National Advertising Review Board and the federal courts result in less than 300 adjudicated cases.

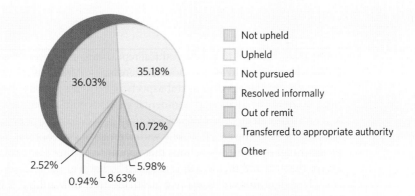

Not upheld
Upheld
Not pursued
Resolved informally
Out of remit
Transferred to appropriate authority
Other

35.18%
36.03%
10.72%
2.52%
0.94%
8.63%
5.98%

Figure 16.4 Outcome of complaints received by EASA members, 2010

Source: from *Statistics Report 2010: European trends in advertising complaints, copy advice and pre-clearance*, European Advertising Standards Alliance (EASA) (2010).

BUSINESS INSIGHT

Code of conduct of the Belgian Association of Communication Companies

Advertisers and communications professionals value freedom in marketing communications as a fundamental principle of a free-market economy. However, responsibility comes with freedom. The Belgian ACC, a professional organisation of communication agencies, adopted a moral code of conduct that encompasses ten principles of ethical communications, above and beyond the legal requirements that are laid down in advertising regulations. All members of the ACC endorse this code. These principles are:

● Marketing communications must not mislead the consumer.

● Marketing communications may not abuse the good faith of the consumer or, particularly in the case of children and youngsters, their lack of knowledge and experience.

● Marketing communications must be recognisable as such, whatever the medium or the format used. It must also be clear who the sender is.

● All marketing communications based on facts must be verifiable.

● Marketing communications may not discriminate against or insult people on the basis of race, nationality, religion, sex, sexual disposition or age.

● Marketing communications must respect people's privacy.

● ACC members always strive for the best possible advice, without fear or prejudice, and always act in the best interest of their customers.

● ACC members always honour their commitments to customers, suppliers and employees.

● ACC members respect other professional codes in the industry, such as the ones of the Jury of Ethical Practices in advertising, the code for sponsoring and advertising on TV and the legal limitations on advertising towards children.

● ACC members respect each other.

Needless to say, this code of conduct is an ambitious one, and can easily conflict with old habits (such as certain types of humour in advertising) and emerging practices (such as data mining and product placement and branded entertainment) in marketing communications.[120]

Corporate social responsibility

Companies that want to build an ethical reputation often invest in **corporate social responsibility (CSR)**, also referred to as 'corporate citizenship'.[121] CSR is an idea that includes the social, the economic and the environmental aspects of business activity ('triple bottom line'). It is the integration of social and environmental values within a company's core business operations and an engagement with stakeholders to improve the well-being of society.[122] It is consistent with the need to engage effectively with a range of stakeholders (stakeholder dialogue). CSR programmes demonstrate actions that appear to further some social good, beyond the interests of the firm and that which is required by law. For instance, embodying the product with socially responsible attributes (e.g. pesticide-free, non-animal-tested ingredients) or signals (e.g. fair trade label) that convey to stakeholders and consumers that the company is concerned about certain social issues. Companies believe that, in developing CSR programmes, they will build a positive image and reputation for themselves and that consumers, by buying their products, will support and reward them. This implies that companies undertake two things: eliminating negatives and doing positives (Table 16.2).[123] Companies communicate about their CSR initiatives as a means to defend their reputation. For instance, an experimental study showed that the use of a CSR claim in times of crisis is more effective, i.e. counters negative publicity, reduces consumer scepticism and leads to better attitudes towards a company and its products, the longer a company is involved in CSR matters.[124] Effective CSR programmes combine sound business and social responsibility. This implies that a company should identify areas in which it can make a positive difference, make (local) media aware of efforts in order to enhance the chances of positive publicity, inform employees with the goal of having them report the company's good deeds to their families, friends and neighbours, and invest in advertising to highlight company efforts.[125]

Well-known CSR areas or techniques are cause-related marketing, green marketing and socially responsible or fair trade marketing. **Cause-related marketing** is the support of a social cause that a firm generates through financial interactions with its customers. For instance, a firm donates a certain percentage of its income or profits to a specific non-profit cause. Carefully selecting causes can have a positive impact on a firm's sales. The impact can be even greater if a firm can find ways to utilise its products and services in the programme (see, for instance, the Procter–UNICEF case at the end of this chapter). **Green marketing** is the development and promotion of products that are environmentally safe: biodegradable, recycled, etc. **Socially responsible marketing** implies selling products that embody certain social ethical values, such as products free of child labour, produced in companies where trade unions are allowed, in decent social circumstances, and at fair wages.

Table 16.2 Building an ethical reputation: do's and don'ts

Image-destroying activities	Image-building activities
Discrimination	Empowerment of employees
Harassment	Charitable contributions
Pollution	Sponsoring local events
Misleading communications	Selling environmentally safe products
Deceptive communications	Outplacement programmes
Offensive communications	Support community events

RESEARCH INSIGHT
Corporate social responsibility in Cyprus

Corporate social responsibility refers to a company's obligation, beyond that required by law or economics, to pursue long-term goals that are good for society. CSR refers to various types of activities and behaviours, such as ethical behaviour, sustainable development, environmentally-friendly behaviour and philanthropic activity. CSR is a synonym for 'good citizenship'. Social responsibility can be used to build strong brands and a positive corporate image and reputation. In a pilot study involving 40 managers and directors of Cypriot companies, the CSR practices were identified. They are summarised in the following table. The figures refer to the percentage of respondents indicating that they practise the principle. Although, on the basis of these results, CSR appears to be of major concern to companies in Cyprus, the low response rate of 1% in this study seems to indicate the opposite.[126]

General	
Engages in fair and honest business	68
Sets high standards of behaviour for all employees	54
Exercises ethical oversight of the executive and board levels	37
Initiates and engages in genuine dialogue with stakeholders	32
Develops and publishes both internally and externally a Code of Conduct	37
Applies confidentiality and anonymity with regard to privileged information	54
Community	
Fosters a reciprocal relationship between the corporation and the community	73
Invests in the communities in which the corporation operates	51
Launches community development activities	27
Encourages employee participation in community projects	42
Consumers	
Respects the rights of consumers	68
Offers quality products and services	83
Provides information that is truthful, honest and useful	76
Avoids false and misleading advertising	68
Discloses all substantial risks associated with product or service usage	34
Avoids engaging in price fixing	37
Employees	
Provides a family-friendly work environment	63
Provides an equitable reward and wage system for employees	61
Engages in open and flexible communication with employees	54
Engages in employment diversity in hiring and promoting women	46
Encourages employees to treat one another with dignity and fairness	59
Investors	
Strives for a competitive return on investments	37
Engages in fair and honest business practices in the relationship with stakeholders	54
Suppliers	
Engages in fair trading transactions with suppliers	76
Environment commitment	
Demonstrates a commitment to sustainable development	54
Demonstrates a commitment to the environment	73

Source: After Doukakis, I., Krambia-Kapardis, M. and Katsioloudes, M. (2003), 'Corporate Social Responsibility: A Pilot Study into the Realities of the Business Sector in Cyprus', in Bennett, R. (ed.), *New Challenges for Corporate and Marketing Communications. Proceedings of the Eighth International Conference on Marketing and Corporate Communications*. London: London Metropolitan University, 64–80.

Normally, green marketing and social marketing programmes generate positive publicity and word of mouth for a company. According to a study by Hines and Ames, 51% of the population had the feeling of being able to make a difference to a company's behaviour and 68% claimed to have bought a product or a service because of a company's responsible reputation.[127] On average, 46% of European consumers also claimed to be willing to pay substantially more for ethical products.[128] However, there are differences as to the reported willingness to pay a price premium for different types of ethical products. For instance, American consumers agreed with a price increase of 6.6% for green products,[129] while French consumers were willing to pay 10% to 25% more for apparel not made by children.[130] With these studies in mind, one could expect a high demand for ethical products. However, the opposite seems to be the case. People do not always put their money where their mouth is: there is often a substantial 'attitude–behaviour' gap: consumers like the idea of ethical products, but they do not always buy them. Most of the ethical labelling initiatives with respect to, for instance, organic food, products free from child labour, legally logged wood and fair trade products often have market shares of less than 1%.[131]

RESEARCH INSIGHT
Determinants of willingness to pay for fair trade products

Fair trade can be described as an alternative approach to a trading partnership that aims for sustainable development of excluded and/or disadvantaged producers. It seeks to do so by providing better trading conditions, raising awareness and campaigning. In the broadest sense, the concept incorporates environmental as well as social issues. Apart from paying fair wages in a local context and providing a safe and clean workplace (mainstream business), maximum fair trade practices should also encompass the development of sustainable businesses, empowerment of artisans, fostering well-being, establishing political and social justice, and developing equitable trade. In a narrow sense, fair trade means fair prices for the products of farmers in developing countries. In essence, it means buying products from farmers in developing countries on terms that are relatively more favourable than commercial terms, and marketing them in developed countries at an ethical premium. This higher price to the consumer is warranted by the higher price that farmers receive for their products and by the fair trade control mechanisms in the trade channel. Companies generally demonstrate their fair trade behaviour to consumers by means of marketing fair trade brands or by means of co-operating with fair trade organisations that accredit their fair trade products and allow them to market these products using a fair trade label.

In 2005, a conjoint analytic study was conducted to estimate the willingness to pay a price premium for fair-trade-labelled coffee by Belgian consumers, and to identify the characteristics of those consumer segments who were willing to pay a substantial fair trade premium. In general, the brand appeared to be the most important attribute of the coffee, closely followed by flavour with fair trade label in third place. The willingness to pay for a fair trade label on coffee of the respondents indicated that about 10% of the sample wanted to pay the current price premium in Belgium of 27%. Clusters based on differences in preference were defined to estimate market opportunities for fairly traded coffee and to profile potential consumers. Profiling was done by means of demographic features: age, gender and education level, as well as personal values. Four clusters were identified. The fair trade lovers accounted for 11% of the sample and were predominantly aged 31–45 years. They were more idealistic and less conventional compared with other groups. The fair trade likers represented the largest group. They did not differ significantly from the rest of the sample in terms of demographic characteristics, but they were relatively more idealistic. The flavour lovers and the brand lovers each accounted for one-quarter of the total sample and were less idealistic and more conventional. In addition, brand lovers were more likely to be women. The fair trade lovers constituted the group that was most prepared to pay the actual price premium (slightly over 50% of them). Of the flavour lovers and the brand lovers, who account for 50% of the sample, only a small minority were prepared to pay the sample average price premium of 10% for fair trade coffee. The 11% fair trade lovers cannot be considered equivalent to actual market share, because the amount of coffee they buy relative to the total population is unknown. However, the authors concluded that, compared with the 1% market share held by fair trade coffee at that time, the 11% fair trade lovers constituted a substantially larger potential market than actually reached.[132]

Summary

Marketing communications professionals should act ethically because it is in their best long-term business interest to be perceived as decent corporate citizens that are sensitive to the moral codes in the society where they market their products. Therefore they should set ethical standards and rules for themselves and follow them in every communications campaign and communications instrument. They should refrain from using controversial and shocking messages such as fear appeals and provocative ads just for the sake of gaining attention. Covert marketing techniques, such as stealth and buzz marketing and certain forms of brand placement, should be used with care and under full disclosure, so that the consumers are not deceived or misled. Men and women, elderly people and sub-culture groups should be portrayed in advertising with due care, in order not to stimulate discriminating or offensive stereotypes. Especially when targeting children, marketing communicators should take into account that they are often cognitively not developed enough to recognise the persuasive attempts of creative marketers, and can therefore be misled in an unacceptable way. Public relations officers, sales managers, salespeople and direct marketers should take care that they do not invade the privacy of customers and that they do not use unfair or deceptive practices. At the minimum, marketing professionals should strictly follow the legal and regulatory guidelines in the countries in which they operate, and should fully co-operate with the self-regulatory bodies and procedures that are in place. They may also become actively socially responsible by engaging in corporate social responsibility projects.

REVIEW QUESTIONS

1. When setting ethical standards, individuals and companies can follow different principles such as the deontological, teleological, distributive justice and 'common decency' principles. In what way are they different and how could they lead to different marketing communications decisions?

2. When laying the groundwork for ethical decision-making, several rules and models can be used, such as the *caveat emptor* and *caveat venditor* rules, and the consumer sovereignty rule. Explain the difference between these rules. How would your decisions be different when you applied these different rules?

3. What are the main ethical concerns with marketing (communications)? To what extent are they correct or exaggerated?

4. What are the most important reasons to be careful with targeting marketing communications at children?

5. Controversial and shocking images are often considered as ethically problematic. What can be considered controversial in marketing communications and when would you consider it an ethical problem?

6. Give examples of covert marketing. When and why can it be unethical? What could a marketing communications professional do to make these techniques and formats ethically acceptable?

7. Give examples of ethical problems in personal selling, direct marketing, public relations and packaging.

8. What are self-regulation procedures based on and how do they function?

9. What are corporate social responsibility programmes? Give examples.

Further reading

Brenkert, G.G. (2008), *Marketing Ethics (Foundations of Business Ethics)*. Hoboken, NJ: Wiley-Blackwell.

Hartley, R.F. (2004), *Business Ethics: Mistakes and Successes*. Hoboken, NJ: Wiley.

Murphy, P.E. and Laczniak, G.R. (2006), *Marketing Ethics: Cases and Readings*. Upper Saddle River, NJ: Pearson Education.

Murphy, P.E., Laczniak, G.E., Bowie, N.E. and Klein, T.E. (2004), *Ethical Marketing (Basic Ethics in Action)*. Upper Saddle River, NJ: Pearson Education.

Saucier, R.D. and Folkers, K.K. (2008), *Marketing Ethics*. Lewiston, NY: Edwin Mellen Pr.

Business Ethics: A European Review, http://www.wiley.com/bw/journal.asp?ref=0962-8770.

Business Ethics Quarterly, https://secure.pdcnet.org/pdc/bvdb.nsf/journal?openform&journal= pdc_beq.

Journal of Business Research, http://www.elsevier.com/wps/find/journaldescription.cws_ home/505722/description#description.

Journal of Consumer Affairs, http://www.wiley.com/bw/journal.asp?ref=0022-0078.

CASE 16:
Pampers and UNICEF: helping protect babies together

Procter & Gamble: branded consumer products help children in need

William Procter and James Gamble formed a humble, small, family-operated soap and candle company, inspired by the purpose of providing products and services of superior quality and value, in 1837. Today, Procter & Gamble is one of the leading global manufacturers and marketers of branded consumer goods. P&G commits itself to providing branded products and services of superior quality and value that improve the lives of the world's consumers. As a result,

it strives for leadership sales, profit and value creation, allowing employees, shareholders and the communities to prosper.

In 2008, P&G employed approximately 135 000 employees working in about 80 countries worldwide and provided products and services in over 180 countries. In 2007, sales were almost $55 000 million. Brands worth $23 billion are the core of the company's product portfolio, and account for almost two-thirds of annual sales. They are in beauty, health care, fabric and home care, baby and family care, snacks, razors and blades, etc. The company has one of the strongest portfolios of trusted, quality, leadership brands, including Pampers®, Tide®, Ariel®, Always®, Whisper®, Pantene®, Mach3®, Bounty®, Dawn®, Gain®, Pringles®, Charmin®, Downy®, Lenor®, Iams®, Crest®, Oral-B®, Actonel®, Duracell®, Olay®, Head & Shoulders®, Wella®, Gillette®, Braun® and Fusion®.

One of the core values of P&G is to help to solve the world's sustainability challenges. It does so through innovations that enhance the environmental profile of products, by reducing the environmental footprint of their operations, and through contributions to help children in need. Indeed, in recent years, P&G decided to focus upon a corporate cause where the need is great and there is a clear fit with P&G's strengths, brands and current programmes, i.e. improving life for children in need, ages 0–13, through the P&G Live, Learn and Thrive programme. This programme entails helping children in need to live by:

- helping to ensure they get off to a healthy start;
- providing them with places, tools and programmes that enhance their ability to learn; and
- giving them access to programmes that help develop the self-esteem and life skills that they need to thrive.

P&G believes that this is both a worthy cause that is of interest to many of its stakeholders, and one for which it can offer expertise. Indeed, P&G has many existing programmes in children's education and development as well as deep expertise in health and hygiene. One of these programmes is a long-term co-operation with UNICEF.

UNICEF: Unite for children

UNICEF, the United Nations Children's (Emergency) Fund, provides help and support to children in need around the world. The organisation focuses on areas that relate to helping children in need, such as child survival and development, child protection, basic education and gender equality, HIV/AIDS and children, and policy advocacy and partnerships. UNICEF works on projects related to child survival, nutrition and environmental interventions, quality education for children, protecting children from violence, exploitation and abuse, prevention and paediatric treatment of HIV and AIDS, and policy analysis, leveraging of resources, and child participation. UNICEF, a Nobel Peace Prize winner, works in 158 countries and territories and is present in 36 industrialised countries. Ninety-three per cent of funds go directly to serve children.

One of the ways in which the organisation tries to achieve its goals is by teaming up with partners in joint support projects. This case describes the co-operation between UNICEF and Pampers in a maternal and neonatal tetanus vaccination programme.

Pampers and UNICEF: protecting vulnerable babies from neonatal tetanus

P&G's Live, Learn and Thrive children support programme is brought to life through partnerships between Pampers, P&G's leading brand of disposable diapers, and sub-brands like Kandoo, and organisations such as UNICEF. The brand–good-cause fit is obvious. UNICEF is the world's leading children's organisation that tries to advance humanity through programmes that ensure every child's right to health, education, equality and protection. Improving the health of children is one responsibility among many in the fight against poverty. Healthy children become healthy adults: people who create better lives for themselves, their communities and their countries. Improving the health of the world's children is a core UNICEF objective.

Pampers is the world's biggest children's brand. Pampers is sold in over 100 countries around the world. Each day Pampers are used by more than 35 million babies. The brand's appeal is beyond functional benefits, and is awarded by mothers all over the world. Mums, Pampers and UNICEF help babies in need and care for babies' development.

Of every 100 children born today, 26 will miss out on immunisations against basic childhood diseases. One of these basic immunisations is against tetanus. Maternal and newborn tetanus (MNT) are often a tale of two worlds. In the industrialised world, most mothers give birth in a medical facility and are routinely immunised both in their first year of life and, through booster doses, periodically. To them tetanus is a thing of the past (unless they step on a rusty nail and require a booster shot of the vaccine). But in the less developed countries, the disease remains endemic. Newborn tetanus is one of the leading causes of newborn mortality in the poorest areas of the world where most women do not have access to health facilities or immunisation services. Newborn (neonatal) tetanus occurs when newborns are infected as a direct result of unhygienic birthing practices, such as cutting the umbilical cord with unsterile instruments, handling it with dirty hands or treating it with contaminated dressings and traditional substances such as ghee, cow dung, ashes and mud. Mothers can also be infected with maternal tetanus during an unsafe or unsanitary delivery.

Once newborn tetanus has been contracted there is no real cure. In rural areas of less developed countries, almost all infants that are infected with newborn tetanus die. Even today over 95% of the babies that suffer from newborn tetanus and who have no access to treatment facilities will die. Over 80 years after the vaccine became available, some 100 million women and thousands of unborn babies are still at risk from one of the most painful deaths known to medicine. About 5% to 7% of infant deaths or approximately 128 000 newborns die annually from newborn tetanus, and thousands of women →

from maternal tetanus. Almost all these deaths occur in just 44 countries.

Between October and December every year, for each specially marked '1 pack = 1 life-saving vaccine' pack of Pampers diaper and wipe product bought, Pampers provides UNICEF with funding for one life-saving tetanus vaccine. Two doses of the tetanus vaccine are needed to protect a woman and any baby born to her during a three-year period. The baby is protected for the first two months of its life.

The partnership between Pampers and UNICEF rests upon common objectives and mutually agreed strategies. The two organisations help babies in need, aim to build a sustainable long-term relationship, and benefit from each other's brand equity and from the broad range of channel outreach (i.e. media, stores, Internet, direct-to-consumer, etc.). The partnership focuses on a key idea that can make the difference in disadvantageous babies' lives, and it nurtures both brands' equity and strengthens the relationship with consumers and the public. Consumers are open to charity, especially at Christmas and other giving periods. The project offers a mechanism that overcomes consumers' concern of 'where does all this money generated actually go?'

The relationship with UNICEF started in 2004 in Latin America with the 'Mothers of the Heart' campaign in Argentina, Venezuela and Mexico. For every pack of Pampers purchased, Pampers and UNICEF donated in support of nutrition and education programmes for babies in need. This programme demonstrated the fit between Pampers and UNICEF values and a common vision of happy healthy children.

The idea of working with UNICEF then travelled to Belgium in 2005 when Pampers teamed up with UNICEF in the fight against polio. Consumers were an integral part of the success of this programme. With every purchase of a Pampers Jumbo pack or Mega pack a polio vaccination was

Photo 16.3 Pampers and UNICEF join forces to help protect babies

Source: Pampers.

donated. Over 200 000 children could be vaccinated as a result of this campaign. The programme also benefited Pampers, mainly in confirming with Pampers consumers the Pampers equity of caring for babies around the world (Photo 16.3).

The UK/Ireland 2006 campaign

Campaign

In November–December 2006, the Pampers/UNICEF tetanus vaccination project started in the UK and Ireland, with the selling line: 'Helping protect babies together'. The campaign was supported by TV, radio, print, direct-to-consumer and Internet advertising and by in-store activity. The key visual of the campaign is shown in Photo 16.4. Thirty-second TV commercials were used during the whole campaign period to create awareness, drive an emotional bond with consumers and invite broad-scale participation. At the end of the campaign a 60-second commercial was aired to thank the consumers for their participation. Also, print was used to convey these messages. Further, in-store communications were used to create an experience with the initiative at the local level. Posters were put up at shop entrances, hanging banners were used to connect with the consumers' emotionality and make the vaccination drive credible, and shelf cards were used to help drive sales. There was massive support from retailers, resulting in unprecedented in-store support, visibility and amplification, with extra displays in most stores despite of difficult Christmas period with its traditional in-store communications overload. On-pack stickers were used to communicate the partnership and the mechanics and to drive the purchase decision. The campaign was further supported by direct mailings, both from Pampers and from retailers, to drive the emotional bond via personalised communications, to drive consumers to the website for more information, and to enhance credibility. In that way, 1 million contacts with the campaign were included in the ongoing e-mail campaigns. Banners were used to leverage the programme by building credibility and by encouraging longer-term participation via interaction and updates and by showing results and impact. Finally, public relations efforts were made to create buzz and awareness and to leverage on UNICEF PR activities.

Results

The campaign was a big success for UNICEF. A total number of 7.5 million vaccines were funded, versus the 6 million estimated from both Pampers sales and the participation of the trade.

Pampers also benefited from the programme from both the consumer support and sales. Figure 16.5 shows that Pampers brand equity was strengthened considerably as a result of the UNICEF campaign: scores on all

Photo 16.4 Key visual of the 2006 Pampers/UNICEF campaign in the UK and Ireland
Source: Pampers.

important brand attributes increased during the period of the campaign.

The 2007–8 global campaign

In 2007 Pampers expanded its partnership with UNICEF to Western Europe, Japan and North America.

In 2008, Pampers committed to a three-year global partnership, expanding the tetanus vaccination programme between Pampers and UNICEF to Western Europe, the Middle East and Africa, Central and Eastern Europe and North America (Japan and China came in 2009) to help eliminate maternal and neonatal tetanus in the 44 remaining countries by 2012. To accomplish that, funding ➜

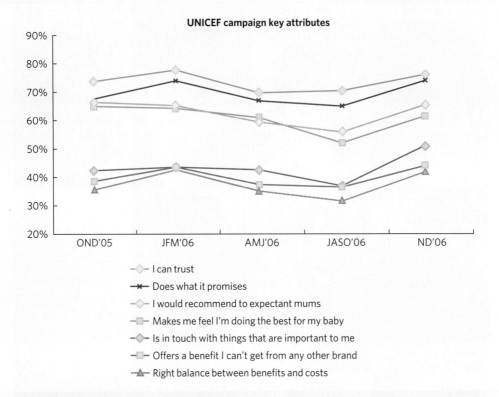

Figure 16.5 Evolution of Pampers brand equity in 2006

for over 300 million vaccines was procured (by 2008–9, 200 million vaccines were procured). Over the 2009–10 campaign, Pampers raised an additional 100 million vaccines. The basic simple mechanism remained the same: for every marked pack shipped P&G donated the cost of one tetanus vaccination at 7 cents. The global Pampers business unit provides global marketing direction, full advertising and PR templates and in-store materials, and support (as needed/appropriate) that has been closely worked out and cleared with UNICEF International. Local customisation and exploitation of these materials are worked out between local P&G subsidiaries and UNICEF National Committees. Local country branches could also engage local ambassadors to build ambassador-endorsed campaigns. P&G and UNICEF have also started a multi-brand initiative under the umbrella of the Pampers–UNICEF partnership to support the maternal and neonatal tetanus vaccination programme.

The 2008 campaign started in October 2008. The communications platform was: 'Together we can help give millions of babies in need a brighter tomorrow.' The business objective was to drive the total Pampers product line (diapers, wipes), putting mums at the heart of the campaign. The creative material for Europe was updated. Again, a mix of various above- and below-the-line communications tools was used, leveraging the P&G marketing tools: 30-second television ads, print campaigns, in-store posters, banners and shelf cards, direct mailings and the

Internet. This time, direct mails were used to thank the consumers for their support at the end of the campaign in January 2009. Public relations materials and the website Pampers Village were used to create extra buzz when celebrating the results in March 2009.

A public relations campaign was set up, with organised field visits with the media to developing countries to witness the campaign's progress and the support of a celebrity mum as the spokesperson for the campaign. To create synergies between these PR initiatives and other instruments of the marketing communications mix, different elements were integrated, to bring to life the campaign in a truly holistic way and make mums in Europe experience the campaign through digital means:

- Make blogs from the press trips to the field.
- Make different reports and videos for the website to bring the initiative to life.
- Collect facts and figures on UNICEF and tetanus around the world for the website.
- Make a website section on the regional ambassador.
- Build relationships with top broadcasters.
- Arrange broadcast press trips for live interviews.
- Regional ambassador to be featured within broadcast.
- Develop additional POS materials featuring the Euro ambassador to leverage the ambassador in-store.

The campaign provided funds for more than 50 million doses of vaccine in 2007. By mid-2009, another 150 million vaccines for women and babies in 27 target countries were provided for.

In the UK 10.08 million vaccines were donated, 6.12 million in France and 7.26 million in Germany. Also, since 2006 the UNICEF campaign has been implemented in the UK. Further, retail support was mixed.

The Pampers–UNICEF campaign also benefited the Pampers brand image. A study among 300 mums of 0–3 year old babies in France revealed that those aware of the campaign scored Pampers considerably higher on various brand image attributes. Also in the UK, four key components of brand equity substantially improved vis-à-vis the competition.

Preparing the fifth anniversary of UNICEF–P&G co-operation in Belgium

In 2008–9 the co-operation between P&G and UNICEF celebrated its fifth anniversary. Plans were made not only to continue the co-operation, but also to include campaign elements that would stress the long-standing joint campaign. In September–October the campaign kicked off with a field trip to Ethiopia with the local ambassador Khadja Nin (a Belgian singer of Burundese descent) and press conferences and releases featuring, among others, Salma Hayek, the campaign ambassador for 2008. Press releases continued to appear in November and December 2008. The new Pampers Village magazine format was used for on- and offline relationship marketing. A Pampers–UNICEF micro-site was launched on which consumers could upload their own birthday song and win one vaccine per song. A professional toolkit for hospitals, paediatricians, gynaecologists, and the national organisation for childhood was produced and distributed. As usual, the campaign was supported through mass media advertising. In November–December, 'Happy birthday' TV commercials were on air, and print was used at the end of the campaign to thank the consumers and to communicate the number of vaccines donated.

'Pampers has already exceeded the three-year MNT target, and pledges to raise additional 100 million vaccines needed to help eliminate MNT by 2012.' Since 2006 Pampers has successfully donated 200 million tetanus vaccines, protecting a total of 45.5 million women and their babies around the world from MNT. Pampers has committed to donate a further 100 million vaccines up to 2010, which will allow the target and protection of an additional 33 million women and their babies in at least 32 countries around the world. Pampers' support for the global elimination of MNT began in 2006, and Pampers will continue to support the global initiative to eliminate MNT in at least 32 countries where newborns still suffer from this deadly, but preventable disease.

Four[†] countries have now completed vaccination activities with the help of the Pampers funds, including Central African Republic, Cote d'Ivoire, Myanmar and Timor Leste. A further 16 countries are expected to complete activities with Pampers funds raised to date, namely: Burkina Faso, Burundi, Cambodia, Cameroon, DR Congo, Ethiopia, Equatorial Guinea, Gabon, Indonesia, Kenya, Lao PDR, Mauritania, Niger, Senegal, Tanzania and Uganda.

Every two seconds since the start of the campaign, Pampers has provided a protective dose of the Tetanus Toxoid vaccine for a woman and her baby.

Since 2006, UNICEF has helped eliminate MNT in five countries, namely Egypt, Zambia, Bangladesh, Republic of Congo and Turkey.

Pampers and UNICEF are aiming for no country to have MNT as a public health problem, where babies die from a completely preventable disease. One case of newborn tetanus is one too many.

QUESTIONS

1. Do you believe there is a good fit between UNICEF and Pampers/P&G? What other companies could be good corporate partners of UNICEF? What other organisations could be appropriate 'good-cause' partners of P&G?

2. Do you think the UK/Ireland campaign of 2006 was well integrated? What could have been done more to make it a better integrated campaign?

3. Do you think it was a good idea also to use Lenor and Ariel to support the vaccination campaign in Germany? Why or why not? What other P&G products would be suitable to include in the campaign? Which ones would you certainly not include?

4. Who would be suitable ambassadors of a UNICEF–Pampers campaign in your own country and why? How would you use them in an integrated communications campaign?

5. Can you think of other ideas for an integrated marketing communications campaign, except for the ones that were used in the 2007–8 campaign?

6. Do you have any other integrated marketing communications ideas to celebrate the fifth anniversary of the P&G–UNICEF co-operation?

Sources: www.pg.com (accessed 27 December 2008), www.unicef.org (accessed 27 December 2008), www.pampers.com (accessed 27 December 2008), www.uk.pg.com (accessed 27 December 2008); Nicolas Frèrejean, P&G Belgium; Luc Suykens, P&G Belgium.

*Christine Edier, UNICEF International, http://www.who.int/immunization_monitoring/diseases/MNTE_initiative/en/i (as at July 2009).

†Activities have been completed but a pre-validation data review may identify the need for small-scale targeted tests before claiming elimination, in which case they may join the list of 16 countries expected to complete activities soon.

References

[1] Clow, K.E. and Baack, D. (2001), *Integrated Advertising, Promotion & Marketing Communications*. Upper Saddle River, NJ: Prentice Hall.

[2] Duncan, T. (2002), *IMC: Using Advertising & Promotion to Build Brands*. Boston, MA: McGraw-Hill Irwin.

[3] Fill, C. (2006), *Marketing Communications: Engagement, Strategies and Practice*. Harlow: Pearson Education; Rossiter, J.R. and Bellman, S. (2005), *Marketing Communications: Theory and Applications*. French Forest, NSW: Pearson Education Australia.

[4] McIntyre, R.P., Capen, M.M. and Minton, A.P. (1995), 'Exploring the Psychological Foundations of Ethical Positions in Marketing', *Psychology & Marketing*, 12(6), 569–82.

[5] Snipes, R.L., LaTour, M. and Bliss, S.J. (1999), 'A Model of the Effects of Self-efficacy on the Perceived Ethicality and Performance of Fear Appeals in Advertising', *Journal of Business Ethics*, 19, 273–85.

[6] Shimp, T.A. (2000), *Advertising, Promotion, Supplemental Aspects of Integrated Marketing Communications*. Fort Worth, TX: Dryden Press.

[7] Duncan, T. (2002), *IMC: Using Advertising & Promotion to Build Brands*. Boston, MA: McGraw-Hill Irwin.

[8] Duncan, T. (2002), *IMC: Using Advertising & Promotion to Build Brands*. Boston, MA: McGraw-Hill Irwin.

[9] Beard, F.K. (2003), 'College Student Attitudes Toward Advertising's Ethical, Economic, and Social Consequences', *Journal of Business Ethics*, 48, 217–28.

[10] Fam, K.S. and Waller, D.S. (2003), 'Advertising Controversial Products in the Asia Pacific: What Makes them Offensive?', *Journal of Business Ethics*, 48, 237–50.

[11] Vitell, S.J., Paolillo, J.G.P. and Thomas, J.L. (2003), 'The Perceived Role of Ethics and Social Responsibility: A Study of Marketing Professionals', *Business Ethics Quarterly*, 13(1), 63–86.

[12] Pickton, D. and Broderick, A. (2005), *Integrated Marketing Communications*. Harlow: Pearson Education.

[13] Galloni, A. (2001), 'In New Global Campaign, Durex Maker Uses Humor to Sell Condoms', *Wall Street Journal*, 27 July.

[14] Pickton, D. and Broderick, A. (2005), *Integrated Marketing Communications*. Harlow: Pearson Education.

[15] Davies, J.J. (1995), 'Ethics in Advertising Decision Making: Implications for Reducing the Incidence of Deceptive Advertising', *Journal of Consumer Affairs*, 28(2), 380–402.

[16] Coutinho de Arruda, M.C. and Leme de Arruda, M. (1999), 'Ethical Standards in Advertising: A Worldwide Perspective', *Journal of Business Ethics*, 19, 159–69.

[17] Pickton, D. and Broderick, A. (2005), *Integrated Marketing Communications*. Harlow: Pearson Education.

[18] Laczniak, G.R. and Murphy, P.E. (1991), 'Fostering Ethical Marketing Decisions', *Journal of Business Ethics*, 10, 259–71.

[19] See, among others, Pickton, D. and Broderick, A. (2005), *Integrated Marketing Communications*. Harlow: Pearson Education; Shimp, T.A. (2000), *Advertising, Promotion, Supplemental Aspects of Integrated Marketing Communications*.

Fort Worth, TX: Dryden Press; Clow, K.E. and Baack, D. (2001), *Integrated Advertising, Promotion & Marketing Communications*. Upper Saddle River, NJ: Prentice Hall.

[20] Plakoyiannaki, E., Mathioudaki, K., Dimitratos, P. and Zotos, Y. (2008), 'Images of Women in Online Advertisements of Global Products: Does Sexism Exist?', *Journal of Business Ethics*, 83(1), 111–12.

[21] Lin, C.-L. (2008), 'Sexual Issues: The Analysis of Female Role Portrayal Preferences in Taiwanese Print Ads', *Journal of Business Ethics*, 83(3), 409–18.

[22] Kramer, Z.A. (2004), 'The Ultimate Gender Stereotype: Equalizing Gender-conforming and Gender-nonconforming Homosexuals under Title VII', *University of Illinois Law Review*, 2004, 465–500; Eisend, M. (2010), 'A Meta-analysis of Gender Roles in Advertising', *Journal of the Academy of Marketing Science*, 38, 418–40.

[23] Ford, J.B., Kramer Voli, P., Honeycutt, E.D. Jr and Casey, S.L. (1998), 'Gender Role Portrayals in Japanese Advertising: A Magazine Content Analysis', *Journal of Advertising*, 27(1), 113–24.

[24] Harker, M., Harker, D. and Svensen, S. (2005), 'Attitudes towards Gender Portrayal in Advertising: An Australian Perspective', *Journal of Marketing Management*, 21, 251–64.

[25] Lindner, K. (2004), 'Images of Women in General Interest and Fashion Magazine Advertisements from 1955 to 2002', *Sex Roles: A Journal of Research*, 51(7), 409–21.

[26] Deachun, A. and Sanghoon, K. (2007), 'Relating Hofstede's Masculinity Dimension to Gender Role Portrayals in Advertising', *International Marketing Review*, 24(2), 181–207.

[27] Reichert, T., Lambiase, J., Morgan, S., Carstarphen, M. and Zavoina, S. (1999), 'Cheesecake and Beefcake: No Matter How You Slice it, Sexual Explicitness in Advertising Continues to Increase', *Journalism & Mass Communication Quarterly*, 76(1), 7–20.

[28] Courtney, A.E. and Whipple, T.W. (1983), *Sex Stereotyping in Advertising*. Lexington, KY: Lexington Books.

[29] Harker, M., Harker, D. and Svensen, S. (2005), 'Attitudes towards Gender Portrayal in Advertising: An Australian Perspective', *Journal of Marketing Management*, 21, 251–64.

[30] Verhellen, Y., Dens, N. and De Pelsmacker, P. (2011), 'A Content Analysis of Gender Role Depiction in Belgian Television Advertising', *Proceedings of the 2011 Icoria Conference, Berlin*, CD-ROM.

[31] Tiggemann, M. and McGill, B. (2004), 'The Role of Social Comparison in the Effect of Magazine Advertisements on Women's Mood and Body Dissatisfaction', *Journal of Social and Clinical Psychology*, 23, 23–44.

[32] Bessenoff, G.R. (2006), 'Can the Media Affect Us? Social Comparison, Self-discrepancy and the Thin Ideal', *Psychology of Women Quarterly*, 30, 239–51.

[33] Spurgin, E.W. (2003), 'What's Wrong with Computer-generated Images of Perfection in Advertising?', *Journal of Business Ethics*, 45, 257–68.

[34] Waller, D.S. (2004), 'What Factors Make Controversial Advertising Offensive? A Preliminary Study', *Australia/*

New Zealand Communication Association (ANZCA) Conference, Sydney; Fam, K.-S., Waller, D. and Yang, Z. (2009), 'Addressing the Advertising of Controversial Products in China: An Empirical Approach', *Journal of Business Ethics*, 88(1), 43–58.

35 Dahl, D.W., Frankenberger, K.D. and Manchanda, R.V. (2003), 'Does it Pay to Shock? Reactions to Shocking and Nonshocking Advertising Content Among University Students', *Journal of Advertising Research*, 43(3), 268–80; Waller, D.S., Fam, K.S. and Erdogan, Z. (2005), 'Advertising of Controversial Products: A Cross-Cultural Study', *Journal of Consumer Marketing*, 22(1), 6–13.

36 Clow, K.E. and Baack, D. (2001), *Integrated Advertising, Promotion & Marketing Communications*. Upper Saddle River, NJ: Prentice Hall.

37 Wilson, A. and West, C. (1981), 'The Marketing of "Unmentionables"', *Harvard Business Review*, 59(1), 91–102; Rehman, S.N. and Brooks, J.R. (1987), 'Attitudes Toward Television Advertising for Controversial Products', *Journal of Healthcare Marketing*, 7(3), 78–83; Triff, M., Benningfield, D. and Murphy, J. (1987), 'Advertising Ethics: A Study of Public Attitudes and Perceptions', *Proceedings of the 1987 Conference of the American Academy of Advertising*. Columbia, SC: AAA.

38 Waller, D.S. (1999), 'Attitudes Towards Offensive Advertising: An Australian Study', *Journal of Consumer Marketing*, 16(3), 288–94.

39 Shimp, T.A. and Stuart, E.W. (2004), 'The Role of Disgust as an Emotional Mediator of Advertising Effects', *Journal of Advertising*, 33 (Spring), 43–53.

40 Dens, N., De Pelsmacker, P. and Janssens, W. (2008), 'Disgust or Conquer? Exploring Consumer Reactions to Incongruent Mild Disgust Appeals', *Journal of Marketing Communications*, 14(4), 269–89; Pope, N.K.L., Voges, K.E. and Brown, M.R. (2004), 'The Effect of Provocation in the Form of Mild Erotica on Attitude to the Ad and Corporate Image: Differences Between Cause-Related and Product-Based Advertising', *Journal of Advertising*, 33(1), 69–82.

41 Dahl, D.W., Frankenberger, K.D. and Manchanda, R.V. (2003), 'Does it Pay to Shock? Reactions to Shocking and Nonshocking Advertising Content Among University Students', *Journal of Advertising Research*, 43(3), 268–80.

42 Dens, N., De Pelsmacker, P. and Janssens, W. (2008), 'Disgust or Conquer? Exploring Consumer Reactions to Incongruent Mild Disgust Appeals', *Journal of Marketing Communications*, 14(4), 269–89.

43 www.unicef.org, Cuckoo Awards, 2006.

44 Reichert, T. and Carpenter, C. (2004), 'An Update on Sex in Magazine Advertising: 1983 to 2003', *Journalism and Mass Communication Quarterly*, 81, 823–37.

45 Dens, N., De Pelsmacker, P. and Janssens, W. (2007), 'The Differential Effects of Scarcely Dressed Male and Female Models in Advertising'. *Proceedings of the SCP Annual Conference*. Las Vegas, NV: SCP; LaTour, M.S. and Henthorne, T.L. (2003), 'Nudity and Sexual Appeals: Understanding the Arousal Process and Advertising Response', in Reichert, T. and Lambiase, J. (eds), *Sex in Advertising: Perspectives on the Erotic Appeals*. Mahwah, NJ: Lawrence Erlbaum Associates, 91–106; Reichert, T. and Lambiase, J. (eds) (2003), *Sex in Advertising: Perspectives on the Erotic Appeals*. Mahwah, NJ: Lawrence Erlbaum Associates; Saad, G. (2004), 'Applying Evolutionary Psychology in Understanding the Representation of Women in Advertisements', *Psychology & Marketing*, 21, 593–612.

46 Dens, N., De Pelsmacker, P. and Janssens, W. (2009), 'Effects of Scarcely Dressed Models in Advertising on Body Esteem for Belgian Men and Women', *Sex Roles: A Journal of Research*, 60(516), 366–78.

47 Martin, K.D. and Smith, N.C. (2008), 'Commercializing Social Interaction: The Ethics of Stealth Marketing', *Journal of Public Policy and Marketing*, 27(1), 45–56.

48 Sprott, D.E. (2008), 'The Policy, Consumer and Ethical Dimensions of Covert Marketing: An Introduction to the Special Section', *Journal of Public Policy and Marketing*, 27(1), 4–6; Martin, K.D. and Smith, N.C. (2008), 'Commercializing Social Interaction: The Ethics of Stealth Marketing', *Journal of Public Policy and Marketing*, 27(1), 45–56.

49 Martin, K.D. and Smith, C. (2008), 'Commercializing Social Interaction: The Ethics of Stealth Marketing', *Journal of Public Policy and Marketing*, 27(1), 45–56.

50 Karrh, J.A. (1998), 'Brand Placement: A Review', *Journal of Current Issues and Research in Advertising*, 20(2), 31–49.

51 PQ Media (2008), 'Exclusive PQ Media Research: Branded Entertainment Market Defies Slowing Economy, Expands 14.7% to $22.3 bil. in 2007', http://www.pqmedia.com/about-press-20080212-bemf.html (accessed June 2009).

52 PQMedia (2010), 'Global Branded Entertainment Marketing Forecast 2010–2014', http://www.pqmedia.com/brandedentertainmentforecast2010-read.html (accessed 3 October 2012).

53 Nebenzahl, I.D. and Jaffe, E.D. (1998), 'Ethical Dimensions of Advertising Executions', *Journal of Business Ethics*, 17, 805–15; Law, S. and Braun, K.A. (2000), 'I'll Have What She's Having: Gauging the Impact of Product Placements on Viewers', *Psychology & Marketing*, 17(12), 1059–75.

54 Bhatnagar, N., Aksoy, L. and Malkoc, S.A. (2004), 'Embedding Brands within Media Content: The Impact of Message, Media, and Consumer Characteristics on Placement Efficacy', in Shrum, L.J. (ed.), *The Psychology of Entertainment Media*. Mahwah, NJ: Lawrence Erlbaum Associates, 99–116.

55 Lindstrom, M. and Seybold, P.B. (2003), *Brand Child*. London: Kogan Page.

56 Eagle, L.C. and de Bruin, A.M. (2000), *Advertising Restrictions: Protection of the Young and Vulnerable?* Auckland, Massey University: Working paper 00.06; Gardner, C. (2004), 'Industry Update', *International Journal of Advertising and Marketing to Children*, 5(3), 73; Clarke, B. (2003), 'The Complex Issue of Food, Advertising, and Child Health', *International Journal of Advertising and Marketing to Children*, 5(1), 11–16.

57 de Bruin, A.M. and Eagle, L. (2000), *Children, the Medium and the Message: Parental Perceptions of Children Directed Advertising Issues and Regulation*. Auckland, Massey University: Working paper 00.14.

58 Eagle, L.C., Bulmer, S.L., de Bruin, A.M. and Kitchen, J. (2004), 'Exploring the Link between Obesity and Advertising in New Zealand,' *Journal of Marketing Communications*, 10(1), 49–67.

59 Berman, R. (2005), 'Sloth, not Ads, is Responsible for Fat Kids', *Advertising Age*, 76(16), 30.

60 Eagle, L.C., Bulmer, S.L. and Hawkins, J.C. (2003), *The 'Obesity Epidemic': Complex Causes, Controversial Cures – Implications for Marketing Communication*. Auckland, Massey University: Technical report 03.03; Eagle, L.C., Bulmer, S.L., Kitchen, J. and Hawkins, J.C. (2004), 'Complex and Controversial Causes For the "Obesity Epidemic": The Role of Marketing Communications', *International Journal of Medical Marketing*, 4(3), 271–87.

61 Burr, L. and Burr, R.M. (1976), 'Television Advertising to Children: What Parents are Saying About Government Control', *Journal of Advertising*, 5(4), 37–41.

62 Chan, K. and McNeal, J.U. (2003), 'Parental Concern about Television Viewing and Children's Advertising in China', *International Journal for Public Opinion Research*, 15(2), 151–66.

63 Spungin, P. (2004), 'Parent Power, Not Pester Power', *International Journal of Advertising and Marketing to Children*, 5(3), 37–40.

64 Nathanson, A.I., Eveland, W. Jr, Park, H.S. and Paul, B. (2002), 'Perceived Media Influence and Efficacy as Predictors of Caregivers' Protective Behaviors', *Journal of Broadcasting and Electronic Media*, 46(3), 385–410.

65 Gray, O. (2005), 'Responsible Advertising in Europe', *Young Consumers*, 6(4), 19–23.

66 Lascoutx, E. (2005), *Food Marketing to Kids*. New York: Children's Advertising Review Unit (CARU), http://www.caru.org.

67 Burr, L. and Burr, R.M. (1976), 'Television Advertising to Children: What Parents Are Saying about Government Control', *Journal of Advertising*, 5(4), 37–41.

68 de Bruin, A.M. and Eagle, L. (2000), *Children, the Medium and the Message: Parental Perceptions of Children Directed Advertising Issues and Regulation*. Auckland, Massey University: Working paper 00.14; Eagle, L.C. and de Bruin, A.M. (2000), *Advertising Restrictions: Protection of the Young and Vulnerable?* Auckland, Massey University: Working paper 00.06; Eagle, L.C. and de Bruin, A.M. (2001), *Marketing Communication Implications of Children's New Electronic Media Use*. Auckland, Massey University: Working paper 01.24.

69 Walsh, A.D., Laczniak, R.N. and Carlson, L. (1998), 'Mothers' Preferences for Regulating Children's Television', *Journal of Advertising*, 27(3), 23–36.

70 Moore, E.S. (2004), 'Children and the Changing World of Advertising', *Journal of Business Ethics*, 52, 161–7.

71 Hudson, S., Hudson, D. and Peloza, J. (2008), 'Meet the Parents: A Parents' Perspective on Product Placement in Children's Films', *Journal of Business Ethics*, 80(2), 289–304.

72 Grossbart, S.L. and Crosby, L.A. (1984), 'Understanding the Bases of Parental Concern and Reaction to Children's Food Advertising', *Journal of Marketing*, 48(3), 79–92; Chan, K. and McNeal, J.U. (2003), 'Parental Concern about Television Viewing and Children's Advertising in China', *International Journal for Public Opinion Research*, 15(2), 151–66; Spungin, P. (2004), 'Parent Power, not Pester Power', *International Journal of Advertising and Marketing to Children*, 5(3), 37–40.

73 Burr, P.L. and Burr, R.M. (1976), 'Television Advertising to Children: What Parents Are Saying about Government Control', *Journal of Advertising*, 5(4), 37–41.

74 Spungin, P. (2004), 'Parent Power, not Pester Power', *International Journal of Advertising and Marketing to Children*, 5(3), 37–40; Buijzen, M. and Valkenburg, P.M. (2003), 'The Unintended Effects of Television Advertising', *Communication Research*, 30(5), 483–503.

75 Burr, P.L. and Burr, R.M. (1977), 'Parental Responses to Child Marketing', *Journal of Advertising Research*, 17(6), 17–20.

76 Young, B. (2003), 'Does Food Advertising Make Children Obese?', *International Journal of Advertising and Marketing to Children*, 4 (April/June), 19–26; Clarke, B. (2005), 'Responsible Marketing,' *Young Consumers*, 6(4), 3–4; Spungin, P. (2004), 'Parent Power, not Pester Power', *International Journal of Advertising and Marketing to Children*, 5(3), 37–40.

77 Spungin, P. (2004), 'Parent Power, not Pester Power', *International Journal of Advertising and Marketing to Children*, 5(3), 37–40.

78 Clarke, B. (2005), 'Responsible Marketing,' *Young Consumers*, 6(4), 3–4.

79 Zappa, J.A., Morton, H. and Mehta, K. (2003), 'Television Food Advertising: Counterproductive to Children's Health? A Content Analysis Using the Australian Guide to Healthy Eating', *Nutrition and Dietics*, 60(2), 78–84; Kunkel, D., Wilcox, B.L., Cantor, J., Palmer, E., Linn, S. and Dowrick, P. (2004), 'Report of the APA Task Force on Advertising to Children', http://www.apa.org/releases/childrenads.pdf (accessed June 2009).

80 Chan, K. and McNeal, J.U. (2003), 'Parental Concern about Television Viewing and Children's Advertising in China', *International Journal for Public Opinion Research*, 15(2), 151–66.

81 Bijmolt, T.H.A., Claassen, W. and Brus, B. (1998), 'Children's Understanding of TV Advertising: Effects of Age, Gender and Parental Influence', *Journal of Consumer Policy*, 21(2), 171–94; Clarke, B. (2005), 'Responsible Marketing,' *Young Consumers*, 6(4), 3–4.

82 Bulmer, S.L. (2001), *Children's Perceptions of Advertising*. Auckland, Massey University: Working paper 01.05; Preston, C. (2005), 'Advertising to Children and Social Responsibility', *Young Consumers*, 6(4), 61–7; Wright, P., Friestad, M. and Boush, D.M. (2005), 'The Development of Marketplace Persuasion Knowledge in Children, Adolescents, and Young Adults', *Journal of Public Policy and Marketing*, 24(2), 222–33; Kunkel, D., Wilcox, B.L., Cantor, J., Palmer, E., Linn, S. and Dowrick, P. (2004), 'Report of the APA Task Force on Advertising to Children', http://www.apa.org/releases/childrenads.pdf (accessed June 2009).

[83] Halford, J.C.G., Gillespie, J., Brown, V., Pontin, E. and Dovey, T.M. (2004), 'Effect of Television Advertisements for Foods on Food Consumption in Children,' *Appetite*, 42, 221–5.

[84] Lvovich, S. (2003), 'Advertising and Obesity: The Research Evidence', *International Journal of Advertising and Marketing to Children*, 4 (January/March), 35–40.

[85] Clarke, B. (2005), 'Responsible Marketing,' *Young Consumers*, 6(4), 3–4.

[86] Young, B. (2003), 'Does Food Advertising Make Children Obese?', *International Journal of Advertising and Marketing to Children*, 4 (April/June), 19–26.

[87] Lyna, A. (2005), 'TV Confuses Children about which Foods Are Healthy, New Study Finds', University of Illinois at Urbana–Champaign news release (6 June 2005), http://www.news.uiuc.edu/news/05/0606kidfood.htm (accessed June 2009).

[88] Zappa, J.A., Morton, H. and Mehta, K. (2003), 'Television Food Advertising: Counterproductive to Children's Health? A Content Analysis Using the Australian Guide to Healthy Eating', *Nutrition and Dietics*, 60(2), 78–84.

[89] Grossbart, S.L. and Crosby, L.A. (1984), 'Understanding the Bases of Parental Concern and Reaction to Children's Food Advertising', *Journal of Marketing*, 48(3), 79–92.

[90] Spungin, P. (2004), 'Parent Power, not Pester Power', *International Journal of Advertising and Marketing to Children*, 5(3), 37–40.

[91] Nathanson, A.I. (2001), 'Parent and Child Perspectives on the Presence and Meaning of Parental Television Mediation', *Journal of Broadcasting and Electronic Media*, 45(2), 210–20; Nathanson, A.I., Eveland, W.P. Jr, Park, H.S. and Paul, B. (2002), 'Perceived Media Influence and Efficacy as Predictors of Caregivers' Protective Behaviours', *Journal of Broadcasting and Electronic Media*, 46(3), 385–410; Grossbart, S.L. and Crosby, L.A. (1984), 'Understanding the Bases of Parental Concern and Reaction to Children's Food Advertising', *Journal of Marketing*, 48(3), 79–92.

[92] Chan, K. and McNeal, J.U. (2003), 'Parental Concern about Television Viewing and Children's Advertising in China', *International Journal for Public Opinion Research*, 15(2), 151–66.

[93] Sneddon, A. (2001), 'Advertising and Deep Autonomy', *Journal of Business Ethics*, 33, 15–28.

[94] Rice, F. (2001), 'Superstars of Spending: Marketers Clamor for Kids', *Advertising Age*, 1 February, S1; Kunkel, D., Wilcox, B.L., Cantor, J., Palmer, E., Linn, S. and Dowrick, P. (2004), 'Report of the APA Task Force on Advertising to Children', http://www.apa.org/releases/childrenads.pdf (accessed June 2009).

[95] McNeal, J. (1998), 'Tapping the Three Kids' Markets', *American Demographics*, 20(4), 37–41.

[96] Furnham, A., Abramski, S. and Gunter, B. (1997), 'A Cross-cultural Content Analysis of Children's Television Advertisements', *Sex Roles*, 37, 91–9.

[97] Lyna, A. (2005), 'TV Confuses Children about which Foods Are Healthy, New Study Finds', University of Illinois at Urbana-Champaign news release (6 June 2005), http://www.news.uiuc.edu/news/05/0606kidfood.htm (accessed 28 July 2005).

[98] Bijmolt, T.H.A., Claassen, W. and Brus, B. (1998), 'Children's Understanding of TV Advertising: Effects of Age, Gender and Parental Influence', *Journal of Consumer Policy*, 21(2), 171–94; Clarke, B. (2003) 'The Complex Issue of Food, Advertising, and Child Health', *International Journal of Advertising and Marketing to Children*, 5(1), 11–16; Clarke, B. (2005) 'Responsible Marketing,' *Young Consumers*, 6(4), 3–4.

[99] Eagle, L.C., Bulmer, S.L., de Bruin, A.M. and Kitchen, P.J. (2004), 'Exploring the Link between Obesity and Advertising in New Zealand', *Journal of Marketing Communications*, 10(1), 49–67.

[100] Lvovich, S. (2003), 'Advertising and Obesity: The Research Evidence', *International Journal of Advertising and Marketing to Children*, 4 (January/March), 35–40; Young, B. (2003) 'Does Food Advertising Make Children Obese?', *International Journal of Advertising and Marketing to Children*, 4 (April/June), 19–26; Eagle, L.C., Bulmer, S.L., de Bruin, A.M. and Kitchen, P.J. (2004), 'Exploring the Link between Obesity and Advertising in New Zealand', *Journal of Marketing Communications*, 10(1), 49–67.

[101] Vandewater, E.A., Shim, M. and Caplovitz, A.G. (2004), 'Linking Obesity and Activity Level with Children's Television and Video Game Use', *Journal of Adolescence*, 27, 71–85.

[102] Eagle, L.C., Bulmer, S.L. and Hawkins, J.C. (2003), *The 'Obesity Epidemic': Complex Causes, Controversial Cures – Implications for Marketing Communication.* Auckland, Massey University: Technical report, 3 March; Eagle, L.C., Bulmer, S.L., Kitchen, P.J. and Hawkins, J.C. (2004) 'Complex and Controversial Causes for the "Obesity Epidemic": The role of Marketing Communications', *International Journal of Medical Marketing*, 4(3), 271–87.

[103] Vandewater, E.A., Shim, M. and Caplovitz, A.G. (2004), 'Linking Obesity and Activity Level with Children's Television and Video Game Use', *Journal of Adolescence*, 27, 71–85.

[104] Clarke, B. (2003), 'The Complex Issue of Food, Advertising, and Child Health', *International Journal of Advertising and Marketing to Children*, 5(1), 11–16; Young, B. (2005) 'The Obesity Epidemic Reviewed', *Young Consumers*, 6(3), 50–5.

[105] Hastings, G., Stead, M. and Webb, J. (2004), 'Fear Appeals in Social Marketing: Strategic and Ethical Reasons for Concern', *Psychology & Marketing*, 21(11), 961–86.

[106] Snipes, R.L., LaTour, M. and Bliss, S.J. (1999), 'A Model of the Effects of Self-efficacy on the Perceived Ethicality and Performance of Fear Appeals in Advertising', *Journal of Business Ethics*, 19, 273–85.

[107] Rossiter, J.R. and Bellman, S. (2005), *Marketing Communications: Theory and Applications.* French Forest, NSW: Pearson Education Australia.

[108] Attas, D. (1999), 'What Is Wrong with "Deceptive" Advertising?', *Journal of Business Ethics*, 21, 49–59.

109 Koslow, S. (2000), 'Can the Truth Hurt? How Honest and Persuasive Advertising Can Unintentionally Lead to Increased Consumer Skepticism', *Journal of Consumer Affairs*, 34(2), 245–68.

110 Fill, C. (2006), *Marketing Communications; Engagement, Strategies and Practice*, Harlow: Pearson Education.

111 http://groups.yahoo.com/group/brandhut/ (accessed May 2003).

112 Shimp, T.A. (2000), *Advertising, Promotion, Supplemental Aspects of Integrated Marketing Communications*, Fort Worth, TX: Dryden Press.

113 Shimp, T.A. (2000), *Advertising, Promotion, Supplemental Aspects of Integrated Marketing Communications*, Fort Worth, TX: Dryden Press.

114 http://www.easa-alliance.org (accessed 3 October 2012).

115 EASA (2003), *Advertising Self-regulation: The Essentials*. Brussels: European Advertising Standards Alliance.

116 http://www.easa-alliance.org (accessed 3 October 2012).

117 EASA (2005), *Advertising Self-Regulation in Europe, The Blue Book, 2005*. Brussels: European Advertising Standards Alliance.

118 'EU Enlargement Expands Opportunities for Advertising Self-Regulation', Press release of 20 May 2003 (www.easa.iccwlo.org).

119 http://www.easa-alliance.org/Publications/Statistics/page.aspx/375 (accessed 3 October 2012).

120 ACC (2006), Code of Conduct.

121 Van Oosterhout, J.H. (2008), 'Transcending the Confines of Economic and Political Organization? The Misguided Metaphor of Corporate Citizenship', *Business Ethics Quarterly*, 18(1), 35–42.

122 O'Riordan, L. and Fairbrass, J. (2008), 'Corporate Social Responsibility (CSR): Models and Theories in Stakeholder Dialogue', *Journal of Business Ethics*, 83(4), 745–58.

123 Clow, K.E. and Baack, D. (2001), *Integrated Advertising, Promotion & Marketing Communications*. Upper Saddle River, NJ: Prentice Hall.

124 Vanhamme, J. and Grobben, B. (2008), 'Too Good to Be True! The Effectiveness of CSR History in Countering Negative Publicity', *Journal of Business Ethics*, 85(2), 273–83.

125 Clow, K.E. and Baack, D. (2001), *Integrated Advertising, Promotion & Marketing Communications*. Upper Saddle River, NJ: Prentice Hall.

126 Doukakis, I., Krambia-Kapardis, M. and Katsioloudes, M. (2003), 'Corporate Responsibility: A Pilot Study into the Realities of the Business Sector in Cyprus', in Bennett, R. (ed.), *New Challenges for Corporate and Marketing Communications. Proceedings of the Eighth International Conference on Marketing and Corporate Communications*. London: London Metropolitan University, 64–80.

127 Hines, C. and Ames, A. (2000), *Ethical Consumerism: A Research Study Conducted for the Co-operative Bank by MORI*. London: MORI.

128 MORI (2000), *European Attitudes towards Corporate Social Responsibility: Research for CSR Europe*. London: MORI.

129 The Roper Organization Inc. (1990), *The Environment: Public Attitudes and Individual Behavior*. Research report commissioned by S.C. Johnson & Son, Inc.

130 CRC-Consommation (1998), *Commerce Ethique: les Consommateurs Solidaires*. Paris: CRC.

131 MacGillivray, A. (2000), *The Fair Share: The Growing Market Share of Green and Ethical Products*. London: New Economics Foundation.

132 De Pelsmacker, P., Driessen, L. and Rayp, G. (2005), 'Do Consumers Care about Ethics? Willingness to Pay for Fair Trade Coffee', *Journal of Consumer Affairs*, 39(2), 361–83.

GLOSSARY

Ability (MAO factor): the resources needed to achieve a particular goal.

Achievement indicators of public relations effectiveness: measure the extent to which a pre-specified objective has been met with a public of interest. Examples include the share of the target audience that has been reached, changes in awareness and knowledge, changes in opinions and attitudes, evolution of the image and goodwill of the company, and the extent to which behaviour has changed.

Action advertising: tries to stimulate consumers to buy a product immediately.

Action communications: seek to influence the buying behaviour of target groups and to persuade the consumer to purchase the product. The primary goal is to stimulate purchases.

Action costing budgeting: a budgeting method in which a programme or activity is planned, and the cost to carry it out is calculated.

Activation measures: measure the extent to which people actively react to advertising by, for instance, looking up further information, talking to friends (buzz) and going to a store.

Addressable media: media by means of which it is possible to communicate individually with each customer or prospect.

Advergames: a rich media type of brand-related online entertainment used as a tool for brand interaction and experience. Advergames use interactive game technology to deliver embedded messages to consumers. The advertising message can then become an integral part of playing the game.

Advertising: any paid, non-personal communication through various media by an identified company, non-profit organisation or individual.

Advertising clutter: the percentage of a medium vehicle that is advertising.

Advertising/performance allowances: monetary incentives aimed at encouraging the retailer to advertise the manufacturer's brand and provided when proof of the ad is produced.

Advertorials: informative ads with an editorial approach but also a clearly identified advertiser.

Affect-as-Information model: a model that posits that consumers may use feelings as a source of information to form an overall evaluation of a product or brand, not by means of a simple association, but through a controlled inferential process or, in other words, in an informed, deliberate manner.

Affiliate marketing or **affiliate networking:** performance-based marketing technique on the Internet in which a business rewards one or more affiliates for each visitor brought about by the affiliate's own marketing efforts.

Affordability budgeting method: 'leftover' resources, after all input costs (i.e. human resources, operational and financial costs) are invested in communications.

Aided brand awareness: the percentage of people that indicate a brand as one that they know in a certain product category.

Ambush or parasitic marketing: an organisation deliberately seeking an association with a particular event without being an official sponsor of the event to persuade the audience that the ambusher is a legitimate or major sponsor. A company may be a minor sponsor of an event but, by spending considerable budgets on advertising support, it creates the impression of being an important sponsor.

Anchor deals: the presence of a brand on certain content sites and portals as a supplier of brand-related content continuously for a long period.

Apps or mobile applications: software applications, usually designed to run on smart phones and tablet computers.

Arbitrary budgeting method: whatever the general manager or managing director decides will be implemented.

ATR model: **A**wareness→**T**rial→**R**einforcement. Marketing communications first arouse awareness, then induce consumers towards a first trial purchase and then reassure and reinforce those users after their first purchase.

Attitude: a person's overall evaluation of an object, a product, a person, an organisation, an ad, etc. An attitude towards a particular brand (Ab) can be considered as a measure of how much a person likes or dislikes the brand, or of the extent to which he or she holds a favourable or unfavourable view of it.

Augmented product: the 'service layer' on top of the tangible product. It includes elements such as prompt delivery, installation service, after-sales service and management of complaints.

Banner ads: graphic images (animated gifs or Java applets) used as advertisements.

Bastion brand: flagship brand of a company that provides most profit for the company, often follows a premium price strategy, is characterised by a high level of psycho-social meaning and is generally considered as a high-performance brand.

Behavioural segmentation: dividing the market into segments referring to product or brand preferences or use, or involvement with product categories.

β-coefficient analysis: analysis by means of which the relationship between the number of exposures to an advertisement and the degree of memorisation (i.e. the percentage of the target group that remembers the ad) is studied.

Billboarding: mentioning the name of a sponsor in or near a television programme.

Brand: a name, term, sign, symbol or design, or a combination of these, intended to identify the goods or services of one seller or group of sellers, and to differentiate them from those of a competitor. A brand is a set of verbal and/or visual cues, and as such it is a part of a product's tangible features. It is an identifier that adds either rational and tangible dimensions (related to product performance) or symbolic, emotional and intangible dimensions (related to what the brand represents) that differentiate it from other products designed to fulfill the same need.

Brand activation: the seamless integration of all available communication means in a creative platform in order to activate consumers by stimulating interest, initiating trial and eventually securing consumer loyalty through interaction with target audiences. It is a marketing process of bringing a brand to life through creating brand experience.

Brand attitude: the perceived value of a brand to a consumer.

Brand awareness: the association of some physical characteristics such as a brand name, logo, package, style, etc., with a category need.

Brand community: a specialised, non-geographically bound community, based on a structured set of social relationships among users of a brand.

Brand confusion: the fact that a communication for brand X is regarded by the consumer as being a communication for a different brand, Y.

Brand dilution: when the brand name is used for so many different product categories that the brand personality becomes fuzzy and the brand's value deteriorates.

Brand equity: the value of a brand, the value added to a product by virtue of its brand name.

Brand experience: sensations, feelings, cognitions and behavioural responses evoked by brand-related stimuli that are part of a brand's design and identity, packaging, communications and environments.

Brand extension or **brand stretching:** when an existing brand is used to market products in a different product category.

Brand feelings: consumers' emotional responses to the brand.

Brand imagery: how consumers think about a brand in an abstract way rather than to what consumers believe the brand really does. Brand imagery pertains to intangible brand aspects that can become linked to the brand by customer experience, marketing communications, word of mouth, etc.

Brand knowledge: target consumers are aware of the most essential brand characteristics, features and benefits.

Brand loyalty: the mental commitment or relation between a consumer and a brand.

Brand mark: the element of a brand that cannot be spoken, often a symbol, design or specific packaging.

Brand name: that part of a brand that can be spoken, including letters, words and numbers.

Brand personality: the set of human personality traits that are both applicable to and relevant for brands.

Brand placement: the paid inclusion of branded products or brand identifiers through audio and/or visual means within mass media programmes.

Brand portfolio: the set of all brands and brand lines that a company possesses.

Brand websites: sites with specific brand-related information and/or services.

Broad brand awareness: the brand comes to mind often, in different usage situations.

Broadcast or programme sponsorship: a brand can sponsor a sports programme, the weather forecast or a 'soap'.

Buttons: very small banner ads, rectangles or squares.

Buy-back allowance: to stimulate the retailer to put a new brand or a renewed version of the product on the shelves, the manufacturer sometimes offers to buy back the 'old' product, or commits to buying back the stock of the new product that is not sold during a specific period of time.

Buzz marketing: giving people a reason to talk about your products or services and making it easier for that conversation to take place.

Campaign evaluation research: advertising tests that focus on the effectiveness of a whole advertising campaign.

Capitation rating or achievement targeting budgeting: audiences to be reached and objectives to be achieved are defined. Experience with previous campaigns are used to calculate the budget required to achieve these objectives.

Cash refunds: discounts offered to the consumer by means of refunding part of the purchase price after sending a proof of purchase.

Catalogue: a list of products or services presented in a visual and/or verbal way. It may be printed or electronically stored on a disk, a CD-ROM or a database, or even be visualized on a website, where the pages can be virtually turned.

Categorical imperative: the philosopher Kant's ethical principle that one should act in such a way that the action taken under the circumstances could be a universal law of behaviour for everyone facing those same circumstances.

Category spending: the advertising spending in a product category.

Cause-related marketing or sponsorship: the support of a social cause that a firm generates through financial interactions with its customers.

Caveat emptor: an ethical view that any marketing action that is legal is also ethical.

Caveat venditor: an ethical view which implies that the maximisation of consumer satisfaction or well-being should be the ultimate aim of marketing action.

Celebrity endorsement: Celebrities are used in marketing communications to endorse a product.

Central-route processing: if motivation, ability and opportunity to process a message are all high, the elaboration likelihood is said to be high and consumers are expected to engage in central route processing. This means that they are willing to elaborate on the information, evaluate the arguments and find out what the information really has to offer.

Co-branding: two or more brands are simultaneously presented on one product.

Co-creation: soliciting input from customers for new products.

Collaborative projects: social media type, the main idea of which is that the joint effort of many actors leads to a better outcome than any actor could achieve individually; also referred to as 'the wisdom of crowds' (e.g. Wikipedia).

Collective advertising: when a government takes the initiative for a campaign.

Collectivistic culture: culture in which people belong to strong, cohesive in-groups (often extended families) who look after and protect each other in exchange for unquestioning loyalty.

Communications audit: all forms of internal and external communications are studied to assess their consistency with overall strategy, as well as their internal consistency.

Communications content research: used to help communications creatives generate ideas about the content of new communications stimuli.

Comparative advertising: an advertisement that directly or indirectly compares one brand with others. A direct comparative ad explicitly names the comparison brand (often a well-known competitive brand) and claims that the comparison brand is inferior to the advertised brand with respect to a specific attribute. An indirect comparative ad does not explicitly mention a comparison brand, but argues to be superior on a certain attribute compared with other brands.

Competitive parity budgeting analysis: companies look at the amount of money that competitors spend on communications and then copy their budgets.

Competitive tendering budgeting: a marketing communications programme is decided on and different agencies are requested to file a proposal and a budget.

Competitor communications strategy research: competitive ads, promotions, budgets and shares of voice, target groups, positioning, communications strategies, media strategies, PR material, etc., are collected and analysed to judge competitive (communications) strategies in order to define target groups and positioning strategies more clearly for the company's own products.

Conference-bound exhibitions: small exhibitions linked to a conference. They have a low reach, but may be highly effective as a result of their high selectivity on the target group.

Confusing positioning: inconsistent communications or an inconsistent choice of distribution channels would give a customer a confused image of a company or brand.

Consistency in marketing communications: marketing instruments combined in such a way that the company's offering is consistently marketed. In other words, all marketing instruments have to work in the same direction, and not conflict with each other.

Consumer brand equity: the underlying customer- and marketing-related components of brand equity.

Consumer promotions: sales promotions by manufacturers or retailers targeted at end-consumers.

Consumer sovereignty: an ethical view that ethical marketing decisions are determined by the answer to three important questions. Is the target market vulnerable in ways that limit consumer decision-making (consumer capability) and are consumers' expectations at purchase likely to be realised? Do consumers have sufficient information to judge (consumer information) and can consumers go elsewhere? Would they incur substantial costs or inconvenience by transferring their loyalty (consumer choice)?

Content communities: the main objective of content communities is sharing content between users. Content communities share different media types, such as text, photos, videos and presentations (e.g. YouTube, Flickr, Instagram).

Content sponsorship: placing an advertiser's message in an area on a website that stands out from other advertisements, for instance a fixed and exclusive presence in a chosen section that is relevant to the advertiser's brand.

Continuous advertising schedule: the advertiser spends a continuous amount of money throughout the whole campaign period.

Contractualism: an ethical principle that focuses upon implied obligation, contracts, duties and rules.

Controversial or shock advertising: advertising that deliberately startles and offends its audience, by means of deliberate norm violation – transgression of law or custom (obscenity) or moral/social code (vulgarity) – or by showing things that outrage the moral or physical senses (e.g. provocative or disgusting images).

Co-operative advertising: two manufacturing companies, or a retailer and a manufacturer, jointly develop an advertising campaign.

Core product: the unique benefit that is being marketed. It is the position, the unique place in the mind of the consumer, that will be focused upon.

Corporate behaviour: the way in which the employees of a company behave. It is an important factor in making the corporate identity visible.

Corporate branding: the name of the company used for all the company's products.

Corporate communications: the total integrated approach to the communications activity generated by all functional departments of a company, targeted at all stakeholders of the company, and aimed at establishing and maintaining the link between strategic objectives, the corporate identity and the corporate image in line.

Corporate culture: the deeper level of basic assumptions and beliefs that are shared by members of an organisation, that operate unconsciously and define in a basic 'taken-for-granted' fashion an organisation's view of itself and its environment.

Corporate design: see **Corporate symbolism**.

Corporate identity: the set of meanings by which a company allows itself to be known and through which it allows people to describe, remember and relate to it. It is the way the company chooses to present itself to its relevant target audiences by means of symbolism, communications and behaviour.

Corporate image: the stakeholder's perception of the way an organisation presents itself. It is the result of the interaction of all experiences, beliefs, feelings, knowledge and impressions of each stakeholder about an organisation. It is a subjective and multidimensional impression of the organisation.

Corporate personality: the values held by personnel within the organisation, the collective, commonly shared understanding of the organisation's distinctive values and characteristics. It encompasses corporate philosophy, mission, strategy and principles.

Corporate public relations: mainly maintaining good relations and creating goodwill with all kinds of audiences who may be important for the company in the long run.

Corporate reputation: the evaluation or esteem in which an organisation's image is held. It is based on experience with the company and/or exposure to communications, behaviour and symbolism. While corporate image can be quite transient and short-term in nature, corporate reputation is more firmly embedded in the mind of an individual.

Corporate social responsibility (CSR): also referred to as 'corporate citizenship'. CSR is an idea that includes the social, the economic and the environmental aspects of business activity ('triple bottom line'). It is the integration of social and environmental values within a company's core business operations and an engagement with stakeholders to improve the well-being of society.

Corporate strategy: long-term strategic objectives of a company.

Corporate structure: organisational structure and brand structure. Organisational structure is concerned with the lines of communication and reporting responsibilities within the organisation. It relates to the degree of centralisation and decentralisation, and often has a major influence on brand structure.

Corporate symbolism or corporate design: a consistent house style on business cards, letter heads, vehicles, gifts, clothes, equipment, packaging, etc. It is an integral part of the corporate identity, or at least of the way in which it is made visible.

Cost per thousand: calculated by dividing the cost of the medium (the air cost of a 15- or 30-second commercial, the cost of a one-page magazine ad, etc.) by the medium's total reach, expressed in thousands of contacts.

Cost per thousand in the target market: calculated by dividing the cost of the medium (the air cost of a 15- or 30-second commercial, the cost of a one-page magazine ad, etc.) by the medium's useful reach in thousands contacts.

Coupons: vouchers representing a monetary value with which the consumer can get a discount on a specific product.

Creative brief: a document provided by the advertiser that forms the starting point for the advertising agency to develop a campaign.

Creative idea: an original and imaginative thought designed to produce goal-directed and problem-solving advertisements and commercials, a proposition which makes it possible to communicate a brand's position in an original, attention-getting, but easy-to-catch way.

Culture: the collective programming of the mind which distinguishes the members of one group or category of people from those of another.

DAGMAR model: a model that describes nine effects of marketing communications that should be reached consecutively: category need, brand awareness, brand knowledge, brand attitude, purchase intention, purchase facilitation, purchase, satisfaction, brand loyalty.

Database: a collection of interrelated data of customers and prospects which can be used for different applications such as analysis, individual selection, segmentation and customer retention, loyalty and service supports.

Day After Recall (DAR) test: advertising post-test by means of a telephone interview. A number of consumers are called. They are asked to indicate which ads they saw on television or heard on the radio the day before, within a certain product category. Brand names are mentioned, and the respondent has to indicate if he or she remembers having seen or heard an ad for the brand. Additionally, a number of questions about the ad content are asked.

Dealer loaders: additional materials are offered to the retailer during a promotional campaign, for instance a refrigerator during a soft drinks promotion. After the promotion, the retailer can keep the extra equipment.

Decent marketing communications: those that do not contain anything that is likely to cause widespread offence, fear or distress.

Deceptive marketing communications: consumers are deceived when there is a claim–fact discrepancy and the false claim is believed by customers. Moreover, the message must be misleading, i.e. representation, omission or practice that is likely to mislead the customer, from the perspective of a reasonable consumer, i.e. by a reasonable number of the group to which the practice is targeted, and the deceptive practice must be material, i.e. important and likely to impact on consumers' choice or conduct regarding the product and thus relate to a central characteristic.

Deep brand awareness: the brand comes to mind easily and enjoys high top-of-mind awareness.

Demographic segmentation: divides the market on the basis of sex, age, family size, religion, birthplace, race, education, income or social class.

Demonstration advertising: an advertisement in which consumers are shown how a product works.

Deontological approach (idealism): ethical principle that focuses upon duties. Some actions are intrinsically right or wrong.

Direct mail: written commercial messages, personally addressed and sent by mail.

Direct marketing communications: contacting customers and prospects in a direct way with the intention of generating an immediate and measurable response or reaction. 'Direct' means using direct media such as mailings (including e-mailings), catalogues, telephone or brochures, and not through intermediaries such as dealers, retailers or sales staff.

An immediate response is possible via the Internet (e-mail/website/social media), answering coupons, phone or a personal visit of the customer to the store or retailer.

Direct opinion measurement test: a jury of customers is exposed to a number of ads and asked to rate the ads on a number of characteristics.

Direct public relations: aimed directly at the stakeholders of interest.

Direct response print advertising or **coupon advertising:** placing an advertisement in a newspaper or a magazine with the following characteristics: direct feedback from the reader (respondent) to the advertiser by returning a coupon, calling a phone number, visiting a website, participating in a contest; a clear link between the response (feedback) and the message advertised; identification of the respondent.

Direct response television (DRTV): television used as a medium to generate reactions.

Distributive justice: ethical principle that holds that rewards are allocated in proportion to the contribution made to organisational ends.

Double-spotting: two spots are placed within the same programme to increase the likelihood of obtaining the effective frequency.

Dramatisation advertising: an advertisement similar to slice-of-life advertising. Both first present a problem and afterwards the solution, but a dramatisation builds suspense and leads consumers to a climax.

Dual branding strategy: a branding strategy in which two brand names are used.

Dual mediation model: the evaluation of an ad has not only an immediate impact on the evaluation of the brand, but also an indirect effect on brand attitude via brand cognitions. The reasoning behind this model is that consumers who hold a positive attitude towards the communication are more likely to be receptive to arguments in favour of the brand advertised.

Dual or second screening: when people interact with their TV via their PC.

E-communications: electronic ways to communicate interactively with different stakeholders.

Effective frequency: the minimum number of exposures, within a purchase cycle, considered necessary to motivate the average prospect in the target audience to accomplish an advertising objective.

Effective reach: the number of target consumers of an advertising campaign who are expected to be exposed to the advertiser's message at an effective frequency level.

Effectiveness goals of communication: goals that should be reached at the brand level: awareness, knowledge, brand attitudes, buying intentions, sales, market share.

Elaboration Likelihood model (ELM): a model that explains how a message can lead to attitude change. The model is a dual-processing model in that it distinguishes two routes to persuasion, a central and a peripheral one, based on motivation, ability and opportunity to process the message.

Emotional advertising appeals: advertisements whose main purpose is to elicit affective responses and to convey an image.

Emotional selling proposition (ESP): A non-functional benefit used in marketing communications, usually a unique psychological association to consumers.

Endorsement branding: two brand names of the same company are used, one of them serving as a quality label or endorsement.

Erotic advertising: an appeal that contains one or more of the following elements: partial or complete nudity, physical contact between two adults, sexy or provocatively dressed person(s), provocative or seductive facial expression, suggestive words or sexually laden music.

Ethics: principles that serve as operational guidelines for both individuals and organisations.

Ethics code: an ethical view that strives for standards on the basis of which companies' and industries' ethical performance is judged, or at least to which they aspire. This set of standards often contains ethical guidelines that go further than the law.

Event marketing: using a number of elements of the communications mix to create an event for the purpose of reaching strategic marketing objectives.

Event-related sponsorship: sponsoring various types of event-related phenomena, such as a soccer competition, a team, an athlete, shirts, a golf tournament, skiing, a baseball game, an exhibition, a series of concerts, a philharmonic orchestra, an artist, a rock concert, a beach festival or an annual traditional crafts exhibition.

Experiential hierarchy-of-effects model: consumers' affective responses towards a product lead them to buy it and, if necessary, reflect on it later. This leads to an affective–conative–cognitive sequence.

Expert endorsement: an advertising format in which an expert appears who endorses and commends a product.

External public relations: directed towards various types of external target groups. Three important types of external corporate PR and PR target groups can be distinguished: public affairs, financial and media PR.

Extra volume or BOGOF (Buy One Get One Free) promotion: an extra quantity of the product is temporarily offered at the same price.

Fear appeal advertising: an advertisement that refers the consumer to a certain type of risk (threat) that he or she might be exposed to and which he or she usually can reduce by buying the product or avoiding the behaviour (coping efficacy).

Feminine culture: culture in which caring for others and quality of life are central values.

Fighter brand: a brand sold at a lower price, situated between the price of the bastion and discount brands. Its quality perception is usually lower than that of the bastion and flanker brands.

Financial brand equity: the financial value of the brand for the company.

Financial public relations: directed towards financial audiences, those groups that are potential shareholders, investors or (potential) advisers to shareholders and investors, such as financial consultants and banks. They are vital for the establishment of the long-term money-raising potential of a company. A crucial objective towards these audiences is to build and maintain the confidence that is necessary to give the company an image of an interesting investment.

Fishbein model: a model of attitude formation in which brand attitudes are made up of three elements: relevant product attributes, the extent to which one believes the brand possesses these attributes, and the evaluation of these attributes or how good/bad one thinks it is for a brand to possess these attributes. More specifically, brand attitude is represented by the weighted sum of the products of brand beliefs and attribute evaluations.

Flanker brand: follows a similar price–profit ratio as the bastion brand, is also characterised by a high psycho-social meaning and perceived performance level, but usually appeals to a different, smaller market segment (niche).

Flighting advertising schedule: advertising concentrated in only a few periods and not during the whole campaign period.

Flog: fake weblog, when firms develop a fake consumer blog about the consumption of some product or service without stating the company's role in the communication.

Foot-Cone-Belding (FCB) grid: buying behaviour model in which four different buying situations are distinguished, based on two dimensions, i.e. the high–low involvement and the think–feel dimension.

Free in-mail promotion: the customer receives a (nearly) free gift in return for a proof of purchase which has to be sent to the manufacturer.

Frequency: indicates how many times a consumer of the target group, on average, is expected to be exposed to the advertiser's message within a specified time period.

Full market coverage: a company tries to target all customer groups with all the products they need.

Gallup–Robinson Impact test: a recall test for print ads. People are called and asked to recall as many ads as they can. After that, a number of questions about the content of the ads are asked: proved name registration, idea penetration and conviction.

Generic advertising: campaigns that promote a whole product category.

Generic brands: indicate the product category. In fact, the concept is a contradiction in terms. Generics are in fact brandless products.

Geographic segments: divides the market based on continents, climate, nations, regions or neighbourhoods.

Globalised communication campaign: see **Standardised campaign**.

Glocalisation: 'think global, act local'. The marketer has a global vision and positioning, but adapts certain aspects of the communications mix to the local context.

Golden rule: when faced with a decision that appears to have ethical implications, act in a way that you would expect others to act towards you.

Green marketing: the development and promotion of products that are environmentally safe: biodegradable, recycled, etc.

Gross Rating Points (GRP): gross reach of an advertising campaign expressed as a percentage of the target group. The weight of a campaign is typically expressed by GRP.

Gross reach: the sum of the number of contacts in the target group that an advertising campaign reaches, regardless of how many times an individual is reached. In other words, a person who is reached by medium x and medium y counts as two.

Heuristic evaluation: when consumers do not have the time to compare all available brands on relevant attributes, they may infer from one specific attribute that the brand is a high-quality brand and therefore form a positive attitude towards it.

Hierarchy-of-effects model: a model of consumer behaviour that assumes that things have to happen in a certain order, implying that the earlier effects form necessary conditions in order for the later effects to occur. According to the traditional hierarchy-of-effects models, consumers go through three different stages in responding to marketing communications, namely a cognitive, an affective and a conative stage, or a think–feel–do sequence.

High-context cultures: cultures in which words are one part of the message, the other part is formed by body language and the context, i.e. the social setting, the importance and knowledge of the person.

Historical comparison budgeting: budgeting based on what has been spent in previous periods, possibly adjusted as a function of changed circumstances.

Honest and truthful marketing communications: those that do not exploit inexperience or lack of knowledge of consumers; no claims should be made which are inaccurate, ambiguous or intended to mislead whether through explicit statement or through omission.

Horizontal trade fairs: exhibitors from one single industry exhibit their products and services to professional target groups, such as sales agents or distributors, from different industries.

Humorous advertising: an appeal created with the intent to make people laugh, irrespective of the fact that the humour is successful (people indeed perceive the ad as humorous) or unsuccessful (people do not think the ad is funny).

Idea advertising: when mostly not-for-profit organisations promote ideas.

Image or theme communications: the advertiser tries to improve relations with target groups, increase customer satisfaction or reinforce brand awareness, brand attitude, brand image and brand preference.

Inbound telemarketing: interested customers or prospects use the phone to contact the company and ask for product information, order a product, ask for help with a problem or file a complaint (incoming calls).

Income proportion budgeting: a pre-specified proportion of margin or sales is devoted to marketing communications.

Indirect public relations: tries to reach stakeholders of interest indirectly through other publics. In that respect, employees, consultants and especially the media can be considered as indirect PR audiences.

Individualist culture: culture in which there are loose ties between people and in which people look after themselves and their immediate family only.

Industrial advertising: aimed at a company that buys the products to use in its own production process.

Industry comparison budgeting: the industry average is used as a benchmark to decide the marketing communications budget.

Industry identity: underlying economic and technical characteristics of an industry, such as industry size, growth, competitiveness, culture and technology levels.

Inertia budgeting analysis: keeping budgets constant year on year, while ignoring the market, competitive actions or consumer opportunities.

Informational buying motives: buying motivations that are aimed at reducing or reversing negative motivations such as solving or avoiding a problem, or normal depletion.

Ingredient branding: a brand of a basic ingredient of a product is mentioned next to the actual product's brand name.

Input indicators of public relations effectiveness: measure PR efforts, such as the number of news stories disseminated, the number of interviews given, trade meetings organised, supermarkets visited or brochures sent. Input indicators measure efforts and not results.

In-script sponsoring: a specific form of product placement in which the sponsoring brand becomes part of the script of the programme.

Institutional advertising: government campaigns.

Integrated marketing communications: a concept of marketing communications planning that recognises the added value of a comprehensive plan that evaluates the strategic roles of a variety of communications disciplines, e.g. general advertising, direct response, sales promotion and public relations – and combines these disciplines to provide clarity, consistency and maximum communications impact.

Interactive (digital) television or i(D)TV: television content that gives viewers the ability to interact with programmes and to use a number of interactive services such as t-government, t-banking, t-commerce, t-learning information, games, video-on-demand and communication (t-mail), all supported by a set-top box.

Internal public relations: aimed at internal stakeholders, such as employees and their families and shareholders. The main purpose of internal public relations is to inform employees about the company's strategic priorities and the role they are playing in them, and to motivate them to carry out these objectives.

Internet: the computer network infrastructure that enables the exchange of digital data on a global scale.

Interstitials: banner ads that appear temporarily when loading a new web page.

Involvement: the importance people attach to a product or a buying decision, the extent to which one has to think it over and the level of perceived risk associated with an inadequate brand choice.

Issues audit: issues are those potential areas that could have an important impact upon the operations of the company. An issues audit identifies all that might be of consequence and helps the company to react and to plan ahead.

Keyword buying: see **Search engine advertising**.

Law of extremes theory: assumes that the relationship between the attitude towards the ad and the attitude towards the brand follows a J-shaped curve. The latter means that not only a very positive, but also a very negative, attitude towards the ad can eventually lead to a positive attitude towards the brand, while communications evoking a moderate instead of an extreme attitude towards the ad result in a less positive brand attitude.

Legal marketing communications: those that are allowed under the current regulations and laws of the country in which the company operates.

Lifestyle segmentation: dividing the market on the basis of how people organise their lives and spend their time and money. Lifestyle measurement is based on the activities, interests and opinions (AIO) of consumers. Activities include how people spend their money and time, e.g. work, leisure, product use, shopping behaviour, etc. Interests can be in fashion, housing, food, cars, culture, etc. Opinions are attitudes, preferences and ideas on general subjects such as politics or economics, on more specific subjects, or on oneself and one's family.

Lifetime value of a customer: the net present value of the profits a company will generate from a customer over a period of time.

Line extension: a new product introduction in an existing product category using the same brand name.

List price: the 'official' price of a product.

Lobbying: the activities that companies undertake to influence decisions of government bodies or the opinion of pressure groups in a positive direction.

Low-context cultures: cultures in which a lot of emphasis is placed on words. One is as accurate, explicit and unambiguous as possible so that the receiver can easily decode the message and understand what is meant.

Low-involvement hierarchy-of-effects model: consumers, after frequent exposure to marketing messages, might buy the product, and decide afterwards how they feel about it (cognitive–conative–affective hierarchy).

Management judgement test: ad execution proposals are presented to a jury of advertising managers, to check whether all the crucial elements of the strategic brief are correctly represented in the execution elements proposed.

Manufacturer advertising: initiated by a manufacturing company that promotes its own brands.

Manufacturer brands: brands developed, owned and marketed by manufacturers of the product.

Marginal budgeting analysis: investing resources as long as extra expenses are compensated by higher extra returns.

Market segmentation: dividing a market into more homogeneous sub-groups on the basis of potentially relevant factors, in that the members of one group share the same need and react in the same way to marketing stimuli and differ in their reactions to these stimuli from the members of other segments.

Market specialisation: a company concentrates on one market segment and sells different products to that group of customers.

Marketing: the process of planning and executing the conception, pricing, promotion and distribution of ideas, goods and services to create and exchange value, and satisfy individual and organisational objectives.

Marketing communications: all instruments by means of which the company communicates with its target groups and stakeholders to promote its products or the company as a whole.

Marketing public relations: targeted at commercial stakeholders, such as distributors, suppliers, competitors and potential customers, and more in direct support of marketing communications than corporate PR.

Masculine culture: culture in which assertiveness, competitiveness and status are valued highly.

Masked identification test: advertising test in which part of a print ad, usually the brand name, is covered. The subject is asked if he or she recognises the ad, and if he or she knows what brand it is for. Recognition and correct attribution scores can then be calculated.

Mass communications: the message transfer takes place with a number of receivers who cannot be identified, using mass media to reach a broad audience.

Media mix: the way advertising spending is allocated across different media.

Media plan: specifies which advertising media and vehicles will be purchased when, at what price and with what expected results. It includes such things as flow charts, the names of specific magazines, reach and frequency estimates and budgets.

Media public relations: developing and maintaining good contacts with radio, television and the (trade) press.

Medium context of advertising: characteristics of the content of the medium in which an ad is inserted, as they are perceived by the individuals who are exposed to the ad.

Medium selectivity: the extent to which a medium is directed towards the target group. Medium selectivity can be represented by a selectivity index showing how well the target group is represented in the medium reach, relative to the universe.

Mere exposure effect: prior mere exposure to stimuli (such as brands) increases positive affect towards these stimuli.

Micro-sites: a temporary brand site that is used for a short period during a product launch.

Mobile marketing or **wireless advertising:** all the activities undertaken to communicate with customers through the use of mobile devices to promote products and services by providing information or offers.

Morals: beliefs or principles that individuals hold concerning what is right and what is wrong.

Motivation (MAO factor): willingness to engage in behaviour, make decisions, pay attention, process information.

Multi-branding: a brand strategy in which different brands are used for products or product ranges in the same product category.

MUSH sponsorship: sponsorship of good causes: Municipal, University, Social, Hospital.

Net promoter score: based on the question 'To what degree would you recommend the following brand to your family or friends?', measured on a 0–10-point scale. The net promoter score is calculated by subtracting the percentage of people scoring 0–6 from the percentage of people who scored 8–10.

Net reach: the sum of all people in the target group reached at least once by an advertising campaign (a person reached by both media x and y counts as one).

Non-addressable media: media by means of which it is not possible to communicate individually with each customer or prospect.

Objective-and-task budgeting analysis: starts from communications objectives and the resources that are needed to reach these planned goals. All needed investments are then added and this will lead to the overall communications budget.

Off-invoice allowances: direct price reductions to the trade during a limited period of time.

One-to-one marketing: getting the right product through the right channel at the right moment to the right customer.

Online advertising: commercial messages on specific rented spaces on websites of other companies.

Opportunity (MAO factor): the extent to which the situation enables a person to obtain the goal set.

Opportunity to see (OTS): the average probability of exposure that an average reached target consumer of an advertising campaign has. It is calculated by dividing gross reach by net reach.

Opt-in: a principle implying that receivers of e-mail have voluntarily agreed to receive commercial e-mails about topics that they find interesting. They do so by subscribing on websites and checking a box.

Opt-out: a principle implying that receivers of e-mail have to uncheck the box on a web page to prevent being put on an e-mail list.

Ordinary decency: an ethical principle that means that lying, cheating and coercion are always considered unethical.

Outbound telemarketing: the marketer is taking the initiative to call clients or prospects (outgoing calls).

Outcomes rule: the ethical quality of a decision is judged in terms of performance, rewards, satisfaction and feedback.

Outdoor advertising: media such as billboards and transit media in the form of messages on buses, trams, in stations, etc.

Output indicators of public relations effectiveness: measure the result of the PR activity in terms of media coverage or publicity. Examples of such measures are the press space or television time devoted to the company, its events or brands, the length of the stories, the tone and news value of the headlines, readership/viewership levels, opportunity to see, tone of coverage.

Overpositioning: extreme positioning on one benefit.

Pay per click advertising model: keyword buying online advertisers only pay for each click-through on their sponsored link.

Perceived behavioural control (PBC): the perceived ease or difficulty of performing a behaviour. It is assumed to reflect past experience as well as anticipated impediments and obstacles.

Percentage of sales budgeting analysis: budgets are defined as a percentage of the projected sales of the next year.

Perception–Experience–Memory model: a model that links the effect of marketing communications to previous and current perception, experience and memory.

Peripheral-route processing: if the motivation, ability or opportunity to process a message is low, consumers are more likely to process the information peripherally. The result of the latter is no real information processing, but an evaluation based on simple, peripheral cues, such as background music, humour, an attractive source or endorser, the number of arguments used, etc.

Personal communications: message transfer directed to certain known and individually addressed persons.

Physiological advertising test: test by means of which the reaction of the body to advertising stimuli is measured. Examples are: pupil dilation, galvanic skin response, heartbeat and voice pitch analysis, and electroencephalography.

Podcast: a sound file with an RSS feed that can be listened to by any MP3 or audio player. This technology makes it easy for people to create their own audio recordings and post them on the Web.

Point-of-purchase communications: communications at the point-of-purchase or point-of-sales (i.e. the shop). They include several communications tools such as displays, advertising within the shop, merchandising, article presentations, store layout, etc.

Pop-unders: banner ads that appear in a separate window beneath the visited website.

Pop-ups: banner ads that appear in a separate window on top of the visited website.

Positioning: defining a unique and relevant position for a product in the mind of the target group, the way a product is perceived by the target group on important attributes, or the 'place in the mind' a product occupies relative to its competitors.

Post-experience model: the model assumes relations between the current purchase on the one hand, and previous purchase, previous advertising, previous promotion, current advertising and current promotion, on the other.

Post-test: a test of the effectiveness of a single ad after placement in the media.

Power distance: the extent to which authority plays an important role, and to what extent less powerful members of the society accept and expect that power is distributed unequally.

Premium: small gifts that come with a product offered in-, on- or near-pack.

Press kit/press release: a set of documentation, containing photos, reports and a press release, which is sent to journalists or presented at a press conference. A press release is a document that contains the material that the company would like to see covered in the press.

Prestige brand: high-quality, luxurious brand targeted at a smaller segment, looking for status and high psycho-social meaning.

Pre-test: advertising stimuli are tested before the ad appears in the media. The general purpose is to test an ad or different ads to assess whether or not they can achieve the purpose for which they are designed.

Pre-test checklists: used to make sure that nothing important is missing in the proposed advertising concept, and that the ad is appealing, powerful and 'on strategy'.

Price cut on the shelf: consumer promotion in which the consumer gets an immediate discount when buying the product.

Private label brands (also called own-label brands, store or dealer brands)**:** brands developed, owned and marketed by wholesalers or retailers.

Problem solution advertising: an advertisement that shows how a problem can be solved or avoided.

Process goals of communication: conditions which should be established before any communication can be effective. All communications should capture the attention of the target group, then appeal or be appreciated, and last but not least be processed and remembered.

Product confusion: attributing a stimulus to a wrong product category.

Product specialisation: a company concentrates on one product and sells it to different market segments.

Professional ethics: only take actions that would be viewed as proper and ethical by an objective panel of professional colleagues.

Psychographic segmentation: segmenting markets using lifestyle or personality criteria.

Public affairs: a management function directed towards the societal and political relations of the company. It is aimed at continuously studying trends and issues related to government decision-making and opinions and attitudes of the general public. Good contacts with the general public and the local community are a part of the public affairs activity.

Public or general fairs: exhibitions and fairs that are open to the general public. There are two kinds of public fairs: general interest fairs and special interest fairs.

Public relations: a communications tool that is used to promote the goodwill of the firm as a whole. It is the projection of the personality of the company, the management of reputation. Public relations is the planned and sustained effort to establish and maintain good relationships, mutual understanding, sympathy and goodwill with publics, audiences or stakeholders. It is those efforts that identify and close the gap between how the organisation is seen by its key publics and how it would like to be seen.

Publics or **stakeholders:** besides customers and potential customers, groups of people that the company is not directly trying to sell products to (that is why these groups are sometimes called secondary target groups), but that are perceived as influencing opinions about the company.

Puffery: the use of hyperbole or exaggeration of attribute and benefit claims in advertising to promote a brand.

Pull advertisements: messages shown to users as they are navigating WAP or wireless sites and properties.

Pulsing advertising schedule: a certain level of advertising takes place during the whole campaign period, but during particular periods higher advertising levels are used.

Purchase facilitation: assuring buyers that there are no barriers hindering product or brand purchase.

Purchase intention: the intention of the buyer to purchase the brand or the product or take other buying-related actions (going to the store, asking for more information).

Push advertising: messages that are proactively sent out to wireless users and devices like alerts, SMS messages or even voice calls.

QR-code: a black and white square on print advertisements (Quick Response code). The QR-code can be scanned by smart phones and provides quick and effortless access to the brand's website.

Rational advertising appeals: advertisements that contain features, practical details and verifiable, factually relevant cues that can serve as evaluative criteria.

Reach goal of communication: how to reach the target groups in an effective and efficient way.

Readability analysis: advertising test that checks whether the advertising copy is simple and easy to understand 'at first glance'.

Recall tests: the extent to which an individual recalls a new ad or a new execution amid existing ads is tested, e.g. the Portfolio test.

Receiver context of advertising: the situational circumstances in which a person is exposed to an advertisement (e.g. at home, in the company of friends, on the way to work, when in a bad mood, etc.).

Recognition test: a sample of ads is presented to a consumer, who is asked to indicate whether he or she recognises the ad or not.

Reinforcement model: according to this model, awareness leads to trial and trial leads to reinforcement. Product experience is the dominant variable in the model, and advertising is supposed to reinforce habits, frame experience and defend consumers' attitudes.

Relationship marketing: brings quality, customer service and marketing into close alignment, leading to long-term and mutually beneficial customer relationships.

Resources costing budgeting: a budgeting method in which management decides what resources are needed (an extra press officer, or an event co-ordinator) and calculates the costs implied.

Retail advertising: when a retailer takes the initiative to advertise to consumers.

RFM-model: a direct marketing response scoring model in which, for all customers in a database, three behavioural response parameters are measured: *Recency*, the time elapsed since the last purchase; *Frequency*, the frequency with which a customer places an order; *Monetary value*, the average amount of money a customer spends per purchase.

Rich media ad: an Internet ad using animated content such as audio/video, Flash, Java, etc., to create special effects, interaction, or moving or floating ads.

Roadblocking: placing the same ad across many channels at the same time.

Rossiter–Percy grid: a buying behaviour model that classifies buying decisions in four categories, based on the dimensions high–low involvement and fulfilling a transformational or informational buying motive.

Routinised response behaviour model: a model that assumes that a large number of product experiences can lead to routinised response behaviour, especially for low-involvement, frequently purchased products.

Sales force promotion: sales promotion targeted at the sales force, offering them incentives to market the product well.

Sales promotions: sales-stimulating campaigns, such as price cuts, coupons, loyalty programmes, competitions, free samples, etc.

Sales response models: depict the relationship between the size of the communications budget and sales.

Sampling: consumer promotion technique that consists of distributing small samples of a product, sometimes in a specially designed package free of charge or at a very low cost.

Savings cards: consumer promotion techniques on the basis of which customers receive a discount provided they have bought a number of units of the brand during a specific period of time.

Search engine advertising (SEA): Internet advertising on large search engines such as Google, Yahoo!, Bing, etc., that is triggered by specific keywords and search terms and which appears alongside and sometimes above or below the search results.

Search engine optimisation (SEO): a number of techniques to improve the listing of a brand or a company in search engines.

Selective advertising: campaigns that promote a specific brand.

Selective specialisation: a company chooses a number of segments that look attractive. There is no synergy between the segments, but every segment looks profitable.

Self-generated persuasion: the consumer is not persuaded by strong brand arguments, but by his or her own thoughts, arguments or imagined consequences. These thoughts go beyond the information offered in the ad. The consumer combines the information in the message with previous experience and knowledge, and tries to imagine him- or herself consuming the product and the consequences thereof.

Self-liquidators or self-liquidating premiums: presents that can be obtained in exchange for a number of proofs of purchase, and an extra amount of money.

Self-reference criterion: our unconscious tendency to refer everything to our own cultural values.

Self-regulation: a process in which the advertising industry regulates itself by establishing codes of practice or sets of guiding principles, the aim of which is ensuring legal, decent, honest and truthful advertising, prepared with a sense of social responsibility to the consumer and society and with proper respect for the rules of fair competition.

Share of voice: the ratio of own communications investments divided by the communications investments of all market players.

Shoskele: a floating Internet ad that moves over the browser in an animated way.

Signalling theory: consumers take advertising repetition as a signal of the quality of a brand.

Skyscrapers: a thin and small banner ad, typically along the right side of a web page.

Slice-of-life advertising: an advertisement that features the product being used in a real-life setting, which usually involves solving a problem.

Slotting allowance: a one-time, upfront fee that is charged by retailers before they allow a new product on their shelves to cover the start-up costs of entering a new product into their system.

Social media: a collection of emerging technologies enabling social networking by offering Internet users the ability to collaborate, add, edit, share and tag content of different kinds (text, sound, video, images).

Social networking sites: applications that enable users to connect on the Internet by creating personal profiles, inviting friends to have access to those profiles, sending e-mails and instant messages between each other. These personal profiles can include photos, video, audio files, blogs, links to websites, and in fact any type of information (e.g. Facebook, Pinterest).

Social TV: given the popularity of social networks, people are frequently talking about TV shows at the same time as they are watching them.

Socially responsible marketing: selling products that embody certain social ethical values, such as products free of child labour, produced in companies where trade unions are allowed, in decent social circumstances, and at fair wages.

Split-scan test: an advertising test procedure in which the television viewing behaviour of a panel of consumers is measured by means of a telemetric device. All members of the panel also receive a store card. By means of a store card, the actual purchases of the panel members can be measured, and in that way the effectiveness of the different commercials can be assessed.

Sponsorship: an investment in cash or kind in an activity, in return for access to the exploitable commercial potential associated with this activity.

Stakeholders: see **Publics**.

Standardised campaign or **globalised communication campaign:** a campaign that is run in different countries, using the same concept, setting, theme, appeal and message, with the possible exception of translations.

Starch test: an advertising recognition post-test for print advertising in which participants are asked to indicate whether they have noticed an ad, associated it with a brand and read most of the text.

Stealth marketing: the use of marketing practices that fail to disclose or reveal the true relationship with the company that produces or sponsors the marketing message.

Stereotyping: an automatic perceptual bias enabling people to construct simplified images of reality.

Store atmospherics: the effort to design buying environments to produce specific emotional effects in the buyers that enhance their purchase probability.

Strategic advertising research: research that is aimed at collecting information about the market environment, the market, the product and consumer behaviour, as preparation for developing an advertising campaign.

Subjective norm: the belief one holds regarding what different reference groups consider as socially desirable behaviour, weighted by the consumer's need or willingness to behave according to the norms of the particular reference group. The latter is referred to as social sensitivity.

Superiority of the pleasant hypothesis: negative ad-evoked feelings, such as irritation, have a negative influence on ad- and brand-related responses.

Superstitials: banner ads in the form of additional pop-up browser windows that are opened when a new web page is opened.

Synergy in marketing communications: marketing mix instruments have to be designed in such a way that the effects of the tools are mutually reinforcing.

SWOT analysis: an internal analysis of the strengths and weaknesses of the company or brand and an external analysis of opportunities and threats in the marketplace.

Talking head advertising: an advertisement in which the characters tell a story in their own words.

Tangible product: the core product is translated into product features, a certain level of quality, the available options, design and packaging.

Targeting: the selection of target groups to focus upon, on the basis of an analysis of market segment attractiveness and for which the company has relevant strengths.

Telemarketing: any measurable activity using the telephone to help find, get, keep and develop customers.

Teleological approach (relativism): ethical principle that focuses on consequences. Good or bad depends on what happens as a result of the action.

Teleprospecting: searching for prospects by phone.

Telesales: actively calling consumers or companies with the purpose of selling products or services.

Testimonial advertising: an advertisement that features ordinary people saying how good a product is.

Theatre test: an indirect advertising opinion test in a theatre setting in which participants are asked to make a brand choice before and after exposure to a tested advertisement.

Theme advertising: attempts to build a reservoir of goodwill for a brand or a product.

Theory of Planned Behaviour (TPB): a model of buying behaviour that, besides attitudes and the subjective norm, also considers perceived behavioural control as a determinant of behaviour. This model is relevant to predict behaviours over which people have incomplete volitional control.

Theory of Reasoned Action (TORA): an extension of the Fishbein model. The model provides a link between attitude and behavioural intention. The latter is determined not only by attitudes, but also by the subjective norm (the influence of relevant others).

Think–feel dimension: the extent to which a decision is made on a cognitive or an affective basis.

Top-of-mind brand awareness (TOMA): the percentage of people for which a brand of a specific product category is the first one that comes to mind.

Top topicals: newspaper ads referring to recent events.

Total reach of a medium vehicle: the number or percentage of people who are expected to be exposed to the advertiser's message in that medium vehicle during a specified period.

Tracking study: advertising effectiveness study in which comparable (random) samples of consumers are asked a standardised set of questions at regular intervals. As a result, the position of a brand and competing products can be tracked over time, and effects of subsequent campaigns can be assessed.

Trade advertising: advertising aimed at a company that buys products to resell them.

Trade fair: exhibitions and trade shows open to people working in a certain field of activity or industry. It is a place where manufacturers and retailers of a certain product category or sector meet each other to talk about trade, to present and demonstrate their products and services, to exchange ideas and network, and actually to buy and sell products.

Trade mart: a hybrid kind of exhibition, i.e. half-exhibition, half-display, with a high frequency. Participants rent a permanent stand and aim to sell. Participants in trade marts have samples permanently on display.

Trade promotions: sales promotions by manufacturers to persuade channel members to include the product in their mix, to give it appropriate shelf space and to assist in promoting the product to the end-consumer.

Trailer test (or coupon-stimulated purchasing test): respondents are randomly recruited in an experimental and a control group. The experimental group is exposed to a new advertisement, while the control group is not. After shopping, the items purchased by the two groups are compared.

Transaction-based sponsorship: cause-related marketing or point-of-purchase politics: a type of sponsorship in which the company invests a pre-specified amount of money in a 'good cause' every time a consumer buys one of the company's products.

Transformational buying motives: positive buying motivations, such as sensory gratification, social approval or intellectual stimulation.

TV test: ethical rule of conduct which implies that a manager should always ask if he or she would feel comfortable explaining his or her action on TV to the general public.

Twitter: a micro-blog and at the same time a free social network service. Twitter enables users to send and read users' updates known as tweets. These are text-based posts of a maximum of 140 characters that are displayed on the user's profile page and delivered to other users (called followers) who subscribe to them.

Two-factor model: an inverted-U relationship exists between the level of exposure to an advertising campaign, on the one hand, and advertising effectiveness (cognitive responses, attitudes, purchase), on the other. Wear-in and wear-out effects explain the nature of this relationship.

Unaided brand awareness: the percentage of consumers that can name a brand in a certain product category.

Uncertainty avoidance culture: the extent to which people feel uncomfortable with uncertainty and ambiguity and have a need for structure and formal rules in their lives.

Underpositioning: a company fails to make a clear differentiation with competitors.

Unfair marketing communications: acts or practices that cause or are likely to cause substantial injury to consumers, which are not reasonably avoidable by consumers themselves and not outweighed by countervailing benefits to consumers or competition. They may go beyond questions of fact and relate merely to public values, e.g. offend public policy as it has been established by statutes, are immoral, unethical, oppressive or unscrupulous, or cause substantial injury to consumers, competitors or other business.

Unique selling proposition (USP): a functional benefit used in marketing communications; usually functional superiority in the sense that the brand offers the best quality, the best service, the lowest price, the most advanced technology.

Useful reach of a medium vehicle: the number or percentage of people from the target group of a campaign who are expected to be exposed to the advertiser's message in that medium vehicle during a specified period.

Useful score: advertising processing measure in which the percentage of the consumer sample that both recognised the ad and attributed it correctly to the brand advertised is measured.

Value marketing: a strategy in which a company links its activities to a philosophy of general societal interest. The company positions itself on the basis of a value system that is often not product-related.

Vertical trade fairs: different industries present their goods and services to target groups belonging to one single field of activity.

Video-on-Demand (VoD): services include the online retail and rental of audio-visual works, primarily feature films, audio-visual fiction, documentaries, educational programmes, cartoons, etc.

Viral marketing: a set of techniques that is used to spur brand users and lovers, game participants or advocate consumers among the target group to promote their favourite brand to friends and relatives. They are put to work to spread the word about the brand or product by using e-mail, SMS, 'tell or send to a friend' buttons or via different social media sites as Facebook, Google+, YouTube, review sites and influential blogs.

Virtual game worlds: games that require their users to behave according to strict rules in the context of a massively multiplayer online role-playing game (MMORPG) (e.g. 'World of Warcraft').

Virtual social worlds: a group of virtual worlds allowing inhabitants to choose their behaviour freely and essentially live a virtual life similar to their real life. Again, virtual social world users appear in the form of avatars and interact in a 3-D virtual environment (e.g. Second Life).

Virtual worlds: Internet platforms that replicate a 3-D environment in which users can appear in the form of personalised avatars and interact with each other as they would in real life.

Warm advertising: an advertising appeal that consists of elements evoking mild, positive feelings such as love, friendship, cosiness, affection and empathy.

Wear-in: at low levels of exposure to advertising, consumers develop negative responses (e.g. counter-arguments) due to the novelty of the stimulus. After a few exposures, the reaction becomes more positive.

Wear-out: at high levels of exposures to advertising, consumers develop negative responses, due to boredom, irritation, etc.

Web 1.0: the World Wide Web as an information source with static websites.

Web 2.0 or **social media (networks):** a concept of the Web as a participation platform on which users participate and connect to each other using services as opposed to sites.

Weblogs, or **blogs:** frequently updated personal web journals that allow owners to publish ideas and information.

Wireless advertising: see **Mobile marketing**.

World Wide Web (WWW): the interactive and graphical communications medium on the Internet. The Web is characterised by the use of hypertext mark-up language (HTML) that allows documents consisting of text, icons, sounds or images to be shared by different users, regardless of the computer operating system they use. The hyperlinks (text- or image-based) make it possible to navigate quickly through documents and pages by simple mouse-clicking.

INDEX